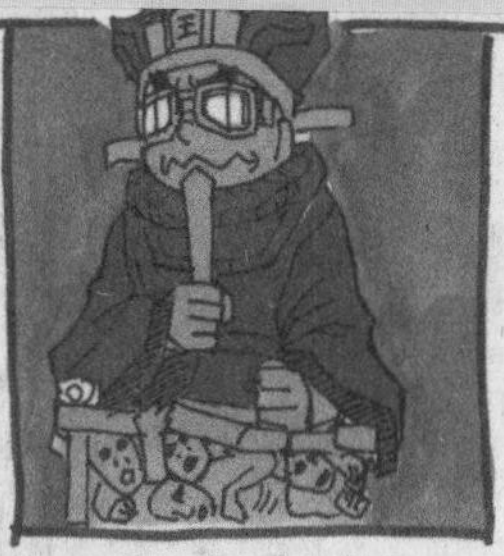
岸本斉史

The ***Naruto*** comics are already at volume 10! In the blink of an eye, we've reached double digits! Although I doubt that triple digits is a milestone we'll ever achieve, it would make me exceedingly happy if all of you would continue to read and enjoy ***Naruto***, without ever getting bored, for the entire run of the series!

—Masashi Kishimoto, 2001

Author/artist Masashi Kishimoto was born in 1974 in rural Okayama Prefecture, Japan. After spending time in art college, he won the Hop Step Award for new manga artists with his manga **Karakuri** (Mechanism). Kishimoto decided to base his next story on traditional Japanese culture. His first version of **Naruto**, drawn in 1997, was a one-shot story about fox spirits; his final version, which debuted in **Weekly Shonen Jump** in 1999, quickly became the most popular ninja manga in Japan.

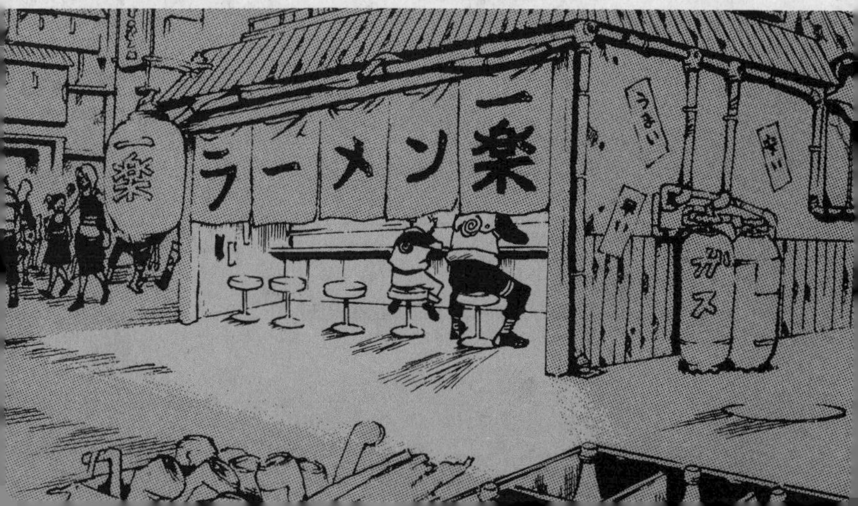
一楽
ラーメン一楽
うまい
ガス

NARUTO

3-in-1 Edition
Volume 4
SHONEN JUMP Manga Omnibus Edition
A compilation of the graphic novel volumes 10–12

STORY AND ART BY MASASHI KISHIMOTO

Translation/Katy Bridges, Mari Morimoto
English Adaptation/Jo Duffy, Mari Morimoto, Frances E. Wall
Touch-up Art & Lettering/Heidi Szykowny
Additional Touch-up/ Josh Simpson
Design/Sean Lee (Manga Edition)
Design/Sam Elzway (Omnibus Edition)
Series Editor/Joel Enos (Manga Edition)
Editor/Frances E. Wall (Manga Edition)
Managing Editor/Erica Yee (Omnibus Edition)

Printed in the U.S.A.

Published by VIZ Media, LLC
P.O. Box 77010
San Francisco, CA 94107

10 9 8 7 6 5 4 3 2
Omnibus edition first printing, February 2013
Second printing, November 2015

www.viz.com

THE WORLD'S
MOST POPULAR MANGA
SHONEN JUMP
www.shonenjump.com

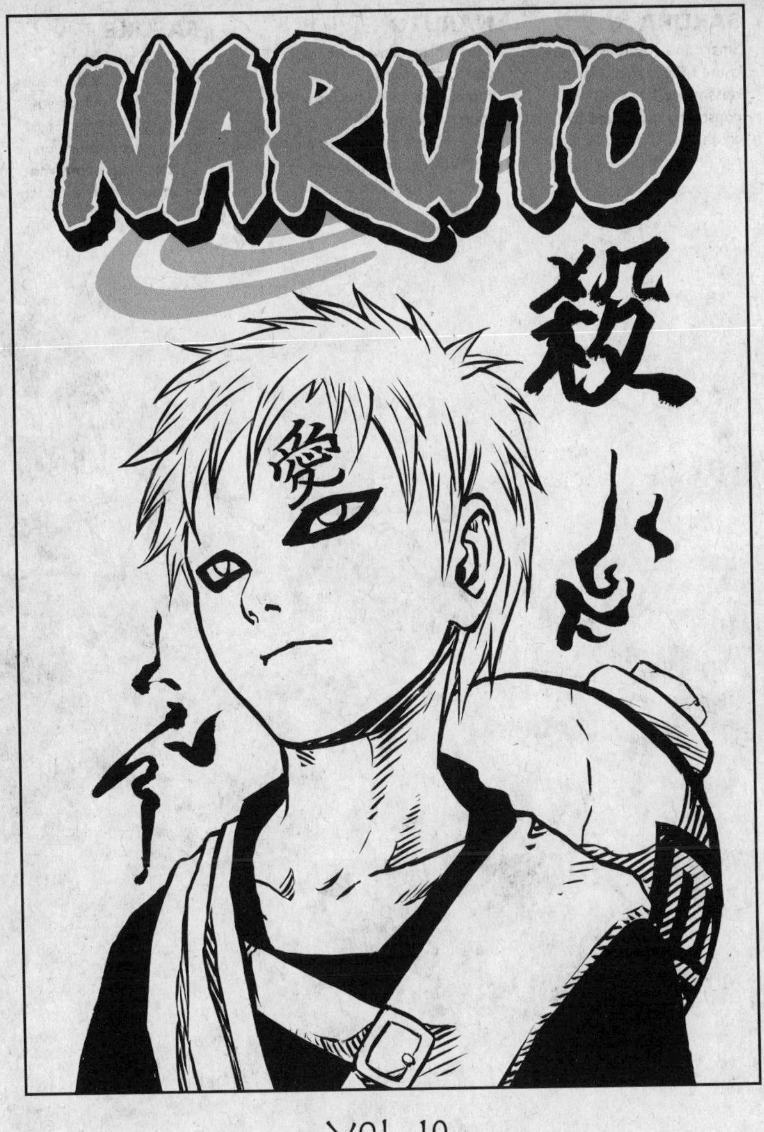
NARUTO
殺
愛

VOL. 10

A SPLENDID NINJA

STORY AND ART BY

MASASHI KISHIMOTO

SAKURA サクラ

Smart and studious, Sakura is the brightest of Naruto's classmates, but she's constantly distracted by her crush on Sasuke. Her goal: to win Sasuke's heart!

NARUTO ナルト

When Naruto was born, a destructive fox spirit was imprisoned inside his body. Spurned by the older villagers, he's grown into an attention-seeking trouble-maker. His goal: to become the village's next *Hokage*.

SASUKE サスケ

The top student in Naruto's class, Sasuke comes from the prestigious Uchiha clan. His goal: to get revenge on a mysterious person who wronged him in the past.

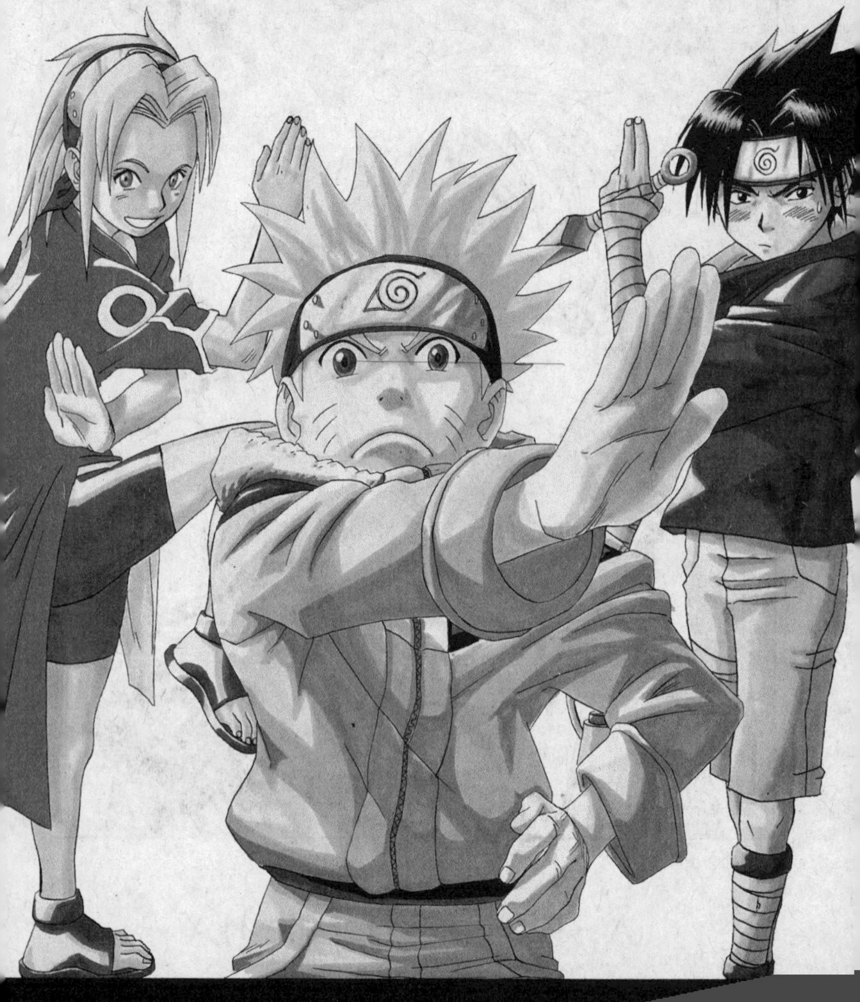

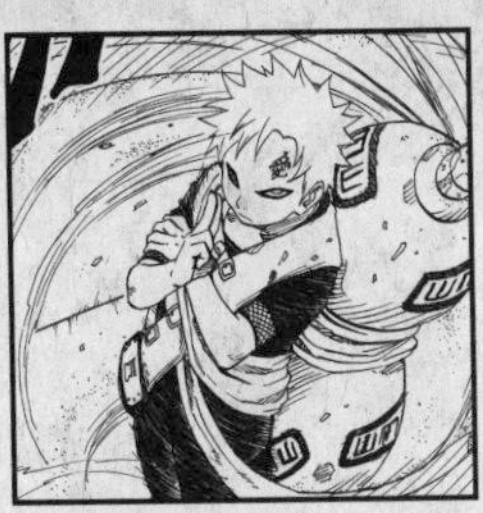

Gaara 我愛羅

Bloodthirsty Gaara is one of the scariest ninja competing in the Chûnin Exams.

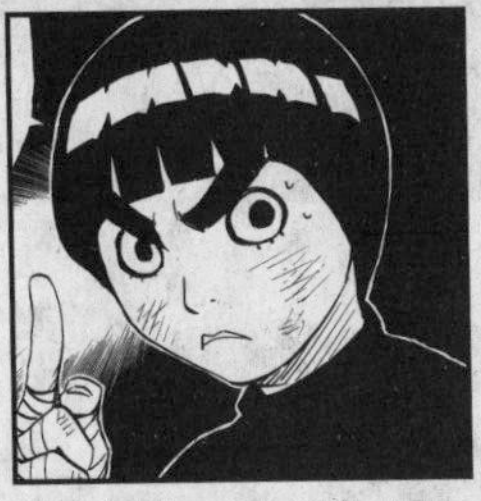

Rock Lee ロック・リー

Lee has been carefully observing the other students' fights while his anticipation for his own battle builds. Now it's about to begin!

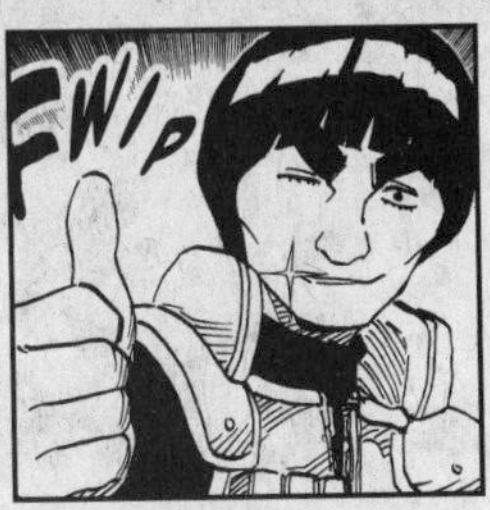
FWIP

Might Guy マイト・ガイ

The flamboyant Master Guy is Lee's idol...and Kakashi's rival!

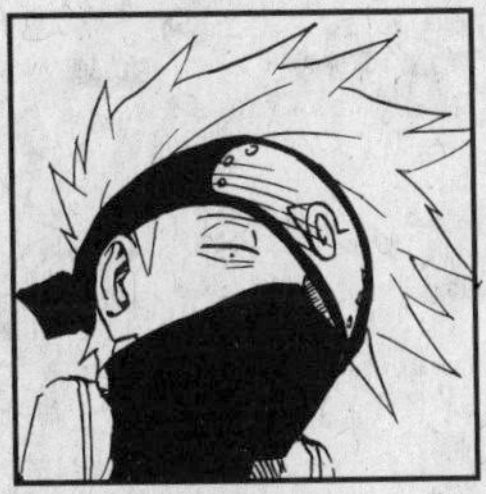

Kakashi カカシ

Although he doesn't have an especially warm personality, Kakashi is protective of his students.

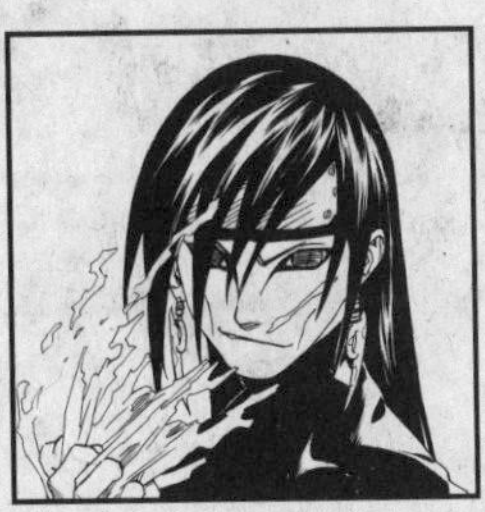

Orochimaru 大蛇丸

This nefarious master of disguise placed a mysterious curse-mark on Sasuke and hopes to mold Sasuke into his successor.

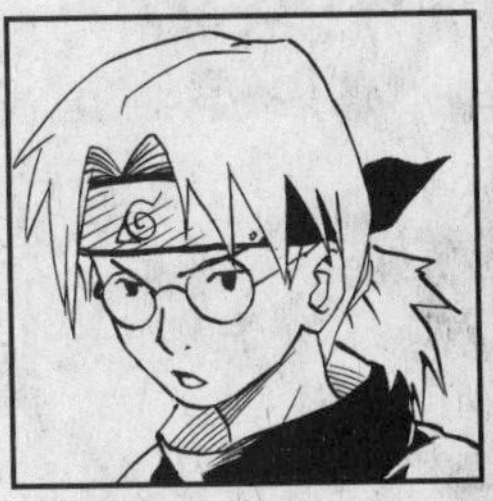

Kabuto カブト

A spy for Orochimaru's village of Otogakure (The Village Hidden in the Sound), Kabuto has been living a double life in Konohagakure since childhood.

THE STORY SO FAR...

Twelve years ago, a destructive nine-tailed fox spirit attacked the ninja village of Konohagakure. The *Hokage*, or village champion, defeated the fox by sealing its soul into the body of a baby boy. Now that boy, Uzumaki Naruto, has grown up to become a ninja-in-training, learning the art of *ninjutsu* with his classmates Sakura and Sasuke.

Naruto, Sasuke and Sakura (along with six other teams of student ninja) have moved on to the third portion of the Chûnin (Journeyman Ninja) Selection Exam—a series of no-holds-barred, one-on-one bouts that begin with a set of preliminary matches. As the preliminaries continue, the battles become increasingly vicious and it's clear that lives are on the line. After the fight between Hyuga Hinata and her cousin Hyuga Neji ends with Hinata being rushed to the emergency room, tensions are at an all-time high. Then the next two combatants are announced: Rock Lee and Gaara!

NARUTO

VOL. 10
A SPLENDID NINJA

CONTENTS

Number 82: Lee's Secret!!

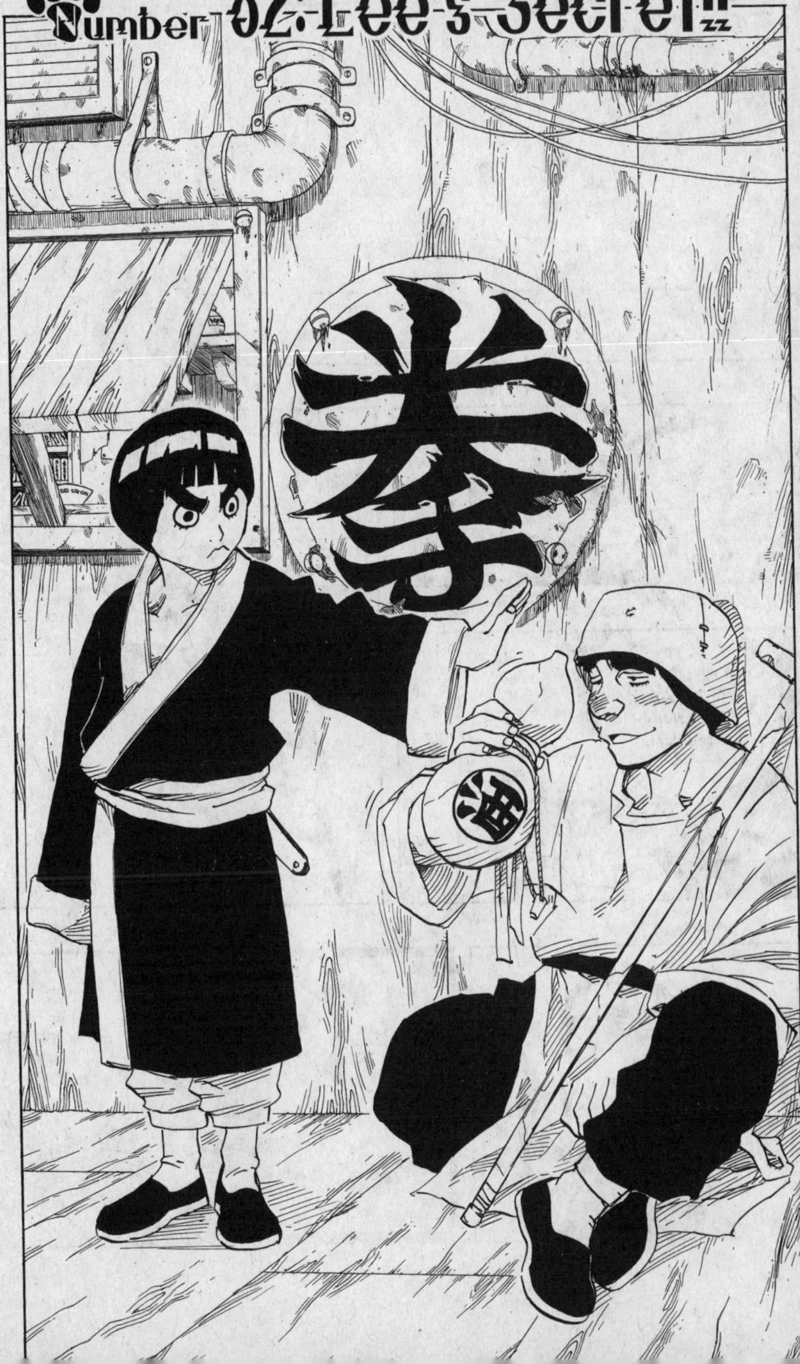
拳
酒

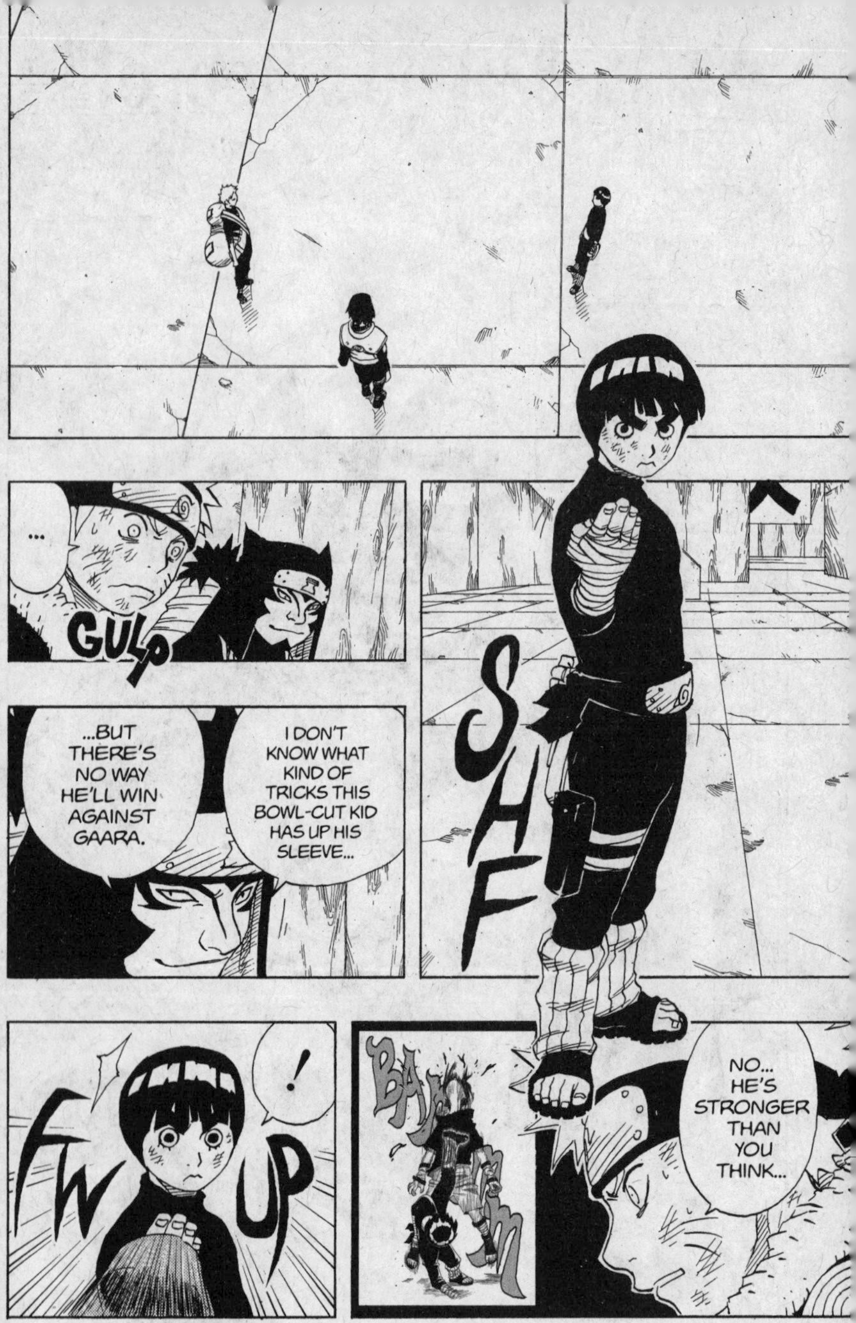
SHF
...
GULP
I DON'T KNOW WHAT KIND OF TRICKS THIS BOWL-CUT KID HAS UP HIS SLEEVE...
...BUT THERE'S NO WAY HE'LL WIN AGAINST GAARA.
NO... HE'S STRONGER THAN YOU THINK...
!
FWUP

READ THIS WAY

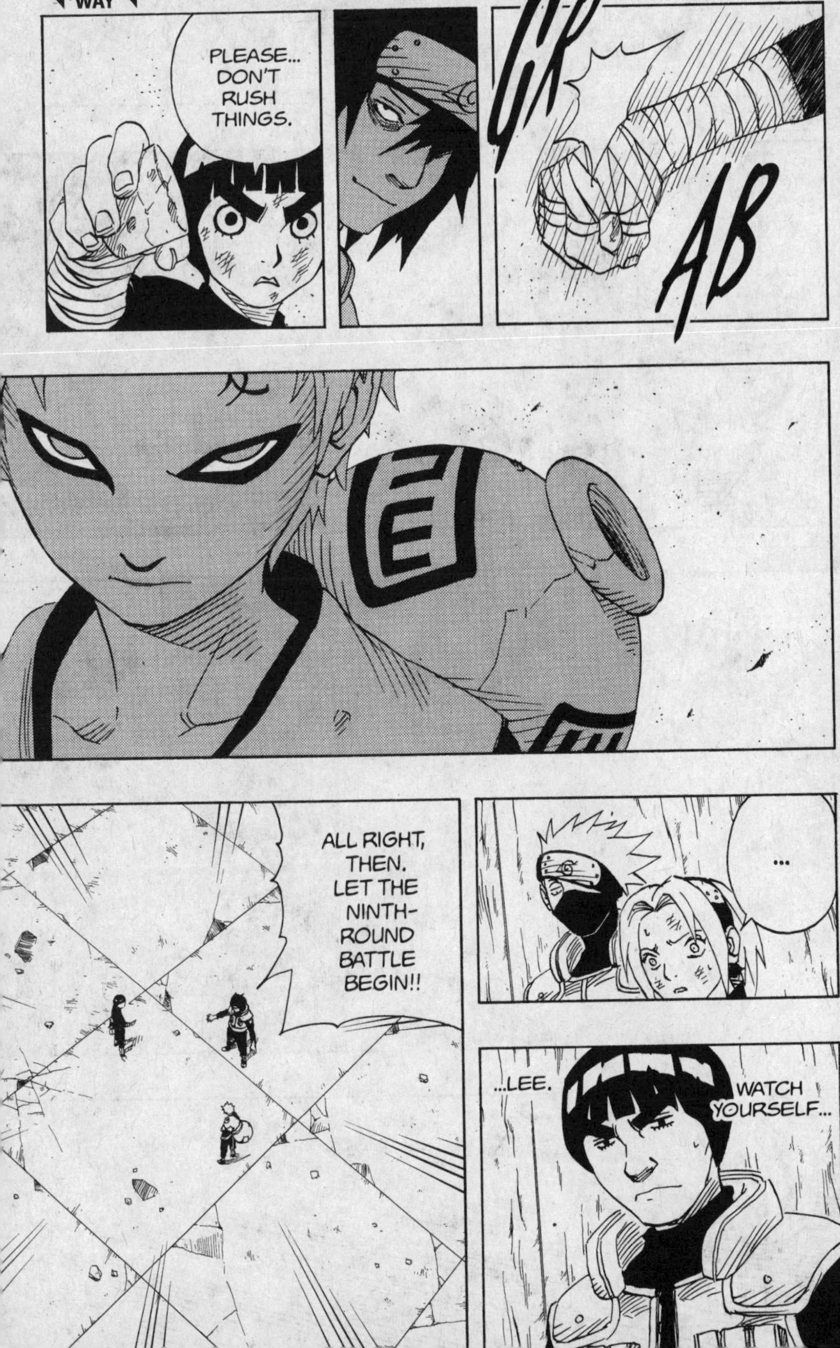
GRAB
PLEASE... DON'T RUSH THINGS.
...
...LEE.
WATCH YOURSELF...
ALL RIGHT, THEN. LET THE NINTH-ROUND BATTLE BEGIN!!

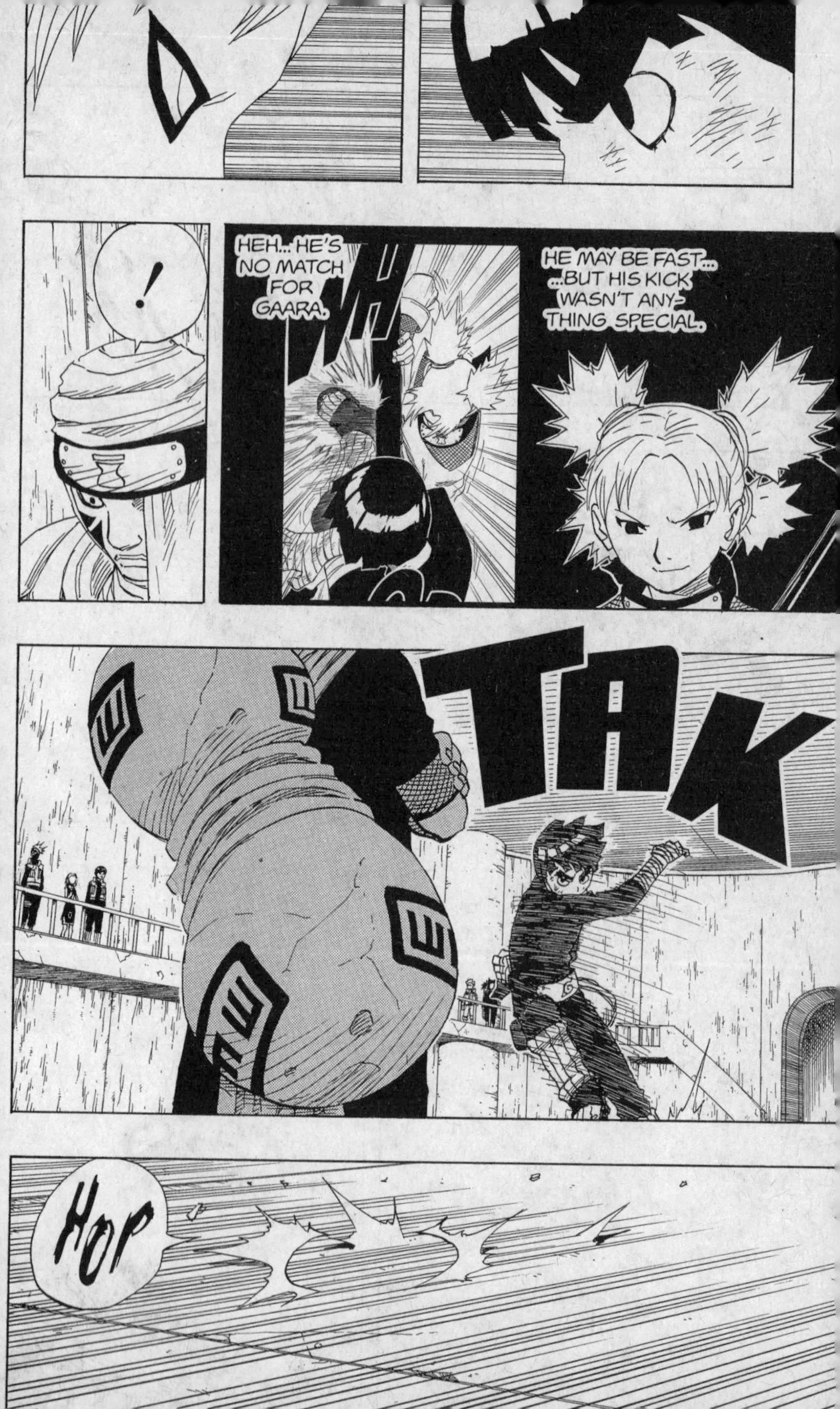

!
HE MAY BE FAST... ...BUT HIS KICK WASN'T ANY-THING SPECIAL.
HEH... HE'S NO MATCH FOR GAARA.
TAK
HOP

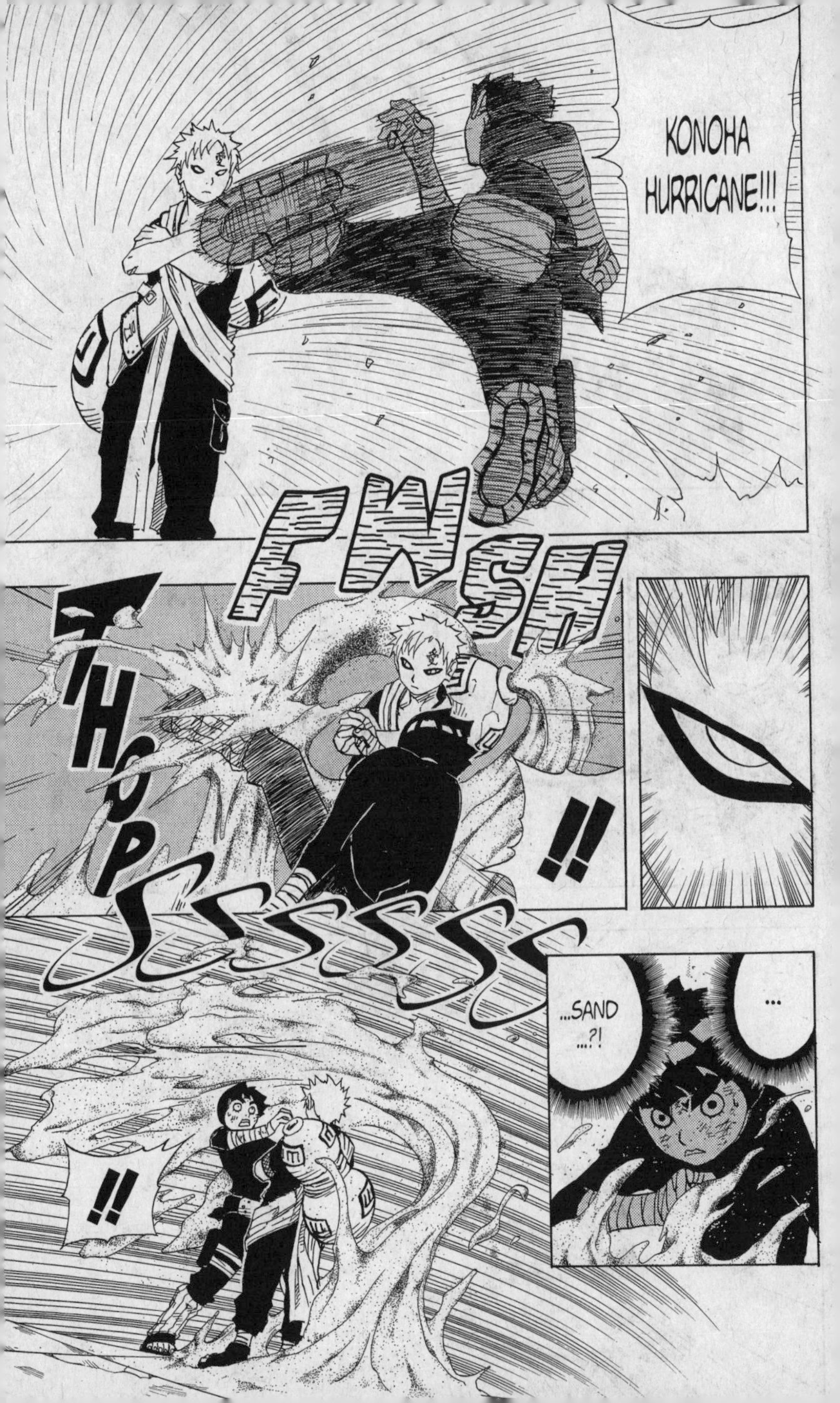
KONOHA HURRICANE!!!
FWSH
THOOP
!!
SSSSSSS
...
...SAND ...?!
!!

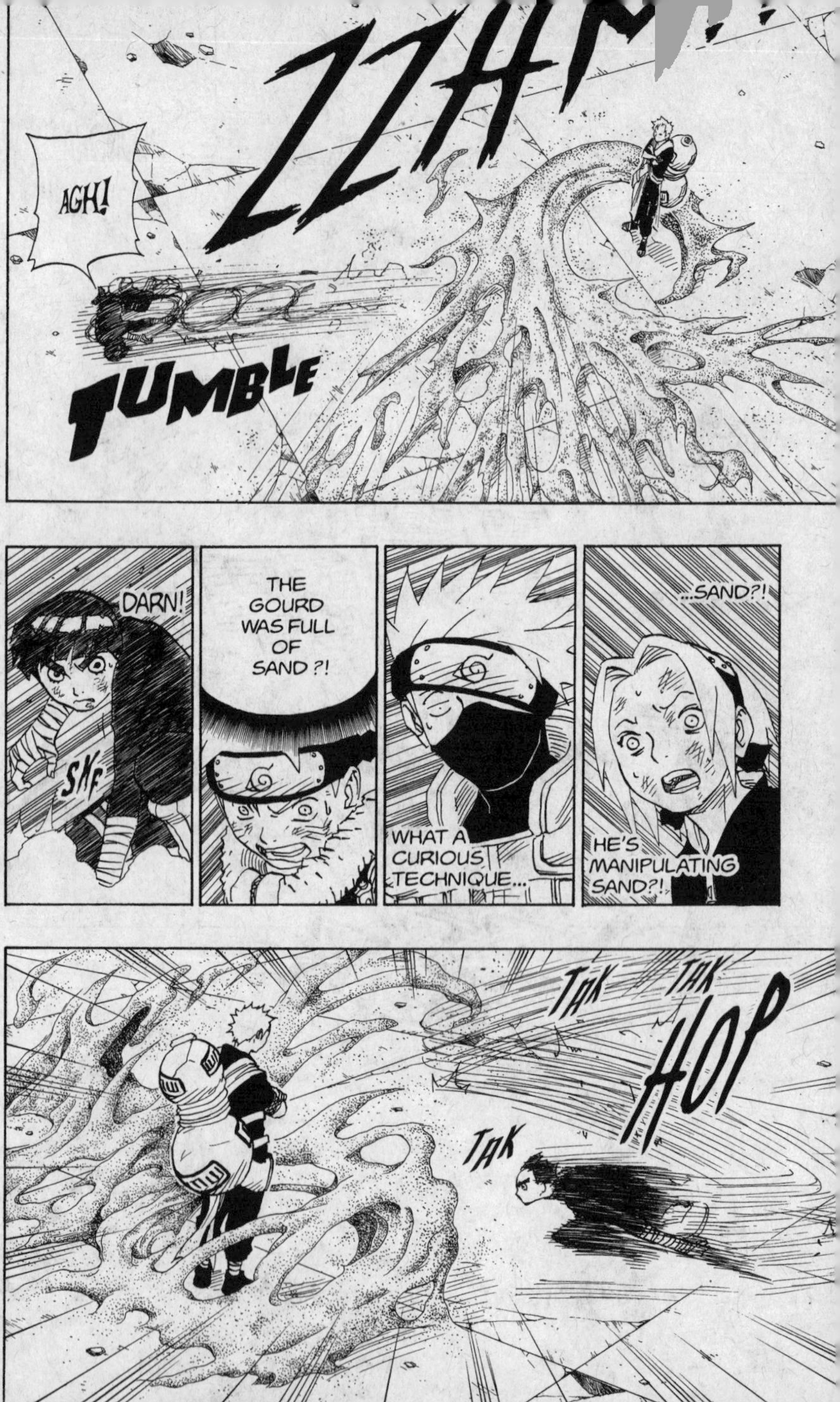
AGH!
TUMBLE
...SAND?!
HE'S MANIPULATING SAND?!
WHAT A CURIOUS TECHNIQUE...
THE GOURD WAS FULL OF SAND?!
DARN!
SKF
TAK
TAK
HOP
TAK

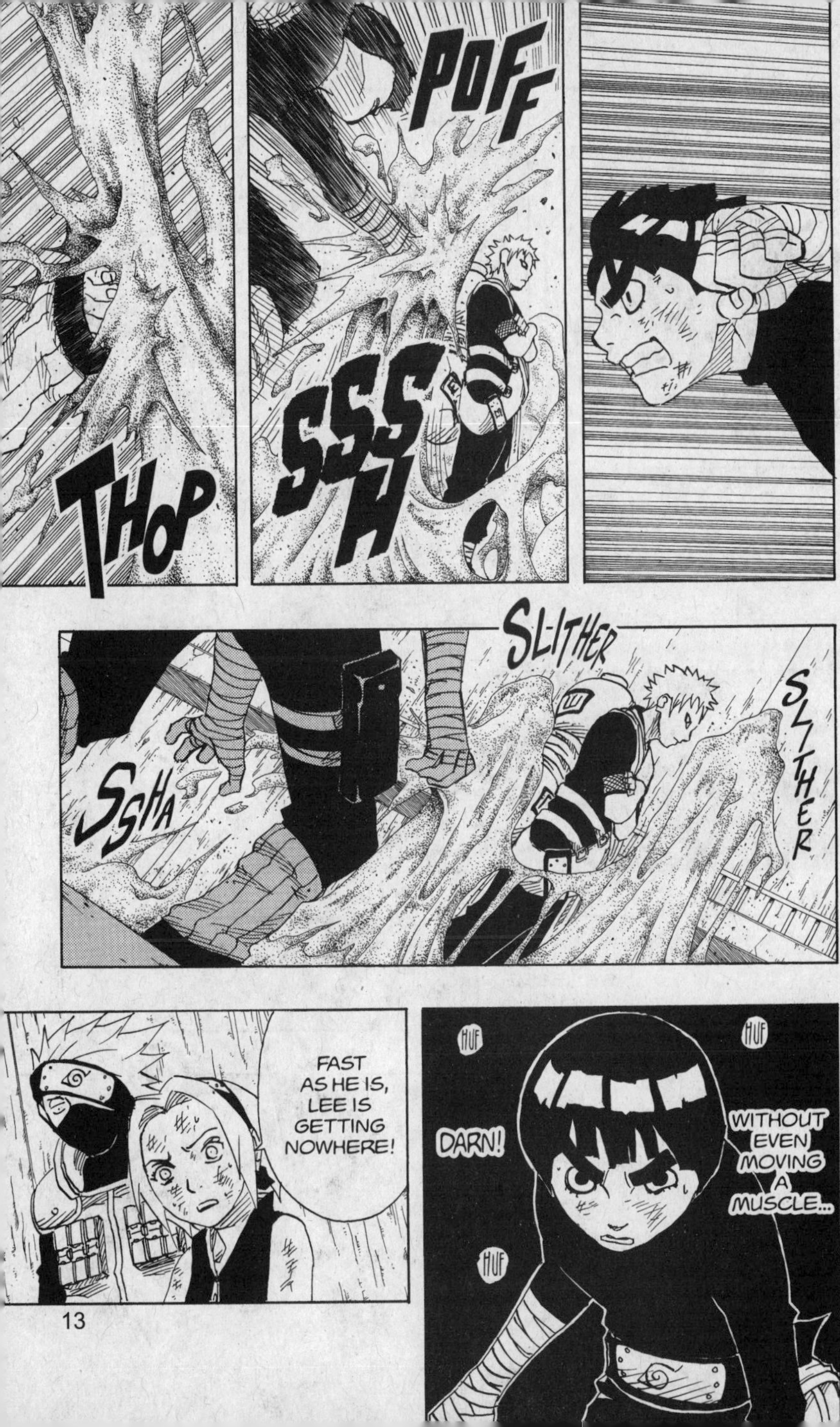
POFF
SSSH
THOP
SLITHER
SLI-THER
SSHA
HUF
HUF
WITHOUT EVEN MOVING A MUSCLE...
DARN!
HUF
FAST AS HE IS, LEE IS GETTING NOWHERE!

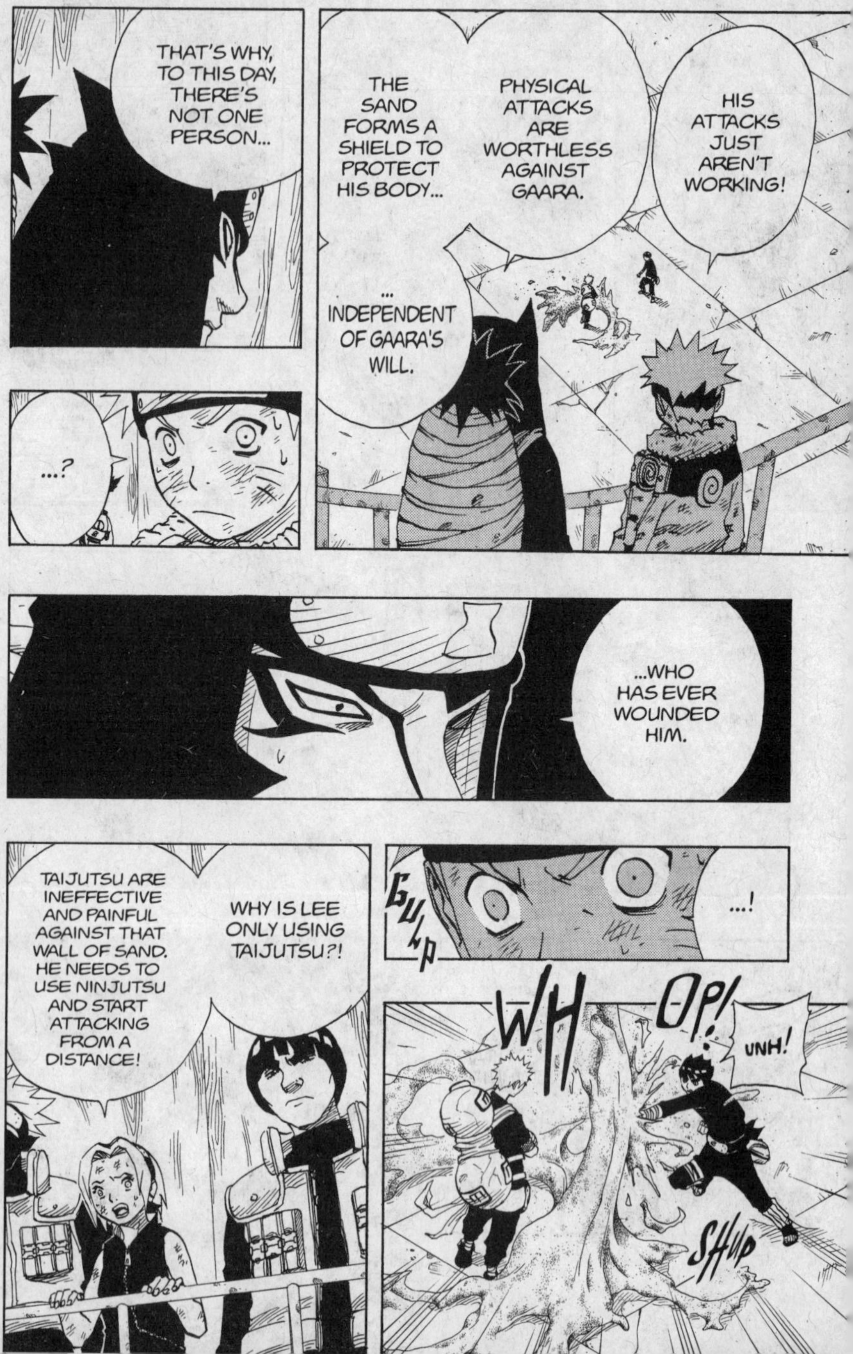
HIS ATTACKS JUST AREN'T WORKING!
PHYSICAL ATTACKS ARE WORTHLESS AGAINST GAARA.
THE SAND FORMS A SHIELD TO PROTECT HIS BODY...
... INDEPENDENT OF GAARA'S WILL.
THAT'S WHY, TO THIS DAY, THERE'S NOT ONE PERSON...
...?
...WHO HAS EVER WOUNDED HIM.
...!
GULP
WHOOP!
UNH!
SHUP
WHY IS LEE ONLY USING TAIJUTSU?!
TAIJUTSU ARE INEFFECTIVE AND PAINFUL AGAINST THAT WALL OF SAND. HE NEEDS TO USE NINJUTSU AND START ATTACKING FROM A DISTANCE!

READ THIS WAY

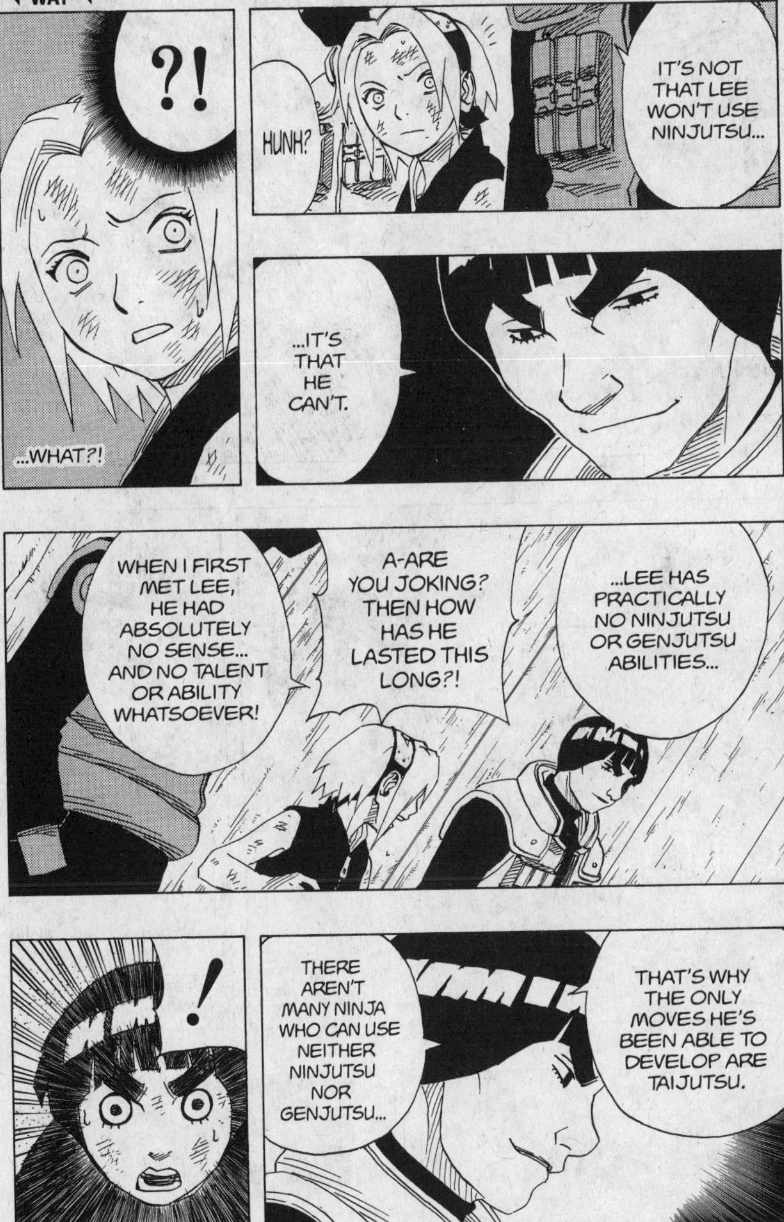

IT'S NOT THAT LEE WON'T USE NINJUTSU...
HUNH?
...IT'S THAT HE CAN'T.
?!
...WHAT?!
...LEE HAS PRACTICALLY NO NINJUTSU OR GENJUTSU ABILITIES...
A-ARE YOU JOKING? THEN HOW HAS HE LASTED THIS LONG?!
WHEN I FIRST MET LEE, HE HAD ABSOLUTELY NO SENSE... AND NO TALENT OR ABILITY WHATSOEVER!
THAT'S WHY THE ONLY MOVES HE'S BEEN ABLE TO DEVELOP ARE TAIJUTSU.
THERE AREN'T MANY NINJA WHO CAN USE NEITHER NINJUTSU NOR GENJUTSU...
!

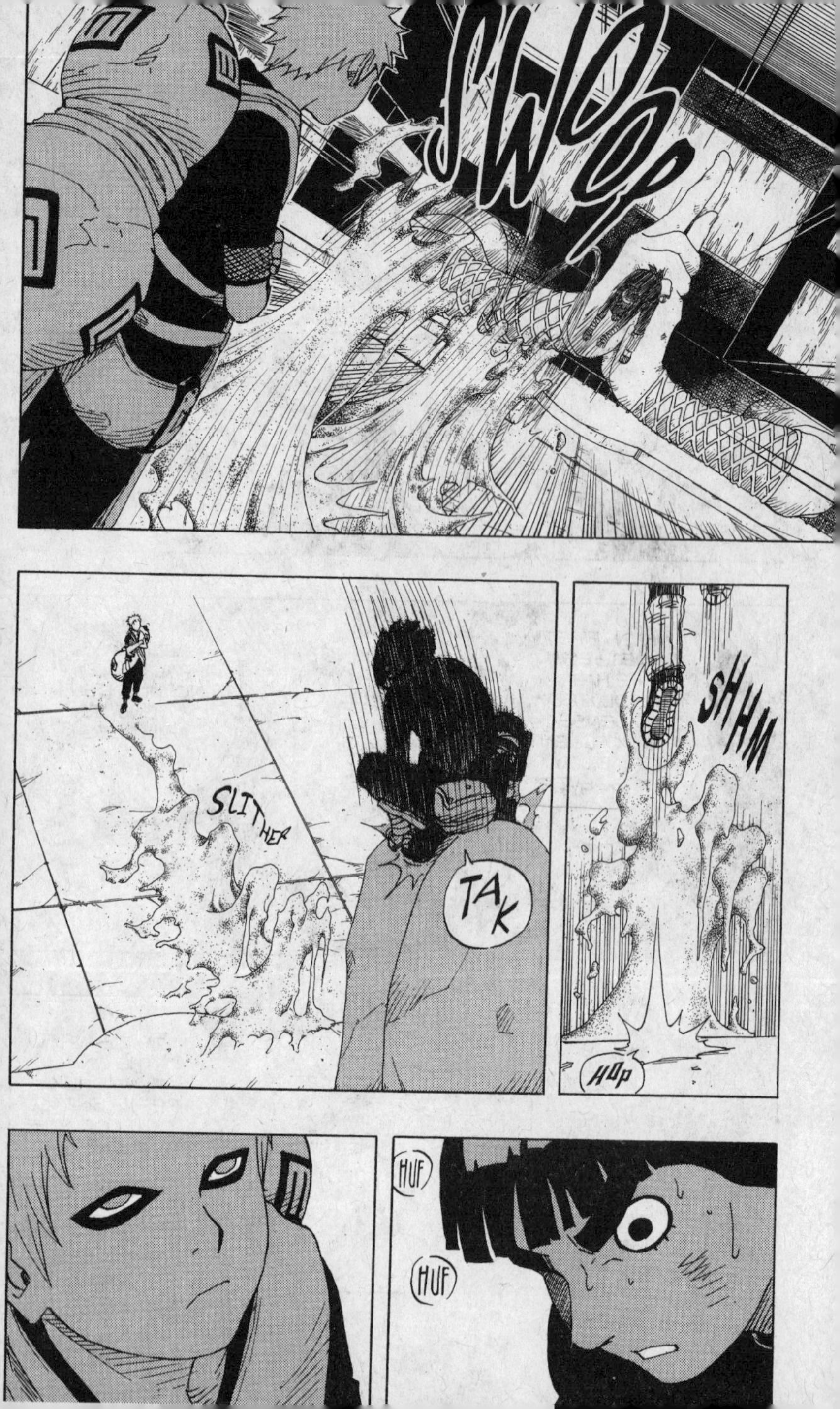
SHHM
HOP
SLITHER
TAK
HUF
HUF

READ THIS WAY

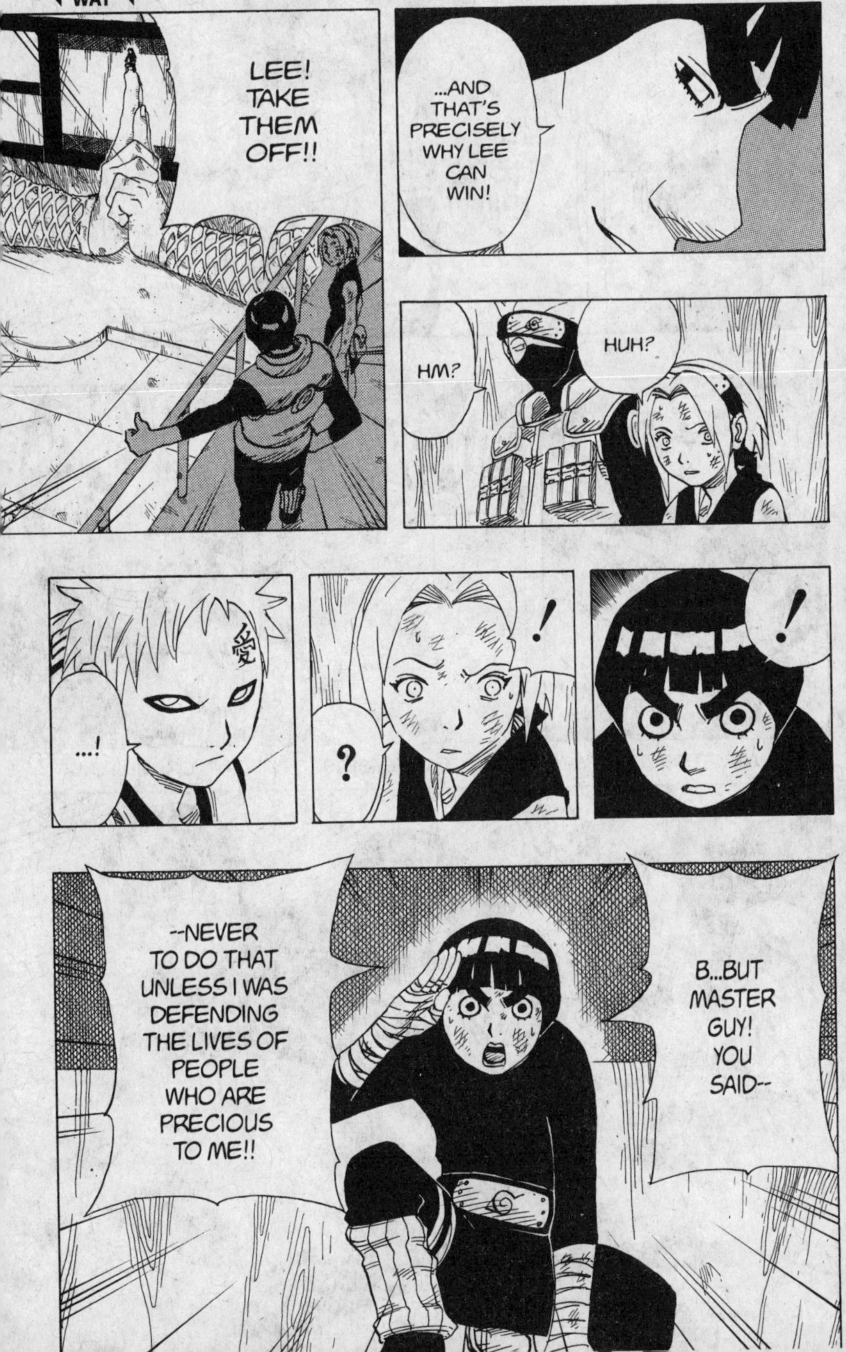
...AND THAT'S PRECISELY WHY LEE CAN WIN!
HUH?
HM?
LEE! TAKE THEM OFF!!
!
!
?
...!
B...BUT MASTER GUY! YOU SAID--
--NEVER TO DO THAT UNLESS I WAS DEFENDING THE LIVES OF PEOPLE WHO ARE PRECIOUS TO ME!!

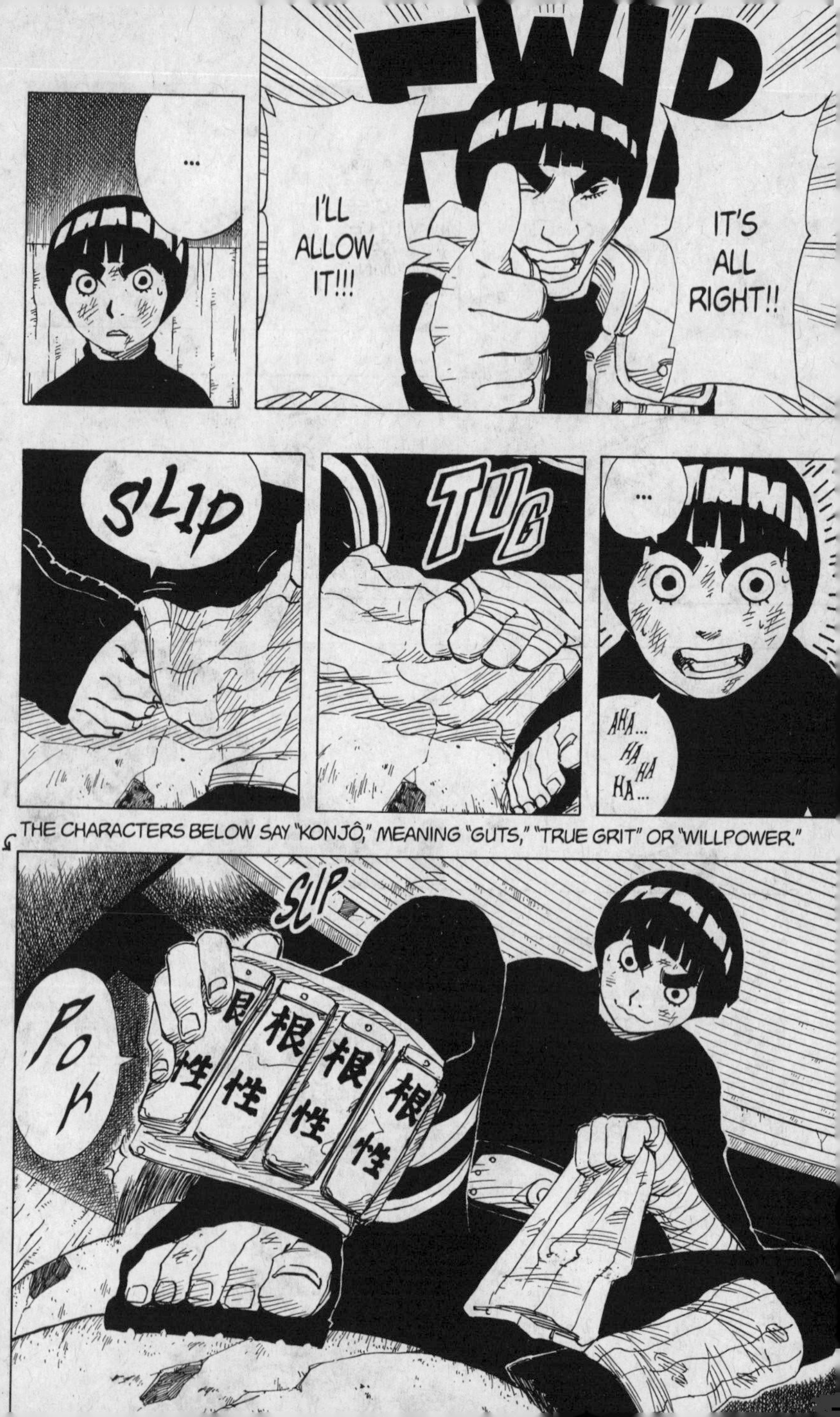
FWIP
IT'S ALL RIGHT!!
I'LL ALLOW IT!!!
...
...
AHA... HA HA HA...
TUG
SLIP
THE CHARACTERS BELOW SAY "KONJÔ," MEANING "GUTS," "TRUE GRIT" OR "WILLPOWER."
SLIP
根性
根性
根性
艮性
POK

READ THIS WAY

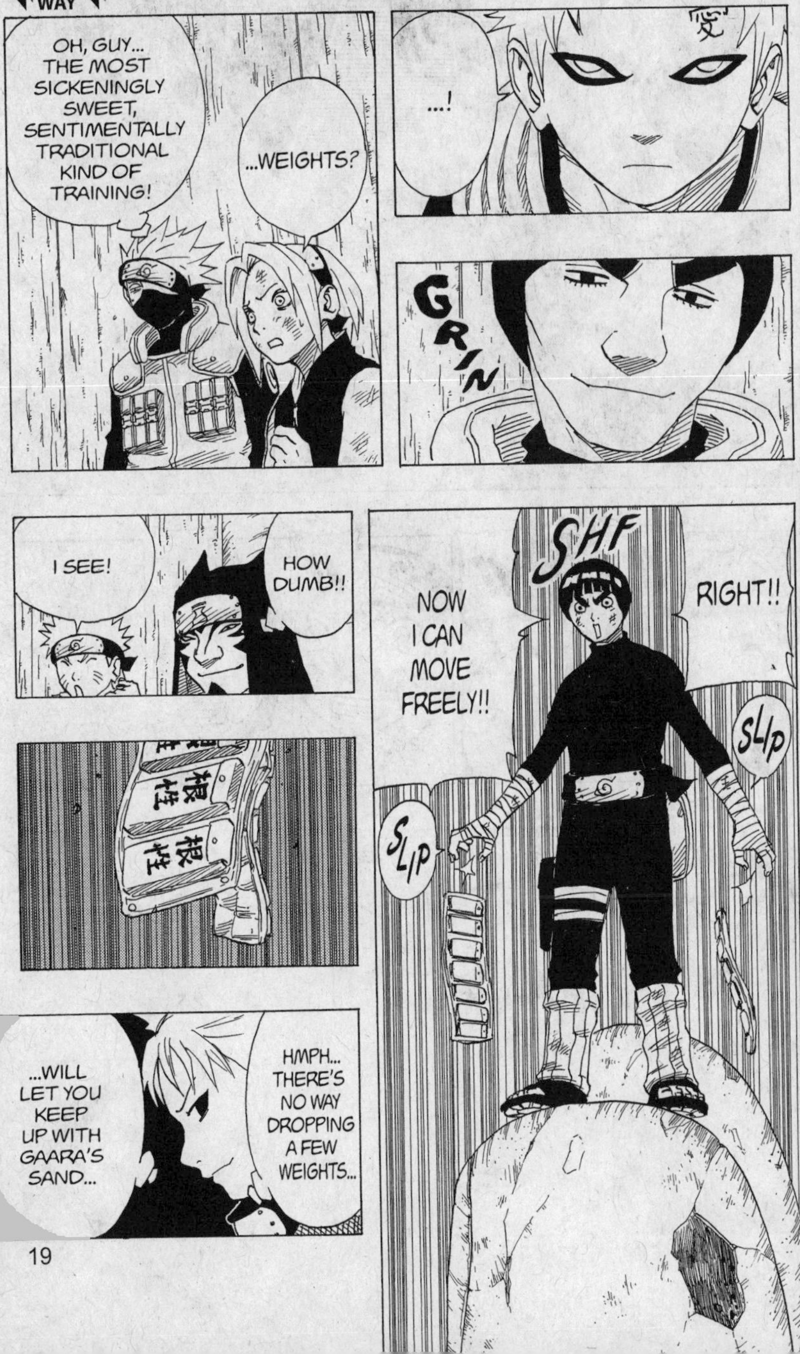
...!
GRIN
...WEIGHTS?
OH, GUY... THE MOST SICKENINGLY SWEET, SENTIMENTALLY TRADITIONAL KIND OF TRAINING!
SHF
RIGHT!!
NOW I CAN MOVE FREELY!!
SLIP
SLIP
HOW DUMB!!
I SEE!
根性
根性
HMPH... THERE'S NO WAY DROPPING A FEW WEIGHTS...
...WILL LET YOU KEEP UP WITH GAARA'S SAND...

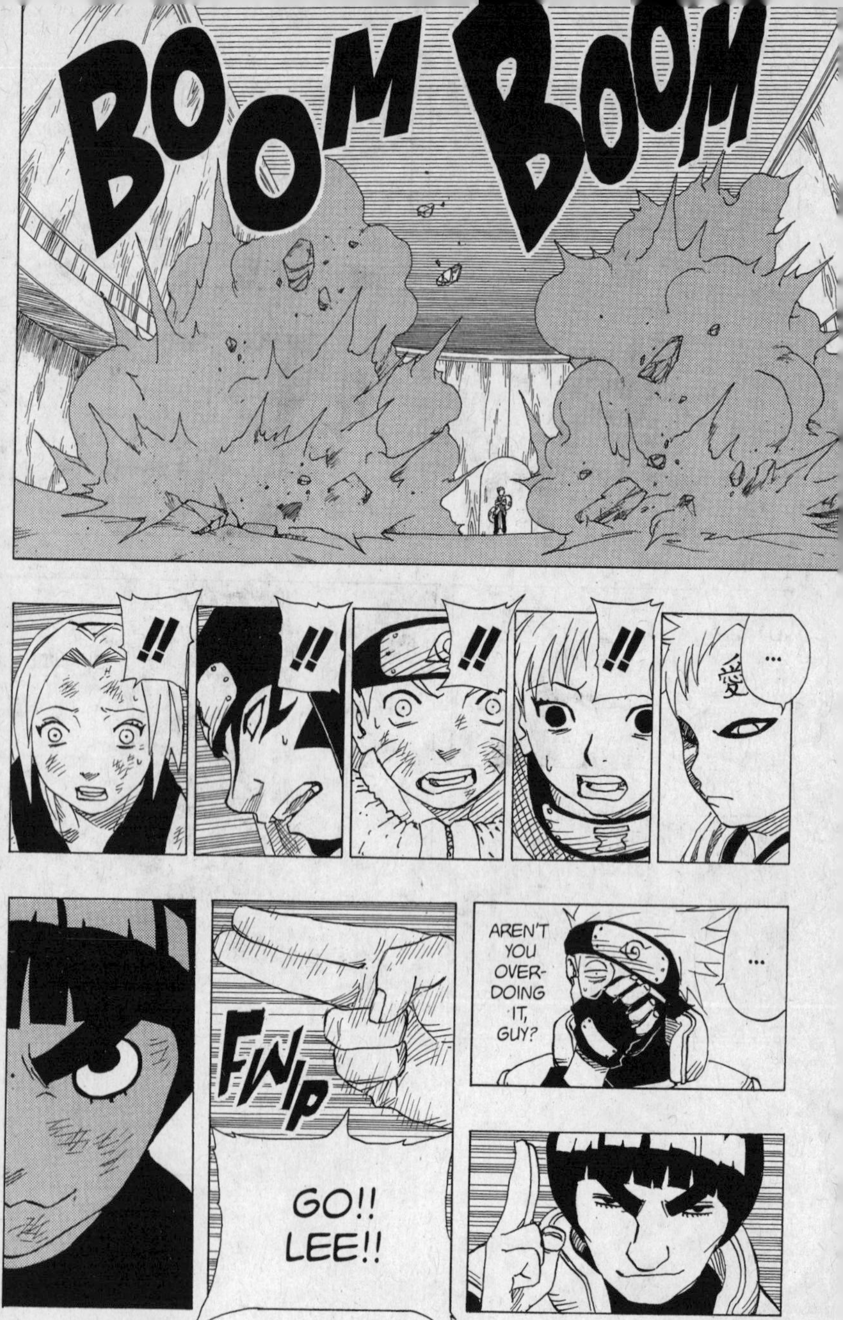
BOOM
BOOM
...
!!
!!
!!
!!
...
AREN'T YOU OVER-DOING IT, GUY?
FWIP
GO!! LEE!!

READ THIS WAY

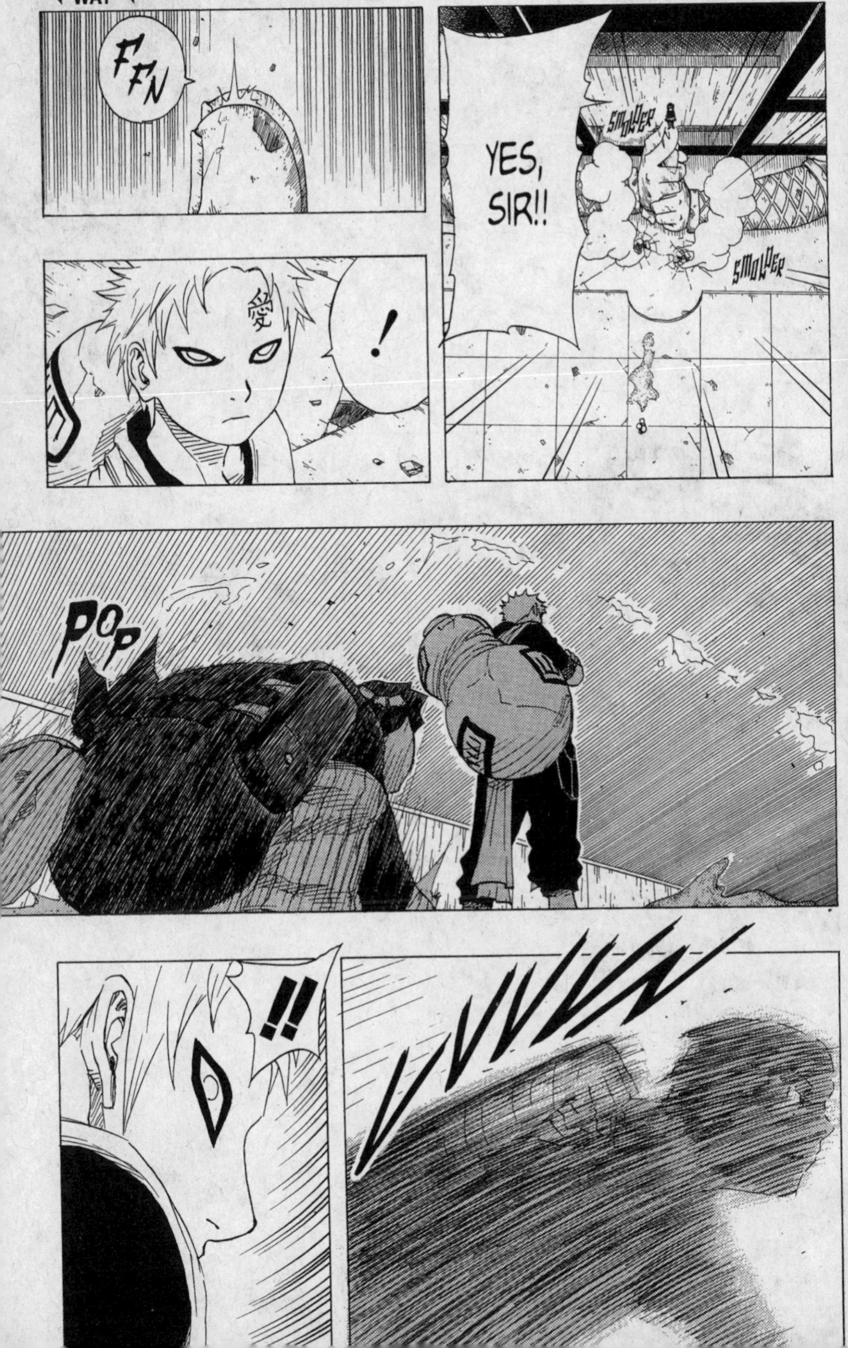
YES, SIR!!
SMOLDER
SMOLDER
FFN
!
POP
VVVVVN
!!

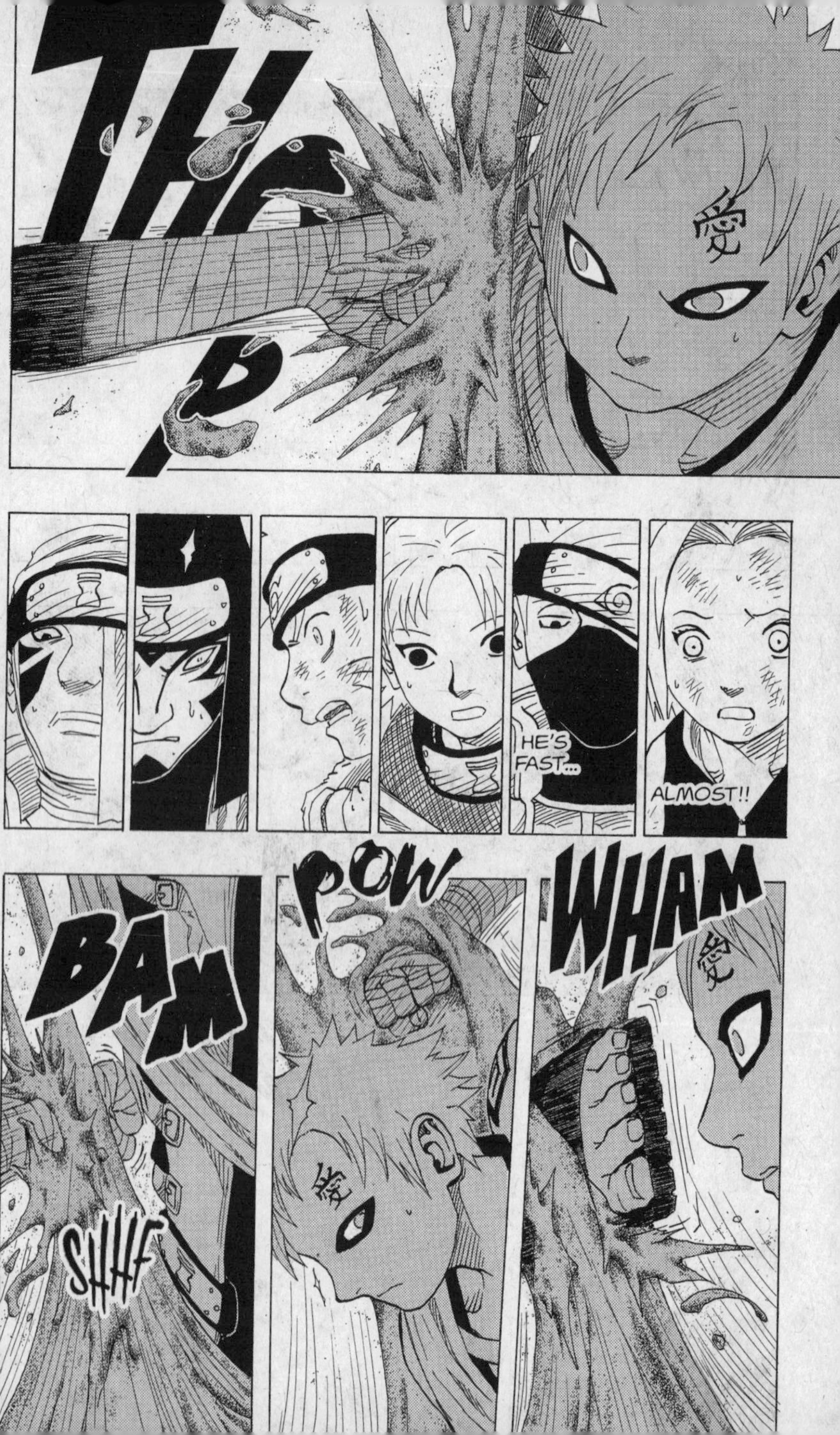
THP
ALMOST!!
HE'S FAST...
WHAM
POW
BAM
SHHF

READ THIS WAY

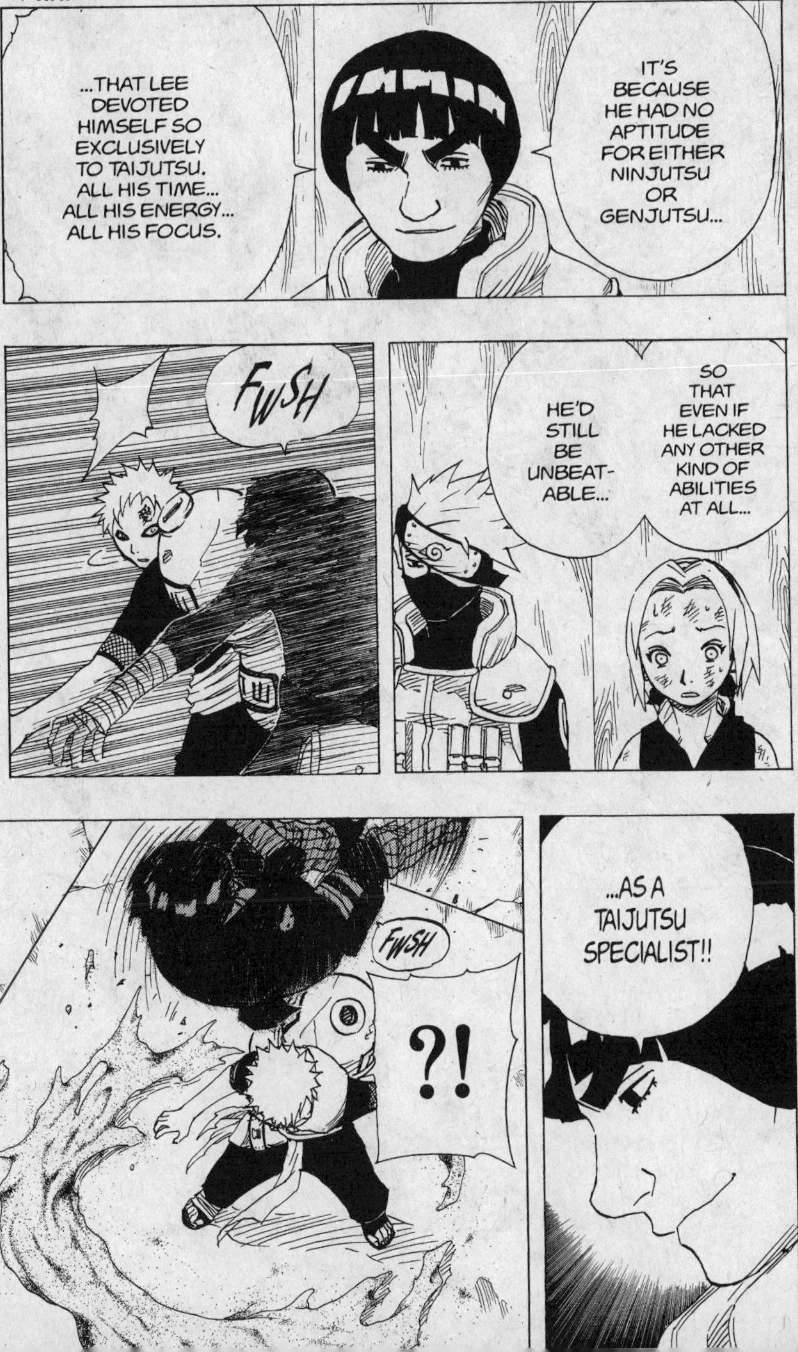
IT'S BECAUSE HE HAD NO APTITUDE FOR EITHER NINJUTSU OR GENJUTSU...
...THAT LEE DEVOTED HIMSELF SO EXCLUSIVELY TO TAIJUTSU. ALL HIS TIME... ALL HIS ENERGY... ALL HIS FOCUS.
SO THAT EVEN IF HE LACKED ANY OTHER KIND OF ABILITIES AT ALL...
HE'D STILL BE UNBEAT-ABLE...
FWSH
...AS A TAIJUTSU SPECIALIST!!
FWSH
?!

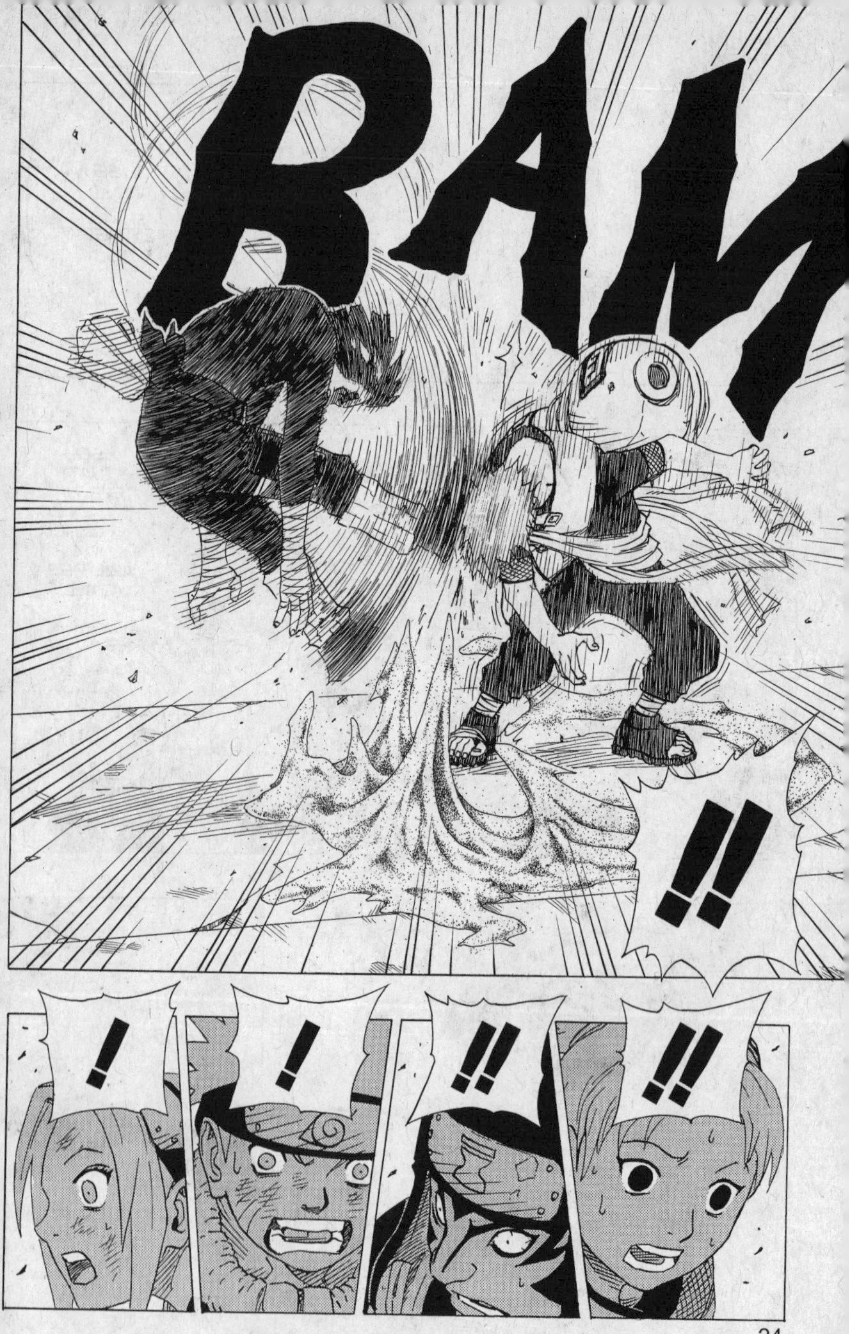
BAM
!!
!!
!!
!
!

READ THIS WAY

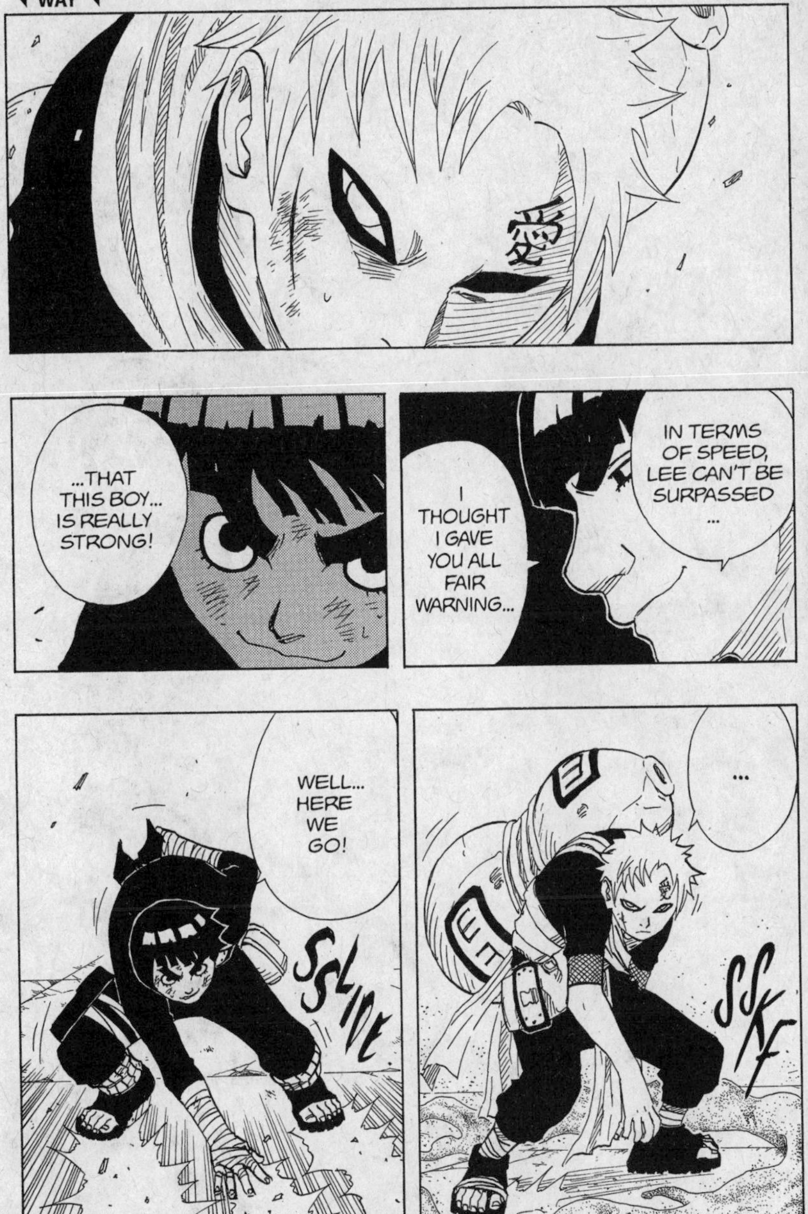

IN TERMS OF SPEED, LEE CAN'T BE SURPASSED ...
I THOUGHT I GAVE YOU ALL FAIR WARNING...
...THAT THIS BOY... IS REALLY STRONG!
...
WELL... HERE WE GO!

Number 83: The Ultimate Defense... Crumbles?!

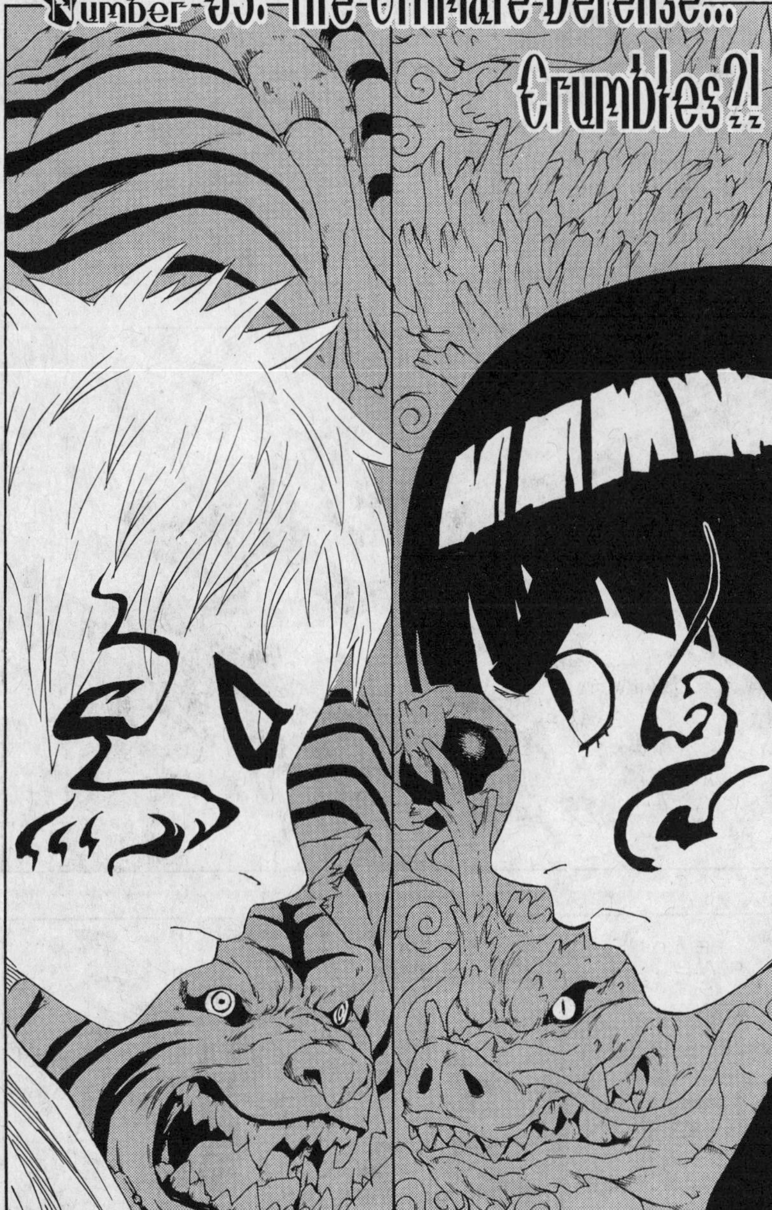

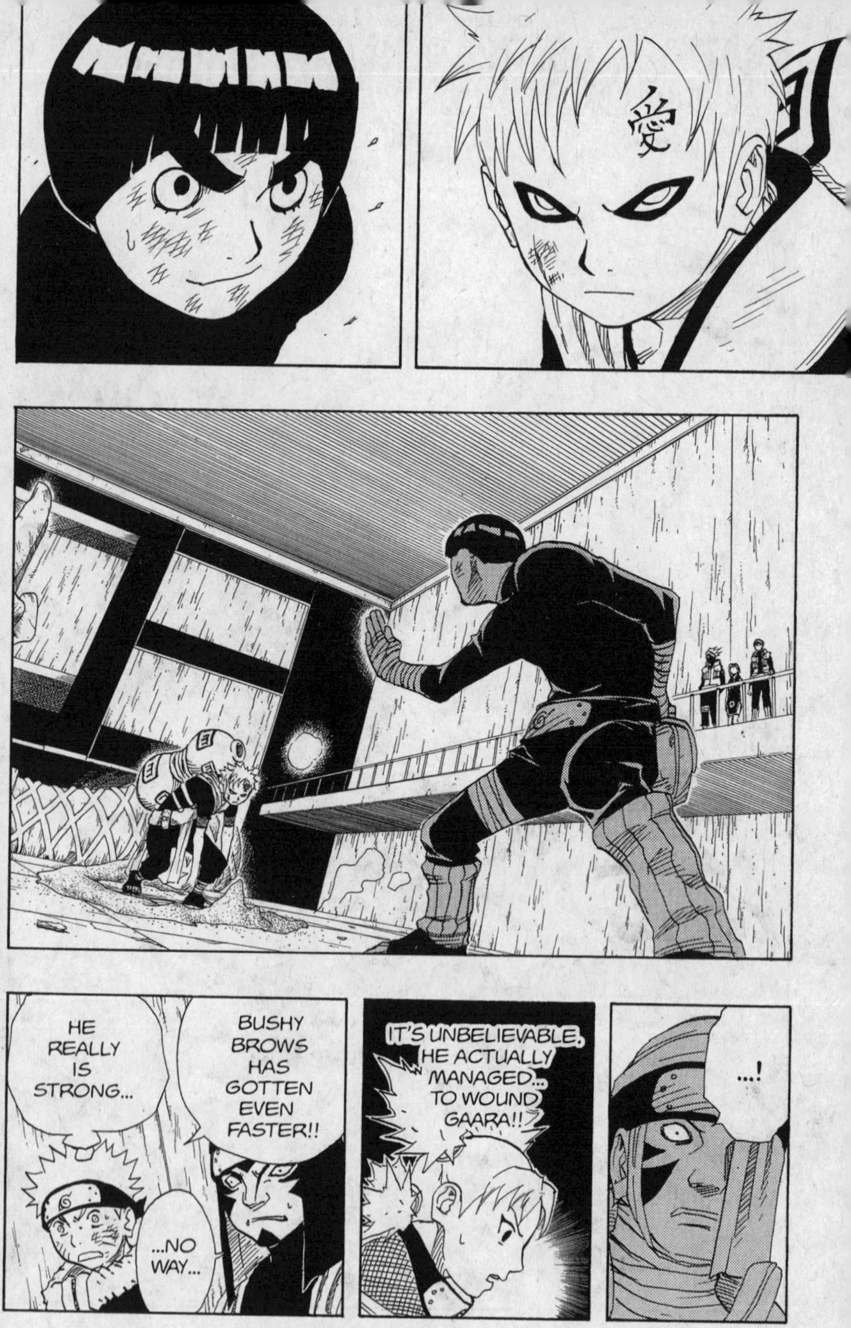
...!
IT'S UNBELIEVABLE. HE ACTUALLY MANAGED... TO WOUND GAARA!!
BUSHY BROWS HAS GOTTEN EVEN FASTER!!
HE REALLY IS STRONG...
...NO WAY...

READ THIS WAY

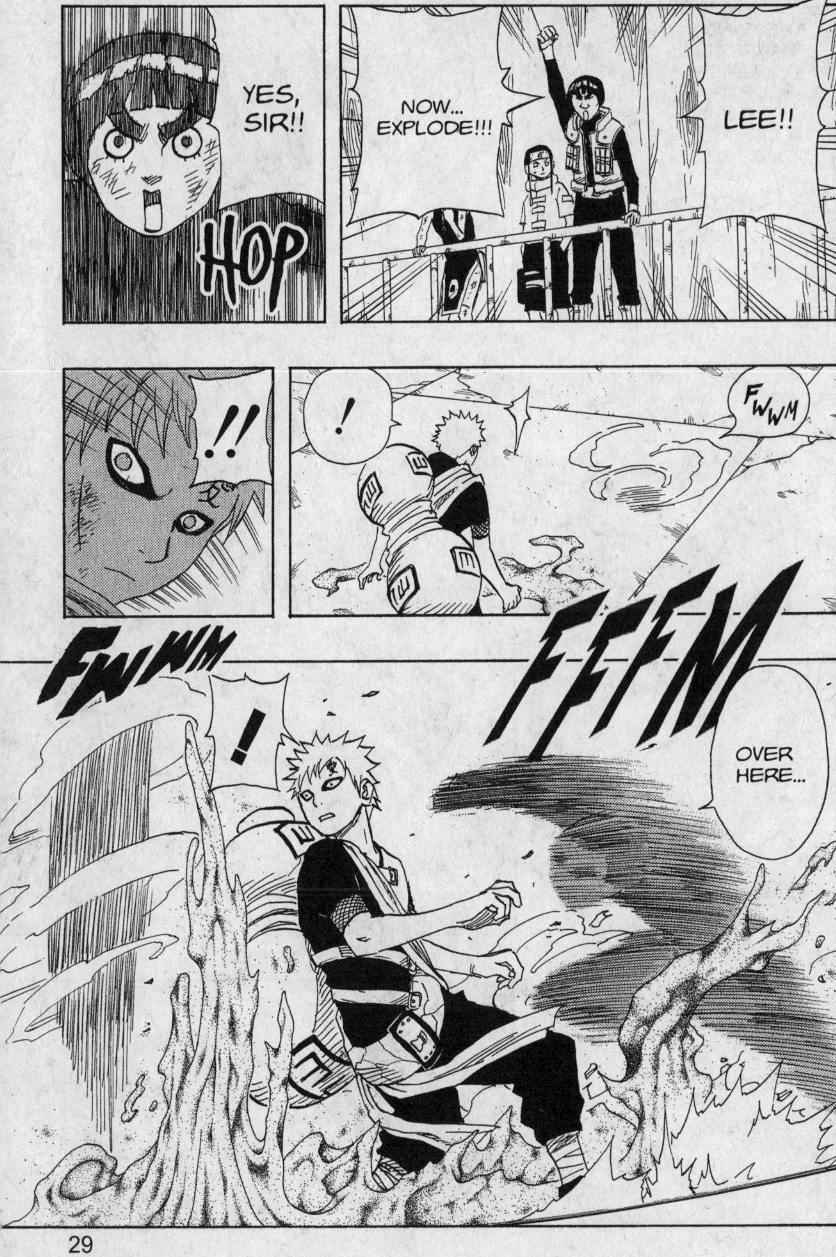
LEE!!
NOW... EXPLODE!!!
YES, SIR!!
HOP
FWWM
!
!!
OVER HERE...
FFFM
!
FWWM

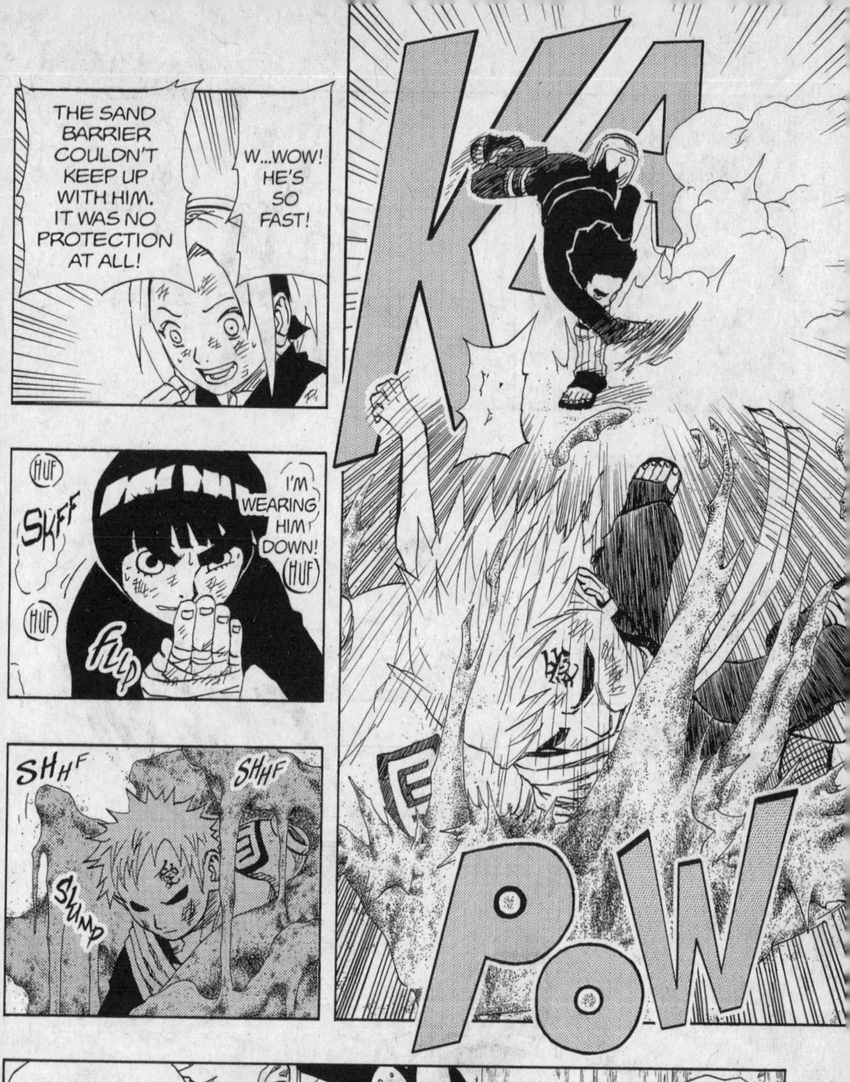
KA
POW
W...WOW! HE'S SO FAST!
THE SAND BARRIER COULDN'T KEEP UP WITH HIM. IT WAS NO PROTECTION AT ALL!
I'M WEARING HIM DOWN!
HUF
HUF
SKFF
HUF
FLLP
SHHF
SHHF
SLUMP
W... WOW...
GULP
HIS MOVES ARE SO FAST, MY EYES CAN'T EVEN TRACK THEM!

READ THIS WAY

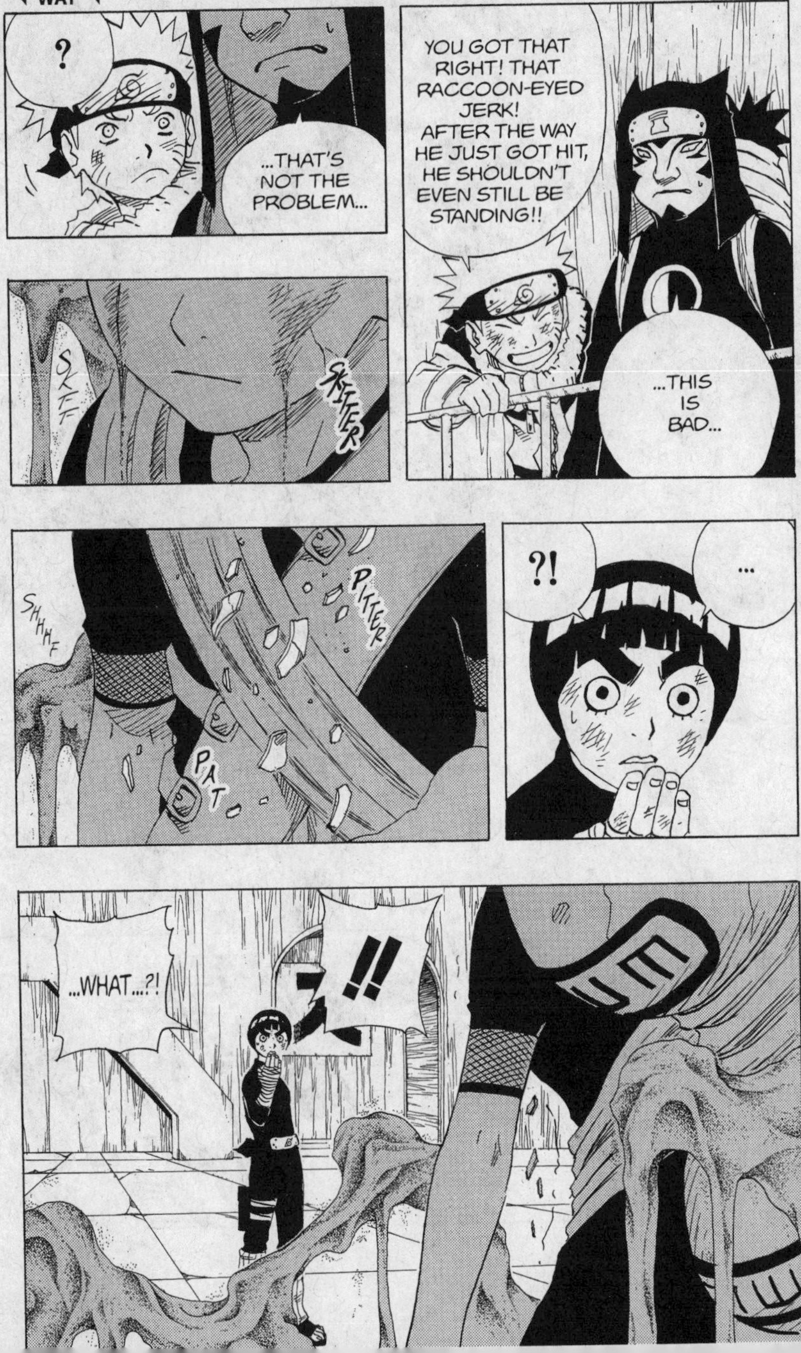
YOU GOT THAT RIGHT! THAT RACCOON-EYED JERK! AFTER THE WAY HE JUST GOT HIT, HE SHOULDN'T EVEN STILL BE STANDING!!
...THIS IS BAD...
?
...THAT'S NOT THE PROBLEM...
SKITTER
SKFF
...
?!
PITTER
SHHHF
PAT
!!
...WHAT...?!

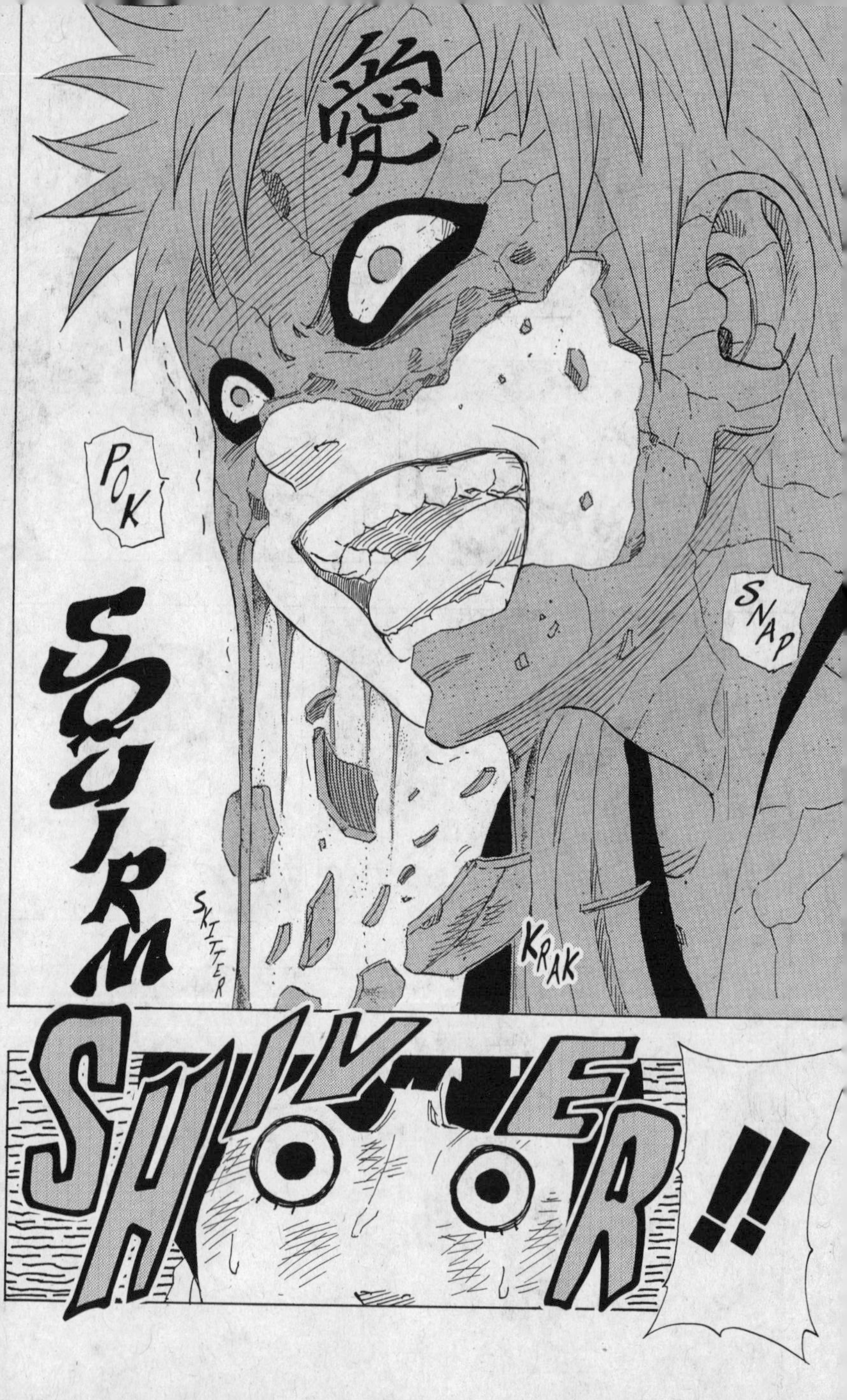

愛
SNAP
POK
SQUIRM
KRAK
SKITTER
SHIVER!!

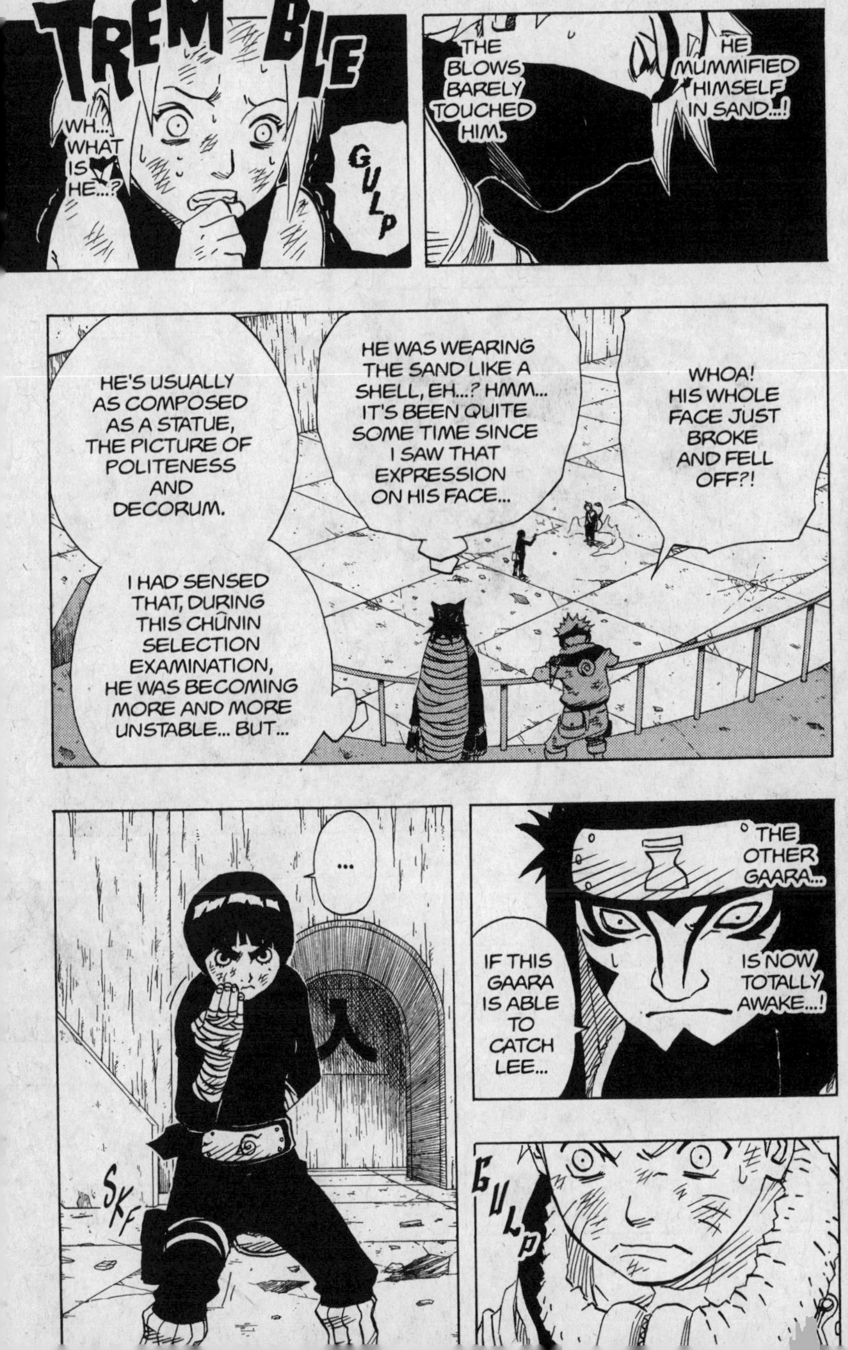
HE MUMMIFIED HIMSELF IN SAND...!
THE BLOWS BARELY TOUCHED HIM.
TREMBLE
GULP
WH... WHAT IS HE...?
WHOA! HIS WHOLE FACE JUST BROKE AND FELL OFF?!
HE WAS WEARING THE SAND LIKE A SHELL, EH...? HMM... IT'S BEEN QUITE SOME TIME SINCE I SAW THAT EXPRESSION ON HIS FACE...
HE'S USUALLY AS COMPOSED AS A STATUE, THE PICTURE OF POLITENESS AND DECORUM.
I HAD SENSED THAT, DURING THIS CHŪNIN SELECTION EXAMINATION, HE WAS BECOMING MORE AND MORE UNSTABLE... BUT...
THE OTHER GAARA...
IS NOW TOTALLY AWAKE...!
IF THIS GAARA IS ABLE TO CATCH LEE...
GULP
...
SKF

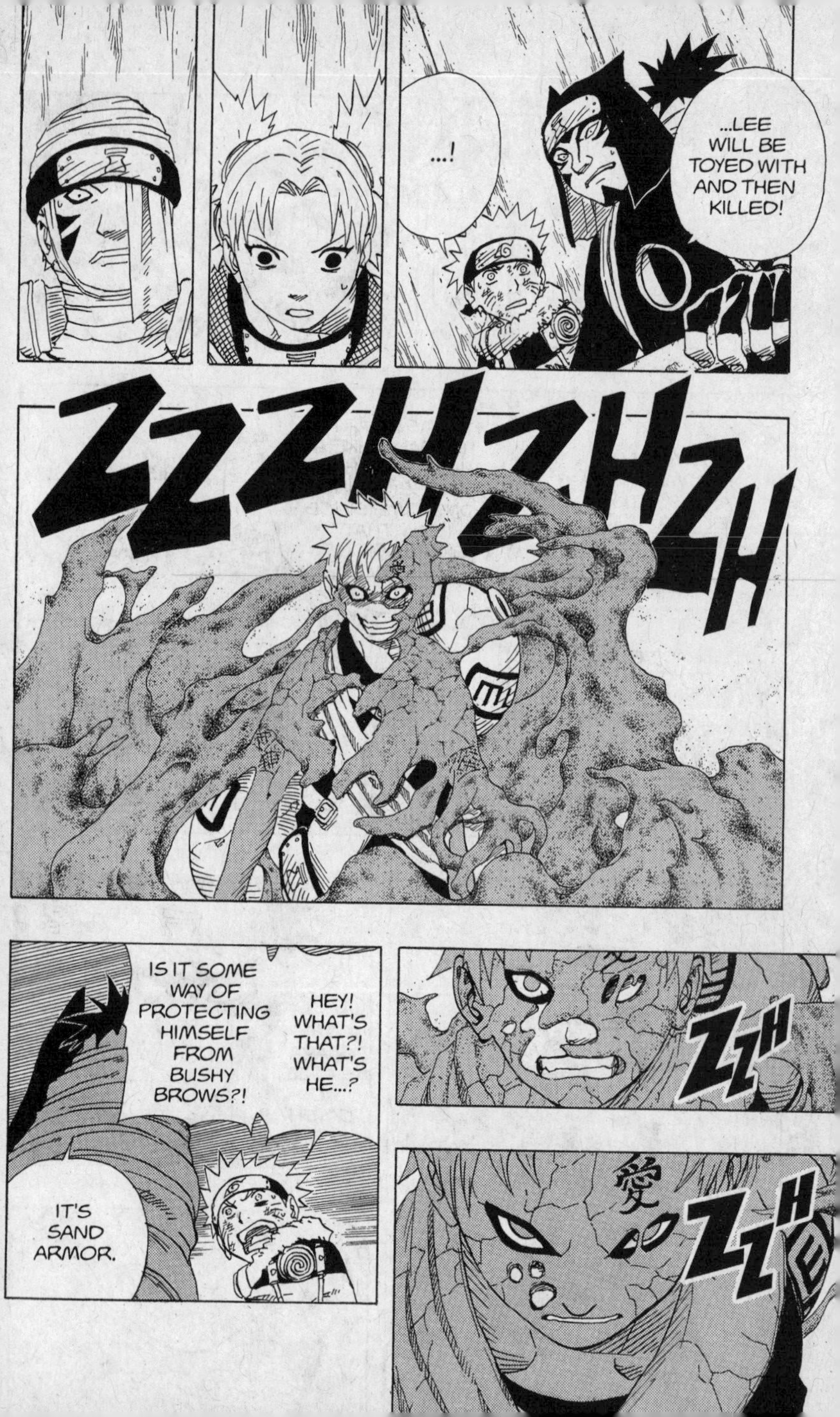
...LEE WILL BE TOYED WITH AND THEN KILLED!
...!
ZZZHZHZHZH
ZZH
ZZH
HEY! WHAT'S THAT?! WHAT'S HE...?
IS IT SOME WAY OF PROTECTING HIMSELF FROM BUSHY BROWS?!
IT'S SAND ARMOR.

READ THIS WAY

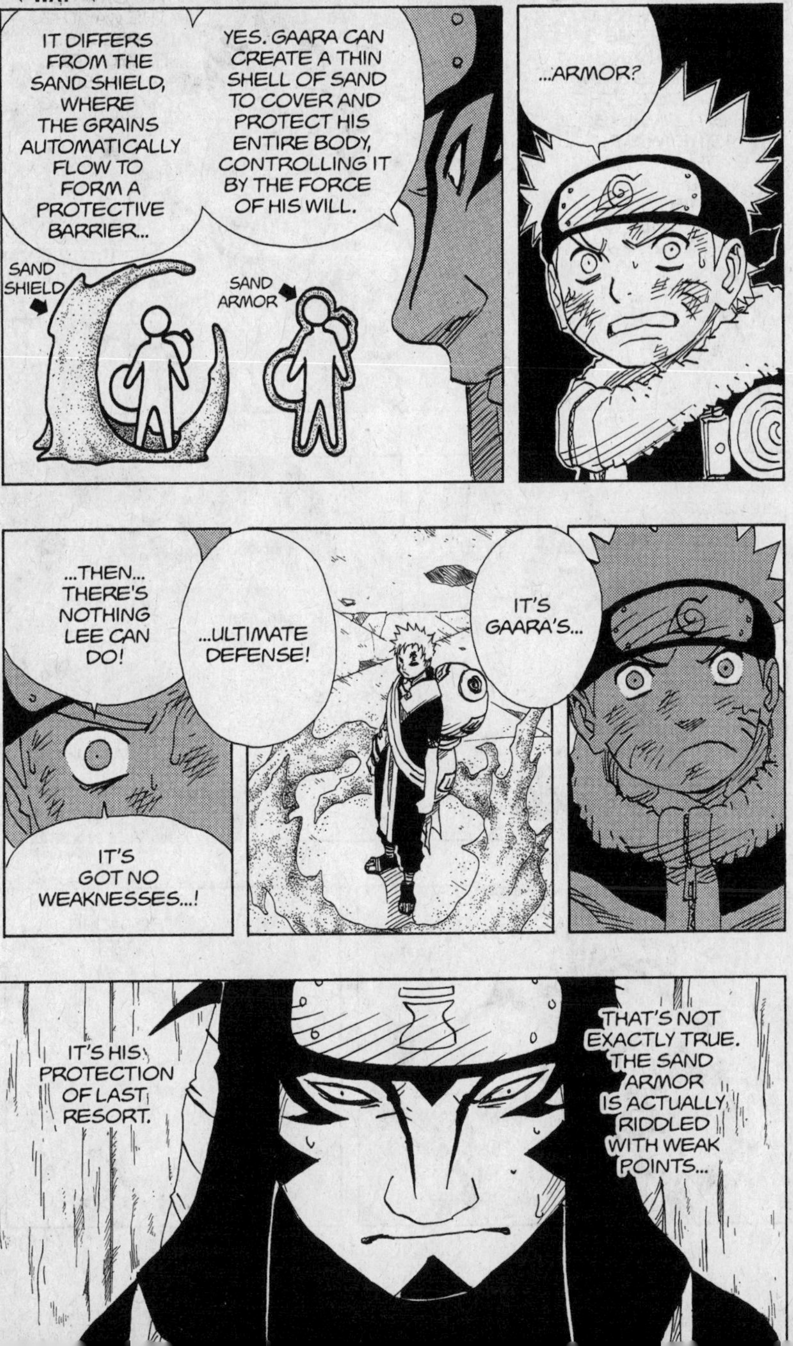
...ARMOR?
YES. GAARA CAN CREATE A THIN SHELL OF SAND TO COVER AND PROTECT HIS ENTIRE BODY, CONTROLLING IT BY THE FORCE OF HIS WILL.
IT DIFFERS FROM THE SAND SHIELD, WHERE THE GRAINS AUTOMATICALLY FLOW TO FORM A PROTECTIVE BARRIER...
SAND ARMOR
SAND SHIELD
IT'S GAARA'S...
...ULTIMATE DEFENSE!
...THEN... THERE'S NOTHING LEE CAN DO!
IT'S GOT NO WEAKNESSES...!
THAT'S NOT EXACTLY TRUE. THE SAND ARMOR IS ACTUALLY RIDDLED WITH WEAK POINTS...
IT'S HIS PROTECTION OF LAST RESORT.

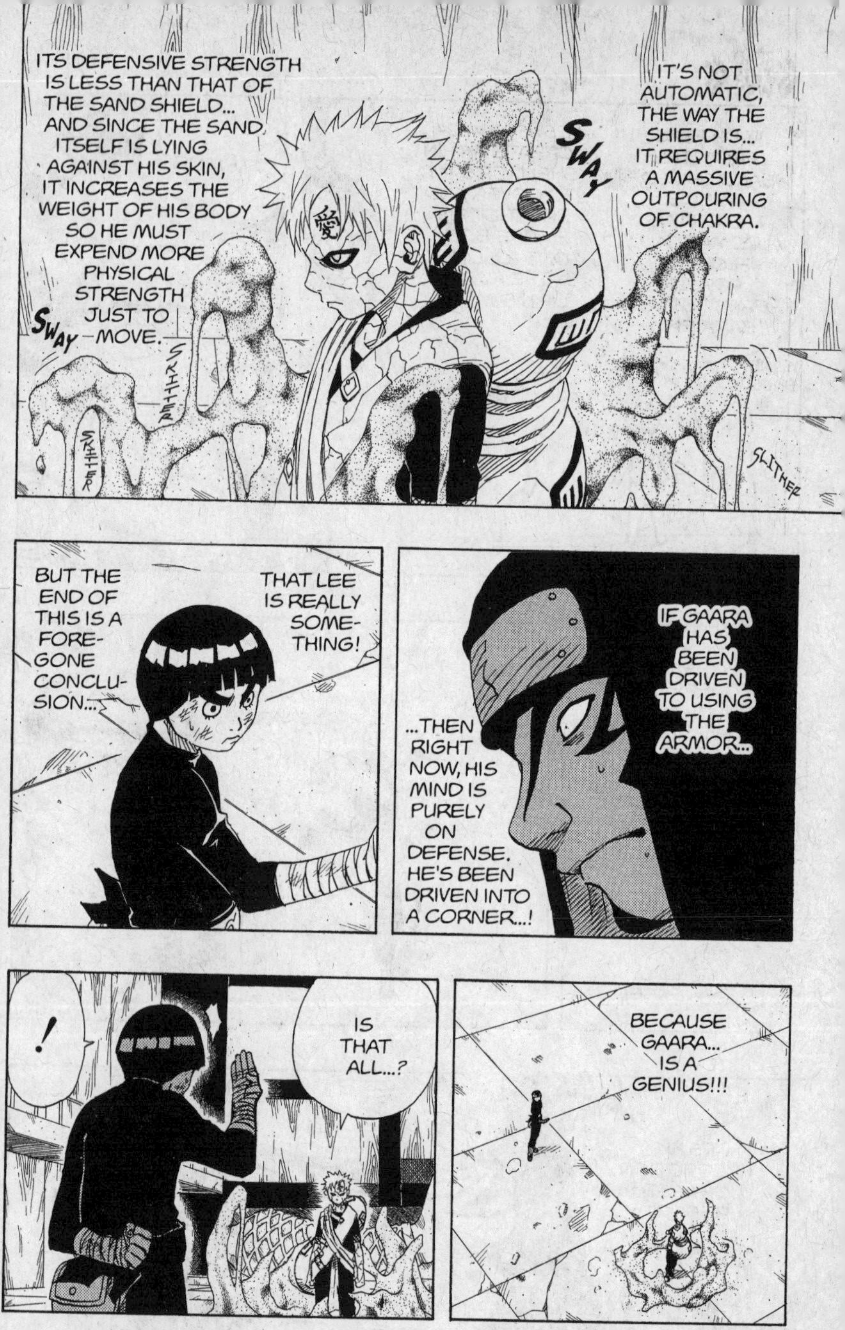
IT'S NOT AUTOMATIC, THE WAY THE SHIELD IS... IT REQUIRES A MASSIVE OUTPOURING OF CHAKRA.
SWAY
ITS DEFENSIVE STRENGTH IS LESS THAN THAT OF THE SAND SHIELD... AND SINCE THE SAND ITSELF IS LYING AGAINST HIS SKIN, IT INCREASES THE WEIGHT OF HIS BODY SO HE MUST EXPEND MORE PHYSICAL STRENGTH JUST TO MOVE.
SWAY
SKITTER
SKITTER
SLITHER
IF GAARA HAS BEEN DRIVEN TO USING THE ARMOR...
...THEN RIGHT NOW, HIS MIND IS PURELY ON DEFENSE. HE'S BEEN DRIVEN INTO A CORNER...!
THAT LEE IS REALLY SOME-THING!
BUT THE END OF THIS IS A FORE-GONE CONCLU-SION...
BECAUSE GAARA... IS A GENIUS!!!
IS THAT ALL...?
!

READ THIS WAY

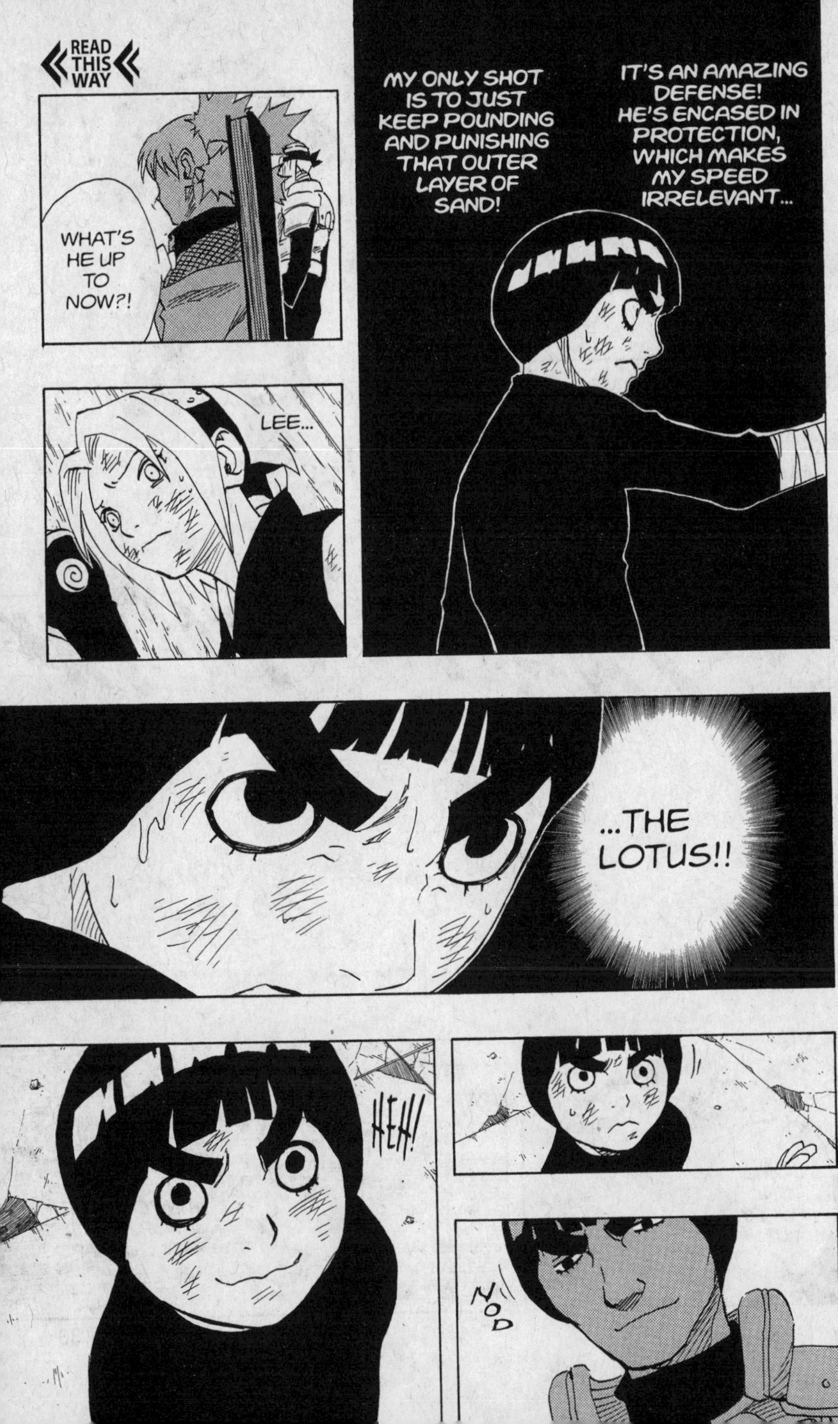

IT'S AN AMAZING DEFENSE! HE'S ENCASED IN PROTECTION, WHICH MAKES MY SPEED IRRELEVANT...
MY ONLY SHOT IS TO JUST KEEP POUNDING AND PUNISHING THAT OUTER LAYER OF SAND!
WHAT'S HE UP TO NOW?!
LEE...
...THE LOTUS!!
NOD
HEH!

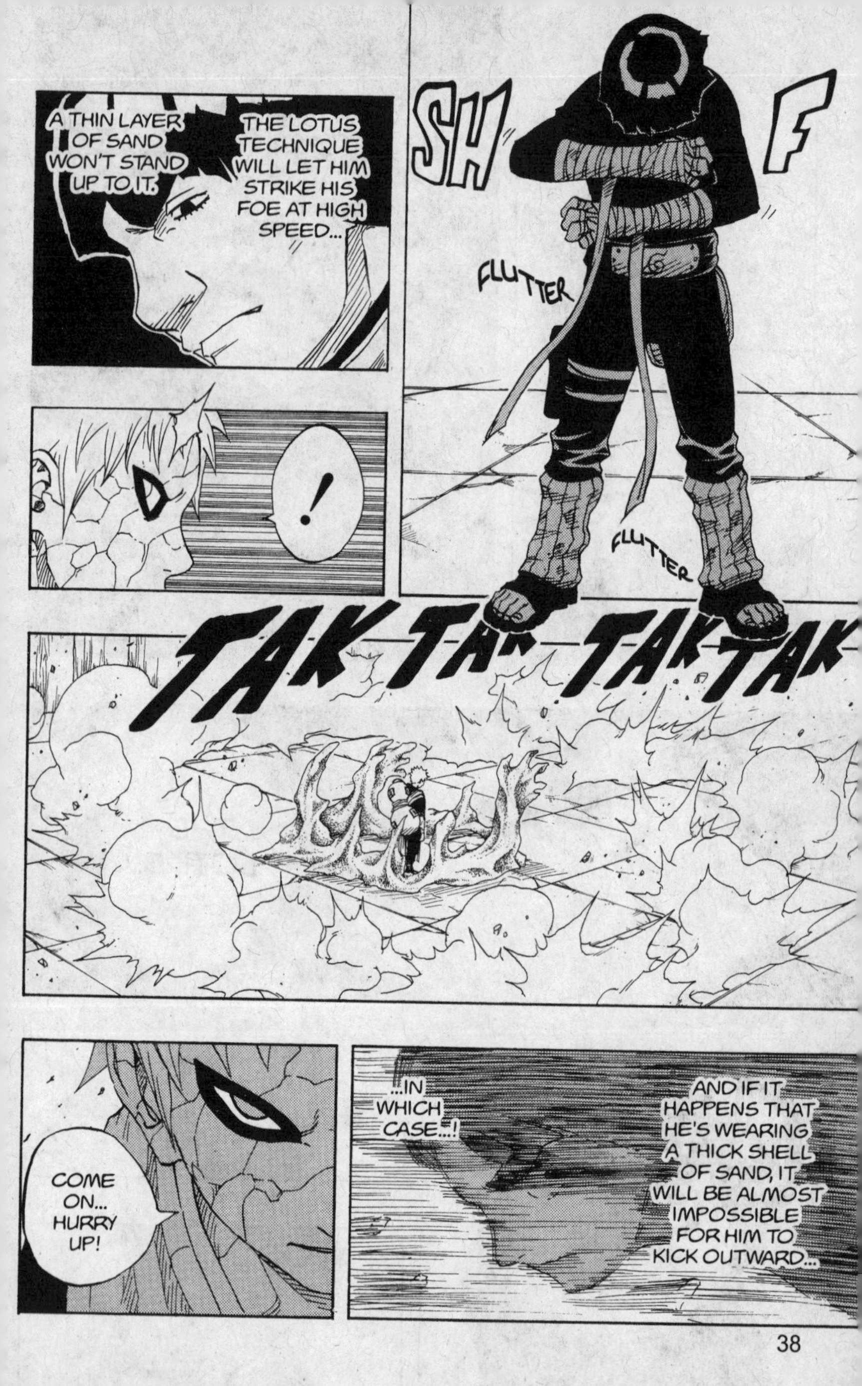
SH F
FLUTTER
FLUTTER
THE LOTUS TECHNIQUE WILL LET HIM STRIKE HIS FOE AT HIGH SPEED...
A THIN LAYER OF SAND WON'T STAND UP TO IT.
!
TAK TAK TAK TAK
AND IF IT HAPPENS THAT HE'S WEARING A THICK SHELL OF SAND, IT WILL BE ALMOST IMPOSSIBLE FOR HIM TO KICK OUTWARD...
...IN WHICH CASE...!
COME ON... HURRY UP!

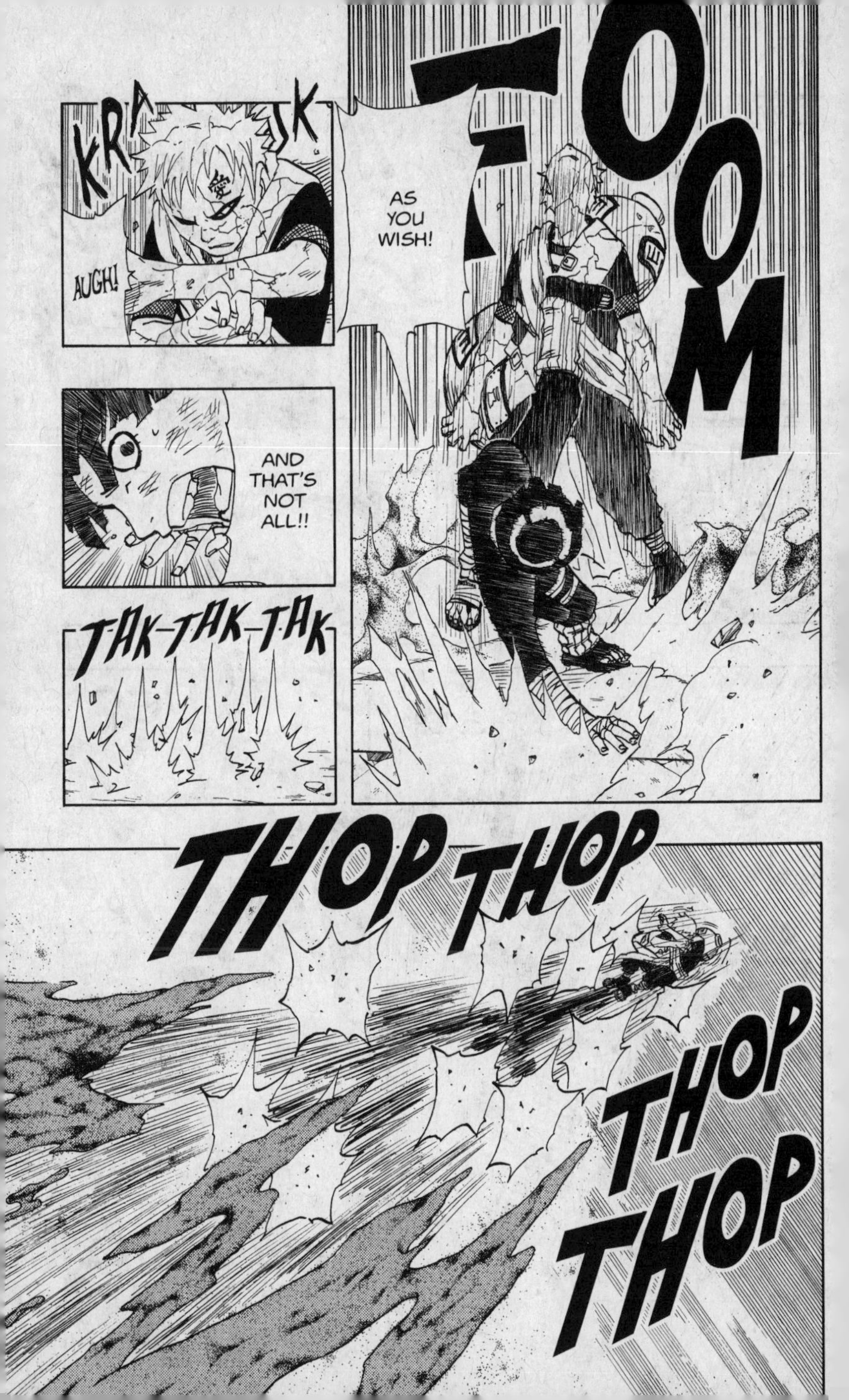
ZOOM
AS YOU WISH!
KRASK
AUGH!
AND THAT'S NOT ALL!!
TAK-TAK-TAK
THOP THOP
THOP THOP

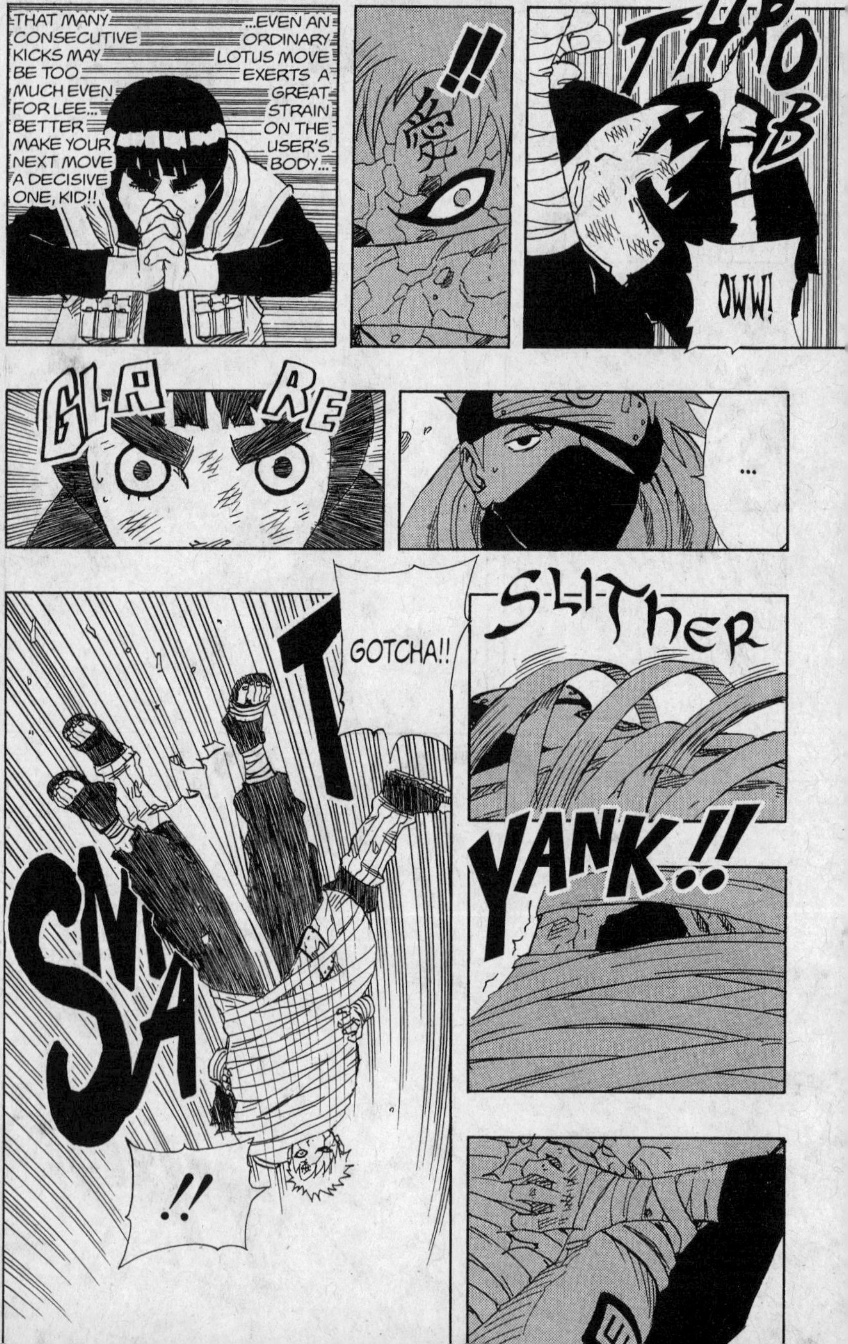
THROB
OWW!
!!
...EVEN AN ORDINARY LOTUS MOVE EXERTS A GREAT STRAIN ON THE USER'S BODY...
THAT MANY CONSECUTIVE KICKS MAY BE TOO MUCH EVEN FOR LEE... BETTER MAKE YOUR NEXT MOVE A DECISIVE ONE, KID!!
...
GLARE
SLITHER
YANK!!
GOTCHA!!
T
SMA
!!

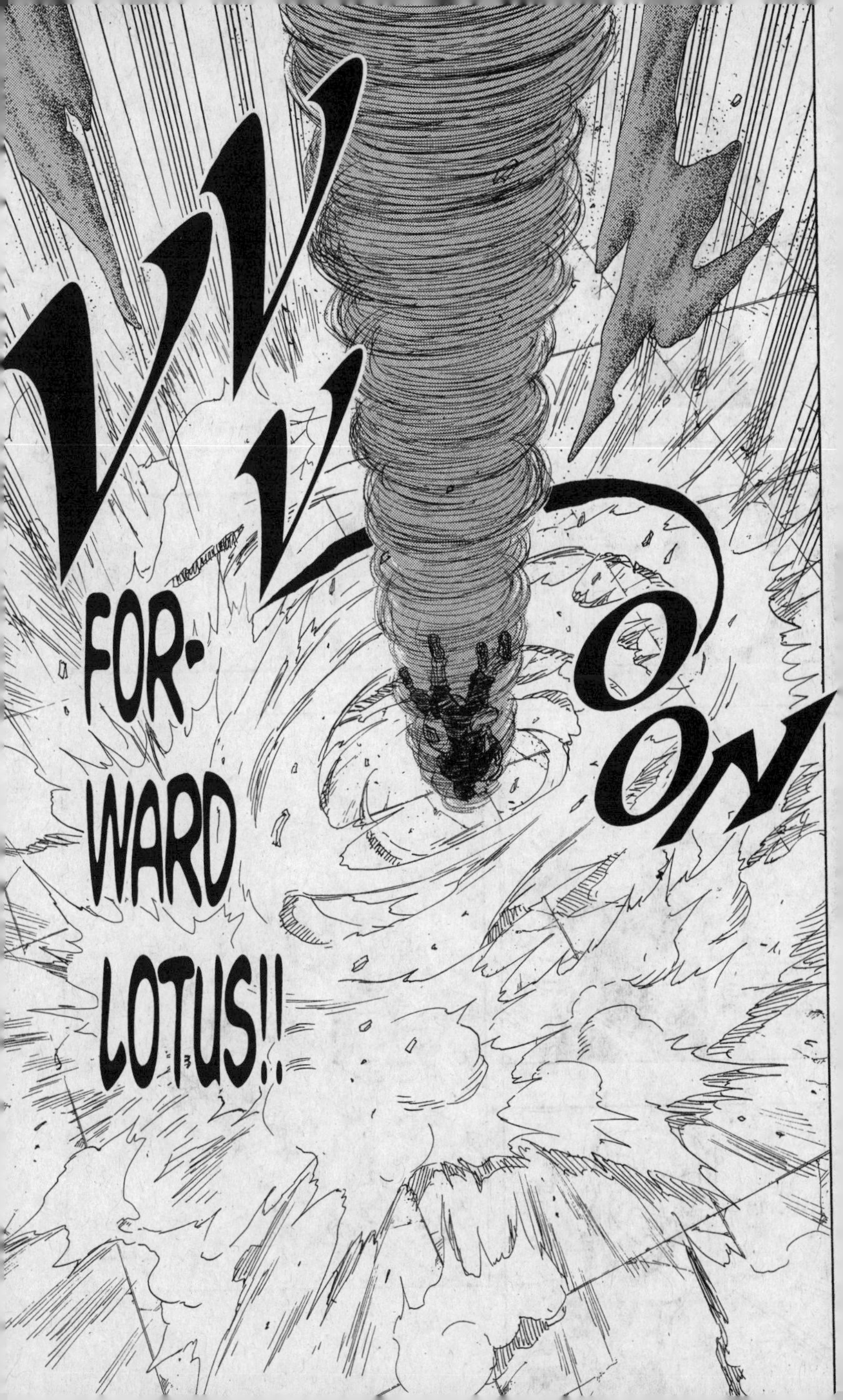
FOR-WARD LOTUS!!

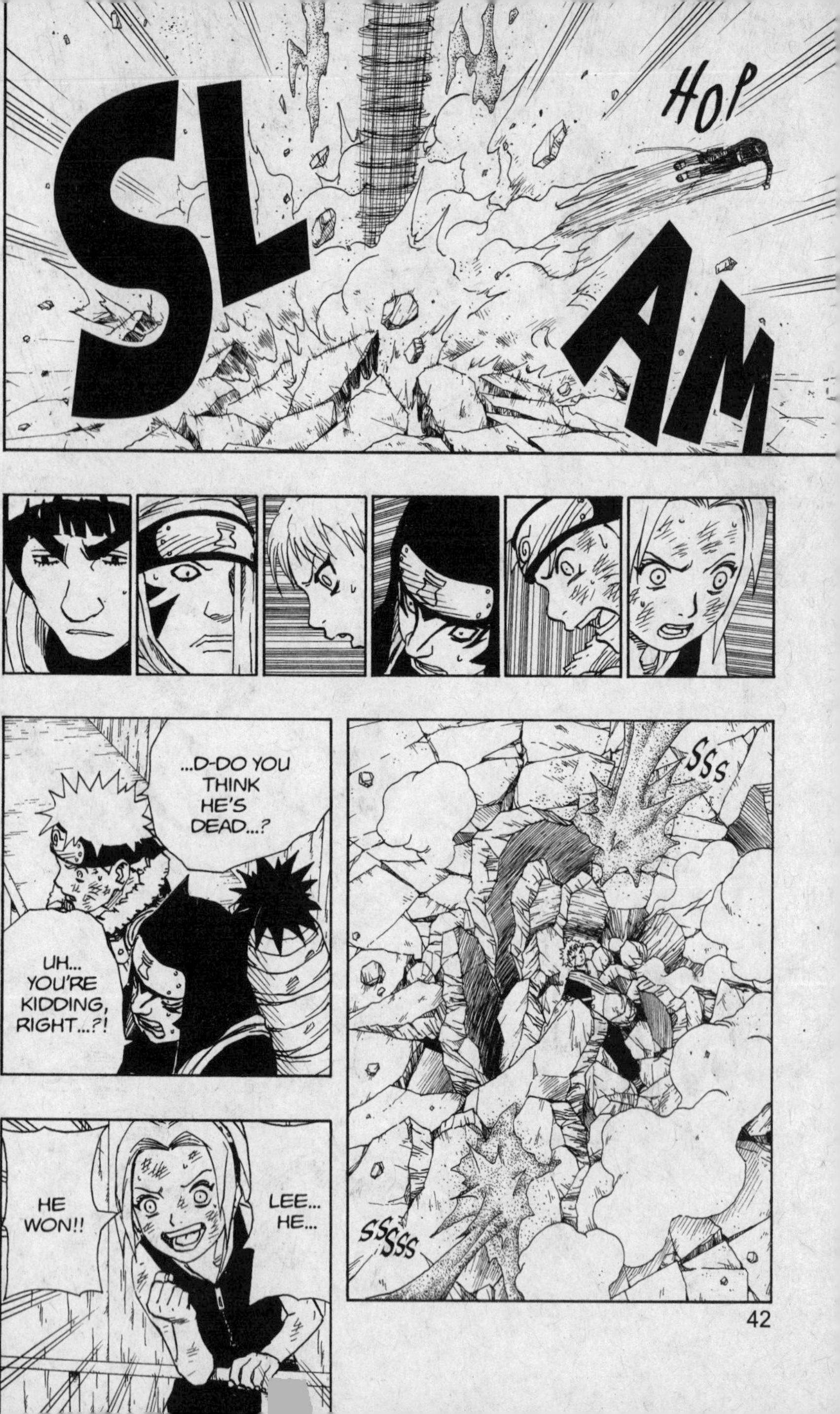
HOP
SLAM
SSS
SSSSS
...D-DO YOU THINK HE'S DEAD...?
UH... YOU'RE KIDDING, RIGHT...?!
LEE... HE...
HE WON!!

READ THIS WAY

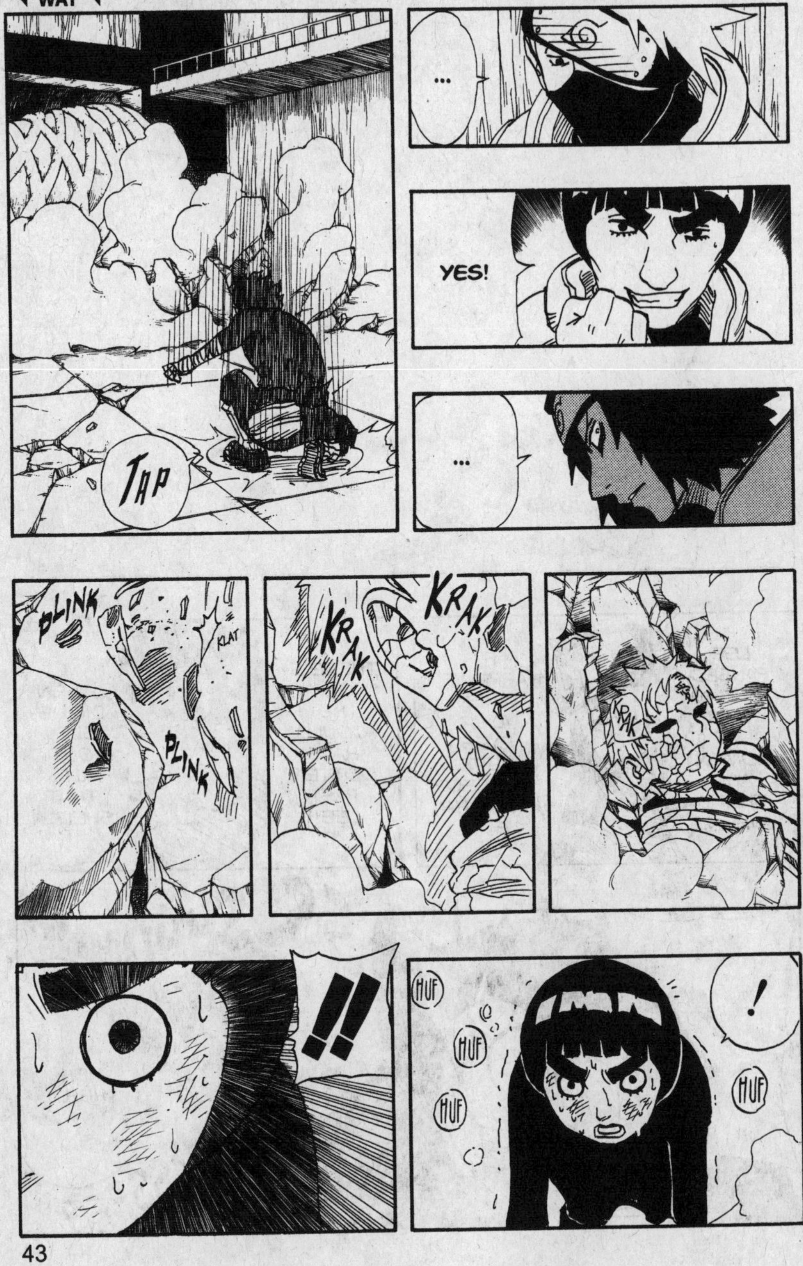
...
YES!
...
TAP
KRAK
KRAK
KRAK
PLINK
KLAT
PLINK
HUF
HUF
HUF
!
HUF
!!

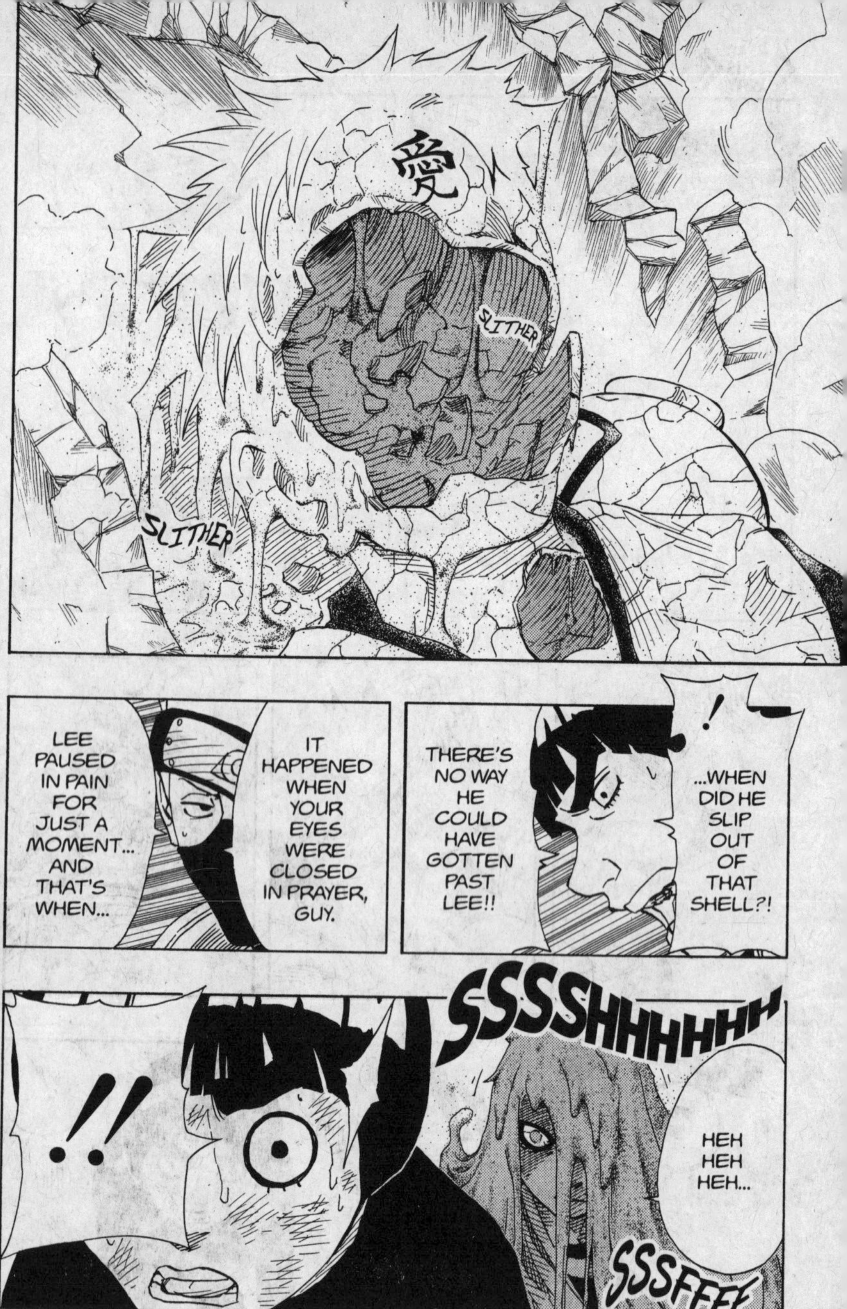

愛
SLITHER
SLITHER
!
...WHEN DID HE SLIP OUT OF THAT SHELL?!
THERE'S NO WAY HE COULD HAVE GOTTEN PAST LEE!!
IT HAPPENED WHEN YOUR EYES WERE CLOSED IN PRAYER, GUY.
LEE PAUSED IN PAIN FOR JUST A MOMENT... AND THAT'S WHEN...
SSSSHHHHHHH
HEH HEH HEH...
SSSFFFF
!!

Number 84: The Genius of Hard Work...!!

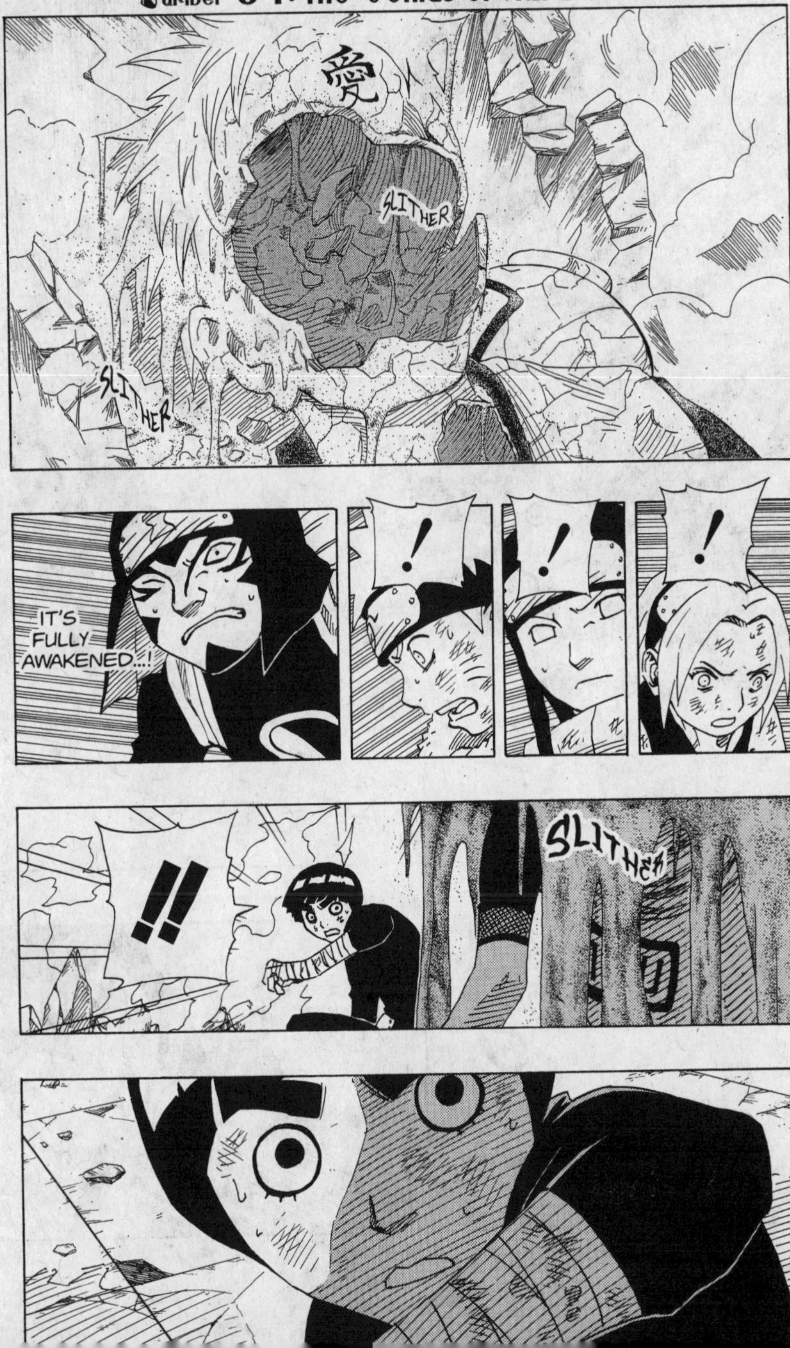
SLITHER
SLITHER
!
!
!
IT'S FULLY AWAKENED...!
SLITHER
!!

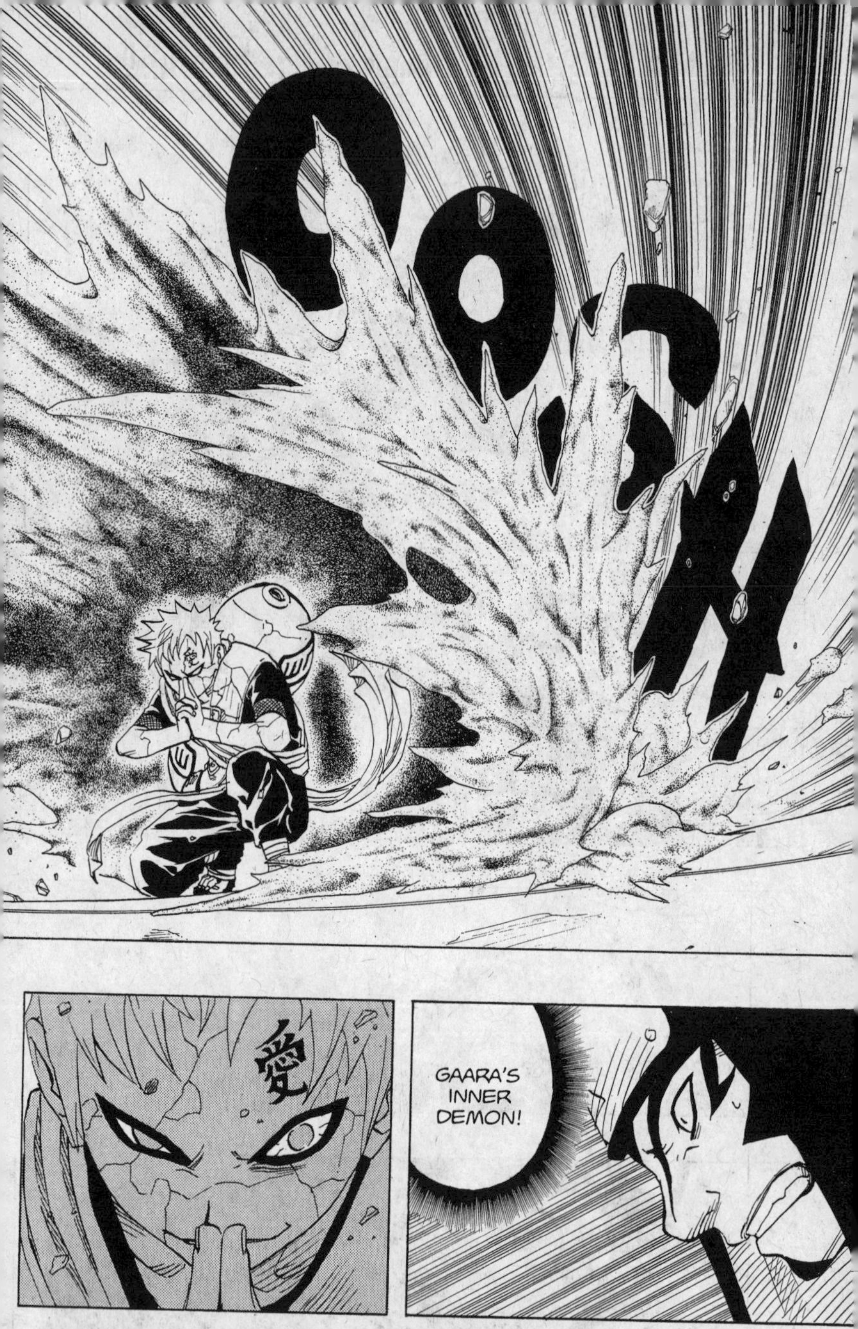
GAARA'S INNER DEMON!

Number 84: The Genius of Hard Work!!

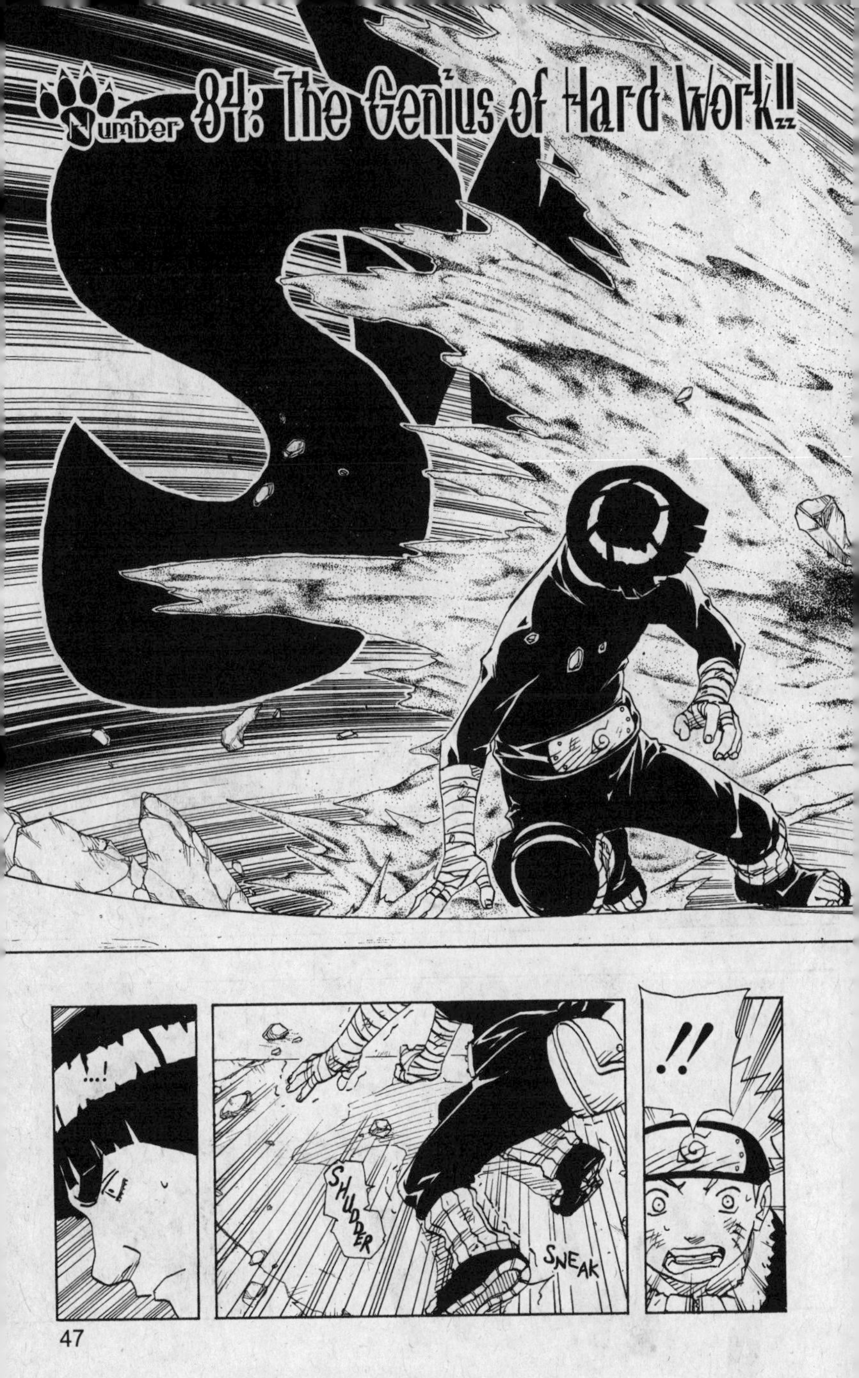
!!
SHUDDER
SNEAK
...!

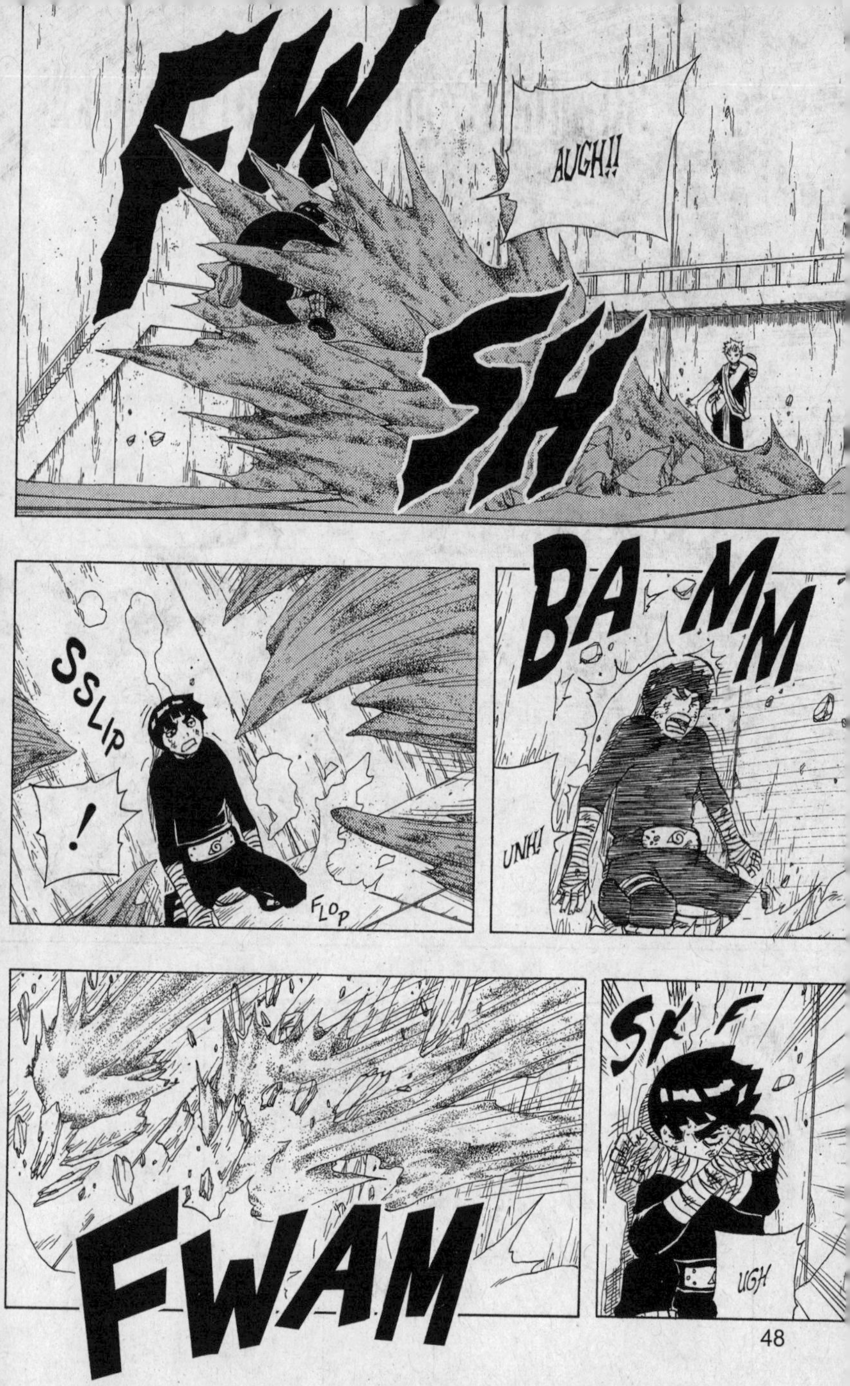

AUGH!!
FW
SH
BAMM
UNH!
SSLIP
!
FLOP
SK F
UGH
FWAM

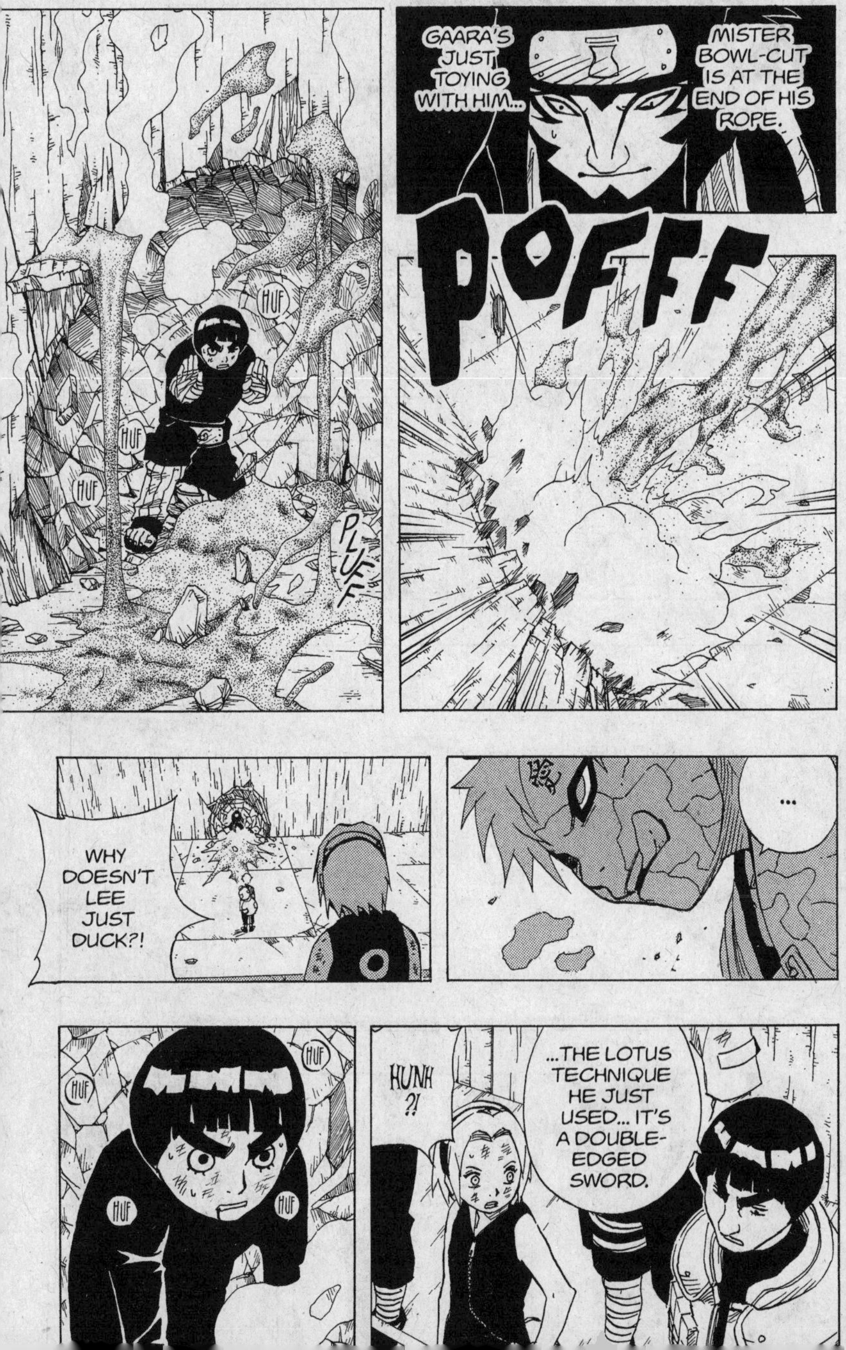
MISTER BOWL-CUT IS AT THE END OF HIS ROPE.
GAARA'S JUST TOYING WITH HIM...
POFFF
HUF
HUF
HUF
PLUFF
...
WHY DOESN'T LEE JUST DUCK?!
...THE LOTUS TECHNIQUE HE JUST USED... IT'S A DOUBLE-EDGED SWORD.
HUNH ?!
HUF
HUF
HUF
HUF

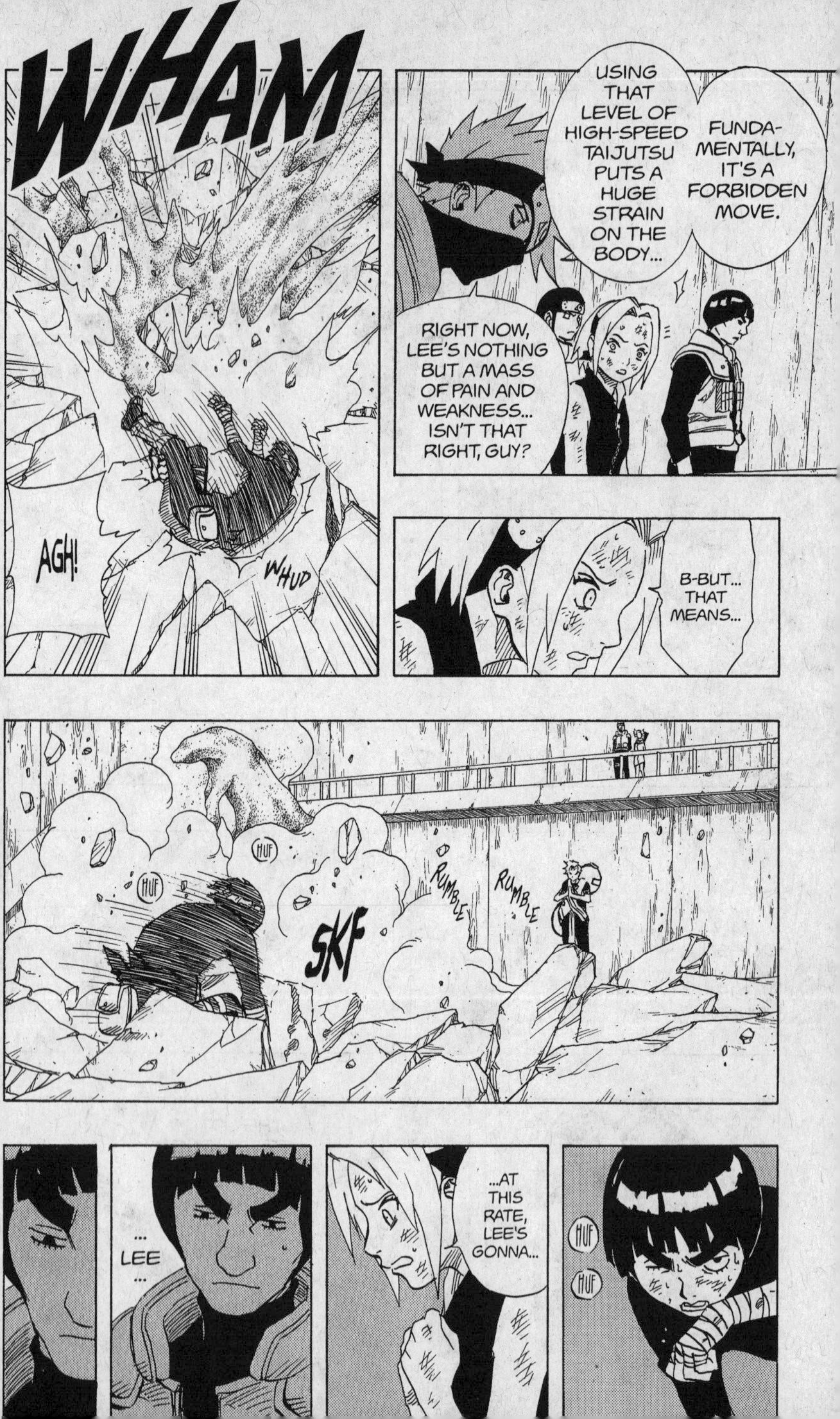
USING THAT LEVEL OF HIGH-SPEED TAIJUTSU PUTS A HUGE STRAIN ON THE BODY...
FUNDAMENTALLY, IT'S A FORBIDDEN MOVE.
RIGHT NOW, LEE'S NOTHING BUT A MASS OF PAIN AND WEAKNESS... ISN'T THAT RIGHT, GUY?
B-BUT... THAT MEANS...
WHAM
WHUD
AGH!
RUMBLE
RUMBLE
HUF
SKF
HUF
HUF
HUF
...AT THIS RATE, LEE'S GONNA...
... LEE ...

READ THIS WAY

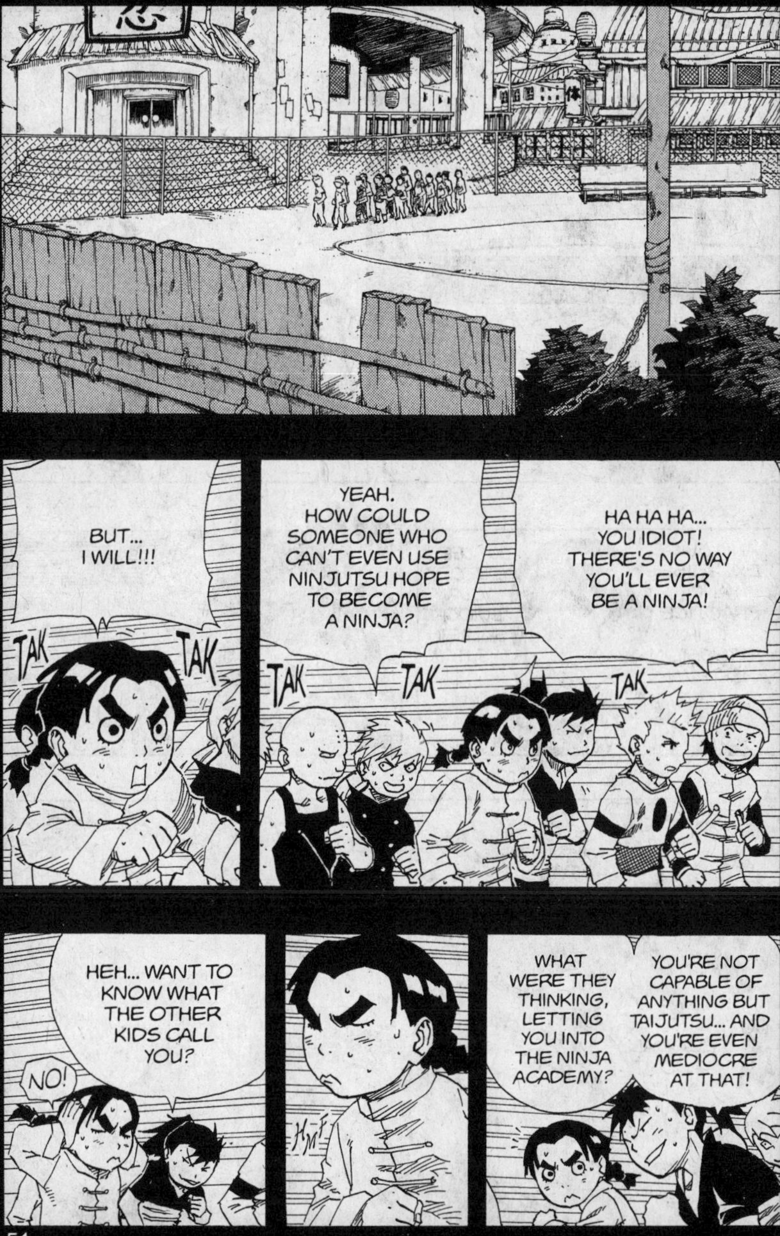

HA HA HA... YOU IDIOT! THERE'S NO WAY YOU'LL EVER BE A NINJA!
TAK
YEAH. HOW COULD SOMEONE WHO CAN'T EVEN USE NINJUTSU HOPE TO BECOME A NINJA?
TAK
TAK
BUT... I WILL!!!
TAK
TAK
YOU'RE NOT CAPABLE OF ANYTHING BUT TAIJUTSU... AND YOU'RE EVEN MEDIOCRE AT THAT!
WHAT WERE THEY THINKING, LETTING YOU INTO THE NINJA ACADEMY?
HMF
HEH... WANT TO KNOW WHAT THE OTHER KIDS CALL YOU?
NO!

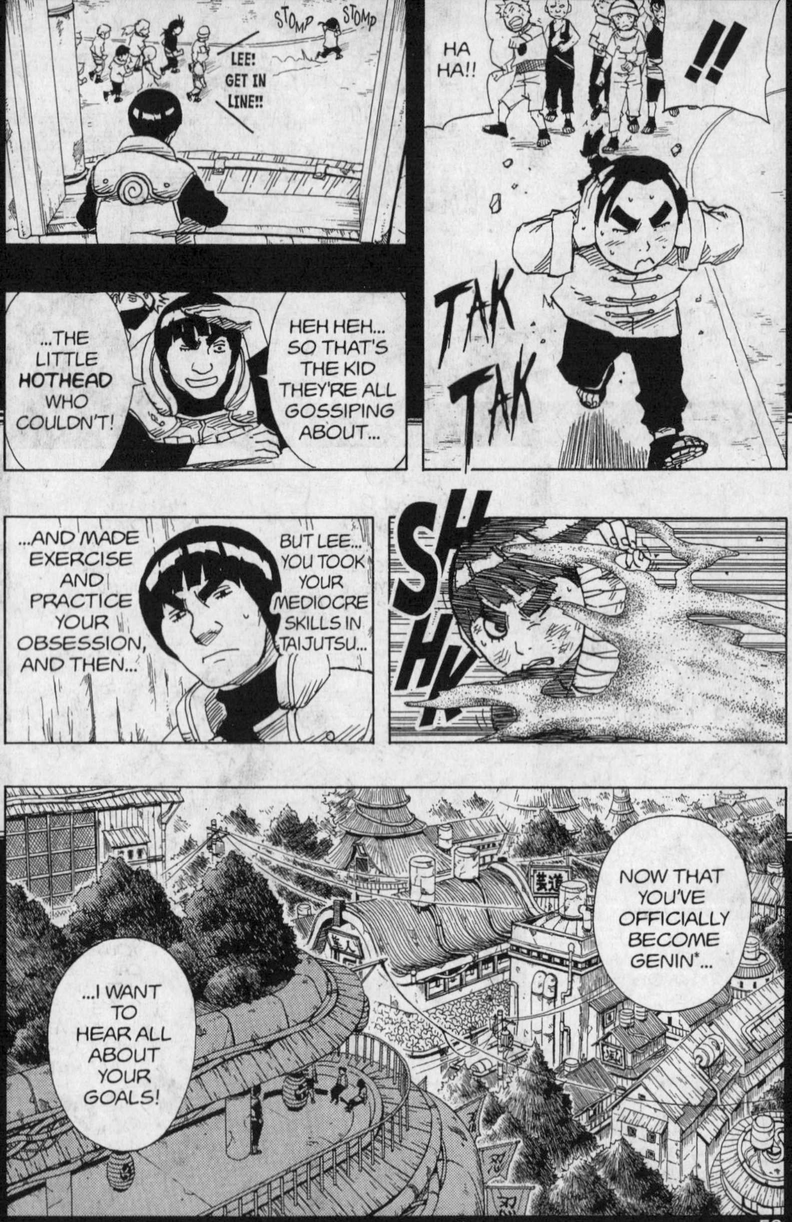
HA HA!!
!!
TAK TAK
STOMP STOMP
LEE! GET IN LINE!!
HEH HEH... SO THAT'S THE KID THEY'RE ALL GOSSIPING ABOUT...
...THE LITTLE **HOTHEAD** WHO COULDN'T!
SHHK
BUT LEE... YOU TOOK YOUR MEDIOCRE SKILLS IN TAIJUTSU...
...AND MADE EXERCISE AND PRACTICE YOUR OBSESSION, AND THEN...
NOW THAT YOU'VE OFFICIALLY BECOME GENIN*...
...I WANT TO HEAR ALL ABOUT YOUR GOALS!

*GENIN = JUNIOR NINJA

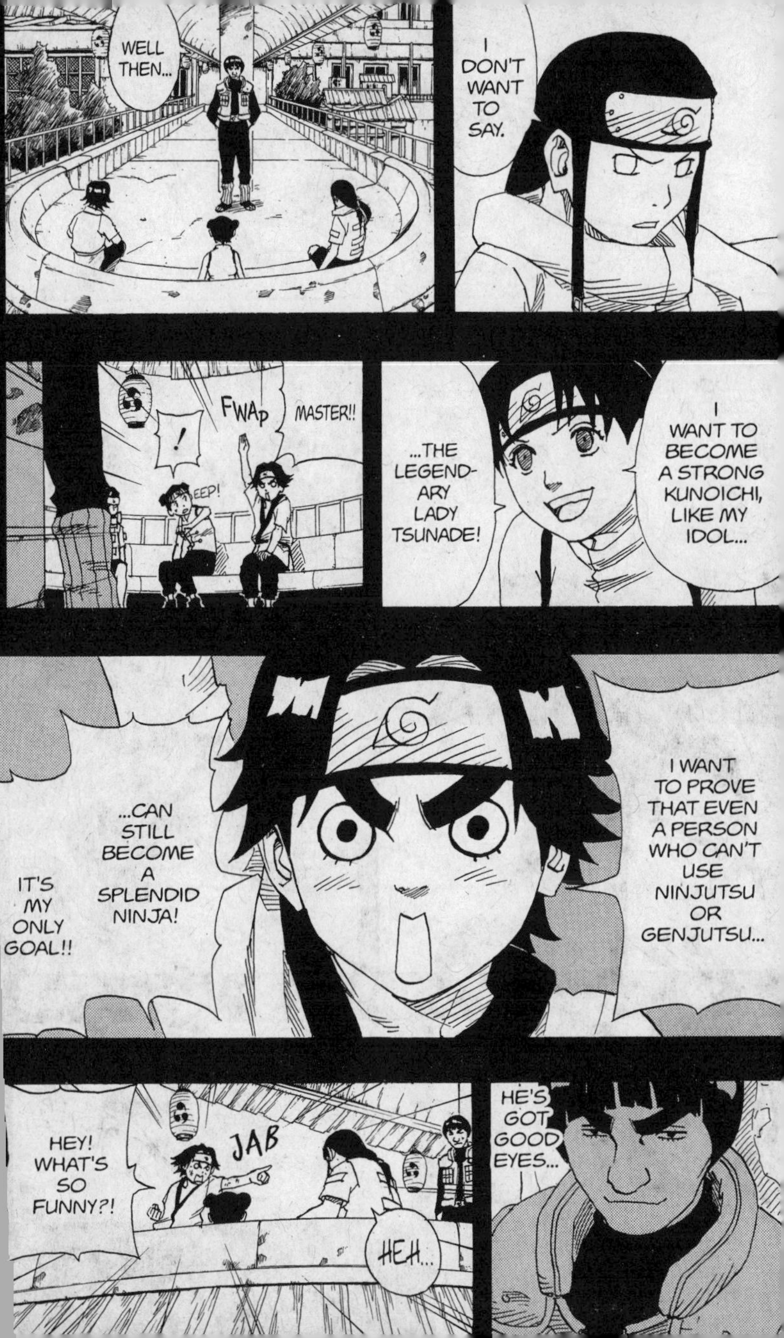

I DON'T WANT TO SAY.
WELL THEN...
I WANT TO BECOME A STRONG KUNOICHI, LIKE MY IDOL...
...THE LEGEND-ARY LADY TSUNADE!
MASTER!!
FWAP
!
EEP!
I WANT TO PROVE THAT EVEN A PERSON WHO CAN'T USE NINJUTSU OR GENJUTSU...
...CAN STILL BECOME A SPLENDID NINJA!
IT'S MY ONLY GOAL!!
HE'S GOT GOOD EYES...
HEH...
JAB
HEY! WHAT'S SO FUNNY?!

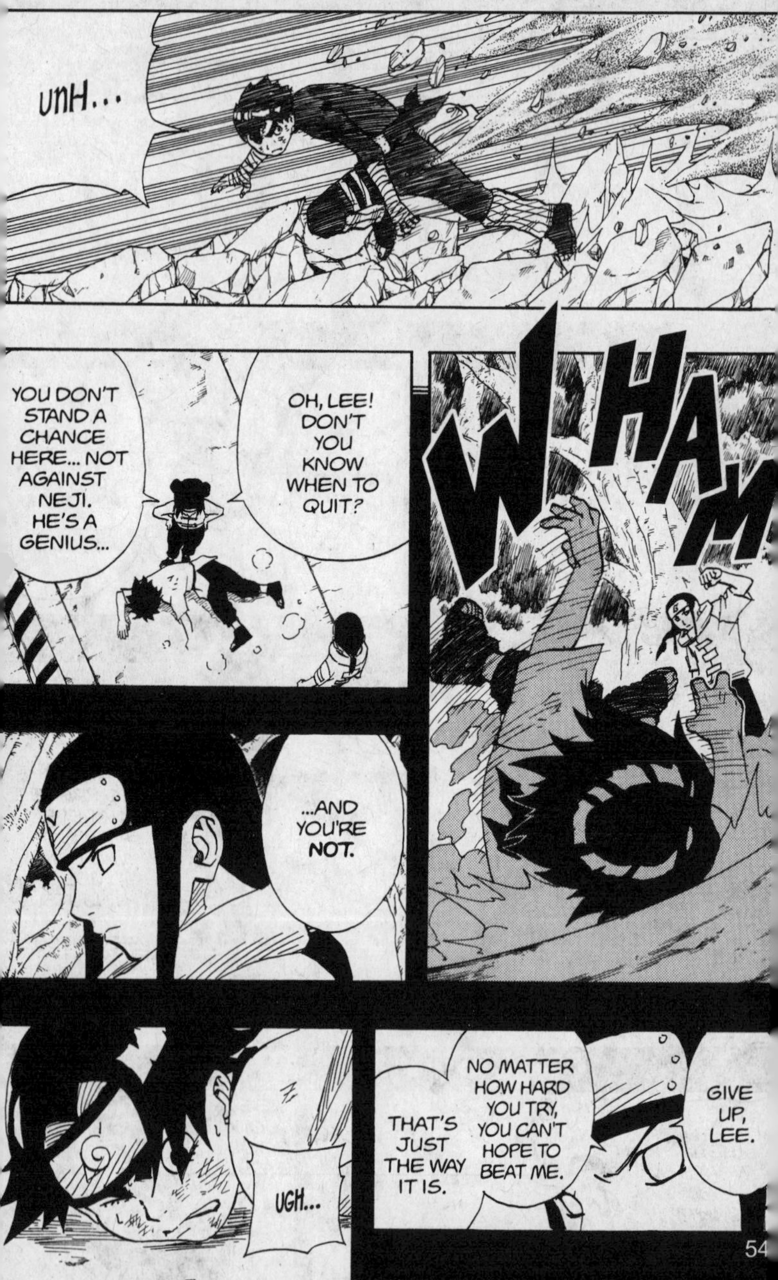
UNH...
WHAM
OH, LEE! DON'T YOU KNOW WHEN TO QUIT?
YOU DON'T STAND A CHANCE HERE... NOT AGAINST NEJI. HE'S A GENIUS...
...AND YOU'RE NOT.
GIVE UP, LEE.
NO MATTER HOW HARD YOU TRY, YOU CAN'T HOPE TO BEAT ME.
THAT'S JUST THE WAY IT IS.
UGH...

READ THIS WAY

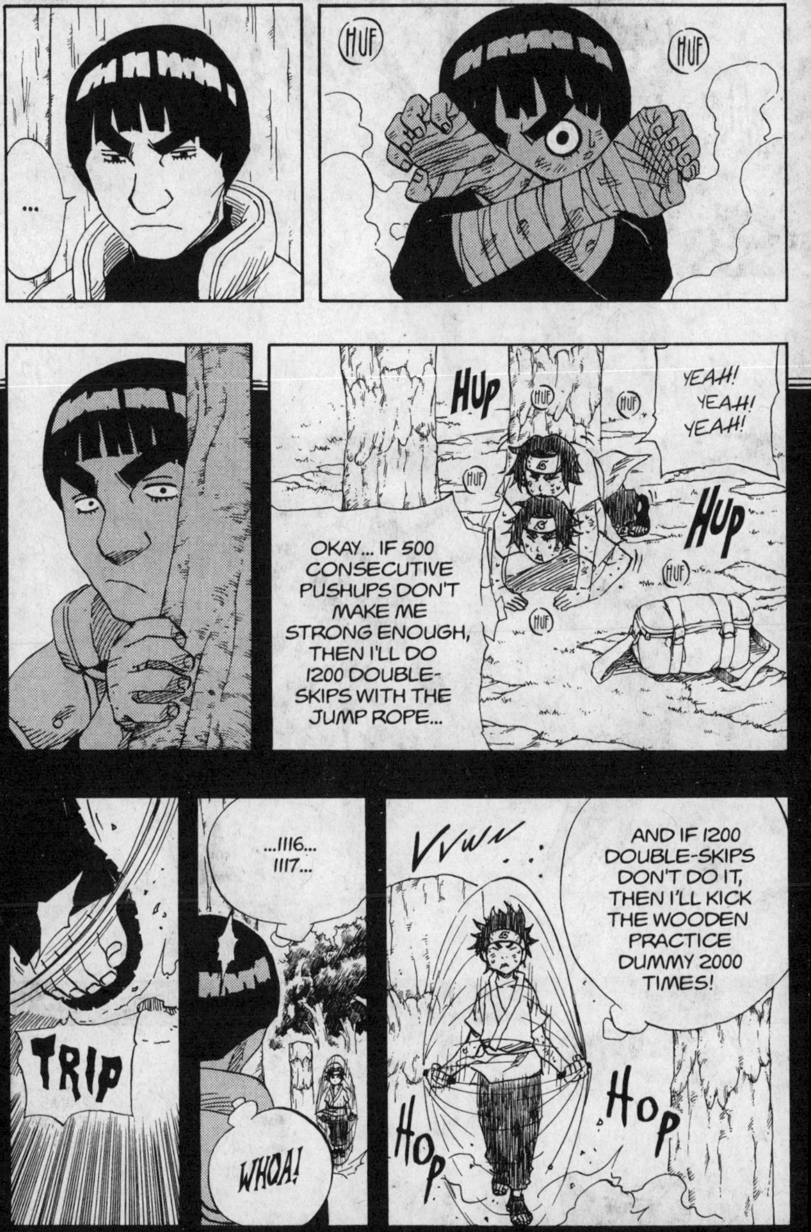

HUF
HUF
...
HUP
HUF
HUF
YEAH! YEAH! YEAH!
HUF
HUP
HUF
HUF
OKAY... IF 500 CONSECUTIVE PUSHUPS DON'T MAKE ME STRONG ENOUGH, THEN I'LL DO 1200 DOUBLE-SKIPS WITH THE JUMP ROPE...
VVWN
AND IF 1200 DOUBLE-SKIPS DON'T DO IT, THEN I'LL KICK THE WOODEN PRACTICE DUMMY 2000 TIMES!
HOP
HOP
...1116... 1117...
WHOA!
TRIP

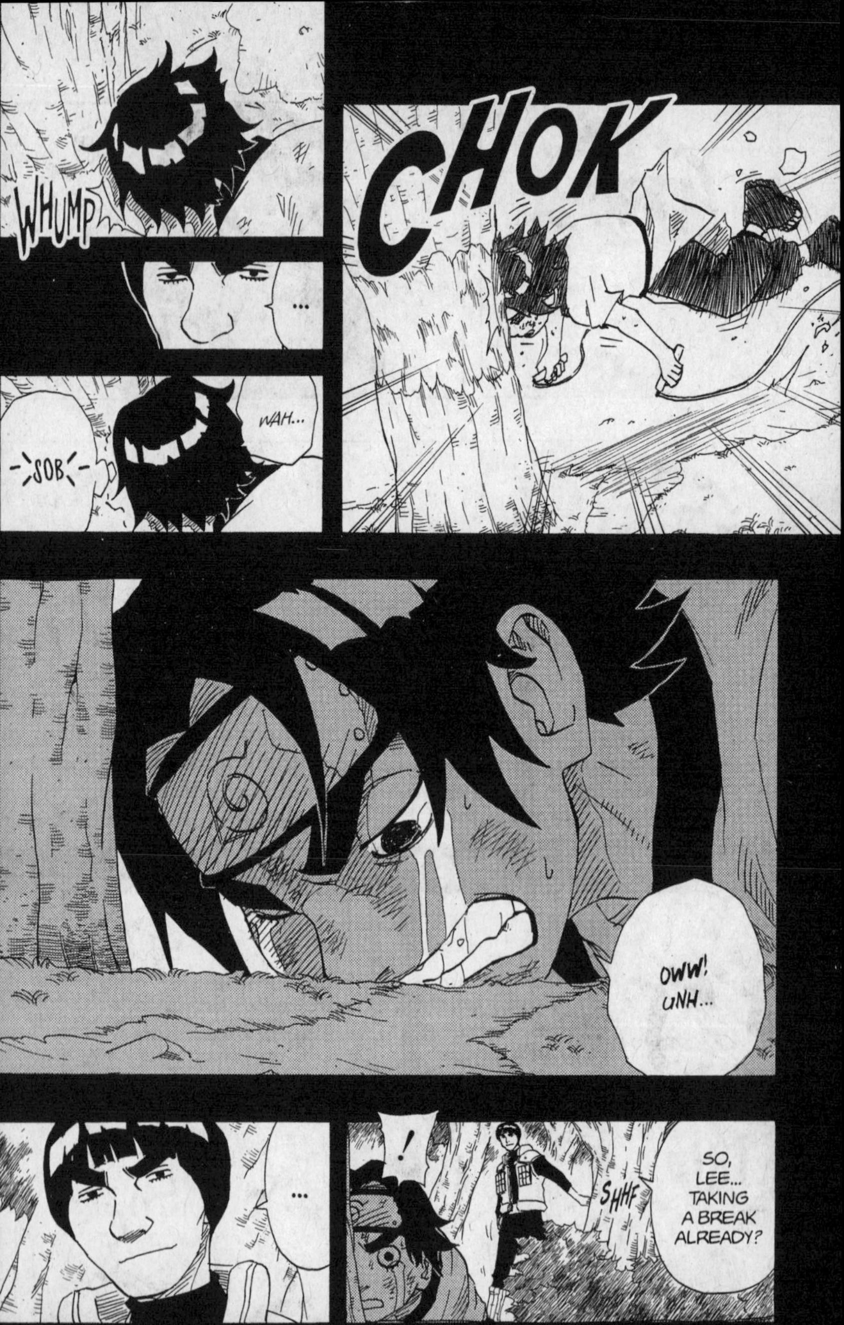
CHOK
WHUMP
...
WAH...
SOB
OWW! UNH...
SO, LEE... TAKING A BREAK ALREADY?
!
SHHF
...

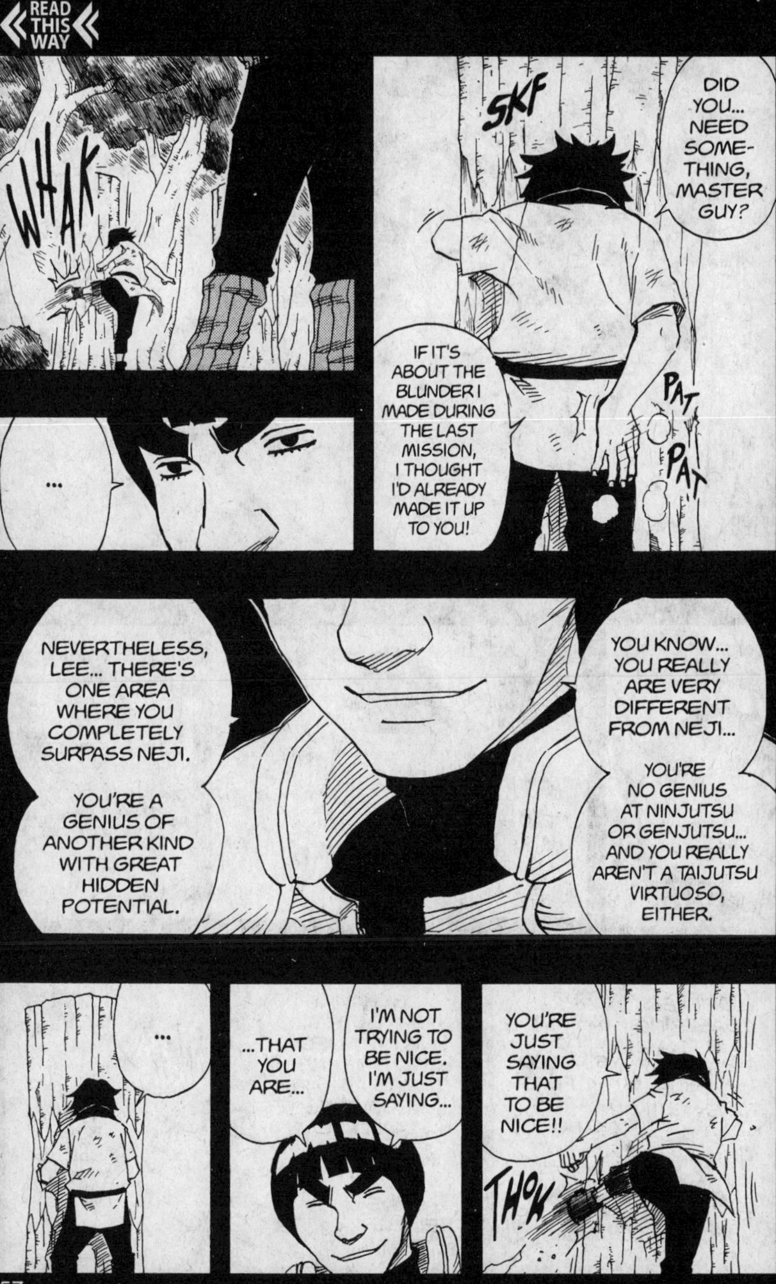
READ THIS WAY
DID YOU... NEED SOMETHING, MASTER GUY?
SKF
IF IT'S ABOUT THE BLUNDER I MADE DURING THE LAST MISSION, I THOUGHT I'D ALREADY MADE IT UP TO YOU!
PAT PAT
WHAK
...
YOU KNOW... YOU REALLY ARE VERY DIFFERENT FROM NEJI...
YOU'RE NO GENIUS AT NINJUTSU OR GENJUTSU... AND YOU REALLY AREN'T A TAIJUTSU VIRTUOSO, EITHER.
NEVERTHELESS, LEE... THERE'S ONE AREA WHERE YOU COMPLETELY SURPASS NEJI.
YOU'RE A GENIUS OF ANOTHER KIND WITH GREAT HIDDEN POTENTIAL.
YOU'RE JUST SAYING THAT TO BE NICE!!
THOK
I'M NOT TRYING TO BE NICE. I'M JUST SAYING...
...THAT YOU ARE...
...

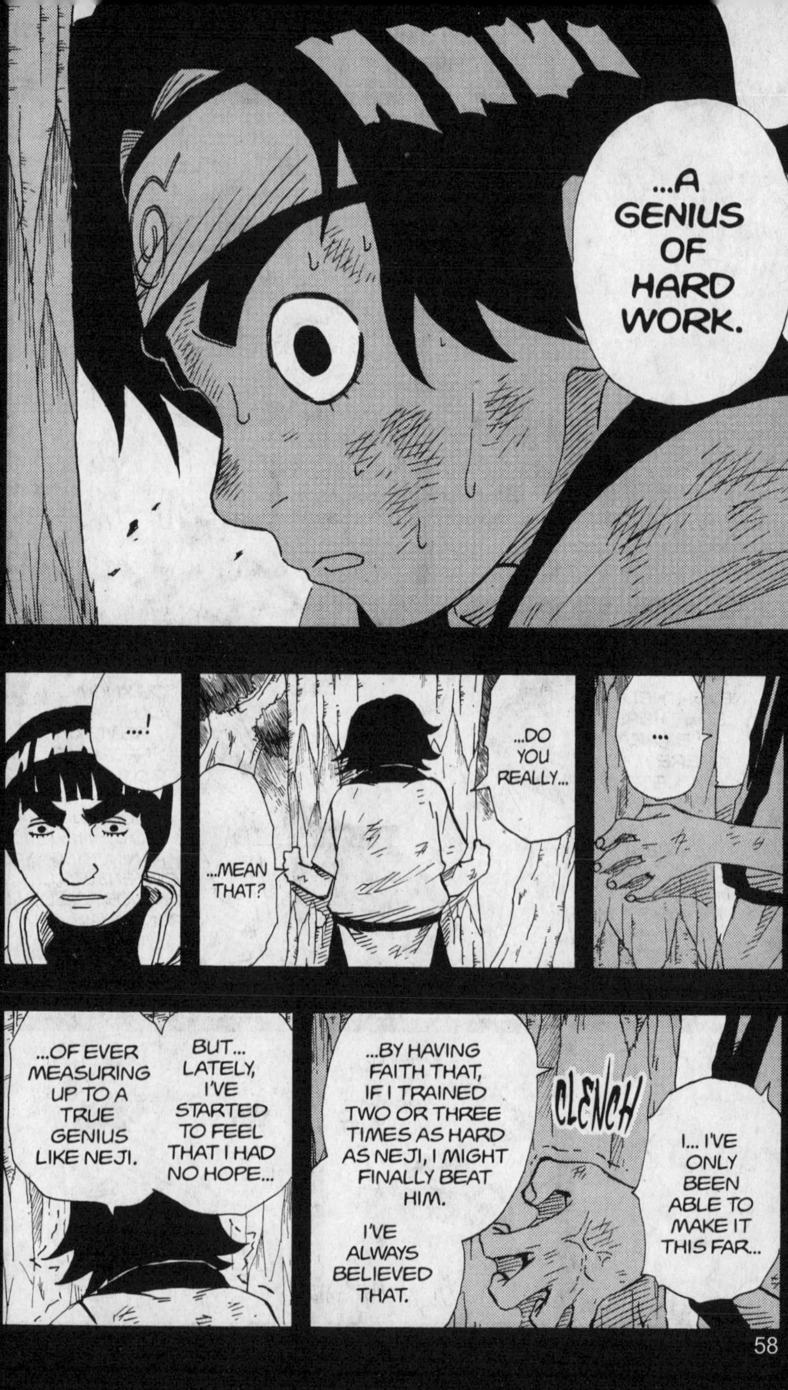
...A GENIUS OF HARD WORK.
...
...DO YOU REALLY...
...MEAN THAT?
...!
I... I'VE ONLY BEEN ABLE TO MAKE IT THIS FAR...
CLENCH
...BY HAVING FAITH THAT, IF I TRAINED TWO OR THREE TIMES AS HARD AS NEJI, I MIGHT FINALLY BEAT HIM.
I'VE ALWAYS BELIEVED THAT.
BUT... LATELY, I'VE STARTED TO FEEL THAT I HAD NO HOPE...
...OF EVER MEASURING UP TO A TRUE GENIUS LIKE NEJI.

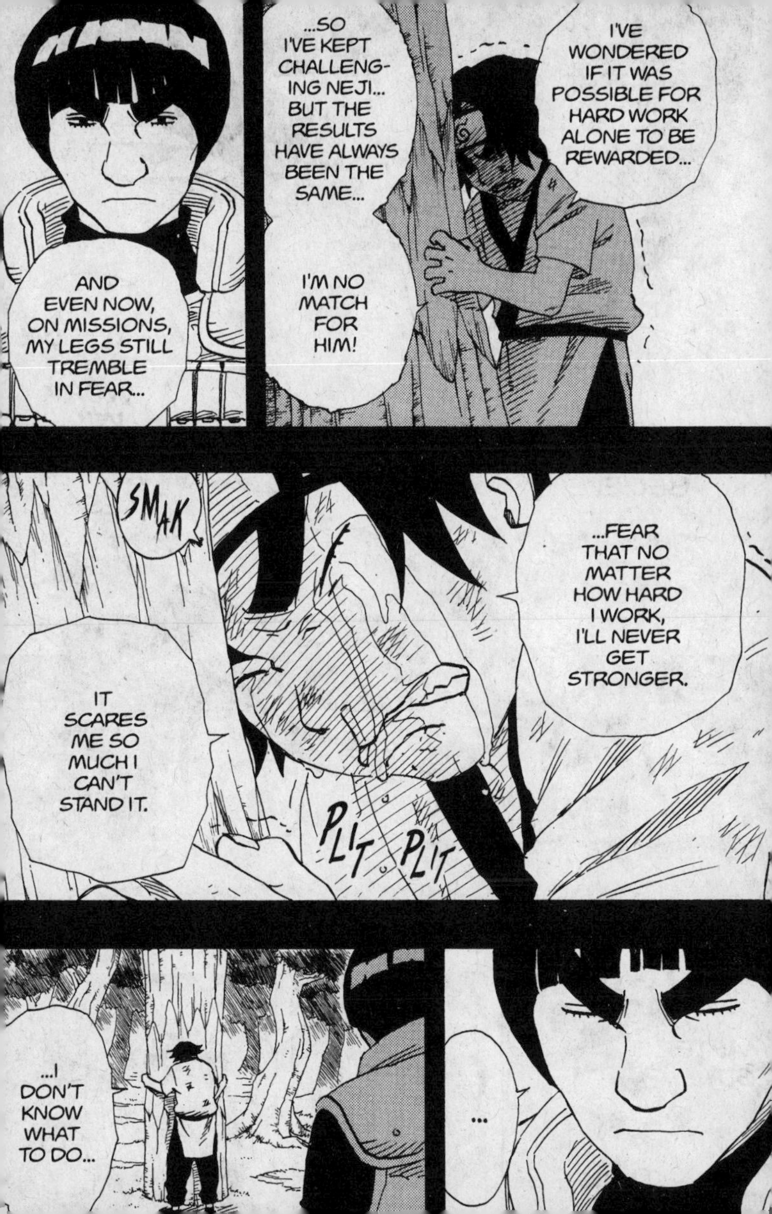
I'VE WONDERED IF IT WAS POSSIBLE FOR HARD WORK ALONE TO BE REWARDED...
...SO I'VE KEPT CHALLENG-ING NEJI... BUT THE RESULTS HAVE ALWAYS BEEN THE SAME...
I'M NO MATCH FOR HIM!
AND EVEN NOW, ON MISSIONS, MY LEGS STILL TREMBLE IN FEAR...
...FEAR THAT NO MATTER HOW HARD I WORK, I'LL NEVER GET STRONGER.
SMAK
IT SCARES ME SO MUCH I CAN'T STAND IT.
PLIT PLIT
...
...I DON'T KNOW WHAT TO DO...

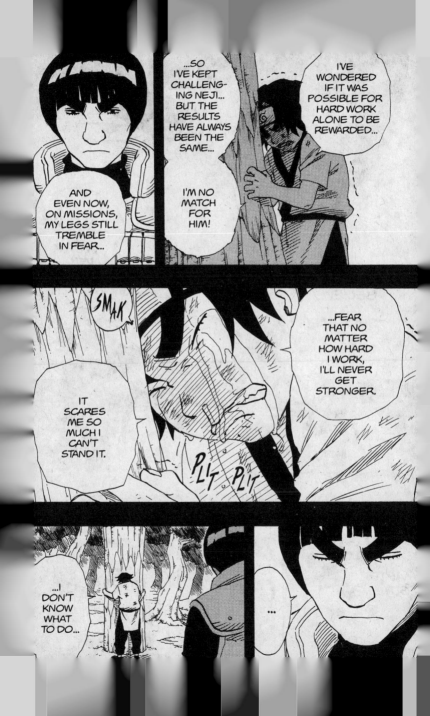

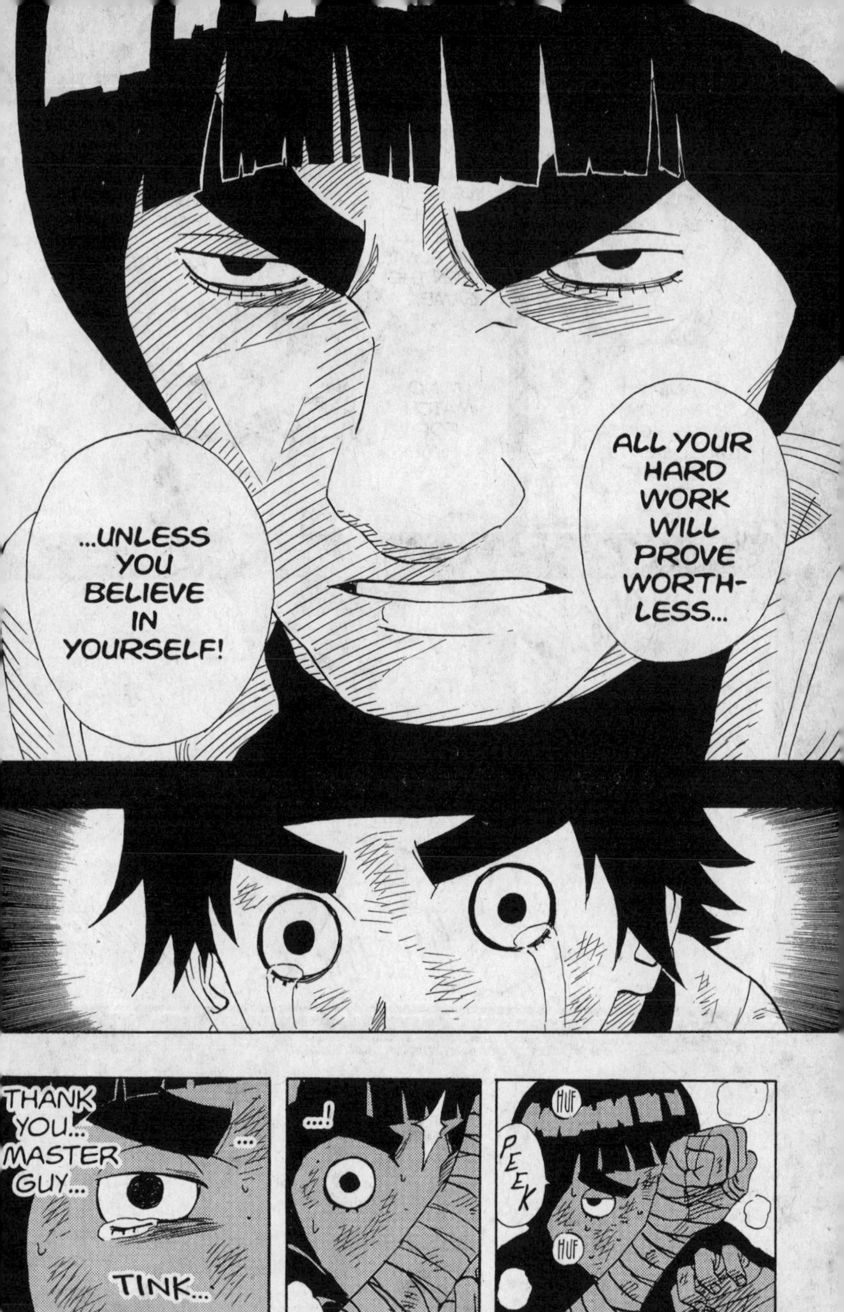
ALL YOUR HARD WORK WILL PROVE WORTH-LESS...
...UNLESS YOU BELIEVE IN YOURSELF!
HUF
PEEK
HUF
...!
...
THANK YOU... MASTER GUY...
TINK...

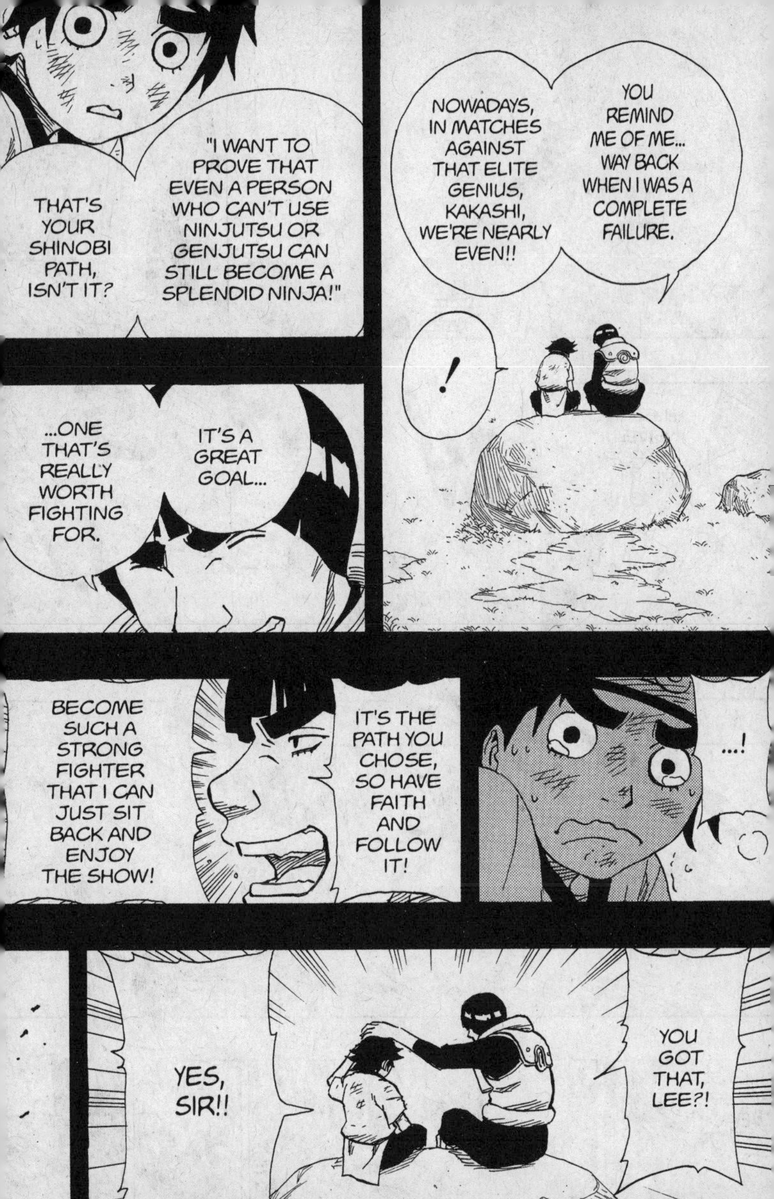
YOU REMIND ME OF ME... WAY BACK WHEN I WAS A COMPLETE FAILURE.
NOWADAYS, IN MATCHES AGAINST THAT ELITE GENIUS, KAKASHI, WE'RE NEARLY EVEN!!
!
"I WANT TO PROVE THAT EVEN A PERSON WHO CAN'T USE NINJUTSU OR GENJUTSU CAN STILL BECOME A SPLENDID NINJA!"
THAT'S YOUR SHINOBI PATH, ISN'T IT?
IT'S A GREAT GOAL...
...ONE THAT'S REALLY WORTH FIGHTING FOR.
...!
IT'S THE PATH YOU CHOSE, SO HAVE FAITH AND FOLLOW IT!
BECOME SUCH A STRONG FIGHTER THAT I CAN JUST SIT BACK AND ENJOY THE SHOW!
YOU GOT THAT, LEE?!
YES, SIR!!

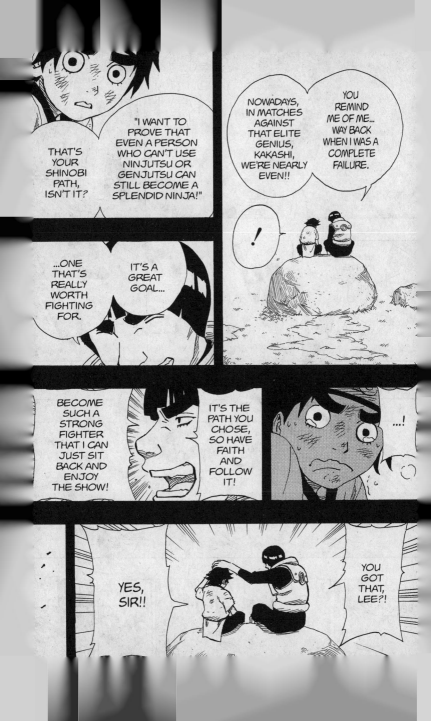

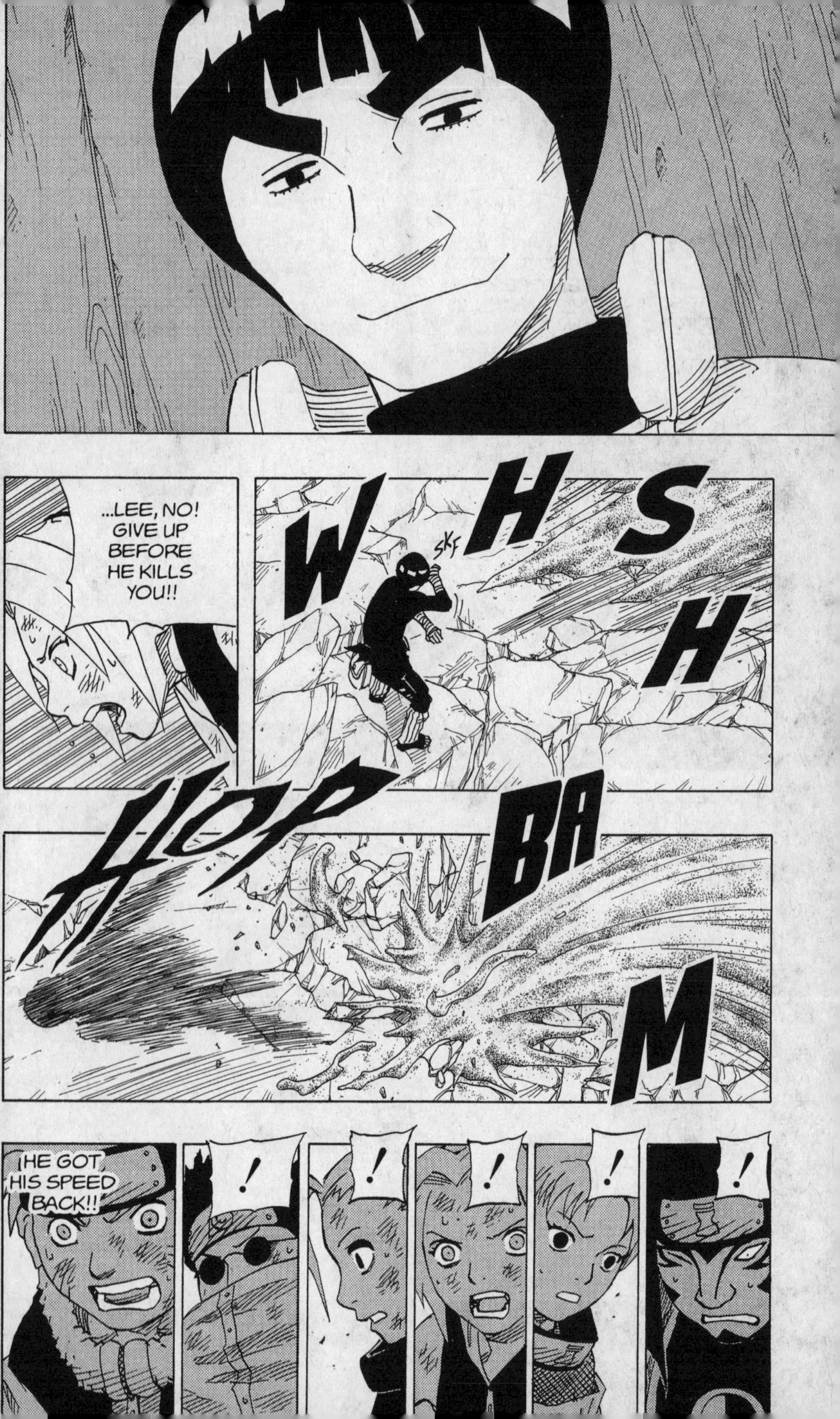
WHSHH
SKF
...LEE, NO! GIVE UP BEFORE HE KILLS YOU!!
HOP
BAM
!
!
!
!
!
HE GOT HIS SPEED BACK!!

READ THIS WAY

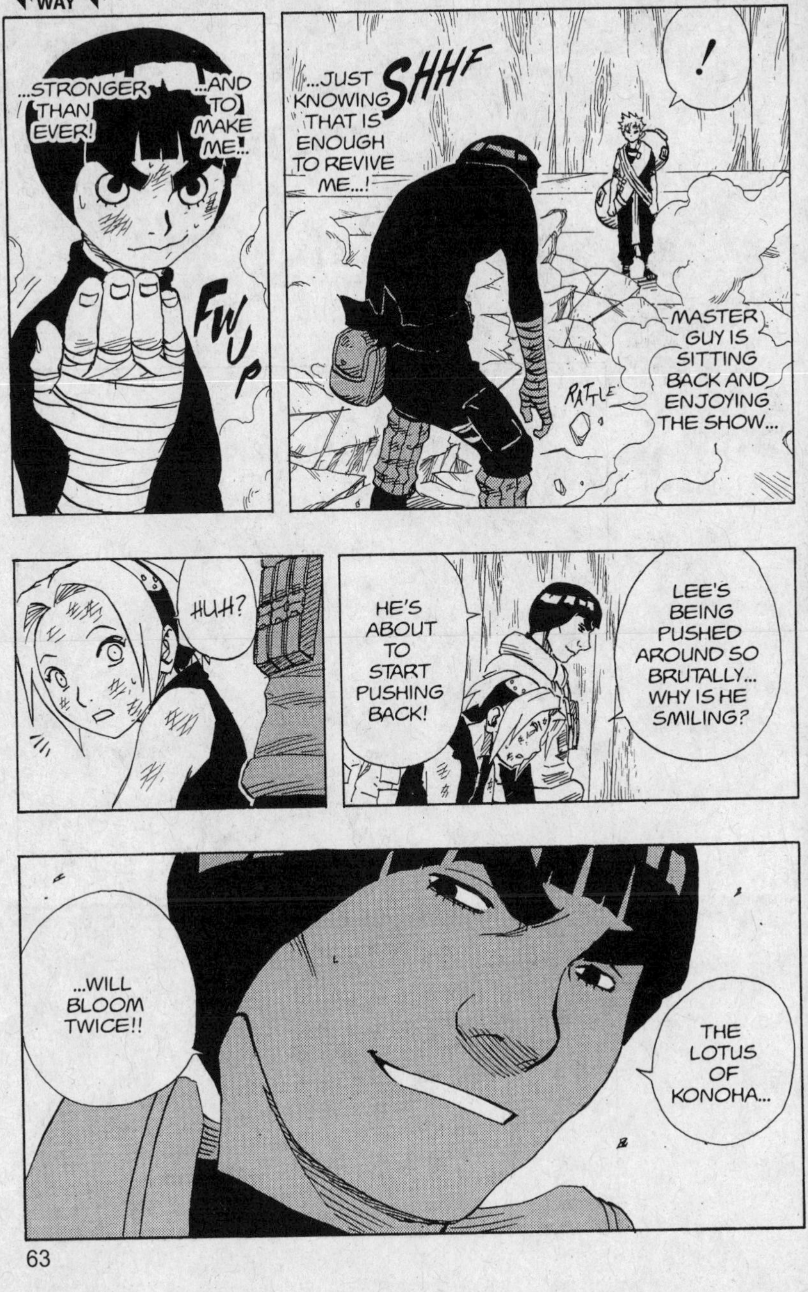
!
MASTER GUY IS SITTING BACK AND ENJOYING THE SHOW...
...JUST KNOWING THAT IS ENOUGH TO REVIVE ME...!
SHHF
RATTLE
...AND TO MAKE ME...
...STRONGER THAN EVER!
FWUP
LEE'S BEING PUSHED AROUND SO BRUTALLY... WHY IS HE SMILING?
HE'S ABOUT TO START PUSHING BACK!
HUH?
THE LOTUS OF KONOHA...
...WILL BLOOM TWICE!!

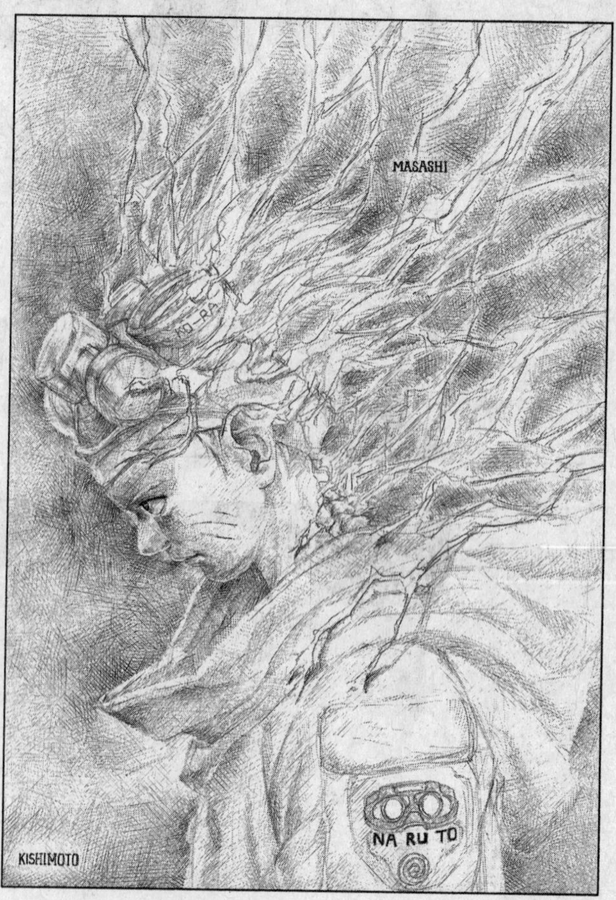
MASASHI
NA RU TO
KISHIMOTO

Number 85: Now, of All Times...!!

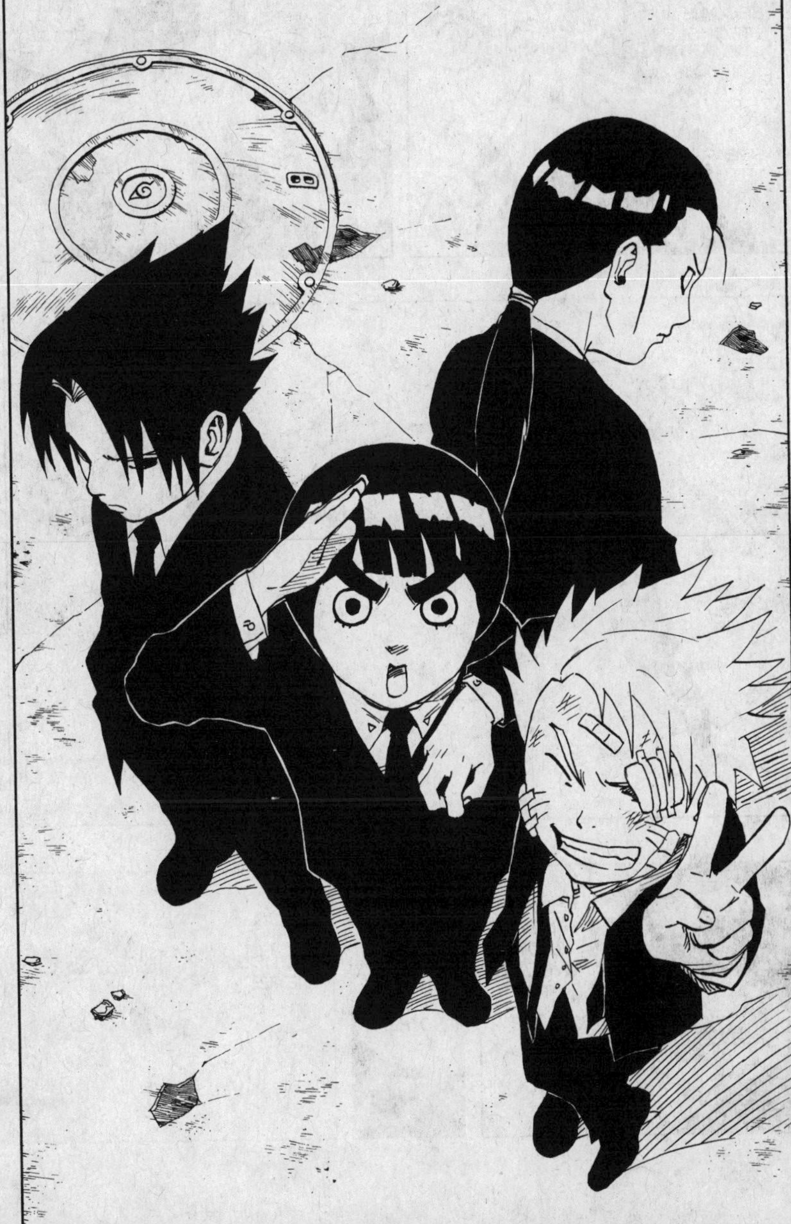

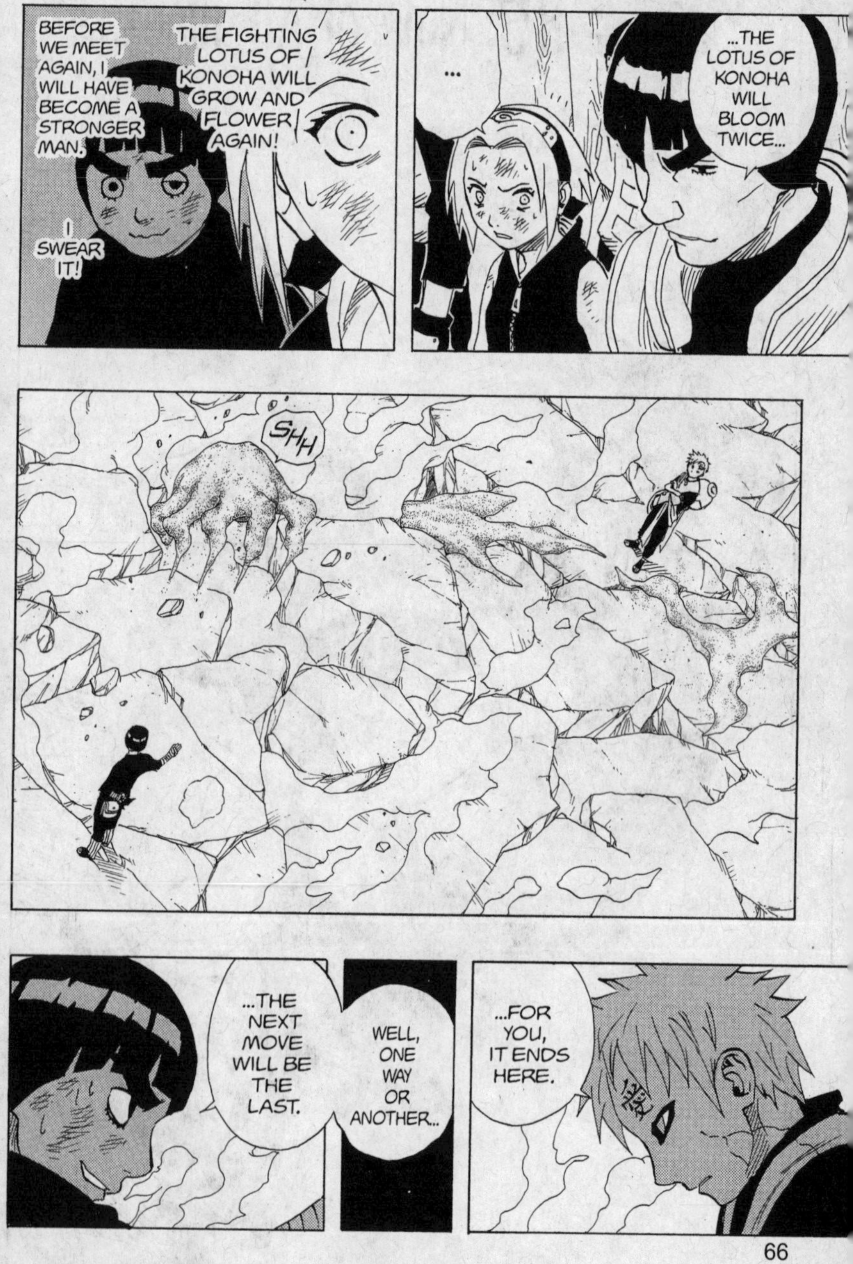
...THE LOTUS OF KONOHA WILL BLOOM TWICE...
...
THE FIGHTING LOTUS OF KONOHA WILL GROW AND FLOWER AGAIN!
BEFORE WE MEET AGAIN, I WILL HAVE BECOME A STRONGER MAN.
I SWEAR IT!
SHH
...FOR YOU, IT ENDS HERE.
WELL, ONE WAY OR ANOTHER...
...THE NEXT MOVE WILL BE THE LAST.

READ THIS WAY

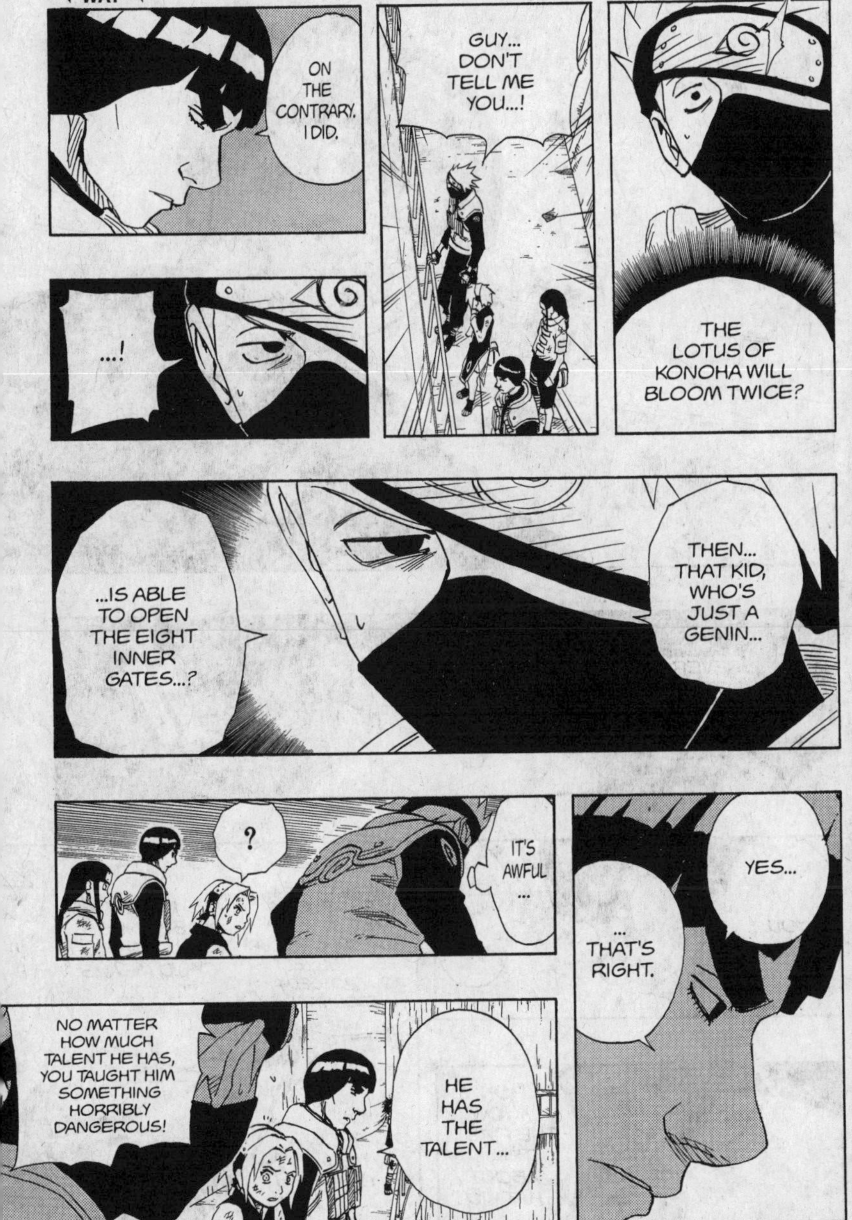

THE LOTUS OF KONOHA WILL BLOOM TWICE?
GUY... DON'T TELL ME YOU...!
ON THE CONTRARY. I DID.
...!
THEN... THAT KID, WHO'S JUST A GENIN...
...IS ABLE TO OPEN THE EIGHT INNER GATES...?
YES...
...THAT'S RIGHT.
IT'S AWFUL...
?
HE HAS THE TALENT...
NO MATTER HOW MUCH TALENT HE HAS, YOU TAUGHT HIM SOMETHING HORRIBLY DANGEROUS!

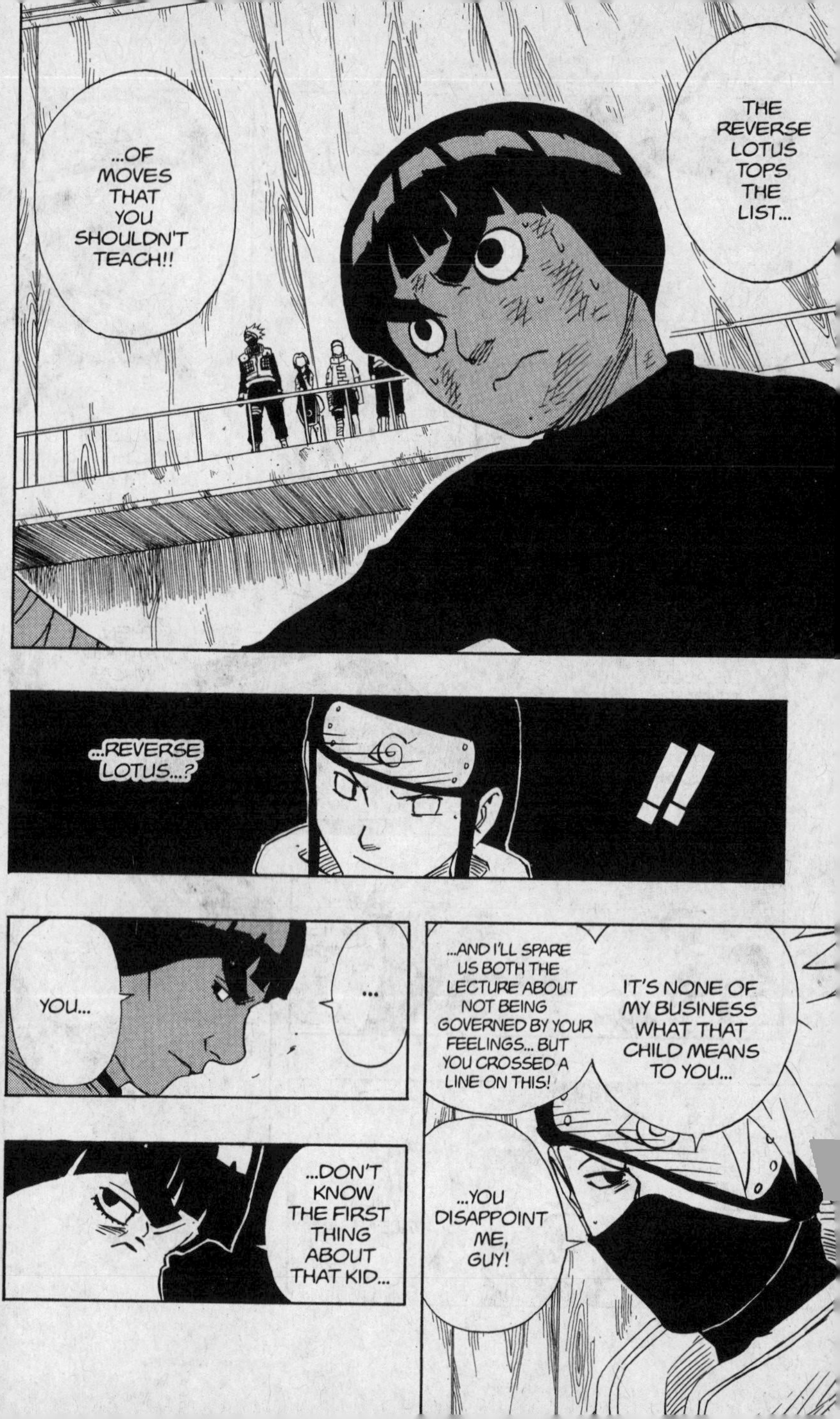
THE REVERSE LOTUS TOPS THE LIST...
...OF MOVES THAT YOU SHOULDN'T TEACH!!
!!
...REVERSE LOTUS...?
IT'S NONE OF MY BUSINESS WHAT THAT CHILD MEANS TO YOU...
...AND I'LL SPARE US BOTH THE LECTURE ABOUT NOT BEING GOVERNED BY YOUR FEELINGS... BUT YOU CROSSED A LINE ON THIS!
...YOU DISAPPOINT ME, GUY!
...
YOU...
...DON'T KNOW THE FIRST THING ABOUT THAT KID...

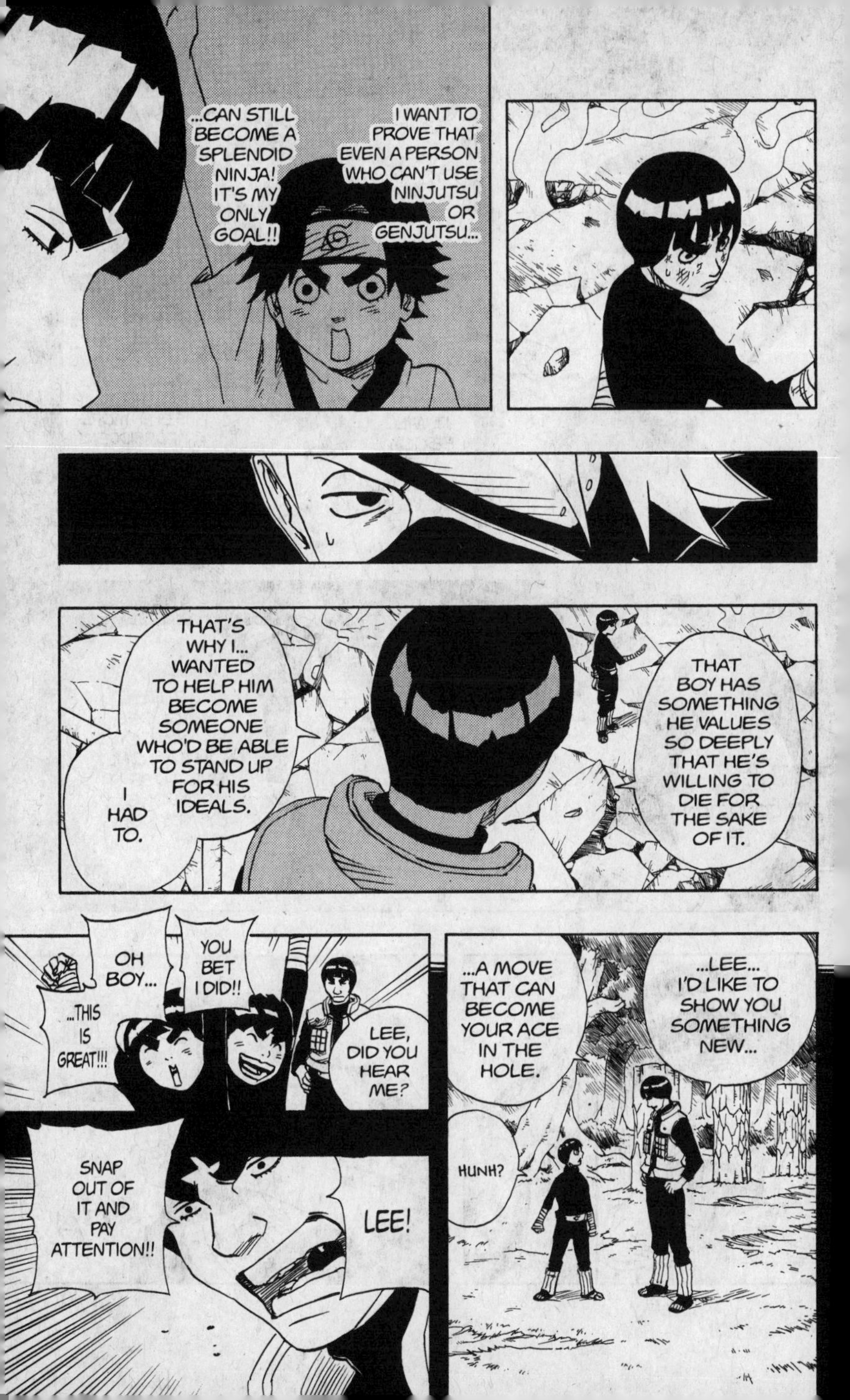
I WANT TO PROVE THAT EVEN A PERSON WHO CAN'T USE NINJUTSU OR GENJUTSU...
...CAN STILL BECOME A SPLENDID NINJA! IT'S MY ONLY GOAL!!
THAT BOY HAS SOMETHING HE VALUES SO DEEPLY THAT HE'S WILLING TO DIE FOR THE SAKE OF IT.
THAT'S WHY I... WANTED TO HELP HIM BECOME SOMEONE WHO'D BE ABLE TO STAND UP FOR HIS IDEALS.
I HAD TO.
...LEE... I'D LIKE TO SHOW YOU SOMETHING NEW...
...A MOVE THAT CAN BECOME YOUR ACE IN THE HOLE.
HUNH?
YOU BET I DID!!
OH BOY...
...THIS IS GREAT!!!
LEE, DID YOU HEAR ME?
LEE!
SNAP OUT OF IT AND PAY ATTENTION!!

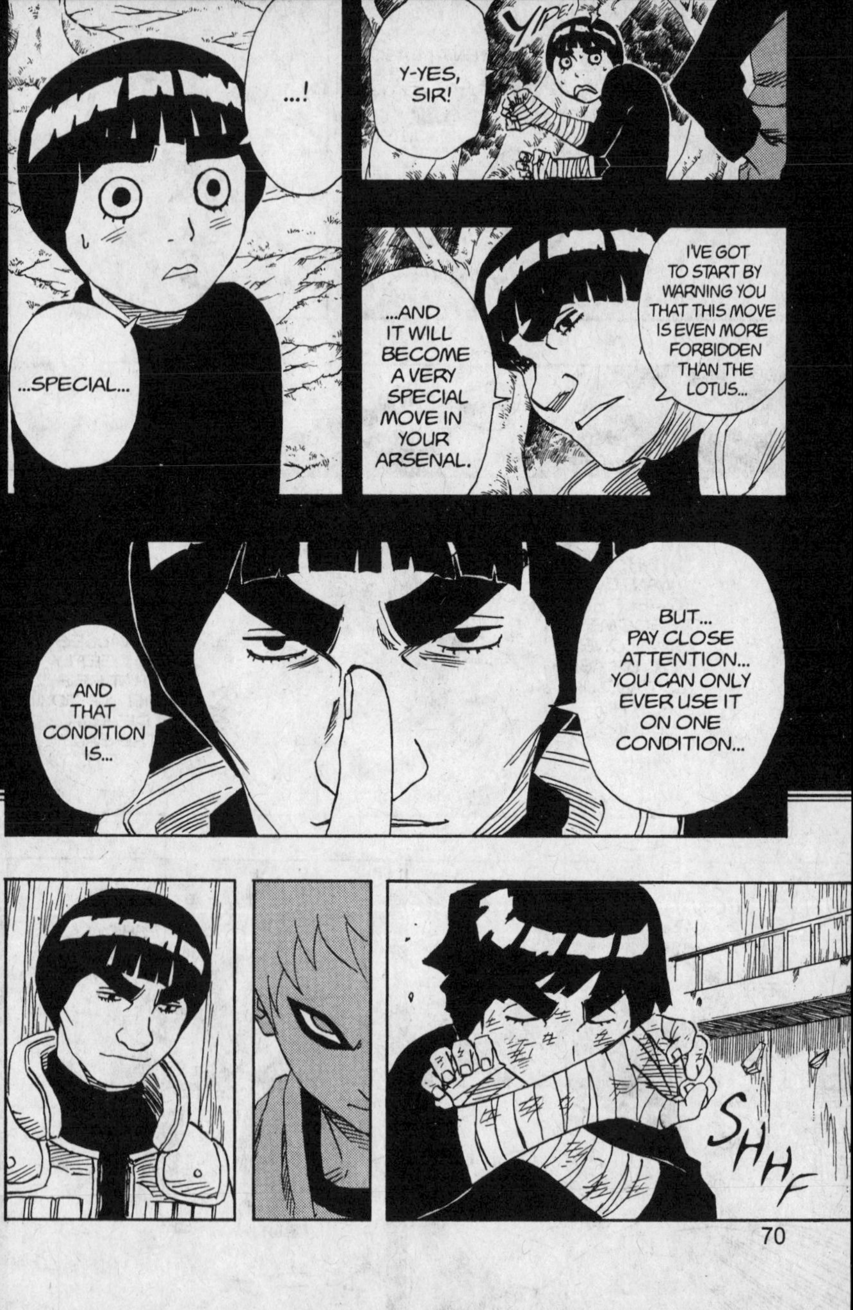
YIPE!
Y-YES, SIR!
I'VE GOT TO START BY WARNING YOU THAT THIS MOVE IS EVEN MORE FORBIDDEN THAN THE LOTUS...
...AND IT WILL BECOME A VERY SPECIAL MOVE IN YOUR ARSENAL.
...!
...SPECIAL...
BUT... PAY CLOSE ATTENTION... YOU CAN ONLY EVER USE IT ON ONE CONDITION...
AND THAT CONDITION IS...
SHHF

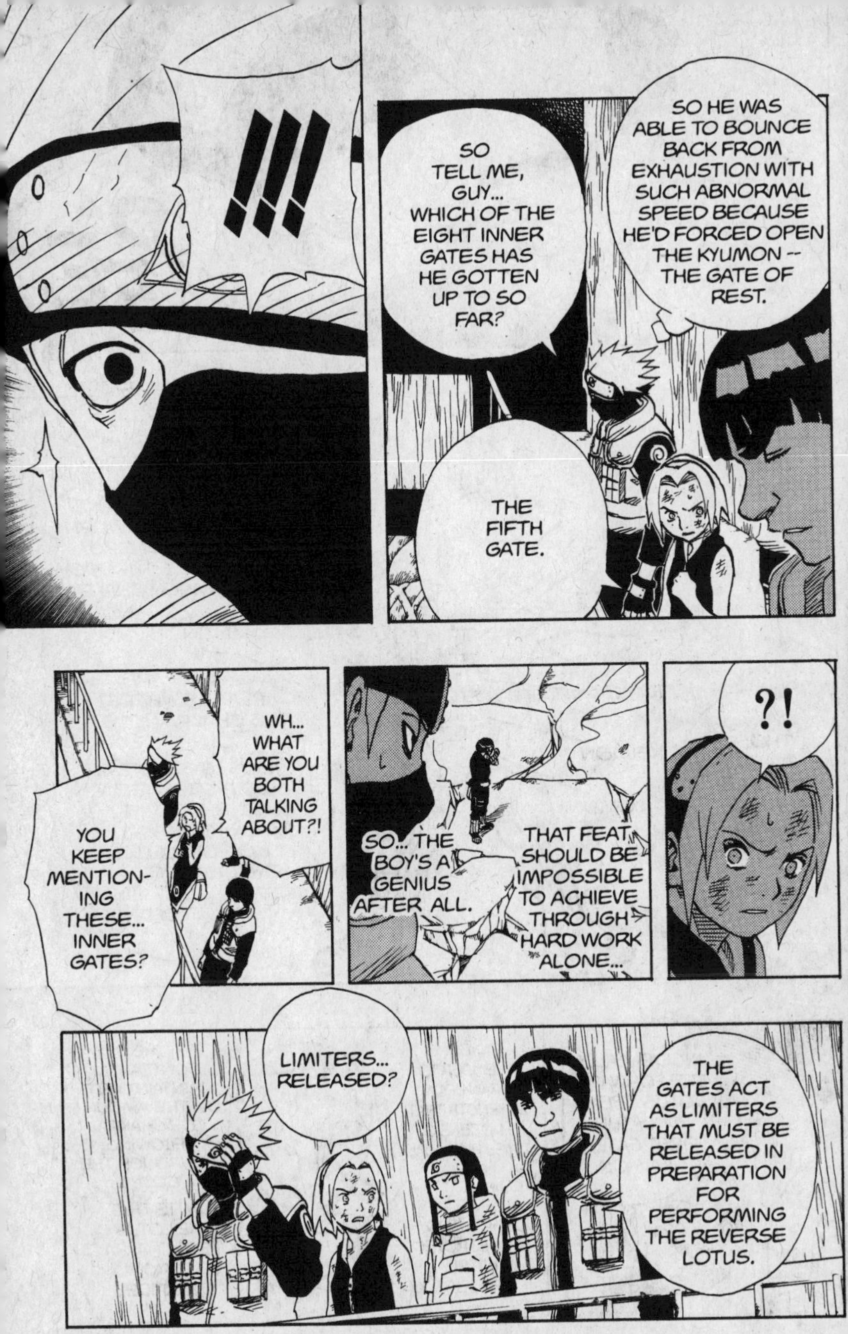
SO HE WAS ABLE TO BOUNCE BACK FROM EXHAUSTION WITH SUCH ABNORMAL SPEED BECAUSE HE'D FORCED OPEN THE KYUMON -- THE GATE OF REST.
SO TELL ME, GUY... WHICH OF THE EIGHT INNER GATES HAS HE GOTTEN UP TO SO FAR?
THE FIFTH GATE.
!!!
?!
THAT FEAT SHOULD BE IMPOSSIBLE TO ACHIEVE THROUGH HARD WORK ALONE...
SO... THE BOY'S A GENIUS AFTER ALL.
WH... WHAT ARE YOU BOTH TALKING ABOUT?!
YOU KEEP MENTIONING THESE... INNER GATES?
THE GATES ACT AS LIMITERS THAT MUST BE RELEASED IN PREPARATION FOR PERFORMING THE REVERSE LOTUS.
LIMITERS... RELEASED?

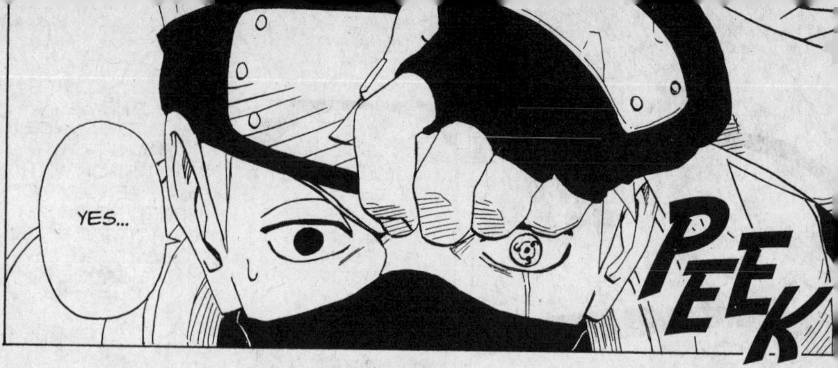
PEEK
YES...

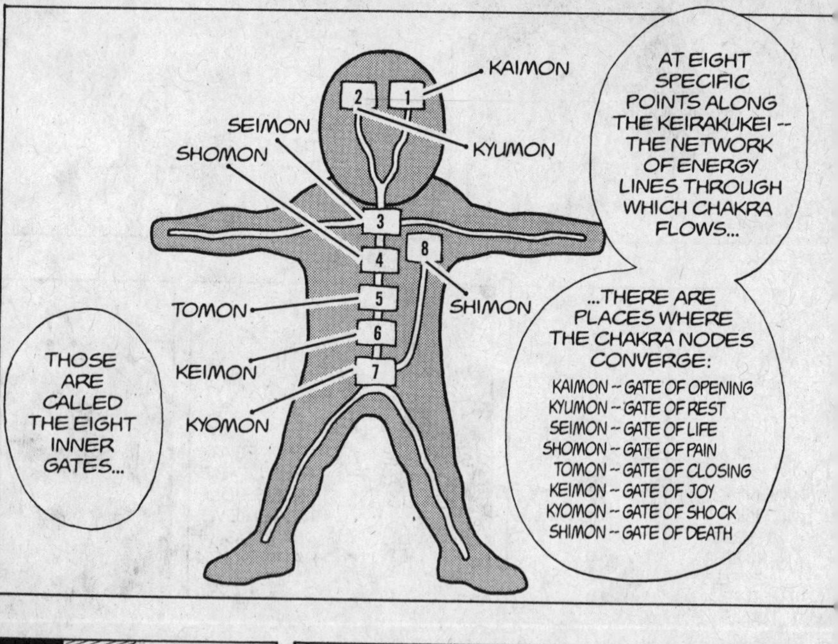
AT EIGHT SPECIFIC POINTS ALONG THE KEIRAKUKEI -- THE NETWORK OF ENERGY LINES THROUGH WHICH CHAKRA FLOWS...
...THERE ARE PLACES WHERE THE CHAKRA NODES CONVERGE:
KAIMON -- GATE OF OPENING
KYUMON -- GATE OF REST
SEIMON -- GATE OF LIFE
SHOMON -- GATE OF PAIN
TOMON -- GATE OF CLOSING
KEIMON -- GATE OF JOY
KYOMON -- GATE OF SHOCK
SHIMON -- GATE OF DEATH
KAIMON
KYUMON
SEIMON
SHOMON
SHIMON
TOMON
KEIMON
KYOMON
1
2
3
4
5
6
7
8
THOSE ARE CALLED THE EIGHT INNER GATES...

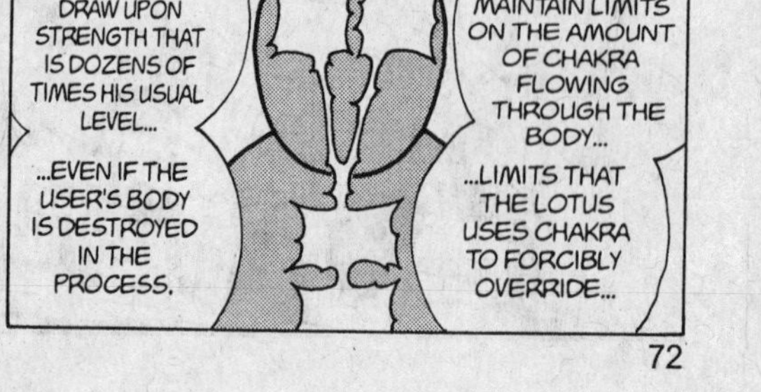
THEY CONSTANTLY MAINTAIN LIMITS ON THE AMOUNT OF CHAKRA FLOWING THROUGH THE BODY...
...LIMITS THAT THE LOTUS USES CHAKRA TO FORCIBLY OVERRIDE...
...ENABLING THE USER TO DRAW UPON STRENGTH THAT IS DOZENS OF TIMES HIS USUAL LEVEL...
...EVEN IF THE USER'S BODY IS DESTROYED IN THE PROCESS.

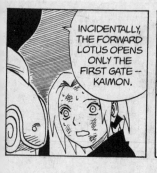

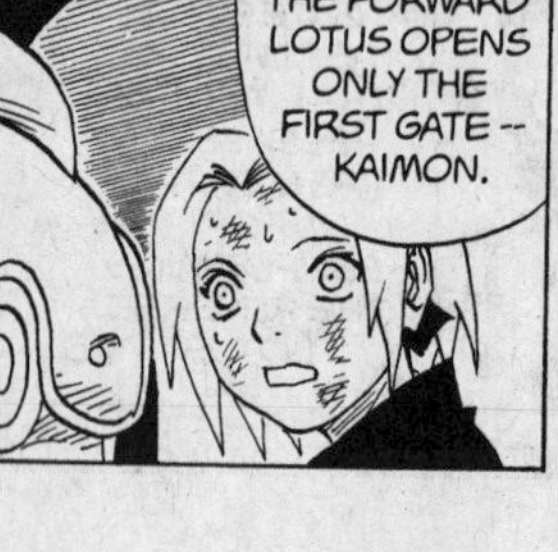
INCIDENTALLY, THE FORWARD LOTUS OPENS ONLY THE FIRST GATE -- KAIMON.

READ THIS WAY

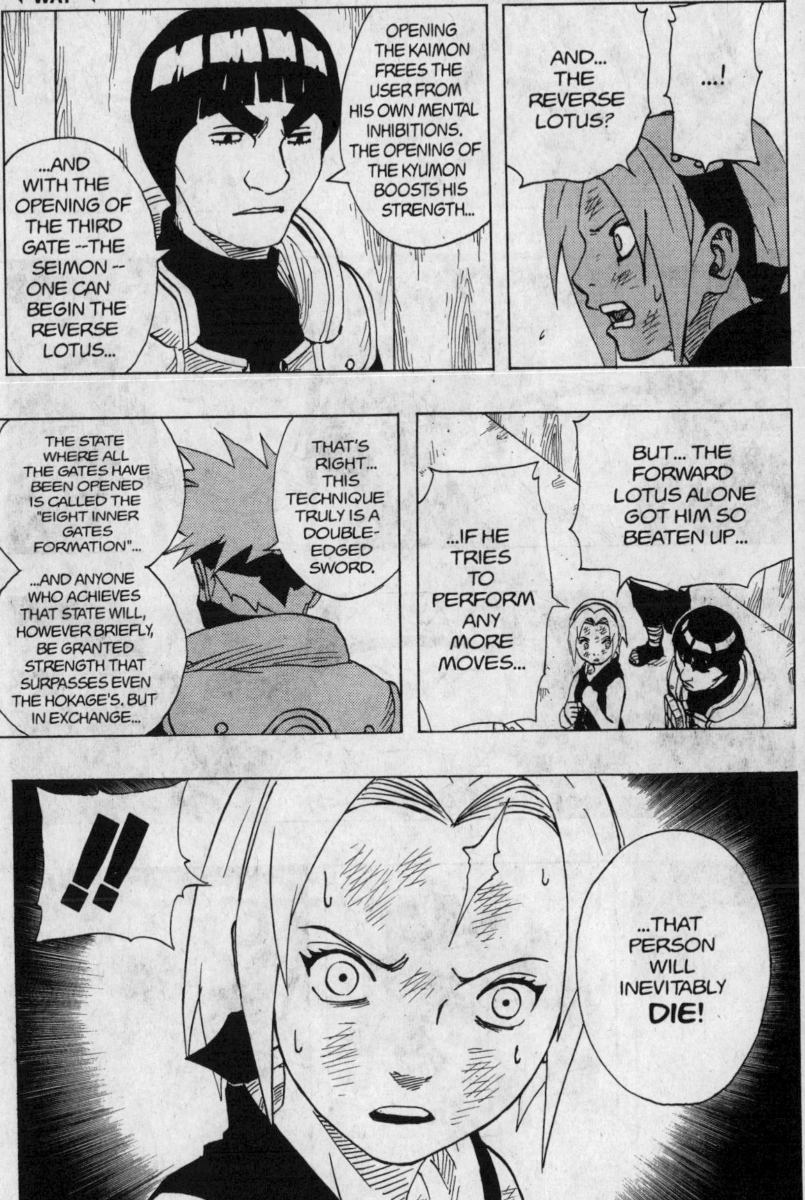

...!
AND... THE REVERSE LOTUS?
OPENING THE KAIMON FREES THE USER FROM HIS OWN MENTAL INHIBITIONS. THE OPENING OF THE KYUMON BOOSTS HIS STRENGTH...
...AND WITH THE OPENING OF THE THIRD GATE --THE SEIMON -- ONE CAN BEGIN THE REVERSE LOTUS...
BUT... THE FORWARD LOTUS ALONE GOT HIM SO BEATEN UP...
...IF HE TRIES TO PERFORM ANY MORE MOVES...
THAT'S RIGHT... THIS TECHNIQUE TRULY IS A DOUBLE-EDGED SWORD.
THE STATE WHERE ALL THE GATES HAVE BEEN OPENED IS CALLED THE "EIGHT INNER GATES FORMATION"...
...AND ANYONE WHO ACHIEVES THAT STATE WILL, HOWEVER BRIEFLY, BE GRANTED STRENGTH THAT SURPASSES EVEN THE HOKAGE'S. BUT IN EXCHANGE...
...THAT PERSON WILL INEVITABLY DIE!
!!

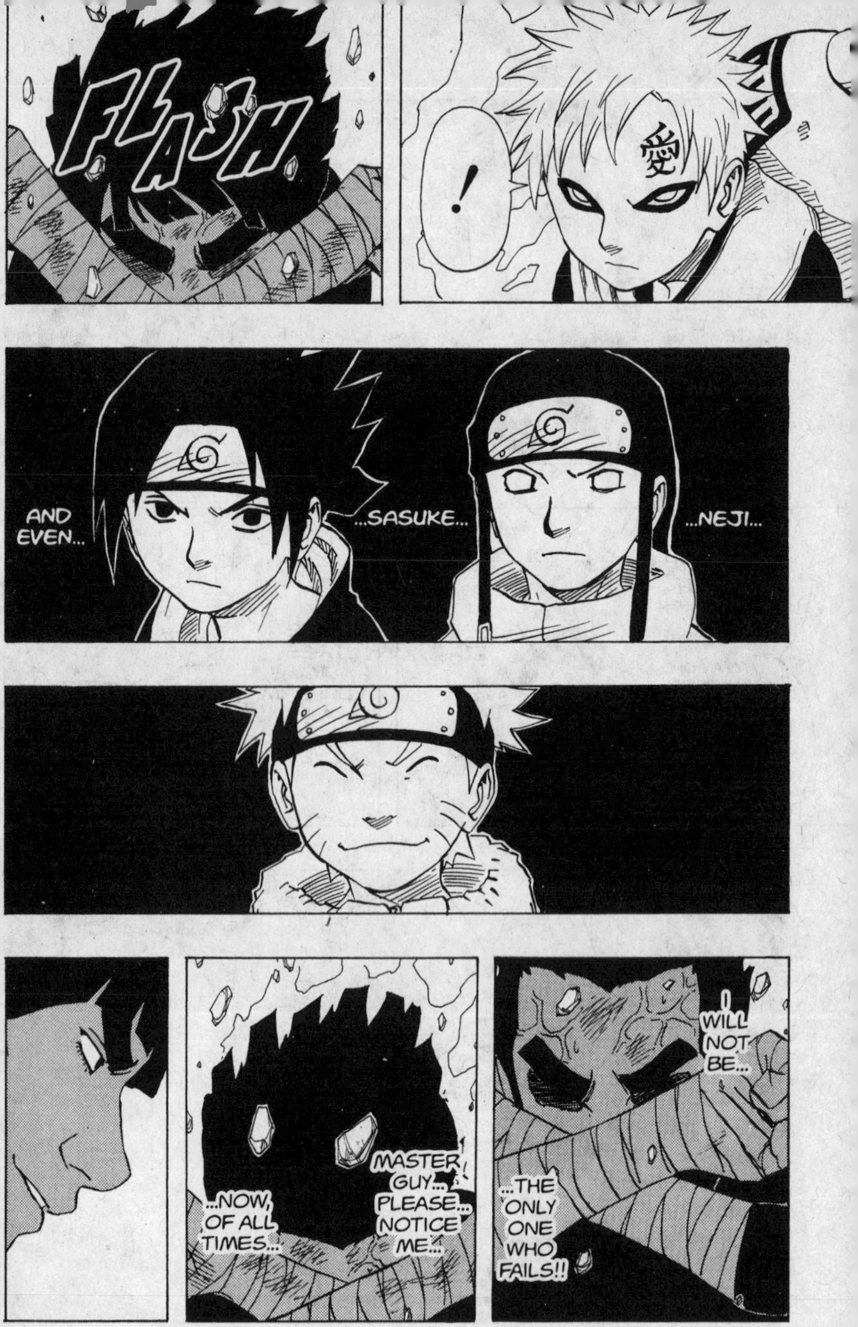
!
FLASH
...NEJI...
...SASUKE...
AND EVEN...
I WILL NOT BE...
...THE ONLY ONE WHO FAILS!!
MASTER GUY... PLEASE... NOTICE ME...
...NOW, OF ALL TIMES...

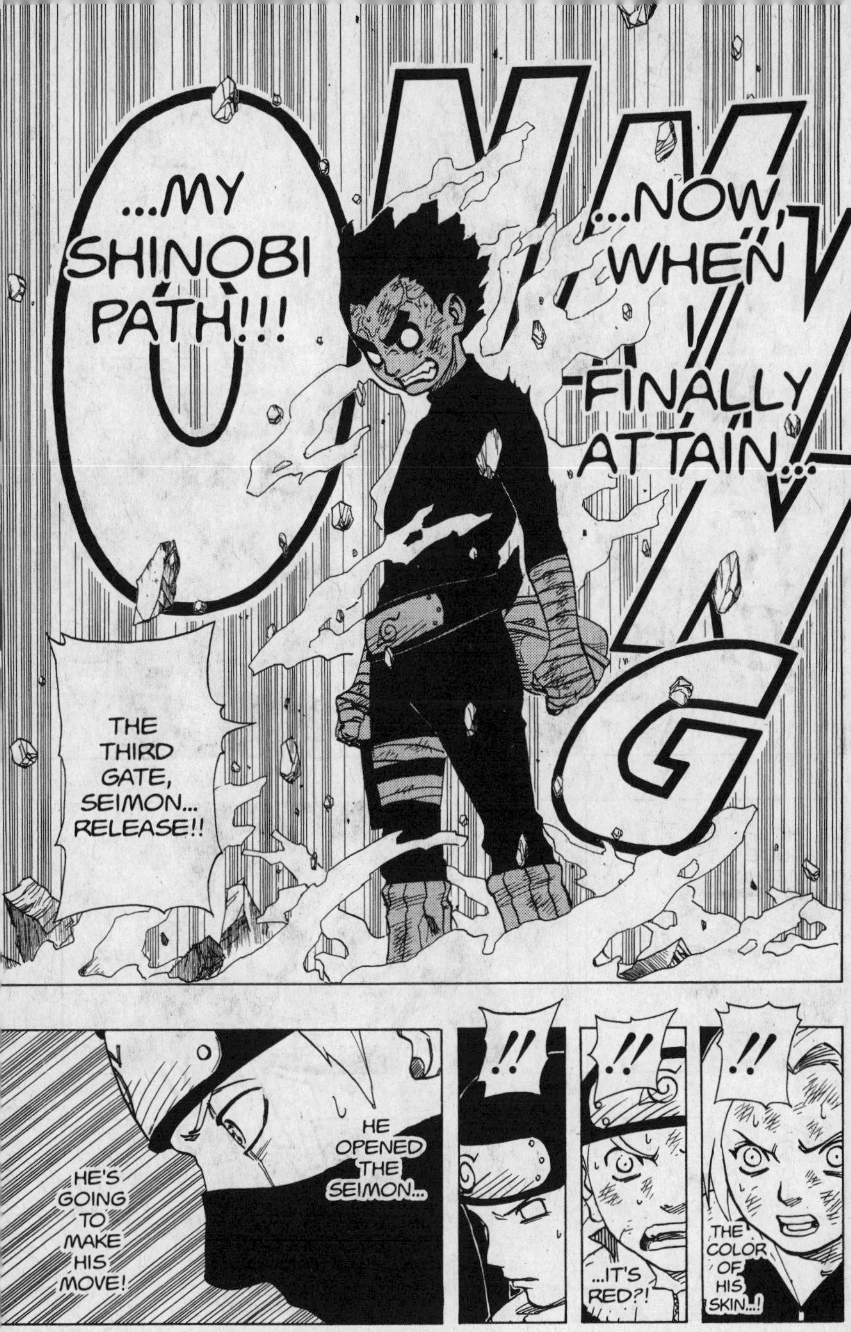
...NOW, WHEN I FINALLY ATTAIN...
...MY SHINOBI PATH!!!
THE THIRD GATE, SEIMON... RELEASE!!
!!
THE COLOR OF HIS SKIN...!
!!
...IT'S RED?!
!!
HE OPENED THE SEIMON...
HE'S GOING TO MAKE HIS MOVE!

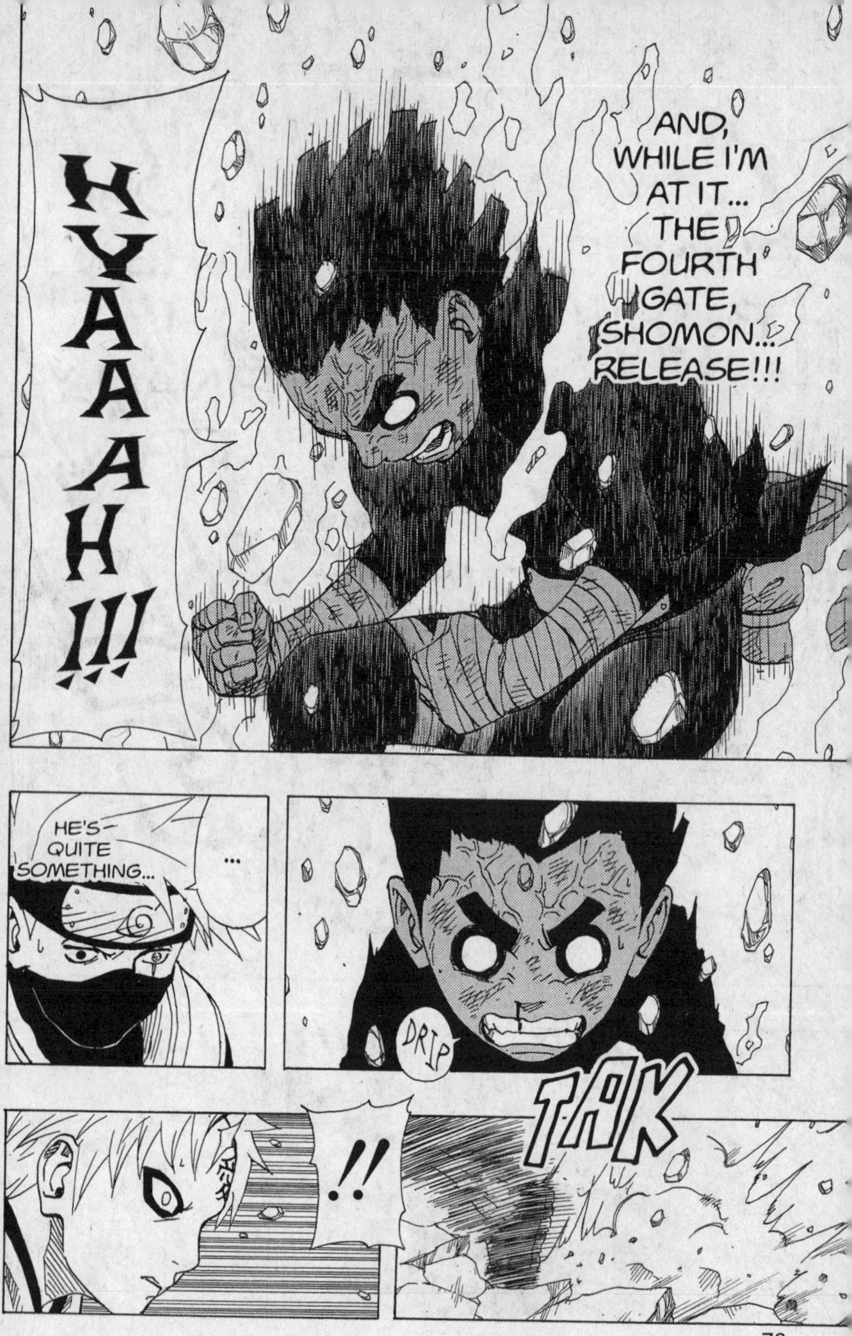
AND, WHILE I'M AT IT... THE FOURTH GATE, SHOMON... RELEASE!!!
HYAAAH!!!
DRIP
HE'S-QUITE SOMETHING...
...
TAK
!!

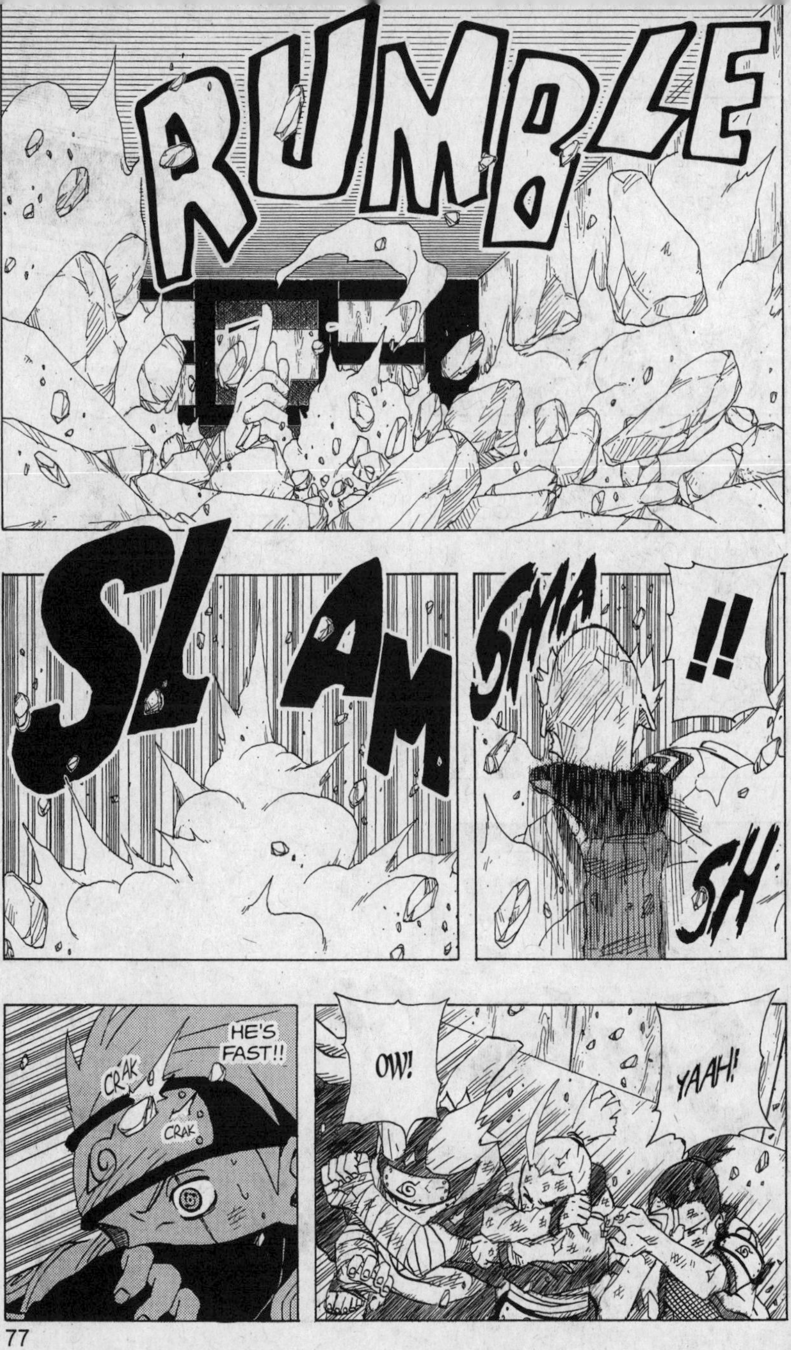

RUMBLE
SMA
!!
SH
SLAM
YAAH!
OW!
HE'S FAST!!
CRAK
CRAK

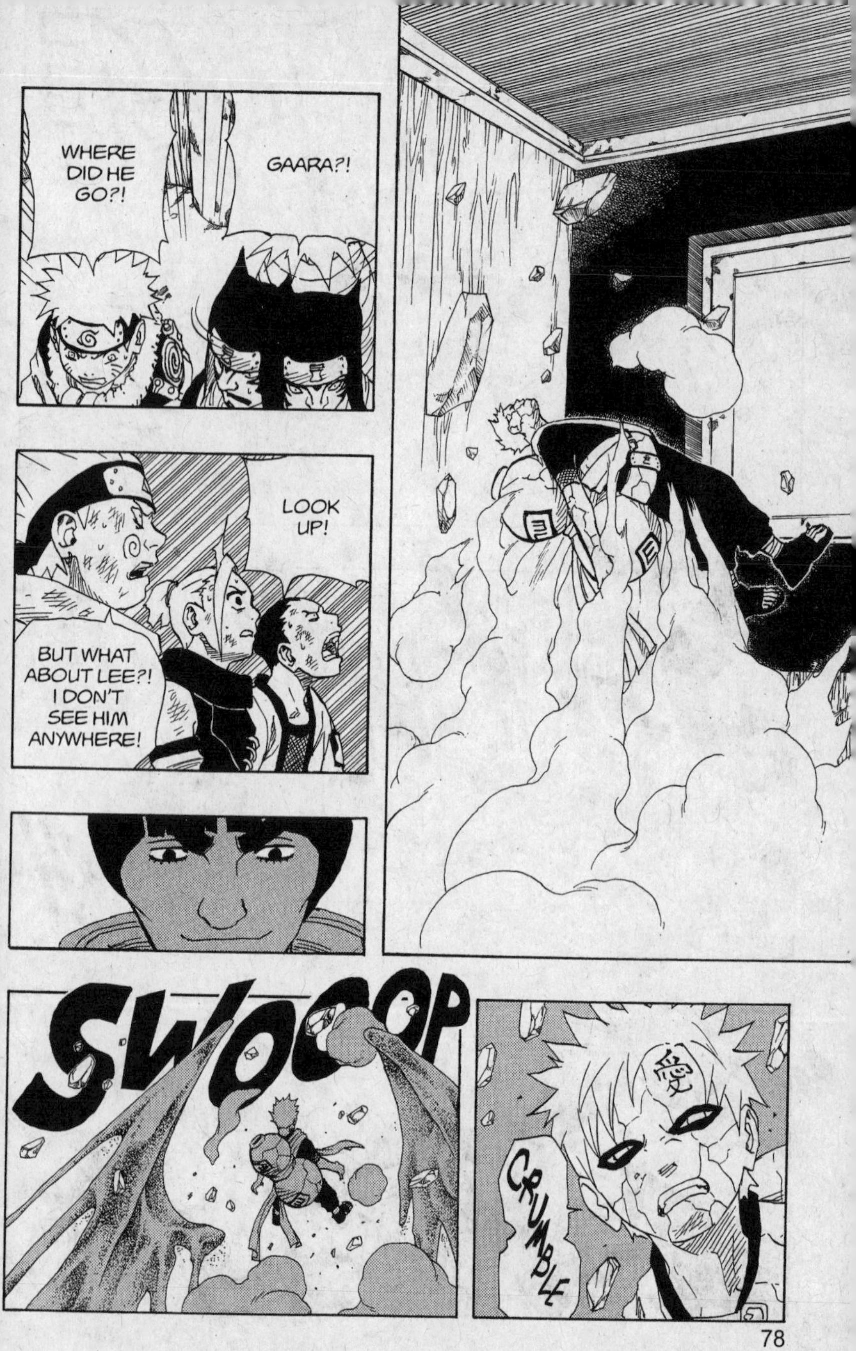
GAARA?!
WHERE DID HE GO?!
LOOK UP!
BUT WHAT ABOUT LEE?! I DON'T SEE HIM ANYWHERE!
CRUMBLE
SWOOOP

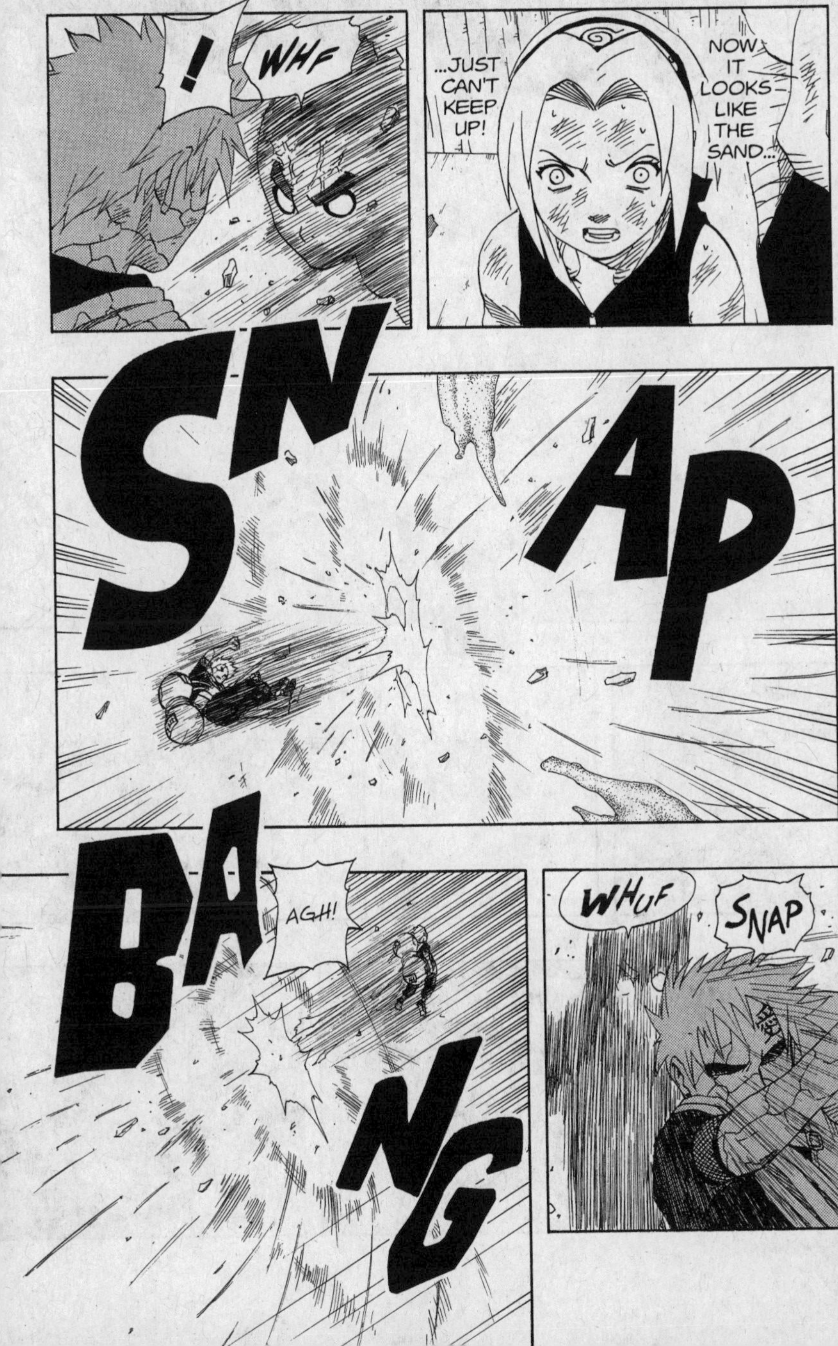
NOW IT LOOKS LIKE THE SAND...
...JUST CAN'T KEEP UP!
!
WHF
SNAP
SNAP
WHUF
AGH!
BANG

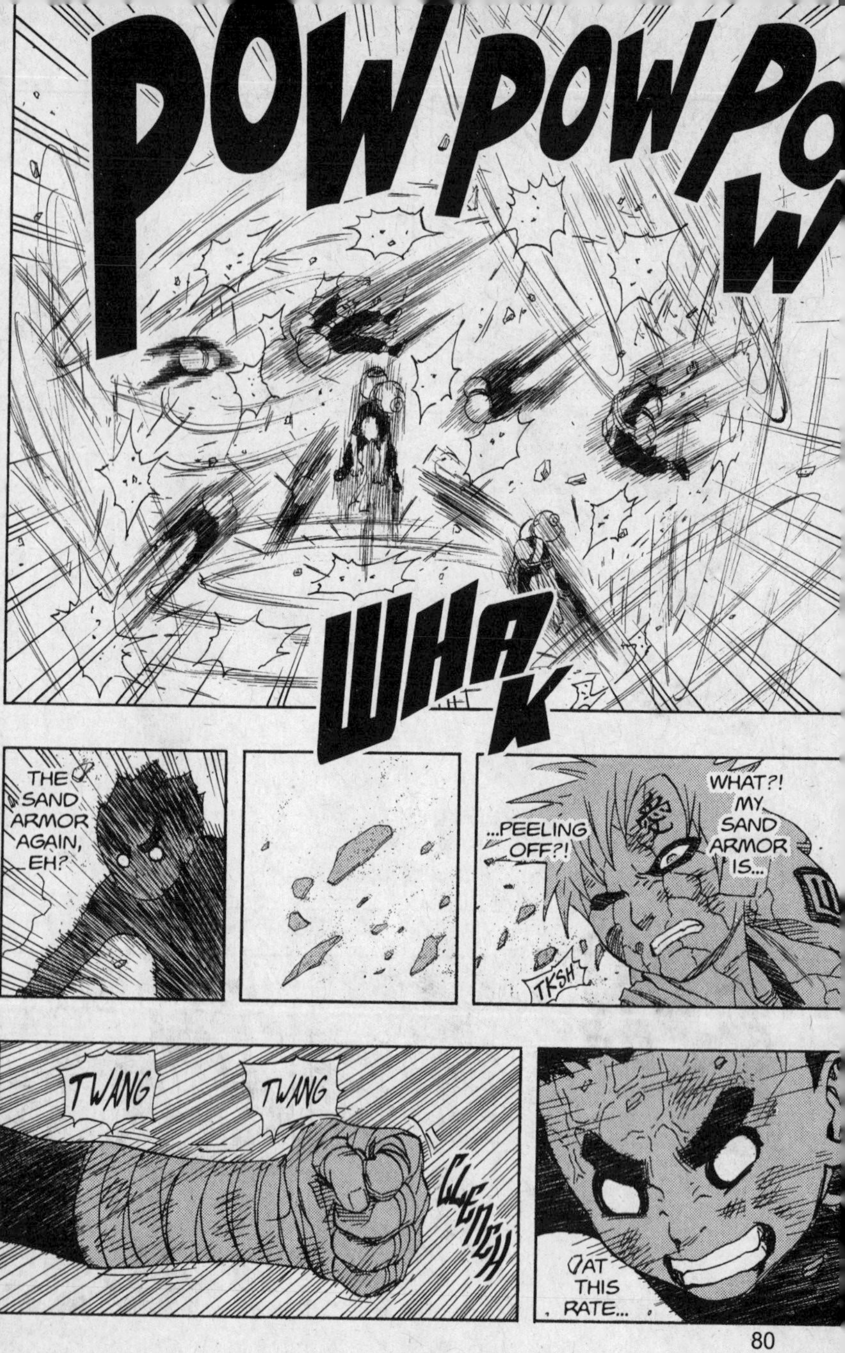
POW POW POW
WHAK
WHAT?! MY SAND ARMOR IS...
...PEELING OFF?!
TKSH
THE SAND ARMOR AGAIN, EH?
AT THIS RATE...
TWANG
TWANG
CLENCH

READ THIS WAY

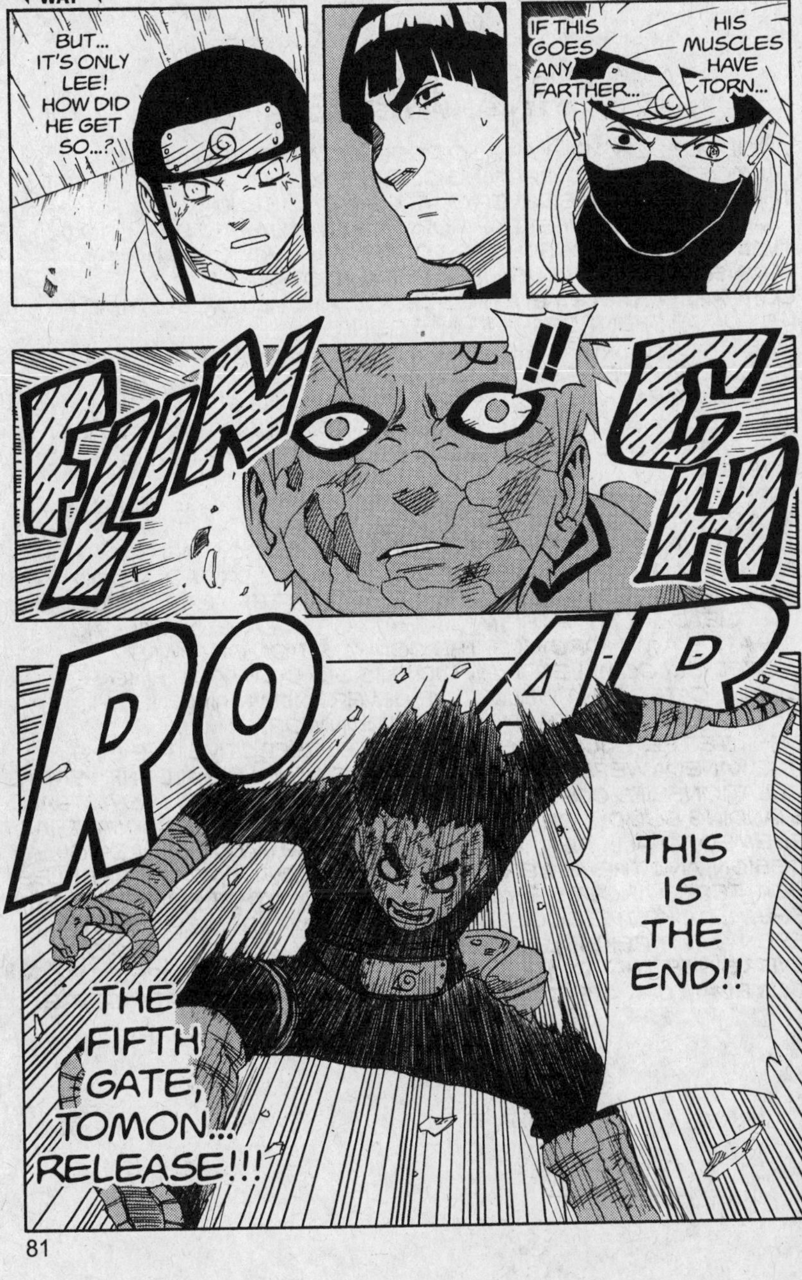

HIS MUSCLES HAVE TORN...
IF THIS GOES ANY FARTHER...
BUT... IT'S ONLY LEE! HOW DID HE GET SO...?
!!
FLINCH
ROAR
THIS IS THE END!!
THE FIFTH GATE, TOMON... RELEASE!!!

THE WORLD OF KISHIMOTO MASASHI
MY PERSONAL HISTORY, PART 12

IN MIDDLE SCHOOL, I WAS SO FOCUSED ON BASEBALL THAT I ALMOST STOPPED DRAWING COMPLETELY.

THERE WERE GAMES EVERY SATURDAY AND SUNDAY, AND PRACTICE EVERY WEEKDAY MORNING. EVEN MY AFTER-SCHOOL TIME WAS FILLED WITH HOURS OF CRAM SCHOOL, SO I WAS ALWAYS INCREDIBLY BUSY. IT WAS LIKE ANOTHER WORLD COMPARED TO ELEMENTARY SCHOOL, AND ALL OF THE TIME I HAD ONCE SPENT DRAWING WAS GONE.

ONE DAY, JUST WHEN I WAS STARTING TO THINK, "MAYBE I'VE OUTGROWN THE URGE TO BE DRAWING ALL THE TIME," I HAD A SUDDEN AND INCREDIBLE REVELATION. IT WAS SO AMAZING THAT I STILL LOOK BACK ON THAT MOMENT AS A HUGE TURNING POINT. THE AMAZING MOMENT OCCURRED WHEN I SAW A MOVIE POSTER.

I WAS ON MY WAY HOME ONE DAY WHEN I HAPPENED TO GLANCE AT A POSTER FOR OTOMO KATSUHIRO'S *AKIRA*.

IN AN INSTANT, THE SIGHT OF IT HAD AN IMPACT ON ME SO POWERFUL THAT EVEN NOW IT'S HARD TO DESCRIBE. I STOOD STARING AT IT FOR OVER AN HOUR. THE POSTER FEATURED AN OVERHEAD SHOT OF THE MAIN CHARACTER, KANEDA, WALKING TOWARDS A MOTORCYCLE. THE COMPOSITION OF IT WAS INCREDIBLY COMPLEX. "HOW DID THIS GUY DRAW ANYTHING SO COMPLICATED THAT WELL?" "I'VE NEVER KNOWN ANYONE WHO COULD HAVE MADE THAT COMPOSITION WORK..."

DESPITE THE TRICKY ANGLES OF THE PERSPECTIVE, THE BIKE AND KANEDA WERE BOTH DRAWN PERFECTLY, WITH ALL THE SPATIAL RELATIONSHIPS CORRECT. THE SENSE THAT KANEDA WAS ACTUALLY STANDING SOLIDLY ON THE GROUND WAS CONVEYED IN A WAY THAT SEEMED TOTALLY REAL AND COOL. THE BIKE HAD AN AMAZING DESIGN, AND THERE WERE CRACKS IN THE GROUND AND PEBBLES SCATTERED ABOUT, SEEMINGLY AT RANDOM. THAT POSTER SEEMED LIKE THE COOLEST, MOST ORIGINAL THING I HAD EVER SEEN AND IT REKINDLED THE FLAME OF MY ARTISTIC PASSION. EVER SINCE THAT DAY, I'VE KEPT DRAWING WITH THE HOPE THAT SOMEDAY I CAN APPROACH THE STANDARD SET BY THAT PICTURE.

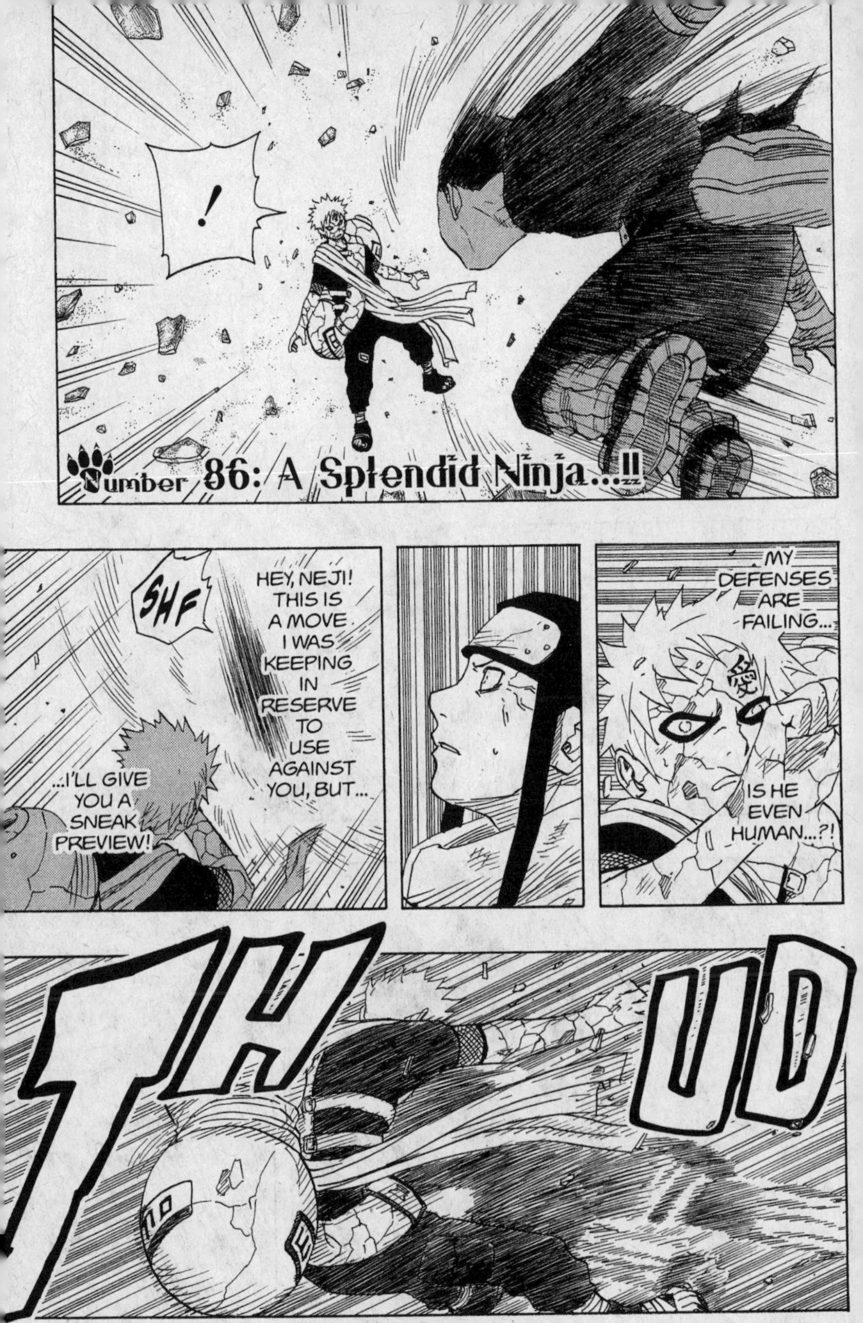
!
Number 86: A Splendid Ninja...!!
MY DEFENSES ARE FAILING...
IS HE EVEN HUMAN...?!
HEY, NEJI! THIS IS A MOVE I WAS KEEPING IN RESERVE TO USE AGAINST YOU, BUT...
SHF
...I'LL GIVE YOU A SNEAK PREVIEW!
THUD

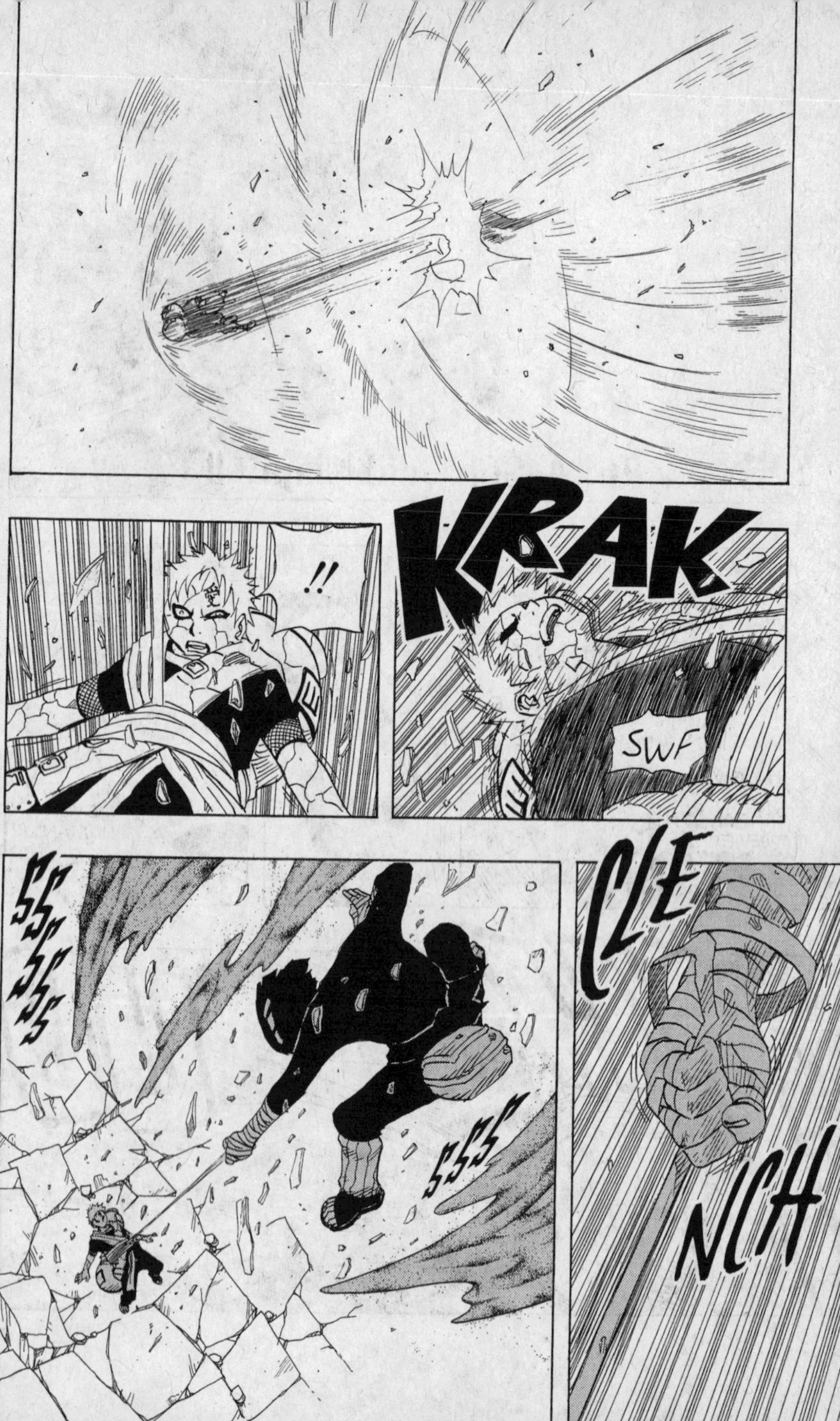
KRAK
SWF
!!
CLE
NCH
SSSSS
SSS

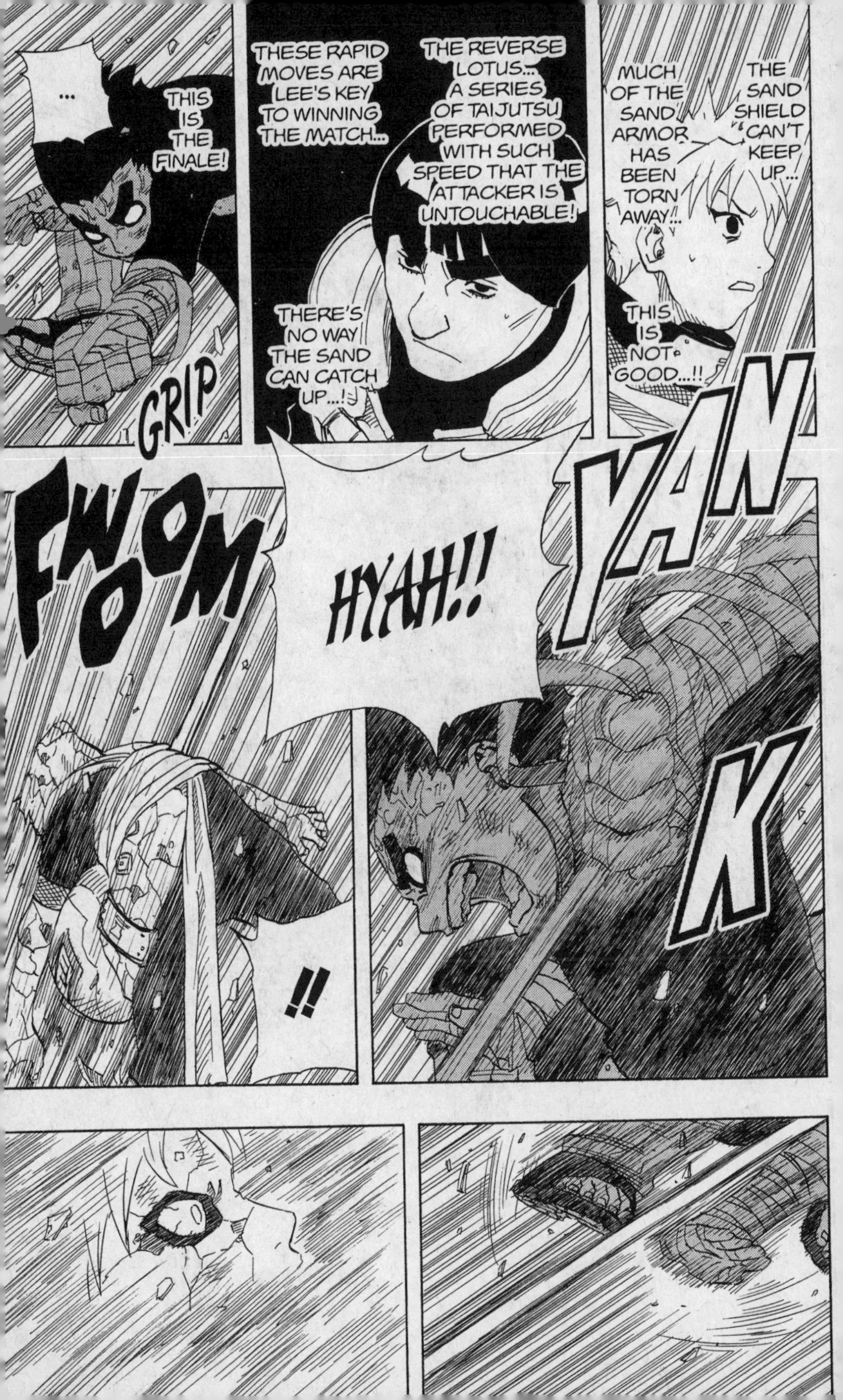
MUCH OF THE SAND ARMOR HAS BEEN TORN AWAY...!!
THE SAND SHIELD CAN'T KEEP UP...
THIS IS NOT GOOD...!!
THE REVERSE LOTUS... A SERIES OF TAIJUTSU PERFORMED WITH SUCH SPEED THAT THE ATTACKER IS UNTOUCHABLE!
THESE RAPID MOVES ARE LEE'S KEY TO WINNING THE MATCH...
THERE'S NO WAY THE SAND CAN CATCH UP...!
...
THIS IS THE FINALE!
GRIP
YANK
HYAH!!
FWOOM
!!

Number 86: A Splendid Ninja...!!

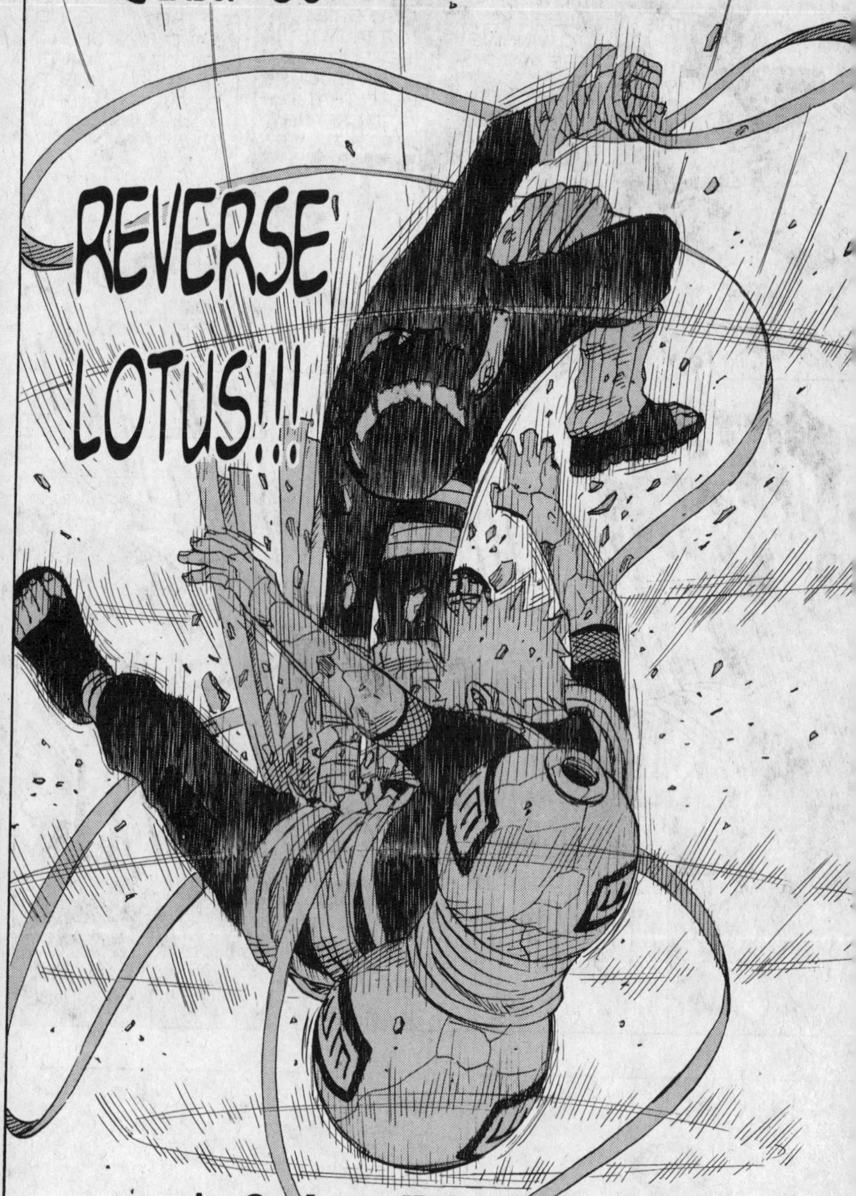
REVERSE LOTUS!!!

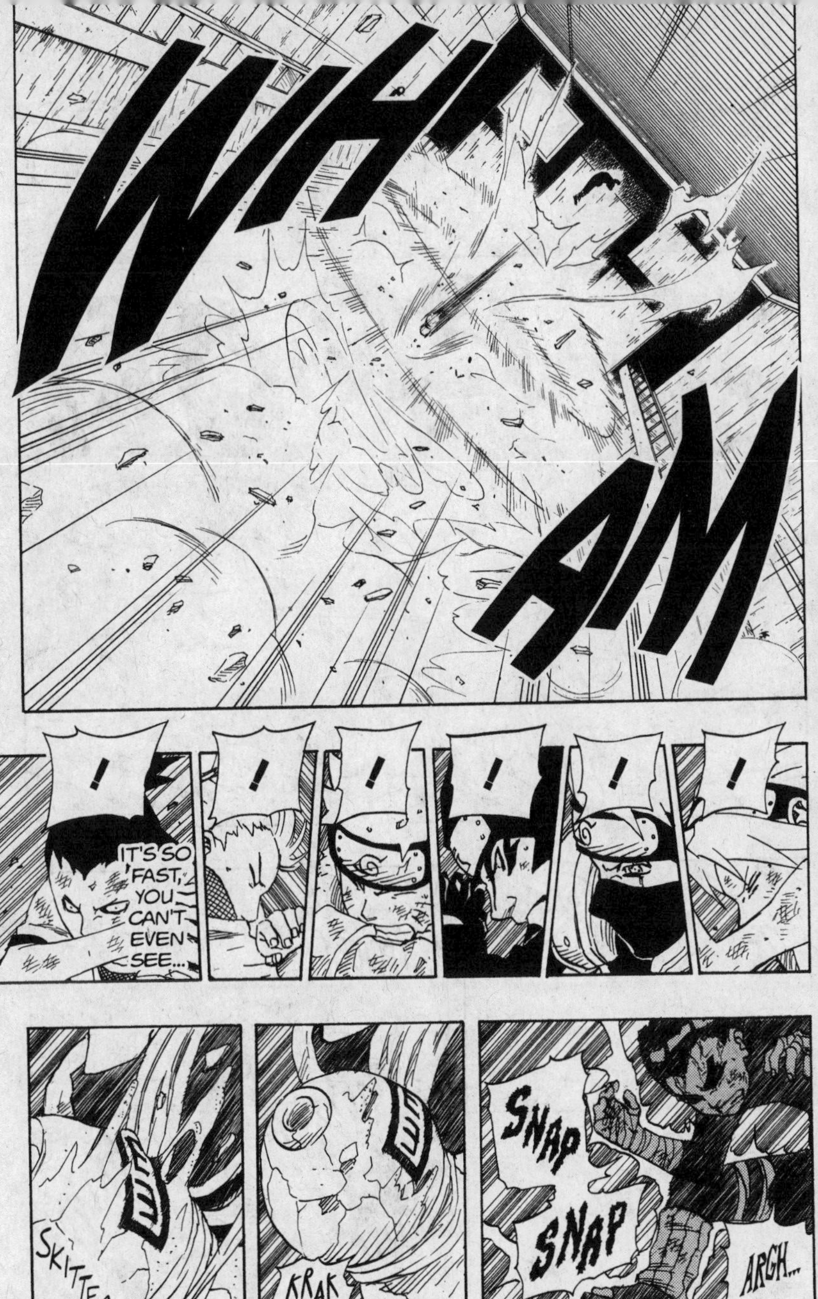
WHAM
!
!
!
!
!
!
IT'S SO FAST, YOU CAN'T EVEN SEE...
SNAP
SNAP
ARGH...
KRAK
SKITTER

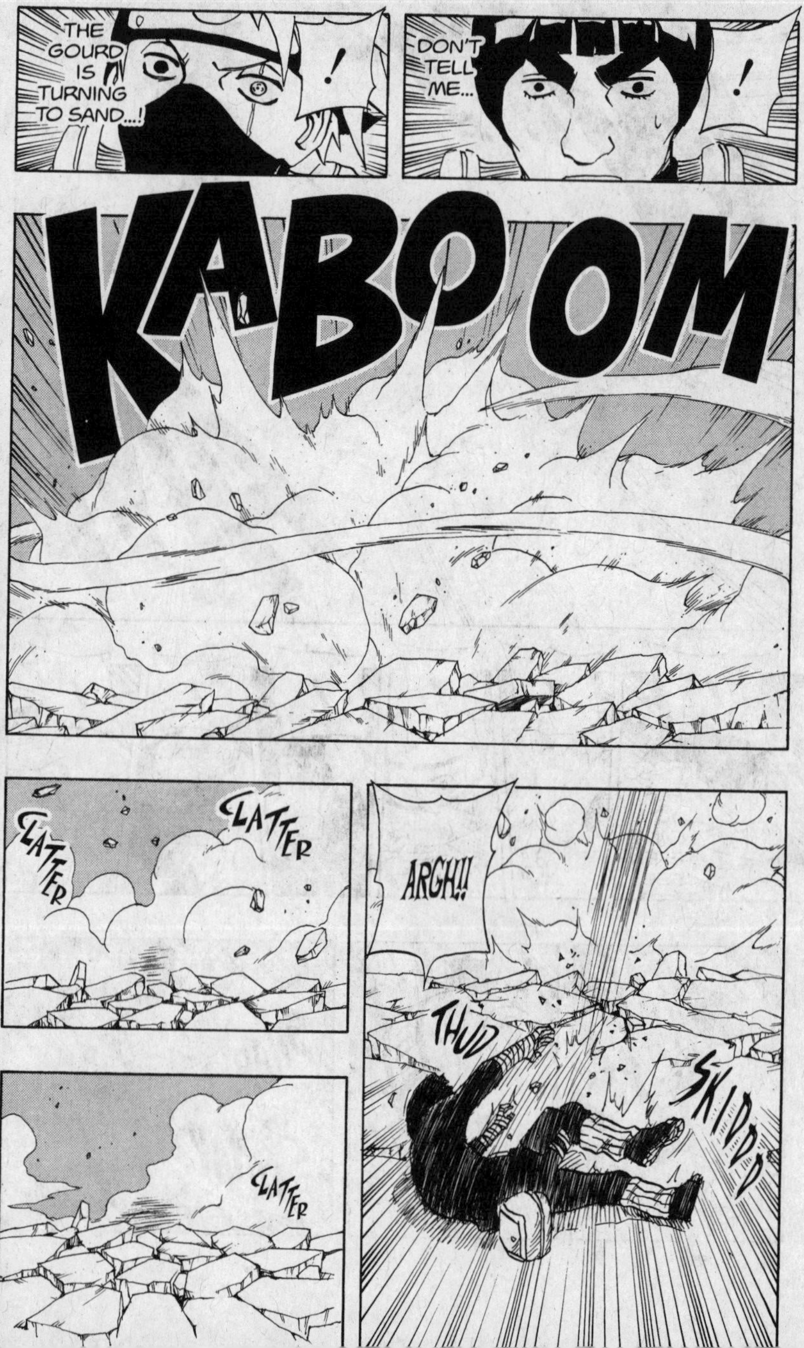
DON'T TELL ME...
!
THE GOURD IS TURNING TO SAND...!
!
KABOOM
ARGH!!
THUD
SKIDDD
CLATTER
CLATTER
CLATTER

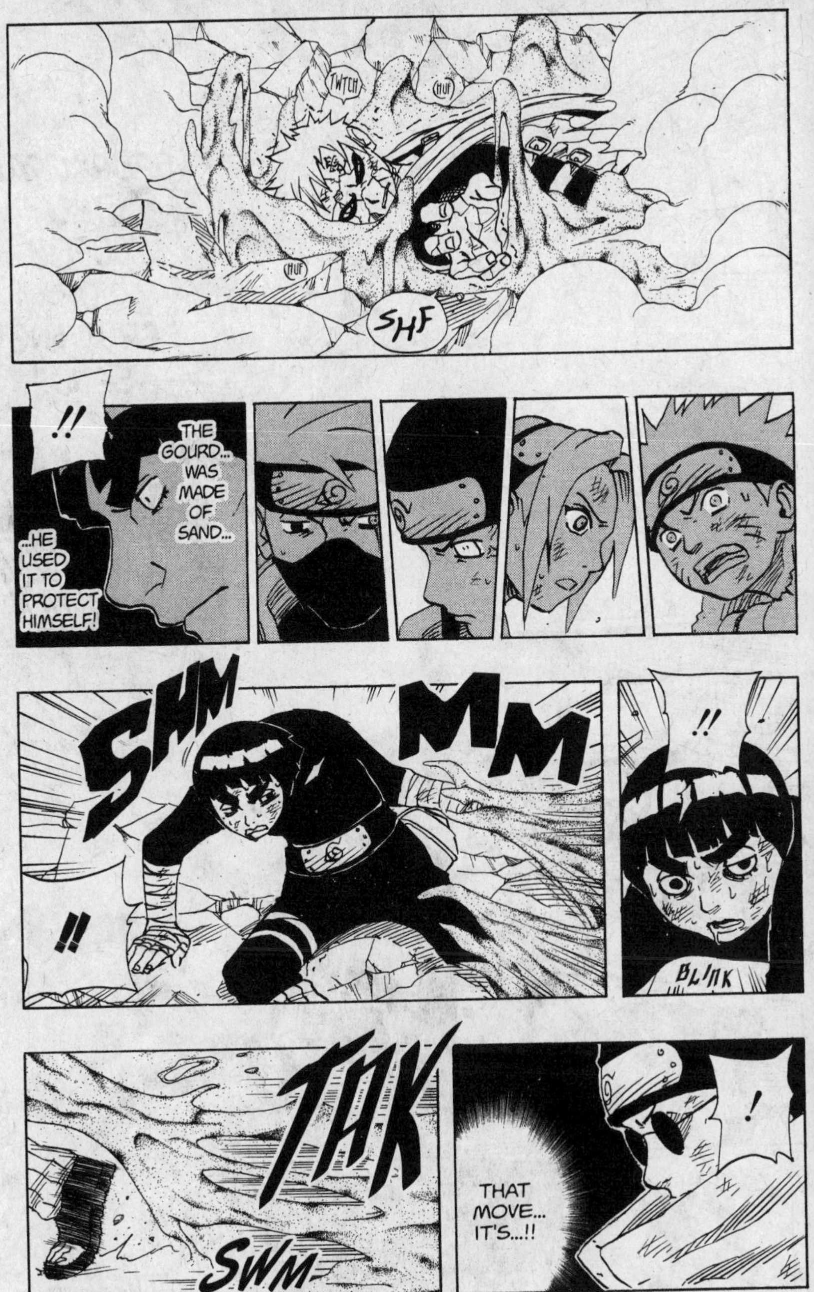
TWTCH
HUF
HUF
SHF
!!
THE GOURD... WAS MADE OF SAND...
...HE USED IT TO PROTECT HIMSELF!
!!
BLINK
SHMMM
!!
!
THAT MOVE... IT'S...!!
TAK
SWM

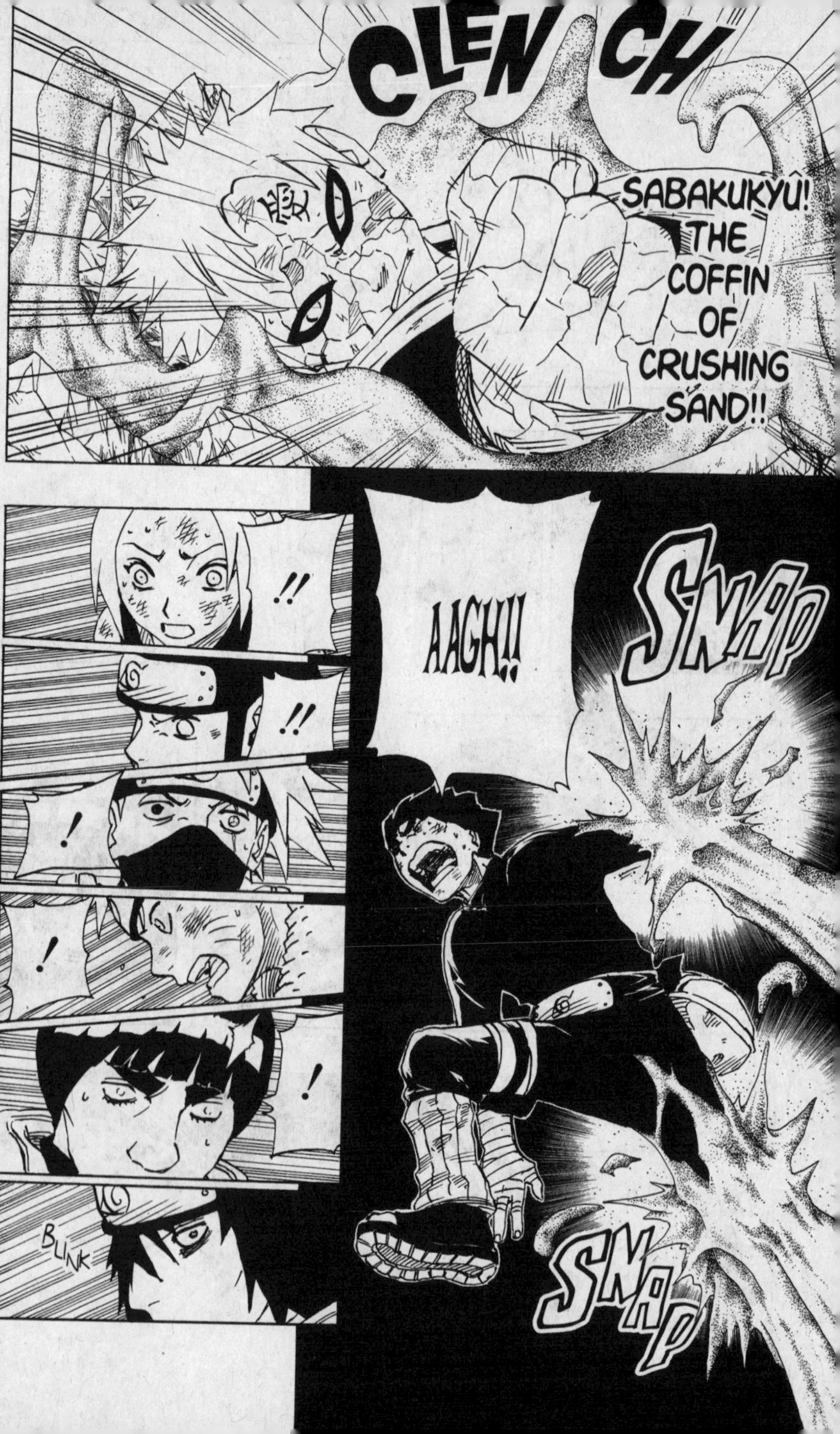
CLENCH
SABAKUKYÛ! THE COFFIN OF CRUSHING SAND!!
AAGH!!
SNAP
SNAP
!!
!!
!
!
!
BLINK

READ THIS WAY

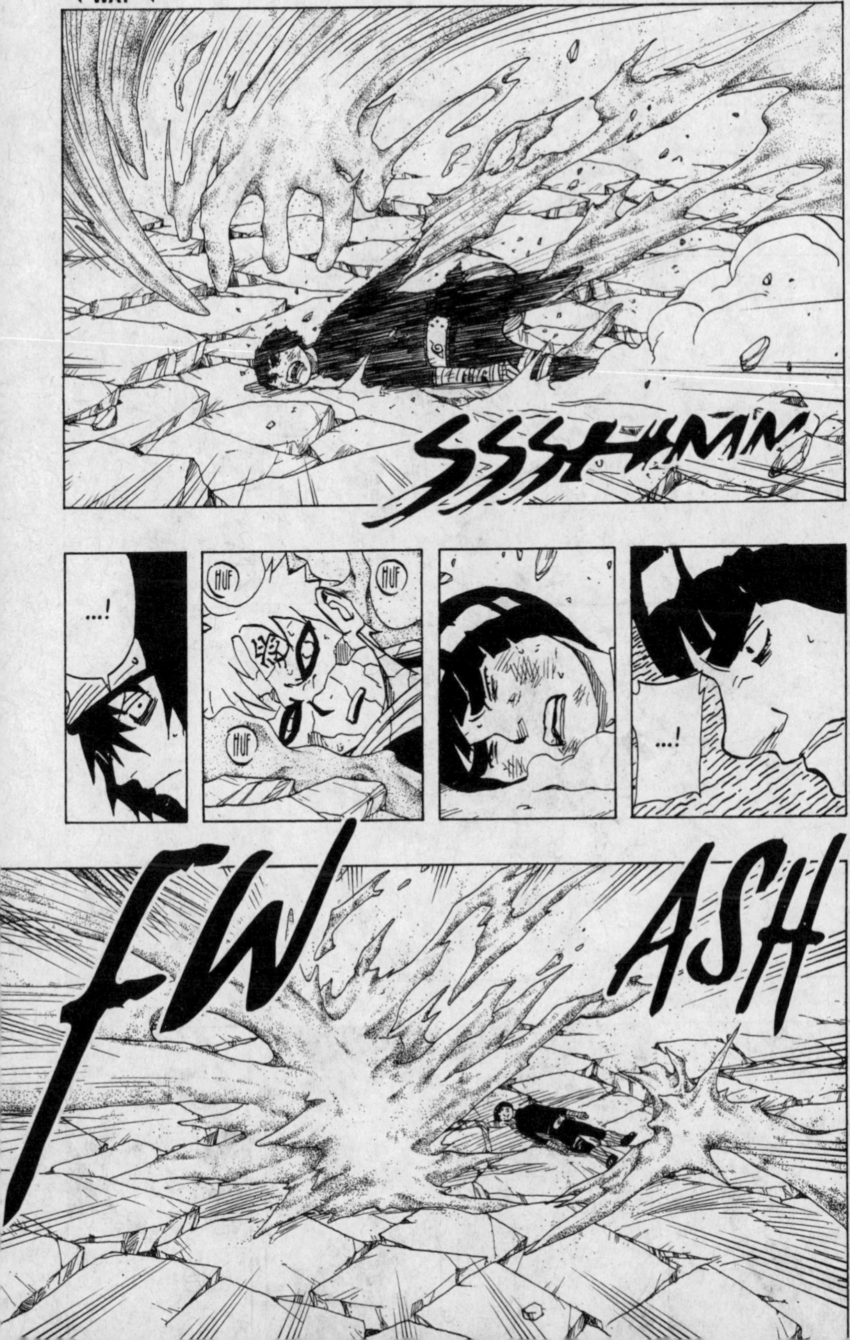
SSSHMMN
...!
HUF
HUF
HUF
...!
FWASH

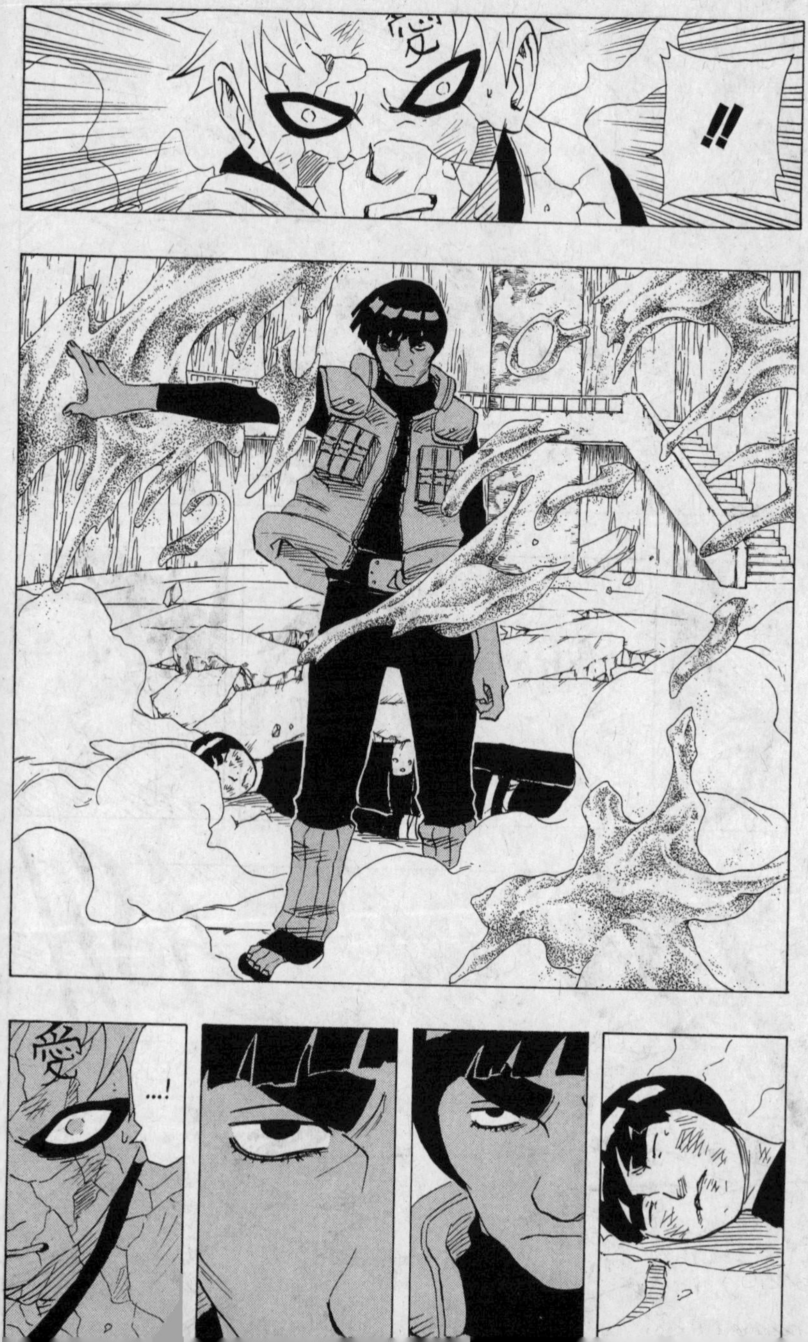

!!
...!

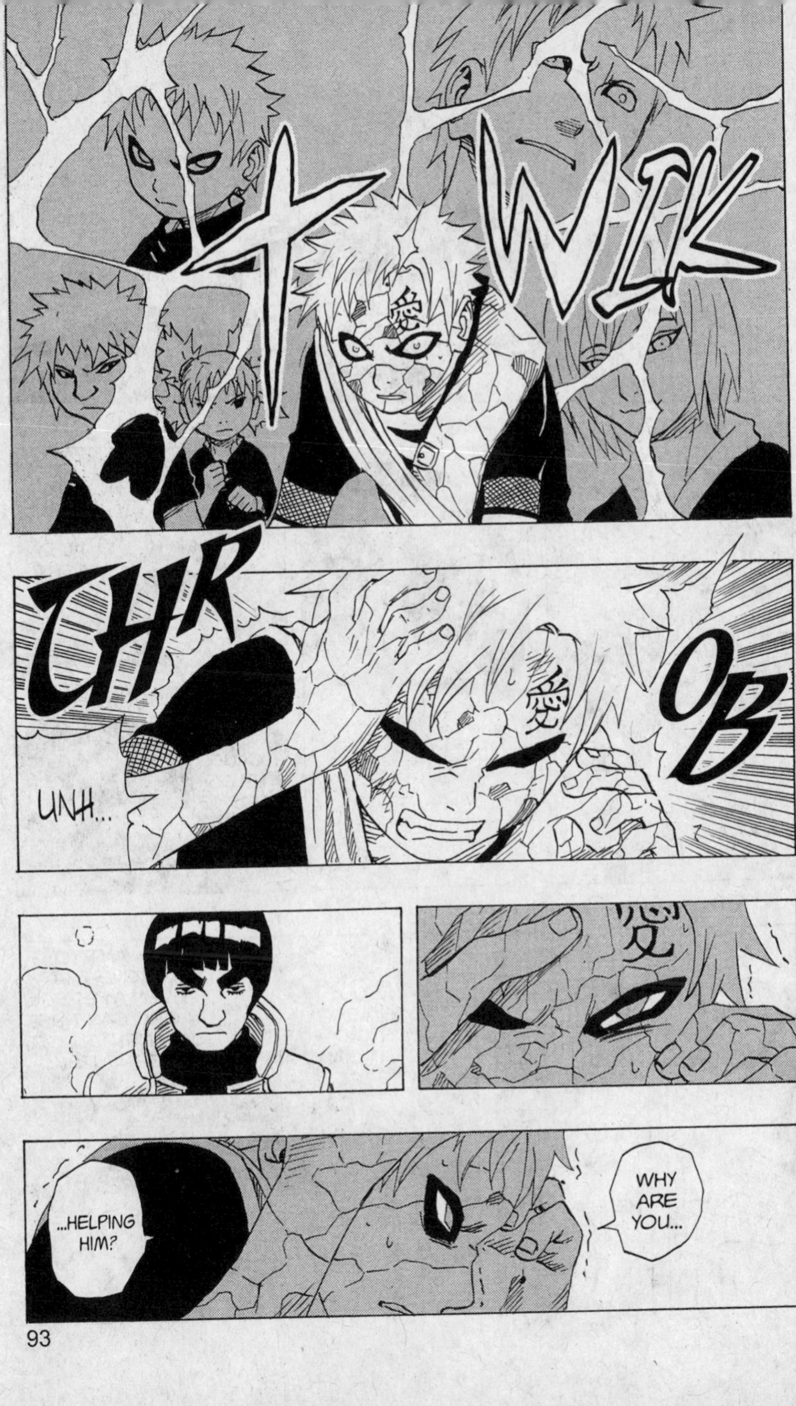
TWIK
CHROB
UNH...
WHY ARE YOU...
...HELPING HIM?

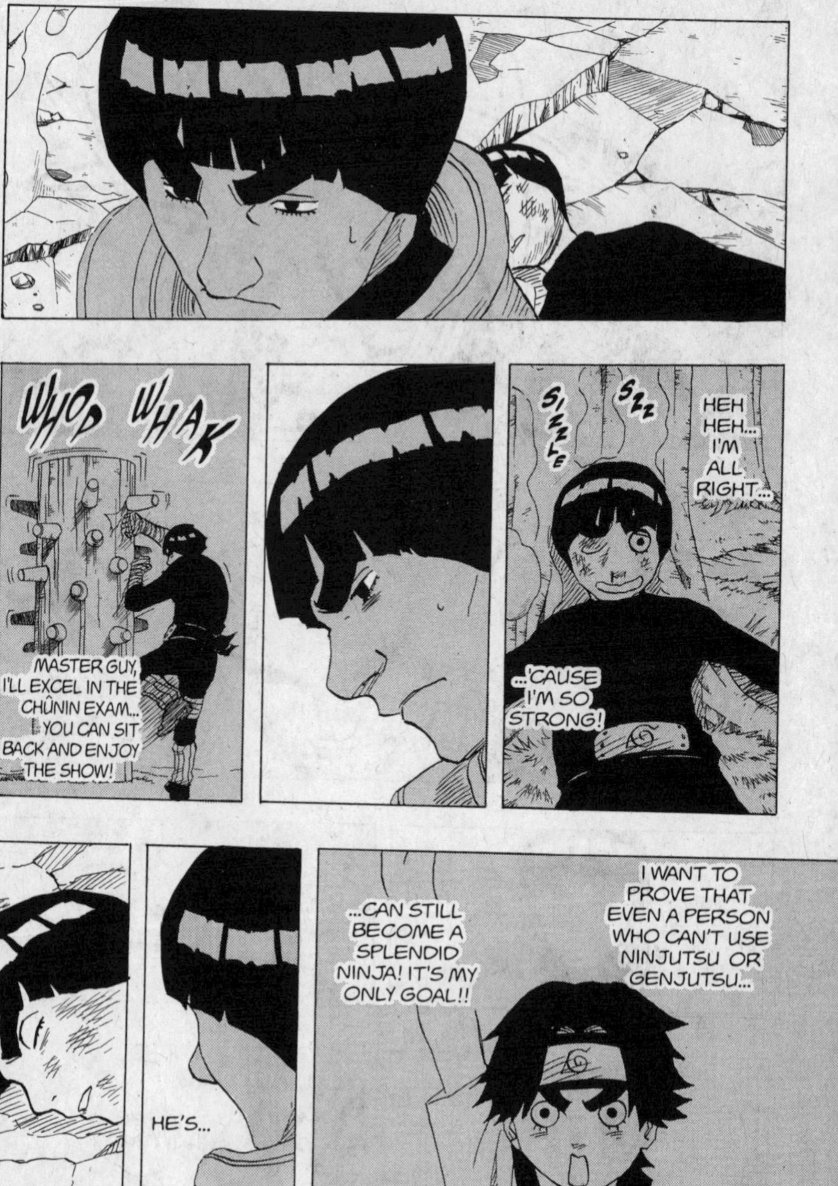
SIZZLE
SZZ
HEH HEH... I'M ALL RIGHT...
...'CAUSE I'M SO STRONG!
WHOP
WHAK
MASTER GUY, I'LL EXCEL IN THE CHÛNIN EXAM... YOU CAN SIT BACK AND ENJOY THE SHOW!
I WANT TO PROVE THAT EVEN A PERSON WHO CAN'T USE NINJUTSU OR GENJUTSU...
...CAN STILL BECOME A SPLENDID NINJA! IT'S MY ONLY GOAL!!
HE'S...

READ THIS WAY

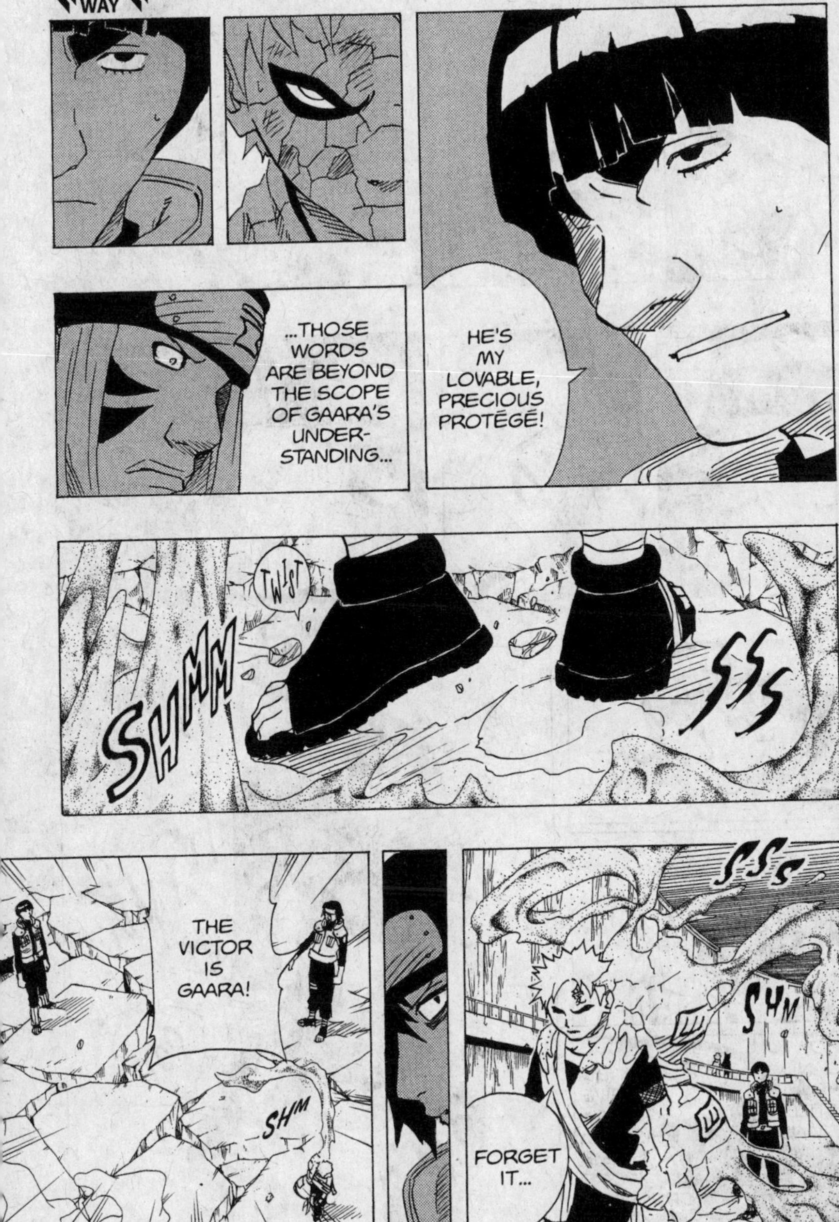
HE'S MY LOVABLE, PRECIOUS PROTÉGÉ!
...THOSE WORDS ARE BEYOND THE SCOPE OF GAARA'S UNDER-STANDING...
SSS
TWIST
SHMM
SSS
SHM
FORGET IT...
THE VICTOR IS GAARA!
SHM

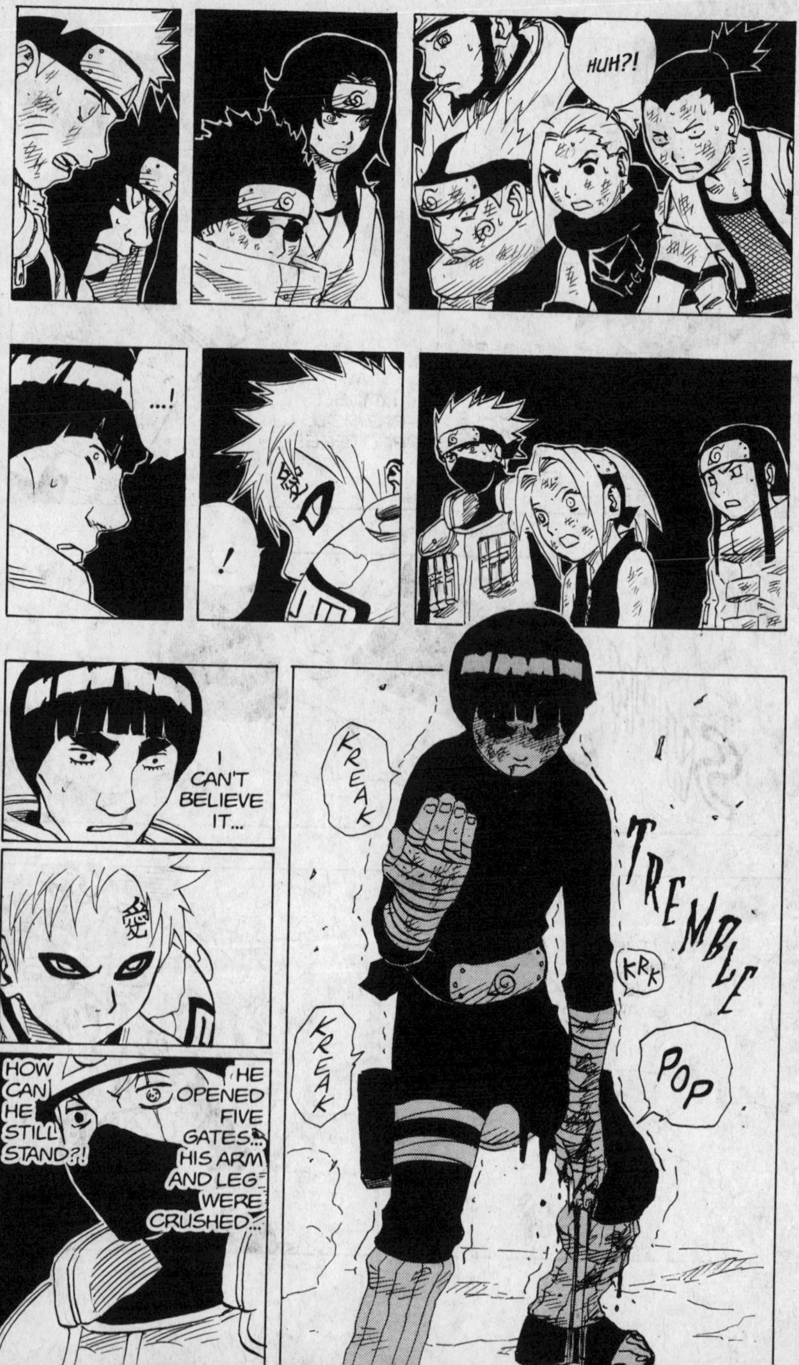
HUH?!
!
...!
KREAK
TREMBLE
KRK
POP
KREAK
I CAN'T BELIEVE IT...
HE OPENED FIVE GATES... HIS ARM AND LEG WERE CRUSHED...
HOW CAN HE STILL STAND?!

READ THIS WAY

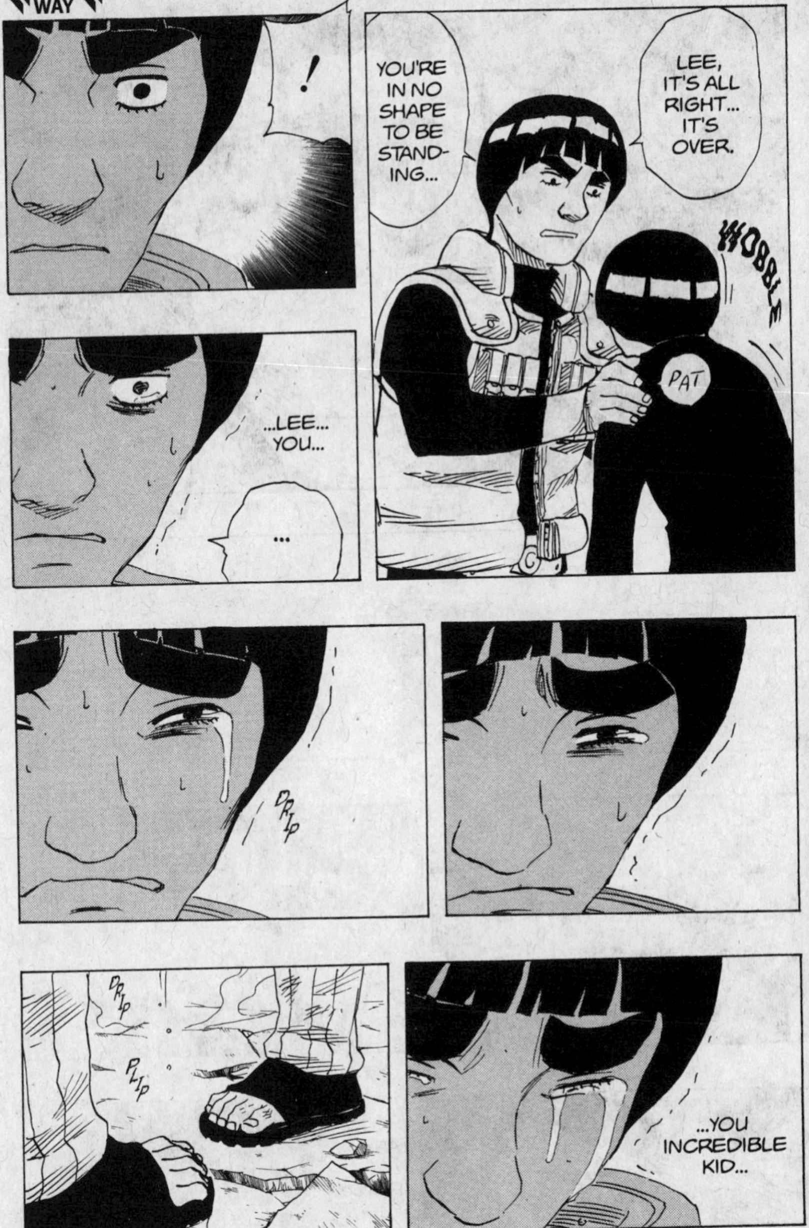
LEE, IT'S ALL RIGHT... IT'S OVER.
YOU'RE IN NO SHAPE TO BE STANDING...
WOBBLE
PAT
!
...LEE... YOU...
...
DRIP
...YOU INCREDIBLE KID...
DRIP
PLIP

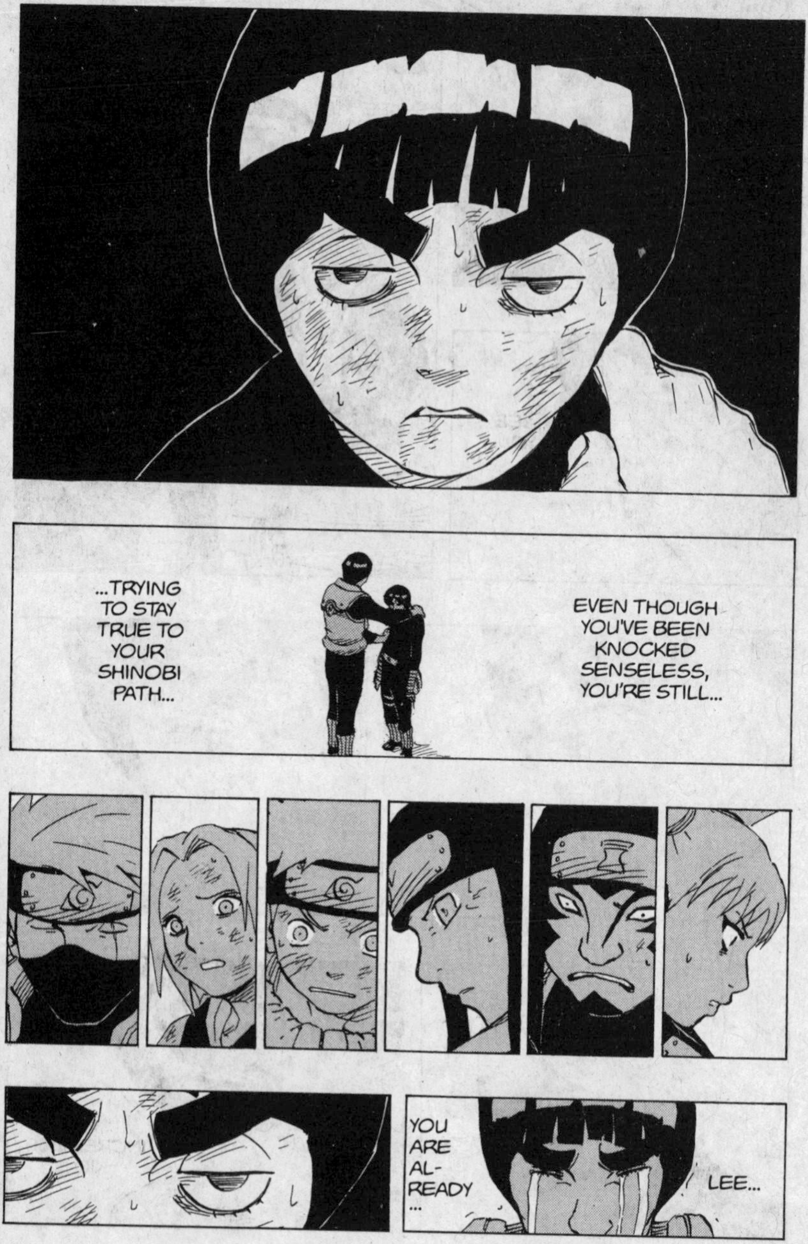

EVEN THOUGH YOU'VE BEEN KNOCKED SENSELESS, YOU'RE STILL...
...TRYING TO STAY TRUE TO YOUR SHINOBI PATH...
YOU ARE AL-READY ...
LEE...

READ THIS WAY

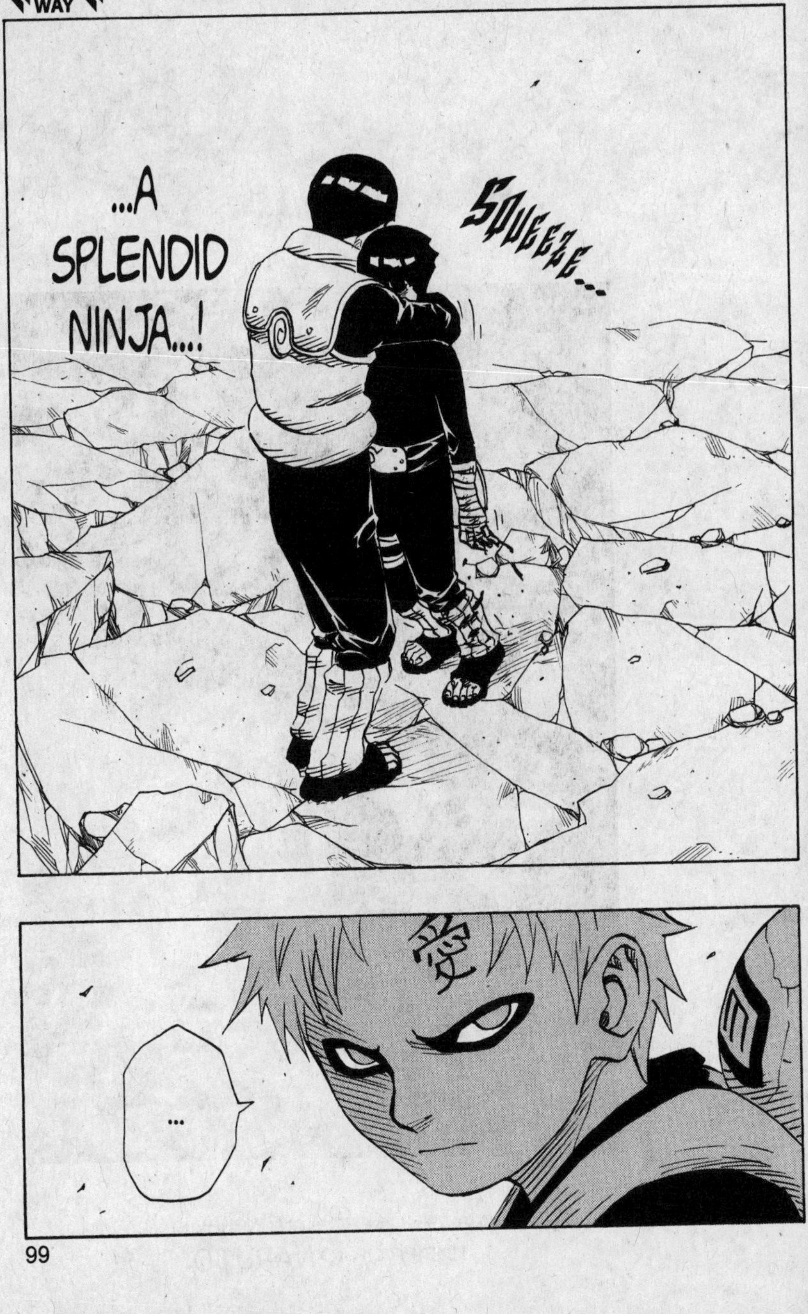

SQUEEZE...
...A SPLENDID NINJA...!
...

• THIS CHARACTER IS FROM AN UNPUBLISHED WORK
I DID PRIOR TO NARUTO.

Number 87: The Preliminaries... Completed!!

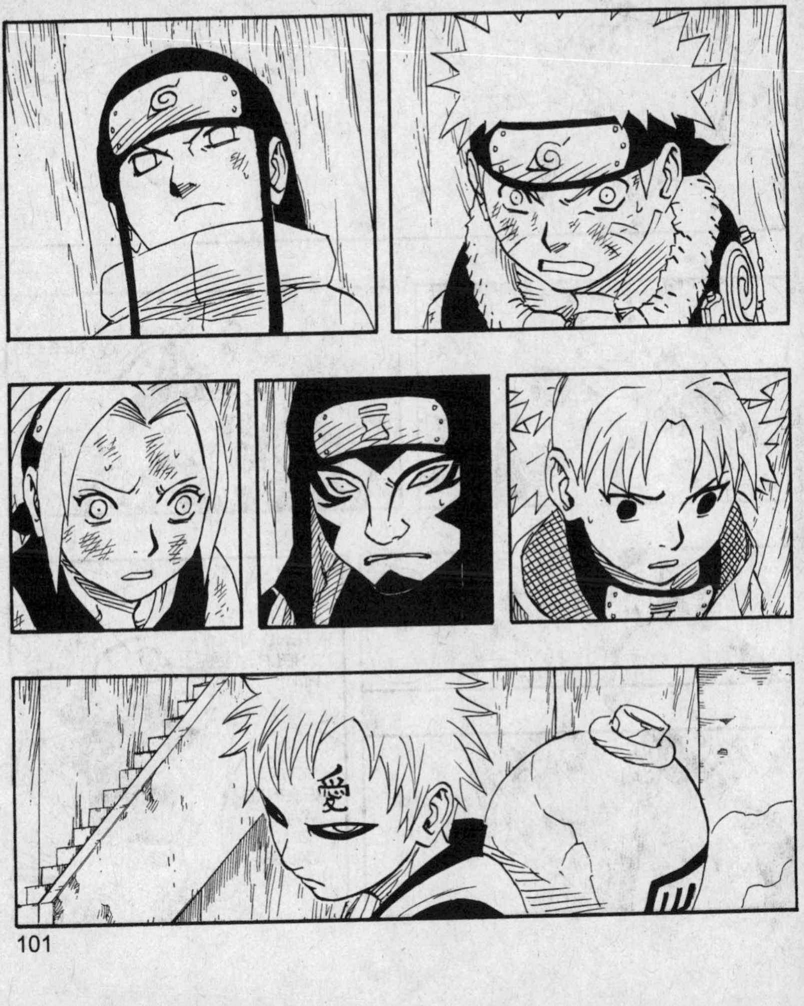

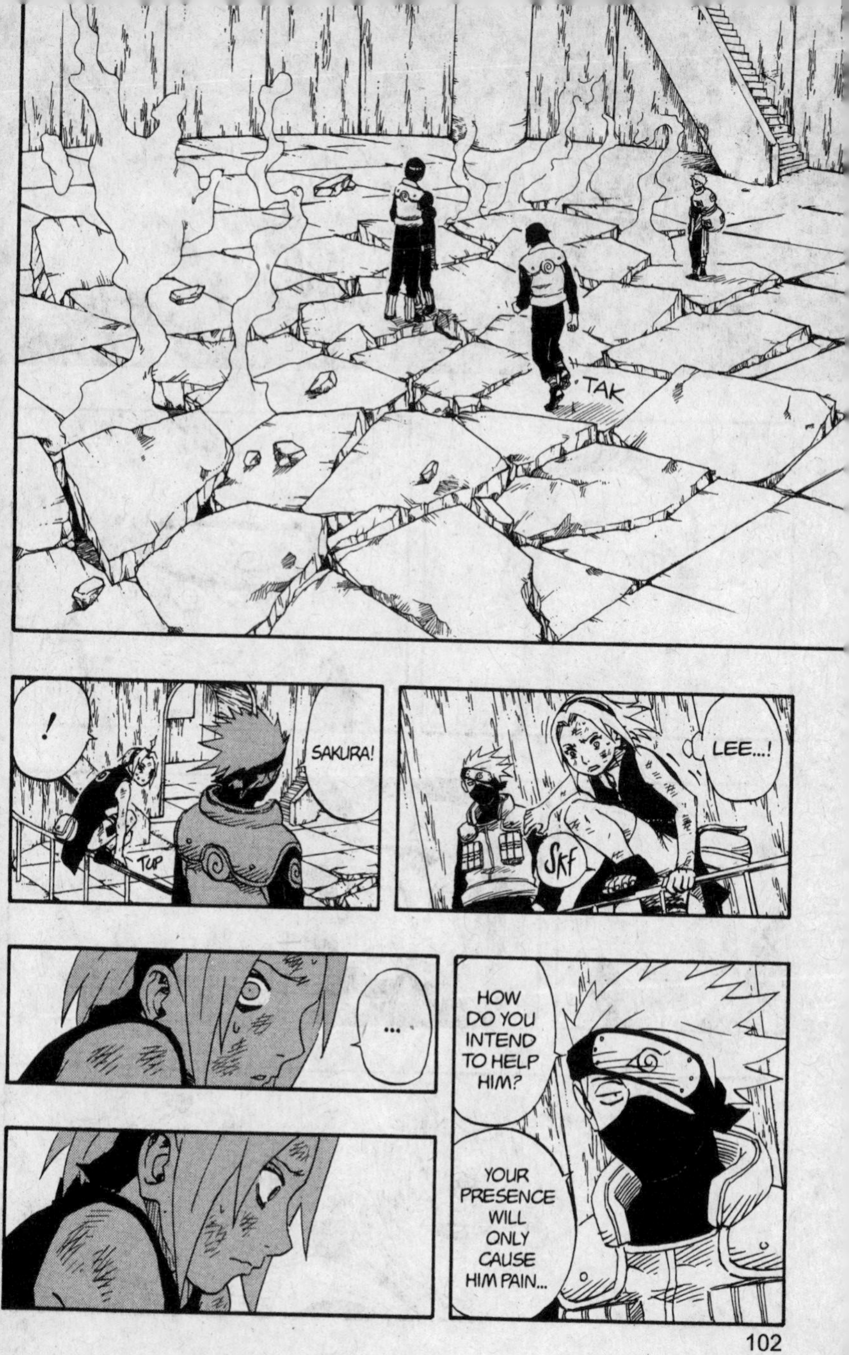
TAK
LEE...!
SKF
SAKURA!
!
TUP
HOW DO YOU INTEND TO HELP HIM?
YOUR PRESENCE WILL ONLY CAUSE HIM PAIN...
...

HOP

!

HMPH! HE NEVER HAD A CHANCE AGAINST GAARA...

SHF

NARUTO...

HOW COULD BUSHY BROWS LOSE TO SUCH A JERK?!

TAK

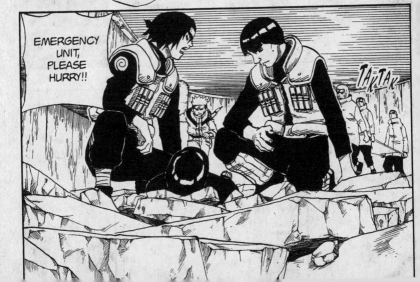

EMERGENCY UNIT, PLEASE HURRY!!

TAK TAK

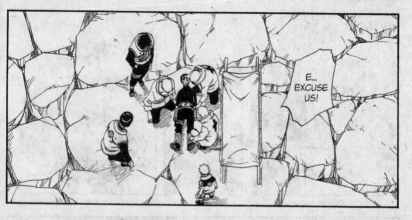

E... EXCUSE US!

...

ARE YOU THE JÔNIN RESPONSIBLE FOR HIM? IF I MAY HAVE A WORD...

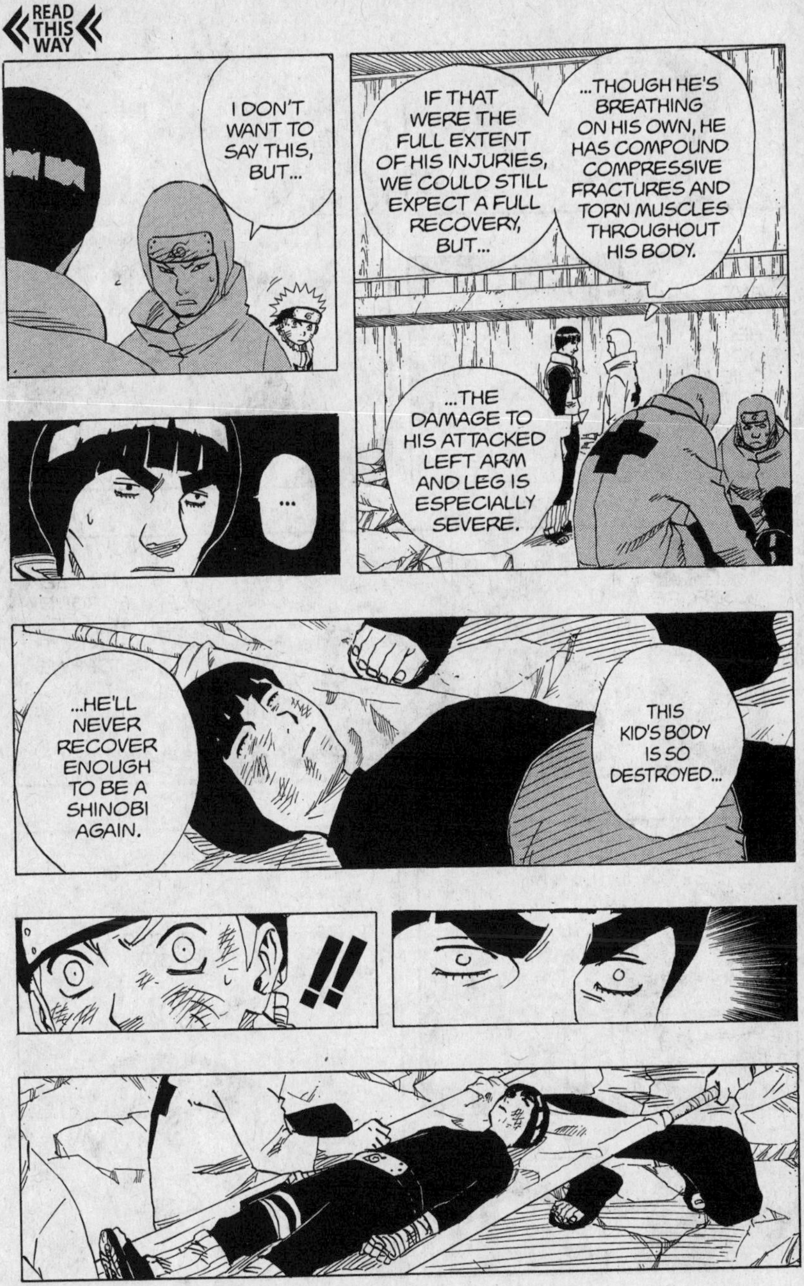
READ THIS WAY
...THOUGH HE'S BREATHING ON HIS OWN, HE HAS COMPOUND COMPRESSIVE FRACTURES AND TORN MUSCLES THROUGHOUT HIS BODY.
IF THAT WERE THE FULL EXTENT OF HIS INJURIES, WE COULD STILL EXPECT A FULL RECOVERY, BUT...
...THE DAMAGE TO HIS ATTACKED LEFT ARM AND LEG IS ESPECIALLY SEVERE.
I DON'T WANT TO SAY THIS, BUT...
...
THIS KID'S BODY IS SO DESTROYED...
...HE'LL NEVER RECOVER ENOUGH TO BE A SHINOBI AGAIN.
!!

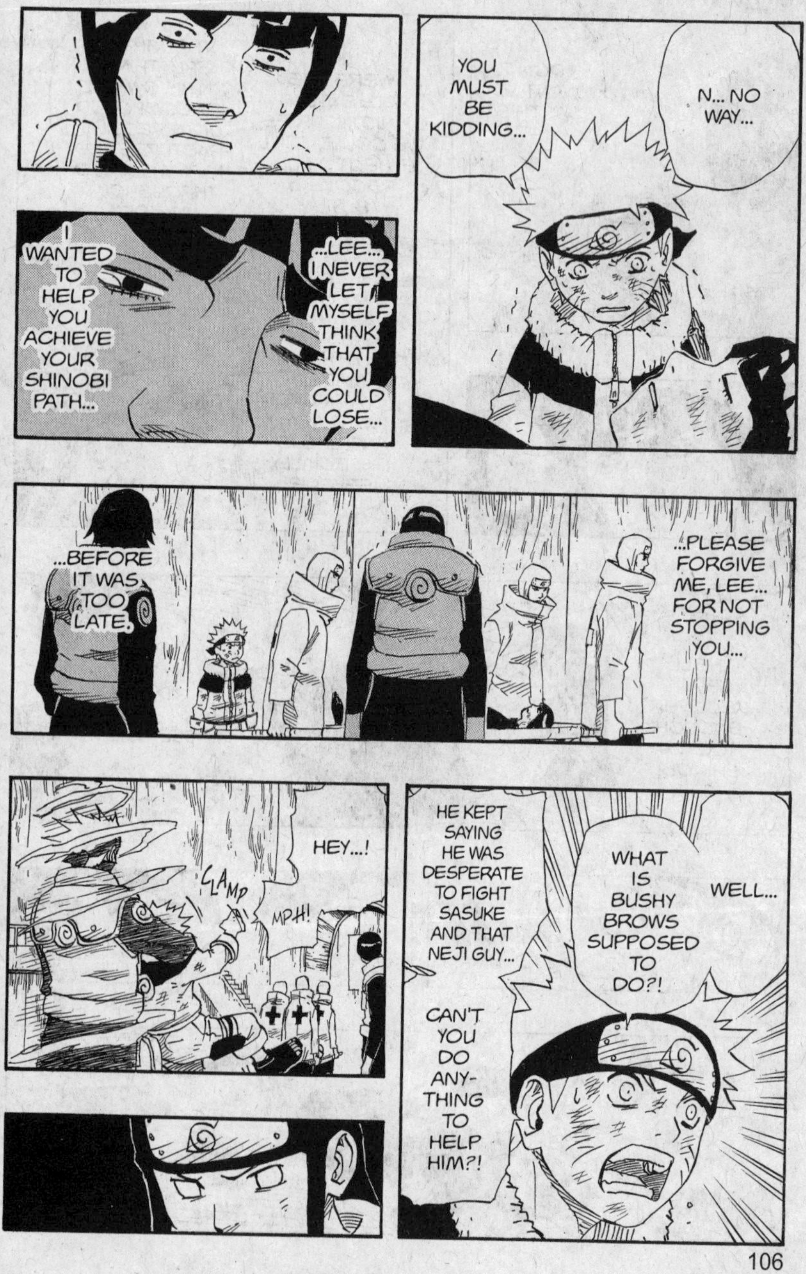
N... NO WAY...
YOU MUST BE KIDDING...
...LEE... I NEVER LET MYSELF THINK THAT YOU COULD LOSE...
I WANTED TO HELP YOU ACHIEVE YOUR SHINOBI PATH...
...PLEASE FORGIVE ME, LEE... FOR NOT STOPPING YOU...
...BEFORE IT WAS TOO LATE.
HE KEPT SAYING HE WAS DESPERATE TO FIGHT SASUKE AND THAT NEJI GUY...
WELL...
WHAT IS BUSHY BROWS SUPPOSED TO DO?!
CAN'T YOU DO ANY-THING TO HELP HIM?!
HEY...!
CLAMP
MPH!

READ THIS WAY

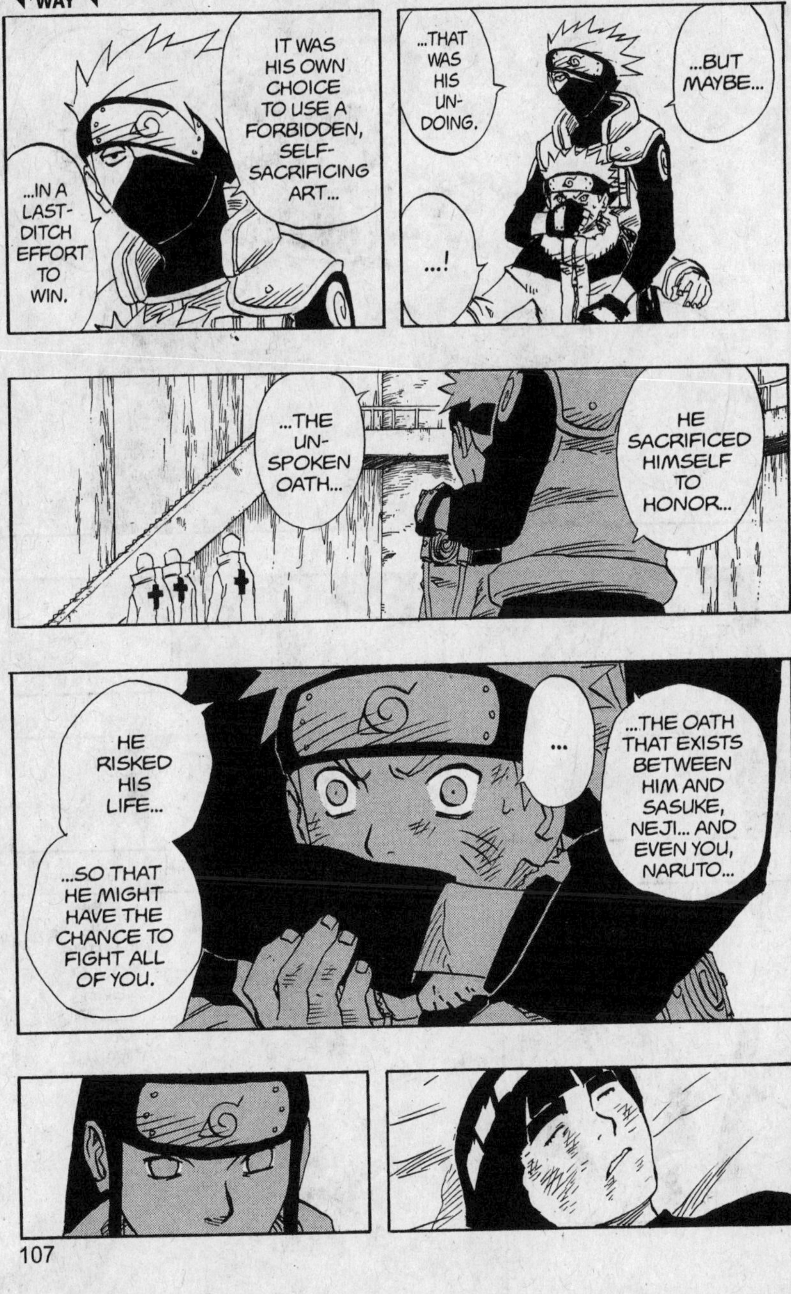
...BUT MAYBE...
...THAT WAS HIS UN-DOING.
...!
IT WAS HIS OWN CHOICE TO USE A FORBIDDEN, SELF-SACRIFICING ART...
...IN A LAST-DITCH EFFORT TO WIN.
HE SACRIFICED HIMSELF TO HONOR...
...THE UN-SPOKEN OATH...
...THE OATH THAT EXISTS BETWEEN HIM AND SASUKE, NEJI... AND EVEN YOU, NARUTO...
...
HE RISKED HIS LIFE...
...SO THAT HE MIGHT HAVE THE CHANCE TO FIGHT ALL OF YOU.

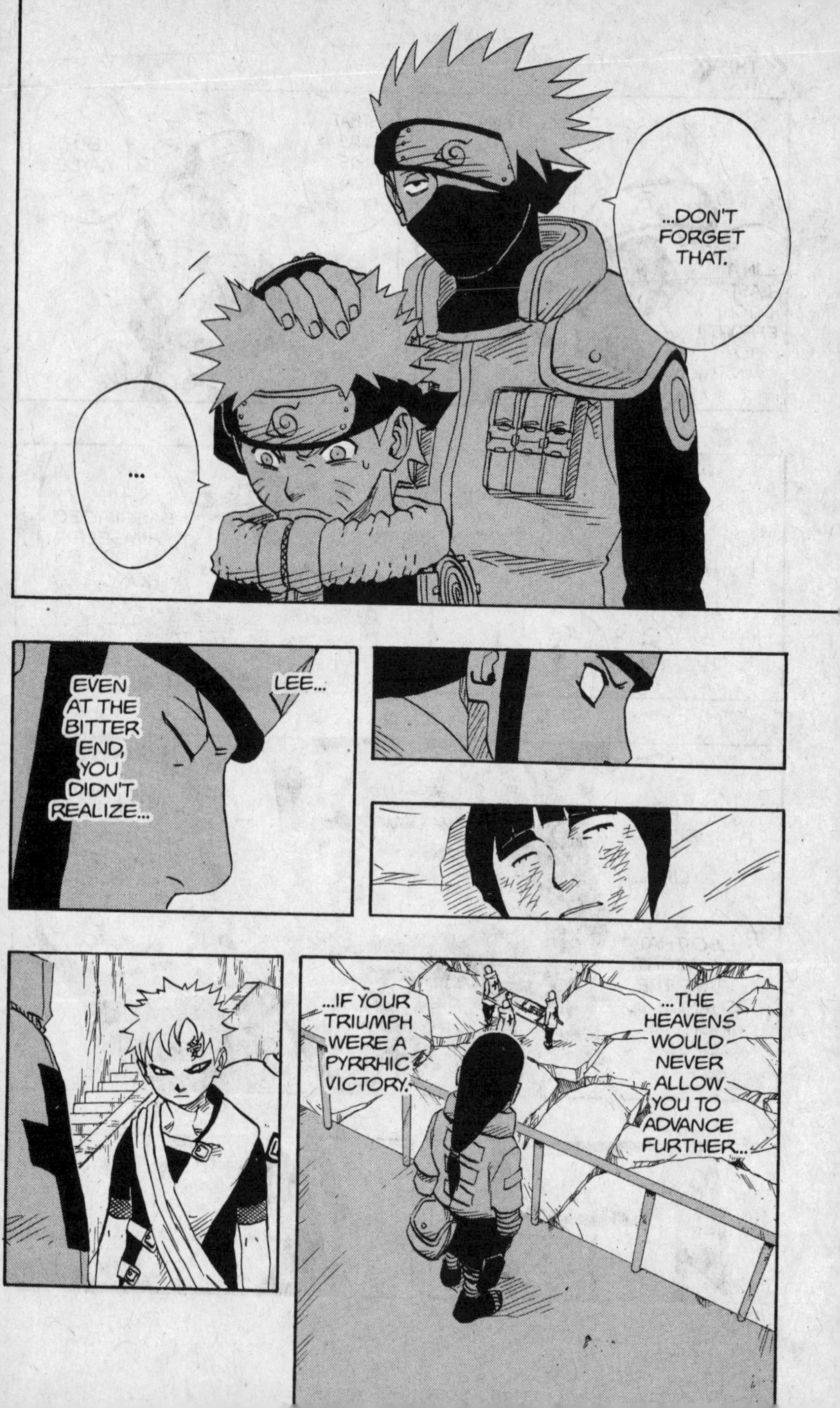
...DON'T FORGET THAT.
...
LEE...
EVEN AT THE BITTER END, YOU DIDN'T REALIZE...
...THE HEAVENS WOULD NEVER ALLOW YOU TO ADVANCE FURTHER...
...IF YOUR TRIUMPH WERE A PYRRHIC VICTORY.

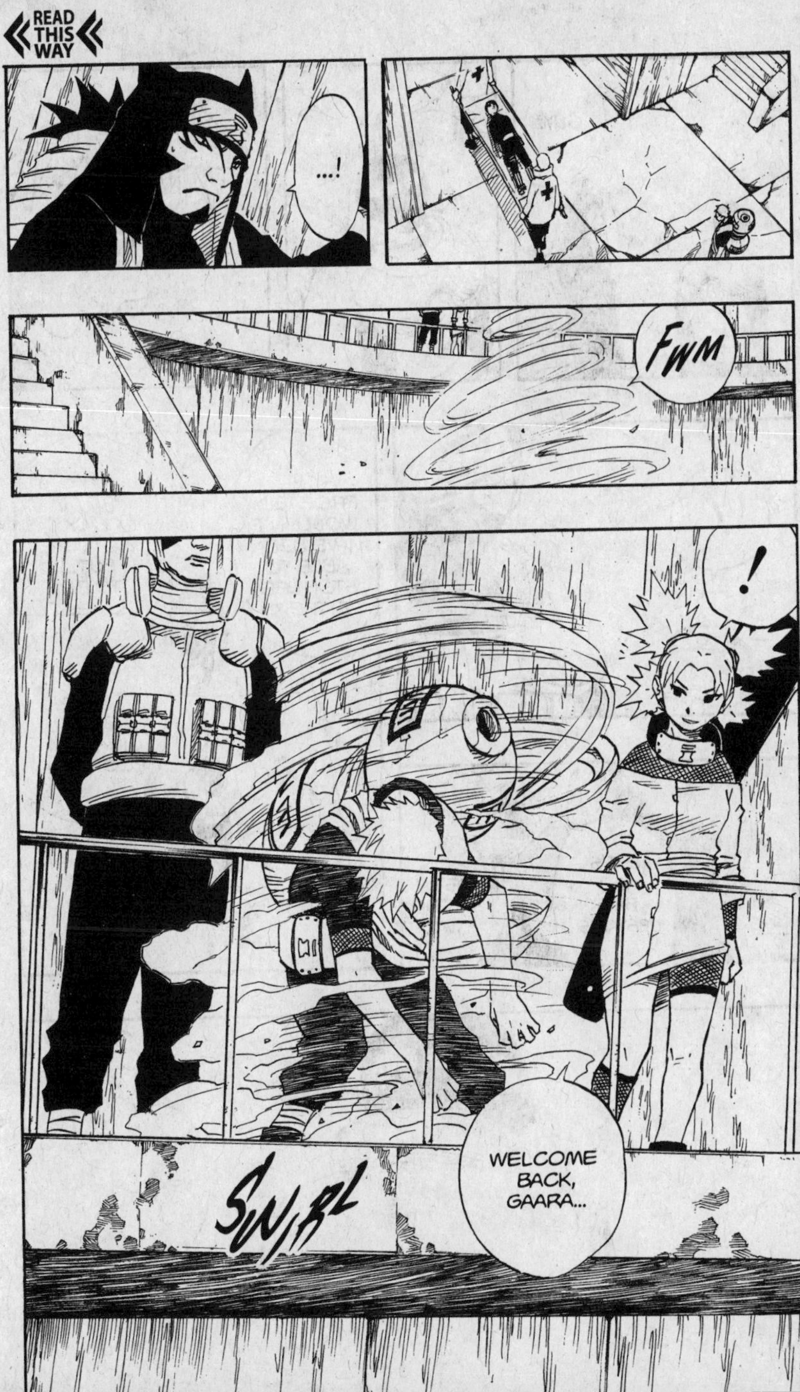
READ THIS WAY
...!
FWM
!
WELCOME BACK, GAARA...
SWIRL

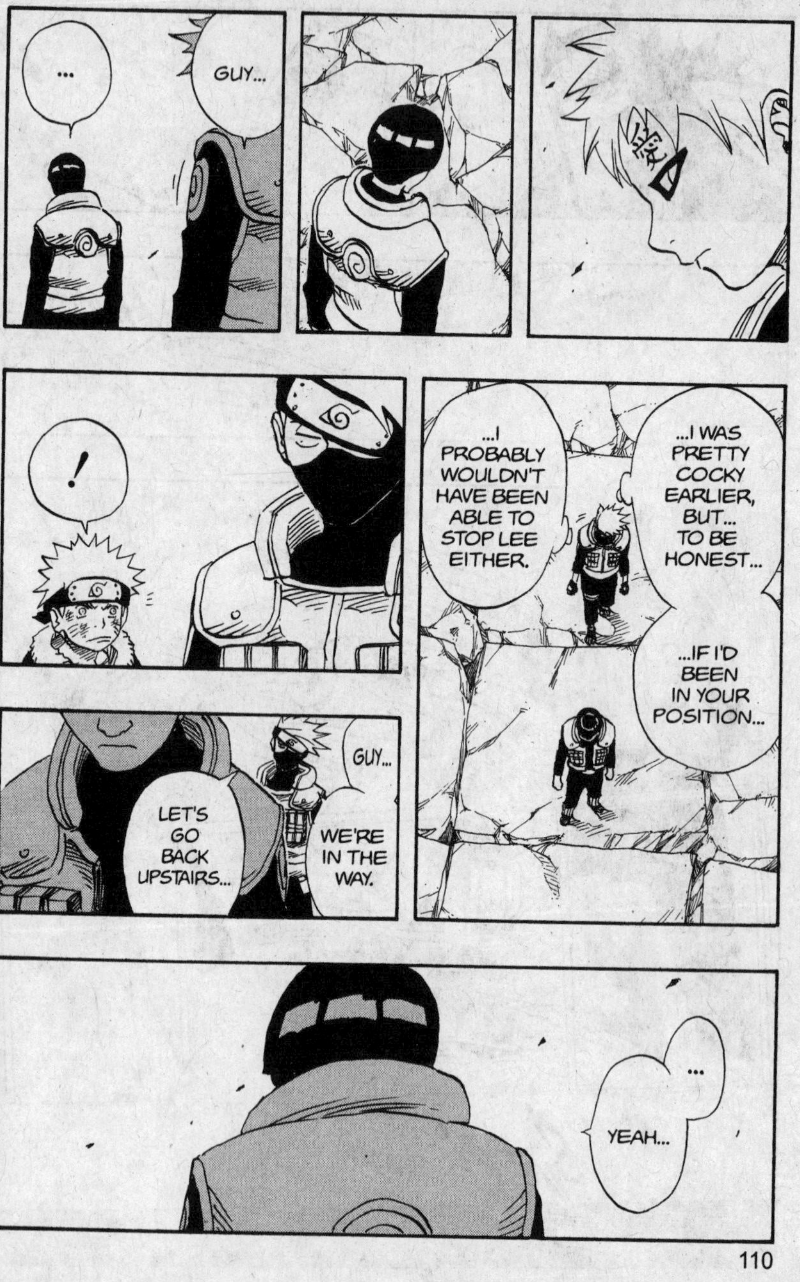
GUY...
...
...I WAS PRETTY COCKY EARLIER, BUT... TO BE HONEST...
...IF I'D BEEN IN YOUR POSITION...
...I PROBABLY WOULDN'T HAVE BEEN ABLE TO STOP LEE EITHER.
!
GUY...
WE'RE IN THE WAY.
LET'S GO BACK UPSTAIRS...
...
YEAH...

READ THIS WAY

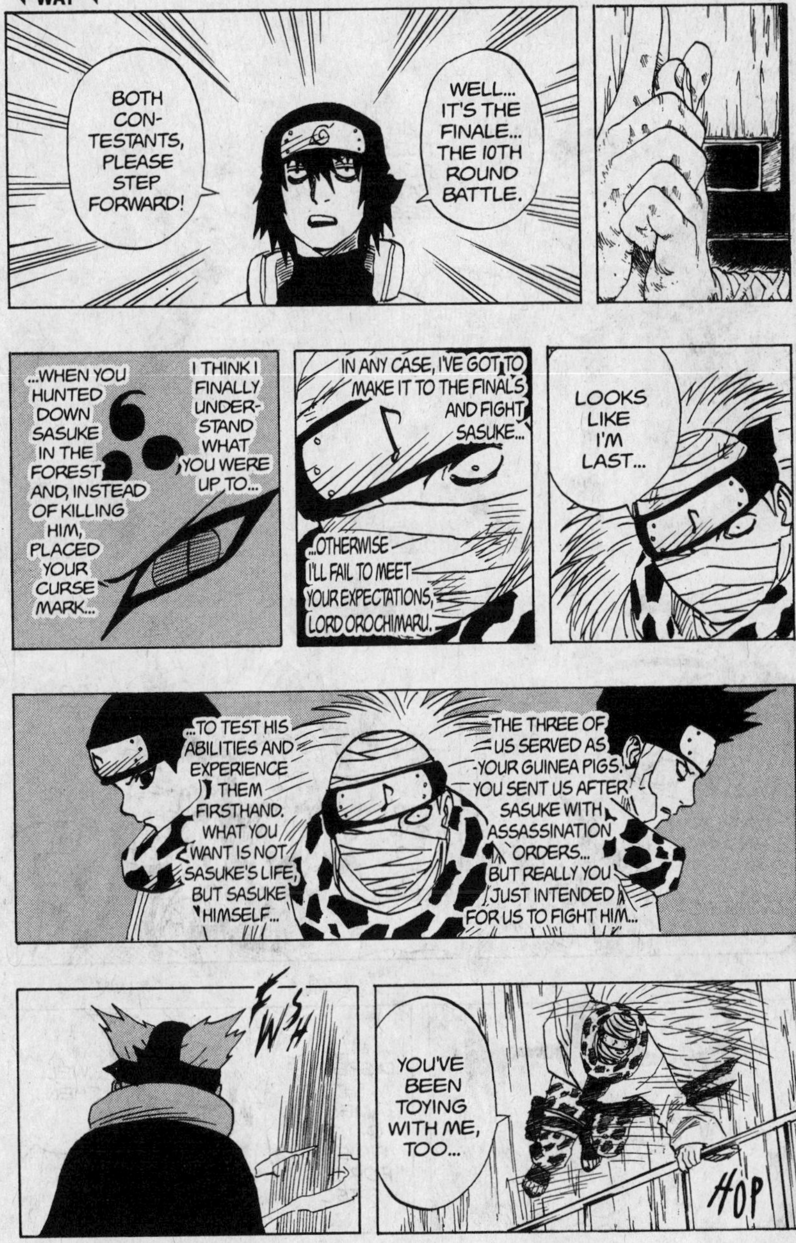

WELL... IT'S THE FINALE... THE 10TH ROUND BATTLE.
BOTH CON-TESTANTS, PLEASE STEP FORWARD!
LOOKS LIKE I'M LAST...
IN ANY CASE, I'VE GOT TO MAKE IT TO THE FINALS AND FIGHT SASUKE...
...OTHERWISE I'LL FAIL TO MEET YOUR EXPECTATIONS, LORD OROCHIMARU.
I THINK I FINALLY UNDER-STAND WHAT YOU WERE UP TO...
...WHEN YOU HUNTED DOWN SASUKE IN THE FOREST AND, INSTEAD OF KILLING HIM, PLACED YOUR CURSE MARK...
THE THREE OF US SERVED AS YOUR GUINEA PIGS. YOU SENT US AFTER SASUKE WITH ASSASSINATION ORDERS... BUT REALLY YOU JUST INTENDED FOR US TO FIGHT HIM...
...TO TEST HIS ABILITIES AND EXPERIENCE THEM FIRSTHAND. WHAT YOU WANT IS NOT SASUKE'S LIFE, BUT SASUKE HIMSELF...
YOU'VE BEEN TOYING WITH ME, TOO...
HOP
FWSH

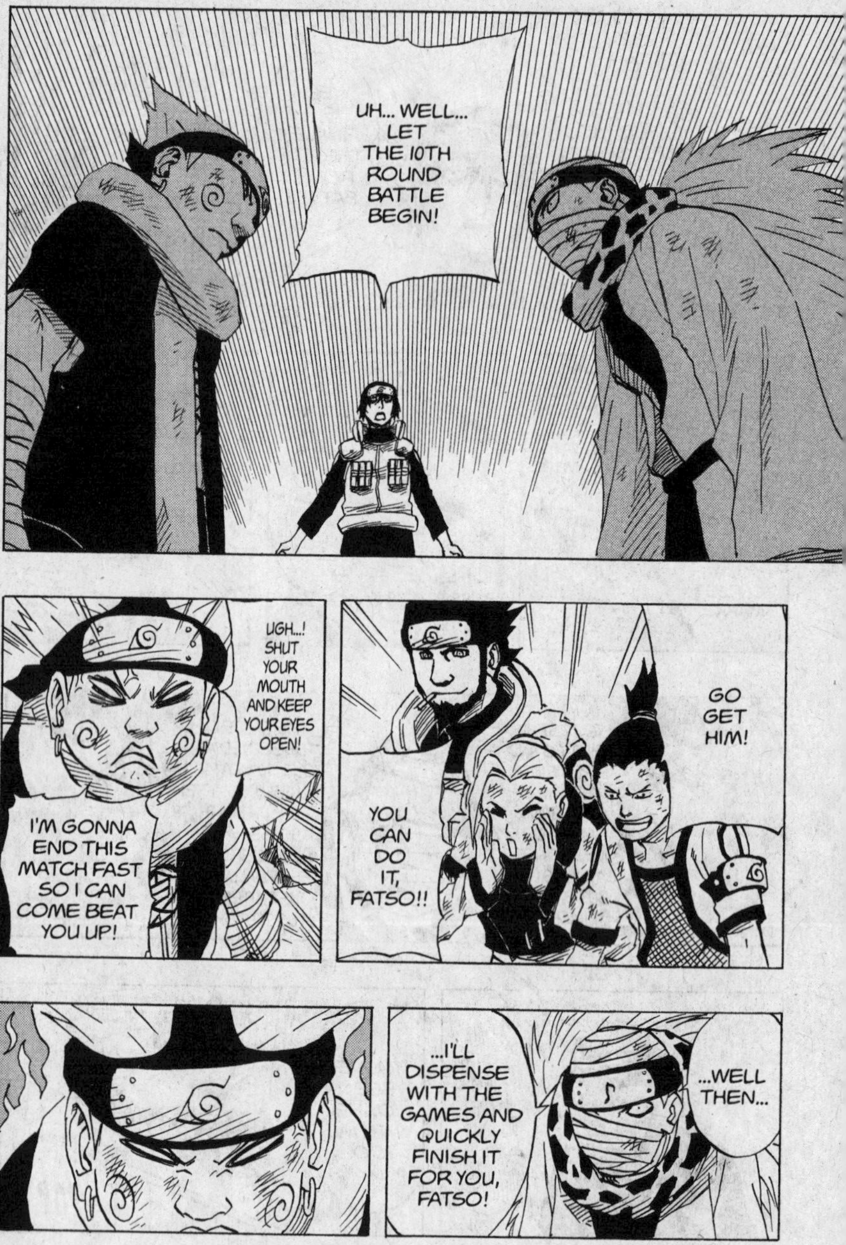
UH... WELL... LET THE 10TH ROUND BATTLE BEGIN!
GO GET HIM!
YOU CAN DO IT, FATSO!!
UGH...! SHUT YOUR MOUTH AND KEEP YOUR EYES OPEN!
I'M GONNA END THIS MATCH FAST SO I CAN COME BEAT YOU UP!
...WELL THEN...
...I'LL DISPENSE WITH THE GAMES AND QUICKLY FINISH IT FOR YOU, FATSO!

READ THIS WAY

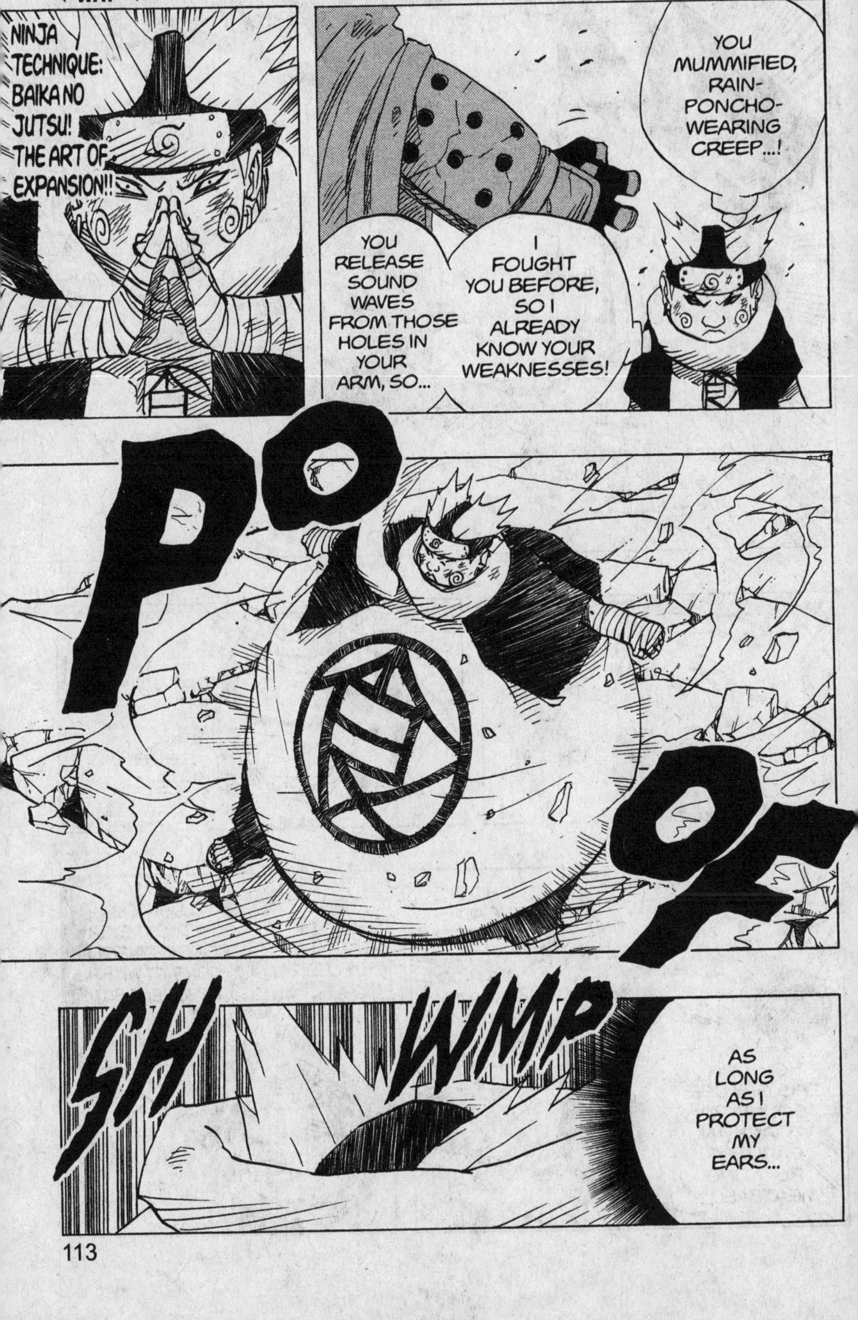
YOU MUMMIFIED, RAIN-PONCHO-WEARING CREEP...!
I FOUGHT YOU BEFORE, SO I ALREADY KNOW YOUR WEAKNESSES!
YOU RELEASE SOUND WAVES FROM THOSE HOLES IN YOUR ARM, SO...
NINJA TECHNIQUE: BAIKA NO JUTSU! THE ART OF EXPANSION!!
POOF
SH WMP
AS LONG AS I PROTECT MY EARS...

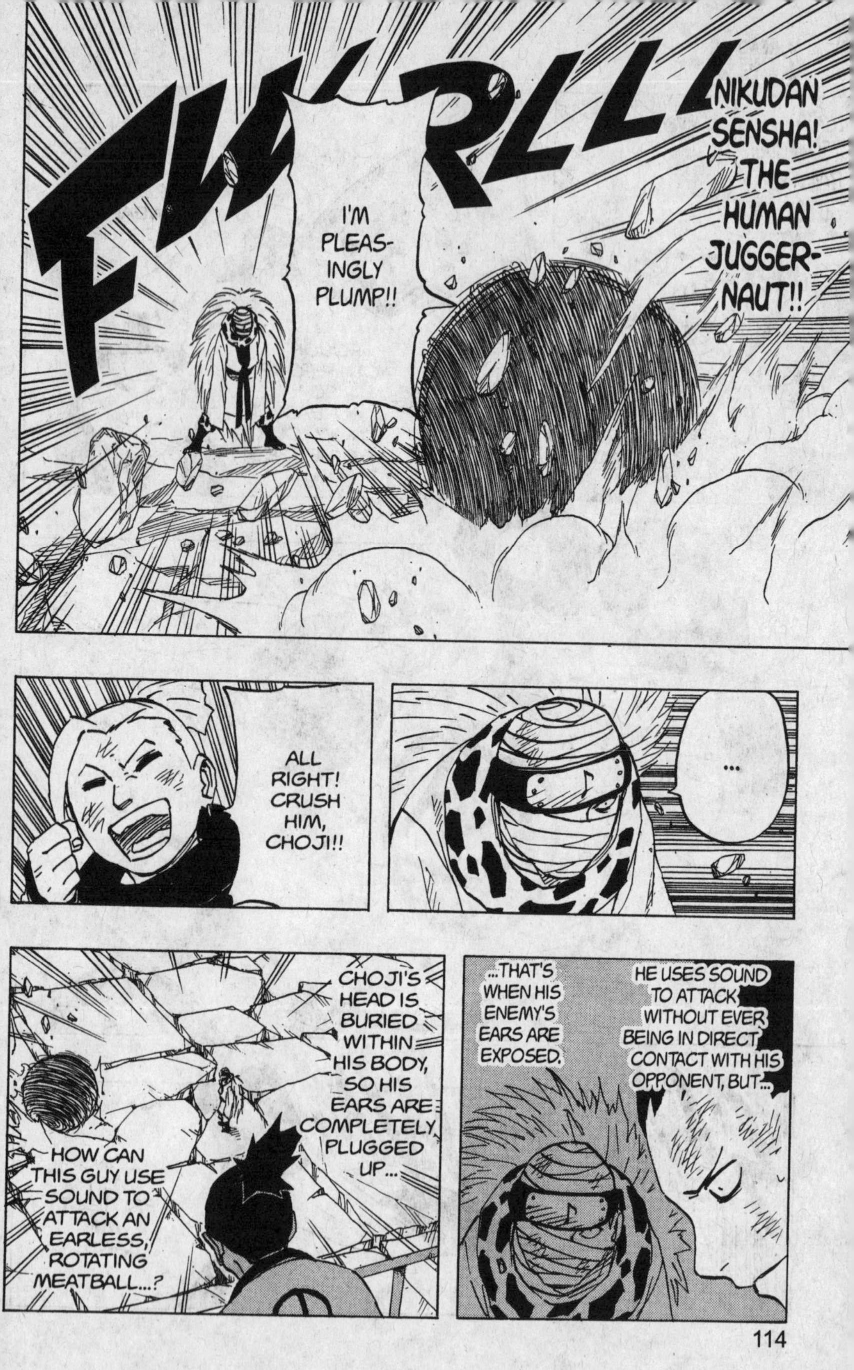
NIKUDAN SENSHA! THE HUMAN JUGGER-NAUT!!
I'M PLEAS-INGLY PLUMP!!
...
ALL RIGHT! CRUSH HIM, CHOJI!!
HE USES SOUND TO ATTACK WITHOUT EVER BEING IN DIRECT CONTACT WITH HIS OPPONENT, BUT...
...THAT'S WHEN HIS ENEMY'S EARS ARE EXPOSED.
CHOJI'S HEAD IS BURIED WITHIN HIS BODY, SO HIS EARS ARE COMPLETELY PLUGGED UP...
HOW CAN THIS GUY USE SOUND TO ATTACK AN EARLESS, ROTATING MEATBALL...?

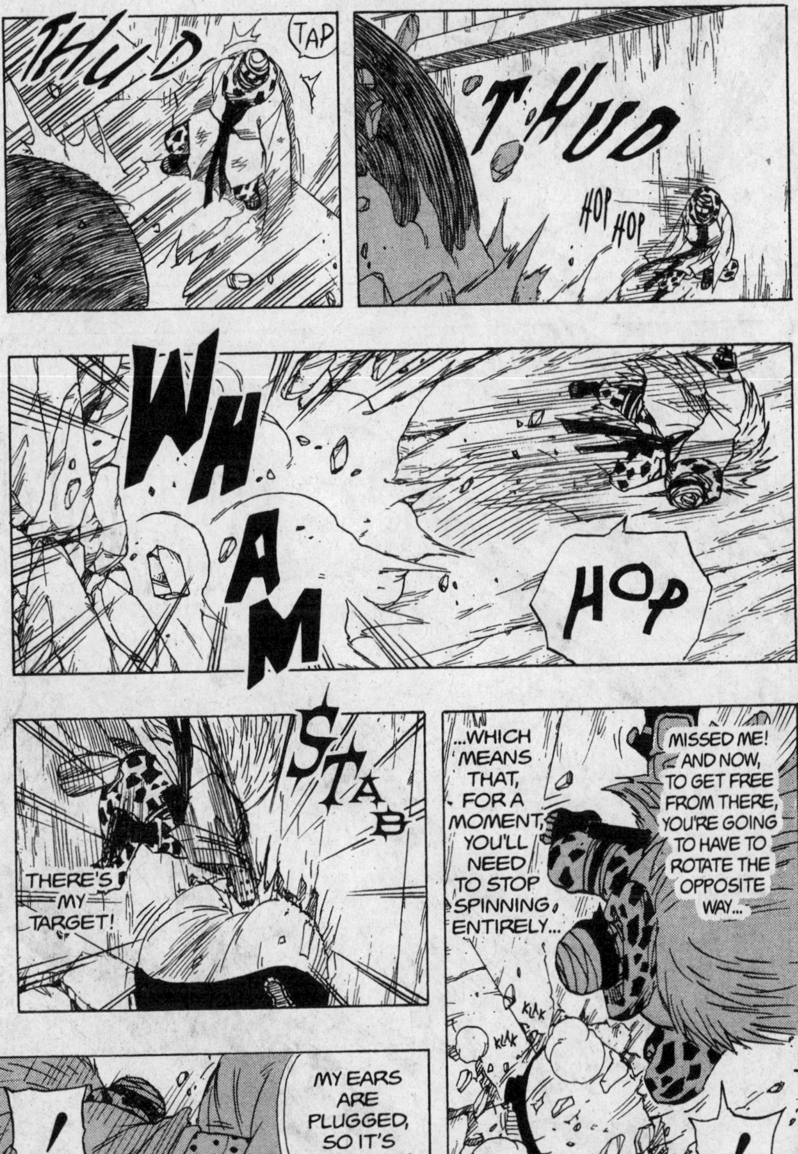
THUD
HOP HOP
THUD
TAP
HOP
WHAM
MISSED ME! AND NOW, TO GET FREE FROM THERE, YOU'RE GOING TO HAVE TO ROTATE THE OPPOSITE WAY...
...WHICH MEANS THAT, FOR A MOMENT, YOU'LL NEED TO STOP SPINNING ENTIRELY...
KLAK
KLAK
!
STAB
THERE'S MY TARGET!
MY EARS ARE PLUGGED, SO IT'S USELESS!
!
TAP

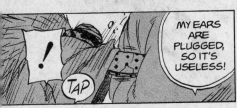

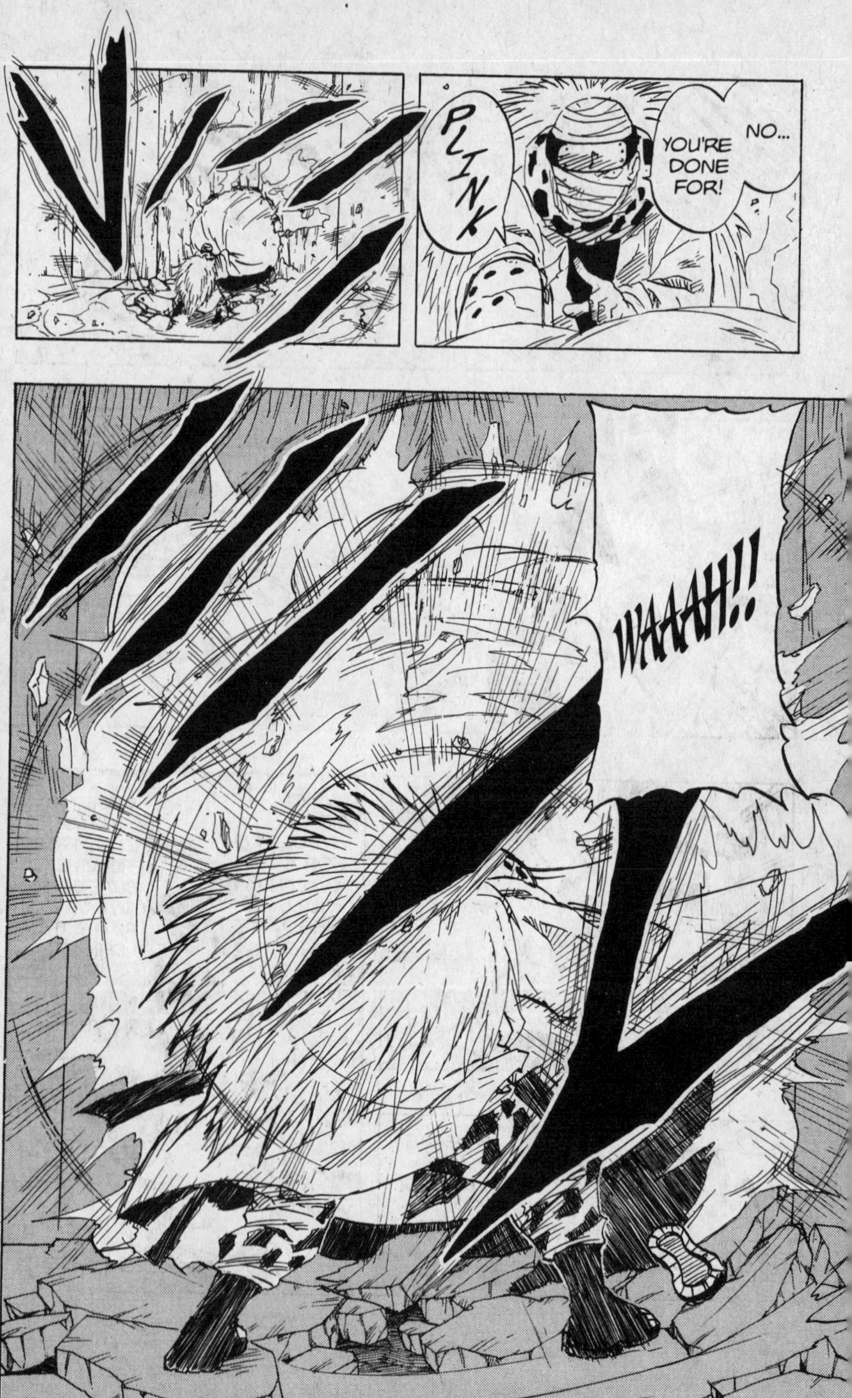

NO... YOU'RE DONE FOR!
PLINK
WAAAH!!

READ THIS WAY

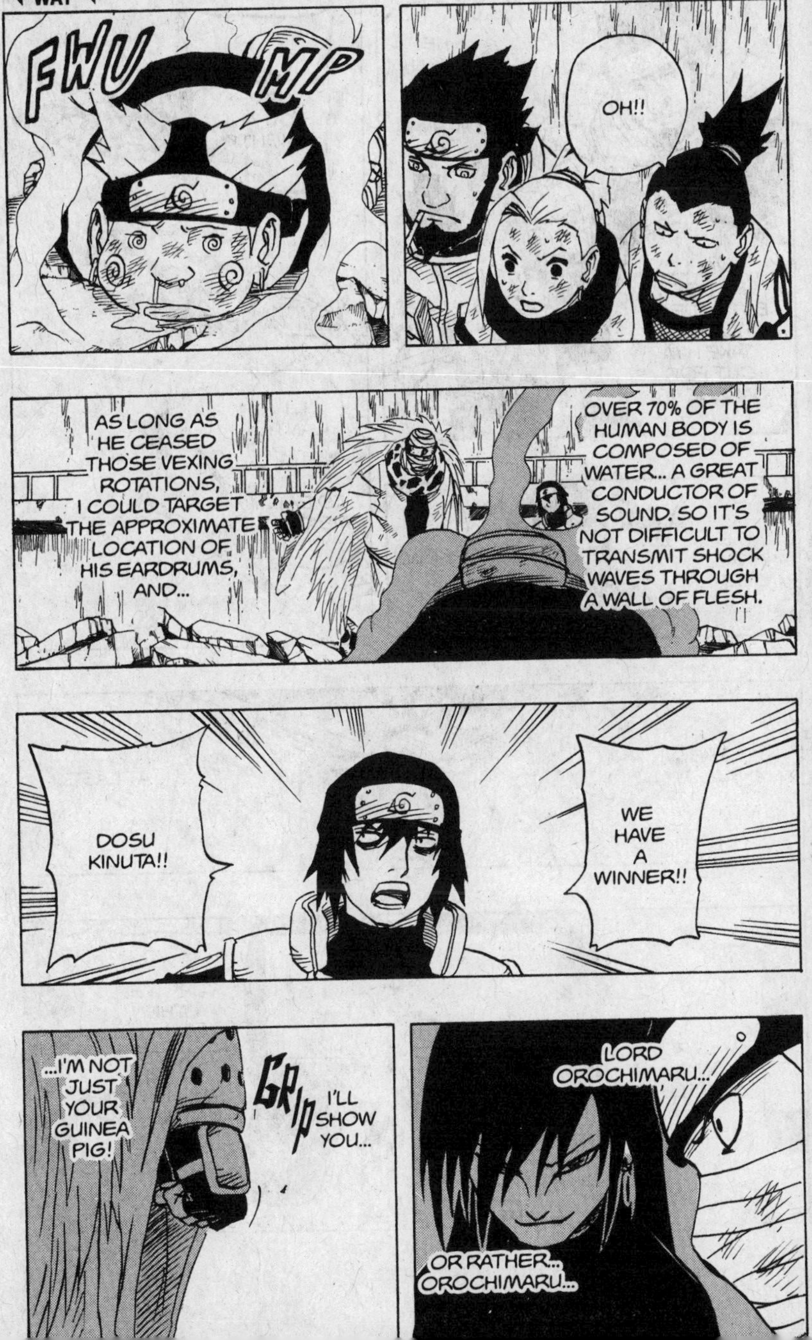

OH!!
FWUMP
OVER 70% OF THE HUMAN BODY IS COMPOSED OF WATER... A GREAT CONDUCTOR OF SOUND. SO IT'S NOT DIFFICULT TO TRANSMIT SHOCK WAVES THROUGH A WALL OF FLESH.
AS LONG AS HE CEASED THOSE VEXING ROTATIONS, I COULD TARGET THE APPROXIMATE LOCATION OF HIS EARDRUMS, AND...
WE HAVE A WINNER!!
DOSU KINUTA!!
LORD OROCHIMARU...
OR RATHER... OROCHIMARU...
I'LL SHOW YOU...
GRIP
...I'M NOT JUST YOUR GUINEA PIG!

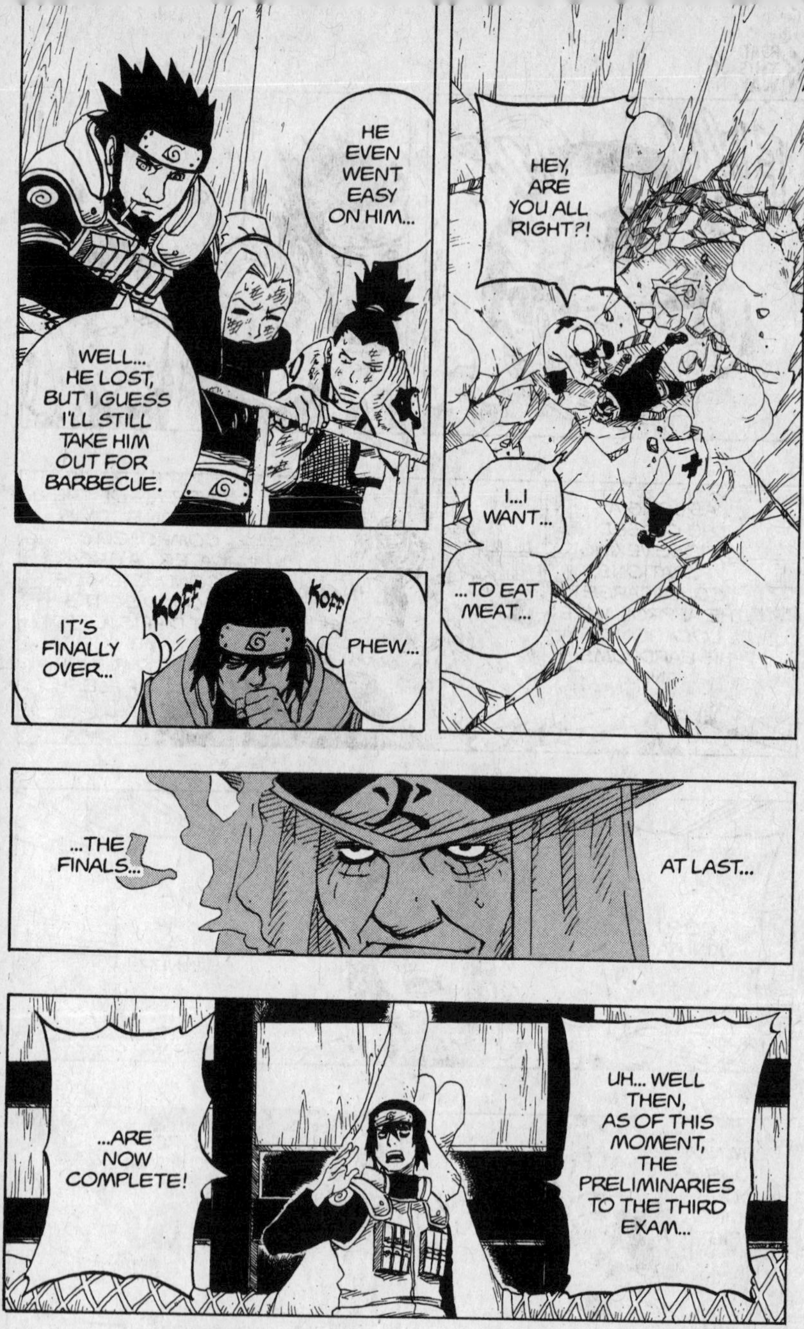
HEY, ARE YOU ALL RIGHT?!
I...I WANT...
...TO EAT MEAT...
HE EVEN WENT EASY ON HIM...
WELL... HE LOST, BUT I GUESS I'LL STILL TAKE HIM OUT FOR BARBECUE.
KOFF
PHEW...
KOFF
IT'S FINALLY OVER...
AT LAST...
...THE FINALS...
UH... WELL THEN, AS OF THIS MOMENT, THE PRELIMINARIES TO THE THIRD EXAM...
...ARE NOW COMPLETE!

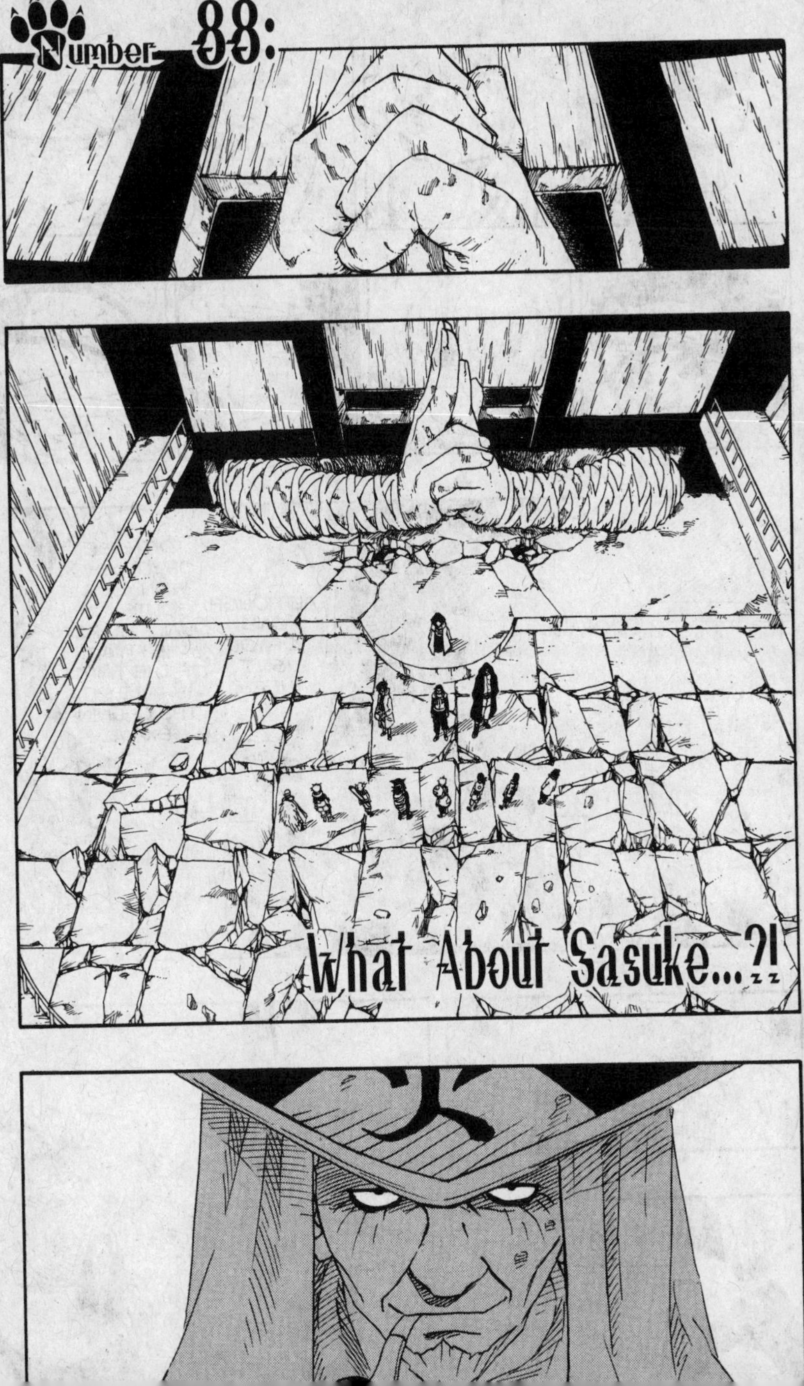
Number 88:
What About Sasuke...?!

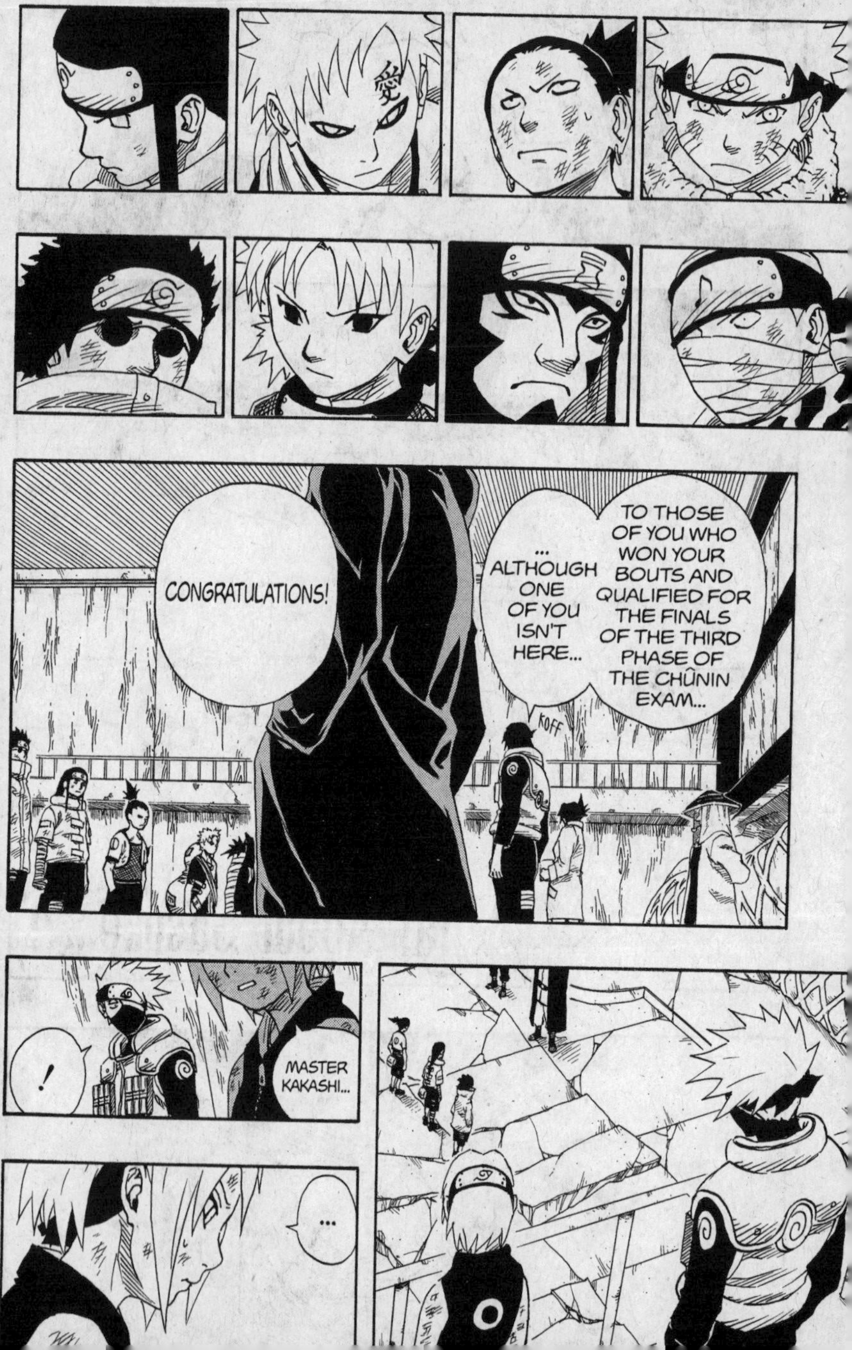
TO THOSE OF YOU WHO WON YOUR BOUTS AND QUALIFIED FOR THE FINALS OF THE THIRD PHASE OF THE CHÛNIN EXAM...
... ALTHOUGH ONE OF YOU ISN'T HERE...
KOFF
CONGRATULATIONS!
MASTER KAKASHI...
!
...

READ THIS WAY

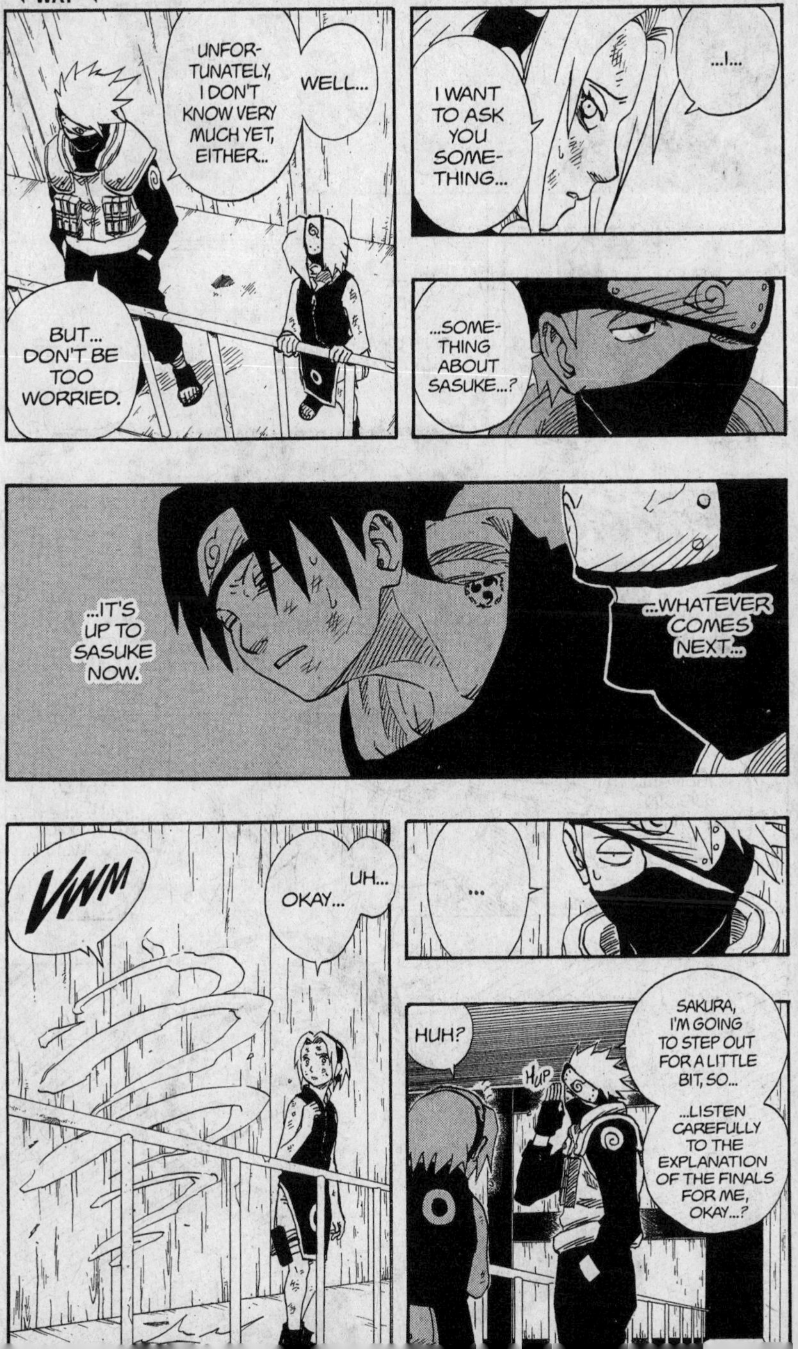
...I...
I WANT TO ASK YOU SOMETHING...
...SOMETHING ABOUT SASUKE...?
WELL...
UNFORTUNATELY, I DON'T KNOW VERY MUCH YET, EITHER...
BUT... DON'T BE TOO WORRIED.
...WHATEVER COMES NEXT...
...IT'S UP TO SASUKE NOW.
...
SAKURA, I'M GOING TO STEP OUT FOR A LITTLE BIT, SO...
...LISTEN CAREFULLY TO THE EXPLANATION OF THE FINALS FOR ME, OKAY...?
HUP
HUH?
UH... OKAY...
VWM

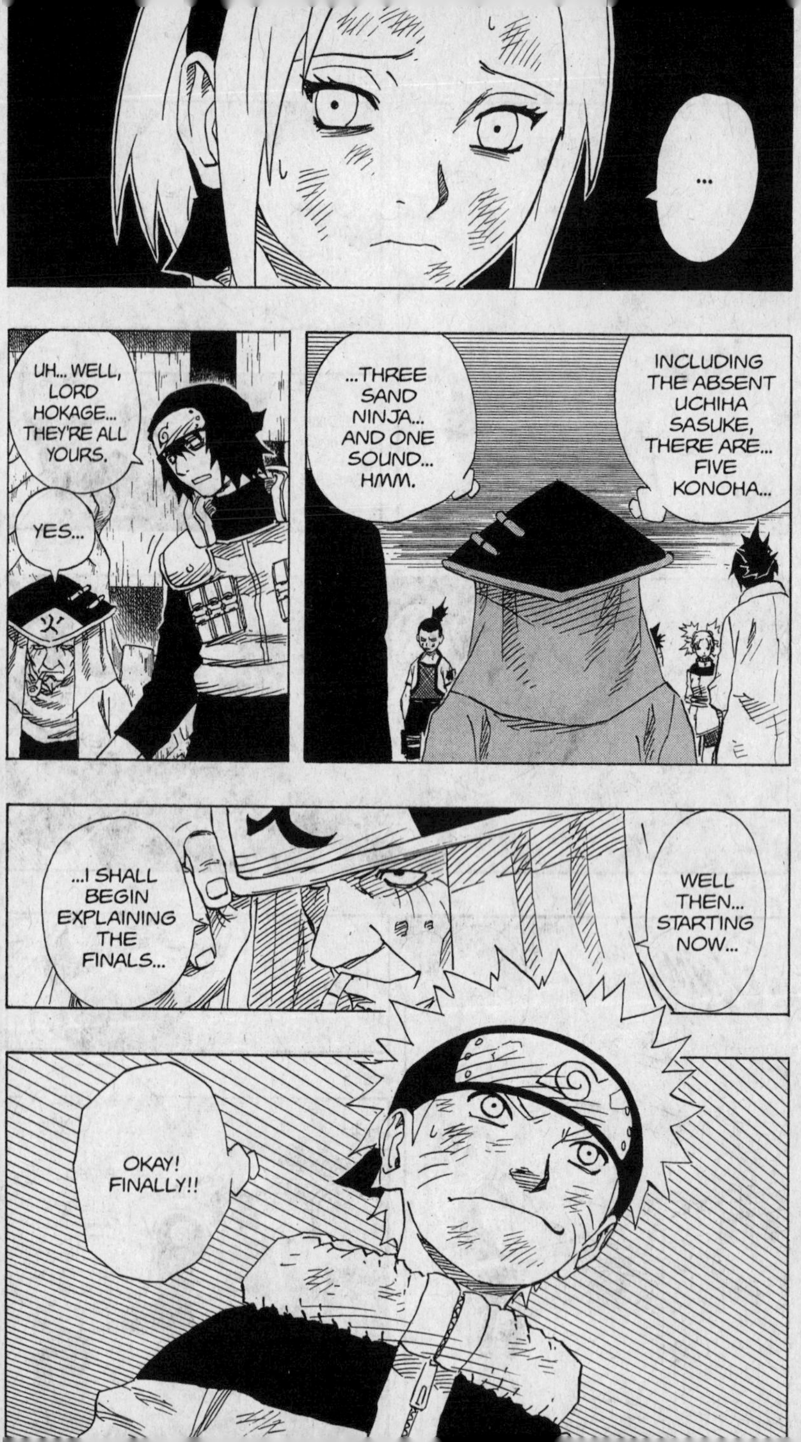
...
INCLUDING THE ABSENT UCHIHA SASUKE, THERE ARE... FIVE KONOHA...
...THREE SAND NINJA... AND ONE SOUND... HMM.
UH... WELL, LORD HOKAGE... THEY'RE ALL YOURS.
YES...
WELL THEN... STARTING NOW...
...I SHALL BEGIN EXPLAINING THE FINALS...
OKAY! FINALLY!!

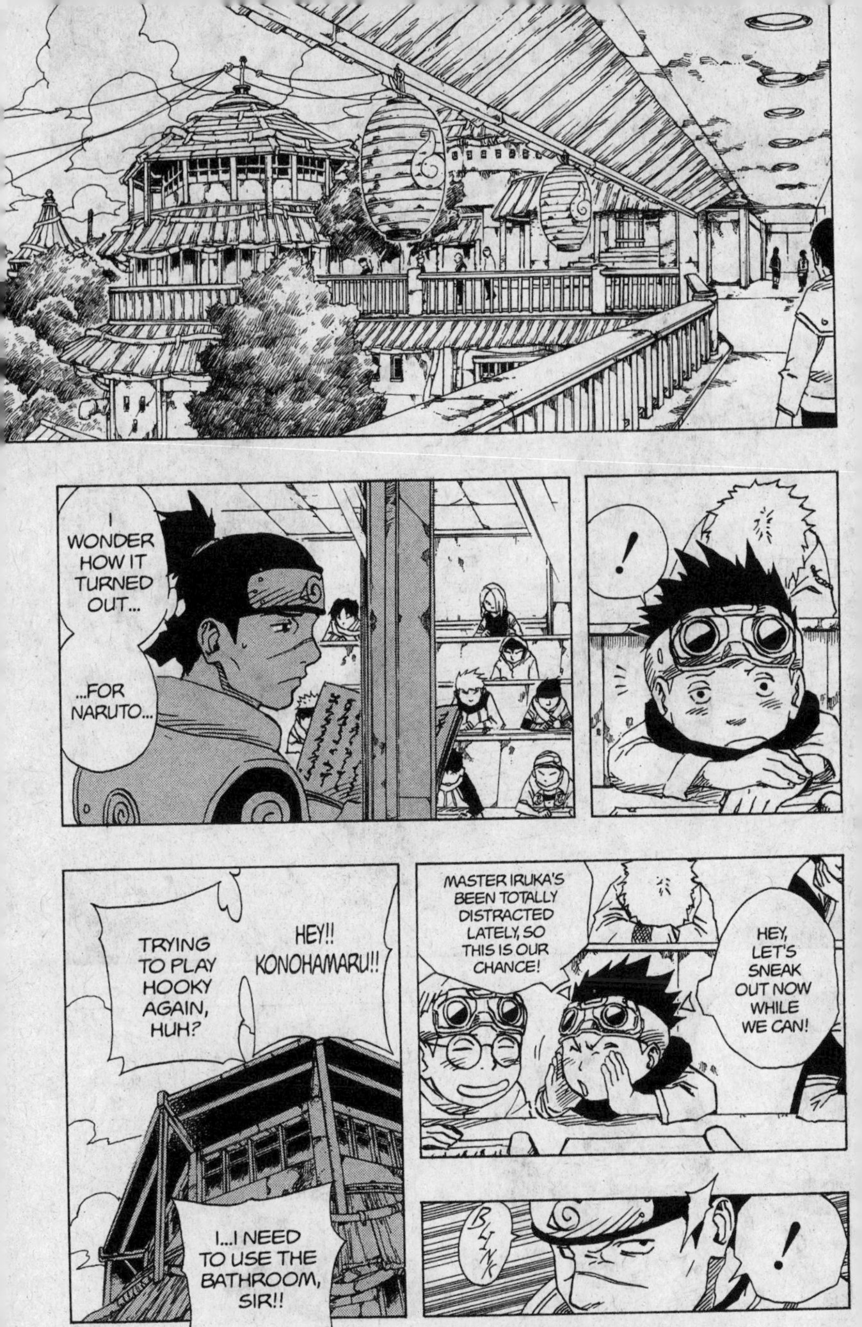
!
I WONDER HOW IT TURNED OUT...
...FOR NARUTO...
HEY, LET'S SNEAK OUT NOW WHILE WE CAN!
MASTER IRUKA'S BEEN TOTALLY DISTRACTED LATELY, SO THIS IS OUR CHANCE!
!
BLINK
HEY!! KONOHAMARU!!
TRYING TO PLAY HOOKY AGAIN, HUH?
I...I NEED TO USE THE BATHROOM, SIR!!

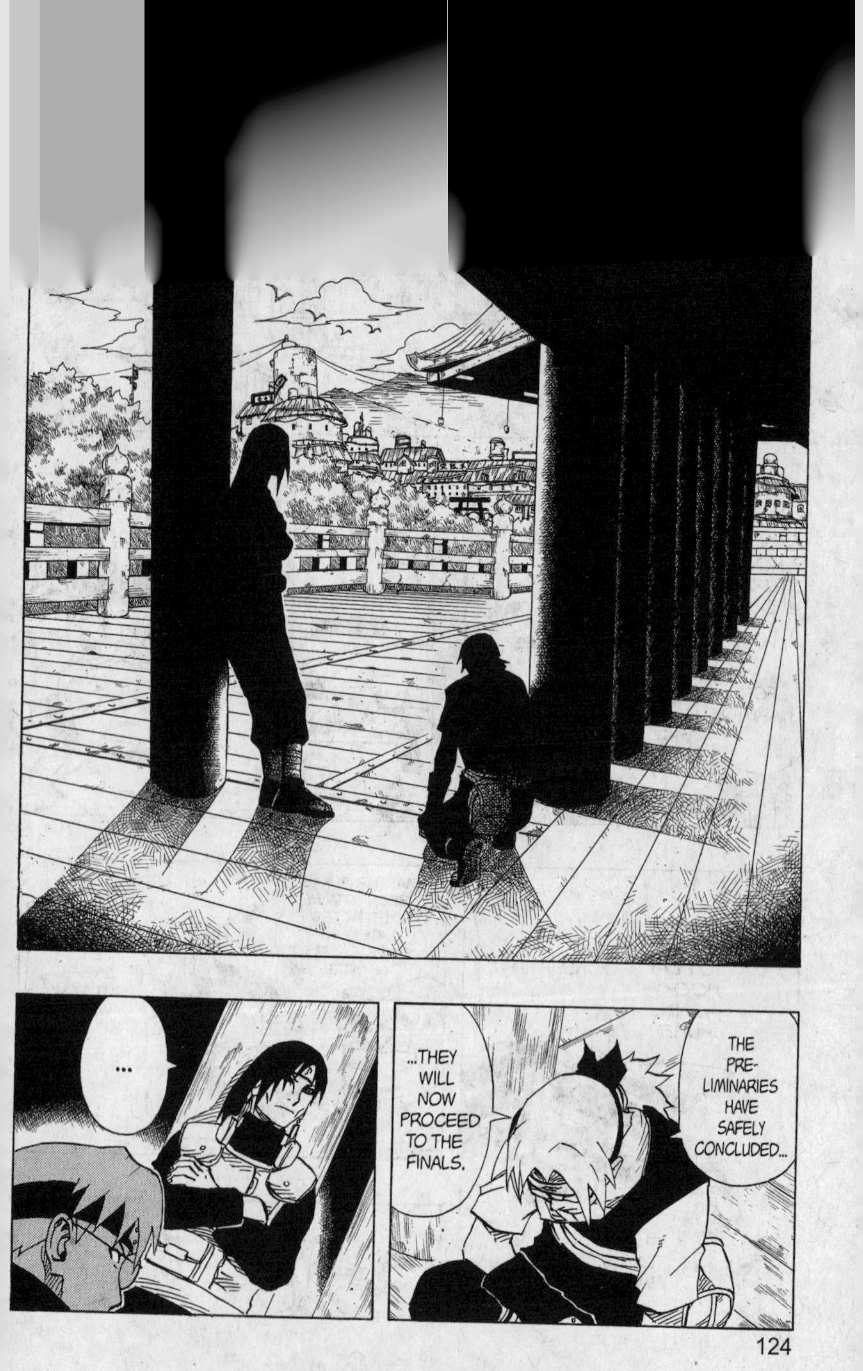
THE PRE-LIMINARIES HAVE SAFELY CONCLUDED...
...THEY WILL NOW PROCEED TO THE FINALS.
...

READ THIS WAY

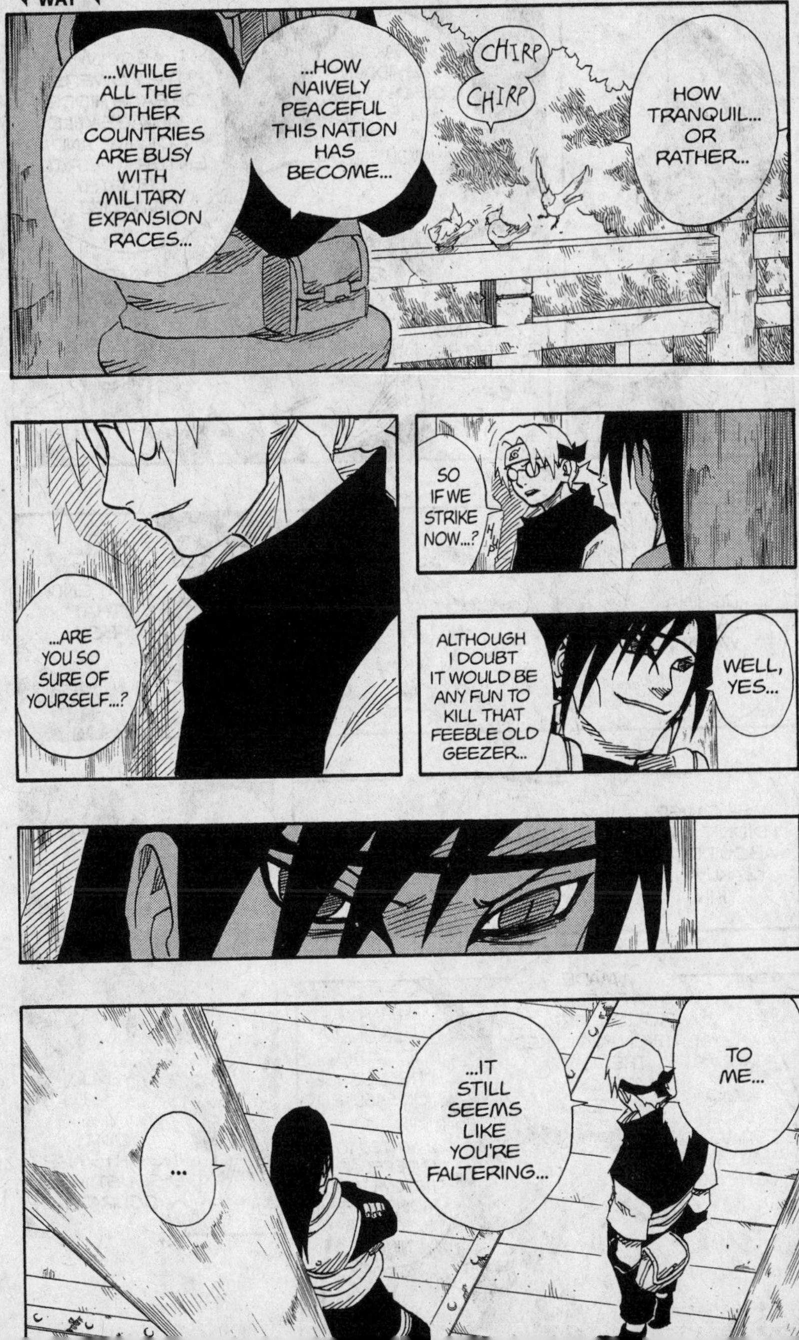
HOW TRANQUIL... OR RATHER...
CHIRP
CHIRP
...HOW NAIVELY PEACEFUL THIS NATION HAS BECOME...
...WHILE ALL THE OTHER COUNTRIES ARE BUSY WITH MILITARY EXPANSION RACES...
SO IF WE STRIKE NOW...?
HUP
WELL, YES...
ALTHOUGH I DOUBT IT WOULD BE ANY FUN TO KILL THAT FEEBLE OLD GEEZER...
...ARE YOU SO SURE OF YOURSELF...?
TO ME...
...IT STILL SEEMS LIKE YOU'RE FALTERING...
...

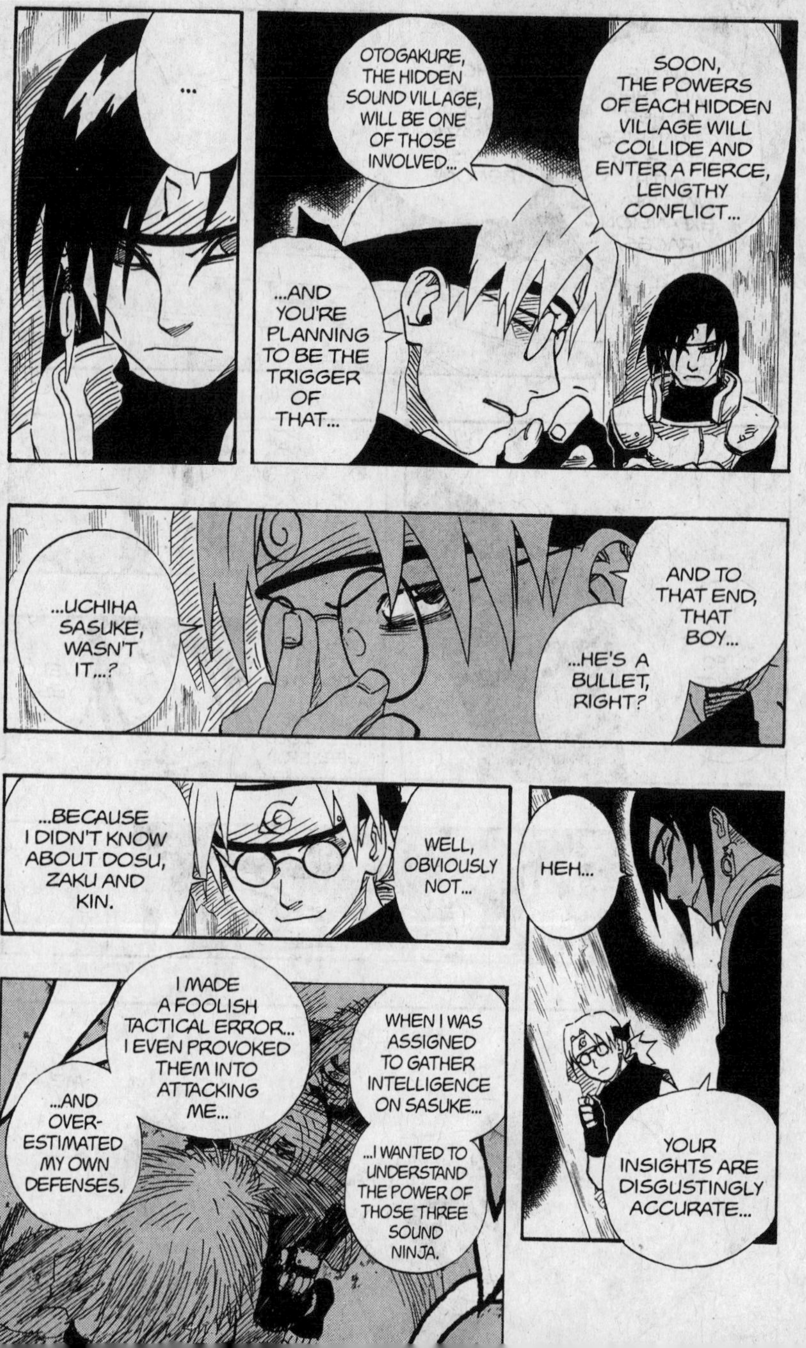
SOON, THE POWERS OF EACH HIDDEN VILLAGE WILL COLLIDE AND ENTER A FIERCE, LENGTHY CONFLICT...
OTOGAKURE, THE HIDDEN SOUND VILLAGE, WILL BE ONE OF THOSE INVOLVED...
...AND YOU'RE PLANNING TO BE THE TRIGGER OF THAT...
...
AND TO THAT END, THAT BOY...
...HE'S A BULLET, RIGHT?
...UCHIHA SASUKE, WASN'T IT...?
HEH...
YOUR INSIGHTS ARE DISGUSTINGLY ACCURATE...
WELL, OBVIOUSLY NOT...
...BECAUSE I DIDN'T KNOW ABOUT DOSU, ZAKU AND KIN.
WHEN I WAS ASSIGNED TO GATHER INTELLIGENCE ON SASUKE...
...I WANTED TO UNDERSTAND THE POWER OF THOSE THREE SOUND NINJA.
I MADE A FOOLISH TACTICAL ERROR... I EVEN PROVOKED THEM INTO ATTACKING ME...
...AND OVER-ESTIMATED MY OWN DEFENSES.

READ THIS WAY

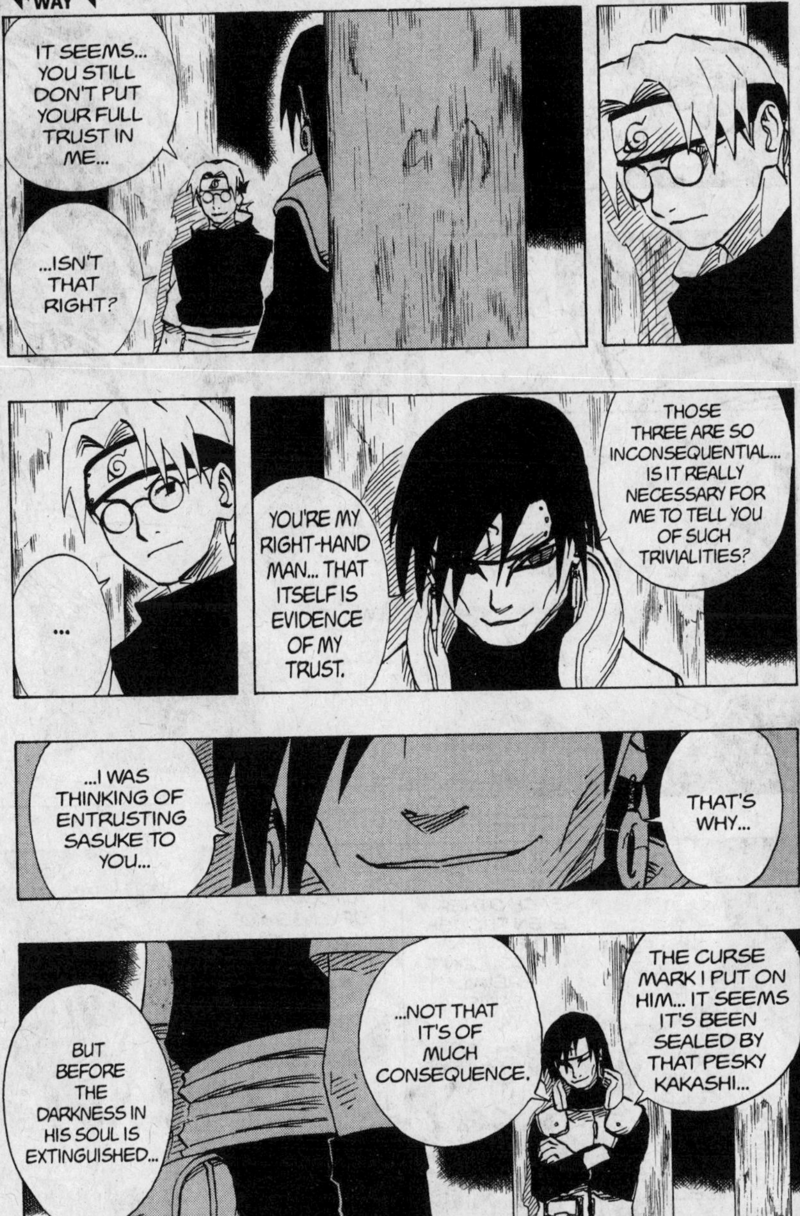
IT SEEMS... YOU STILL DON'T PUT YOUR FULL TRUST IN ME...
...ISN'T THAT RIGHT?
THOSE THREE ARE SO INCONSEQUENTIAL... IS IT REALLY NECESSARY FOR ME TO TELL YOU OF SUCH TRIVIALITIES?
YOU'RE MY RIGHT-HAND MAN... THAT ITSELF IS EVIDENCE OF MY TRUST.
...
THAT'S WHY...
...I WAS THINKING OF ENTRUSTING SASUKE TO YOU...
THE CURSE MARK I PUT ON HIM... IT SEEMS IT'S BEEN SEALED BY THAT PESKY KAKASHI...
...NOT THAT IT'S OF MUCH CONSEQUENCE.
BUT BEFORE THE DARKNESS IN HIS SOUL IS EXTINGUISHED...

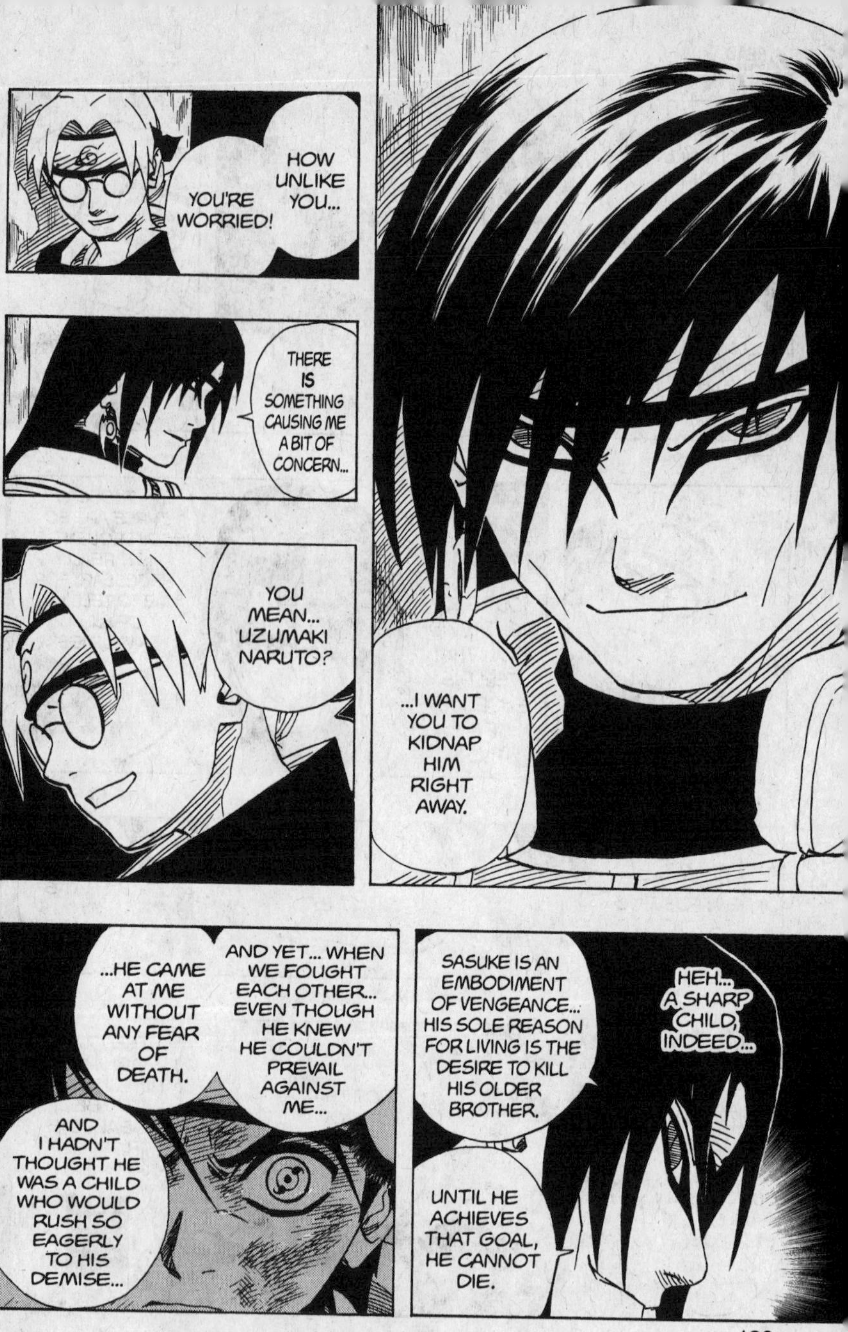
HOW UNLIKE YOU...
YOU'RE WORRIED!
THERE IS SOMETHING CAUSING ME A BIT OF CONCERN...
YOU MEAN... UZUMAKI NARUTO?
...I WANT YOU TO KIDNAP HIM RIGHT AWAY.
AND YET... WHEN WE FOUGHT EACH OTHER... EVEN THOUGH HE KNEW HE COULDN'T PREVAIL AGAINST ME...
...HE CAME AT ME WITHOUT ANY FEAR OF DEATH.
AND I HADN'T THOUGHT HE WAS A CHILD WHO WOULD RUSH SO EAGERLY TO HIS DEMISE...
SASUKE IS AN EMBODIMENT OF VENGEANCE... HIS SOLE REASON FOR LIVING IS THE DESIRE TO KILL HIS OLDER BROTHER.
UNTIL HE ACHIEVES THAT GOAL, HE CANNOT DIE.
HEH... A SHARP CHILD, INDEED...

READ THIS WAY

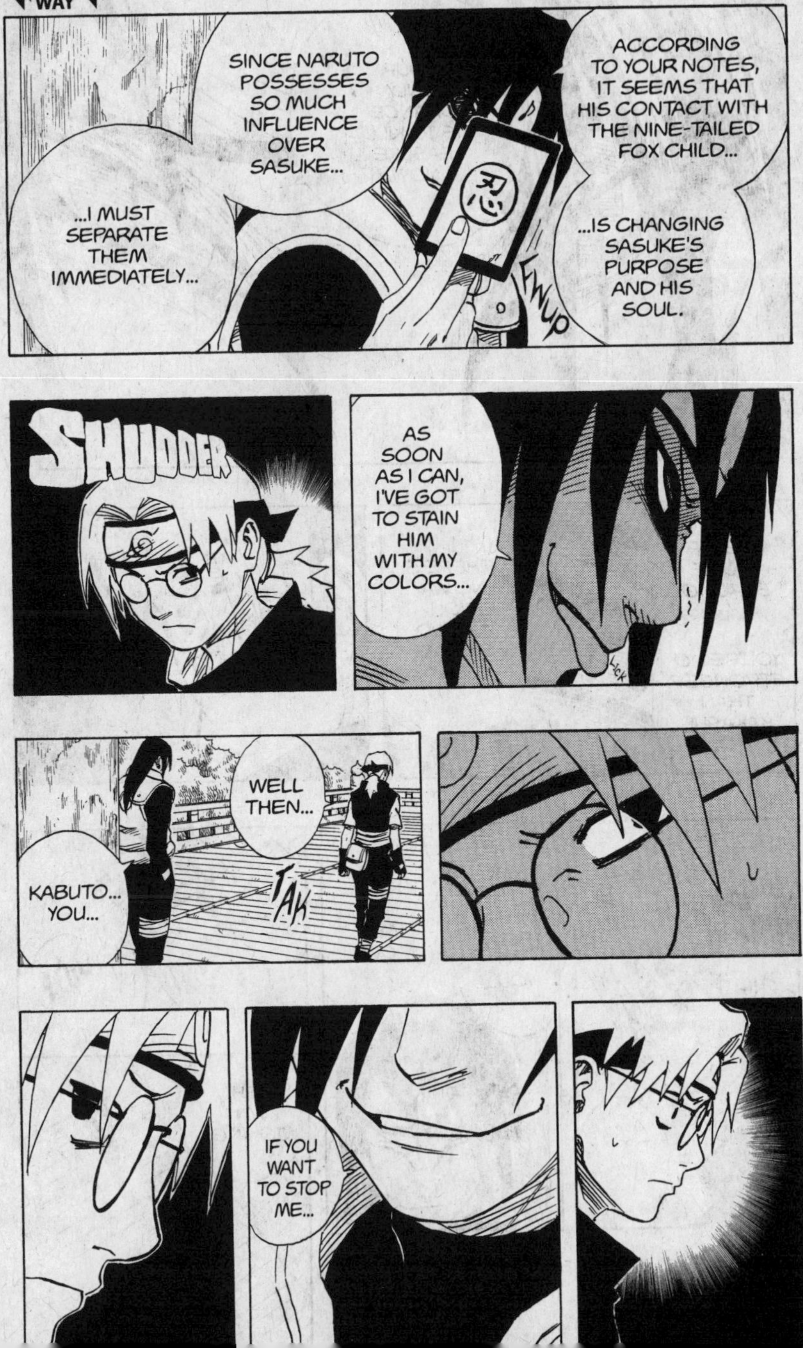

ACCORDING TO YOUR NOTES, IT SEEMS THAT HIS CONTACT WITH THE NINE-TAILED FOX CHILD...
...IS CHANGING SASUKE'S PURPOSE AND HIS SOUL.
FWUP
SINCE NARUTO POSSESSES SO MUCH INFLUENCE OVER SASUKE...
...I MUST SEPARATE THEM IMMEDIATELY...
AS SOON AS I CAN, I'VE GOT TO STAIN HIM WITH MY COLORS...
LICK
SHUDDER
WELL THEN...
TAK
KABUTO... YOU...
IF YOU WANT TO STOP ME...

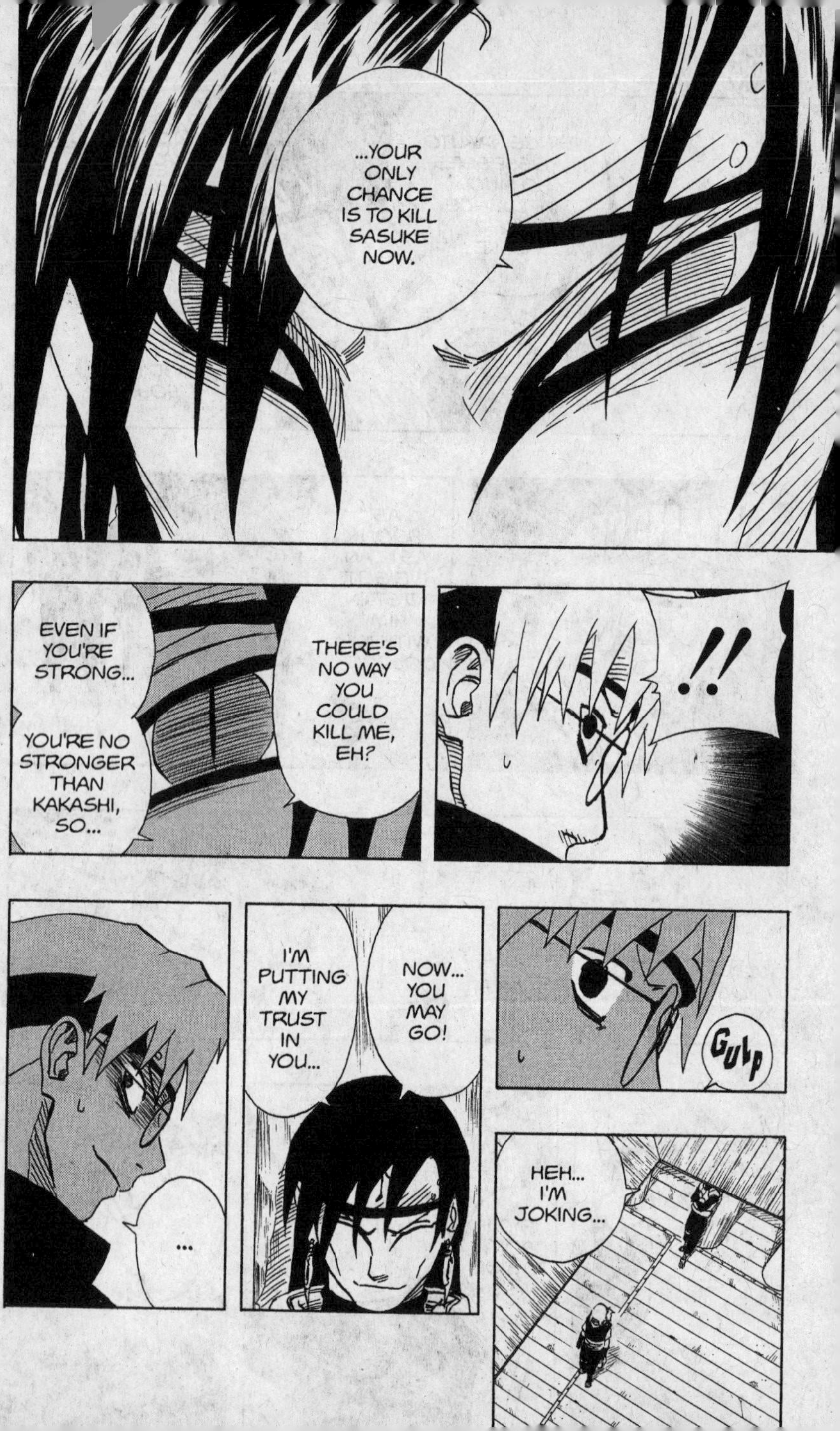
...YOUR ONLY CHANCE IS TO KILL SASUKE NOW.
!!
THERE'S NO WAY YOU COULD KILL ME, EH?
EVEN IF YOU'RE STRONG...
YOU'RE NO STRONGER THAN KAKASHI, SO...
GULP
HEH... I'M JOKING...
NOW... YOU MAY GO!
I'M PUTTING MY TRUST IN YOU...
...

READ THIS WAY

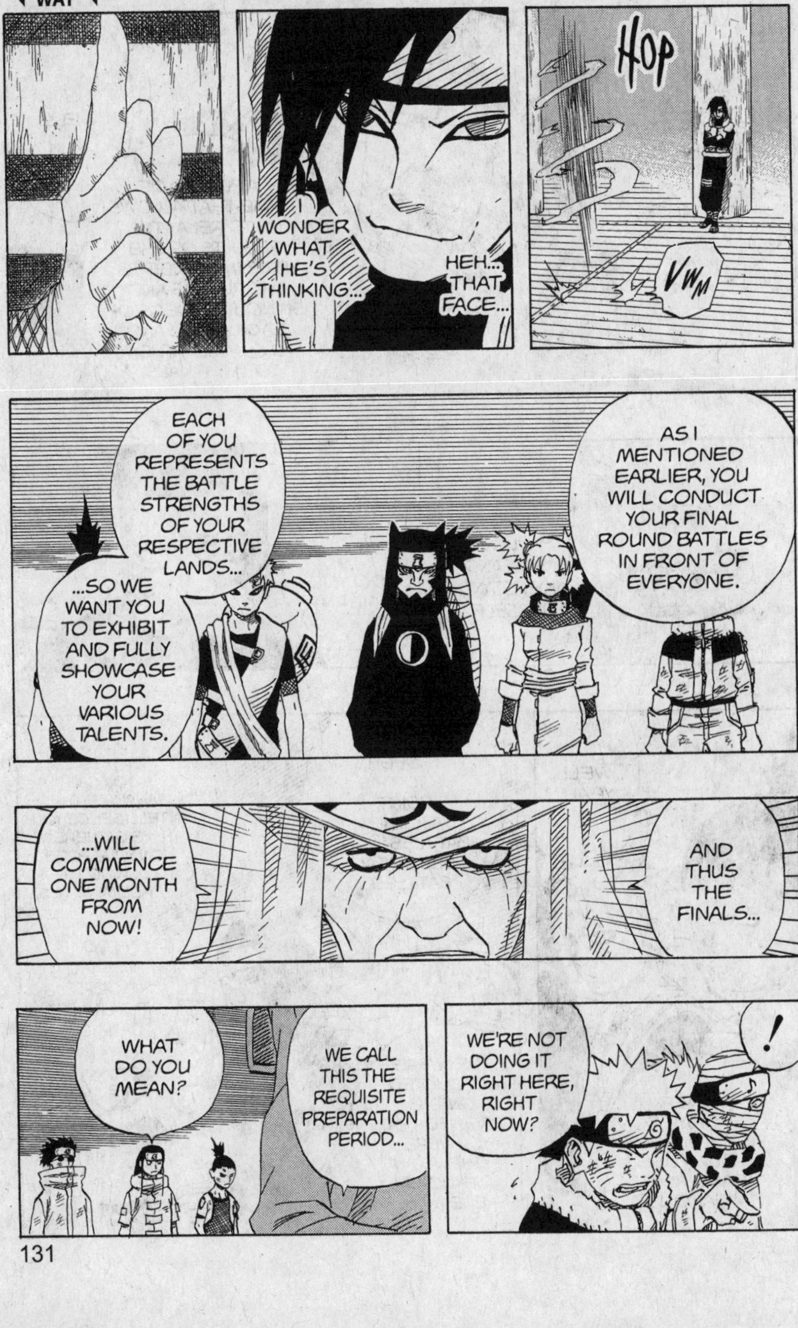
HOP
VWM
HEH... THAT FACE...
I WONDER WHAT HE'S THINKING...
AS I MENTIONED EARLIER, YOU WILL CONDUCT YOUR FINAL ROUND BATTLES IN FRONT OF EVERYONE.
EACH OF YOU REPRESENTS THE BATTLE STRENGTHS OF YOUR RESPECTIVE LANDS...
...SO WE WANT YOU TO EXHIBIT AND FULLY SHOWCASE YOUR VARIOUS TALENTS.
AND THUS THE FINALS...
...WILL COMMENCE ONE MONTH FROM NOW!
!
WE'RE NOT DOING IT RIGHT HERE, RIGHT NOW?
WE CALL THIS THE REQUISITE PREPARATION PERIOD...
WHAT DO YOU MEAN?

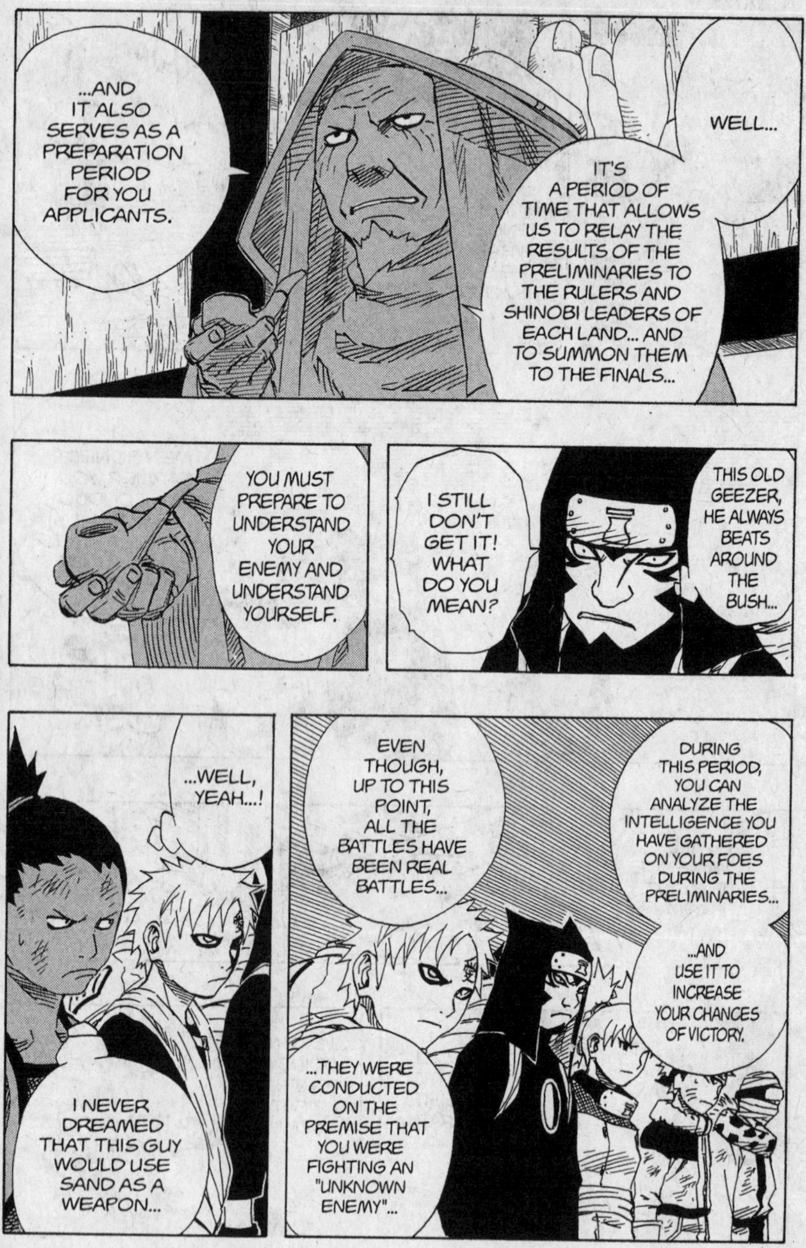
WELL...
IT'S A PERIOD OF TIME THAT ALLOWS US TO RELAY THE RESULTS OF THE PRELIMINARIES TO THE RULERS AND SHINOBI LEADERS OF EACH LAND... AND TO SUMMON THEM TO THE FINALS...
...AND IT ALSO SERVES AS A PREPARATION PERIOD FOR YOU APPLICANTS.
THIS OLD GEEZER, HE ALWAYS BEATS AROUND THE BUSH...
I STILL DON'T GET IT! WHAT DO YOU MEAN?
YOU MUST PREPARE TO UNDERSTAND YOUR ENEMY AND UNDERSTAND YOURSELF.
DURING THIS PERIOD, YOU CAN ANALYZE THE INTELLIGENCE YOU HAVE GATHERED ON YOUR FOES DURING THE PRELIMINARIES...
EVEN THOUGH, UP TO THIS POINT, ALL THE BATTLES HAVE BEEN REAL BATTLES...
...AND USE IT TO INCREASE YOUR CHANCES OF VICTORY.
...THEY WERE CONDUCTED ON THE PREMISE THAT YOU WERE FIGHTING AN "UNKNOWN ENEMY"...
...WELL, YEAH...!
I NEVER DREAMED THAT THIS GUY WOULD USE SAND AS A WEAPON...

READ THIS WAY

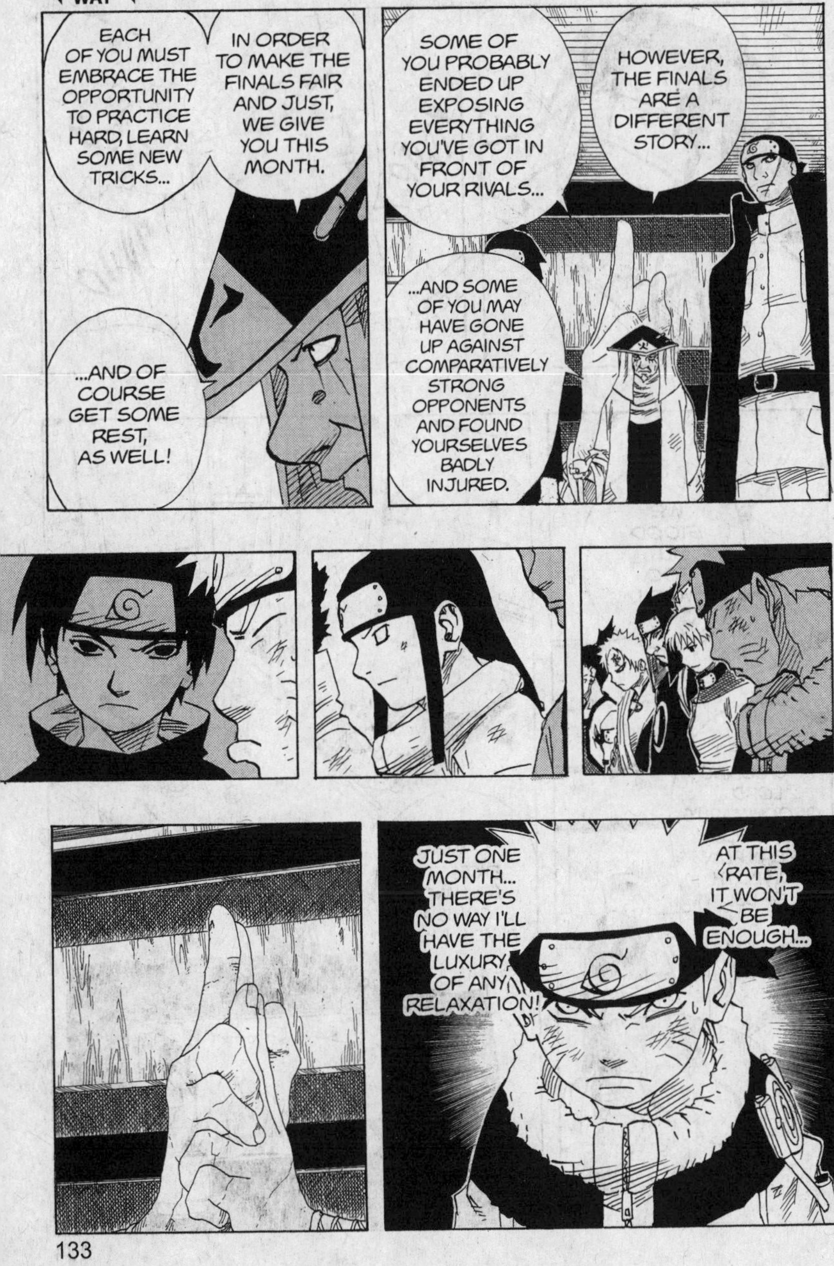

HOWEVER, THE FINALS ARE A DIFFERENT STORY...
SOME OF YOU PROBABLY ENDED UP EXPOSING EVERYTHING YOU'VE GOT IN FRONT OF YOUR RIVALS...
...AND SOME OF YOU MAY HAVE GONE UP AGAINST COMPARATIVELY STRONG OPPONENTS AND FOUND YOURSELVES BADLY INJURED.
IN ORDER TO MAKE THE FINALS FAIR AND JUST, WE GIVE YOU THIS MONTH.
EACH OF YOU MUST EMBRACE THE OPPORTUNITY TO PRACTICE HARD, LEARN SOME NEW TRICKS...
...AND OF COURSE GET SOME REST, AS WELL!
AT THIS RATE, IT WON'T BE ENOUGH...
JUST ONE MONTH... THERE'S NO WAY I'LL HAVE THE LUXURY OF ANY RELAXATION!

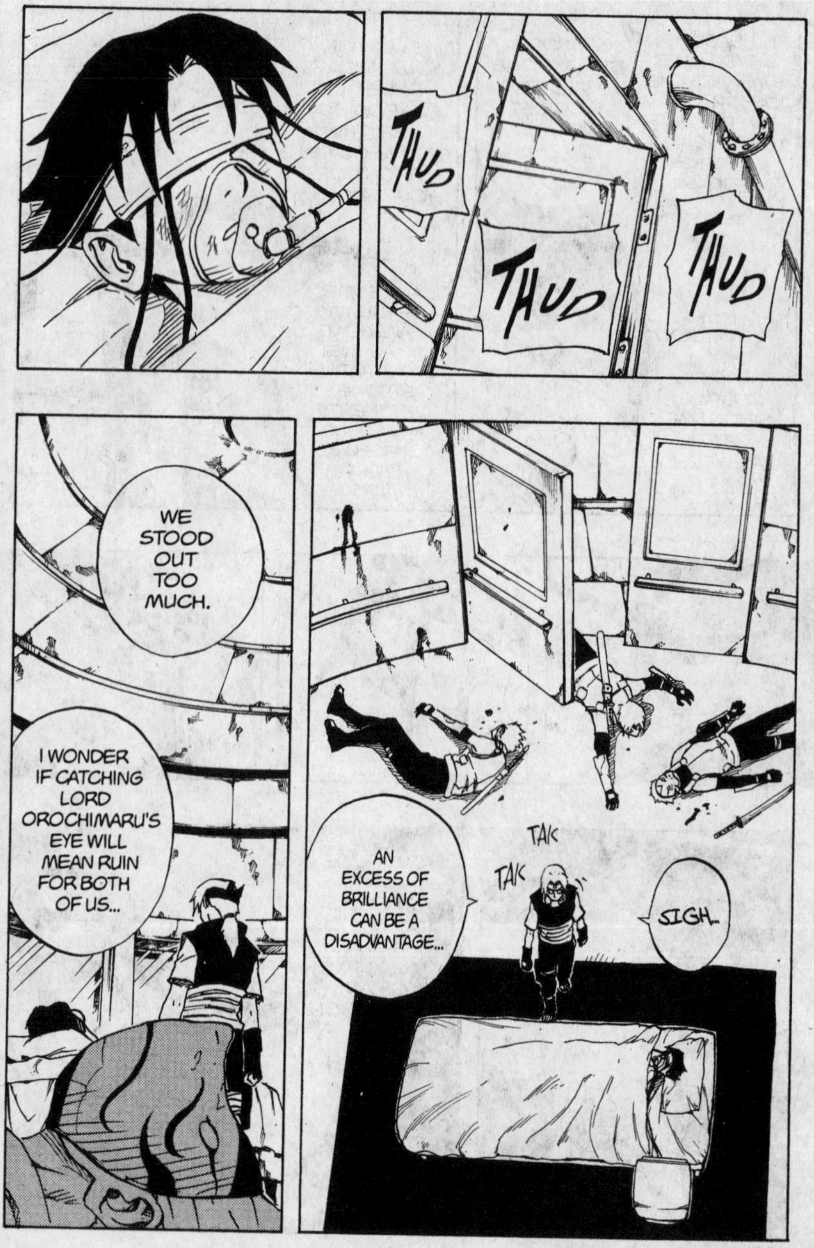
THUD
THUD
THUD
TAK
TAK
AN EXCESS OF BRILLIANCE CAN BE A DISADVANTAGE...
SIGH...
WE STOOD OUT TOO MUCH.
I WONDER IF CATCHING LORD OROCHIMARU'S EYE WILL MEAN RUIN FOR BOTH OF US...

READ THIS WAY

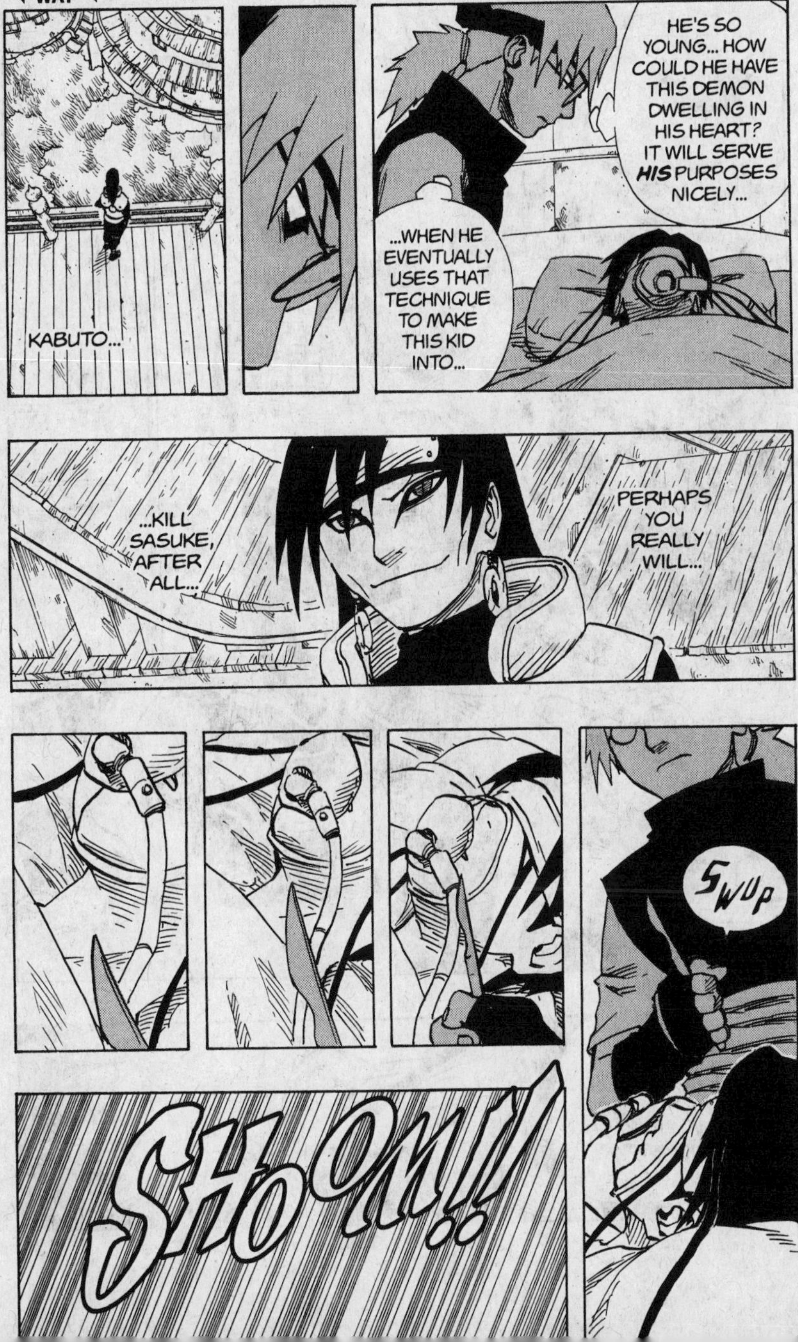

HE'S SO YOUNG... HOW COULD HE HAVE THIS DEMON DWELLING IN HIS HEART? IT WILL SERVE **HIS** PURPOSES NICELY...
...WHEN HE EVENTUALLY USES THAT TECHNIQUE TO MAKE THIS KID INTO...
KABUTO...
PERHAPS YOU REALLY WILL...
...KILL SASUKE, AFTER ALL...
SWUP
SHOOM!!

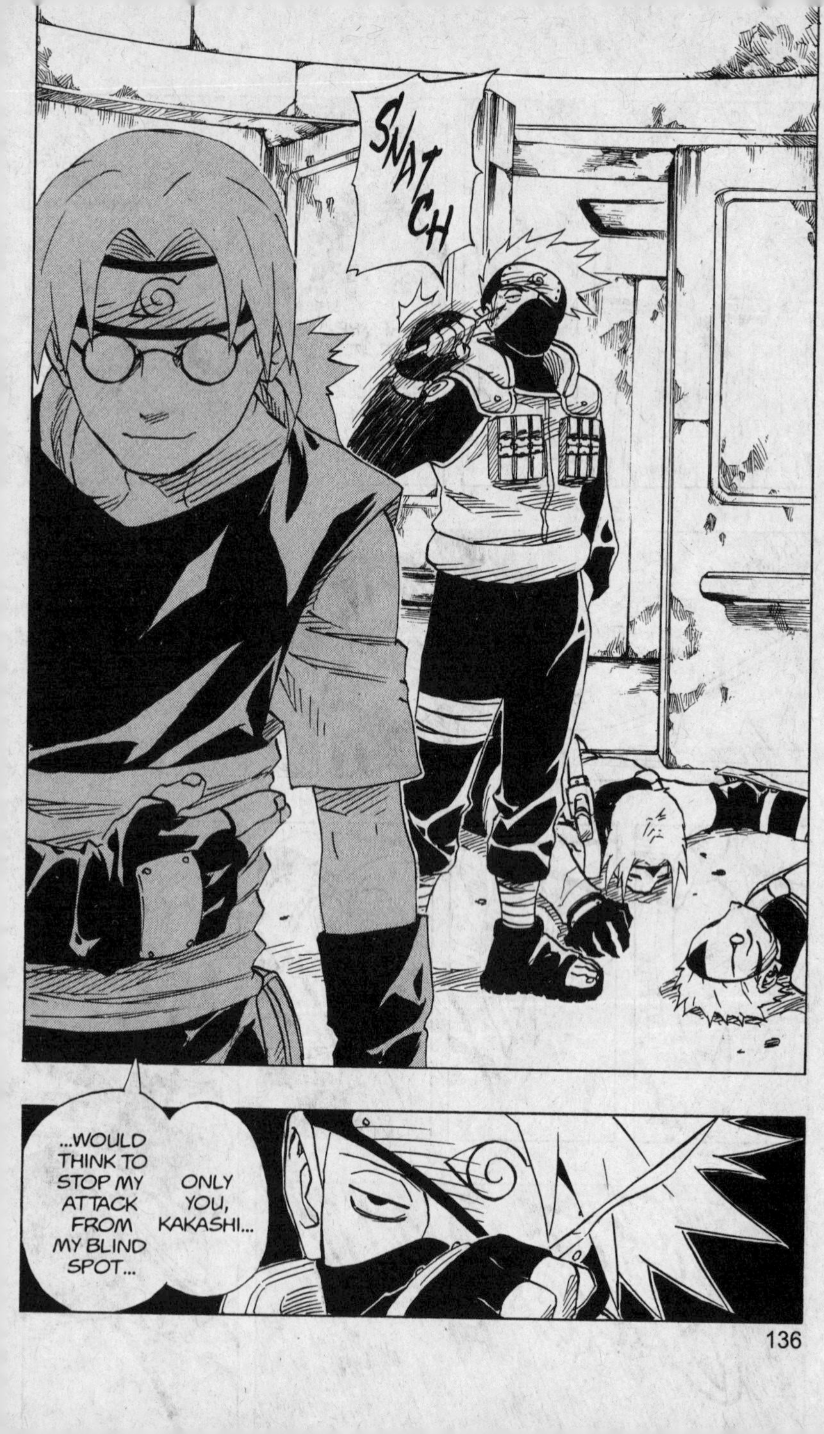
SNATCH
ONLY YOU, KAKASHI...
...WOULD THINK TO STOP MY ATTACK FROM MY BLIND SPOT...

READ THIS WAY

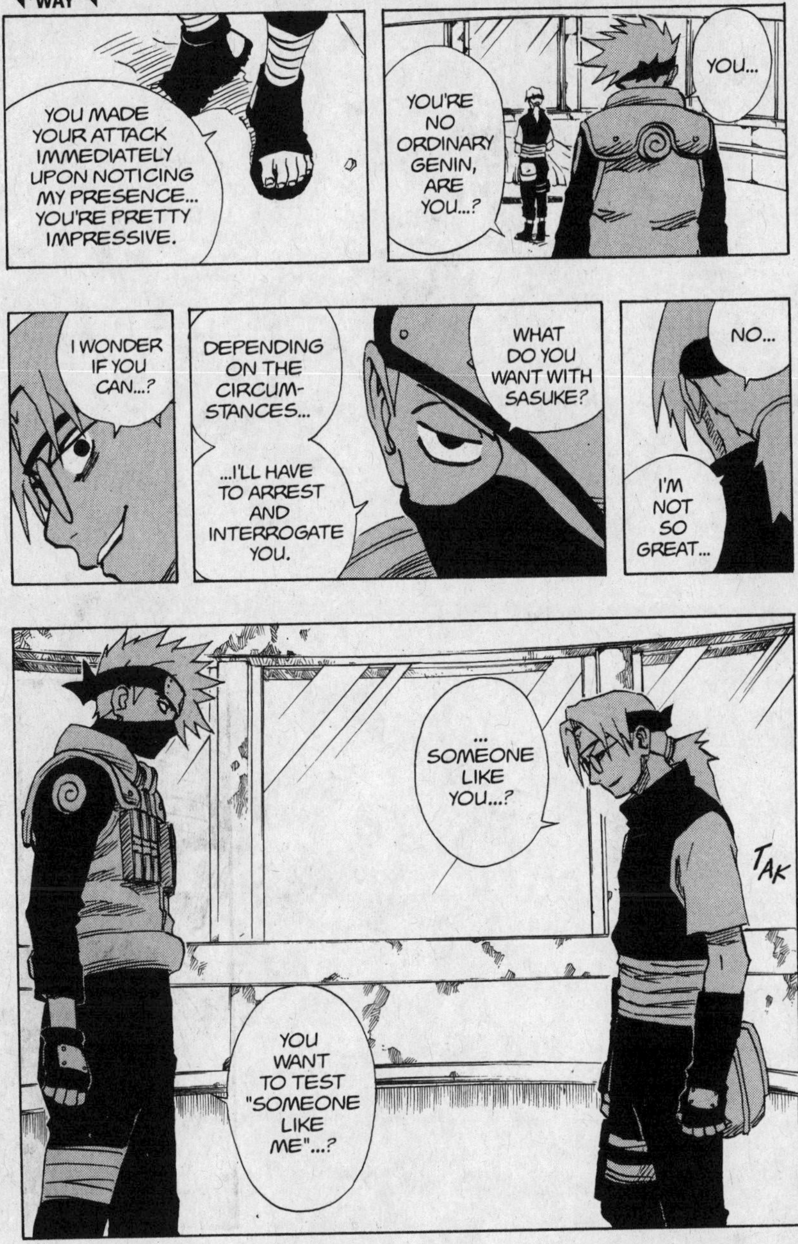
YOU...
YOU'RE NO ORDINARY GENIN, ARE YOU...?
YOU MADE YOUR ATTACK IMMEDIATELY UPON NOTICING MY PRESENCE... YOU'RE PRETTY IMPRESSIVE.
NO...
I'M NOT SO GREAT...
WHAT DO YOU WANT WITH SASUKE?
DEPENDING ON THE CIRCUM-STANCES...
...I'LL HAVE TO ARREST AND INTERROGATE YOU.
I WONDER IF YOU CAN...?
... SOMEONE LIKE YOU...?
TAK
YOU WANT TO TEST "SOMEONE LIKE ME"...?

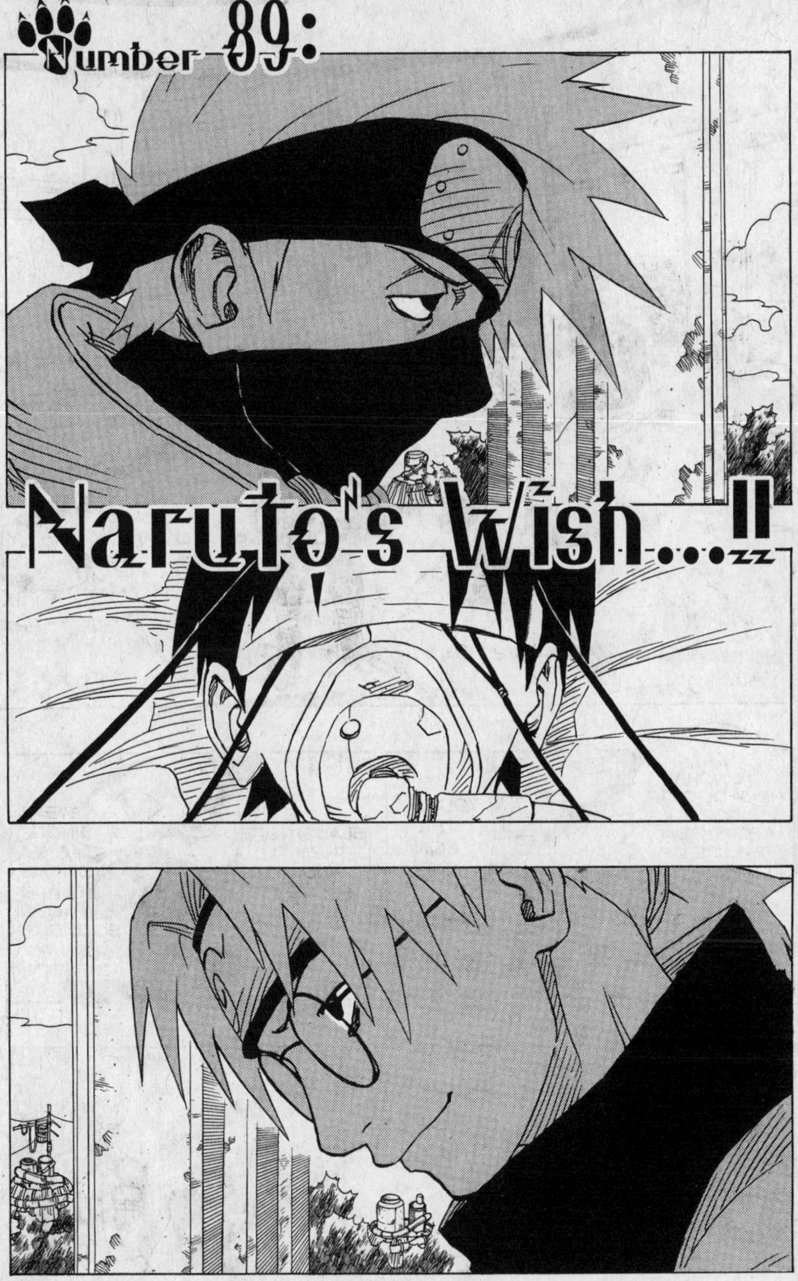

Number 89:
Naruto's Wish...!!

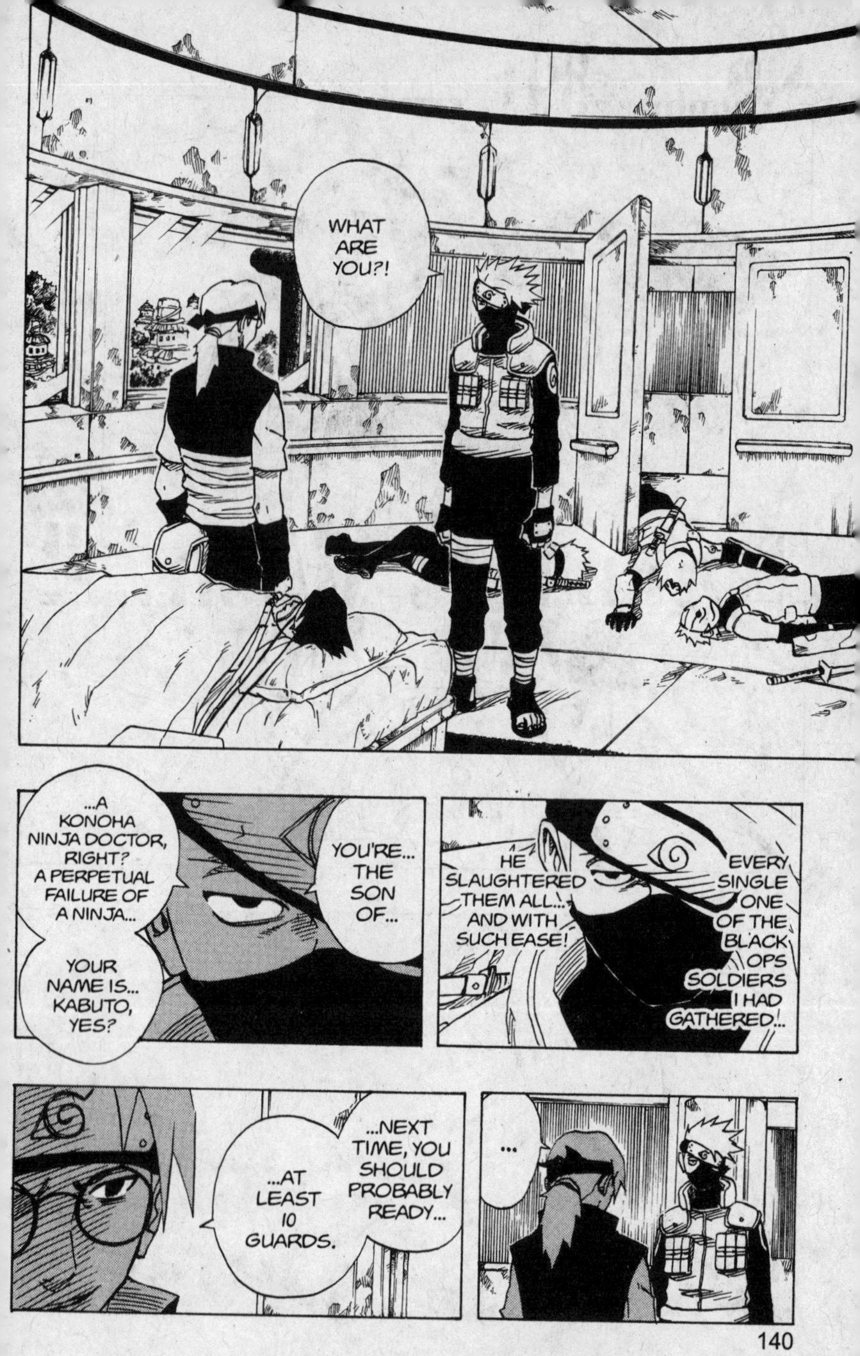
WHAT ARE YOU?!
EVERY SINGLE ONE OF THE BLACK OPS SOLDIERS I HAD GATHERED...
HE SLAUGHTERED THEM ALL... AND WITH SUCH EASE!
YOU'RE... THE SON OF...
...A KONOHA NINJA DOCTOR, RIGHT? A PERPETUAL FAILURE OF A NINJA...
YOUR NAME IS... KABUTO, YES?
...
...NEXT TIME, YOU SHOULD PROBABLY READY...
...AT LEAST 10 GUARDS.

READ THIS WAY

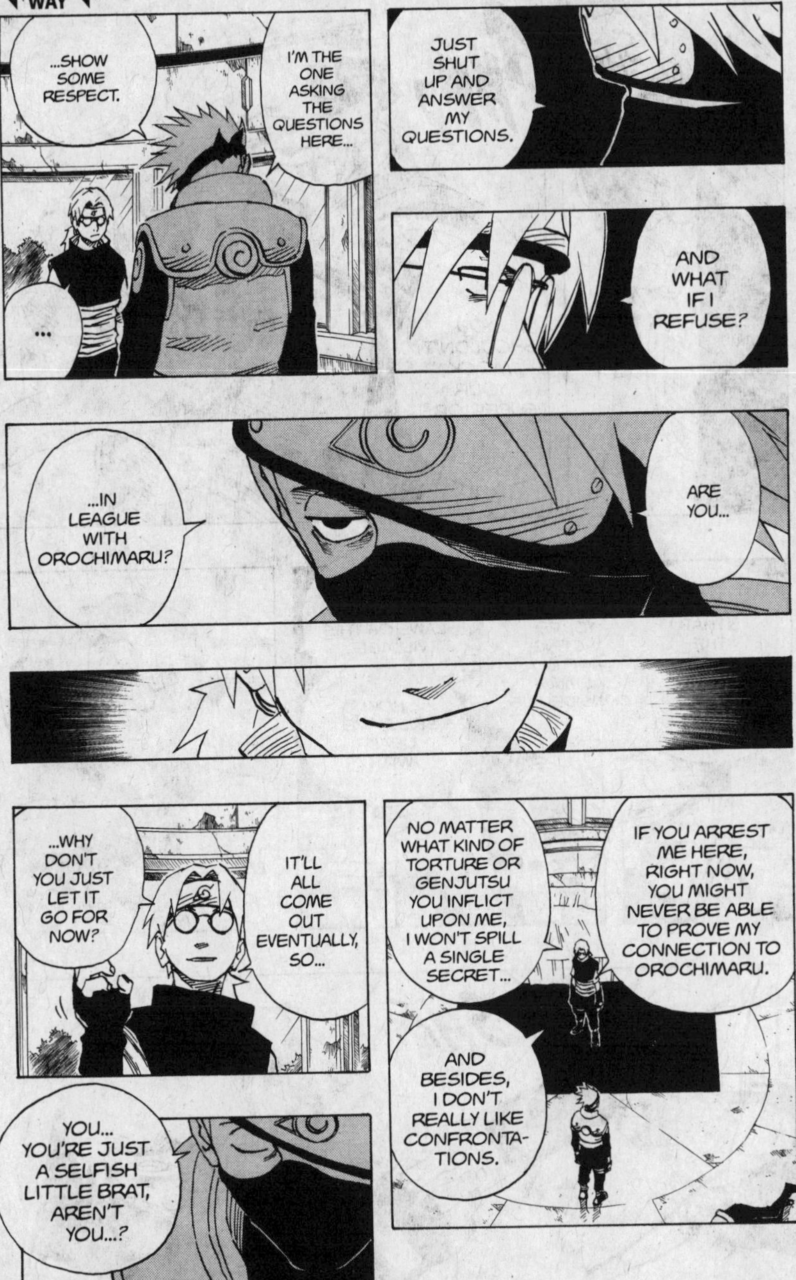
JUST SHUT UP AND ANSWER MY QUESTIONS.
AND WHAT IF I REFUSE?
I'M THE ONE ASKING THE QUESTIONS HERE...
...SHOW SOME RESPECT.
...
ARE YOU...
...IN LEAGUE WITH OROCHIMARU?
IF YOU ARREST ME HERE, RIGHT NOW, YOU MIGHT NEVER BE ABLE TO PROVE MY CONNECTION TO OROCHIMARU.
NO MATTER WHAT KIND OF TORTURE OR GENJUTSU YOU INFLICT UPON ME, I WON'T SPILL A SINGLE SECRET...
AND BESIDES, I DON'T REALLY LIKE CONFRONTA-TIONS.
IT'LL ALL COME OUT EVENTUALLY, SO...
...WHY DON'T YOU JUST LET IT GO FOR NOW?
YOU... YOU'RE JUST A SELFISH LITTLE BRAT, AREN'T YOU...?

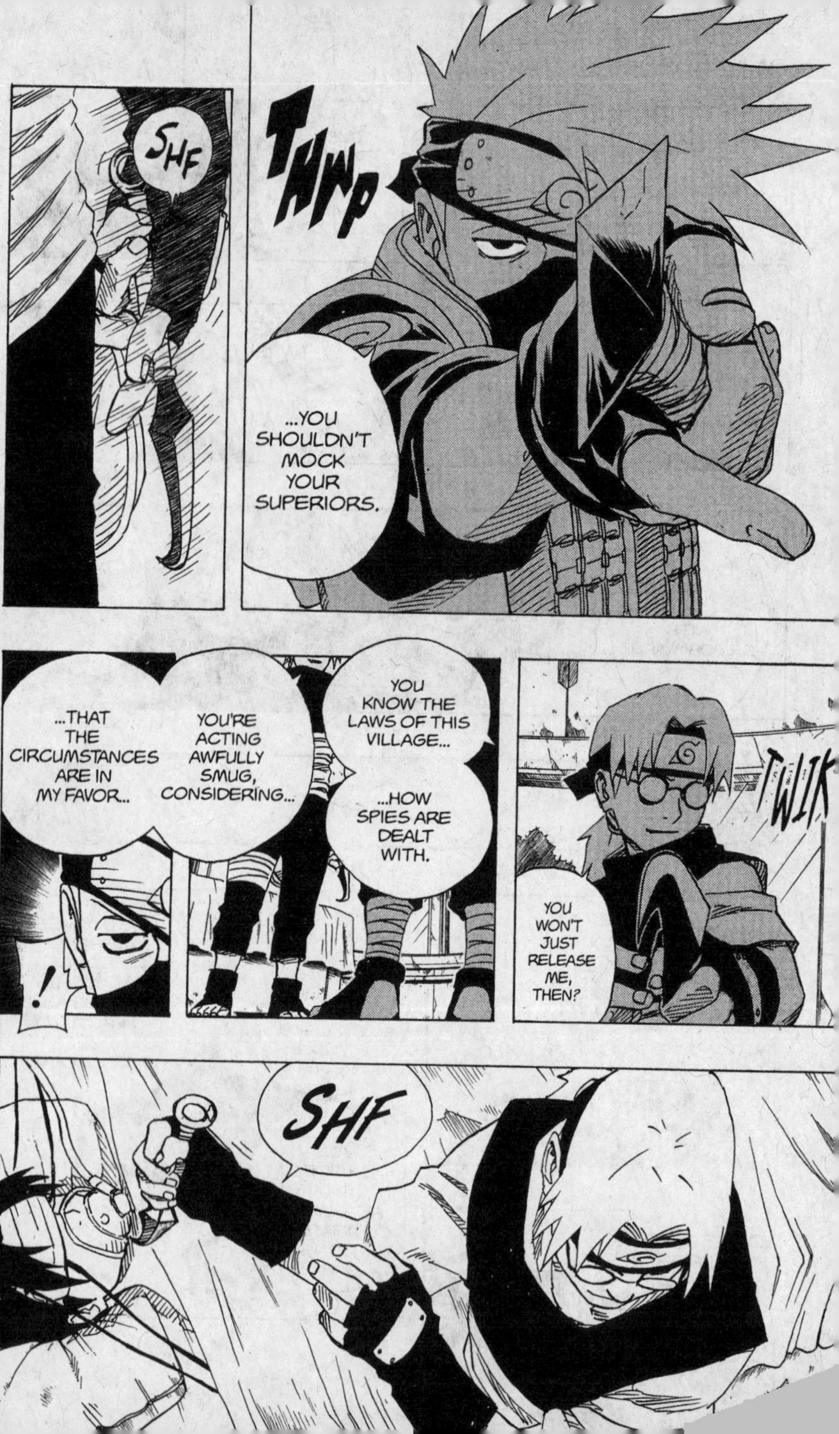
THWP
...YOU SHOULDN'T MOCK YOUR SUPERIORS.
SHF
TWIK
YOU WON'T JUST RELEASE ME, THEN?
YOU KNOW THE LAWS OF THIS VILLAGE...
...HOW SPIES ARE DEALT WITH.
YOU'RE ACTING AWFULLY SMUG, CONSIDERING...
...THAT THE CIRCUMSTANCES ARE IN MY FAVOR...
!
SHF

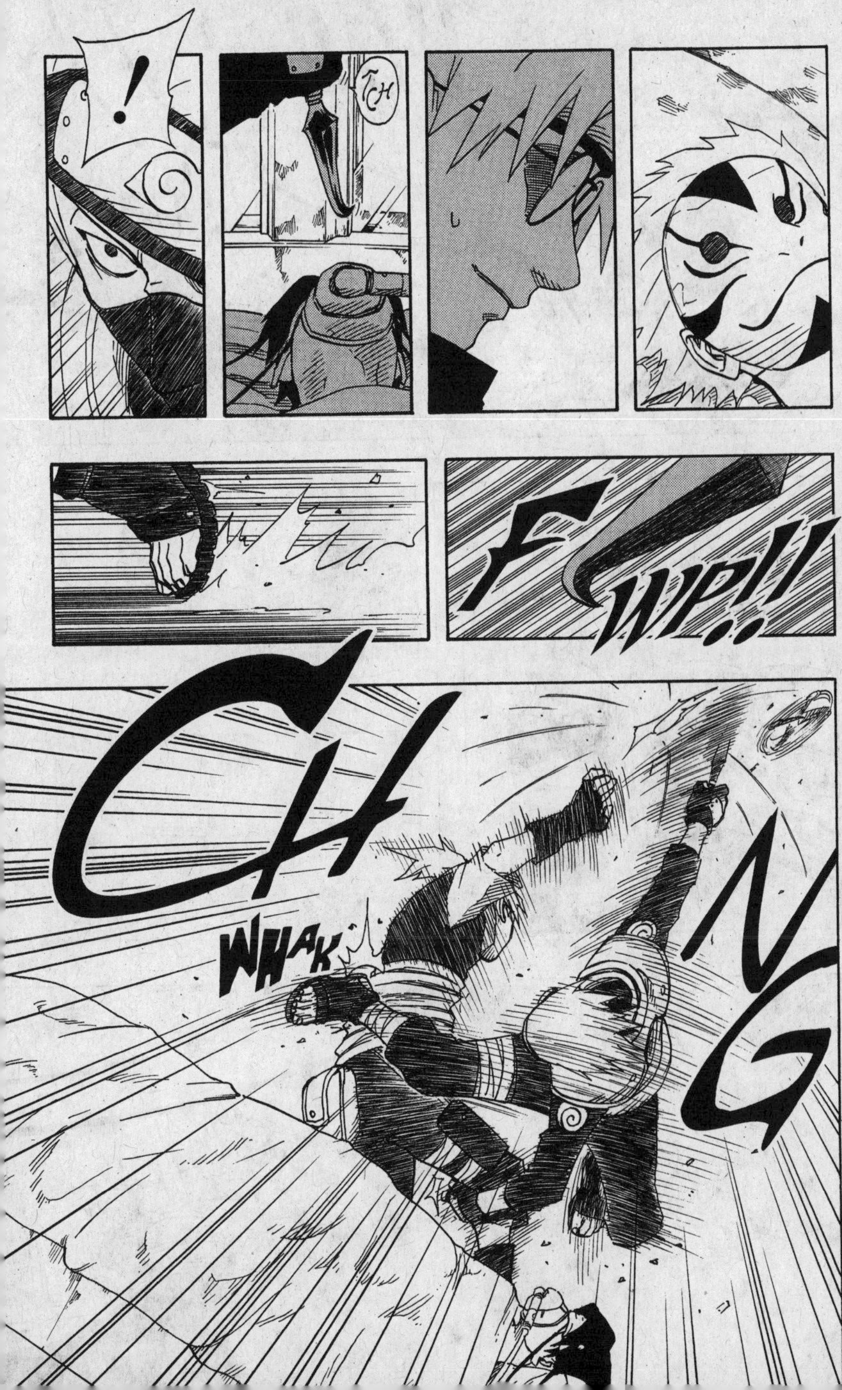
TCH
!
FWIP!!
CHING
WHAK

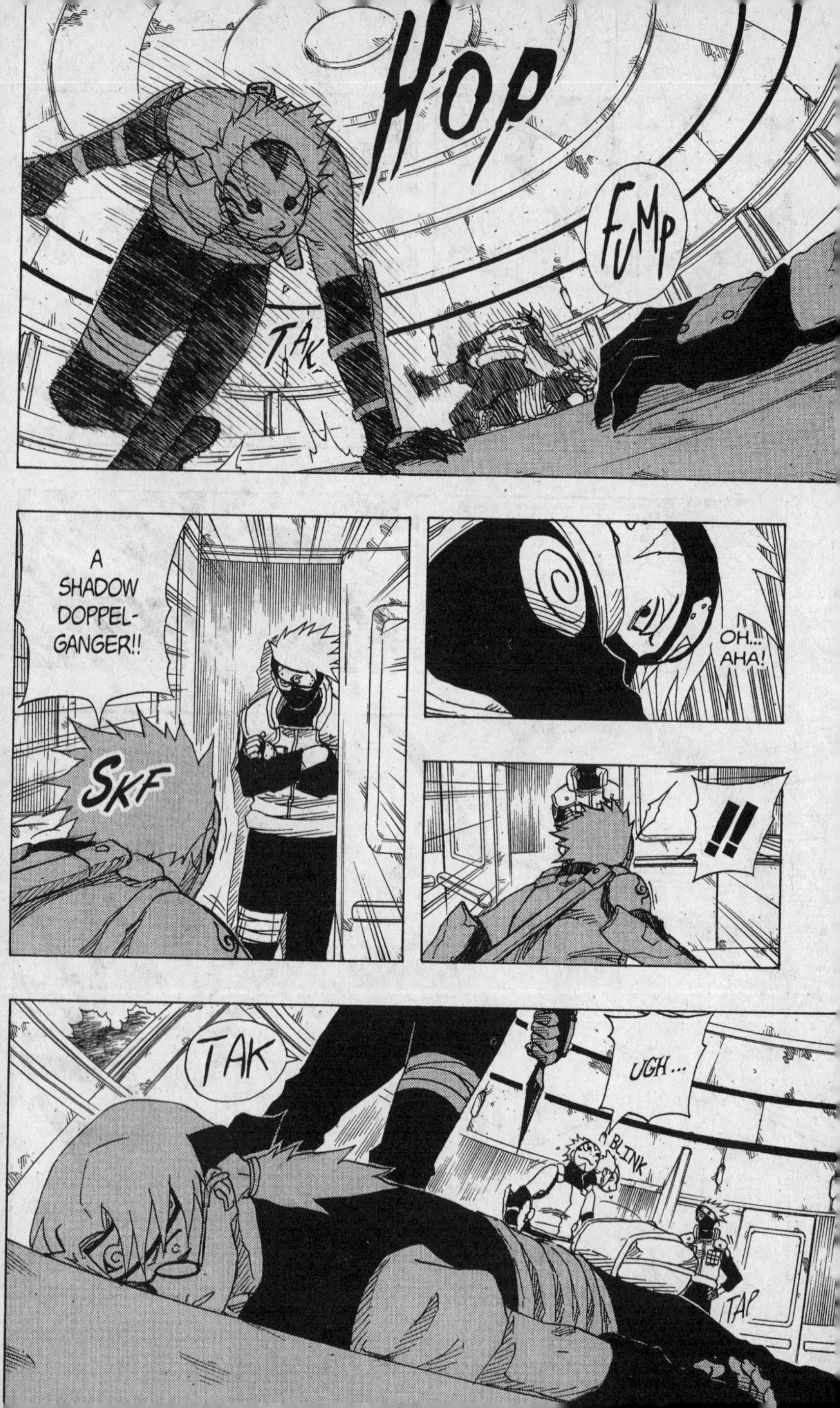
HOP
FUMP
TAK
OH... AHA!
!!
A SHADOW DOPPEL-GANGER!!
SKF
UGH...
BLINK
TAP
TAK

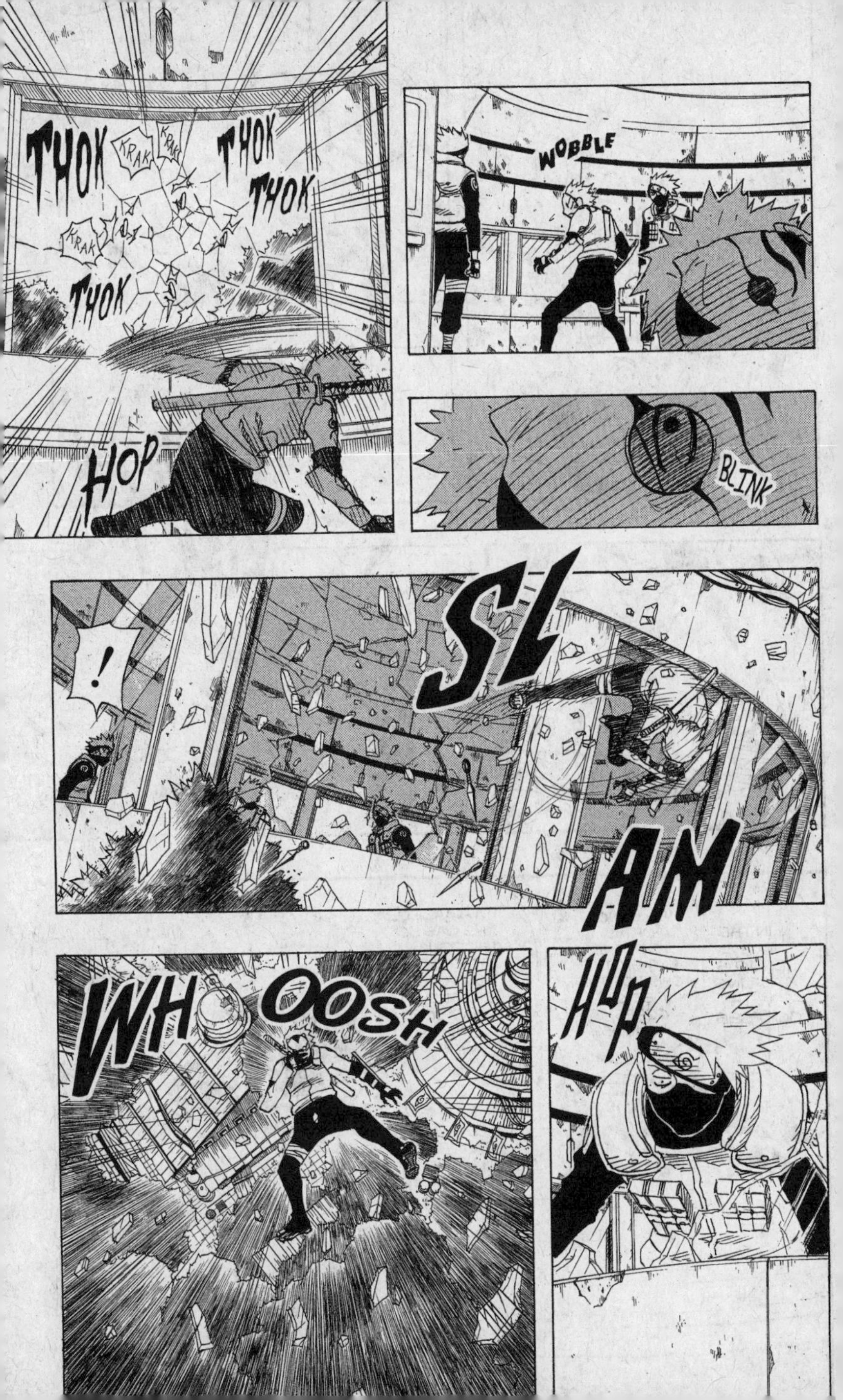
WOBBLE
BLINK
THOK
THOK
KRAK
KRAK
THOK
KRAK
THOK
HOP
!
SLAM
HOP
WHOOSH

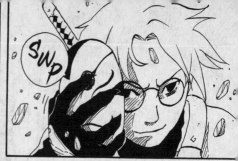

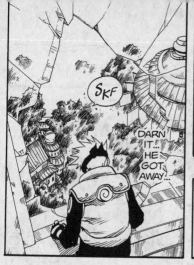

SWP
...!
SKF
DARN IT... HE GOT AWAY...
FUMP-POOF
AMAZ-ING...
TWIST
JUST AS I THOUGHT... SHIKON NO JUTSU... THE ART OF DEAD SOULS, USED TO TEMPORARILY RESTORE A CADAVER'S HEART BEAT AND MANIPULATE THE CORPSE...
HE SURGICALLY ALTERED THE FACE... TO MAKE IT RESEMBLE HIS OWN...!
I'M AMAZED... HE WAS SO THOROUGH IN HIS DECEPTION THAT HE EVEN ERASED THE DEAD BODY'S ODOR...
AND HE STILLED HIS OWN HEARTBEAT... DISGUISING HIMSELF AS ONE OF THE BLACK OPS SOLDIERS HE HAD KILLED... TO ALLOW HIS ESCAPE.
THE INFLUENCE OF HIS ADOPTIVE FATHER, THE CHIEF OF THE MEDICAL CORPS, IS OBVIOUS...
...IN THE WAY HE ENJOYS TRIFLING WITH CORPSES...

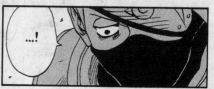

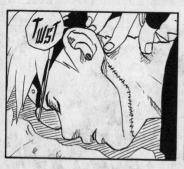

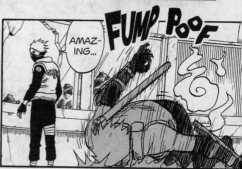

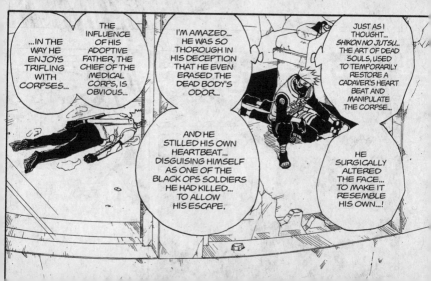

READ THIS WAY

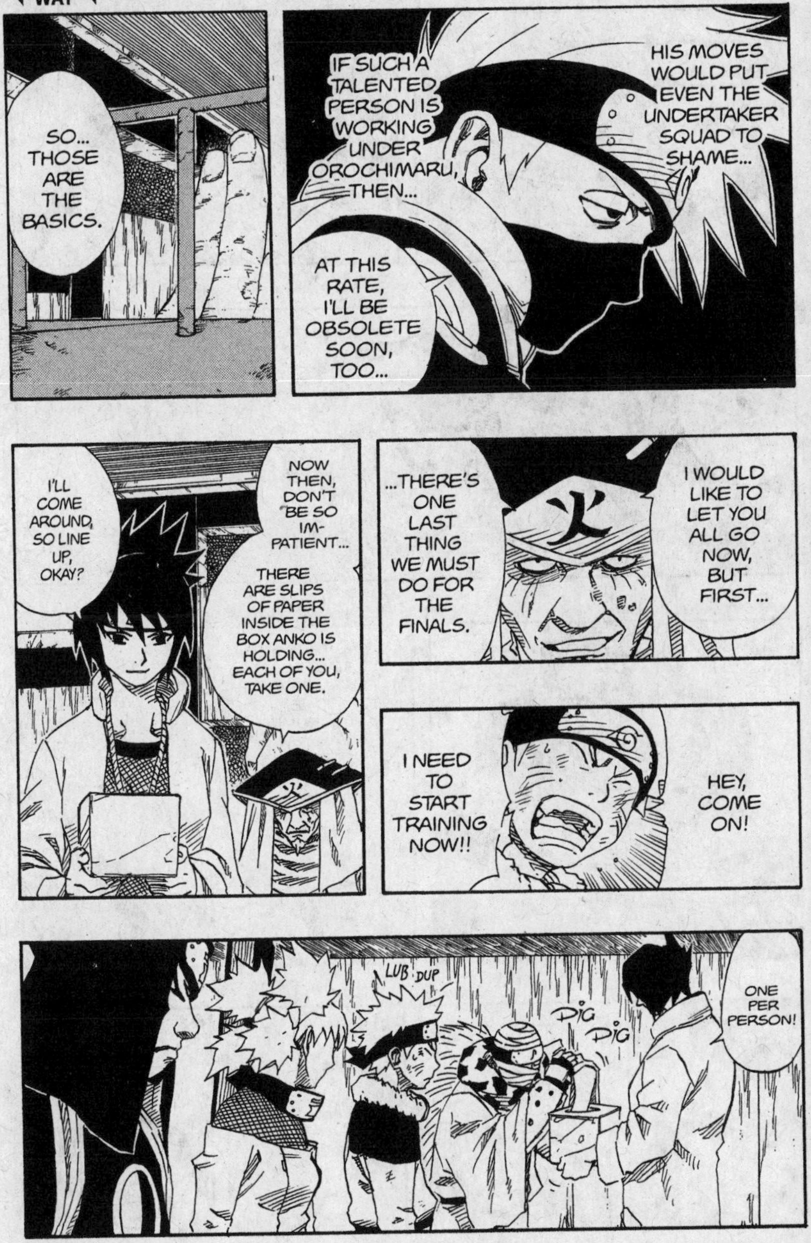
HIS MOVES WOULD PUT EVEN THE UNDERTAKER SQUAD TO SHAME...
IF SUCH A TALENTED PERSON IS WORKING UNDER OROCHIMARU, THEN...
AT THIS RATE, I'LL BE OBSOLETE SOON, TOO...
SO... THOSE ARE THE BASICS.
I WOULD LIKE TO LET YOU ALL GO NOW, BUT FIRST...
...THERE'S ONE LAST THING WE MUST DO FOR THE FINALS.
HEY, COME ON!
I NEED TO START TRAINING NOW!!
NOW THEN, DON'T BE SO IM-PATIENT...
THERE ARE SLIPS OF PAPER INSIDE THE BOX ANKO IS HOLDING... EACH OF YOU, TAKE ONE.
I'LL COME AROUND, SO LINE UP, OKAY?
ONE PER PERSON!
DIG DIG
LUB DUP

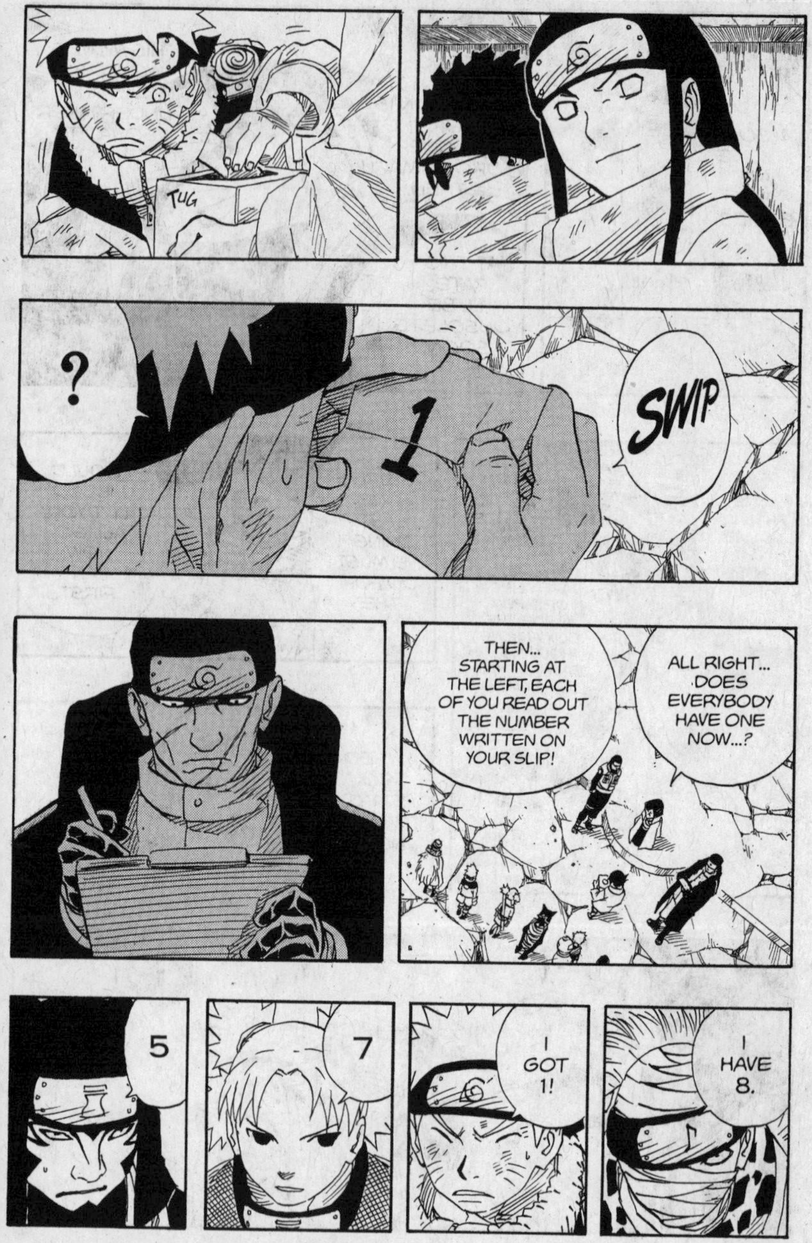
TUG
SWIP
?
ALL RIGHT... DOES EVERYBODY HAVE ONE NOW...?
THEN... STARTING AT THE LEFT, EACH OF YOU READ OUT THE NUMBER WRITTEN ON YOUR SLIP!
I HAVE 8.
I GOT 1!
7
5

READ THIS WAY

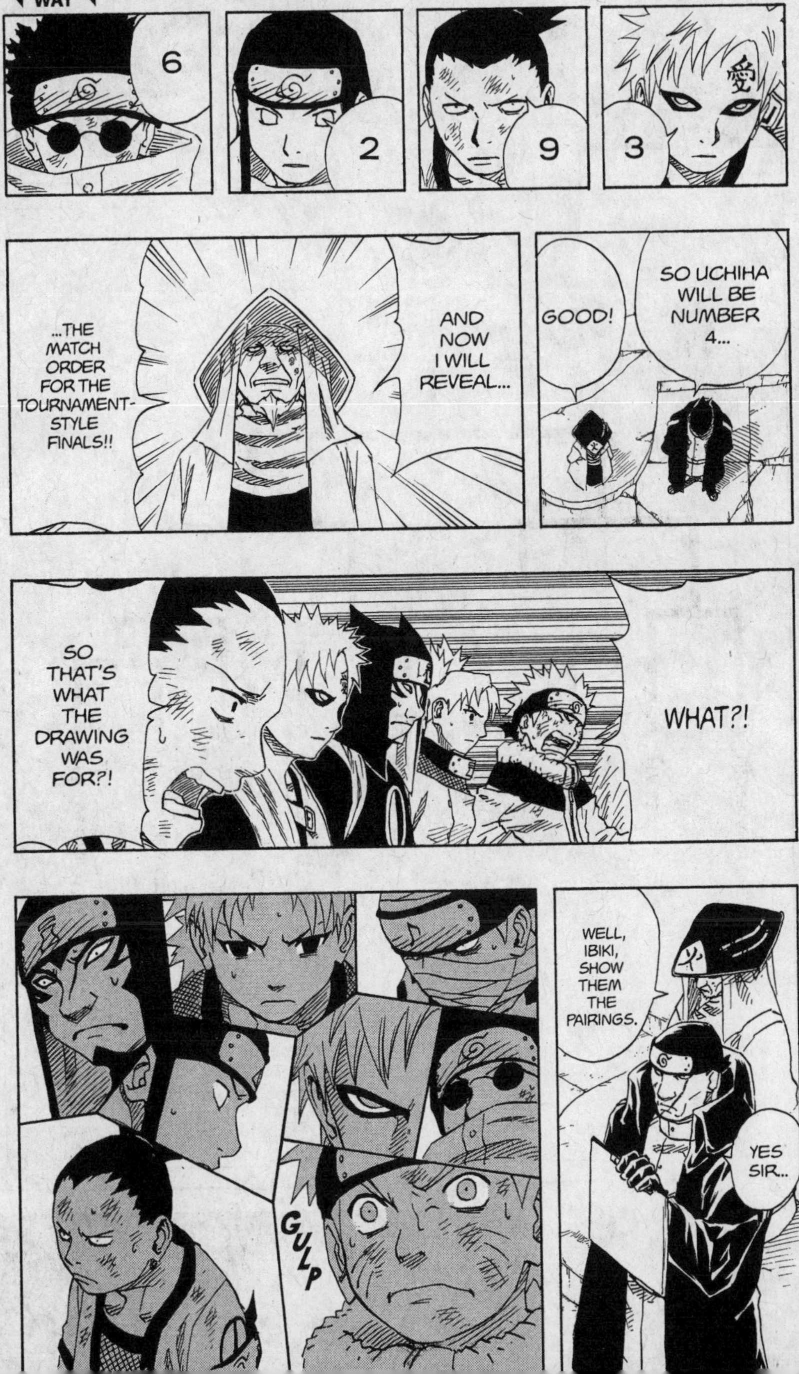
3
9
2
6
SO UCHIHA WILL BE NUMBER 4...
GOOD!
AND NOW I WILL REVEAL...
...THE MATCH ORDER FOR THE TOURNAMENT-STYLE FINALS!!
WHAT?!
SO THAT'S WHAT THE DRAWING WAS FOR?!
WELL, IBIKI, SHOW THEM THE PAIRINGS.
YES SIR...
GULP

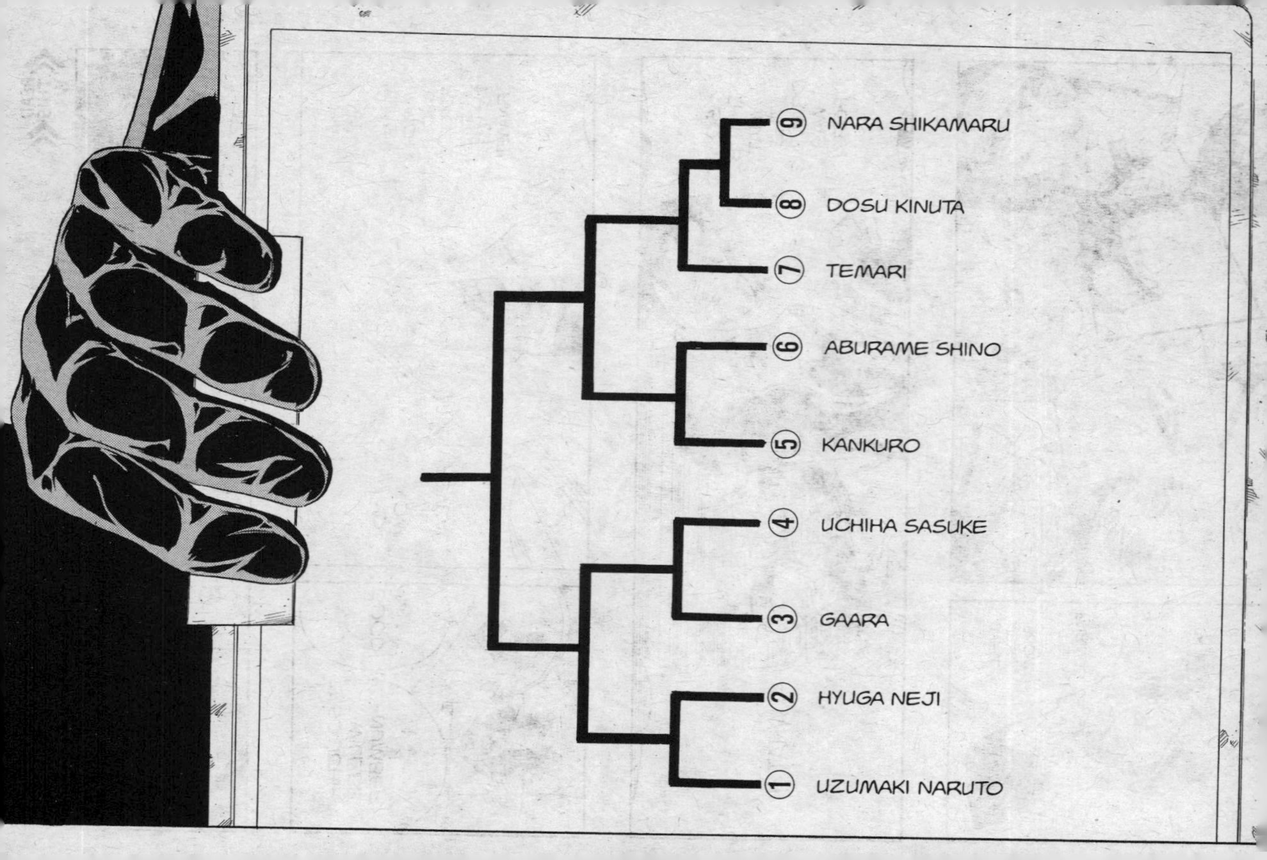

① UZUMAKI NARUTO
② HYUGA NEJI
③ GAARA
④ UCHIHA SASUKE
⑤ KANKURO
⑥ ABURAME SHINO
⑦ TEMARI
⑧ DOSU KINUTA
⑨ NARA SHIKAMARU

READ THIS WAY

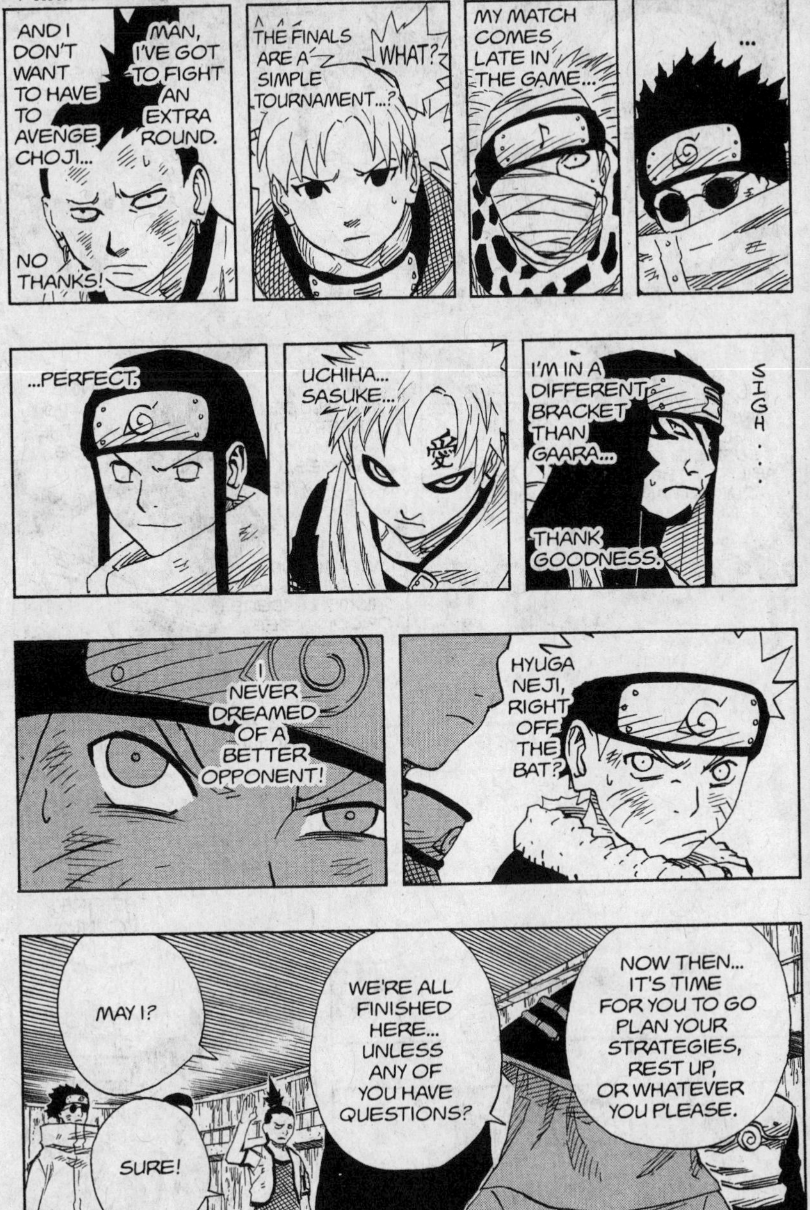
...
MY MATCH COMES LATE IN THE GAME...
THE FINALS ARE A SIMPLE TOURNAMENT...?
WHAT?
MAN, I'VE GOT TO FIGHT AN EXTRA ROUND.
AND I DON'T WANT TO HAVE TO AVENGE CHOJI...
NO THANKS!
I'M IN A DIFFERENT BRACKET THAN GAARA...
SIGH...
THANK GOODNESS.
UCHIHA... SASUKE...
...PERFECT.
HYUGA NEJI, RIGHT OFF THE BAT?
I NEVER DREAMED OF A BETTER OPPONENT!
NOW THEN... IT'S TIME FOR YOU TO GO PLAN YOUR STRATEGIES, REST UP, OR WHATEVER YOU PLEASE.
WE'RE ALL FINISHED HERE... UNLESS ANY OF YOU HAVE QUESTIONS?
MAY I?
SURE!

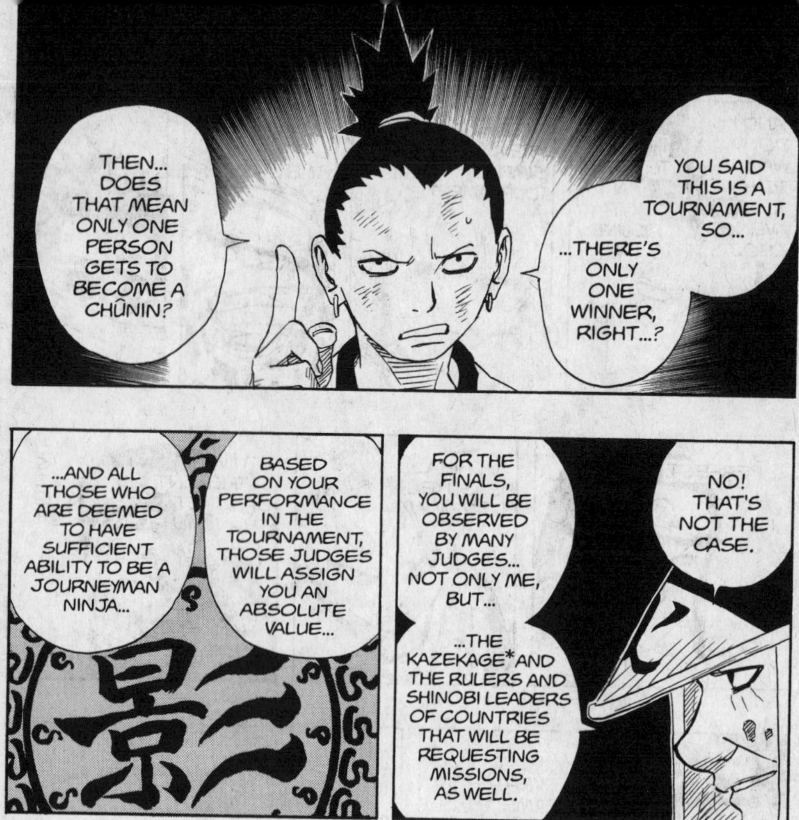
YOU SAID THIS IS A TOURNAMENT, SO...
...THERE'S ONLY ONE WINNER, RIGHT...?
THEN... DOES THAT MEAN ONLY ONE PERSON GETS TO BECOME A CHÛNIN?
NO! THAT'S NOT THE CASE.
FOR THE FINALS, YOU WILL BE OBSERVED BY MANY JUDGES... NOT ONLY ME, BUT...
...THE KAZEKAGE* AND THE RULERS AND SHINOBI LEADERS OF COUNTRIES THAT WILL BE REQUESTING MISSIONS, AS WELL.
BASED ON YOUR PERFORMANCE IN THE TOURNAMENT, THOSE JUDGES WILL ASSIGN YOU AN ABSOLUTE VALUE...
...AND ALL THOSE WHO ARE DEEMED TO HAVE SUFFICIENT ABILITY TO BE A JOURNEYMAN NINJA...

*THE LEADER OF THE VILLAGE OF SUNAGAKURE (THE VILLAGE HIDDEN IN SAND).

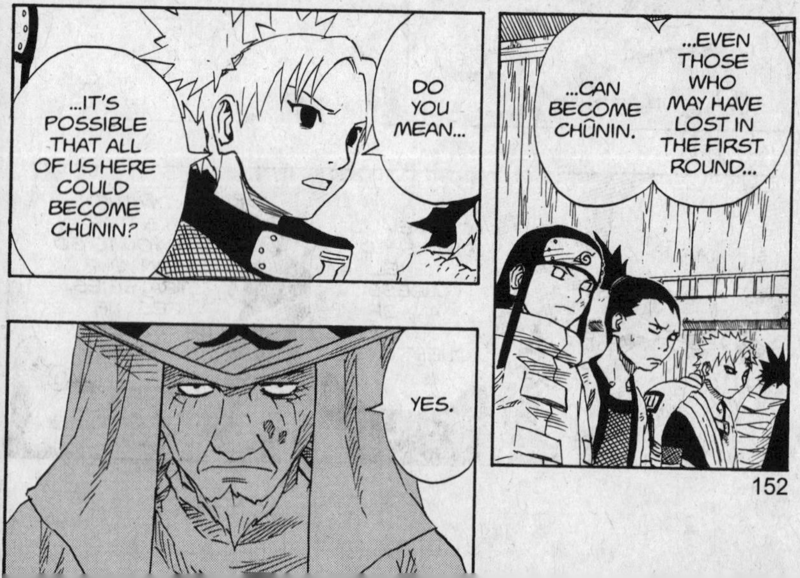
...EVEN THOSE WHO MAY HAVE LOST IN THE FIRST ROUND...
...CAN BECOME CHÛNIN.
DO YOU MEAN...
...IT'S POSSIBLE THAT ALL OF US HERE COULD BECOME CHÛNIN?
YES.

READ THIS WAY

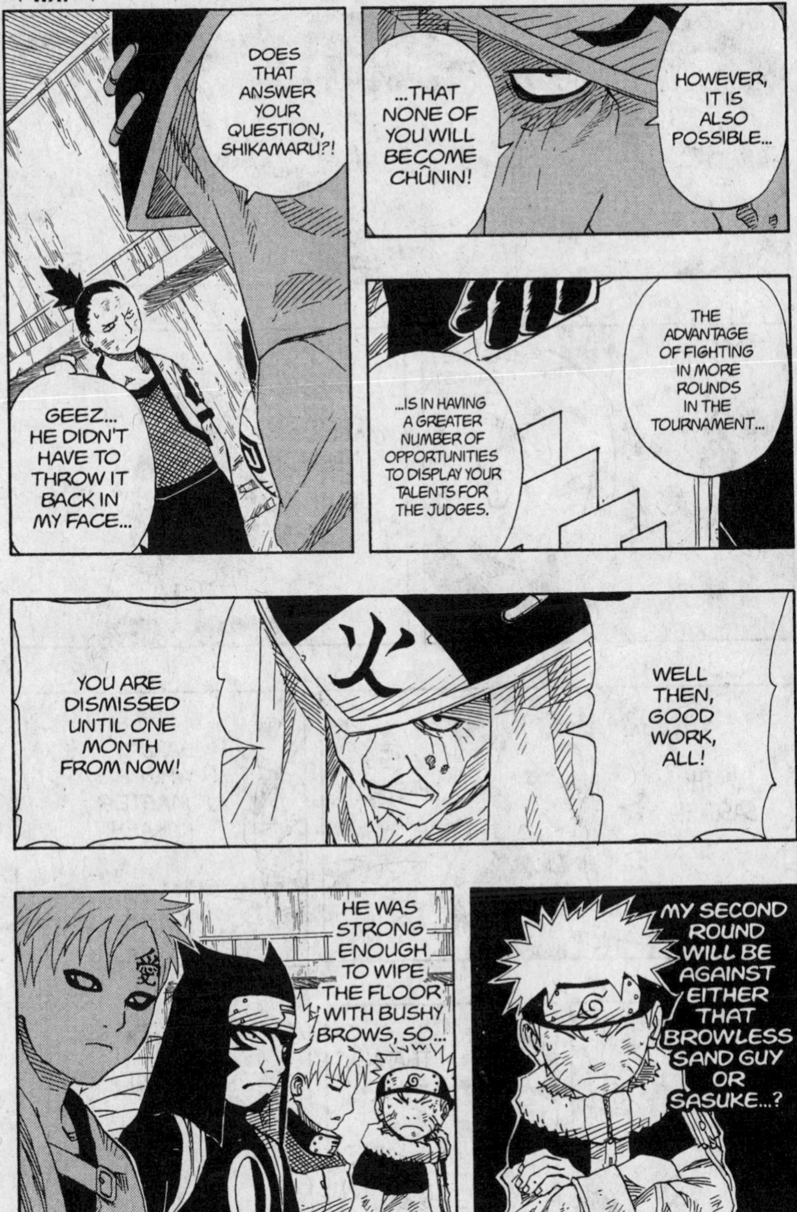
HOWEVER, IT IS ALSO POSSIBLE...
...THAT NONE OF YOU WILL BECOME CHÛNIN!
THE ADVANTAGE OF FIGHTING IN MORE ROUNDS IN THE TOURNAMENT...
...IS IN HAVING A GREATER NUMBER OF OPPORTUNITIES TO DISPLAY YOUR TALENTS FOR THE JUDGES.
DOES THAT ANSWER YOUR QUESTION, SHIKAMARU?!
GEEZ... HE DIDN'T HAVE TO THROW IT BACK IN MY FACE...
WELL THEN, GOOD WORK, ALL!
YOU ARE DISMISSED UNTIL ONE MONTH FROM NOW!
MY SECOND ROUND WILL BE AGAINST EITHER THAT BROWLESS SAND GUY OR SASUKE...?
HE WAS STRONG ENOUGH TO WIPE THE FLOOR WITH BUSHY BROWS, SO...

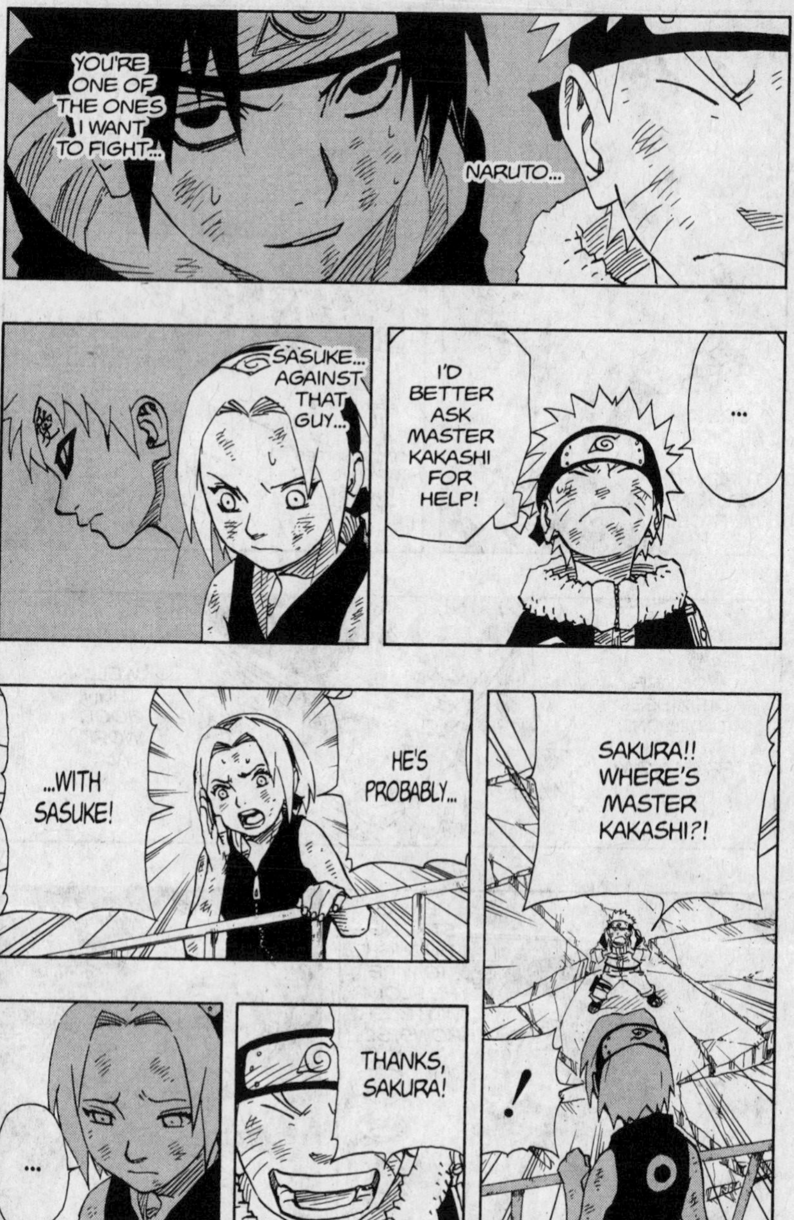
NARUTO...
YOU'RE ONE OF THE ONES I WANT TO FIGHT...
...
I'D BETTER ASK MASTER KAKASHI FOR HELP!
SASUKE... AGAINST THAT GUY...
SAKURA!! WHERE'S MASTER KAKASHI?!
!
HE'S PROBABLY...
...WITH SASUKE!
THANKS, SAKURA!
...

READ THIS WAY

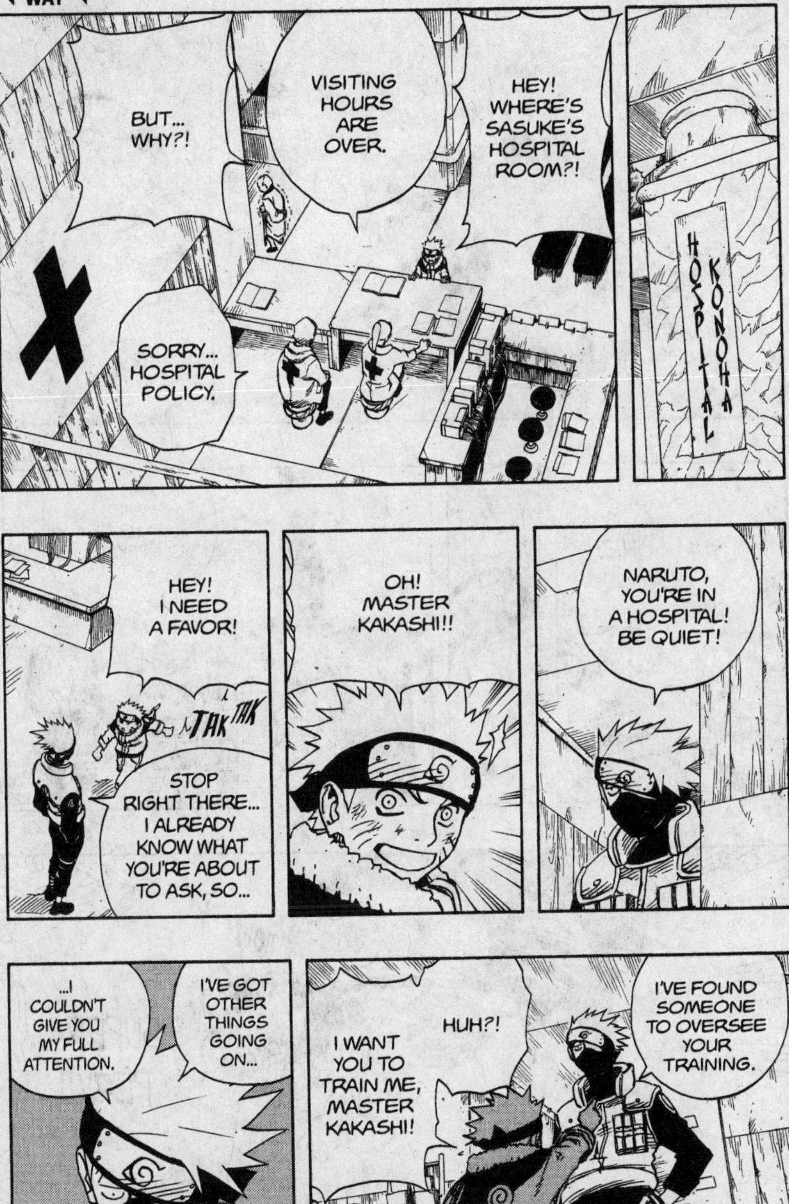
KONOHA
HOSPITAL
HEY! WHERE'S SASUKE'S HOSPITAL ROOM?!
VISITING HOURS ARE OVER.
BUT... WHY?!
SORRY... HOSPITAL POLICY.
NARUTO, YOU'RE IN A HOSPITAL! BE QUIET!
OH! MASTER KAKASHI!!
HEY! I NEED A FAVOR!
TAK TAK
STOP RIGHT THERE... I ALREADY KNOW WHAT YOU'RE ABOUT TO ASK, SO...
I'VE FOUND SOMEONE TO OVERSEE YOUR TRAINING.
HUH?!
I WANT YOU TO TRAIN ME, MASTER KAKASHI!
I'VE GOT OTHER THINGS GOING ON...
...I COULDN'T GIVE YOU MY FULL ATTENTION.

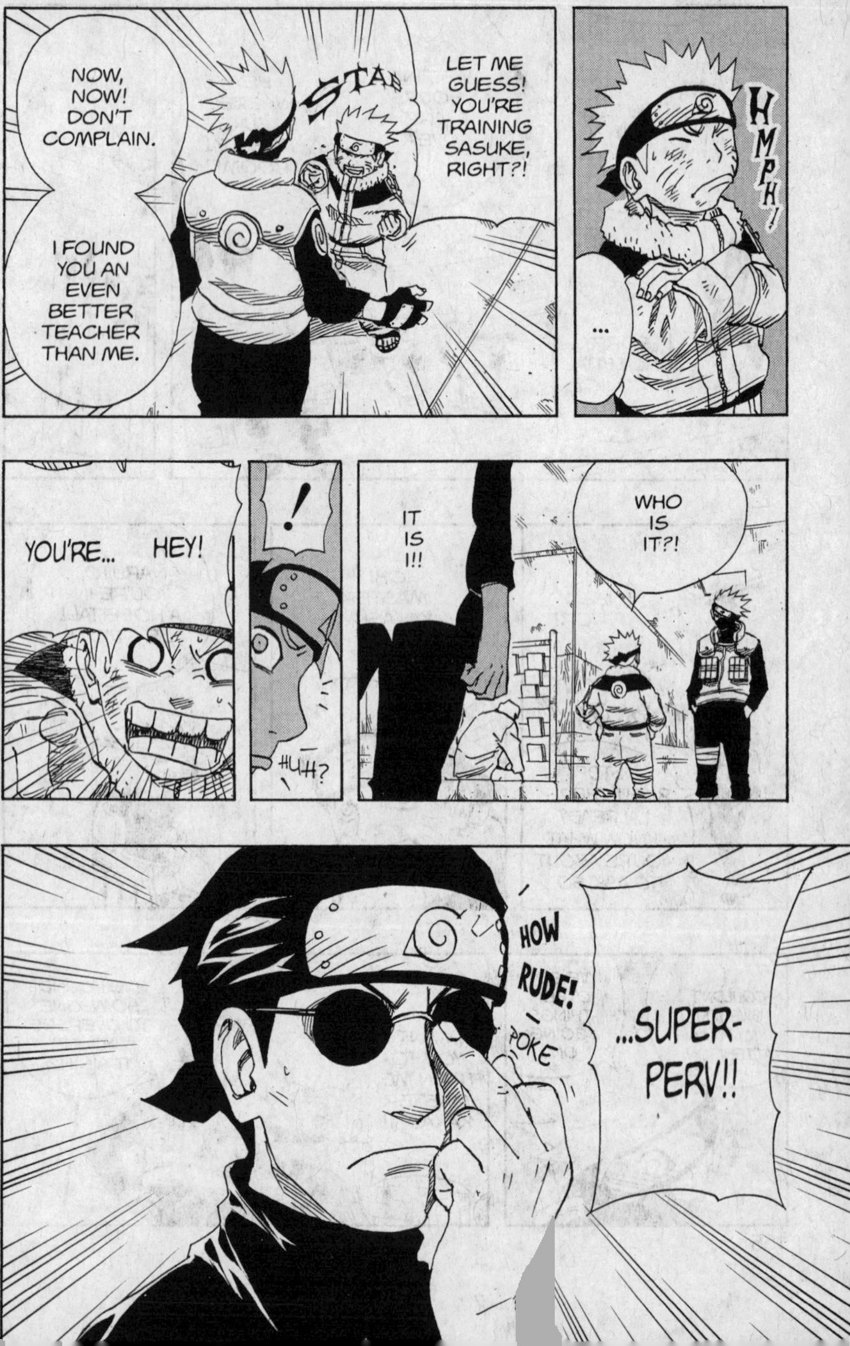
HMPH!
...
LET ME GUESS! YOU'RE TRAINING SASUKE, RIGHT?!
STAB
NOW, NOW! DON'T COMPLAIN.
I FOUND YOU AN EVEN BETTER TEACHER THAN ME.
WHO IS IT?!
IT IS I!!
!
HUH?
HEY!
YOU'RE...
...SUPER-PERV!!
HOW RUDE!
POKE

THE WORLD OF KISHIMOTO MASASHI
MY PERSONAL HISTORY, PART 13

ONCE I WAS EXPOSED TO *AKIRA*, MY ATTITUDE TOWARD ART BEGAN TO CHANGE DRAMATICALLY. I DID SOME RESEARCH ON THE STYLE OF MR. OTOMO, THE AUTHOR AND ARTIST OF *AKIRA*, IN AN ATTEMPT TO LEARN WHICH ARTISTS HAD INFLUENCED HIM... BUT I COULDN'T FIND ANYTHING. SO I CONCLUDED THAT IT WAS COMPLETELY ORIGINAL... AND THAT'S WHEN IT CAME TO ME: "WOW, THIS IS THE FIRST TIME SINCE SEEING MR. TORIYAMA'S WORK THAT I'VE BEEN SO STRONGLY AFFECTED BY SOMEONE'S ART."

I HAD ABSOLUTELY NO IDEA WHY MR. TORIYAMA'S AND MR. OTOMO'S ART WERE BOTH SO FASCINATING, BUT THERE WERE TWO THINGS THAT I WAS SURE OF. BOTH OF THEM DID WORK THAT SEEMED ORIGINAL AND HAD A GREAT SENSE OF STYLE. I HAD THE FEELING THAT THEIR EFFECTS, DESIGN AND ATTENTION TO DETAIL WERE TOTALLY DIFFERENT FROM THOSE OF OTHER PEOPLE. IN OTHER WORDS, I STARTED THINKING THAT WHAT "FASCINATING ART" MEANT TO ME WAS "ORIGINAL ART," AND THAT COPYCAT ART, NO MATTER HOW TECHNICALLY SKILLFUL, WAS MEANINGLESS.

AFTER THAT, I TRIED TO MAKE SURE THAT EVERYTHING I DREW WAS TRULY ORIGINAL... BUT I ALWAYS ENDED UP LETTING OUTSIDE INFLUENCES CREEP IN, AND MY END PRODUCT WASN'T ORIGINAL AFTER ALL. STILL UNSATISFIED WITH MY RESULTS, I BEGAN STUDYING THE WORK OF MANY DIFFERENT MANGA ARTISTS, ONE BY ONE, WONDERING IF I COULD FIND ANY OTHERS WHOSE ART COULD RIVAL THAT OF THE TWO I ALREADY REVERED.

THAT'S WHEN I REALIZED THAT THE ARTISTS WHOSE WORK I FOUND INTERESTING WERE ALL INFLUENCED EITHER BY ONE OR BOTH OF THE ABOVE TWO, OR BY SOMEONE ELSE, AND THAT A TOTALLY ORIGINAL STYLE IS VERY RARE. IN ANY CASE, I THOUGHT MR. OTOMO HAD THE BEST STYLE OF THEM ALL, SO I STARTED IMITATING HIM. IN THE BEGINNING OF EIGHTH OR NINTH GRADE, I BOUGHT ALL THE *AKIRA*-RELATED MATERIALS I COULD FIND -- THE ART BOOK, MANGA AND MOVIE MANGA -- AND FURIOUSLY COPIED THEM. BUT I CONTINUED TO STRIVE FOR MY OWN STYLE AND WORKED HARD AT ALL DIFFERENT SORTS OF ORIGINAL ART AS WELL. (LATER, I WOULD ENCOUNTER TWO OTHER ARTISTS WHOM I CAME TO CONSIDER ORIGINAL AND STYLISH, BUT THAT IS A TALE FOR ANOTHER DAY.)

Number 90: What About My Training?!

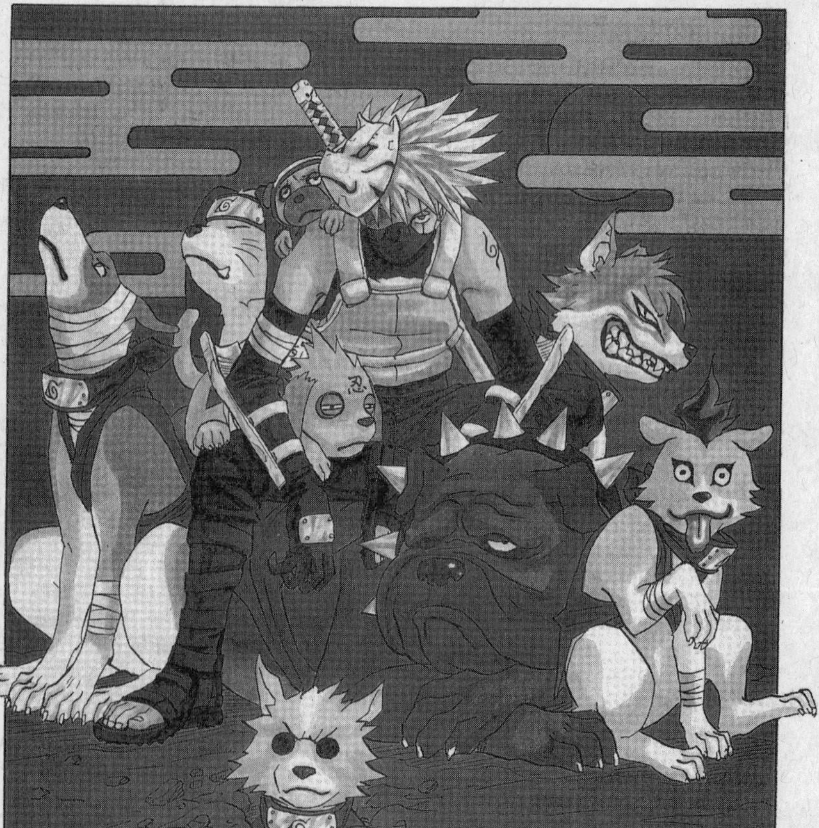

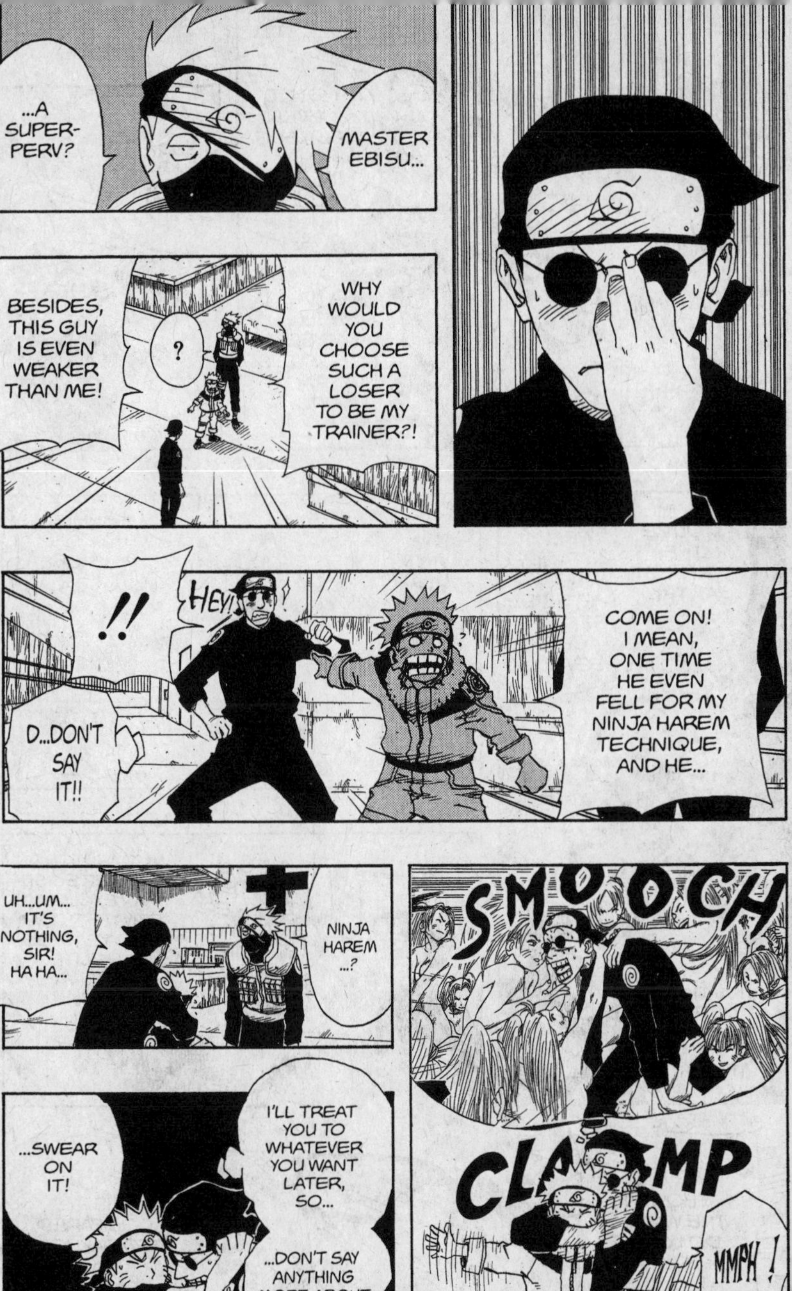
MASTER EBISU...
...A SUPER-PERV?
WHY WOULD YOU CHOOSE SUCH A LOSER TO BE MY TRAINER?!
?
BESIDES, THIS GUY IS EVEN WEAKER THAN ME!
COME ON! I MEAN, ONE TIME HE EVEN FELL FOR MY NINJA HAREM TECHNIQUE, AND HE...
HEY!
!!
D...DON'T SAY IT!!
SMOOCH
CLAMP
MMPH!
NINJA HAREM ...?
UH...UM... IT'S NOTHING, SIR! HA HA...
I'LL TREAT YOU TO WHATEVER YOU WANT LATER, SO...
...DON'T SAY ANYTHING MORE ABOUT IT, OK?!
...SWEAR ON IT!

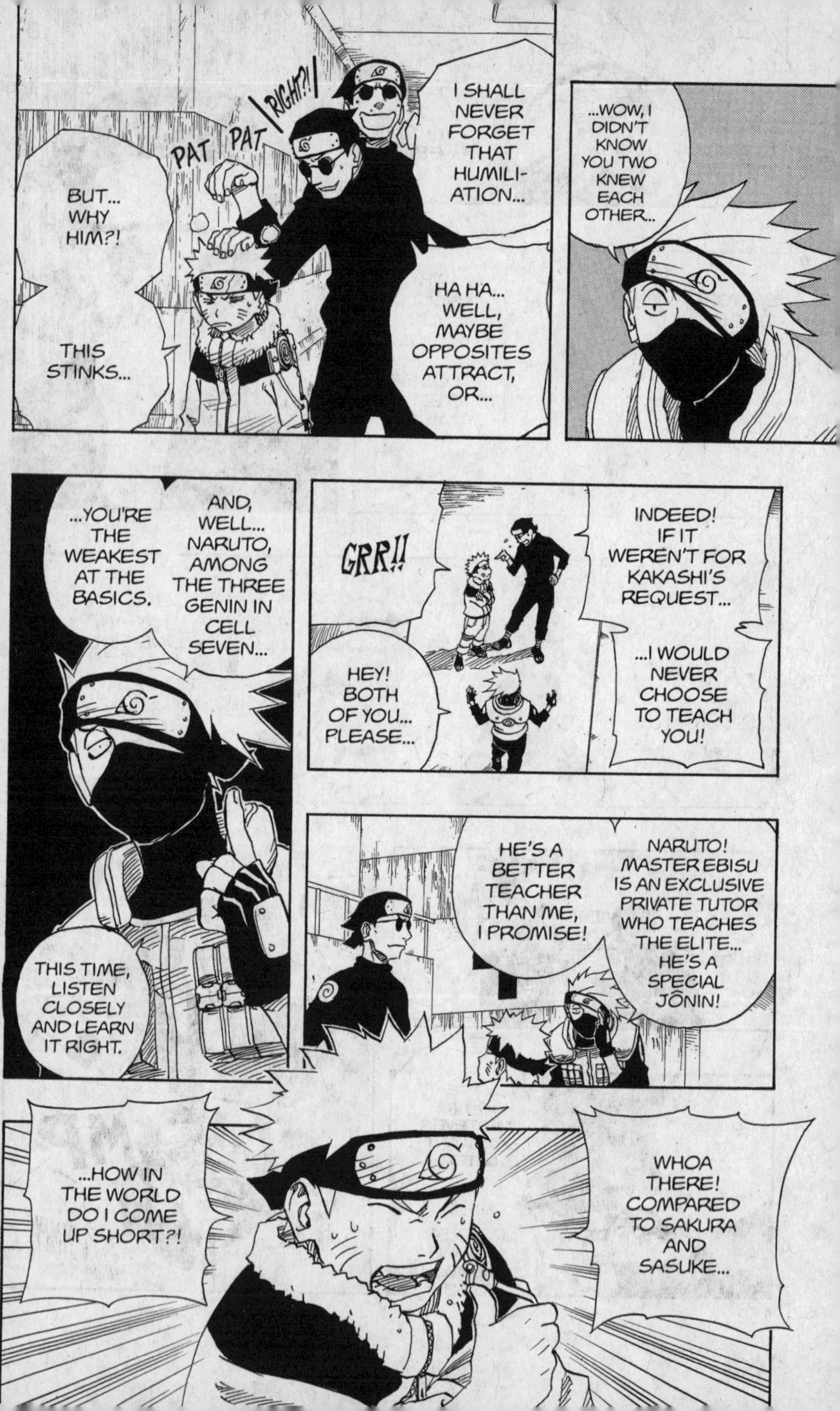
...WOW, I DIDN'T KNOW YOU TWO KNEW EACH OTHER...
I SHALL NEVER FORGET THAT HUMILIATION...
RIGHT?!
PAT PAT
HA HA... WELL, MAYBE OPPOSITES ATTRACT, OR...
BUT... WHY HIM?!
THIS STINKS...
INDEED! IF IT WEREN'T FOR KAKASHI'S REQUEST...
...I WOULD NEVER CHOOSE TO TEACH YOU!
GRR!!
HEY! BOTH OF YOU... PLEASE...
NARUTO! MASTER EBISU IS AN EXCLUSIVE PRIVATE TUTOR WHO TEACHES THE ELITE... HE'S A SPECIAL JŌNIN!
HE'S A BETTER TEACHER THAN ME, I PROMISE!
AND, WELL... NARUTO, AMONG THE THREE GENIN IN CELL SEVEN...
...YOU'RE THE WEAKEST AT THE BASICS.
THIS TIME, LISTEN CLOSELY AND LEARN IT RIGHT.
WHOA THERE! COMPARED TO SAKURA AND SASUKE...
...HOW IN THE WORLD DO I COME UP SHORT?!

READ THIS WAY

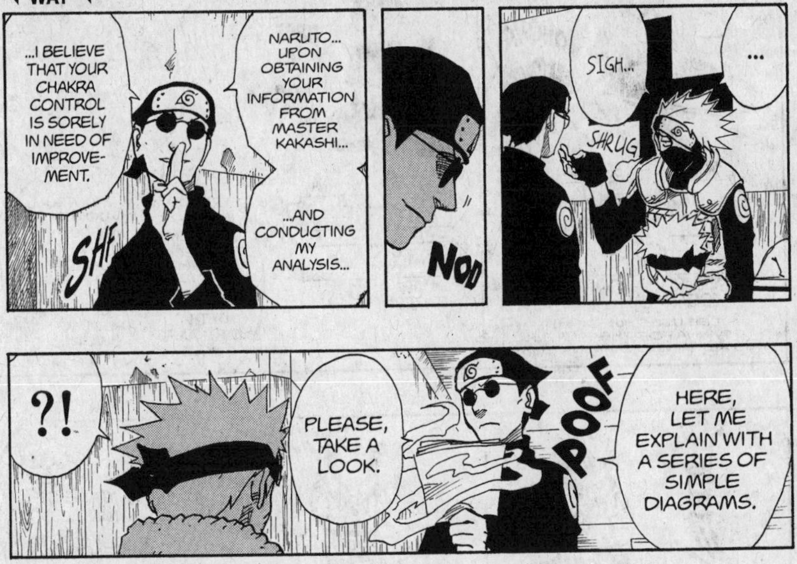
...
SIGH...
SHRUG
NOD
NARUTO... UPON OBTAINING YOUR INFORMATION FROM MASTER KAKASHI...
...AND CONDUCTING MY ANALYSIS...
...I BELIEVE THAT YOUR CHAKRA CONTROL IS SORELY IN NEED OF IMPROVEMENT.
SHF
HERE, LET ME EXPLAIN WITH A SERIES OF SIMPLE DIAGRAMS.
POOF
PLEASE, TAKE A LOOK.
?!

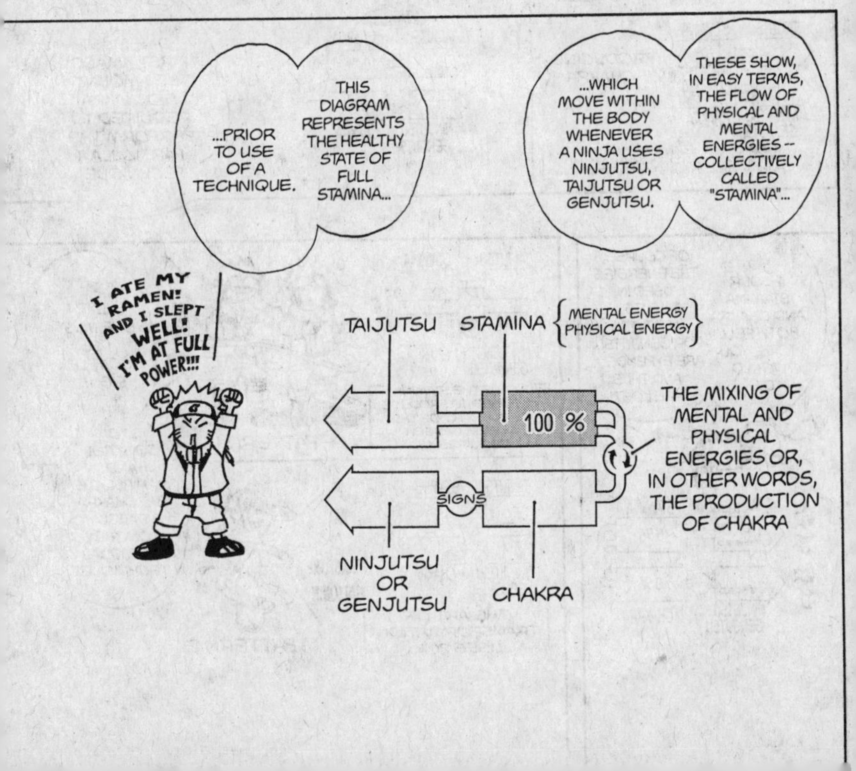
THESE SHOW, IN EASY TERMS, THE FLOW OF PHYSICAL AND MENTAL ENERGIES -- COLLECTIVELY CALLED "STAMINA"...
...WHICH MOVE WITHIN THE BODY WHENEVER A NINJA USES NINJUTSU, TAIJUTSU OR GENJUTSU.
THIS DIAGRAM REPRESENTS THE HEALTHY STATE OF FULL STAMINA...
...PRIOR TO USE OF A TECHNIQUE.
I ATE MY RAMEN! AND I SLEPT WELL! I'M AT FULL POWER!!!
TAIJUTSU
STAMINA
MENTAL ENERGY
PHYSICAL ENERGY
100 %
THE MIXING OF MENTAL AND PHYSICAL ENERGIES OR, IN OTHER WORDS, THE PRODUCTION OF CHAKRA
SIGNS
NINJUTSU OR GENJUTSU
CHAKRA

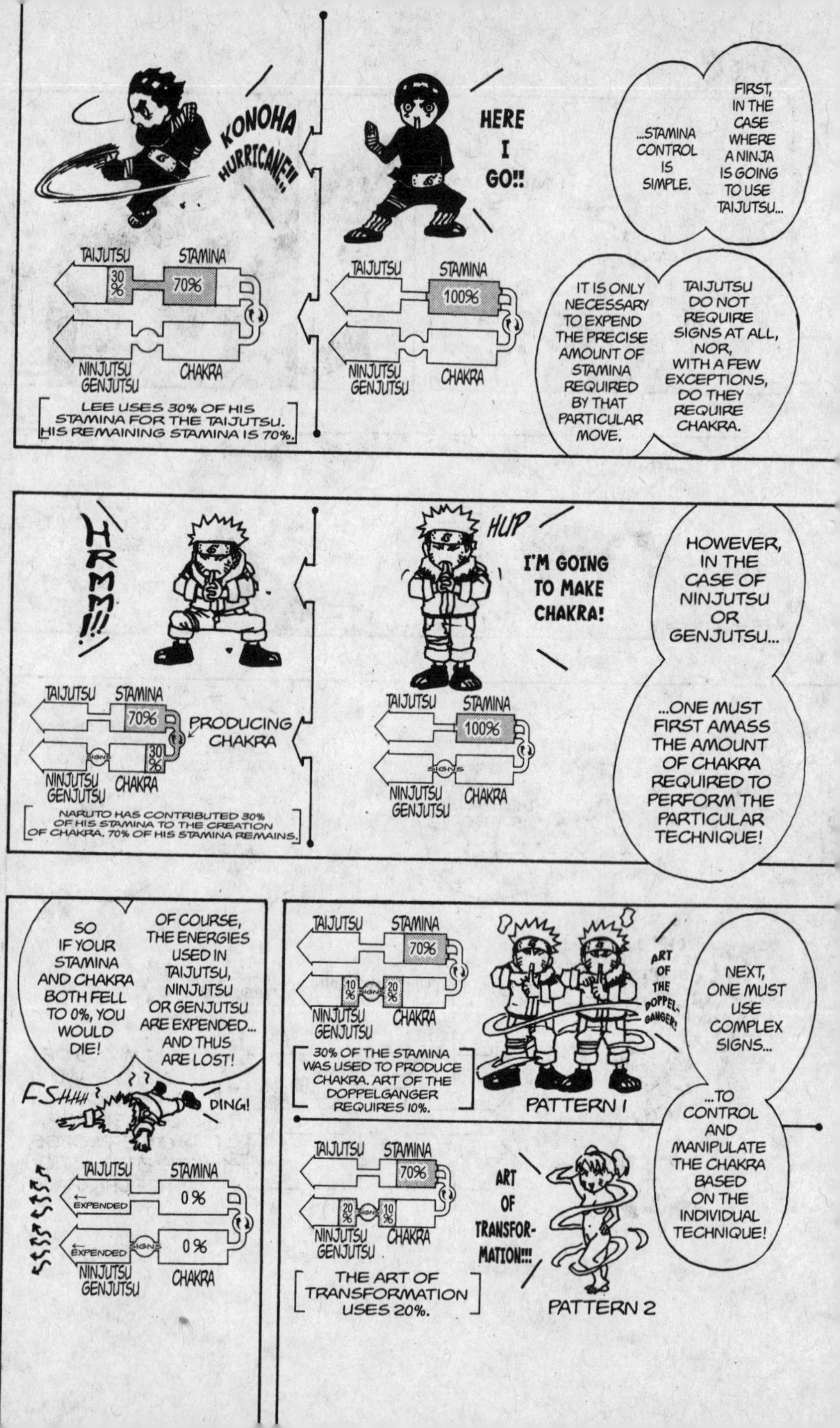

FIRST, IN THE CASE WHERE A NINJA IS GOING TO USE TAIJUTSU...
...STAMINA CONTROL IS SIMPLE.
TAIJUTSU DO NOT REQUIRE SIGNS AT ALL, NOR, WITH A FEW EXCEPTIONS, DO THEY REQUIRE CHAKRA.
IT IS ONLY NECESSARY TO EXPEND THE PRECISE AMOUNT OF STAMINA REQUIRED BY THAT PARTICULAR MOVE.
HERE I GO!!
TAIJUTSU
STAMINA
100%
NINJUTSU GENJUTSU
CHAKRA
KONOHA HURRICANE!!
TAIJUTSU
30%
STAMINA
70%
NINJUTSU GENJUTSU
CHAKRA
LEE USES 30% OF HIS STAMINA FOR THE TAIJUTSU. HIS REMAINING STAMINA IS 70%.
HOWEVER, IN THE CASE OF NINJUTSU OR GENJUTSU...
...ONE MUST FIRST AMASS THE AMOUNT OF CHAKRA REQUIRED TO PERFORM THE PARTICULAR TECHNIQUE!
HUP
I'M GOING TO MAKE CHAKRA!
TAIJUTSU
STAMINA
100%
SIGNS
NINJUTSU GENJUTSU
CHAKRA
HRMMM!!!
TAIJUTSU
STAMINA
70%
PRODUCING CHAKRA
SIGNS
30%
NINJUTSU GENJUTSU
CHAKRA
NARUTO HAS CONTRIBUTED 30% OF HIS STAMINA TO THE CREATION OF CHAKRA. 70% OF HIS STAMINA REMAINS.
NEXT, ONE MUST USE COMPLEX SIGNS...
...TO CONTROL AND MANIPULATE THE CHAKRA BASED ON THE INDIVIDUAL TECHNIQUE!
ART OF THE DOPPEL-GANGER!
PATTERN 1
TAIJUTSU
STAMINA
70%
10%
SIGNS
20%
NINJUTSU GENJUTSU
CHAKRA
30% OF THE STAMINA WAS USED TO PRODUCE CHAKRA. ART OF THE DOPPELGANGER REQUIRES 10%.
ART OF TRANSFOR-MATION!!!
PATTERN 2
TAIJUTSU
STAMINA
70%
20%
SIGNS
10%
NINJUTSU GENJUTSU
CHAKRA
THE ART OF TRANSFORMATION USES 20%.
OF COURSE, THE ENERGIES USED IN TAIJUTSU, NINJUTSU OR GENJUTSU ARE EXPENDED... AND THUS ARE LOST!
SO IF YOUR STAMINA AND CHAKRA BOTH FELL TO 0%, YOU WOULD DIE!
FSHHH
DING!
TAIJUTSU
STAMINA
EXPENDED
0%
EXPENDED
SIGNS
0%
NINJUTSU GENJUTSU
CHAKRA

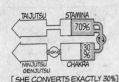

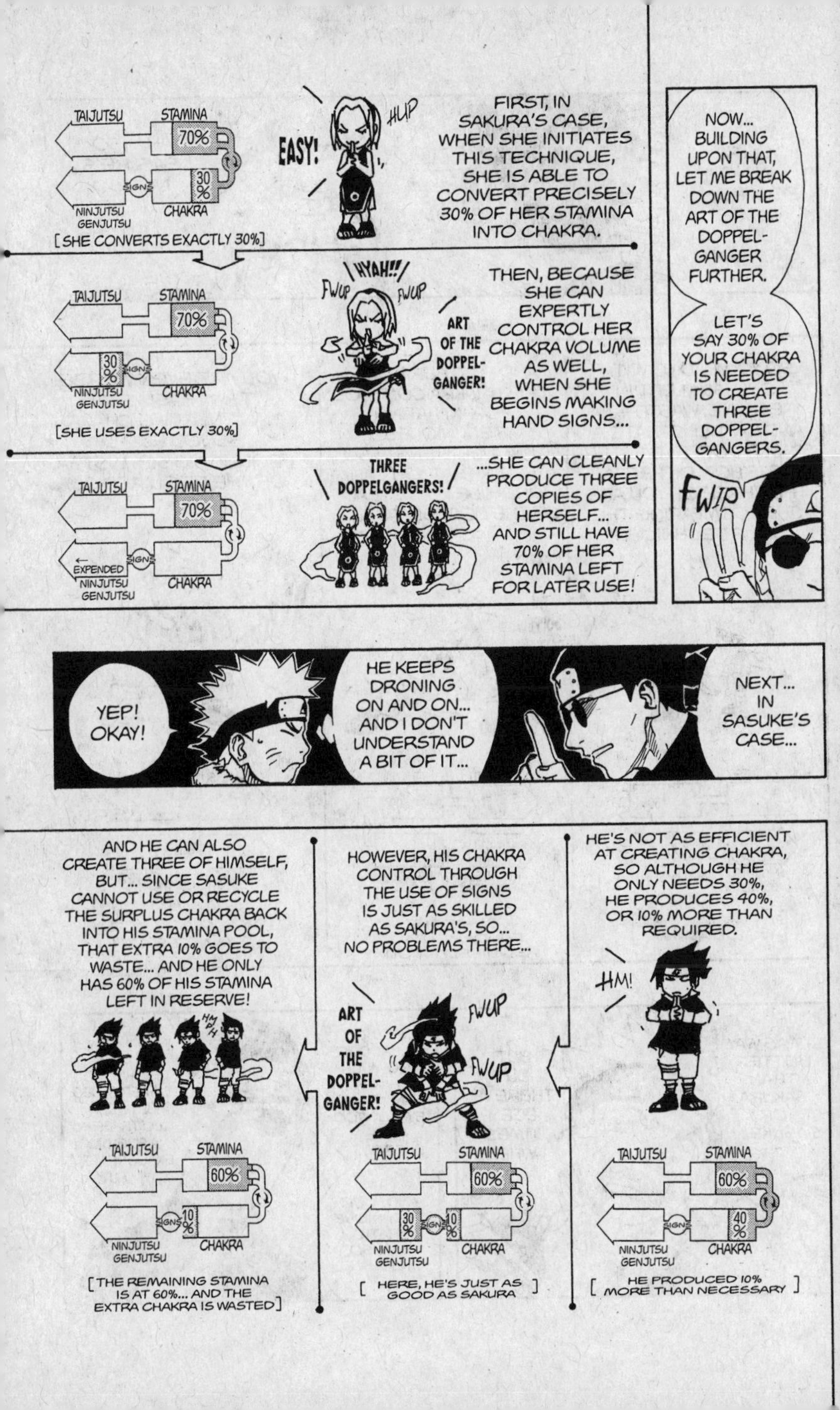

NOW... BUILDING UPON THAT, LET ME BREAK DOWN THE ART OF THE DOPPEL-GANGER FURTHER.
LET'S SAY 30% OF YOUR CHAKRA IS NEEDED TO CREATE THREE DOPPEL-GANGERS.
FWIP
FIRST, IN SAKURA'S CASE, WHEN SHE INITIATES THIS TECHNIQUE, SHE IS ABLE TO CONVERT PRECISELY 30% OF HER STAMINA INTO CHAKRA.
HUP
EASY!
TAIJUTSU
STAMINA
70%
30%
SIGNS
NINJUTSU GENJUTSU
CHAKRA
[SHE CONVERTS EXACTLY 30%]
THEN, BECAUSE SHE CAN EXPERTLY CONTROL HER CHAKRA VOLUME AS WELL, WHEN SHE BEGINS MAKING HAND SIGNS...
ART OF THE DOPPEL-GANGER!
HYAH!!
FWUP
FWUP
TAIJUTSU
STAMINA
70%
30%
SIGNS
NINJUTSU GENJUTSU
CHAKRA
[SHE USES EXACTLY 30%]
...SHE CAN CLEANLY PRODUCE THREE COPIES OF HERSELF... AND STILL HAVE 70% OF HER STAMINA LEFT FOR LATER USE!
THREE DOPPELGANGERS!
TAIJUTSU
STAMINA
70%
SIGNS
← EXPENDED
NINJUTSU GENJUTSU
CHAKRA
NEXT... IN SASUKE'S CASE...
HE KEEPS DRONING ON AND ON... AND I DON'T UNDERSTAND A BIT OF IT...
YEP! OKAY!
HE'S NOT AS EFFICIENT AT CREATING CHAKRA, SO ALTHOUGH HE ONLY NEEDS 30%, HE PRODUCES 40%, OR 10% MORE THAN REQUIRED.
HM!
TAIJUTSU
STAMINA
60%
40%
SIGNS
NINJUTSU GENJUTSU
CHAKRA
[HE PRODUCED 10% MORE THAN NECESSARY]
HOWEVER, HIS CHAKRA CONTROL THROUGH THE USE OF SIGNS IS JUST AS SKILLED AS SAKURA'S, SO... NO PROBLEMS THERE...
ART OF THE DOPPEL-GANGER!
FWUP
FWUP
TAIJUTSU
STAMINA
60%
30%
SIGNS
10%
NINJUTSU GENJUTSU
CHAKRA
[HERE, HE'S JUST AS GOOD AS SAKURA]
AND HE CAN ALSO CREATE THREE OF HIMSELF, BUT... SINCE SASUKE CANNOT USE OR RECYCLE THE SURPLUS CHAKRA BACK INTO HIS STAMINA POOL, THAT EXTRA 10% GOES TO WASTE... AND HE ONLY HAS 60% OF HIS STAMINA LEFT IN RESERVE!
HMPH
TAIJUTSU
STAMINA
60%
SIGNS
10%
NINJUTSU GENJUTSU
CHAKRA
[THE REMAINING STAMINA IS AT 60%... AND THE EXTRA CHAKRA IS WASTED]

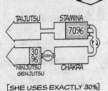

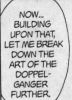

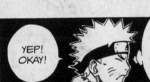

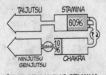

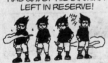

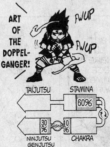

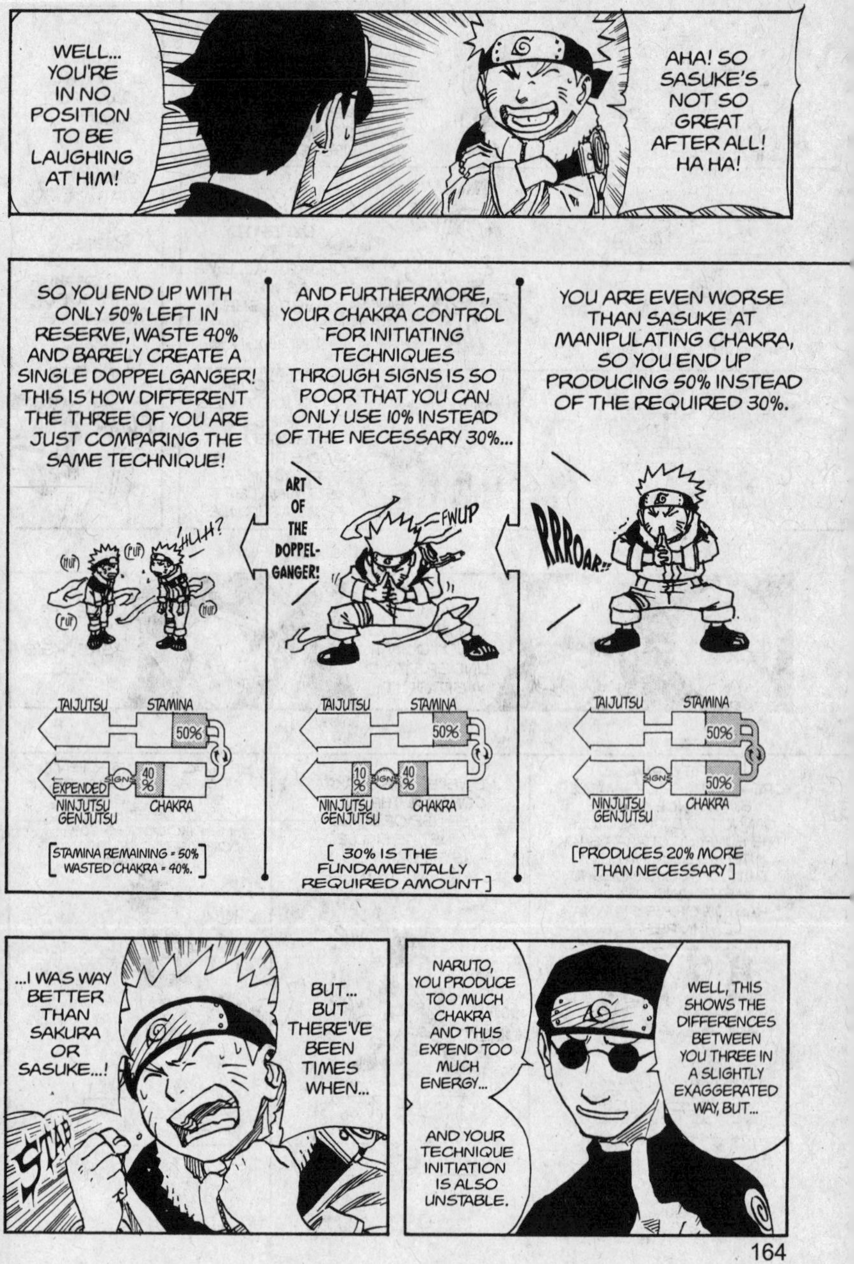
AHA! SO SASUKE'S NOT SO GREAT AFTER ALL! HA HA!
WELL... YOU'RE IN NO POSITION TO BE LAUGHING AT HIM!
YOU ARE EVEN WORSE THAN SASUKE AT MANIPULATING CHAKRA, SO YOU END UP PRODUCING 50% INSTEAD OF THE REQUIRED 30%.
RRROAR!!
TAIJUTSU
STAMINA
50%
SIGNS
50%
NINJUTSU GENJUTSU
CHAKRA
[PRODUCES 20% MORE THAN NECESSARY]
AND FURTHERMORE, YOUR CHAKRA CONTROL FOR INITIATING TECHNIQUES THROUGH SIGNS IS SO POOR THAT YOU CAN ONLY USE 10% INSTEAD OF THE NECESSARY 30%...
ART OF THE DOPPEL-GANGER!
FWUP
TAIJUTSU
STAMINA
50%
10%
SIGNS
40%
NINJUTSU GENJUTSU
CHAKRA
[30% IS THE FUNDAMENTALLY REQUIRED AMOUNT]
SO YOU END UP WITH ONLY 50% LEFT IN RESERVE, WASTE 40% AND BARELY CREATE A SINGLE DOPPELGANGER! THIS IS HOW DIFFERENT THE THREE OF YOU ARE JUST COMPARING THE SAME TECHNIQUE!
HUH?
TAIJUTSU
STAMINA
50%
EXPENDED
SIGNS
40%
NINJUTSU GENJUTSU
CHAKRA
[STAMINA REMAINING = 50% WASTED CHAKRA = 40%.]
WELL, THIS SHOWS THE DIFFERENCES BETWEEN YOU THREE IN A SLIGHTLY EXAGGERATED WAY, BUT...
NARUTO, YOU PRODUCE TOO MUCH CHAKRA AND THUS EXPEND TOO MUCH ENERGY...
AND YOUR TECHNIQUE INITIATION IS ALSO UNSTABLE.
BUT... BUT THERE'VE BEEN TIMES WHEN...
...I WAS WAY BETTER THAN SAKURA OR SASUKE...!
STAB

READ THIS WAY

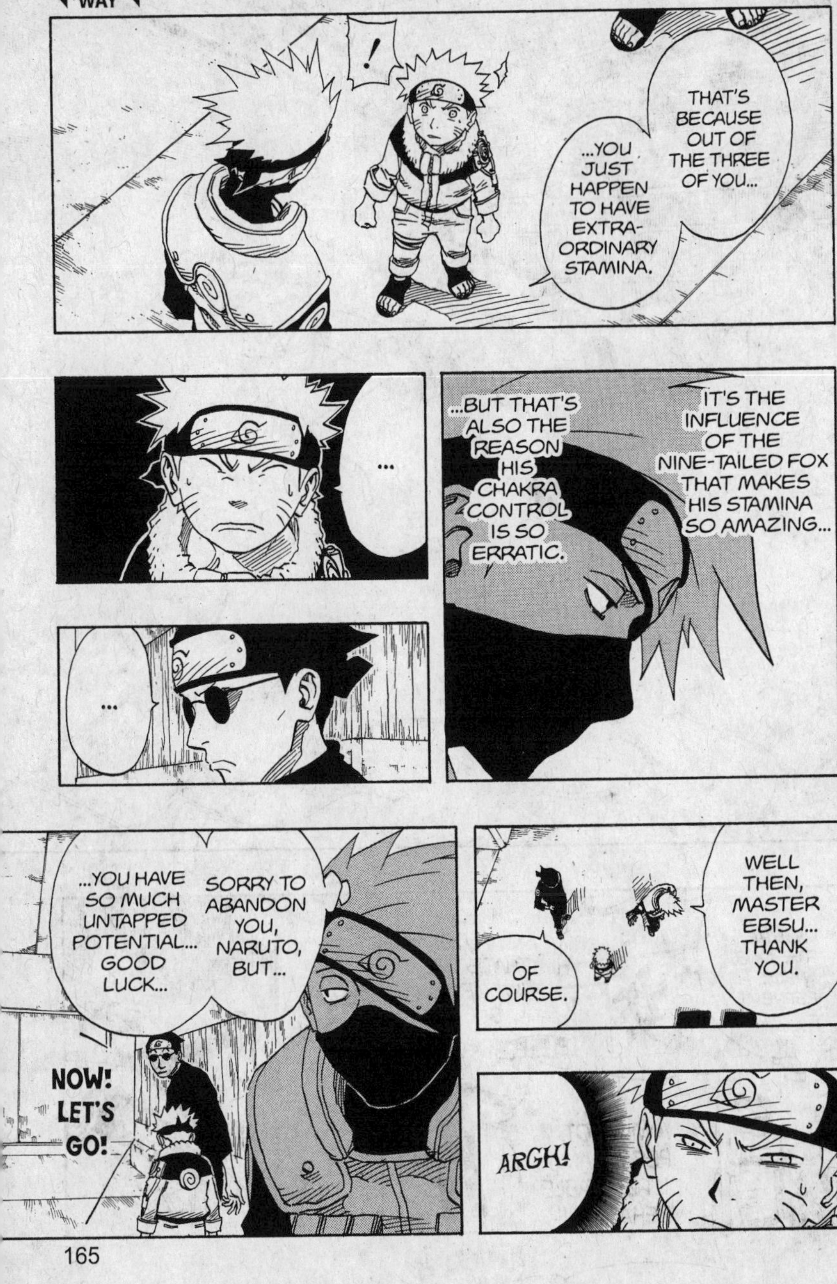
!
THAT'S BECAUSE OUT OF THE THREE OF YOU...
...YOU JUST HAPPEN TO HAVE EXTRA-ORDINARY STAMINA.
IT'S THE INFLUENCE OF THE NINE-TAILED FOX THAT MAKES HIS STAMINA SO AMAZING...
...BUT THAT'S ALSO THE REASON HIS CHAKRA CONTROL IS SO ERRATIC.
...
...
WELL THEN, MASTER EBISU... THANK YOU.
OF COURSE.
ARGH!
SORRY TO ABANDON YOU, NARUTO, BUT...
...YOU HAVE SO MUCH UNTAPPED POTENTIAL... GOOD LUCK...
NOW! LET'S GO!

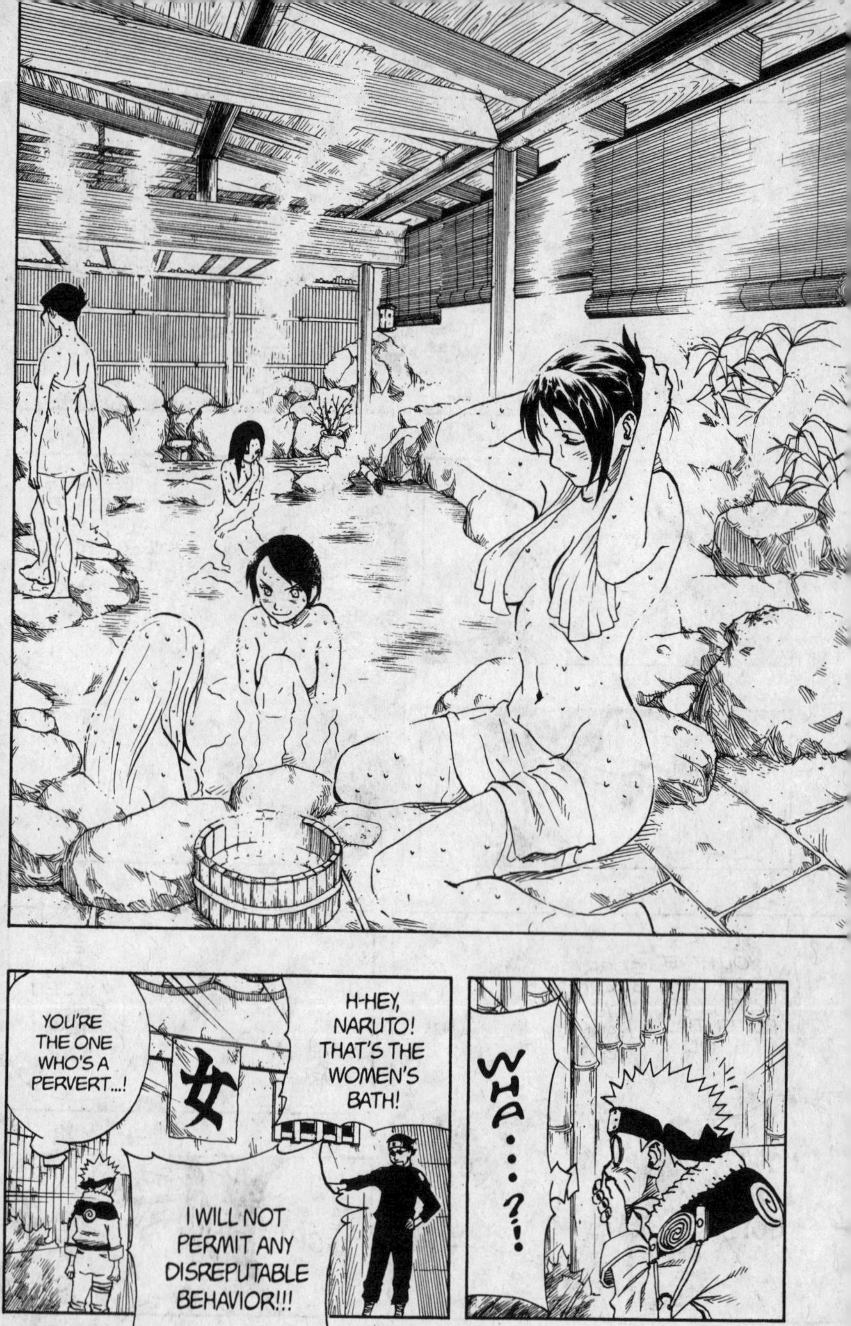
WHA...?!
H-HEY, NARUTO! THAT'S THE WOMEN'S BATH!
女
YOU'RE THE ONE WHO'S A PERVERT...!
I WILL NOT PERMIT ANY DISREPUTABLE BEHAVIOR!!!

READ THIS WAY

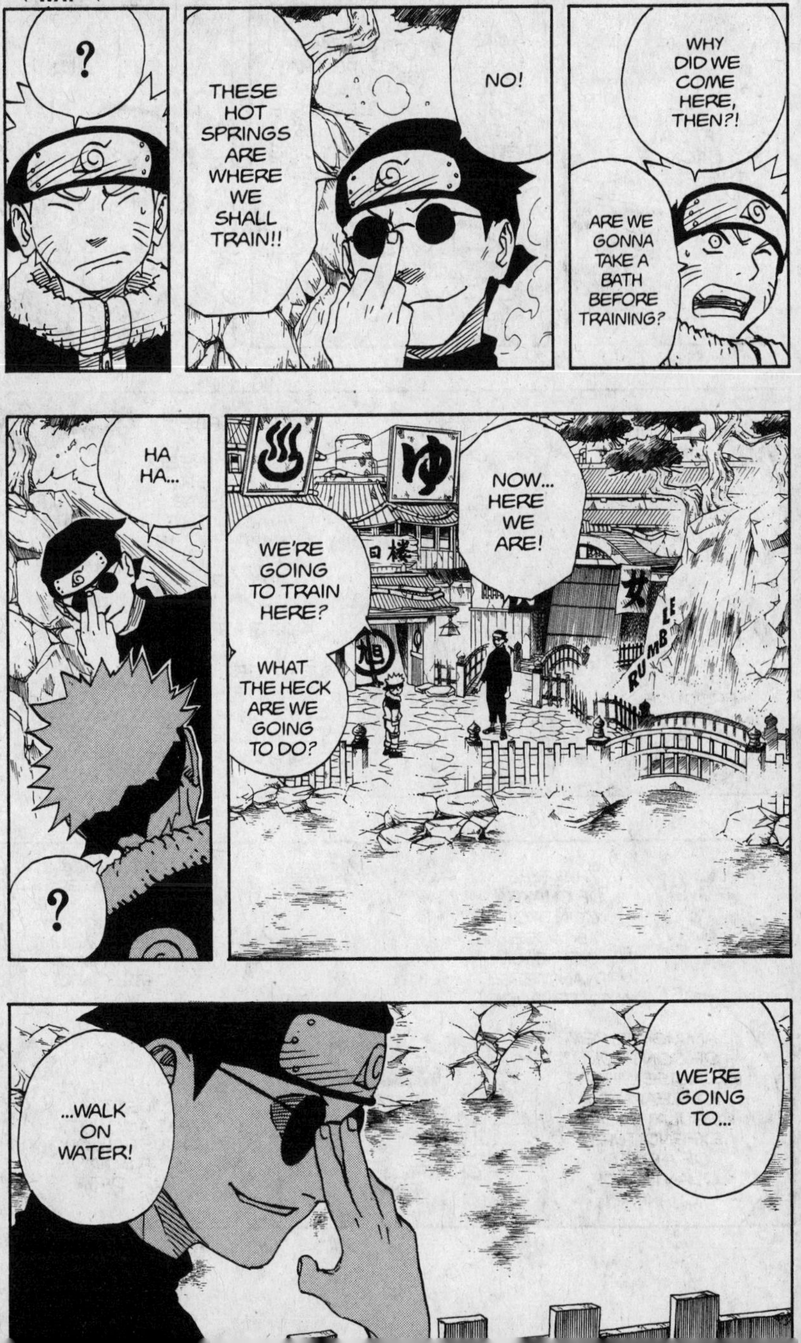
WHY DID WE COME HERE, THEN?!
ARE WE GONNA TAKE A BATH BEFORE TRAINING?
NO!
THESE HOT SPRINGS ARE WHERE WE SHALL TRAIN!!
?
NOW... HERE WE ARE!
WE'RE GOING TO TRAIN HERE?
WHAT THE HECK ARE WE GOING TO DO?
RUMBLE
HA HA...
?
WE'RE GOING TO...
...WALK ON WATER!

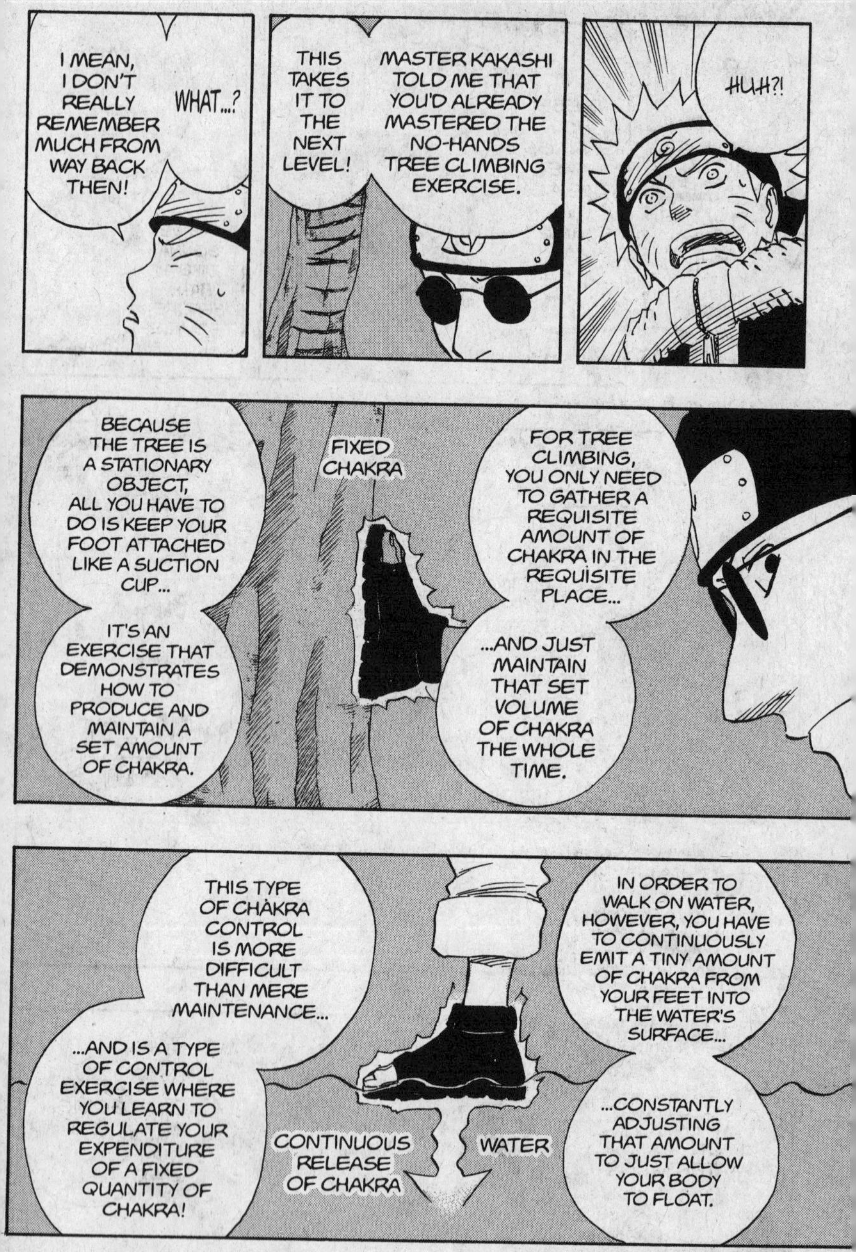
HUH?!
MASTER KAKASHI TOLD ME THAT YOU'D ALREADY MASTERED THE NO-HANDS TREE CLIMBING EXERCISE.
THIS TAKES IT TO THE NEXT LEVEL!
WHAT...?
I MEAN, I DON'T REALLY REMEMBER MUCH FROM WAY BACK THEN!
FOR TREE CLIMBING, YOU ONLY NEED TO GATHER A REQUISITE AMOUNT OF CHAKRA IN THE REQUISITE PLACE...
...AND JUST MAINTAIN THAT SET VOLUME OF CHAKRA THE WHOLE TIME.
FIXED CHAKRA
BECAUSE THE TREE IS A STATIONARY OBJECT, ALL YOU HAVE TO DO IS KEEP YOUR FOOT ATTACHED LIKE A SUCTION CUP...
IT'S AN EXERCISE THAT DEMONSTRATES HOW TO PRODUCE AND MAINTAIN A SET AMOUNT OF CHAKRA.
IN ORDER TO WALK ON WATER, HOWEVER, YOU HAVE TO CONTINUOUSLY EMIT A TINY AMOUNT OF CHAKRA FROM YOUR FEET INTO THE WATER'S SURFACE...
...CONSTANTLY ADJUSTING THAT AMOUNT TO JUST ALLOW YOUR BODY TO FLOAT.
WATER
CONTINUOUS RELEASE OF CHAKRA
THIS TYPE OF CHAKRA CONTROL IS MORE DIFFICULT THAN MERE MAINTENANCE...
...AND IS A TYPE OF CONTROL EXERCISE WHERE YOU LEARN TO REGULATE YOUR EXPENDITURE OF A FIXED QUANTITY OF CHAKRA!

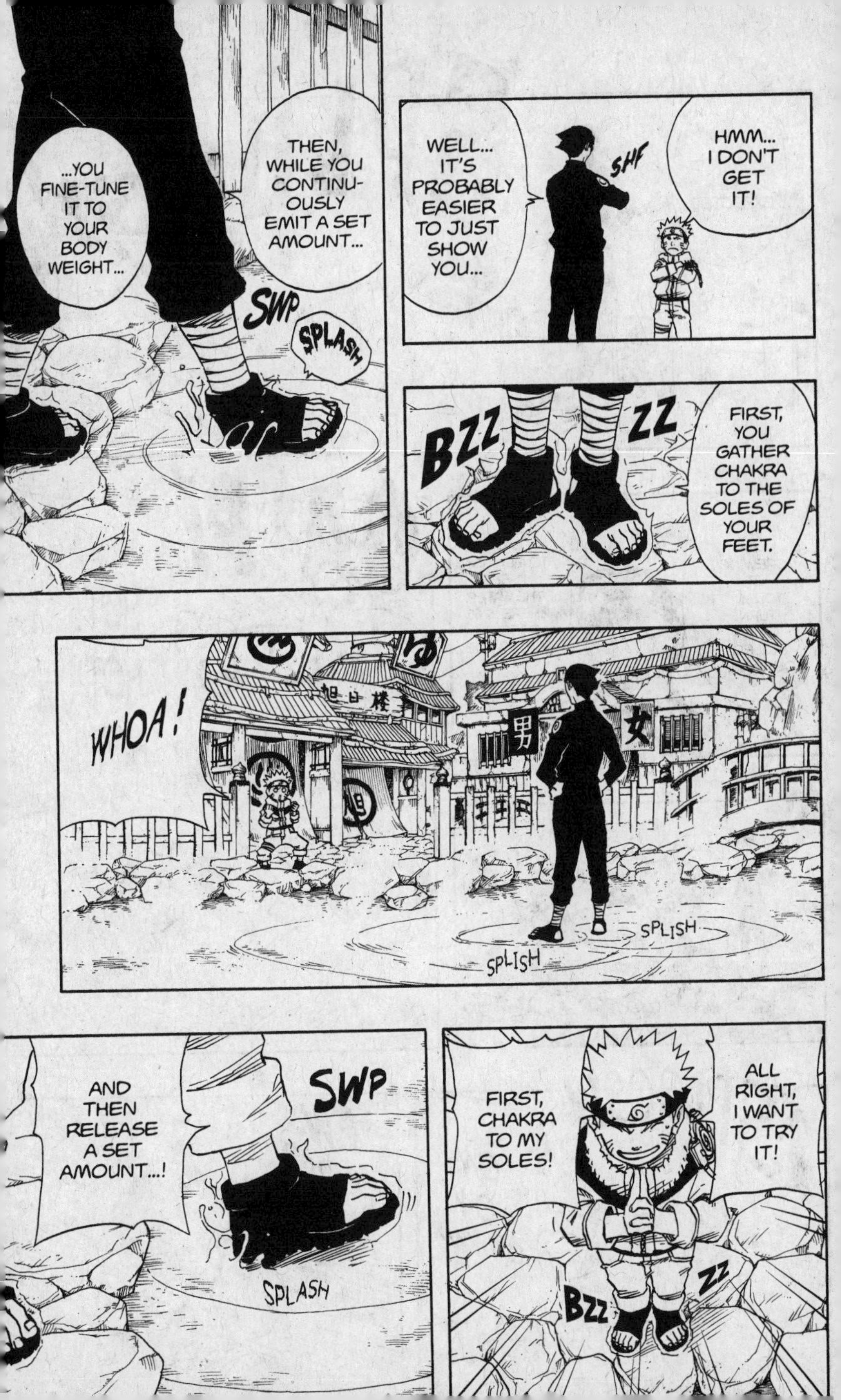
HMM... I DON'T GET IT!
SHF
WELL... IT'S PROBABLY EASIER TO JUST SHOW YOU...
FIRST, YOU GATHER CHAKRA TO THE SOLES OF YOUR FEET.
BZZ ZZ
THEN, WHILE YOU CONTINU-OUSLY EMIT A SET AMOUNT...
...YOU FINE-TUNE IT TO YOUR BODY WEIGHT...
SWP
SPLASH
女
男
WHOA!
SPLISH
SPLISH
ALL RIGHT, I WANT TO TRY IT!
FIRST, CHAKRA TO MY SOLES!
ZZ
BZZ
SWP
AND THEN RELEASE A SET AMOUNT...!
SPLASH

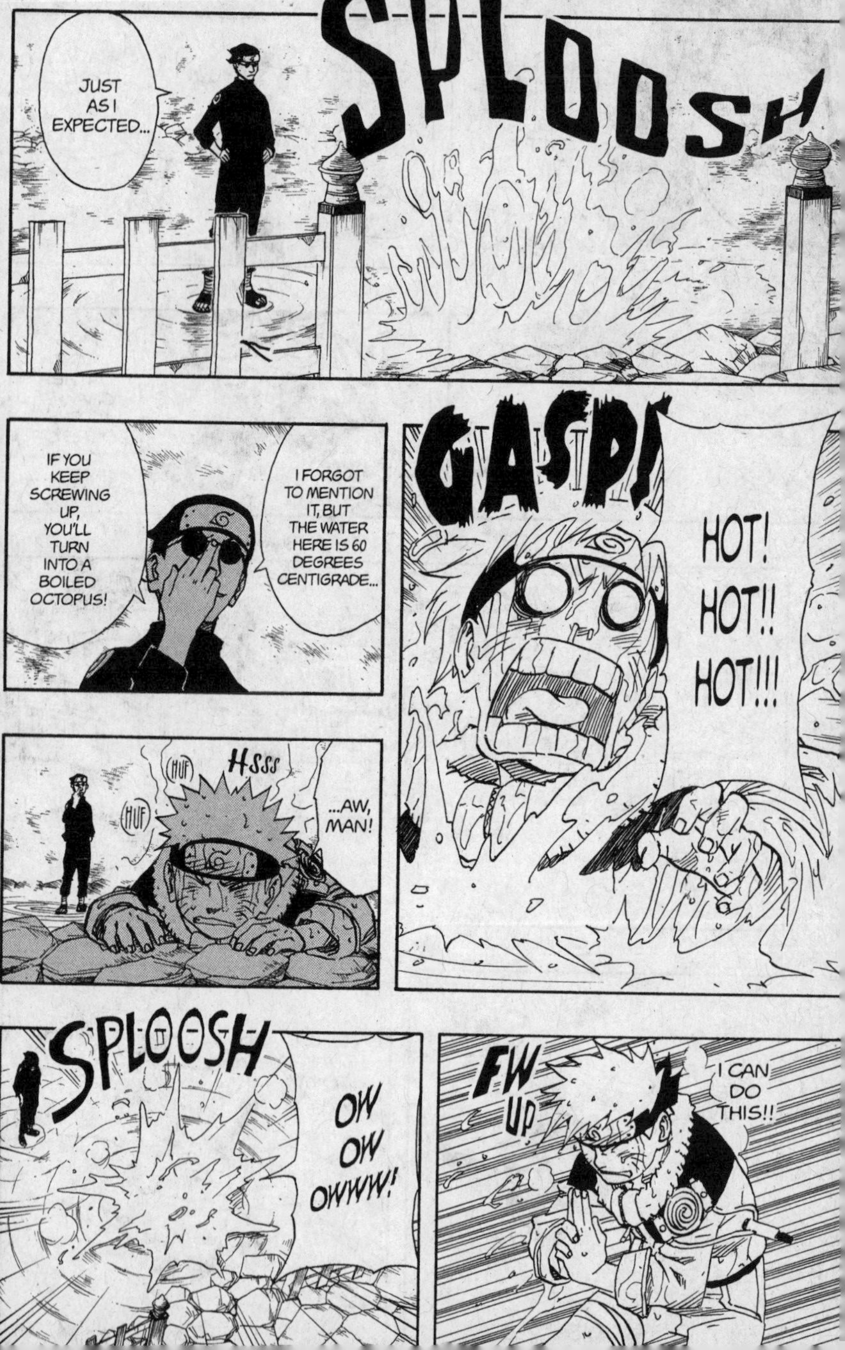
SPLOOSH
JUST AS I EXPECTED...
GASP!
HOT! HOT!! HOT!!!
I FORGOT TO MENTION IT, BUT THE WATER HERE IS 60 DEGREES CENTIGRADE...
IF YOU KEEP SCREWING UP, YOU'LL TURN INTO A BOILED OCTOPUS!
...AW, MAN!
HSSS
(HUF)
(HUF)
I CAN DO THIS!!
FWUP
OW OW OWWW!
SPLOOSH

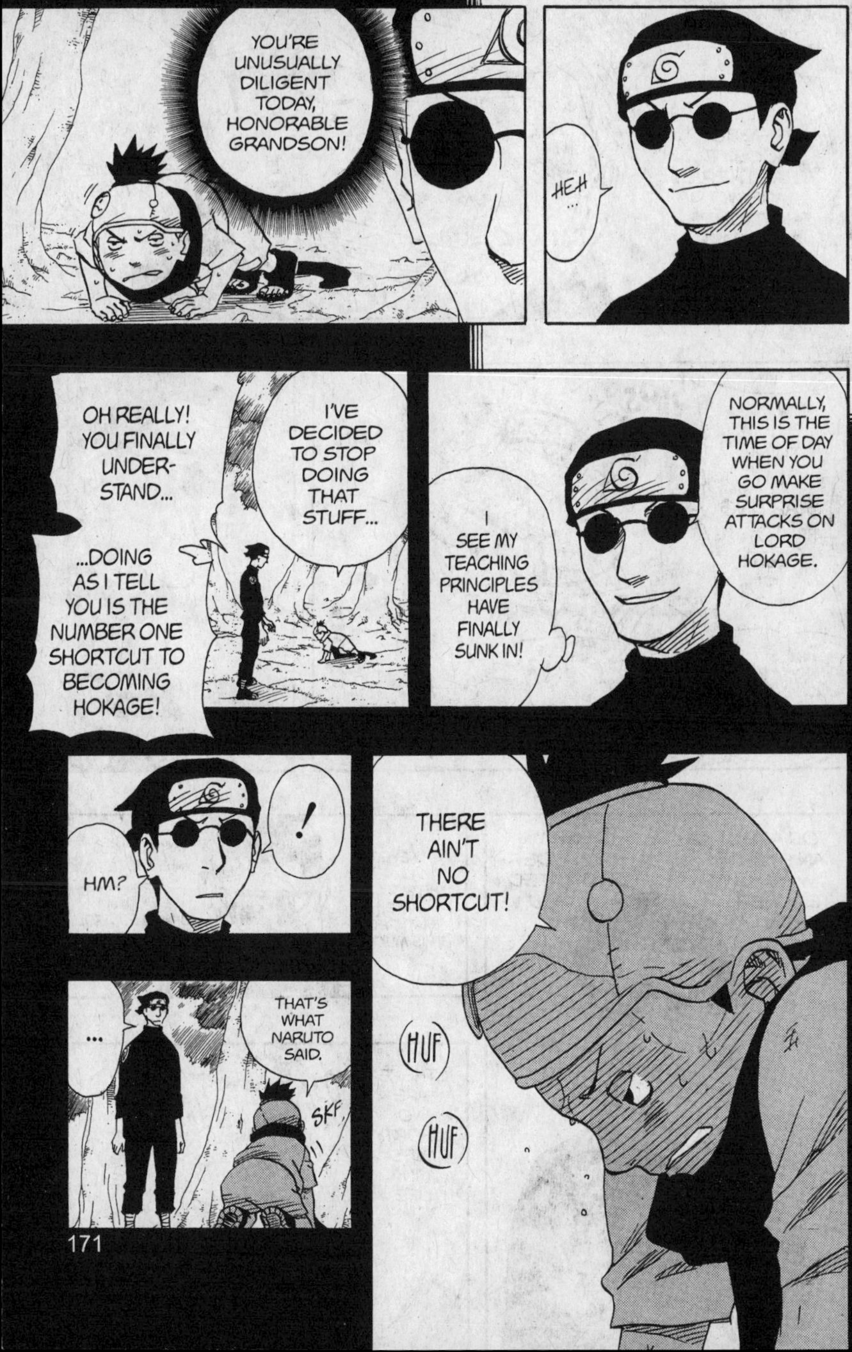
HEH ...
YOU'RE UNUSUALLY DILIGENT TODAY, HONORABLE GRANDSON!
NORMALLY, THIS IS THE TIME OF DAY WHEN YOU GO MAKE SURPRISE ATTACKS ON LORD HOKAGE.
I SEE MY TEACHING PRINCIPLES HAVE FINALLY SUNK IN!
I'VE DECIDED TO STOP DOING THAT STUFF...
OH REALLY! YOU FINALLY UNDER-STAND...
...DOING AS I TELL YOU IS THE NUMBER ONE SHORTCUT TO BECOMING HOKAGE!
THERE AIN'T NO SHORTCUT!
HUF
HUF
!
HM?
THAT'S WHAT NARUTO SAID.
SKF
...

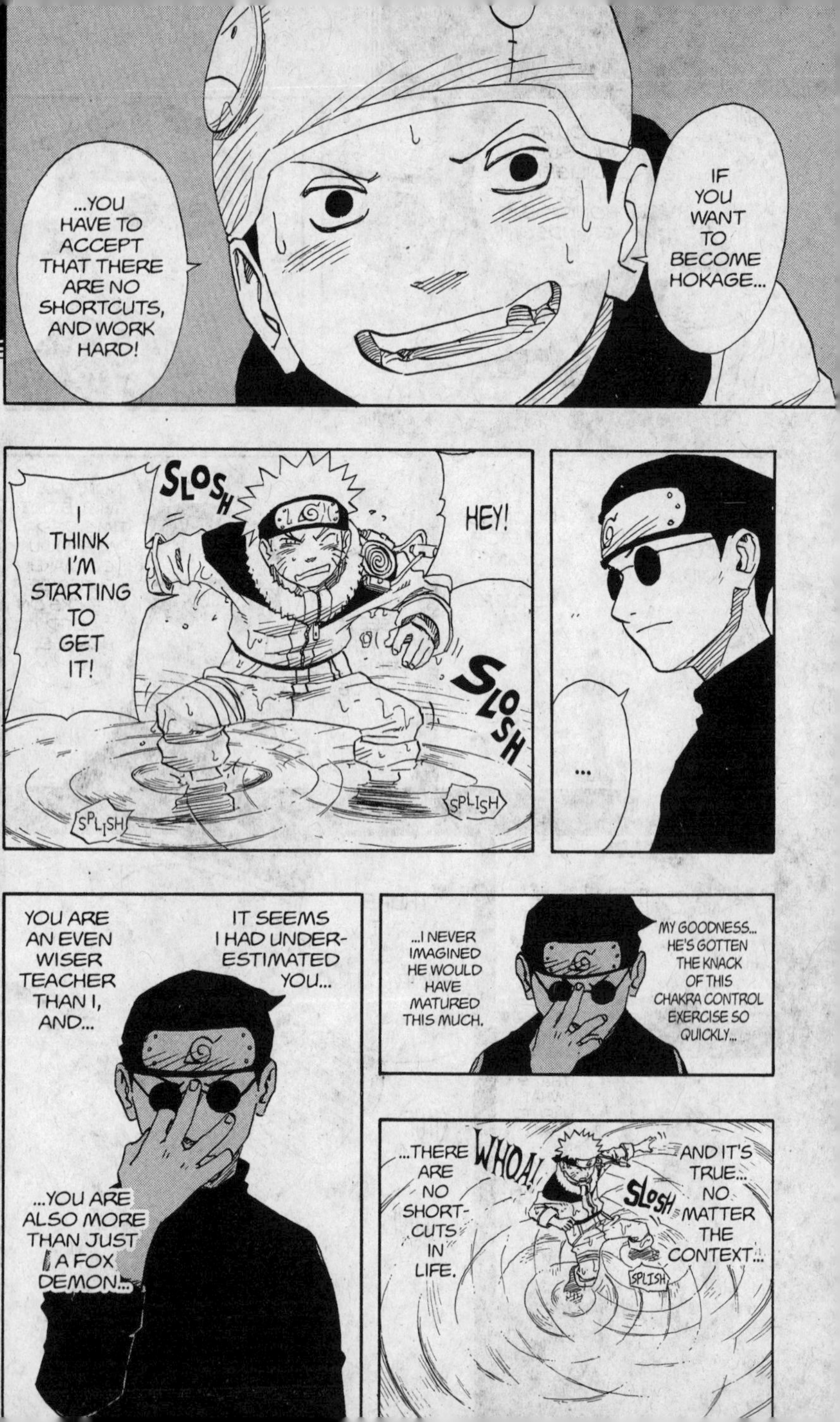
IF YOU WANT TO BECOME HOKAGE...
...YOU HAVE TO ACCEPT THAT THERE ARE NO SHORTCUTS, AND WORK HARD!
...
HEY!
SLOSH
I THINK I'M STARTING TO GET IT!
SLOSH
SPLISH
SPLISH
MY GOODNESS... HE'S GOTTEN THE KNACK OF THIS CHAKRA CONTROL EXERCISE SO QUICKLY...
...I NEVER IMAGINED HE WOULD HAVE MATURED THIS MUCH.
AND IT'S TRUE... NO MATTER THE CONTEXT...
SLOSH
WHOA!
...THERE ARE NO SHORT-CUTS IN LIFE.
SPLISH
IT SEEMS I HAD UNDER-ESTIMATED YOU...
YOU ARE AN EVEN WISER TEACHER THAN I, AND...
...YOU ARE ALSO MORE THAN JUST A FOX DEMON...

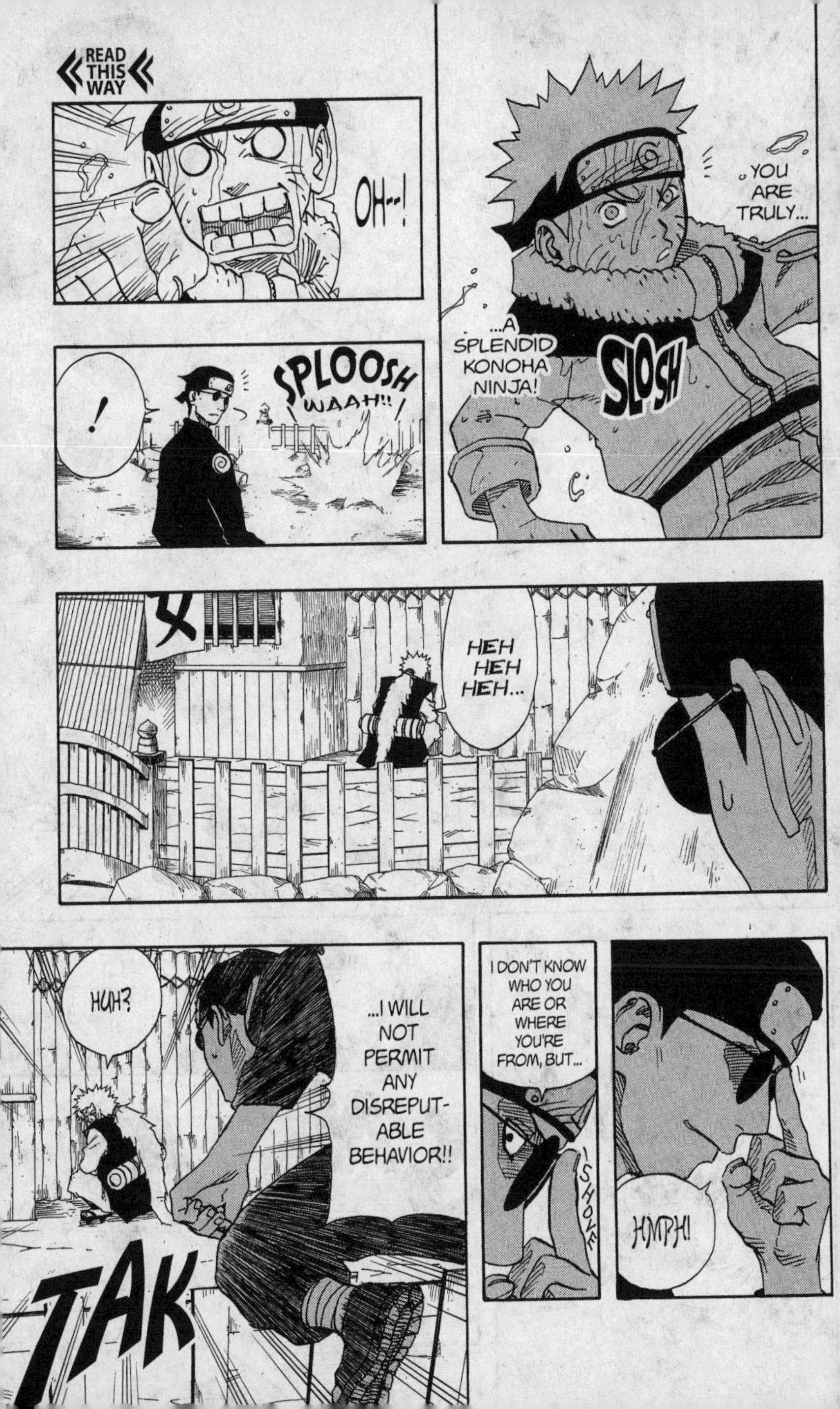
READ THIS WAY
YOU ARE TRULY...
...A SPLENDID KONOHA NINJA!
SLOSH
OH--!
!
SPLOOSH
WAAH!!
HEH HEH HEH...
HMPH!
I DON'T KNOW WHO YOU ARE OR WHERE YOU'RE FROM, BUT...
SHOVE
...I WILL NOT PERMIT ANY DISREPUT-ABLE BEHAVIOR!!
HUH?
TAK

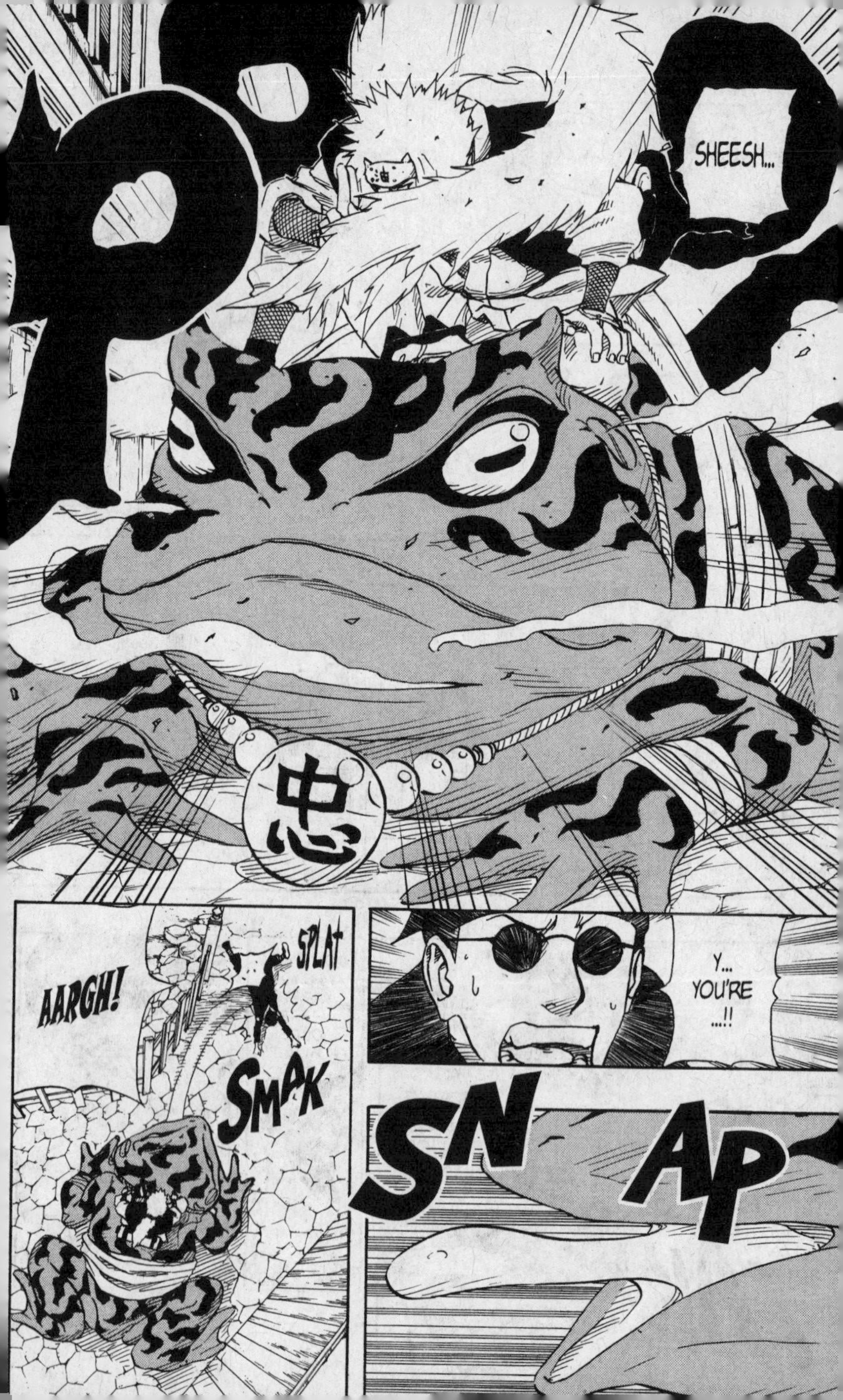
SHEESH...
忠
Y... YOU'RE ...!!
SNAP
SPLAT
AARGH!
SMAK

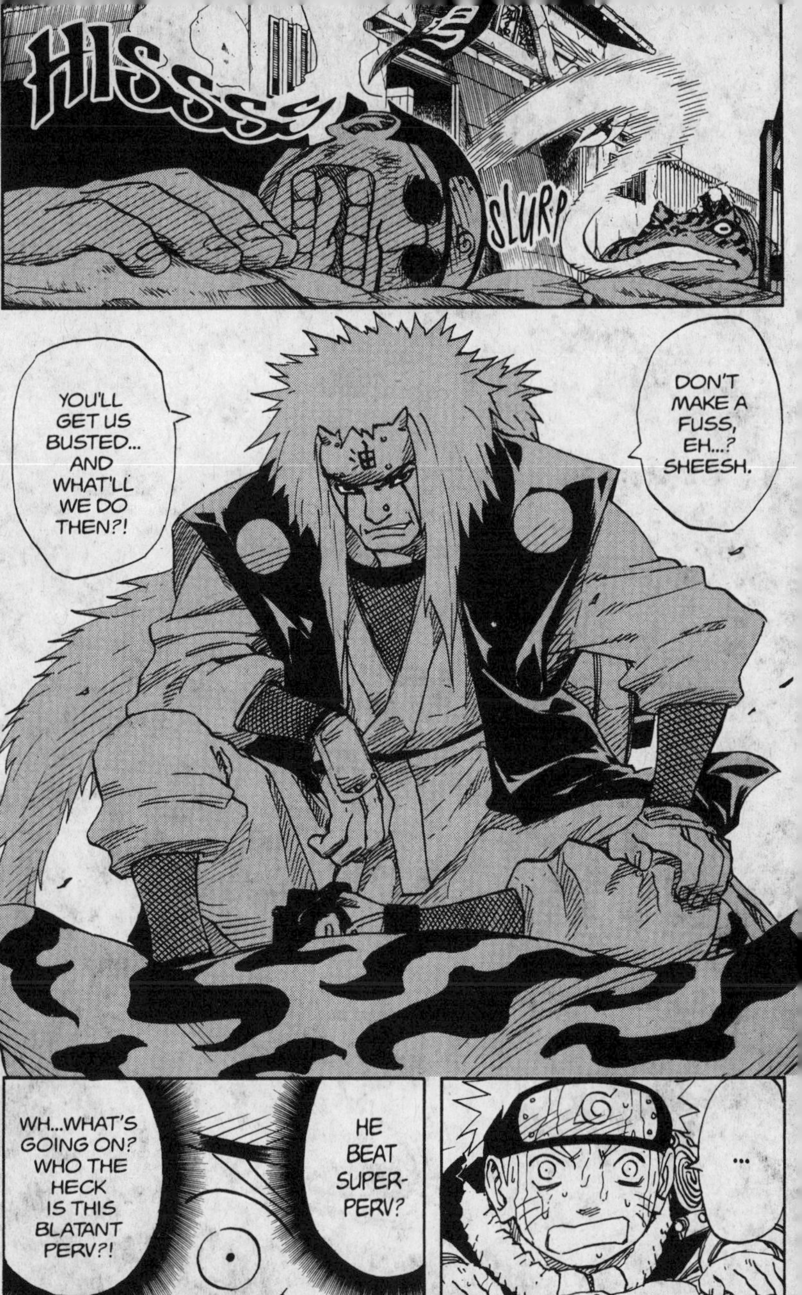
HISSSS
SLURP
DON'T MAKE A FUSS, EH...? SHEESH.
YOU'LL GET US BUSTED... AND WHAT'LL WE DO THEN?!
...
HE BEAT SUPER-PERV?
WH...WHAT'S GOING ON? WHO THE HECK IS THIS BLATANT PERV?!

NARUTO

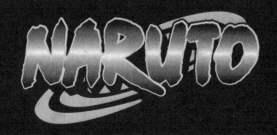

岸本斉史

Recently, my editor has been taking me out to really tasty eateries more and more often. I ate fugu (blowfish) for the first time in my life, and I've gotta tell you, it's real yummy, everybody! Next time, I want to spin my plate of fugu on top of my chopsticks before I eat it!

—*Masashi Kishimoto, 2002*

NARUTO

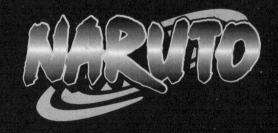

SHONEN JUMP MANGA

NARUTO

VOL. 11
IMPASSIONED EFFORTS

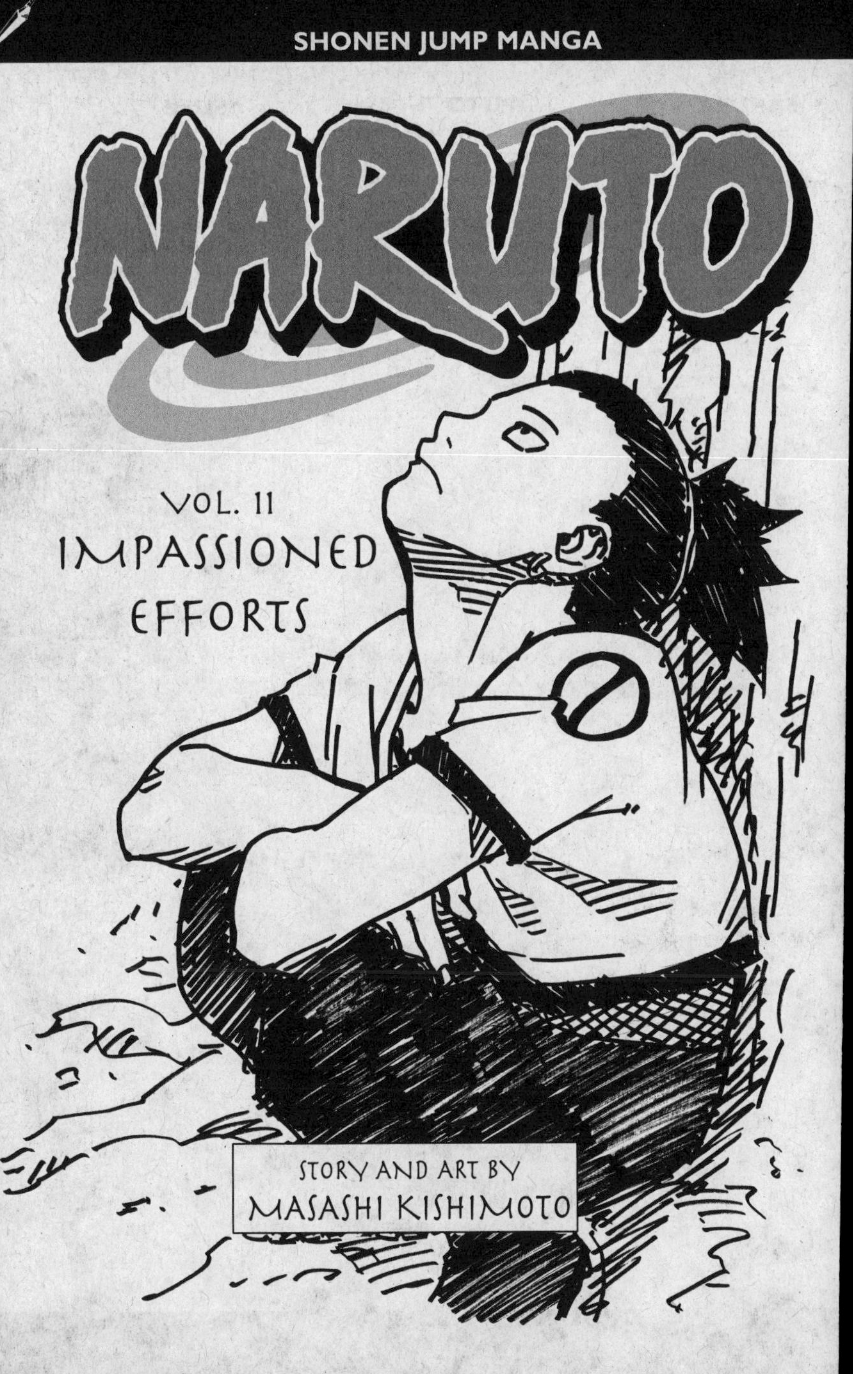

STORY AND ART BY
MASASHI KISHIMOTO

SAKURA サクラ

Smart and studious, Sakura is the brightest of Naruto's classmates, but she's constantly distracted by her crush on Sasuke. Her goal: to win Sasuke's heart!

NARUTO ナルト

When Naruto was born, a destructive fox spirit was imprisoned inside his body. Spurned by the older villagers, he's grown into an attention-seeking trouble-maker. His goal: to become the village's next *Hokage*.

SASUKE サスケ

The top student in Naruto's class, Sasuke comes from the prestigious Uchiha clan. His goal: to get revenge on a mysterious person who wronged him in the past.

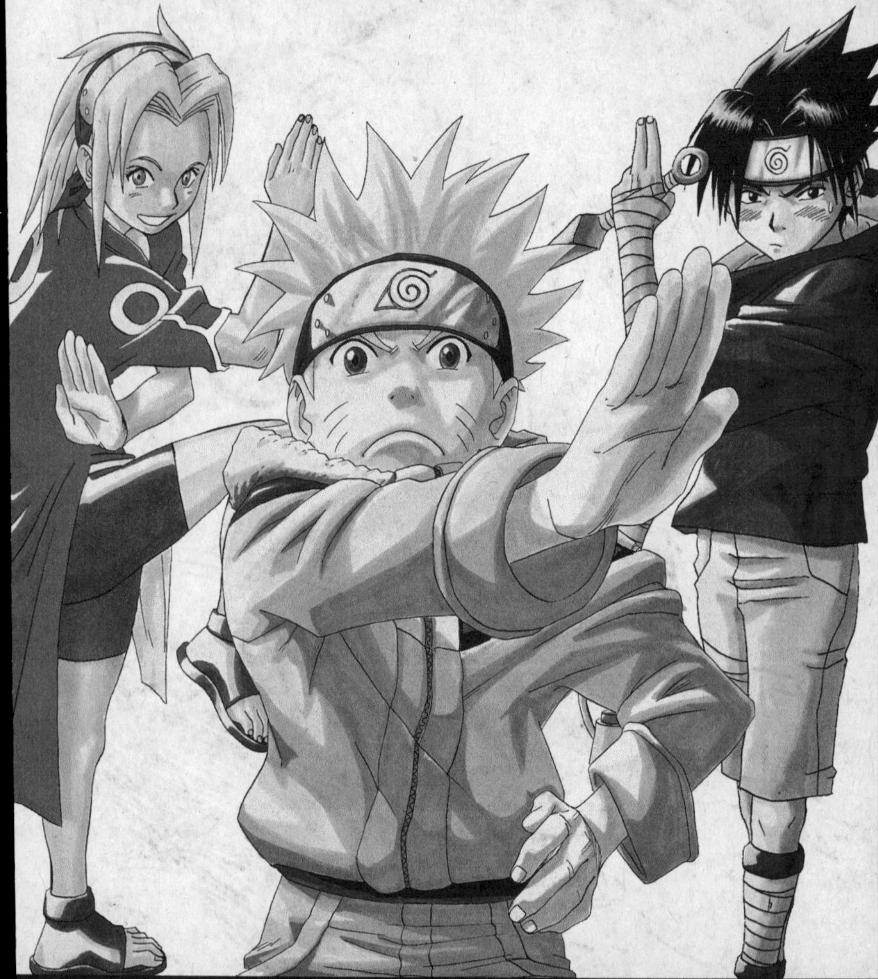

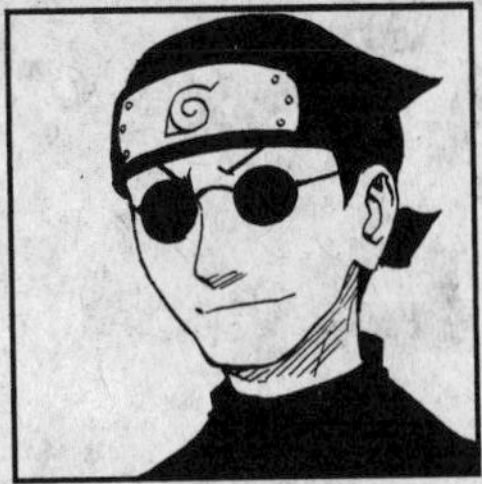

Ebisu エビス

Once tutor to Konohamaru (the Honorable Grandson of the Hokage), Ebisu has now been assigned to train Naruto for the final phase of the Chûnin Exam.

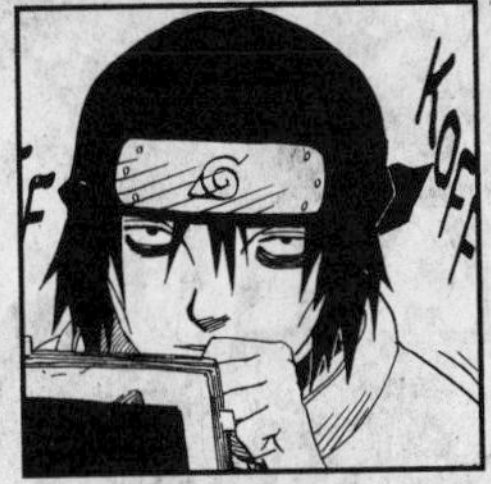
KOFF

Hayate ハヤテ

A jônin from Konohagakure and proctor of the third stage of the Chûnin Exam.

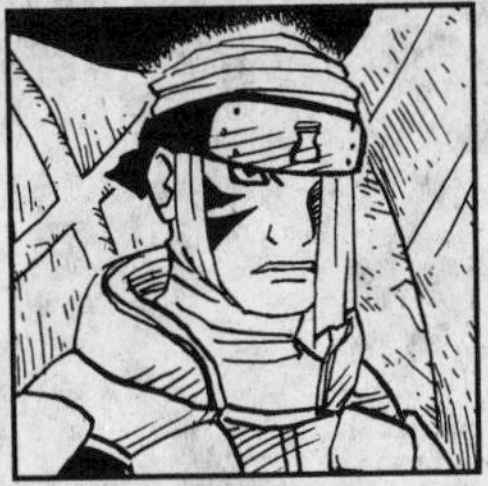

Baki バキ

Jônin leader of Gaara, Kankuro and Temari — the trio of ninja from Sunagakure (The Village Hidden in Sand).

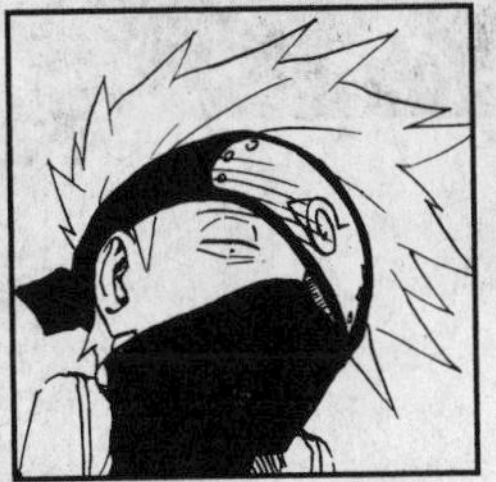

Kakashi カカシ

Although he doesn't have an especially warm personality, Kakashi is protective of his students.

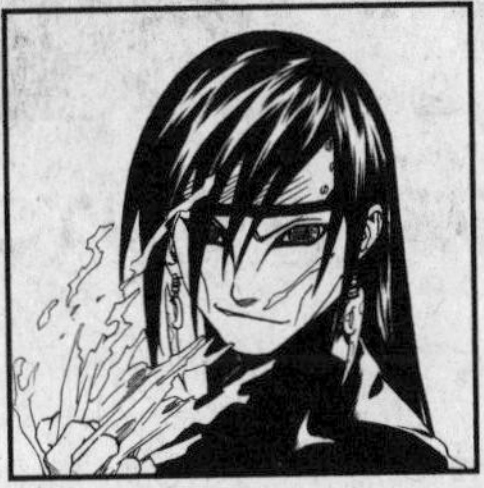

Orochimaru 大蛇丸

This nefarious master of disguise placed a mysterious curse-mark on Sasuke and hopes to mold Sasuke into his successor.

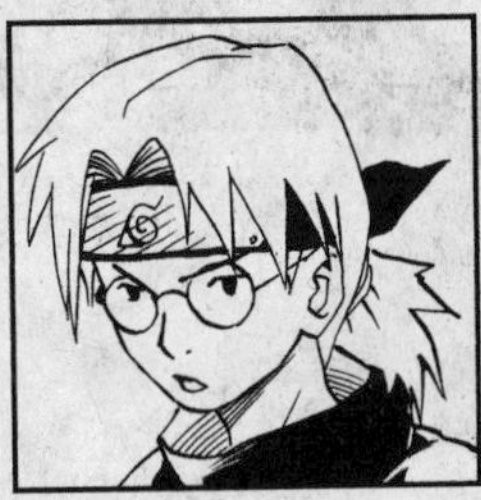

Kabuto カブト

A spy for Orochimaru's village of Otogakure (The Village Hidden in the Sound), Kabuto has been living a double life in Konohagakure since childhood.

THE STORY SO FAR...

Twelve years ago, a destructive nine-tailed fox spirit attacked the ninja village of Konohagakure. The *Hokage*, or village champion, defeated the fox by sealing its soul into the body of a baby boy. Now that boy, Uzumaki Naruto, has grown up to become a ninja-in-training, learning the art of *ninjutsu* with his teammates Sakura and Sasuke.

Nine candidates — including Naruto and Sasuke — have made it past the preliminary rounds of the third Chûnin Exam, and they begin a month-long period of preparation for the finals. Meanwhile, Orochimaru orders Kabuto to kidnap Sasuke...but Kakashi catches Kabuto in the act. Although Sasuke is safe, Kabuto escapes — but not before his true identity is revealed. Now training with elite tutor Ebisu, Naruto practices a water-walking exercise at the local hot spring. But when a peeping tom and a giant toad knock out his instructor, what's Naruto to do?!

CONTENTS

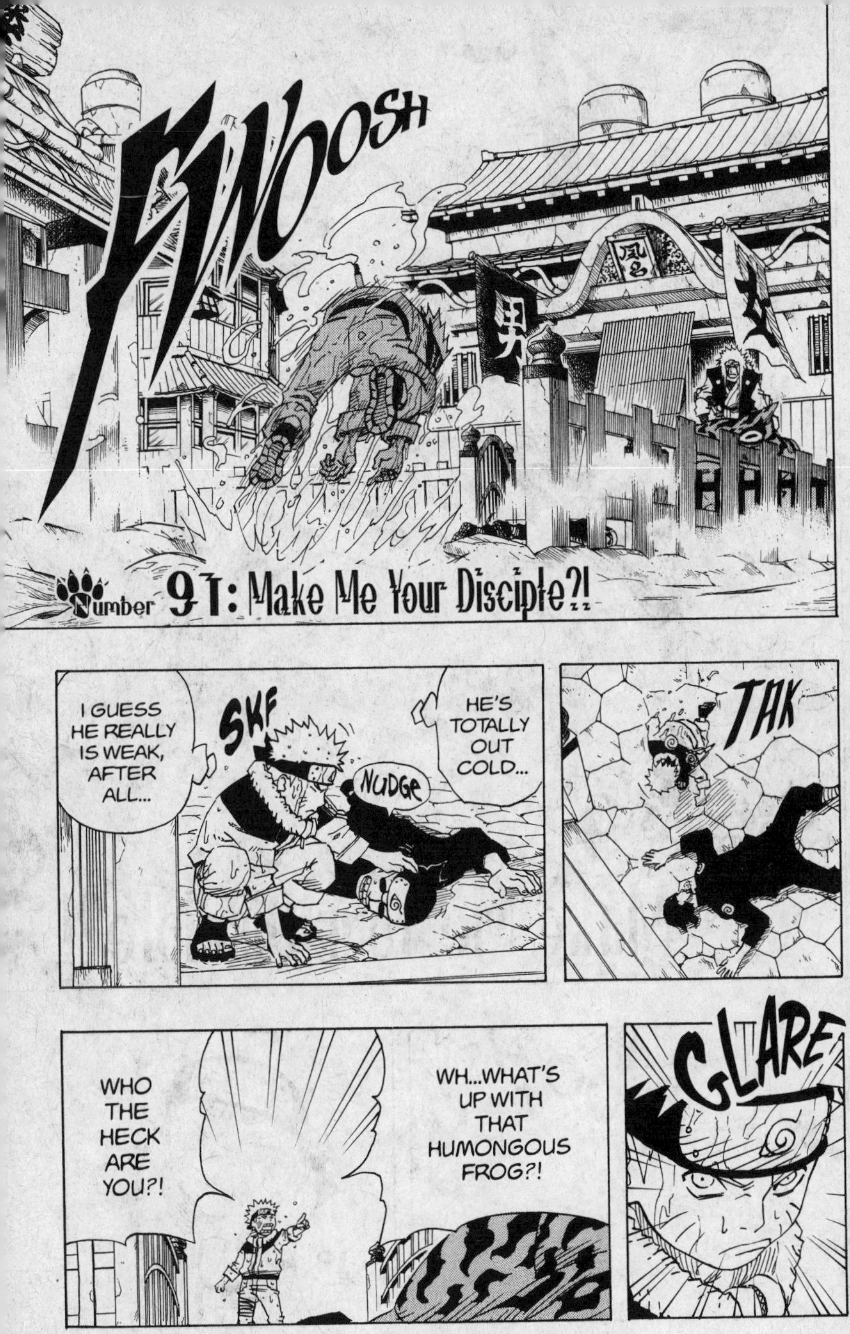
WHOOSH
Number 91: Make Me Your Disciple?!
TAK
HE'S TOTALLY OUT COLD...
SKF
NUDGE
I GUESS HE REALLY IS WEAK, AFTER ALL...
GLARE
WH...WHAT'S UP WITH THAT HUMONGOUS FROG?!
WHO THE HECK ARE YOU?!

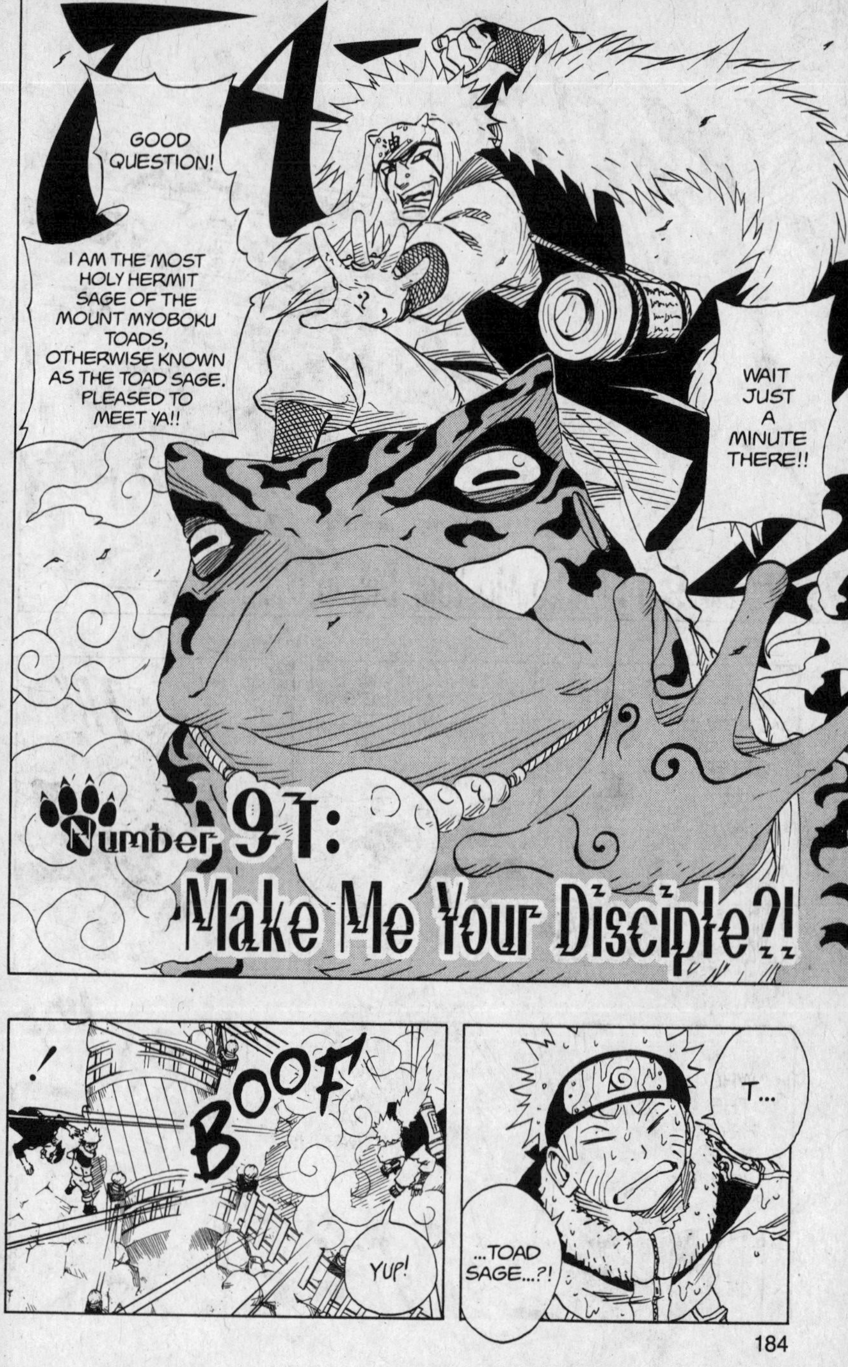

GOOD QUESTION!
I AM THE MOST HOLY HERMIT SAGE OF THE MOUNT MYOBOKU TOADS, OTHERWISE KNOWN AS THE TOAD SAGE. PLEASED TO MEET YA!!
WAIT JUST A MINUTE THERE!!
Number 91:
Make Me Your Disciple?!
T...
...TOAD SAGE...?!
!
BOOF
YUP!

READ THIS WAY

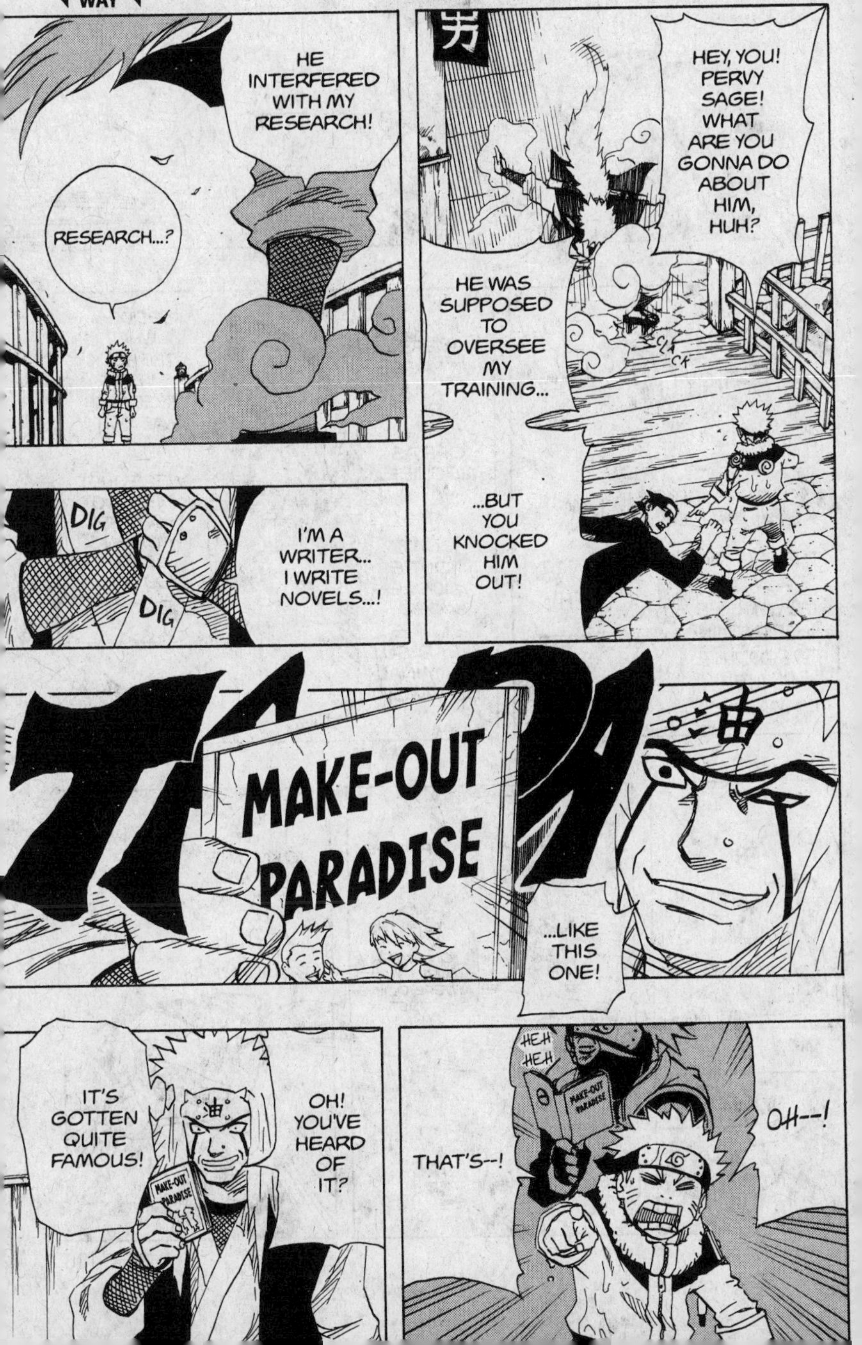

HEY, YOU! PERVY SAGE! WHAT ARE YOU GONNA DO ABOUT HIM, HUH?
HE WAS SUPPOSED TO OVERSEE MY TRAINING...
CLACK
...BUT YOU KNOCKED HIM OUT!
HE INTERFERED WITH MY RESEARCH!
RESEARCH...?
I'M A WRITER... I WRITE NOVELS...!
DIG
DIG
MAKE-OUT PARADISE
...LIKE THIS ONE!
HEH HEH
MAKE-OUT PARADISE
OH--!
THAT'S--!
OH! YOU'VE HEARD OF IT?
IT'S GOTTEN QUITE FAMOUS!
MAKE-OUT PARADISE

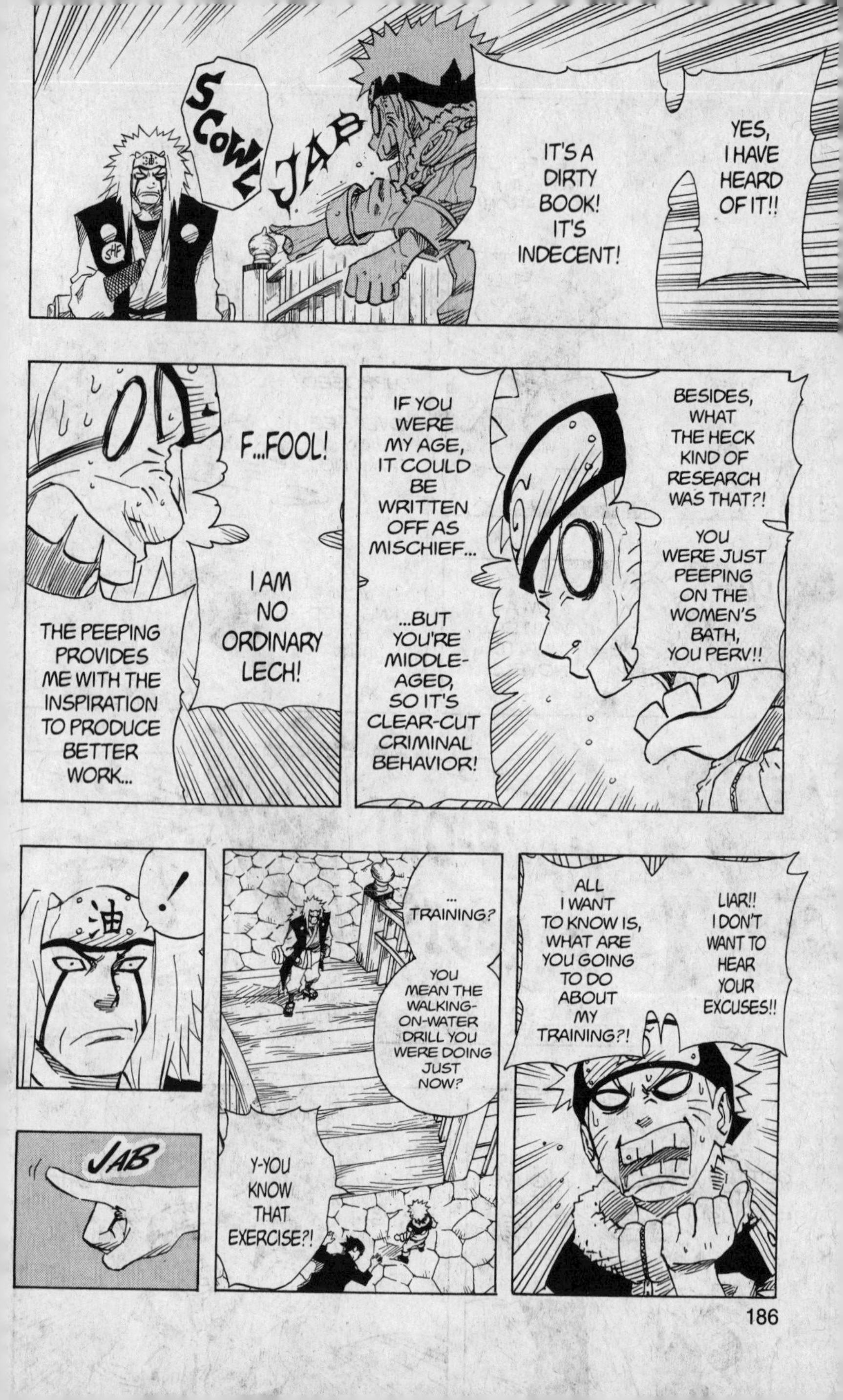
YES, I HAVE HEARD OF IT!!
IT'S A DIRTY BOOK! IT'S INDECENT!
SCOWL
JAB
BESIDES, WHAT THE HECK KIND OF RESEARCH WAS THAT?!
YOU WERE JUST PEEPING ON THE WOMEN'S BATH, YOU PERV!!
IF YOU WERE MY AGE, IT COULD BE WRITTEN OFF AS MISCHIEF...
...BUT YOU'RE MIDDLE-AGED, SO IT'S CLEAR-CUT CRIMINAL BEHAVIOR!
F...FOOL!
I AM NO ORDINARY LECH!
THE PEEPING PROVIDES ME WITH THE INSPIRATION TO PRODUCE BETTER WORK...
LIAR!! I DON'T WANT TO HEAR YOUR EXCUSES!!
ALL I WANT TO KNOW IS, WHAT ARE YOU GOING TO DO ABOUT MY TRAINING?!
... TRAINING?
YOU MEAN THE WALKING-ON-WATER DRILL YOU WERE DOING JUST NOW?
Y-YOU KNOW THAT EXERCISE?!
!
JAB

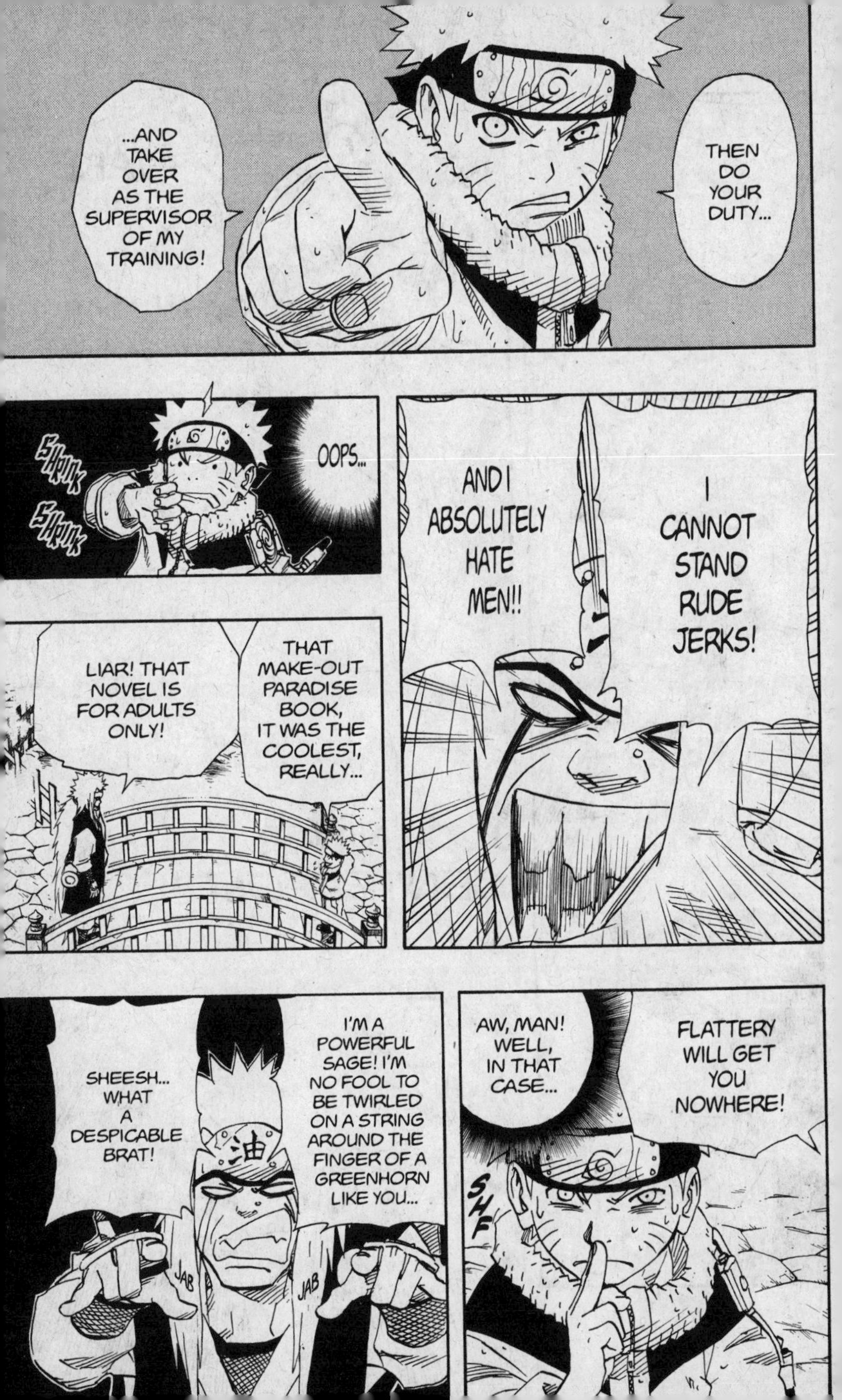
THEN DO YOUR DUTY...
...AND TAKE OVER AS THE SUPERVISOR OF MY TRAINING!
I CANNOT STAND RUDE JERKS!
AND I ABSOLUTELY HATE MEN!!
OOPS...
SHRINK
SHRINK
THAT MAKE-OUT PARADISE BOOK, IT WAS THE COOLEST, REALLY...
LIAR! THAT NOVEL IS FOR ADULTS ONLY!
FLATTERY WILL GET YOU NOWHERE!
AW, MAN! WELL, IN THAT CASE...
SHF
I'M A POWERFUL SAGE! I'M NO FOOL TO BE TWIRLED ON A STRING AROUND THE FINGER OF A GREENHORN LIKE YOU...
SHEESH... WHAT A DESPICABLE BRAT!
油
JAB
JAB

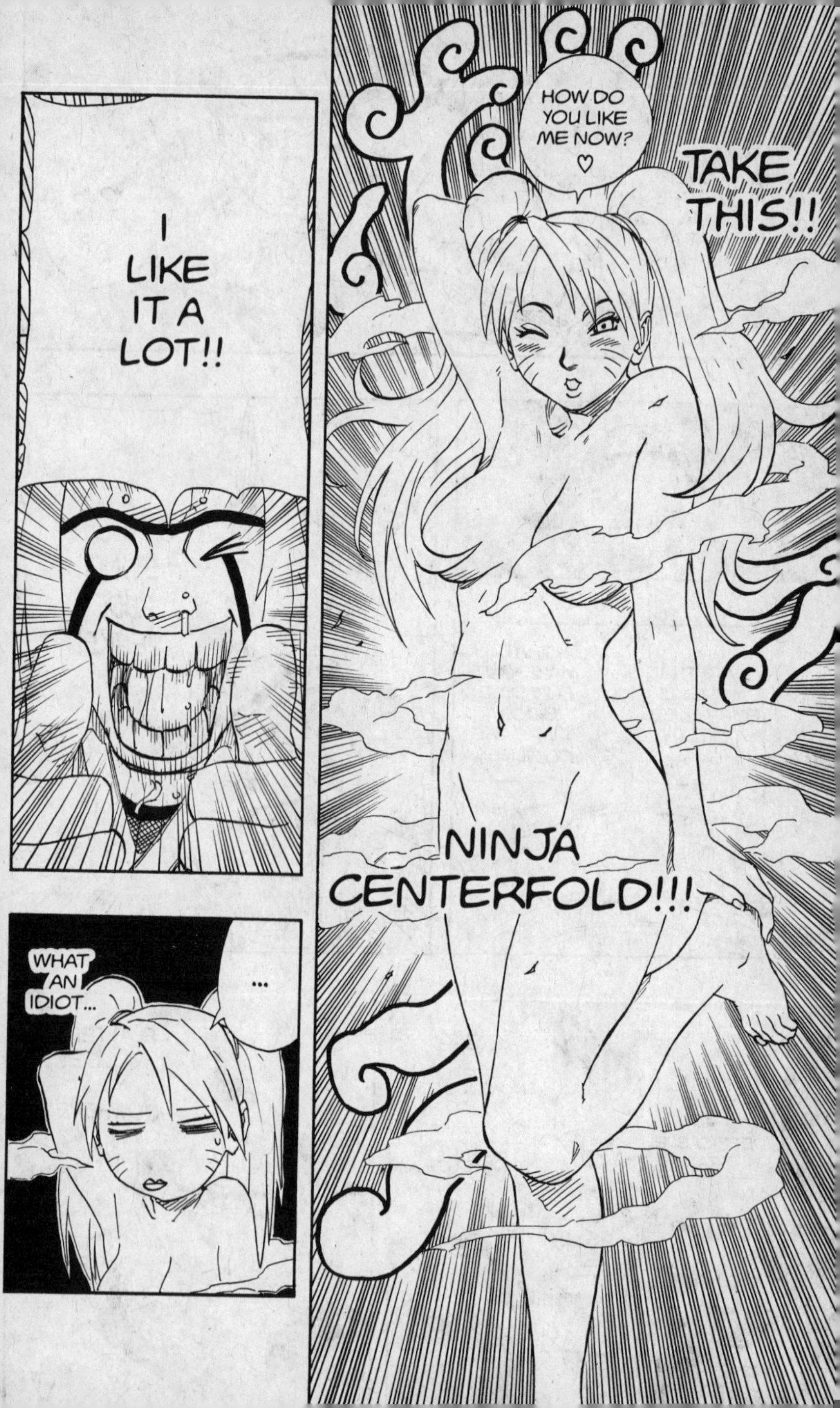
TAKE THIS!!
HOW DO YOU LIKE ME NOW? ♡
NINJA CENTERFOLD!!!
I LIKE IT A LOT!!
...
WHAT AN IDIOT...

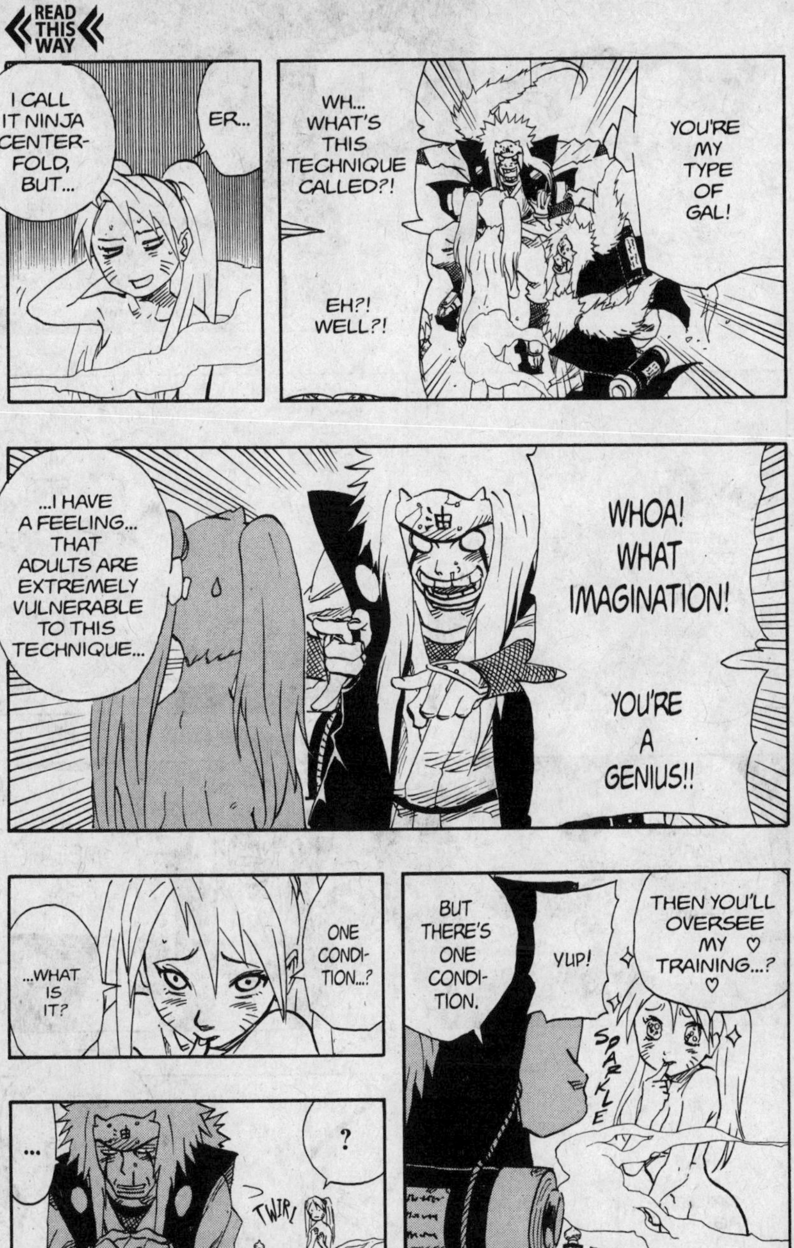
READ THIS WAY
YOU'RE MY TYPE OF GAL!
WH... WHAT'S THIS TECHNIQUE CALLED?!
EH?! WELL?!
ER...
I CALL IT NINJA CENTERFOLD, BUT...
WHOA! WHAT IMAGINATION!
YOU'RE A GENIUS!!
...I HAVE A FEELING... THAT ADULTS ARE EXTREMELY VULNERABLE TO THIS TECHNIQUE...
THEN YOU'LL OVERSEE MY ♡ TRAINING...? ♡
YUP!
BUT THERE'S ONE CONDITION.
SPARKLE
ONE CONDITION...?
...WHAT IS IT?
?
TWIRL
...

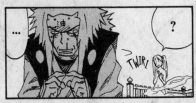

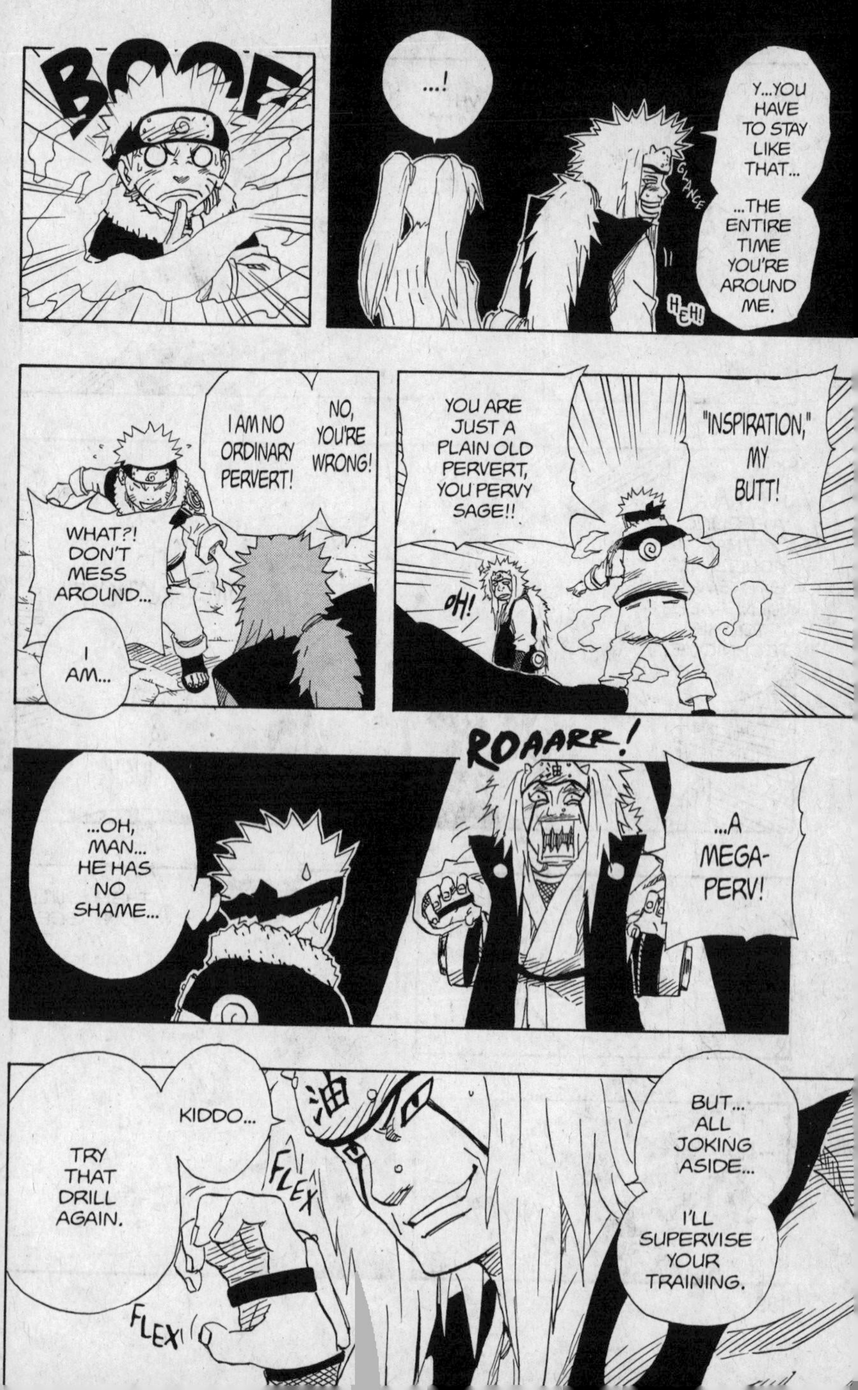
Y...YOU HAVE TO STAY LIKE THAT...
...THE ENTIRE TIME YOU'RE AROUND ME.
GLANCE
HEH!
...!
BOOF
"INSPIRATION," MY BUTT!
YOU ARE JUST A PLAIN OLD PERVERT, YOU PERVY SAGE!!
OH!
NO, YOU'RE WRONG!
I AM NO ORDINARY PERVERT!
WHAT?! DON'T MESS AROUND...
I AM...
ROAARR!
...A MEGA-PERV!
...OH, MAN... HE HAS NO SHAME...
BUT... ALL JOKING ASIDE...
I'LL SUPERVISE YOUR TRAINING.
KIDDO...
TRY THAT DRILL AGAIN.
FLEX
FLEX

READ THIS WAY

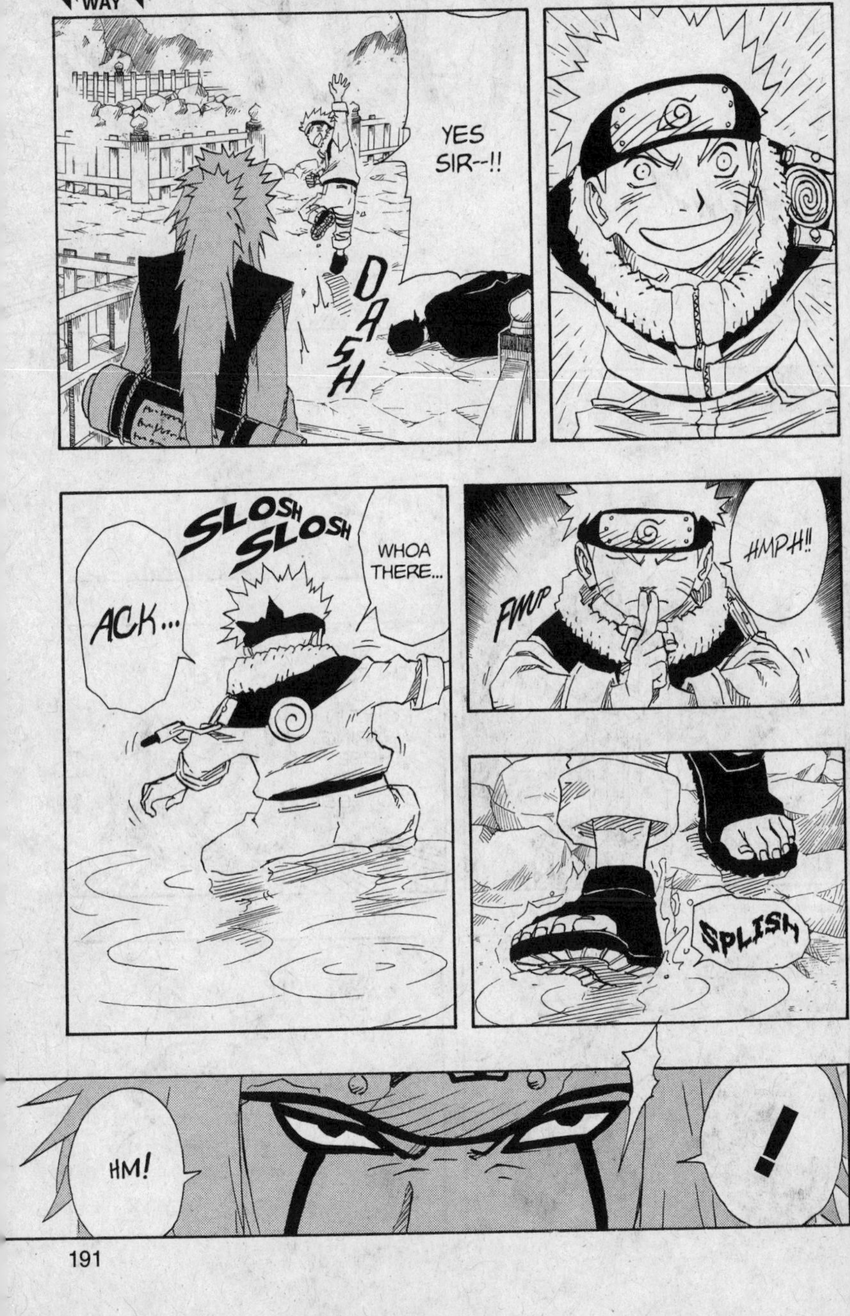

YES SIR--!!
DASH
HMPH!!
FWUP
SPLISH
WHOA THERE...
SLOSH SLOSH
ACK...
!
HM!

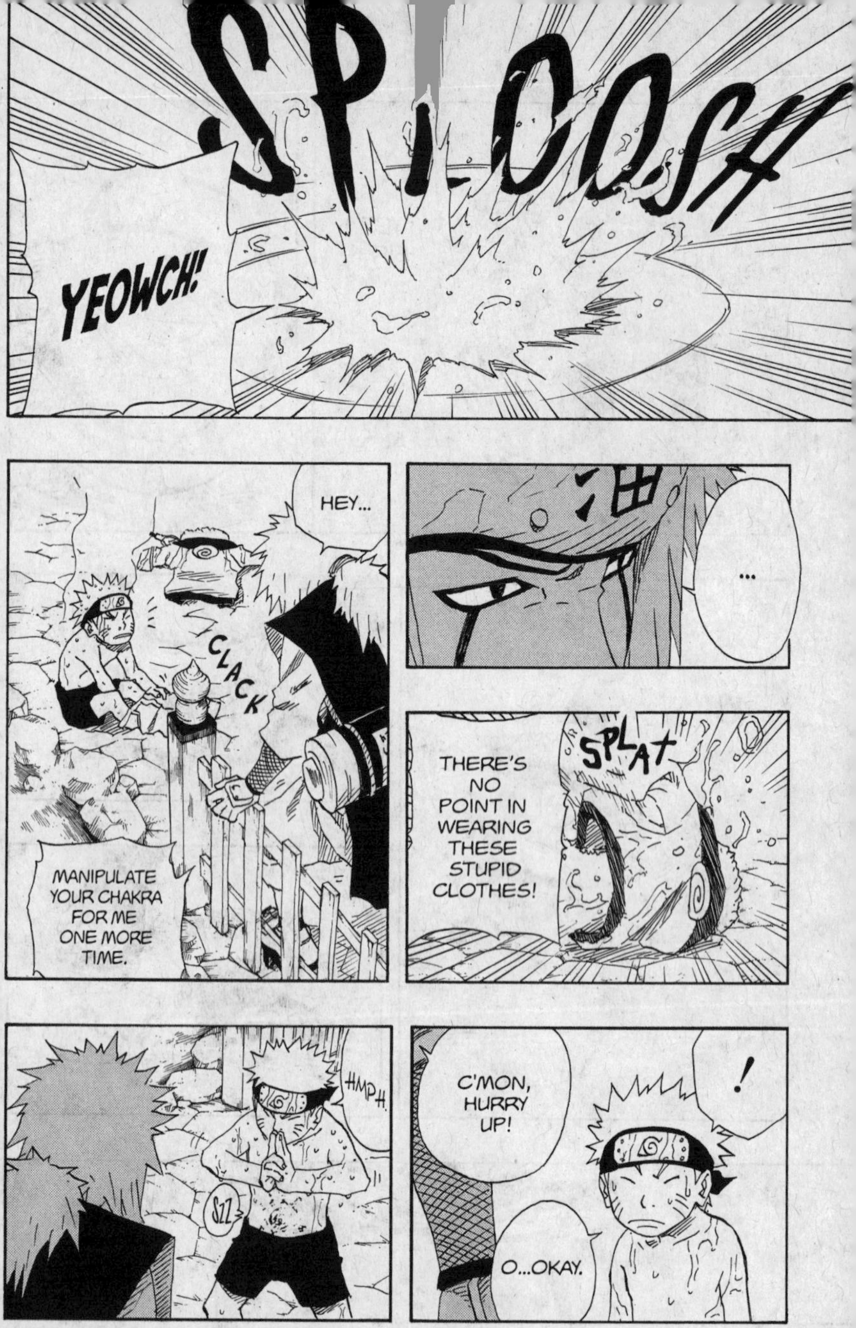

SPLOOSH
YEOWCH!
...
SPLAT
THERE'S NO POINT IN WEARING THESE STUPID CLOTHES!
HEY...
CLACK
MANIPULATE YOUR CHAKRA FOR ME ONE MORE TIME.
!
C'MON, HURRY UP!
O...OKAY.
HMPH
SZZ

READ THIS WAY

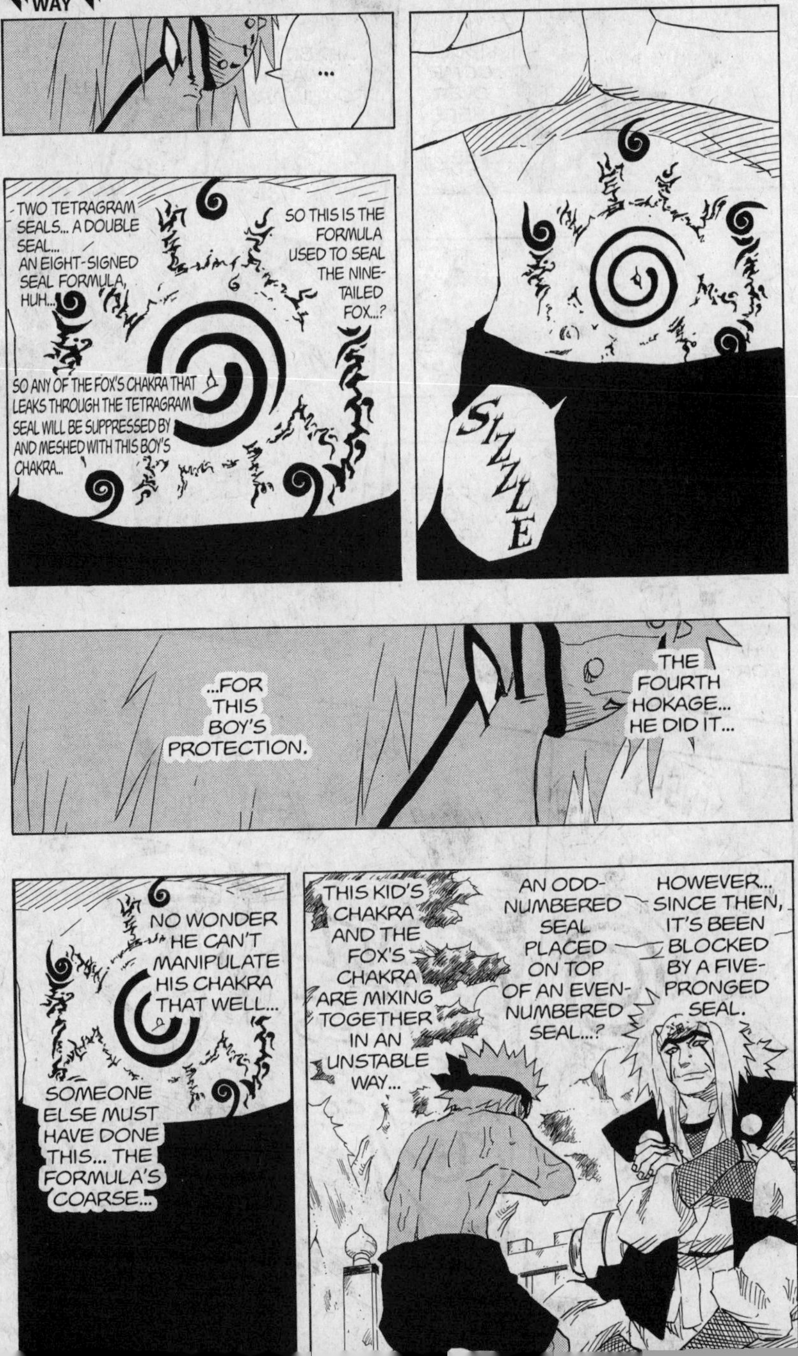
SIZZLE
...
SO THIS IS THE FORMULA USED TO SEAL THE NINE-TAILED FOX...?
TWO TETRAGRAM SEALS... A DOUBLE SEAL... AN EIGHT-SIGNED SEAL FORMULA, HUH...
SO ANY OF THE FOX'S CHAKRA THAT LEAKS THROUGH THE TETRAGRAM SEAL WILL BE SUPPRESSED BY AND MESHED WITH THIS BOY'S CHAKRA...
THE FOURTH HOKAGE... HE DID IT...
...FOR THIS BOY'S PROTECTION.
HOWEVER... SINCE THEN, IT'S BEEN BLOCKED BY A FIVE-PRONGED SEAL.
AN ODD-NUMBERED SEAL PLACED ON TOP OF AN EVEN-NUMBERED SEAL...?
THIS KID'S CHAKRA AND THE FOX'S CHAKRA ARE MIXING TOGETHER IN AN UNSTABLE WAY...
NO WONDER HE CAN'T MANIPULATE HIS CHAKRA THAT WELL...
SOMEONE ELSE MUST HAVE DONE THIS... THE FORMULA'S COARSE...

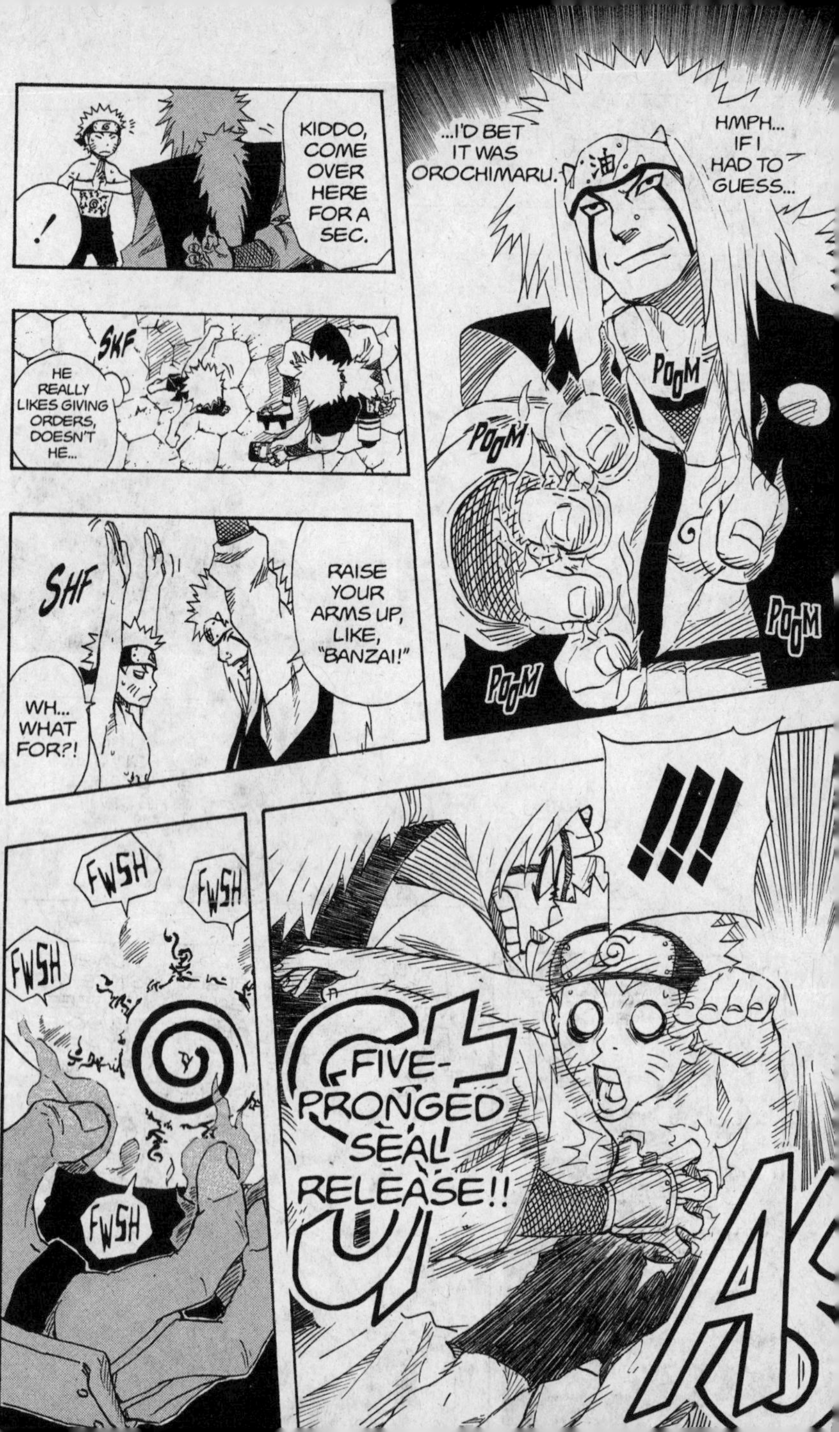
HMPH... IF I HAD TO GUESS...
...I'D BET IT WAS OROCHIMARU.
POOM
POOM
POOM
POOM
KIDDO, COME OVER HERE FOR A SEC.
!
SKF
HE REALLY LIKES GIVING ORDERS, DOESN'T HE...
RAISE YOUR ARMS UP, LIKE, "BANZAI!"
SHF
WH... WHAT FOR?!
!!!
FIVE-PRONGED SEAL RELEASE!!
FWSH
FWSH
FWSH
FWSH

READ THIS WAY

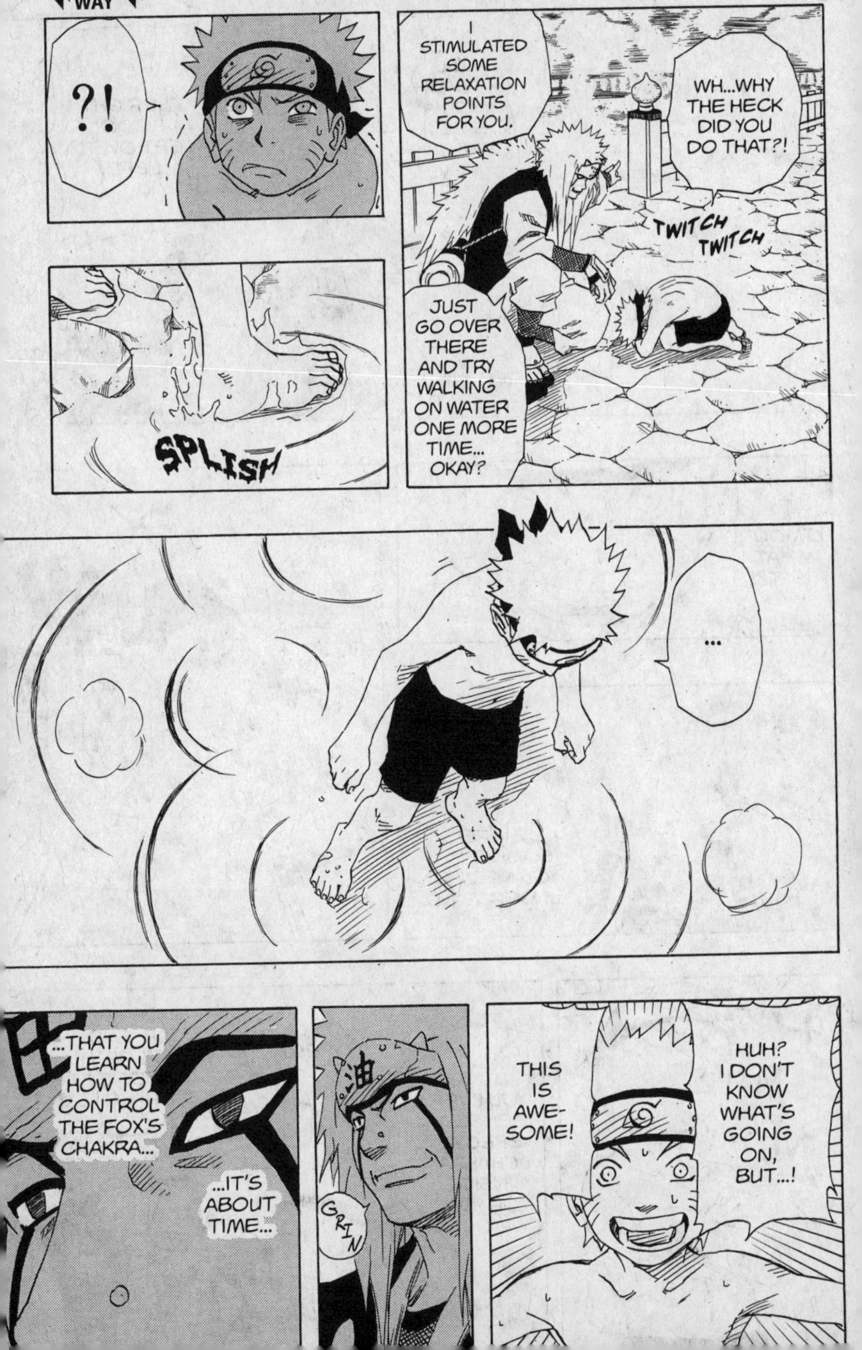
WH...WHY THE HECK DID YOU DO THAT?!
I STIMULATED SOME RELAXATION POINTS FOR YOU.
TWITCH TWITCH
JUST GO OVER THERE AND TRY WALKING ON WATER ONE MORE TIME... OKAY?
?!
SPLISH
...
HUH? I DON'T KNOW WHAT'S GOING ON, BUT...!
THIS IS AWE-SOME!
GRIN
...THAT YOU LEARN HOW TO CONTROL THE FOX'S CHAKRA...
...IT'S ABOUT TIME...

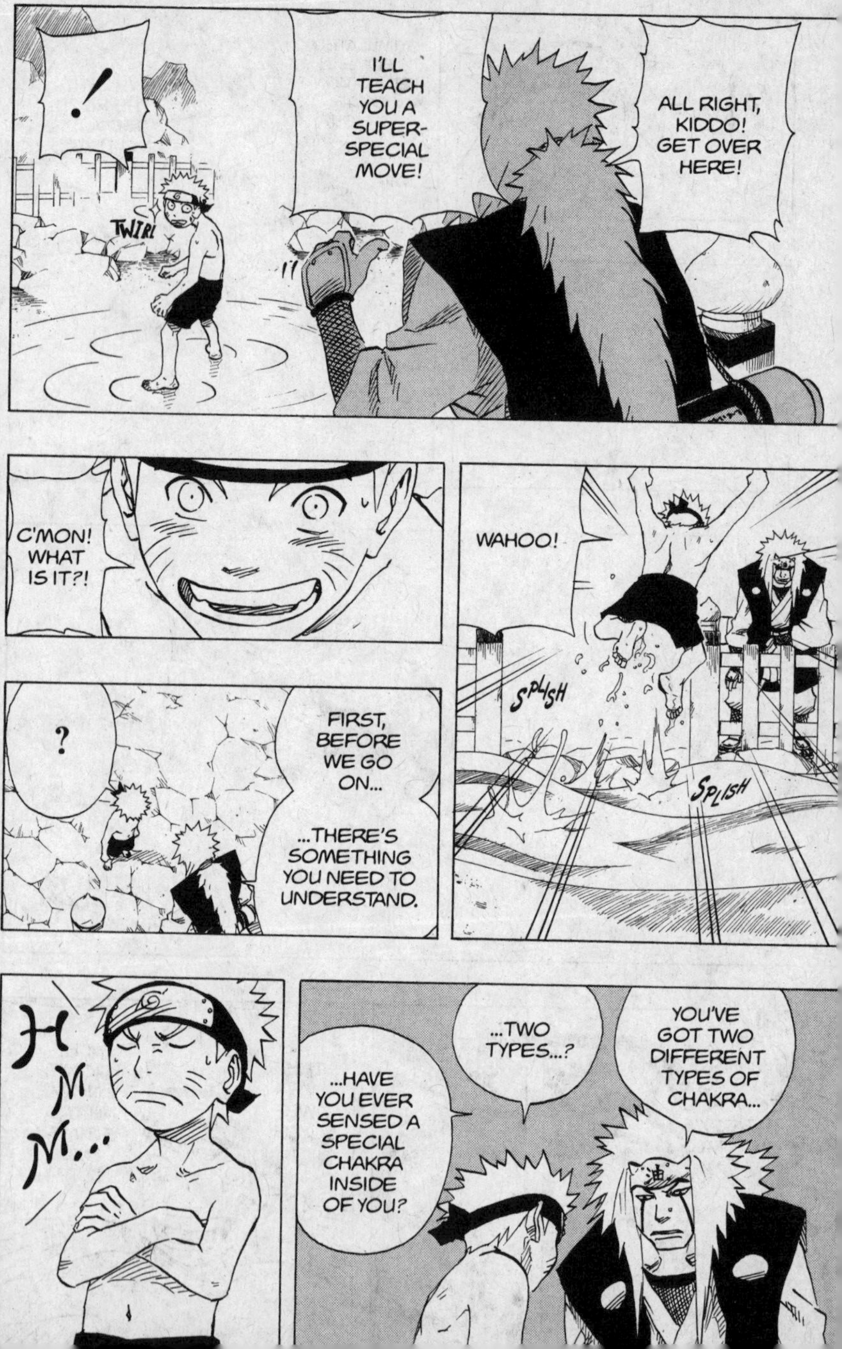
ALL RIGHT, KIDDO! GET OVER HERE!
I'LL TEACH YOU A SUPER-SPECIAL MOVE!
!
TWIRL
WAHOO!
SPLISH
SPLISH
C'MON! WHAT IS IT?!
FIRST, BEFORE WE GO ON...
...THERE'S SOMETHING YOU NEED TO UNDERSTAND.
?
YOU'VE GOT TWO DIFFERENT TYPES OF CHAKRA...
...TWO TYPES...?
...HAVE YOU EVER SENSED A SPECIAL CHAKRA INSIDE OF YOU?
HMM...

READ THIS WAY

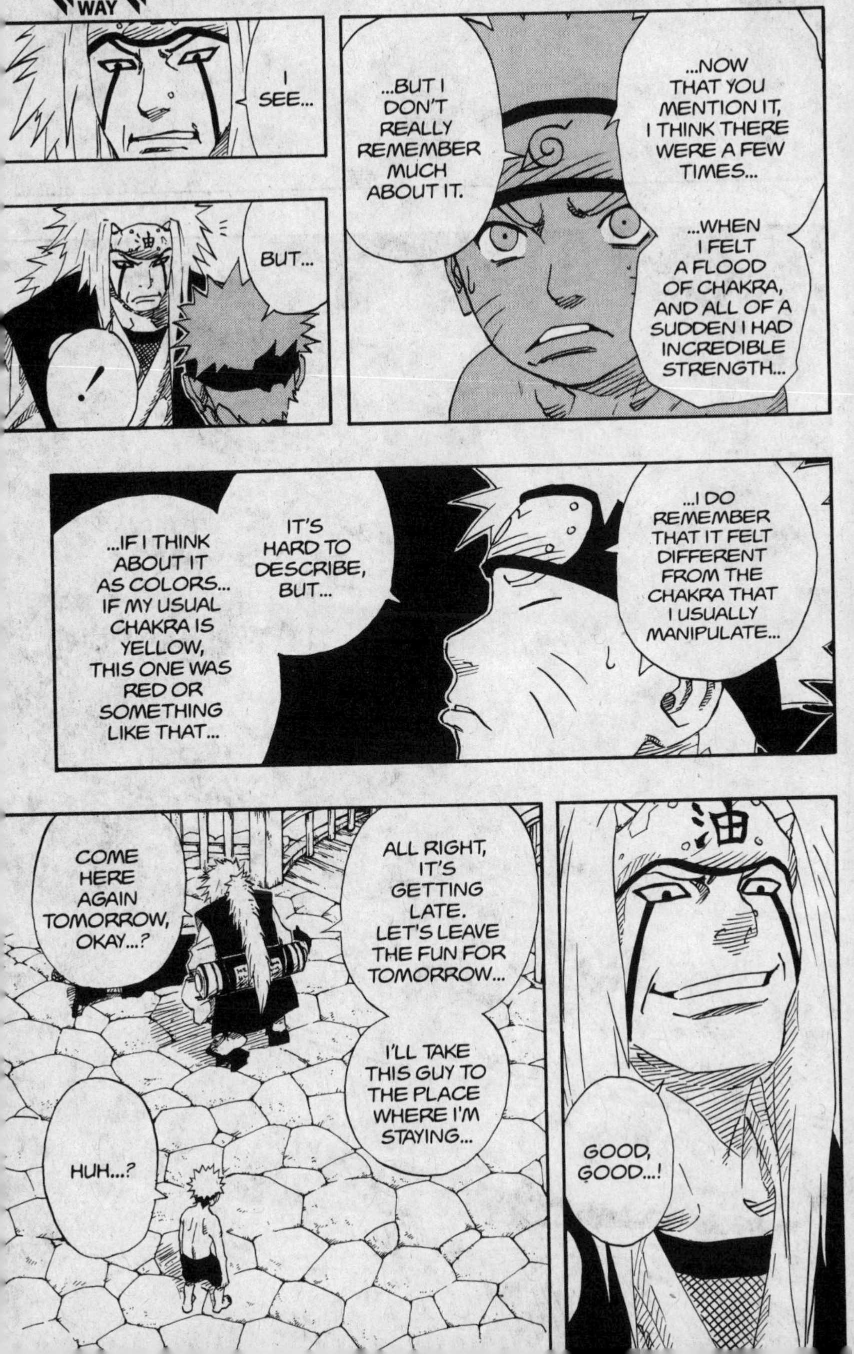
...NOW THAT YOU MENTION IT, I THINK THERE WERE A FEW TIMES...
...WHEN I FELT A FLOOD OF CHAKRA, AND ALL OF A SUDDEN I HAD INCREDIBLE STRENGTH...
...BUT I DON'T REALLY REMEMBER MUCH ABOUT IT.
I SEE...
BUT...
!
...I DO REMEMBER THAT IT FELT DIFFERENT FROM THE CHAKRA THAT I USUALLY MANIPULATE...
IT'S HARD TO DESCRIBE, BUT...
...IF I THINK ABOUT IT AS COLORS... IF MY USUAL CHAKRA IS YELLOW, THIS ONE WAS RED OR SOMETHING LIKE THAT...
GOOD, GOOD...!
ALL RIGHT, IT'S GETTING LATE. LET'S LEAVE THE FUN FOR TOMORROW...
I'LL TAKE THIS GUY TO THE PLACE WHERE I'M STAYING...
COME HERE AGAIN TOMORROW, OKAY...?
HUH...?

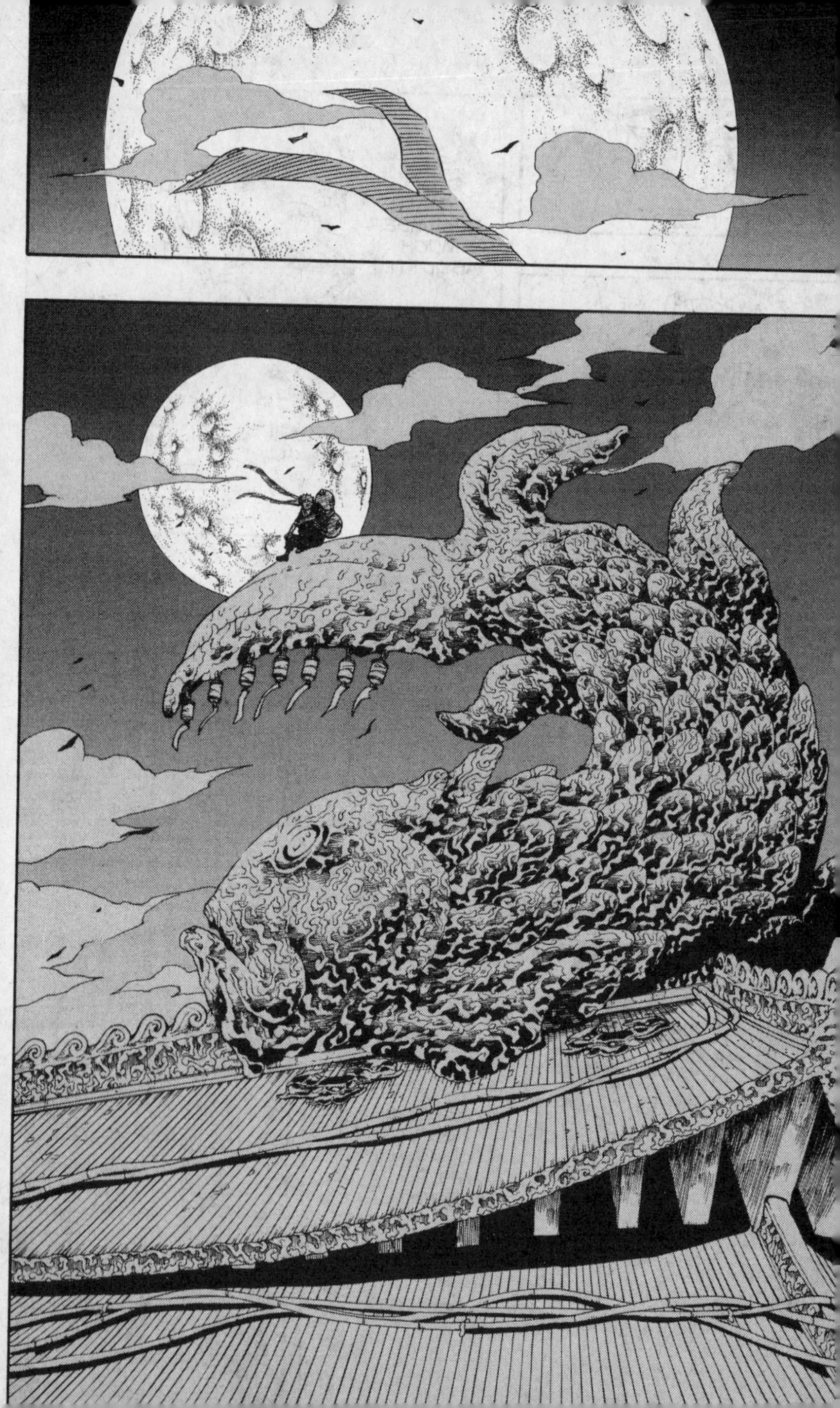

READ THIS WAY

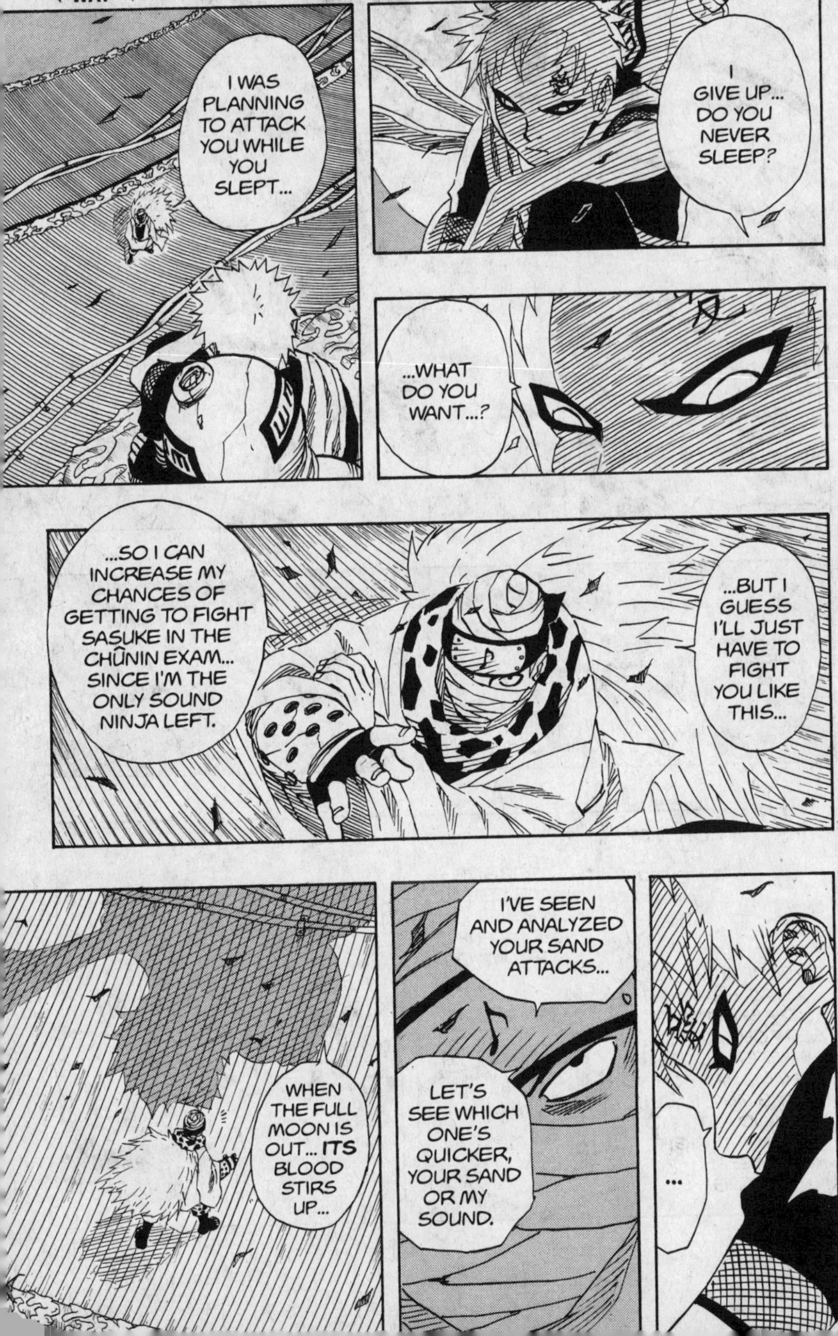
I GIVE UP... DO YOU NEVER SLEEP?
...WHAT DO YOU WANT...?
I WAS PLANNING TO ATTACK YOU WHILE YOU SLEPT...
...SO I CAN INCREASE MY CHANCES OF GETTING TO FIGHT SASUKE IN THE CHŪNIN EXAM... SINCE I'M THE ONLY SOUND NINJA LEFT.
...BUT I GUESS I'LL JUST HAVE TO FIGHT YOU LIKE THIS...
...
I'VE SEEN AND ANALYZED YOUR SAND ATTACKS...
LET'S SEE WHICH ONE'S QUICKER, YOUR SAND OR MY SOUND.
WHEN THE FULL MOON IS OUT... **ITS** BLOOD STIRS UP...

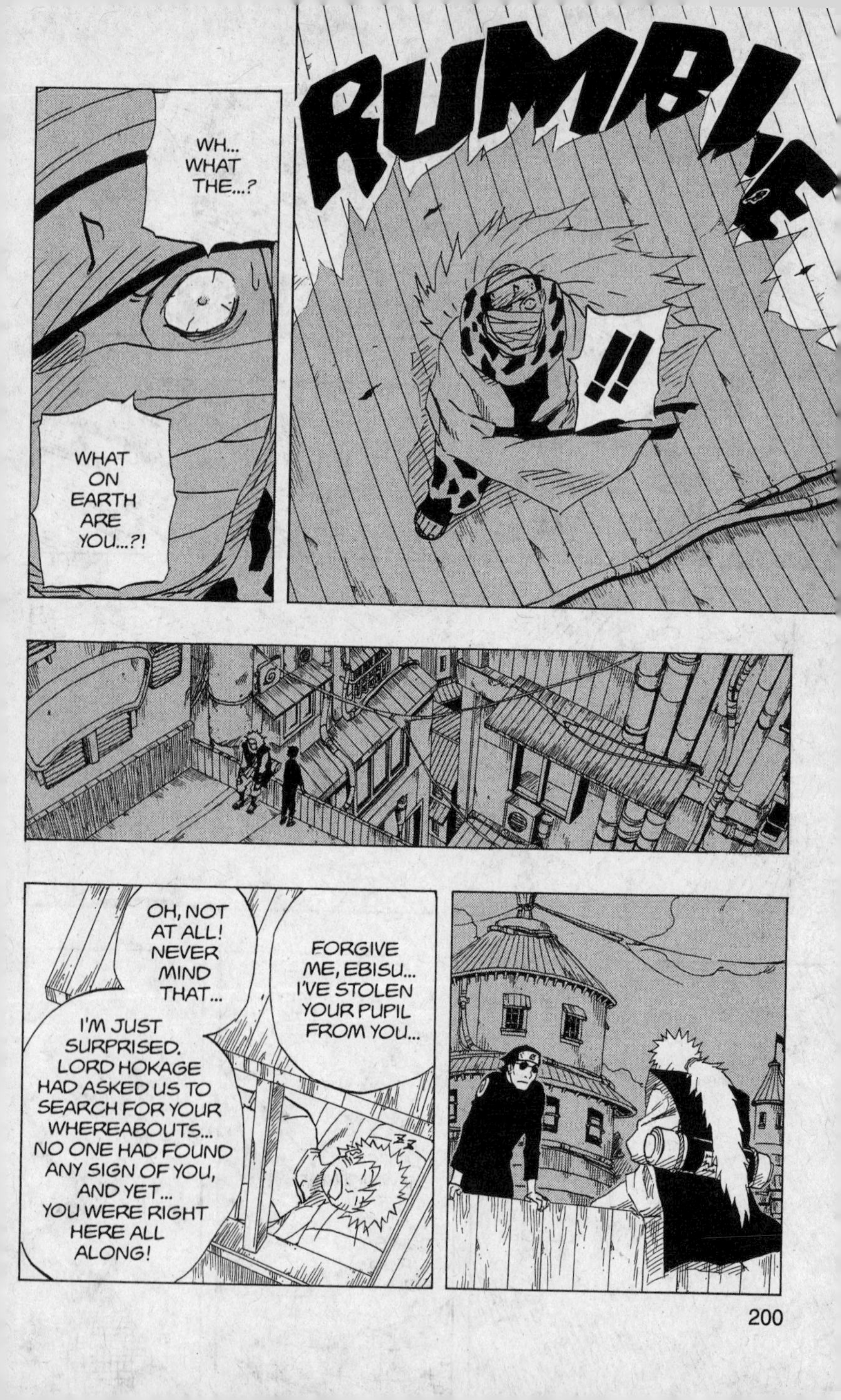
RUMBLE
!!
WH... WHAT THE...?
WHAT ON EARTH ARE YOU...?!
FORGIVE ME, EBISU... I'VE STOLEN YOUR PUPIL FROM YOU...
OH, NOT AT ALL! NEVER MIND THAT...
I'M JUST SURPRISED. LORD HOKAGE HAD ASKED US TO SEARCH FOR YOUR WHEREABOUTS... NO ONE HAD FOUND ANY SIGN OF YOU, AND YET... YOU WERE RIGHT HERE ALL ALONG!

READ THIS WAY

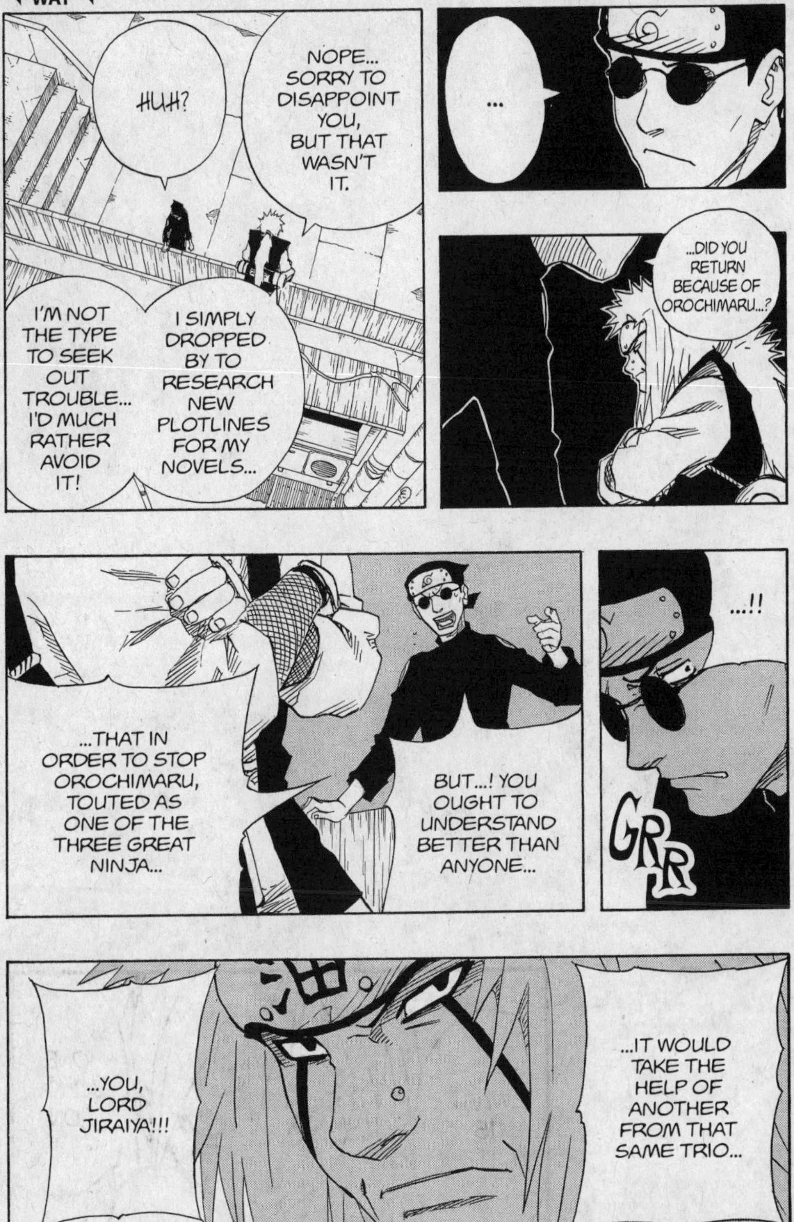
...
...DID YOU RETURN BECAUSE OF OROCHIMARU...?
NOPE... SORRY TO DISAPPOINT YOU, BUT THAT WASN'T IT.
HUH?
I SIMPLY DROPPED BY TO RESEARCH NEW PLOTLINES FOR MY NOVELS...
I'M NOT THE TYPE TO SEEK OUT TROUBLE... I'D MUCH RATHER AVOID IT!
...!!
GRR
BUT...! YOU OUGHT TO UNDERSTAND BETTER THAN ANYONE...
...THAT IN ORDER TO STOP OROCHIMARU, TOUTED AS ONE OF THE THREE GREAT NINJA...
...IT WOULD TAKE THE HELP OF ANOTHER FROM THAT SAME TRIO...
...YOU, LORD JIRAIYA!!!

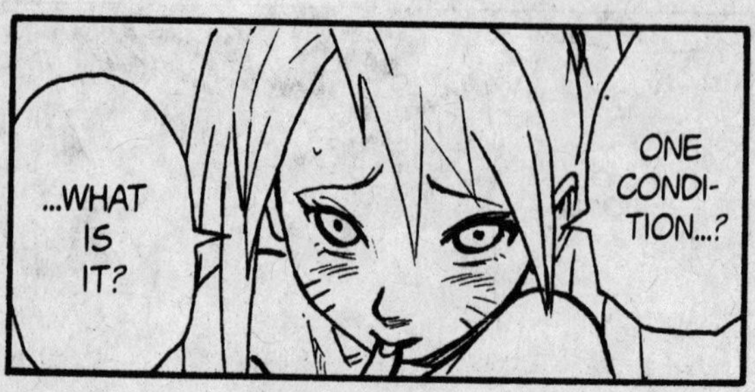
ONE CONDI-TION...?
...WHAT IS IT?

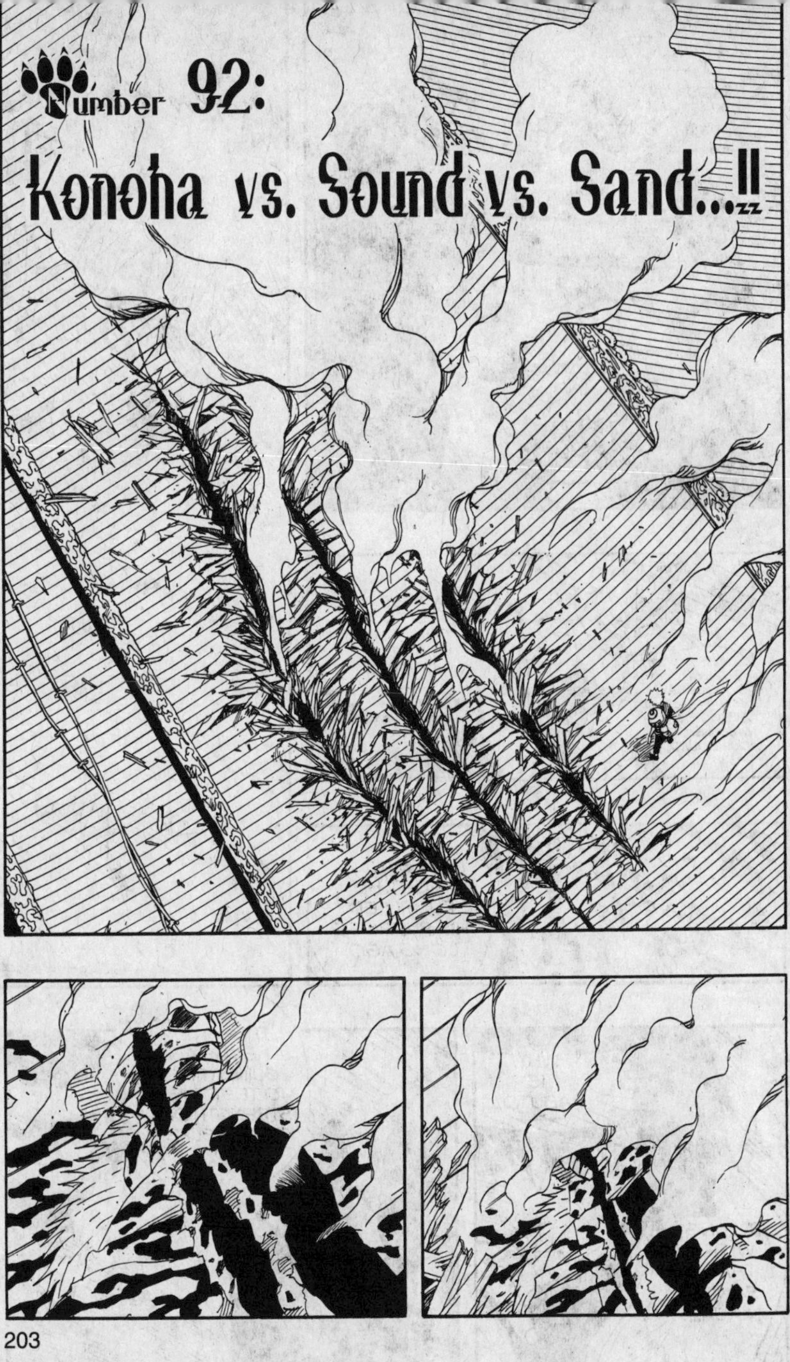
Number 92:
Konoha vs. Sound vs. Sand...!!

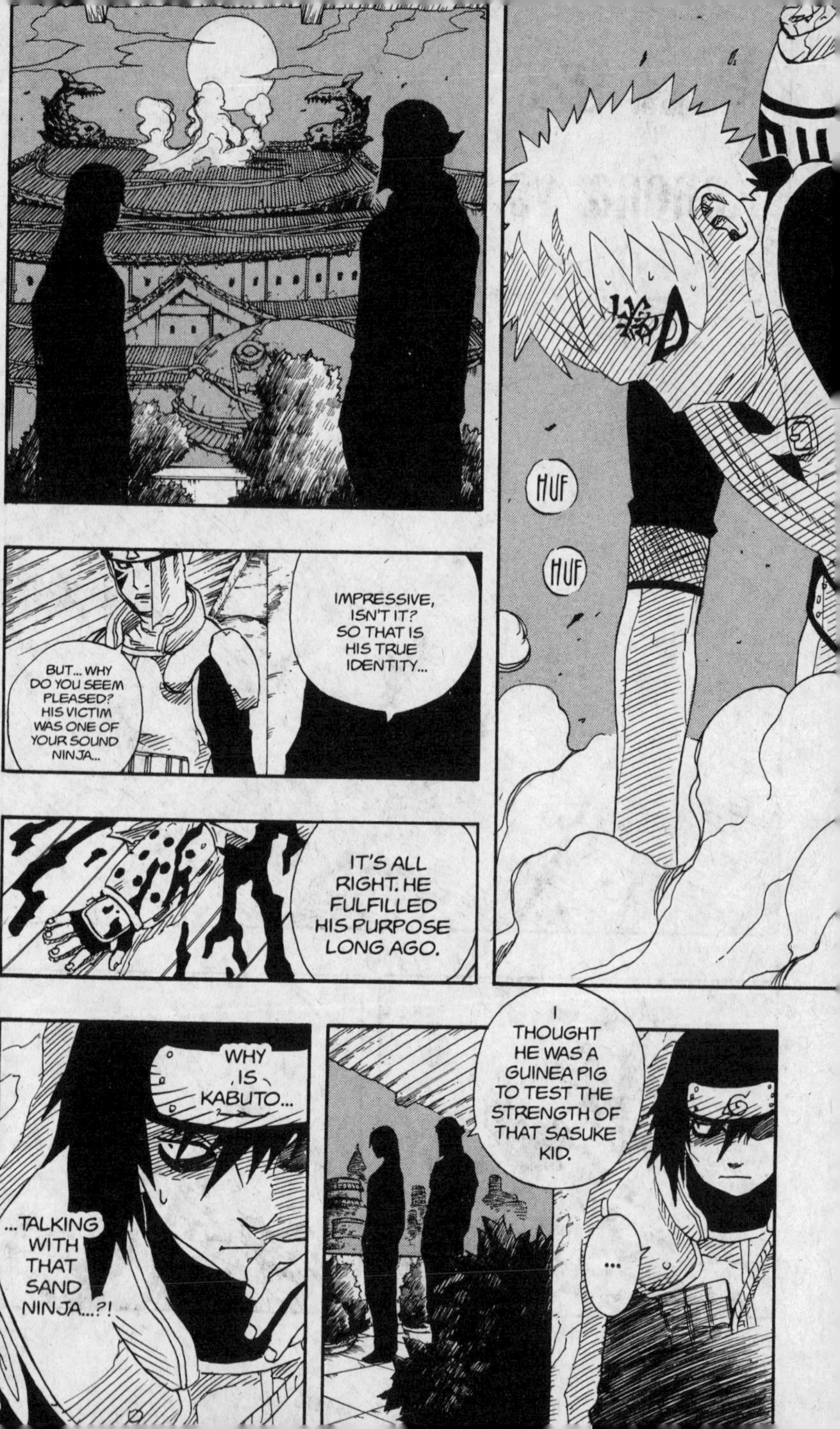
HUF
HUF
IMPRESSIVE, ISN'T IT? SO THAT IS HIS TRUE IDENTITY...
BUT... WHY DO YOU SEEM PLEASED? HIS VICTIM WAS ONE OF YOUR SOUND NINJA...
IT'S ALL RIGHT. HE FULFILLED HIS PURPOSE LONG AGO.
I THOUGHT HE WAS A GUINEA PIG TO TEST THE STRENGTH OF THAT SASUKE KID.
...
WHY IS KABUTO...
...TALKING WITH THAT SAND NINJA...?!

READ THIS WAY

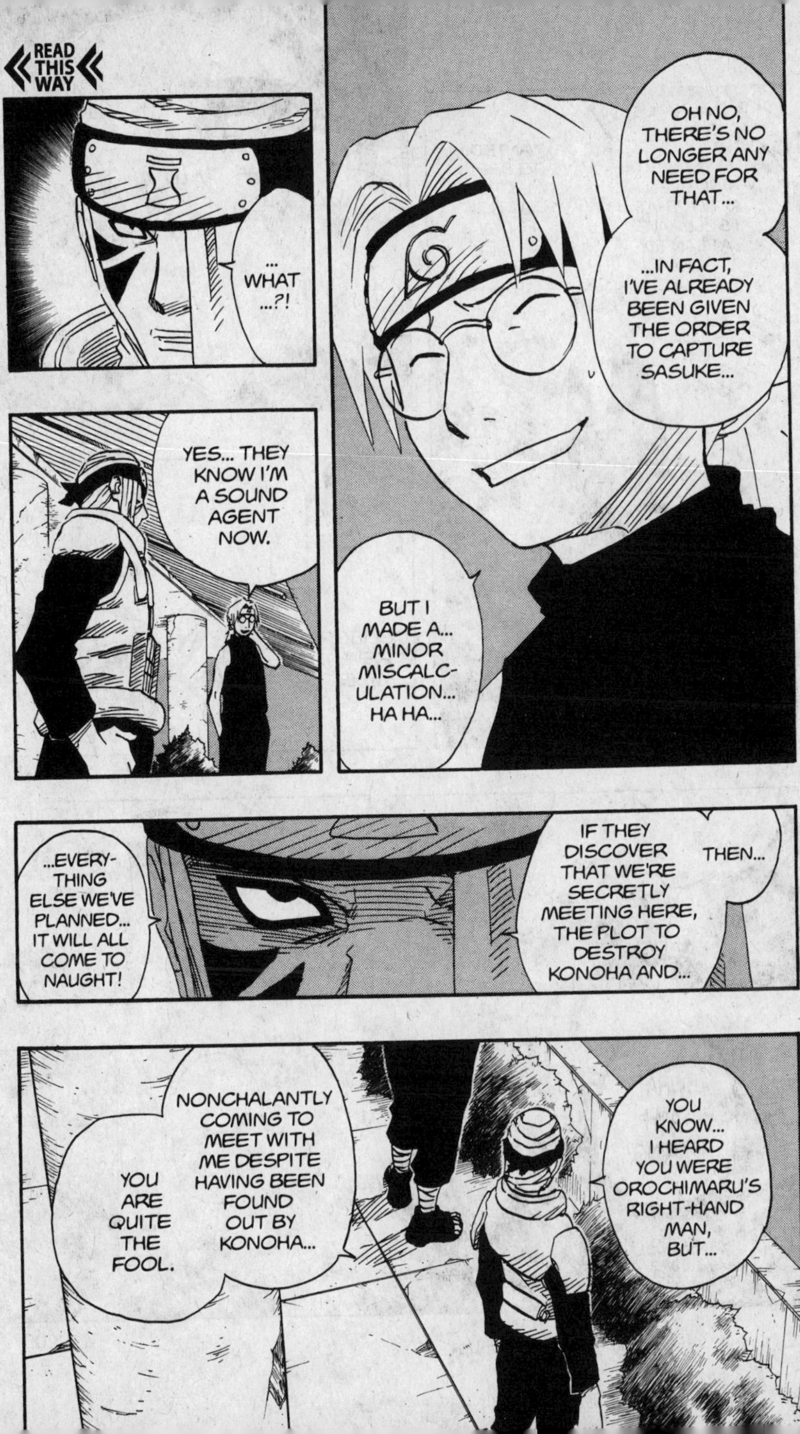
OH NO, THERE'S NO LONGER ANY NEED FOR THAT...
...IN FACT, I'VE ALREADY BEEN GIVEN THE ORDER TO CAPTURE SASUKE...
BUT I MADE A... MINOR MISCALC-ULATION... HA HA...
...WHAT...?!
YES... THEY KNOW I'M A SOUND AGENT NOW.
IF THEY DISCOVER THAT WE'RE SECRETLY MEETING HERE, THE PLOT TO DESTROY KONOHA AND... THEN...
...EVERY-THING ELSE WE'VE PLANNED... IT WILL ALL COME TO NAUGHT!
YOU KNOW... I HEARD YOU WERE OROCHIMARU'S RIGHT-HAND MAN, BUT...
NONCHALANTLY COMING TO MEET WITH ME DESPITE HAVING BEEN FOUND OUT BY KONOHA...
YOU ARE QUITE THE FOOL.

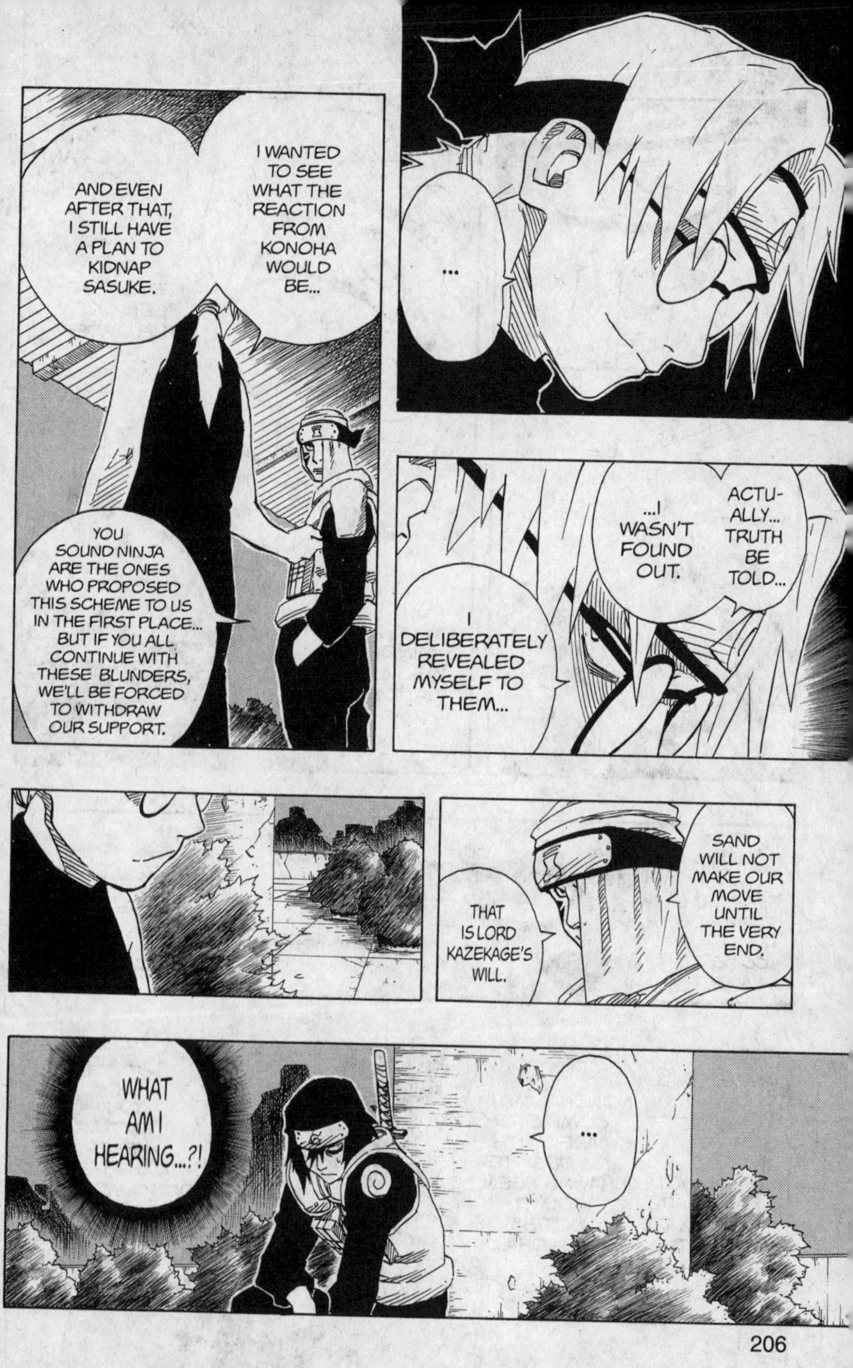
...
ACTU-ALLY... TRUTH BE TOLD...
...I WASN'T FOUND OUT.
I DELIBERATELY REVEALED MYSELF TO THEM...
I WANTED TO SEE WHAT THE REACTION FROM KONOHA WOULD BE...
AND EVEN AFTER THAT, I STILL HAVE A PLAN TO KIDNAP SASUKE.
YOU SOUND NINJA ARE THE ONES WHO PROPOSED THIS SCHEME TO US IN THE FIRST PLACE... BUT IF YOU ALL CONTINUE WITH THESE BLUNDERS, WE'LL BE FORCED TO WITHDRAW OUR SUPPORT.
SAND WILL NOT MAKE OUR MOVE UNTIL THE VERY END.
THAT IS LORD KAZEKAGE'S WILL.
...
WHAT AM I HEARING...?!

READ THIS WAY

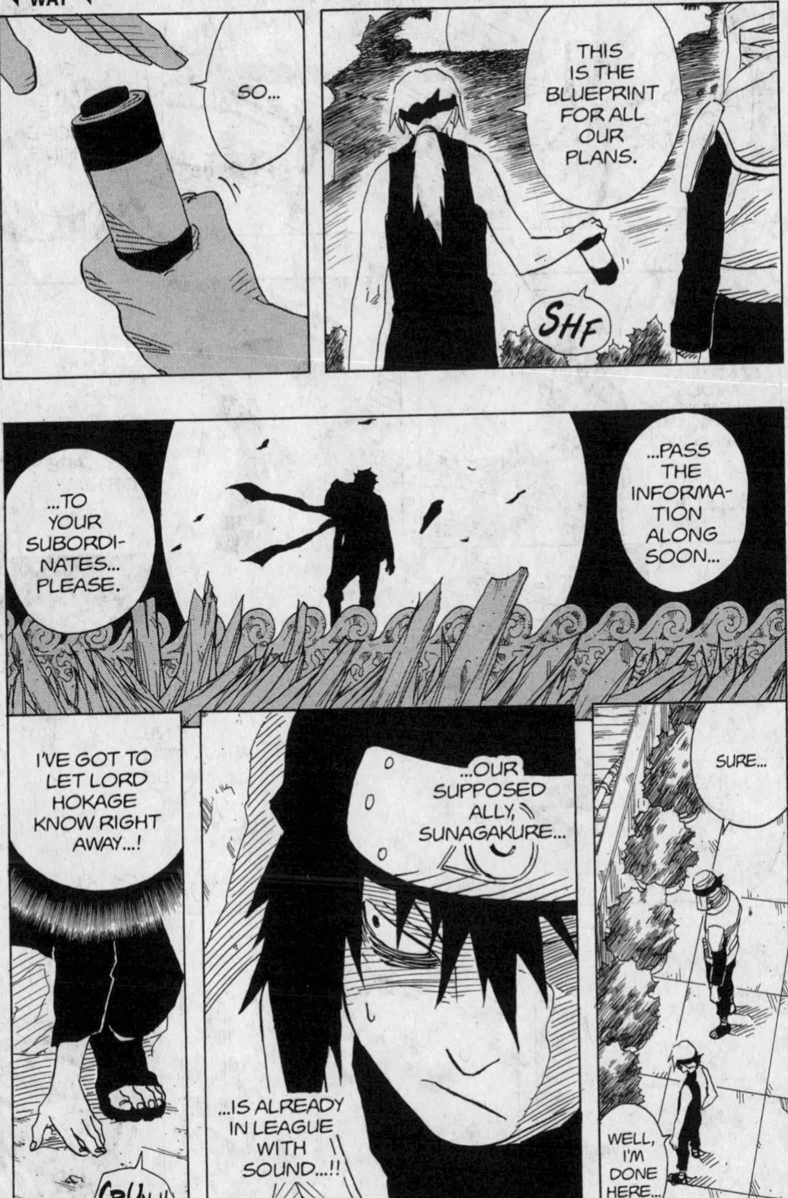
THIS IS THE BLUEPRINT FOR ALL OUR PLANS.
SHF
SO...
...PASS THE INFORMATION ALONG SOON...
...TO YOUR SUBORDINATES... PLEASE.
SURE...
WELL, I'M DONE HERE...
...OUR SUPPOSED ALLY, SUNAGAKURE...
...IS ALREADY IN LEAGUE WITH SOUND...!!
I'VE GOT TO LET LORD HOKAGE KNOW RIGHT AWAY...!
CRUNCH

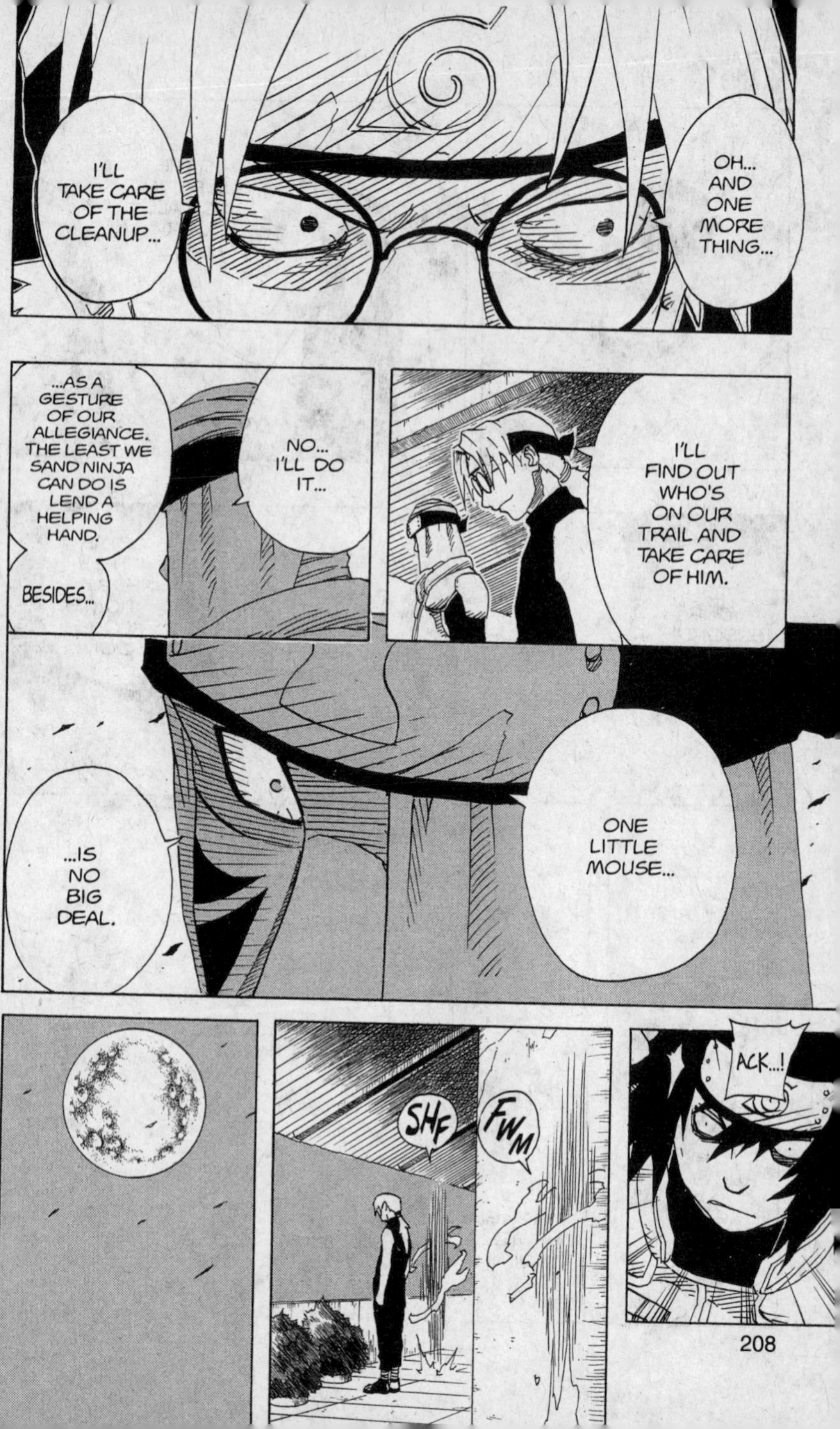
OH... AND ONE MORE THING...
I'LL TAKE CARE OF THE CLEANUP...
I'LL FIND OUT WHO'S ON OUR TRAIL AND TAKE CARE OF HIM.
NO... I'LL DO IT...
...AS A GESTURE OF OUR ALLEGIANCE. THE LEAST WE SAND NINJA CAN DO IS LEND A HELPING HAND.
BESIDES...
ONE LITTLE MOUSE...
...IS NO BIG DEAL.
ACK...!
FWM
SHF

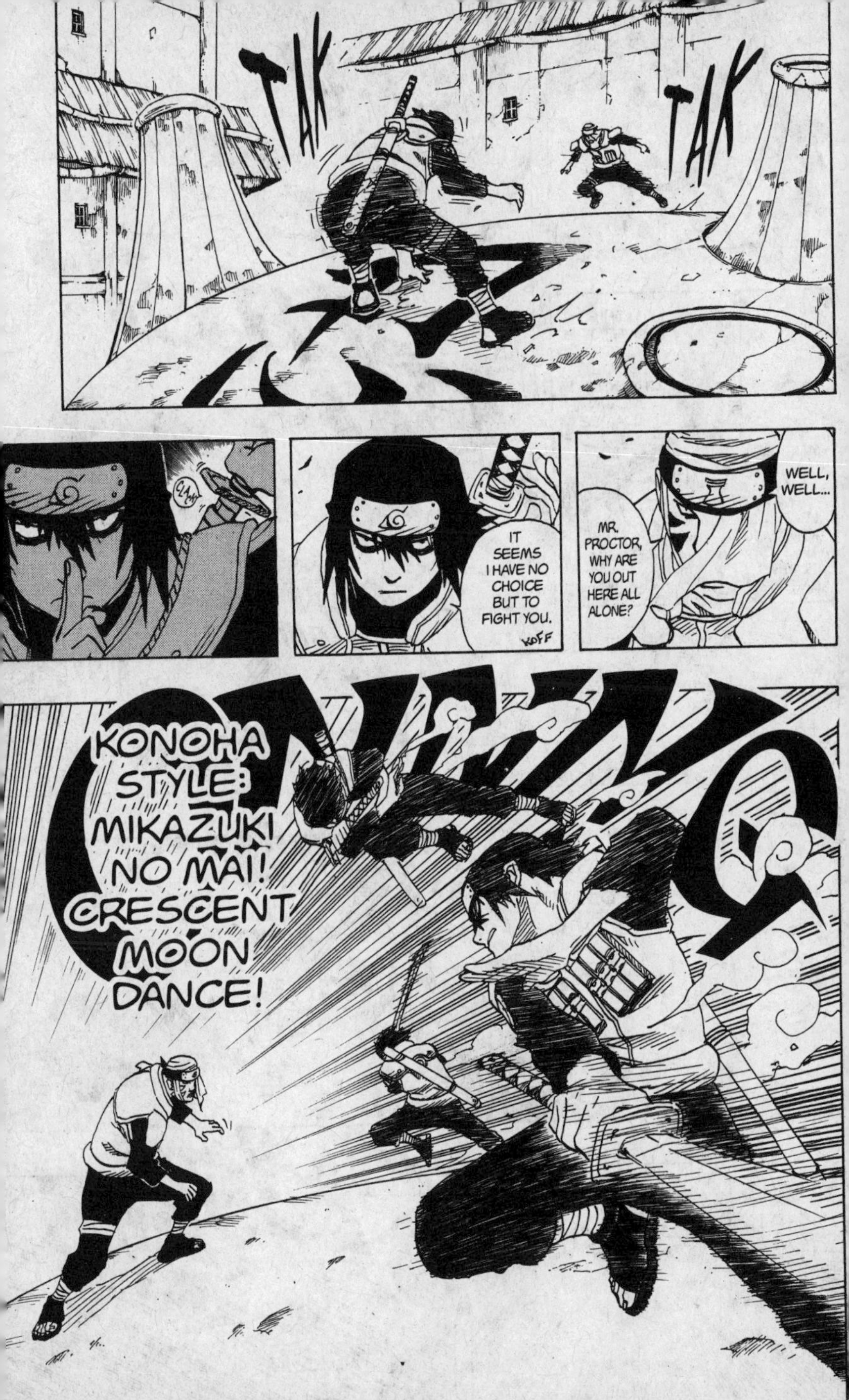
TAK
TAK
WELL, WELL...
MR. PROCTOR, WHY ARE YOU OUT HERE ALL ALONE?
IT SEEMS I HAVE NO CHOICE BUT TO FIGHT YOU.
KOFF
CLAK
KONOHA STYLE: MIKAZUKI NO MAI! CRESCENT MOON DANCE!

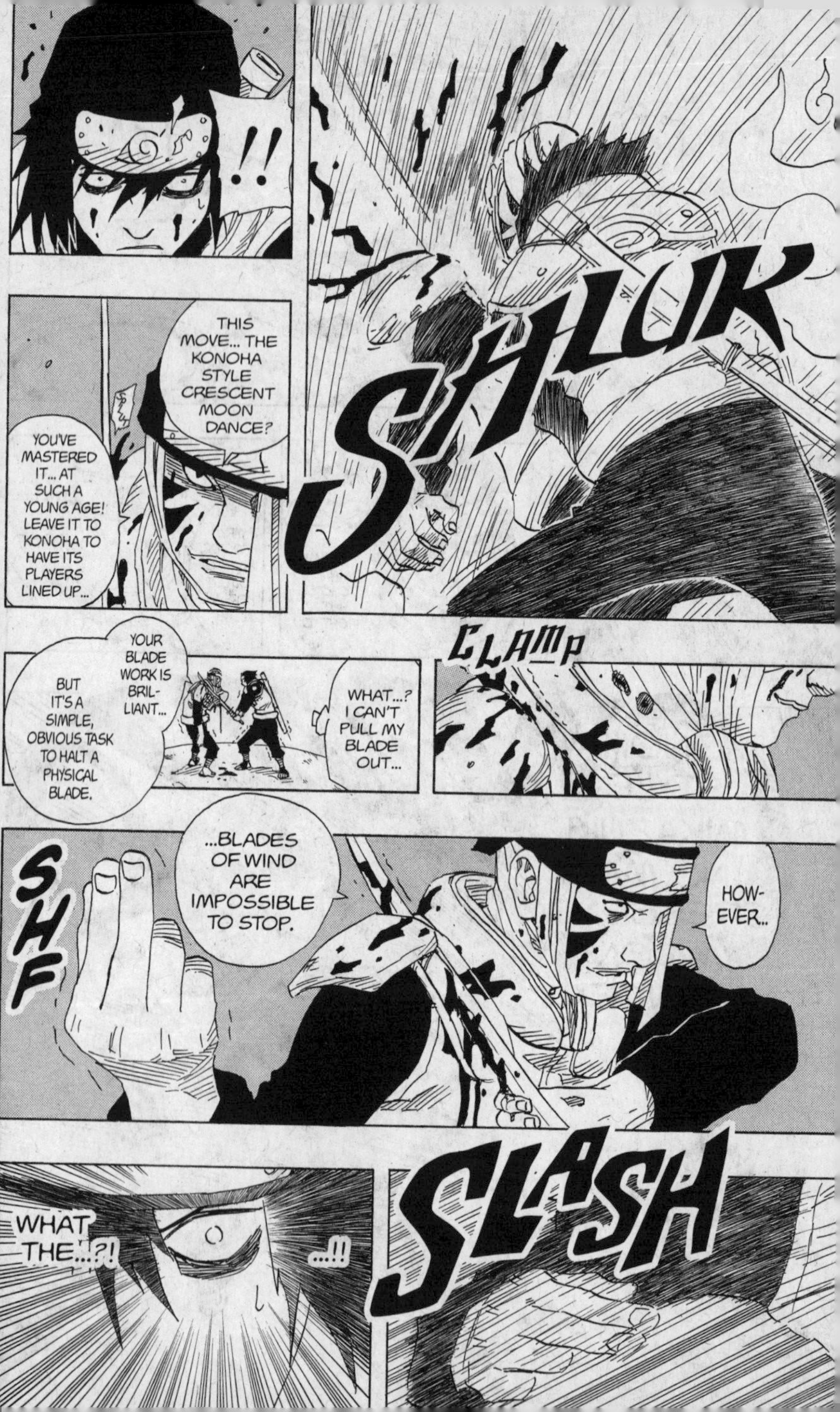
SHLUK
!!
THIS MOVE... THE KONOHA STYLE CRESCENT MOON DANCE?
YOU'VE MASTERED IT... AT SUCH A YOUNG AGE! LEAVE IT TO KONOHA TO HAVE ITS PLAYERS LINED UP...
CLAMP
WHAT...? I CAN'T PULL MY BLADE OUT...
YOUR BLADE WORK IS BRIL-LIANT...
BUT IT'S A SIMPLE, OBVIOUS TASK TO HALT A PHYSICAL BLADE.
HOW-EVER...
...BLADES OF WIND ARE IMPOSSIBLE TO STOP.
SHF
SLASH
...!!
WHAT THE...?!

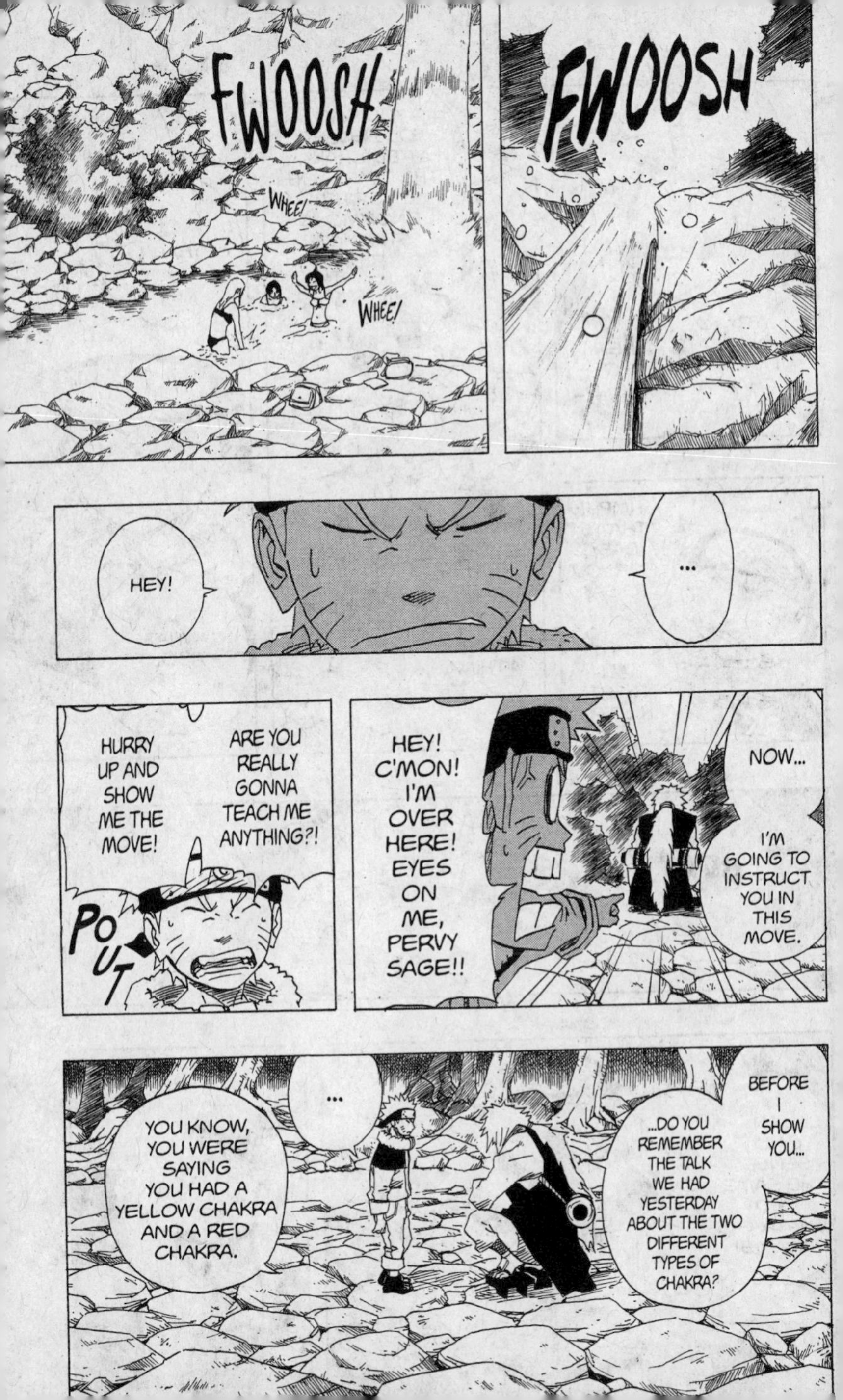
FWOOSH
FWOOSH
WHEE!
WHEE!
...
HEY!
NOW...
I'M GOING TO INSTRUCT YOU IN THIS MOVE.
HEY! C'MON! I'M OVER HERE! EYES ON ME, PERVY SAGE!!
ARE YOU REALLY GONNA TEACH ME ANYTHING?!
HURRY UP AND SHOW ME THE MOVE!
POUT
BEFORE I SHOW YOU...
...DO YOU REMEMBER THE TALK WE HAD YESTERDAY ABOUT THE TWO DIFFERENT TYPES OF CHAKRA?
...
YOU KNOW, YOU WERE SAYING YOU HAD A YELLOW CHAKRA AND A RED CHAKRA.

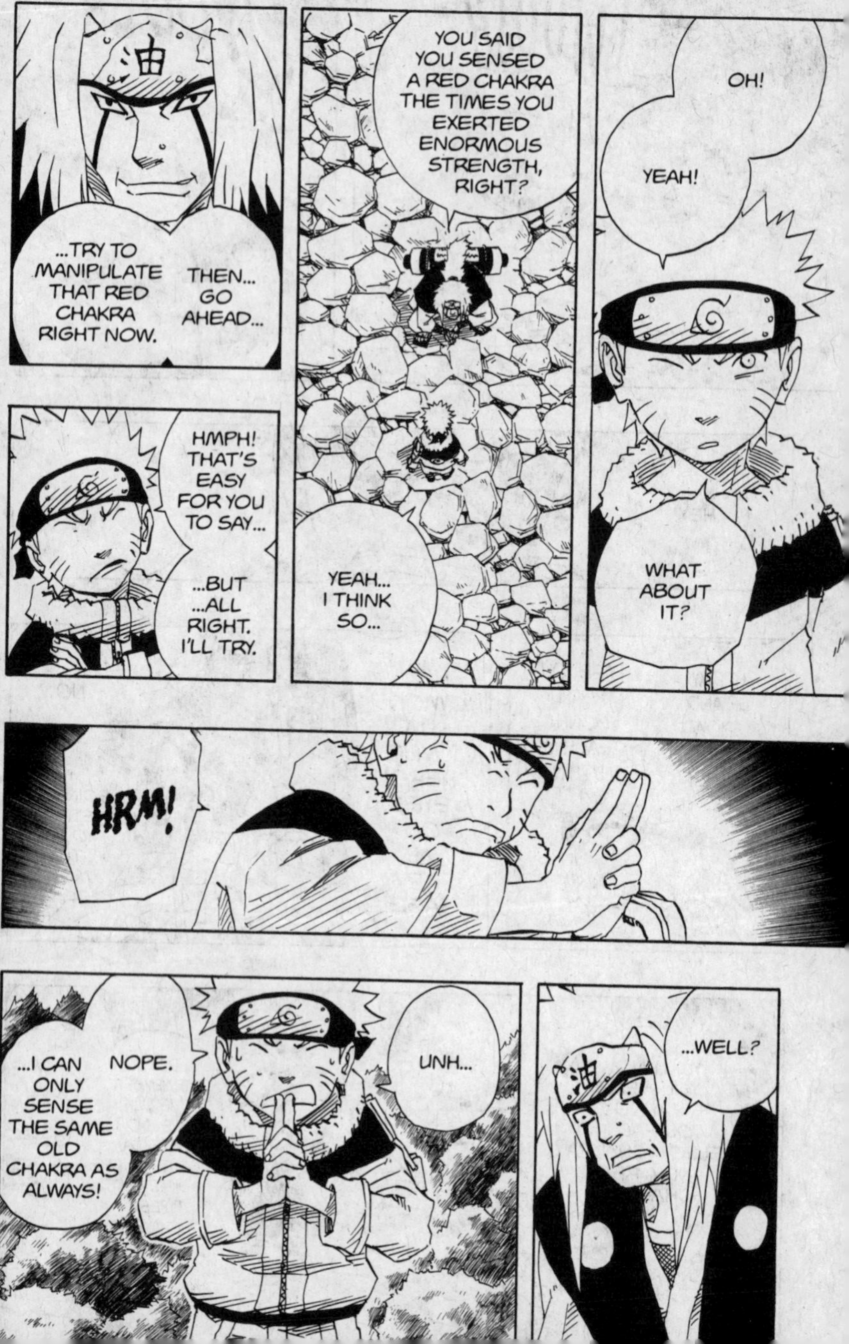
OH!
YEAH!
WHAT ABOUT IT?
YOU SAID YOU SENSED A RED CHAKRA THE TIMES YOU EXERTED ENORMOUS STRENGTH, RIGHT?
YEAH... I THINK SO...
THEN... GO AHEAD...
...TRY TO MANIPULATE THAT RED CHAKRA RIGHT NOW.
HMPH! THAT'S EASY FOR YOU TO SAY...
...BUT ...ALL RIGHT. I'LL TRY.
HRM!
...WELL?
UNH...
NOPE.
...I CAN ONLY SENSE THE SAME OLD CHAKRA AS ALWAYS!

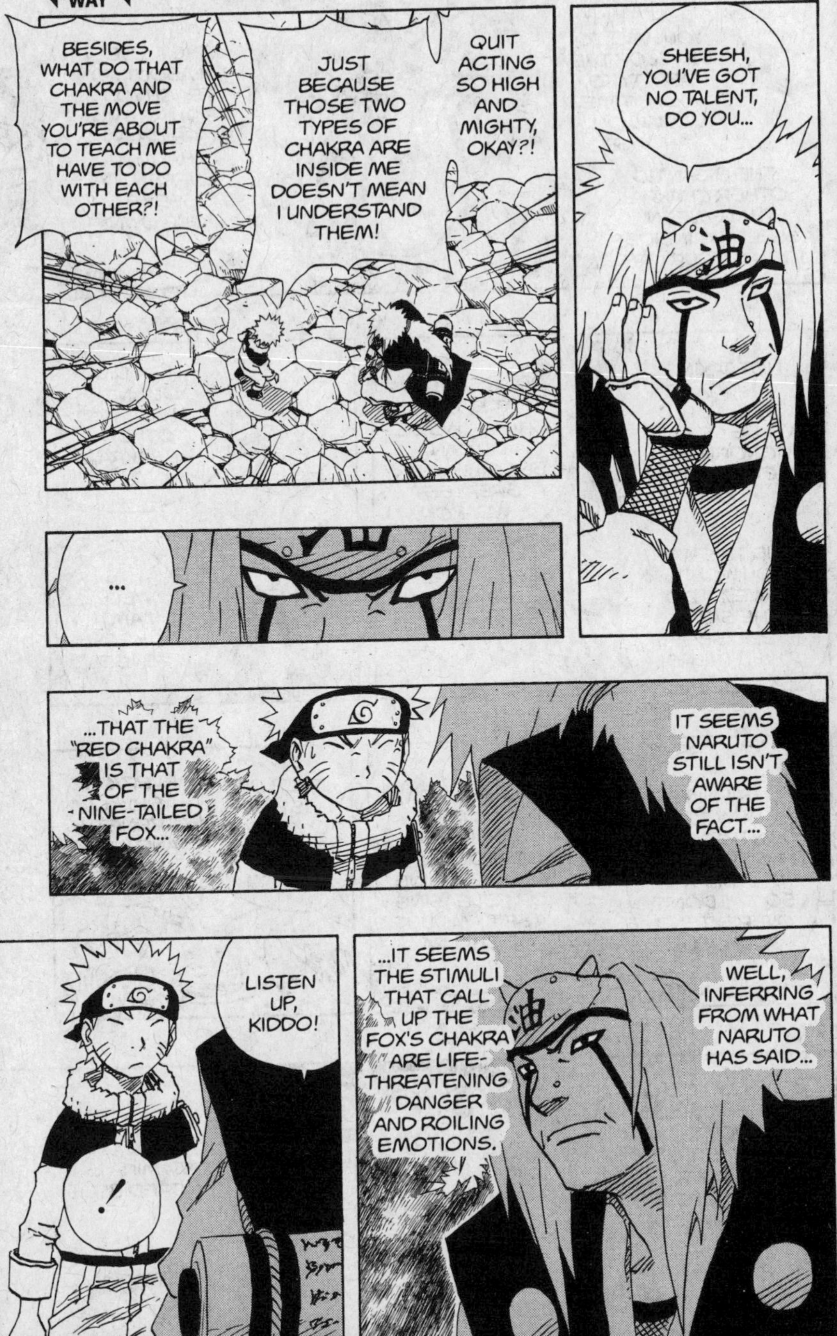

READ THIS WAY
SHEESH, YOU'VE GOT NO TALENT, DO YOU...
QUIT ACTING SO HIGH AND MIGHTY, OKAY?!
JUST BECAUSE THOSE TWO TYPES OF CHAKRA ARE INSIDE ME DOESN'T MEAN I UNDERSTAND THEM!
BESIDES, WHAT DO THAT CHAKRA AND THE MOVE YOU'RE ABOUT TO TEACH ME HAVE TO DO WITH EACH OTHER?!
...
IT SEEMS NARUTO STILL ISN'T AWARE OF THE FACT...
...THAT THE "RED CHAKRA" IS THAT OF THE NINE-TAILED FOX...
WELL, INFERRING FROM WHAT NARUTO HAS SAID...
...IT SEEMS THE STIMULI THAT CALL UP THE FOX'S CHAKRA ARE LIFE-THREATENING DANGER AND ROILING EMOTIONS.
LISTEN UP, KIDDO!
!

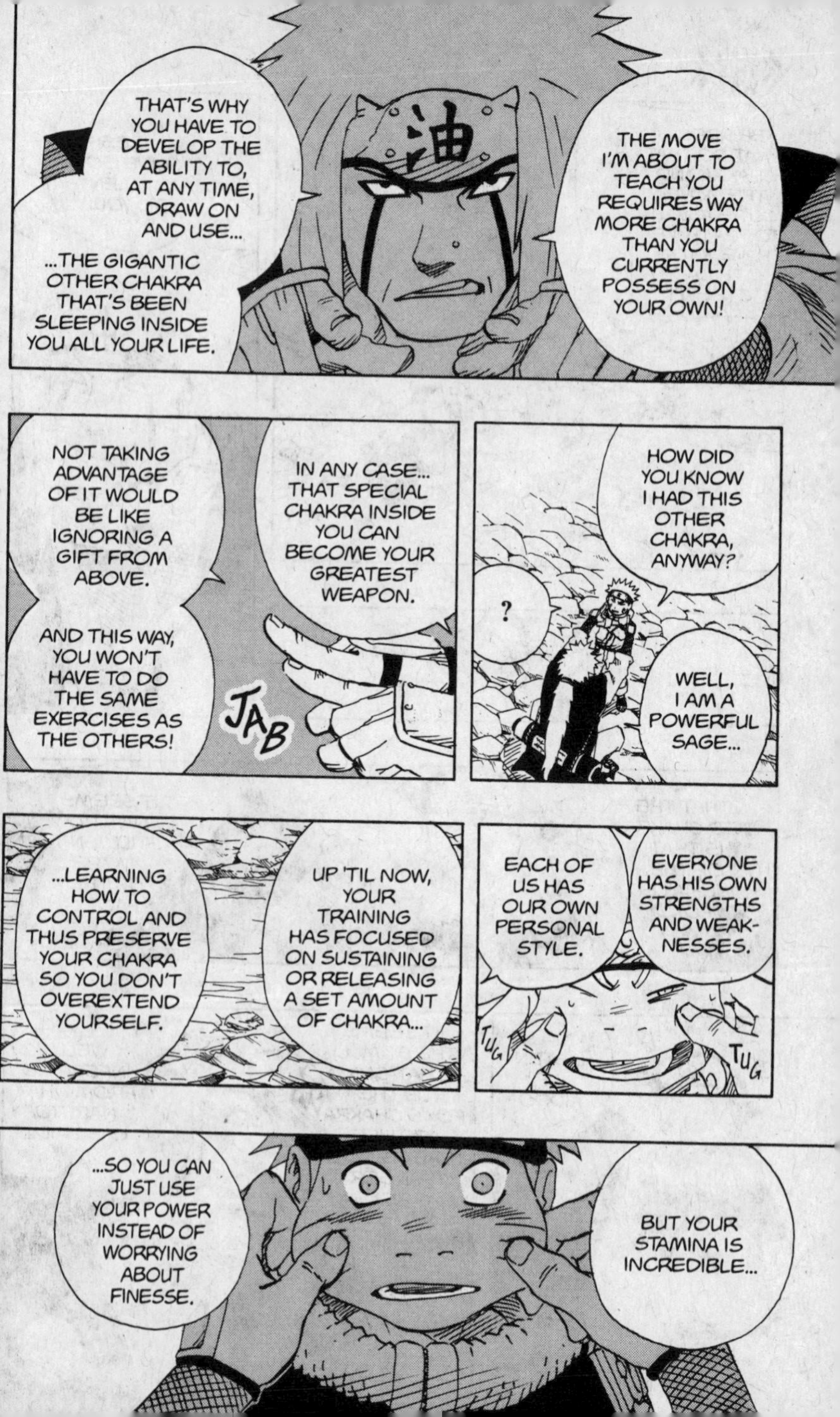
THE MOVE I'M ABOUT TO TEACH YOU REQUIRES WAY MORE CHAKRA THAN YOU CURRENTLY POSSESS ON YOUR OWN!
THAT'S WHY YOU HAVE TO DEVELOP THE ABILITY TO, AT ANY TIME, DRAW ON AND USE...
...THE GIGANTIC OTHER CHAKRA THAT'S BEEN SLEEPING INSIDE YOU ALL YOUR LIFE.
HOW DID YOU KNOW I HAD THIS OTHER CHAKRA, ANYWAY?
?
WELL, I AM A POWERFUL SAGE...
IN ANY CASE... THAT SPECIAL CHAKRA INSIDE YOU CAN BECOME YOUR GREATEST WEAPON.
NOT TAKING ADVANTAGE OF IT WOULD BE LIKE IGNORING A GIFT FROM ABOVE.
AND THIS WAY, YOU WON'T HAVE TO DO THE SAME EXERCISES AS THE OTHERS!
JAB
EVERYONE HAS HIS OWN STRENGTHS AND WEAK-NESSES.
EACH OF US HAS OUR OWN PERSONAL STYLE.
TUG
TUG
UP 'TIL NOW, YOUR TRAINING HAS FOCUSED ON SUSTAINING OR RELEASING A SET AMOUNT OF CHAKRA...
...LEARNING HOW TO CONTROL AND THUS PRESERVE YOUR CHAKRA SO YOU DON'T OVEREXTEND YOURSELF.
BUT YOUR STAMINA IS INCREDIBLE...
...SO YOU CAN JUST USE YOUR POWER INSTEAD OF WORRYING ABOUT FINESSE.

READ THIS WAY

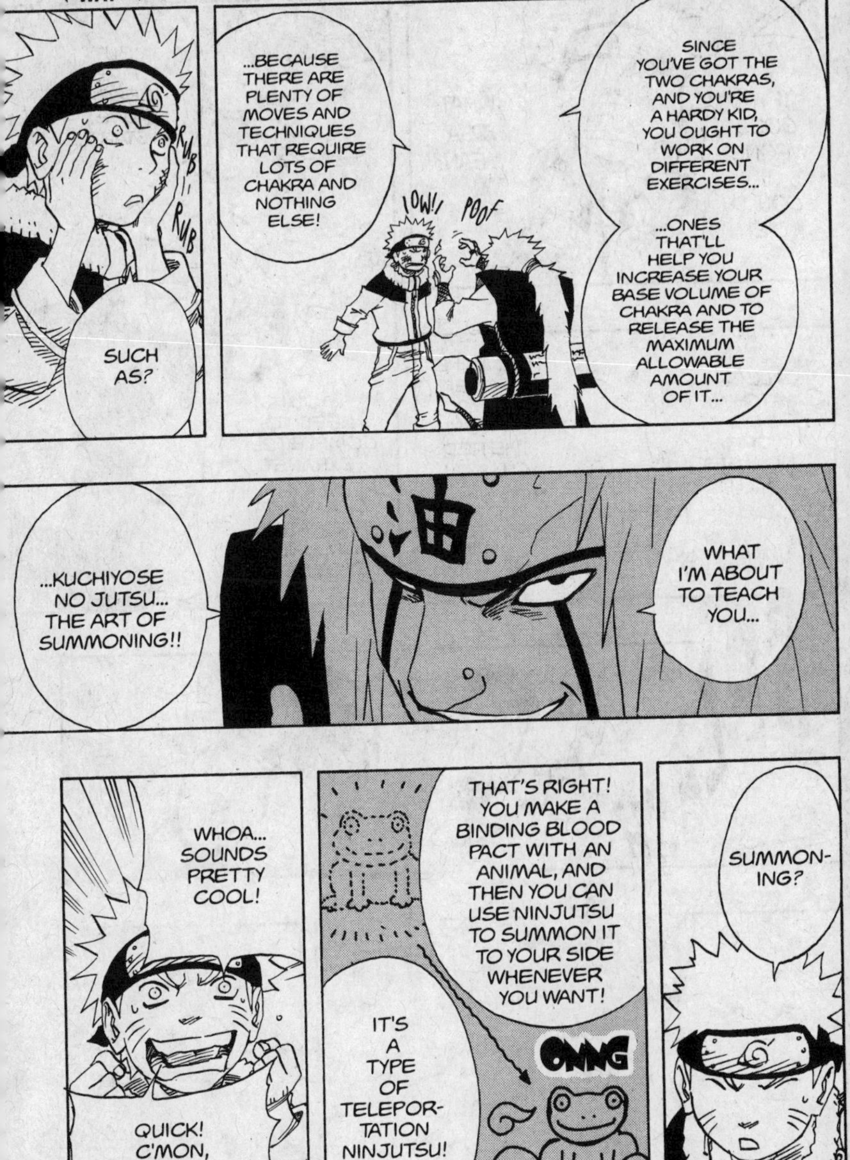
SINCE YOU'VE GOT THE TWO CHAKRAS, AND YOU'RE A HARDY KID, YOU OUGHT TO WORK ON DIFFERENT EXERCISES...
...ONES THAT'LL HELP YOU INCREASE YOUR BASE VOLUME OF CHAKRA AND TO RELEASE THE MAXIMUM ALLOWABLE AMOUNT OF IT...
POOF
OW!!
...BECAUSE THERE ARE PLENTY OF MOVES AND TECHNIQUES THAT REQUIRE LOTS OF CHAKRA AND NOTHING ELSE!
RUB
RUB
SUCH AS?
WHAT I'M ABOUT TO TEACH YOU...
...KUCHIYOSE NO JUTSU... THE ART OF SUMMONING!!
SUMMON-ING?
THAT'S RIGHT! YOU MAKE A BINDING BLOOD PACT WITH AN ANIMAL, AND THEN YOU CAN USE NINJUTSU TO SUMMON IT TO YOUR SIDE WHENEVER YOU WANT!
ONNG
IT'S A TYPE OF TELEPOR-TATION NINJUTSU!
WHOA... SOUNDS PRETTY COOL!
QUICK! C'MON, TEACH IT TO ME!

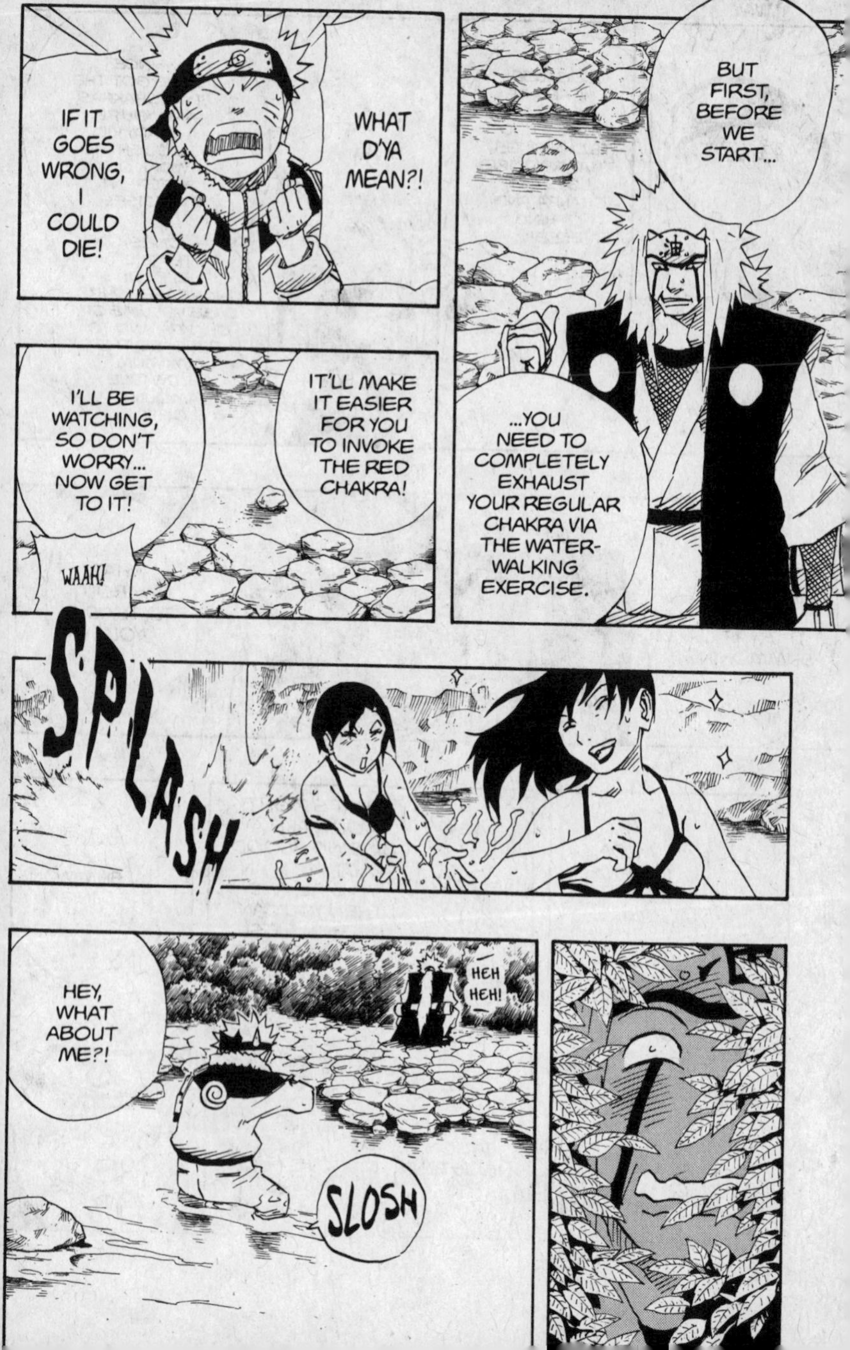
BUT FIRST, BEFORE WE START...
...YOU NEED TO COMPLETELY EXHAUST YOUR REGULAR CHAKRA VIA THE WATER-WALKING EXERCISE.
WHAT D'YA MEAN?!
IF IT GOES WRONG, I COULD DIE!
IT'LL MAKE IT EASIER FOR YOU TO INVOKE THE RED CHAKRA!
I'LL BE WATCHING, SO DON'T WORRY... NOW GET TO IT!
WAAH!
SPLASH
HEH HEH!
HEY, WHAT ABOUT ME?!
SLOSH

READ THIS WAY

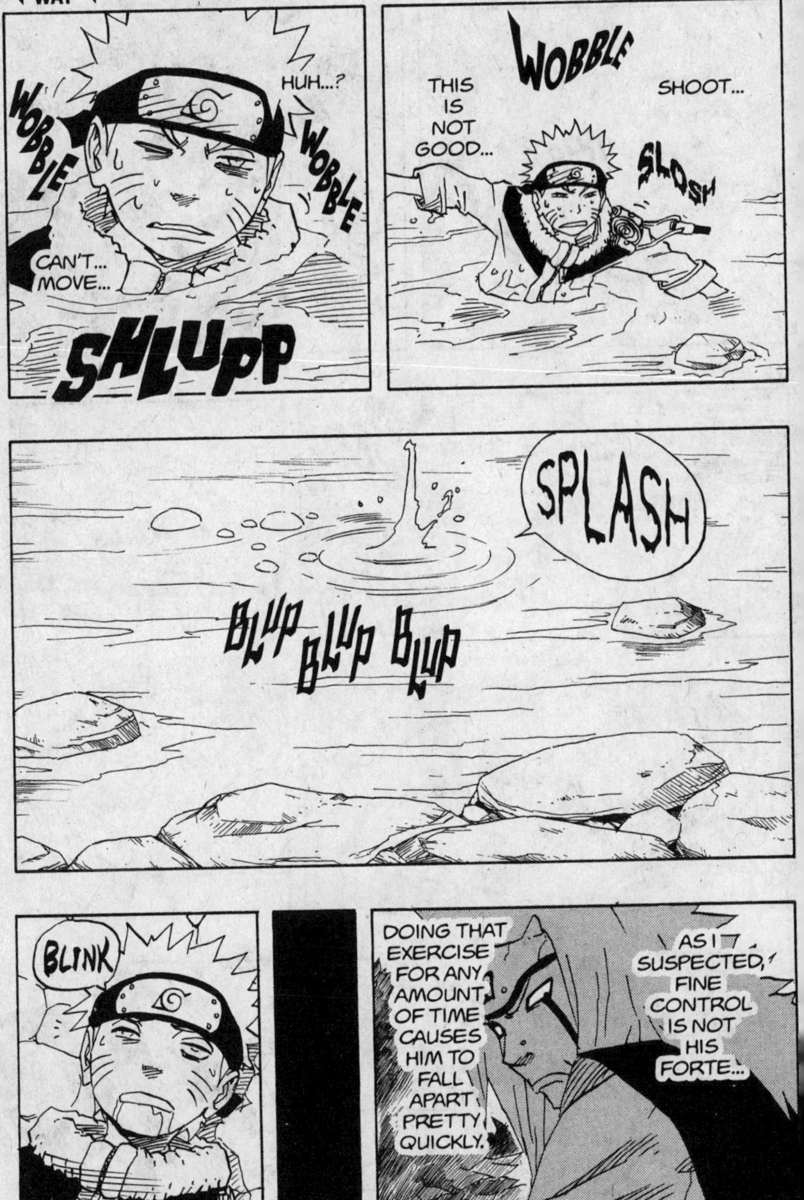
WOBBLE
SHOOT...
THIS IS NOT GOOD...
SLOSH
HUH...?
WOBBLE
WOBBLE
CAN'T... MOVE...
SHLUPP
SPLASH
BLUP BLUP BLUP
AS I SUSPECTED, FINE CONTROL IS NOT HIS FORTE...
DOING THAT EXERCISE FOR ANY AMOUNT OF TIME CAUSES HIM TO FALL APART PRETTY QUICKLY.
BLINK

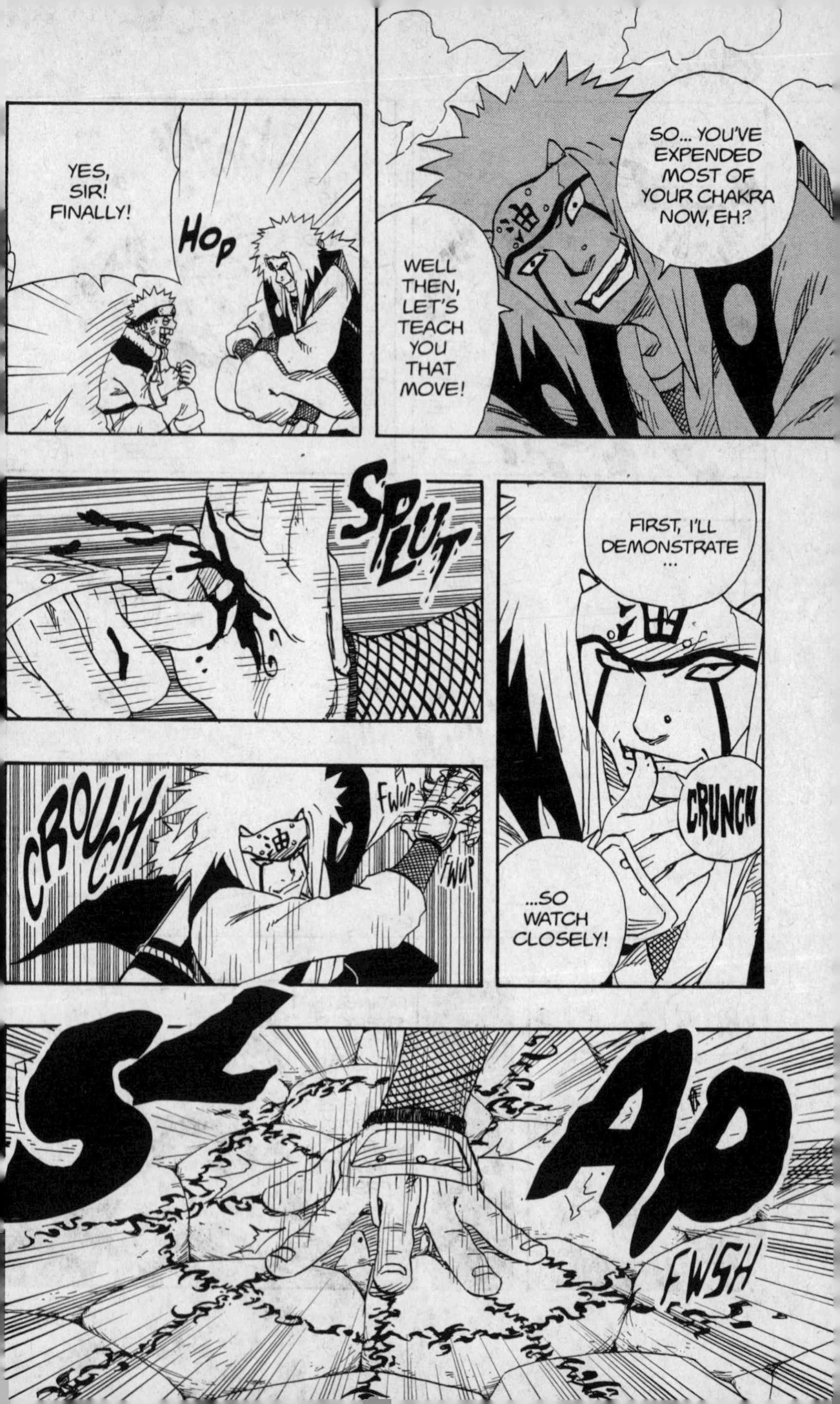
SO... YOU'VE EXPENDED MOST OF YOUR CHAKRA NOW, EH?
WELL THEN, LET'S TEACH YOU THAT MOVE!
YES, SIR! FINALLY!
HOP
FIRST, I'LL DEMONSTRATE ...
CRUNCH
...SO WATCH CLOSELY!
SPLUT
FWUP
FWUP
CROUCH
SLAP
FWSH

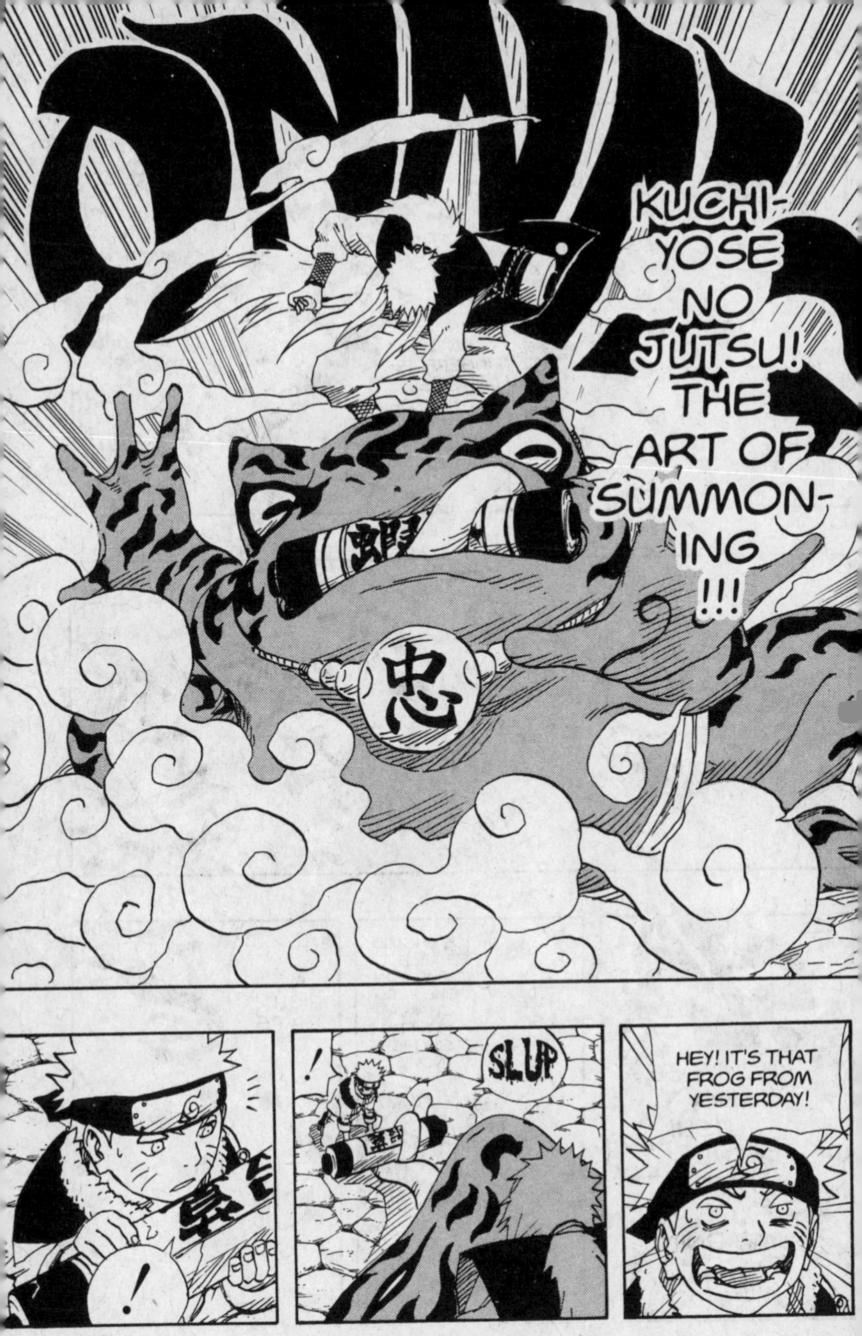

KUCHI-YOSE NO JUTSU! THE ART OF SUMMON-ING!!!
忠
HEY! IT'S THAT FROG FROM YESTERDAY!
SLUP
!
!

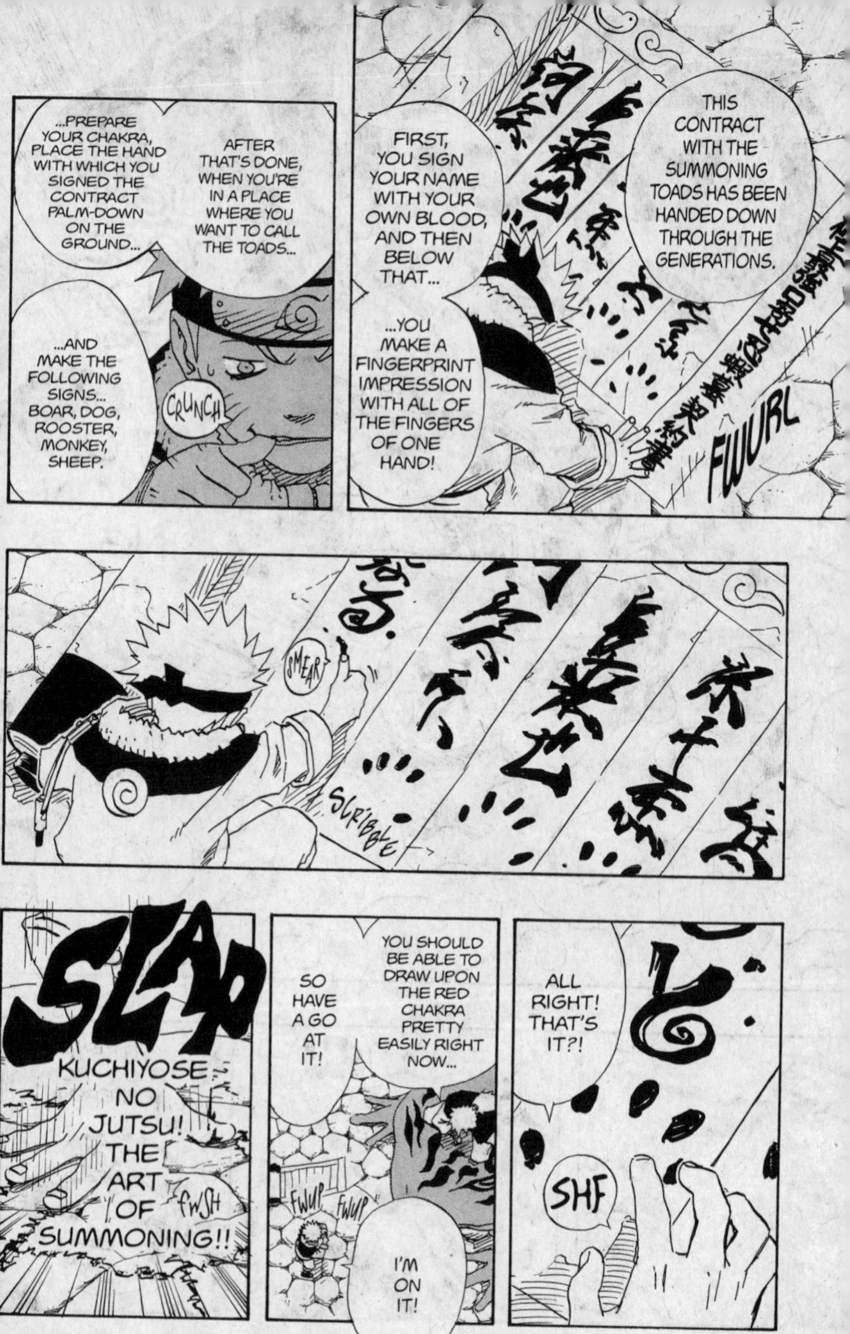
THIS CONTRACT WITH THE SUMMONING TOADS HAS BEEN HANDED DOWN THROUGH THE GENERATIONS.
FIRST, YOU SIGN YOUR NAME WITH YOUR OWN BLOOD, AND THEN BELOW THAT...
...YOU MAKE A FINGERPRINT IMPRESSION WITH ALL OF THE FINGERS OF ONE HAND!
FWUURL
AFTER THAT'S DONE, WHEN YOU'RE IN A PLACE WHERE YOU WANT TO CALL THE TOADS...
...PREPARE YOUR CHAKRA, PLACE THE HAND WITH WHICH YOU SIGNED THE CONTRACT PALM-DOWN ON THE GROUND...
CRUNCH
...AND MAKE THE FOLLOWING SIGNS... BOAR, DOG, ROOSTER, MONKEY, SHEEP.
SMEAR
SCRIBBLE
ALL RIGHT! THAT'S IT?!
SHF
YOU SHOULD BE ABLE TO DRAW UPON THE RED CHAKRA PRETTY EASILY RIGHT NOW...
SO HAVE A GO AT IT!
FWUP
FWUP
I'M ON IT!
SLAP
KUCHIYOSE NO JUTSU! THE ART OF SUMMONING!!
FWSH

READ THIS WAY

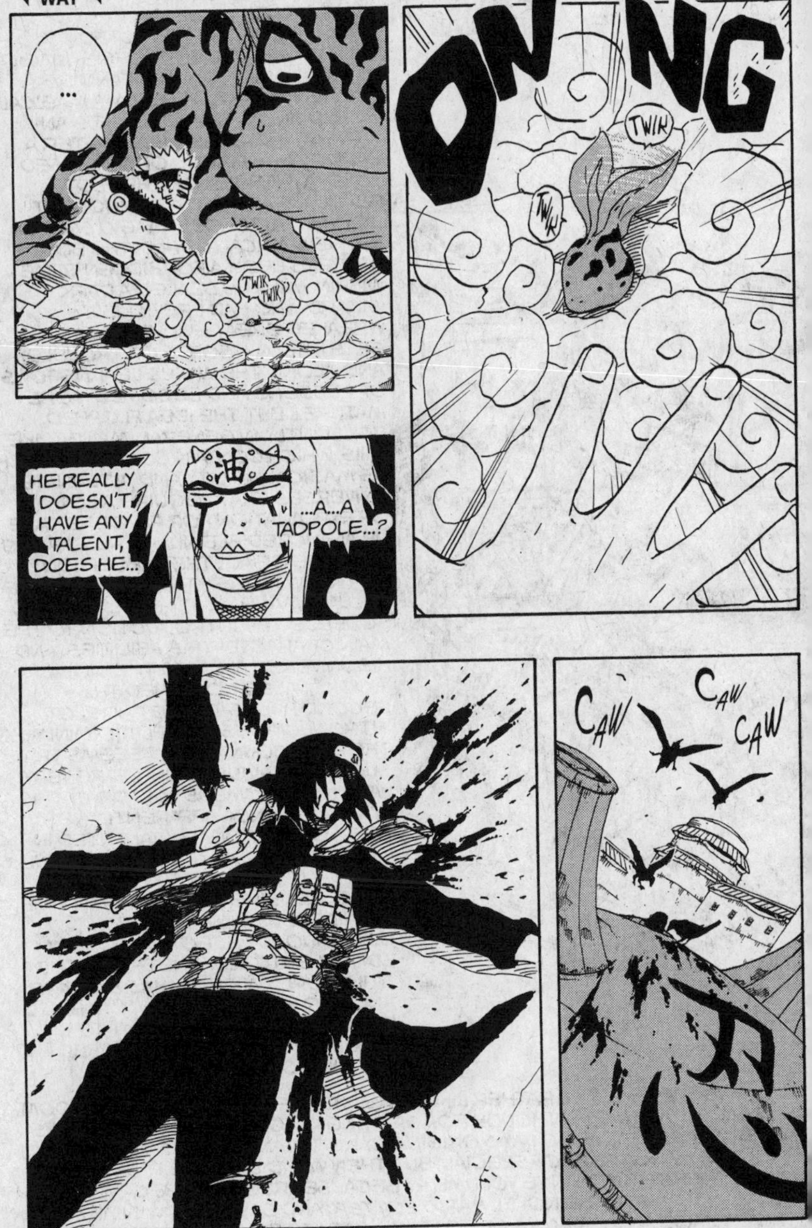

ON NG
TWIK
TWIK
...
TWIK TWIK
...A...A TADPOLE...?
HE REALLY DOESN'T HAVE ANY TALENT, DOES HE...
CAW
CAW
CAW

KISHIMOTO MASASHI'S MANGA REJECT SPECIAL NO. 4!

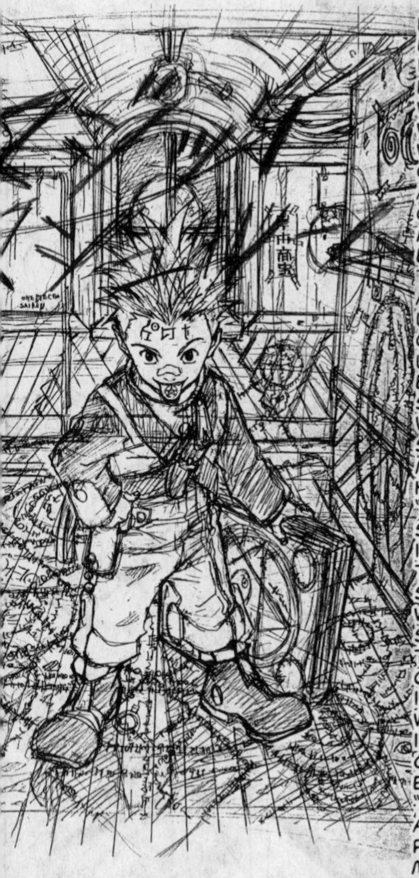

I'M GOING TO DO A MANGA REJECT SPECIAL FOR THE FIRST TIME IN A LONG WHILE!
THE TITLE OF THE REJECTED MANGA PANEL TO THE LEFT IS "MAGIC MUSHROOM," AND IT'S A FANTASY-ADVENTURE MANGA SET IN A MAGICAL WORLD (IN OTHER WORDS, IT'S AN OTAKU MANGA). I NAMED IT AFTER A BAND THAT A FRIEND OF MINE USED TO BE A MEMBER OF. THE PLOT REVOLVES AROUND A DELINQUENT BOY WHO ATTENDS A MAGIC SCHOOL IN THIS MAGICAL WORLD. THE BOY HAPPENS UPON A FORBIDDEN TOME WITHIN WHICH IS SEALED A DARK WIZARD WHO HAD PREVIOUSLY WREAKED GREAT EVIL. THE BOY GETS INTO ALL SORTS OF TROUBLE, AND ALONG THE WAY HE LEARNS TONS OF LESSONS AND BECOMES MORE MATURE... BUT THE IDEA FLOPPED BRILLIANTLY. IN GENERAL, MANGA LIKE THIS, WHICH CONTAIN CONCEPTS SUCH AS MAGICAL ABILITY AND ALTERNATE UNIVERSES THAT REQUIRE A LOT OF EXPLANATION FOR READERS, TAKE UP AN INCREDIBLE NUMBER OF PAGES BECAUSE OF ALL THE EXPOSITION. SO I KNEW IT WASN'T IDEAL FOR A ONE-VOLUME MANGA, BUT I STILL TRIED TO SQUEEZE THE INTRODUCTION TO THE MAIN CHARACTER, HIS ABILITIES, AND HIS UNIVERSE ALL INTO THE INITIAL "HOOK." I ALSO COMBINED THE SECOND HALF'S THEME AND PLOT INTRODUCTIONS AS WELL TO MINIMIZE THE PAGE COUNT, BUT IT SEEMS THAT SUCH MANGA JUST DON'T FARE VERY WELL... NEWCOMERS WHO DRAW THIS SORT OF MANGA APPARENTLY NEED TO BE EXCEPTIONALLY TALENTED IN ORDER TO PULL IT OFF SUCCESSFULLY. I ACTUALLY PERSISTED FOR QUITE A WHILE, REVISING AND RESUBMITTING IT NUMEROUS TIMES DESPITE CONTINUOUS REJECTION FROM MY EDITOR. BUT THEN ONE DAY HE SAID, "THIS WORLD ALREADY HAS *BASTARD* AND *BERSERK*, YOU KNOW?!" "OH, ALL RIGHT! I GIVE UP!" I THOUGHT TO MYSELF, AND PROMPTLY STOPPED WORKING ON IT.

HOWEVER, WELL, I STILL RATHER LIKED THE IDEA OF THIS "MAGIC MUSHROOM," SO I ENTERTAINED THE THOUGHT OF DRAWING IT AGAIN SOME DAY, PERHAPS AFTER *NARUTO* ENDS, SO I WAS ORIGINALLY NOT PLANNING TO SUBMIT IT TO THE MANGA REJECT SPECIAL. BUT THEN WHY DID I BRING IT UP NOW, FOR THE FIRST TIME SINCE VOLUME 4? BECAUSE I RECENTLY BECAME ACQUAINTED WITH THE NOVEL *HARRY POTTER*, AND SEEING HOW SIMILAR THE PREMISE AND STORY WERE TO IT, I'M LOATH TO BE CALLED A COPYCAT. SO I LOST INTEREST IN DRAWING IT, AND DECIDED TO SHOWCASE IT HERE.

Number 93: Impassioned Efforts... Each and Every One!!

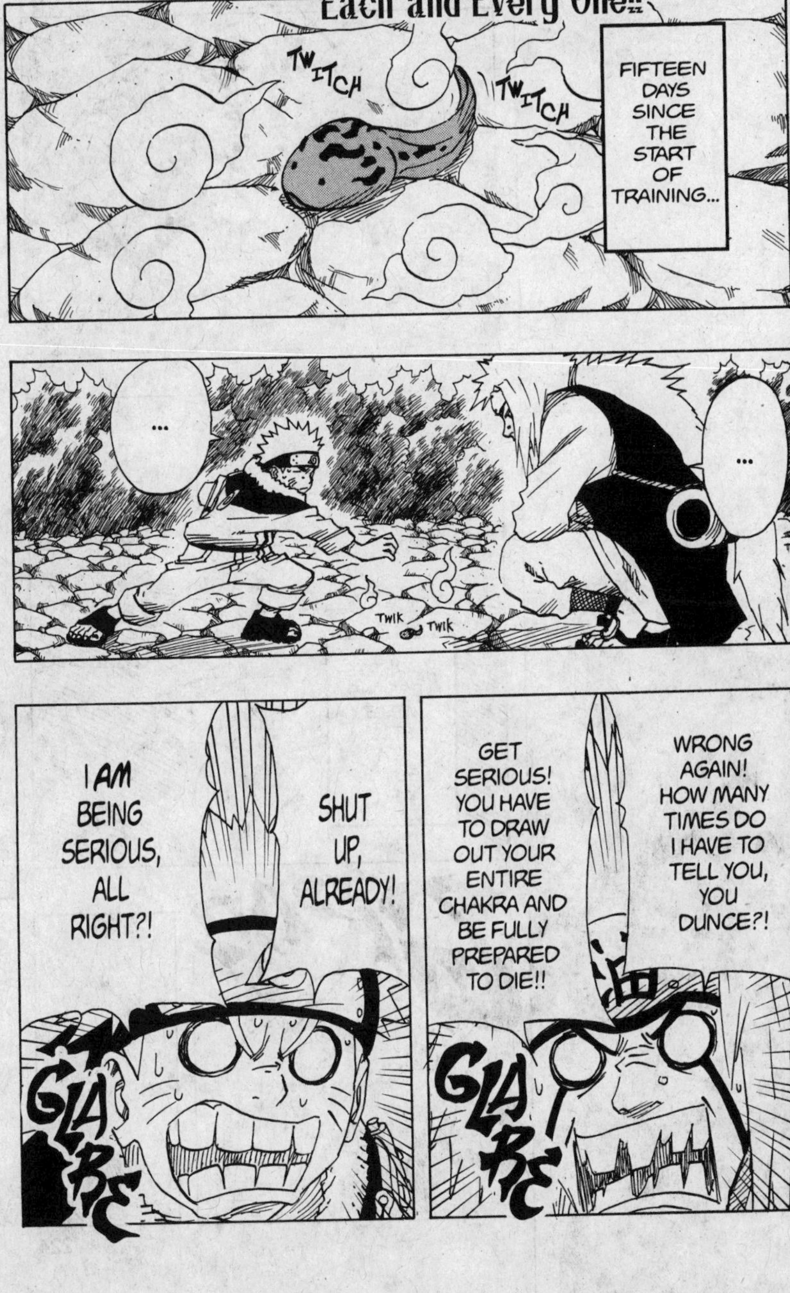
FIFTEEN DAYS SINCE THE START OF TRAINING...
TWITCH
TWITCH
...
...
TWIK TWIK
WRONG AGAIN! HOW MANY TIMES DO I HAVE TO TELL YOU, YOU DUNCE?!
GET SERIOUS! YOU HAVE TO DRAW OUT YOUR ENTIRE CHAKRA AND BE FULLY PREPARED TO DIE!!
GLARE
SHUT UP, ALREADY!
I AM BEING SERIOUS, ALL RIGHT?!
GLARE

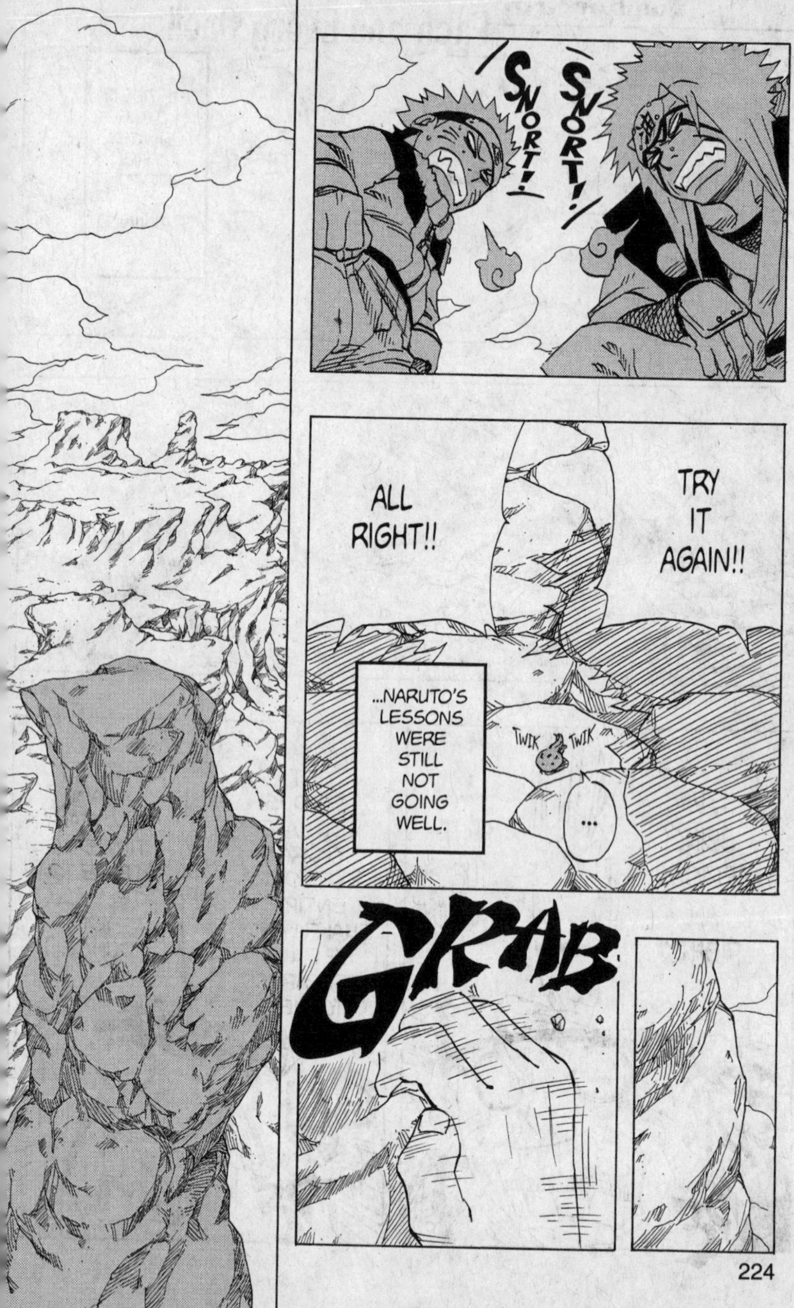
SNORT!!
SNORT!!
TRY IT AGAIN!!
ALL RIGHT!!
...NARUTO'S LESSONS WERE STILL NOT GOING WELL.
TWIK TWIK
...
GRAB

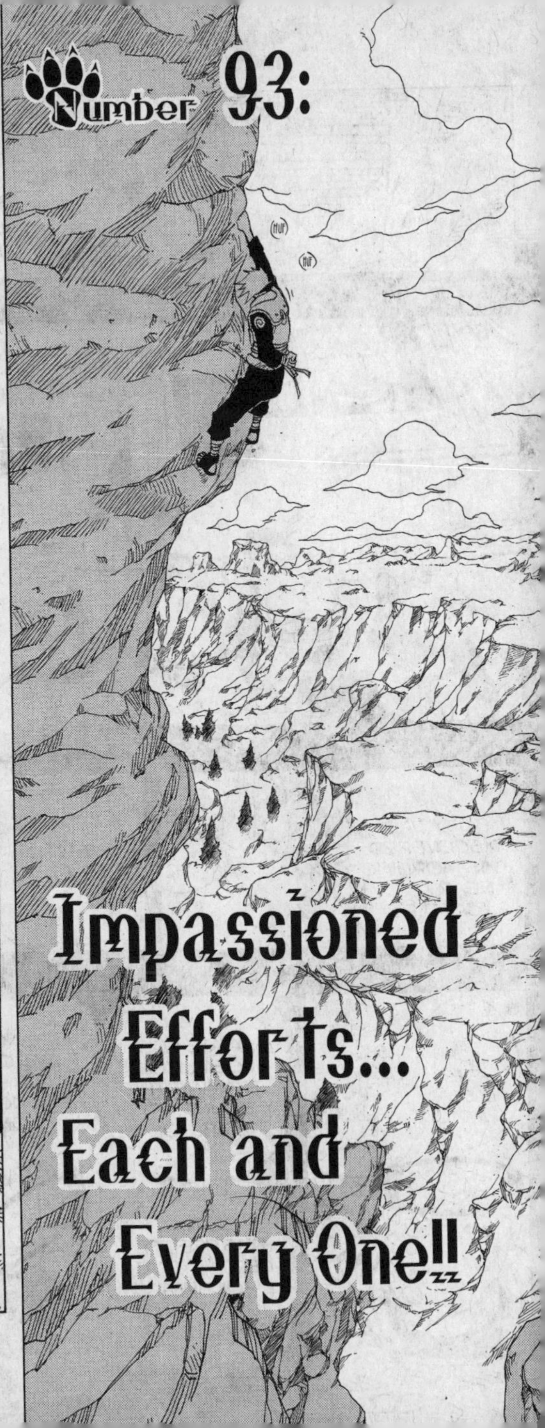
Number 93:
HUF
HUF
Impassioned Efforts... Each and Every One!!

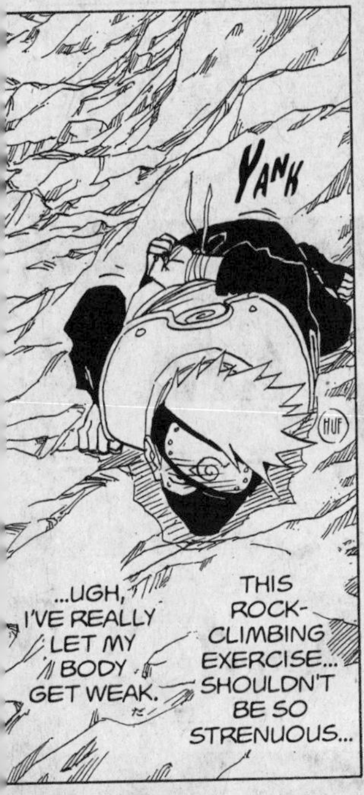
YANK
HUF
THIS ROCK-CLIMBING EXERCISE... SHOULDN'T BE SO STRENUOUS...
...UGH, I'VE REALLY LET MY BODY GET WEAK.

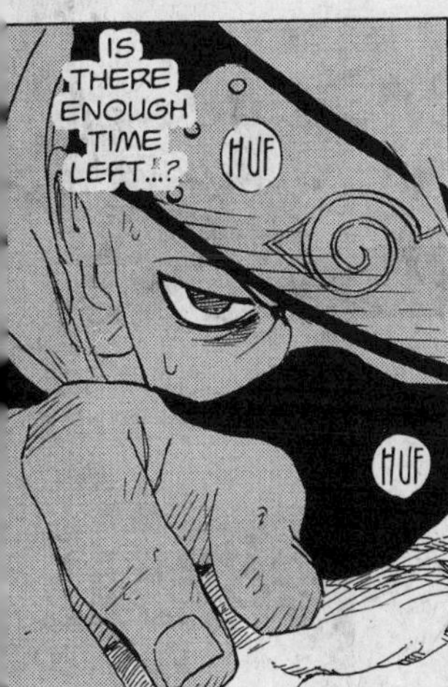
HUF
IS THERE ENOUGH TIME LEFT...?
HUF

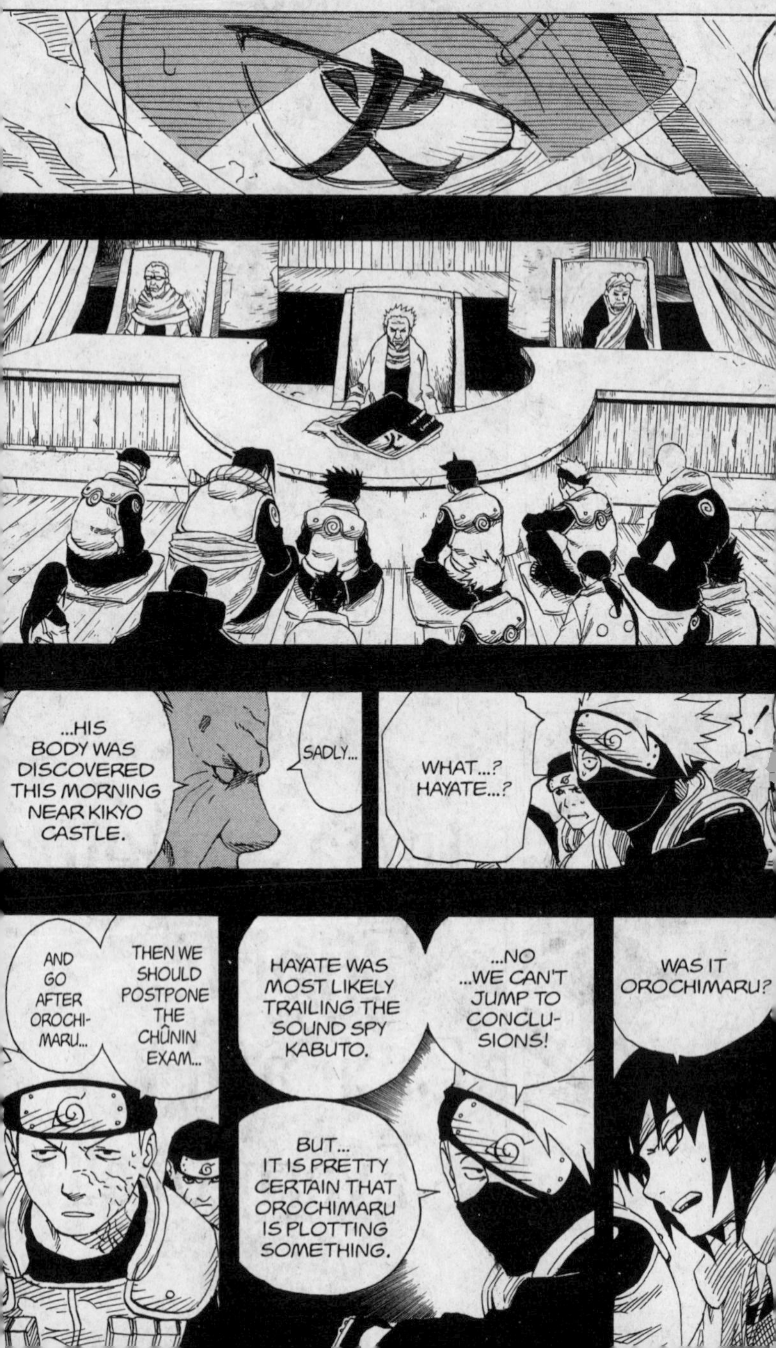
WHAT...? HAYATE...?
SADLY...
...HIS BODY WAS DISCOVERED THIS MORNING NEAR KIKYO CASTLE.
WAS IT OROCHIMARU?
...NO ...WE CAN'T JUMP TO CONCLUSIONS!
HAYATE WAS MOST LIKELY TRAILING THE SOUND SPY KABUTO.
BUT... IT IS PRETTY CERTAIN THAT OROCHIMARU IS PLOTTING SOMETHING.
THEN WE SHOULD POSTPONE THE CHÛNIN EXAM...
AND GO AFTER OROCHIMARU...

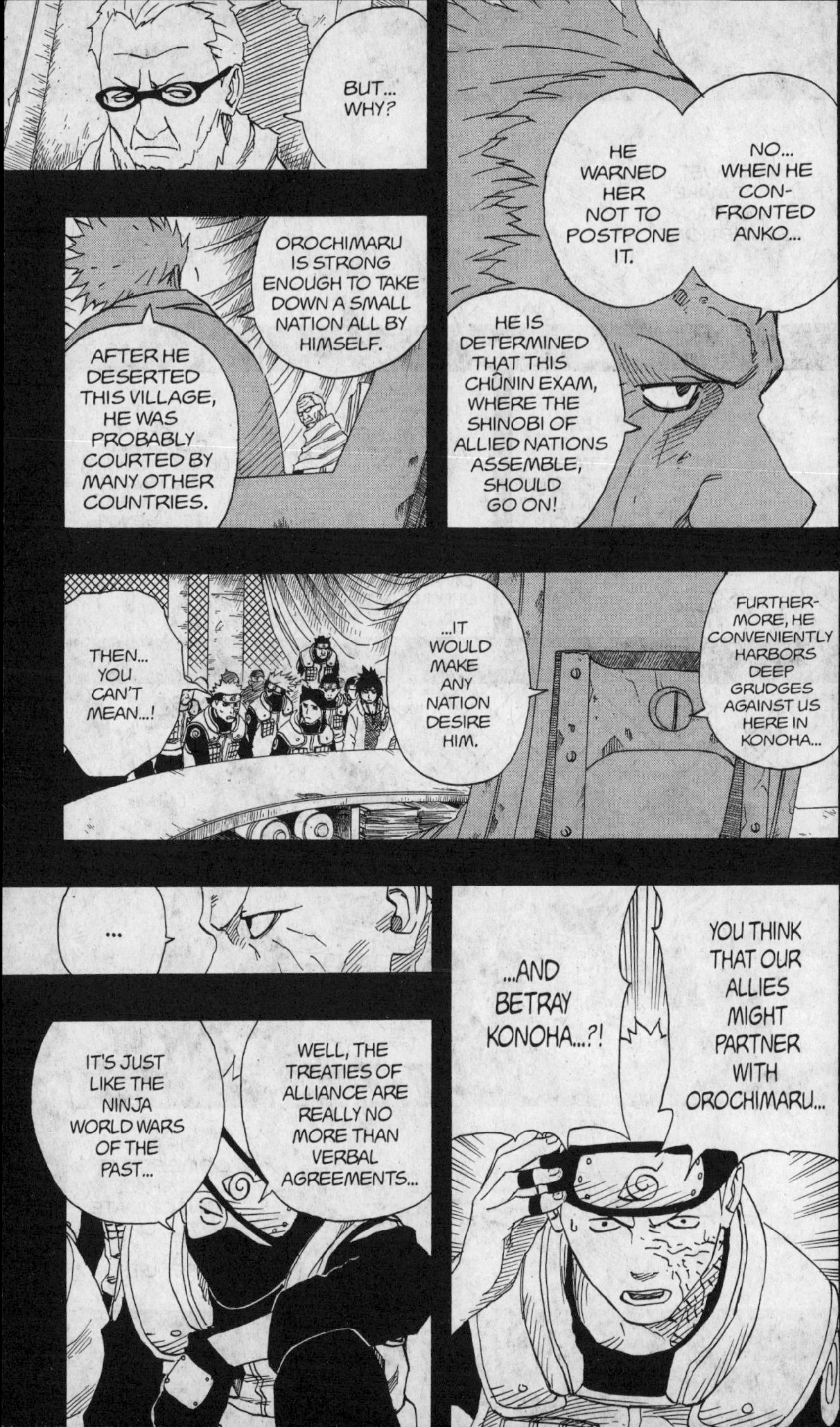
NO... WHEN HE CONFRONTED ANKO...
HE WARNED HER NOT TO POSTPONE IT.
HE IS DETERMINED THAT THIS CHÛNIN EXAM, WHERE THE SHINOBI OF ALLIED NATIONS ASSEMBLE, SHOULD GO ON!
BUT... WHY?
OROCHIMARU IS STRONG ENOUGH TO TAKE DOWN A SMALL NATION ALL BY HIMSELF.
AFTER HE DESERTED THIS VILLAGE, HE WAS PROBABLY COURTED BY MANY OTHER COUNTRIES.
FURTHERMORE, HE CONVENIENTLY HARBORS DEEP GRUDGES AGAINST US HERE IN KONOHA...
...IT WOULD MAKE ANY NATION DESIRE HIM.
THEN... YOU CAN'T MEAN...!
YOU THINK THAT OUR ALLIES MIGHT PARTNER WITH OROCHIMARU...
...AND BETRAY KONOHA...?!
...
WELL, THE TREATIES OF ALLIANCE ARE REALLY NO MORE THAN VERBAL AGREEMENTS...
IT'S JUST LIKE THE NINJA WORLD WARS OF THE PAST...

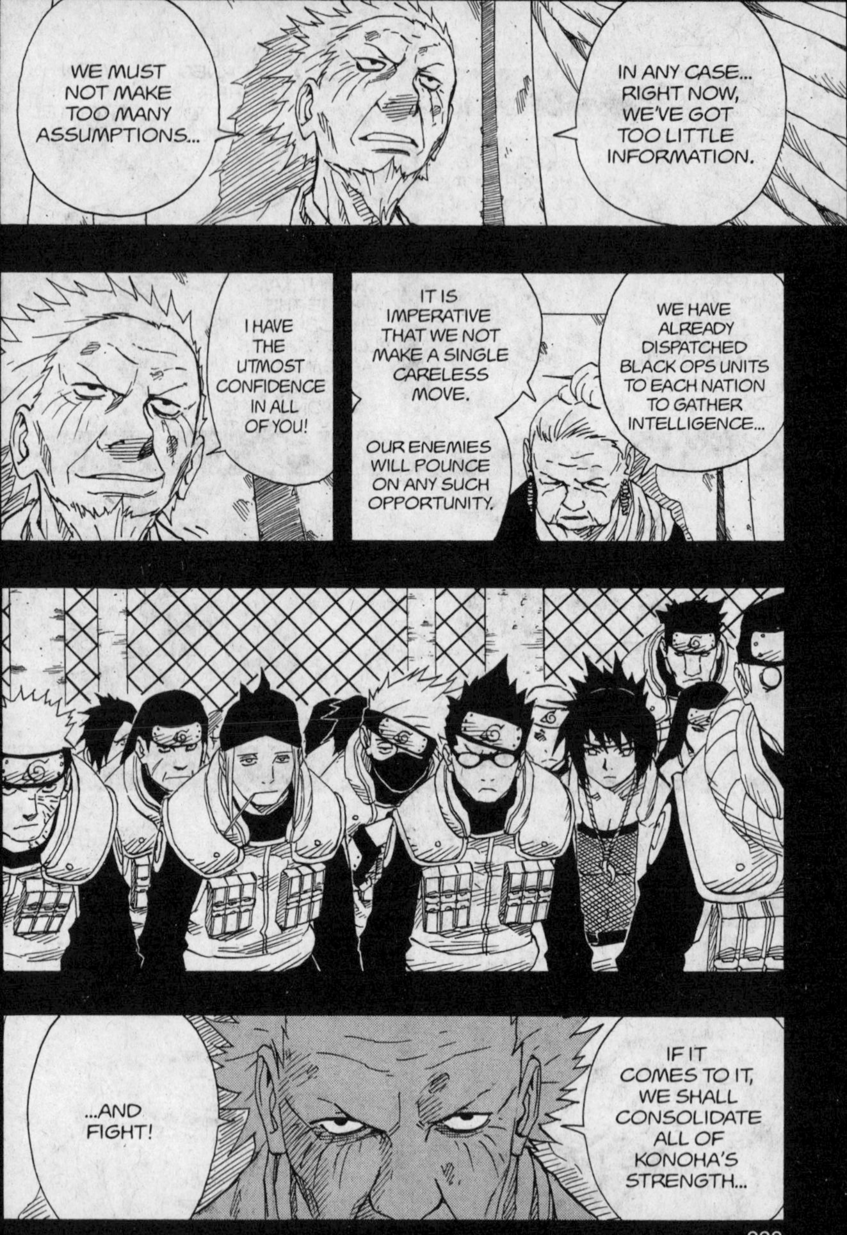
IN ANY CASE... RIGHT NOW, WE'VE GOT TOO LITTLE INFORMATION.
WE MUST NOT MAKE TOO MANY ASSUMPTIONS...
WE HAVE ALREADY DISPATCHED BLACK OPS UNITS TO EACH NATION TO GATHER INTELLIGENCE...
IT IS IMPERATIVE THAT WE NOT MAKE A SINGLE CARELESS MOVE.
OUR ENEMIES WILL POUNCE ON ANY SUCH OPPORTUNITY.
I HAVE THE UTMOST CONFIDENCE IN ALL OF YOU!
IF IT COMES TO IT, WE SHALL CONSOLIDATE ALL OF KONOHA'S STRENGTH...
...AND FIGHT!

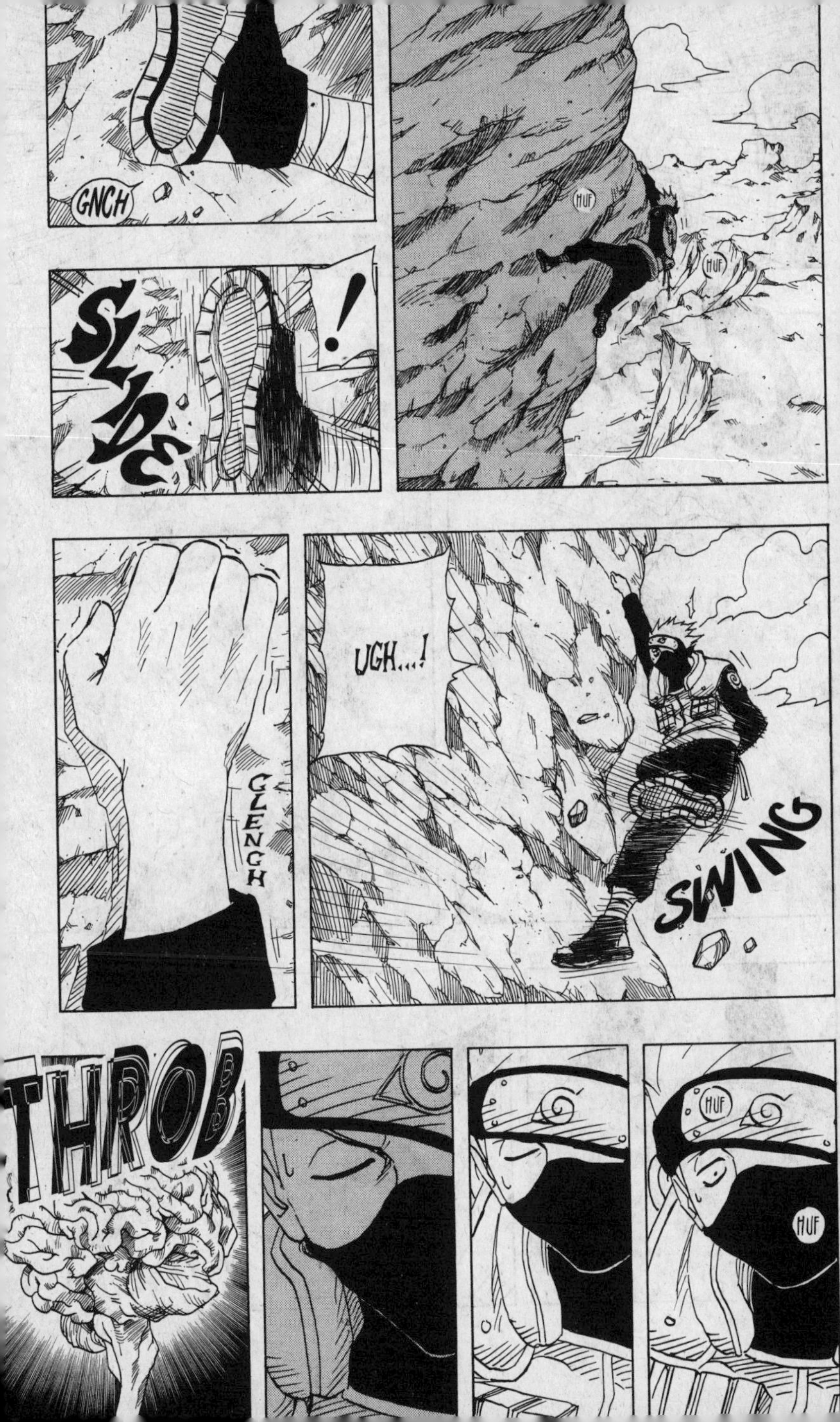
HUF
HUF
GNCH
SLIDE
!
UGH...!
SWING
CLENCH
HUF
HUF
THROB

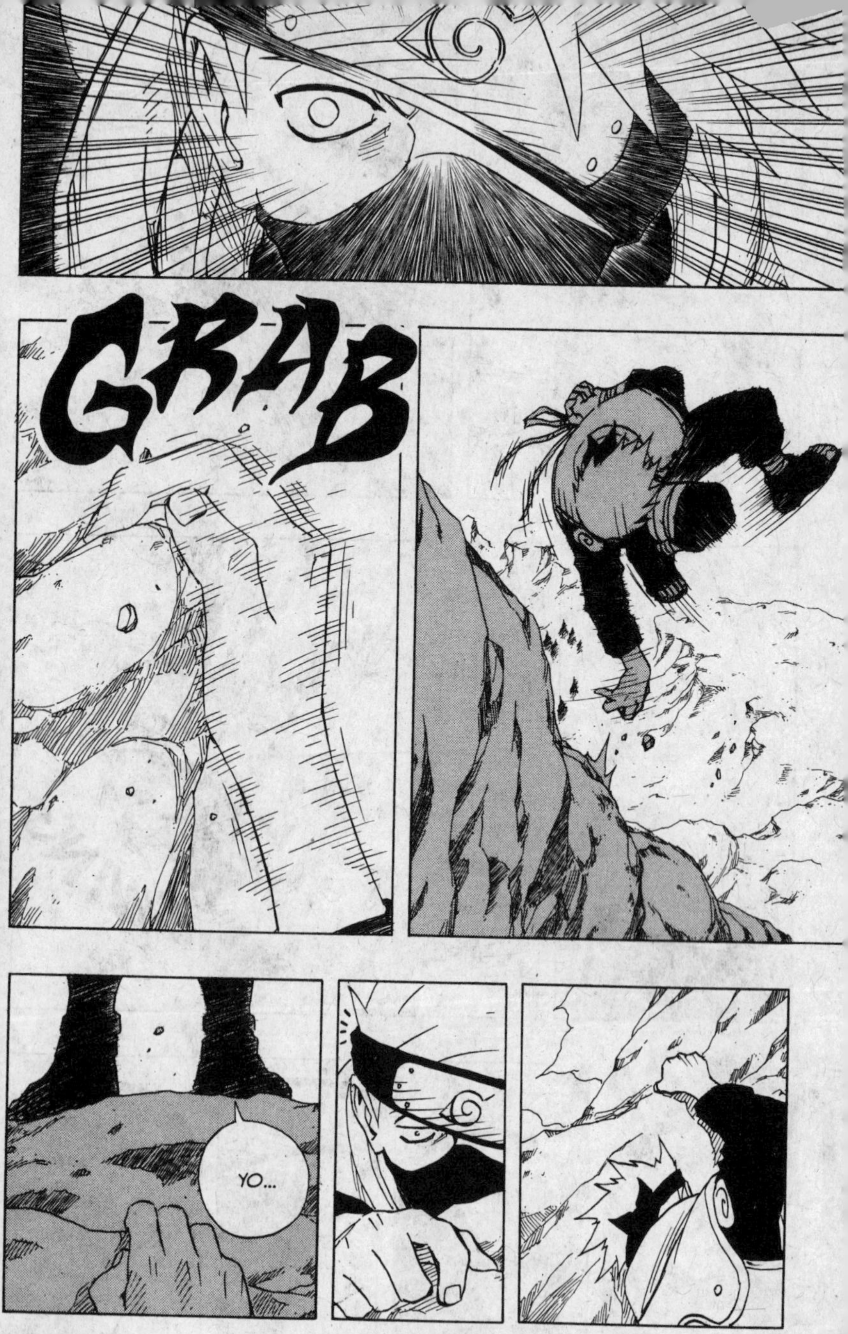
GRAB
YO...

READ THIS WAY

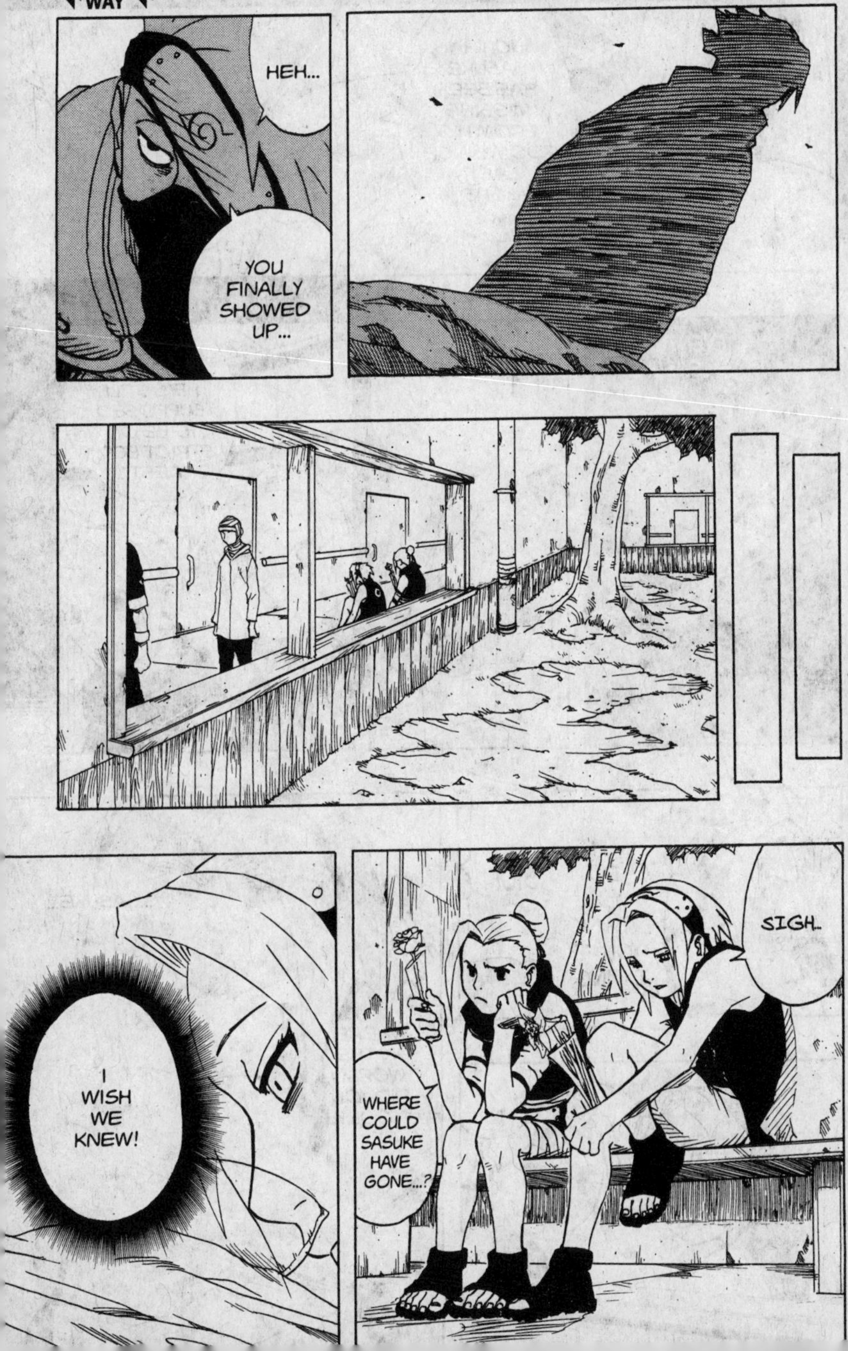
HEH...
YOU FINALLY SHOWED UP...
SIGH..
WHERE COULD SASUKE HAVE GONE...?
I WISH WE KNEW!

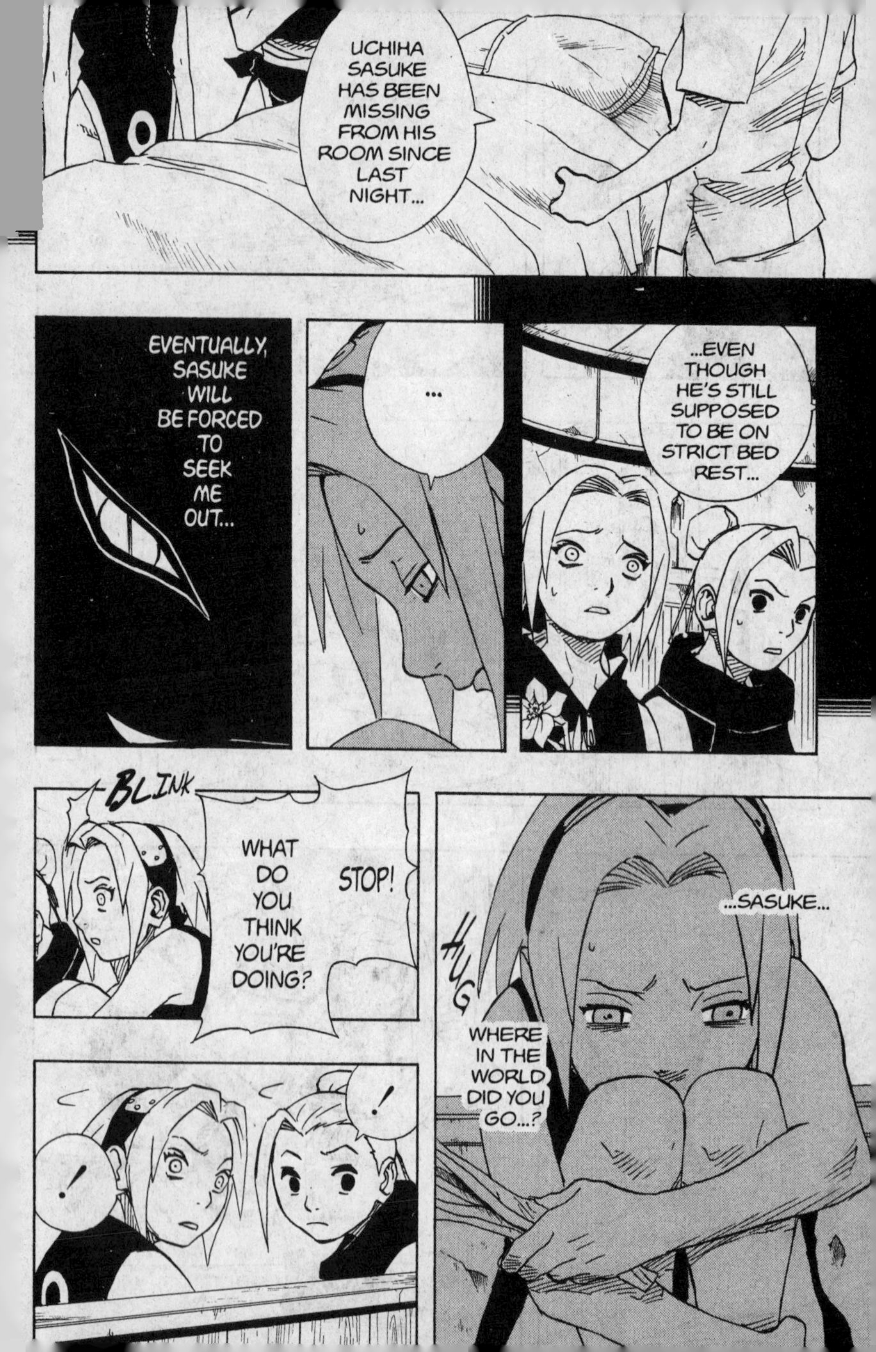
UCHIHA SASUKE HAS BEEN MISSING FROM HIS ROOM SINCE LAST NIGHT...
...EVEN THOUGH HE'S STILL SUPPOSED TO BE ON STRICT BED REST...
...
EVENTUALLY, SASUKE WILL BE FORCED TO SEEK ME OUT...
...SASUKE...
HUG
WHERE IN THE WORLD DID YOU GO...?
BLINK
STOP!
WHAT DO YOU THINK YOU'RE DOING?
!
!

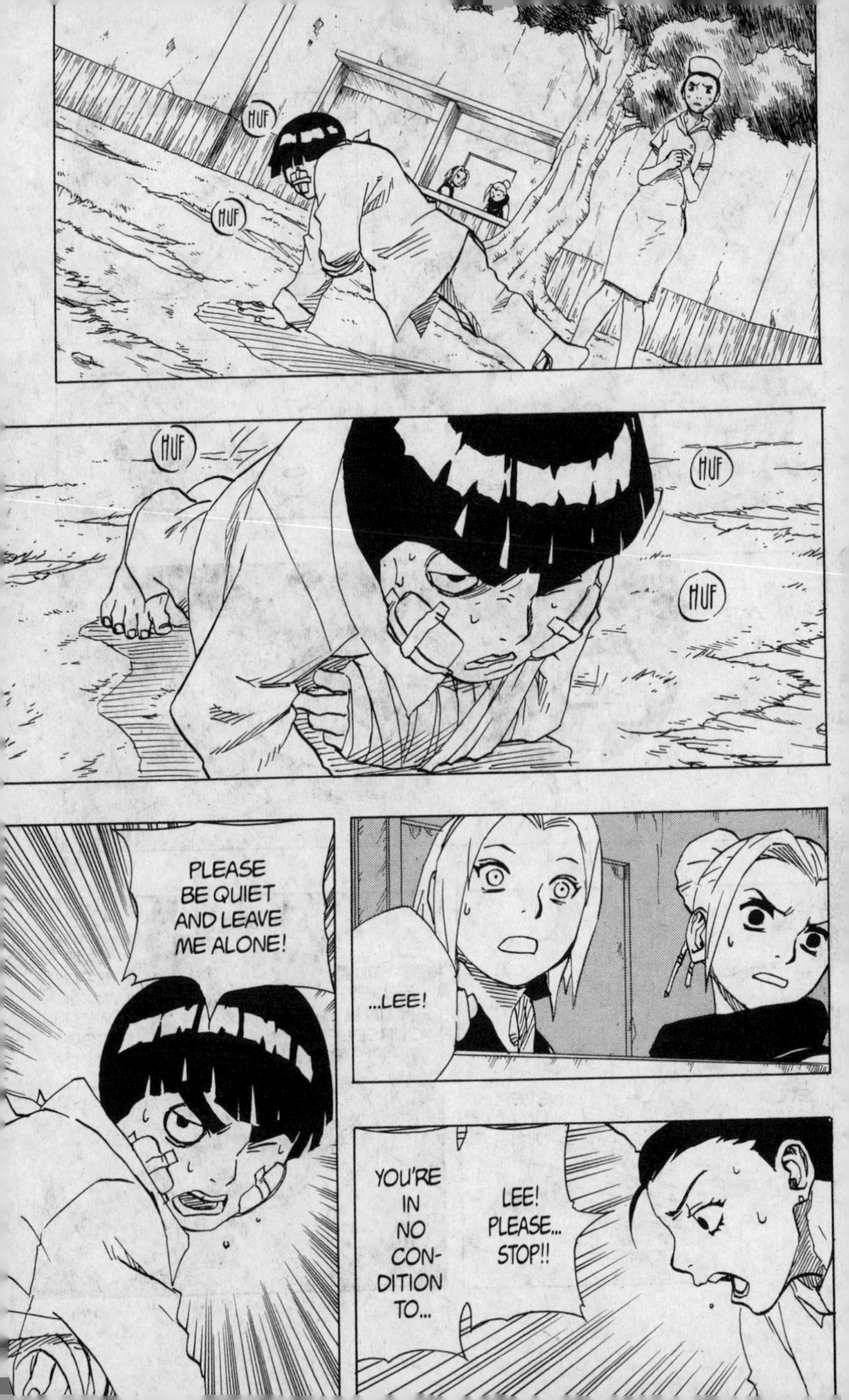
HUF
HUF
HUF
HUF
HUF
...LEE!
LEE! PLEASE... STOP!!
YOU'RE IN NO CON-DITION TO...
PLEASE BE QUIET AND LEAVE ME ALONE!

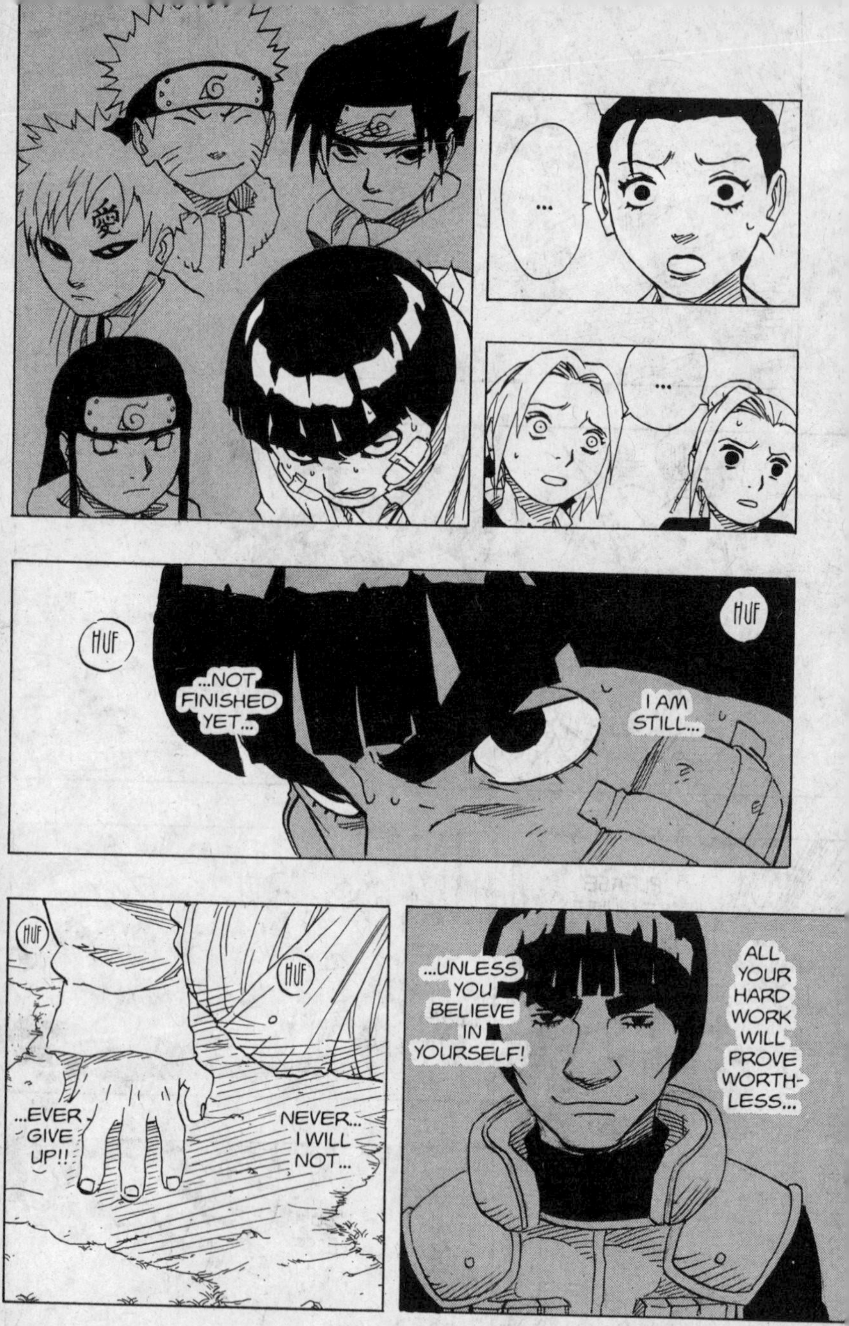
...
...
HUF
I AM STILL...
...NOT FINISHED YET...
HUF
ALL YOUR HARD WORK WILL PROVE WORTH-LESS...
...UNLESS YOU BELIEVE IN YOURSELF!
HUF
HUF
NEVER... I WILL NOT...
...EVER GIVE UP!!

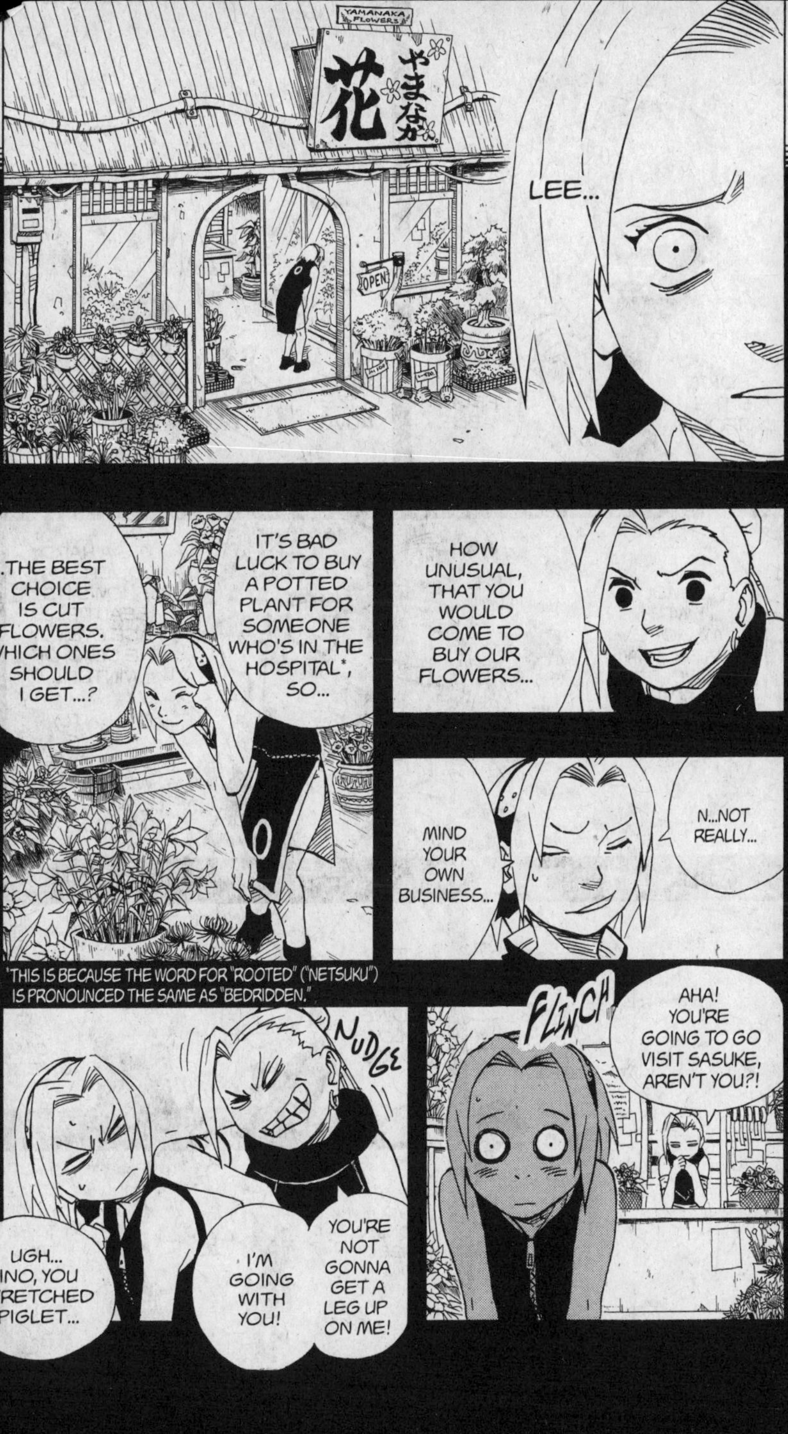
YAMANAKA FLOWERS
花 やまなか
OPEN
LEE...
HOW UNUSUAL, THAT YOU WOULD COME TO BUY OUR FLOWERS...
N...NOT REALLY...
MIND YOUR OWN BUSINESS...
IT'S BAD LUCK TO BUY A POTTED PLANT FOR SOMEONE WHO'S IN THE HOSPITAL*, SO...
...THE BEST CHOICE IS CUT FLOWERS. WHICH ONES SHOULD I GET...?
*THIS IS BECAUSE THE WORD FOR "ROOTED" ("NETSUKU") IS PRONOUNCED THE SAME AS "BEDRIDDEN."
FLINCH
AHA! YOU'RE GOING TO GO VISIT SASUKE, AREN'T YOU?!
NUDGE
YOU'RE NOT GONNA GET A LEG UP ON ME!
I'M GOING WITH YOU!
UGH... INO, YOU WRETCHED PIGLET...

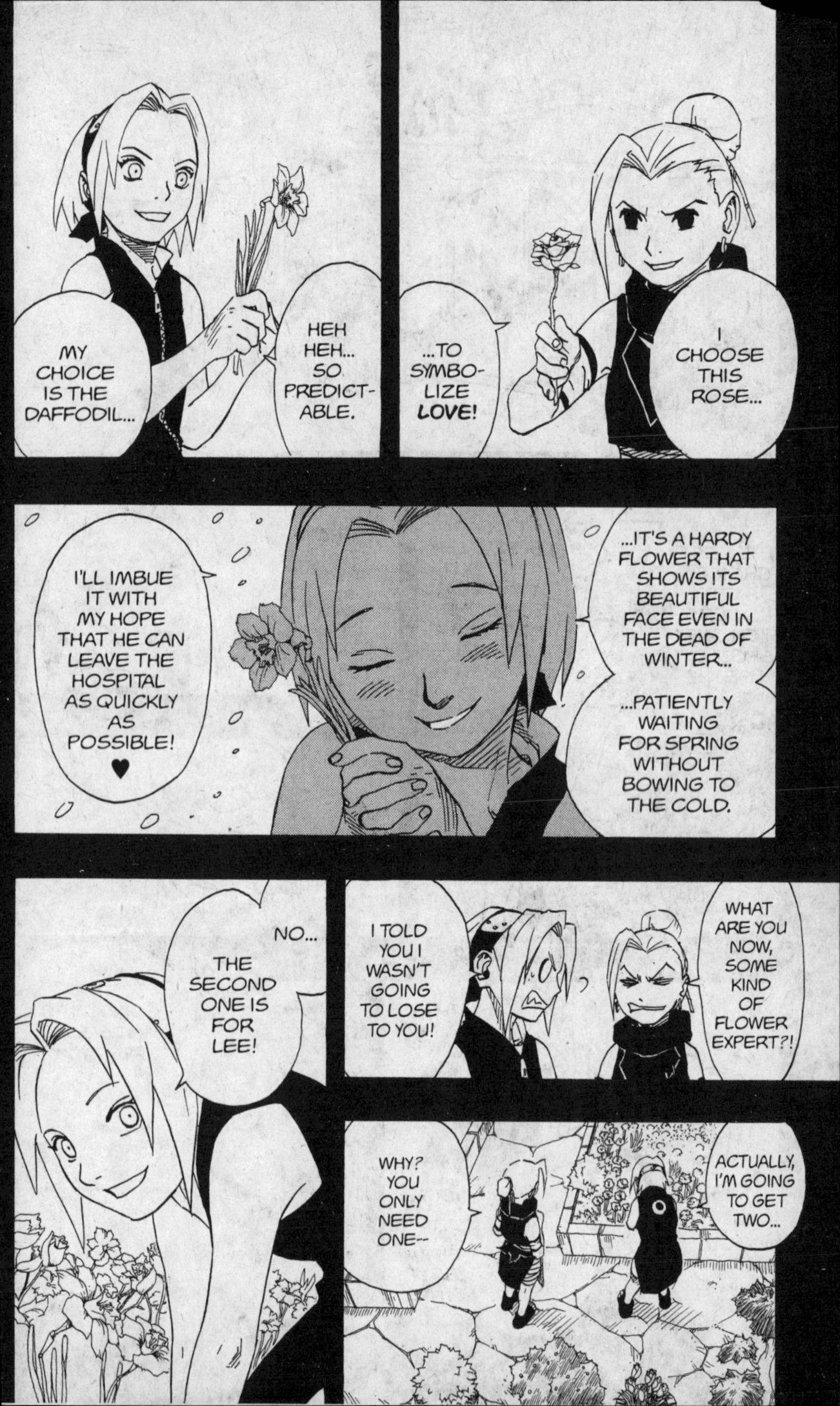
I CHOOSE THIS ROSE...
...TO SYMBOLIZE **LOVE**!
HEH HEH... SO PREDICTABLE.
MY CHOICE IS THE DAFFODIL...
...IT'S A HARDY FLOWER THAT SHOWS ITS BEAUTIFUL FACE EVEN IN THE DEAD OF WINTER...
...PATIENTLY WAITING FOR SPRING WITHOUT BOWING TO THE COLD.
I'LL IMBUE IT WITH MY HOPE THAT HE CAN LEAVE THE HOSPITAL AS QUICKLY AS POSSIBLE! ♥
WHAT ARE YOU NOW, SOME KIND OF FLOWER EXPERT?!
I TOLD YOU I WASN'T GOING TO LOSE TO YOU!
ACTUALLY, I'M GOING TO GET TWO...
WHY? YOU ONLY NEED ONE--
NO...
THE SECOND ONE IS FOR LEE!

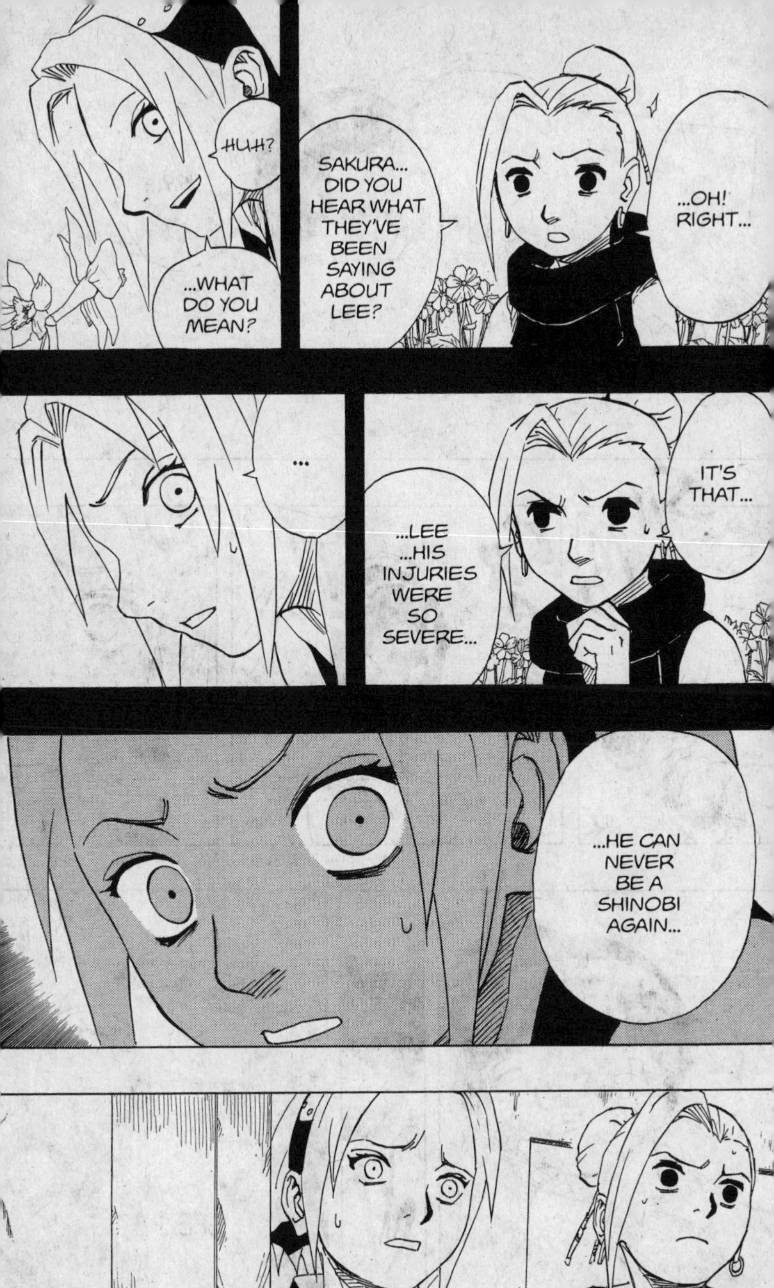
...OH! RIGHT...
SAKURA... DID YOU HEAR WHAT THEY'VE BEEN SAYING ABOUT LEE?
HUH?
...WHAT DO YOU MEAN?
IT'S THAT...
...LEE ...HIS INJURIES WERE SO SEVERE...
...
...HE CAN NEVER BE A SHINOBI AGAIN...

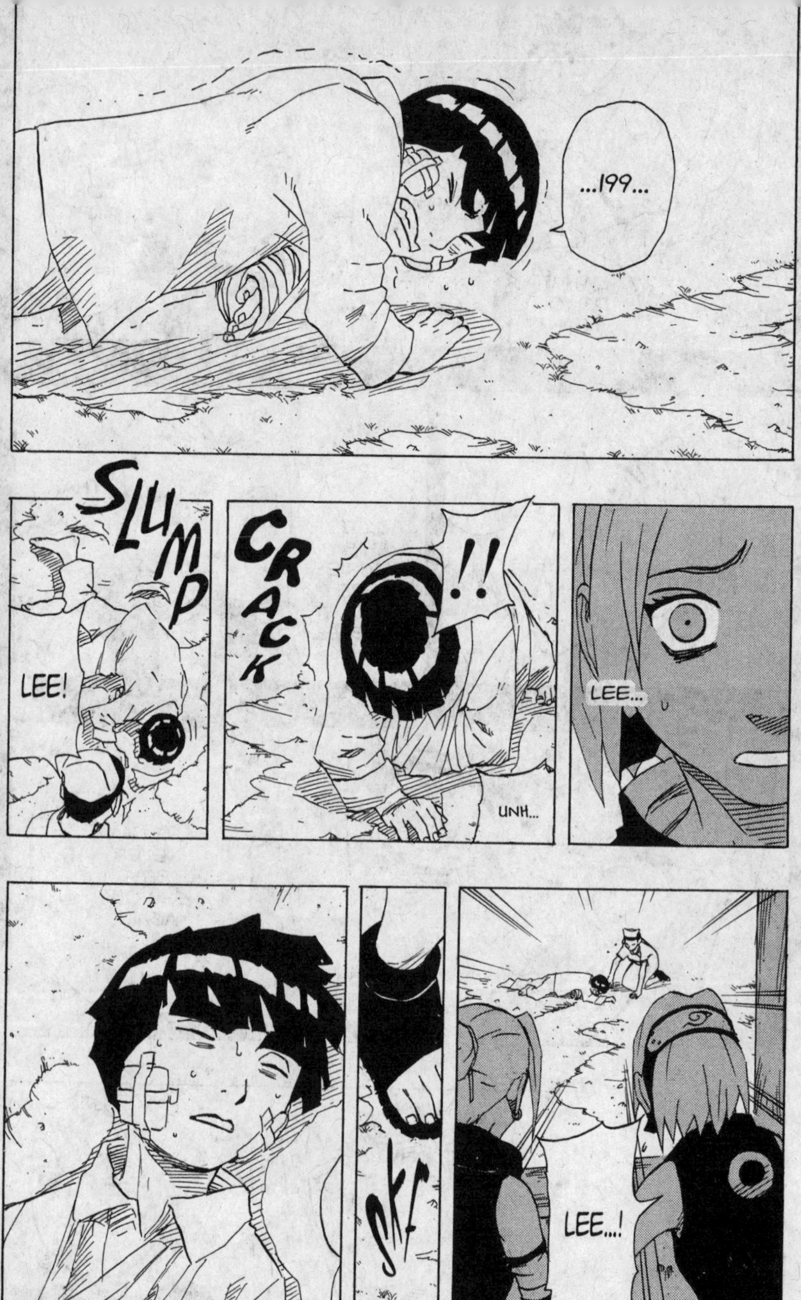
...199...
LEE...
!!
CRACK
UNH...
SLUMP
LEE!
LEE...!
SKF

READ THIS WAY

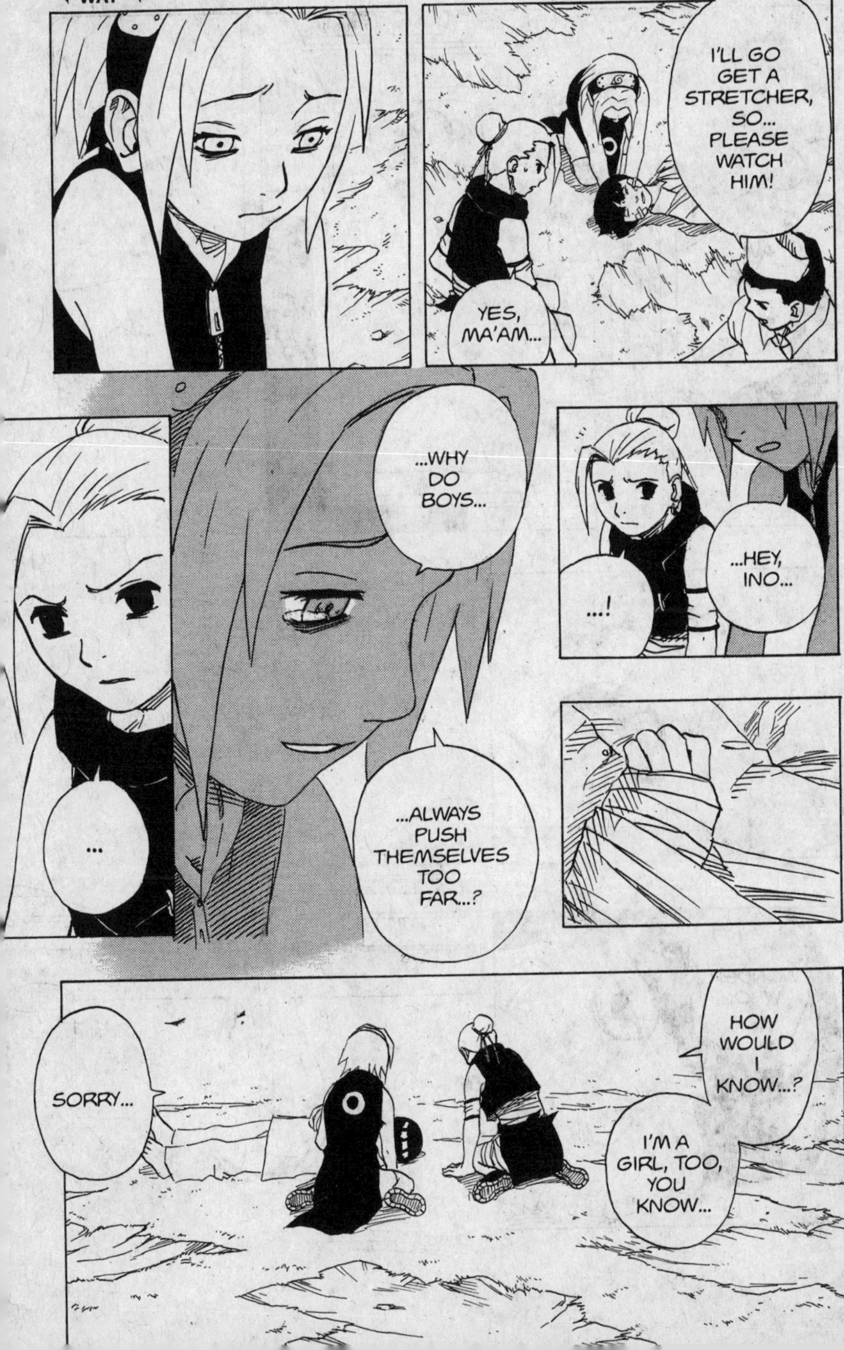
I'LL GO GET A STRETCHER, SO... PLEASE WATCH HIM!
YES, MA'AM...
...HEY, INO...
...!
...WHY DO BOYS...
...ALWAYS PUSH THEMSELVES TOO FAR...?
...
HOW WOULD I KNOW...?
I'M A GIRL, TOO, YOU KNOW...
SORRY...

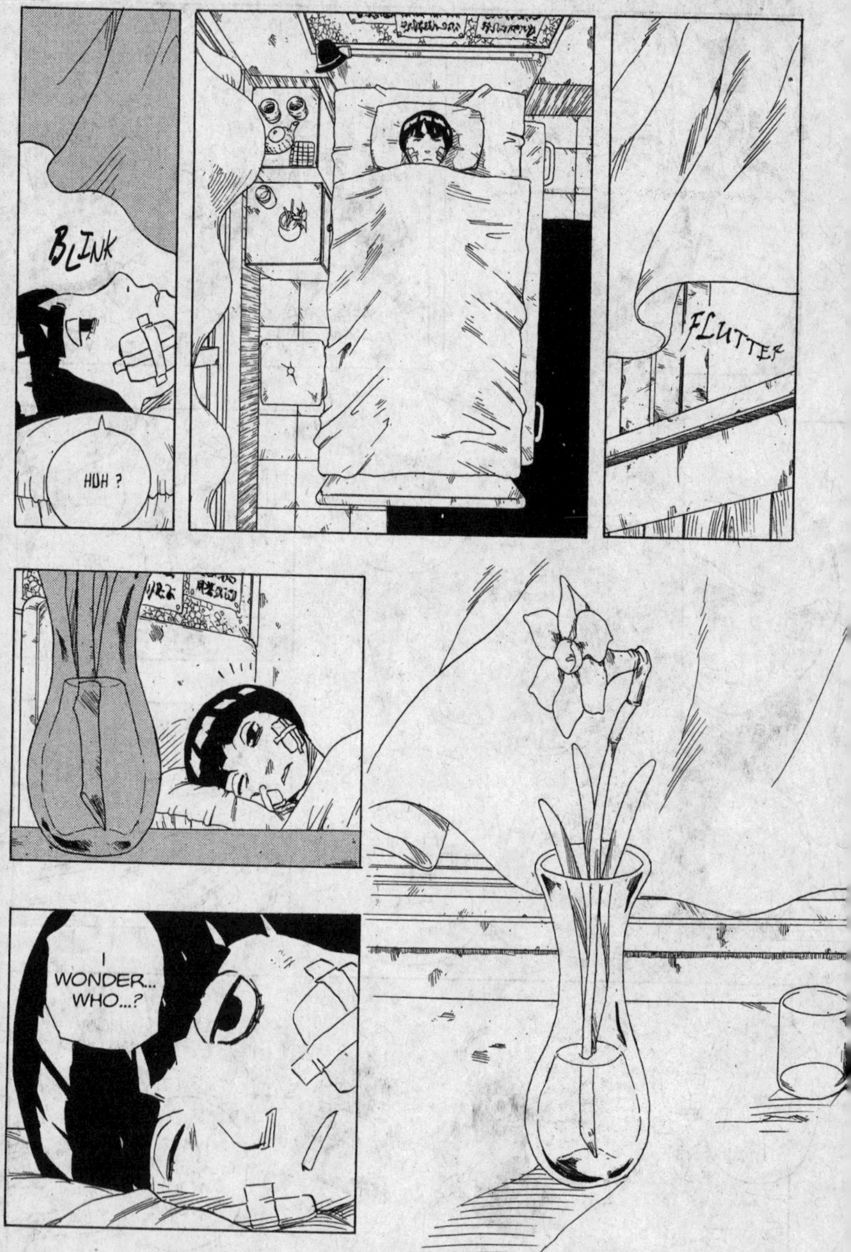
FLUTTER
BLINK
HUH ?
I WONDER... WHO...?

READ THIS WAY

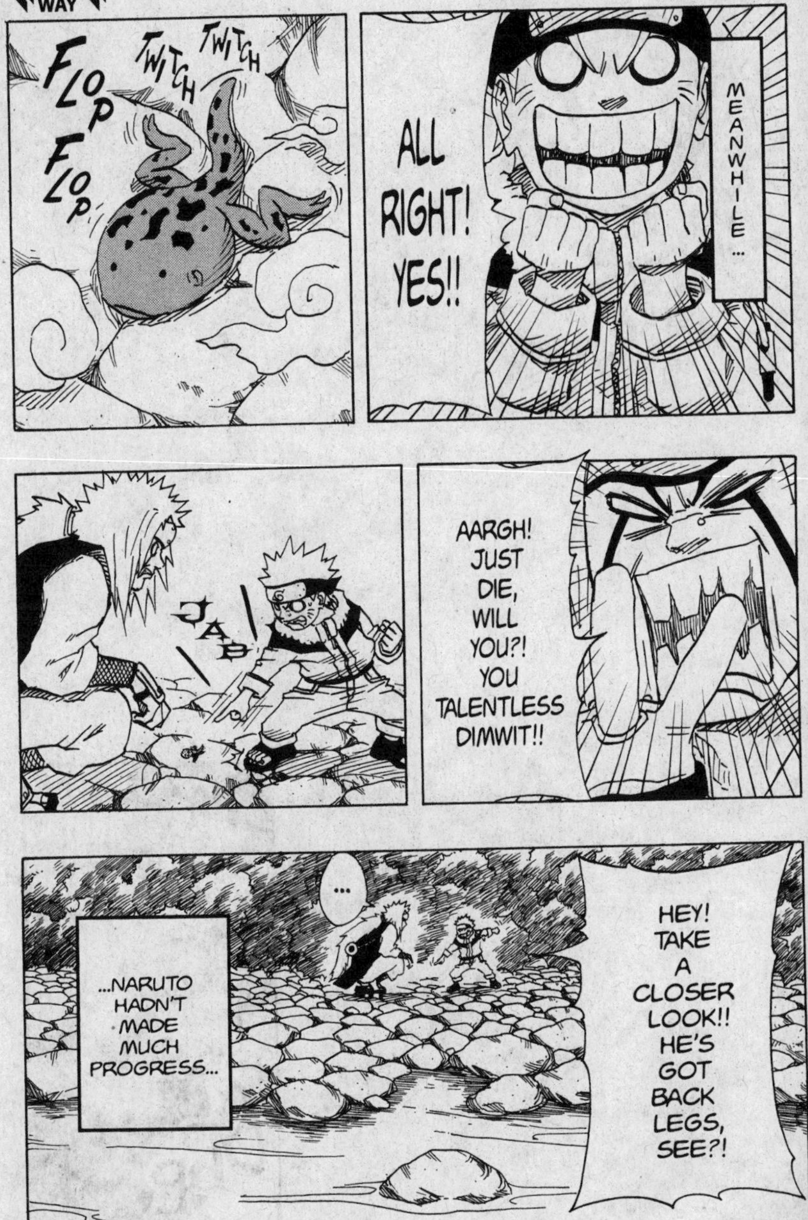
MEANWHILE...
ALL RIGHT! YES!!
TWITCH TWITCH
FLOP FLOP
AARGH! JUST DIE, WILL YOU?! YOU TALENTLESS DIMWIT!!
JAB
HEY! TAKE A CLOSER LOOK!! HE'S GOT BACK LEGS, SEE?!
...
...NARUTO HADN'T MADE MUCH PROGRESS...

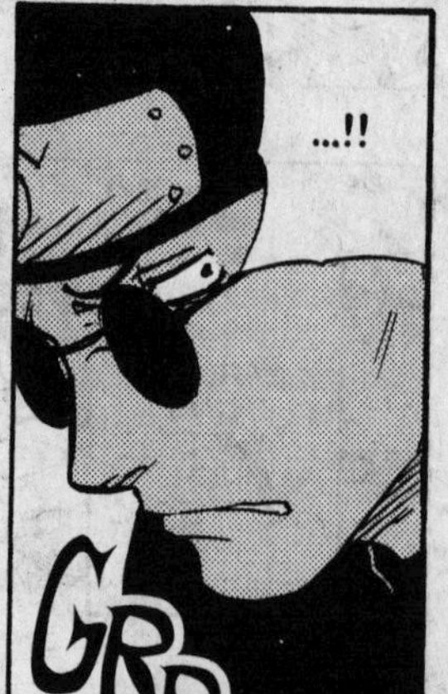
...!!
GRR

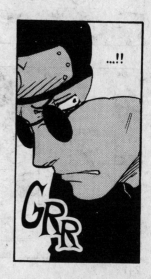

Number 94: The Key...!!

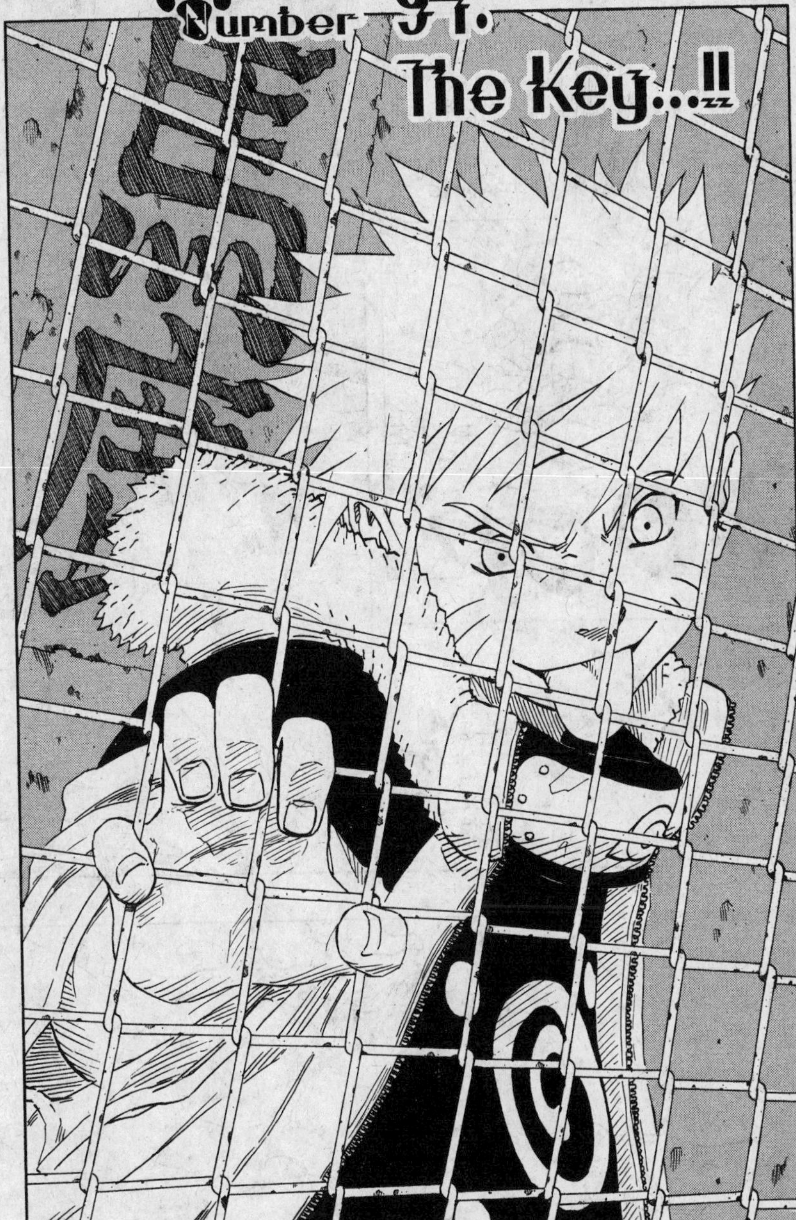

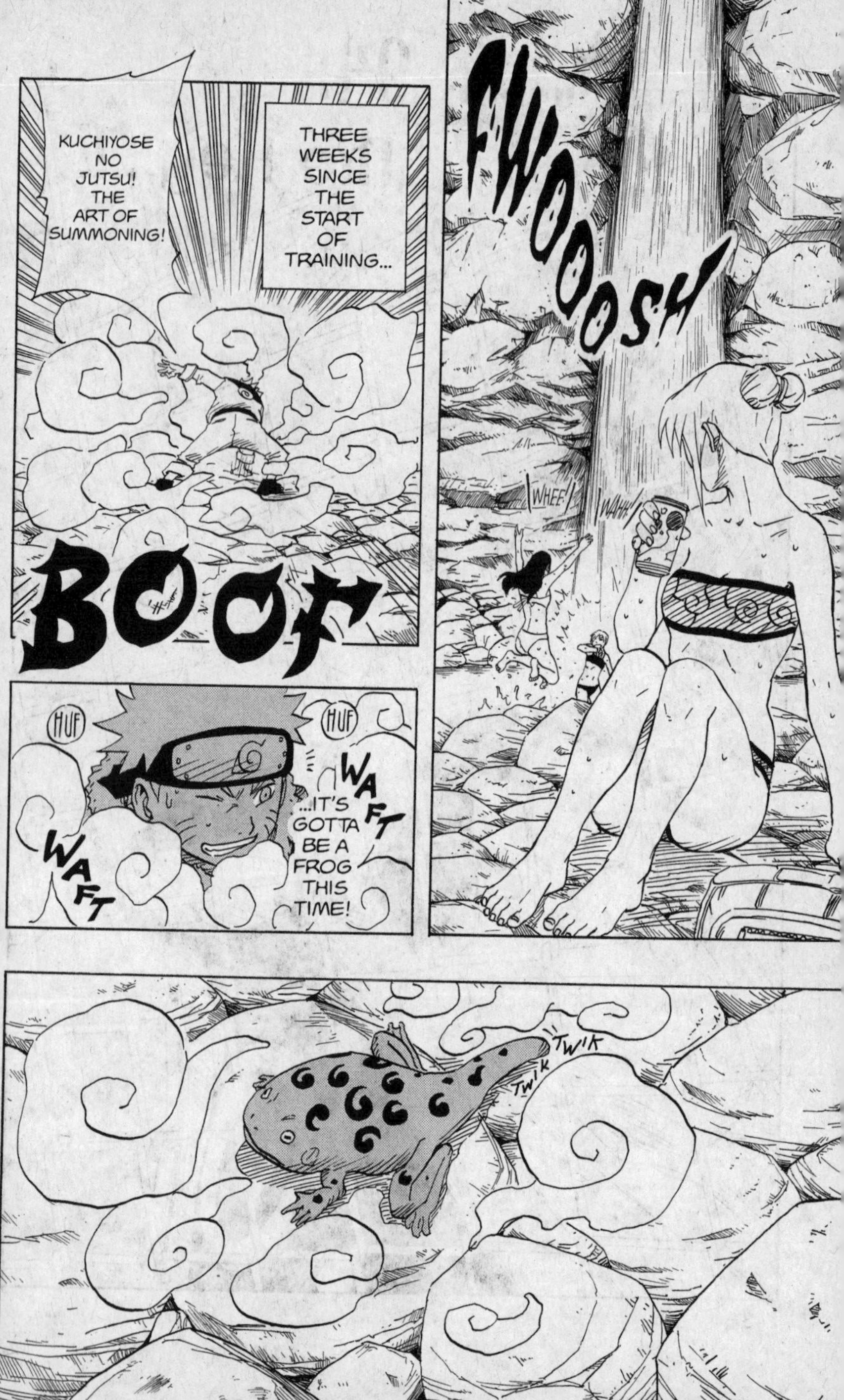
FWOOOSH
WAHH!
WHEE!
THREE WEEKS SINCE THE START OF TRAINING...
KUCHIYOSE NO JUTSU! THE ART OF SUMMONING!
BOOF
HUF
WAFT
...IT'S GOTTA BE A FROG THIS TIME!
HUF
WAFT
TWIK
TWIK

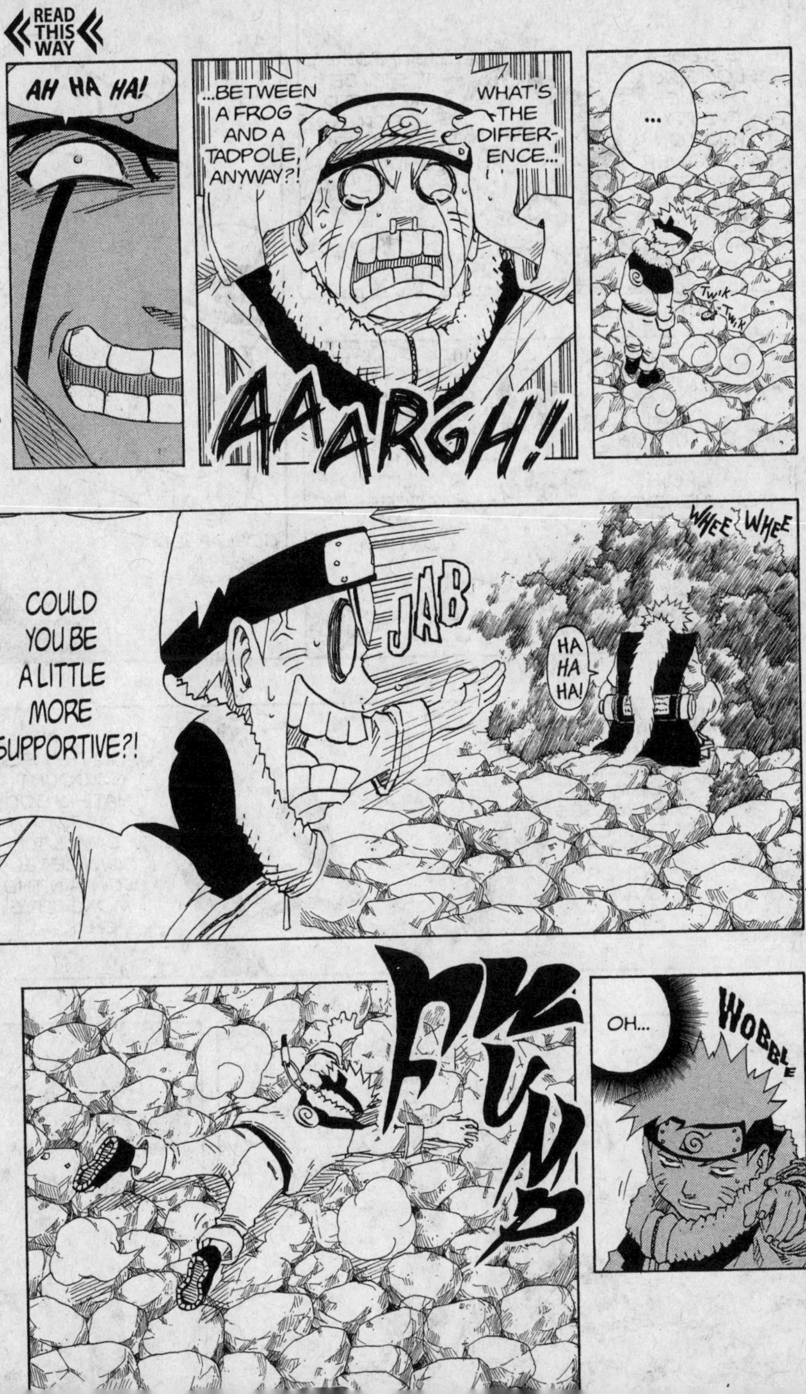
READ THIS WAY
...
TWIK TWIK
WHAT'S THE DIFFERENCE...
...BETWEEN A FROG AND A TADPOLE, ANYWAY?!
AAARGH!
AH HA HA!
WHEE WHEE
HA HA HA!
JAB
COULD YOU BE A LITTLE MORE SUPPORTIVE?!
OH...
WOBBLE

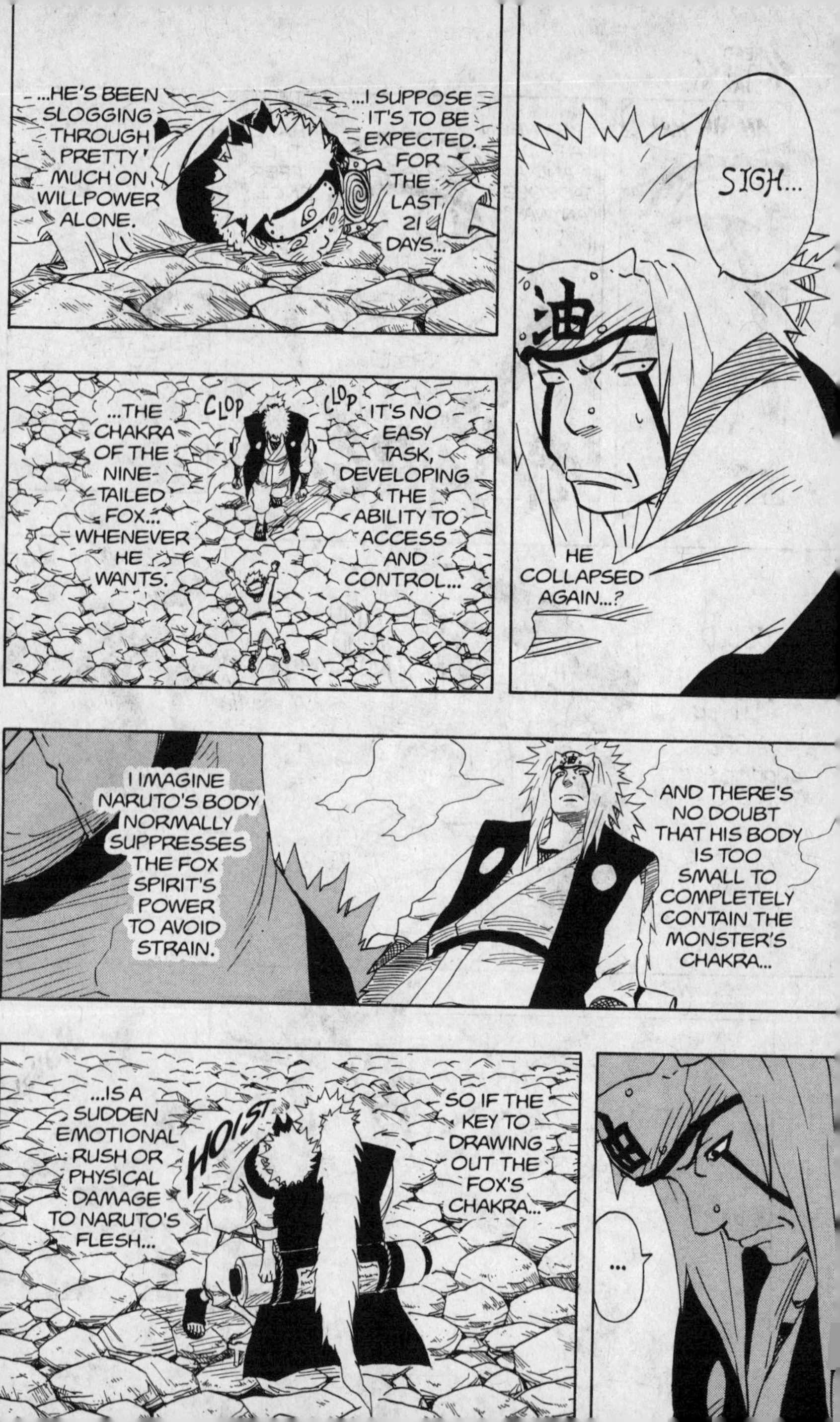
SIGH...
HE COLLAPSED AGAIN...?
...I SUPPOSE IT'S TO BE EXPECTED. FOR THE LAST 21 DAYS...
...HE'S BEEN SLOGGING THROUGH PRETTY MUCH ON WILLPOWER ALONE.
IT'S NO EASY TASK, DEVELOPING THE ABILITY TO ACCESS AND CONTROL...
CLOP
CLOP
...THE CHAKRA OF THE NINE-TAILED FOX... WHENEVER HE WANTS.
AND THERE'S NO DOUBT THAT HIS BODY IS TOO SMALL TO COMPLETELY CONTAIN THE MONSTER'S CHAKRA...
I IMAGINE NARUTO'S BODY NORMALLY SUPPRESSES THE FOX SPIRIT'S POWER TO AVOID STRAIN.
...
SO IF THE KEY TO DRAWING OUT THE FOX'S CHAKRA...
HOIST
...IS A SUDDEN EMOTIONAL RUSH OR PHYSICAL DAMAGE TO NARUTO'S FLESH...

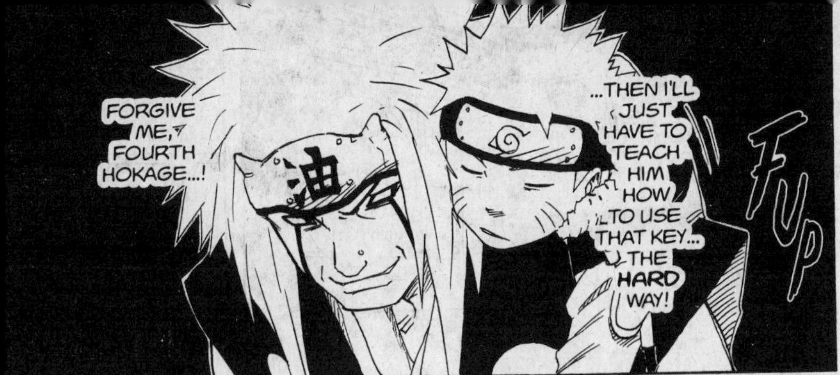
FUP
...THEN I'LL JUST HAVE TO TEACH HIM HOW TO USE THAT KEY... THE HARD WAY!
FORGIVE ME, FOURTH HOKAGE...!
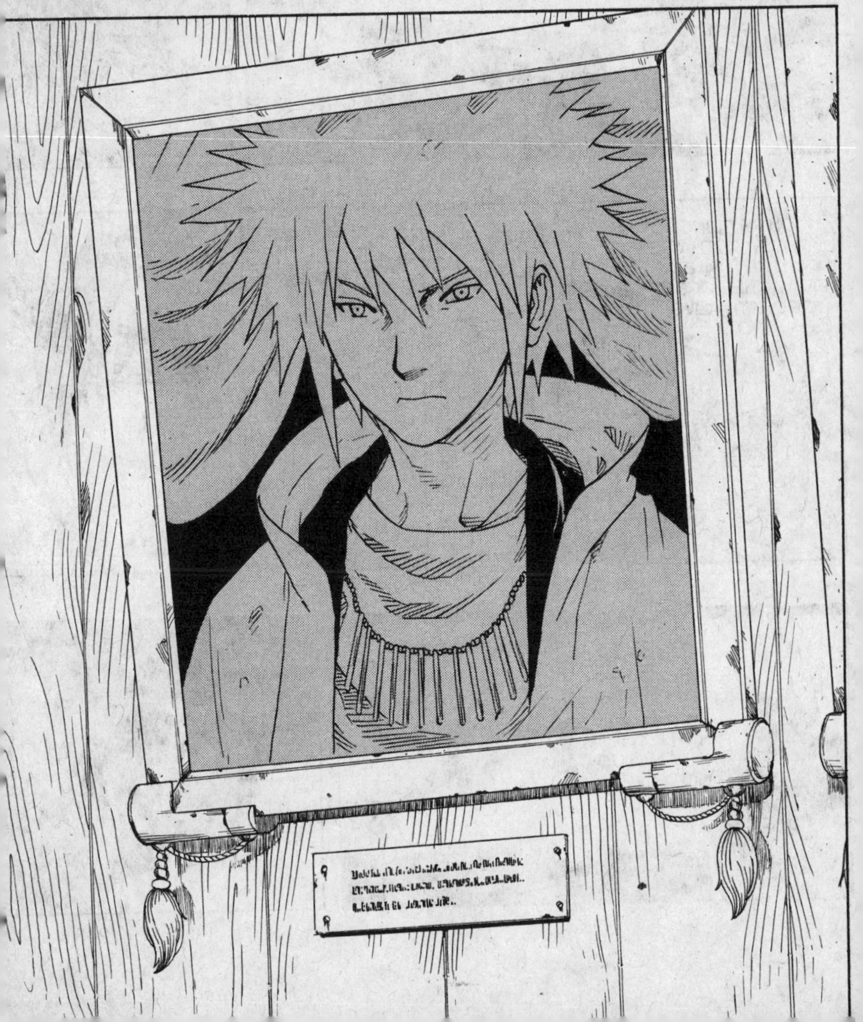

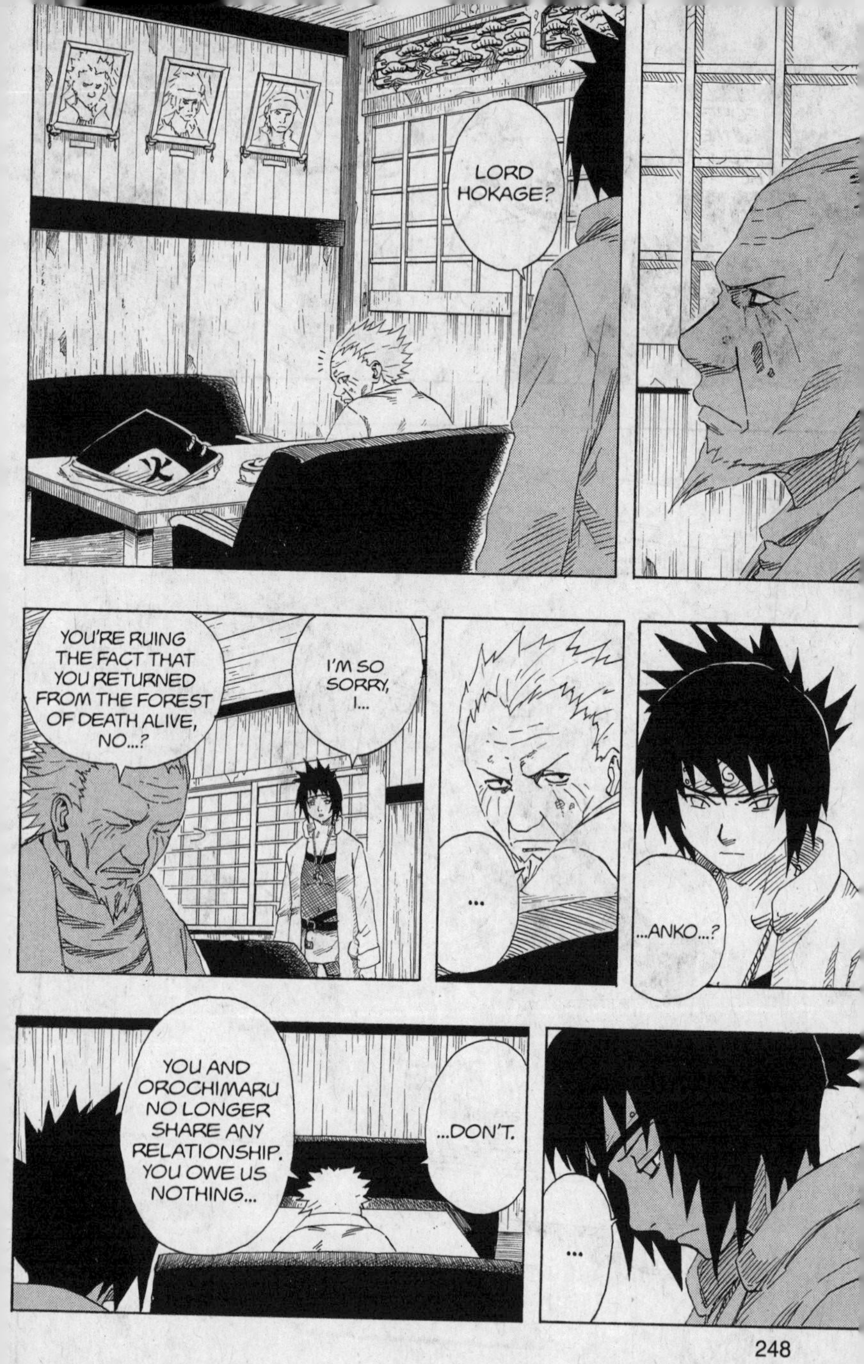
LORD HOKAGE?
...ANKO...?
...
I'M SO SORRY, I...
YOU'RE RUINING THE FACT THAT YOU RETURNED FROM THE FOREST OF DEATH ALIVE, NO...?
...
...DON'T.
YOU AND OROCHIMARU NO LONGER SHARE ANY RELATIONSHIP. YOU OWE US NOTHING...

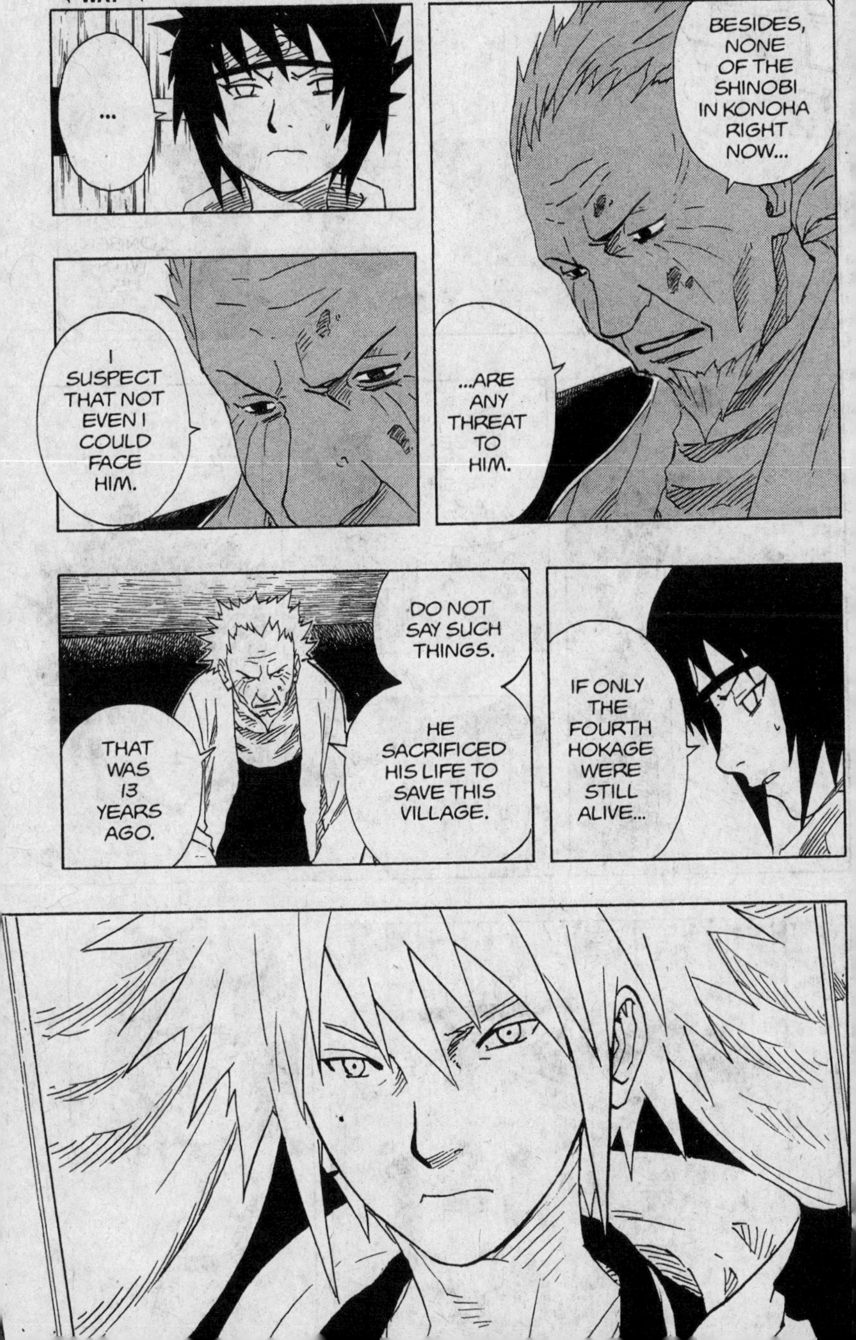
READ THIS WAY
BESIDES, NONE OF THE SHINOBI IN KONOHA RIGHT NOW...
...ARE ANY THREAT TO HIM.
...
I SUSPECT THAT NOT EVEN I COULD FACE HIM.
IF ONLY THE FOURTH HOKAGE WERE STILL ALIVE...
DO NOT SAY SUCH THINGS.
HE SACRIFICED HIS LIFE TO SAVE THIS VILLAGE.
THAT WAS 13 YEARS AGO.

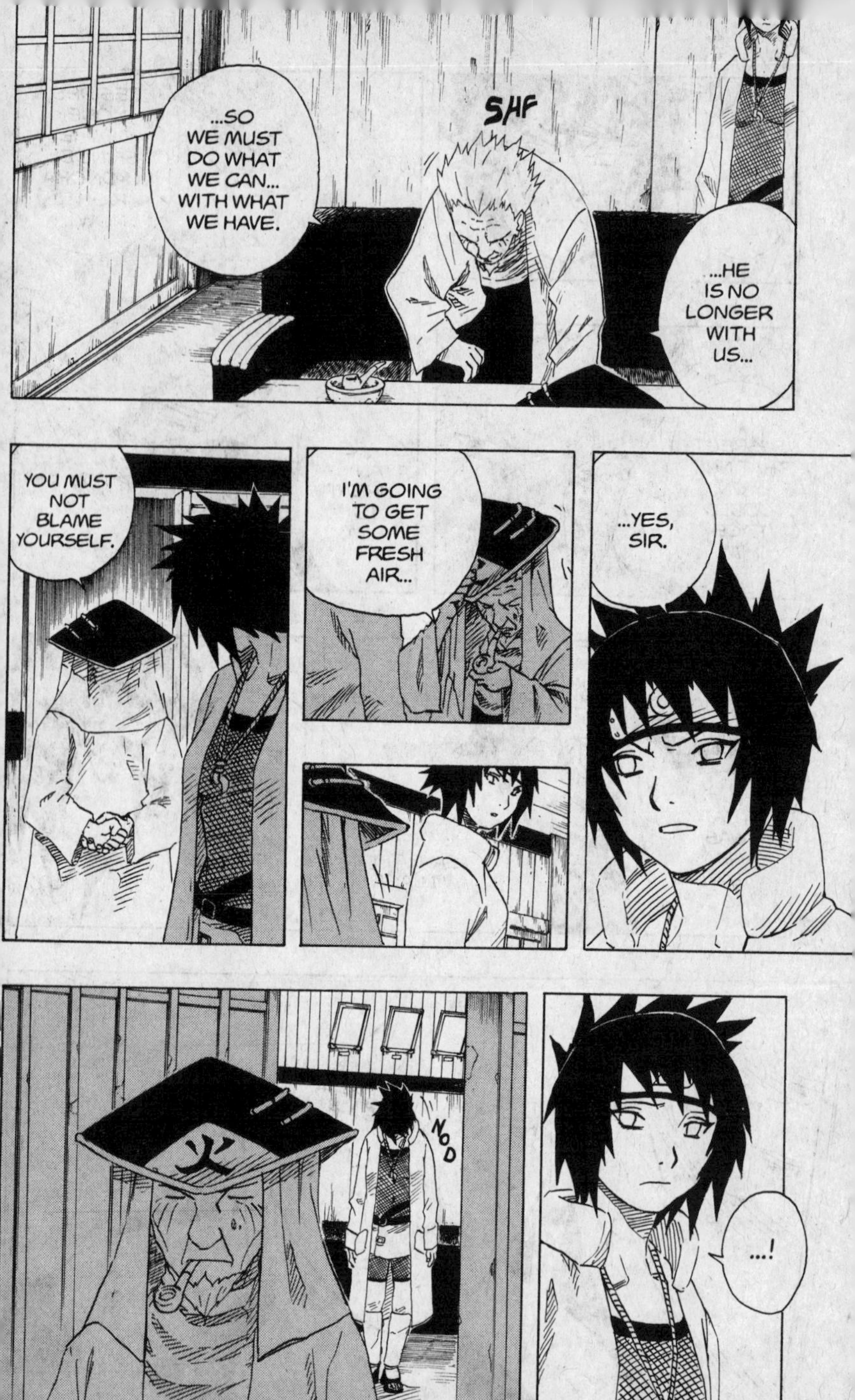
...HE IS NO LONGER WITH US...
SHF
...SO WE MUST DO WHAT WE CAN... WITH WHAT WE HAVE.
...YES, SIR.
I'M GOING TO GET SOME FRESH AIR...
YOU MUST NOT BLAME YOURSELF.
...!
NOD

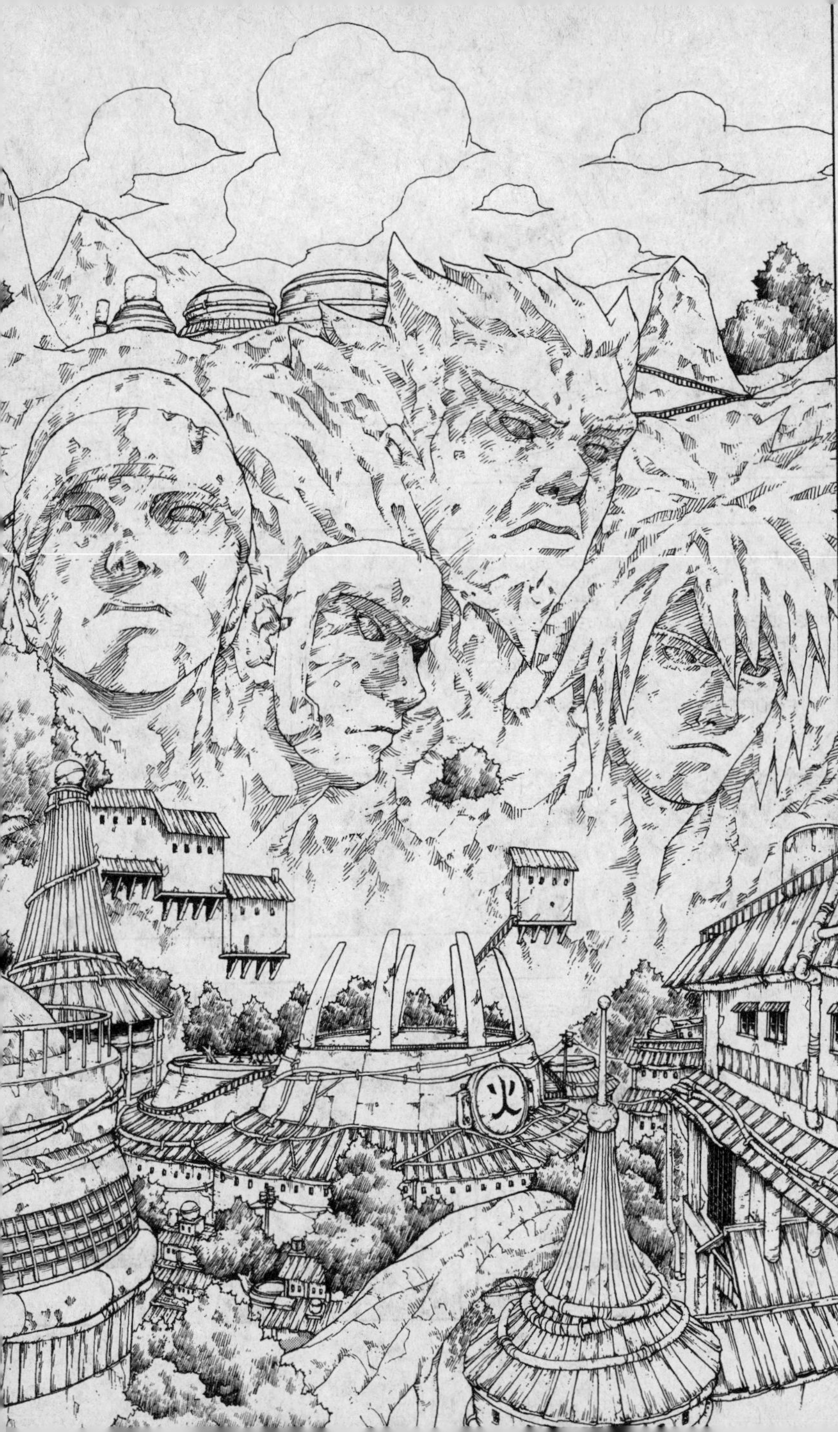
火

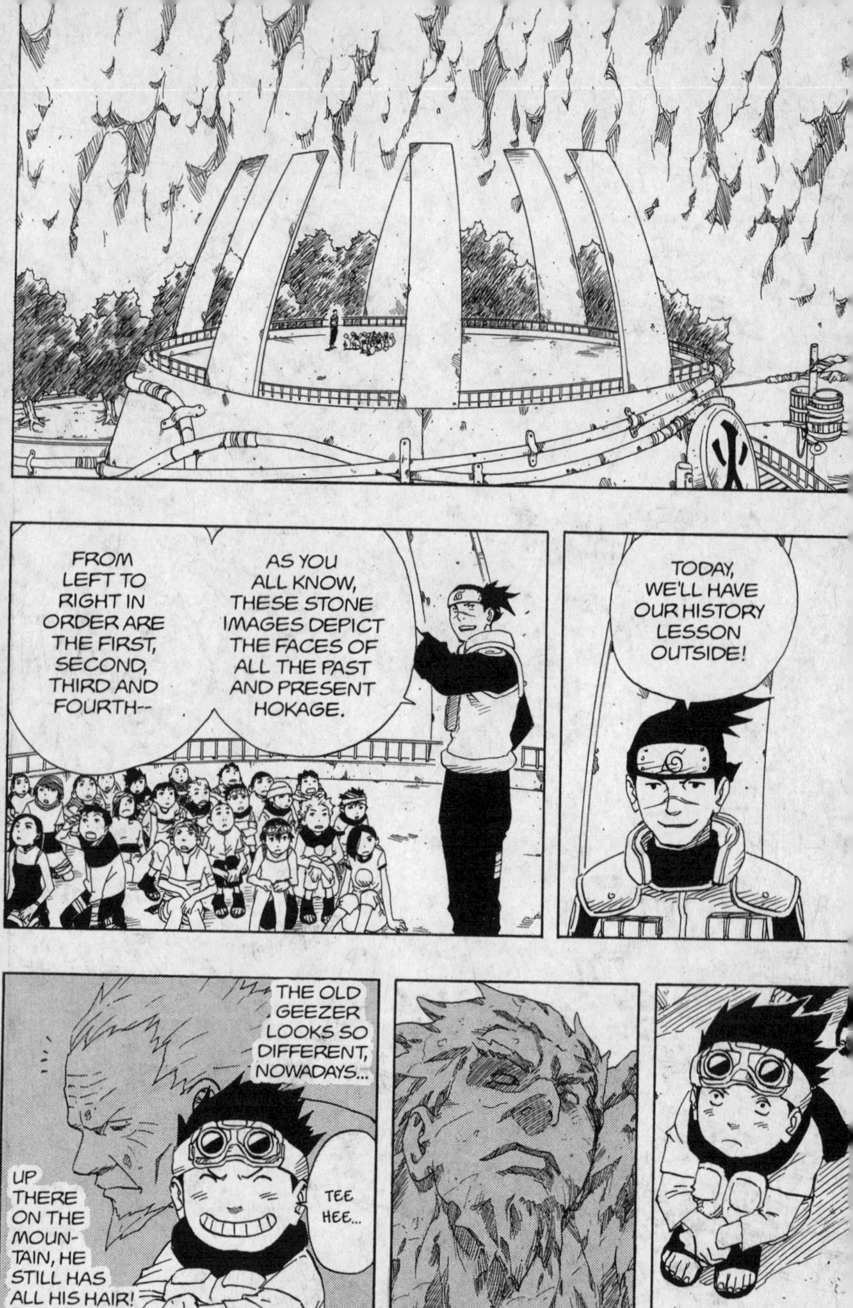
TODAY, WE'LL HAVE OUR HISTORY LESSON OUTSIDE!
AS YOU ALL KNOW, THESE STONE IMAGES DEPICT THE FACES OF ALL THE PAST AND PRESENT HOKAGE.
FROM LEFT TO RIGHT IN ORDER ARE THE FIRST, SECOND, THIRD AND FOURTH--
THE OLD GEEZER LOOKS SO DIFFERENT, NOWADAYS...
TEE HEE...
UP THERE ON THE MOUNTAIN, HE STILL HAS ALL HIS HAIR!

READ THIS WAY

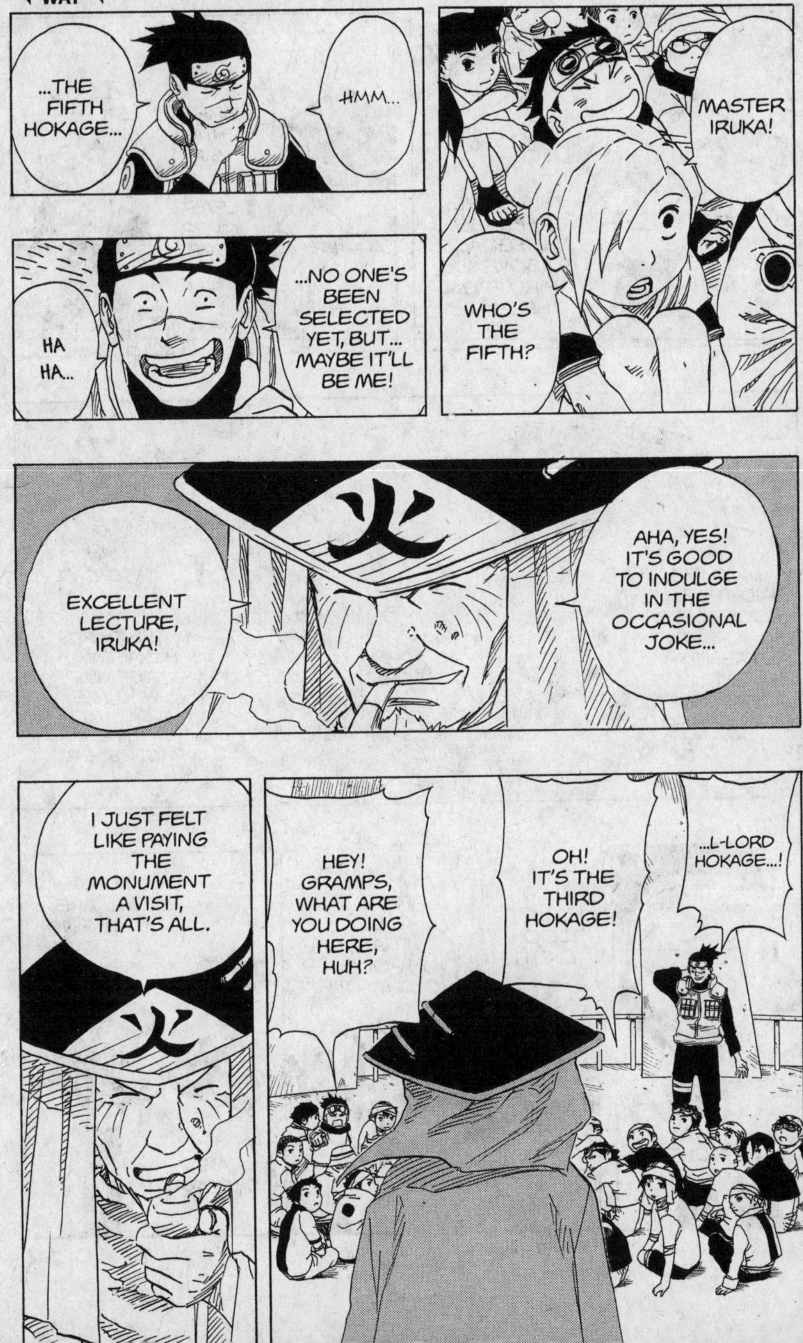
MASTER IRUKA!
WHO'S THE FIFTH?
HMM...
...THE FIFTH HOKAGE...
...NO ONE'S BEEN SELECTED YET, BUT... MAYBE IT'LL BE ME!
HA HA...
AHA, YES! IT'S GOOD TO INDULGE IN THE OCCASIONAL JOKE...
EXCELLENT LECTURE, IRUKA!
...L-LORD HOKAGE...!
OH! IT'S THE THIRD HOKAGE!
HEY! GRAMPS, WHAT ARE YOU DOING HERE, HUH?
I JUST FELT LIKE PAYING THE MONUMENT A VISIT, THAT'S ALL.

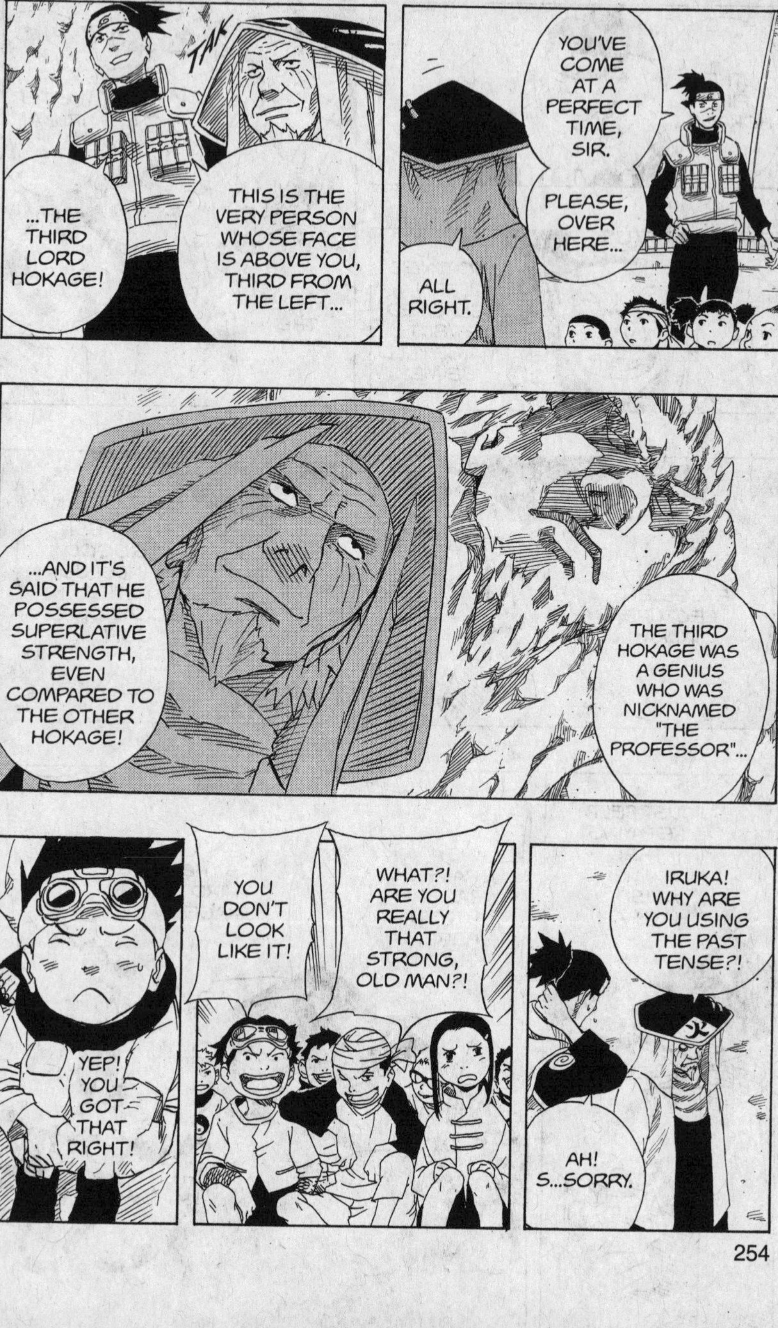
YOU'VE COME AT A PERFECT TIME, SIR.
PLEASE, OVER HERE...
ALL RIGHT.
TAK
THIS IS THE VERY PERSON WHOSE FACE IS ABOVE YOU, THIRD FROM THE LEFT...
...THE THIRD LORD HOKAGE!
THE THIRD HOKAGE WAS A GENIUS WHO WAS NICKNAMED "THE PROFESSOR"...
...AND IT'S SAID THAT HE POSSESSED SUPERLATIVE STRENGTH, EVEN COMPARED TO THE OTHER HOKAGE!
IRUKA! WHY ARE YOU USING THE PAST TENSE?!
AH! S...SORRY.
WHAT?! ARE YOU REALLY THAT STRONG, OLD MAN?!
YOU DON'T LOOK LIKE IT!
YEP! YOU GOT THAT RIGHT!

READ THIS WAY

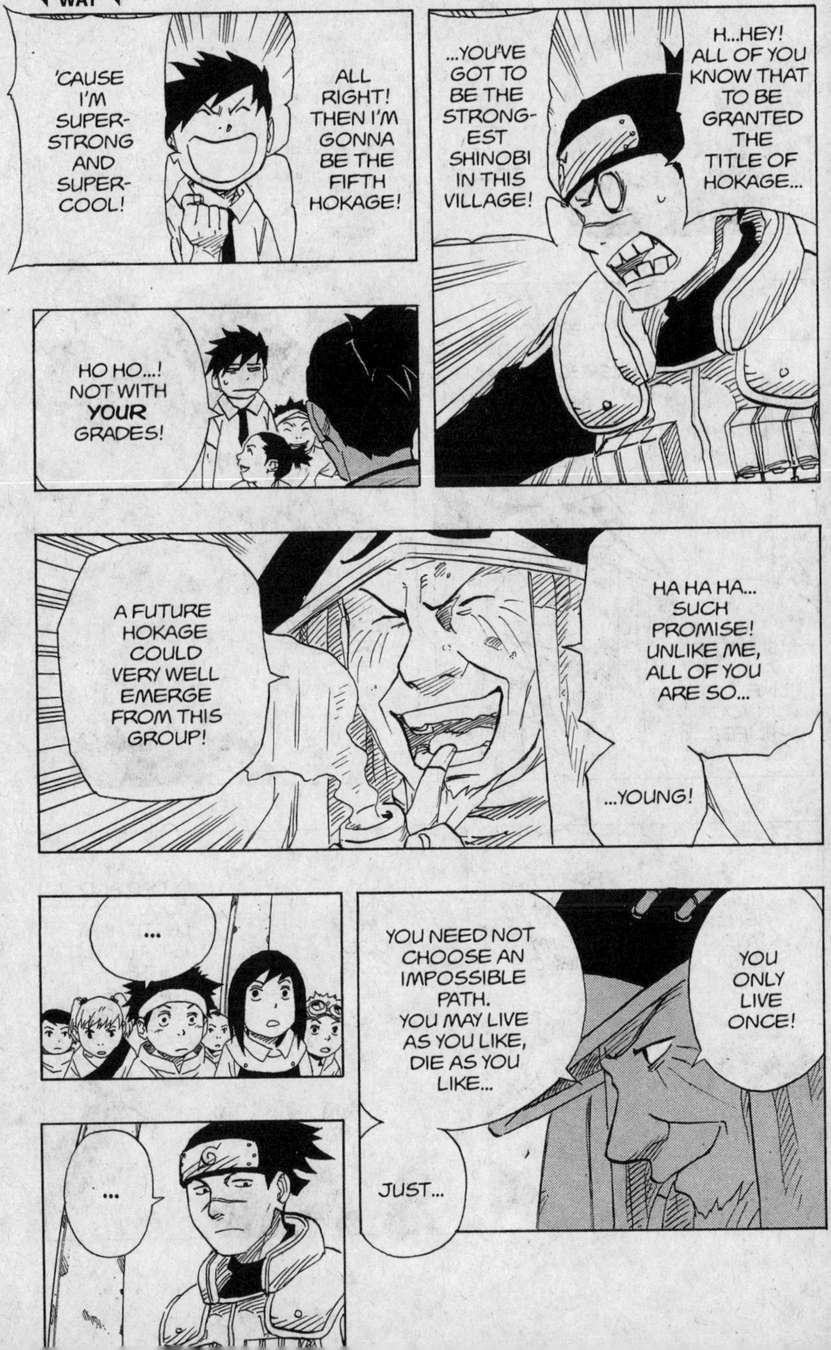
H...HEY! ALL OF YOU KNOW THAT TO BE GRANTED THE TITLE OF HOKAGE...
...YOU'VE GOT TO BE THE STRONGEST SHINOBI IN THIS VILLAGE!
ALL RIGHT! THEN I'M GONNA BE THE FIFTH HOKAGE!
'CAUSE I'M SUPER-STRONG AND SUPER-COOL!
HO HO...! NOT WITH **YOUR** GRADES!
HA HA HA... SUCH PROMISE! UNLIKE ME, ALL OF YOU ARE SO...
...YOUNG!
A FUTURE HOKAGE COULD VERY WELL EMERGE FROM THIS GROUP!
YOU ONLY LIVE ONCE!
YOU NEED NOT CHOOSE AN IMPOSSIBLE PATH. YOU MAY LIVE AS YOU LIKE, DIE AS YOU LIKE...
JUST...
...
...

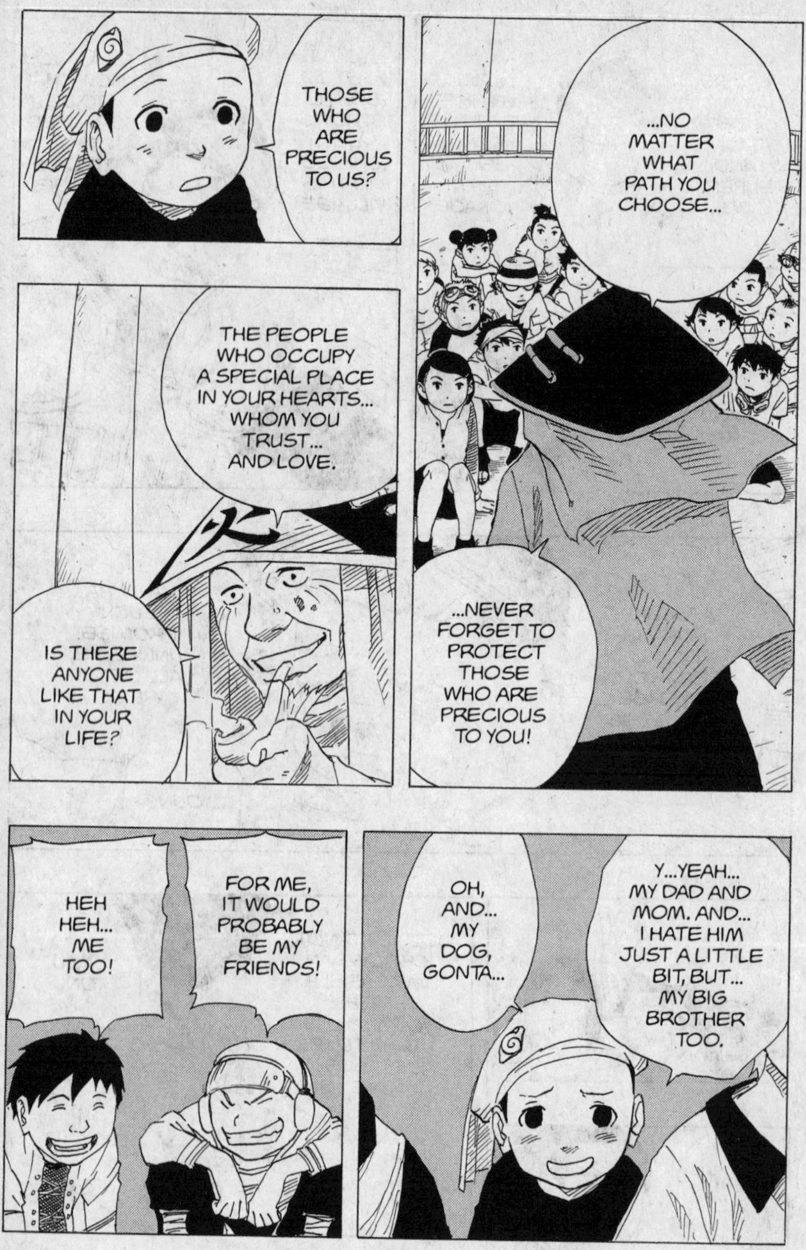
...NO MATTER WHAT PATH YOU CHOOSE...
...NEVER FORGET TO PROTECT THOSE WHO ARE PRECIOUS TO YOU!
THOSE WHO ARE PRECIOUS TO US?
THE PEOPLE WHO OCCUPY A SPECIAL PLACE IN YOUR HEARTS... WHOM YOU TRUST... AND LOVE.
IS THERE ANYONE LIKE THAT IN YOUR LIFE?
Y...YEAH... MY DAD AND MOM. AND... I HATE HIM JUST A LITTLE BIT, BUT... MY BIG BROTHER TOO.
OH, AND... MY DOG, GONTA...
FOR ME, IT WOULD PROBABLY BE MY FRIENDS!
HEH HEH... ME TOO!

READ THIS WAY

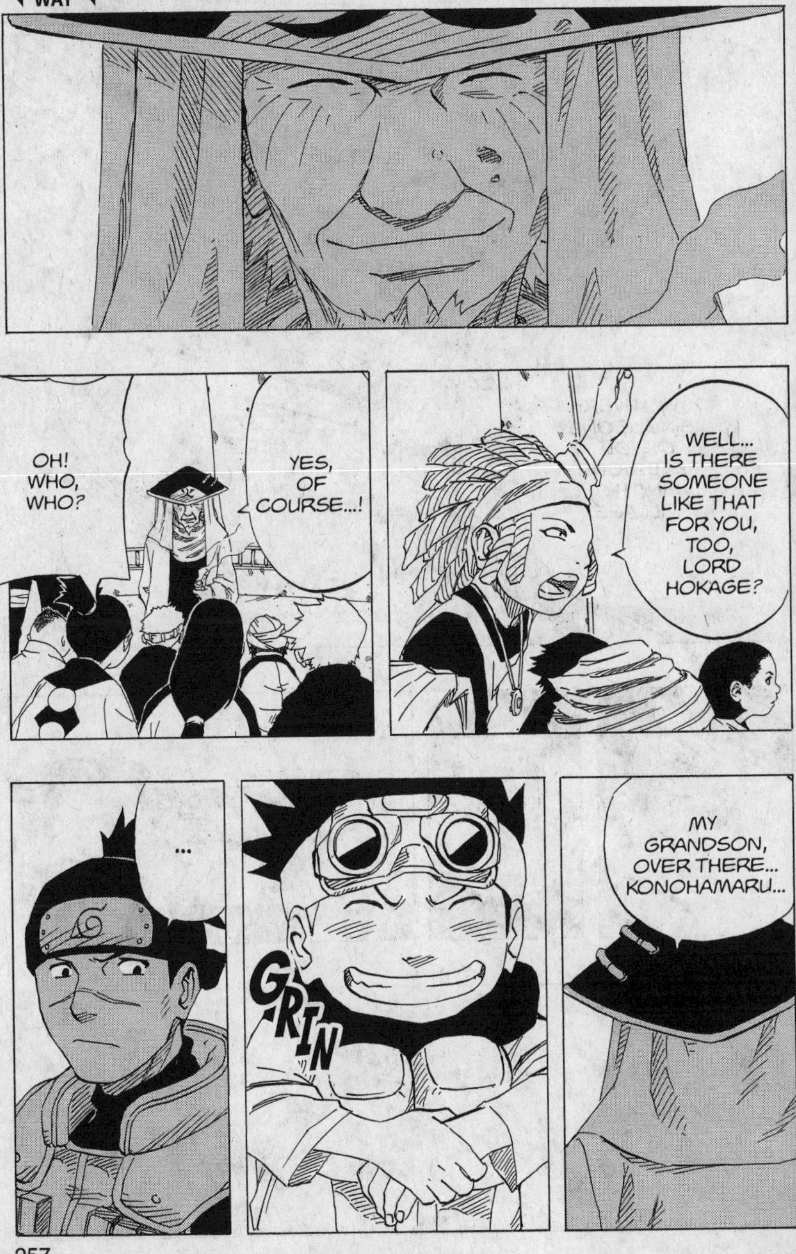

WELL... IS THERE SOMEONE LIKE THAT FOR YOU, TOO, LORD HOKAGE?
YES, OF COURSE...!
OH! WHO, WHO?
MY GRANDSON, OVER THERE... KONOHAMARU...
GRIN
...

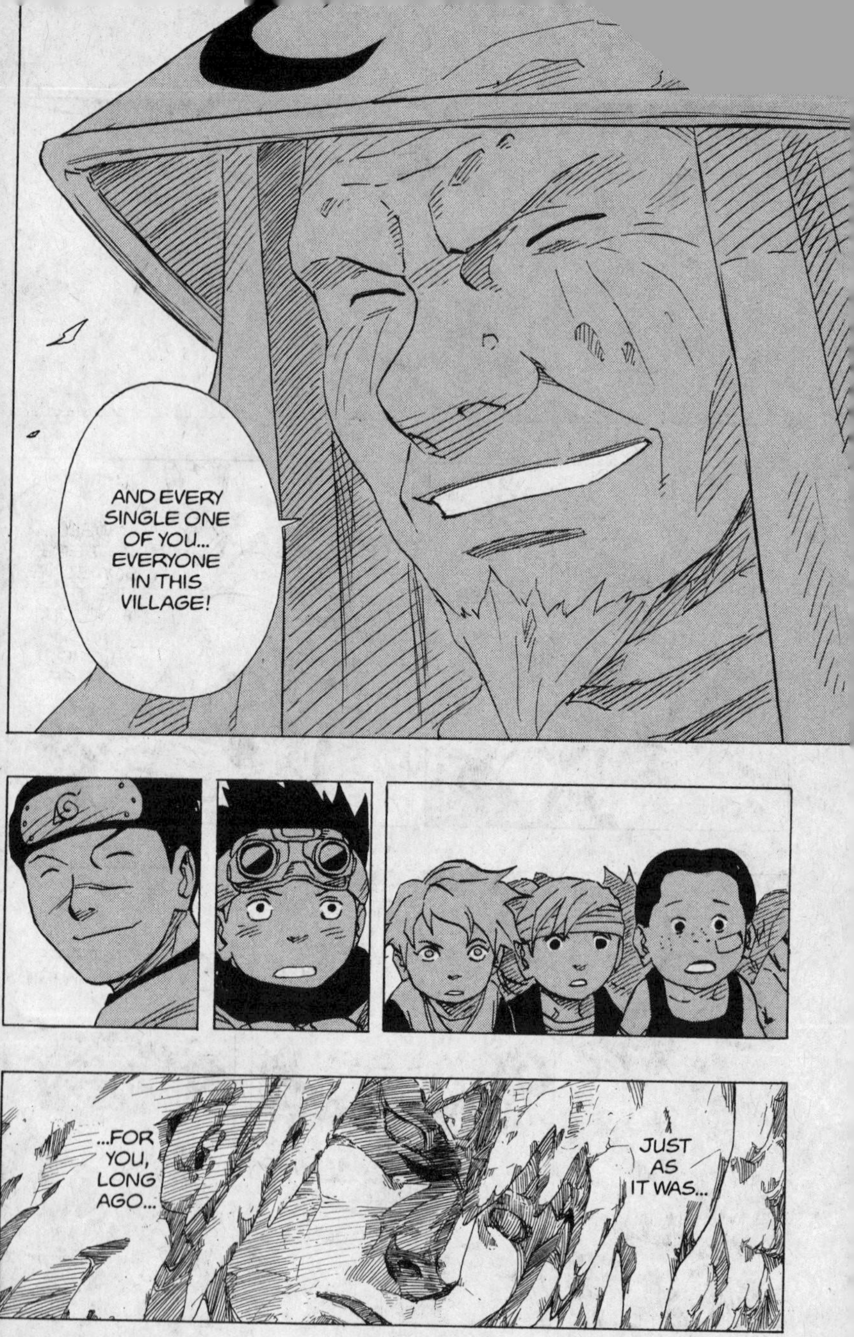
AND EVERY SINGLE ONE OF YOU... EVERYONE IN THIS VILLAGE!
JUST AS IT WAS...
...FOR YOU, LONG AGO...

READ THIS WAY

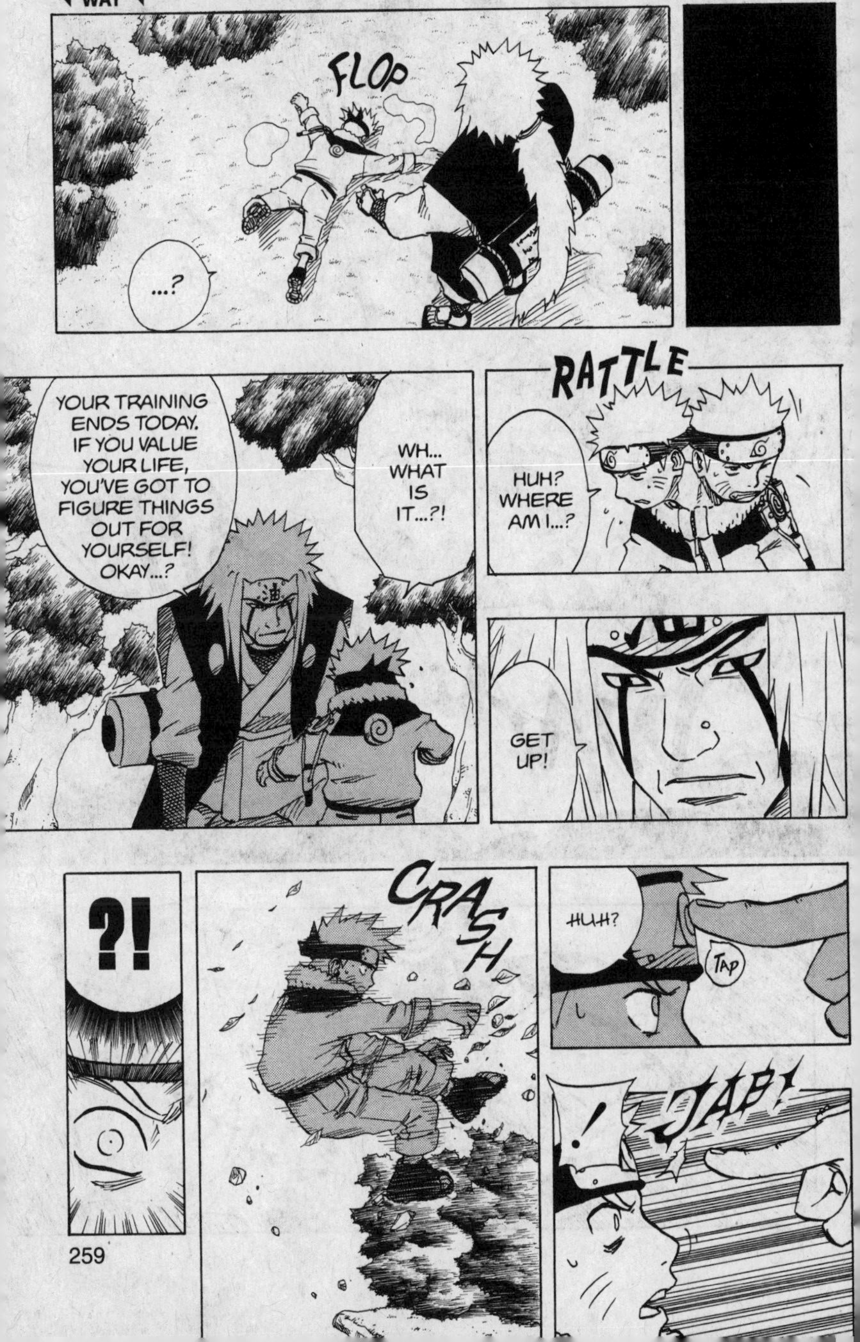

FLOP
...?
RATTLE
HUH? WHERE AM I...?
GET UP!
WH... WHAT IS IT...?!
YOUR TRAINING ENDS TODAY. IF YOU VALUE YOUR LIFE, YOU'VE GOT TO FIGURE THINGS OUT FOR YOURSELF! OKAY...?
HUH?
TAP
!
JAB!
CRASH
?!

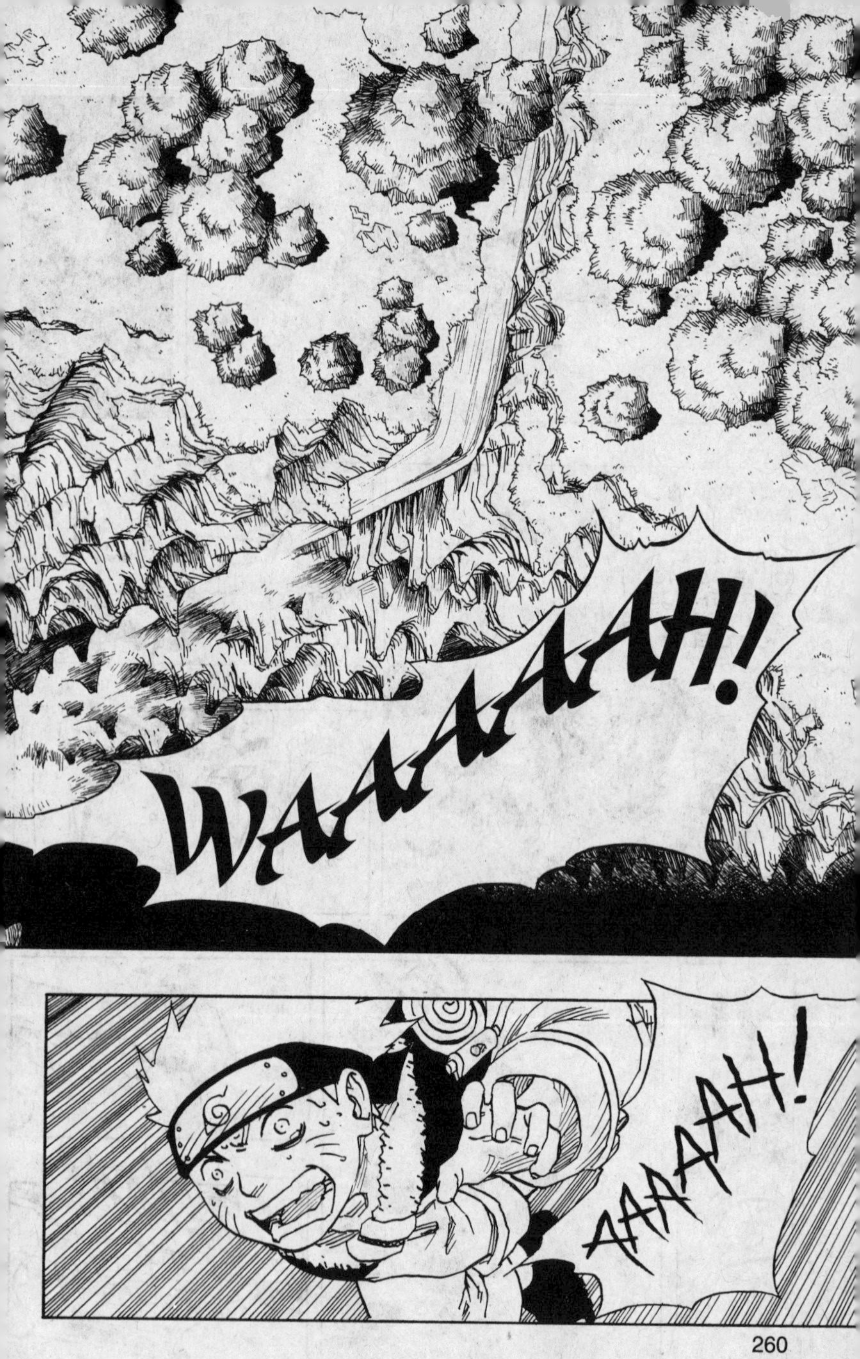
WAAAAAH!
AAAAAH!

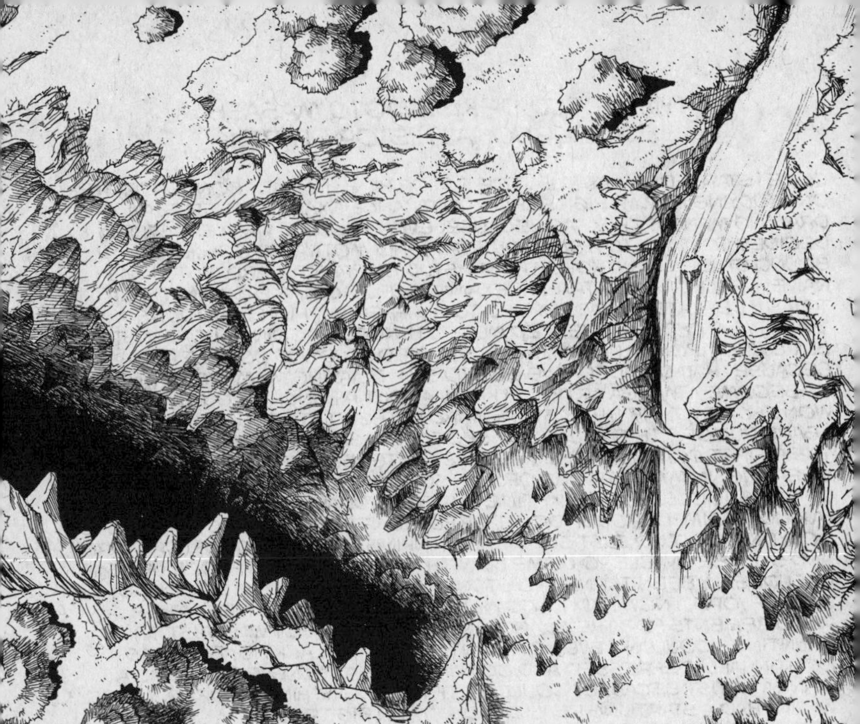

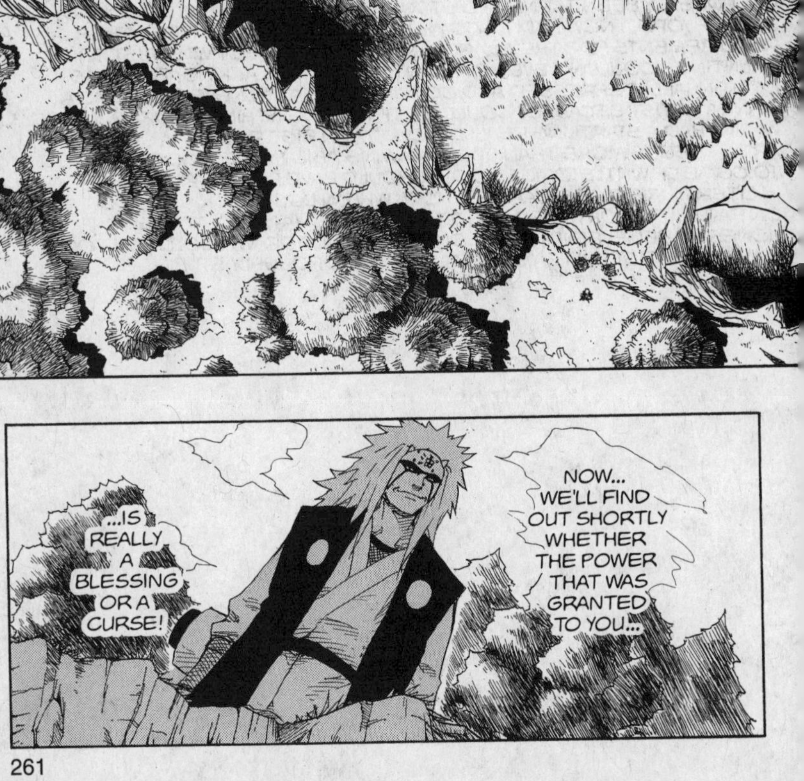
NOW... WE'LL FIND OUT SHORTLY WHETHER THE POWER THAT WAS GRANTED TO YOU...
...IS REALLY A BLESSING OR A CURSE!

THE WORLD OF KISHIMOTO MASASHI
MY PERSONAL HISTORY, PART 14

ONCE I STARTED MY LAST YEAR OF JUNIOR HIGH, I HAD TO CONCENTRATE ON STUDYING FOR MY HIGH SCHOOL ENTRANCE EXAMS RATHER THAN DRAWING MANGA. THIS WAS BECAUSE, EVEN THOUGH I WAS VERY STUPID, I DECIDED TO APPLY TO A SCHOOL FOR HIGHLY MOTIVATED COLLEGE-BOUND STUDENTS. I THOUGHT I HAD STUDIED PRETTY HARD, BUT... I WAS NAIVE! I FAILED THE ENTRANCE EXAM IN SPECTACULAR FASHION. I FELT TOTALLY DEFLATED. I HAD APPLIED TO A DIFFERENT HIGH SCHOOL AS A "SAFETY," AND THEY ACCEPTED ME, SO I ENDED UP GOING THERE INSTEAD. BUT BY THAT POINT I PRETTY MUCH STOPPED STUDYING COMPLETELY BECAUSE I HAD DECIDED, "I'VE GOT TO START MAKING MY MOVE IF I'M GOING TO BECOME A MANGA ARTIST!" I KNEW ABOUT A BUNCH OF GUYS WHO HAD WON *SHONEN JUMP*'S HOP STEP AWARD IN THEIR LATE TEENS, AND I HAD HEARD RUMORS THAT PLENTY OF SHOJO MANGA ARTISTS PUBLISHED THEIR FIRST COMICS BY THE TIME THEY ENTERED HIGH SCHOOL, SO I WAS SWEATING. IN MY FIRST YEAR OF HIGH SCHOOL, I BOUGHT A SET OF MANGA DRAWING TOOLS, BUT EVERY TIME I TRIED TO DRAW A "NAME" FOR A STORY (A KIND OF SIMPLE ROUGH DRAFT OF PLOTLINES AND CHARACTERS), I JUST COULDN'T DO IT. I'D JUST SIT THERE THINKING FOR FIVE HOURS (OR MORE!) AND STILL BE UNABLE TO COME UP WITH A SINGLE PAGE... I FROZE UP AS IF I'D SUDDENLY BEEN TURNED TO STONE. UNLIKE MY RANDOM DOODLING DAYS OF YORE, I NOW HAD TO COME UP WITH 31 PAGES TO MEET THE REQUIREMENTS FOR THE AWARD, AND THAT PROSPECT WAS JUST TOO DAUNTING. I COULDN'T EVEN PINPOINT WHAT I WAS LACKING, BUT I WAS CONTINUALLY DEPRESSED AND CONVINCED THAT I'D NEVER BECOME A MANGA ARTIST BECAUSE I COULDN'T THINK OF ANYTHING TO DRAW. THAT'S WHEN I HAD A STARTLING REALIZATION. "I'M IN BIG TROUBLE! A MANGA ARTIST NEEDS MORE THAN JUST DRAWING ABILITY... HE'S GOT TO BE ABLE TO COME UP WITH STORIES, TOO! I SHOULD HAVE PAID MORE ATTENTION IN LITERATURE CLASS. DARN IT!" NOW, WHEN I LOOK BACK, I WONDER WHY ON EARTH IT TOOK ME SO LONG TO REALIZE THAT! BUT AT THE TIME, I HONESTLY BELIEVED THAT AS LONG AS I COULD DRAW, I COULD BECOME A MANGA ARTIST. AS I SAID, I REALLY WAS THOROUGHLY STUPID.

Number 95: A Chance Encounter...!!

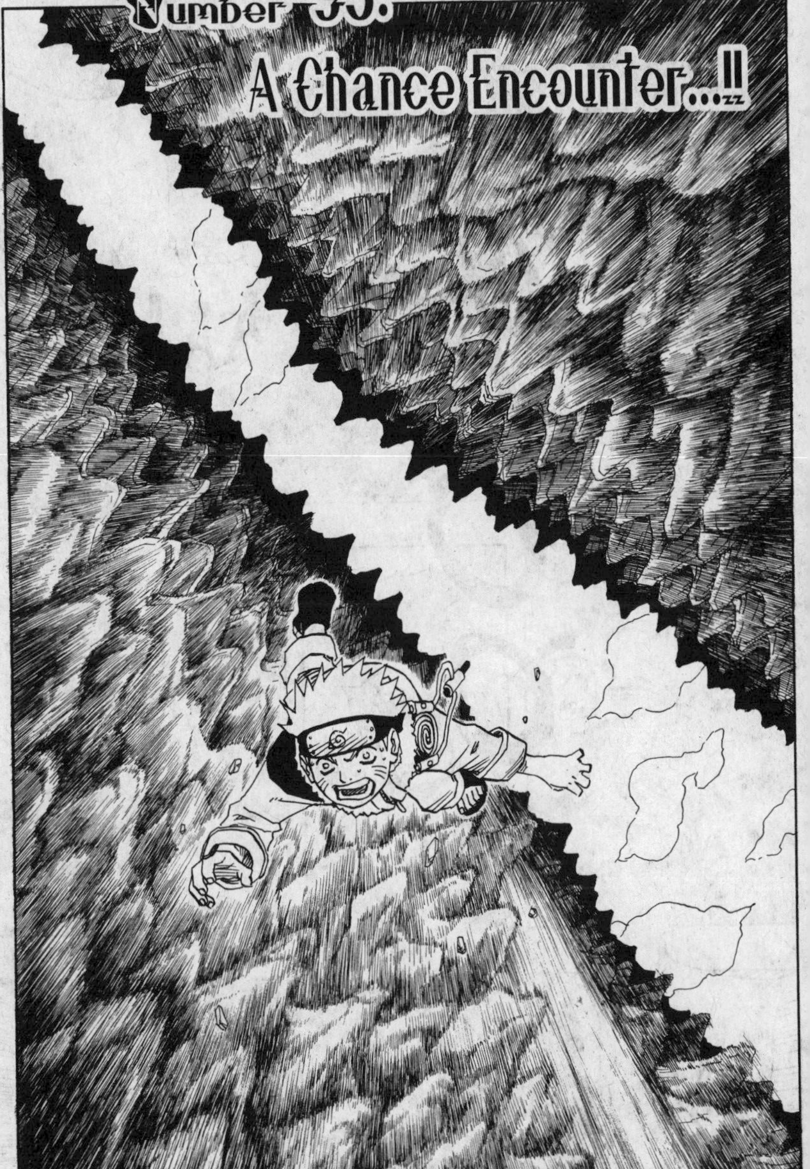

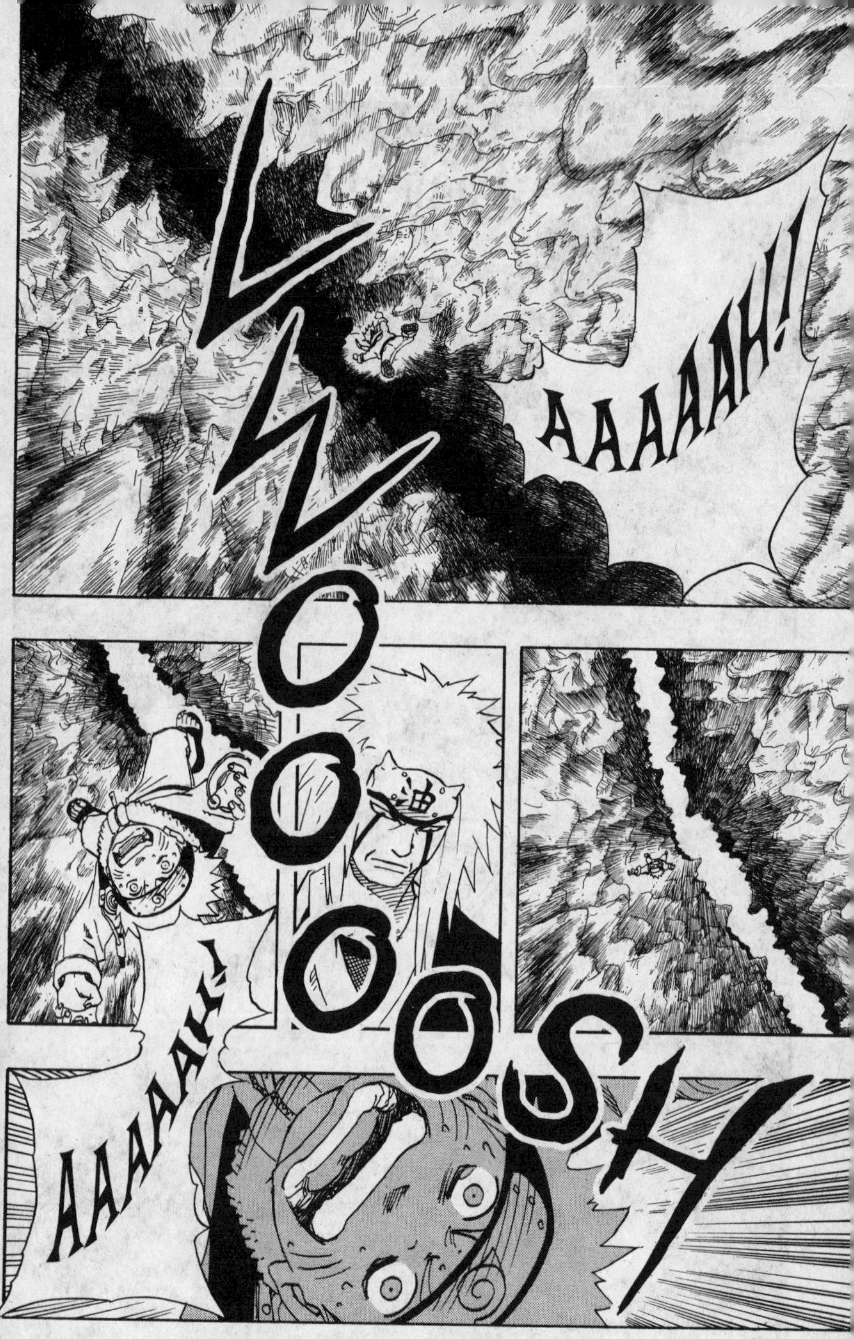
AAAAAH!!
WOOOOSH
AAAAAH!

READ THIS WAY
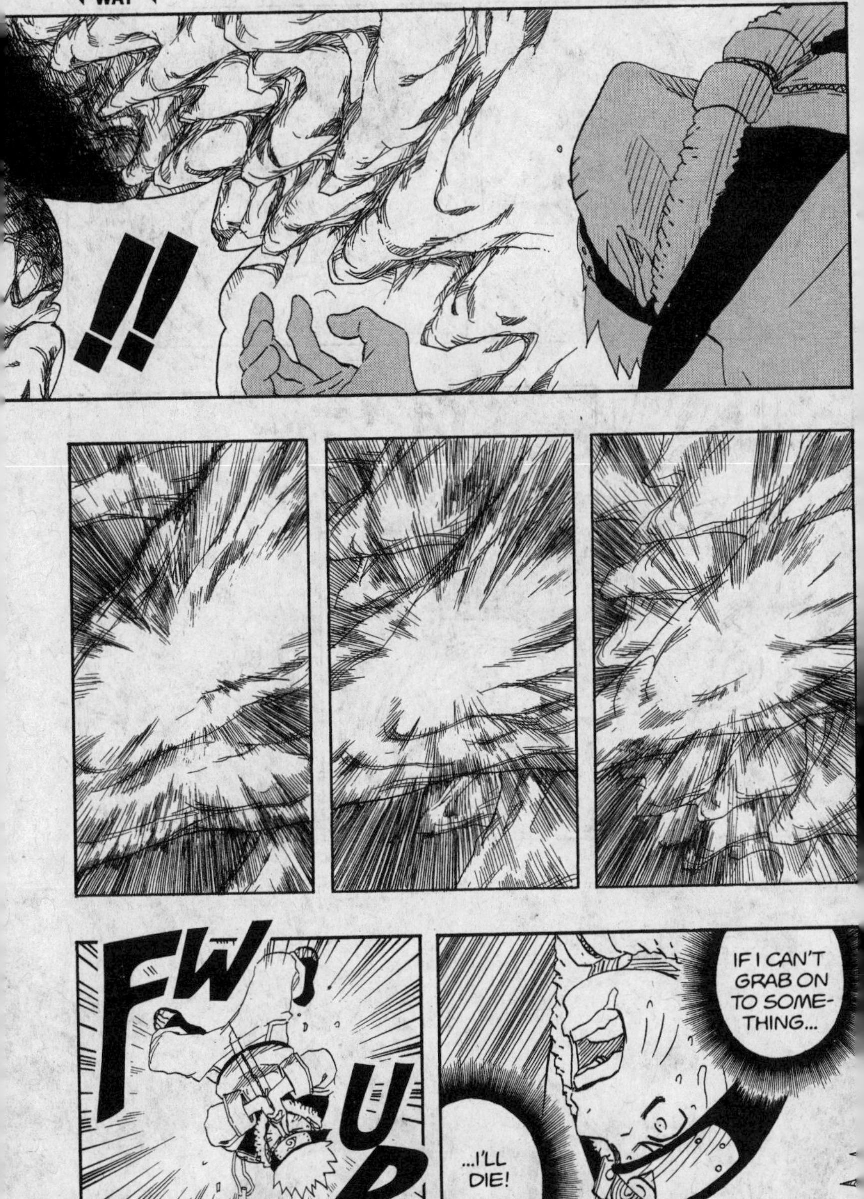
!!
FWUP
IF I CAN'T GRAB ON TO SOMETHING...
...I'LL DIE!

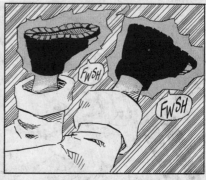
FWSH
FWSH
FWSH

!

SNATCH

NOW!

SLIP
WAAH!

READ THIS WAY

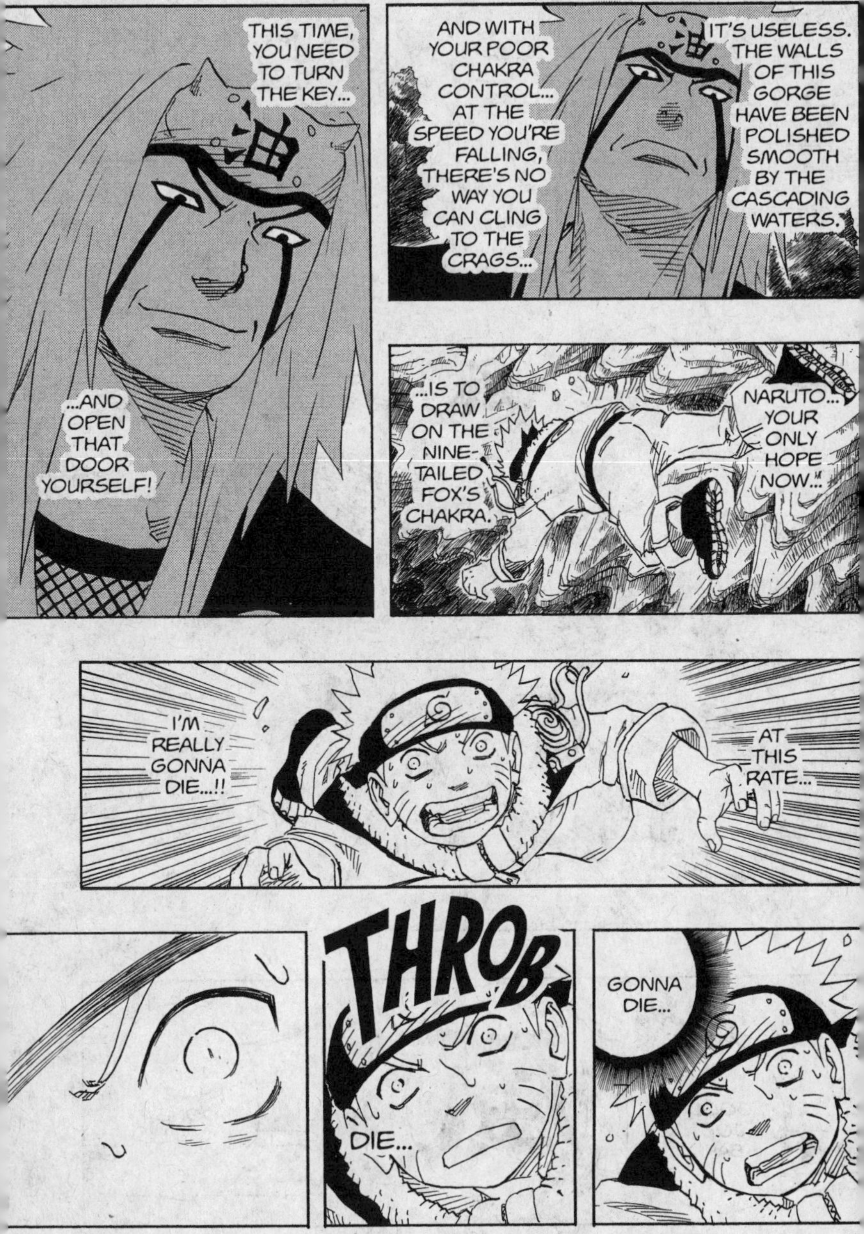

IT'S USELESS. THE WALLS OF THIS GORGE HAVE BEEN POLISHED SMOOTH BY THE CASCADING WATERS.
AND WITH YOUR POOR CHAKRA CONTROL... AT THE SPEED YOU'RE FALLING, THERE'S NO WAY YOU CAN CLING TO THE CRAGS...
NARUTO... YOUR ONLY HOPE NOW...
...IS TO DRAW ON THE NINE-TAILED FOX'S CHAKRA.
THIS TIME, YOU NEED TO TURN THE KEY...
...AND OPEN THAT DOOR YOURSELF!
AT THIS RATE...
I'M REALLY GONNA DIE...!!
GONNA DIE...
THROB
DIE...

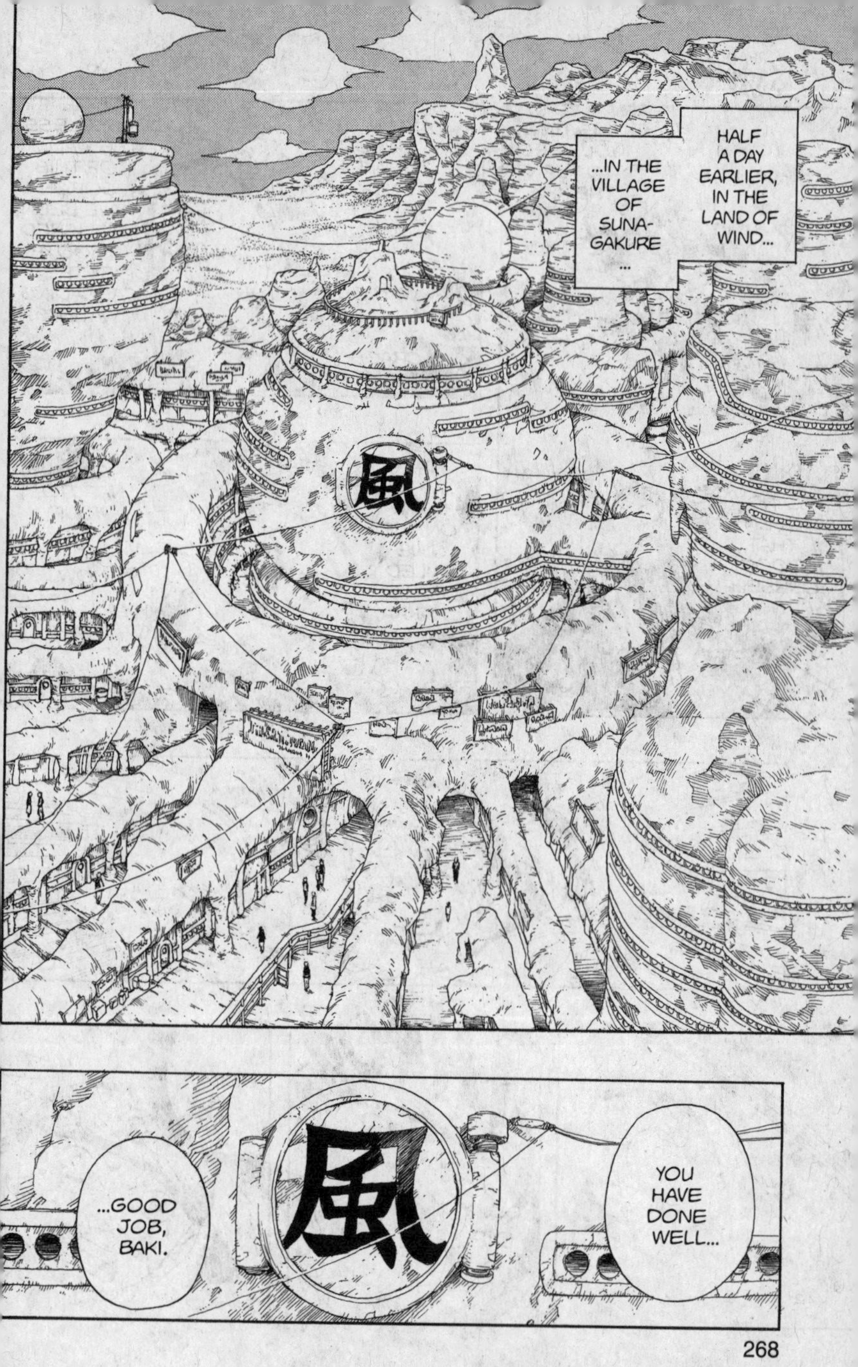
HALF A DAY EARLIER, IN THE LAND OF WIND...
...IN THE VILLAGE OF SUNA-GAKURE ...
風
YOU HAVE DONE WELL...
風
...GOOD JOB, BAKI.

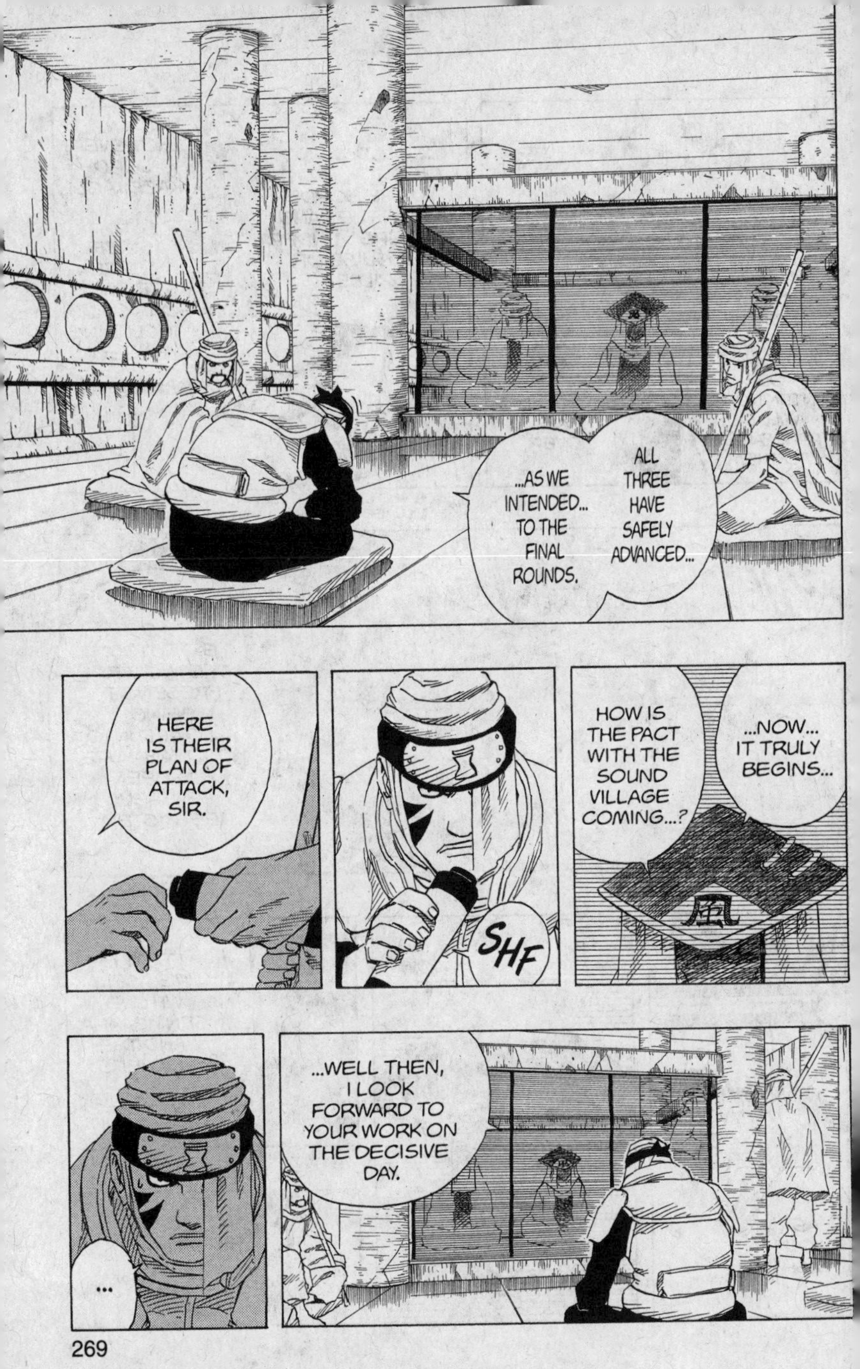
ALL THREE HAVE SAFELY ADVANCED...
...AS WE INTENDED... TO THE FINAL ROUNDS.
...NOW... IT TRULY BEGINS...
HOW IS THE PACT WITH THE SOUND VILLAGE COMING...?
SHF
HERE IS THEIR PLAN OF ATTACK, SIR.
...WELL THEN, I LOOK FORWARD TO YOUR WORK ON THE DECISIVE DAY.
...

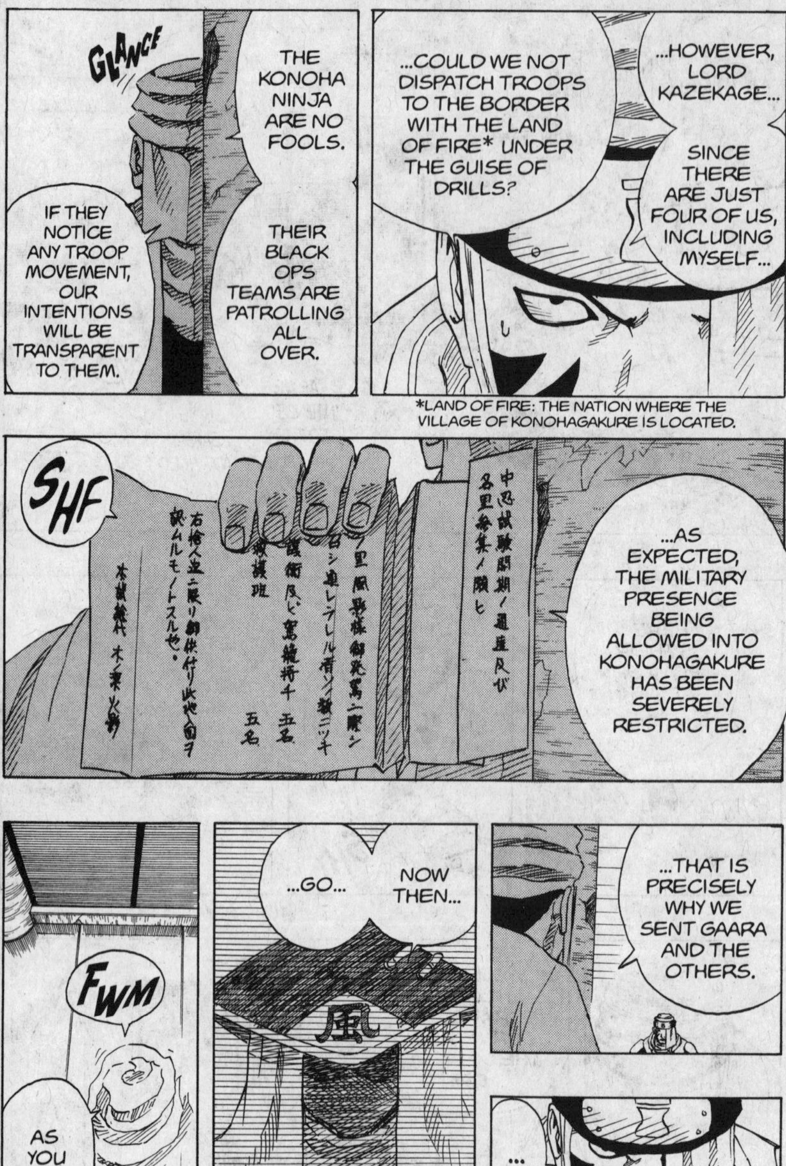
...HOWEVER, LORD KAZEKAGE...
SINCE THERE ARE JUST FOUR OF US, INCLUDING MYSELF...
...COULD WE NOT DISPATCH TROOPS TO THE BORDER WITH THE LAND OF FIRE* UNDER THE GUISE OF DRILLS?
THE KONOHA NINJA ARE NO FOOLS.
GLANCE
THEIR BLACK OPS TEAMS ARE PATROLLING ALL OVER.
IF THEY NOTICE ANY TROOP MOVEMENT, OUR INTENTIONS WILL BE TRANSPARENT TO THEM.
*LAND OF FIRE: THE NATION WHERE THE VILLAGE OF KONOHAGAKURE IS LOCATED.
...AS EXPECTED, THE MILITARY PRESENCE BEING ALLOWED INTO KONOHAGAKURE HAS BEEN SEVERELY RESTRICTED.
SHF
...THAT IS PRECISELY WHY WE SENT GAARA AND THE OTHERS.
...
NOW THEN...
...GO...
FWM
AS YOU WISH.

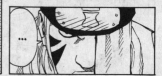

READ THIS WAY

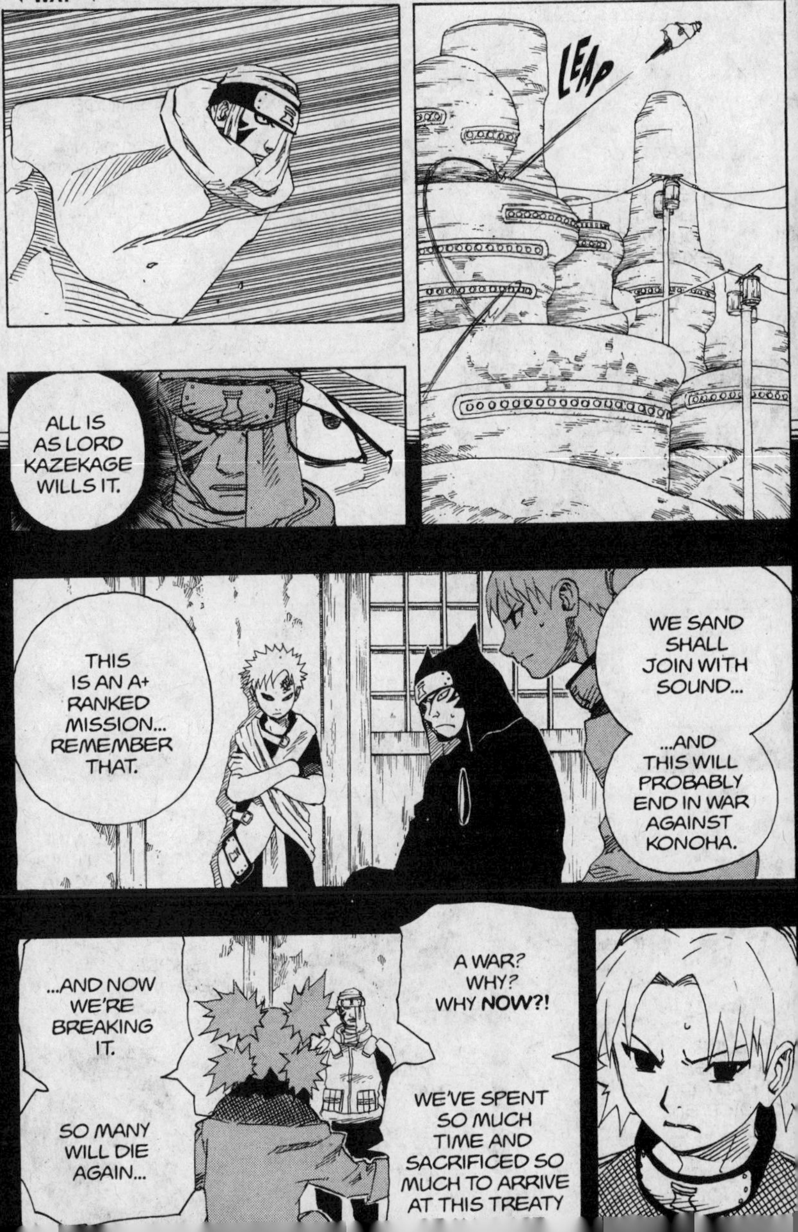

LEAP
ALL IS AS LORD KAZEKAGE WILLS IT.
WE SAND SHALL JOIN WITH SOUND...
...AND THIS WILL PROBABLY END IN WAR AGAINST KONOHA.
THIS IS AN A+ RANKED MISSION... REMEMBER THAT.
A WAR? WHY? WHY **NOW**?!
WE'VE SPENT SO MUCH TIME AND SACRIFICED SO MUCH TO ARRIVE AT THIS TREATY
...AND NOW WE'RE BREAKING IT.
SO MANY WILL DIE AGAIN...

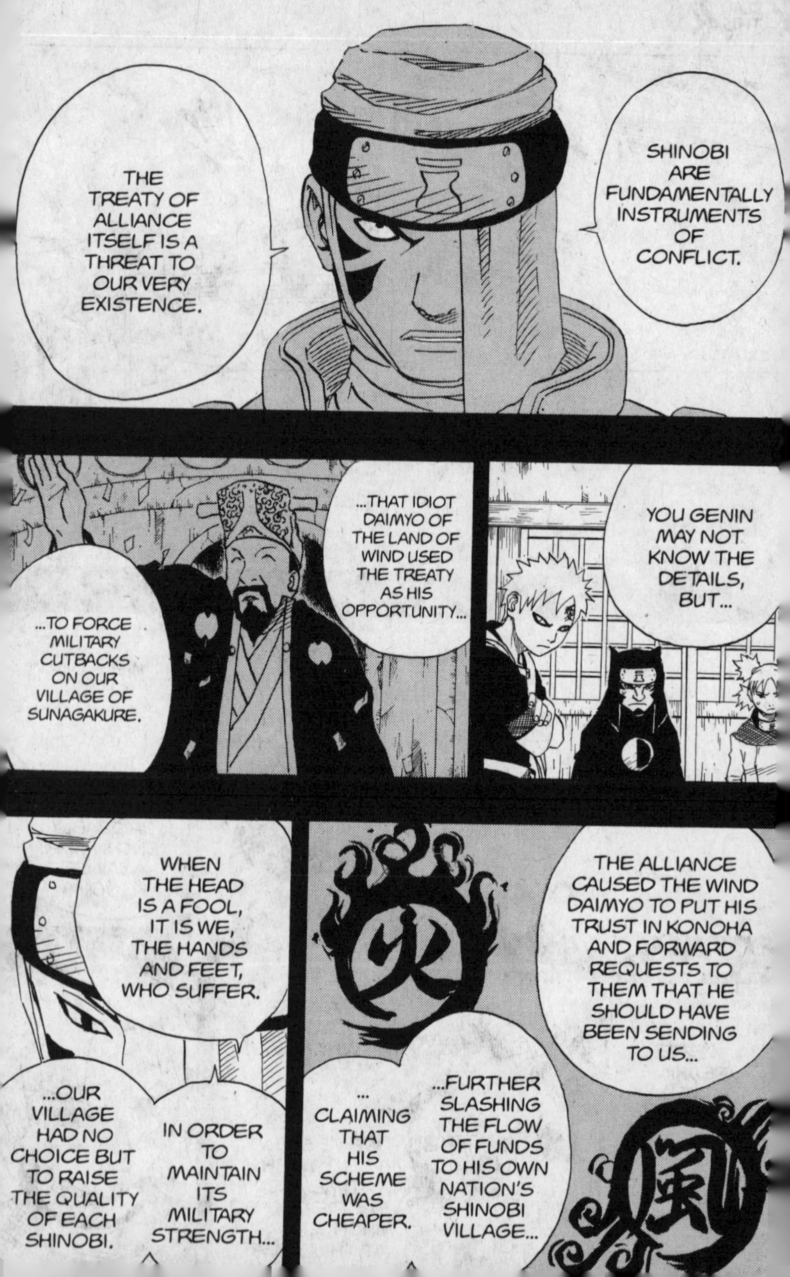
SHINOBI ARE FUNDAMENTALLY INSTRUMENTS OF CONFLICT.
THE TREATY OF ALLIANCE ITSELF IS A THREAT TO OUR VERY EXISTENCE.
YOU GENIN MAY NOT KNOW THE DETAILS, BUT...
...THAT IDIOT DAIMYO OF THE LAND OF WIND USED THE TREATY AS HIS OPPORTUNITY...
...TO FORCE MILITARY CUTBACKS ON OUR VILLAGE OF SUNAGAKURE.
THE ALLIANCE CAUSED THE WIND DAIMYO TO PUT HIS TRUST IN KONOHA AND FORWARD REQUESTS TO THEM THAT HE SHOULD HAVE BEEN SENDING TO US...
...FURTHER SLASHING THE FLOW OF FUNDS TO HIS OWN NATION'S SHINOBI VILLAGE...
...CLAIMING THAT HIS SCHEME WAS CHEAPER.
WHEN THE HEAD IS A FOOL, IT IS WE, THE HANDS AND FEET, WHO SUFFER.
IN ORDER TO MAINTAIN ITS MILITARY STRENGTH...
...OUR VILLAGE HAD NO CHOICE BUT TO RAISE THE QUALITY OF EACH SHINOBI.

READ THIS WAY

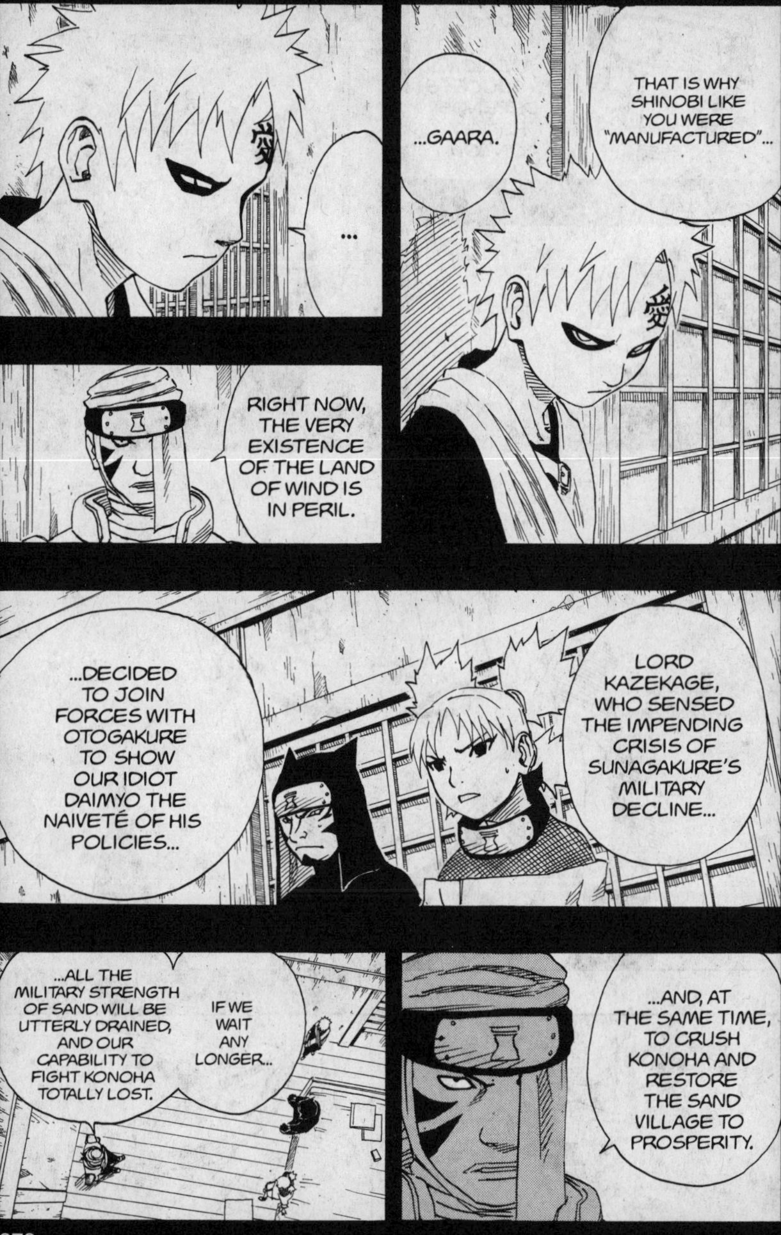
THAT IS WHY SHINOBI LIKE YOU WERE "MANUFACTURED"...
...GAARA.
...
RIGHT NOW, THE VERY EXISTENCE OF THE LAND OF WIND IS IN PERIL.
LORD KAZEKAGE, WHO SENSED THE IMPENDING CRISIS OF SUNAGAKURE'S MILITARY DECLINE...
...DECIDED TO JOIN FORCES WITH OTOGAKURE TO SHOW OUR IDIOT DAIMYO THE NAIVETÉ OF HIS POLICIES...
...AND, AT THE SAME TIME, TO CRUSH KONOHA AND RESTORE THE SAND VILLAGE TO PROSPERITY.
IF WE WAIT ANY LONGER...
...ALL THE MILITARY STRENGTH OF SAND WILL BE UTTERLY DRAINED, AND OUR CAPABILITY TO FIGHT KONOHA TOTALLY LOST.

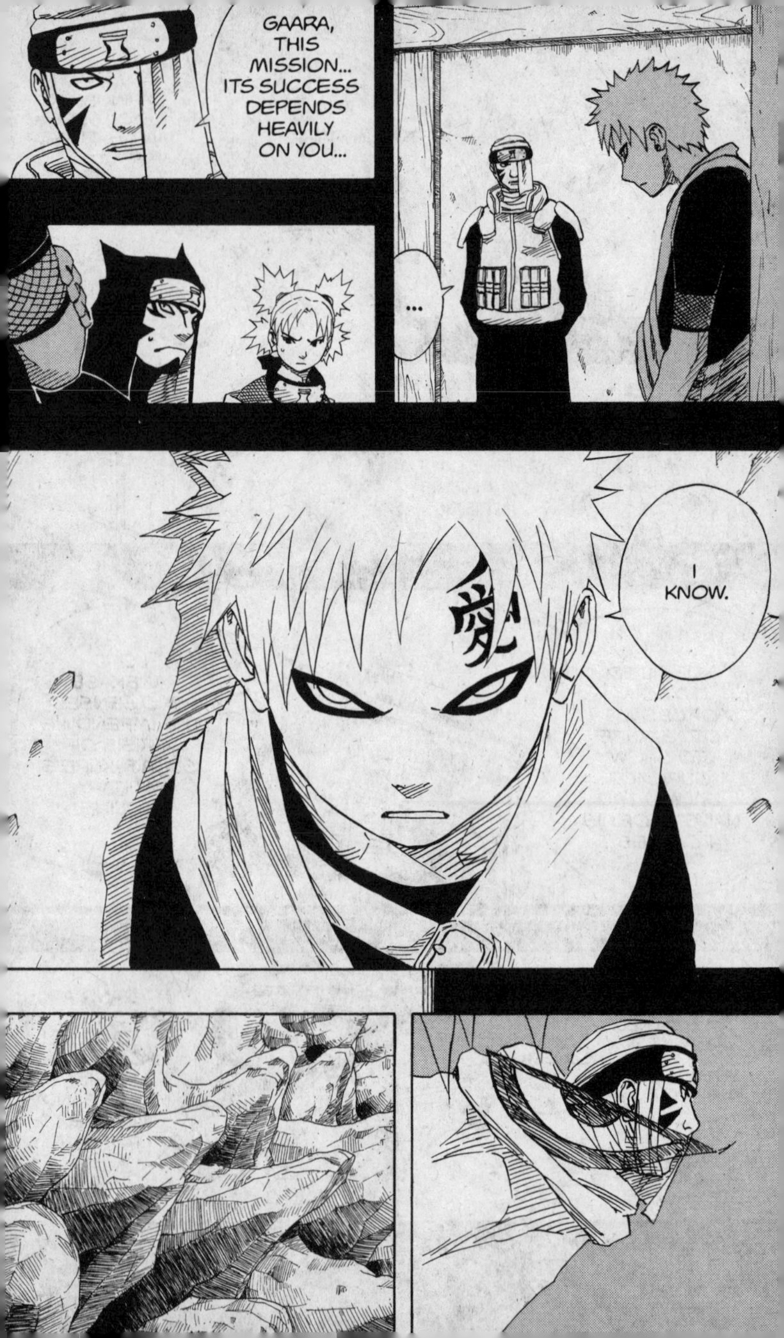
...
GAARA, THIS MISSION... ITS SUCCESS DEPENDS HEAVILY ON YOU...
I KNOW.

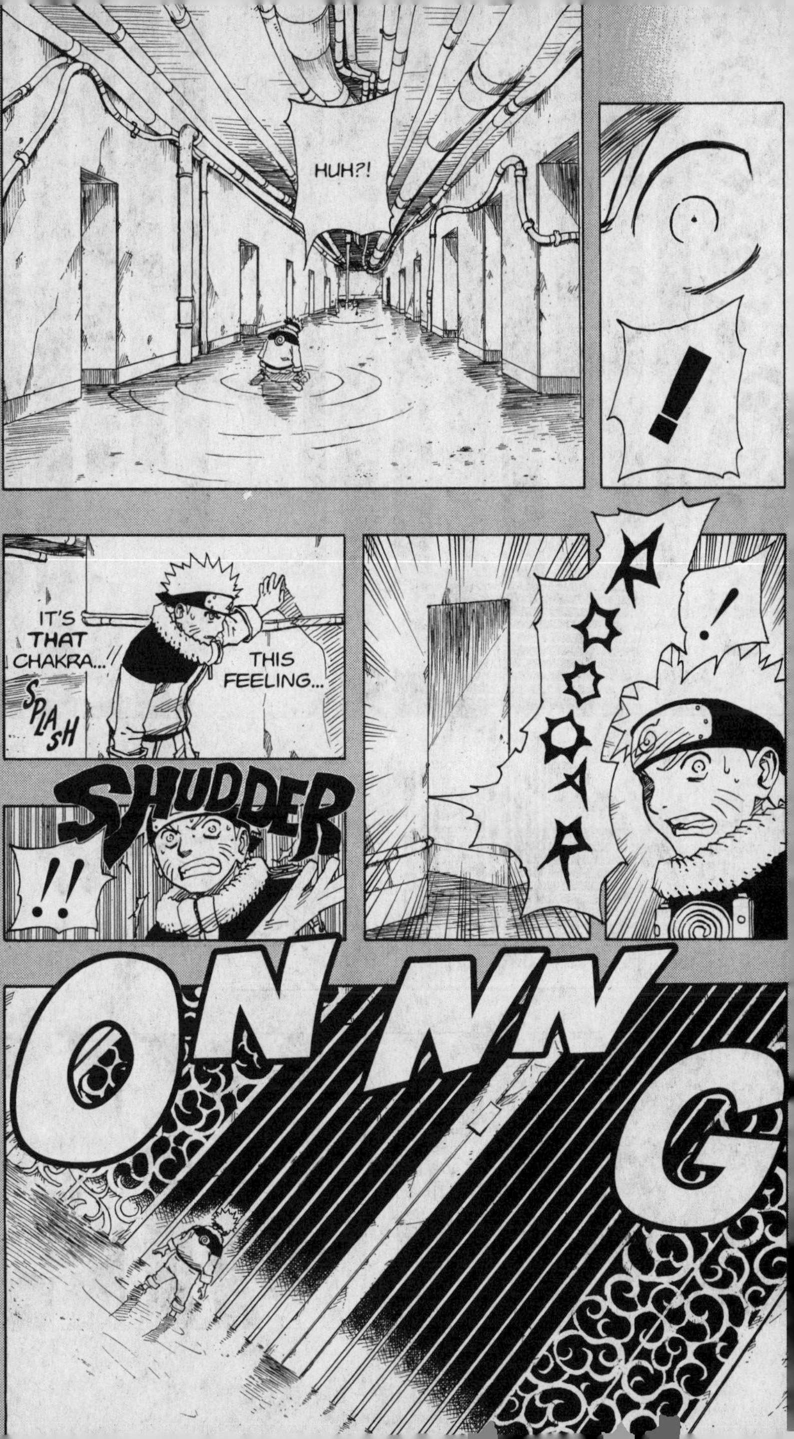
!
HUH?!
!
THIS FEELING...
IT'S THAT CHAKRA...
SPLASH
SHUDDER
!!
ONNNG

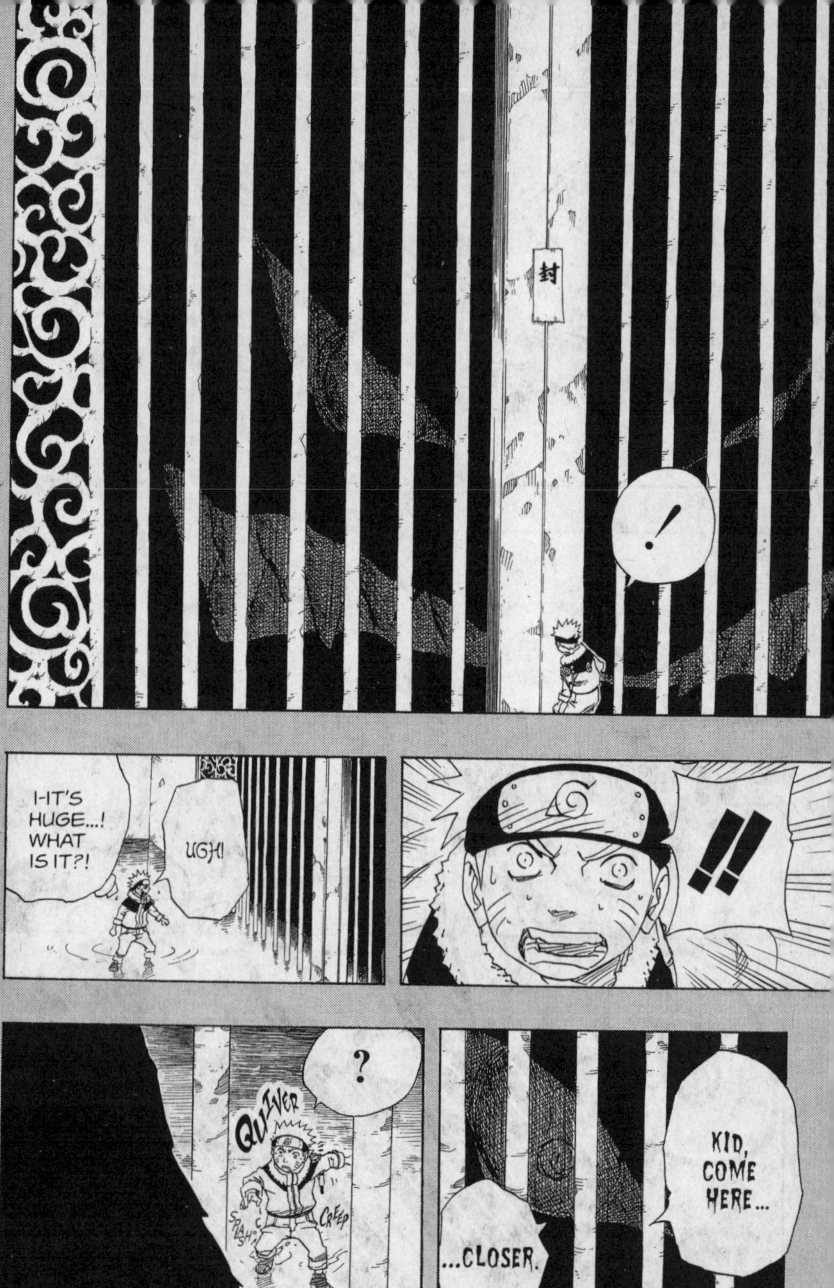
封
!
!!
UGH!
I-IT'S HUGE...! WHAT IS IT?!
KID, COME HERE...
...CLOSER.
?
QUIVER
CREEP
SPLASH

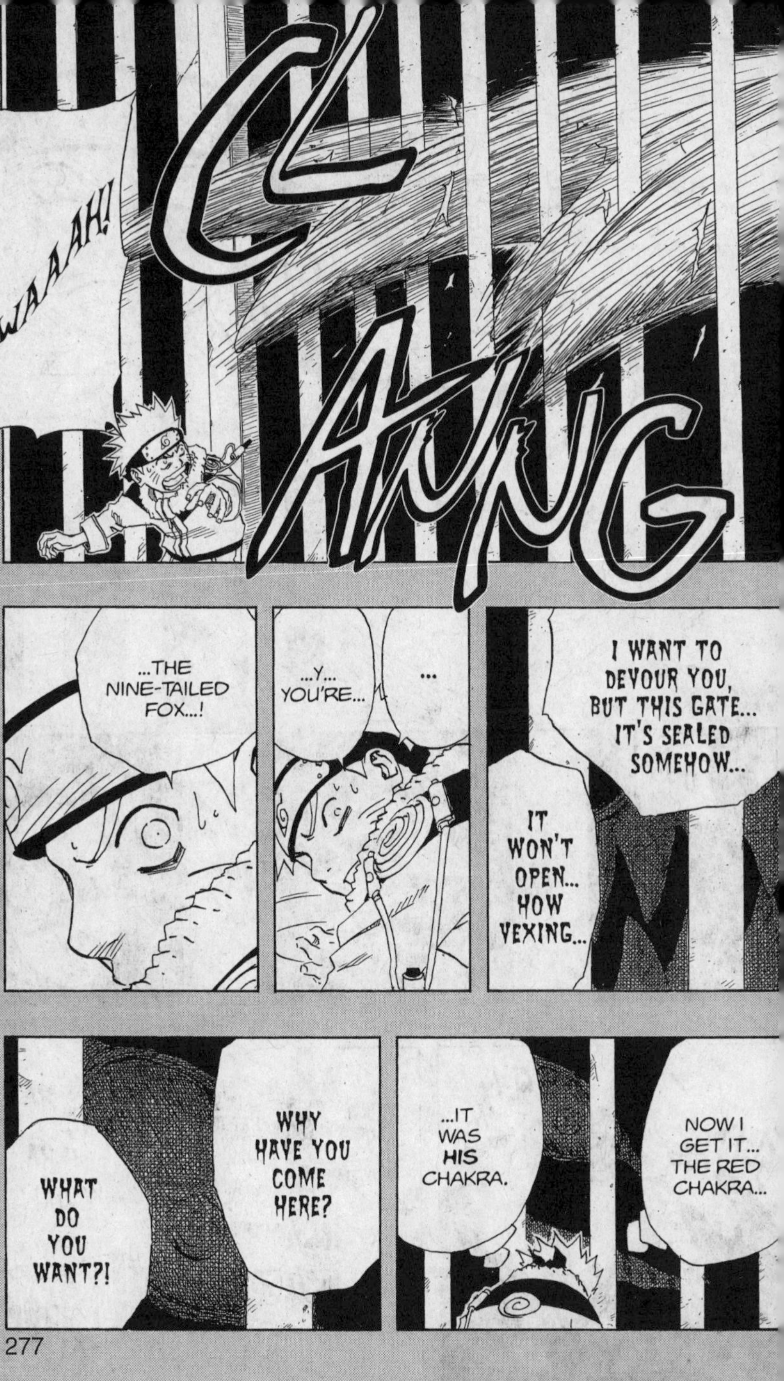
CLANG
WAAAH!
I WANT TO DEVOUR YOU, BUT THIS GATE... IT'S SEALED SOMEHOW...
IT WON'T OPEN... HOW VEXING...
...
...Y... YOU'RE...
...THE NINE-TAILED FOX...!
NOW I GET IT... THE RED CHAKRA...
...IT WAS **HIS** CHAKRA.
WHY HAVE YOU COME HERE?
WHAT DO YOU WANT?!

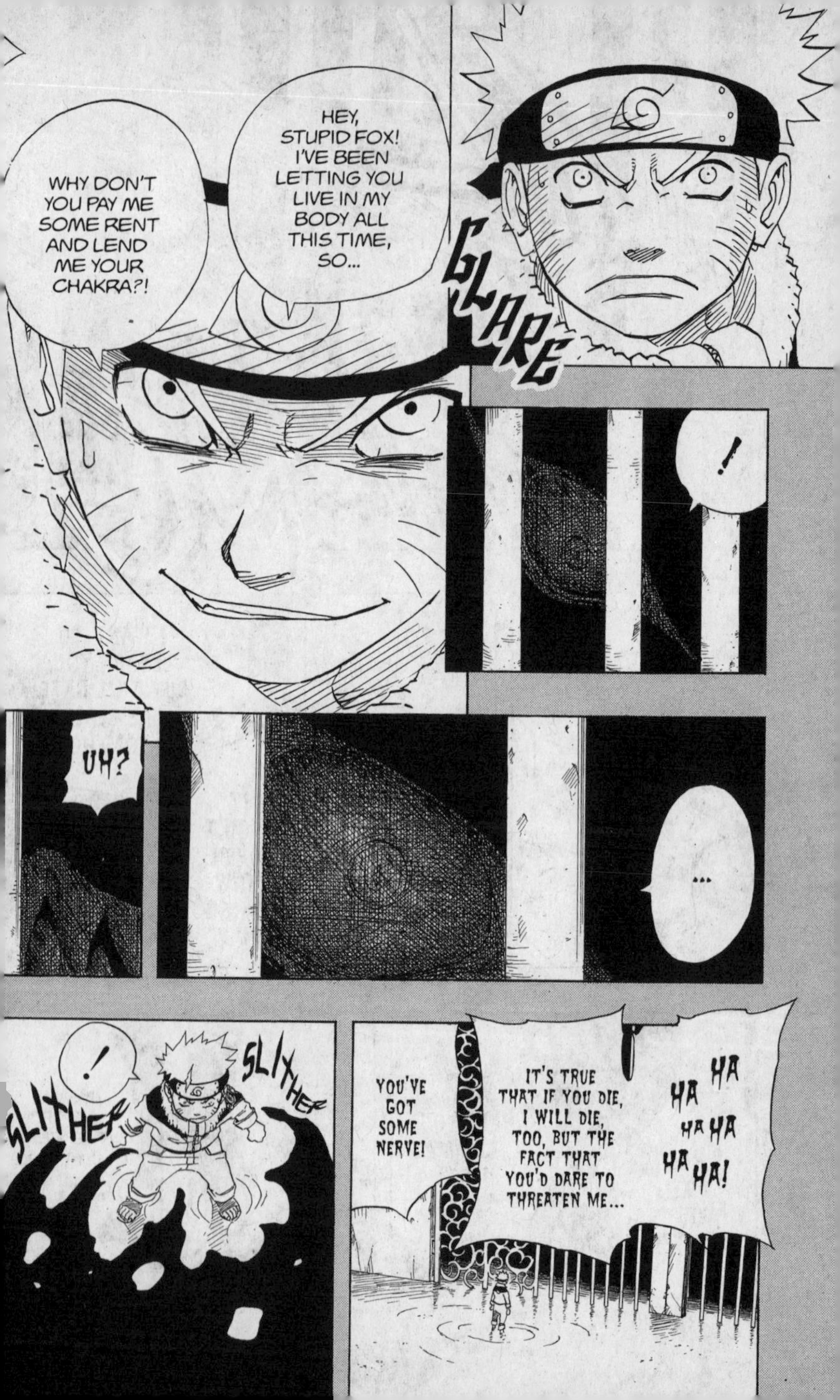
GLARE
!
HEY, STUPID FOX! I'VE BEEN LETTING YOU LIVE IN MY BODY ALL THIS TIME, SO...
WHY DON'T YOU PAY ME SOME RENT AND LEND ME YOUR CHAKRA?!
...
UH?
IT'S TRUE THAT IF YOU DIE, I WILL DIE, TOO, BUT THE FACT THAT YOU'D DARE TO THREATEN ME...
HA HA HA HA HA HA!
YOU'VE GOT SOME NERVE!
!
SLITHER
SLITHER

READ THIS WAY

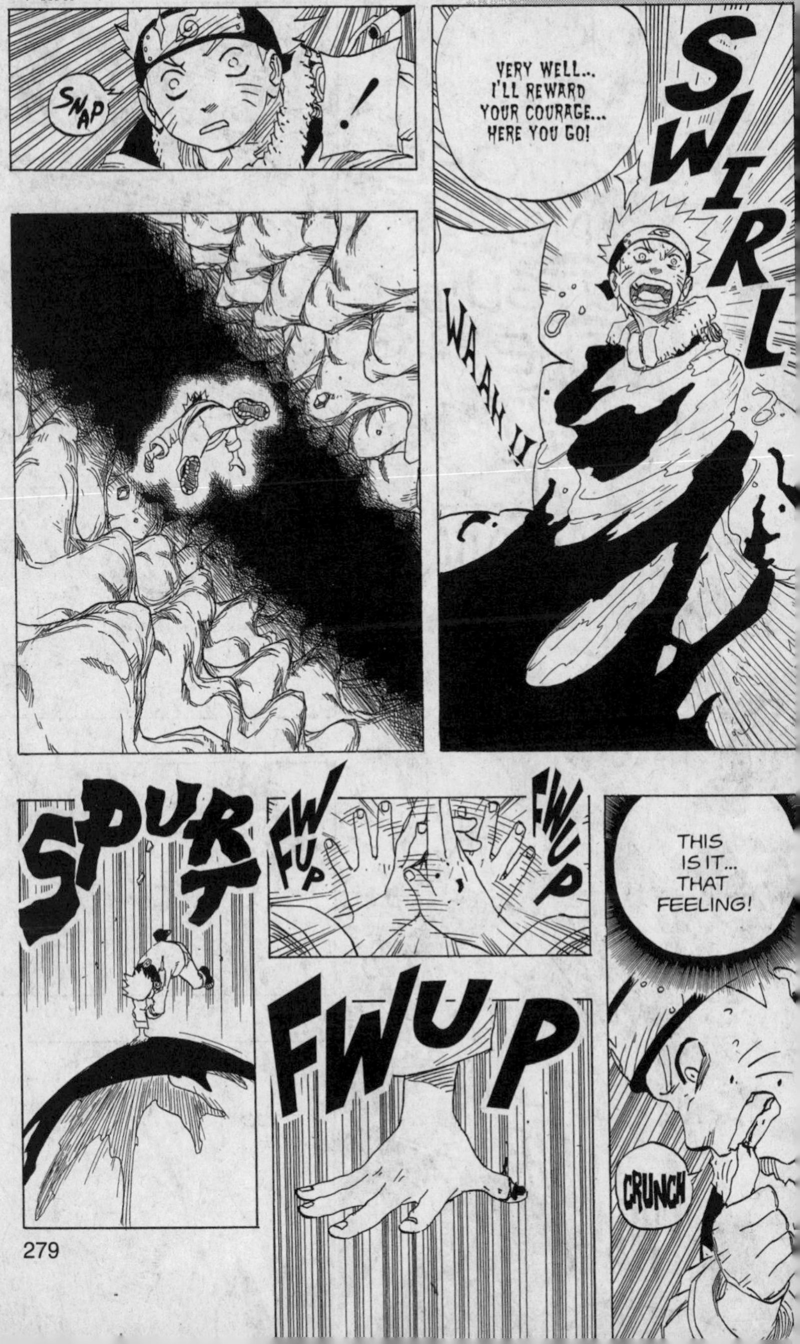

SWIRL
VERY WELL... I'LL REWARD YOUR COURAGE... HERE YOU GO!
WAAAH!!
SNAP
!
THIS IS IT... THAT FEELING!
CRUNCH
FWUP
FWUP
FWUP
SPURT

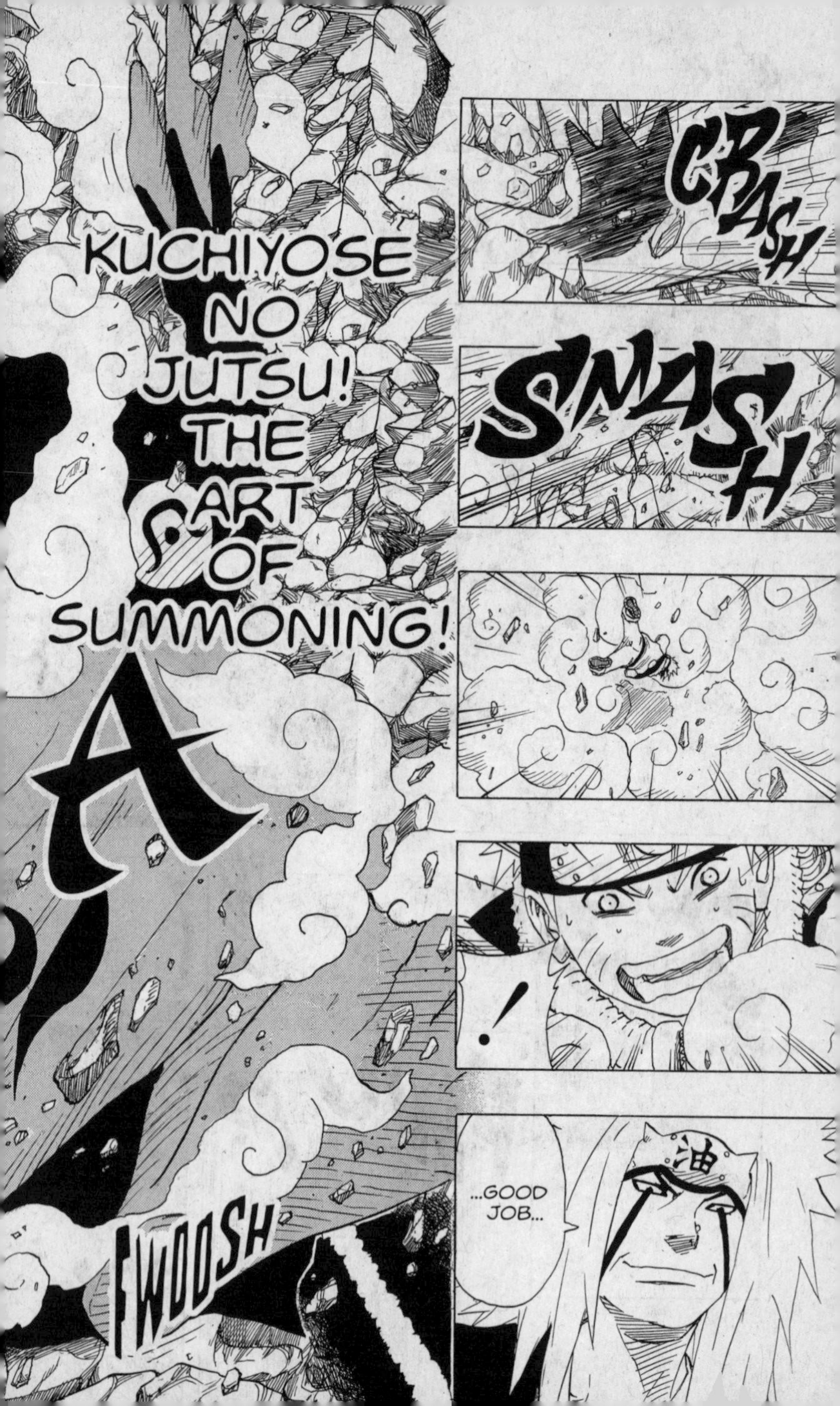
CRASH
SMASH
!
油
...GOOD JOB...
KUCHIYOSE NO JUTSU! THE ART OF SUMMONING!
FWOOSH

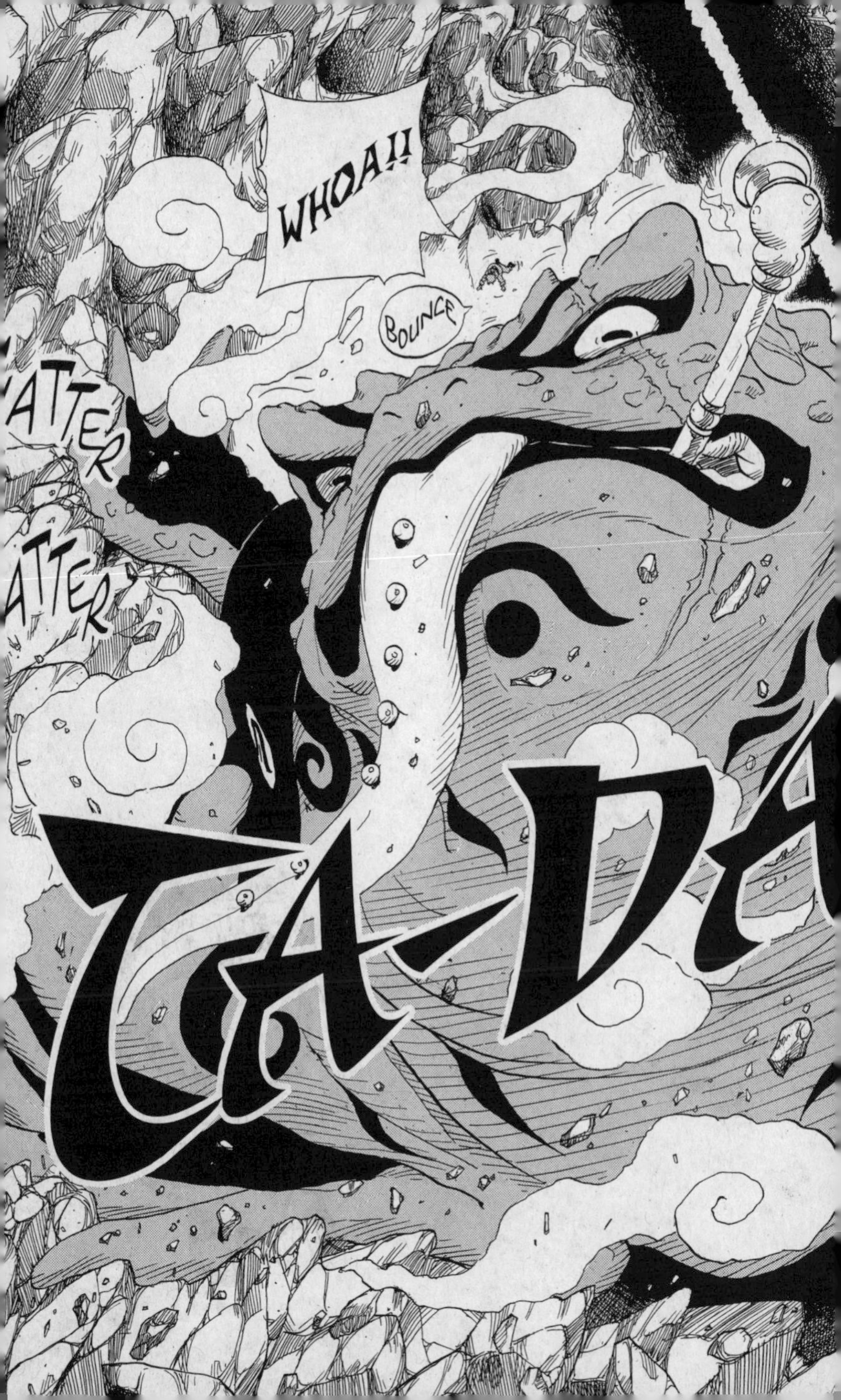

WHOA!!
BOUNCE
ATTER
ATTER
TA-DA

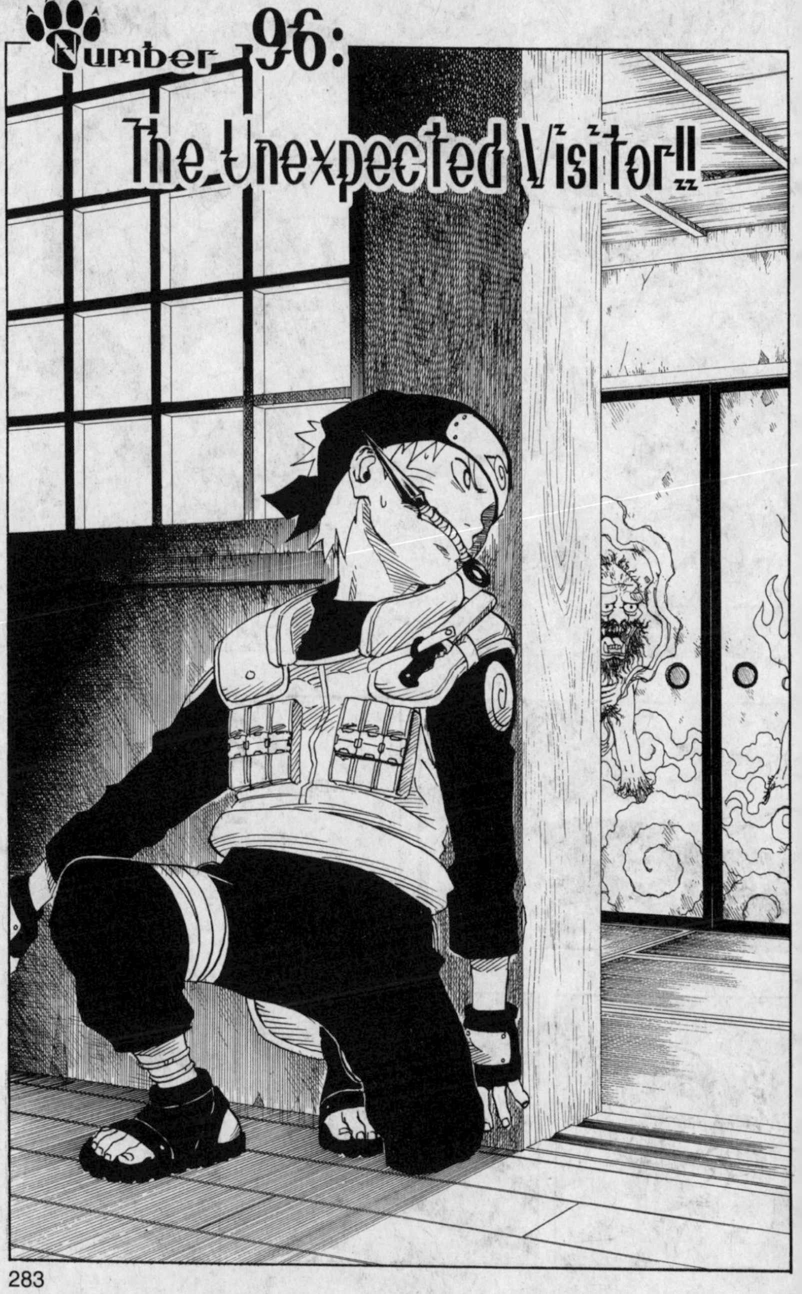
Number 96:
The Unexpected Visitor!!

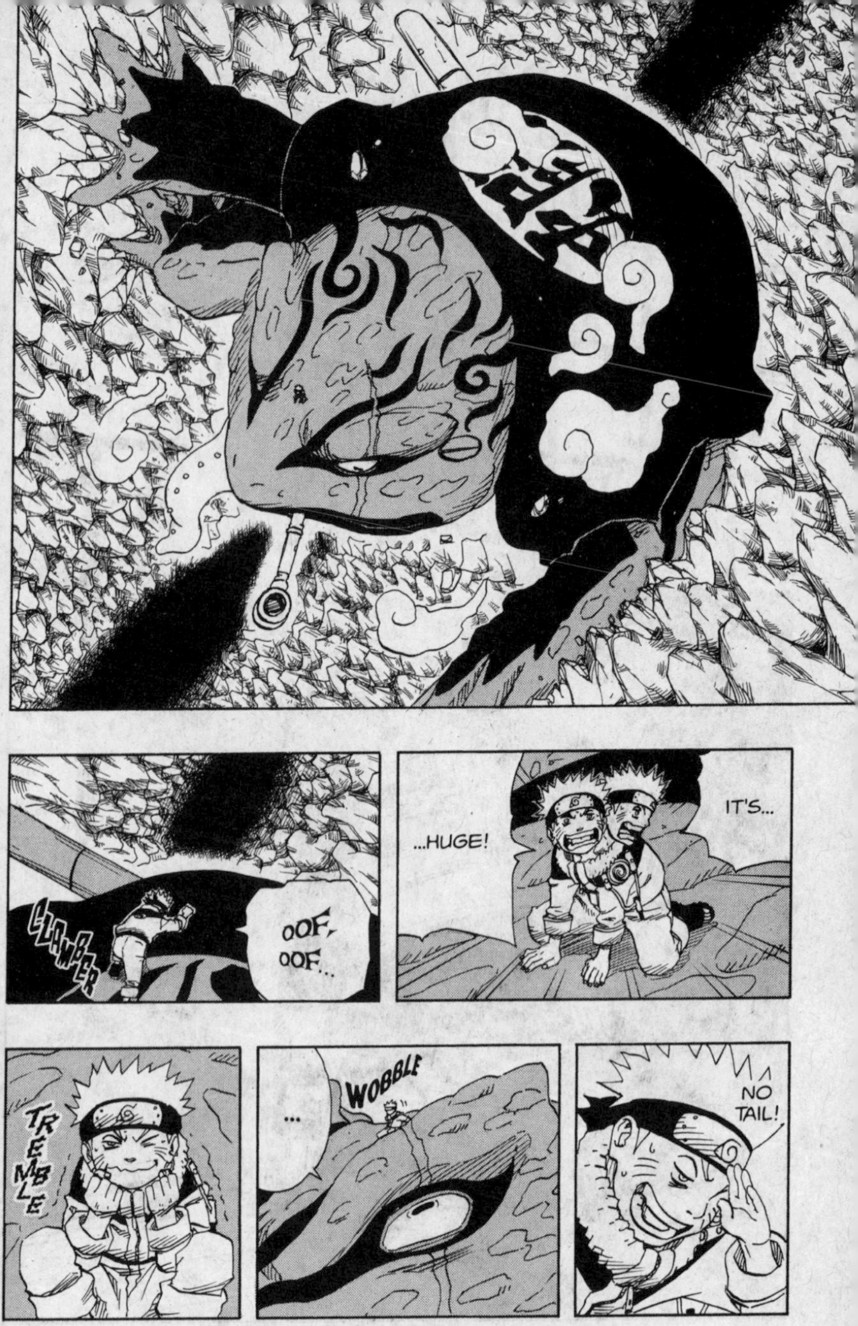
IT'S...
...HUGE!
OOF, OOF...
CLAMBER
NO TAIL!
WOBBLE
...
TREMBLE

READ THIS WAY

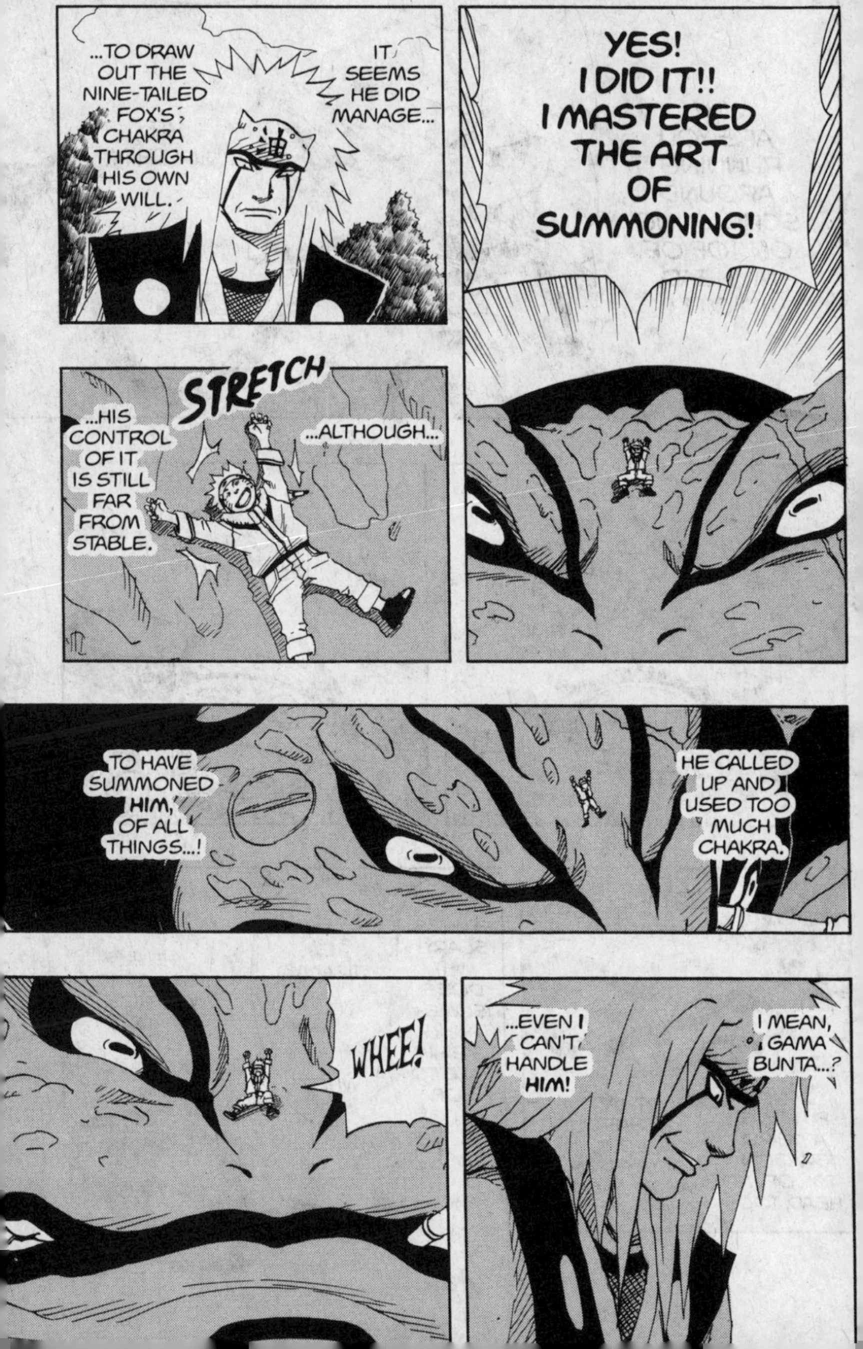
YES! I DID IT!! I MASTERED THE ART OF SUMMONING!
IT SEEMS HE DID MANAGE...
...TO DRAW OUT THE NINE-TAILED FOX'S CHAKRA THROUGH HIS OWN WILL.
...ALTHOUGH...
STRETCH
...HIS CONTROL OF IT IS STILL FAR FROM STABLE.
HE CALLED UP AND USED TOO MUCH CHAKRA.
TO HAVE SUMMONED HIM, OF ALL THINGS...!
I MEAN, GAMA BUNTA...?
...EVEN I CAN'T HANDLE HIM!
WHEE!

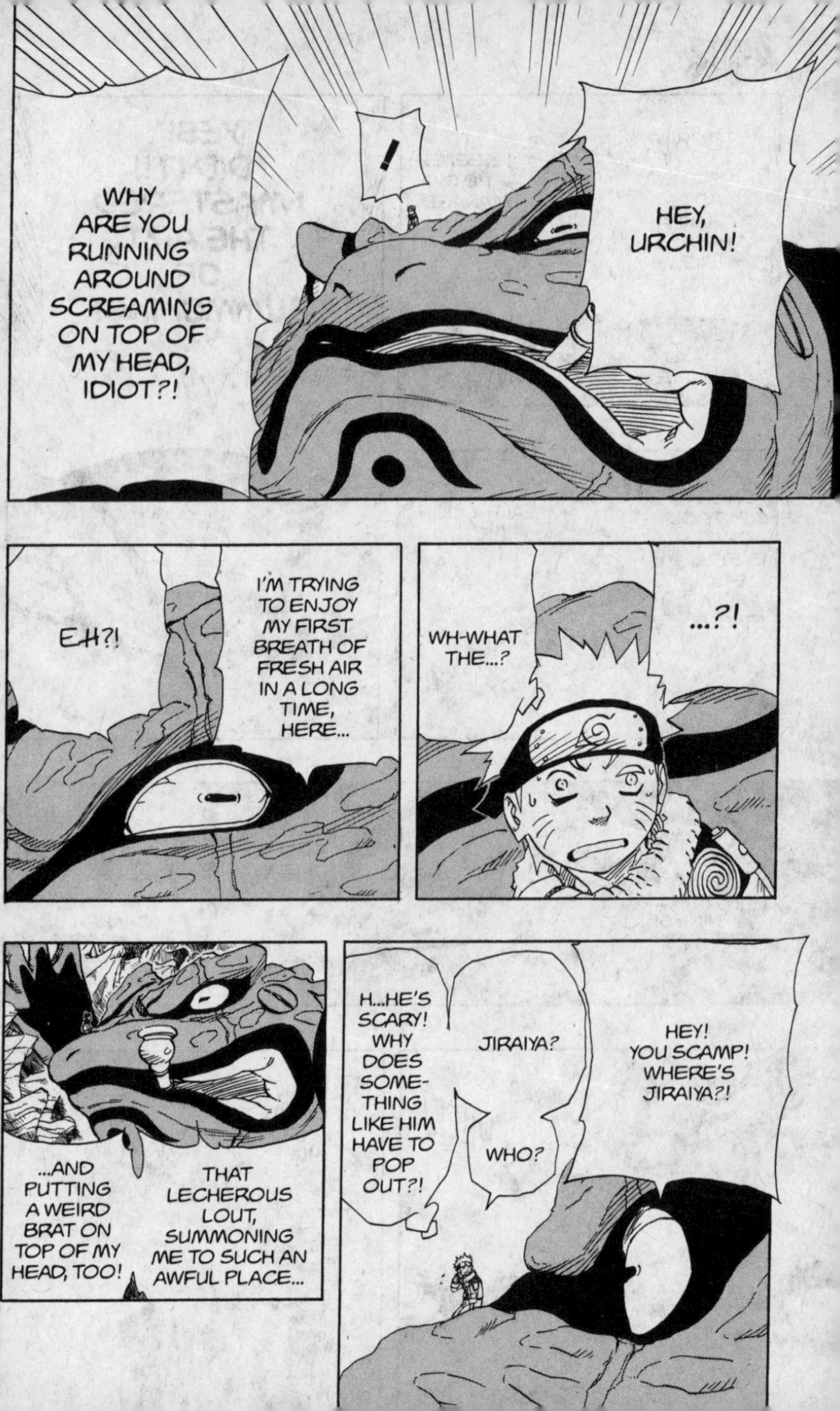
HEY, URCHIN!
!
WHY ARE YOU RUNNING AROUND SCREAMING ON TOP OF MY HEAD, IDIOT?!
...?!
WH-WHAT THE...?
I'M TRYING TO ENJOY MY FIRST BREATH OF FRESH AIR IN A LONG TIME, HERE...
EH?!
HEY! YOU SCAMP! WHERE'S JIRAIYA?!
JIRAIYA?
WHO?
H...HE'S SCARY! WHY DOES SOME-THING LIKE HIM HAVE TO POP OUT?!
THAT LECHEROUS LOUT, SUMMONING ME TO SUCH AN AWFUL PLACE...
...AND PUTTING A WEIRD BRAT ON TOP OF MY HEAD, TOO!

READ THIS WAY

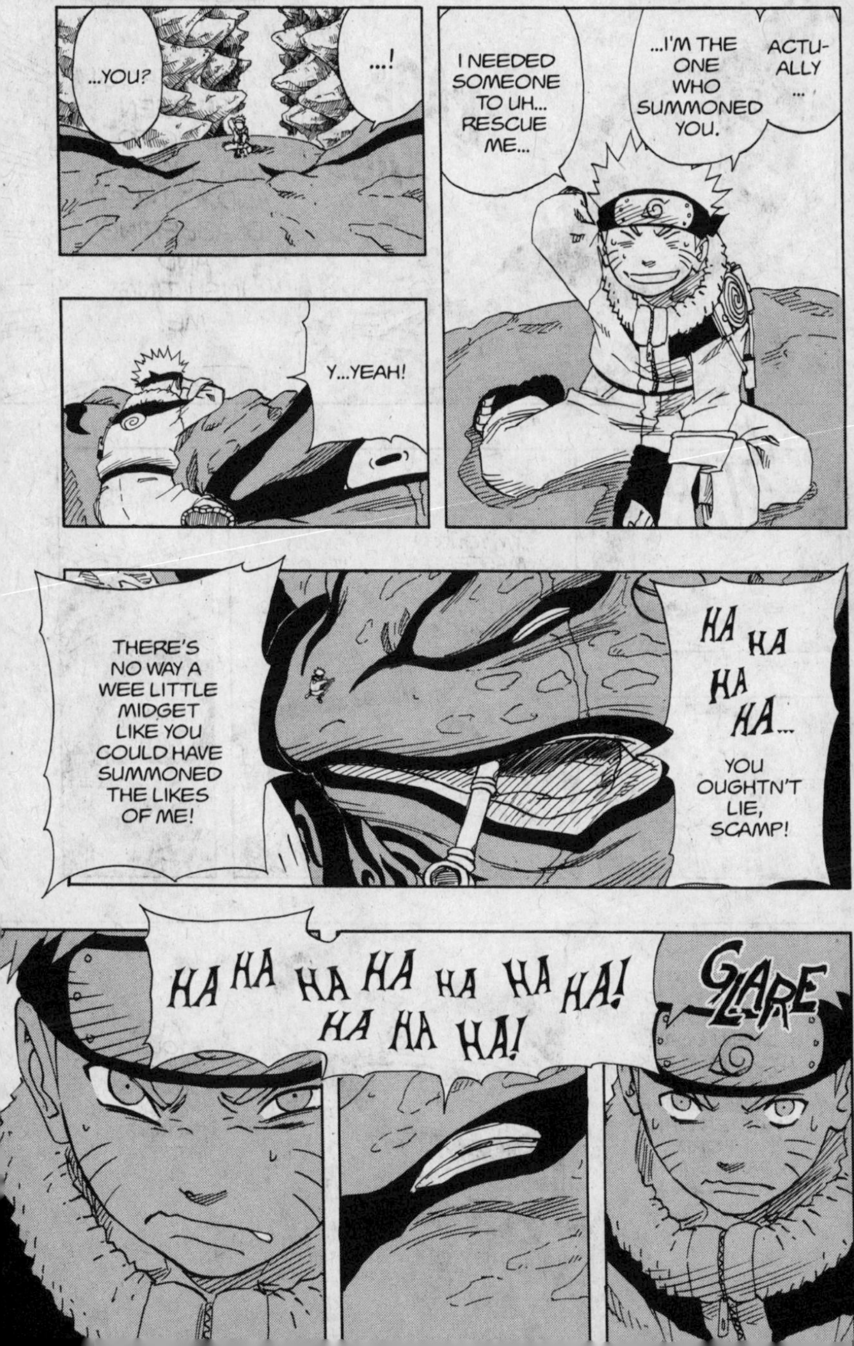
ACTUALLY...
...I'M THE ONE WHO SUMMONED YOU.
I NEEDED SOMEONE TO UH... RESCUE ME...
...!
...YOU?
Y...YEAH!
HA HA HA HA...
YOU OUGHTN'T LIE, SCAMP!
THERE'S NO WAY A WEE LITTLE MIDGET LIKE YOU COULD HAVE SUMMONED THE LIKES OF ME!
HA HA HA HA HA HA HA! HA HA HA!
GLARE

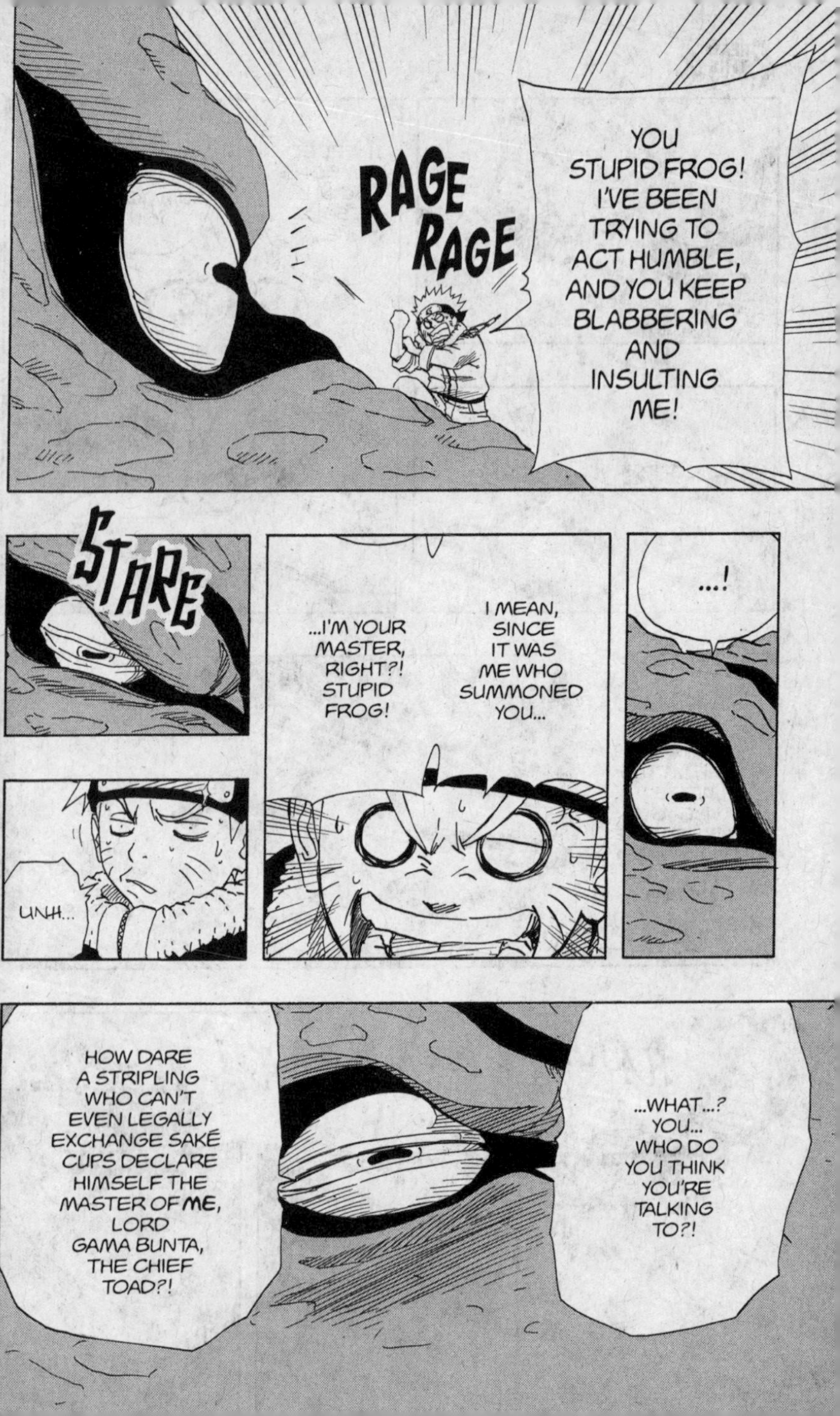
YOU STUPID FROG! I'VE BEEN TRYING TO ACT HUMBLE, AND YOU KEEP BLABBERING AND INSULTING ME!
RAGE RAGE
...!
I MEAN, SINCE IT WAS ME WHO SUMMONED YOU...
...I'M YOUR MASTER, RIGHT?! STUPID FROG!
STARE
UNH...
...WHAT...? YOU... WHO DO YOU THINK YOU'RE TALKING TO?!
HOW DARE A STRIPLING WHO CAN'T EVEN LEGALLY EXCHANGE SAKÉ CUPS DECLARE HIMSELF THE MASTER OF ME, LORD GAMA BUNTA, THE CHIEF TOAD?!

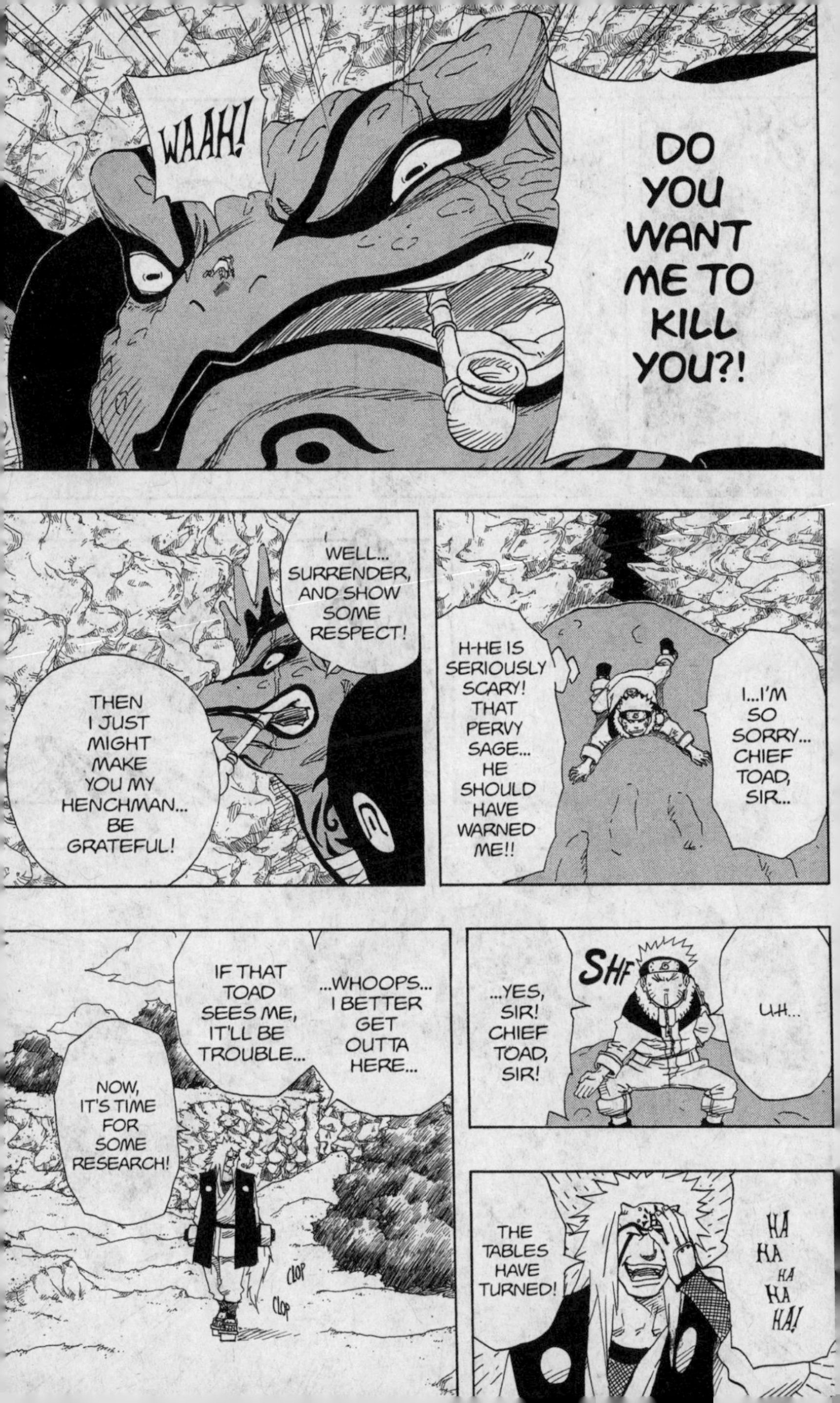
DO YOU WANT ME TO KILL YOU?!
WAAH!
I...I'M SO SORRY... CHIEF TOAD, SIR...
H-HE IS SERIOUSLY SCARY! THAT PERVY SAGE... HE SHOULD HAVE WARNED ME!!
I WELL... SURRENDER, AND SHOW SOME RESPECT!
THEN I JUST MIGHT MAKE YOU MY HENCHMAN... BE GRATEFUL!
UH...
SHF
...YES, SIR! CHIEF TOAD, SIR!
HA HA HA HA HA!
THE TABLES HAVE TURNED!
...WHOOPS... I BETTER GET OUTTA HERE...
IF THAT TOAD SEES ME, IT'LL BE TROUBLE...
NOW, IT'S TIME FOR SOME RESEARCH!
CLOP
CLOP

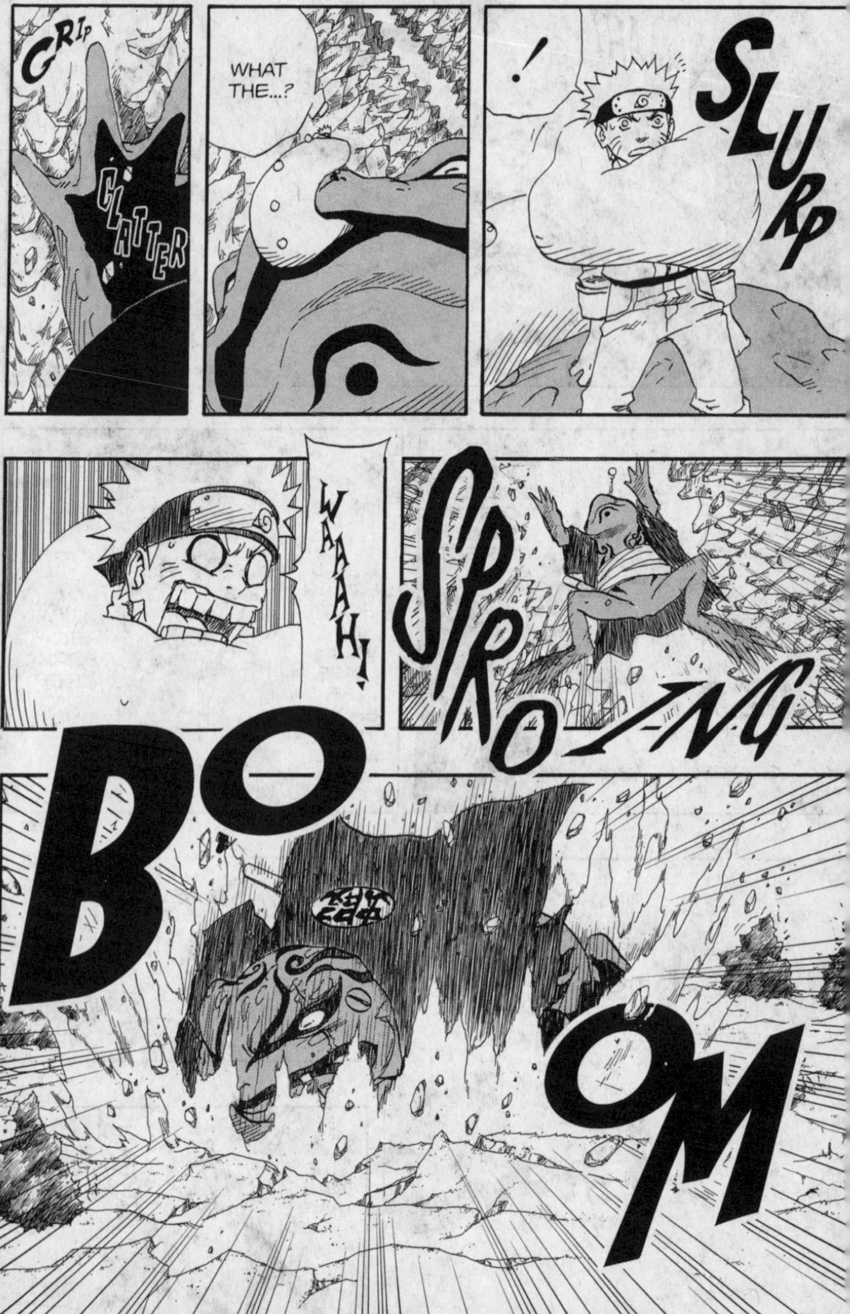
!
SLURP
WHAT THE...?
GRIP
CLATTER
SPROING
WAAAH!
BOOM

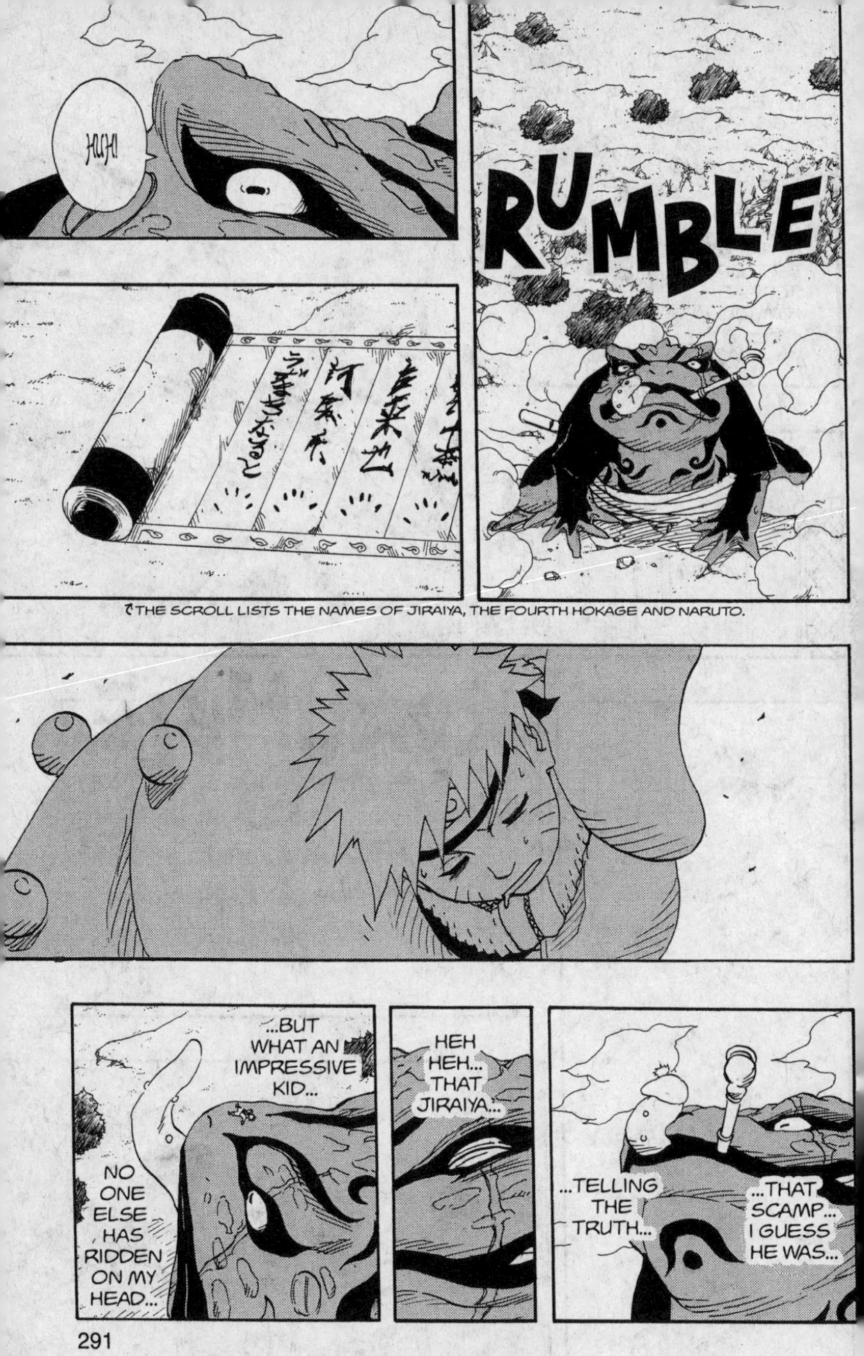
RUMBLE
HUH!
THE SCROLL LISTS THE NAMES OF JIRAIYA, THE FOURTH HOKAGE AND NARUTO.
...THAT SCAMP... I GUESS HE WAS...
...TELLING THE TRUTH...
HEH HEH... THAT JIRAIYA...
...BUT WHAT AN IMPRESSIVE KID...
NO ONE ELSE HAS RIDDEN ON MY HEAD...

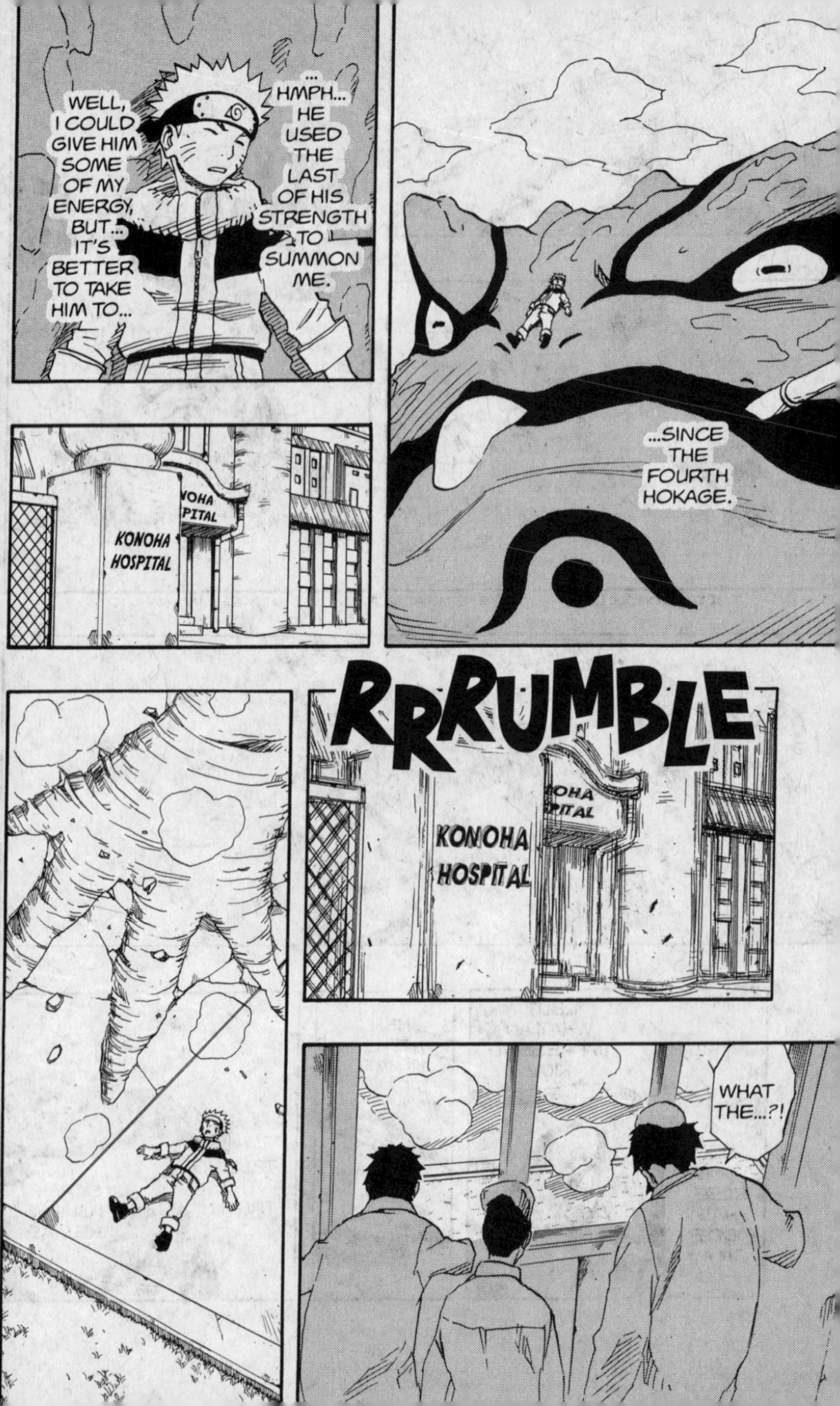
...SINCE THE FOURTH HOKAGE.
... HMPH... HE USED THE LAST OF HIS STRENGTH TO SUMMON ME.
WELL, I COULD GIVE HIM SOME OF MY ENERGY, BUT... IT'S BETTER TO TAKE HIM TO...
KONOHA HOSPITAL
RRRUMBLE
KONOHA HOSPITAL
WHAT THE...?!

READ THIS WAY

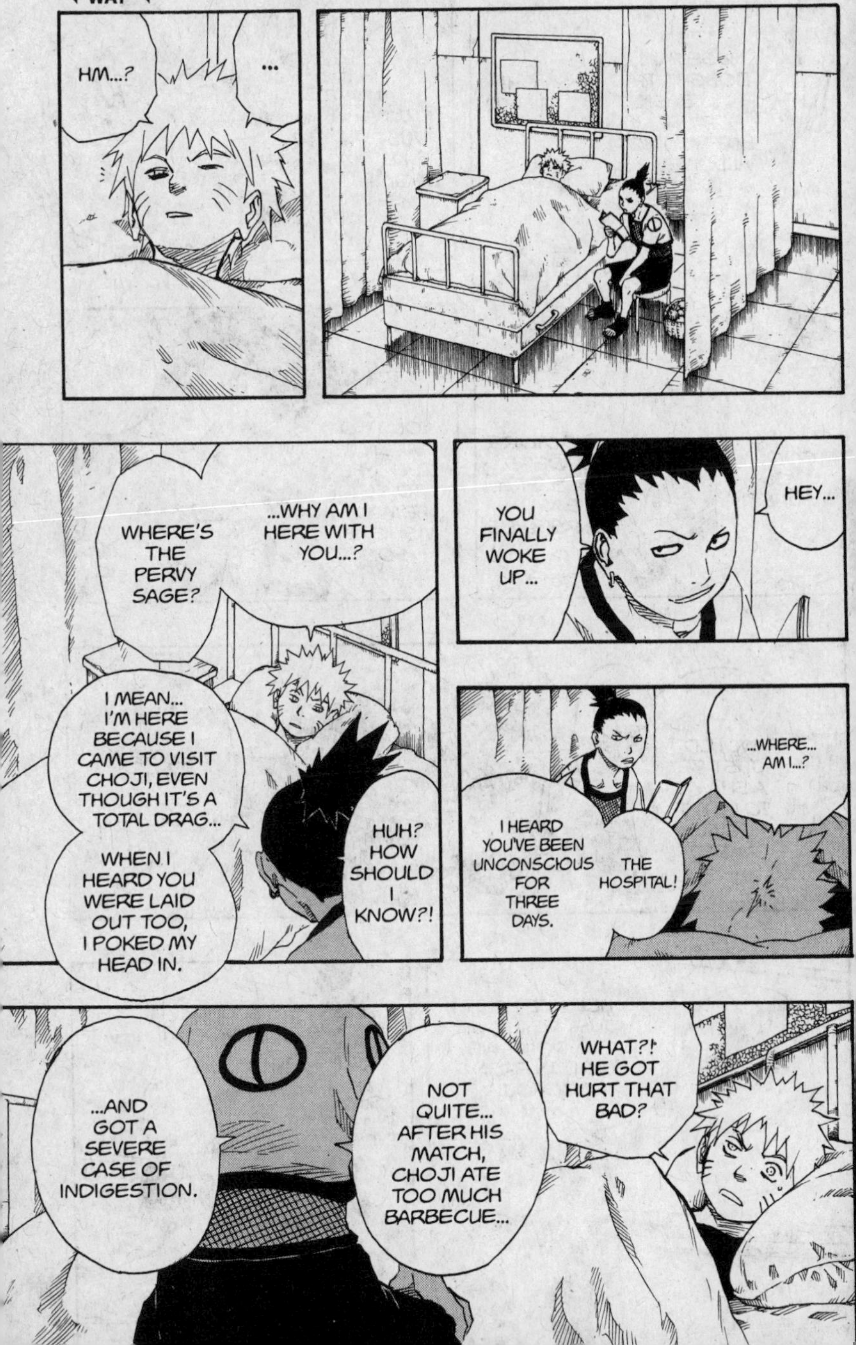
...
HM...?
HEY...
YOU FINALLY WOKE UP...
...WHERE... AM I...?
THE HOSPITAL!
I HEARD YOU'VE BEEN UNCONSCIOUS FOR THREE DAYS.
...WHY AM I HERE WITH YOU...?
WHERE'S THE PERVY SAGE?
HUH? HOW SHOULD I KNOW?!
I MEAN... I'M HERE BECAUSE I CAME TO VISIT CHOJI, EVEN THOUGH IT'S A TOTAL DRAG...
WHEN I HEARD YOU WERE LAID OUT TOO, I POKED MY HEAD IN.
WHAT?! HE GOT HURT THAT BAD?
NOT QUITE... AFTER HIS MATCH, CHOJI ATE TOO MUCH BARBECUE...
...AND GOT A SEVERE CASE OF INDIGESTION.

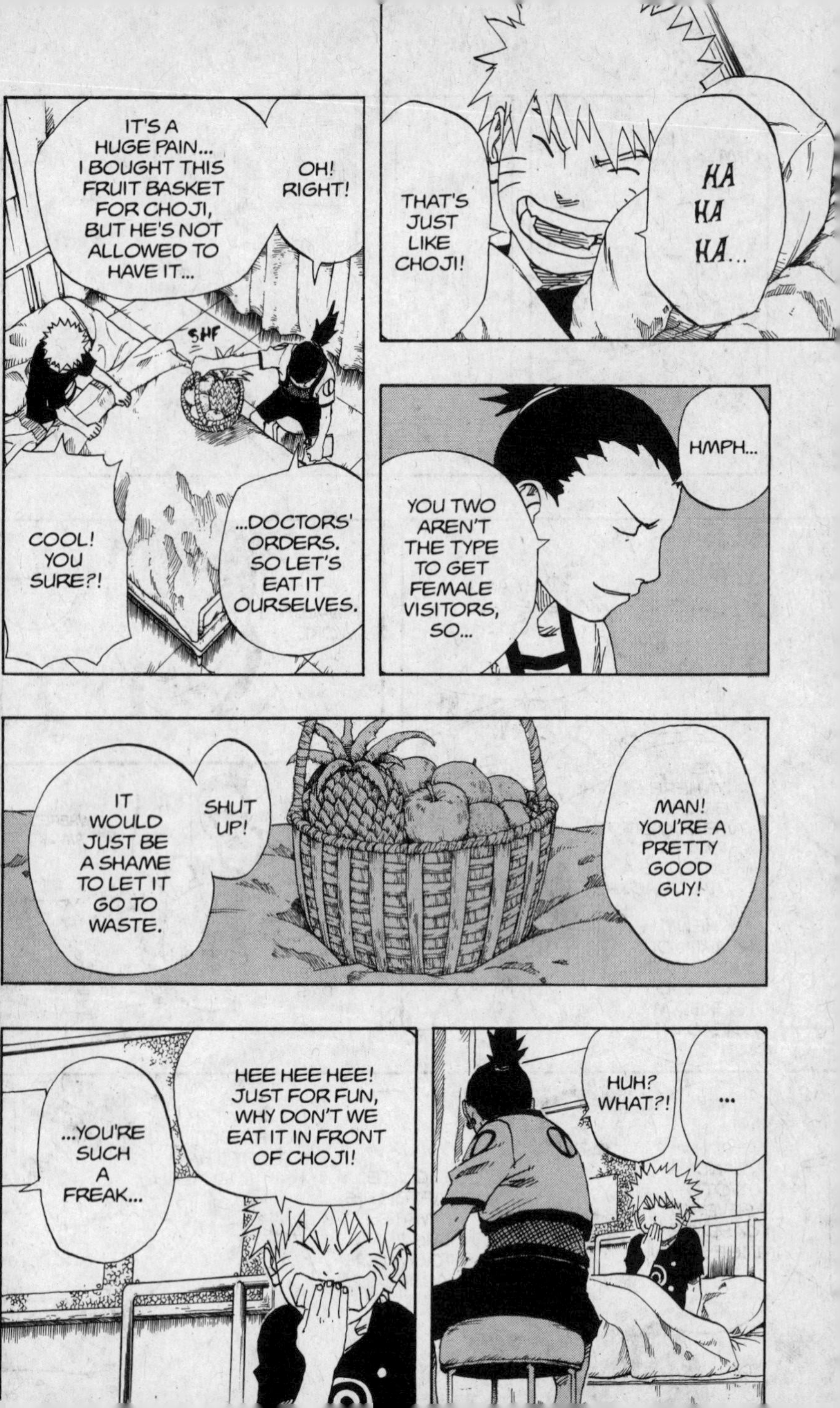
HA HA HA...
THAT'S JUST LIKE CHOJI!
HMPH...
YOU TWO AREN'T THE TYPE TO GET FEMALE VISITORS, SO...
IT'S A HUGE PAIN... I BOUGHT THIS FRUIT BASKET FOR CHOJI, BUT HE'S NOT ALLOWED TO HAVE IT...
OH! RIGHT!
SHF
...DOCTORS' ORDERS. SO LET'S EAT IT OURSELVES.
COOL! YOU SURE?!
MAN! YOU'RE A PRETTY GOOD GUY!
SHUT UP!
IT WOULD JUST BE A SHAME TO LET IT GO TO WASTE.
...
HUH? WHAT?!
HEE HEE HEE! JUST FOR FUN, WHY DON'T WE EAT IT IN FRONT OF CHOJI!
...YOU'RE SUCH A FREAK...

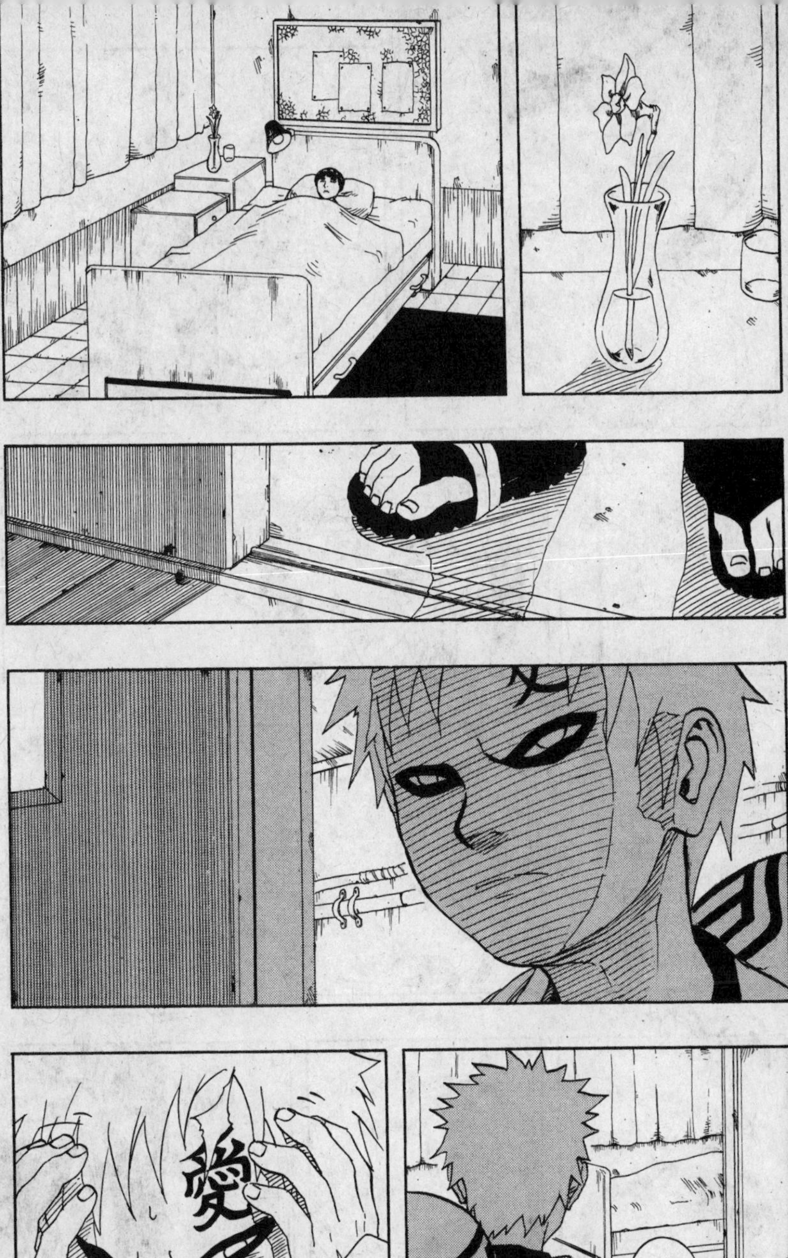
...
UNH...
愛

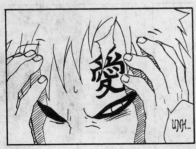

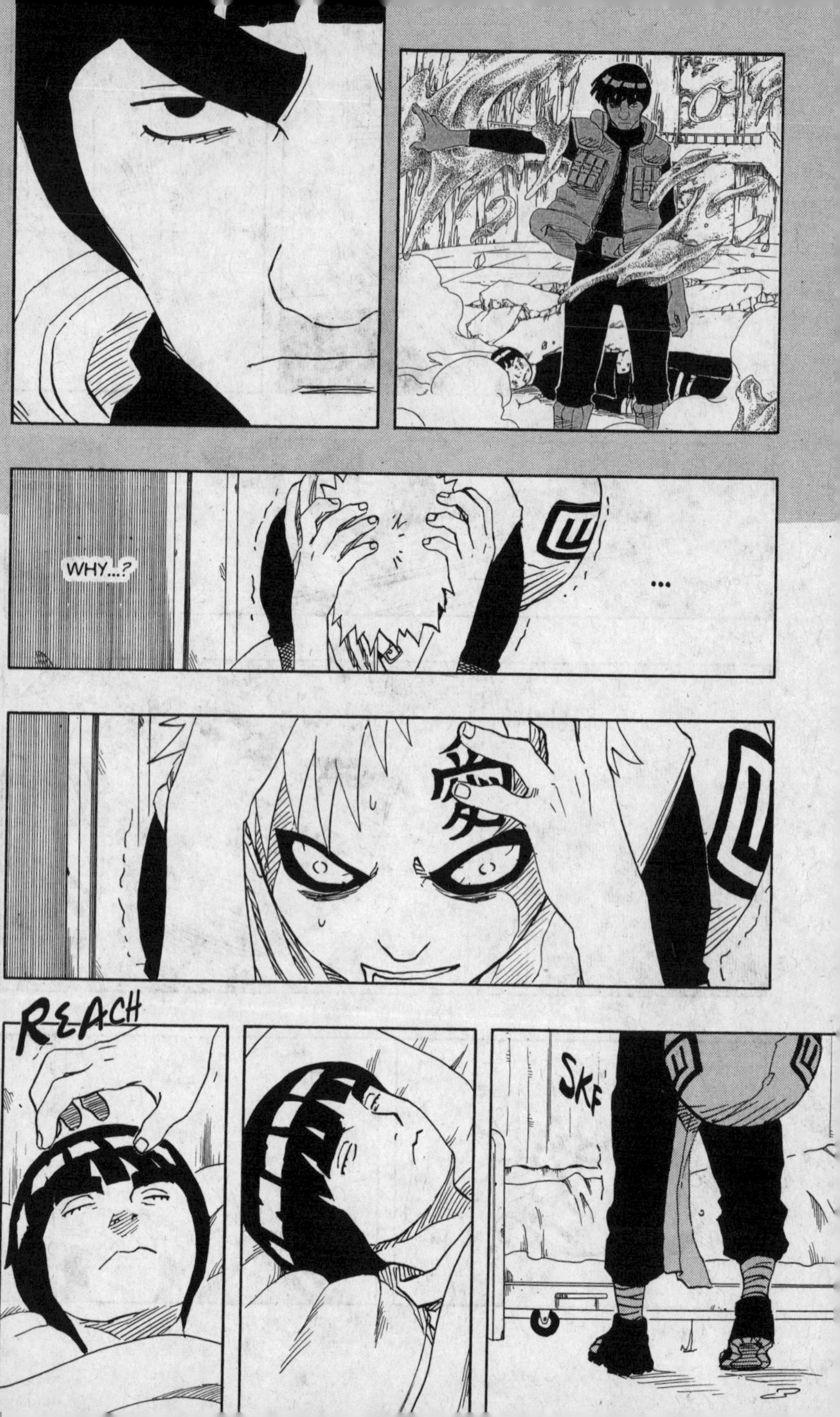
...
WHY...?
SKF
REACH

READ THIS WAY

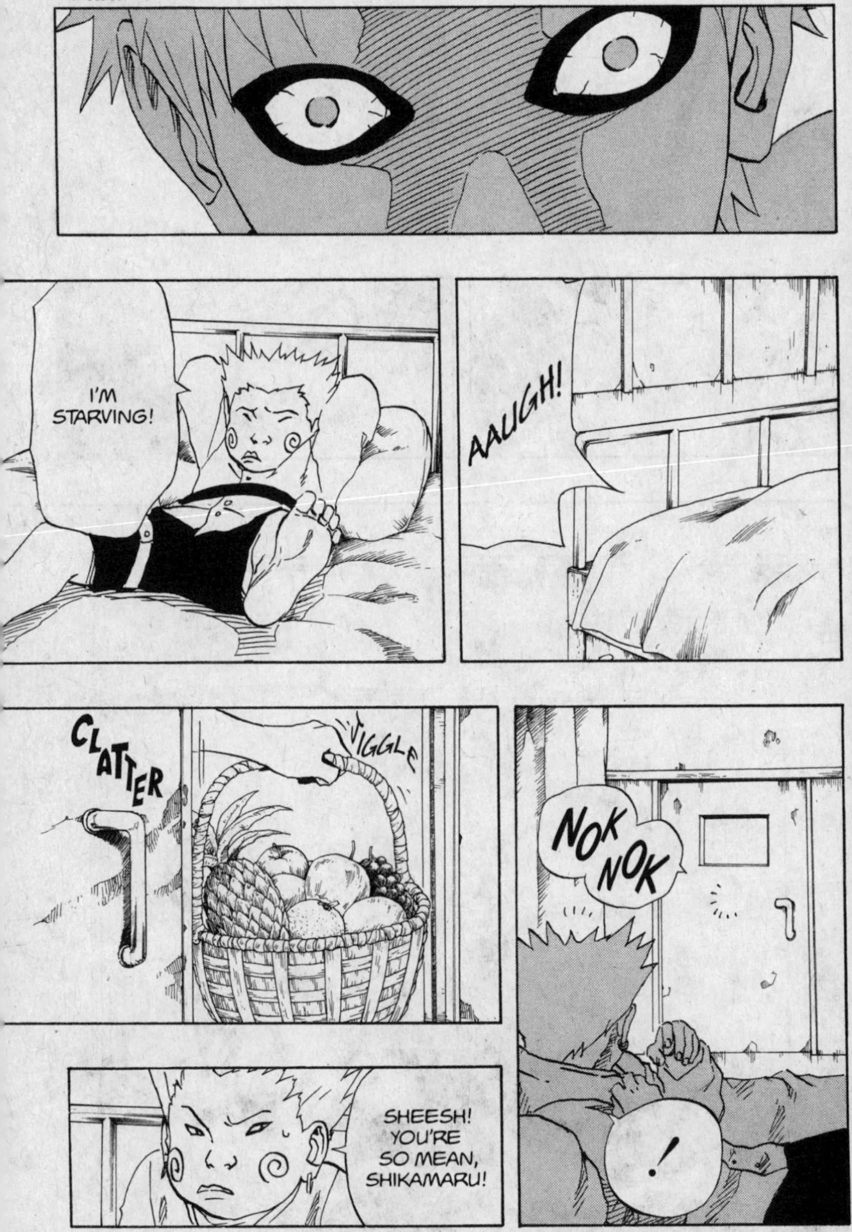

AAUGH!
I'M STARVING!
NOK NOK
!
JIGGLE
CLATTER
SHEESH! YOU'RE SO MEAN, SHIKAMARU!

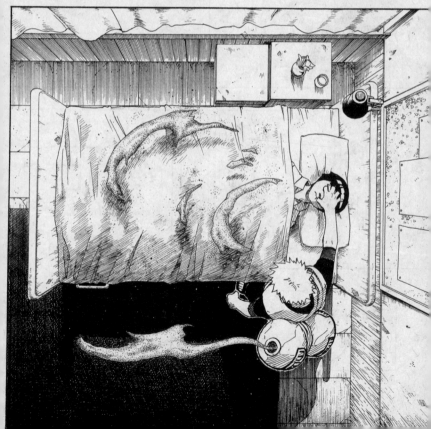

READ THIS WAY

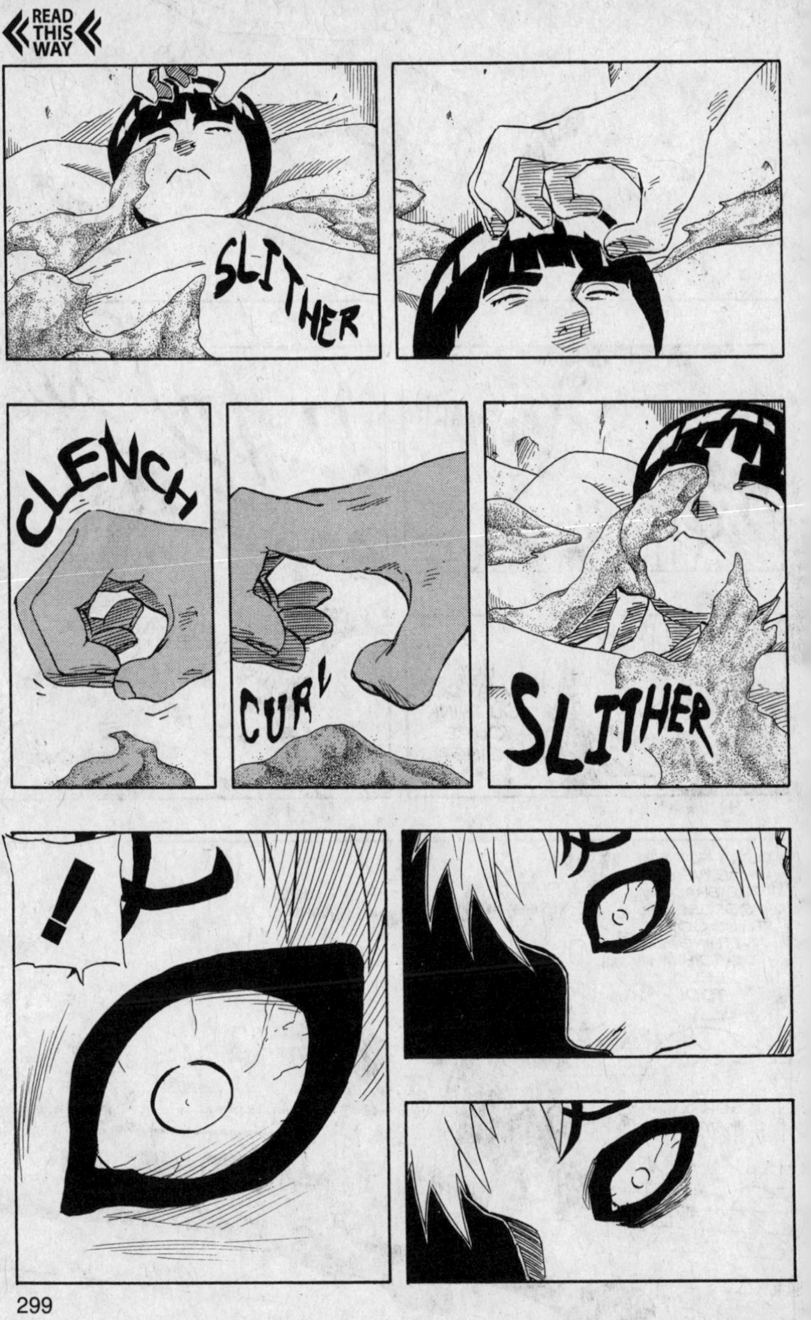

SLITHER
SLITHER
CURL
CLENCH
!

...I CAN'T... MOVE...

QUIVER

QUIVER

WAAH!!

CRACK

!!

POW

HEY, WHAT DO YOU THINK YOU'RE DOING?!

DON'T FORGET, WHILE I'VE GOT THE SHADOW POSSESSION THING GOING, ANYTHING YOU DO TO HIM, I FEEL IT TOO!

...HEY, NARUTO...

SORRY, SHIKAMARU...!

READ THIS WAY

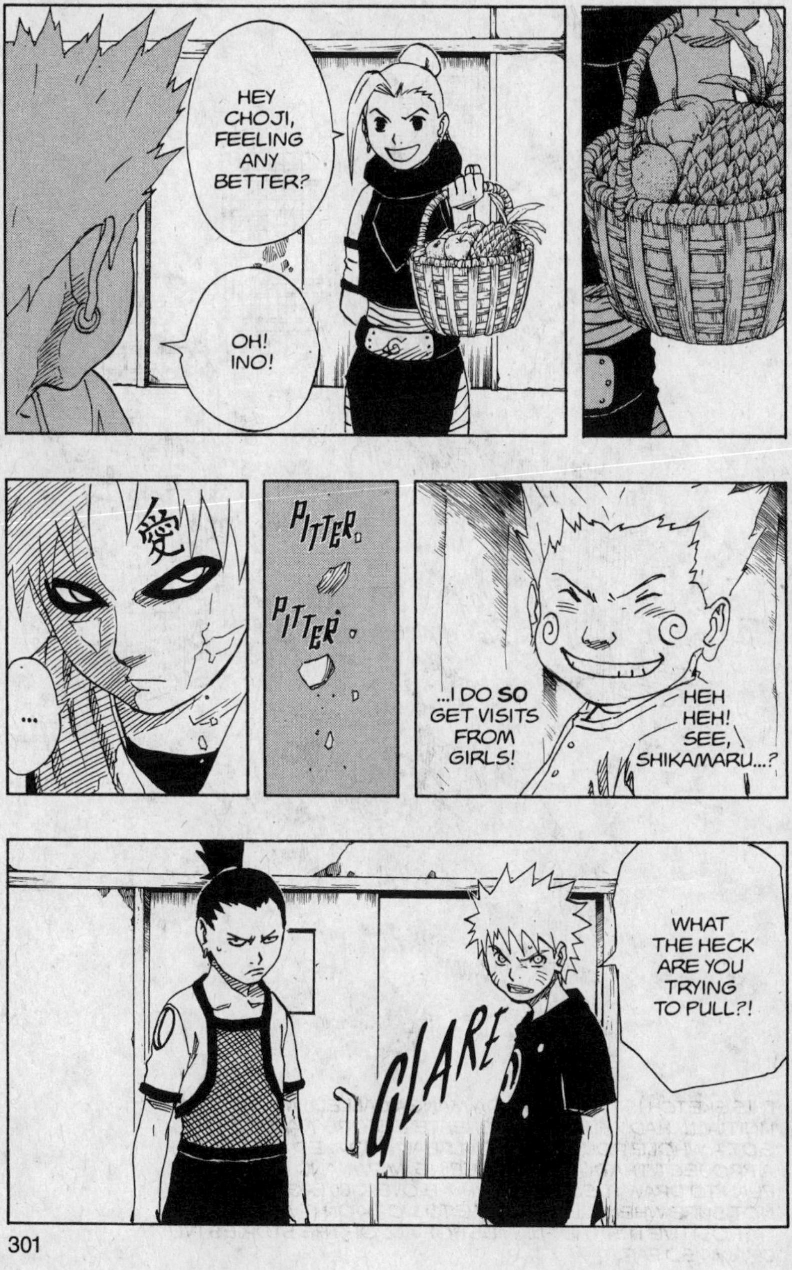
HEY CHOJI, FEELING ANY BETTER?
OH! INO!
HEH HEH! SEE, SHIKAMARU...?
...I DO SO GET VISITS FROM GIRLS!
PITTER
PITTER
...
WHAT THE HECK ARE YOU TRYING TO PULL?!
GLARE

KISHIMOTO MASASHI'S MANGA REJECT SPECIAL NO. 5!

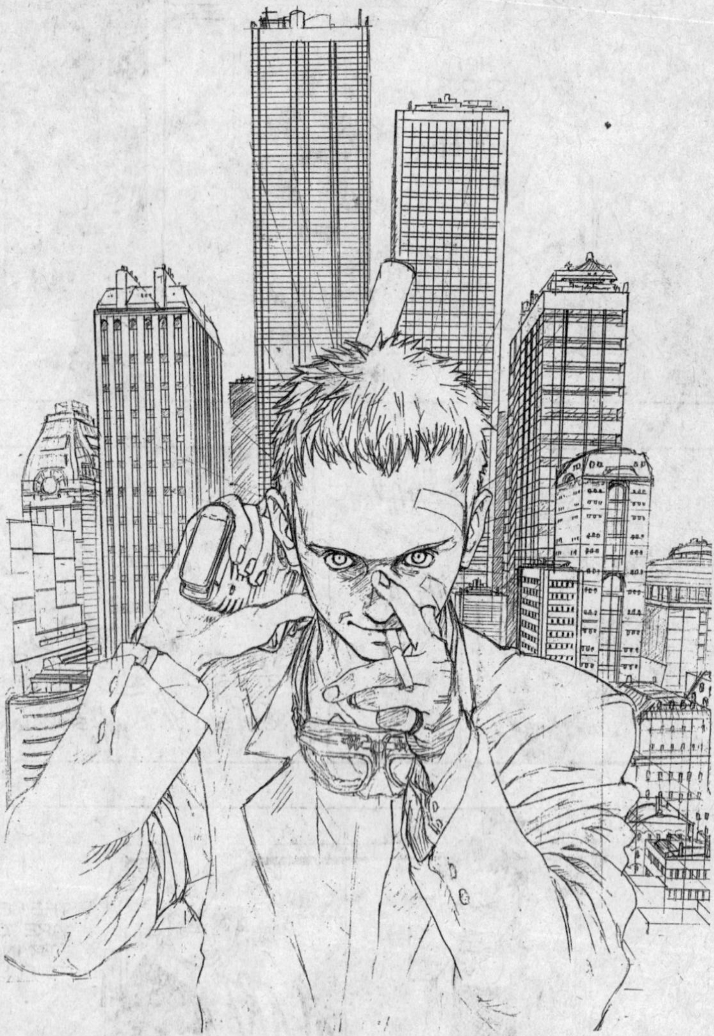

THIS SKETCH IS FROM A MAFIA MANGA CALLED "MARIO" THAT I INITIALLY HAD THE IDEA TO CREATE BEFORE *NARUTO*. I'VE GOT A WHOLE ROUGH DRAFT ALREADY WORKED OUT, SO IT'S A PROJECT THAT I'M STILL KEEPING WARM, AND I DEFINITELY PLAN TO DRAW IT SOME DAY. I HAVE OVER 160 PAGES, AND I'M NOT SURE WHEN I'LL HAVE TIME TO WORK ON IT AGAIN... BUT I'M POSITIVE IT'S THE FUNNIEST OF ALL OF THE STORIES I'VE DRAWN SO FAR.

Number 97:

My Reason for Living...!!

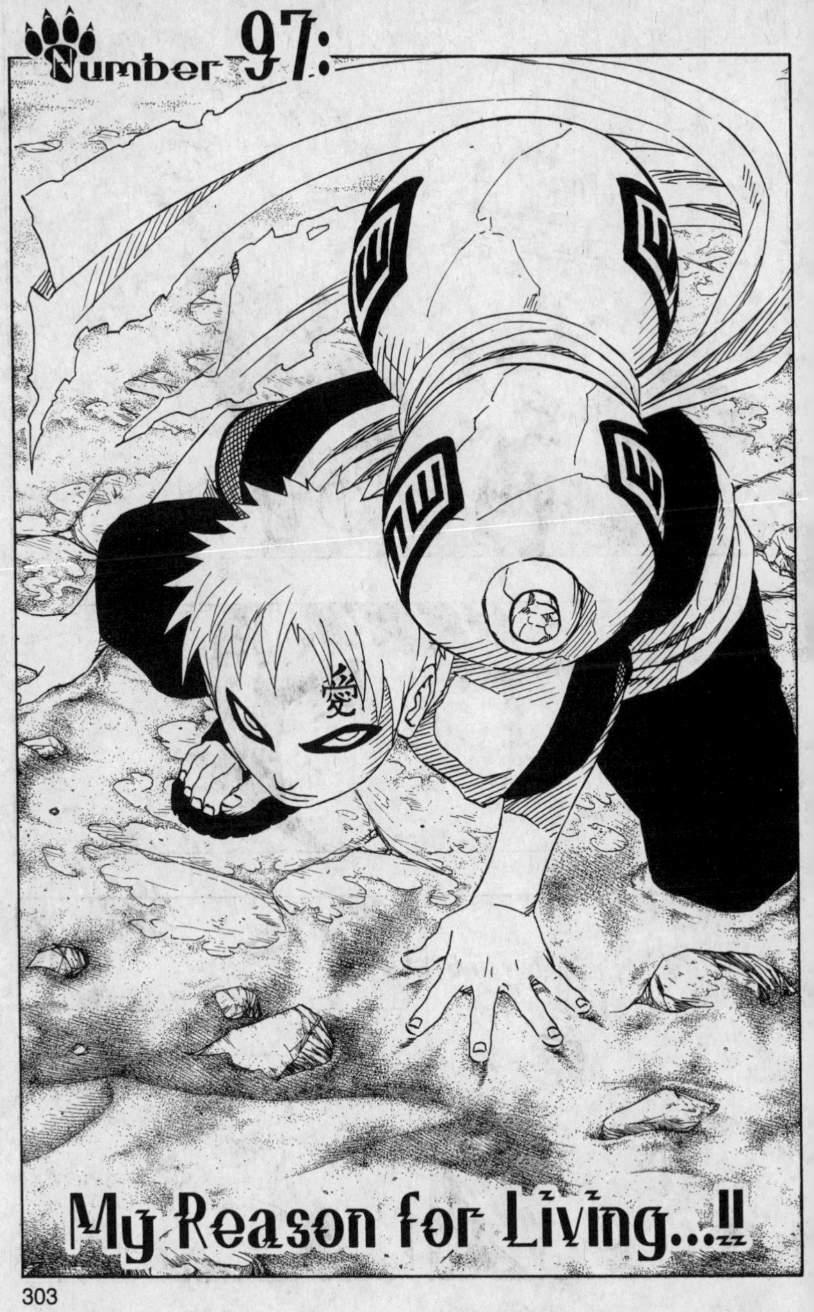

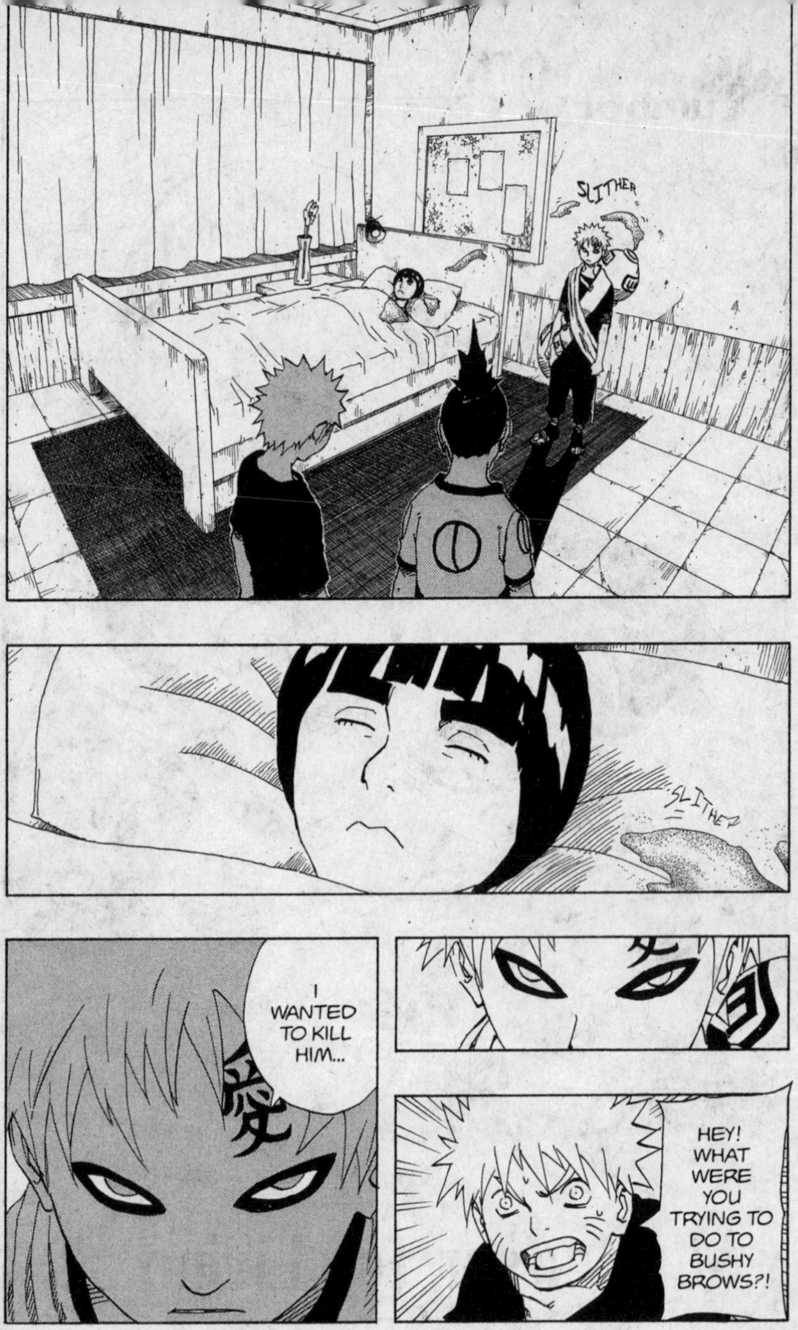
SLITHER
SLITHER
HEY! WHAT WERE YOU TRYING TO DO TO BUSHY BROWS?!
I WANTED TO KILL HIM...

READ THIS WAY

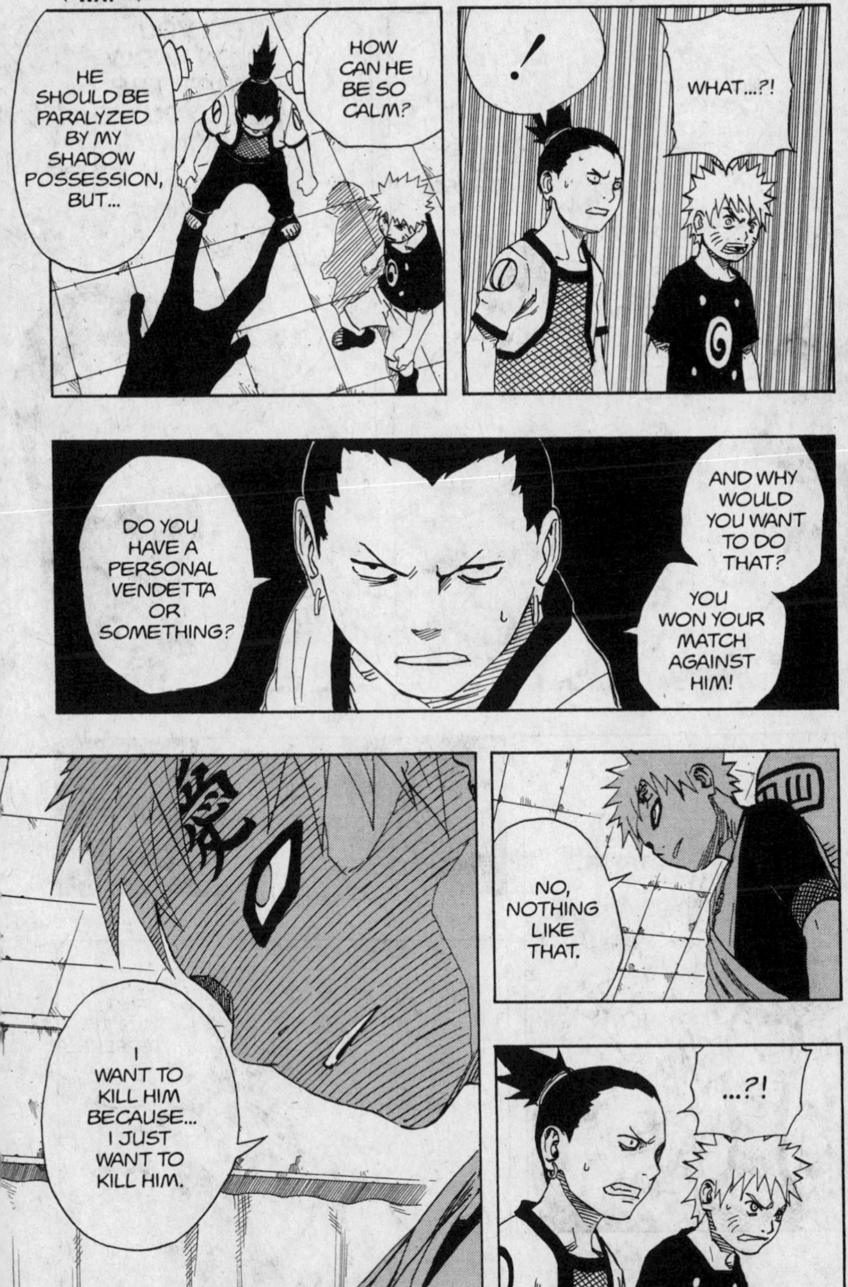
!
WHAT...?!
HOW CAN HE BE SO CALM?
HE SHOULD BE PARALYZED BY MY SHADOW POSSESSION, BUT...
AND WHY WOULD YOU WANT TO DO THAT?
DO YOU HAVE A PERSONAL VENDETTA OR SOMETHING?
YOU WON YOUR MATCH AGAINST HIM!
NO, NOTHING LIKE THAT.
...?!
I WANT TO KILL HIM BECAUSE... I JUST WANT TO KILL HIM.

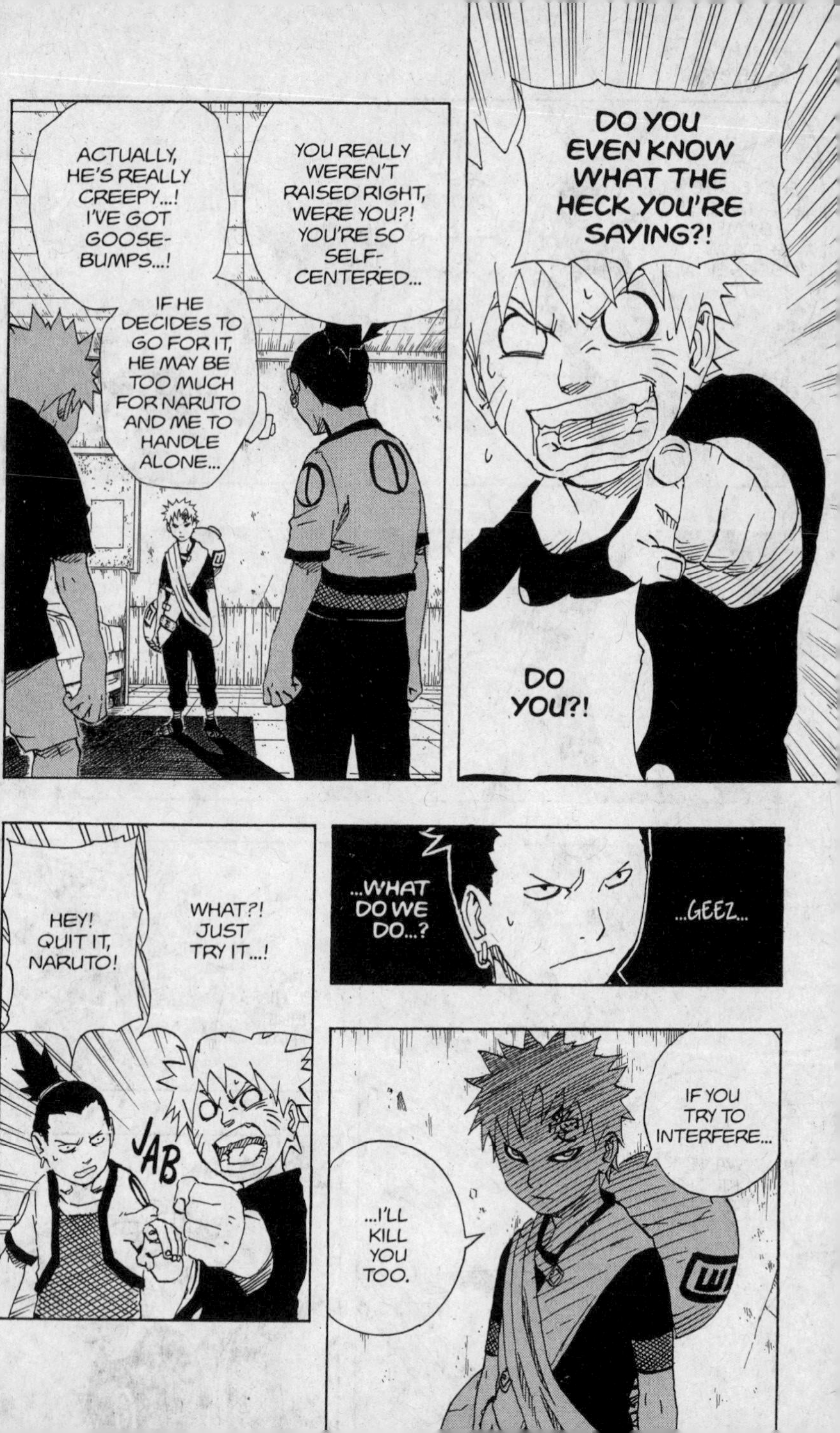
DO YOU EVEN KNOW WHAT THE HECK YOU'RE SAYING?!
DO YOU?!
YOU REALLY WEREN'T RAISED RIGHT, WERE YOU?! YOU'RE SO SELF-CENTERED...
ACTUALLY, HE'S REALLY CREEPY...! I'VE GOT GOOSE-BUMPS...!
IF HE DECIDES TO GO FOR IT, HE MAY BE TOO MUCH FOR NARUTO AND ME TO HANDLE ALONE...
...GEEZ...
...WHAT DO WE DO...?
IF YOU TRY TO INTERFERE...
...I'LL KILL YOU TOO.
WHAT?! JUST TRY IT...!
HEY! QUIT IT, NARUTO!
JAB

READ THIS WAY

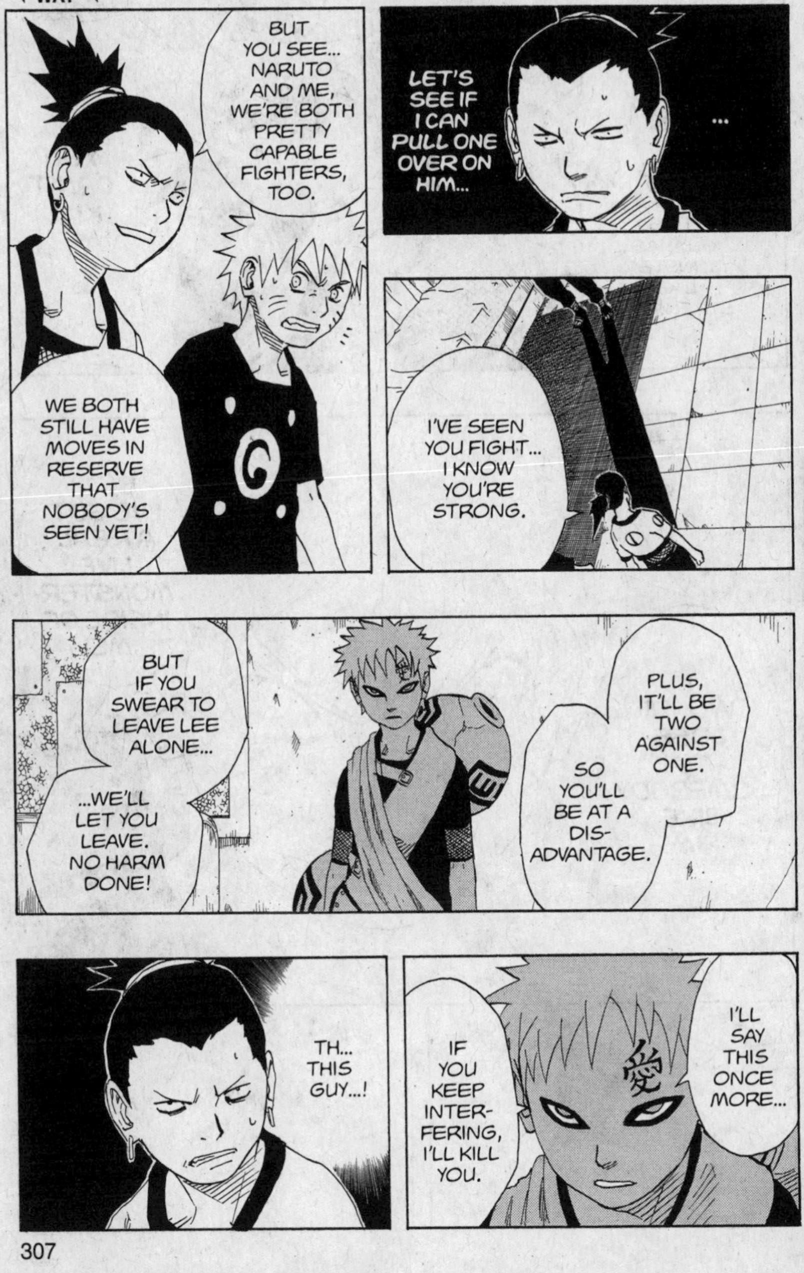
...
LET'S SEE IF I CAN PULL ONE OVER ON HIM...
I'VE SEEN YOU FIGHT... I KNOW YOU'RE STRONG.
BUT YOU SEE... NARUTO AND ME, WE'RE BOTH PRETTY CAPABLE FIGHTERS, TOO.
WE BOTH STILL HAVE MOVES IN RESERVE THAT NOBODY'S SEEN YET!
PLUS, IT'LL BE TWO AGAINST ONE.
SO YOU'LL BE AT A DIS-ADVANTAGE.
BUT IF YOU SWEAR TO LEAVE LEE ALONE...
...WE'LL LET YOU LEAVE. NO HARM DONE!
I'LL SAY THIS ONCE MORE...
IF YOU KEEP INTER-FERING, I'LL KILL YOU.
TH... THIS GUY...!

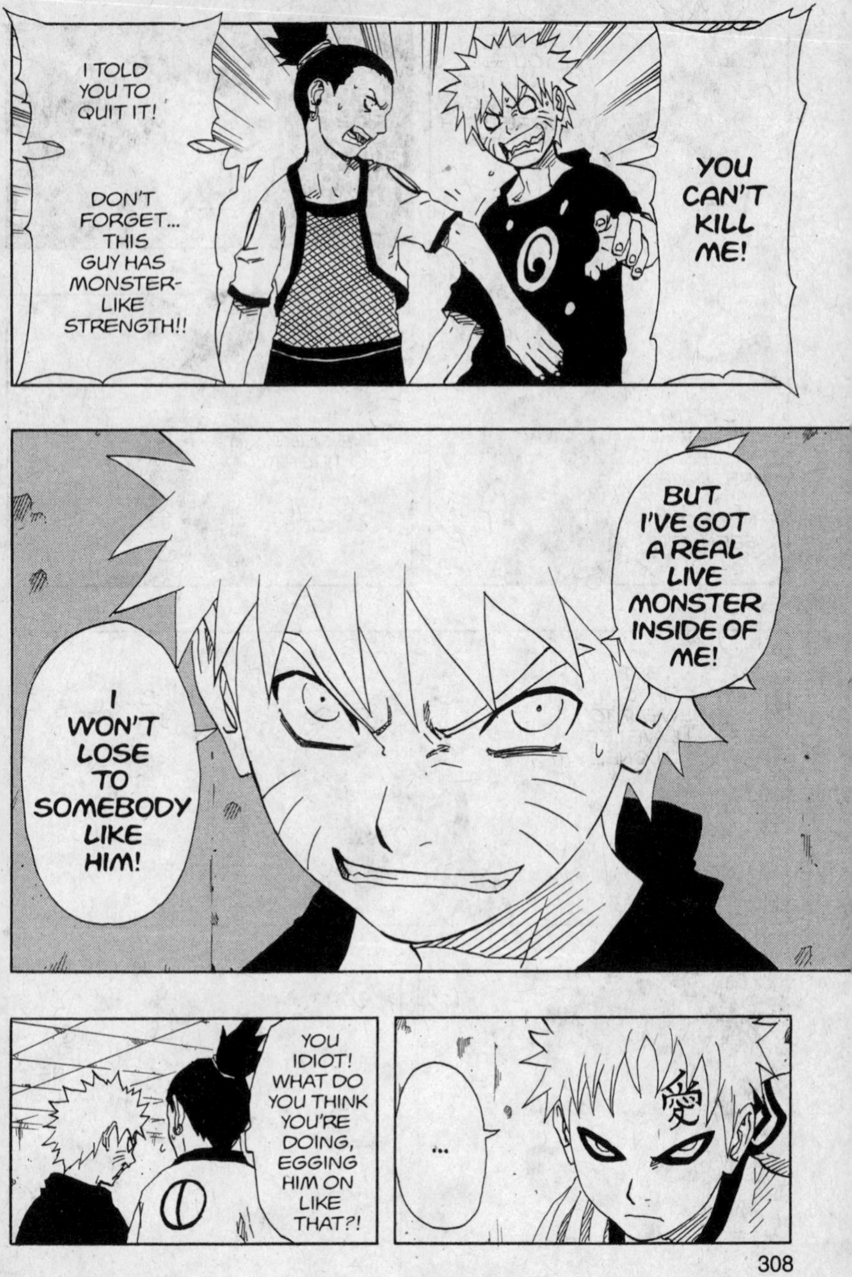
YOU CAN'T KILL ME!
I TOLD YOU TO QUIT IT!
DON'T FORGET... THIS GUY HAS MONSTER-LIKE STRENGTH!!
BUT I'VE GOT A REAL LIVE MONSTER INSIDE OF ME!
I WON'T LOSE TO SOMEBODY LIKE HIM!
...
YOU IDIOT! WHAT DO YOU THINK YOU'RE DOING, EGGING HIM ON LIKE THAT?!

READ THIS WAY

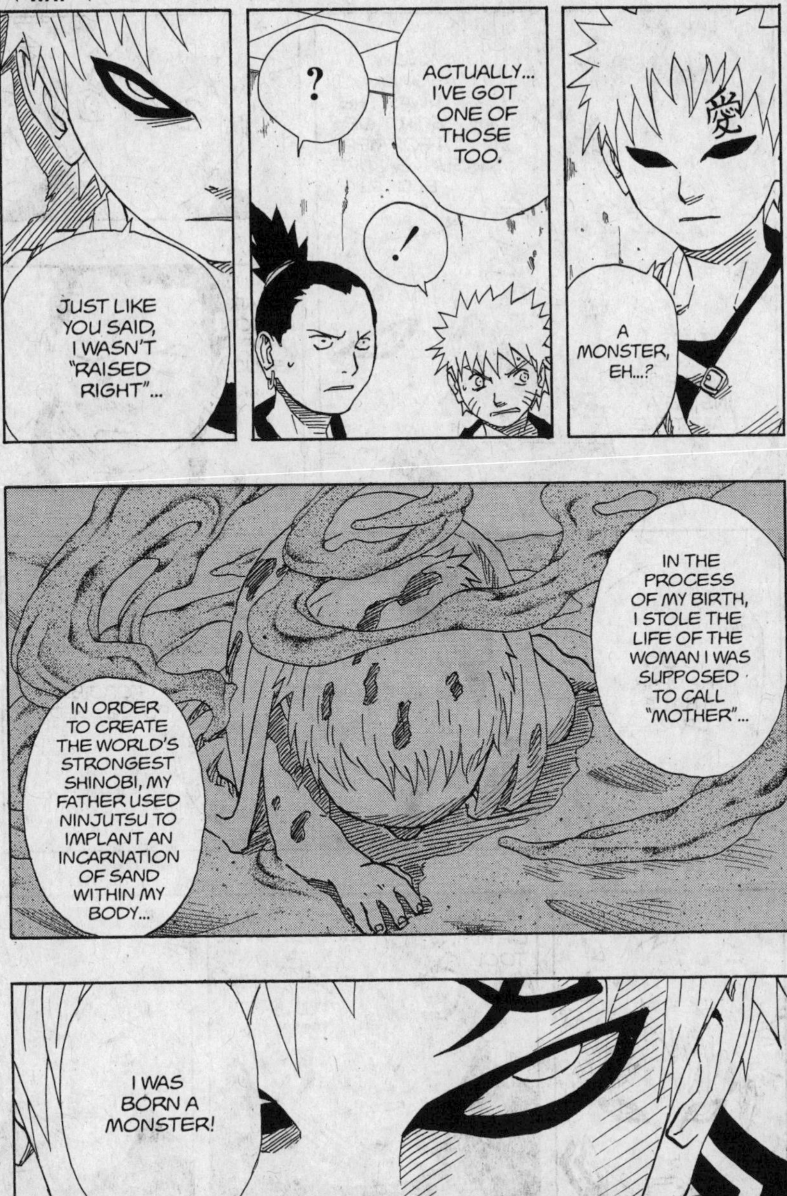
A MONSTER, EH...?
ACTUALLY... I'VE GOT ONE OF THOSE TOO.
?
!
JUST LIKE YOU SAID, I WASN'T "RAISED RIGHT"...
IN THE PROCESS OF MY BIRTH, I STOLE THE LIFE OF THE WOMAN I WAS SUPPOSED TO CALL "MOTHER"...
IN ORDER TO CREATE THE WORLD'S STRONGEST SHINOBI, MY FATHER USED NINJUTSU TO IMPLANT AN INCARNATION OF SAND WITHIN MY BODY...
I WAS BORN A MONSTER!

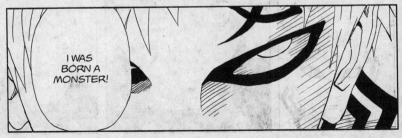

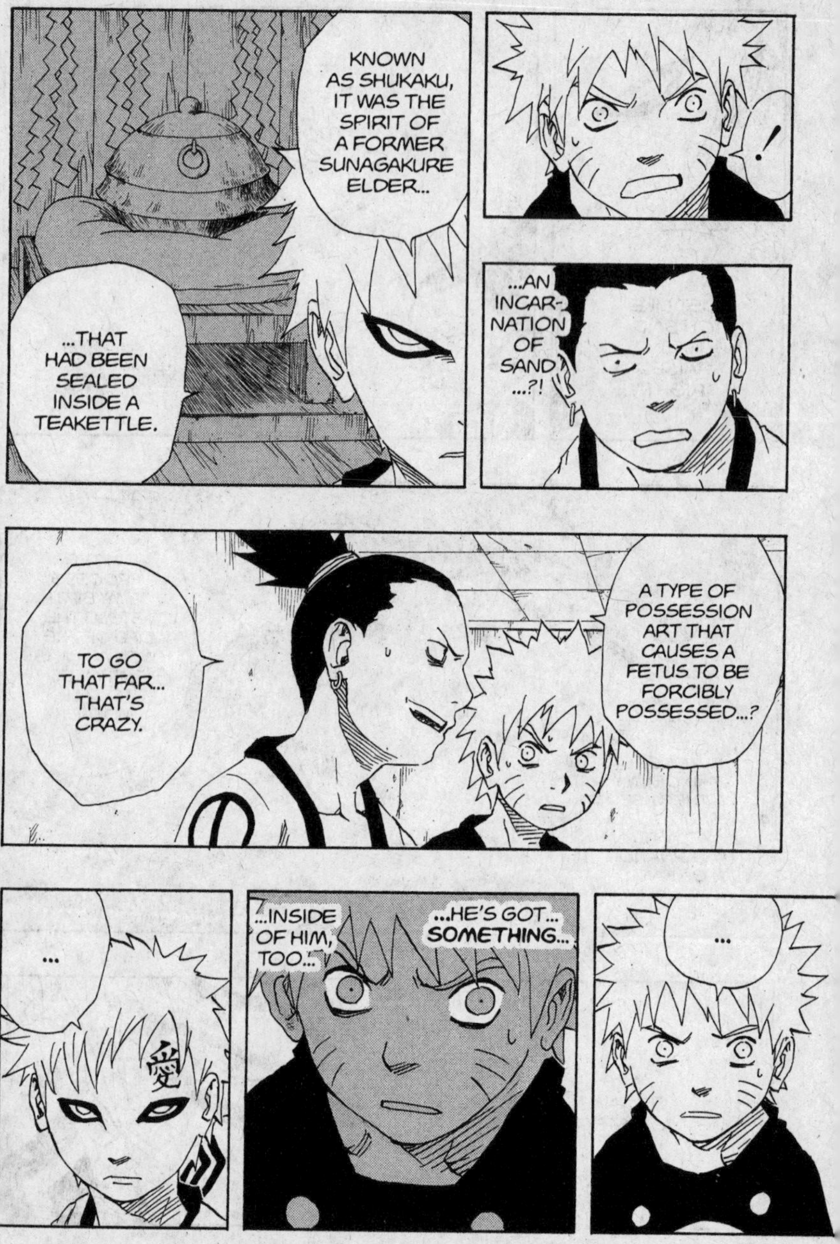
!
...AN INCARNATION OF SAND ...?!
KNOWN AS SHUKAKU, IT WAS THE SPIRIT OF A FORMER SUNAGAKURE ELDER...
...THAT HAD BEEN SEALED INSIDE A TEAKETTLE.
A TYPE OF POSSESSION ART THAT CAUSES A FETUS TO BE FORCIBLY POSSESSED...?
TO GO THAT FAR... THAT'S CRAZY.
...
...HE'S GOT... SOMETHING...
...INSIDE OF HIM, TOO...
...
愛

READ THIS WAY

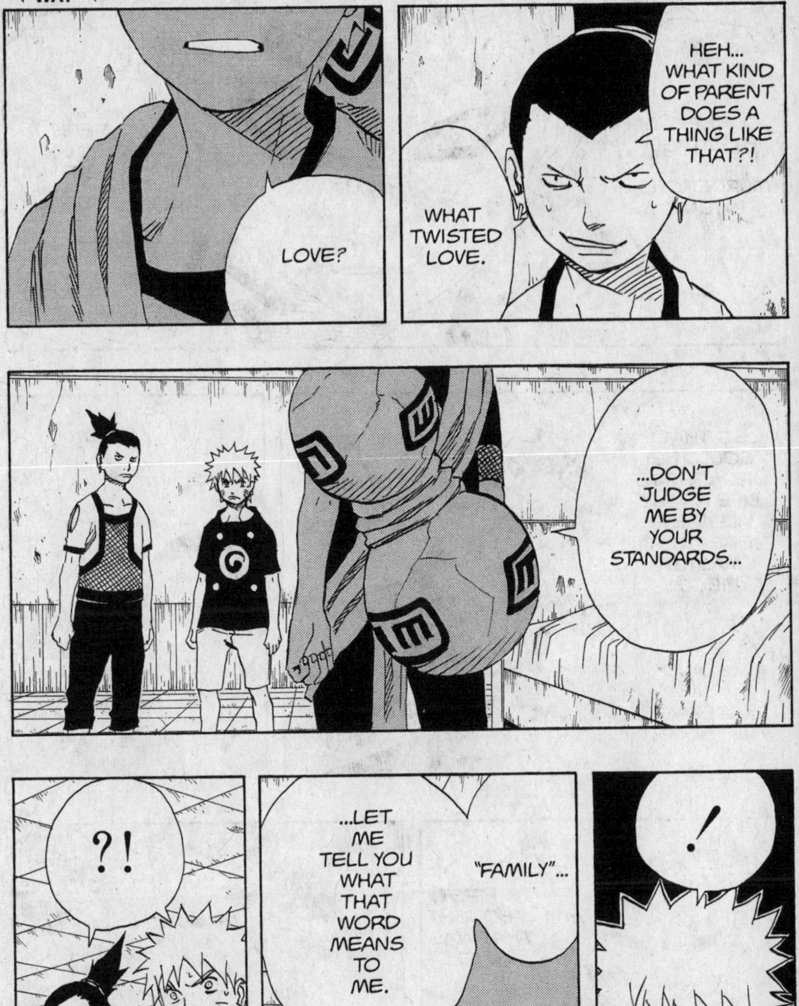

HEH... WHAT KIND OF PARENT DOES A THING LIKE THAT?!
WHAT TWISTED LOVE.
LOVE?
...DON'T JUDGE ME BY YOUR STANDARDS...
!
"FAMILY"...
...LET ME TELL YOU WHAT THAT WORD MEANS TO ME.
?!

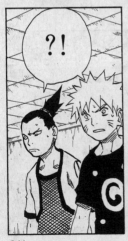

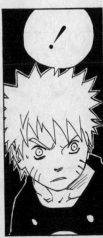

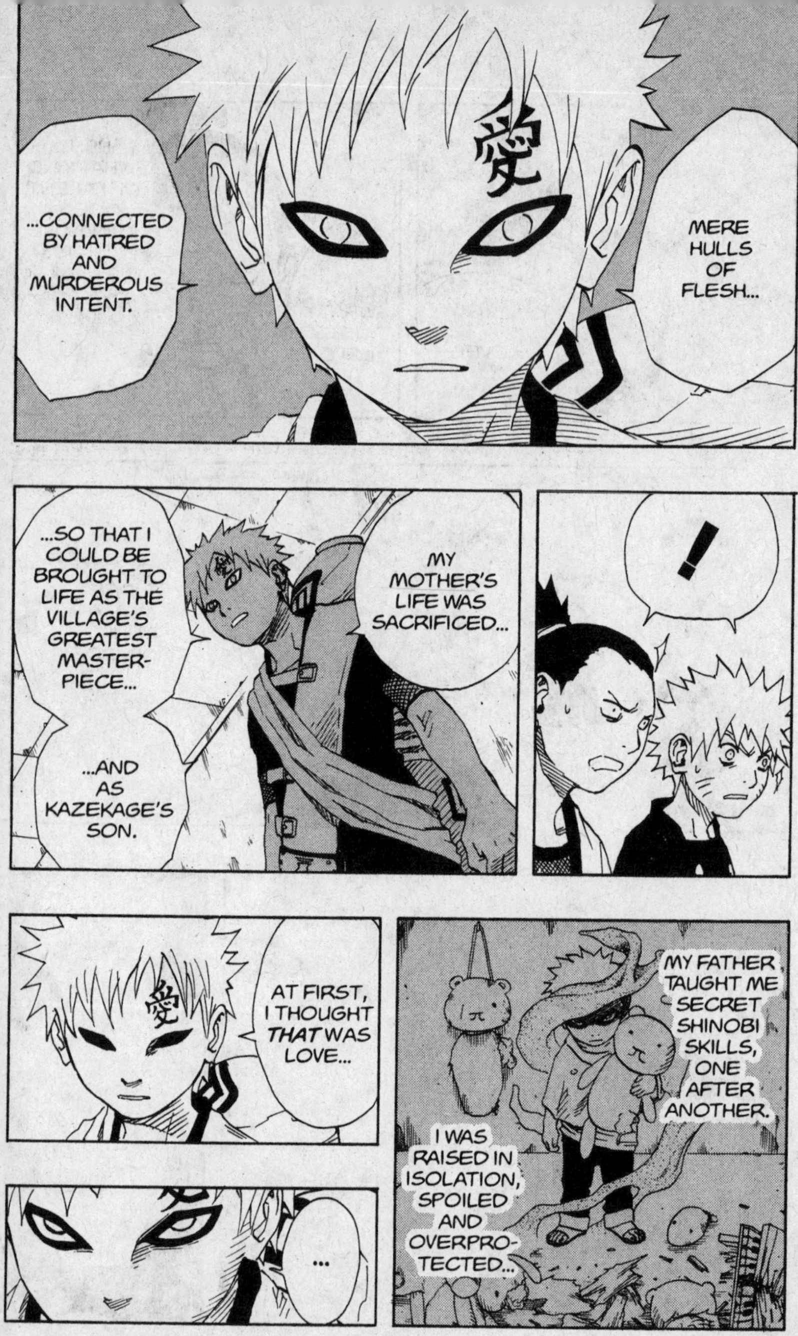
MERE HULLS OF FLESH...
...CONNECTED BY HATRED AND MURDEROUS INTENT.
!
MY MOTHER'S LIFE WAS SACRIFICED...
...SO THAT I COULD BE BROUGHT TO LIFE AS THE VILLAGE'S GREATEST MASTER-PIECE...
...AND AS KAZEKAGE'S SON.
MY FATHER TAUGHT ME SECRET SHINOBI SKILLS, ONE AFTER ANOTHER.
I WAS RAISED IN ISOLATION, SPOILED AND OVERPRO-TECTED...
AT FIRST, I THOUGHT *THAT* WAS LOVE...
...

READ THIS WAY

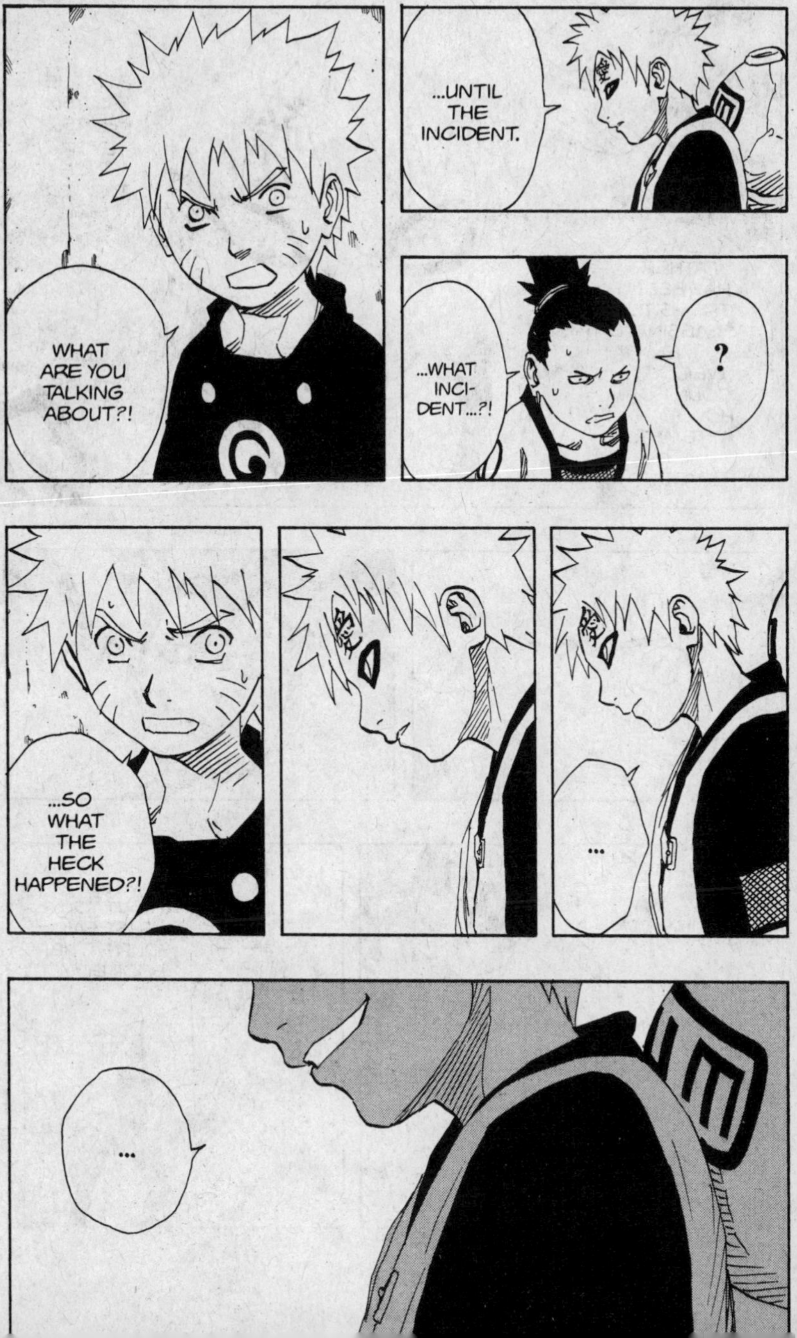

...UNTIL THE INCIDENT.
?
...WHAT INCI-DENT...?!
WHAT ARE YOU TALKING ABOUT?!
...
...SO WHAT THE HECK HAPPENED?!
...

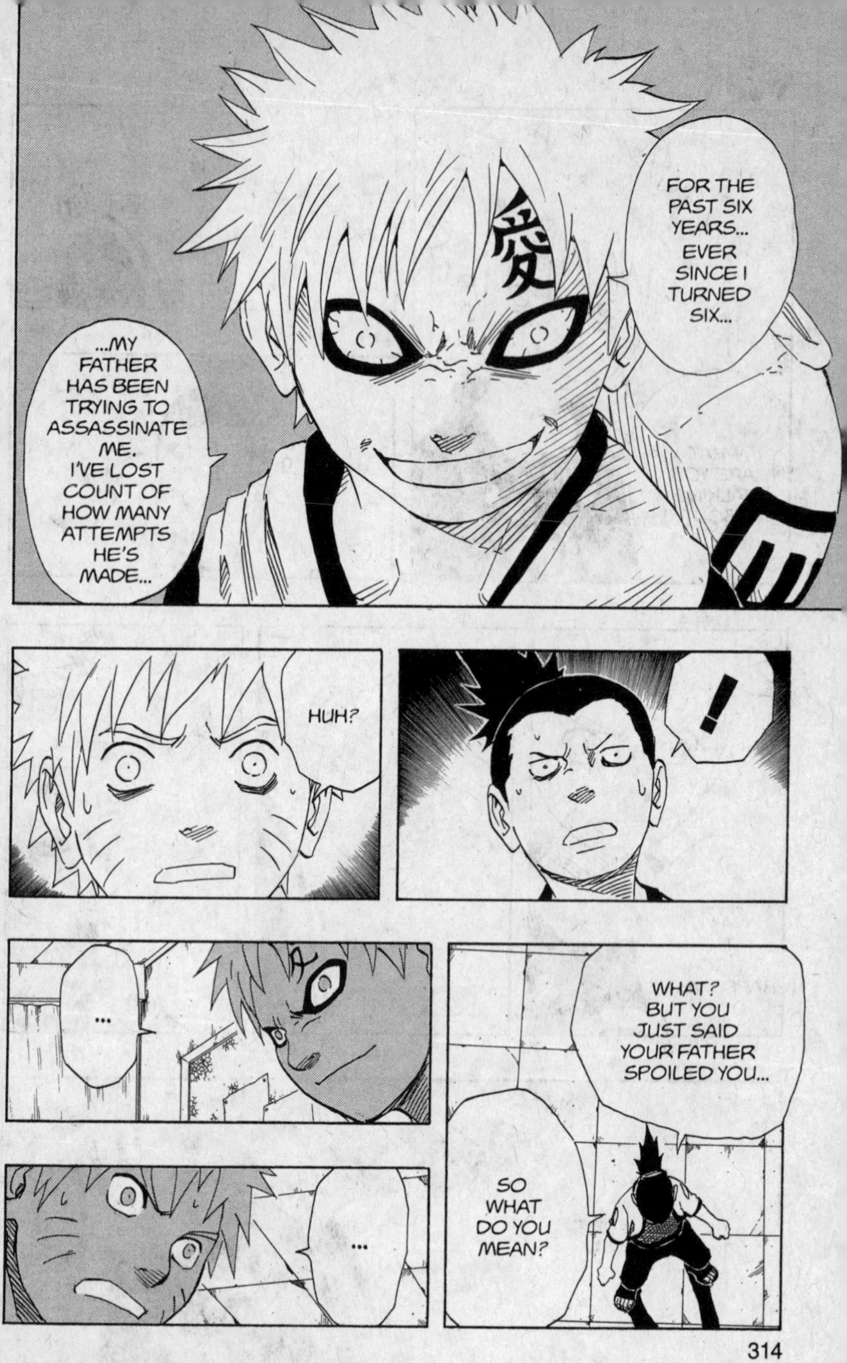
FOR THE PAST SIX YEARS... EVER SINCE I TURNED SIX...
...MY FATHER HAS BEEN TRYING TO ASSASSINATE ME. I'VE LOST COUNT OF HOW MANY ATTEMPTS HE'S MADE...
!
HUH?
WHAT? BUT YOU JUST SAID YOUR FATHER SPOILED YOU...
SO WHAT DO YOU MEAN?
...
...

READ THIS WAY

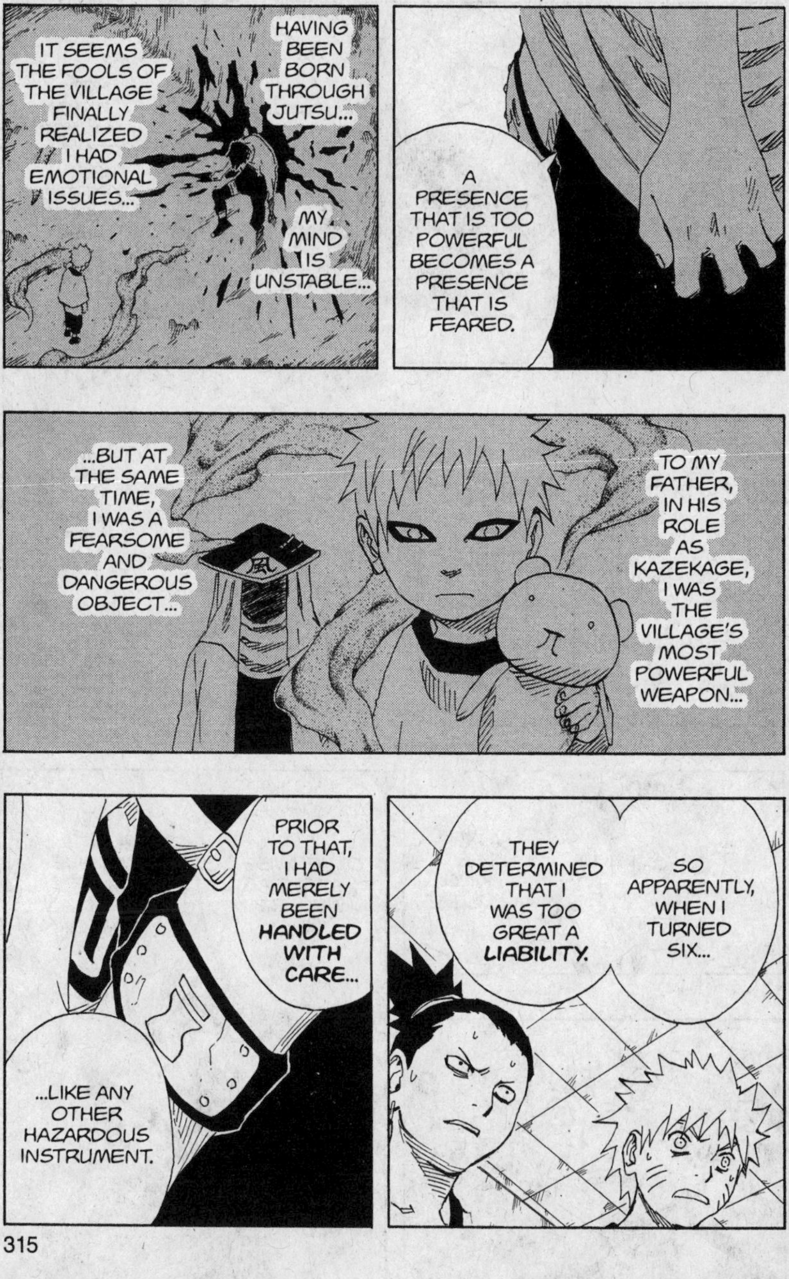

A PRESENCE THAT IS TOO POWERFUL BECOMES A PRESENCE THAT IS FEARED.
HAVING BEEN BORN THROUGH JUTSU...
IT SEEMS THE FOOLS OF THE VILLAGE FINALLY REALIZED I HAD EMOTIONAL ISSUES...
MY MIND IS UNSTABLE...
TO MY FATHER, IN HIS ROLE AS KAZEKAGE, I WAS THE VILLAGE'S MOST POWERFUL WEAPON...
...BUT AT THE SAME TIME, I WAS A FEARSOME AND DANGEROUS OBJECT...
SO APPARENTLY, WHEN I TURNED SIX...
THEY DETERMINED THAT I WAS TOO GREAT A **LIABILITY.**
PRIOR TO THAT, I HAD MERELY BEEN **HANDLED WITH CARE...**
...LIKE ANY OTHER HAZARDOUS INSTRUMENT.

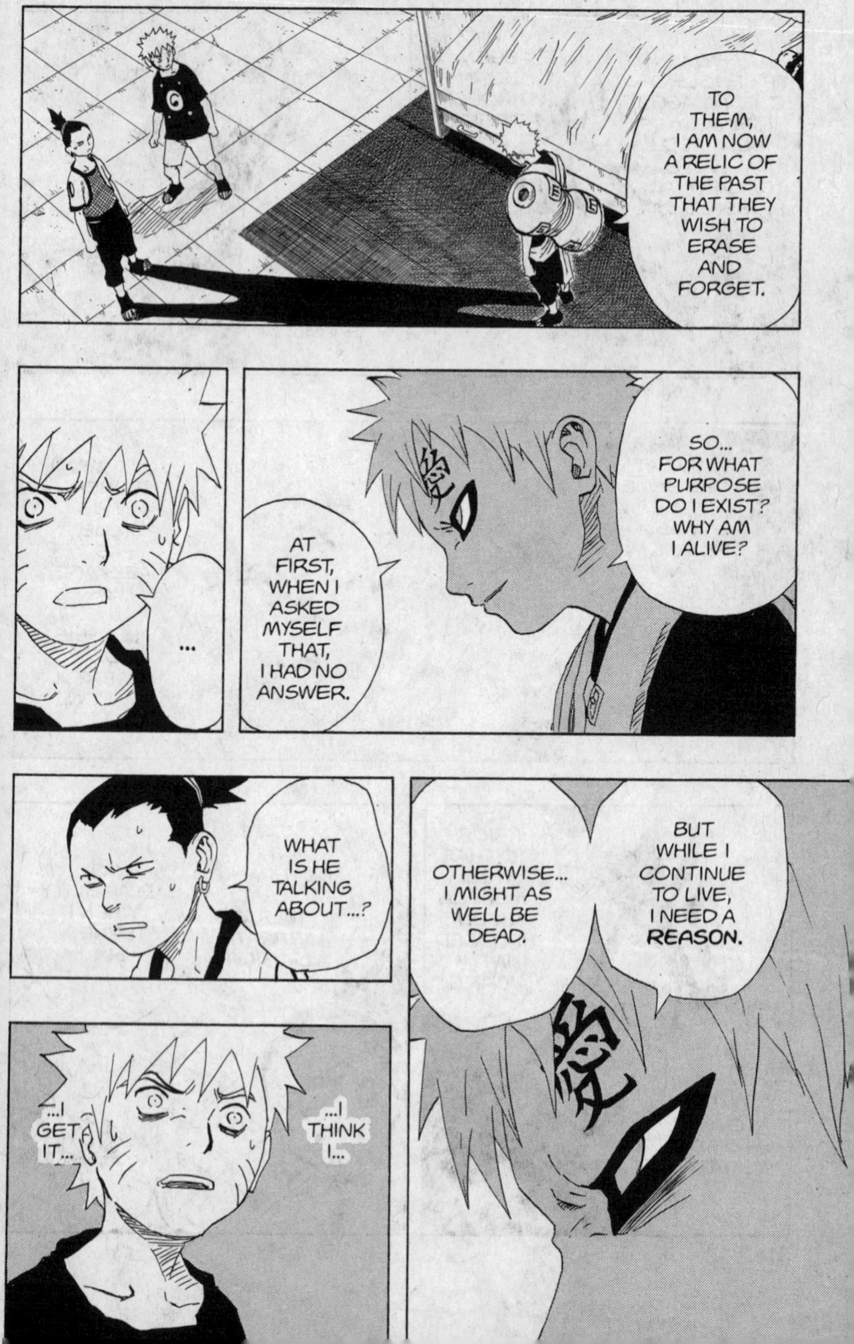
TO THEM, I AM NOW A RELIC OF THE PAST THAT THEY WISH TO ERASE AND FORGET.
SO... FOR WHAT PURPOSE DO I EXIST? WHY AM I ALIVE?
AT FIRST, WHEN I ASKED MYSELF THAT, I HAD NO ANSWER.
...
BUT WHILE I CONTINUE TO LIVE, I NEED A **REASON.**
OTHERWISE... I MIGHT AS WELL BE DEAD.
WHAT IS HE TALKING ABOUT...?
...I THINK I...
...I GET IT...

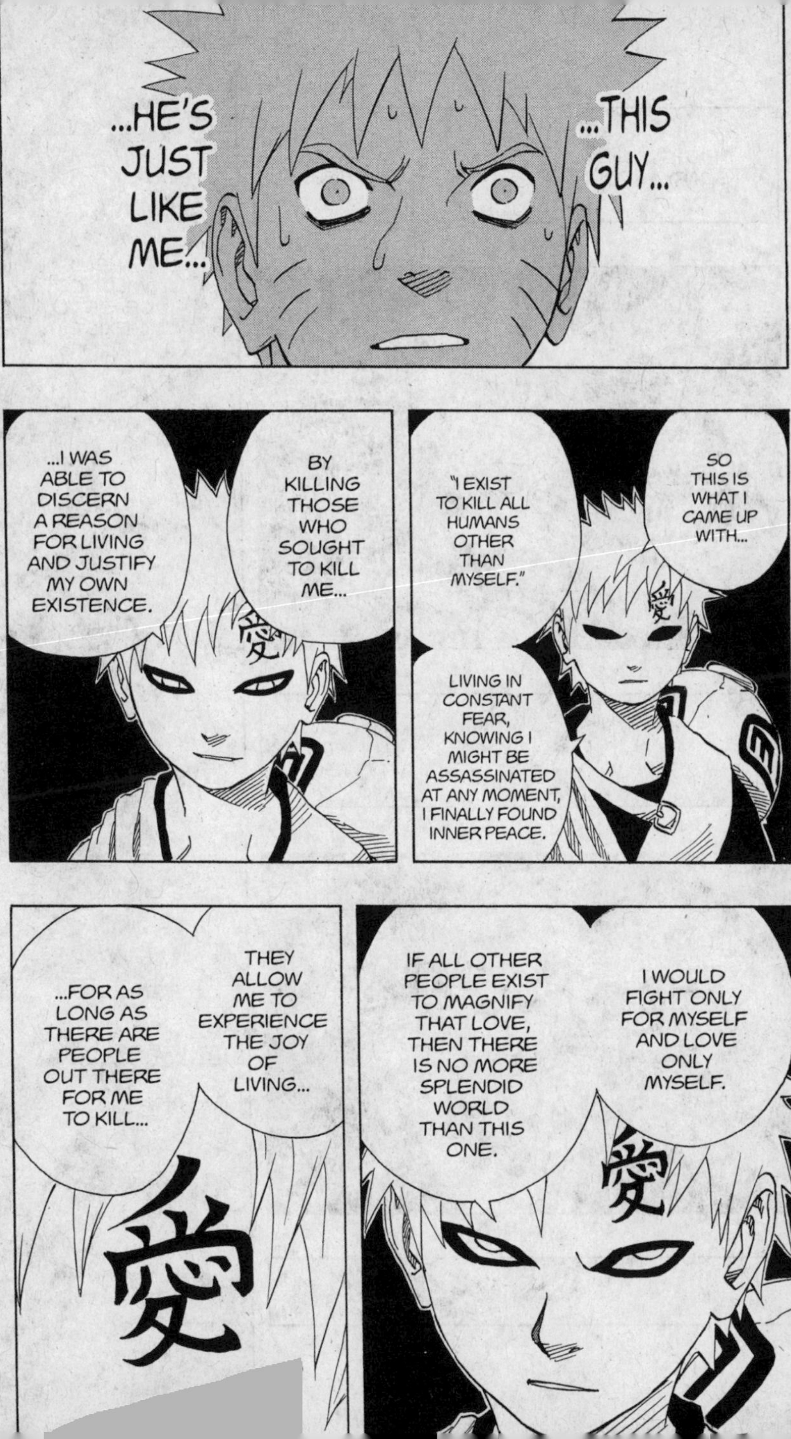
...THIS GUY...
...HE'S JUST LIKE ME...
SO THIS IS WHAT I CAME UP WITH...
"I EXIST TO KILL ALL HUMANS OTHER THAN MYSELF."
LIVING IN CONSTANT FEAR, KNOWING I MIGHT BE ASSASSINATED AT ANY MOMENT, I FINALLY FOUND INNER PEACE.
BY KILLING THOSE WHO SOUGHT TO KILL ME...
...I WAS ABLE TO DISCERN A REASON FOR LIVING AND JUSTIFY MY OWN EXISTENCE.
I WOULD FIGHT ONLY FOR MYSELF AND LOVE ONLY MYSELF.
IF ALL OTHER PEOPLE EXIST TO MAGNIFY THAT LOVE, THEN THERE IS NO MORE SPLENDID WORLD THAN THIS ONE.
THEY ALLOW ME TO EXPERIENCE THE JOY OF LIVING...
...FOR AS LONG AS THERE ARE PEOPLE OUT THERE FOR ME TO KILL...

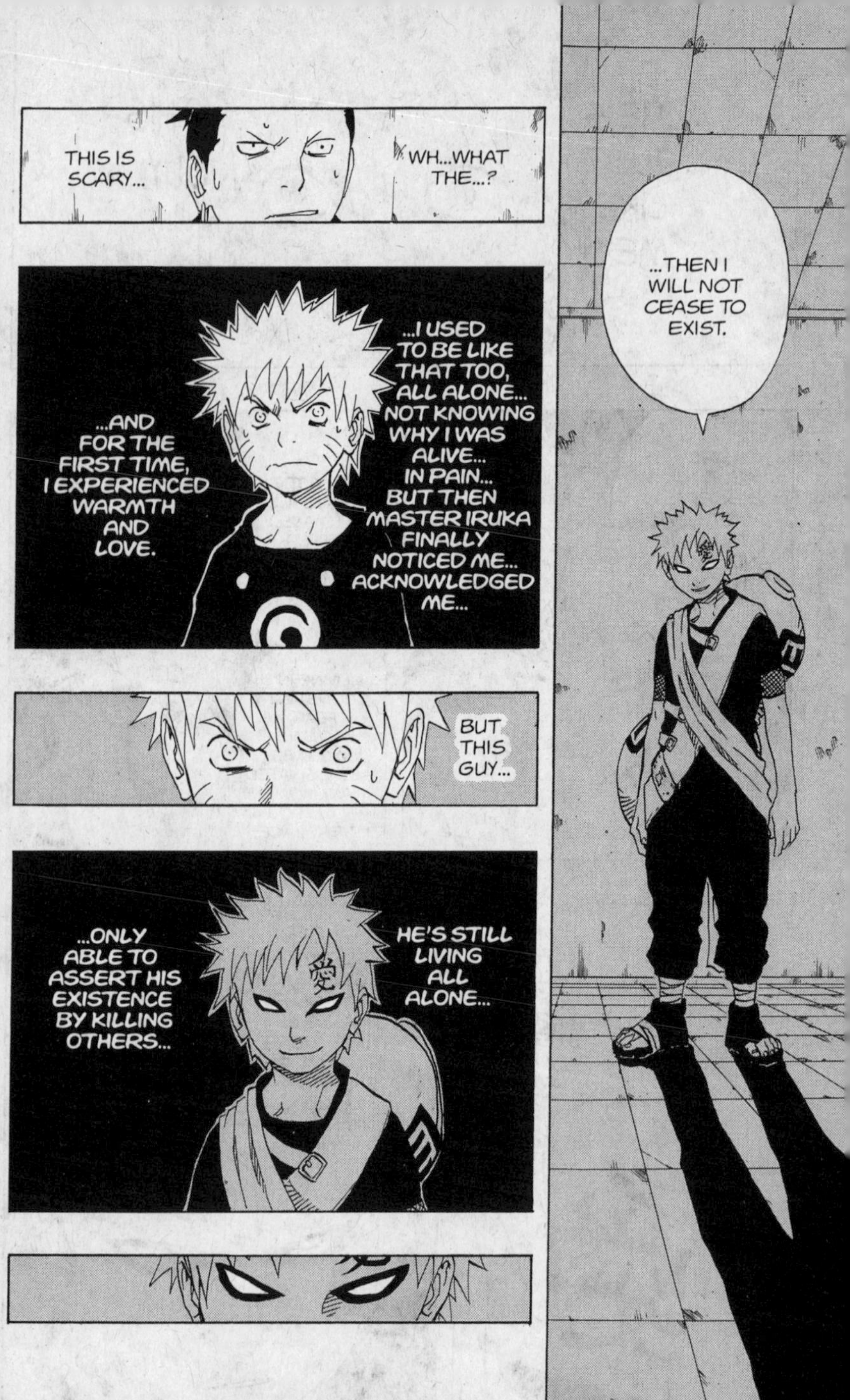
...THEN I WILL NOT CEASE TO EXIST.
WH...WHAT THE...?
THIS IS SCARY...
...I USED TO BE LIKE THAT TOO, ALL ALONE... NOT KNOWING WHY I WAS ALIVE... IN PAIN... BUT THEN MASTER IRUKA FINALLY NOTICED ME... ACKNOWLEDGED ME...
...AND FOR THE FIRST TIME, I EXPERIENCED WARMTH AND LOVE.
BUT THIS GUY...
HE'S STILL LIVING ALL ALONE...
...ONLY ABLE TO ASSERT HIS EXISTENCE BY KILLING OTHERS...

READ THIS WAY

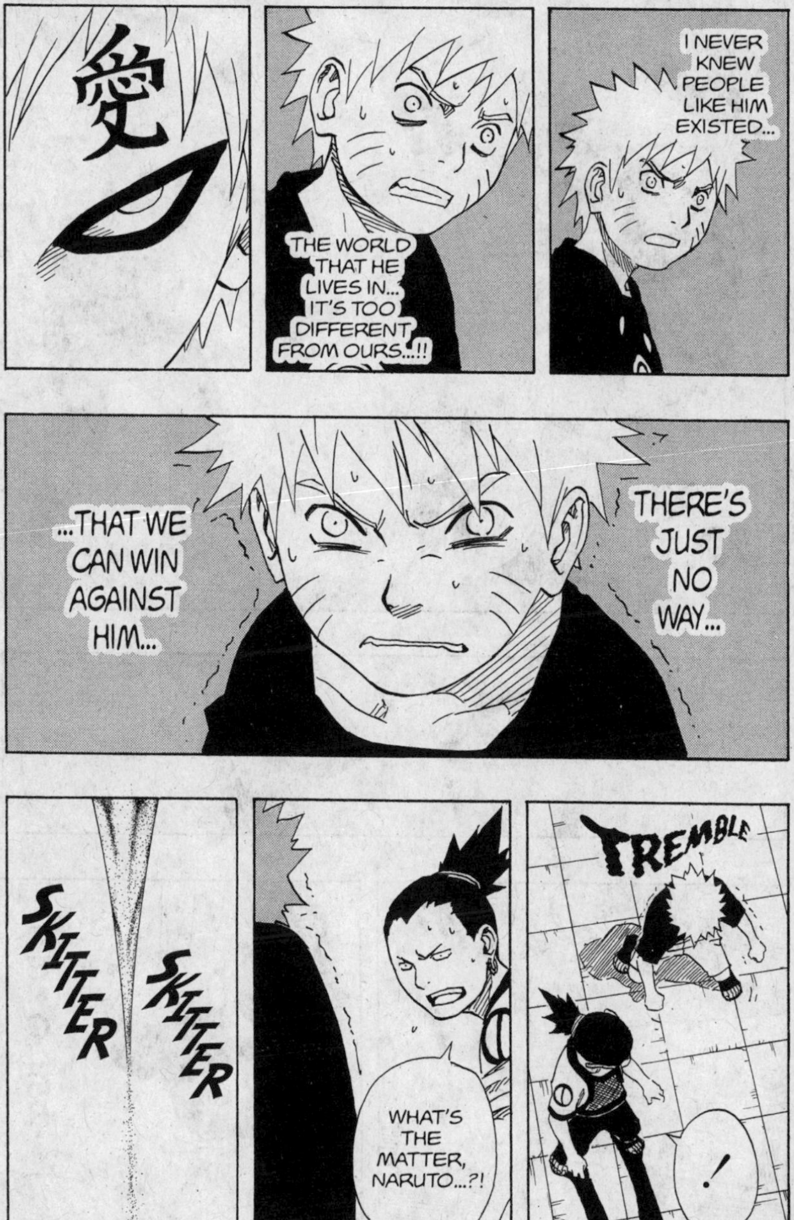

I NEVER KNEW PEOPLE LIKE HIM EXISTED...
THE WORLD THAT HE LIVES IN... IT'S TOO DIFFERENT FROM OURS...!!
愛
THERE'S JUST NO WAY...
...THAT WE CAN WIN AGAINST HIM...
TREMBLE
!
WHAT'S THE MATTER, NARUTO...?!
SKITTER
SKITTER

SSSSSS

!!

...HELP
ME
FEEL
ALIVE!

...NOW...

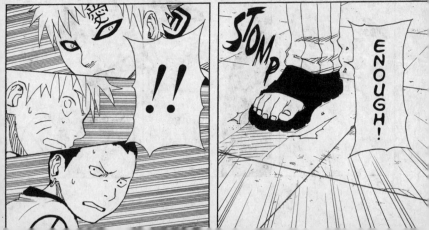

!!

STOMP

ENOUGH!

READ THIS WAY

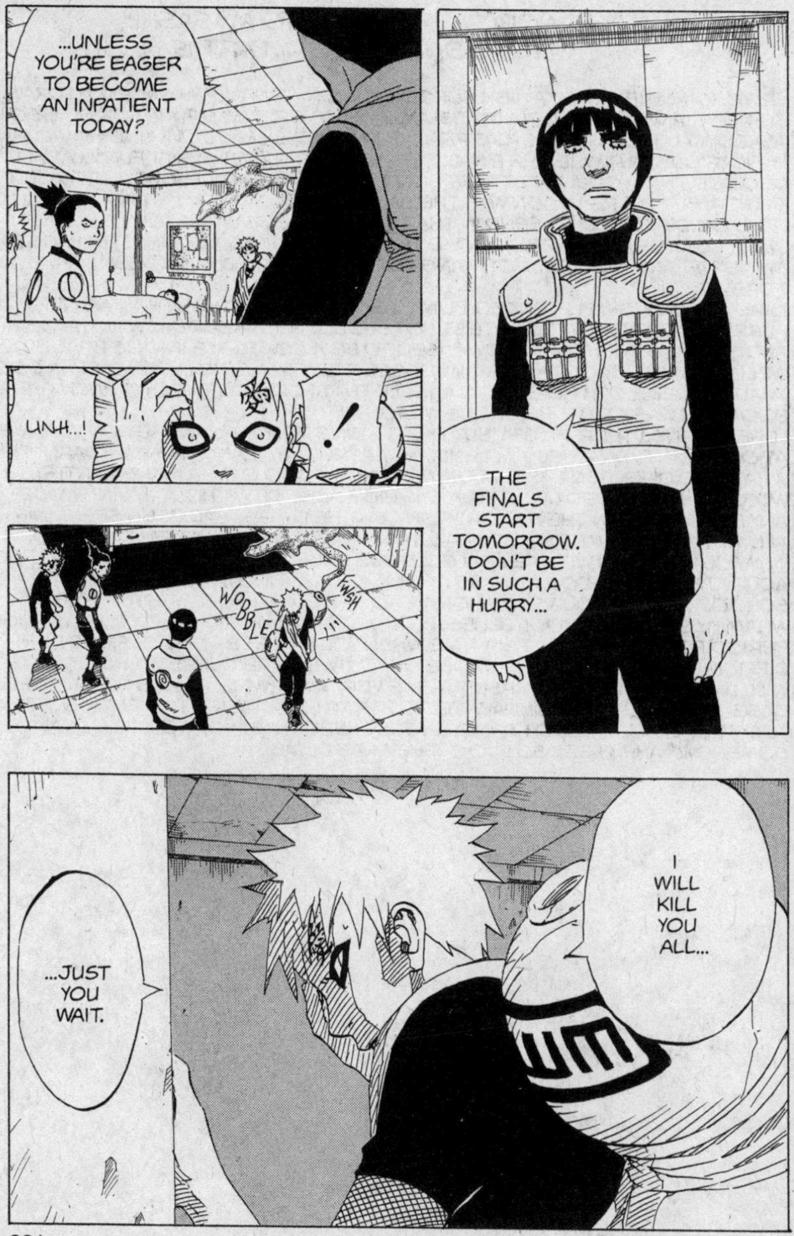
THE FINALS START TOMORROW. DON'T BE IN SUCH A HURRY...
...UNLESS YOU'RE EAGER TO BECOME AN INPATIENT TODAY?
UNH...!
!
WOBBLE
FWSH
I WILL KILL YOU ALL...
...JUST YOU WAIT.

THE WORLD OF KISHIMOTO MASASHI
MY PERSONAL HISTORY, PART 15

SOMEHOW, WHEN I WAS A HIGH SCHOOL JUNIOR, I FINALLY MANAGED TO DRAW A 31-PAGE MANGA, BUT I COULDN'T JUDGE WHETHER IT WAS FUNNY OR NOT, SO I ASKED MY LITTLE BROTHER TO READ IT. I WAITED, SILENTLY WILLING HIM TO FIND IT HILARIOUS, BUT WHEN HE FINALLY SPOKE, HE SAID, "THIS ISN'T FUNNY AT ALL!" I DECIDED THAT I COULDN'T TRUST HIS OPINION, SO NEXT I SHOWED IT TO OUR FATHER, BUT HIS REACTION WAS THE SAME... "IT'S NOT FUNNY!" I HAD BEEN ALL READY AND EXCITED TO SEND IN THAT FIRST 31-PAGE MANGA TO THE *SHONEN JUMP* CONTEST. BUT AFTER THOSE TEPID RESPONSES, I COMPLETELY LOST MY NERVE, AND THAT REJECT MANGA ENDED UP BURIED IN MY DESK DRAWER FOREVER.

I WAS A YOUNG, SIMPLEMINDED, BLINKERED FOOL WHO THOUGHT, "I WANT TO HURRY UP AND WIN THAT CONTEST, SO I SHOULD JUST KEEP DRAWING MANGA AND SENDING THEM IN!" I KNOW I USED TO BE A COMPLETE IDIOTIC BRAT, BUT... WELL, LOOKING BACK, THAT BRAINLESS PERSEVERANCE WAS PROBABLY A GOOD TRAIT TO DEVELOP. I REASON TO MYSELF THAT I COULDN'T HELP IT BACK THEN BECAUSE I WAS AT THE HEIGHT OF MY YOUTH.

I DREW MANY OTHER MANGA, BUT I KEPT BEING TOLD THEY WERE NOT FUNNY, SO AT ONE POINT I SNAPPED AND SAID, "WHY AREN'T MY MANGA FUNNY?! DARN IT! WHAT'S SO DIFFERENT ABOUT THEM COMPARED TO OTHER MANGA ARTISTS' WORK, HUH?!" I ENDED UP GRADUATING HIGH SCHOOL WITHOUT HAVING MADE ANY PROGRESS ON THE MANGA FRONT. BUT BECAUSE I HAD BEEN SPENDING ALL MY TIME ATTEMPTING TO DRAW MANGA, MY GRADES WERE 38TH OUT OF 39 IN MY CLASS. EVEN WITH REVIEW COURSES, IT BECAME CLEAR I WOULD NOT BE ACCEPTED TO ANY COLLEGE. SO I STANK AT CREATING MANGA, I STANK AT SCHOOL, AND OF COURSE MY ROMANTIC LIFE STANK, SO IT WAS A TRIPLE WHAMMY OF HIGH SCHOOL BLUES. BUT I GUESS THAT HIGH SCHOOL IS A ROUGH PERIOD FOR EVERYONE. IT'S A TIME WHEN YOU'RE BESET ON ALL SIDES BY DIFFICULT CIRCUMSTANCES (THOSE OF YOU WHO ARE CURRENTLY STUDENTS WILL UNDERSTAND). FATE WASN'T BEING VERY KIND (WELL, THAT'S USUALLY THE CASE). HOWEVER, I WAS UNDAUNTED... OR RATHER, I WASN'T THE TYPE TO THINK TOO DEEPLY ABOUT SUCH THINGS... I JUST KEPT THINKING, "WELL! I'LL MANAGE SOMEHOW." AHH, I FEEL SO LUCKY THAT I WAS DUMB!

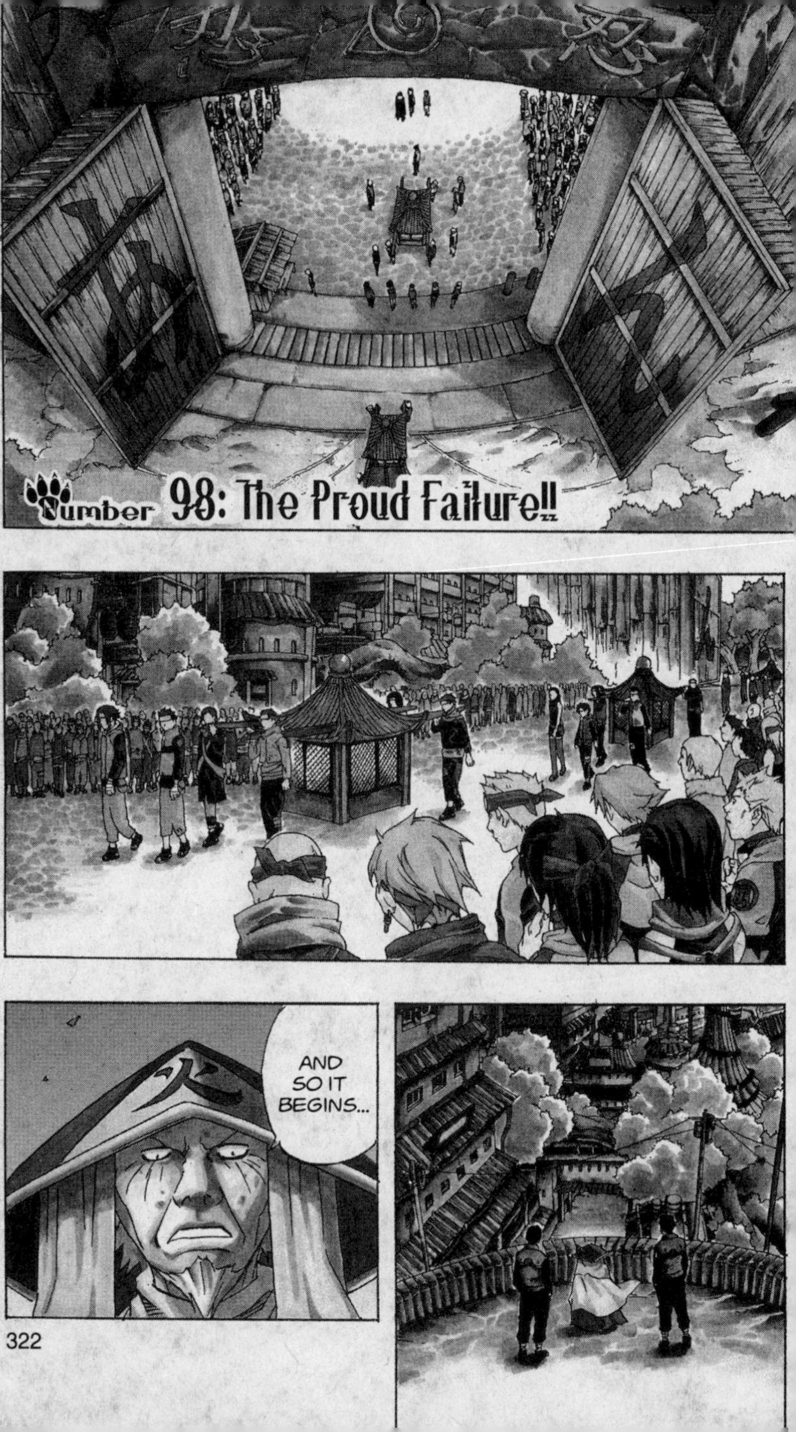
Number 98: The Proud Failure!!
AND SO IT BEGINS...

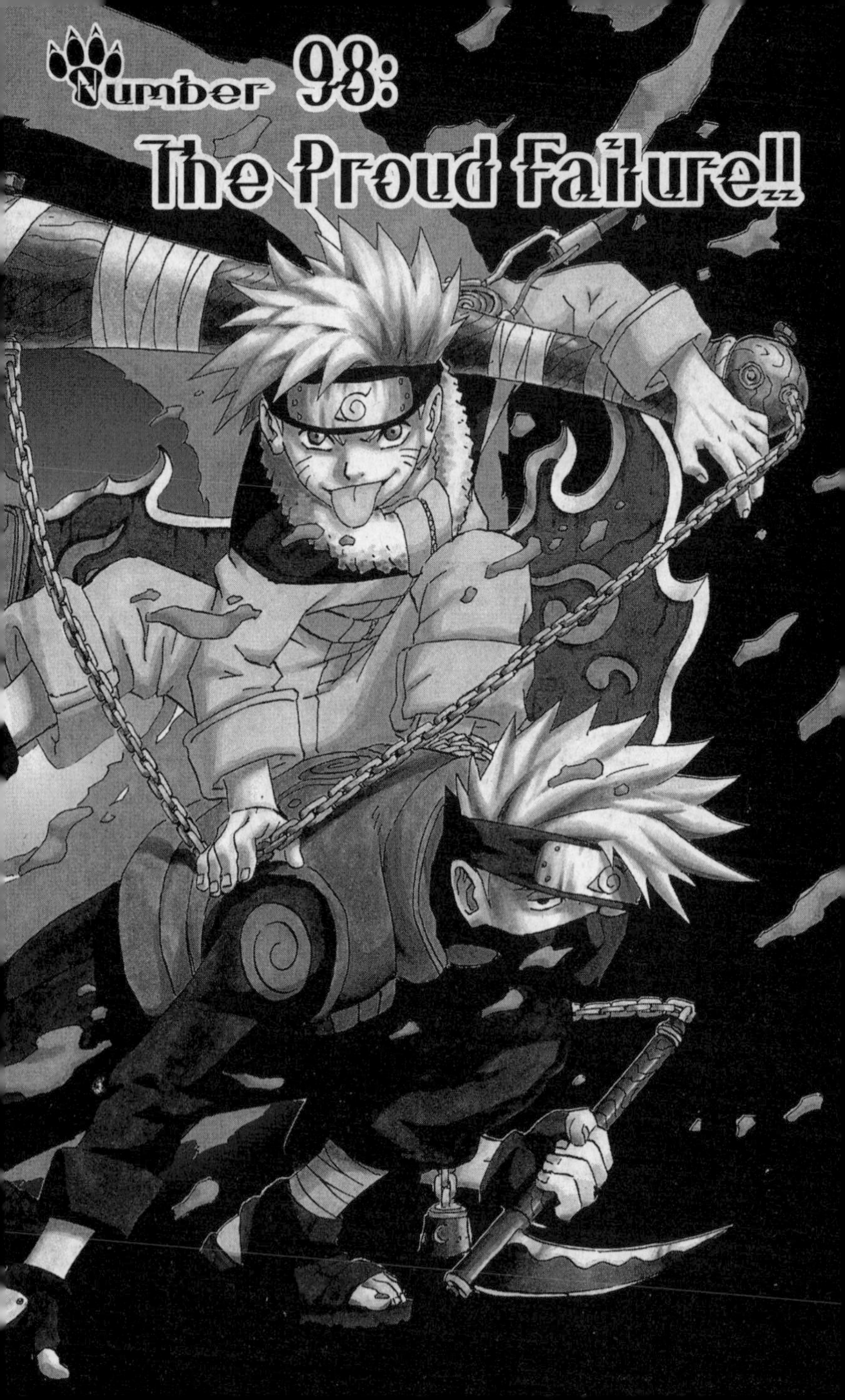
Number 98:
The Proud Failure!!

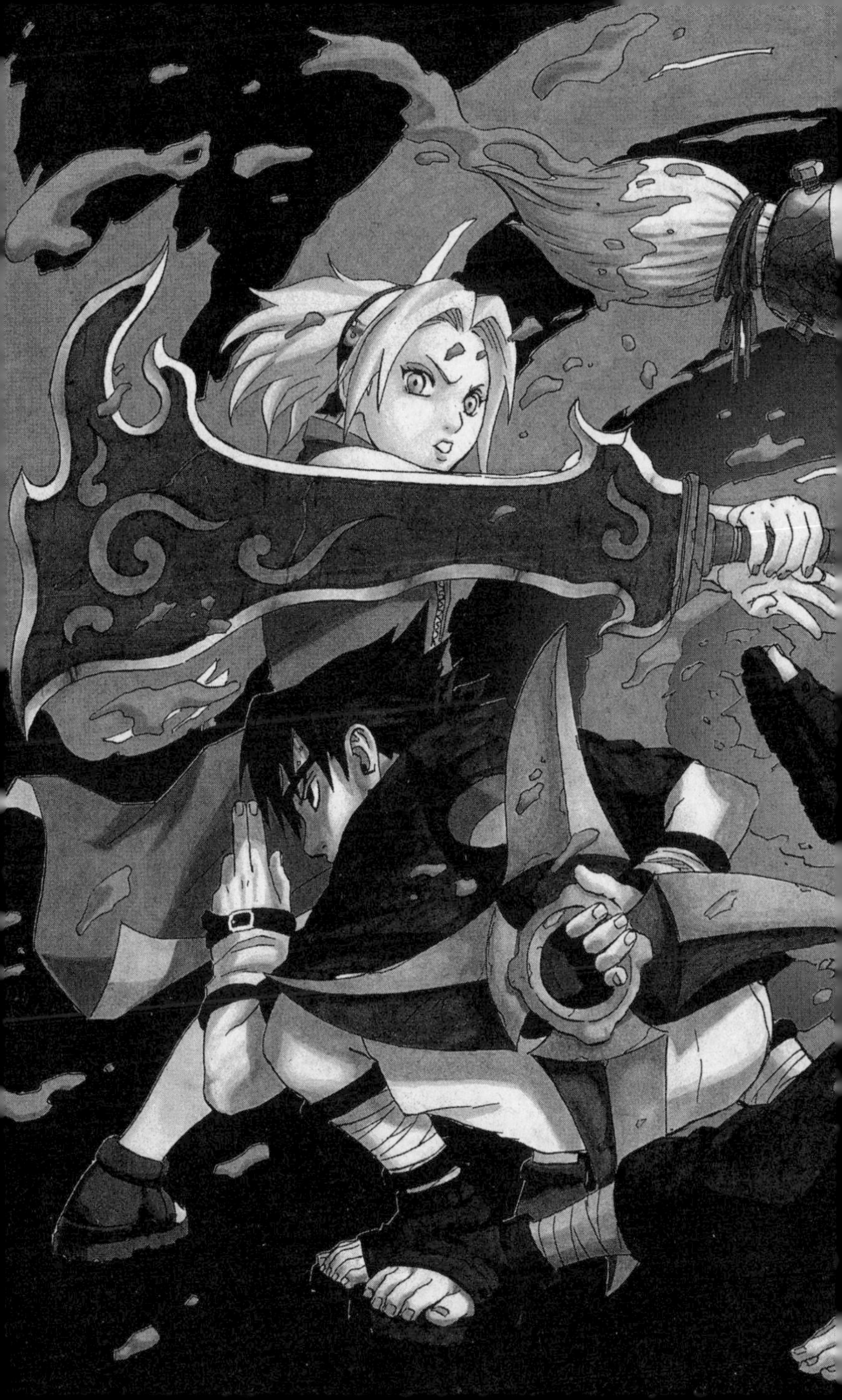

NARUTO

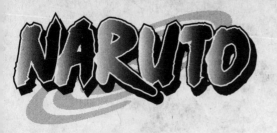

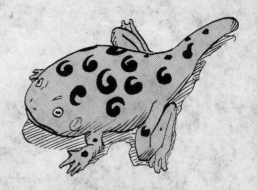

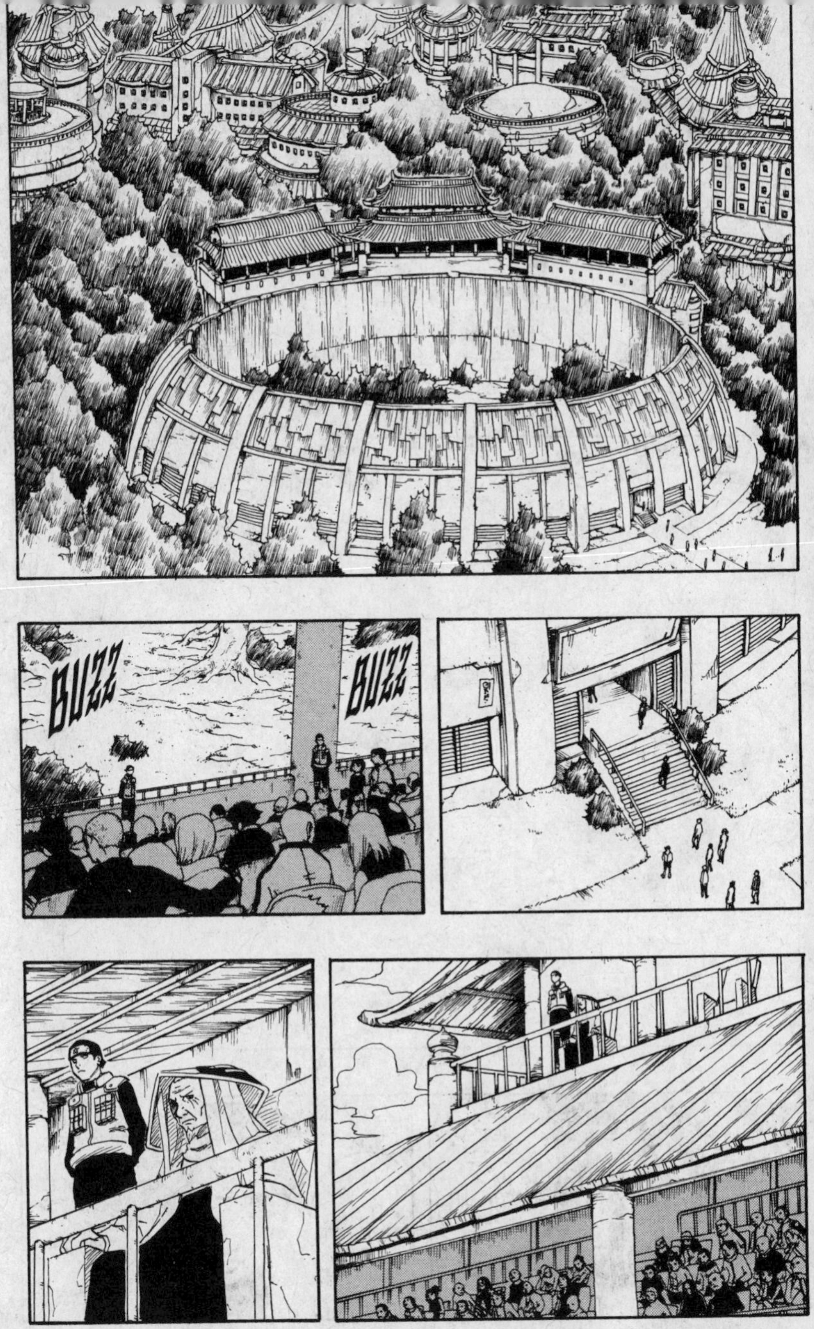
BUZZ
BUZZ

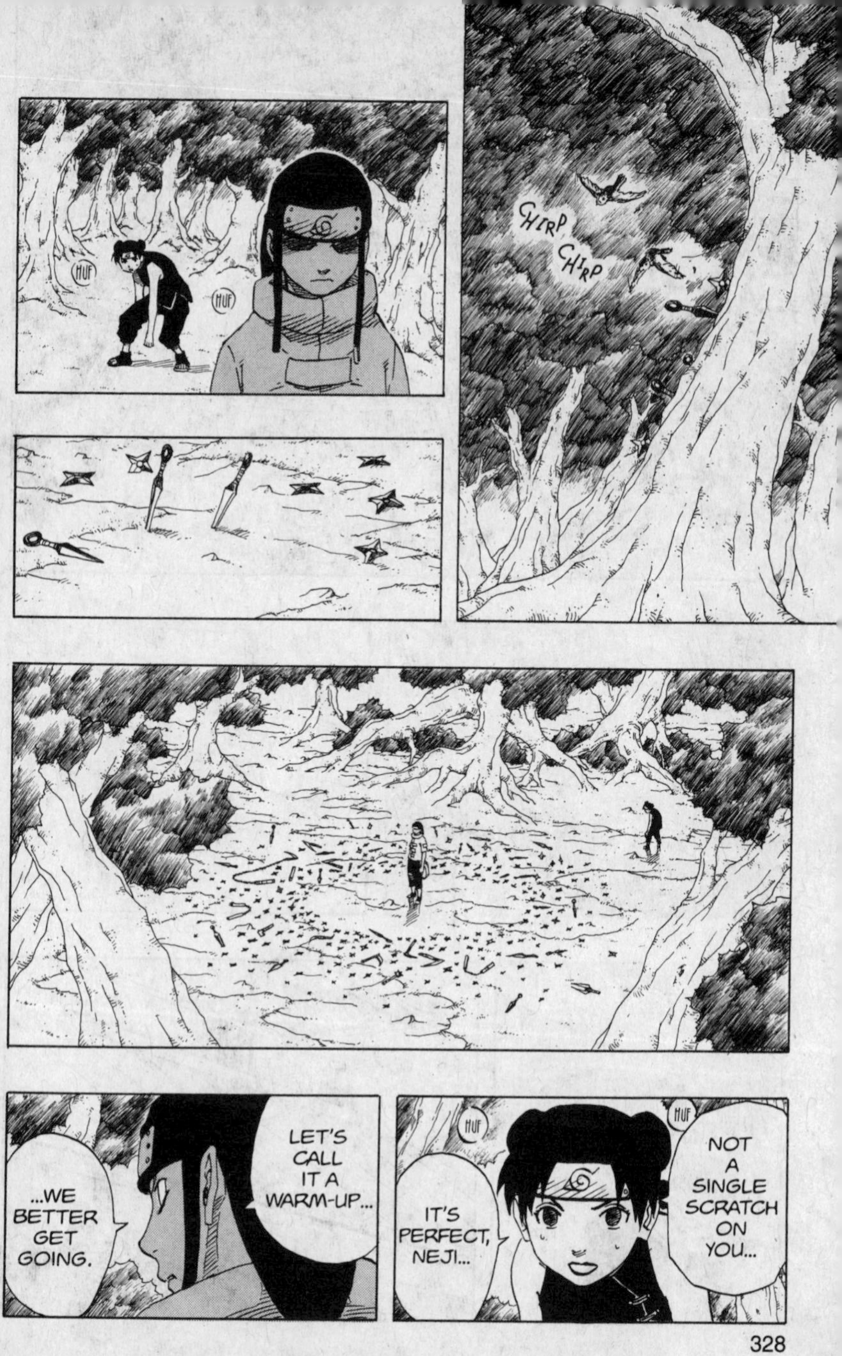
CHIRP CHIRP
HUF
HUF
HUF
NOT A SINGLE SCRATCH ON YOU...
HUF
IT'S PERFECT, NEJI...
LET'S CALL IT A WARM-UP...
...WE BETTER GET GOING.

READ THIS WAY

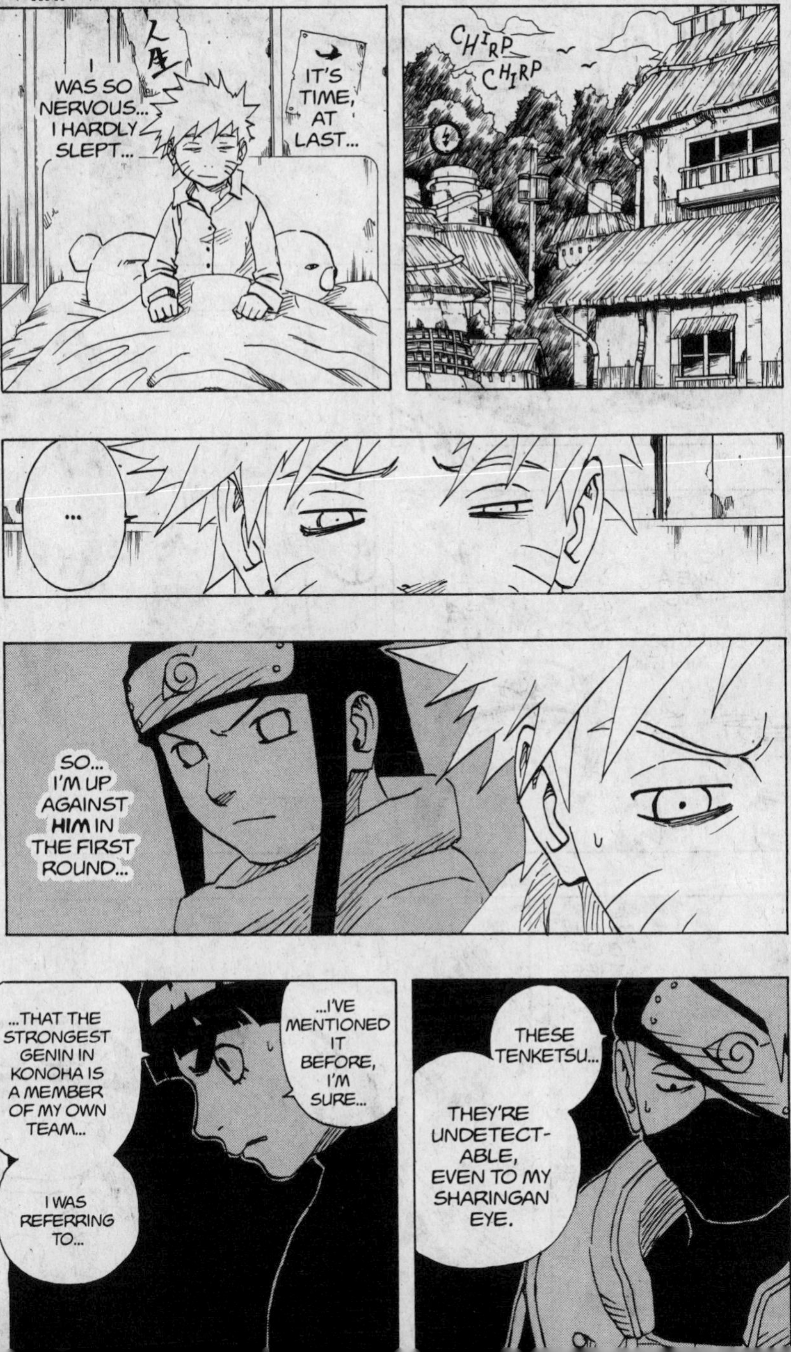
CHIRP
CHIRP
IT'S TIME, AT LAST...
人生
I WAS SO NERVOUS... I HARDLY SLEPT...
...
SO... I'M UP AGAINST **HIM** IN THE FIRST ROUND...
THESE TENKETSU...
THEY'RE UNDETECTABLE, EVEN TO MY SHARINGAN EYE.
...I'VE MENTIONED IT BEFORE, I'M SURE...
...THAT THE STRONGEST GENIN IN KONOHA IS A MEMBER OF MY OWN TEAM...
I WAS REFERRING TO...

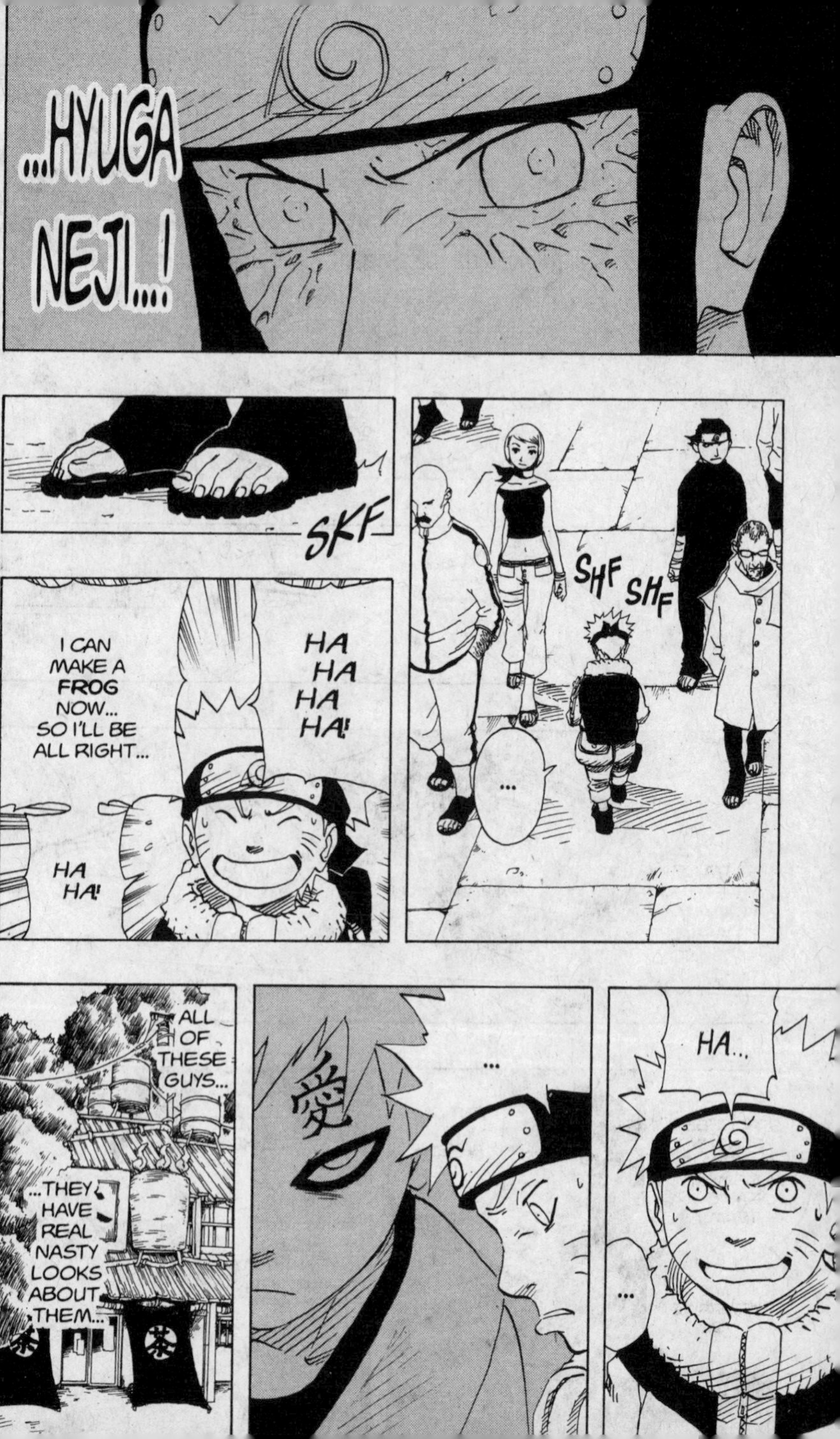

...HYUGA NEJI...!
SHF SHF
...
SKF
HA HA HA HA!
I CAN MAKE A FROG NOW... SO I'LL BE ALL RIGHT...
HA HA!
HA...
...
...
ALL OF THESE GUYS...
...THEY HAVE REAL NASTY LOOKS ABOUT THEM...

READ THIS WAY

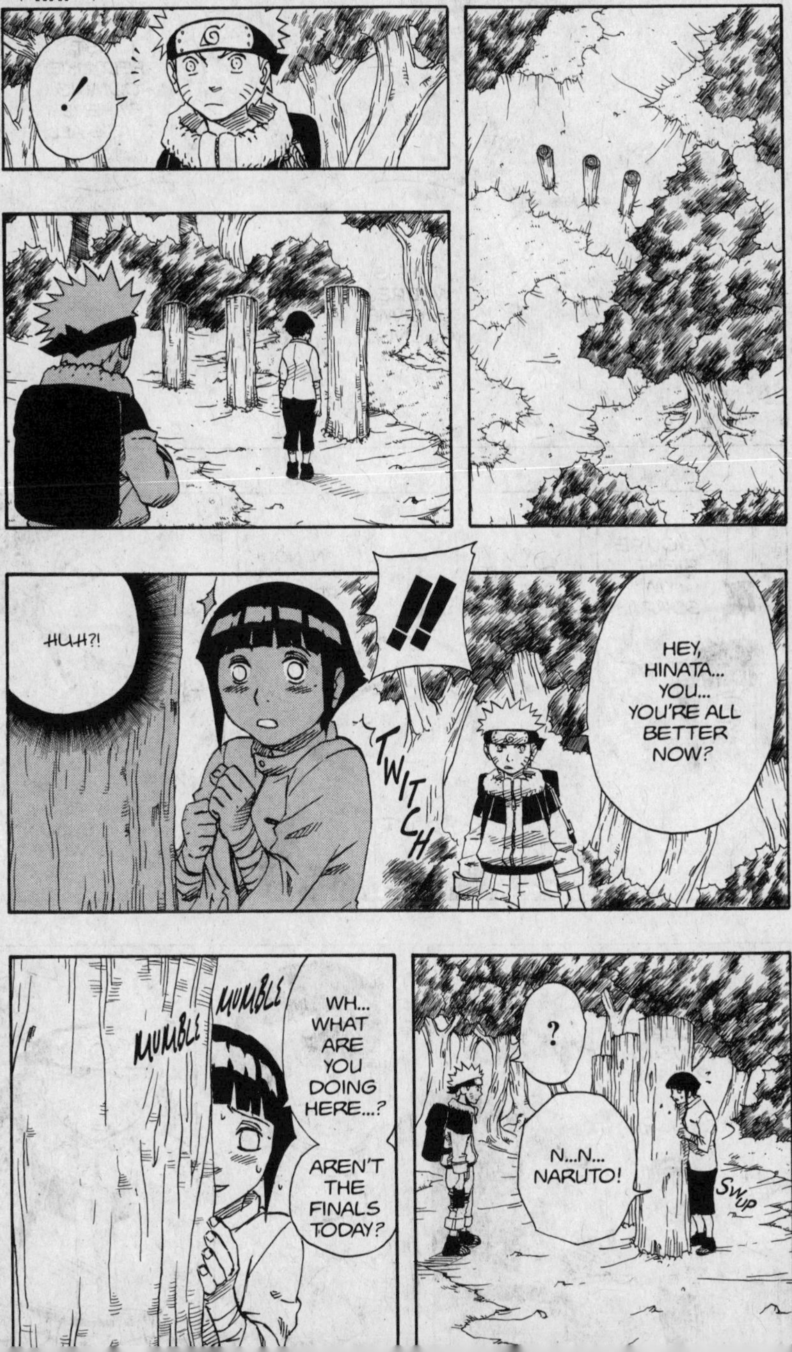

!
HEY, HINATA... YOU... YOU'RE ALL BETTER NOW?
TWITCH
!!
HUH?!
?
N...N... NARUTO!
SWUP
WH... WHAT ARE YOU DOING HERE...?
AREN'T THE FINALS TODAY?
MUMBLE
MUMBLE

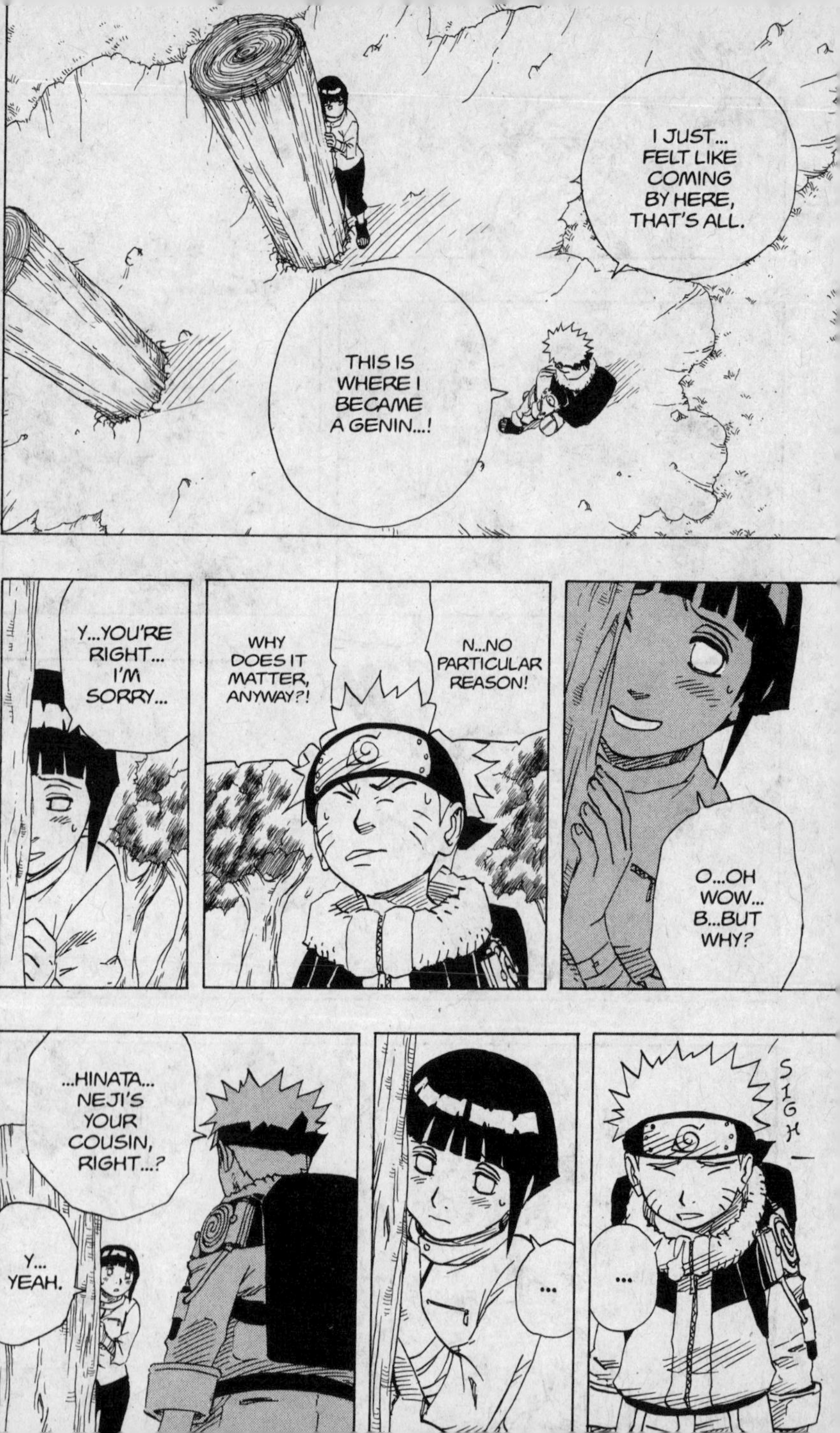

I JUST... FELT LIKE COMING BY HERE, THAT'S ALL.
THIS IS WHERE I BECAME A GENIN...!
O...OH WOW... B...BUT WHY?
N...NO PARTICULAR REASON!
WHY DOES IT MATTER, ANYWAY?!
Y...YOU'RE RIGHT... I'M SORRY...
SIGH
...
...
...HINATA... NEJI'S YOUR COUSIN, RIGHT...?
Y... YEAH.

READ THIS WAY

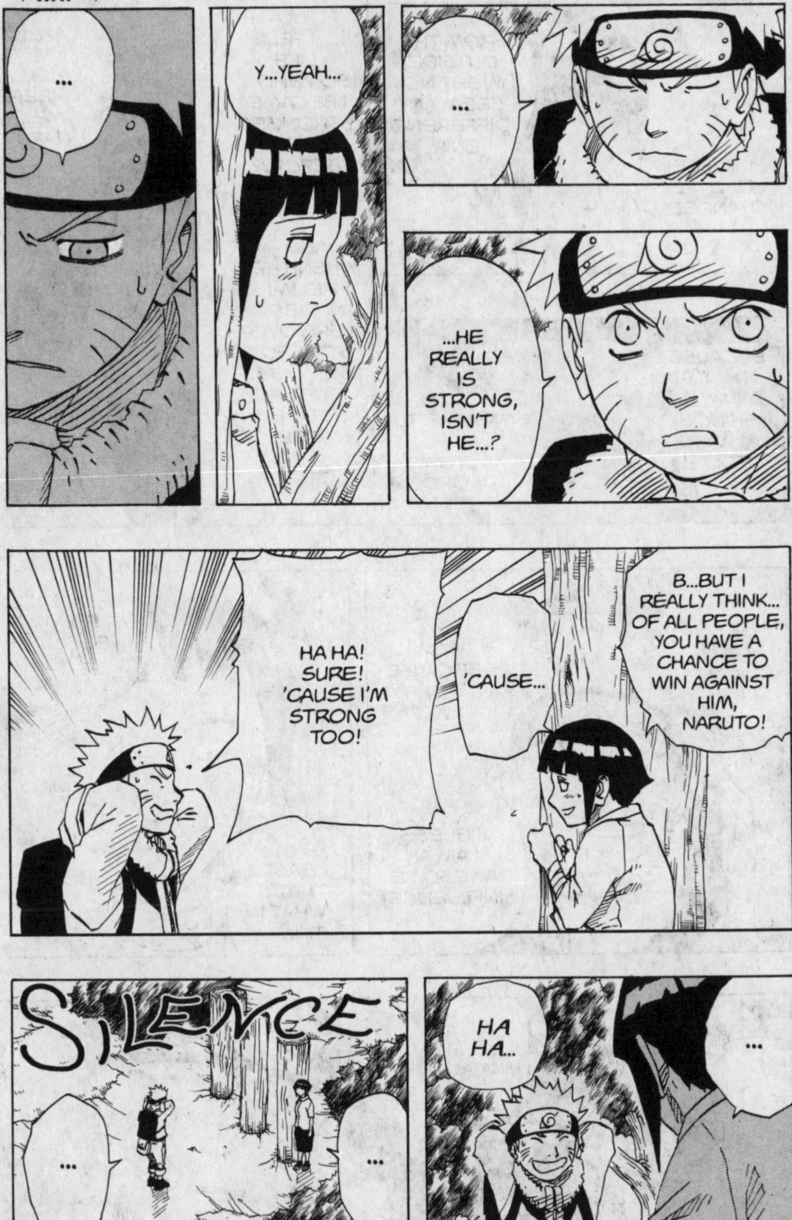
...
...HE REALLY IS STRONG, ISN'T HE...?
Y...YEAH...
...
B...BUT I REALLY THINK... OF ALL PEOPLE, YOU HAVE A CHANCE TO WIN AGAINST HIM, NARUTO!
'CAUSE...
HA HA! SURE! 'CAUSE I'M STRONG TOO!
...
HA HA...
SILENCE
...
...

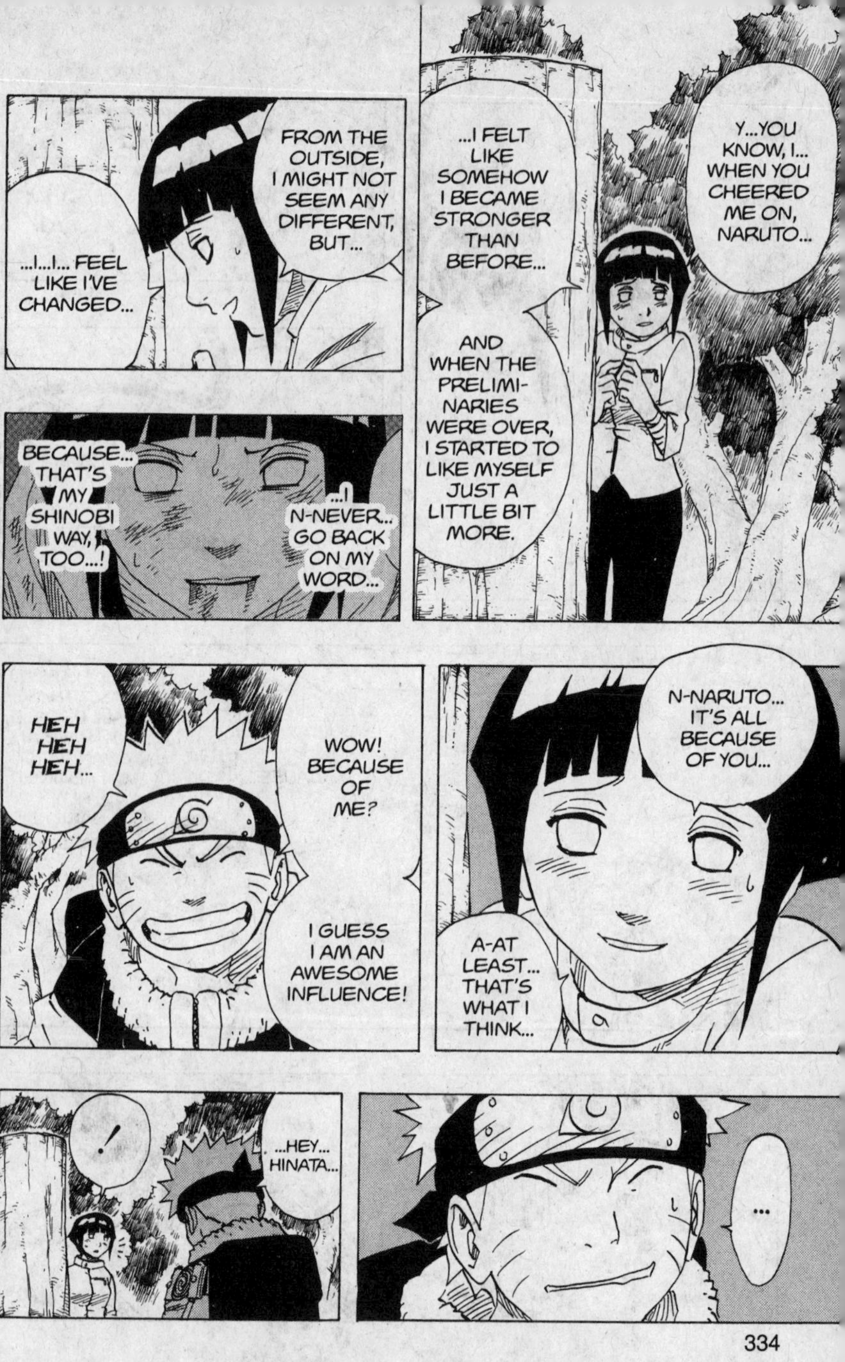
Y...YOU KNOW, I... WHEN YOU CHEERED ME ON, NARUTO...
...I FELT LIKE SOMEHOW I BECAME STRONGER THAN BEFORE...
AND WHEN THE PRELIMI-NARIES WERE OVER, I STARTED TO LIKE MYSELF JUST A LITTLE BIT MORE.
FROM THE OUTSIDE, I MIGHT NOT SEEM ANY DIFFERENT, BUT...
...I...I... FEEL LIKE I'VE CHANGED...
...I N-NEVER... GO BACK ON MY WORD...
BECAUSE... THAT'S MY SHINOBI WAY, TOO...!
N-NARUTO... IT'S ALL BECAUSE OF YOU...
A-AT LEAST... THAT'S WHAT I THINK...
WOW! BECAUSE OF ME?
I GUESS I AM AN AWESOME INFLUENCE!
HEH HEH HEH...
...
...HEY... HINATA...
!

READ THIS WAY

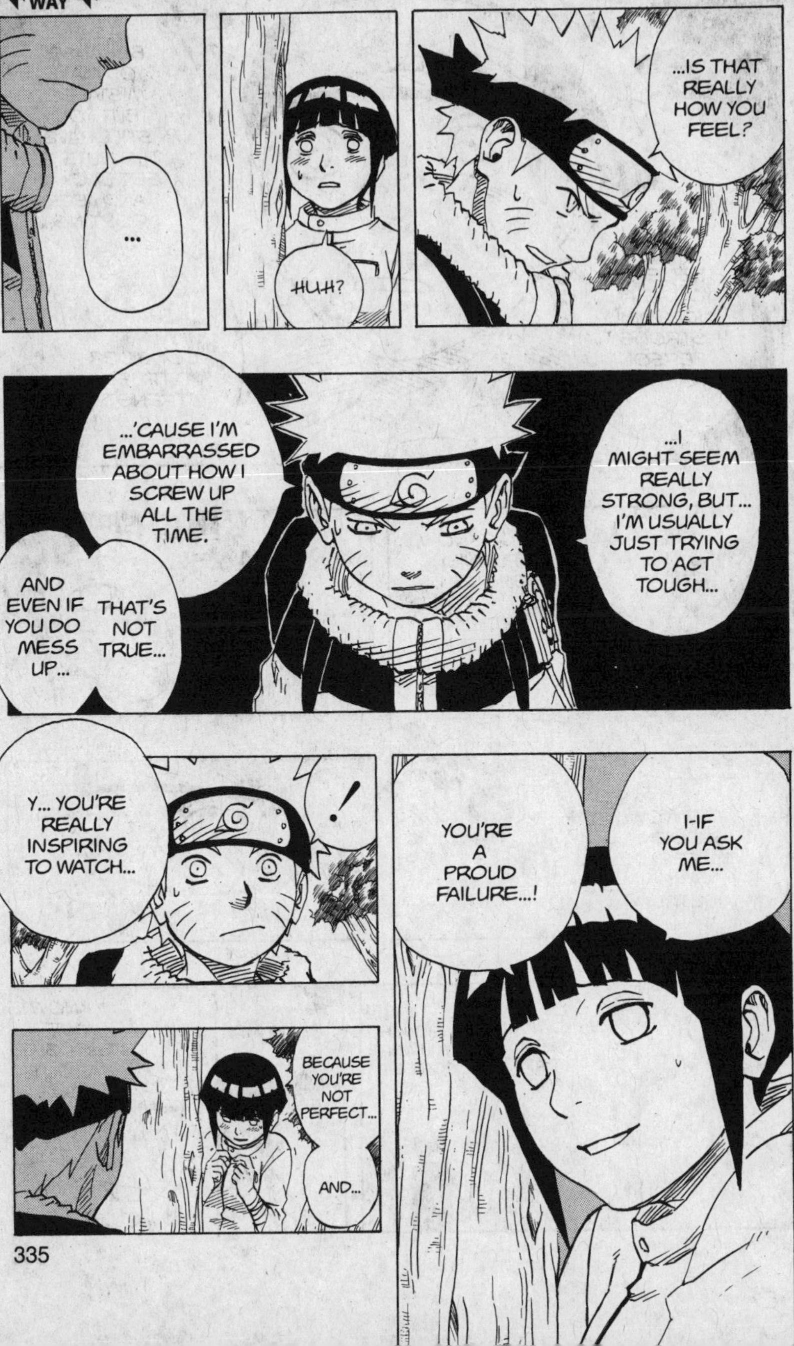
...IS THAT REALLY HOW YOU FEEL?
HUH?
...
...I MIGHT SEEM REALLY STRONG, BUT... I'M USUALLY JUST TRYING TO ACT TOUGH...
...'CAUSE I'M EMBARRASSED ABOUT HOW I SCREW UP ALL THE TIME.
THAT'S NOT TRUE...
AND EVEN IF YOU DO MESS UP...
I-IF YOU ASK ME...
YOU'RE A PROUD FAILURE...!
!
Y... YOU'RE REALLY INSPIRING TO WATCH...
BECAUSE YOU'RE NOT PERFECT...
AND...

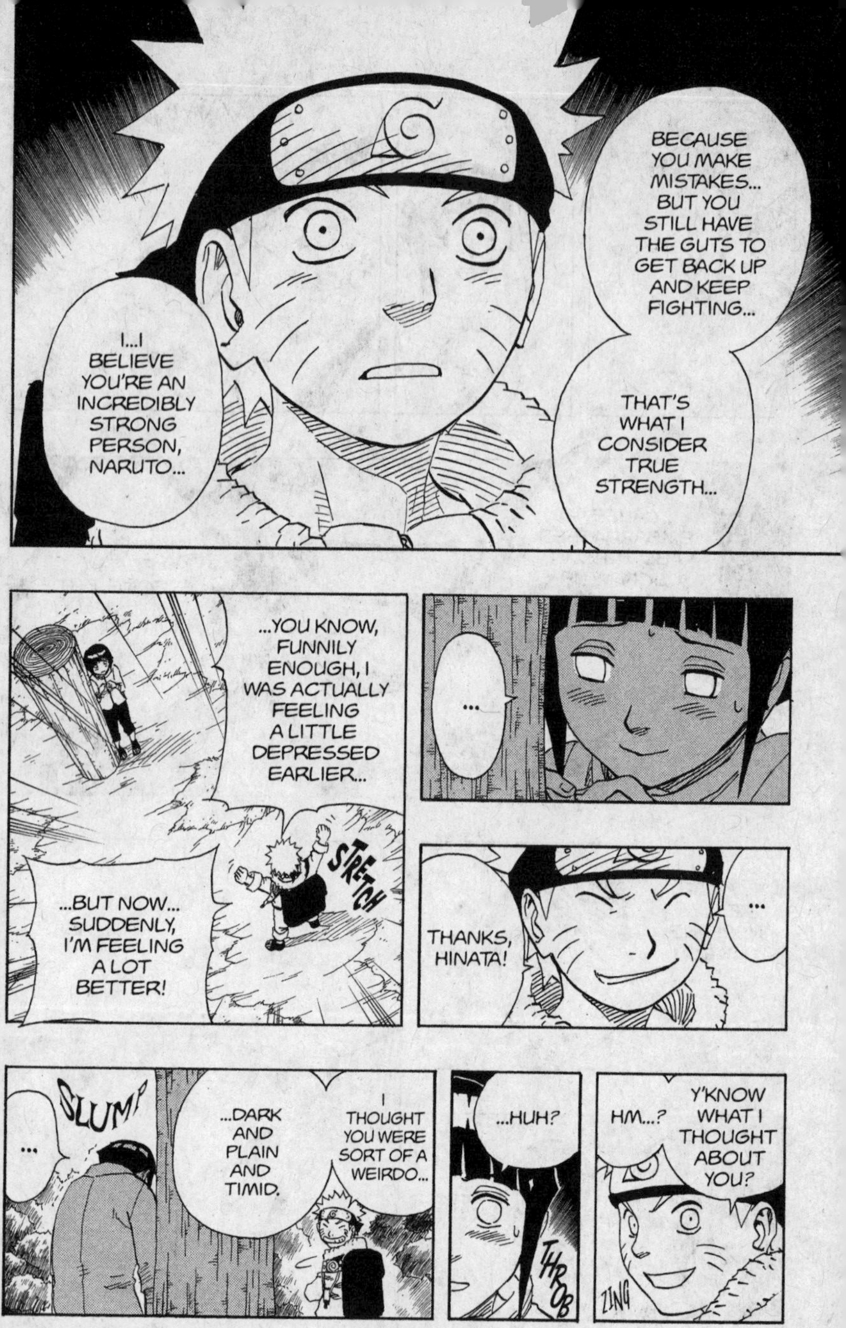
BECAUSE YOU MAKE MISTAKES... BUT YOU STILL HAVE THE GUTS TO GET BACK UP AND KEEP FIGHTING...
I...I BELIEVE YOU'RE AN INCREDIBLY STRONG PERSON, NARUTO...
THAT'S WHAT I CONSIDER TRUE STRENGTH...
...
...
THANKS, HINATA!
...YOU KNOW, FUNNILY ENOUGH, I WAS ACTUALLY FEELING A LITTLE DEPRESSED EARLIER...
STRETCH
...BUT NOW... SUDDENLY, I'M FEELING A LOT BETTER!
Y'KNOW WHAT I THOUGHT ABOUT YOU?
HM...?
ZING
...HUH?
THROB
I THOUGHT YOU WERE SORT OF A WEIRDO...
...DARK AND PLAIN AND TIMID.
SLUMP
...

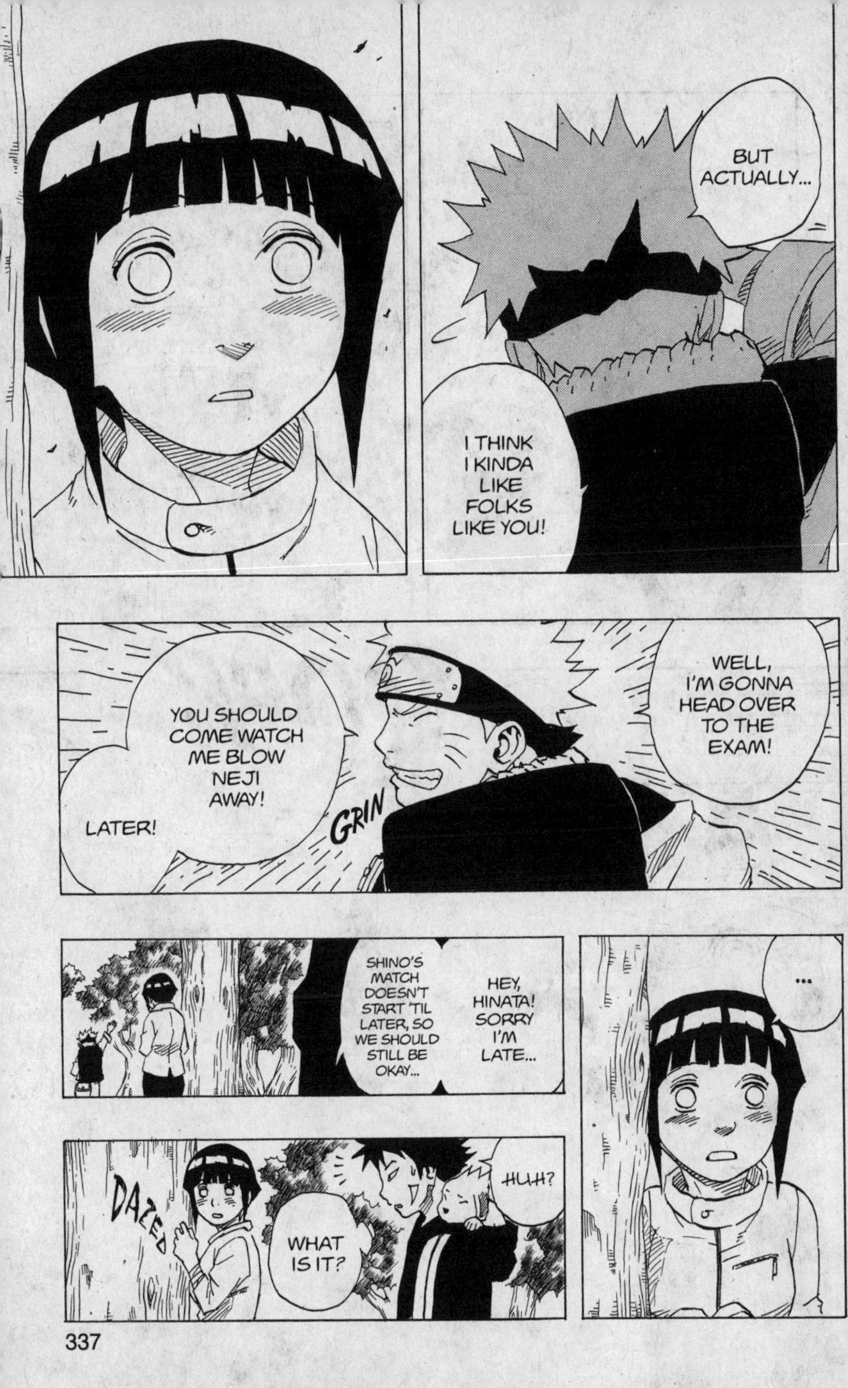
BUT ACTUALLY...
I THINK I KINDA LIKE FOLKS LIKE YOU!
WELL, I'M GONNA HEAD OVER TO THE EXAM!
YOU SHOULD COME WATCH ME BLOW NEJI AWAY!
LATER!
GRIN
...
HEY, HINATA! SORRY I'M LATE...
SHINO'S MATCH DOESN'T START 'TIL LATER, SO WE SHOULD STILL BE OKAY...
HUH?
WHAT IS IT?
DAZED

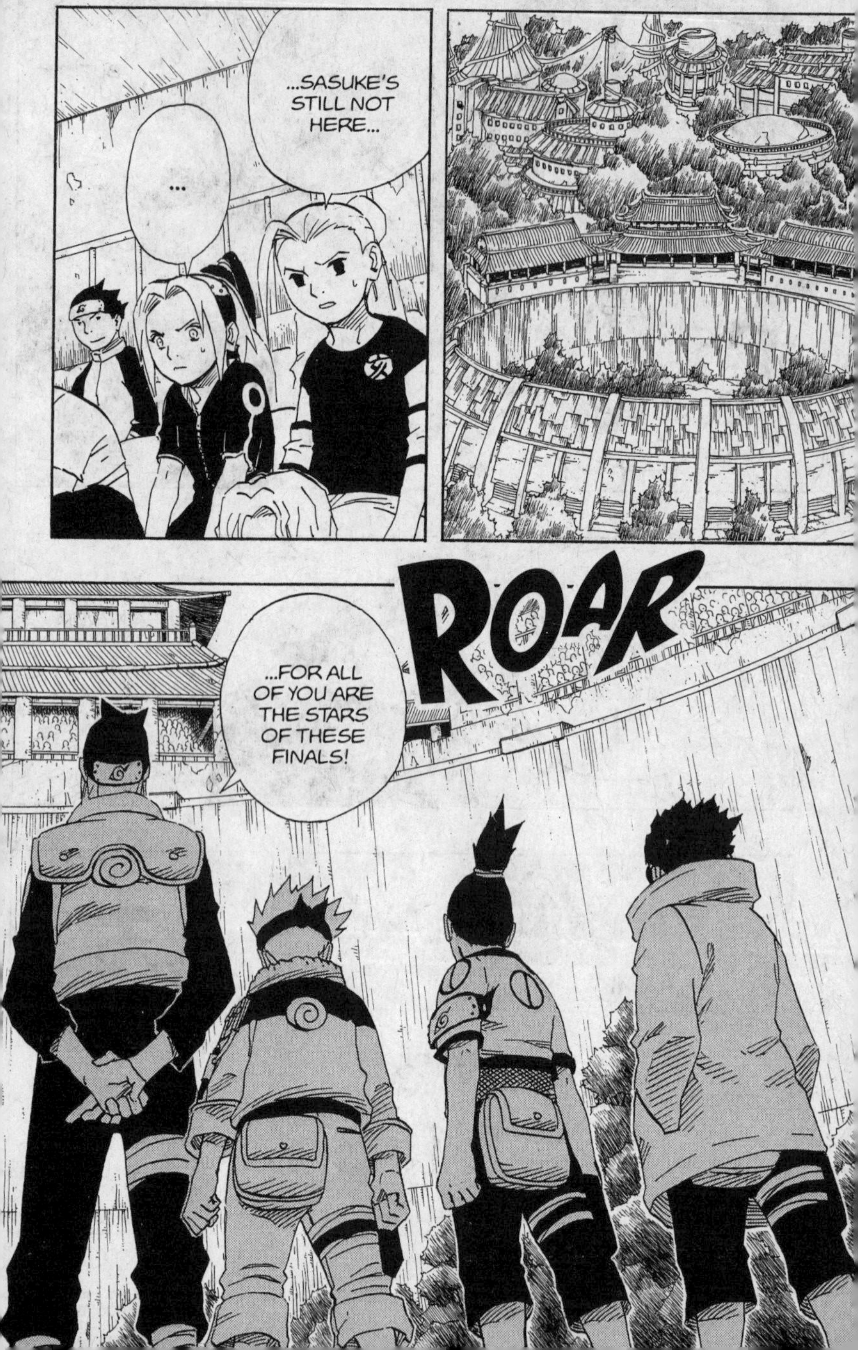
...SASUKE'S STILL NOT HERE...
...
ROAR
...FOR ALL OF YOU ARE THE STARS OF THESE FINALS!

READ THIS WAY

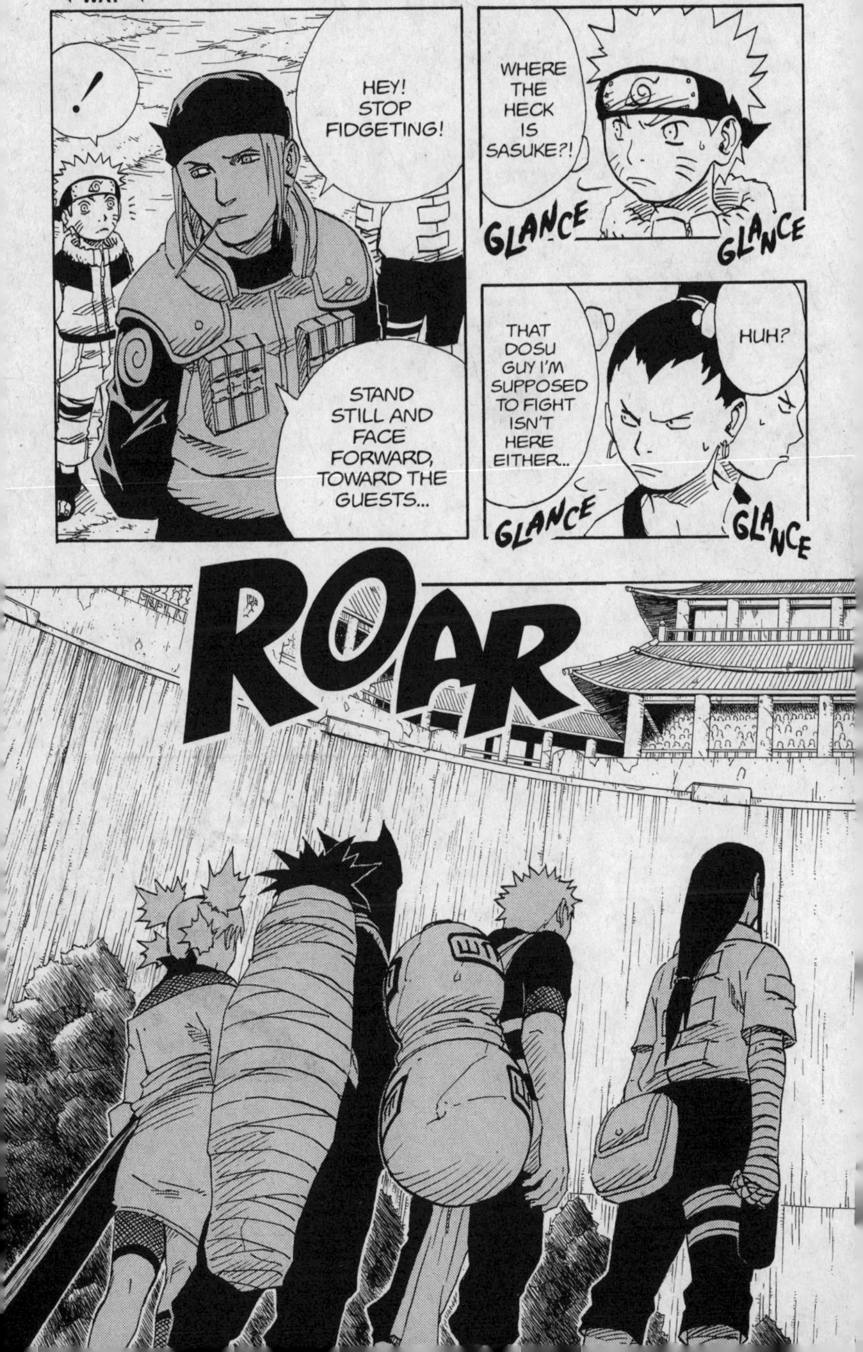
WHERE THE HECK IS SASUKE?!
GLANCE
GLANCE
HUH?
THAT DOSU GUY I'M SUPPOSED TO FIGHT ISN'T HERE EITHER...
GLANCE
GLANCE
HEY! STOP FIDGETING!
!
STAND STILL AND FACE FORWARD, TOWARD THE GUESTS...
ROAR

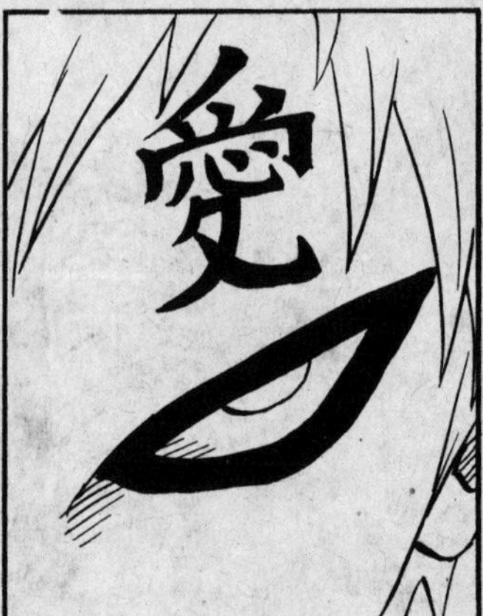
愛

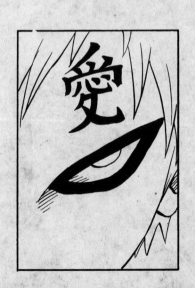

Number 99:

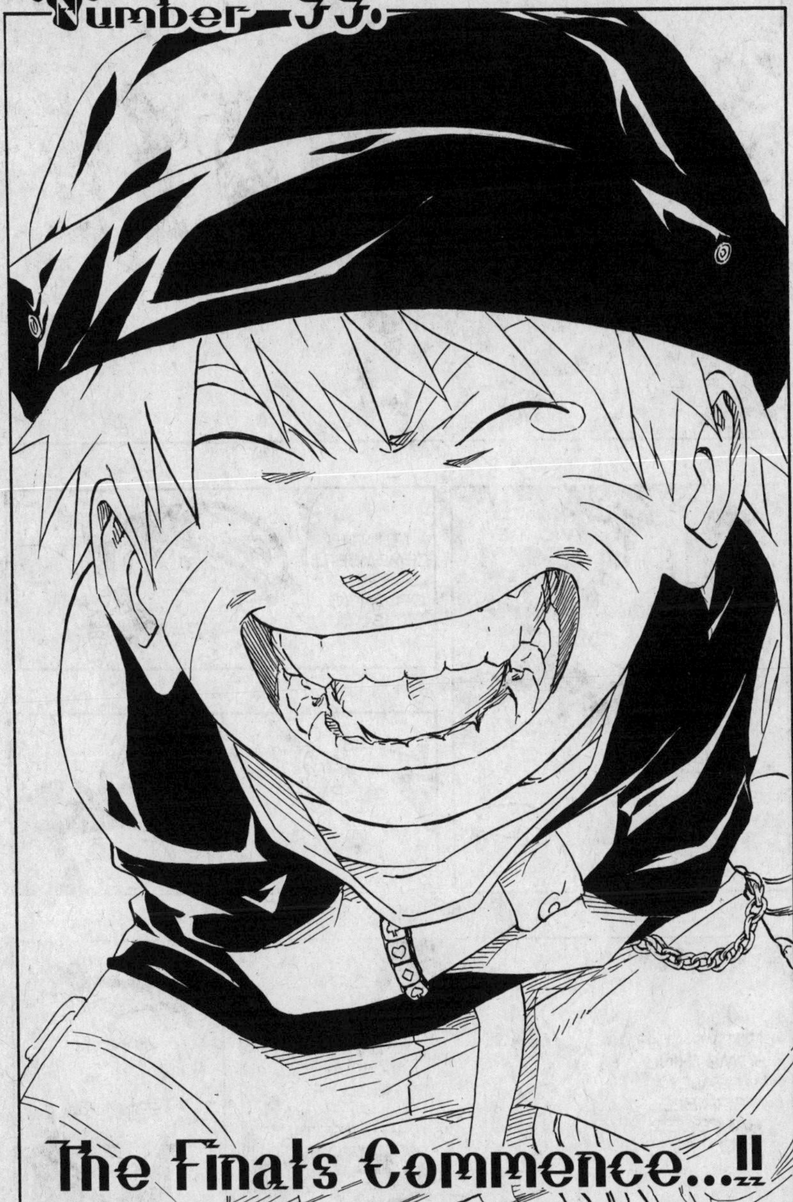
The Finals Commence...!!

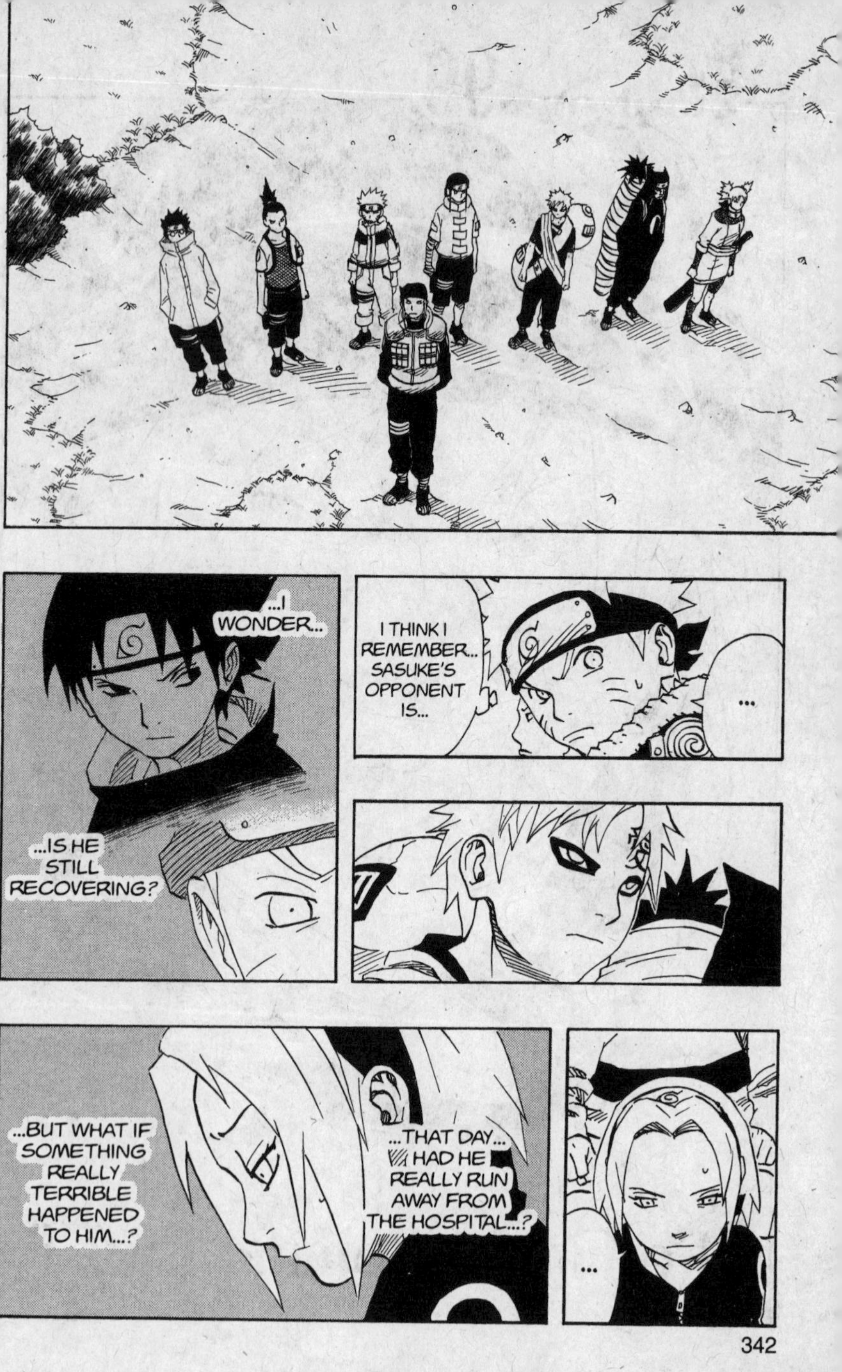
I THINK I REMEMBER... SASUKE'S OPPONENT IS...
...
...I WONDER...
...IS HE STILL RECOVERING?
...
...THAT DAY... HAD HE REALLY RUN AWAY FROM THE HOSPITAL...?
...BUT WHAT IF SOMETHING REALLY TERRIBLE HAPPENED TO HIM...?

READ THIS WAY

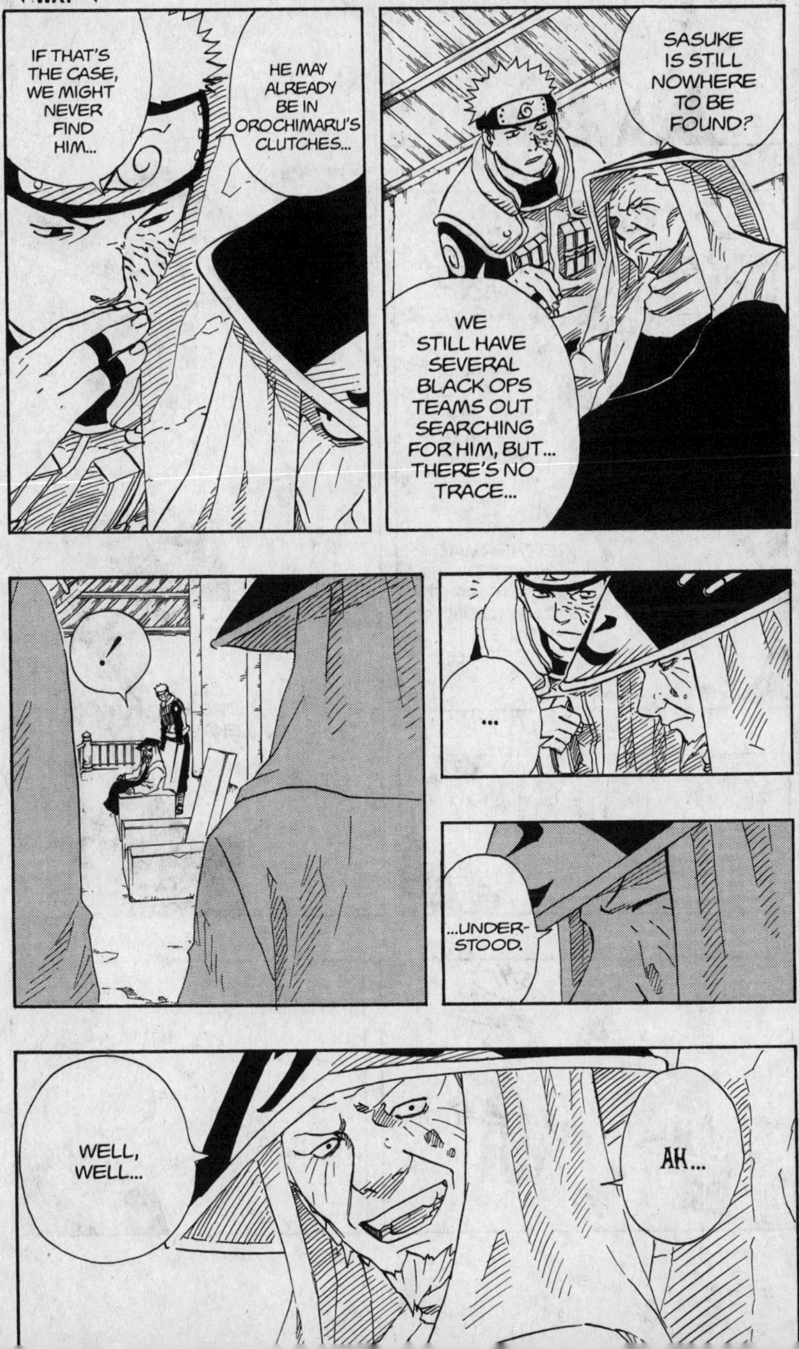

SASUKE IS STILL NOWHERE TO BE FOUND?
WE STILL HAVE SEVERAL BLACK OPS TEAMS OUT SEARCHING FOR HIM, BUT... THERE'S NO TRACE...
HE MAY ALREADY BE IN OROCHIMARU'S CLUTCHES...
IF THAT'S THE CASE, WE MIGHT NEVER FIND HIM...
...
...UNDER-STOOD.
!
AH...
WELL, WELL...

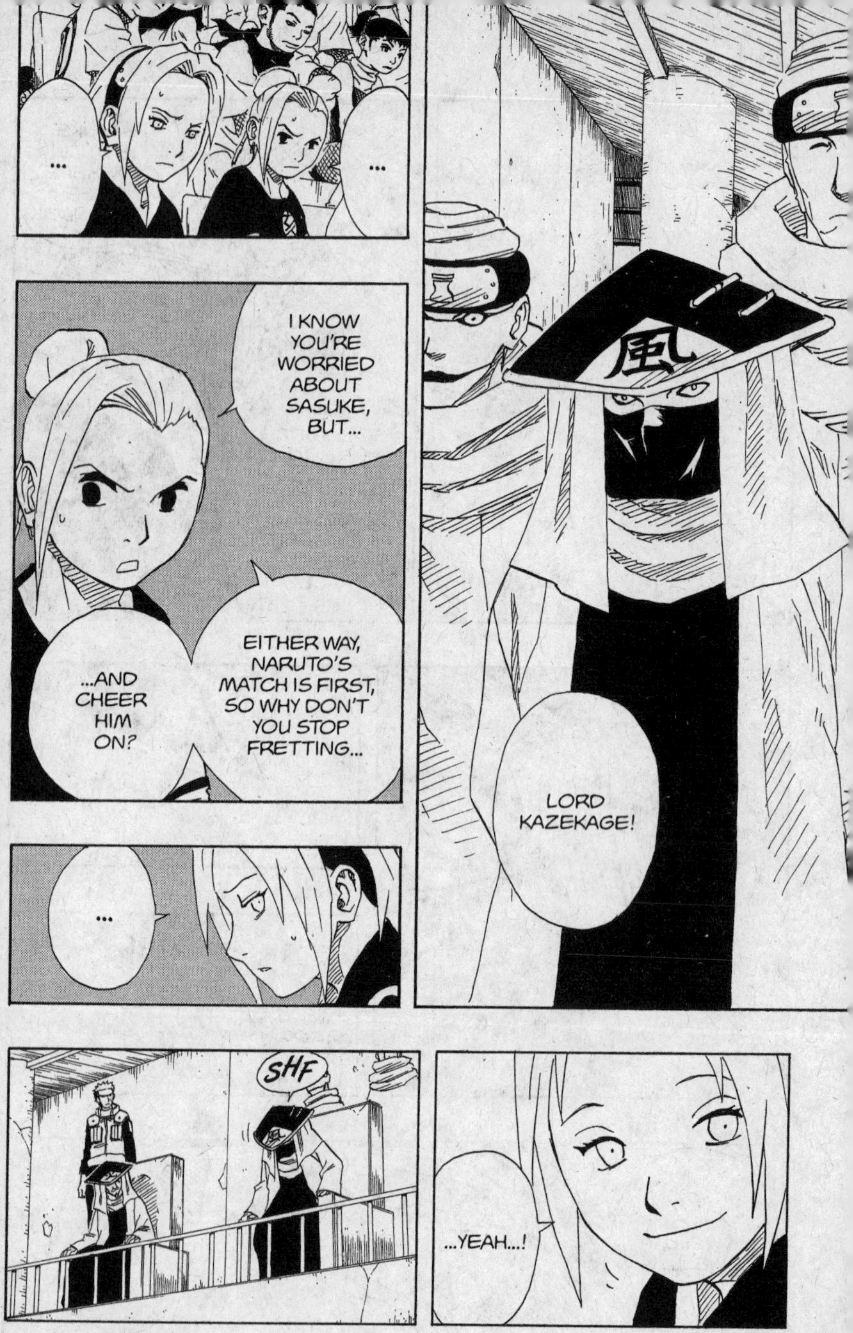
LORD KAZEKAGE!
...
...
I KNOW YOU'RE WORRIED ABOUT SASUKE, BUT...
EITHER WAY, NARUTO'S MATCH IS FIRST, SO WHY DON'T YOU STOP FRETTING...
...AND CHEER HIM ON?
...
...YEAH...!
SHF

READ THIS WAY

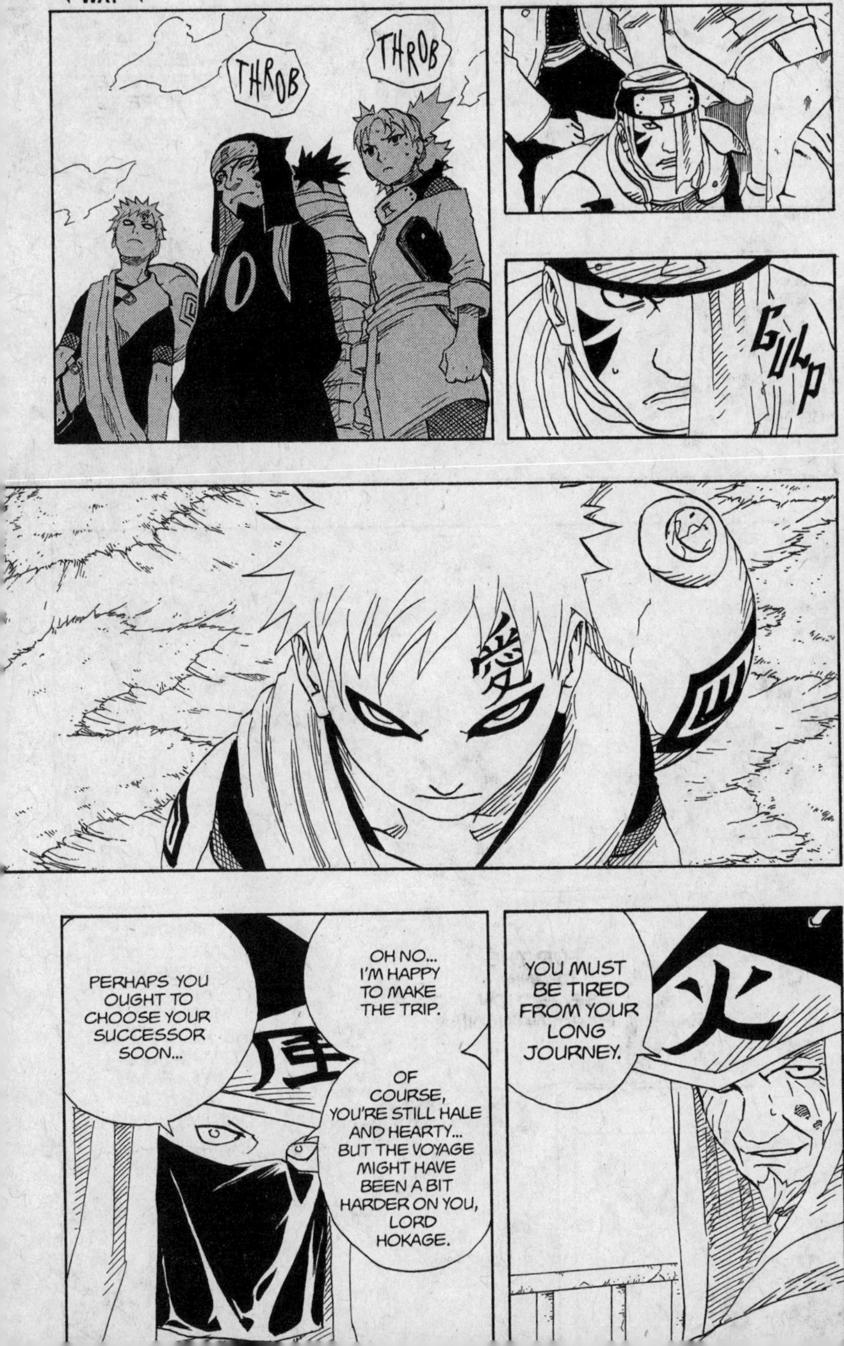
GULP
THROB
THROB
YOU MUST BE TIRED FROM YOUR LONG JOURNEY.
OH NO... I'M HAPPY TO MAKE THE TRIP.
OF COURSE, YOU'RE STILL HALE AND HEARTY... BUT THE VOYAGE MIGHT HAVE BEEN A BIT HARDER ON YOU, LORD HOKAGE.
PERHAPS YOU OUGHT TO CHOOSE YOUR SUCCESSOR SOON...

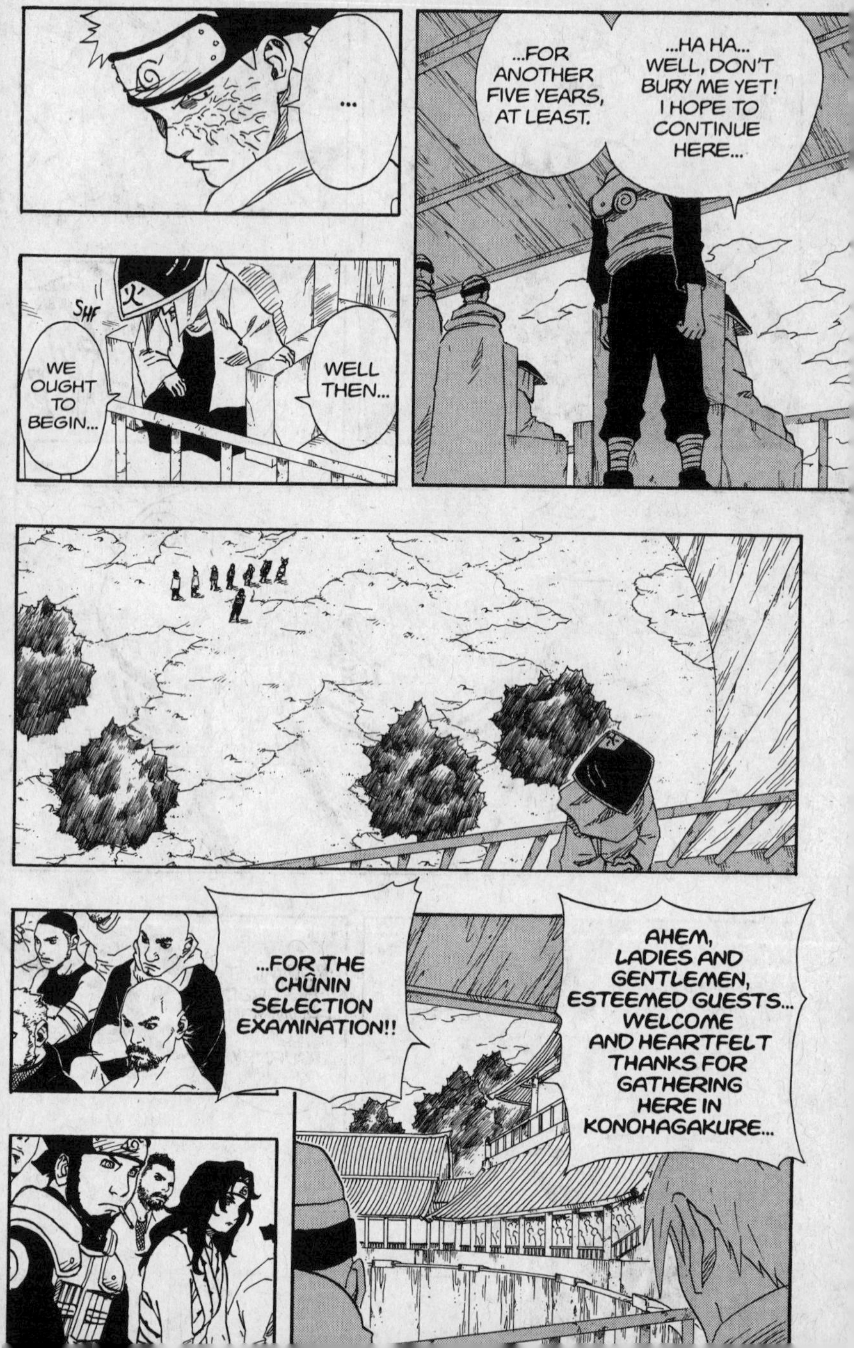
...HA HA... WELL, DON'T BURY ME YET! I HOPE TO CONTINUE HERE...
...FOR ANOTHER FIVE YEARS, AT LEAST.
...
WELL THEN...
SHF
WE OUGHT TO BEGIN...
AHEM, LADIES AND GENTLEMEN, ESTEEMED GUESTS... WELCOME AND HEARTFELT THANKS FOR GATHERING HERE IN KONOHAGAKURE...
...FOR THE CHÛNIN SELECTION EXAMINATION!!

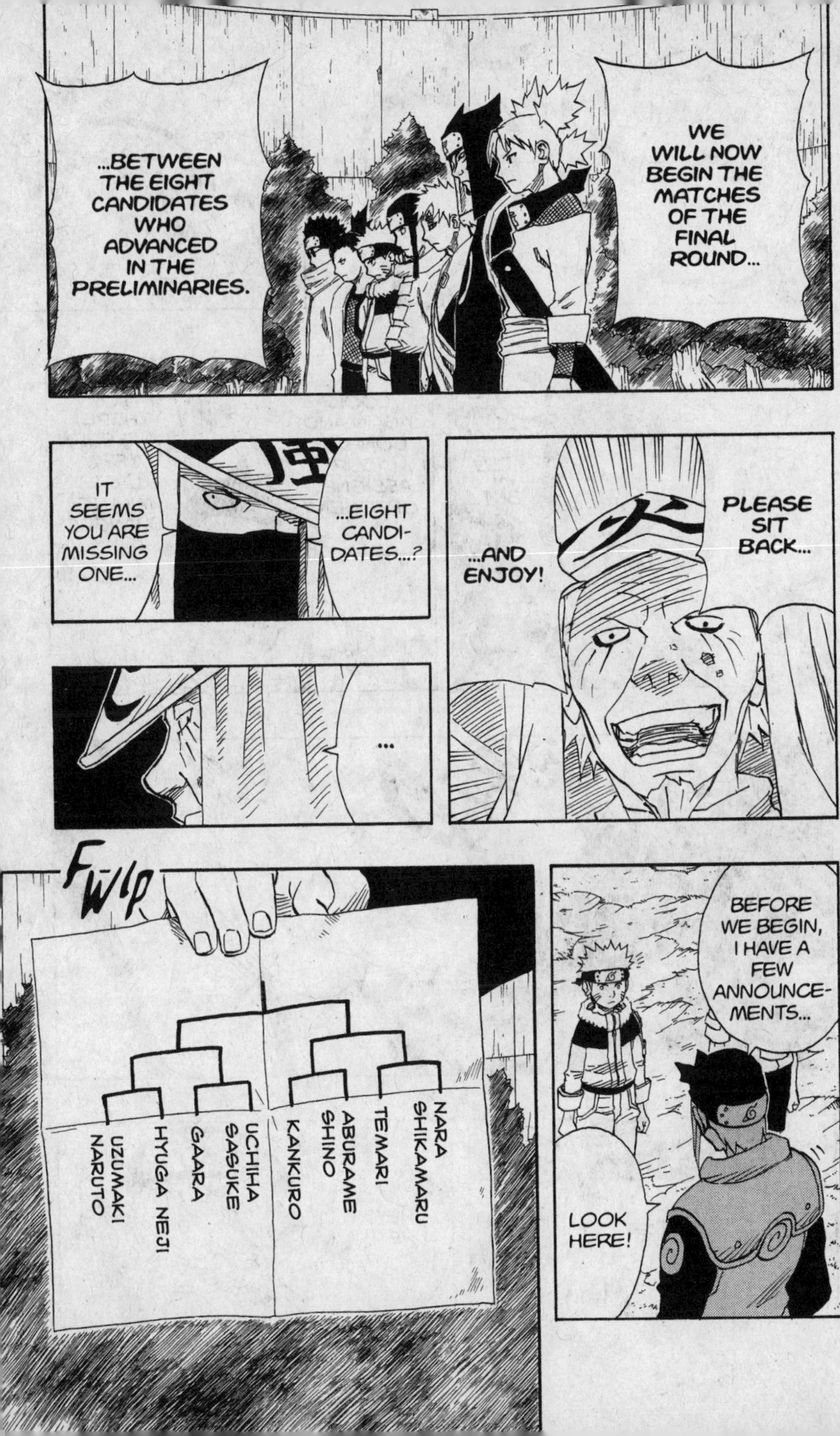
WE WILL NOW BEGIN THE MATCHES OF THE FINAL ROUND...
...BETWEEN THE EIGHT CANDIDATES WHO ADVANCED IN THE PRELIMINARIES.
PLEASE SIT BACK...
...AND ENJOY!
...EIGHT CANDI-DATES...?
IT SEEMS YOU ARE MISSING ONE...
...
BEFORE WE BEGIN, I HAVE A FEW ANNOUNCE-MENTS...
LOOK HERE!
FWIP
NARA SHIKAMARU
TEMARI
ABURAME SHINO
KANKURO
UCHIHA SASUKE
GAARA
HYUGA NEJI
UZUMAKI NARUTO

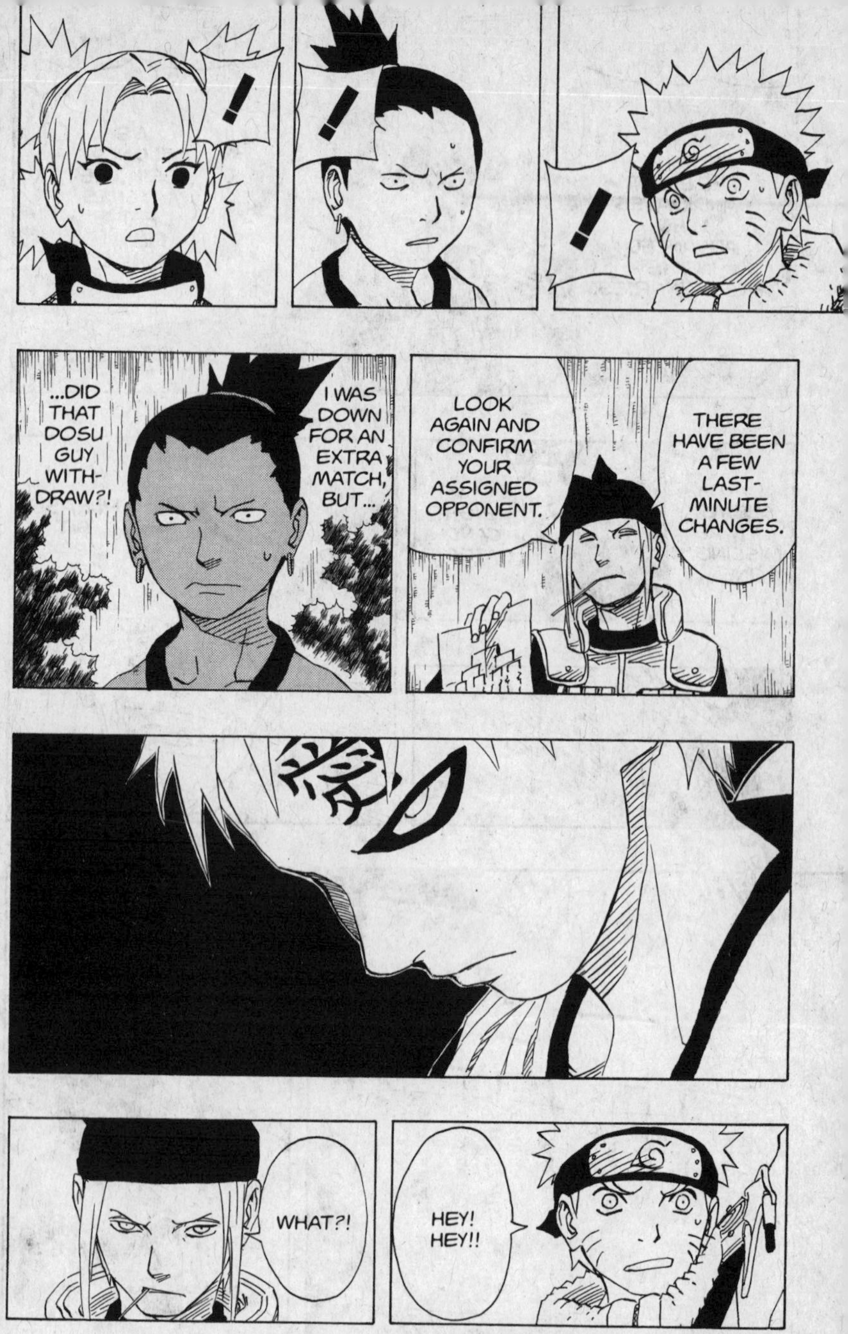
!
!
!
THERE HAVE BEEN A FEW LAST-MINUTE CHANGES.
LOOK AGAIN AND CONFIRM YOUR ASSIGNED OPPONENT.
I WAS DOWN FOR AN EXTRA MATCH, BUT...
...DID THAT DOSU GUY WITH-DRAW?!
HEY! HEY!!
WHAT?!

READ THIS WAY

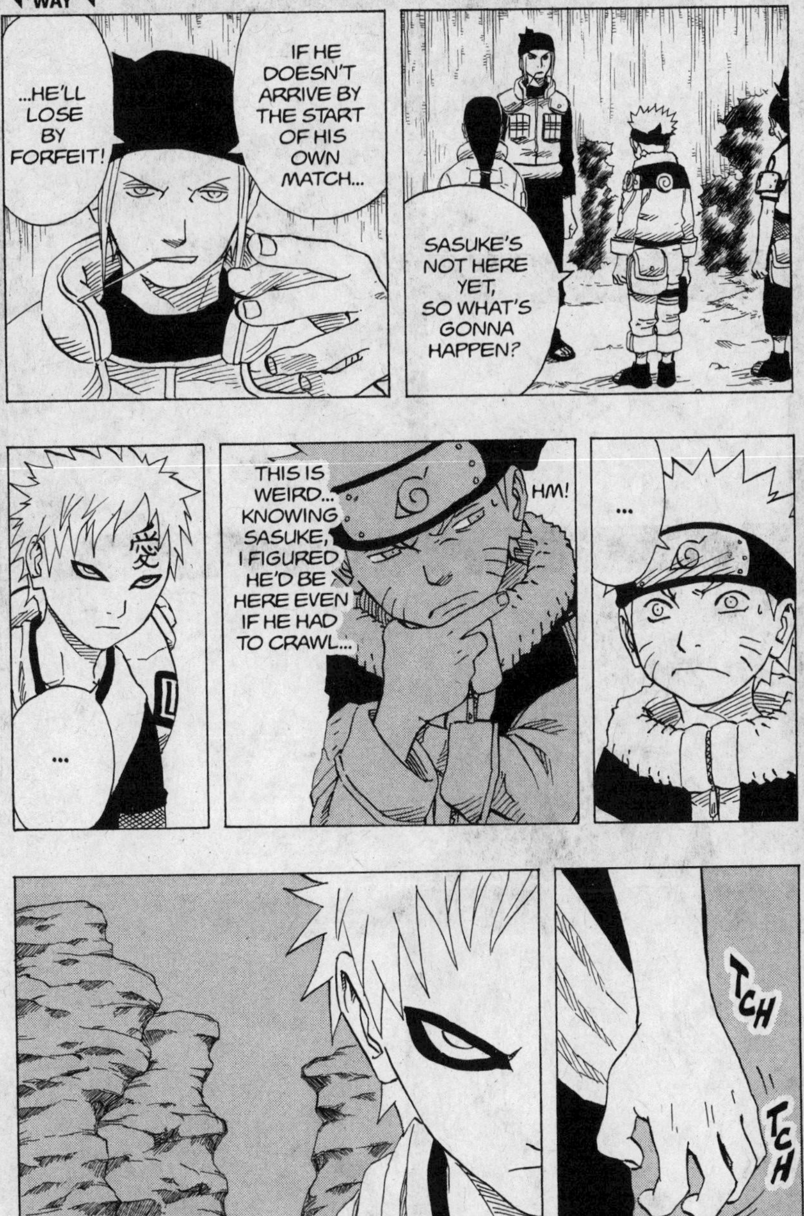
SASUKE'S NOT HERE YET, SO WHAT'S GONNA HAPPEN?
IF HE DOESN'T ARRIVE BY THE START OF HIS OWN MATCH...
...HE'LL LOSE BY FORFEIT!
...
HM!
THIS IS WEIRD... KNOWING SASUKE, I FIGURED HE'D BE HERE EVEN IF HE HAD TO CRAWL...
...
TCH
TCH

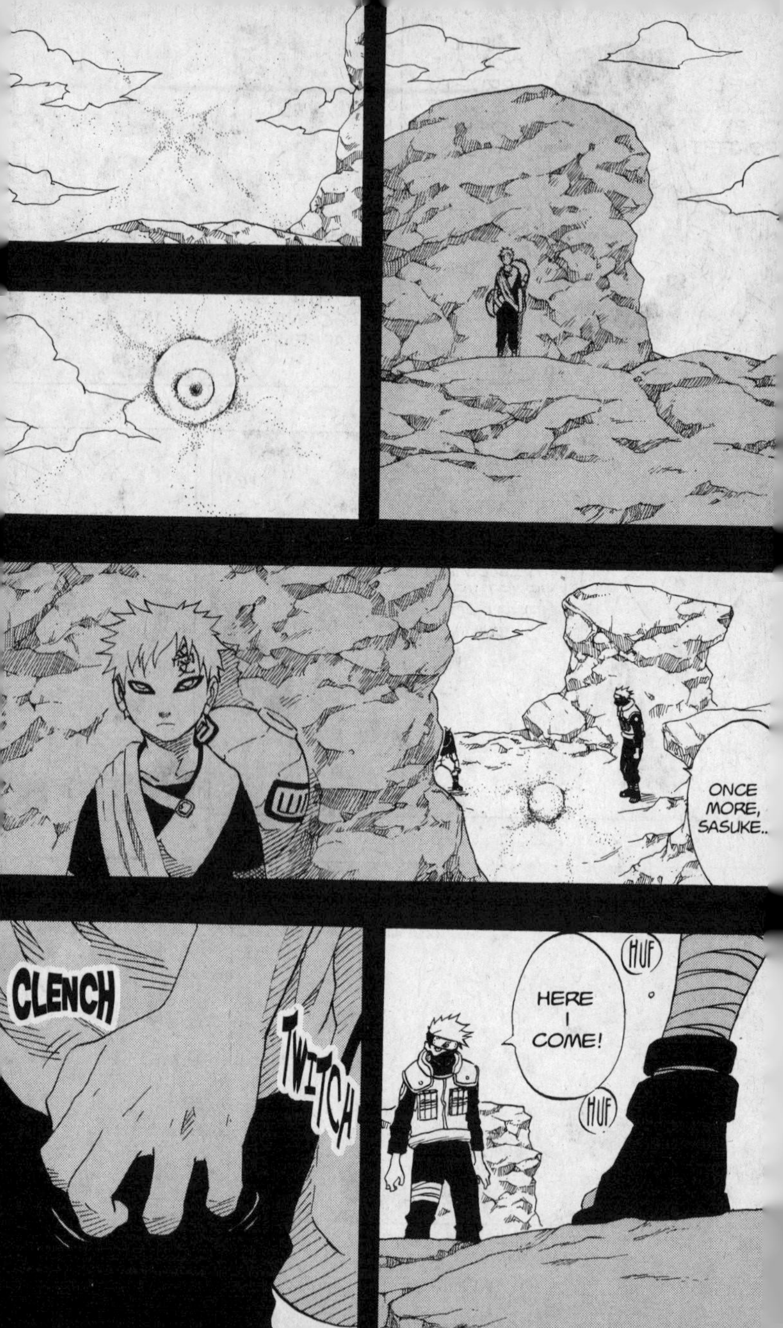
ONCE MORE, SASUKE..
HUF
HERE I COME!
HUF
CLENCH
TWITCH

READ THIS WAY

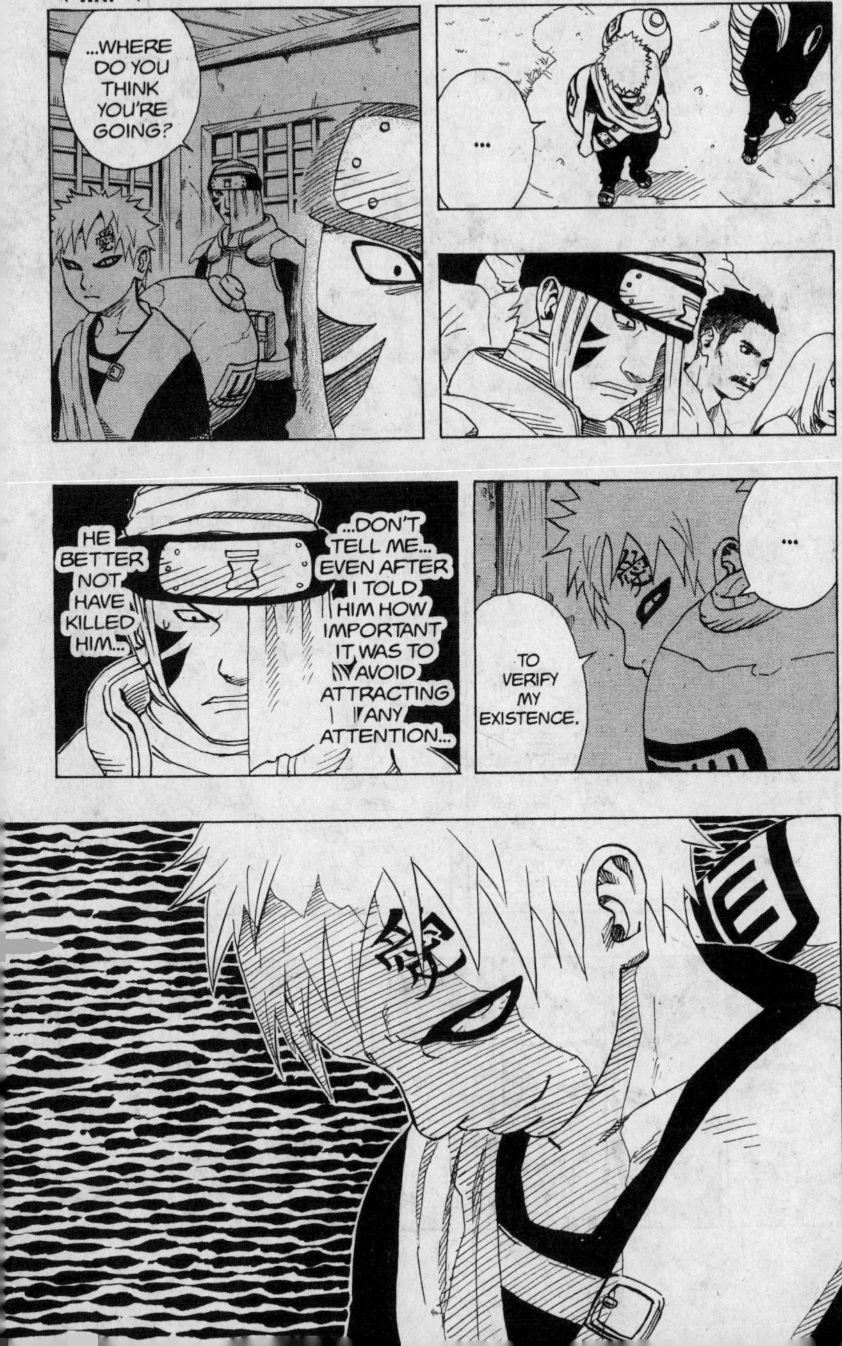
...
...WHERE DO YOU THINK YOU'RE GOING?
...
TO VERIFY MY EXISTENCE.
...DON'T TELL ME... EVEN AFTER I TOLD HIM HOW IMPORTANT IT WAS TO AVOID ATTRACTING ANY ATTENTION...
HE BETTER NOT HAVE KILLED HIM...

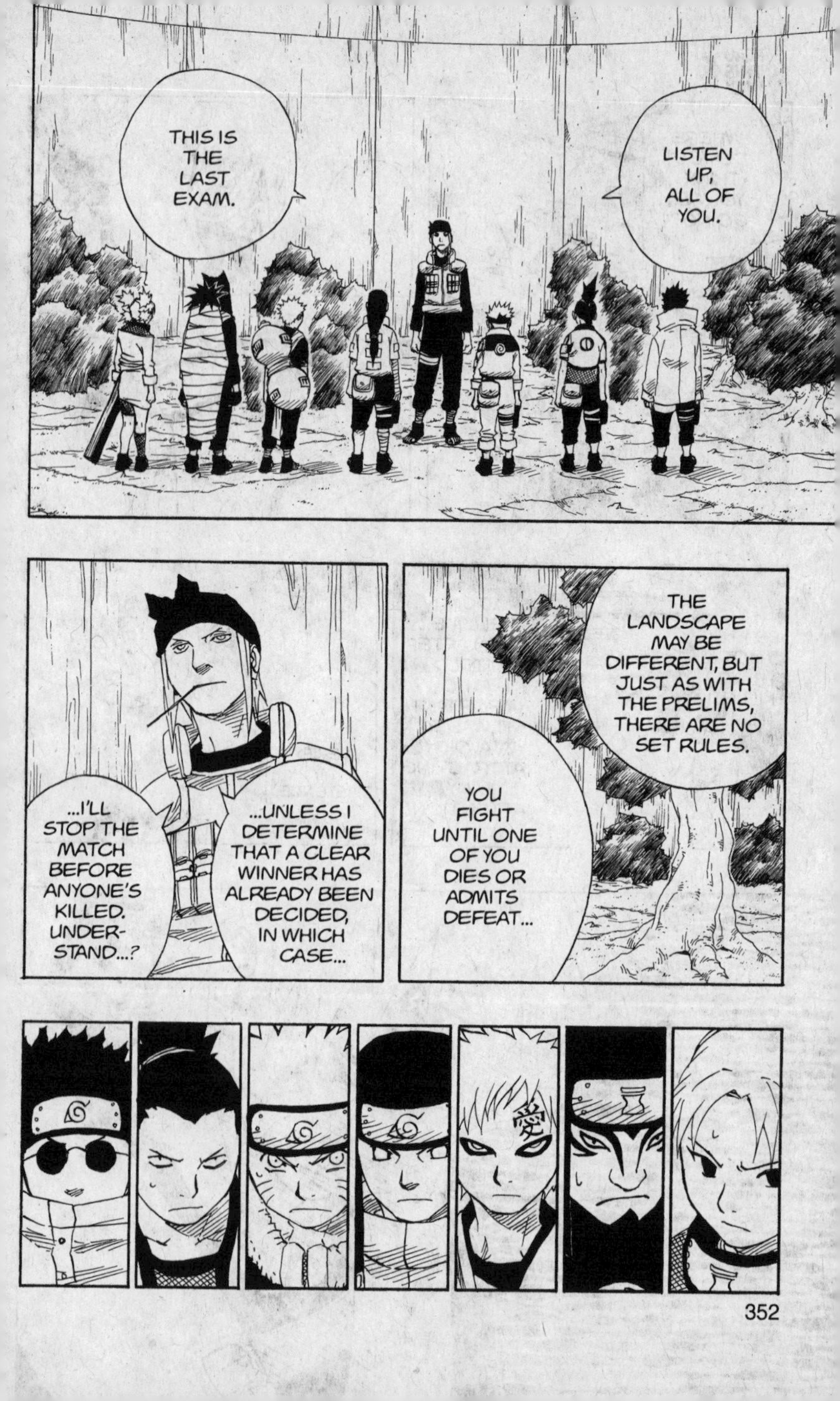
LISTEN UP, ALL OF YOU.
THIS IS THE LAST EXAM.
THE LANDSCAPE MAY BE DIFFERENT, BUT JUST AS WITH THE PRELIMS, THERE ARE NO SET RULES.
YOU FIGHT UNTIL ONE OF YOU DIES OR ADMITS DEFEAT...
...UNLESS I DETERMINE THAT A CLEAR WINNER HAS ALREADY BEEN DECIDED, IN WHICH CASE...
...I'LL STOP THE MATCH BEFORE ANYONE'S KILLED. UNDER-STAND...?

READ THIS WAY

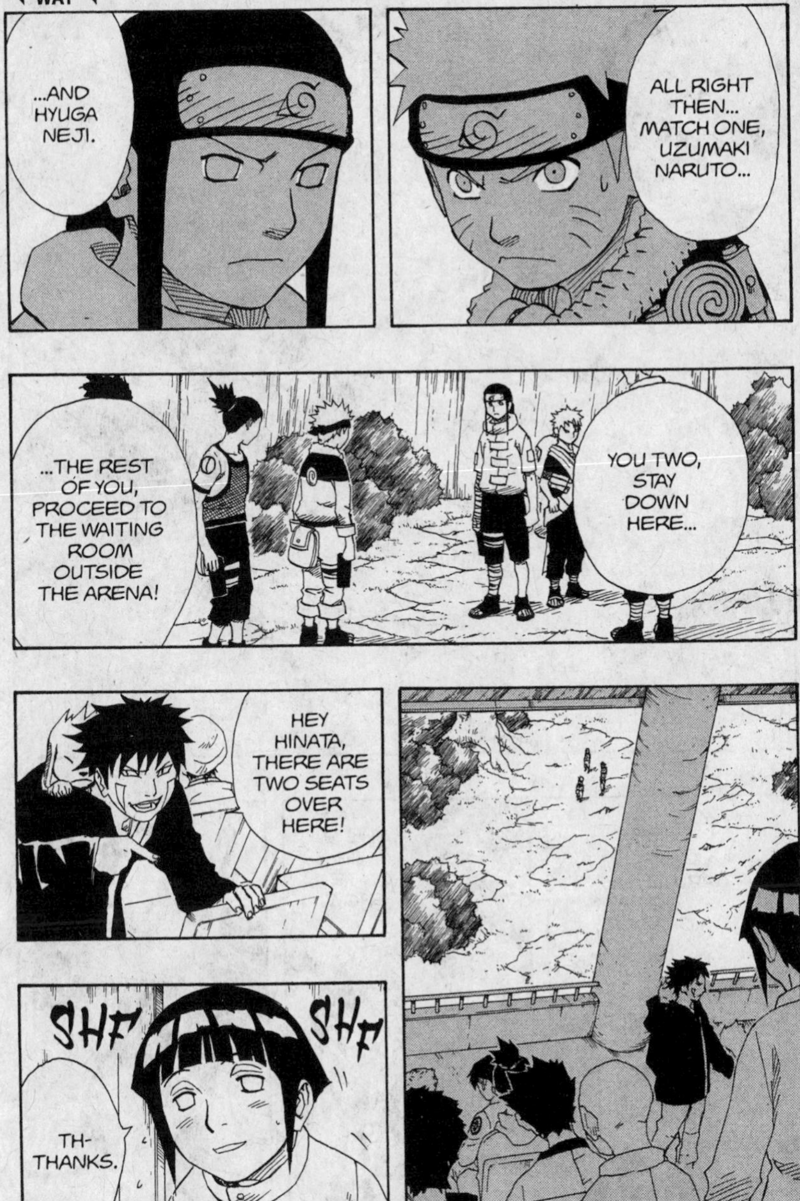
ALL RIGHT THEN... MATCH ONE, UZUMAKI NARUTO...
...AND HYUGA NEJI.
YOU TWO, STAY DOWN HERE...
...THE REST OF YOU, PROCEED TO THE WAITING ROOM OUTSIDE THE ARENA!
HEY HINATA, THERE ARE TWO SEATS OVER HERE!
SHF
SHF
TH-THANKS.

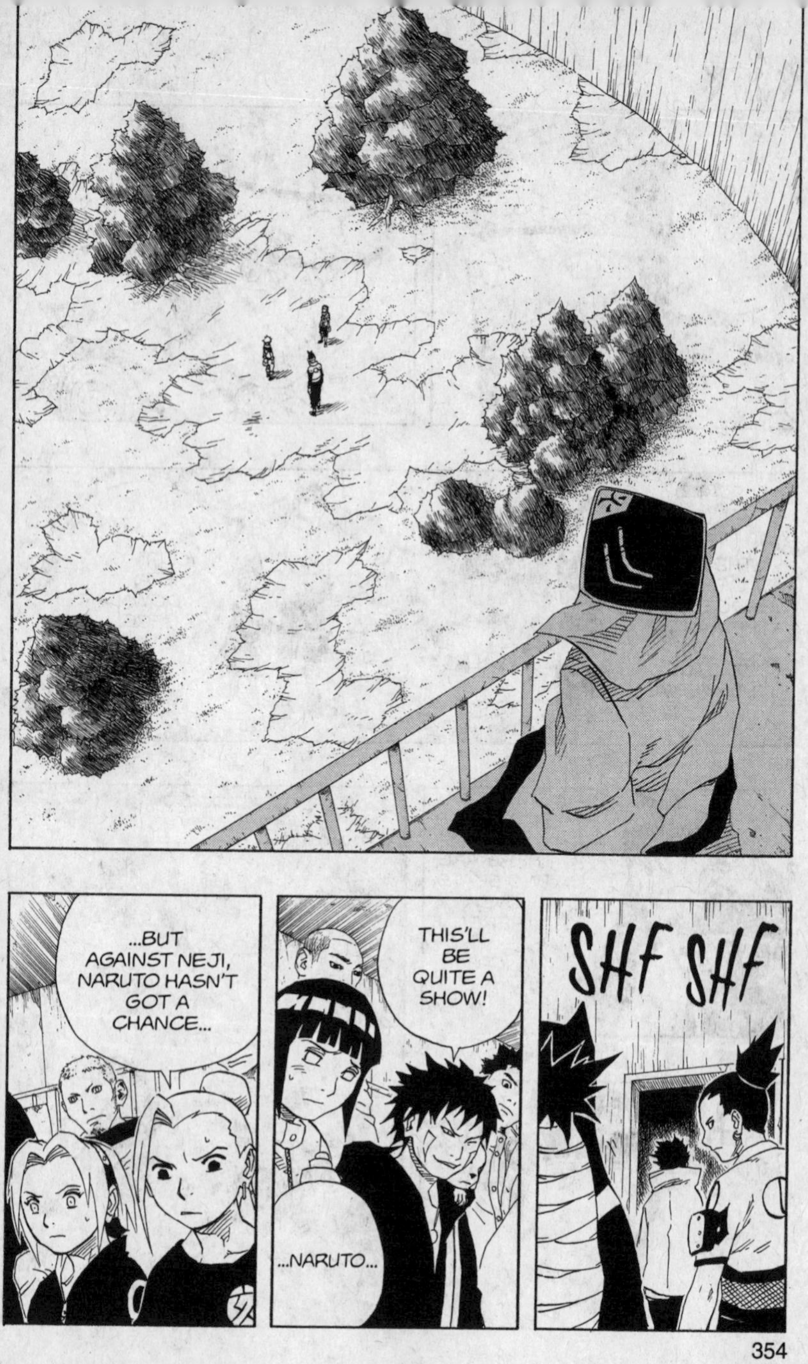
SHF SHF
THIS'LL BE QUITE A SHOW!
...NARUTO...
...BUT AGAINST NEJI, NARUTO HASN'T GOT A CHANCE...

READ THIS WAY

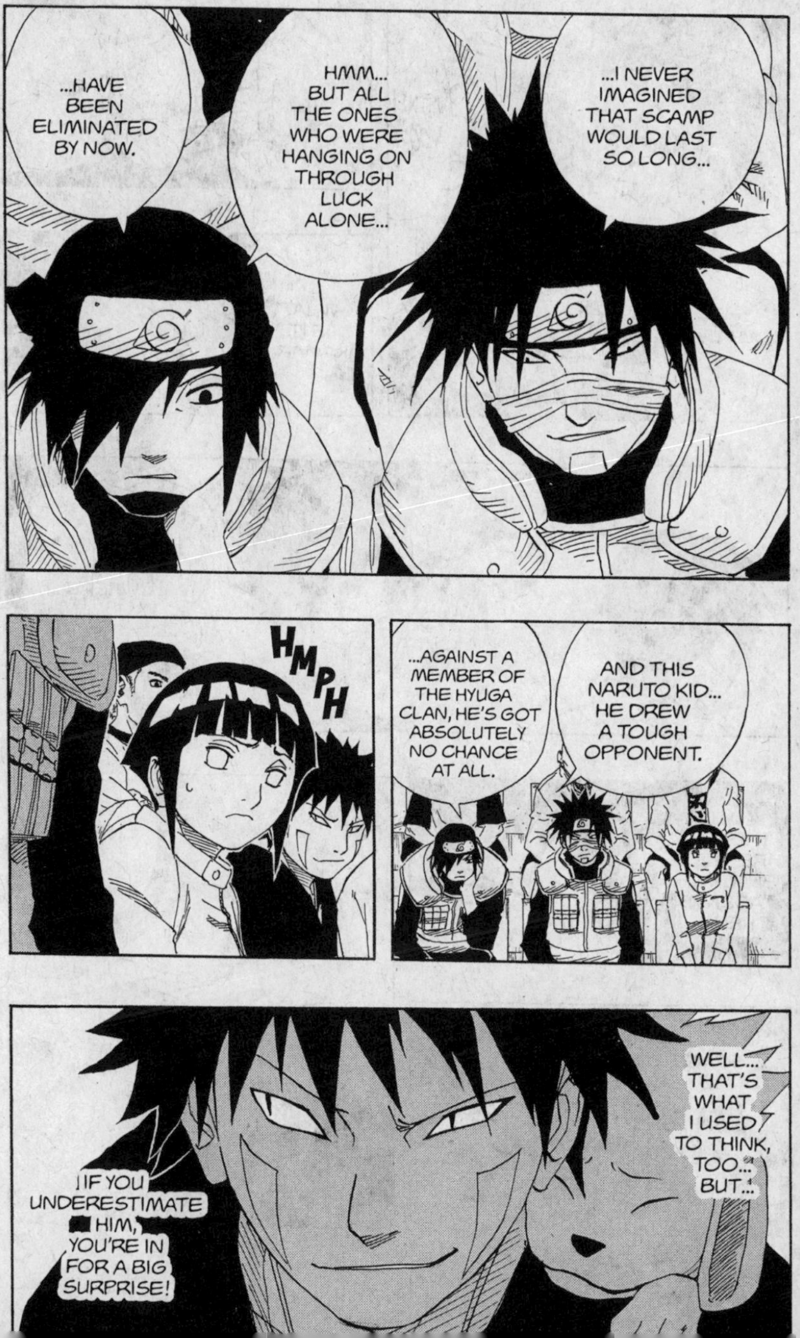
...I NEVER IMAGINED THAT SCAMP WOULD LAST SO LONG...
HMM... BUT ALL THE ONES WHO WERE HANGING ON THROUGH LUCK ALONE...
...HAVE BEEN ELIMINATED BY NOW.
AND THIS NARUTO KID... HE DREW A TOUGH OPPONENT.
...AGAINST A MEMBER OF THE HYUGA CLAN, HE'S GOT ABSOLUTELY NO CHANCE AT ALL.
HMPH
WELL... THAT'S WHAT I USED TO THINK, TOO... BUT...
IF YOU UNDERESTIMATE HIM, YOU'RE IN FOR A BIG SURPRISE!

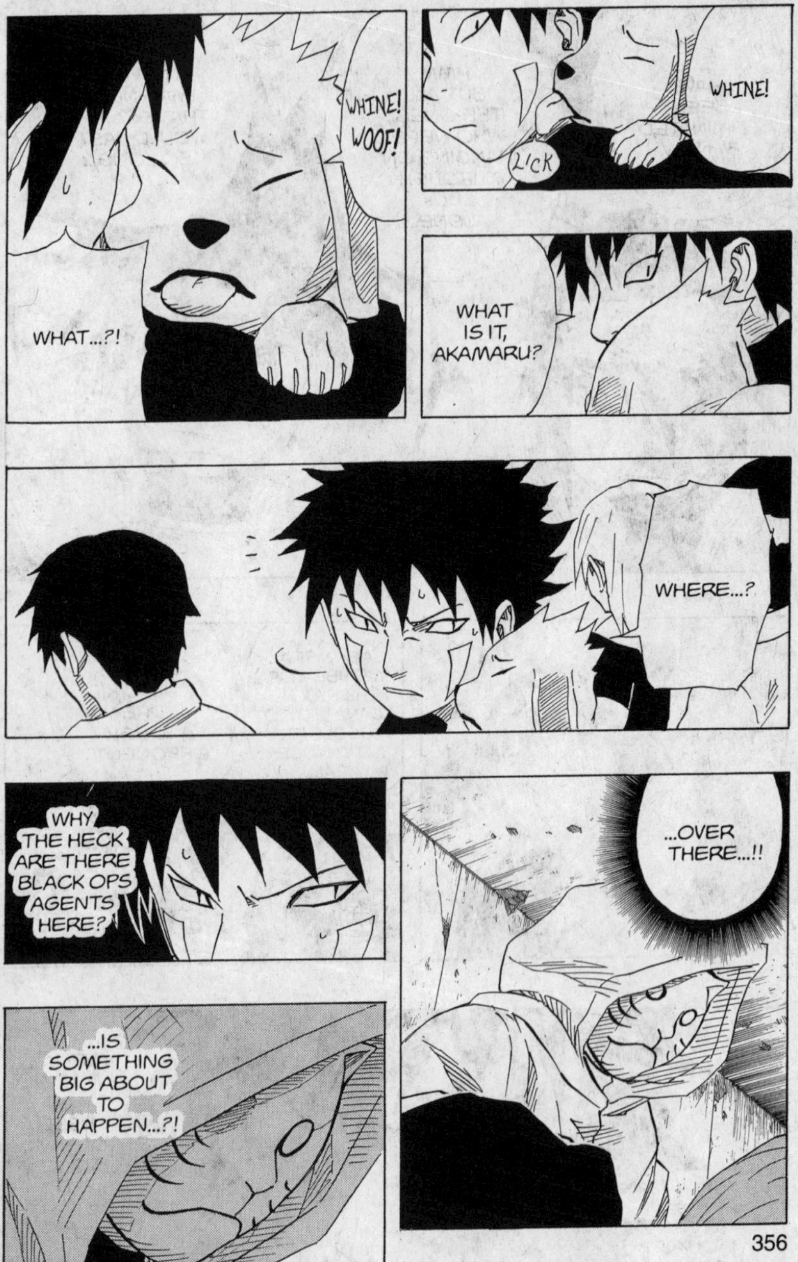
WHINE!
LICK
WHAT IS IT, AKAMARU?
WHINE! WOOF!
WHAT...?!
WHERE...?
...OVER THERE...!!
WHY THE HECK ARE THERE BLACK OPS AGENTS HERE?
...IS SOMETHING BIG ABOUT TO HAPPEN...?!

READ THIS WAY

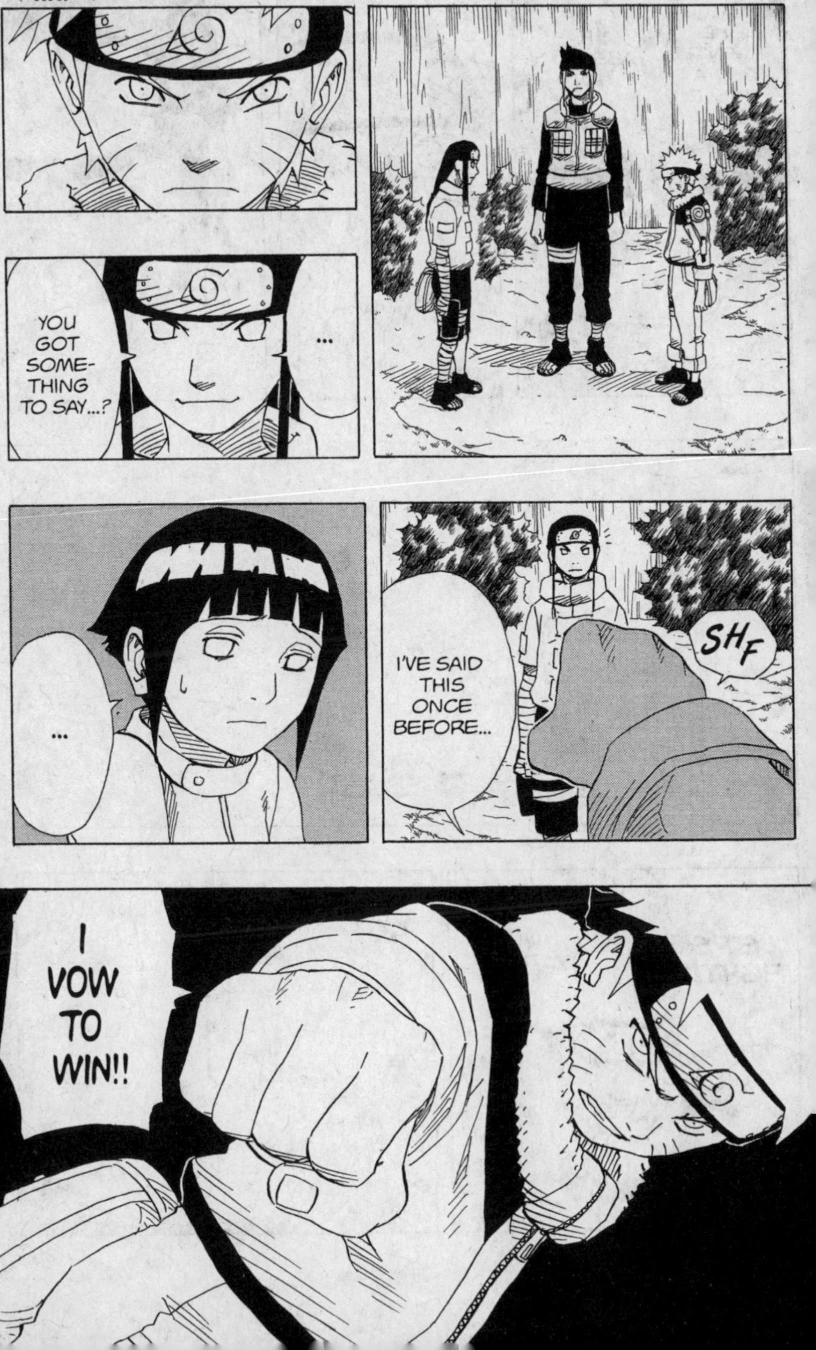
...
YOU GOT SOMETHING-THING TO SAY...?
SHF
I'VE SAID THIS ONCE BEFORE...
...
I VOW TO WIN!!

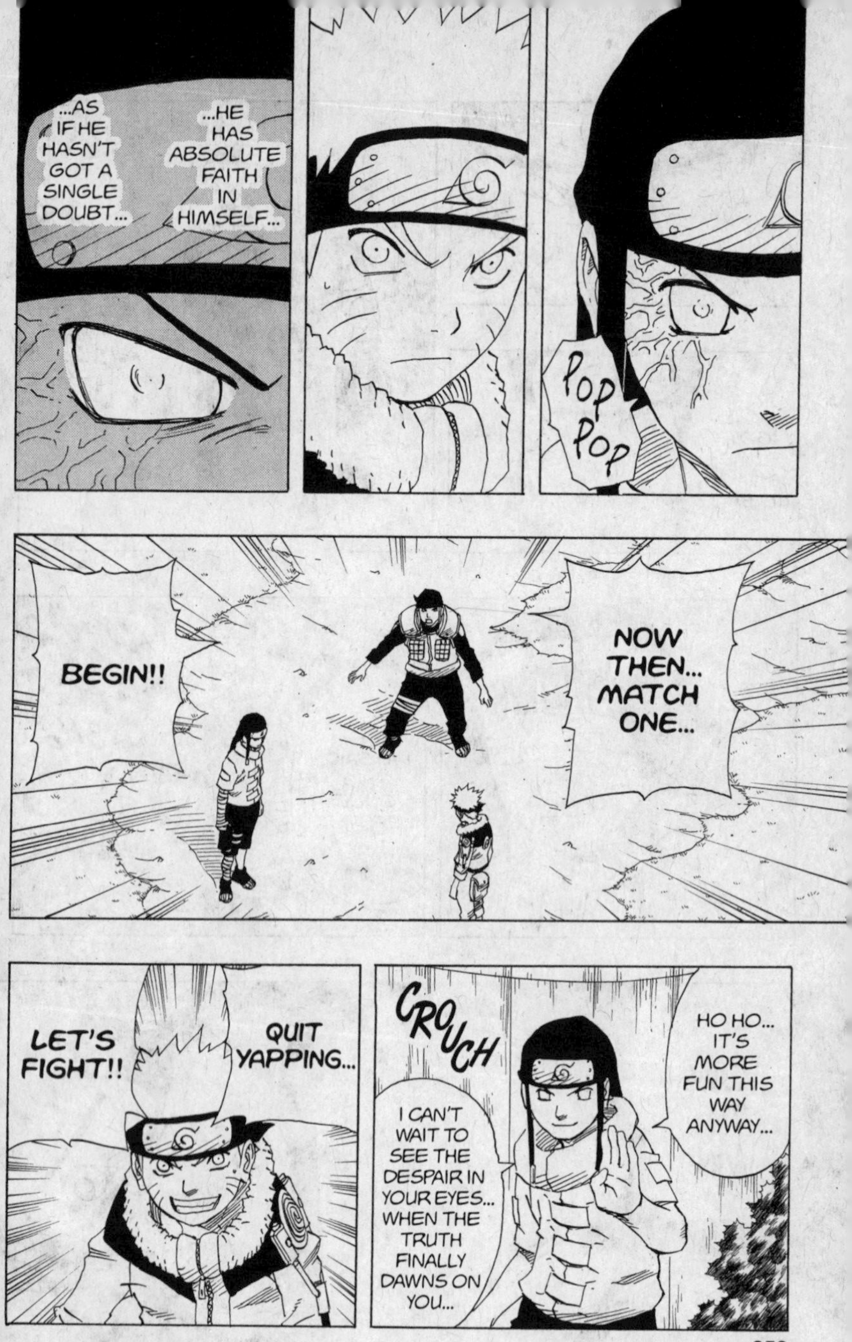
POP POP
...HE HAS ABSOLUTE FAITH IN HIMSELF...
...AS IF HE HASN'T GOT A SINGLE DOUBT...
NOW THEN... MATCH ONE...
BEGIN!!
HO HO... IT'S MORE FUN THIS WAY ANYWAY...
CROUCH
I CAN'T WAIT TO SEE THE DESPAIR IN YOUR EYES... WHEN THE TRUTH FINALLY DAWNS ON YOU...
QUIT YAPPING...
LET'S FIGHT!!

READ THIS WAY

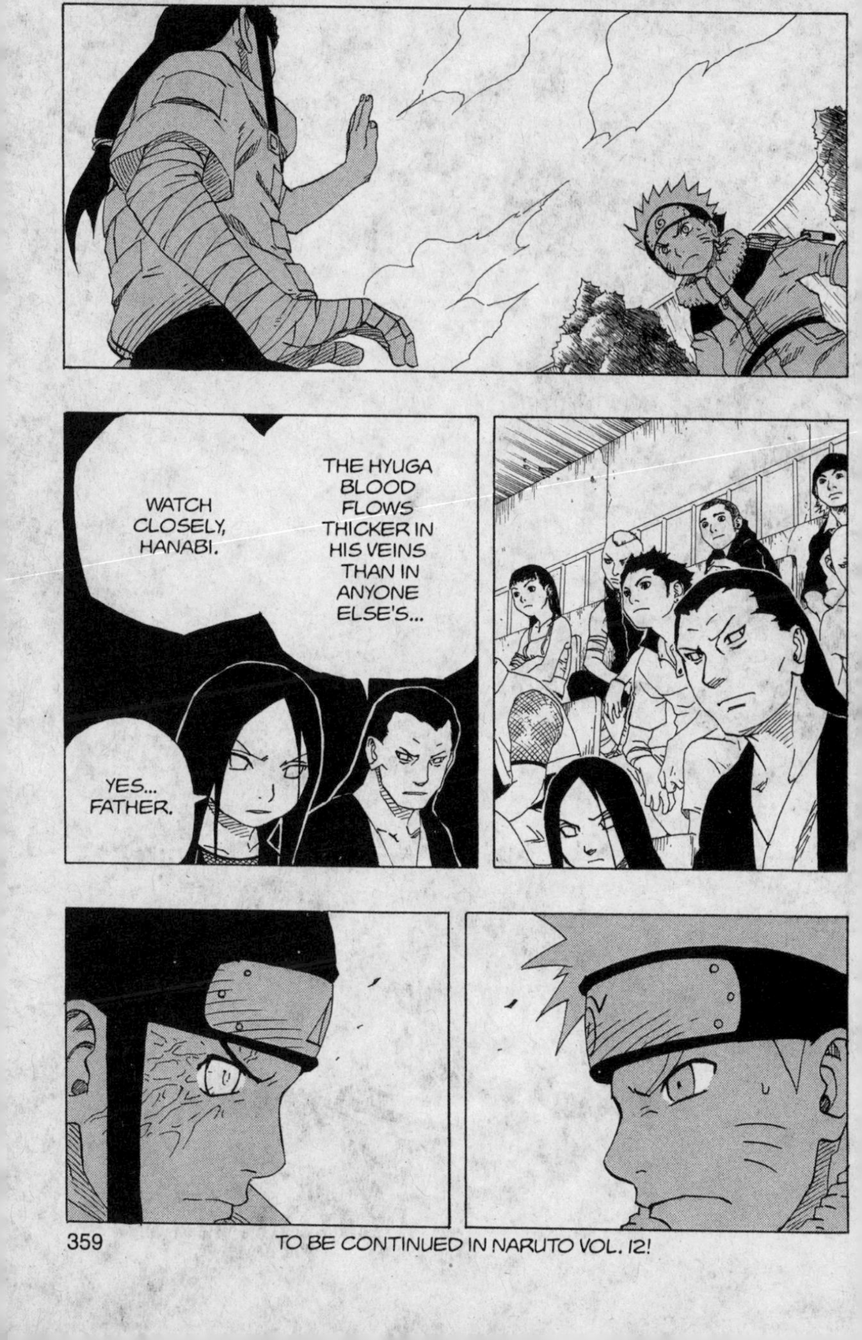
THE HYUGA BLOOD FLOWS THICKER IN HIS VEINS THAN IN ANYONE ELSE'S...
WATCH CLOSELY, HANABI.
YES... FATHER.

TO BE CONTINUED IN NARUTO VOL. 12!

NARUTO

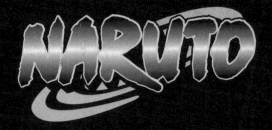

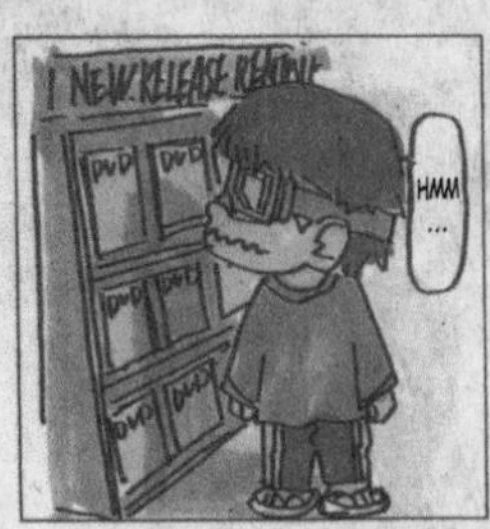
HMM
...

岸本斉史

Recently, DVDs have become prominent at movie rental stores. Certainly, DVDs are nice because unlike videotapes, you can just rent one disc and not have to choose what kind of audio track you want or whether you want subtitles or not until right when you watch it. That's really great, but...DVDs don't include coming attractions before the main feature. That's what I was looking forward to...

—Masashi Kishimoto, 2002

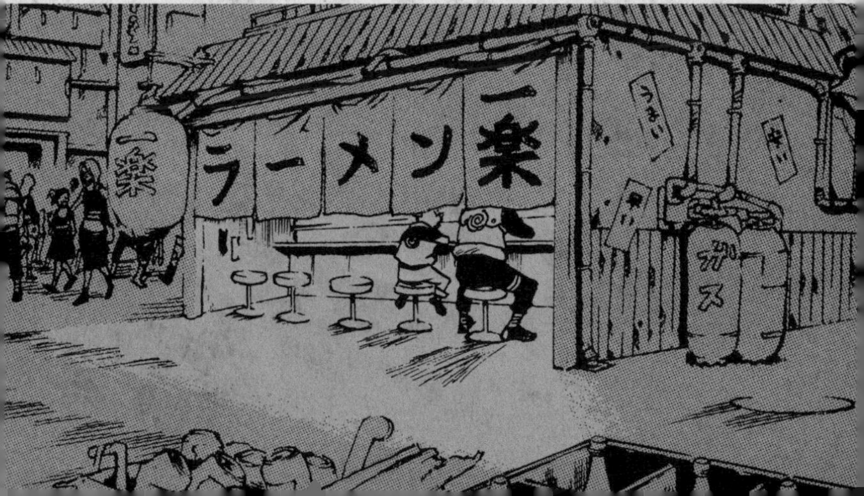
一楽
ラーメン一楽
うまい
ガス

NARUTO

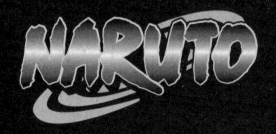

SHONEN JUMP MANGA

NARUTO

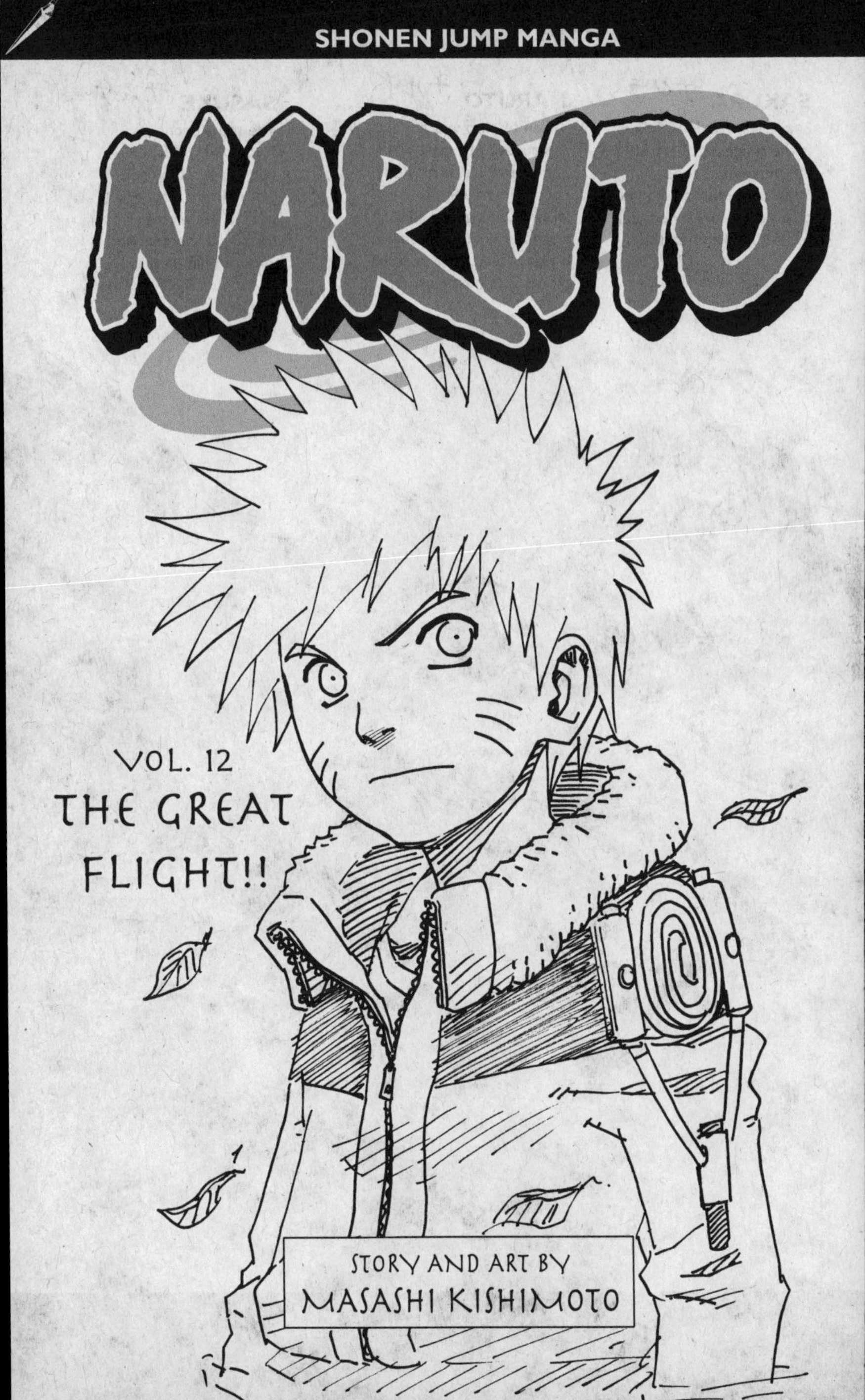

VOL. 12

THE GREAT FLIGHT!!

STORY AND ART BY
MASASHI KISHIMOTO

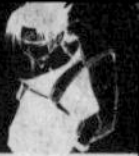

SAKURA サクラ

Smart and studious, Sakura is the brightest of Naruto's classmates, but she's constantly distracted by her crush on Sasuke. Her goal: to win Sasuke's heart!

NARUTO ナルト

When Naruto was born, a destructive fox spirit was imprisoned inside his body. Spurned by the older villagers, he's grown into an attention-seeking trouble-maker. His goal: to become the village's next *Hokage*.

SASUKE サスケ

The top student in Naruto's class, Sasuke comes from the prestigious Uchiha clan. His goal: to get revenge on a mysterious person who wronged him in the past.

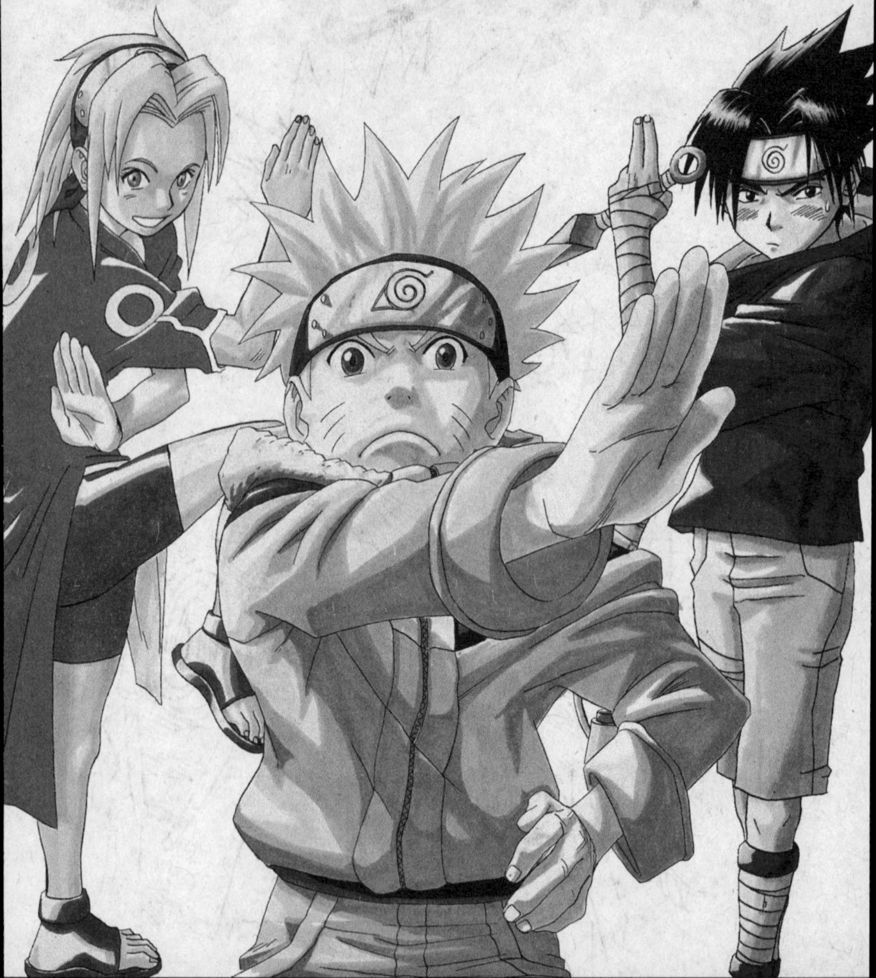

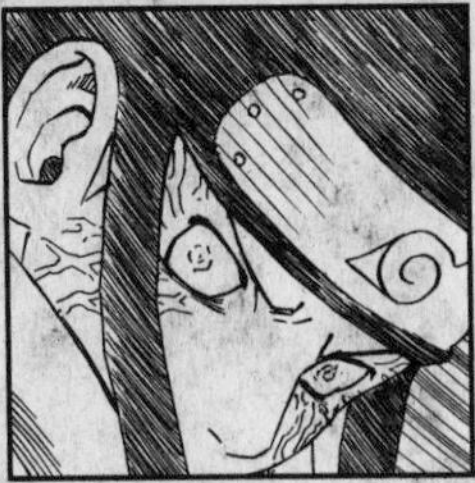

Neji ネジ

Part of the Cadet Branch of the Hyuga Clan, as opposed to the Main Branch to which Hinata belongs. Neji is widely considered to be a genius.

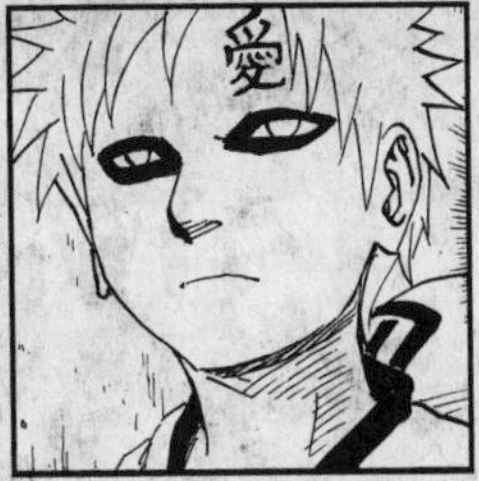
愛

Gaara 我愛羅

Bloodthirsty Gaara is one of the scariest ninja competing in the Chûnin exams.

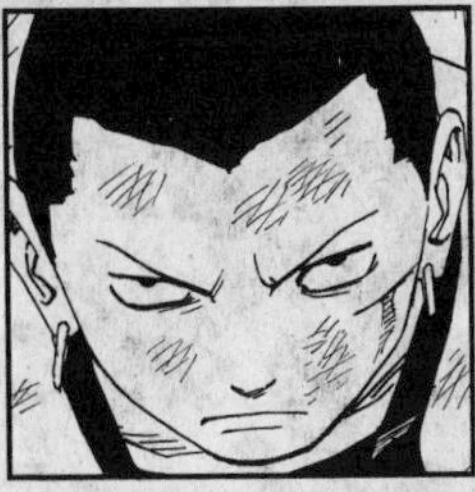

Shikamaru シカマル

One of Naruto's classmates. He specializes in the Shadow Possession jutsu, and is a skilled ninja despite his lazy demeanor.

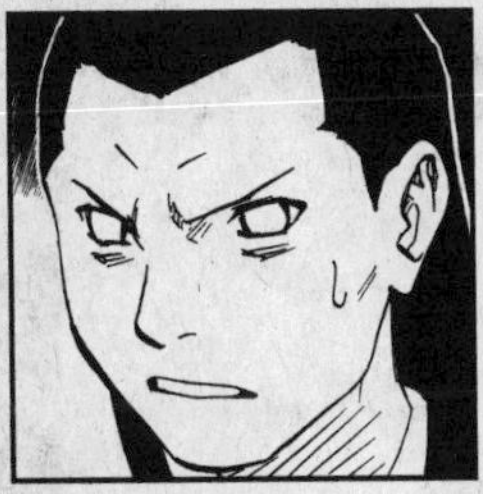

Hyuga Hiashi

日向ヒアシ

The head of the main branch of the Hyuga family and Neji's uncle.

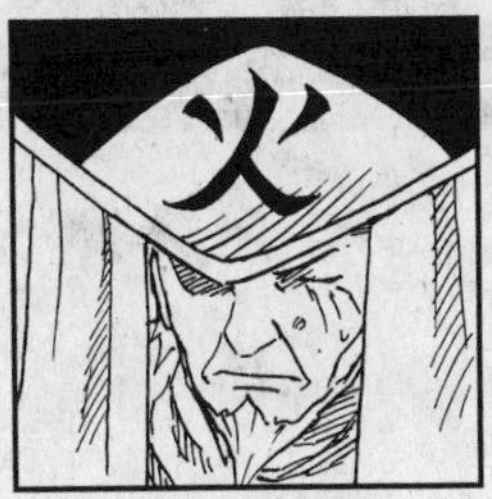
火

Hokage 火影

The leader of Konohagakure. He was retired, but stepped back into the position when the fourth Hokage was killed by the nine-tailed fox spirit.

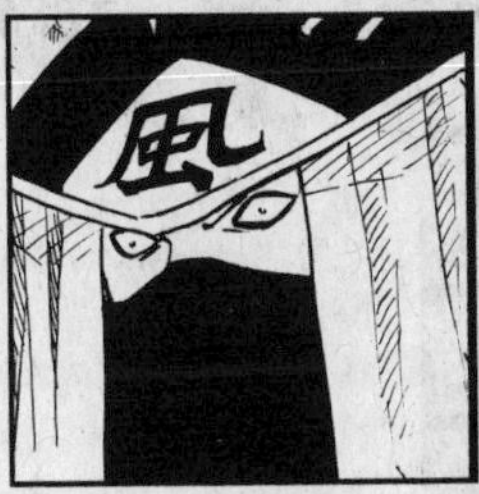
風

Kazekage 風影

The leader of Sunagakure (the Village Hidden in the Sand) within the Land of Wind.

THE STORY SO FAR...

Twelve years ago, a destructive nine-tailed fox spirit attacked the ninja village of Konohagakure. The *Hokage*, or village champion, defeated the fox by sealing its soul into the body of a baby boy. Now that boy, Uzumaki Naruto, has grown up to become a ninja-in-training, learning the art of *ninjutsu* with his teammates Sakura and Sasuke.

The preliminaries of the Third Exam are over and Sasuke, Shino, Kankuro, Temari, Shikamaru, Naruto, Neji, Gaara and Dosu have all passed and remain in the running. During the month of preparation time before the finals, Naruto trains with Jiraiya and brilliantly manages to draw out the Nine-Tailed Fox's chakra. The final round begins amid the swirling intrigue of Orochimaru and company. In the first battle, Naruto squares off against Neji, but...?!

NARUTO

VOL. 12

THE GREAT FLIGHT!!

CONTENTS

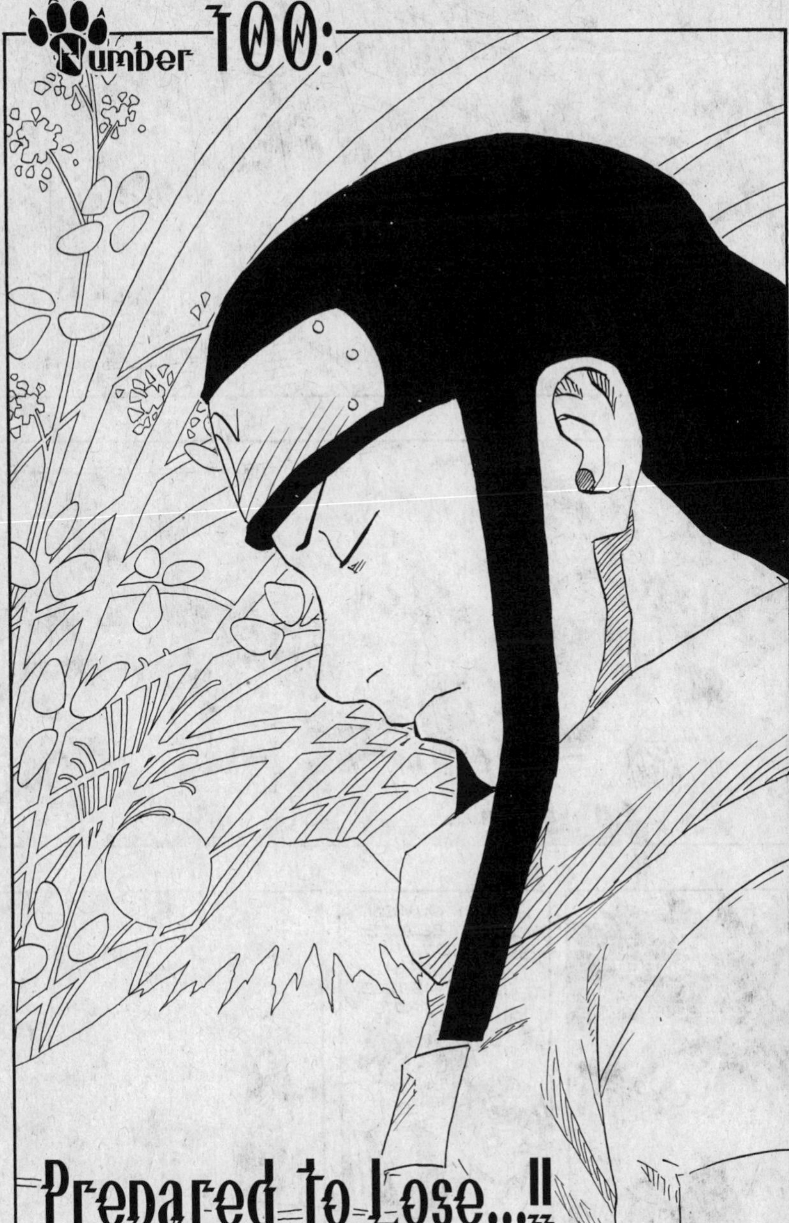
Number 100:
Prepared to Lose...!!

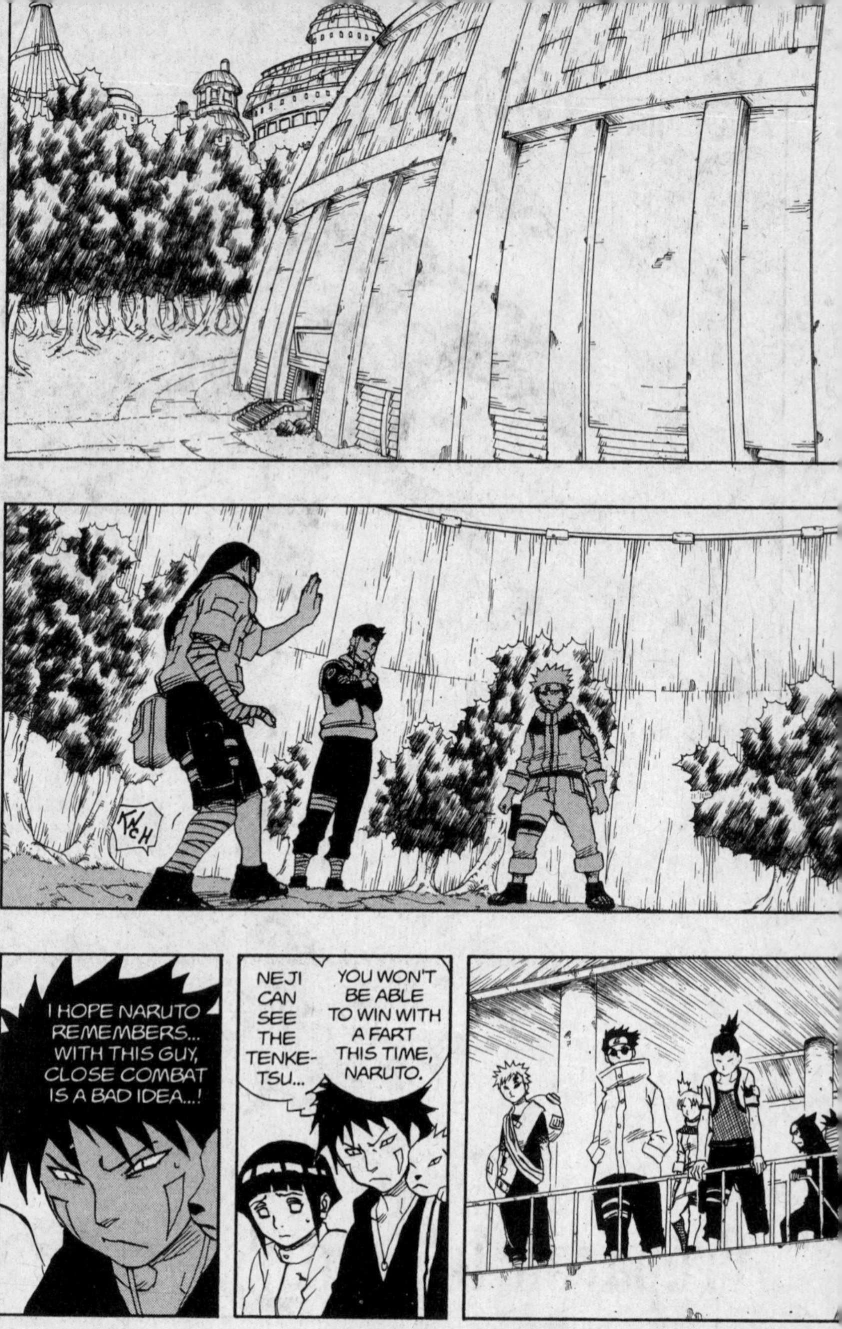
KNCH
YOU WON'T BE ABLE TO WIN WITH A FART THIS TIME, NARUTO.
NEJI CAN SEE THE TENKE-TSU...
I HOPE NARUTO REMEMBERS... WITH THIS GUY, CLOSE COMBAT IS A BAD IDEA...!

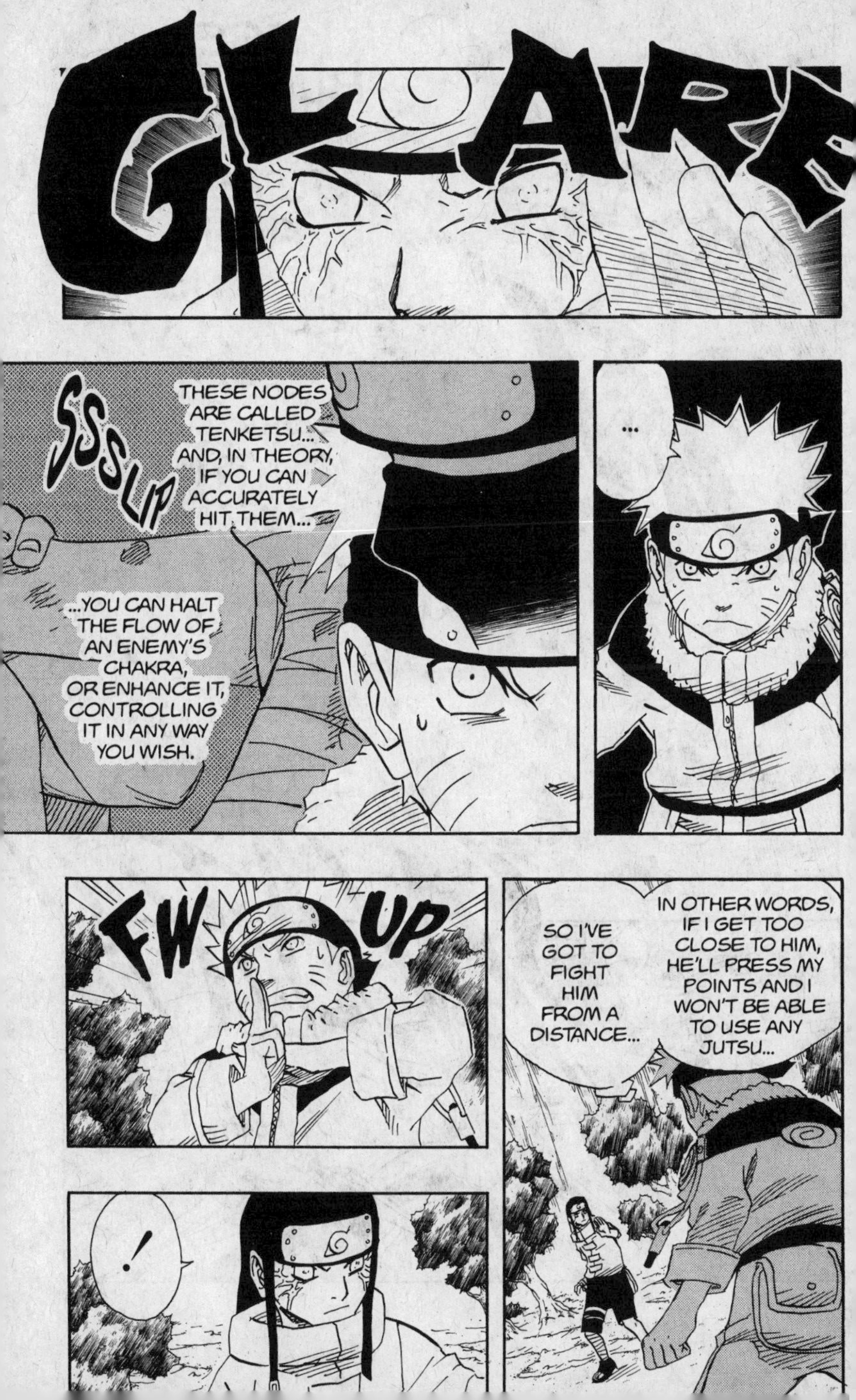
GLARE
...
SSSLIP
THESE NODES ARE CALLED TENKETSU... AND, IN THEORY, IF YOU CAN ACCURATELY HIT THEM...
...YOU CAN HALT THE FLOW OF AN ENEMY'S CHAKRA, OR ENHANCE IT, CONTROLLING IT IN ANY WAY YOU WISH.
IN OTHER WORDS, IF I GET TOO CLOSE TO HIM, HE'LL PRESS MY POINTS AND I WON'T BE ABLE TO USE ANY JUTSU...
SO I'VE GOT TO FIGHT HIM FROM A DISTANCE...
FWUP
!

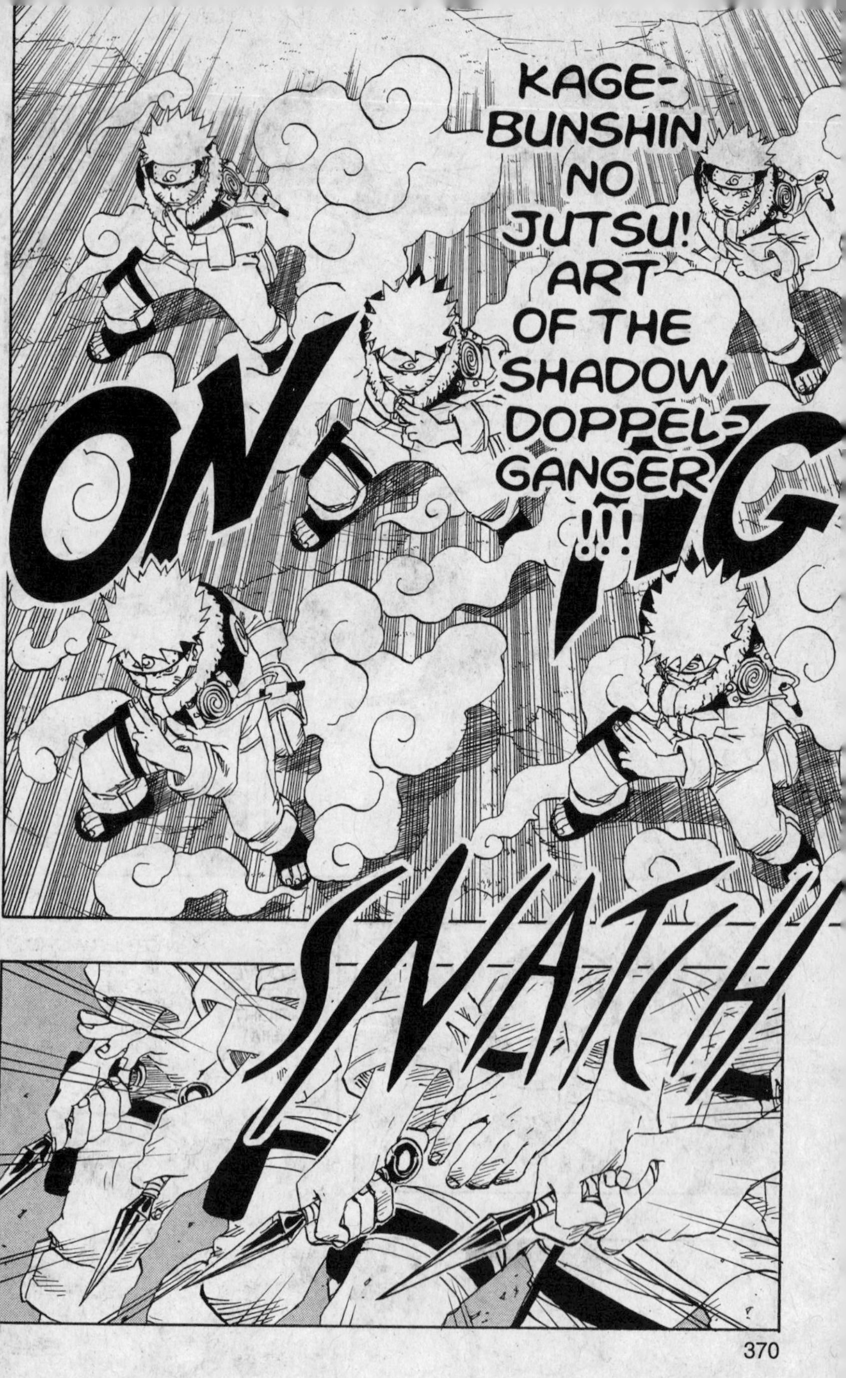
KAGE-BUNSHIN NO JUTSU! ART OF THE SHADOW DOPPEL-GANGER !!!
SNATCH

READ THIS WAY

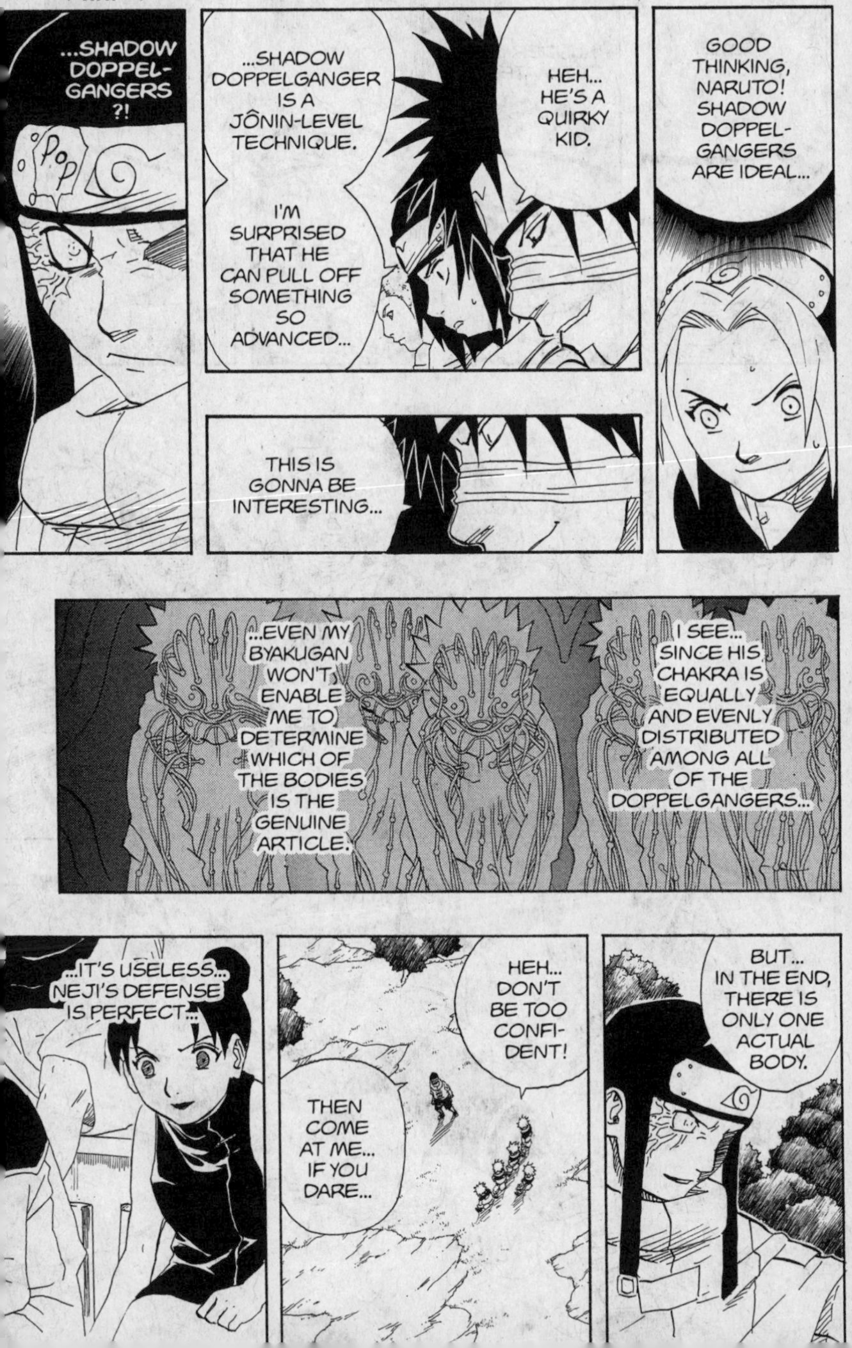
GOOD THINKING, NARUTO! SHADOW DOPPEL-GANGERS ARE IDEAL...
HEH... HE'S A QUIRKY KID.
...SHADOW DOPPELGANGER IS A JÔNIN-LEVEL TECHNIQUE.
I'M SURPRISED THAT HE CAN PULL OFF SOMETHING SO ADVANCED...
THIS IS GONNA BE INTERESTING...
...SHADOW DOPPEL-GANGERS?!
POP
I SEE... SINCE HIS CHAKRA IS EQUALLY AND EVENLY DISTRIBUTED AMONG ALL OF THE DOPPELGANGERS...
...EVEN MY BYAKUGAN WON'T ENABLE ME TO DETERMINE WHICH OF THE BODIES IS THE GENUINE ARTICLE.
BUT... IN THE END, THERE IS ONLY ONE ACTUAL BODY.
HEH... DON'T BE TOO CONFI-DENT!
THEN COME AT ME... IF YOU DARE...
...IT'S USELESS... NEJI'S DEFENSE IS PERFECT...

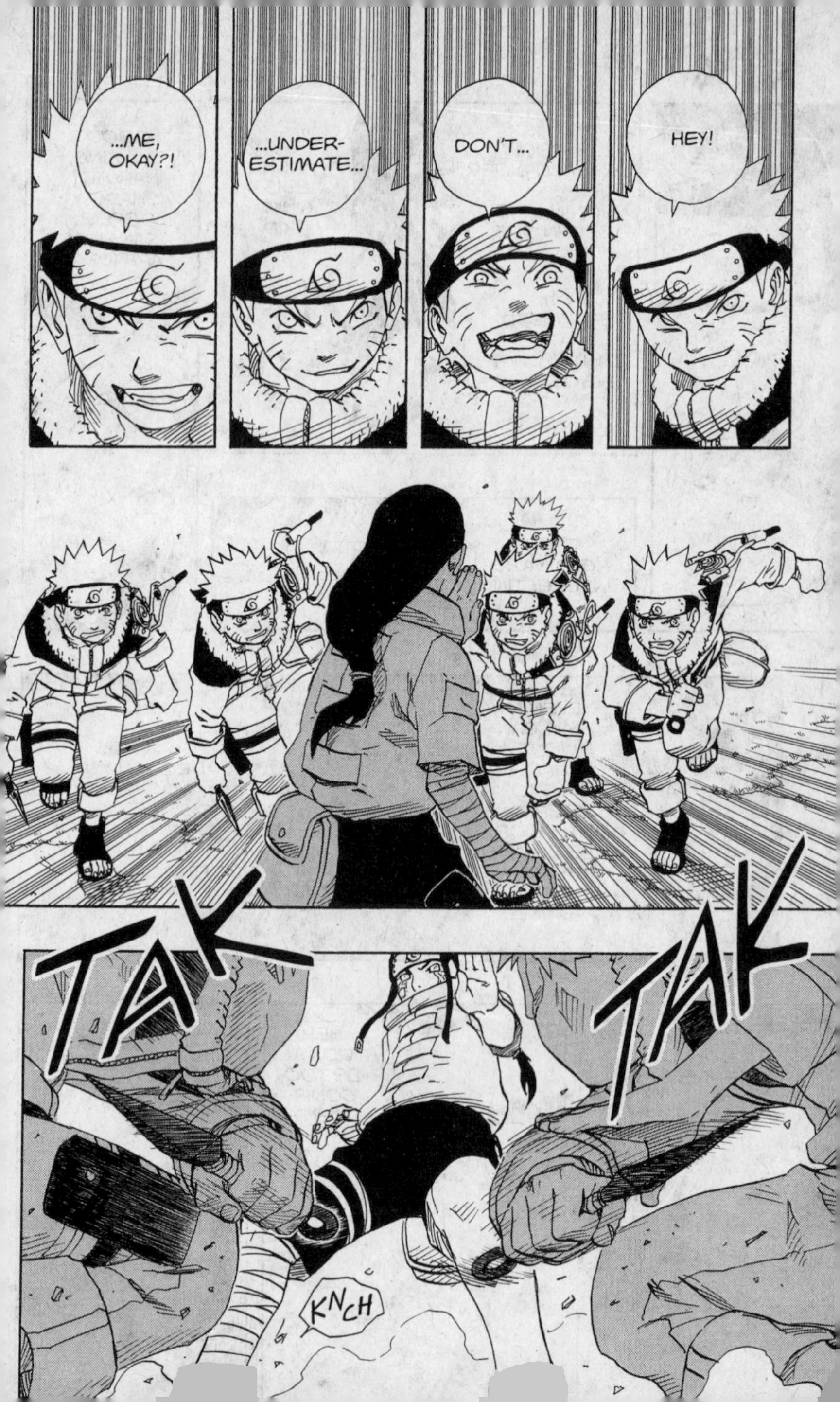
HEY!
DON'T...
...UNDER-ESTIMATE...
...ME, OKAY?!
TAK
TAK
KNCH

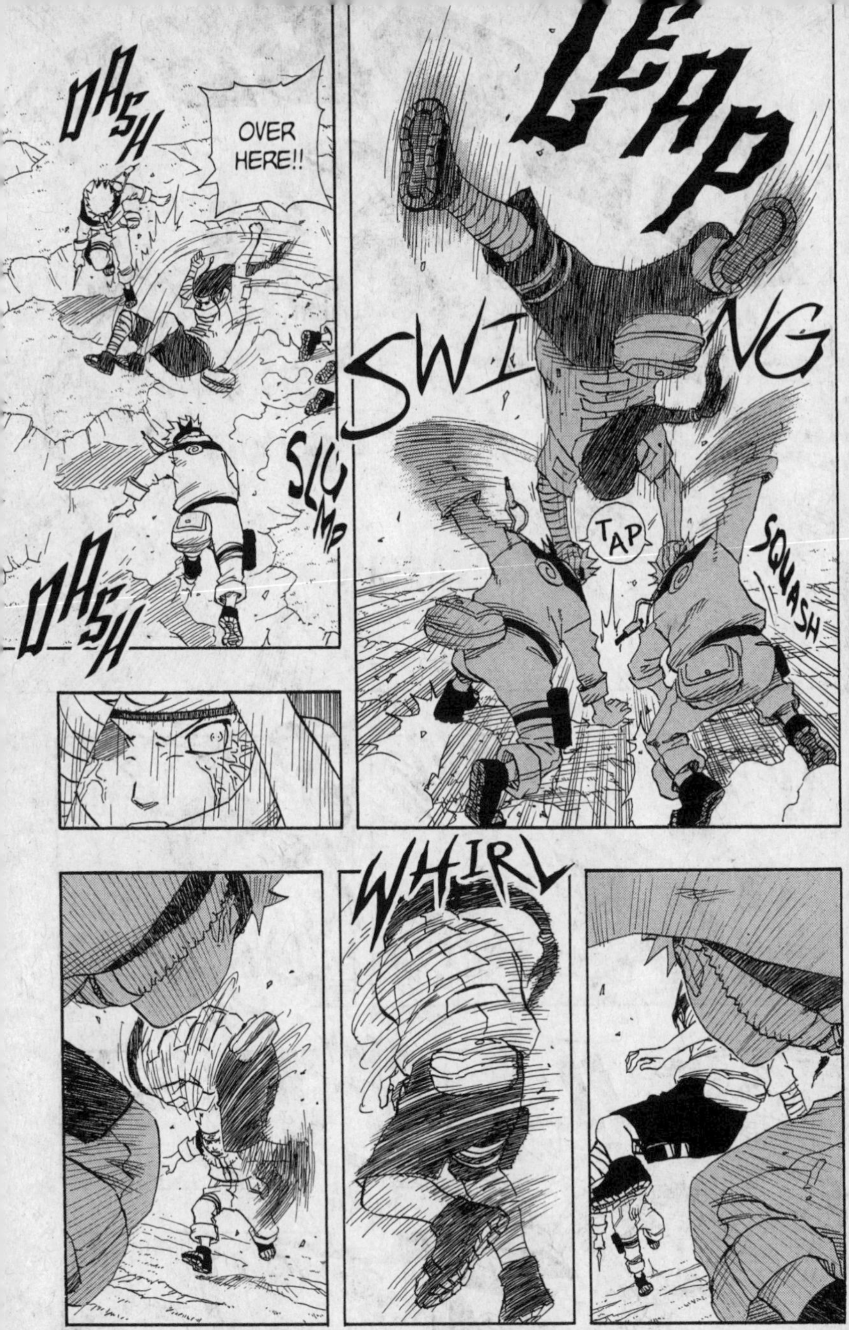
LEAP
SWING
TAP
SQUASH
OVER HERE!!
DASH
SLUMP
DASH
WHIRL

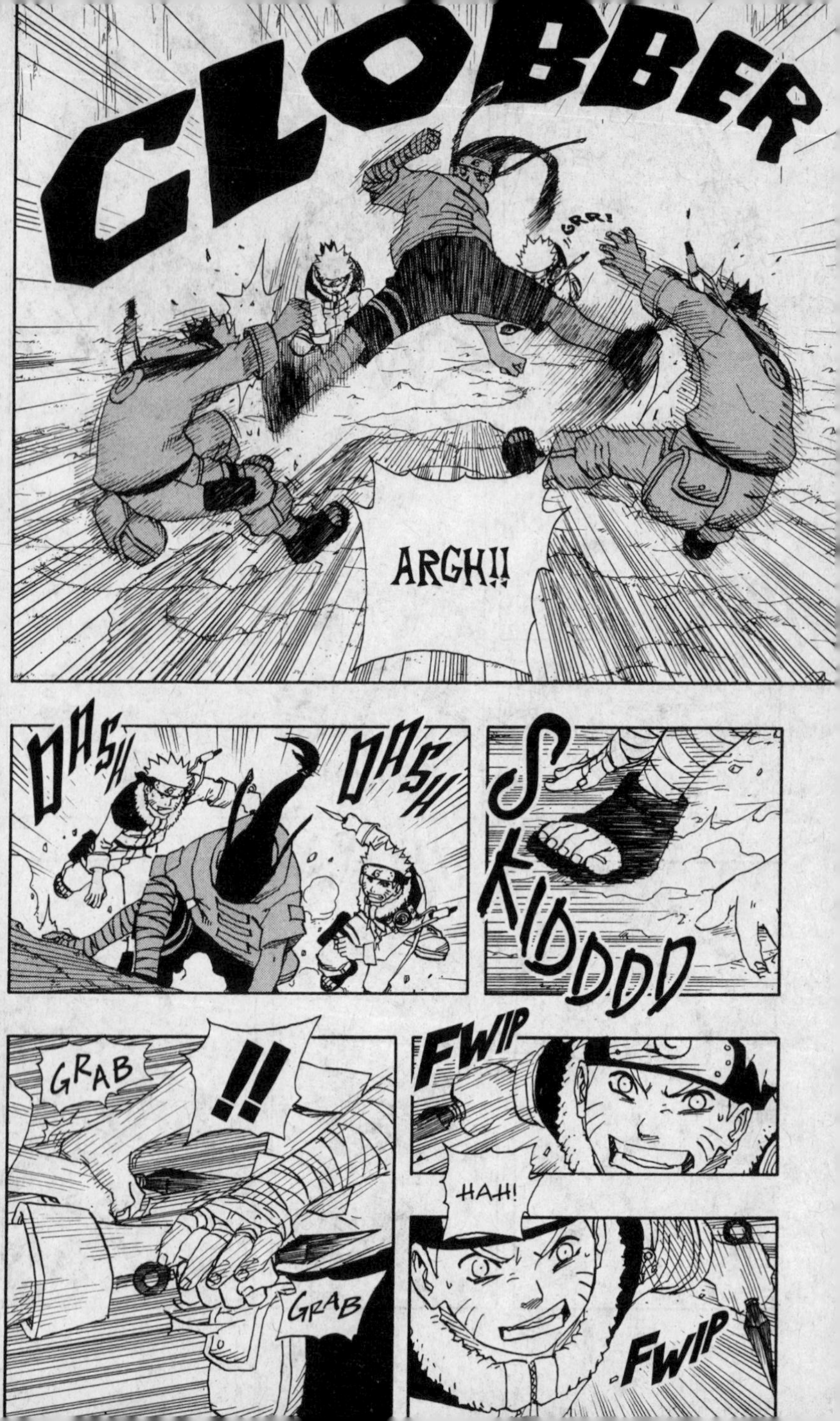
CLOBBER
GRR!
ARGH!!
SKIDDDD
DASH
DASH
FWIP
HAH!
FWIP
!!
GRAB
GRAB

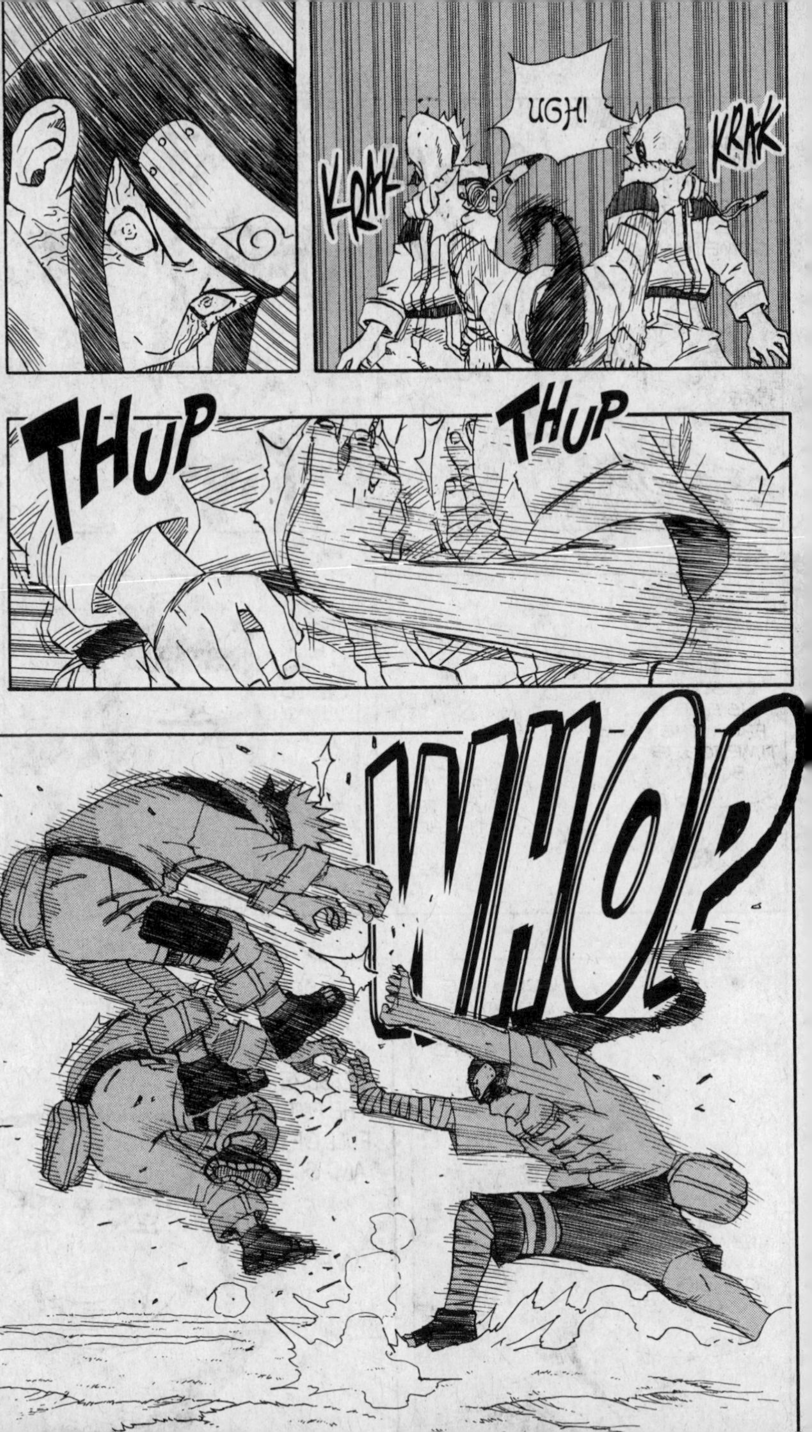
KRAK
UGH!
KRAK
THUP
THUP
WHO?

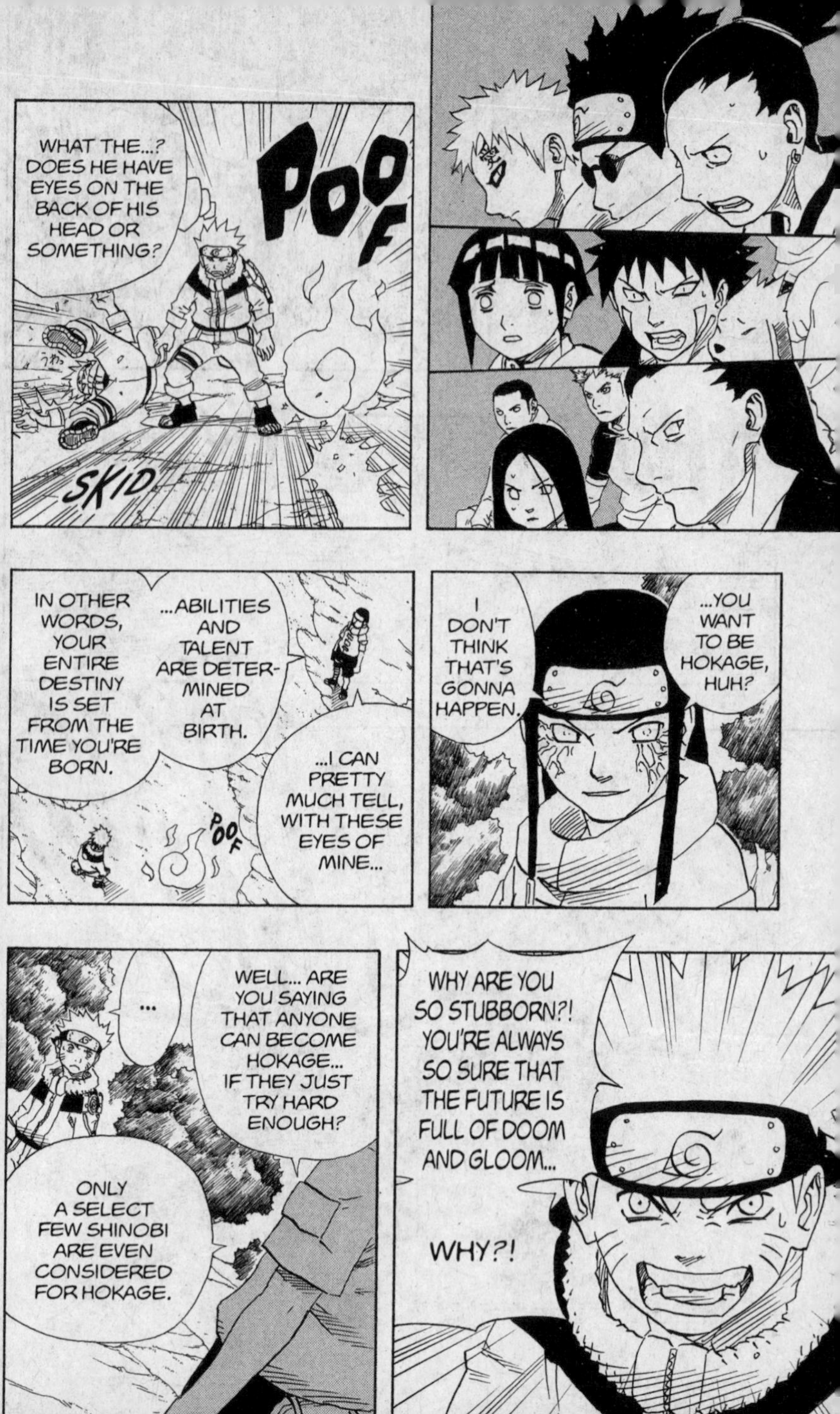

WHAT THE...? DOES HE HAVE EYES ON THE BACK OF HIS HEAD OR SOMETHING?
POOF
SKID
...YOU WANT TO BE HOKAGE, HUH?
I DON'T THINK THAT'S GONNA HAPPEN.
...I CAN PRETTY MUCH TELL, WITH THESE EYES OF MINE...
...ABILITIES AND TALENT ARE DETERMINED AT BIRTH.
IN OTHER WORDS, YOUR ENTIRE DESTINY IS SET FROM THE TIME YOU'RE BORN.
POOF
WHY ARE YOU SO STUBBORN?! YOU'RE ALWAYS SO SURE THAT THE FUTURE IS FULL OF DOOM AND GLOOM...
WHY?!
WELL... ARE YOU SAYING THAT ANYONE CAN BECOME HOKAGE... IF THEY JUST TRY HARD ENOUGH?
...
ONLY A SELECT FEW SHINOBI ARE EVEN CONSIDERED FOR HOKAGE.

READ THIS WAY

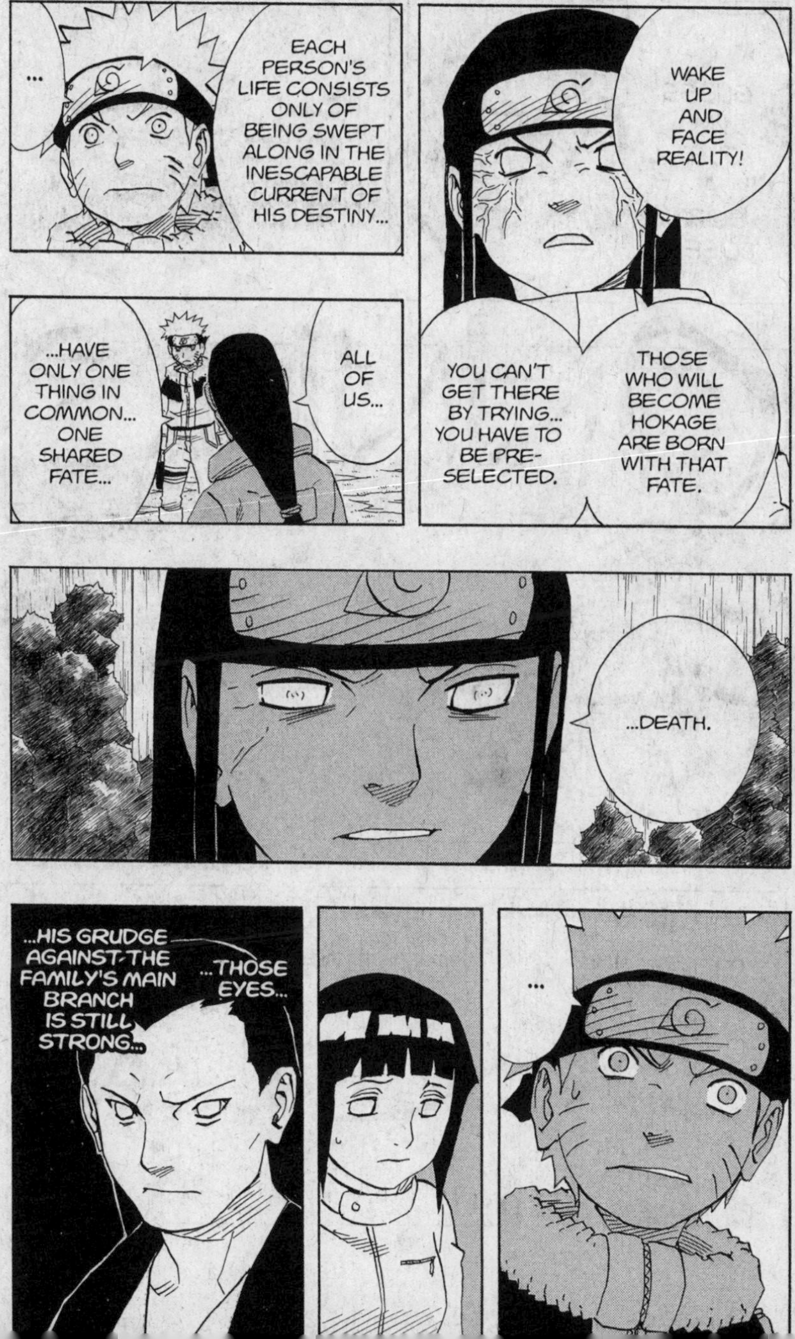
WAKE UP AND FACE REALITY!
THOSE WHO WILL BECOME HOKAGE ARE BORN WITH THAT FATE.
YOU CAN'T GET THERE BY TRYING... YOU HAVE TO BE PRE-SELECTED.
EACH PERSON'S LIFE CONSISTS ONLY OF BEING SWEPT ALONG IN THE INESCAPABLE CURRENT OF HIS DESTINY...
...
ALL OF US...
...HAVE ONLY ONE THING IN COMMON... ONE SHARED FATE...
...DEATH.
...
...THOSE EYES...
...HIS GRUDGE AGAINST THE FAMILY'S MAIN BRANCH IS STILL STRONG...

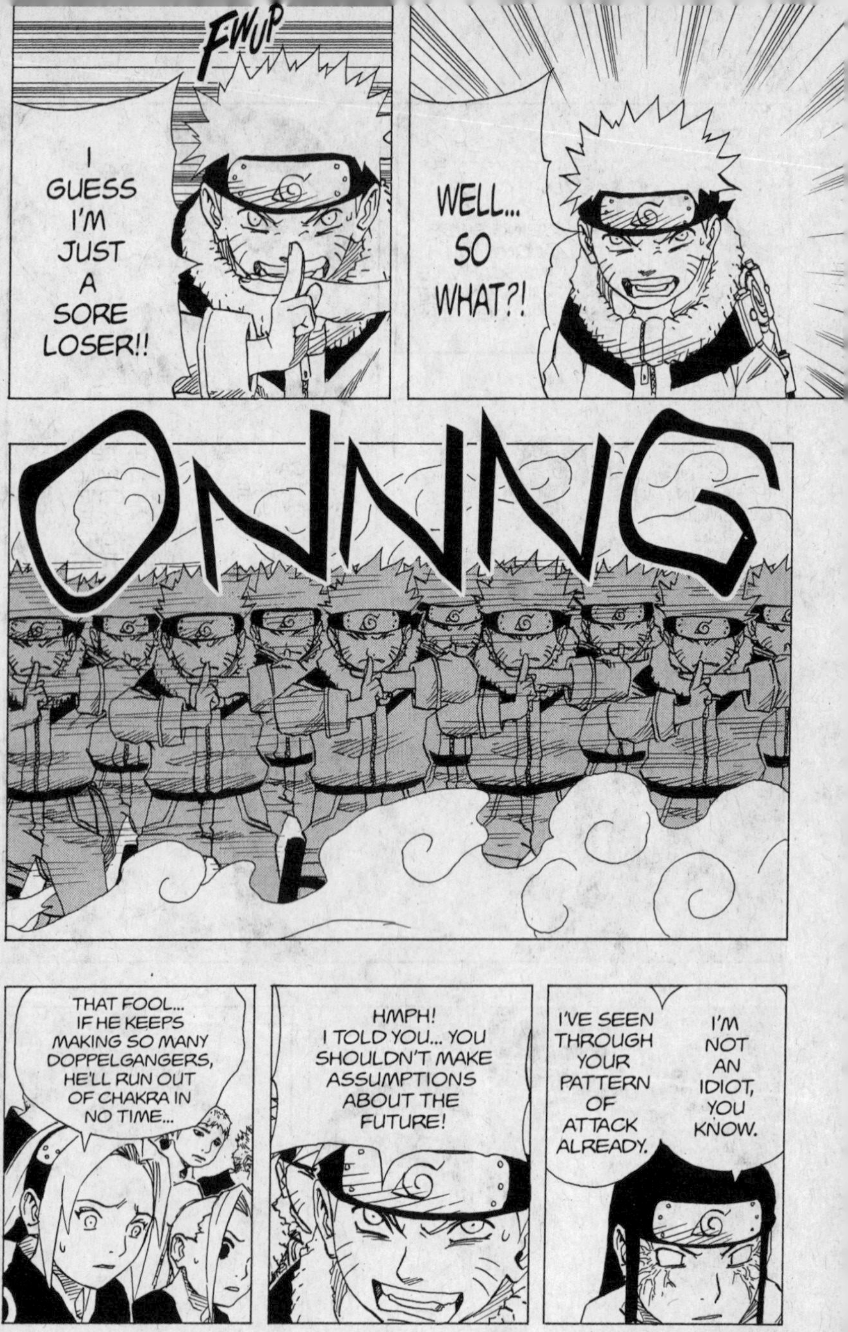
WELL... SO WHAT?!
FWUP
I GUESS I'M JUST A SORE LOSER!!
ONNNG
I'M NOT AN IDIOT, YOU KNOW.
I'VE SEEN THROUGH YOUR PATTERN OF ATTACK ALREADY.
HMPH! I TOLD YOU... YOU SHOULDN'T MAKE ASSUMPTIONS ABOUT THE FUTURE!
THAT FOOL... IF HE KEEPS MAKING SO MANY DOPPELGANGERS, HE'LL RUN OUT OF CHAKRA IN NO TIME...

READ THIS WAY

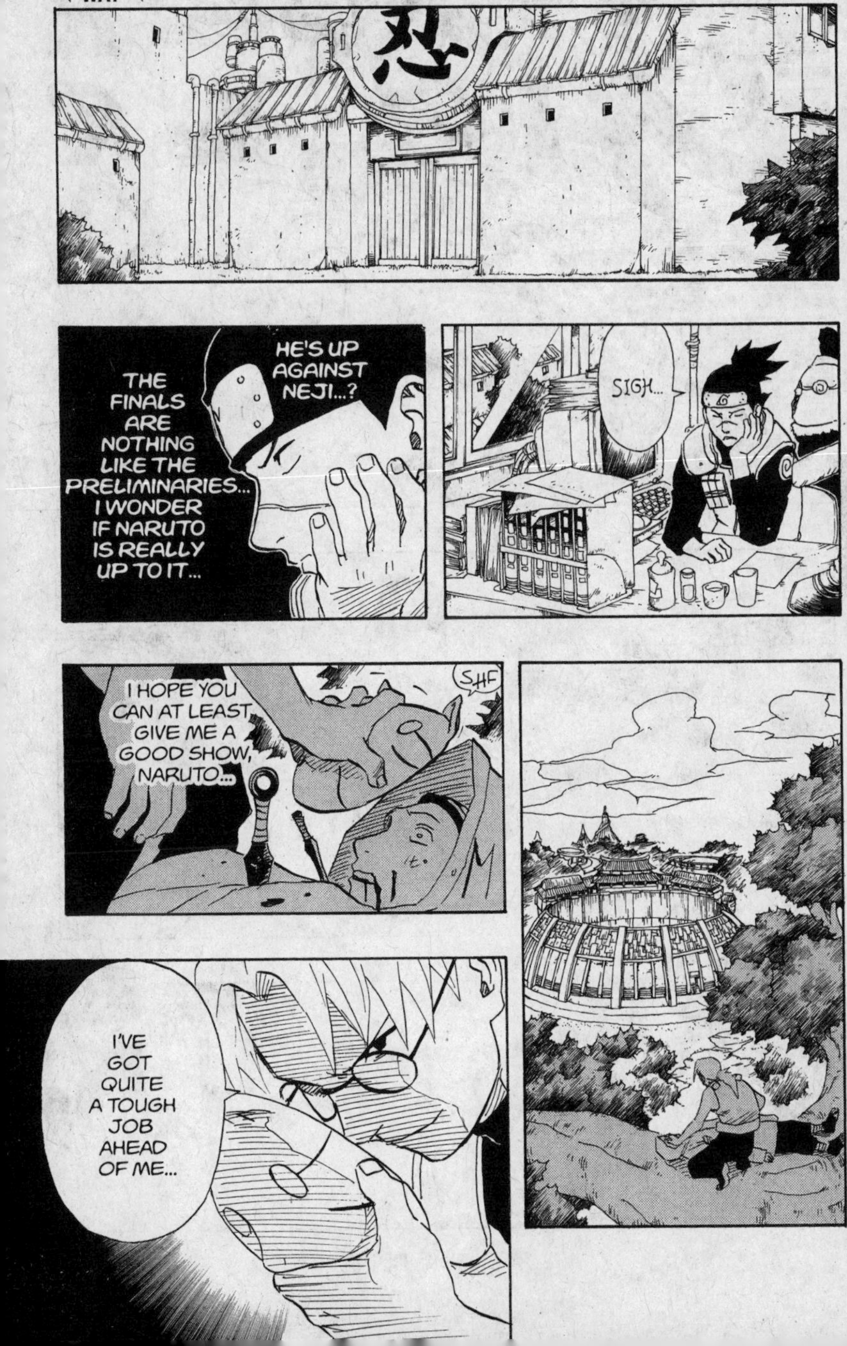
SIGH...
HE'S UP AGAINST NEJI...?
THE FINALS ARE NOTHING LIKE THE PRELIMINARIES... I WONDER IF NARUTO IS REALLY UP TO IT...
SHF
I HOPE YOU CAN AT LEAST GIVE ME A GOOD SHOW, NARUTO...
I'VE GOT QUITE A TOUGH JOB AHEAD OF ME...

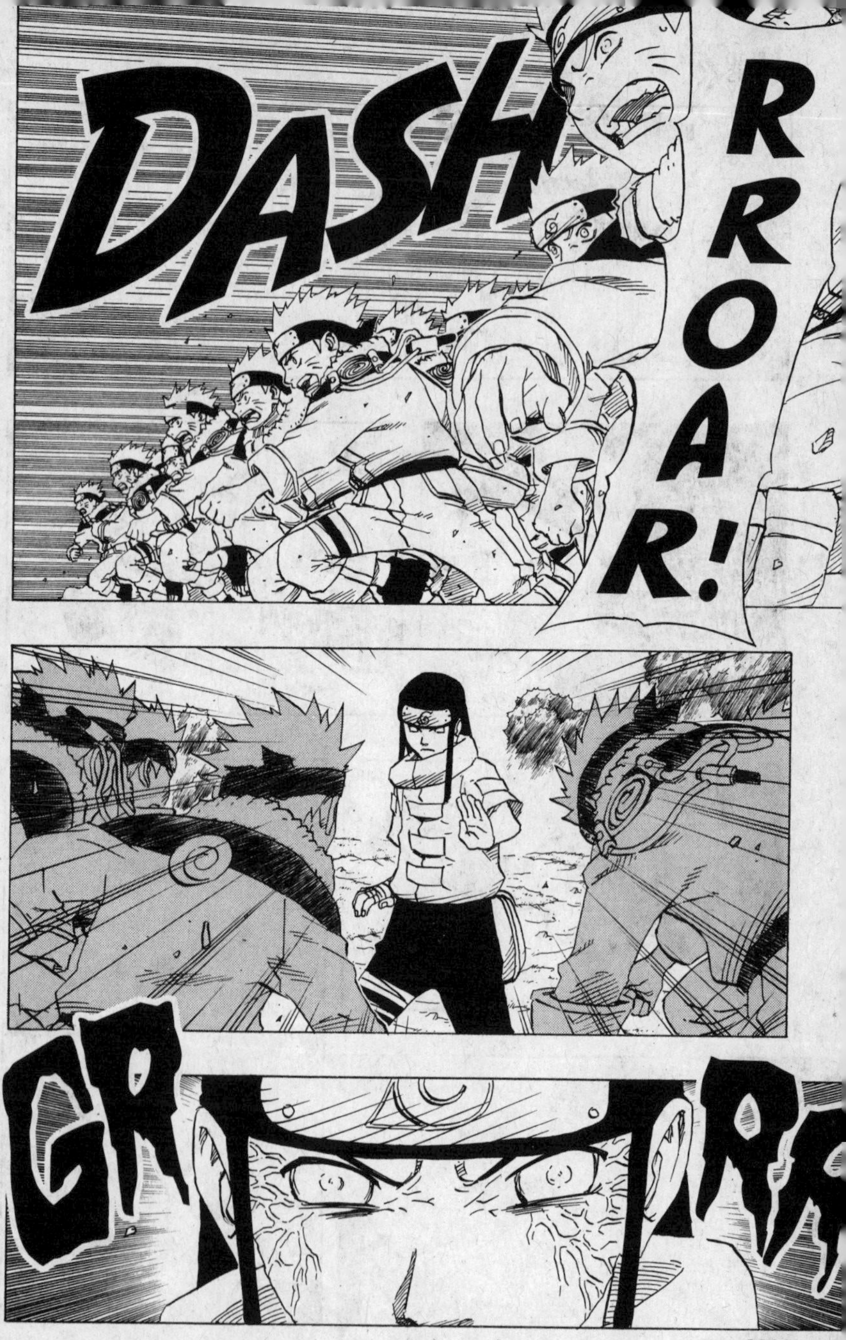
RROAR!
DASH
GRRR

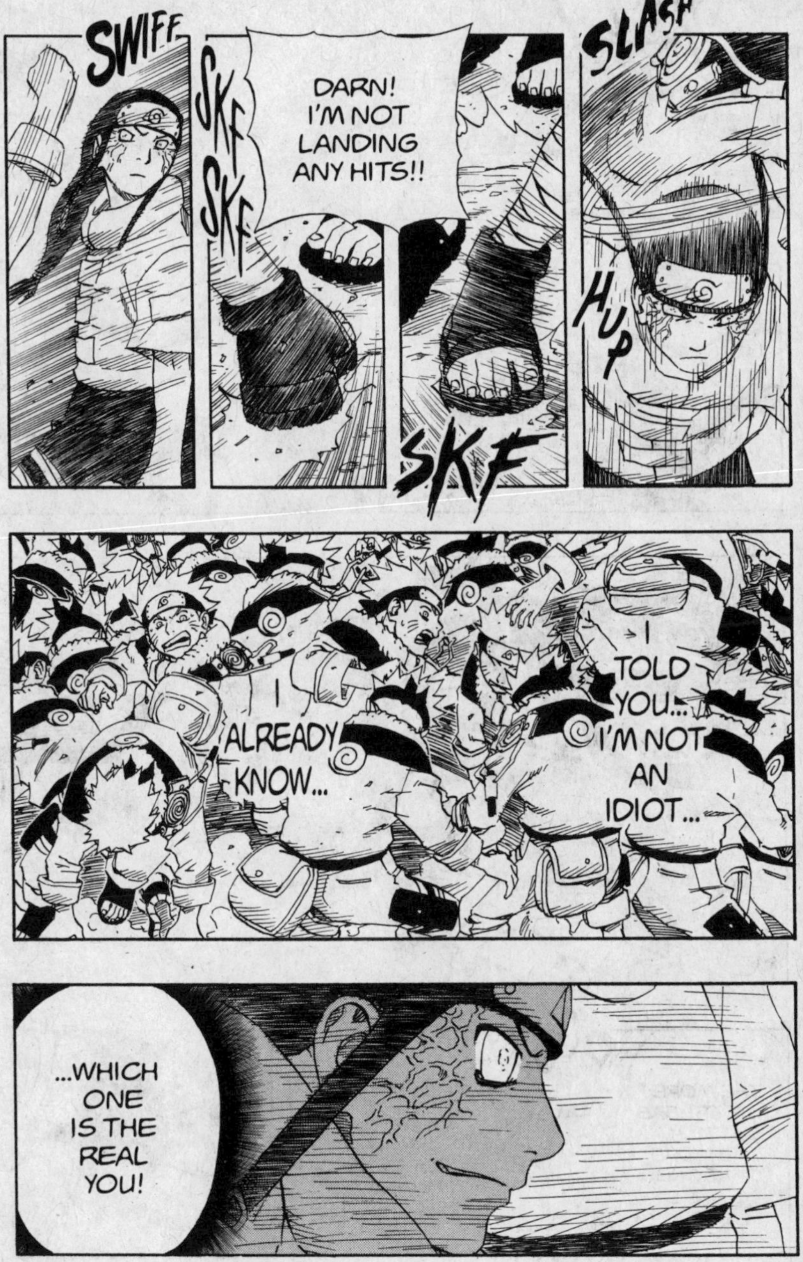
SLASH
HUP
SKF
DARN! I'M NOT LANDING ANY HITS!!
SKF SKF
SWIFF
I TOLD YOU... I'M NOT AN IDIOT...
I ALREADY KNOW...
...WHICH ONE IS THE REAL YOU!

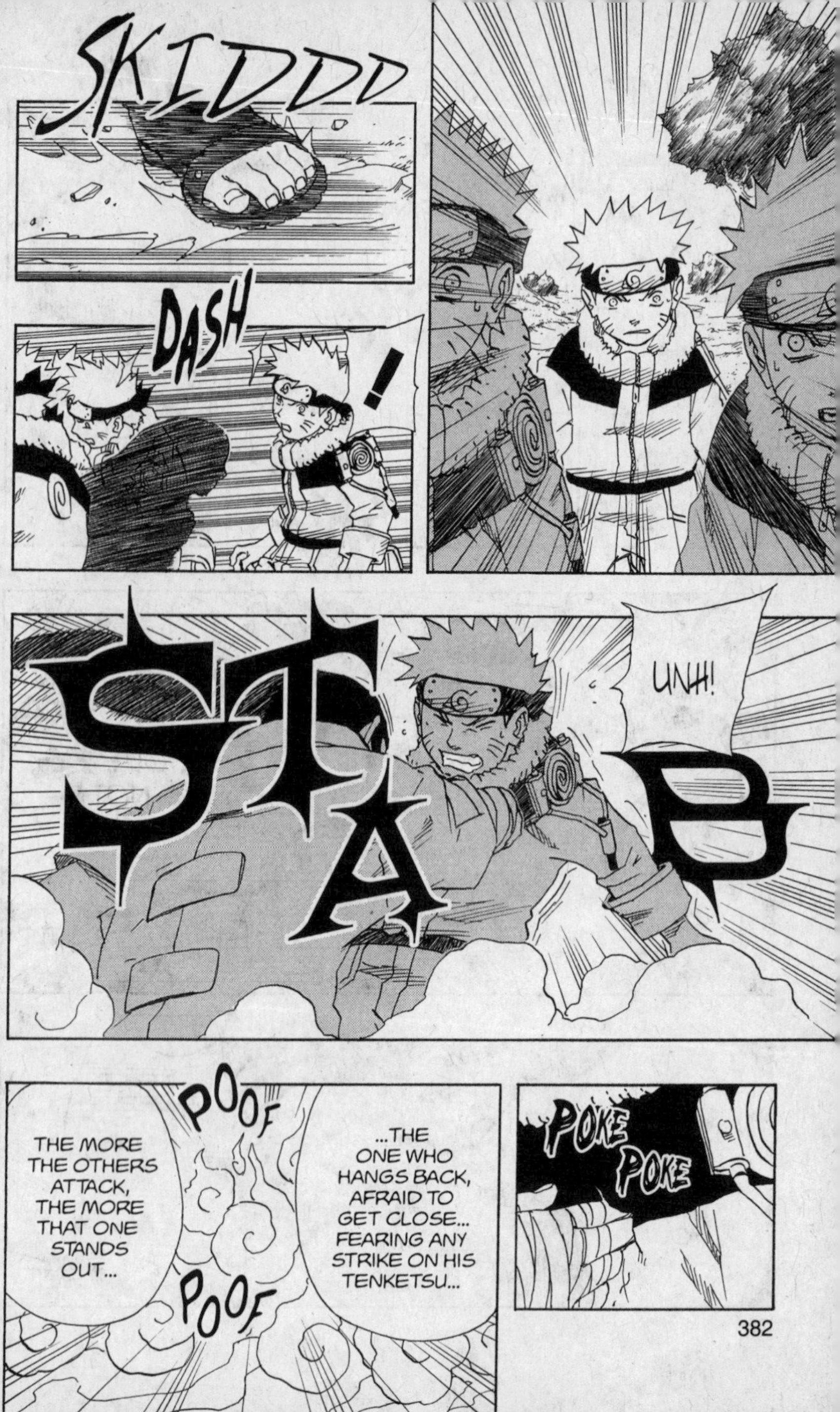
SKIDDD
DASH
!
STAB
UNH!
POKE POKE
POOF
...THE ONE WHO HANGS BACK, AFRAID TO GET CLOSE... FEARING ANY STRIKE ON HIS TENKETSU...
THE MORE THE OTHERS ATTACK, THE MORE THAT ONE STANDS OUT...
POOF

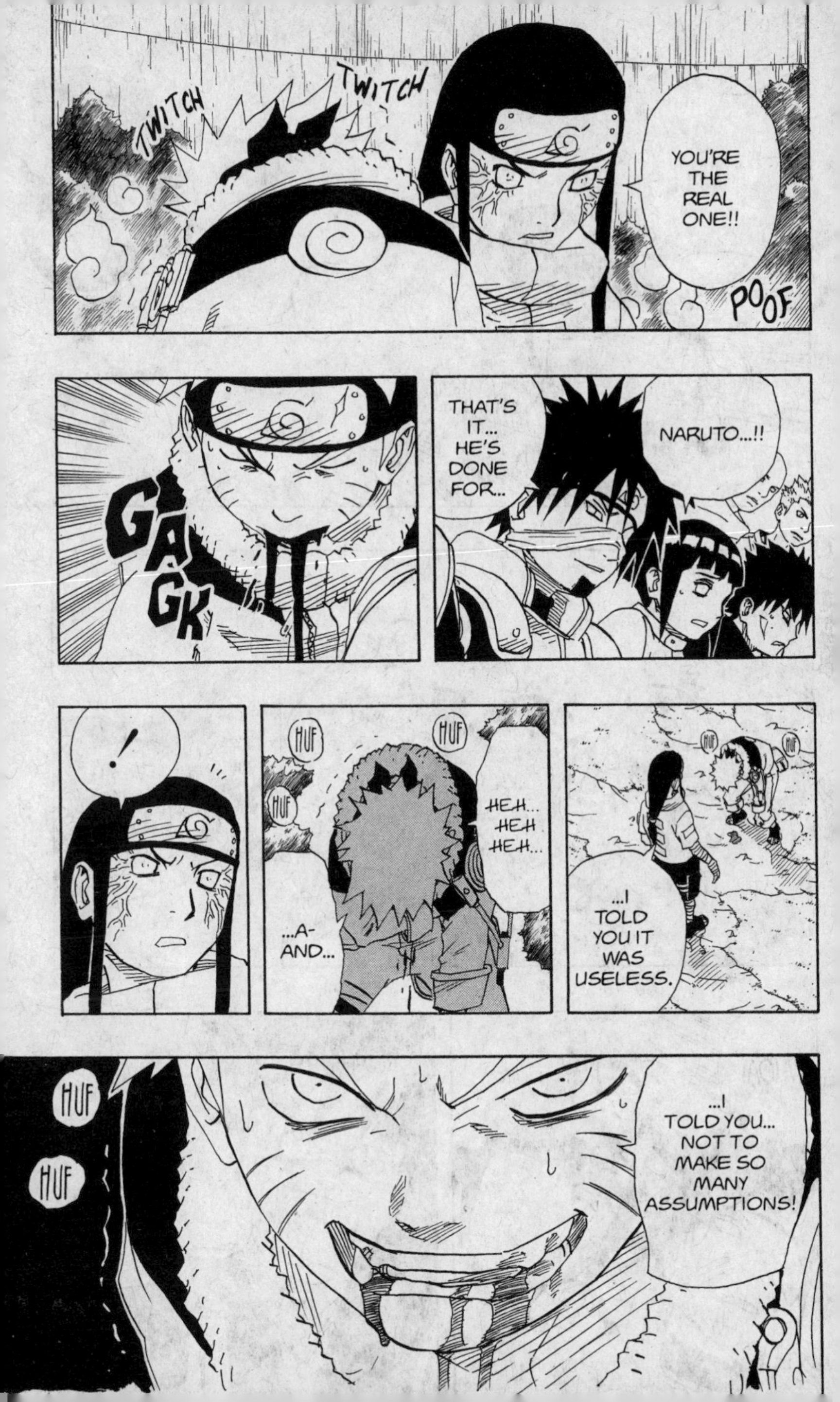
YOU'RE THE REAL ONE!!
TWITCH
TWITCH
POOF
NARUTO...!!
THAT'S IT... HE'S DONE FOR...
GAGK
HUF
HUF
...I TOLD YOU IT WAS USELESS.
HUF
HUF
HUF
HEH... HEH HEH...
...A- AND...
!
...I TOLD YOU... NOT TO MAKE SO MANY ASSUMPTIONS!
HUF
HUF

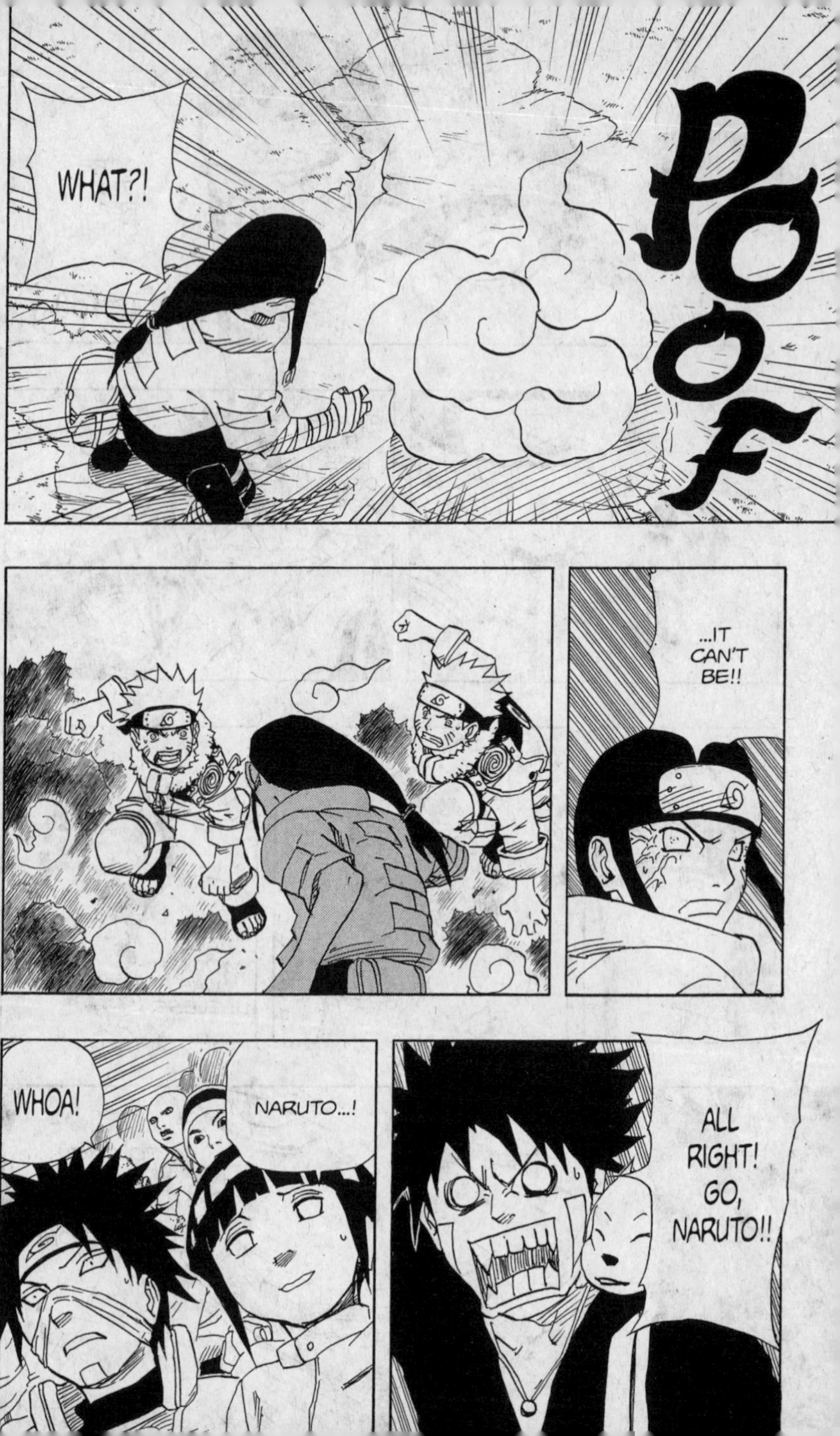
POOF
WHAT?!
...IT CAN'T BE!!
ALL RIGHT! GO, NARUTO!!
NARUTO...!
WHOA!

READ THIS WAY

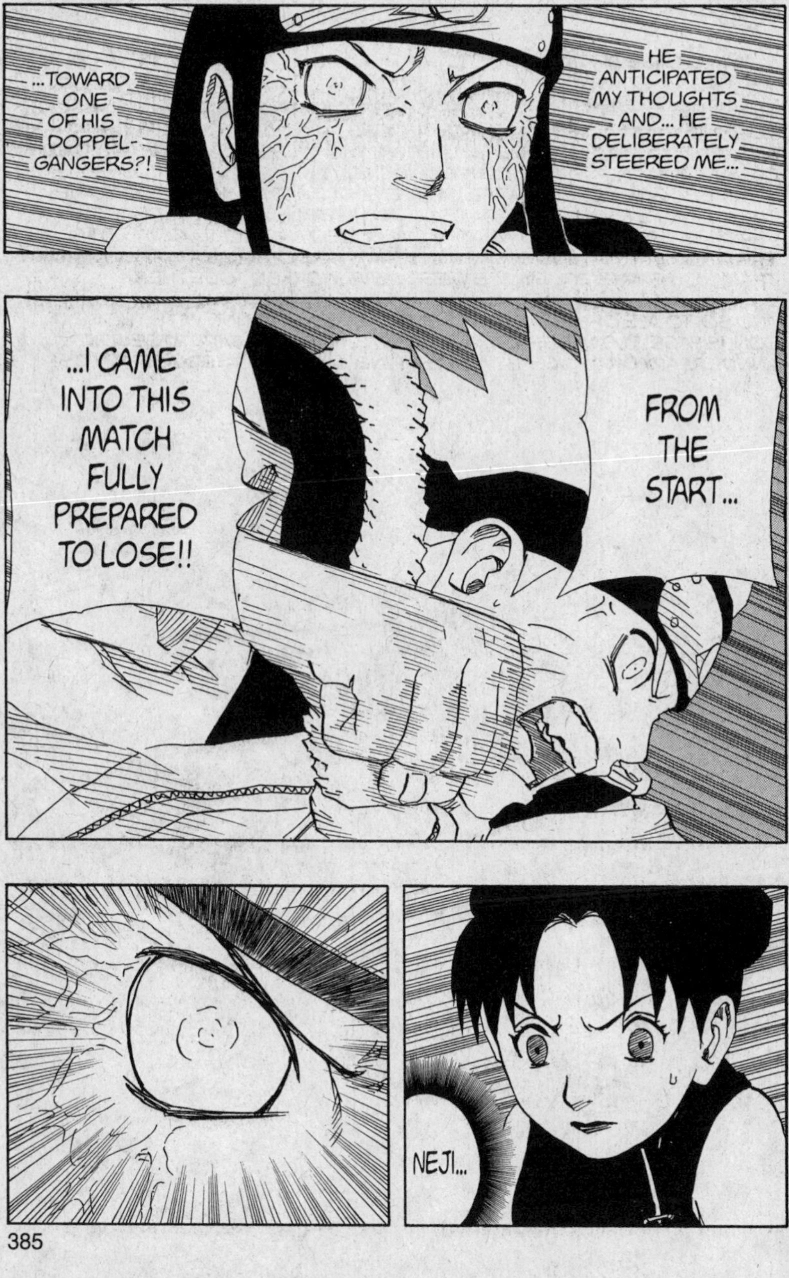

HE ANTICIPATED MY THOUGHTS AND... HE DELIBERATELY STEERED ME...
...TOWARD ONE OF HIS DOPPEL-GANGERS?!
FROM THE START...
...I CAME INTO THIS MATCH FULLY PREPARED TO LOSE!!
NEJI...

A MESSAGE FROM KISHIMOTO MASASHI TO ALL OF HIS ASSISTANTS

I CAN'T BELIEVE IT'S ALREADY BEEN OVER TWO YEARS SINCE WE STARTED WORKING ON *NARUTO*! I WANT TO EXPRESS MY SINCERE GRATITUDE TO ALL OF YOU, WHO ALWAYS LISTEN SILENTLY TO MY SELFISH, UNREASONABLE DEMANDS AND CATER TO MY EVERY WHIM.
I HAVE BECOME KEENLY AWARE OF THE FACT THAT MANGA IS NOT SOME-THING ONE PERSON CAN CREATE ALL BY HIMSELF. I HONESTLY BELIEVE THAT YOUR HARD WORK IS WHAT HAS ALLOWED *NARUTO* TO COME THIS FAR WHILE MAINTAINING SUCH HIGH STANDARDS OF QUALITY. I TRULY THANK YOU FOR EVERY SINGLE WEEK WE'VE WORKED TOGETHER!!

AND SO, TO ALL OF YOU READERS OUT THERE... STARTING WITH THE NEXT BONUS PAGE, PLEASE ENJOY THE COMMEMORATIVE *NARUTO* SECOND ANNIVERSARY DRAWINGS BY MY INSPIRING AND DEDICATED ASSISTANTS!

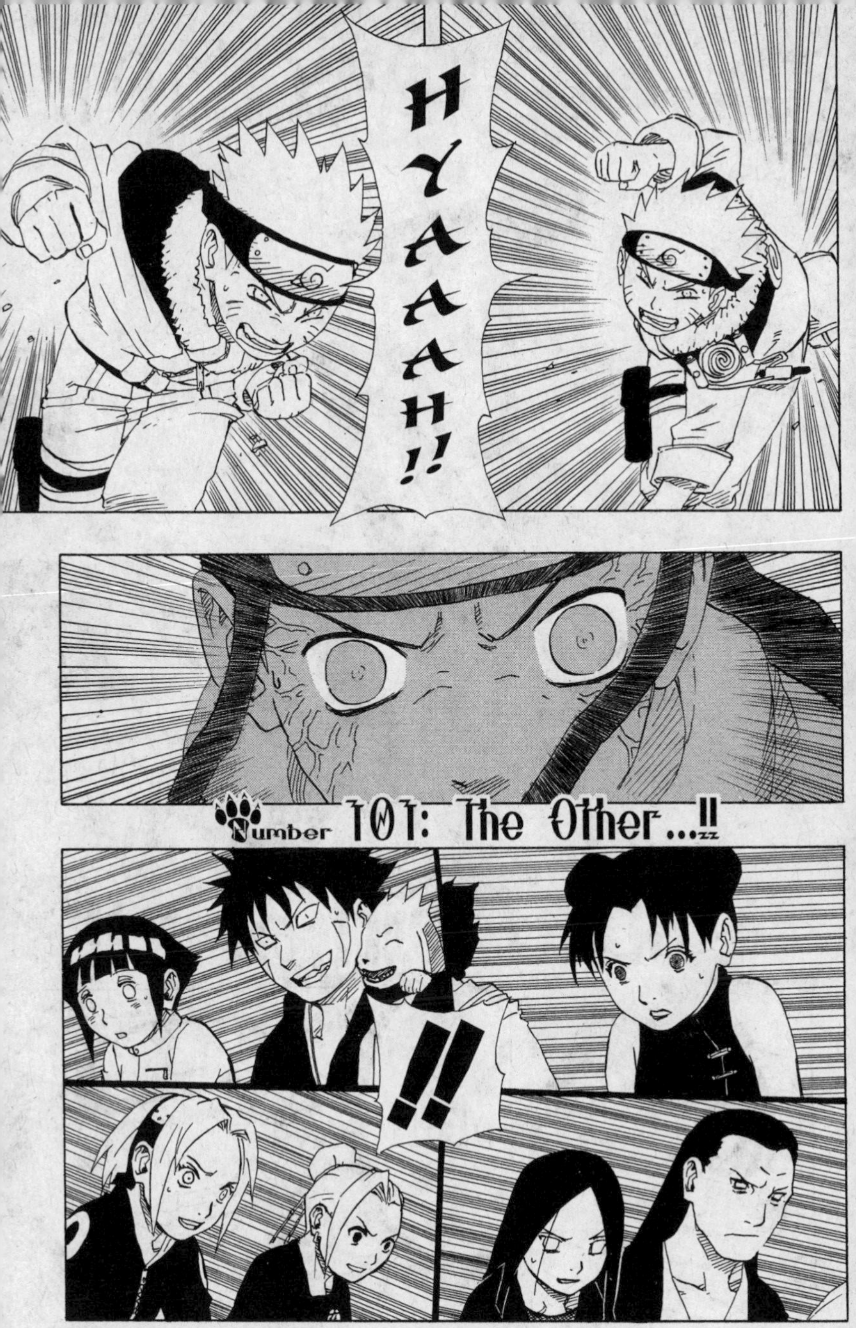
HYAAAAH!!
Number 101: The Other...!!
!!

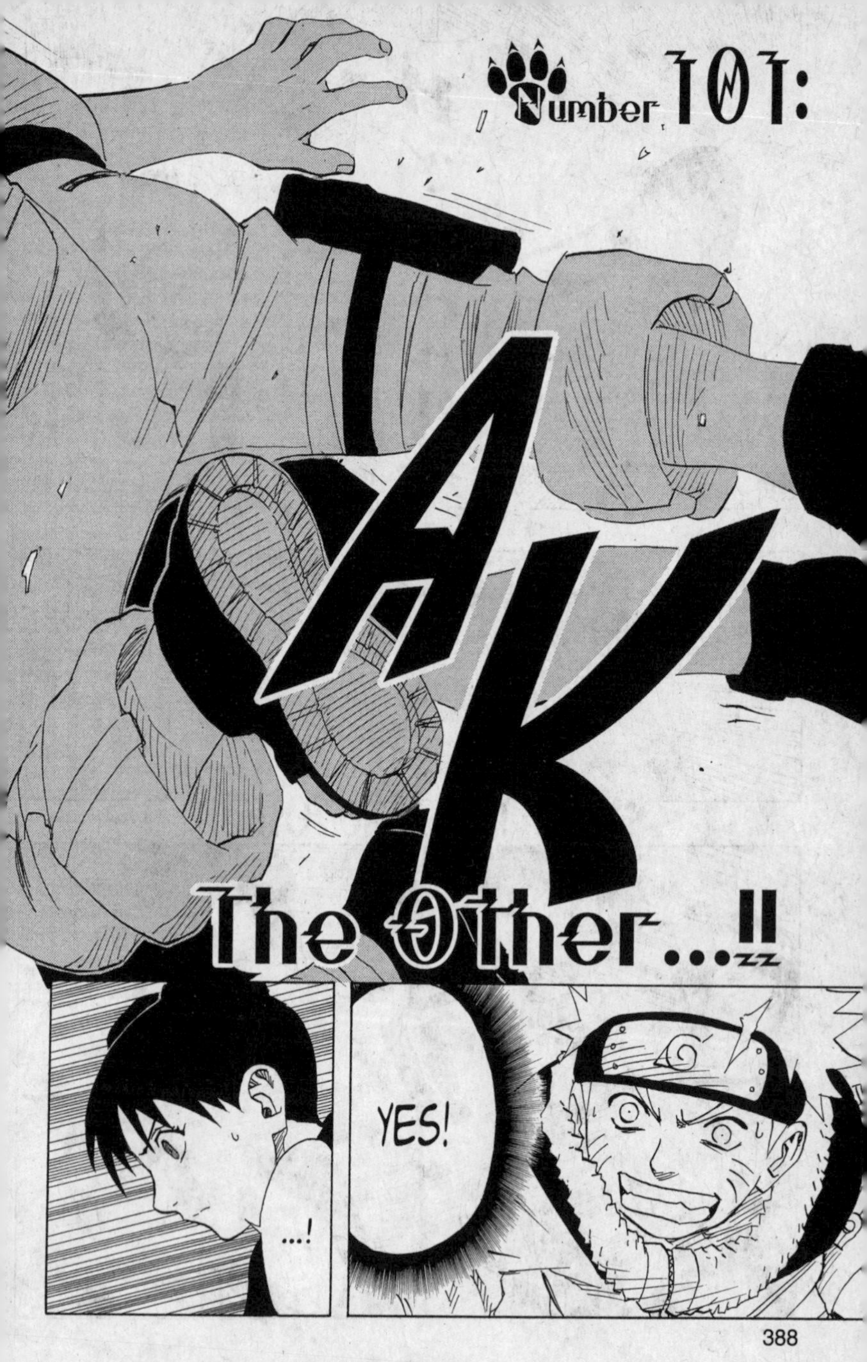
Number 101:
The Other...!!
TAK
YES!
...!

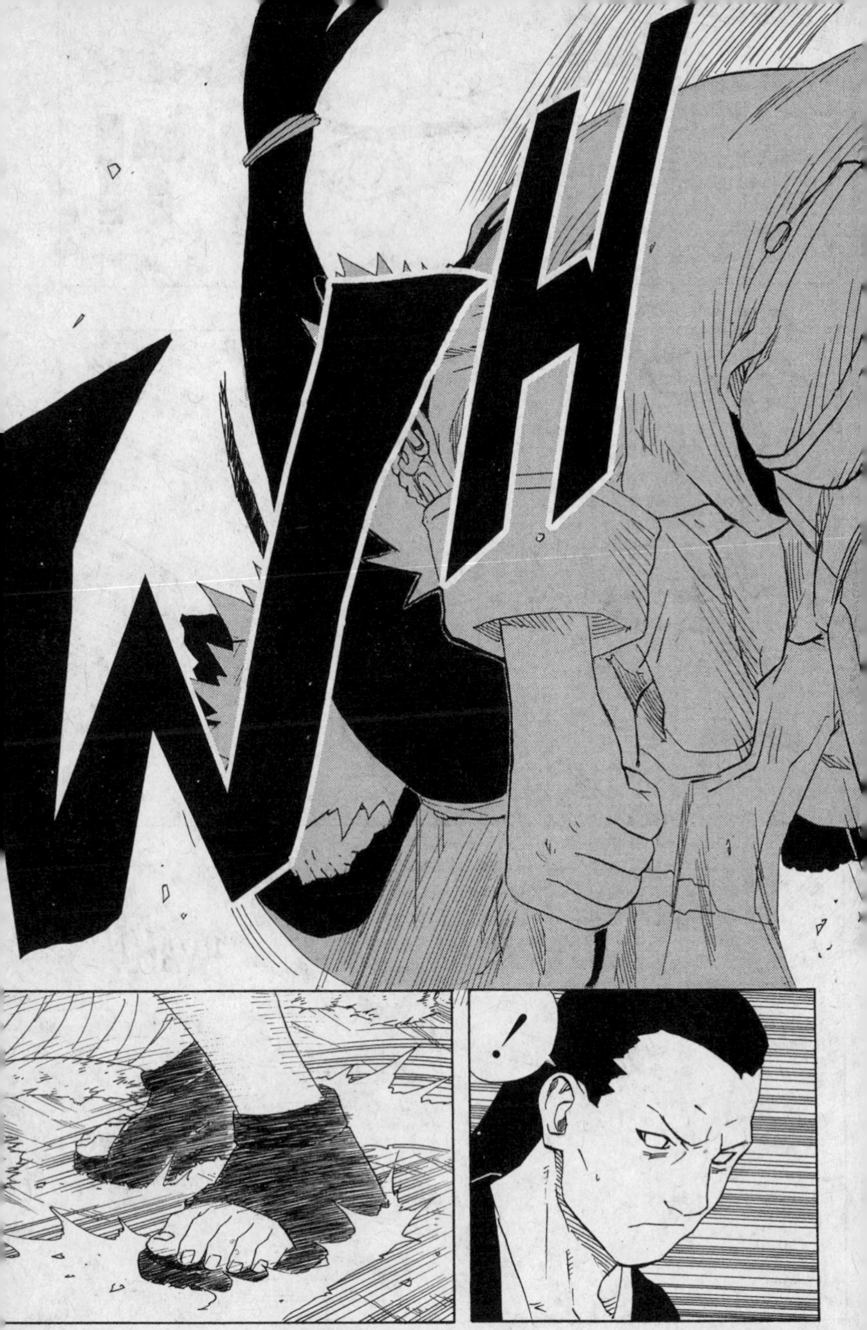
!

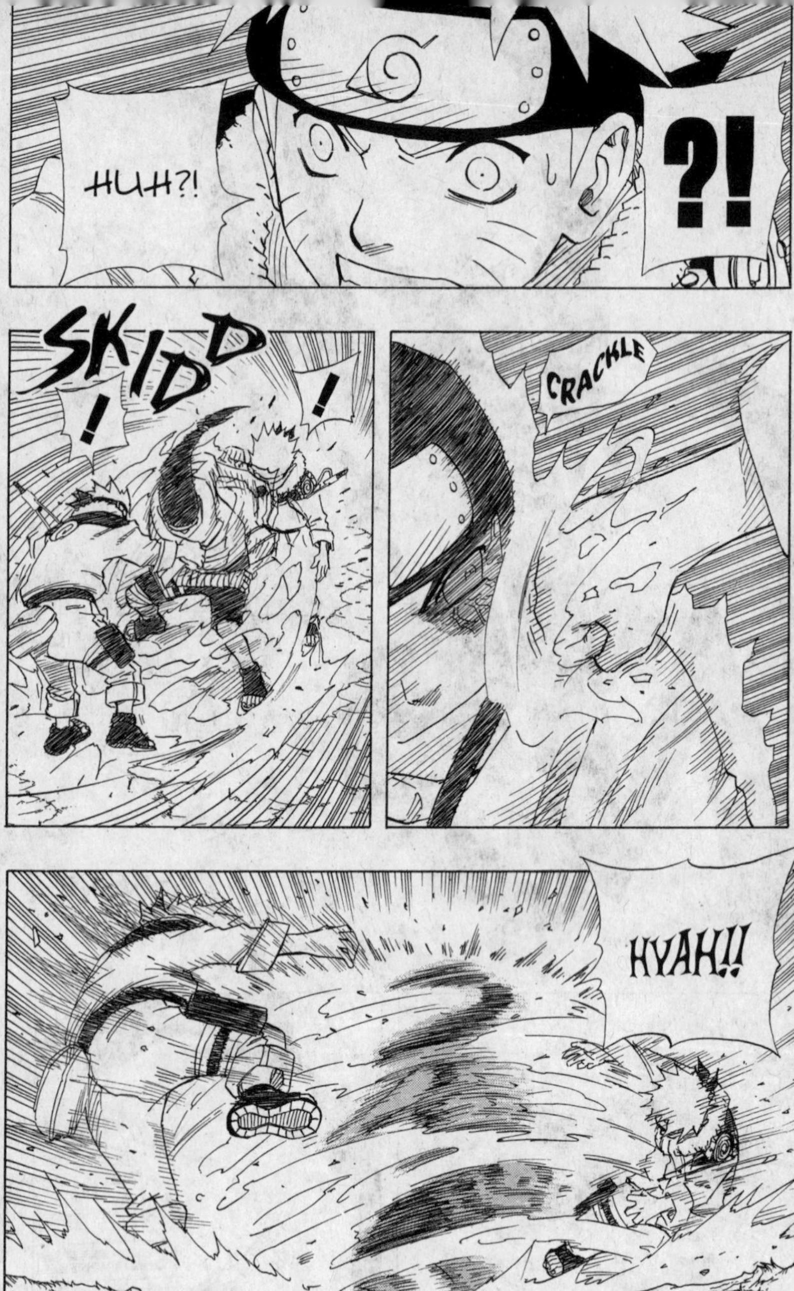
?!
HUH?!
CRACKLE
!
!
SKIDD
HYAH!!

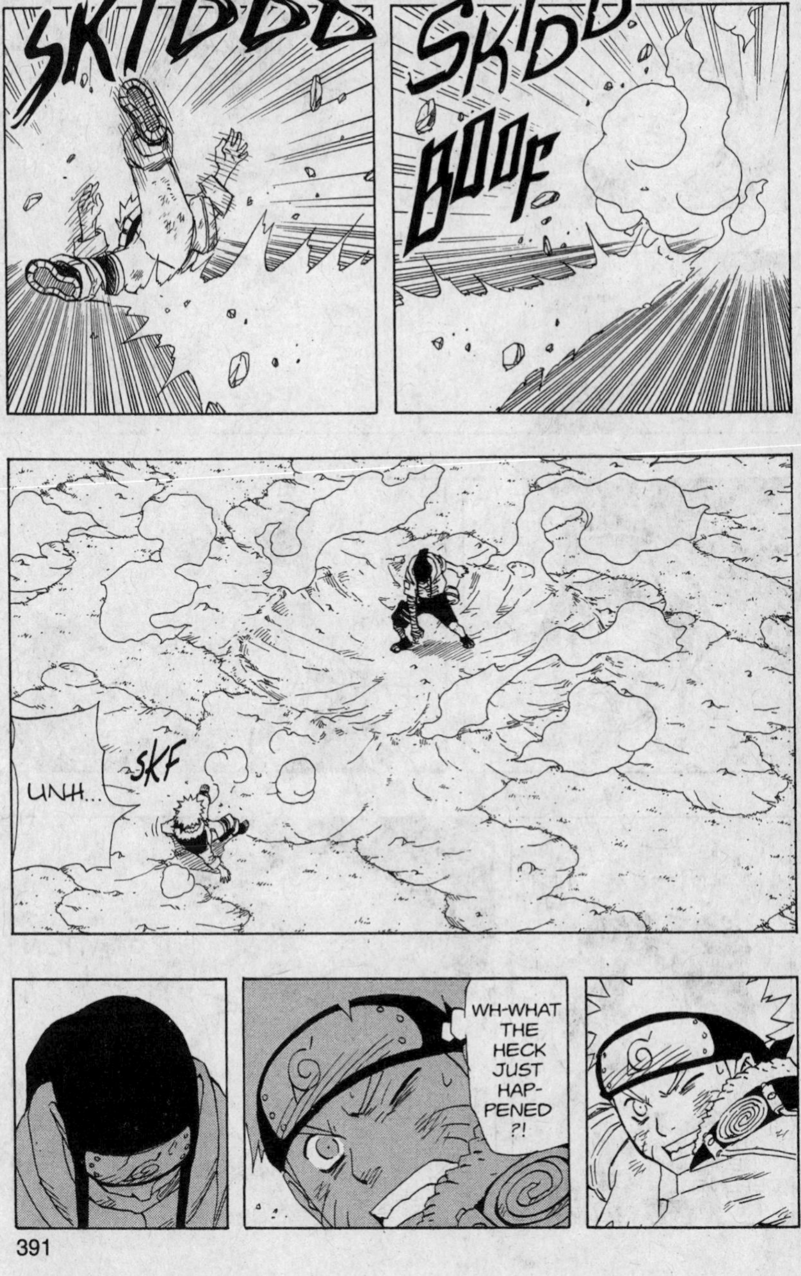
SKIDD
BOOF
SKIDDD
SKF
UNH...
WH-WHAT THE HECK JUST HAP-PENED?!

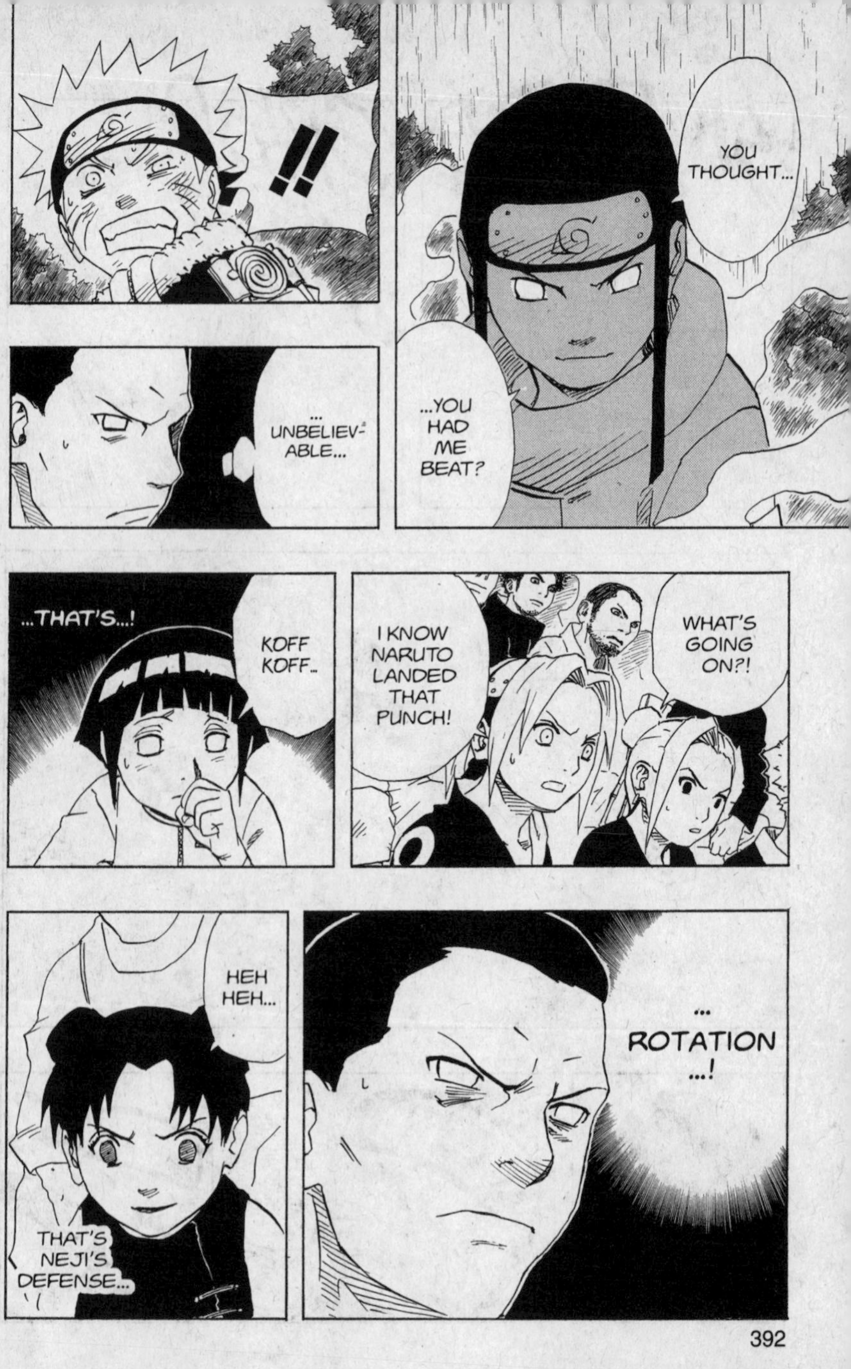

YOU THOUGHT...
...YOU HAD ME BEAT?
!!
...UNBELIEVABLE...
WHAT'S GOING ON?!
I KNOW NARUTO LANDED THAT PUNCH!
KOFF KOFF..
...THAT'S...!
...ROTATION...!
HEH HEH...
THAT'S NEJI'S DEFENSE...

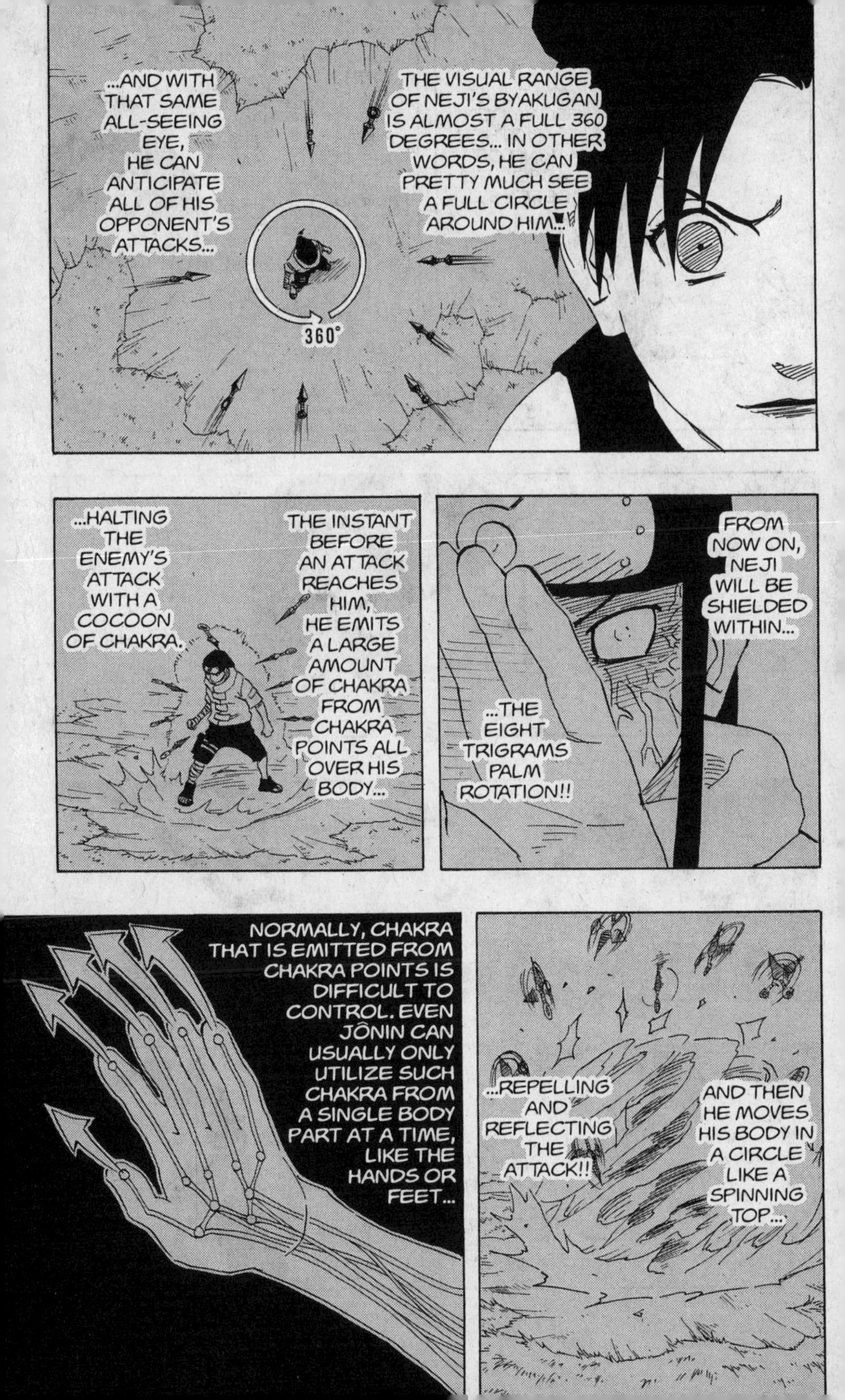
THE VISUAL RANGE OF NEJI'S BYAKUGAN IS ALMOST A FULL 360 DEGREES... IN OTHER WORDS, HE CAN PRETTY MUCH SEE A FULL CIRCLE AROUND HIM!!...
...AND WITH THAT SAME ALL-SEEING EYE, HE CAN ANTICIPATE ALL OF HIS OPPONENT'S ATTACKS...
360°
FROM NOW ON, NEJI WILL BE SHIELDED WITHIN...
...THE EIGHT TRIGRAMS PALM ROTATION!!
THE INSTANT BEFORE AN ATTACK REACHES HIM, HE EMITS A LARGE AMOUNT OF CHAKRA FROM CHAKRA POINTS ALL OVER HIS BODY...
...HALTING THE ENEMY'S ATTACK WITH A COCOON OF CHAKRA.
AND THEN HE MOVES HIS BODY IN A CIRCLE LIKE A SPINNING TOP...
...REPELLING AND REFLECTING THE ATTACK!!
NORMALLY, CHAKRA THAT IS EMITTED FROM CHAKRA POINTS IS DIFFICULT TO CONTROL. EVEN JÔNIN CAN USUALLY ONLY UTILIZE SUCH CHAKRA FROM A SINGLE BODY PART AT A TIME, LIKE THE HANDS OR FEET...

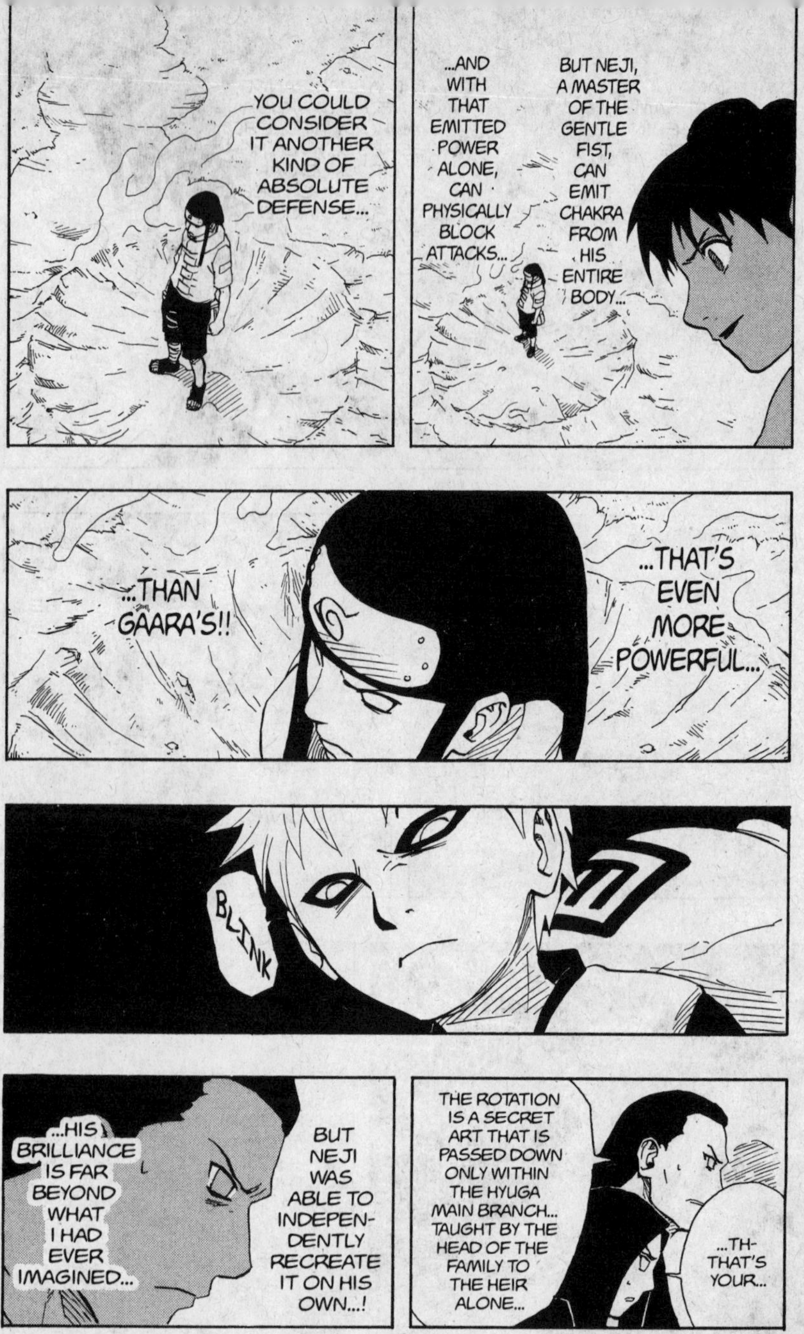
BUT NEJI, A MASTER OF THE GENTLE FIST, CAN EMIT CHAKRA FROM HIS ENTIRE BODY...
...AND WITH THAT EMITTED POWER ALONE, CAN PHYSICALLY BLOCK ATTACKS...
YOU COULD CONSIDER IT ANOTHER KIND OF ABSOLUTE DEFENSE...
...THAT'S EVEN MORE POWERFUL...
...THAN GAARA'S!!
BLINK
THE ROTATION IS A SECRET ART THAT IS PASSED DOWN ONLY WITHIN THE HYUGA MAIN BRANCH... TAUGHT BY THE HEAD OF THE FAMILY TO THE HEIR ALONE...
...TH-THAT'S YOUR...
BUT NEJI WAS ABLE TO INDEPEN-DENTLY RECREATE IT ON HIS OWN...!
...HIS BRILLIANCE IS FAR BEYOND WHAT I HAD EVER IMAGINED...

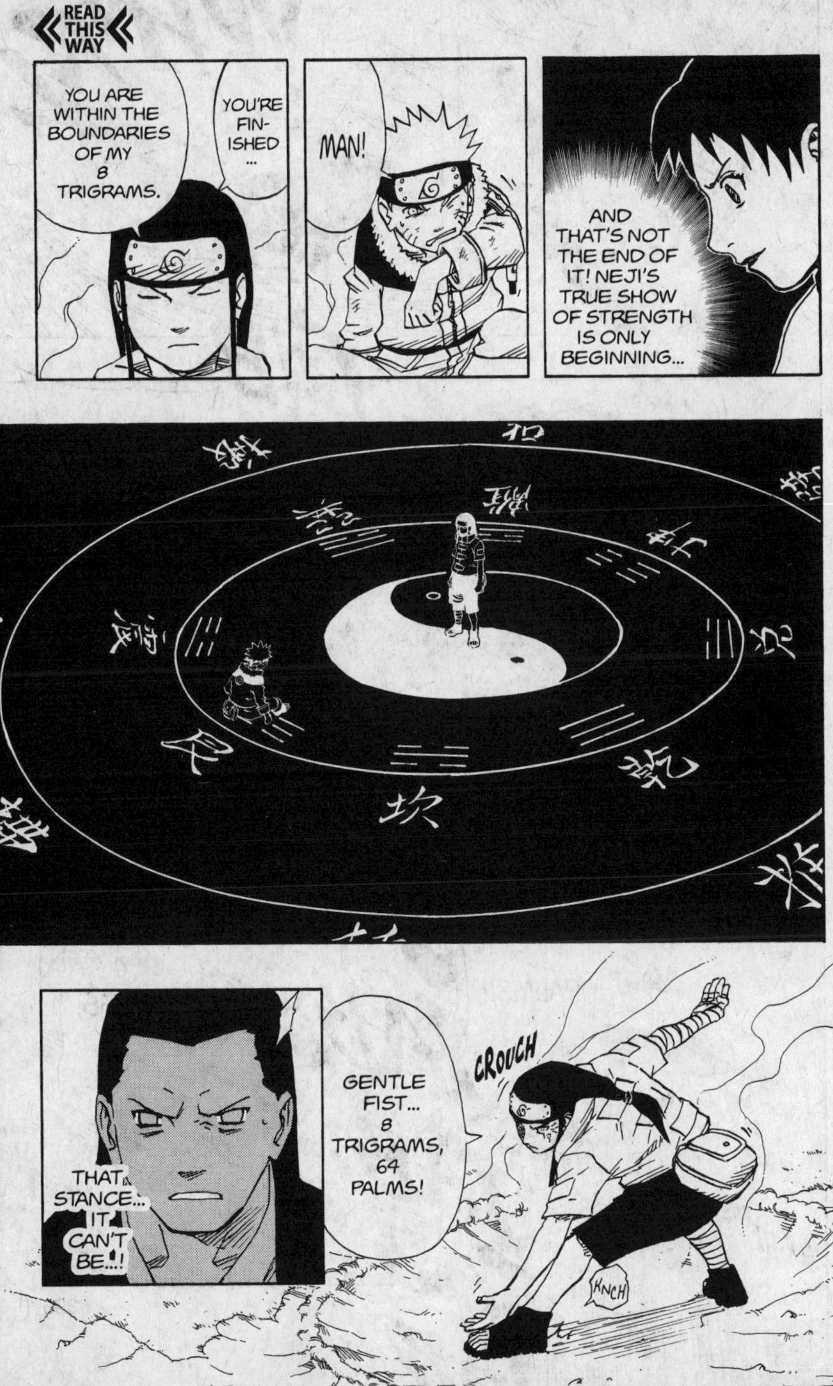
READ THIS WAY
AND THAT'S NOT THE END OF IT! NEJI'S TRUE SHOW OF STRENGTH IS ONLY BEGINNING...
MAN!
YOU'RE FIN-ISHED...
YOU ARE WITHIN THE BOUNDARIES OF MY 8 TRIGRAMS.
CROUCH
GENTLE FIST... 8 TRIGRAMS, 64 PALMS!
KNCH
THAT STANCE... IT CAN'T BE...!

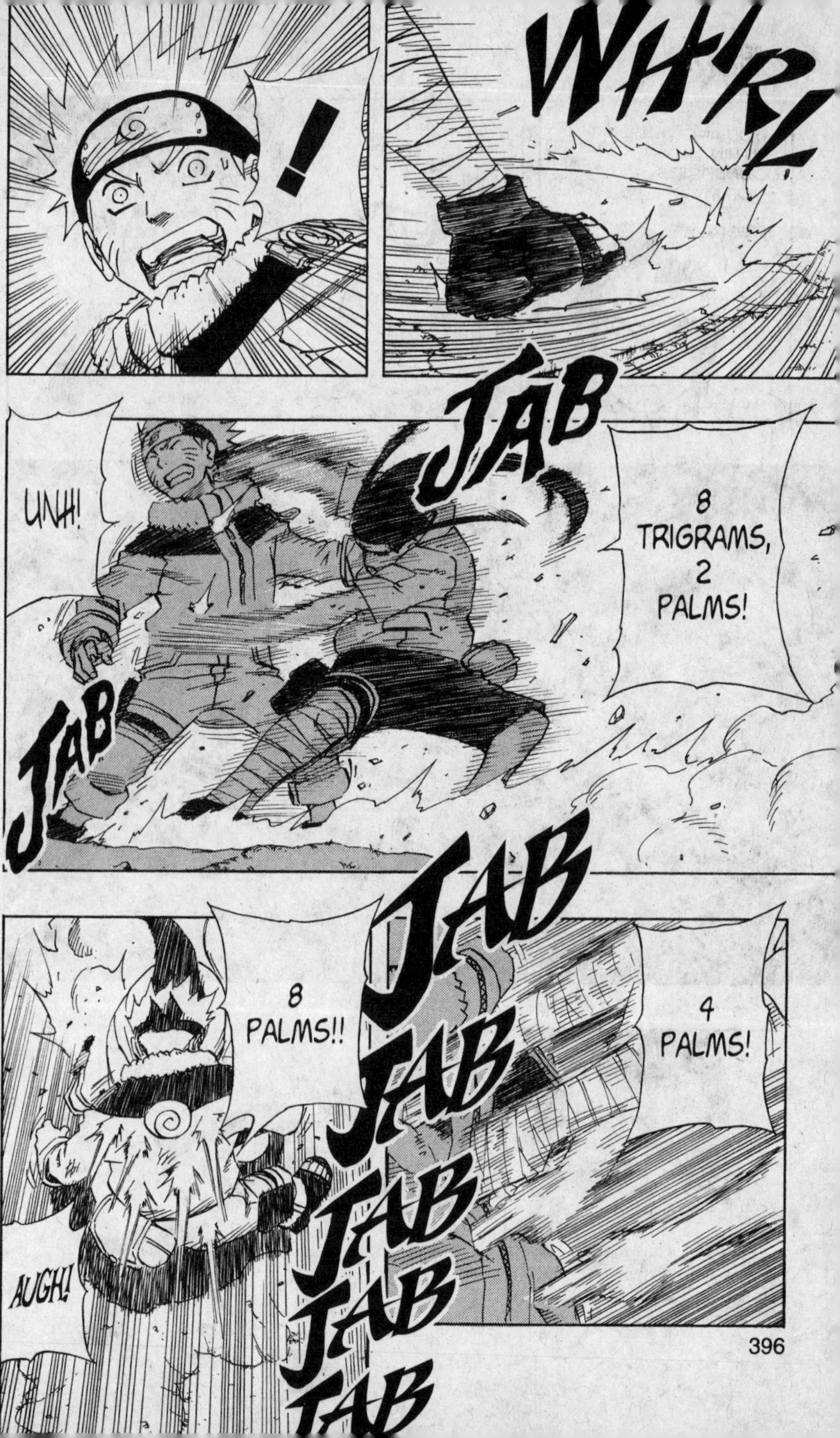
WHIRL
!
JAB
8 TRIGRAMS, 2 PALMS!
UNH!
JAB
4 PALMS!
8 PALMS!!
JAB
JAB
JAB
JAB
JAB
AUGH!

READ THIS WAY

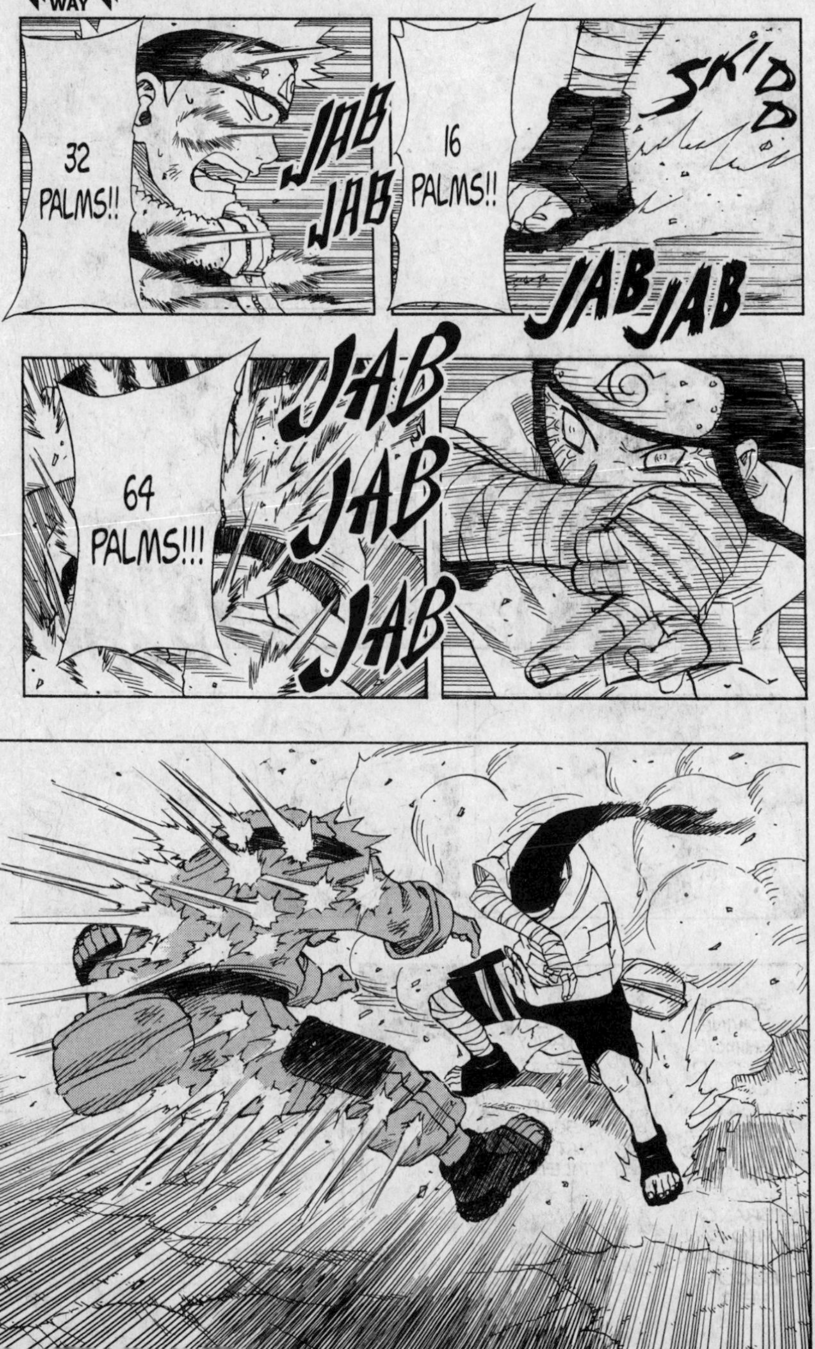
16 PALMS!!
SKIDD
JAB JAB
32 PALMS!!
JAB JAB
64 PALMS!!!
JAB JAB JAB

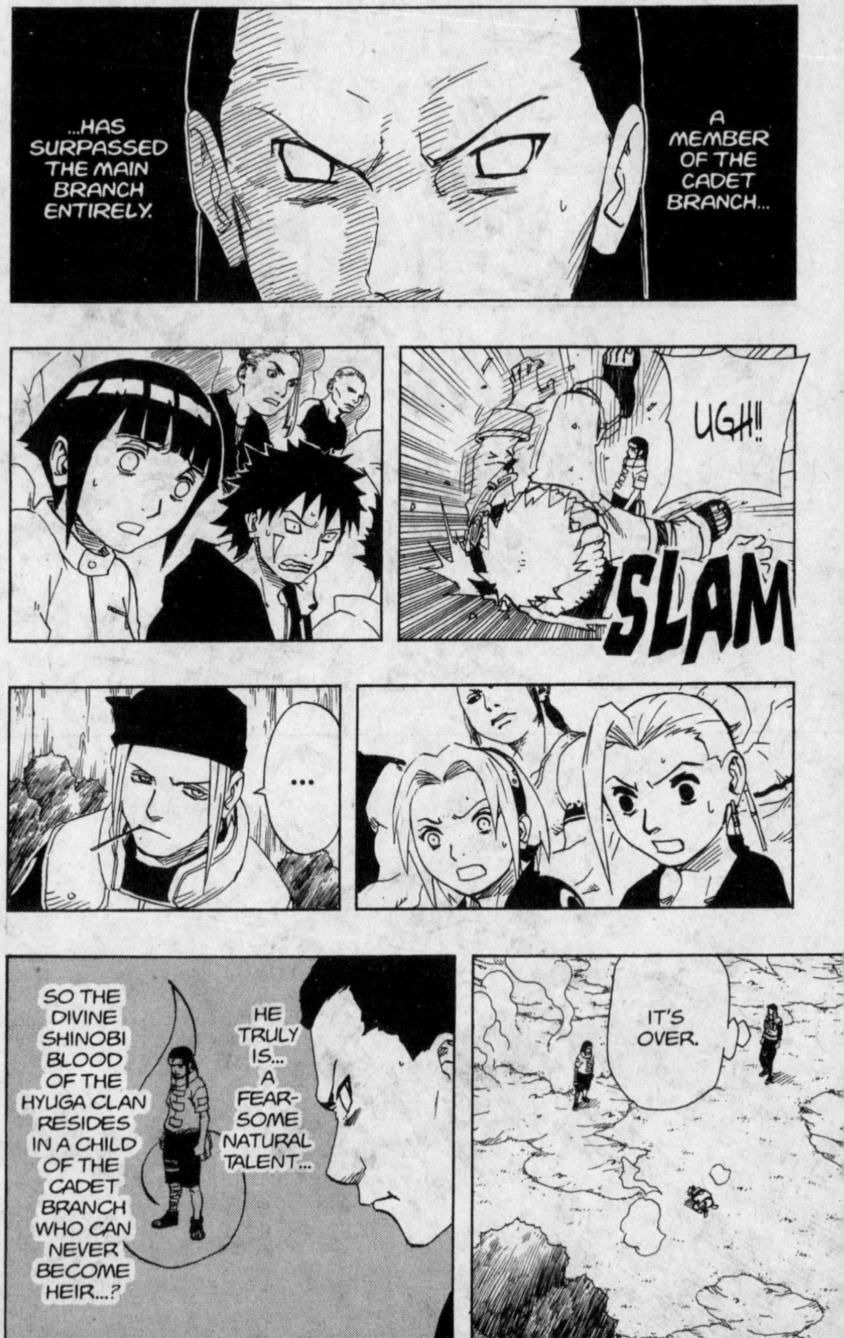
A MEMBER OF THE CADET BRANCH...
...HAS SURPASSED THE MAIN BRANCH ENTIRELY.
UGH!!
SLAM
...
IT'S OVER.
HE TRULY IS... A FEARSOME NATURAL TALENT...
SO THE DIVINE SHINOBI BLOOD OF THE HYUGA CLAN RESIDES IN A CHILD OF THE CADET BRANCH WHO CAN NEVER BECOME HEIR...?

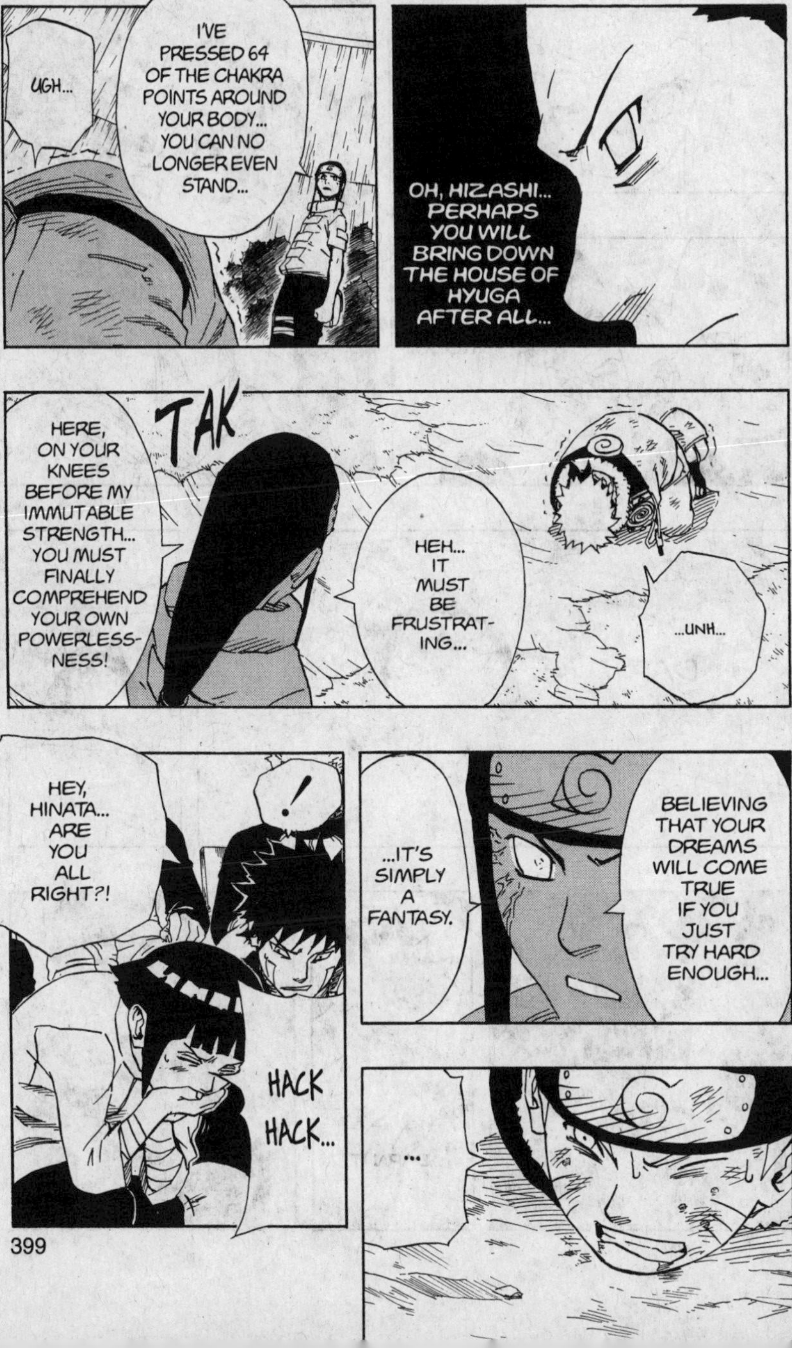
OH, HIZASHI... PERHAPS YOU WILL BRING DOWN THE HOUSE OF HYUGA AFTER ALL...
I'VE PRESSED 64 OF THE CHAKRA POINTS AROUND YOUR BODY... YOU CAN NO LONGER EVEN STAND...
UGH...
...UNH...
HEH... IT MUST BE FRUSTRATING...
TAK
HERE, ON YOUR KNEES BEFORE MY IMMUTABLE STRENGTH... YOU MUST FINALLY COMPREHEND YOUR OWN POWERLESSNESS!
BELIEVING THAT YOUR DREAMS WILL COME TRUE IF YOU JUST TRY HARD ENOUGH...
...IT'S SIMPLY A FANTASY.
...
!
HEY, HINATA... ARE YOU ALL RIGHT?!
HACK
HACK...

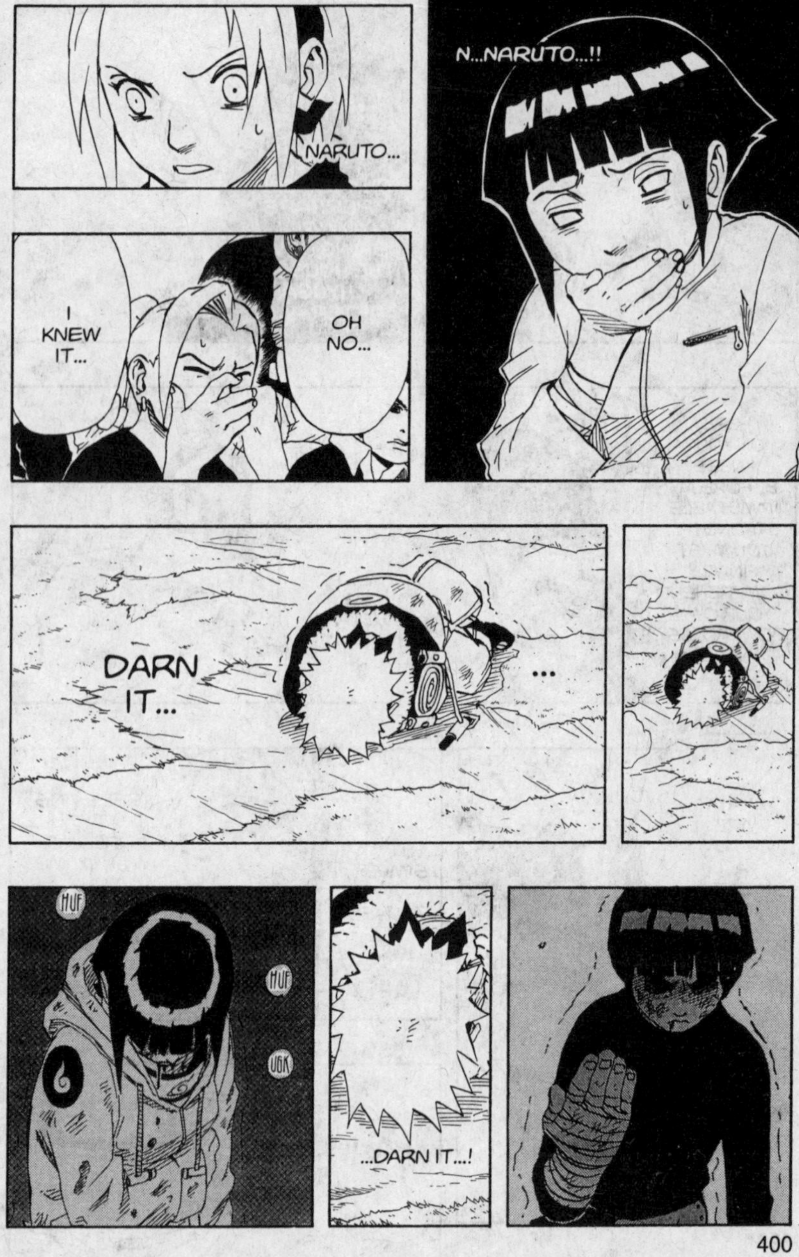
N...NARUTO...!!
NARUTO...
OH NO...
I KNEW IT...
...
DARN IT...
...DARN IT...!
HUF
HUF
UGK

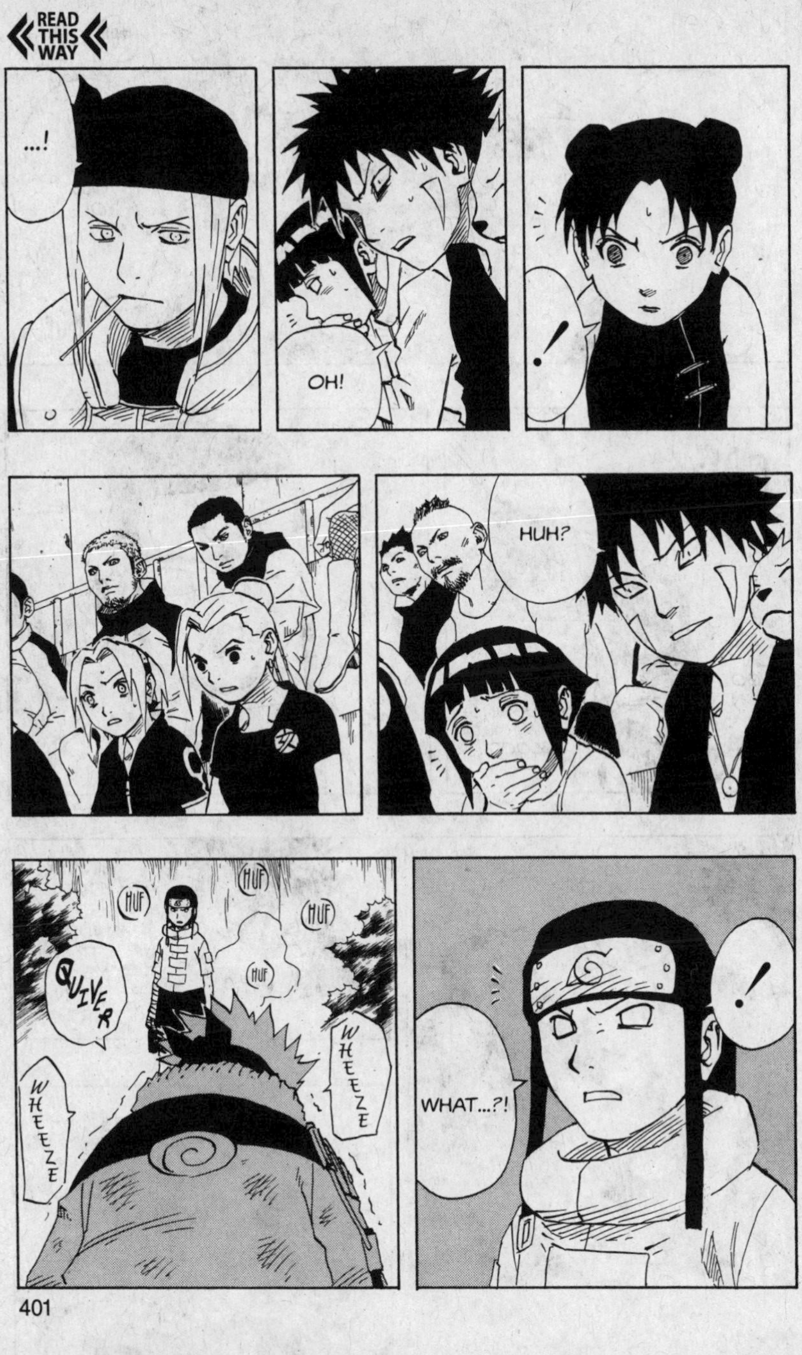
READ THIS WAY
!
OH!
...!
HUH?
!
WHAT...?!
HUF
HUF
HUF
HUF
WHEEZE
QUIVER
WHEEZE

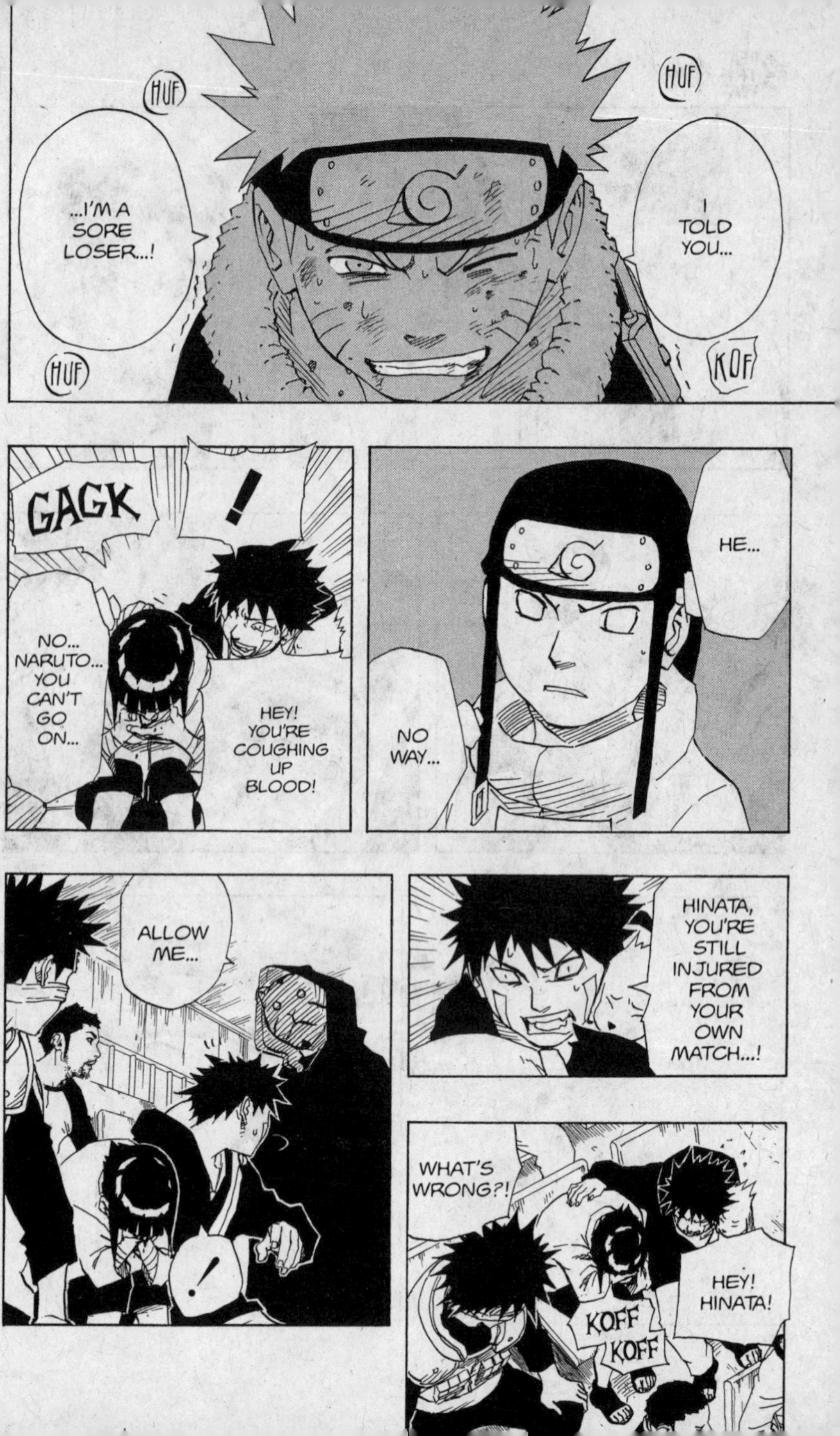
HUF
I TOLD YOU...
KOF
HUF
...I'M A SORE LOSER...!
HUF
HE...
NO WAY...
!
GAGK
HEY! YOU'RE COUGHING UP BLOOD!
NO... NARUTO... YOU CAN'T GO ON...
HINATA, YOU'RE STILL INJURED FROM YOUR OWN MATCH...!
HEY! HINATA!
WHAT'S WRONG?!
KOFF KOFF
ALLOW ME...
!

READ THIS WAY

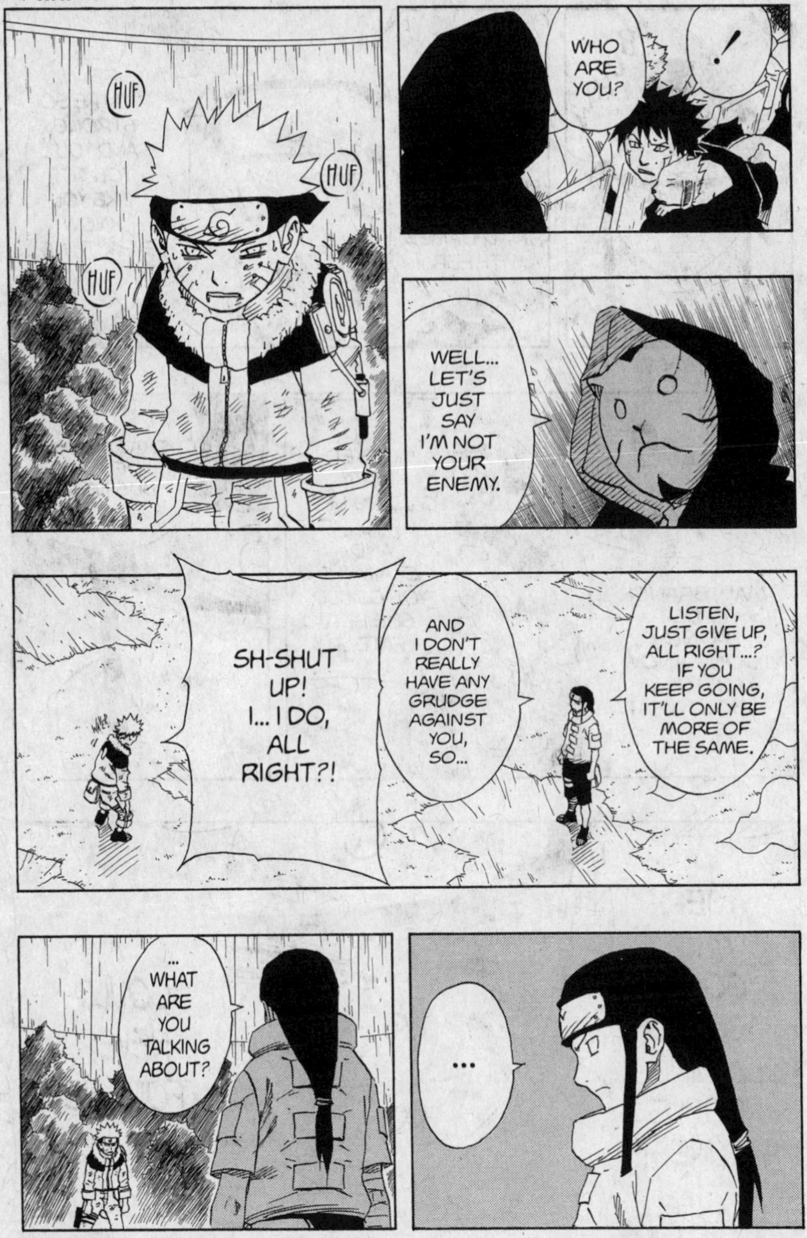
!
WHO ARE YOU?
WELL... LET'S JUST SAY I'M NOT YOUR ENEMY.
HUF
HUF
HUF
LISTEN, JUST GIVE UP, ALL RIGHT...? IF YOU KEEP GOING, IT'LL ONLY BE MORE OF THE SAME.
AND I DON'T REALLY HAVE ANY GRUDGE AGAINST YOU, SO...
SH-SHUT UP! I... I DO, ALL RIGHT?!
...
... WHAT ARE YOU TALKING ABOUT?

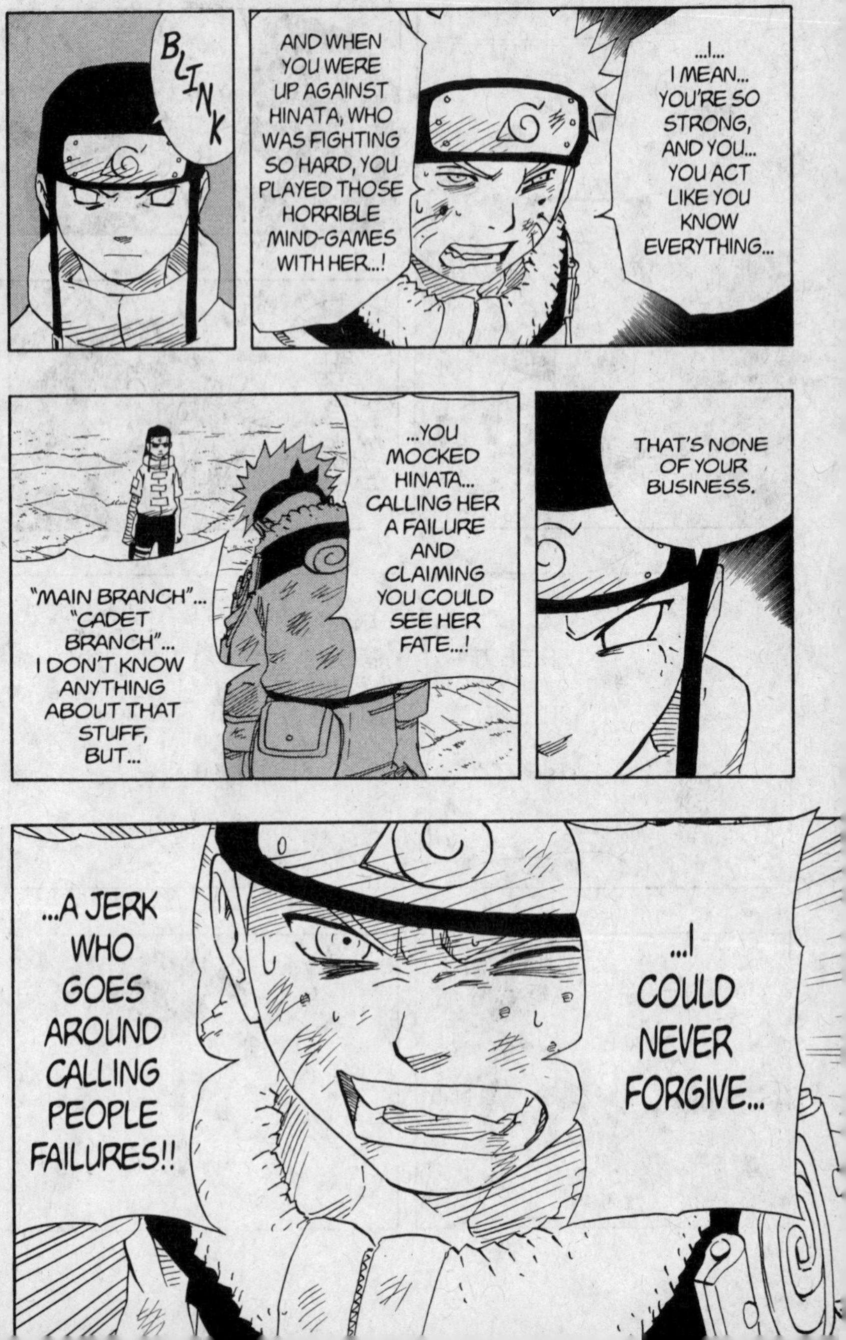
...I... I MEAN... YOU'RE SO STRONG, AND YOU... YOU ACT LIKE YOU KNOW EVERYTHING...
AND WHEN YOU WERE UP AGAINST HINATA, WHO WAS FIGHTING SO HARD, YOU PLAYED THOSE HORRIBLE MIND-GAMES WITH HER...!
BLINK
THAT'S NONE OF YOUR BUSINESS.
...YOU MOCKED HINATA... CALLING HER A FAILURE AND CLAIMING YOU COULD SEE HER FATE...!
"MAIN BRANCH"... "CADET BRANCH"... I DON'T KNOW ANYTHING ABOUT THAT STUFF, BUT...
...I COULD NEVER FORGIVE...
...A JERK WHO GOES AROUND CALLING PEOPLE FAILURES!!

READ THIS WAY

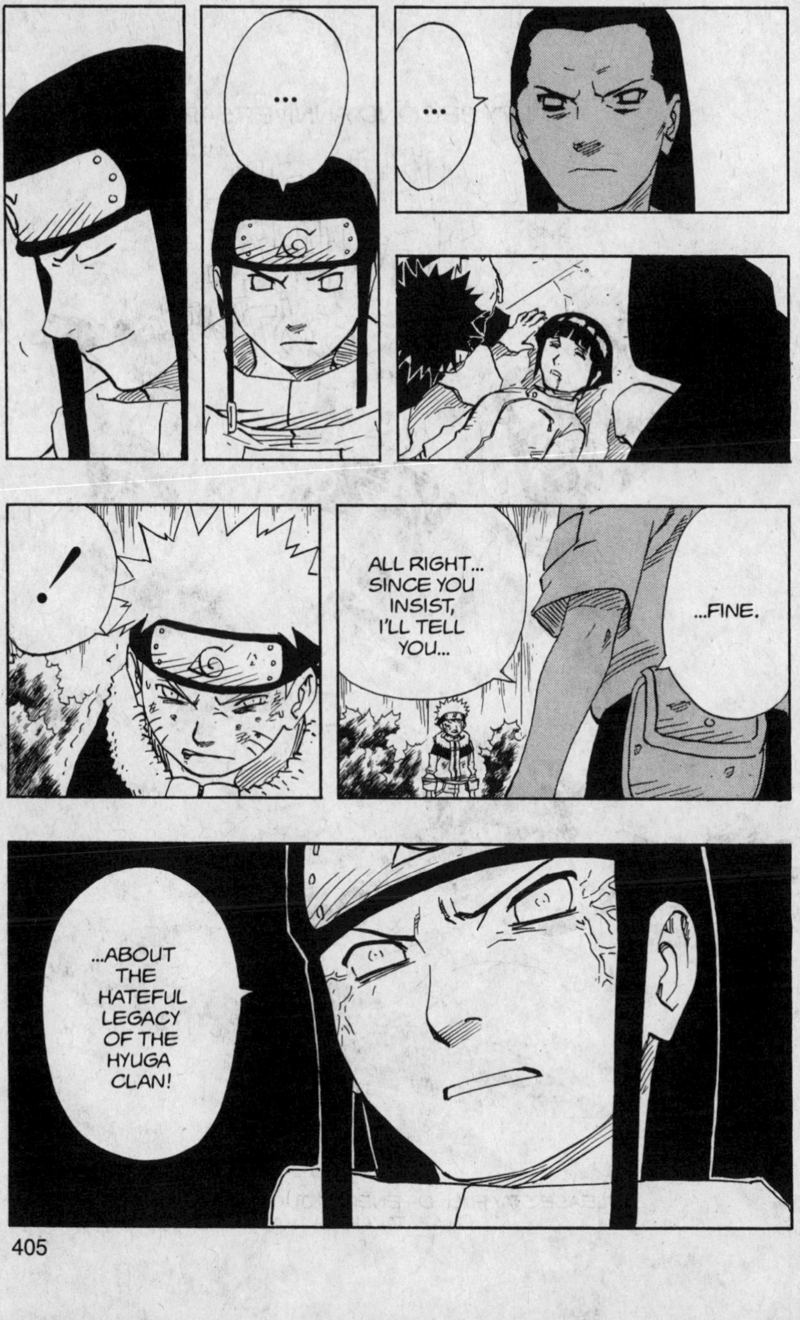
...
...
...FINE.
ALL RIGHT... SINCE YOU INSIST, I'LL TELL YOU...
!
...ABOUT THE HATEFUL LEGACY OF THE HYUGA CLAN!

HAPPY SECOND ANNIVERSARY!!

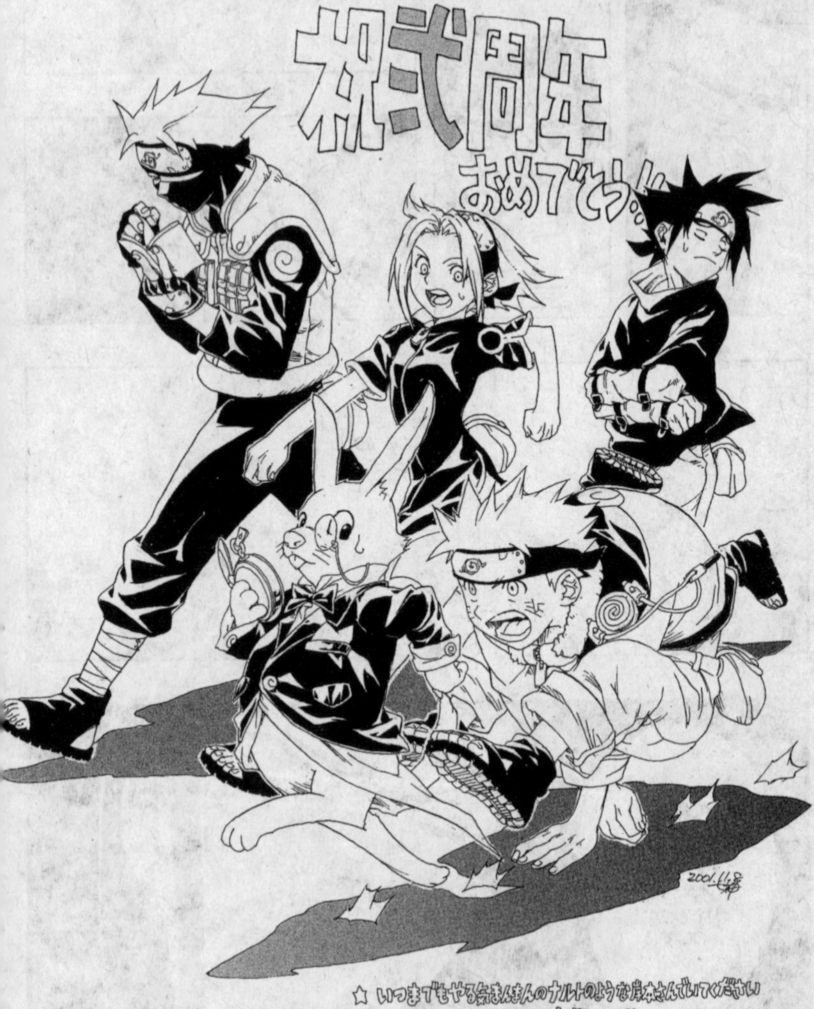
祝弐周年
おめでとう!!
2001.11.8

☆ いつまでもやる気まんまんのナルトのような岸本さんでいてください
高橋 一浩

PLEASE STAY FULL OF ENERGY, JUST LIKE NARUTO, FOREVER!
TAKAHASHI KAZUHIRO

Number 102: The Caged Bird...!!

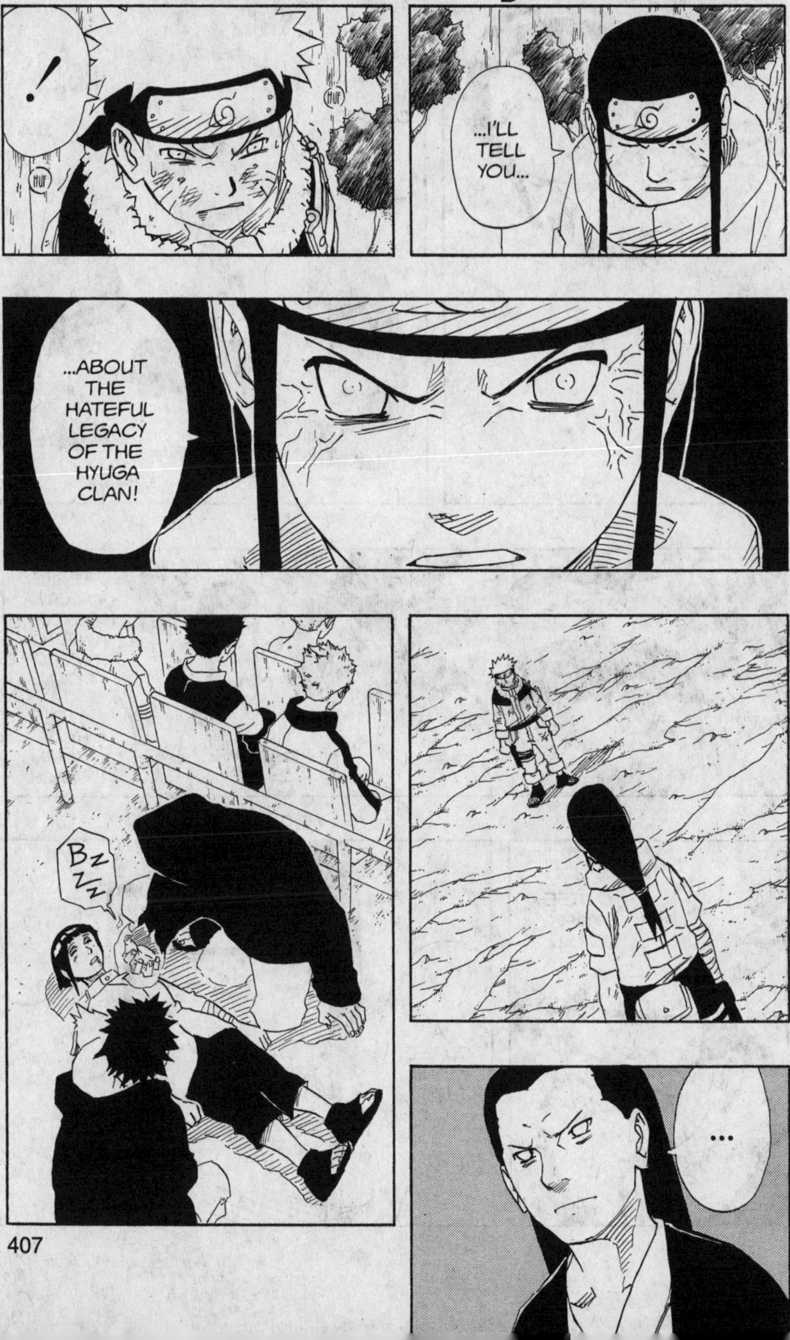

...I'LL TELL YOU...
!
HUF
HUF
...ABOUT THE HATEFUL LEGACY OF THE HYUGA CLAN!
...
BZZZ

...

RELAX, I'M A DOCTOR...

HEY...!

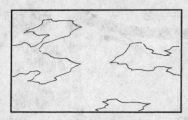

THERE'S A SECRET BIRTHRIGHT NINJUTSU PASSED DOWN...

...IN THE HYUGA MAIN BRANCH.

(HUF)   (HUF)

A CURSE MARK JUTSU...?

(HUF)

...A CURSE MARK JUTSU.

IT'S...

READ THIS WAY

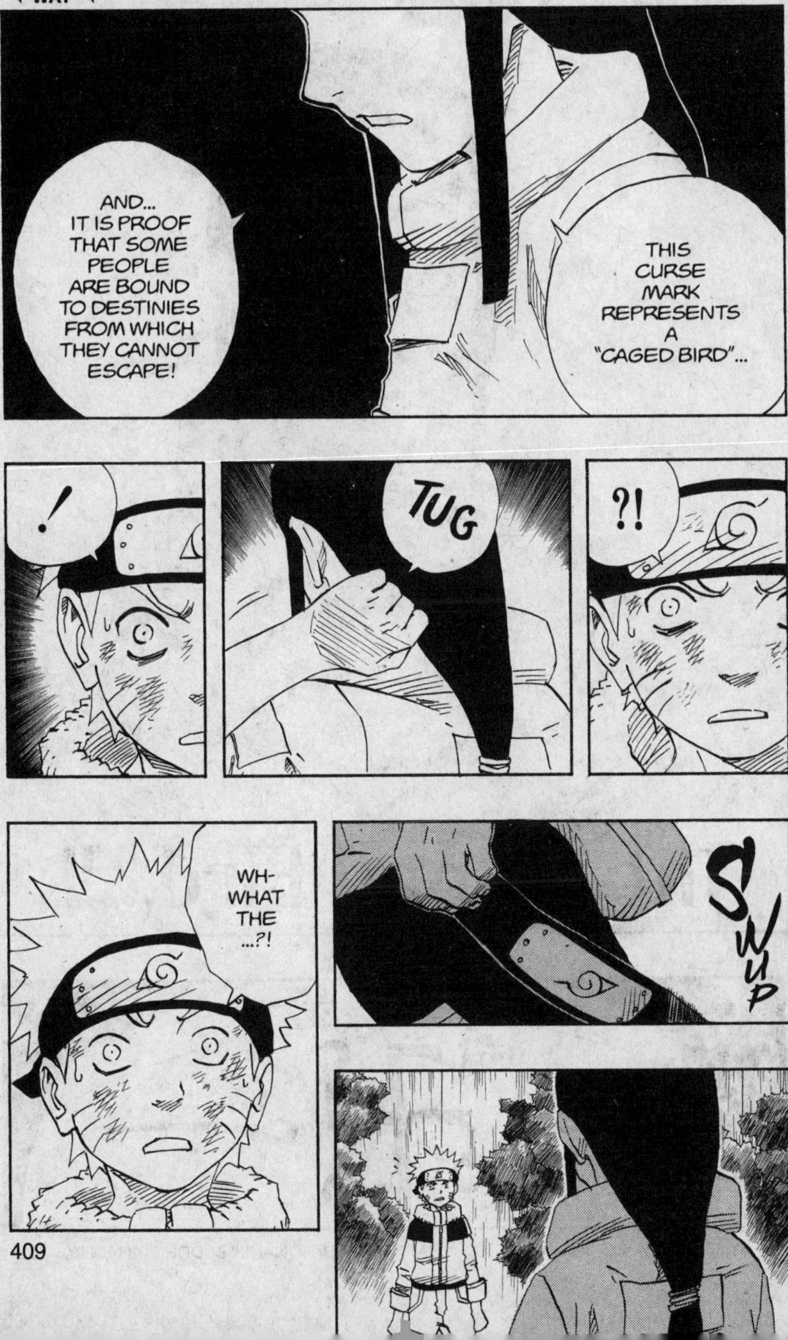
THIS CURSE MARK REPRESENTS A "CAGED BIRD"...
AND... IT IS PROOF THAT SOME PEOPLE ARE BOUND TO DESTINIES FROM WHICH THEY CANNOT ESCAPE!
?!
TUG
!
SWUP
WH- WHAT THE ...?!

Number 102: The Caged Bird...!!

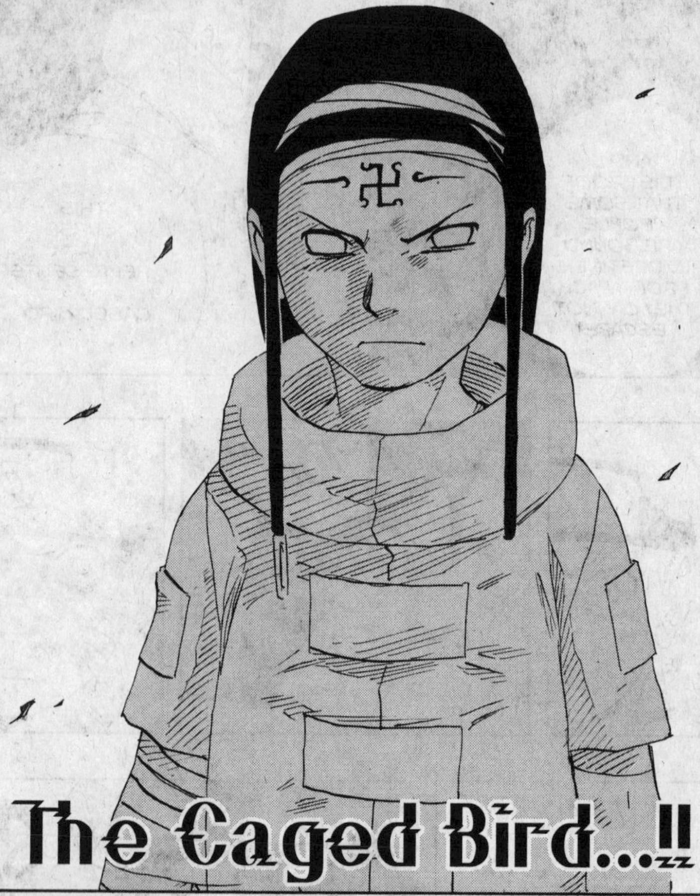

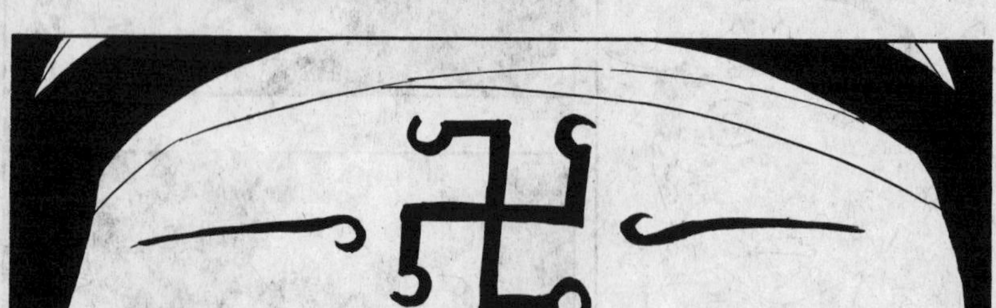

THE SYMBOL PICTURED ABOVE, CALLED A MANJI, IS TRADITIONAL IN BUDDHIST IMAGERY. --ED.

READ THIS WAY

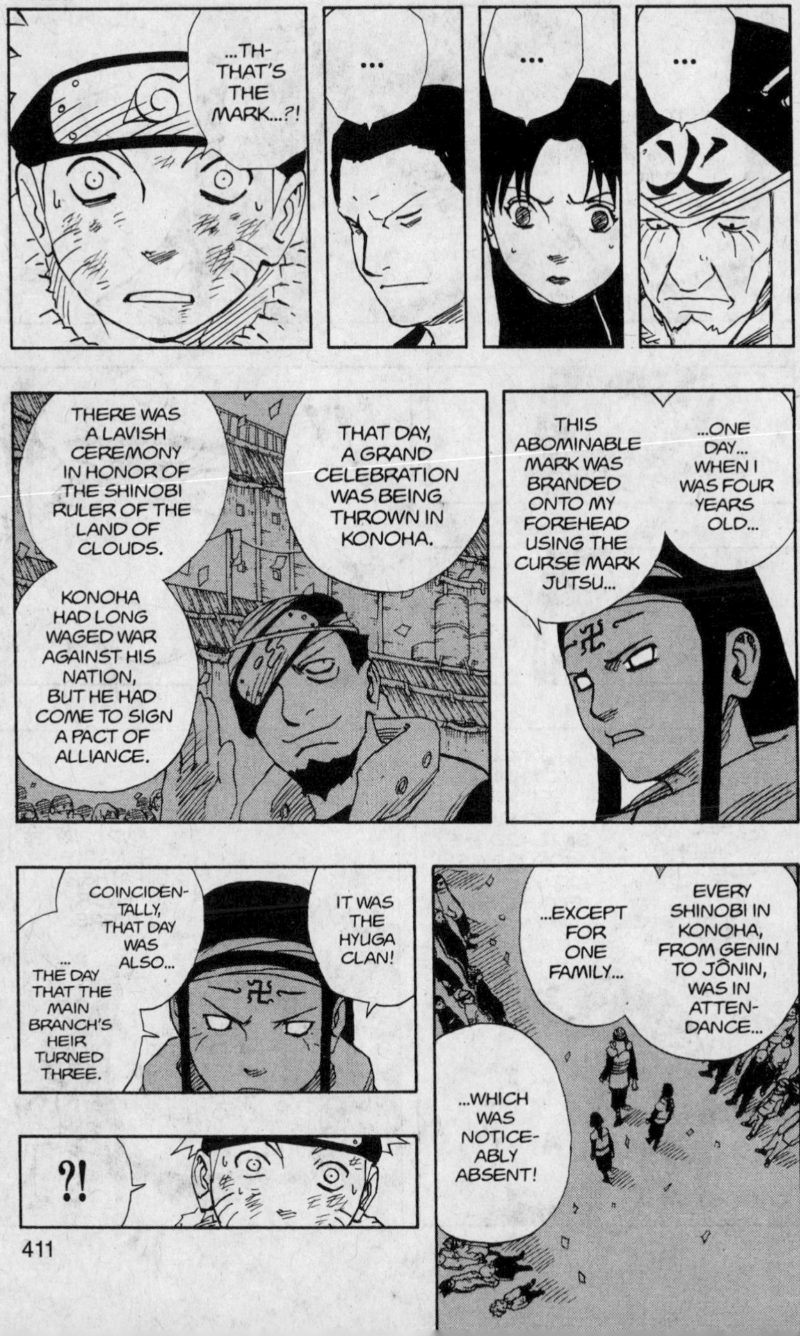
...
...
...
...TH-THAT'S THE MARK...?!
...ONE DAY... WHEN I WAS FOUR YEARS OLD...
THIS ABOMINABLE MARK WAS BRANDED ONTO MY FOREHEAD USING THE CURSE MARK JUTSU...
THAT DAY, A GRAND CELEBRATION WAS BEING THROWN IN KONOHA.
THERE WAS A LAVISH CEREMONY IN HONOR OF THE SHINOBI RULER OF THE LAND OF CLOUDS.
KONOHA HAD LONG WAGED WAR AGAINST HIS NATION, BUT HE HAD COME TO SIGN A PACT OF ALLIANCE.
EVERY SHINOBI IN KONOHA, FROM GENIN TO JÔNIN, WAS IN ATTENDANCE...
...EXCEPT FOR ONE FAMILY...
...WHICH WAS NOTICEABLY ABSENT!
IT WAS THE HYUGA CLAN!
COINCIDENTALLY, THAT DAY WAS ALSO...
...THE DAY THAT THE MAIN BRANCH'S HEIR TURNED THREE.
?!

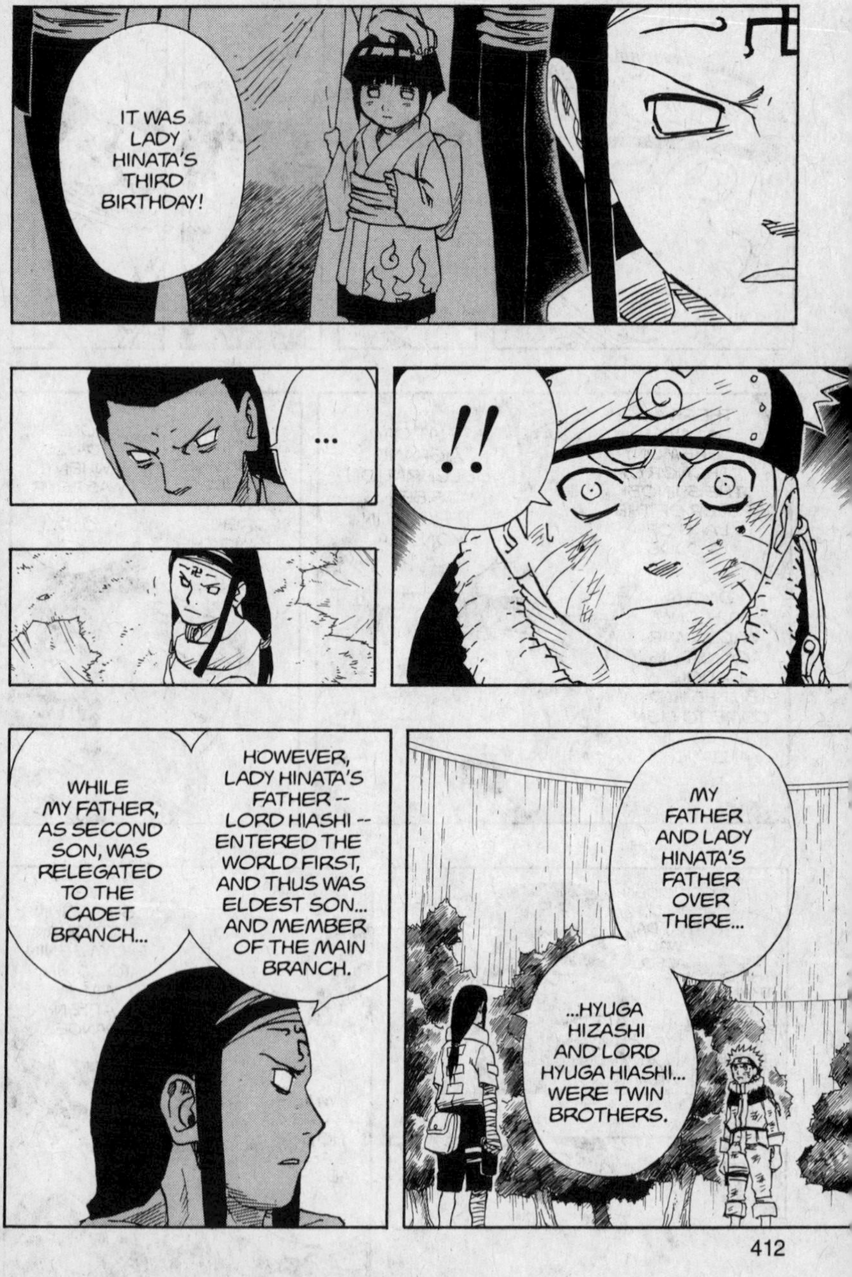
IT WAS LADY HINATA'S THIRD BIRTHDAY!
!!
...
MY FATHER AND LADY HINATA'S FATHER OVER THERE...
...HYUGA HIZASHI AND LORD HYUGA HIASHI... WERE TWIN BROTHERS.
WHILE MY FATHER, AS SECOND SON, WAS RELEGATED TO THE CADET BRANCH...
HOWEVER, LADY HINATA'S FATHER -- LORD HIASHI -- ENTERED THE WORLD FIRST, AND THUS WAS ELDEST SON... AND MEMBER OF THE MAIN BRANCH.

READ THIS WAY

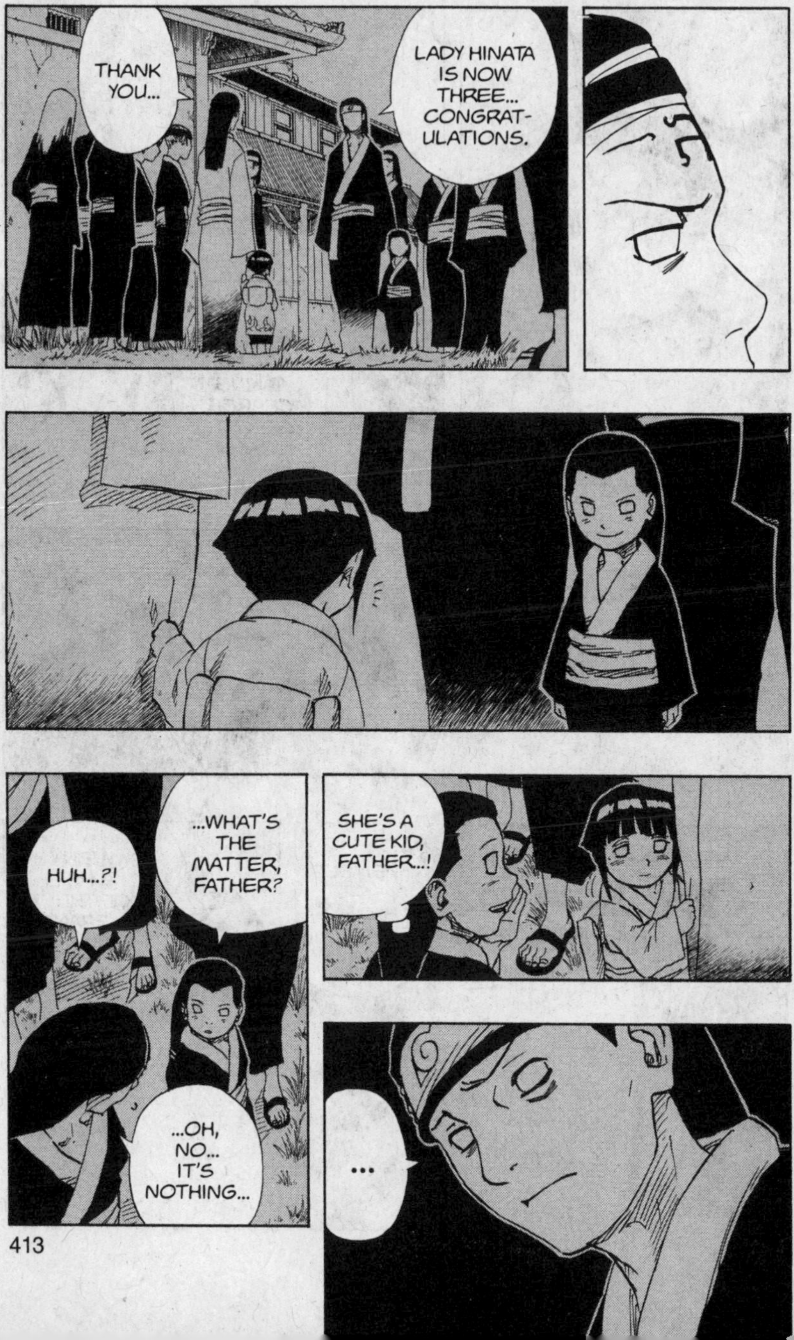

LADY HINATA IS NOW THREE... CONGRAT-ULATIONS.
THANK YOU...
SHE'S A CUTE KID, FATHER...!
...
...WHAT'S THE MATTER, FATHER?
HUH...?!
...OH, NO... IT'S NOTHING...

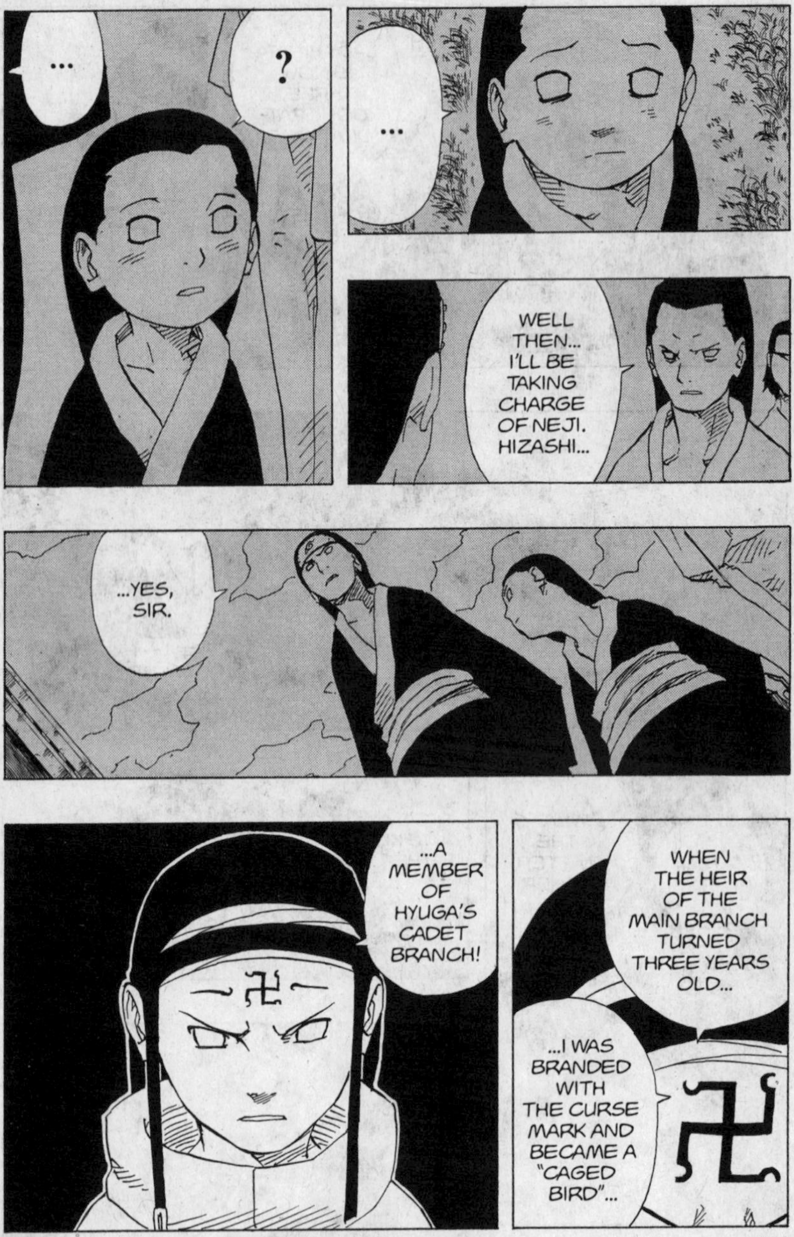
...
WELL THEN... I'LL BE TAKING CHARGE OF NEJI. HIZASHI...
?
...
...YES, SIR.
WHEN THE HEIR OF THE MAIN BRANCH TURNED THREE YEARS OLD...
...I WAS BRANDED WITH THE CURSE MARK AND BECAME A "CAGED BIRD"...
...A MEMBER OF HYUGA'S CADET BRANCH!

READ THIS WAY

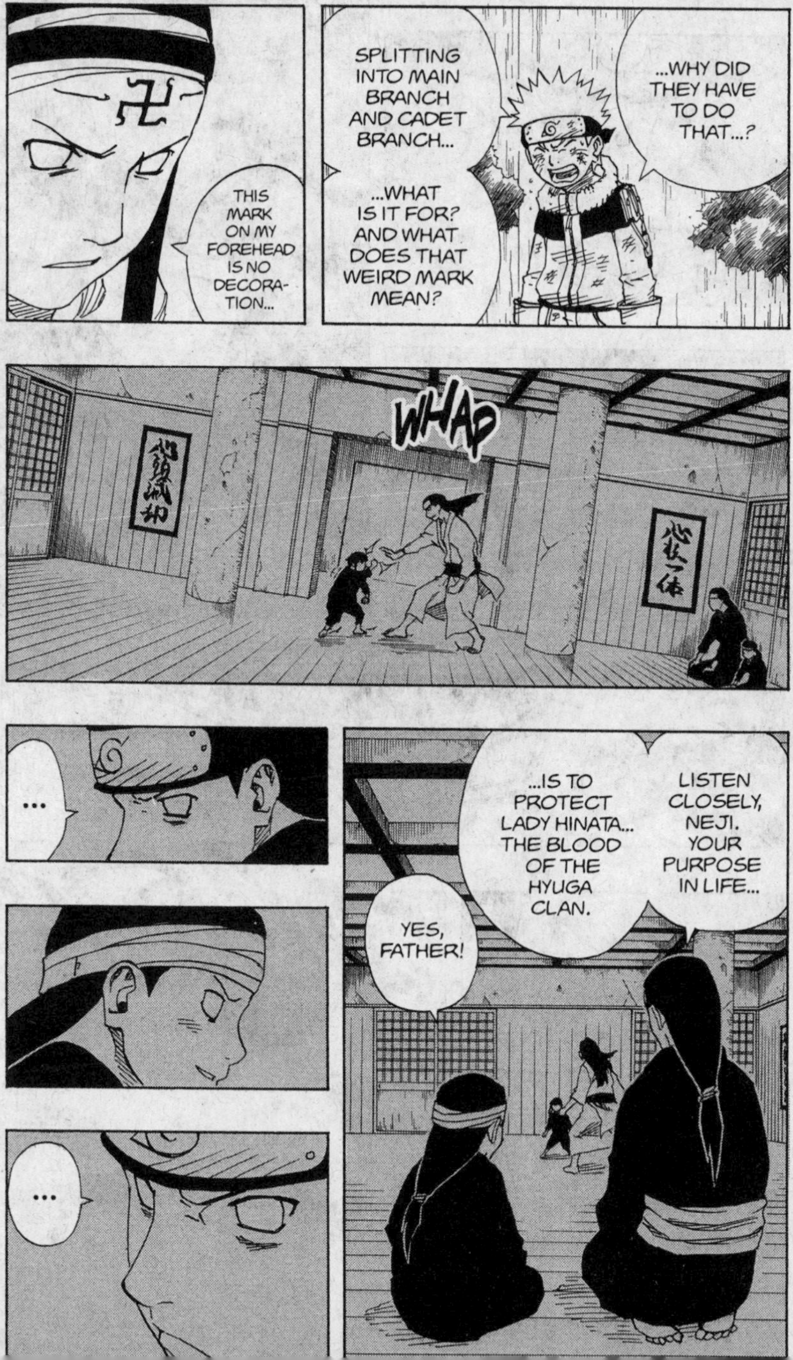
...WHY DID THEY HAVE TO DO THAT...?
SPLITTING INTO MAIN BRANCH AND CADET BRANCH...
...WHAT IS IT FOR? AND WHAT DOES THAT WEIRD MARK MEAN?
THIS MARK ON MY FOREHEAD IS NO DECORA-TION...
WHAP
LISTEN CLOSELY, NEJI. YOUR PURPOSE IN LIFE...
...IS TO PROTECT LADY HINATA... THE BLOOD OF THE HYUGA CLAN.
YES, FATHER!
...
...

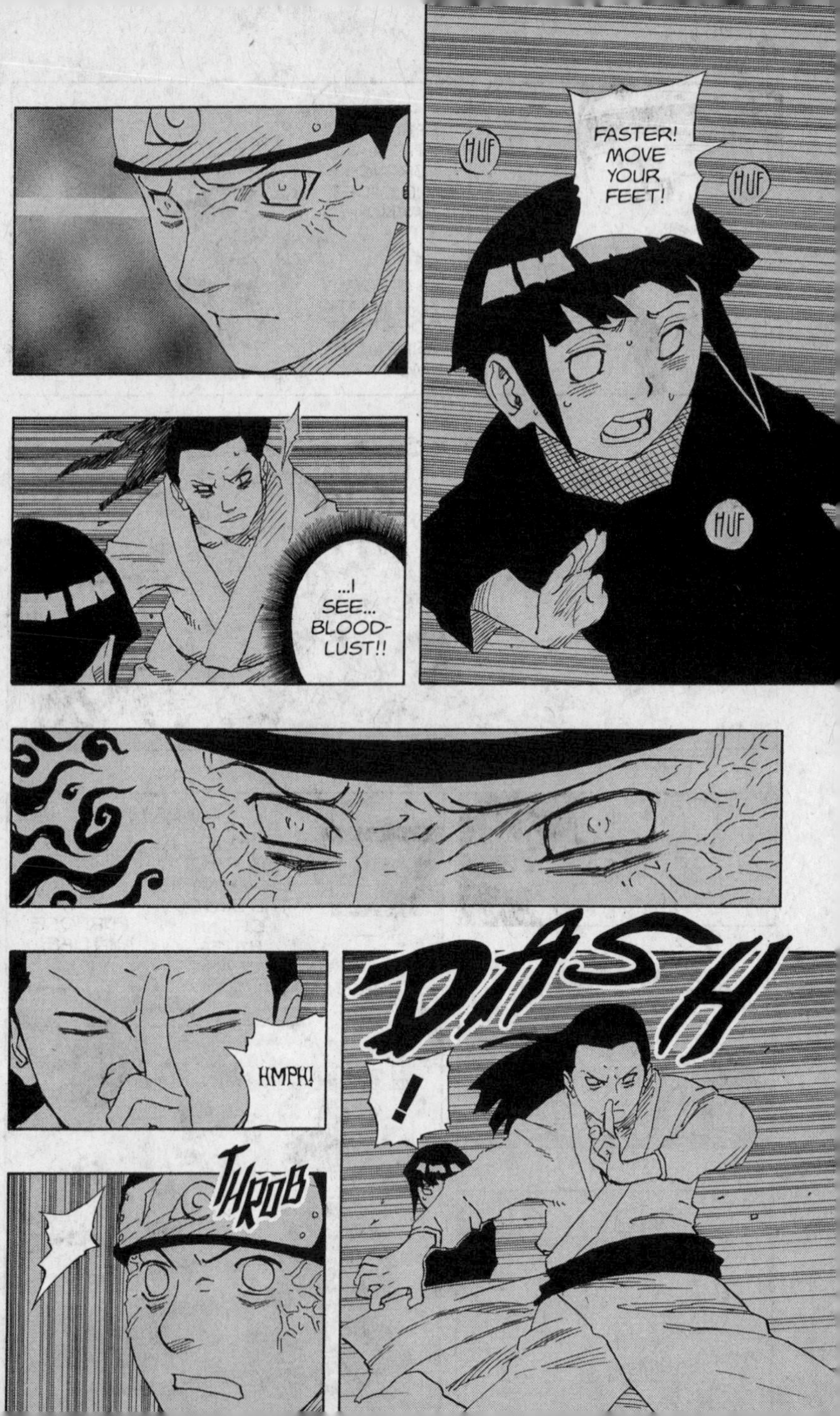
HUF
FASTER! MOVE YOUR FEET!
HUF
HUF
...I SEE... BLOOD-LUST!!
DASH
!
HMPH!
THROB

FATHER! WHAT'S WRONG?!

AAARGH!

!!

GAAH!

FWUMP

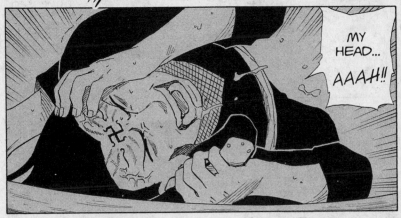

MY HEAD... AAAH!!

I WILL NOT TOLERATE THIS FOOLISH- NESS A SECOND TIME...

GO HOME NOW.

UGH... UNH...

FATHER!!

417

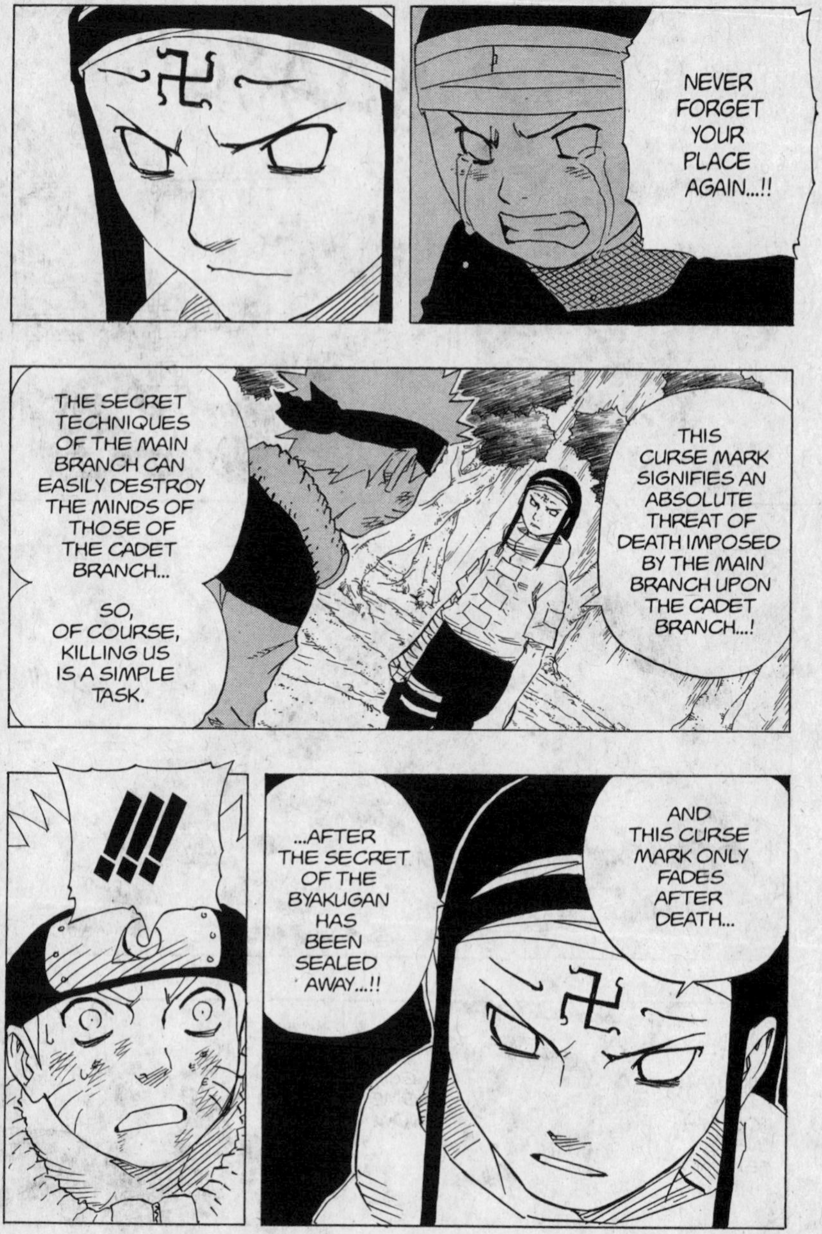
NEVER FORGET YOUR PLACE AGAIN...!!
THIS CURSE MARK SIGNIFIES AN ABSOLUTE THREAT OF DEATH IMPOSED BY THE MAIN BRANCH UPON THE CADET BRANCH...!
THE SECRET TECHNIQUES OF THE MAIN BRANCH CAN EASILY DESTROY THE MINDS OF THOSE OF THE CADET BRANCH...
SO, OF COURSE, KILLING US IS A SIMPLE TASK.
AND THIS CURSE MARK ONLY FADES AFTER DEATH...
...AFTER THE SECRET OF THE BYAKUGAN HAS BEEN SEALED AWAY...!!
!!!

READ THIS WAY

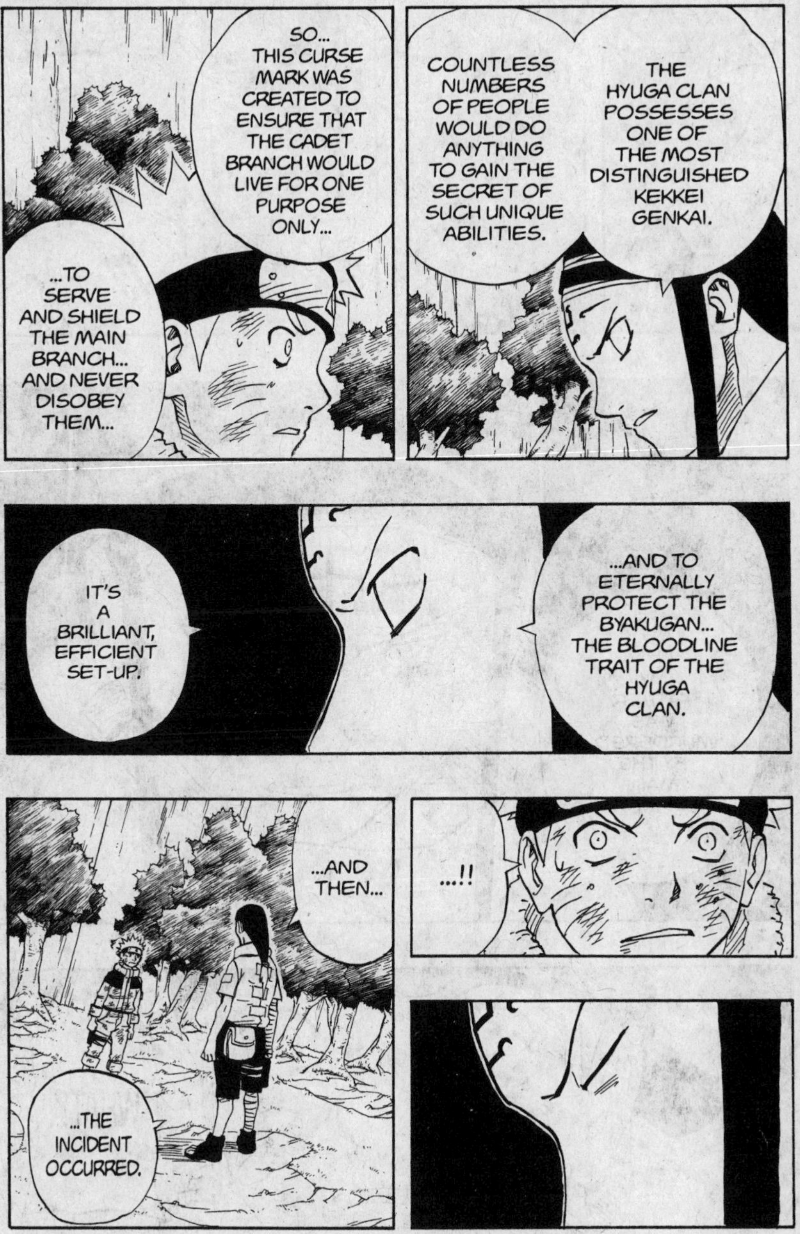
THE HYUGA CLAN POSSESSES ONE OF THE MOST DISTINGUISHED KEKKEI GENKAI.
COUNTLESS NUMBERS OF PEOPLE WOULD DO ANYTHING TO GAIN THE SECRET OF SUCH UNIQUE ABILITIES.
SO... THIS CURSE MARK WAS CREATED TO ENSURE THAT THE CADET BRANCH WOULD LIVE FOR ONE PURPOSE ONLY...
...TO SERVE AND SHIELD THE MAIN BRANCH... AND NEVER DISOBEY THEM...
...AND TO ETERNALLY PROTECT THE BYAKUGAN... THE BLOODLINE TRAIT OF THE HYUGA CLAN.
IT'S A BRILLIANT, EFFICIENT SET-UP.
...!!
...AND THEN...
...THE INCIDENT OCCURRED.

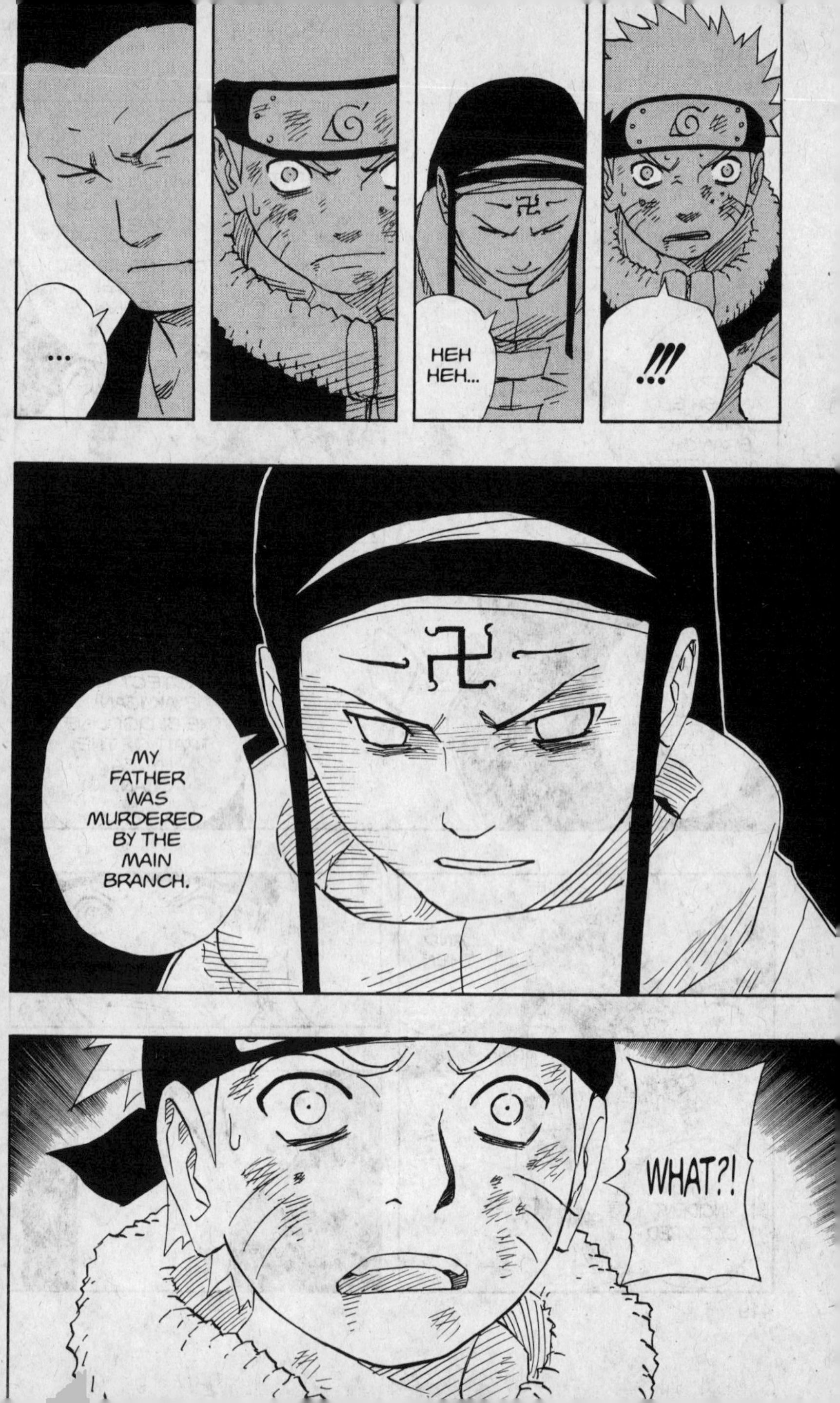
!!!
HEH HEH...
...
MY FATHER WAS MURDERED BY THE MAIN BRANCH.
WHAT?!

READ THIS WAY

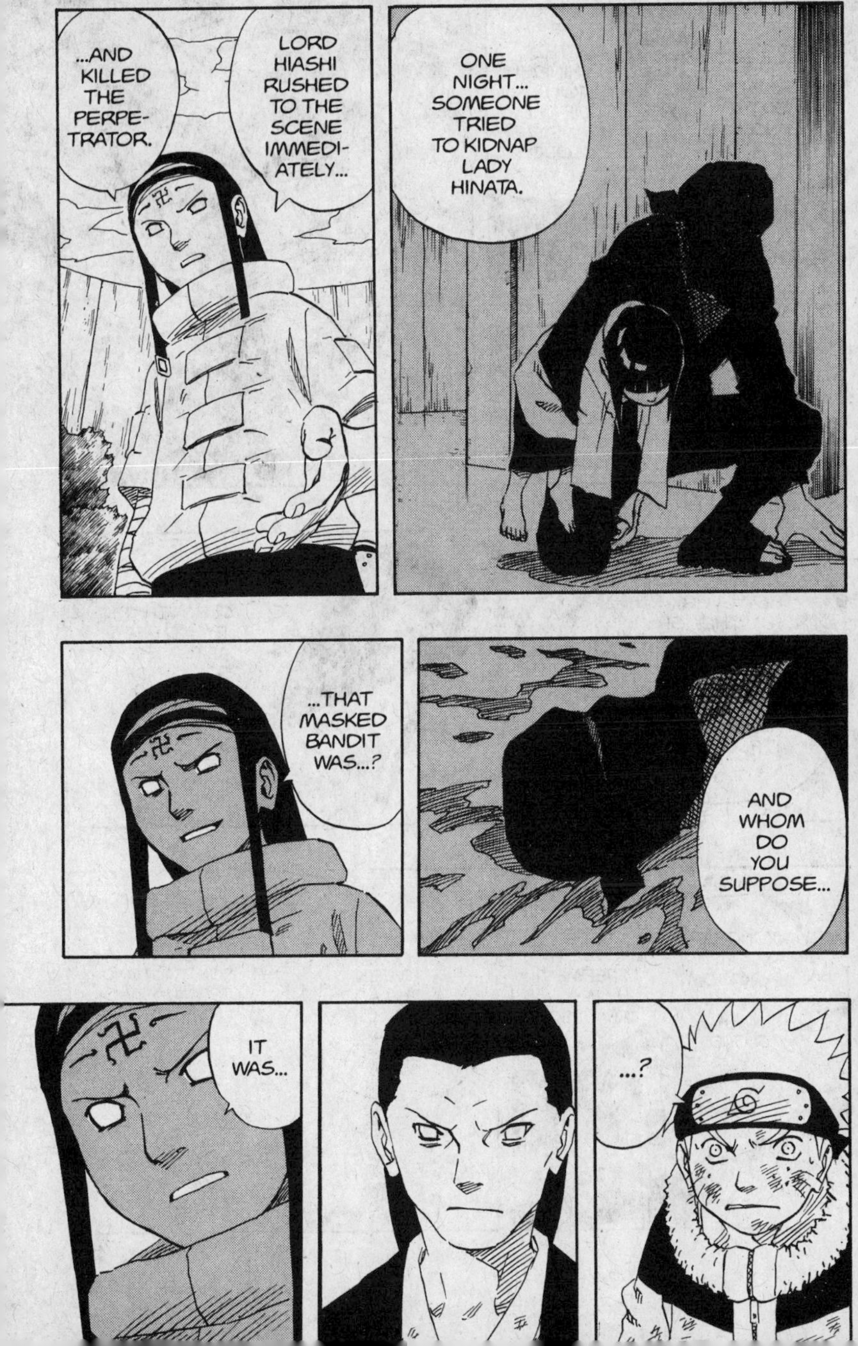
ONE NIGHT... SOMEONE TRIED TO KIDNAP LADY HINATA.
LORD HIASHI RUSHED TO THE SCENE IMMEDI-ATELY...
...AND KILLED THE PERPE-TRATOR.
AND WHOM DO YOU SUPPOSE...
...THAT MASKED BANDIT WAS...?
...?
IT WAS...

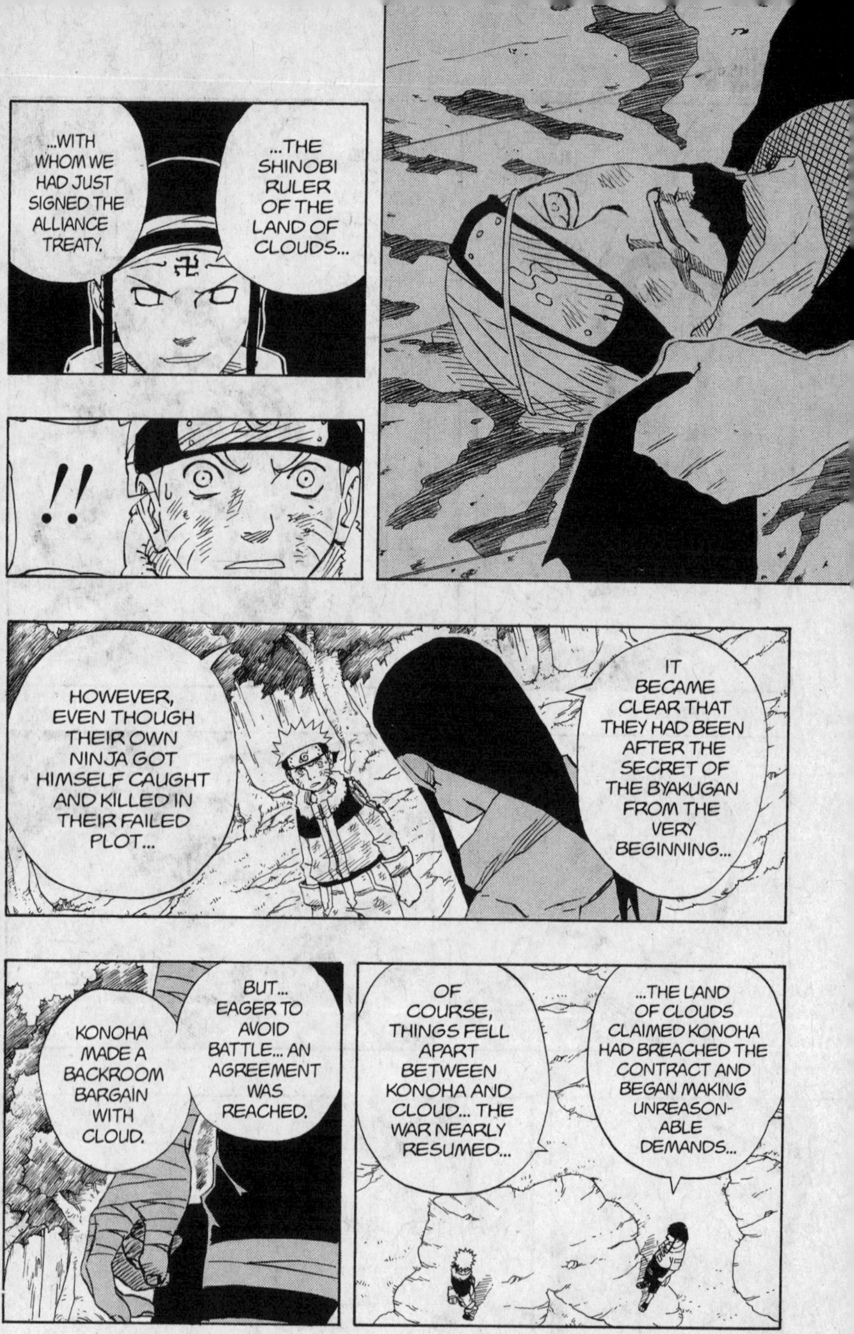
...THE SHINOBI RULER OF THE LAND OF CLOUDS...
...WITH WHOM WE HAD JUST SIGNED THE ALLIANCE TREATY.
!!
IT BECAME CLEAR THAT THEY HAD BEEN AFTER THE SECRET OF THE BYAKUGAN FROM THE VERY BEGINNING...
HOWEVER, EVEN THOUGH THEIR OWN NINJA GOT HIMSELF CAUGHT AND KILLED IN THEIR FAILED PLOT...
...THE LAND OF CLOUDS CLAIMED KONOHA HAD BREACHED THE CONTRACT AND BEGAN MAKING UNREASON-ABLE DEMANDS...
OF COURSE, THINGS FELL APART BETWEEN KONOHA AND CLOUD... THE WAR NEARLY RESUMED...
BUT... EAGER TO AVOID BATTLE... AN AGREEMENT WAS REACHED.
KONOHA MADE A BACKROOM BARGAIN WITH CLOUD.

READ THIS WAY

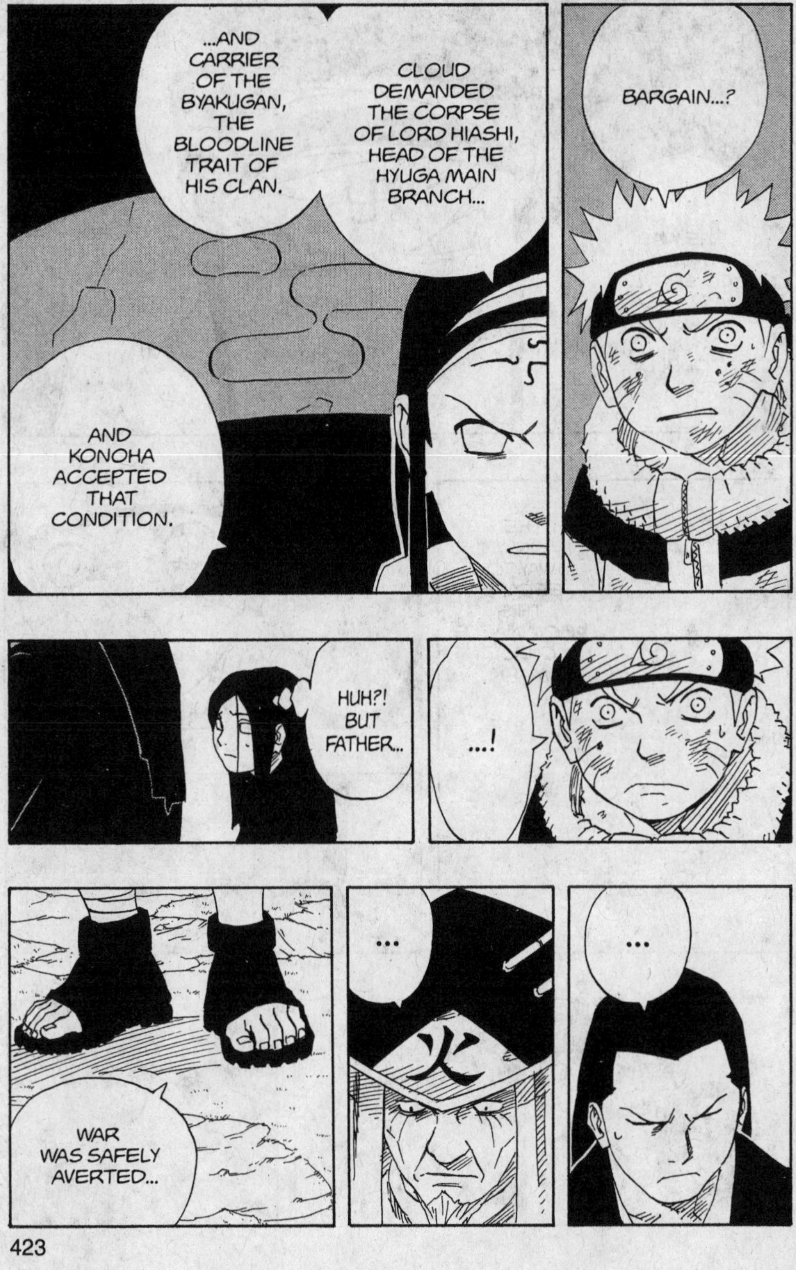
BARGAIN...?
CLOUD DEMANDED THE CORPSE OF LORD HIASHI, HEAD OF THE HYUGA MAIN BRANCH...
...AND CARRIER OF THE BYAKUGAN, THE BLOODLINE TRAIT OF HIS CLAN.
AND KONOHA ACCEPTED THAT CONDITION.
...!
HUH?! BUT FATHER...
...
...
WAR WAS SAFELY AVERTED...

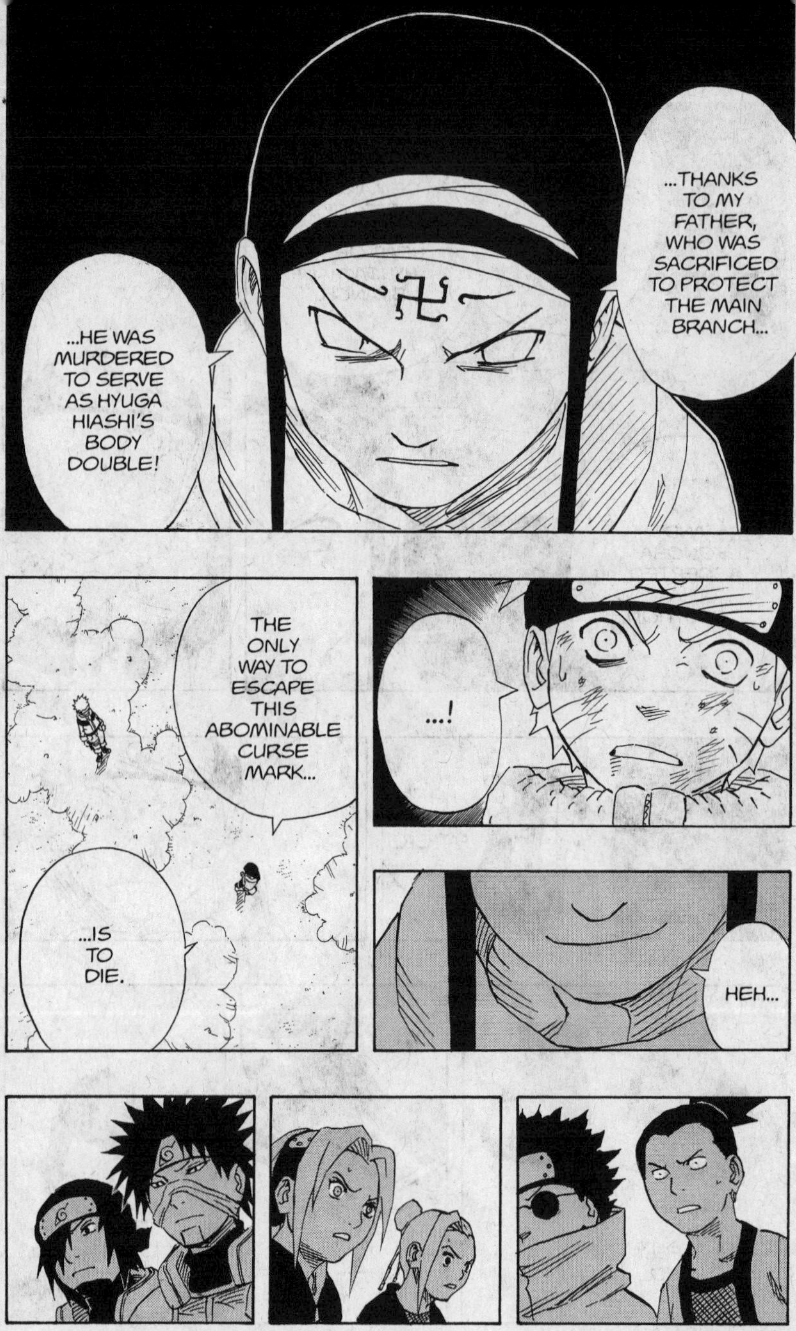
...THANKS TO MY FATHER, WHO WAS SACRIFICED TO PROTECT THE MAIN BRANCH...
...HE WAS MURDERED TO SERVE AS HYUGA HIASHI'S BODY DOUBLE!
...!
HEH...
THE ONLY WAY TO ESCAPE THIS ABOMINABLE CURSE MARK...
...IS TO DIE.

READ THIS WAY

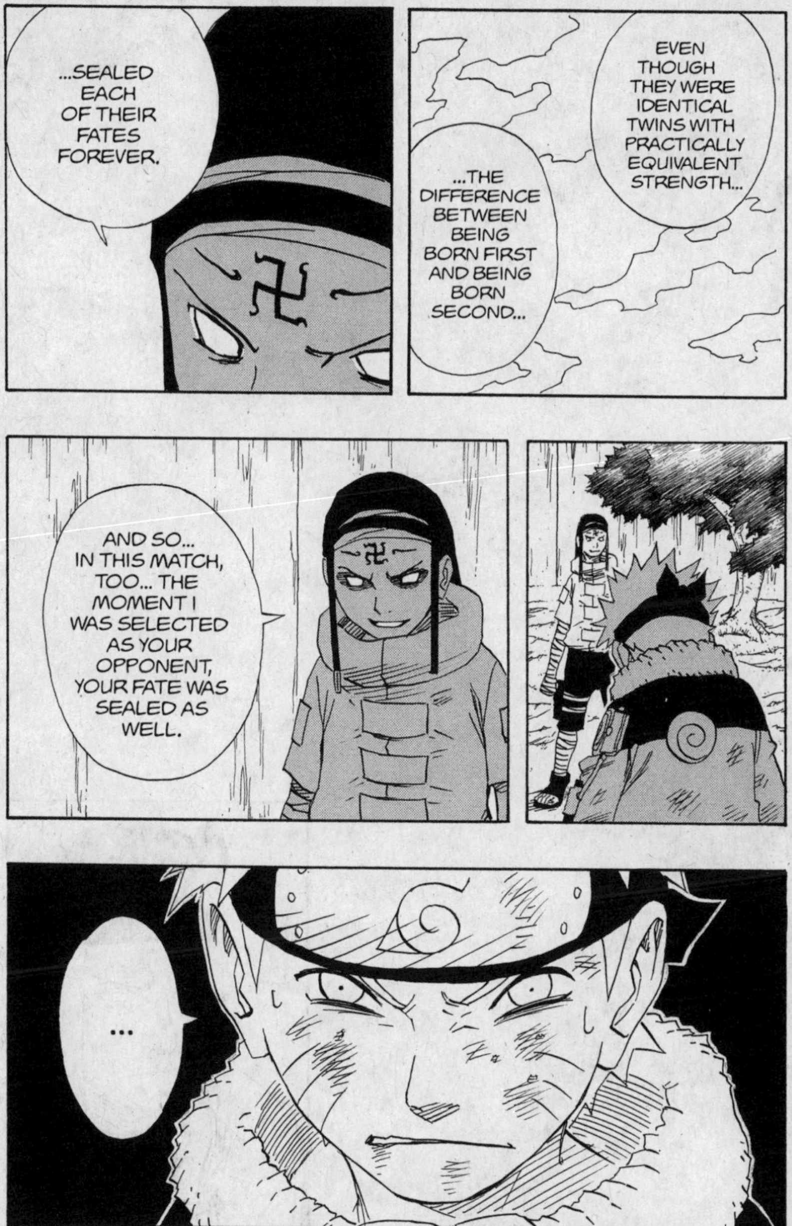

EVEN THOUGH THEY WERE IDENTICAL TWINS WITH PRACTICALLY EQUIVALENT STRENGTH...
...THE DIFFERENCE BETWEEN BEING BORN FIRST AND BEING BORN SECOND...
...SEALED EACH OF THEIR FATES FOREVER.
AND SO... IN THIS MATCH, TOO... THE MOMENT I WAS SELECTED AS YOUR OPPONENT, YOUR FATE WAS SEALED AS WELL.
...

Number 103: The Failure!!

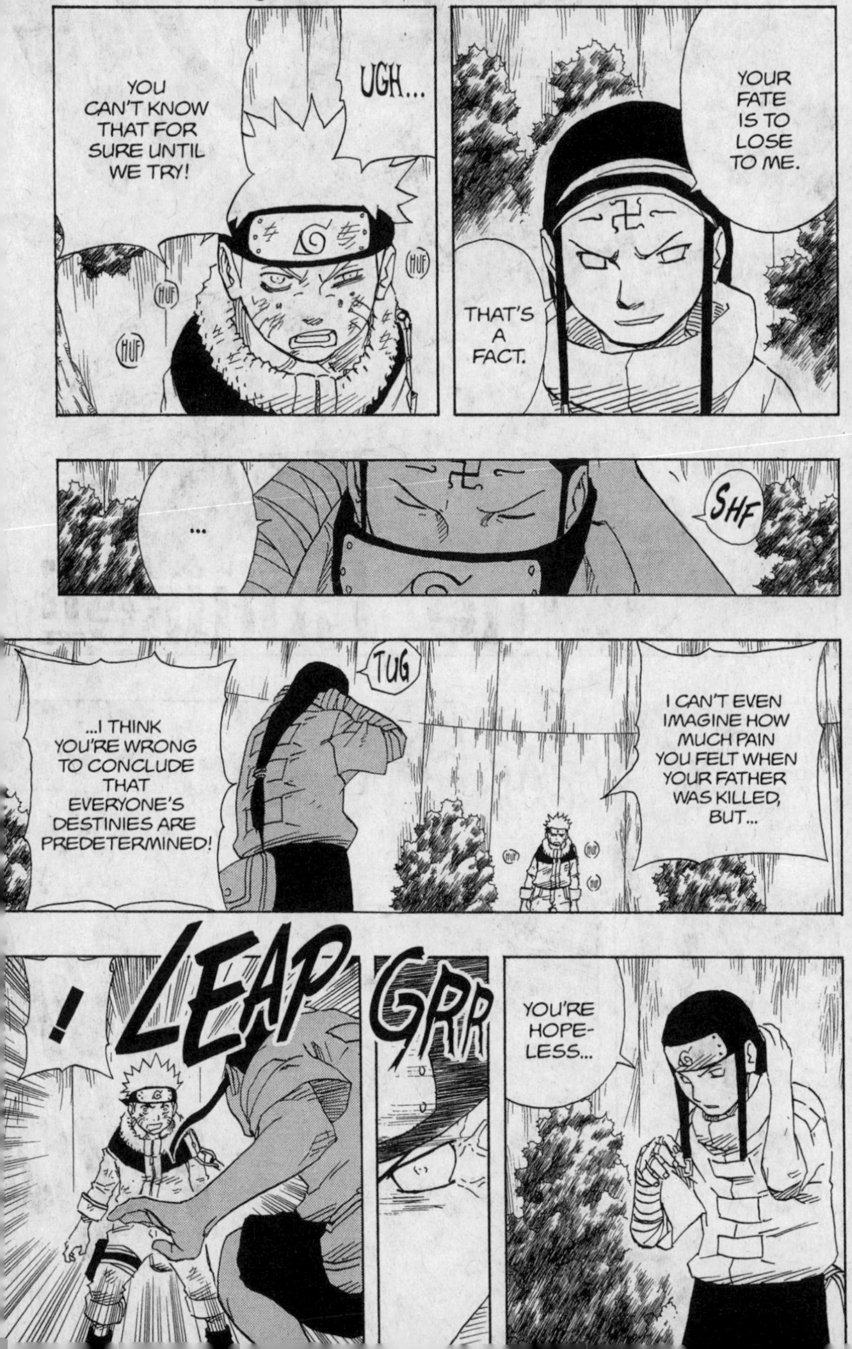
YOUR FATE IS TO LOSE TO ME.
THAT'S A FACT.
UGH...
YOU CAN'T KNOW THAT FOR SURE UNTIL WE TRY!
HUF
HUF
HUF
SHF
...
I CAN'T EVEN IMAGINE HOW MUCH PAIN YOU FELT WHEN YOUR FATHER WAS KILLED, BUT...
TUG
...I THINK YOU'RE WRONG TO CONCLUDE THAT EVERYONE'S DESTINIES ARE PREDETERMINED!
YOU'RE HOPE-LESS...
GRR
LEAP
!

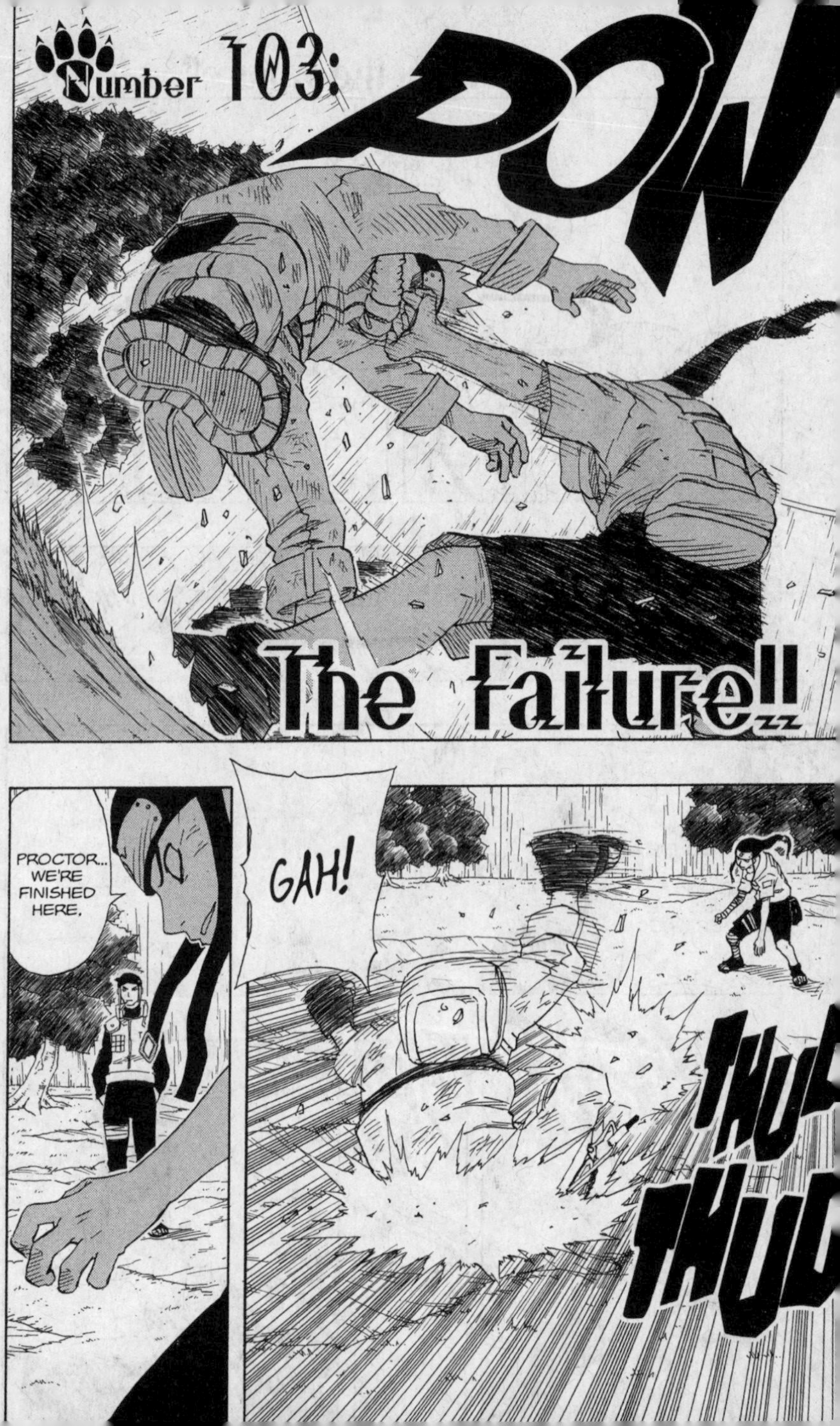
Number 103:
POW
The Failure!!
GAH!
PROCTOR... WE'RE FINISHED HERE.

READ THIS WAY

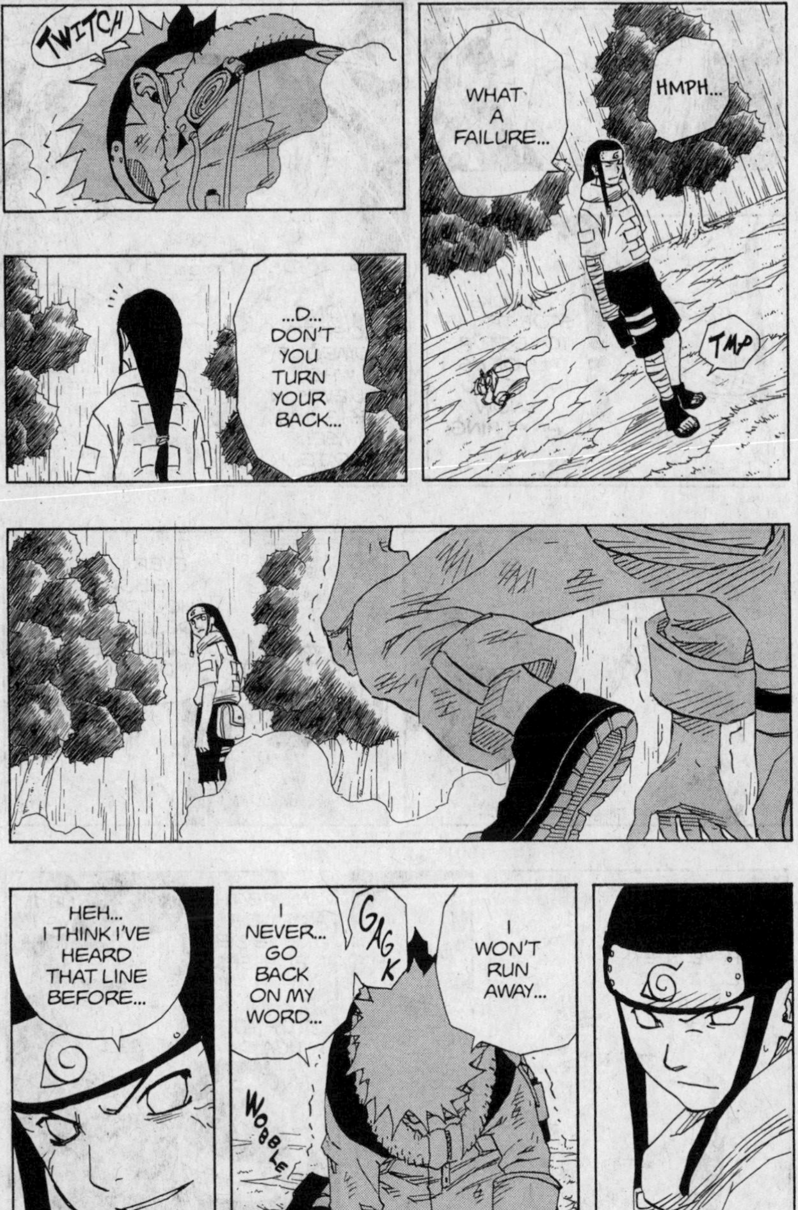
HMPH...
WHAT A FAILURE...
TMP
TWITCH
...D... DON'T YOU TURN YOUR BACK...
I WON'T RUN AWAY...
GAGK
I NEVER... GO BACK ON MY WORD...
WOBBLE
HEH... I THINK I'VE HEARD THAT LINE BEFORE...

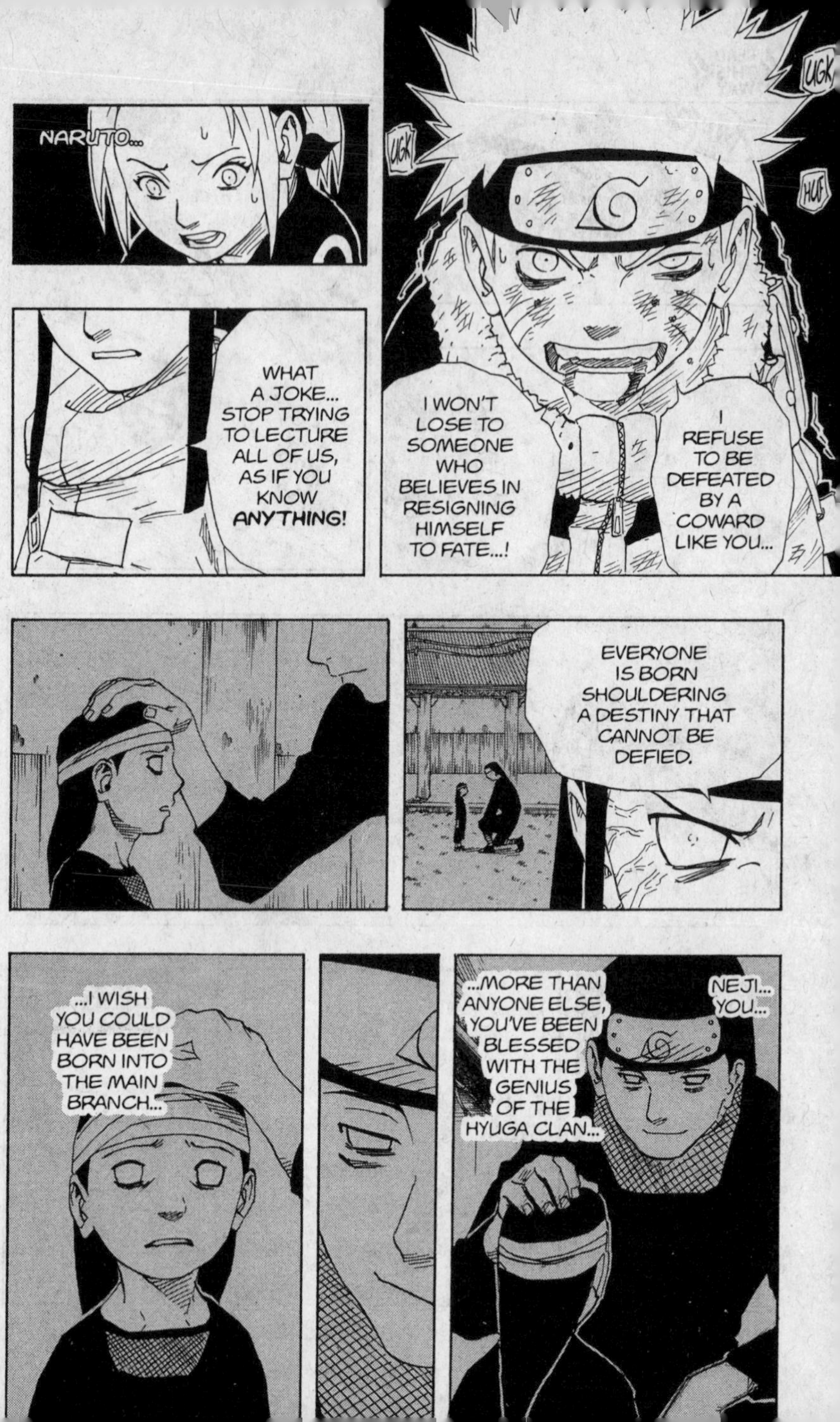
UGK
HUF
UGK
I REFUSE TO BE DEFEATED BY A COWARD LIKE YOU...
I WON'T LOSE TO SOMEONE WHO BELIEVES IN RESIGNING HIMSELF TO FATE...!
NARUTO...
WHAT A JOKE... STOP TRYING TO LECTURE ALL OF US, AS IF YOU KNOW **ANYTHING!**
EVERYONE IS BORN SHOULDERING A DESTINY THAT CANNOT BE DEFIED.
NEJI... YOU...
...MORE THAN ANYONE ELSE, YOU'VE BEEN BLESSED WITH THE GENIUS OF THE HYUGA CLAN...
...I WISH YOU COULD HAVE BEEN BORN INTO THE MAIN BRANCH...

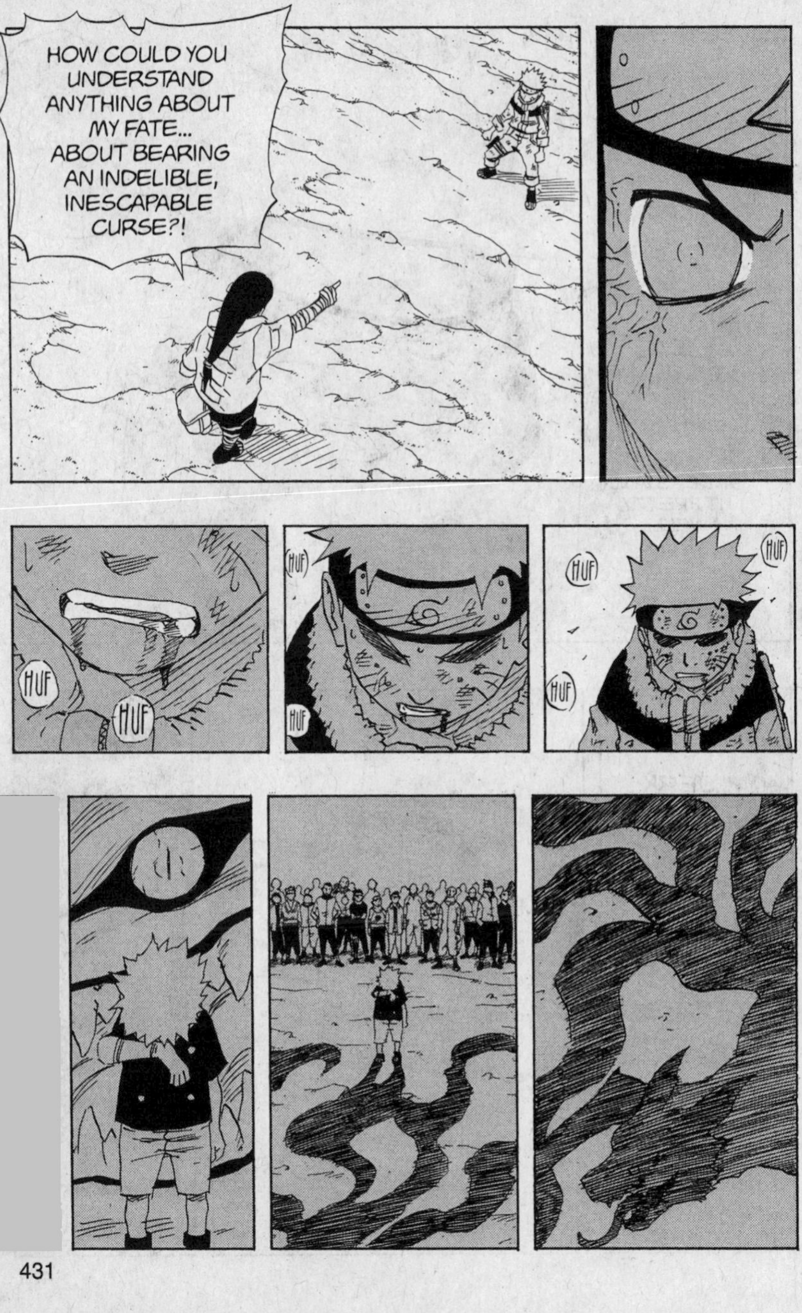
HOW COULD YOU UNDERSTAND ANYTHING ABOUT MY FATE... ABOUT BEARING AN INDELIBLE, INESCAPABLE CURSE?!
HUF
HUF
HUF
HUF
HUF
HUF
HUF

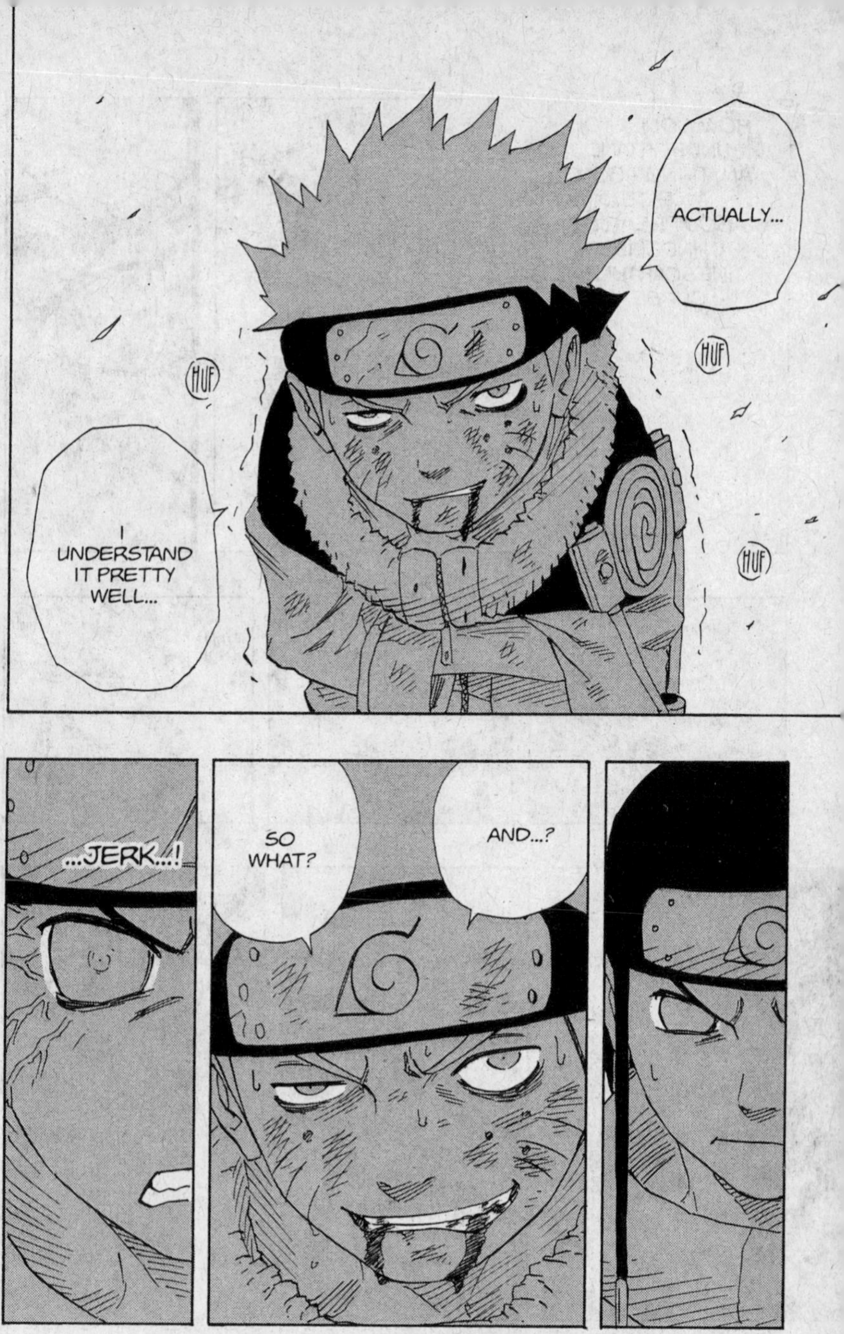
ACTUALLY...
HUF
HUF
HUF
I UNDERSTAND IT PRETTY WELL...
AND...?
SO WHAT?
...JERK...!

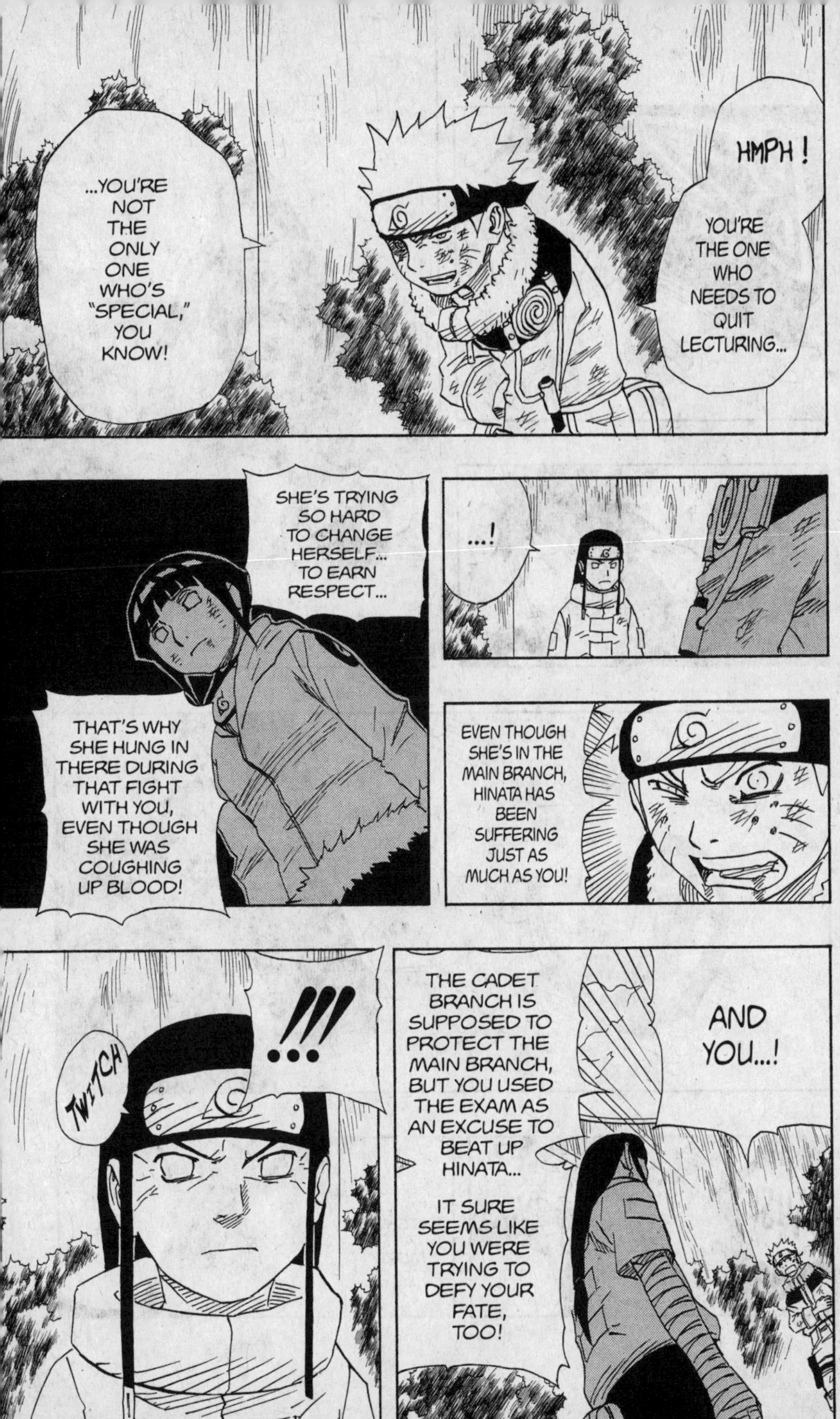
HMPH!
YOU'RE THE ONE WHO NEEDS TO QUIT LECTURING...
...YOU'RE NOT THE ONLY ONE WHO'S "SPECIAL," YOU KNOW!
...!
EVEN THOUGH SHE'S IN THE MAIN BRANCH, HINATA HAS BEEN SUFFERING JUST AS MUCH AS YOU!
SHE'S TRYING SO HARD TO CHANGE HERSELF... TO EARN RESPECT...
THAT'S WHY SHE HUNG IN THERE DURING THAT FIGHT WITH YOU, EVEN THOUGH SHE WAS COUGHING UP BLOOD!
AND YOU...!
THE CADET BRANCH IS SUPPOSED TO PROTECT THE MAIN BRANCH, BUT YOU USED THE EXAM AS AN EXCUSE TO BEAT UP HINATA...
IT SURE SEEMS LIKE YOU WERE TRYING TO DEFY YOUR FATE, TOO!
...!!!
TWITCH

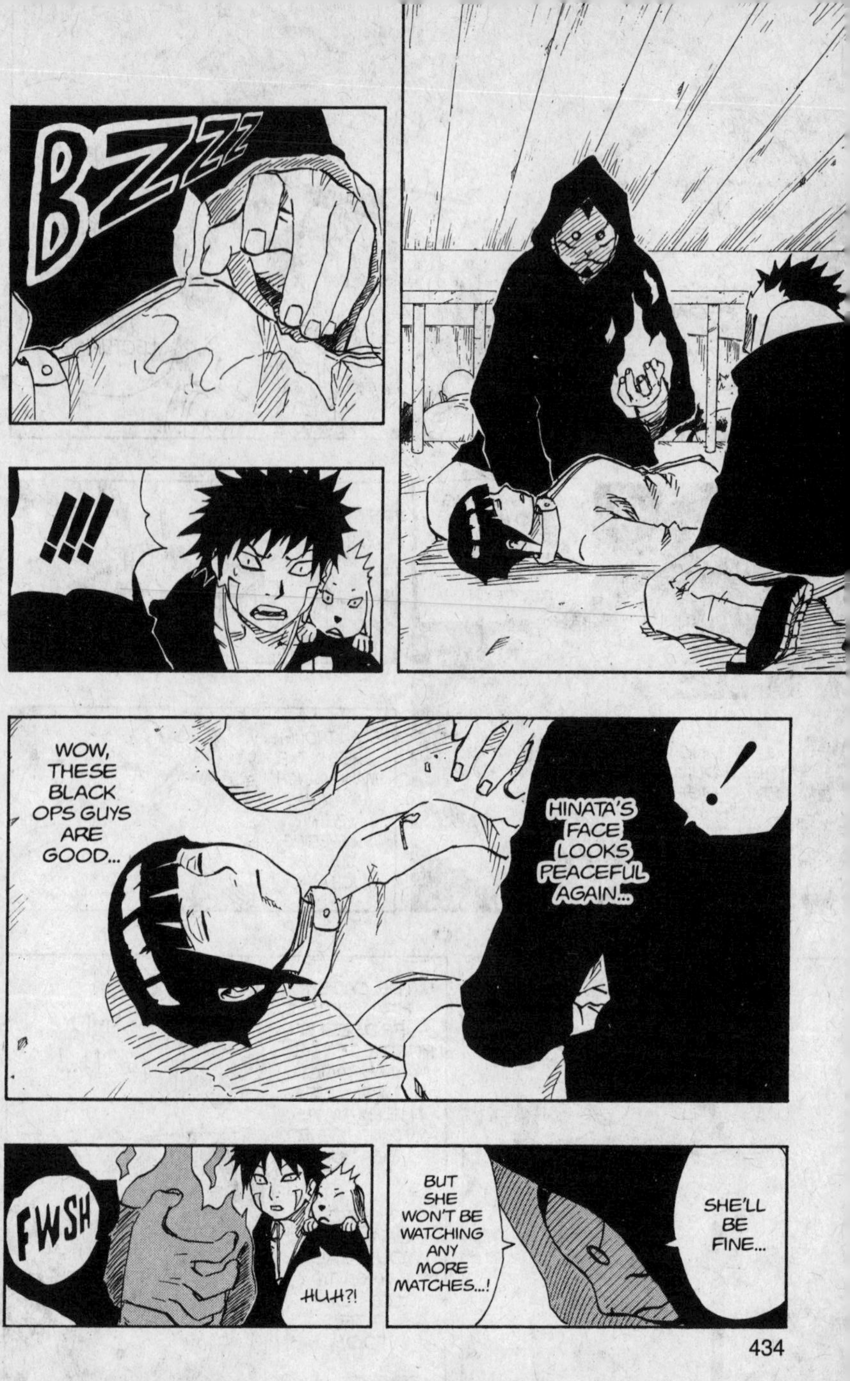
BZZZ
!!!
!
HINATA'S FACE LOOKS PEACEFUL AGAIN...
WOW, THESE BLACK OPS GUYS ARE GOOD...
SHE'LL BE FINE...
BUT SHE WON'T BE WATCHING ANY MORE MATCHES...!
FWSH
HUH?!

READ THIS WAY

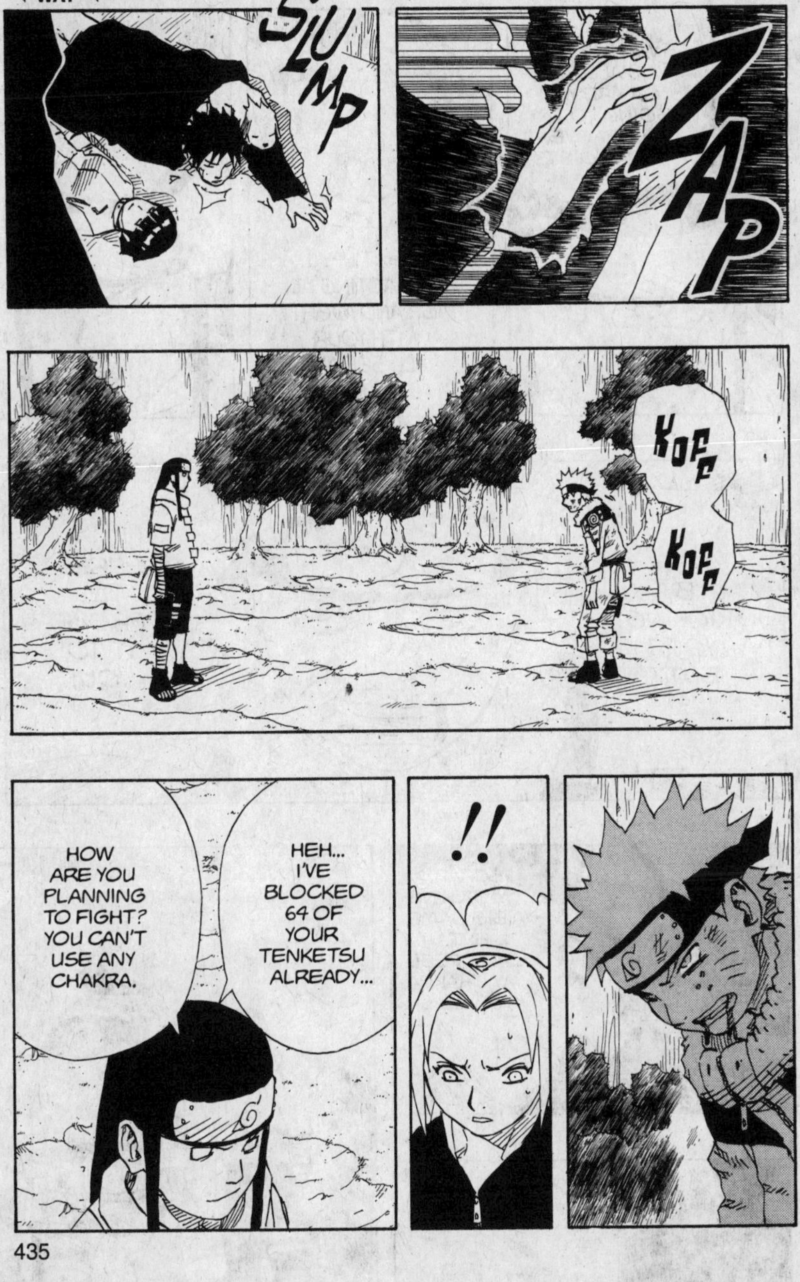
ZAP
SLUMP
KOFF KOFF
!!
HEH... I'VE BLOCKED 64 OF YOUR TENKETSU ALREADY...
HOW ARE YOU PLANNING TO FIGHT? YOU CAN'T USE ANY CHAKRA.

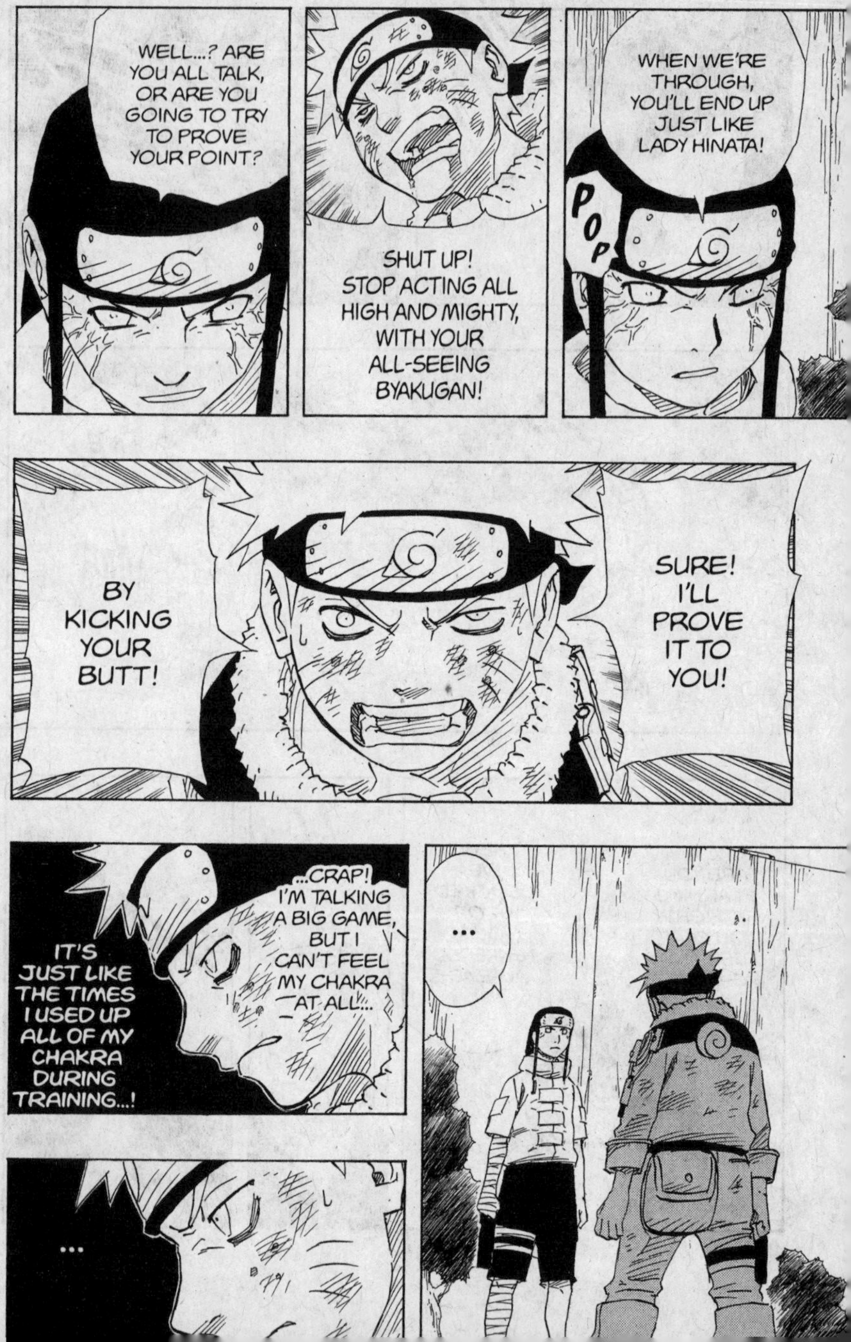
POP
WHEN WE'RE THROUGH, YOU'LL END UP JUST LIKE LADY HINATA!
SHUT UP! STOP ACTING ALL HIGH AND MIGHTY, WITH YOUR ALL-SEEING BYAKUGAN!
WELL...? ARE YOU ALL TALK, OR ARE YOU GOING TO TRY TO PROVE YOUR POINT?
SURE! I'LL PROVE IT TO YOU!
BY KICKING YOUR BUTT!
...
...CRAP! I'M TALKING A BIG GAME, BUT I CAN'T FEEL MY CHAKRA AT ALL...
IT'S JUST LIKE THE TIMES I USED UP ALL OF MY CHAKRA DURING TRAINING...!
...

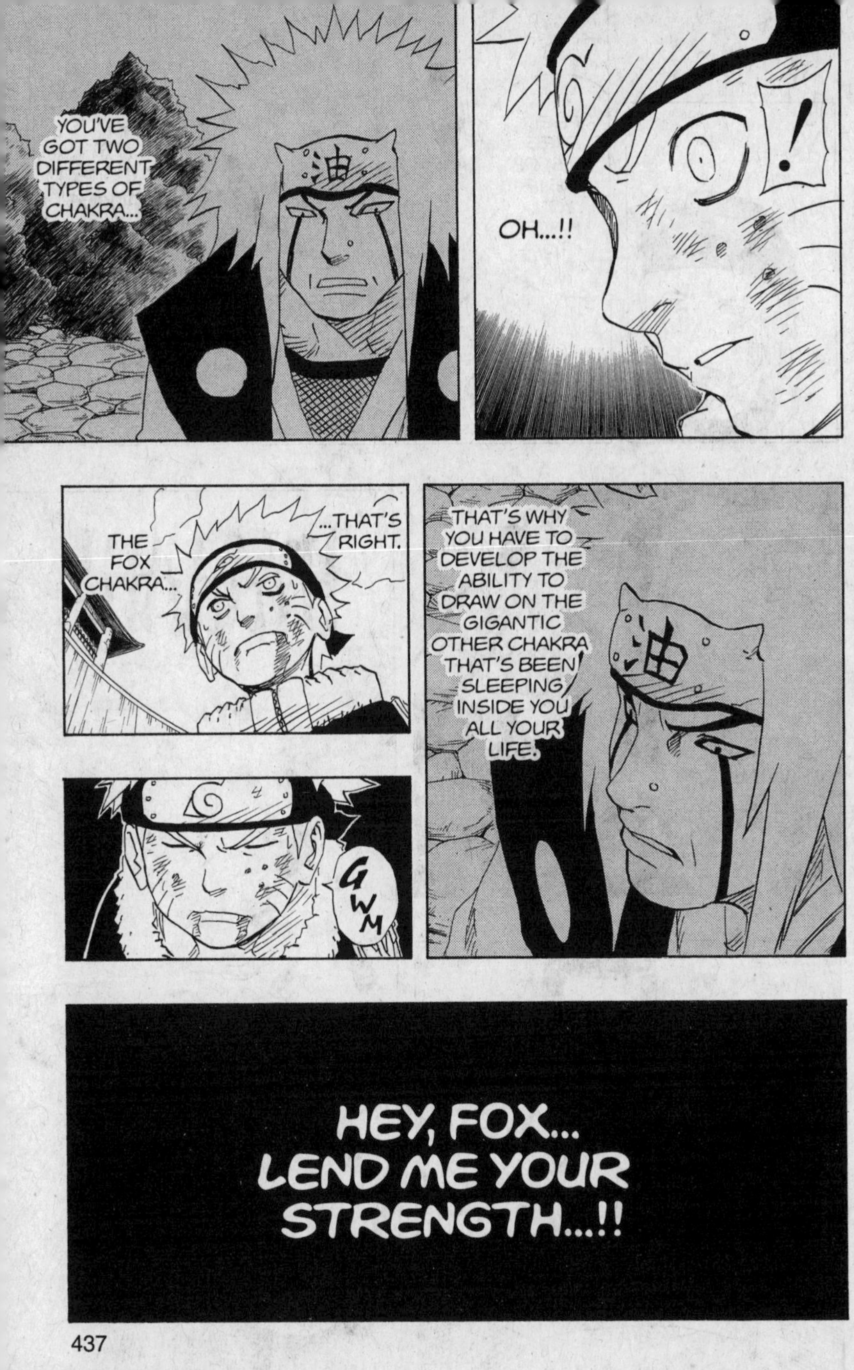
!
OH...!!
YOU'VE GOT TWO DIFFERENT TYPES OF CHAKRA...
THAT'S WHY YOU HAVE TO DEVELOP THE ABILITY TO DRAW ON THE GIGANTIC OTHER CHAKRA THAT'S BEEN SLEEPING INSIDE YOU ALL YOUR LIFE.
...THAT'S RIGHT.
THE FOX CHAKRA...
GWM
HEY, FOX... LEND ME YOUR STRENGTH...!!

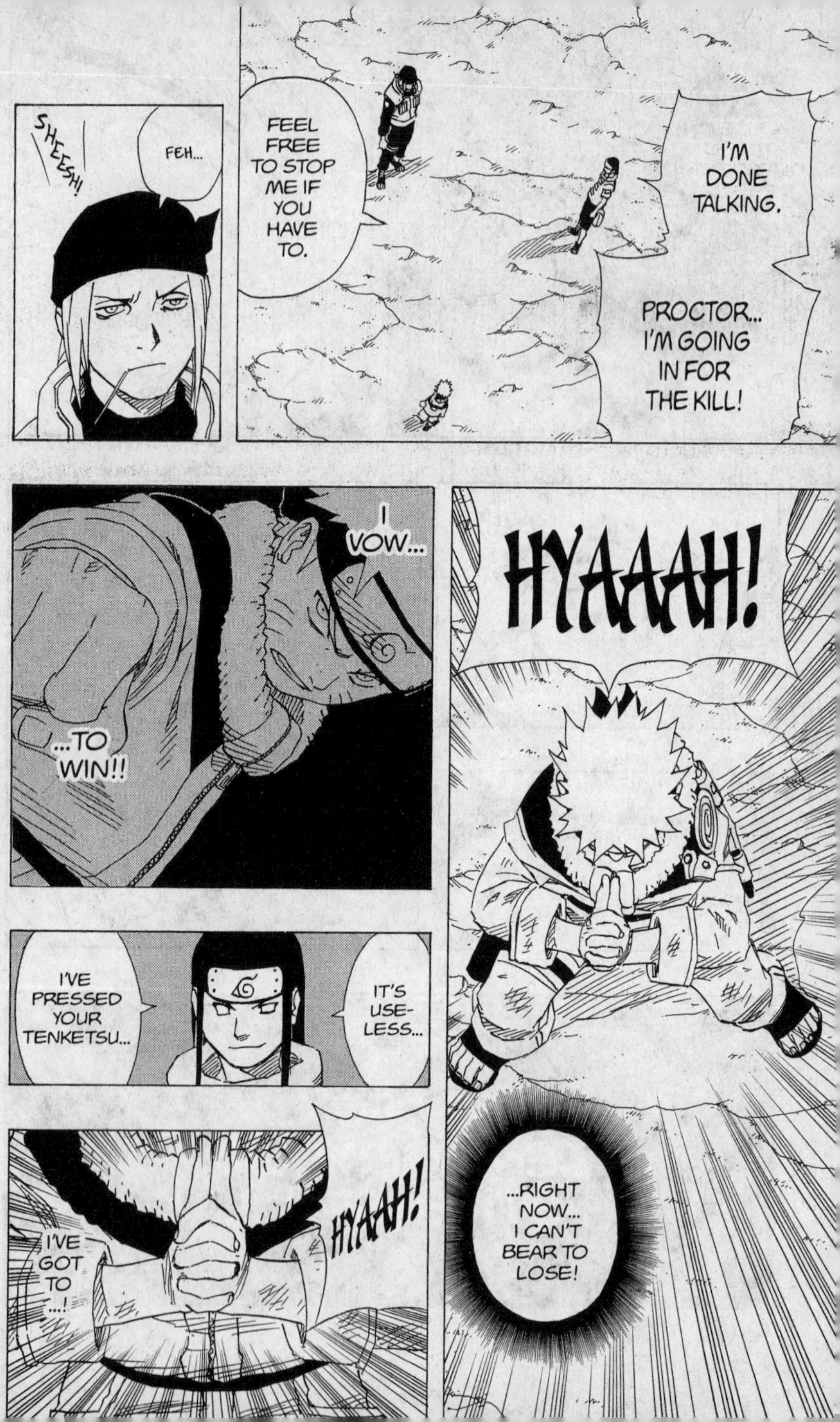
I'M DONE TALKING.
PROCTOR... I'M GOING IN FOR THE KILL!
FEEL FREE TO STOP ME IF YOU HAVE TO.
FEH...
SHEESH!
HYAAAH!
...RIGHT NOW... I CAN'T BEAR TO LOSE!
I VOW...
...TO WIN!!
IT'S USELESS...
I'VE PRESSED YOUR TENKETSU...
HYAAH!
I'VE GOT TO ...!

READ THIS WAY

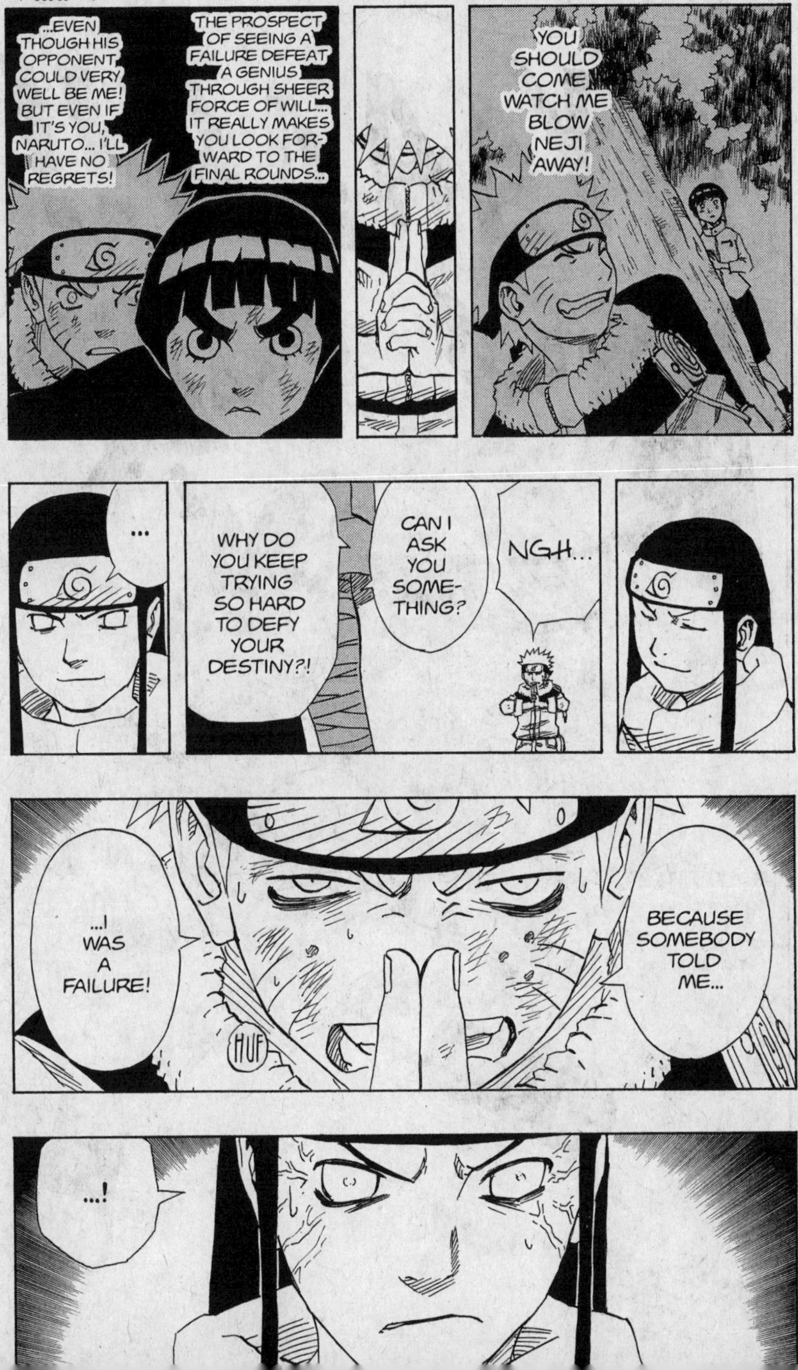
YOU SHOULD COME WATCH ME BLOW NEJI AWAY!
THE PROSPECT OF SEEING A FAILURE DEFEAT A GENIUS THROUGH SHEER FORCE OF WILL... IT REALLY MAKES YOU LOOK FORWARD TO THE FINAL ROUNDS...
...EVEN THOUGH HIS OPPONENT COULD VERY WELL BE ME! BUT EVEN IF IT'S YOU, NARUTO... I'LL HAVE NO REGRETS!
NGH...
CAN I ASK YOU SOMETHING?
WHY DO YOU KEEP TRYING SO HARD TO DEFY YOUR DESTINY?!
...
BECAUSE SOMEBODY TOLD ME...
HUF
...I WAS A FAILURE!
...!

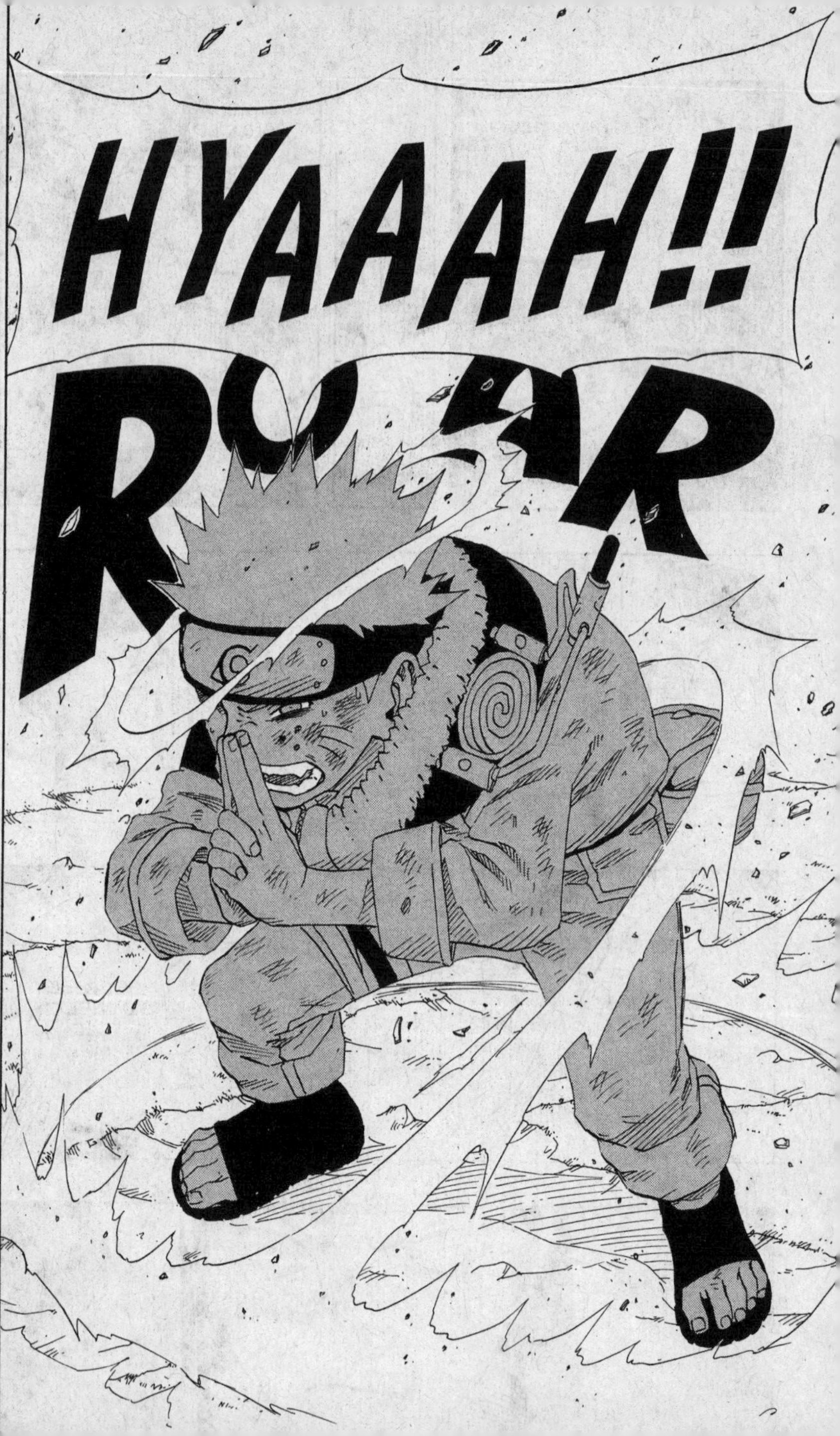
HYAAAH!!
ROAR

 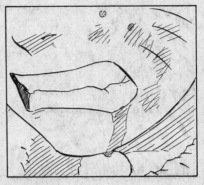

HIS CHAKRA IS OOZING OUT... WHAT'S GOING ON...?

...IMPOSSIBLE!

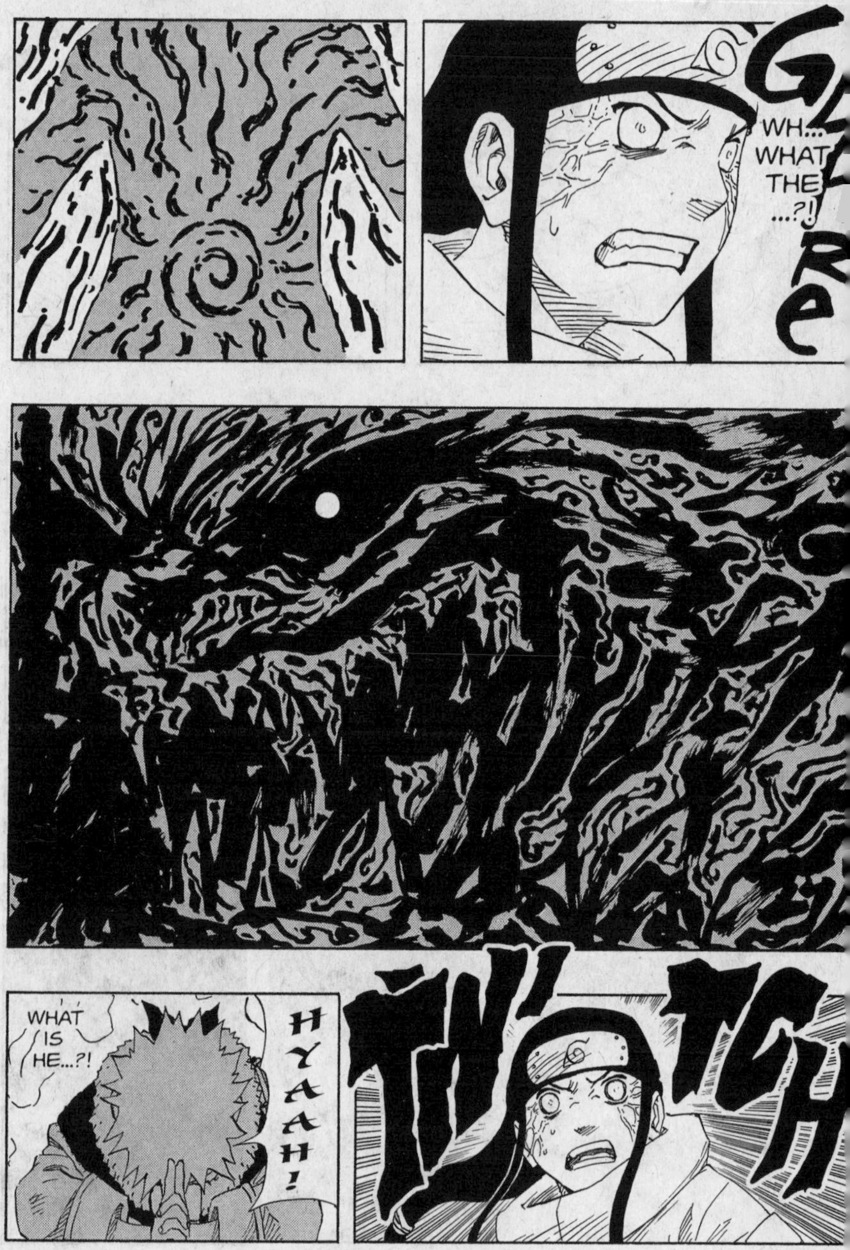
WH... WHAT THE ...?!
HYAAAH!
WHAT IS HE...?!

READ THIS WAY

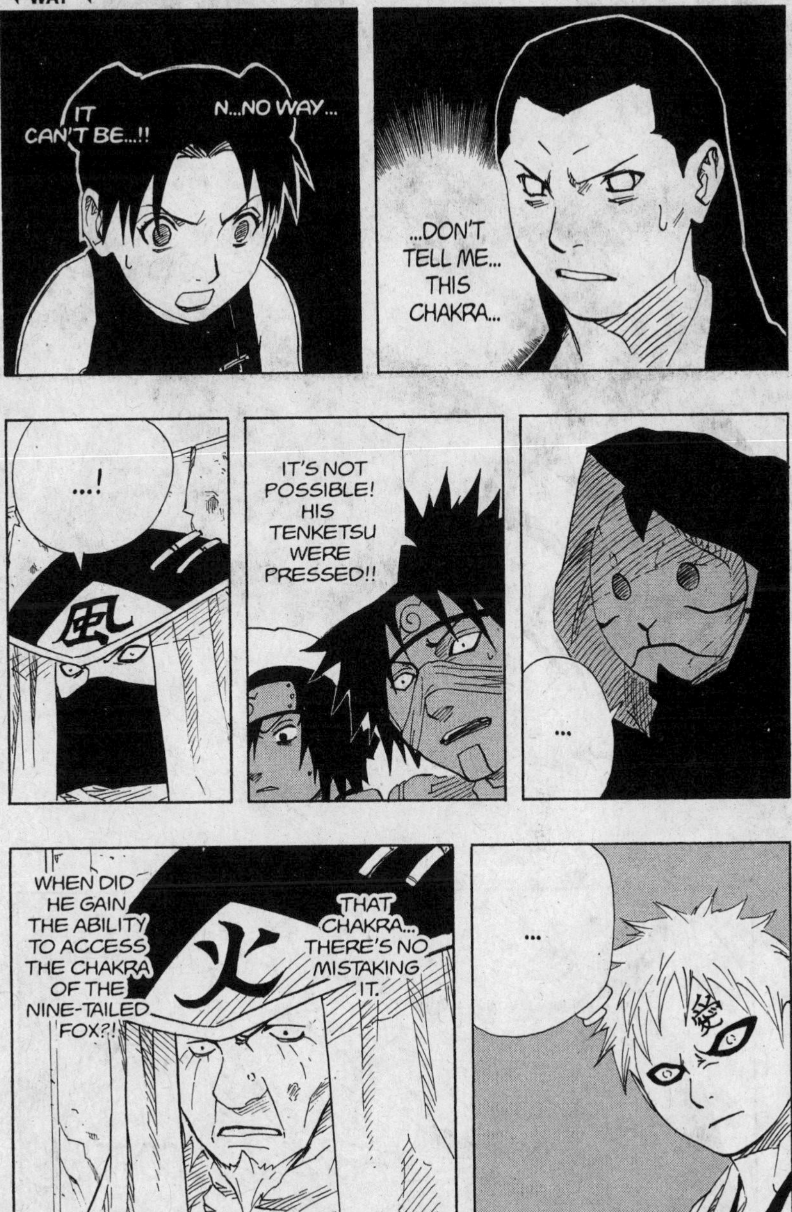
...DON'T TELL ME... THIS CHAKRA...
N...NO WAY...
IT CAN'T BE...!!
...
IT'S NOT POSSIBLE! HIS TENKETSU WERE PRESSED!!
...!
...
THAT CHAKRA... THERE'S NO MISTAKING IT.
WHEN DID HE GAIN THE ABILITY TO ACCESS THE CHAKRA OF THE NINE-TAILED FOX?!

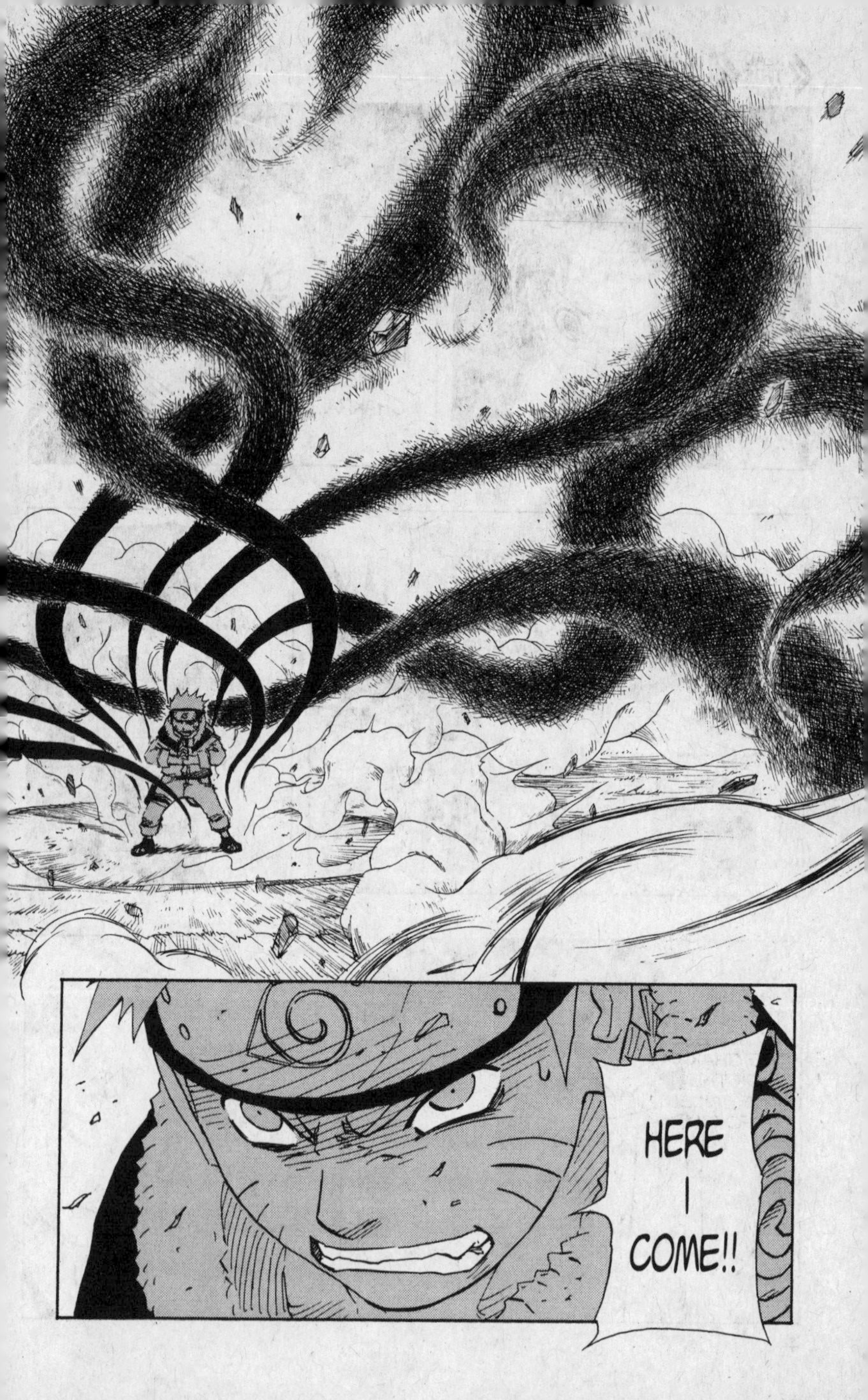
HERE I COME!!

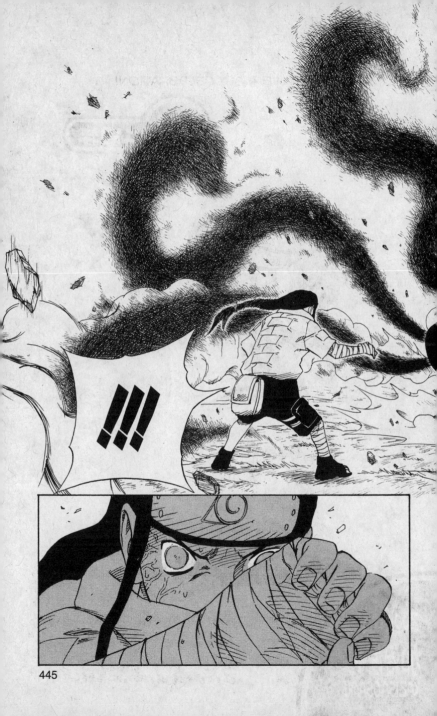

445

SECOND ANNIVERSARY CELEBRATION!

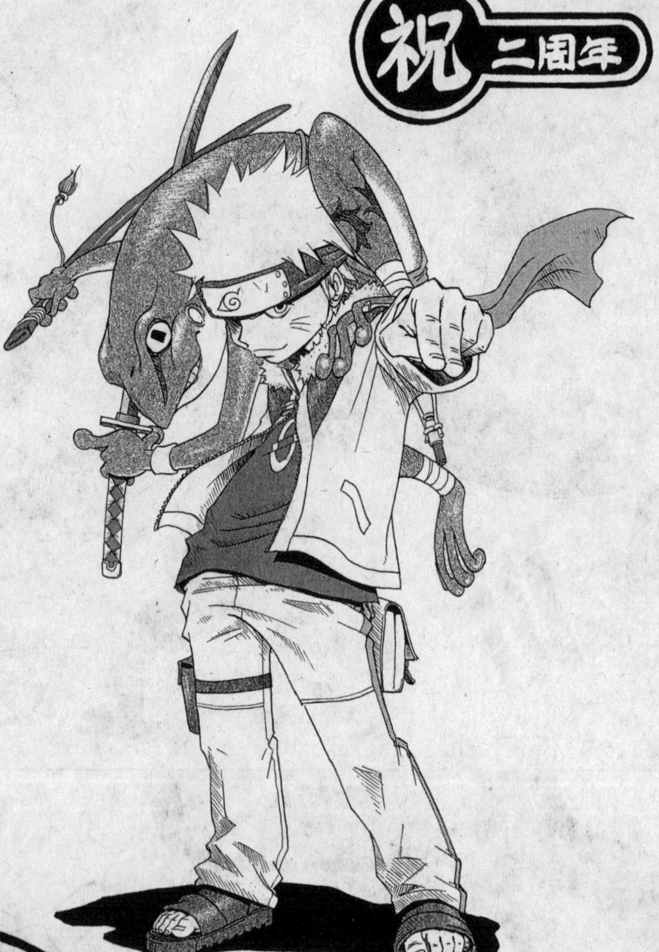
祝 二周年

I CAN'T BELIEVE IT'S ALREADY BEEN TWO YEARS!
I HOPE YOU CAN ALWAYS KEEP DRAWING WITH
THE AMAZING ENERGY YOU HAVE NOW!

はやいもんで もう2年ですね.
これからも 今と変わらぬテンションで描きまくって下さい.

2001.11.8
加治佐 修
KAZISA OSAMU

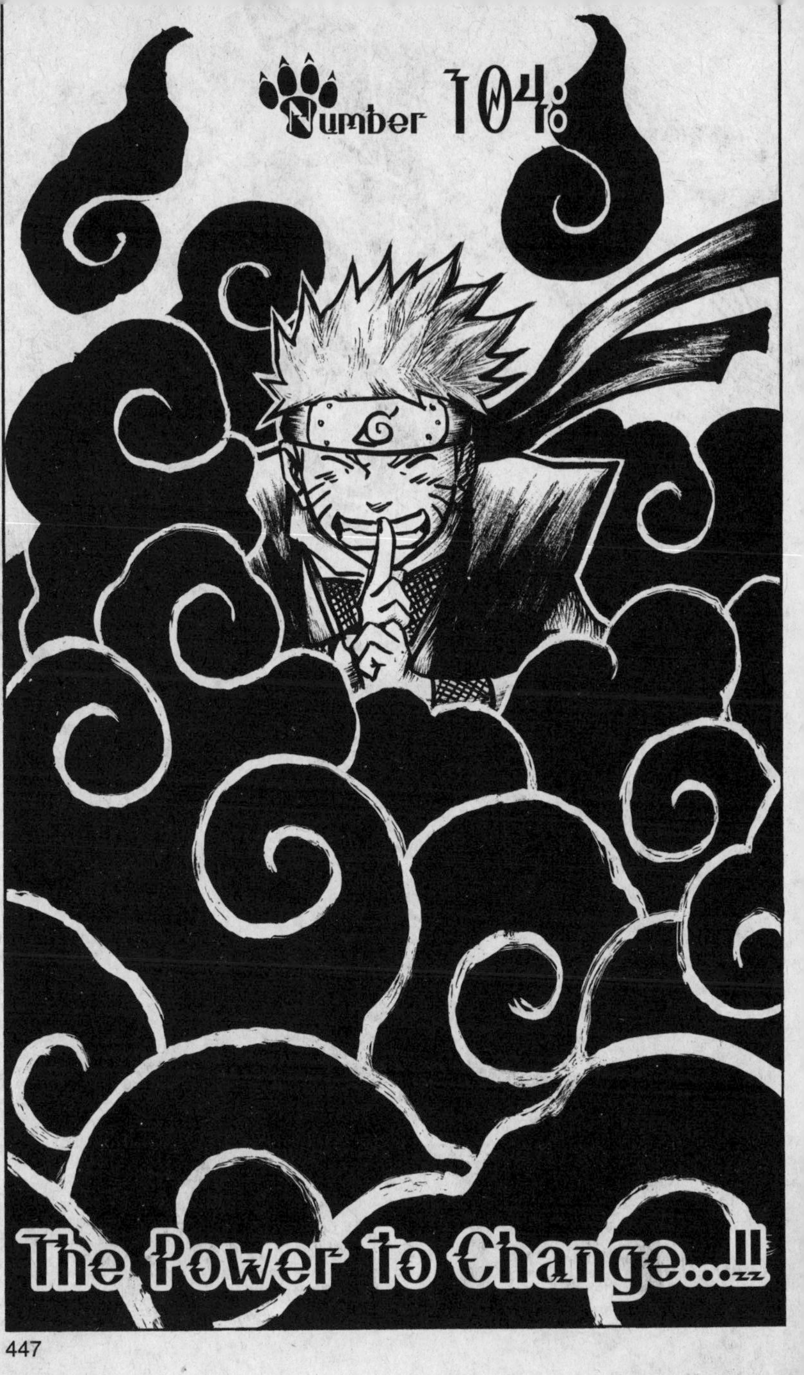
Number 104:
The Power to Change...!!

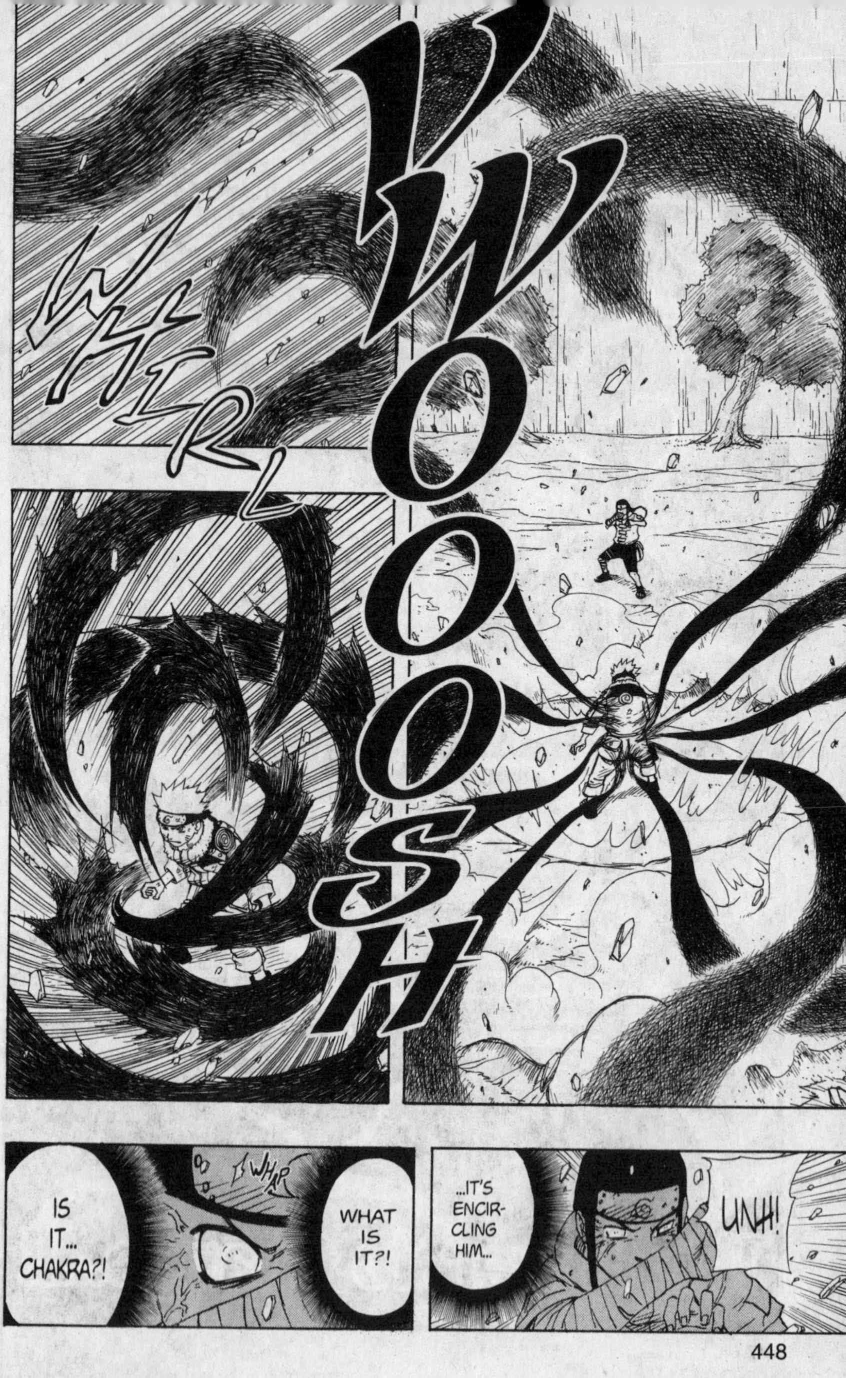
WHOOOOSH
WHIRL
UNH!
...IT'S ENCIR-CLING HIM...
WHAP
WHAT IS IT?!
IS IT... CHAKRA?!

READ THIS WAY

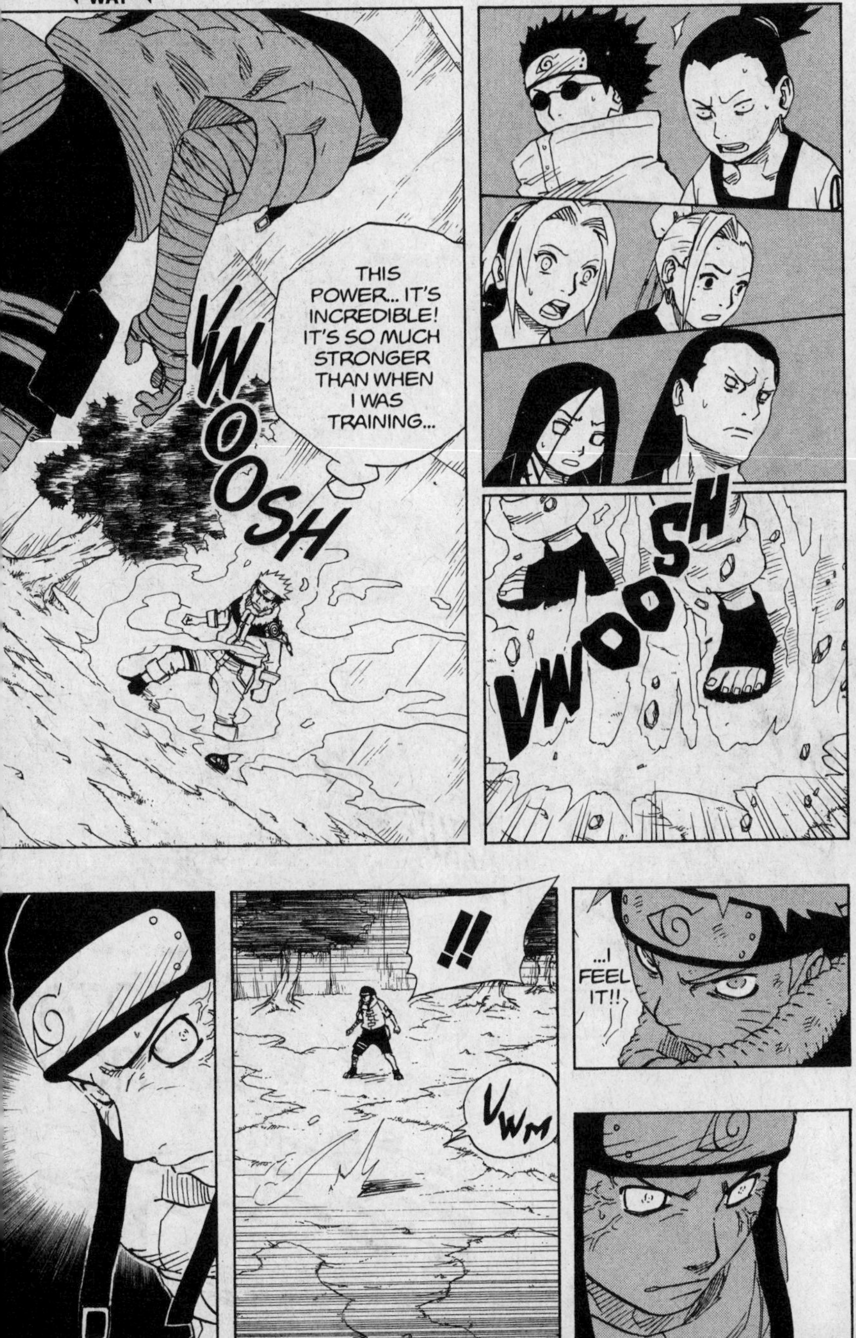
VWOOSH
THIS POWER... IT'S INCREDIBLE! IT'S SO MUCH STRONGER THAN WHEN I WAS TRAINING...
VWOOSH
...I FEEL IT!!
!!
VWM

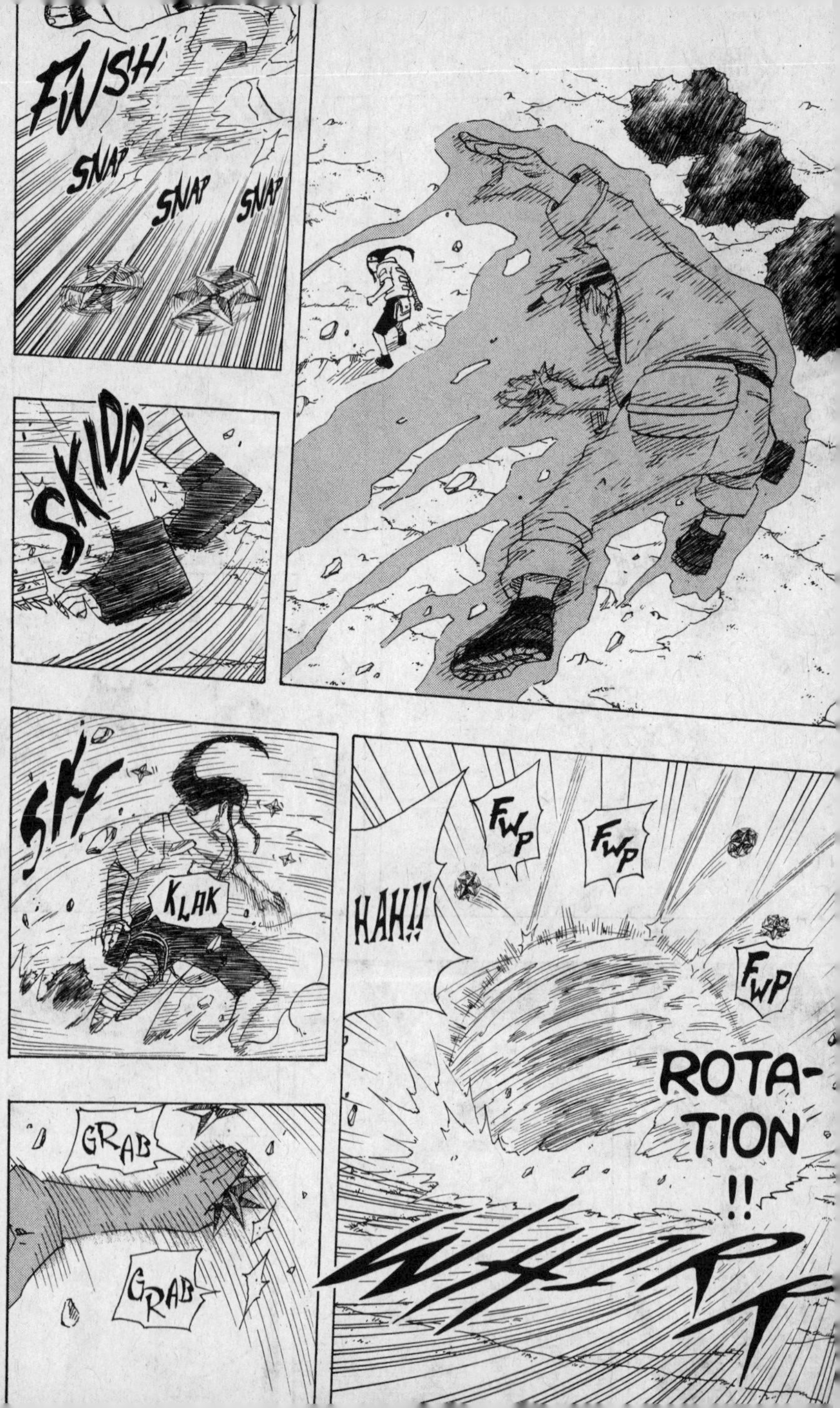
FWSH
SNAP
SNAP
SNAP
SKIDD
FWP
FWP
FWP
HAH!!
ROTATION!!
WHIRR
SKF
KLAK
GRAB
GRAB

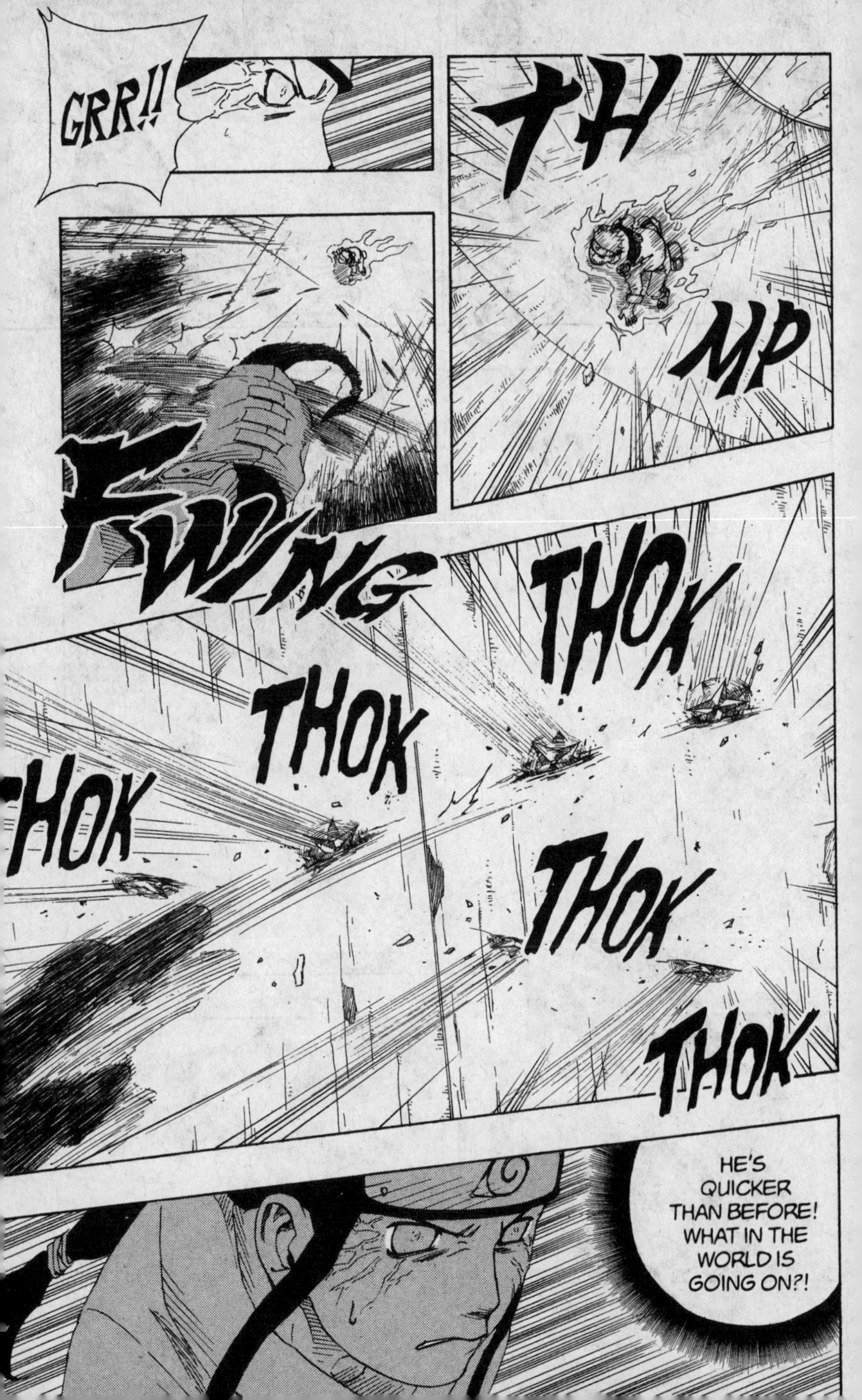
TH
MP
GRR!!
FWING
THOK
THOK
THOK
THOK
HOK
HE'S QUICKER THAN BEFORE! WHAT IN THE WORLD IS GOING ON?!

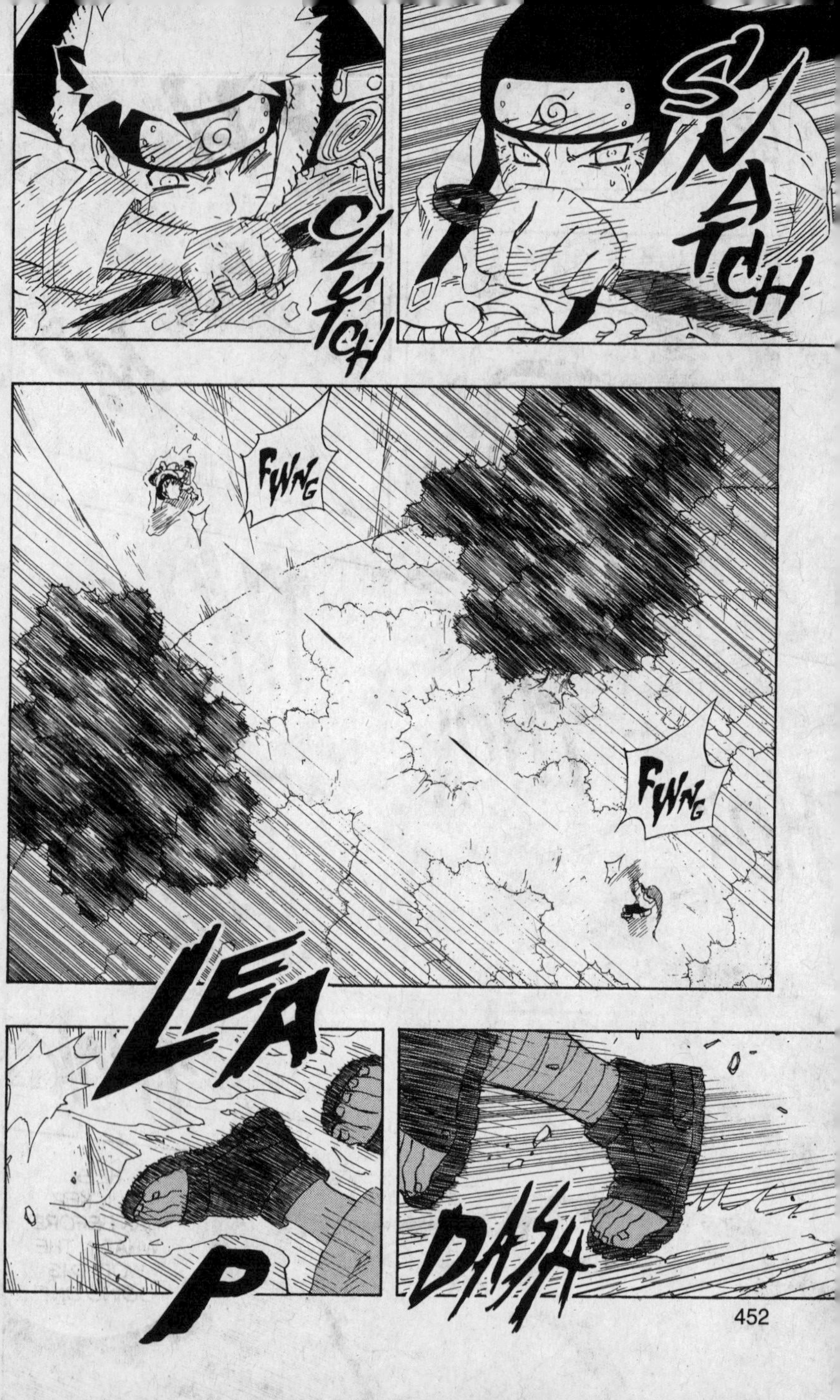
SNATCH
CLUTCH
FWNG
FWNG
DASH
LEAP

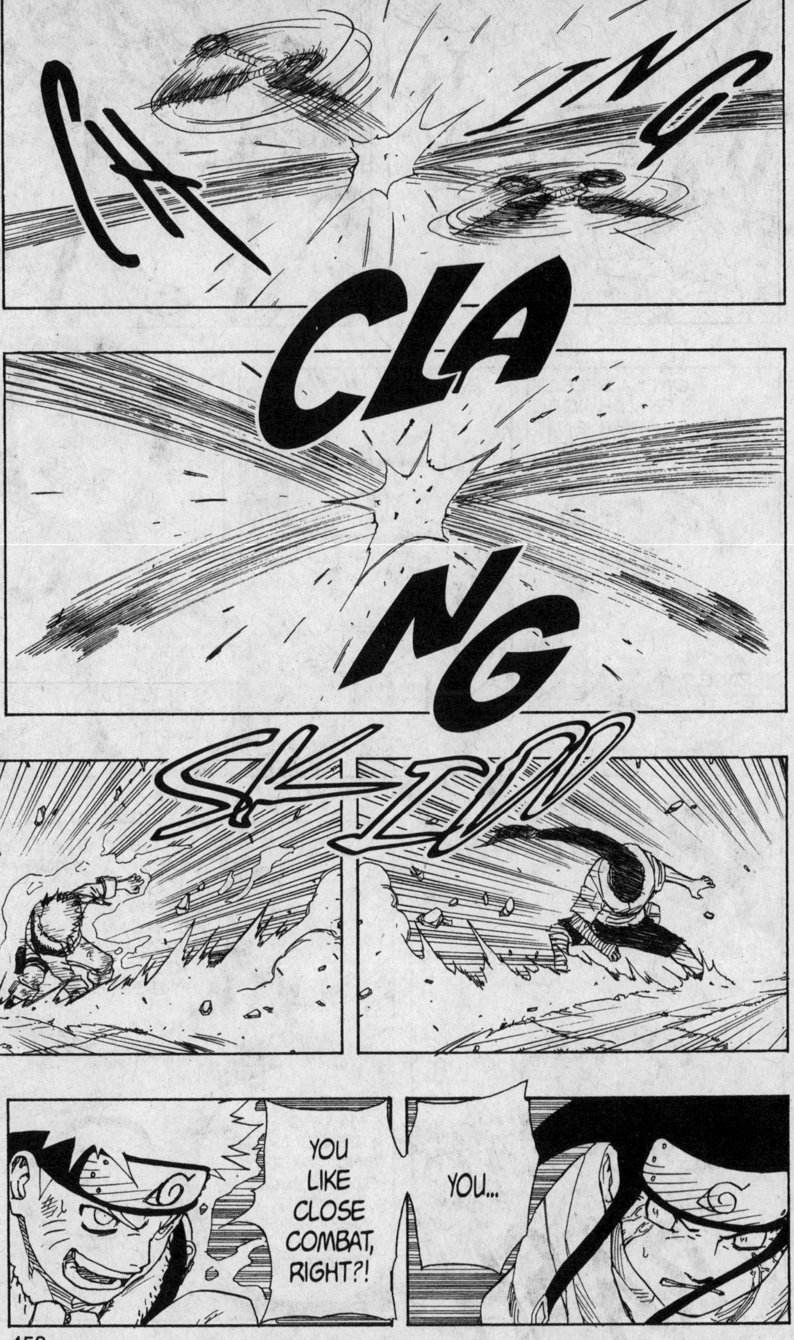
CHING
CLANG
SKIN
YOU...
YOU LIKE CLOSE COMBAT, RIGHT?!

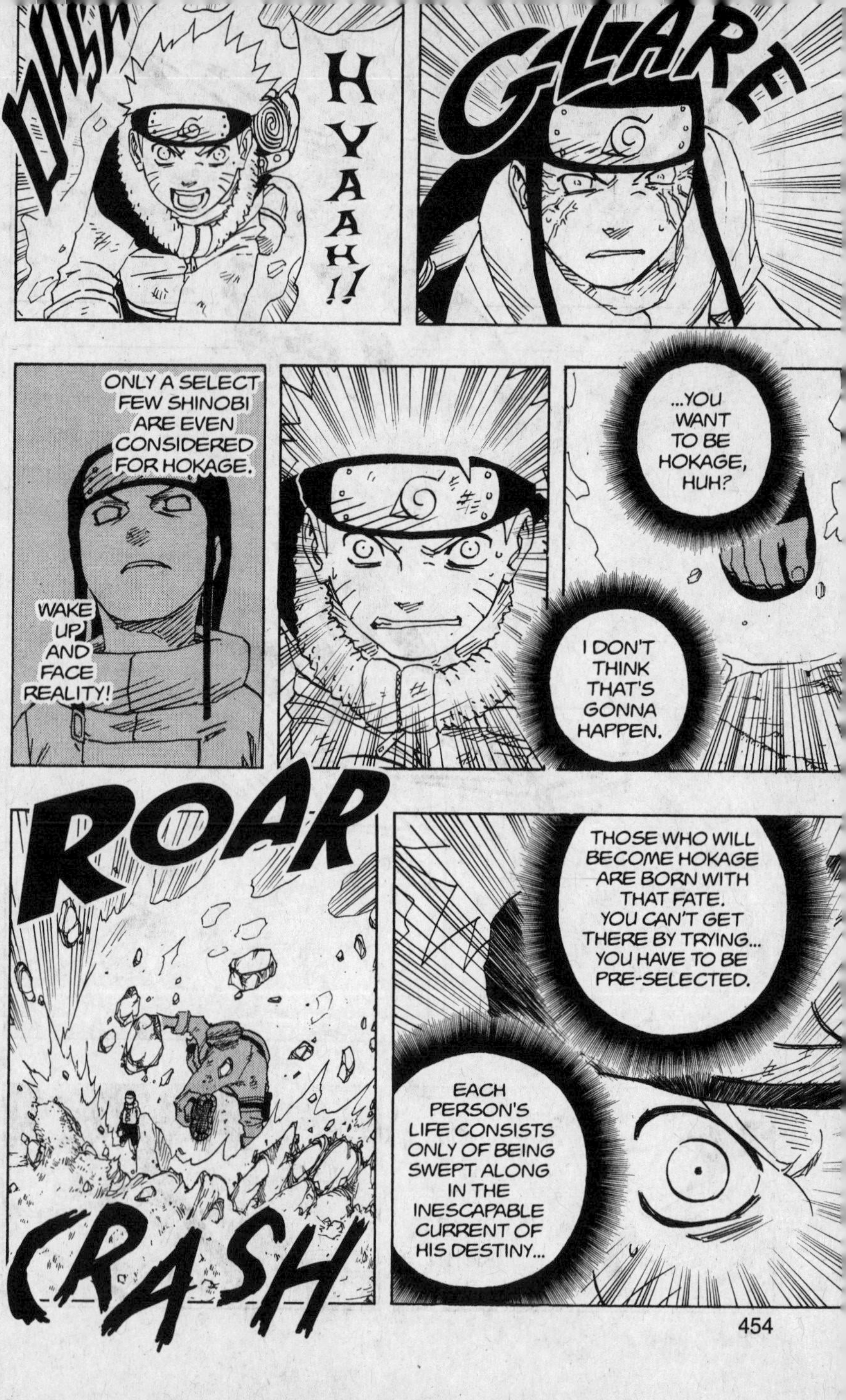
GLARE
HYAAH!!
DASH
...YOU WANT TO BE HOKAGE, HUH?
I DON'T THINK THAT'S GONNA HAPPEN.
ONLY A SELECT FEW SHINOBI ARE EVEN CONSIDERED FOR HOKAGE.
WAKE UP AND FACE REALITY!
THOSE WHO WILL BECOME HOKAGE ARE BORN WITH THAT FATE. YOU CAN'T GET THERE BY TRYING... YOU HAVE TO BE PRE-SELECTED.
EACH PERSON'S LIFE CONSISTS ONLY OF BEING SWEPT ALONG IN THE INESCAPABLE CURRENT OF HIS DESTINY...
ROAR
CRASH

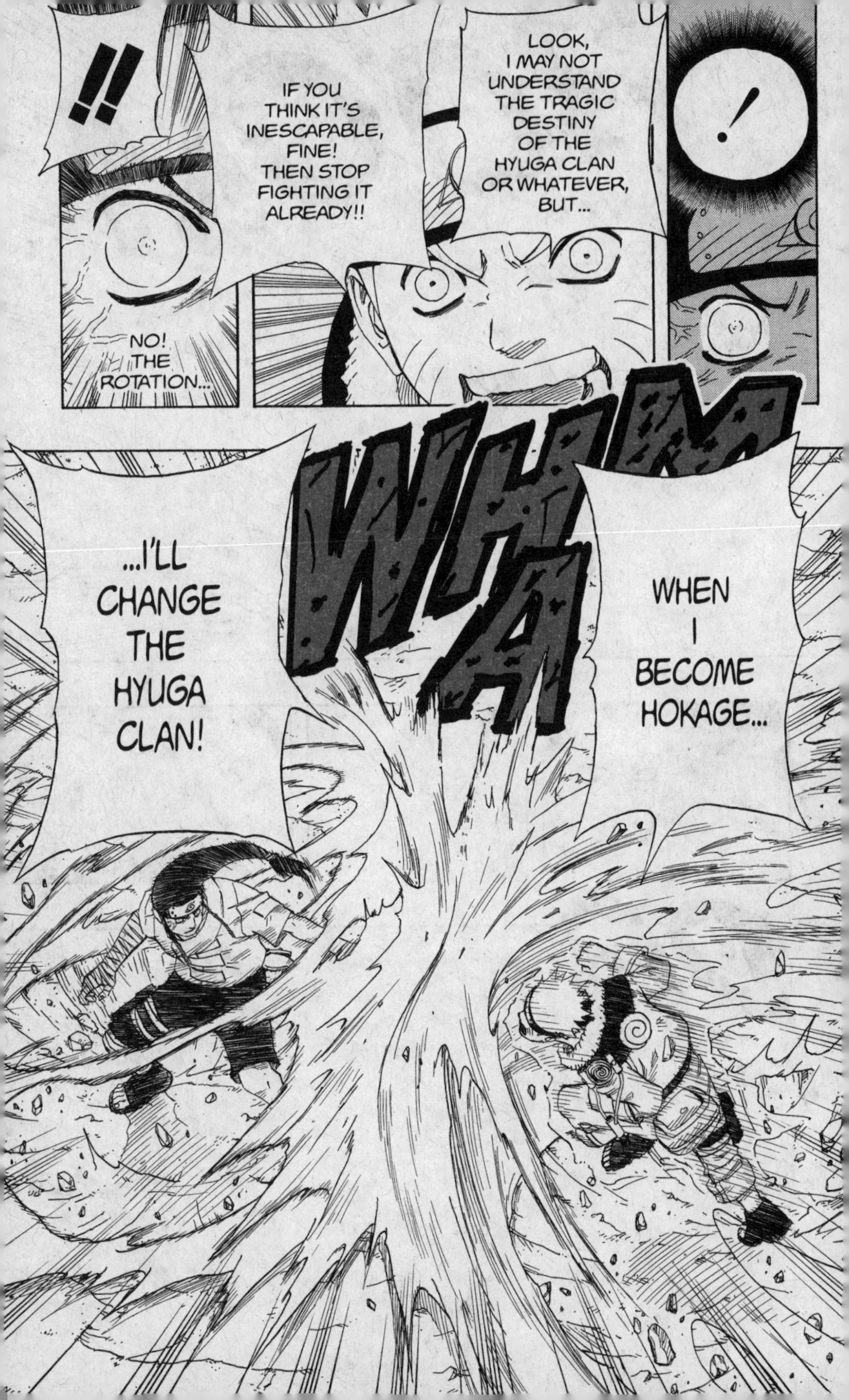
!
IF YOU THINK IT'S INESCAPABLE, FINE! THEN STOP FIGHTING IT ALREADY!!
LOOK, I MAY NOT UNDERSTAND THE TRAGIC DESTINY OF THE HYUGA CLAN OR WHATEVER, BUT...
!!
NO! THE ROTATION...
WHAM
WHEN I BECOME HOKAGE...
...I'LL CHANGE THE HYUGA CLAN!

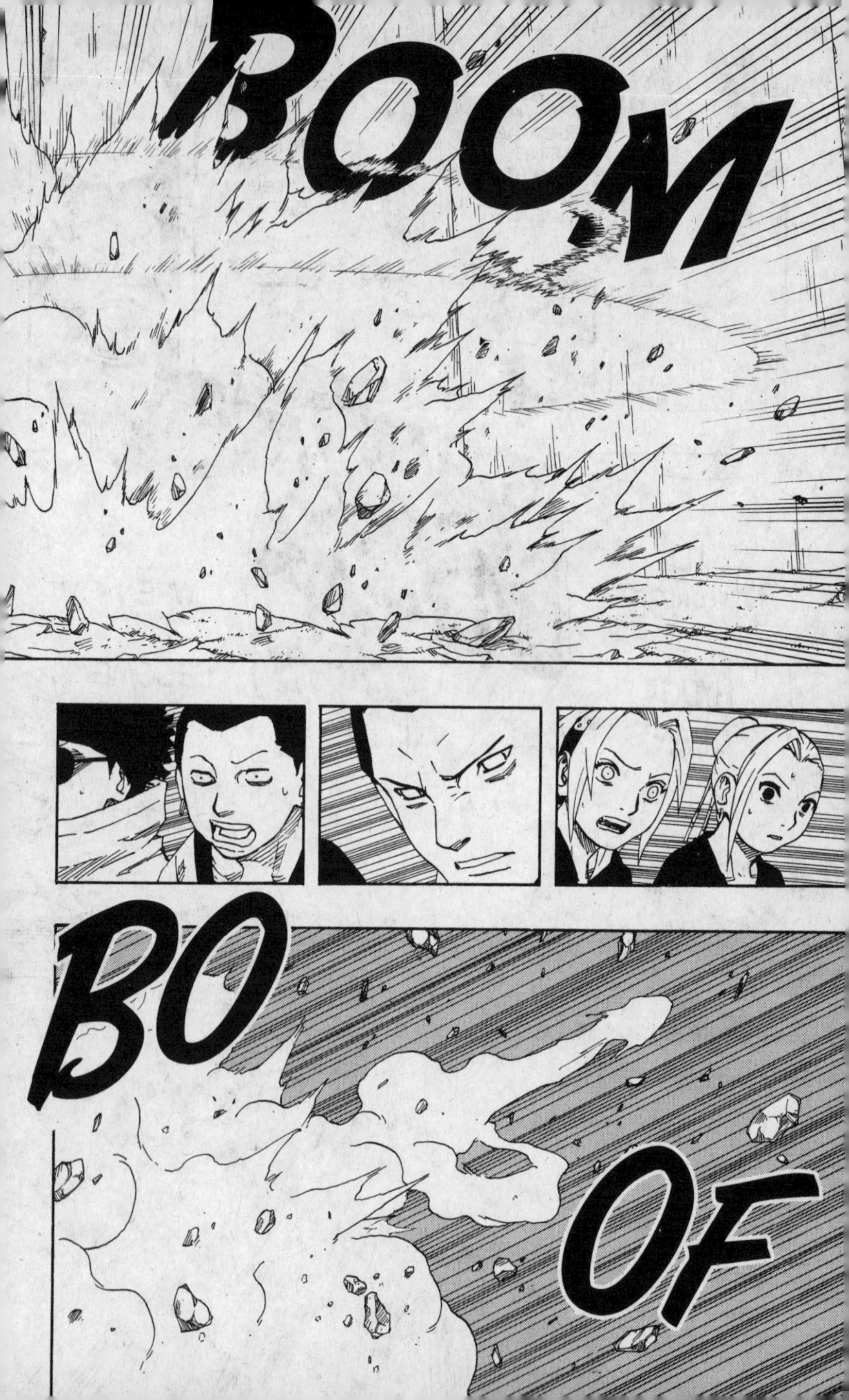
BOOM
BOOF

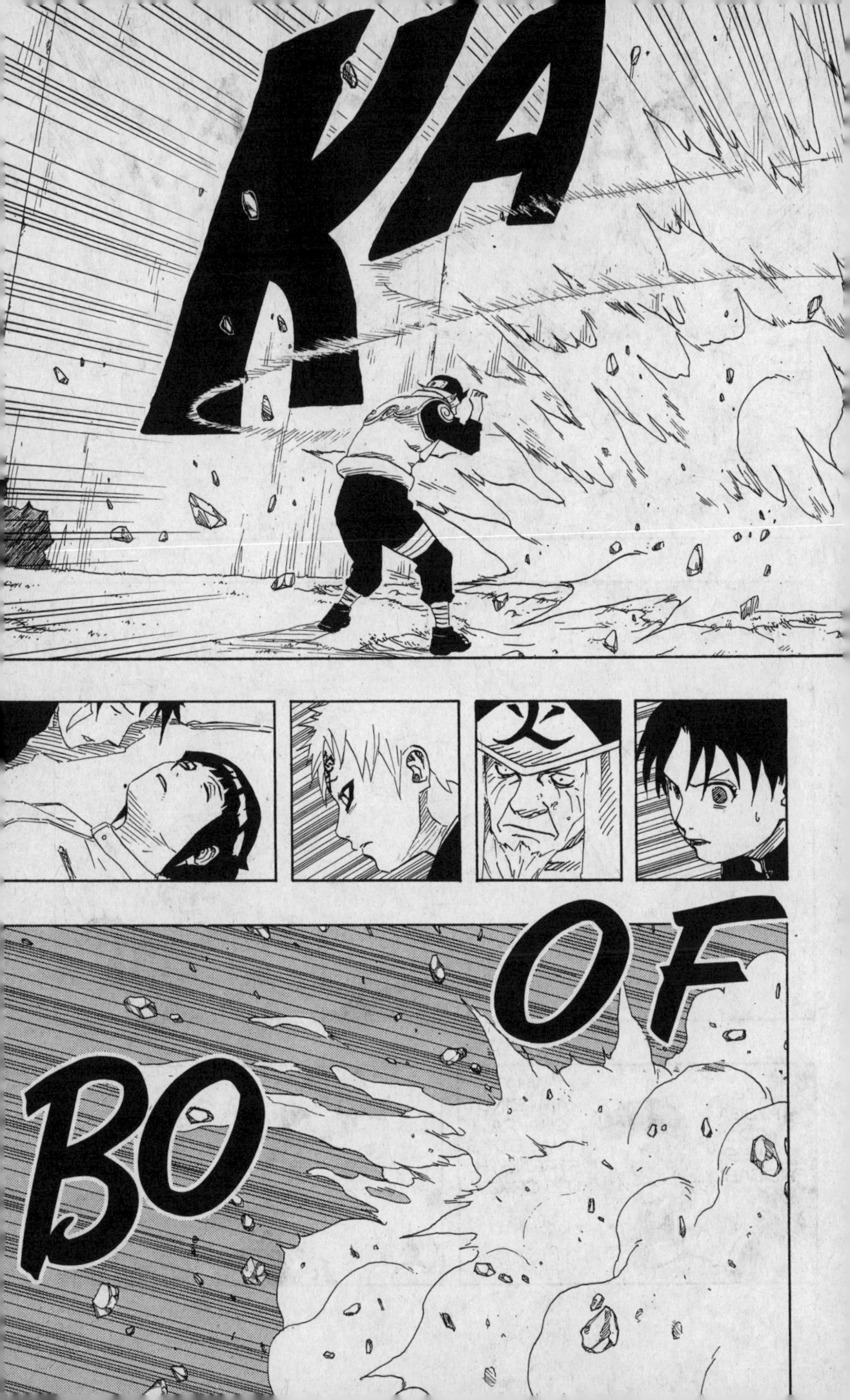
KA
BO
OF

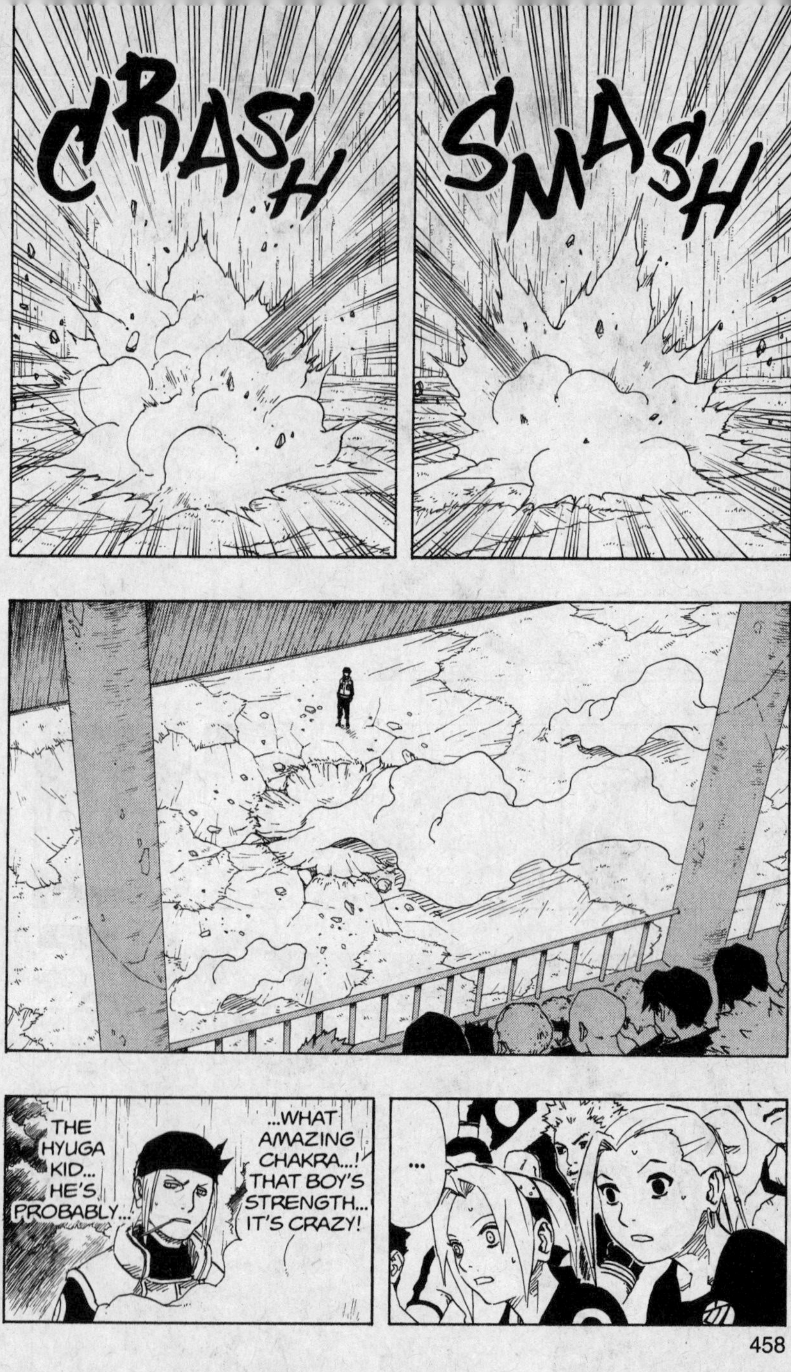
SMASH
CRASH
...
...WHAT AMAZING CHAKRA...! THAT BOY'S STRENGTH... IT'S CRAZY!
THE HYUGA KID... HE'S PROBABLY...

READ THIS WAY

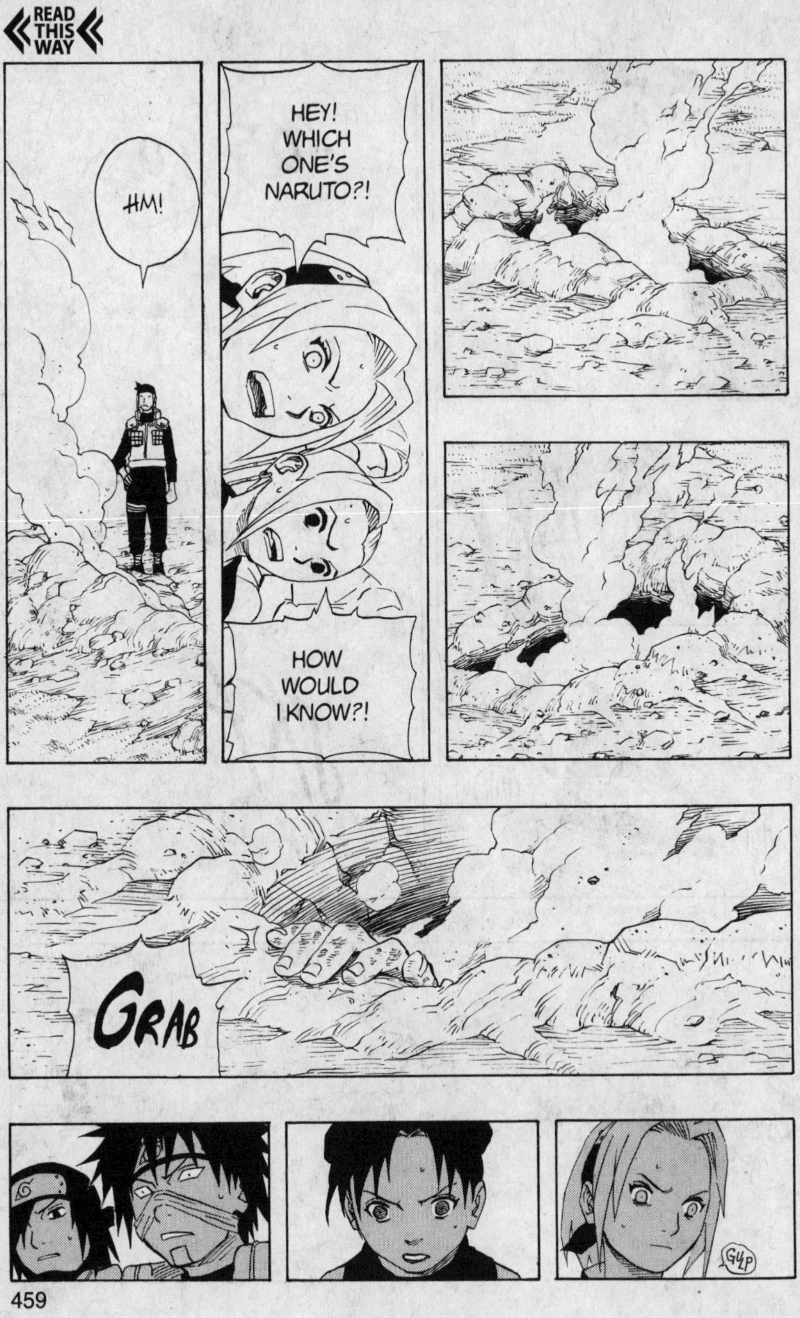
HEY! WHICH ONE'S NARUTO?!
HOW WOULD I KNOW?!
HM!
GRAB
GULP

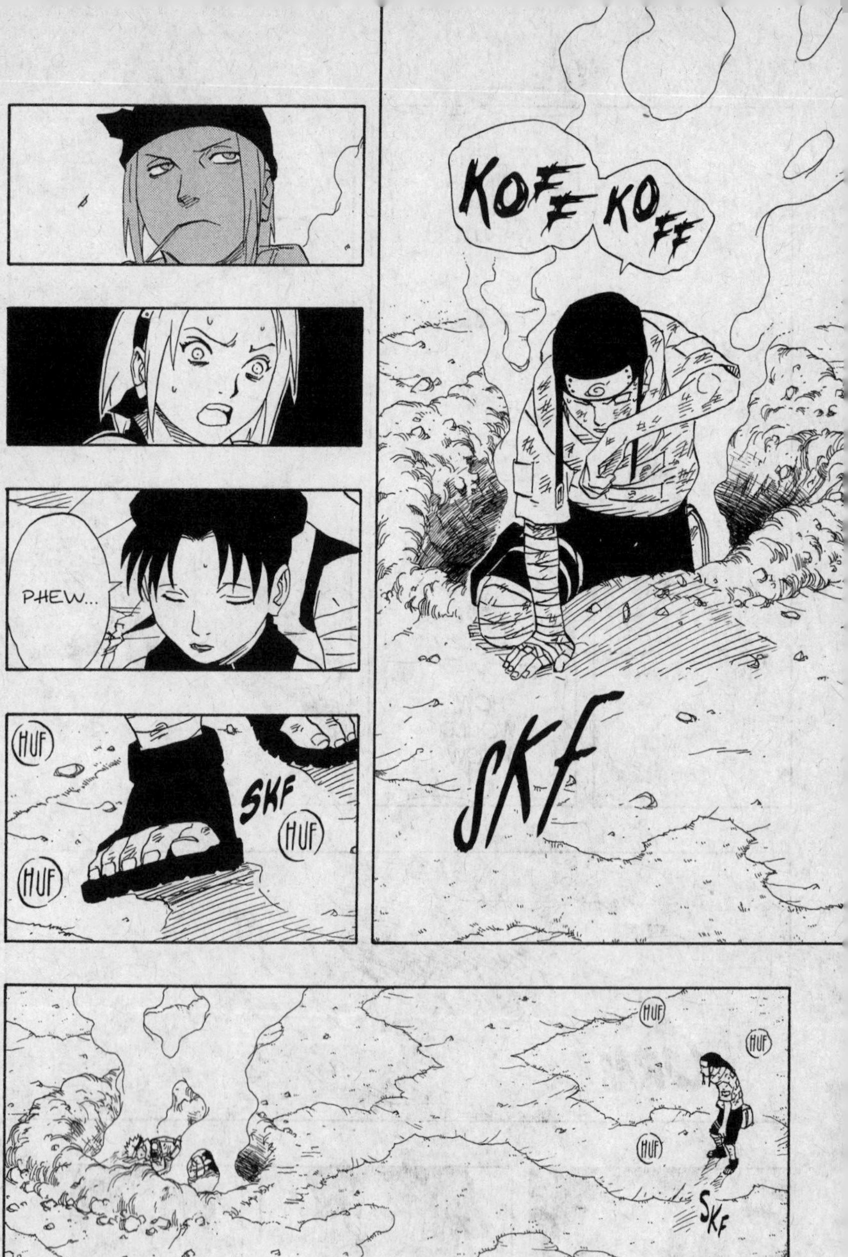
KOFF KOFF
SKF
PHEW...
SKF
HUF
HUF
HUF
HUF
HUF
HUF
SKF

READ THIS WAY

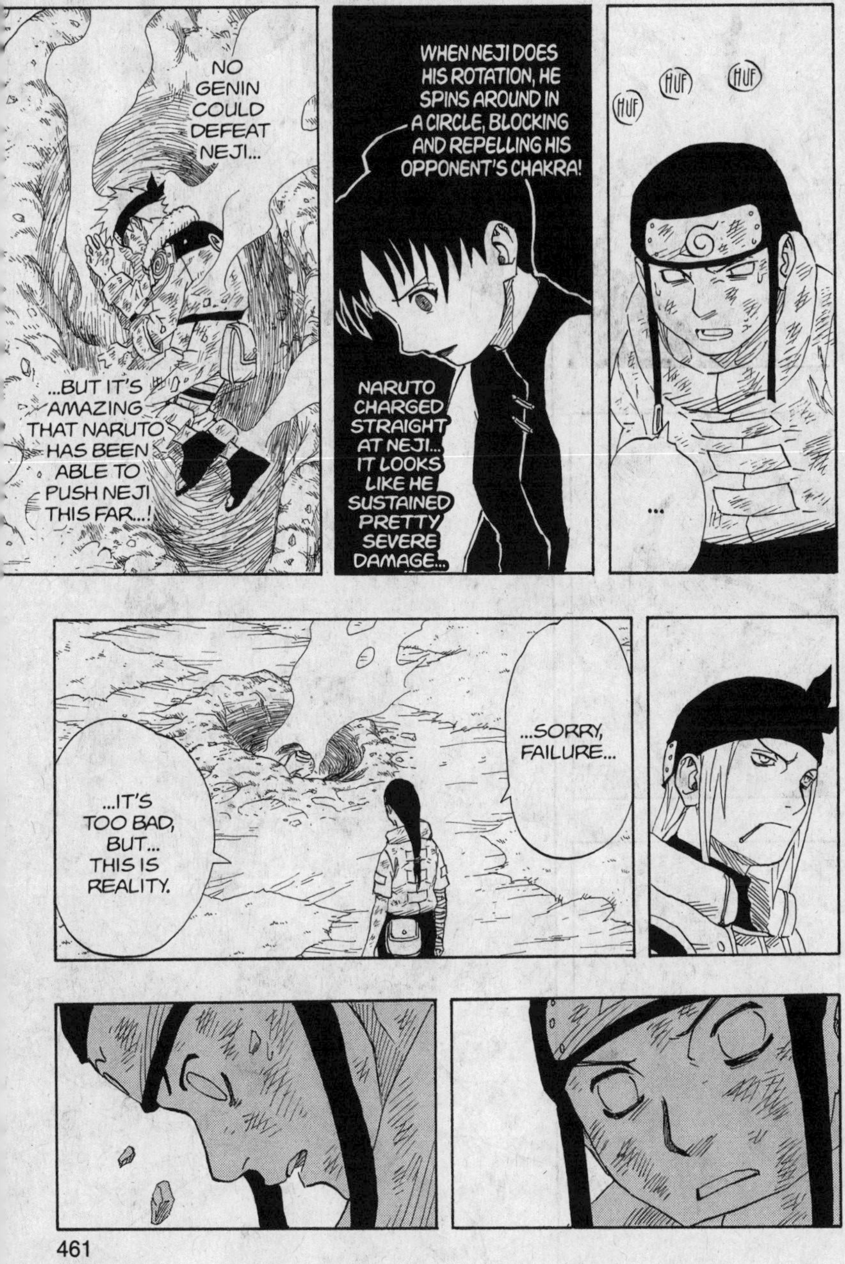
HUF
HUF
HUF
...
WHEN NEJI DOES HIS ROTATION, HE SPINS AROUND IN A CIRCLE, BLOCKING AND REPELLING HIS OPPONENT'S CHAKRA!
NARUTO CHARGED STRAIGHT AT NEJI... IT LOOKS LIKE HE SUSTAINED PRETTY SEVERE DAMAGE...
NO GENIN COULD DEFEAT NEJI...
...BUT IT'S AMAZING THAT NARUTO HAS BEEN ABLE TO PUSH NEJI THIS FAR...!
...SORRY, FAILURE...
...IT'S TOO BAD, BUT... THIS IS REALITY.

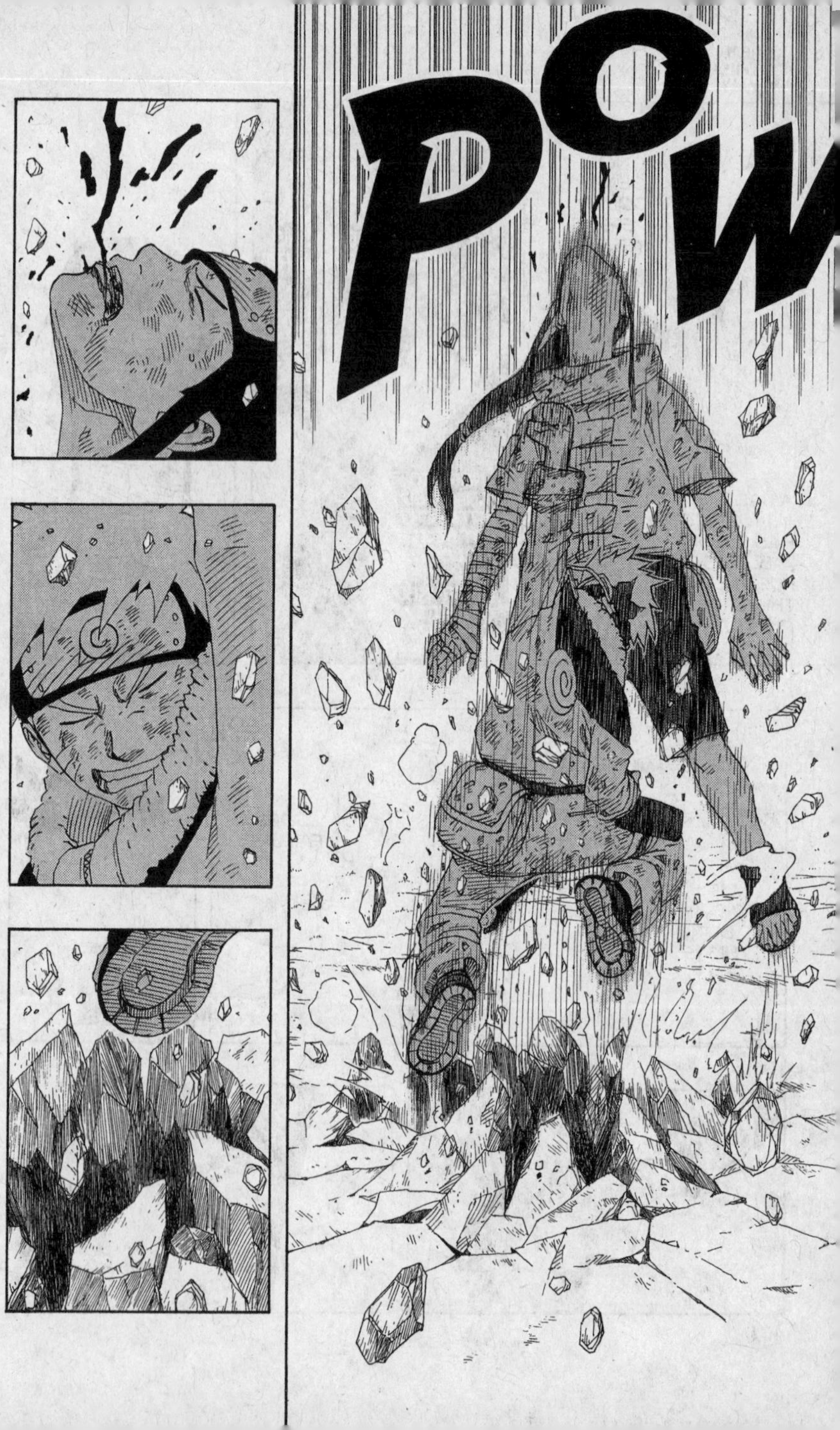
POW

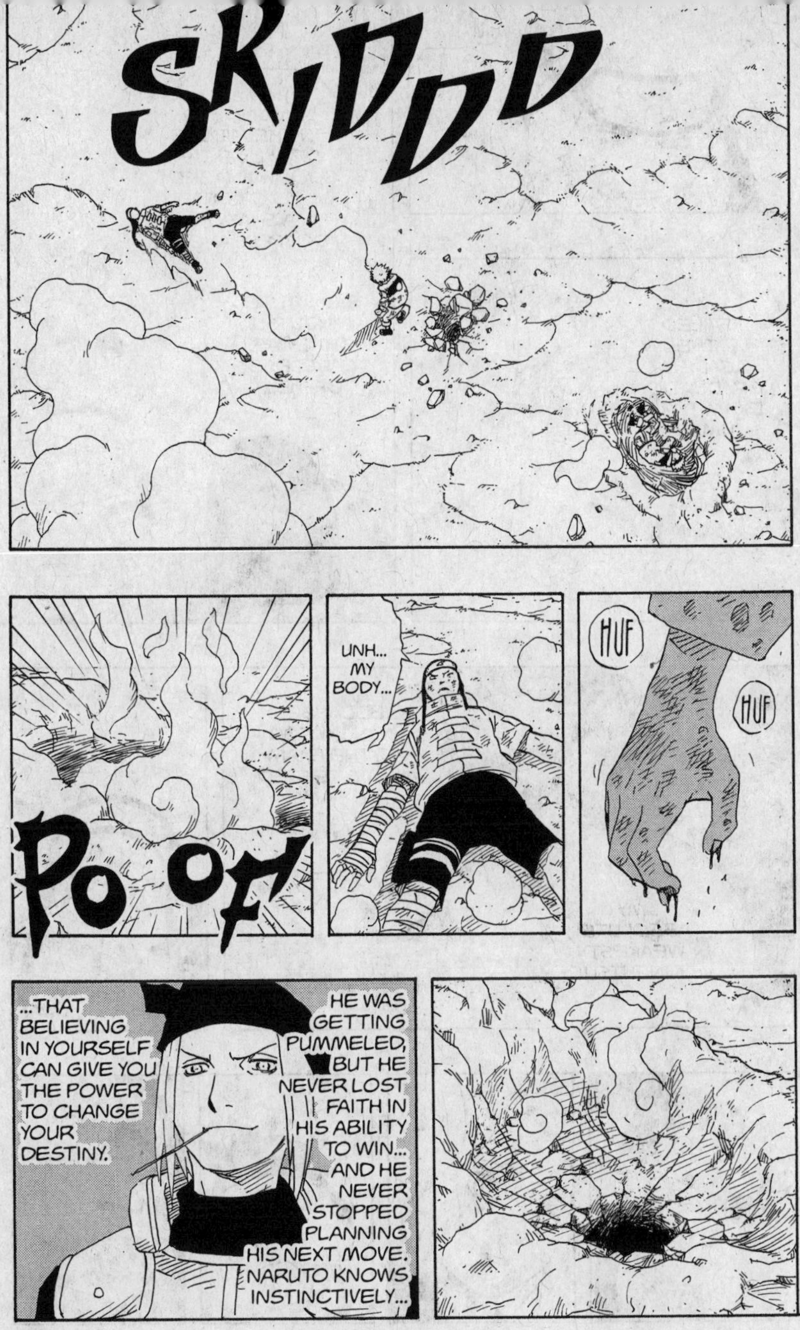
SKIDDD
HUF
HUF
UNH... MY BODY...
POOF
HE WAS GETTING PUMMELED, BUT HE NEVER LOST FAITH IN HIS ABILITY TO WIN... AND HE NEVER STOPPED PLANNING HIS NEXT MOVE. NARUTO KNOWS INSTINCTIVELY...
...THAT BELIEVING IN YOURSELF CAN GIVE YOU THE POWER TO CHANGE YOUR DESTINY.

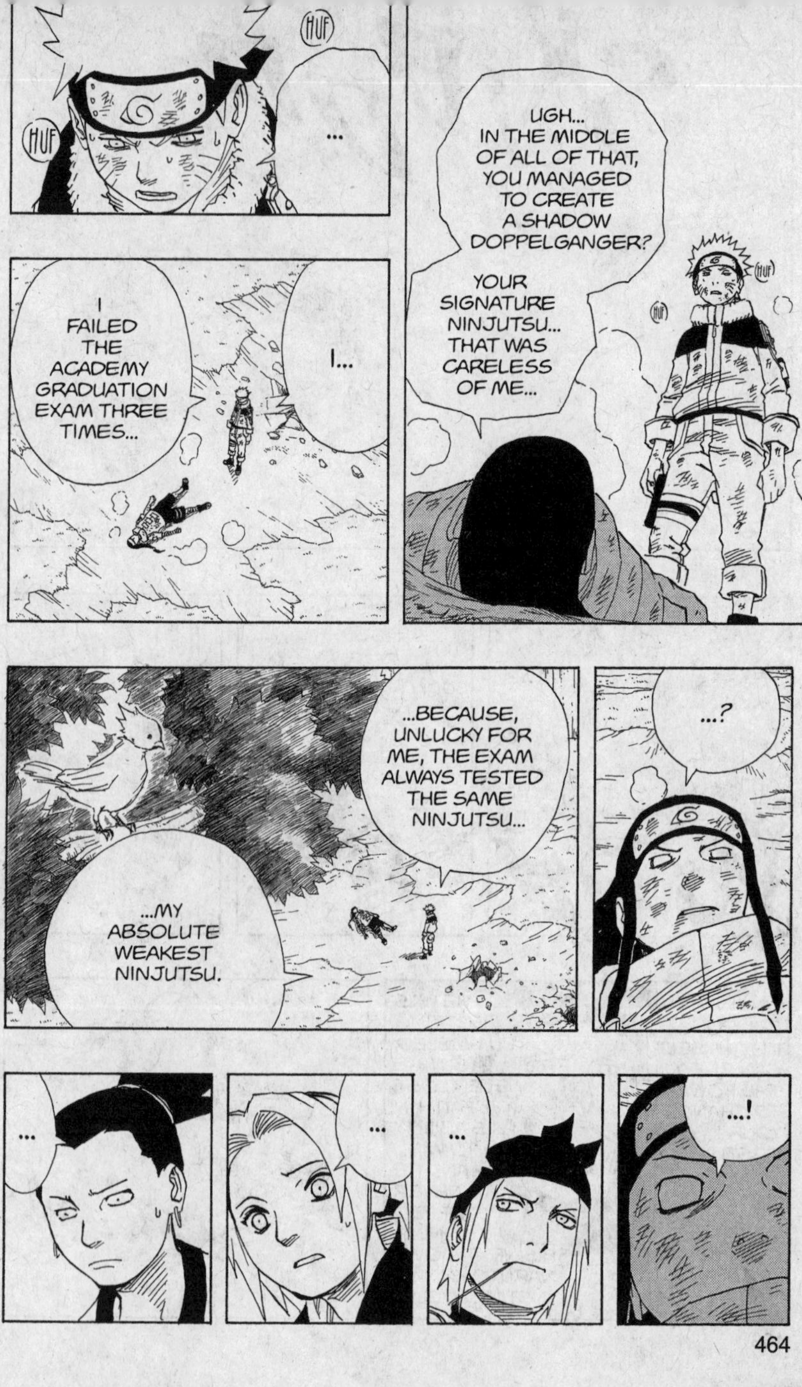

UGH... IN THE MIDDLE OF ALL OF THAT, YOU MANAGED TO CREATE A SHADOW DOPPELGANGER?
YOUR SIGNATURE NINJUTSU... THAT WAS CARELESS OF ME...
HUF
HUF
HUF
...
HUF
I...
I FAILED THE ACADEMY GRADUATION EXAM THREE TIMES...
...?
...BECAUSE, UNLUCKY FOR ME, THE EXAM ALWAYS TESTED THE SAME NINJUTSU...
...MY ABSOLUTE WEAKEST NINJUTSU.
...!
...
...
...

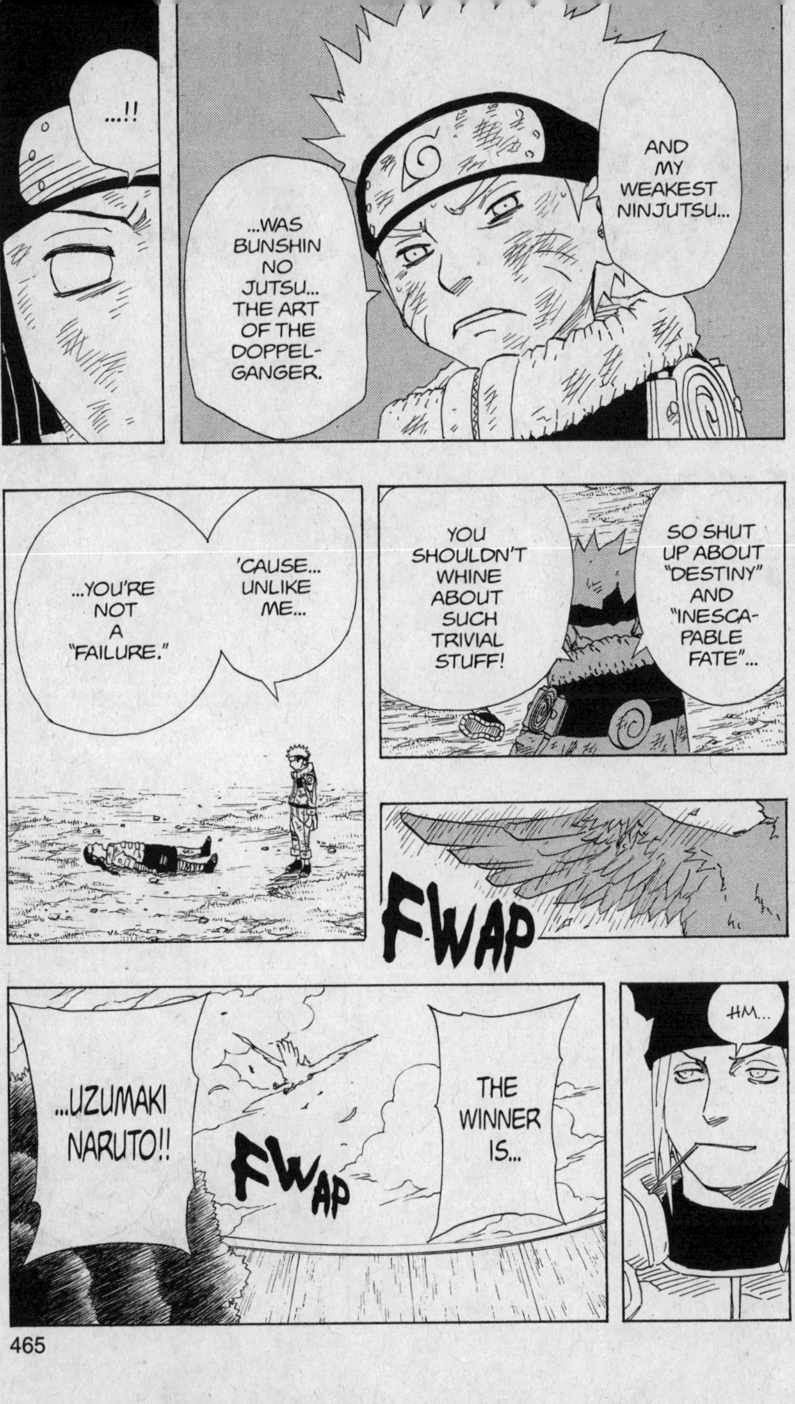
AND MY WEAKEST NINJUTSU...
...WAS BUNSHIN NO JUTSU... THE ART OF THE DOPPEL-GANGER.
...!!
SO SHUT UP ABOUT "DESTINY" AND "INESCA-PABLE FATE"...
YOU SHOULDN'T WHINE ABOUT SUCH TRIVIAL STUFF!
FWAP
'CAUSE... UNLIKE ME...
...YOU'RE NOT A "FAILURE."
HM...
THE WINNER IS...
FWAP
...UZUMAKI NARUTO!!

Number 105: The Great Flight!!

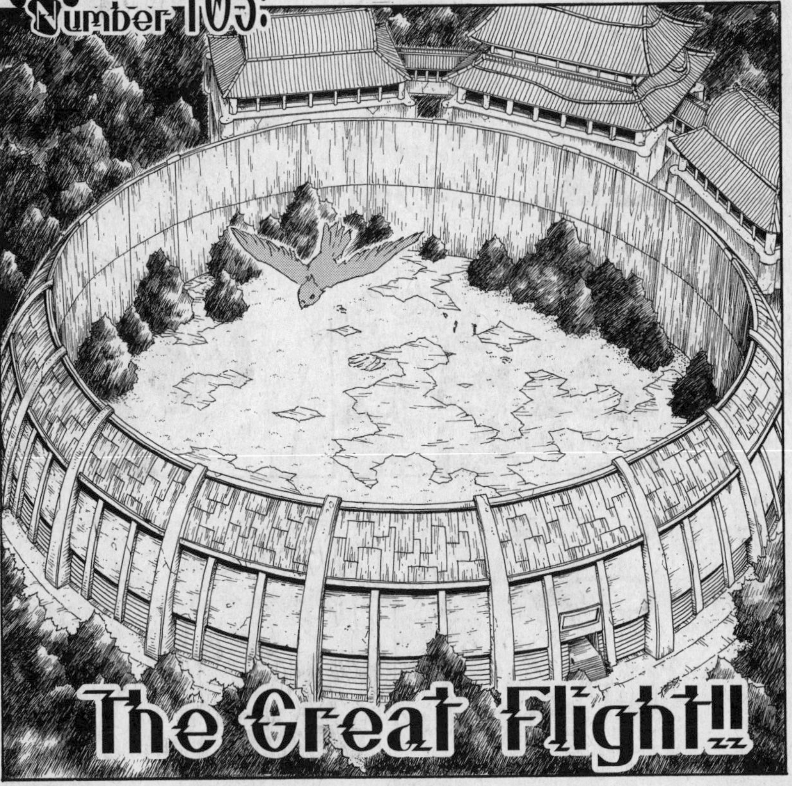

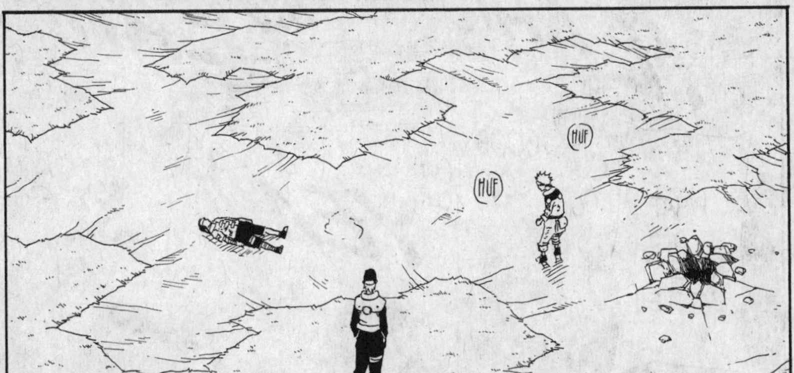
HUF
HUF

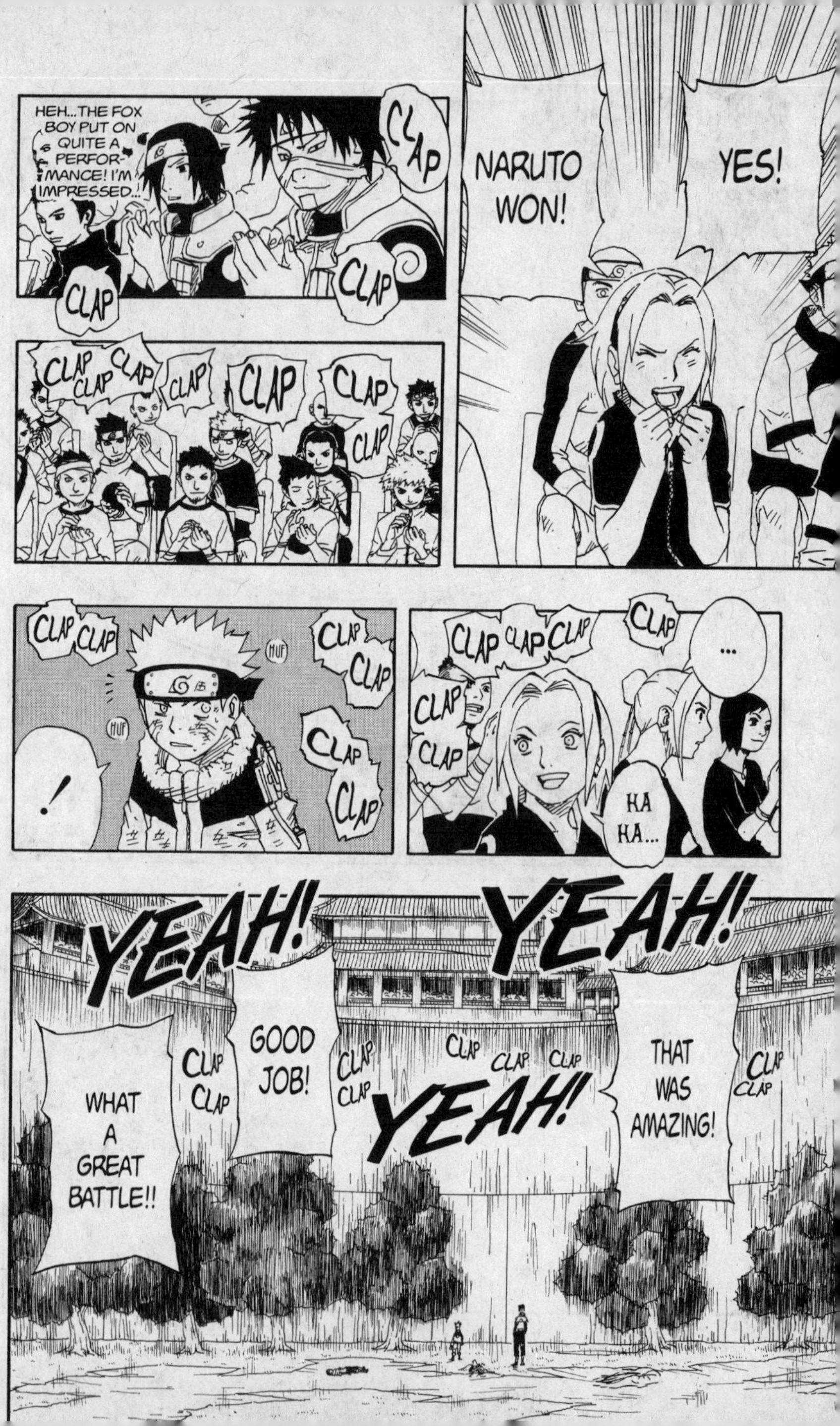
YES!
NARUTO WON!
CLAP
HEH...THE FOX BOY PUT ON QUITE A PERFORMANCE! I'M IMPRESSED...!
CLAP
CLAP
CLAP
CLAP
CLAP
CLAP
CLAP CLAP
CLAP
CLAP
...
CLAP CLAP CLAP
CLAP
CLAP
CLAP
HA HA...
CLAP
CLAP
CLAP
CLAP
HUF
CLAP CLAP
HUF
!
YEAH!
CLAP
CLAP
THAT WAS AMAZING!
CLAP CLAP CLAP
YEAH!
CLAP
CLAP
YEAH!
GOOD JOB!
CLAP
CLAP
WHAT A GREAT BATTLE!!

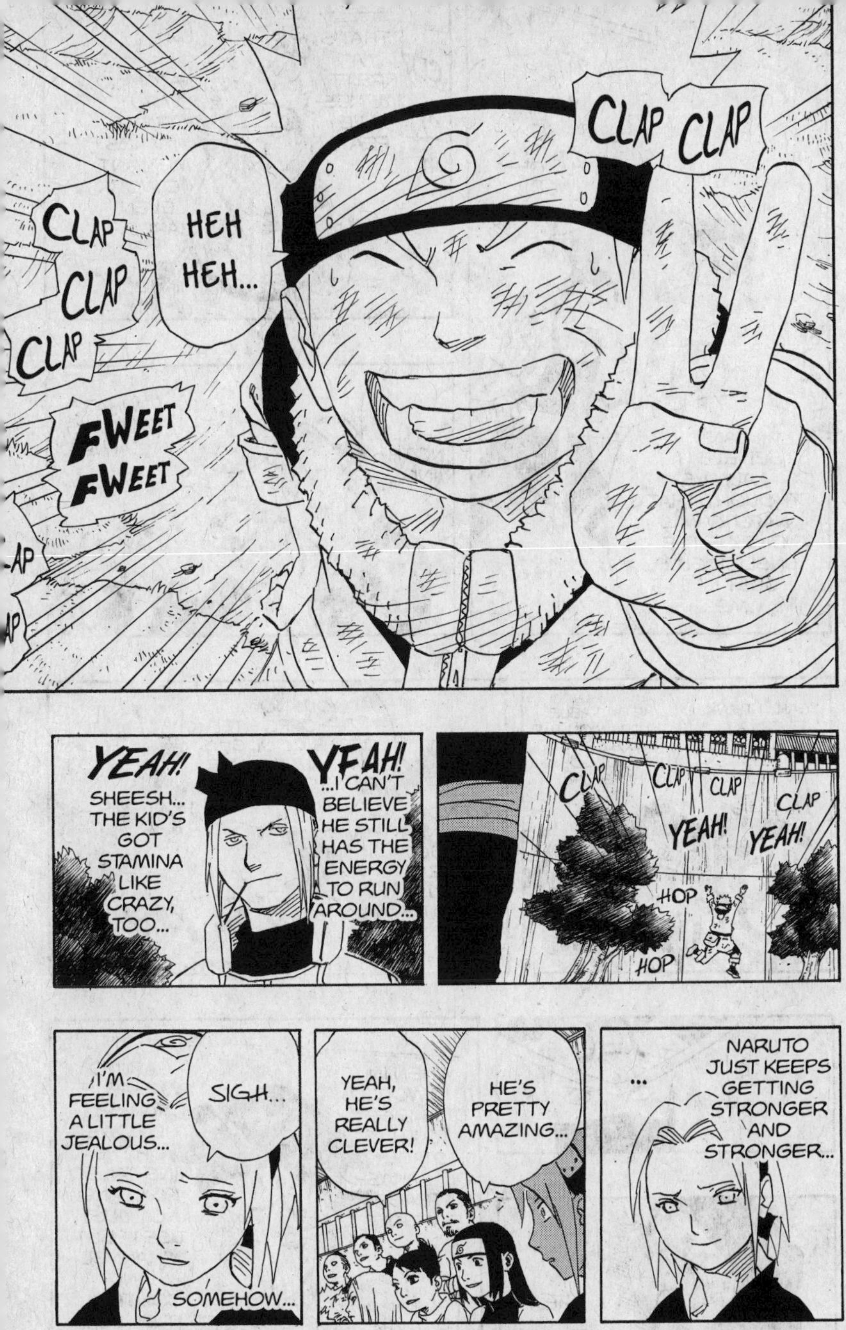
CLAP CLAP
HEH HEH...
CLAP
CLAP
CLAP
FWEET FWEET
CLAP
CLAP
CLAP
CLAP
YEAH!
YEAH!
HOP
HOP
YEAH!
...I CAN'T BELIEVE HE STILL HAS THE ENERGY TO RUN AROUND...
YEAH!
SHEESH... THE KID'S GOT STAMINA LIKE CRAZY, TOO...
NARUTO JUST KEEPS GETTING STRONGER AND STRONGER...
...
HE'S PRETTY AMAZING...
YEAH, HE'S REALLY CLEVER!
SIGH...
I'M FEELING A LITTLE JEALOUS...
SOMEHOW...

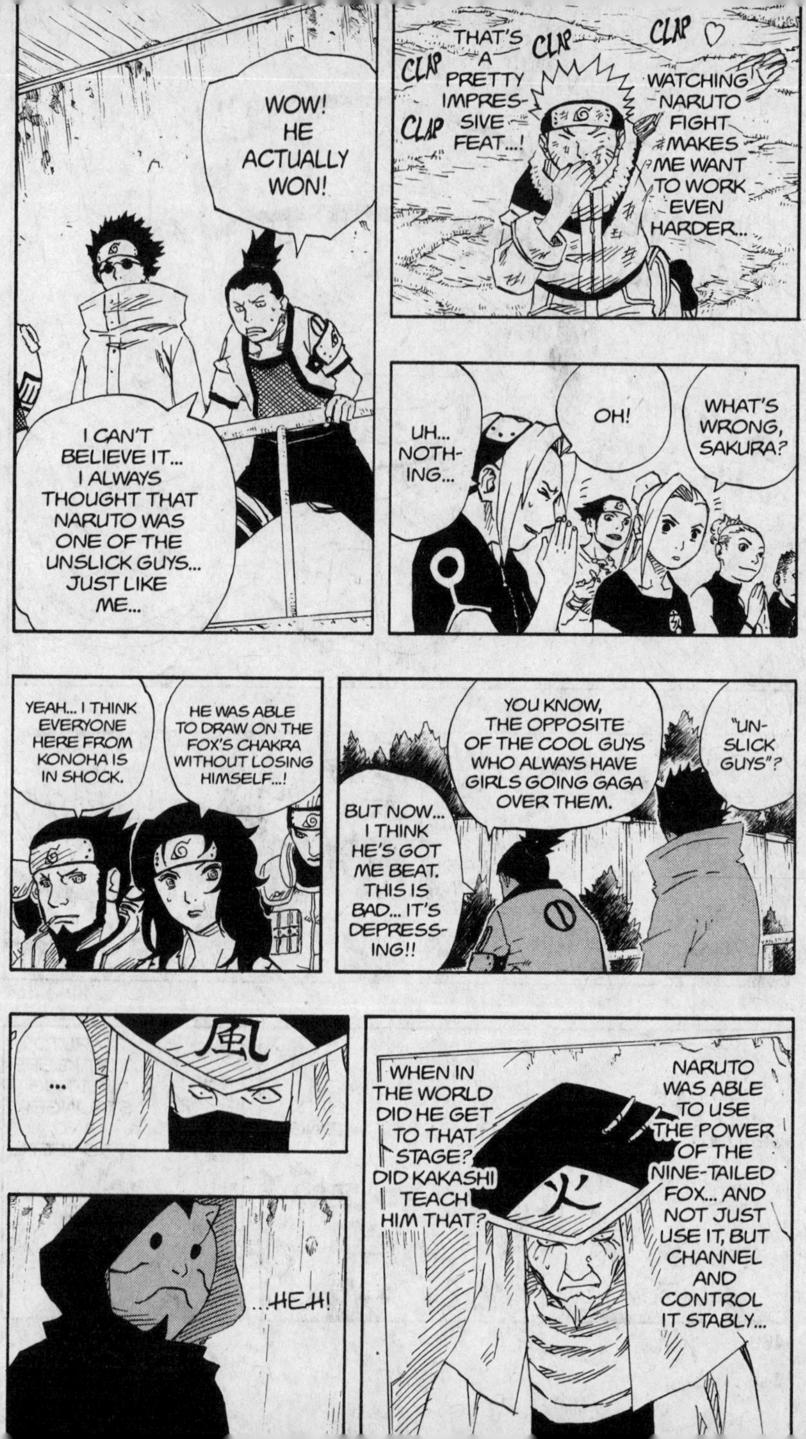
CLAP
CLAP
CLAP
CLAP ♡
THAT'S A PRETTY IMPRES-SIVE FEAT...!
WATCHING NARUTO FIGHT MAKES ME WANT TO WORK EVEN HARDER...
WHAT'S WRONG, SAKURA?
OH!
UH... NOTH-ING...
WOW! HE ACTUALLY WON!
I CAN'T BELIEVE IT... I ALWAYS THOUGHT THAT NARUTO WAS ONE OF THE UNSLICK GUYS... JUST LIKE ME...
"UN-SLICK GUYS"?
YOU KNOW, THE OPPOSITE OF THE COOL GUYS WHO ALWAYS HAVE GIRLS GOING GAGA OVER THEM.
BUT NOW... I THINK HE'S GOT ME BEAT. THIS IS BAD... IT'S DEPRESS-ING!!
HE WAS ABLE TO DRAW ON THE FOX'S CHAKRA WITHOUT LOSING HIMSELF...!
YEAH... I THINK EVERYONE HERE FROM KONOHA IS IN SHOCK.
火
NARUTO WAS ABLE TO USE THE POWER OF THE NINE-TAILED FOX... AND NOT JUST USE IT, BUT CHANNEL AND CONTROL IT STABLY...
WHEN IN THE WORLD DID HE GET TO THAT STAGE? DID KAKASHI TEACH HIM THAT?
風
...
...HEH!

READ THIS WAY

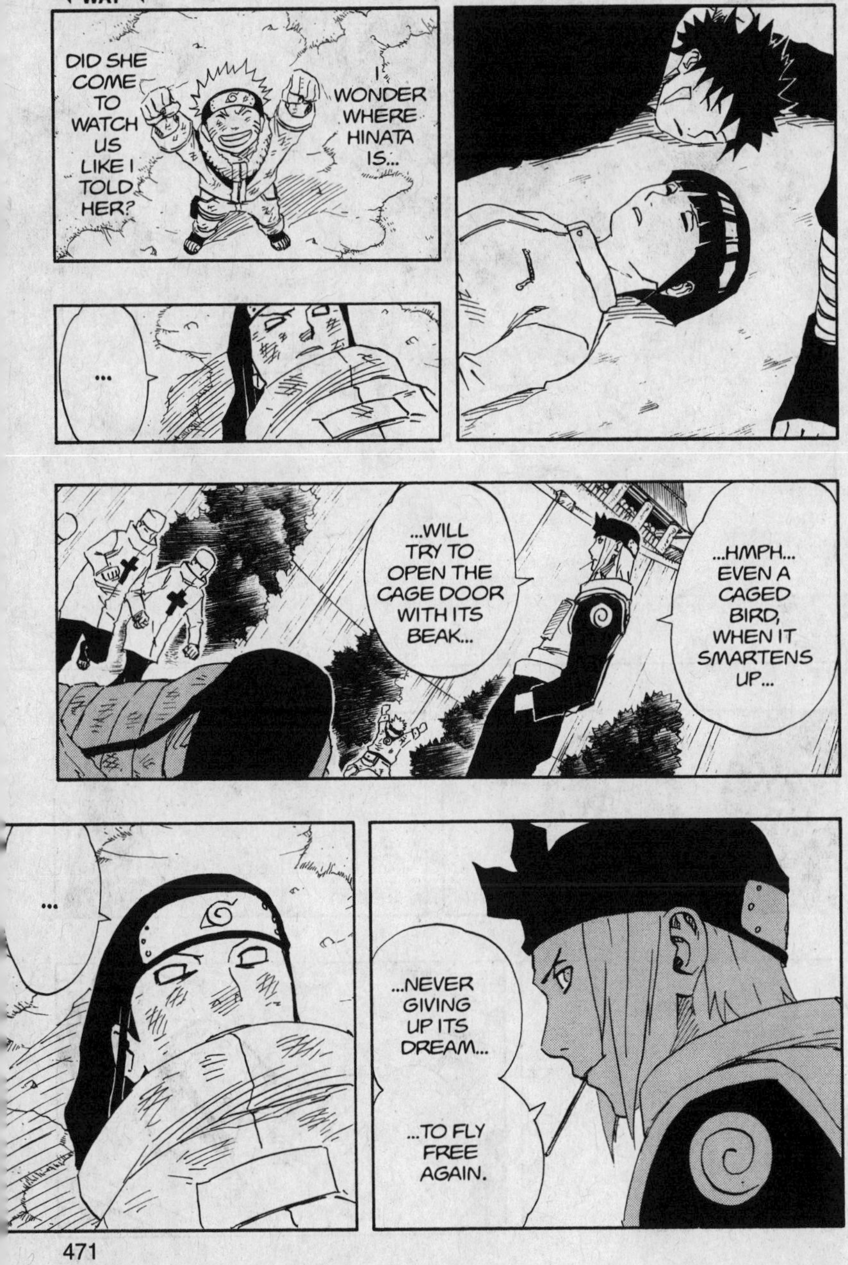
I WONDER WHERE HINATA IS...
DID SHE COME TO WATCH US LIKE I TOLD HER?
...
...HMPH... EVEN A CAGED BIRD, WHEN IT SMARTENS UP...
...WILL TRY TO OPEN THE CAGE DOOR WITH ITS BEAK...
...NEVER GIVING UP ITS DREAM...
...TO FLY FREE AGAIN.
...

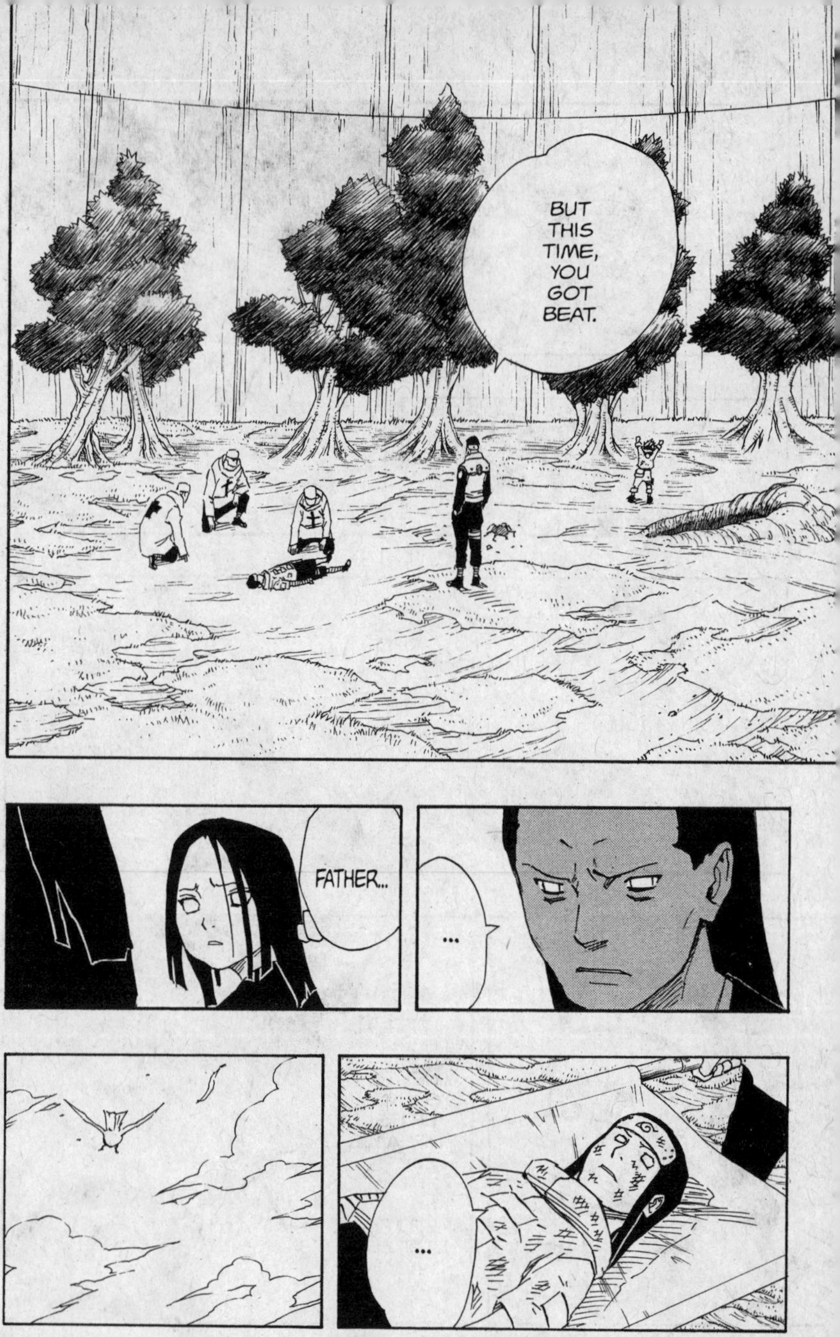
BUT THIS TIME, YOU GOT BEAT.
...
FATHER...
...

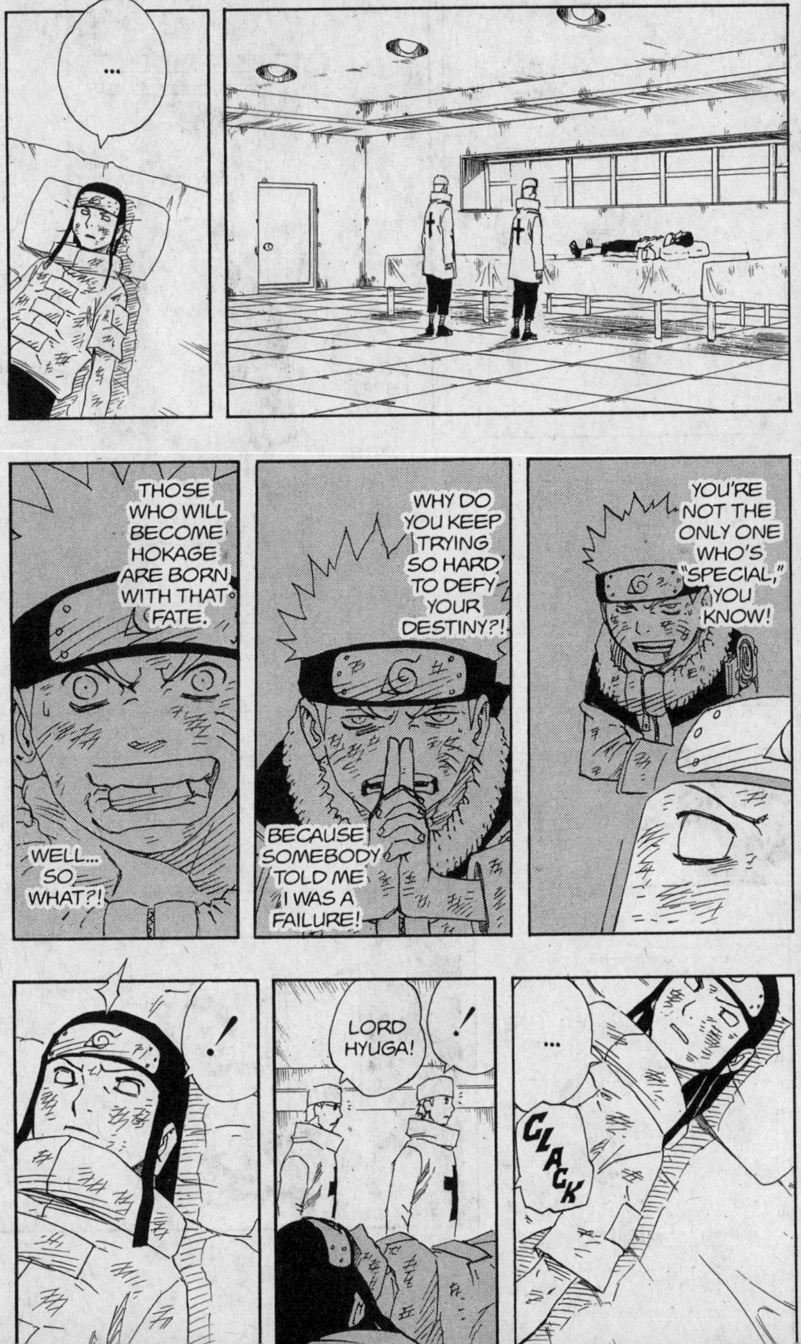
...
YOU'RE NOT THE ONLY ONE WHO'S "SPECIAL," YOU KNOW!
WHY DO YOU KEEP TRYING SO HARD TO DEFY YOUR DESTINY?!
BECAUSE SOMEBODY TOLD ME I WAS A FAILURE!
THOSE WHO WILL BECOME HOKAGE ARE BORN WITH THAT FATE.
WELL... SO WHAT?!
...
CLACK
!
LORD HYUGA!
!

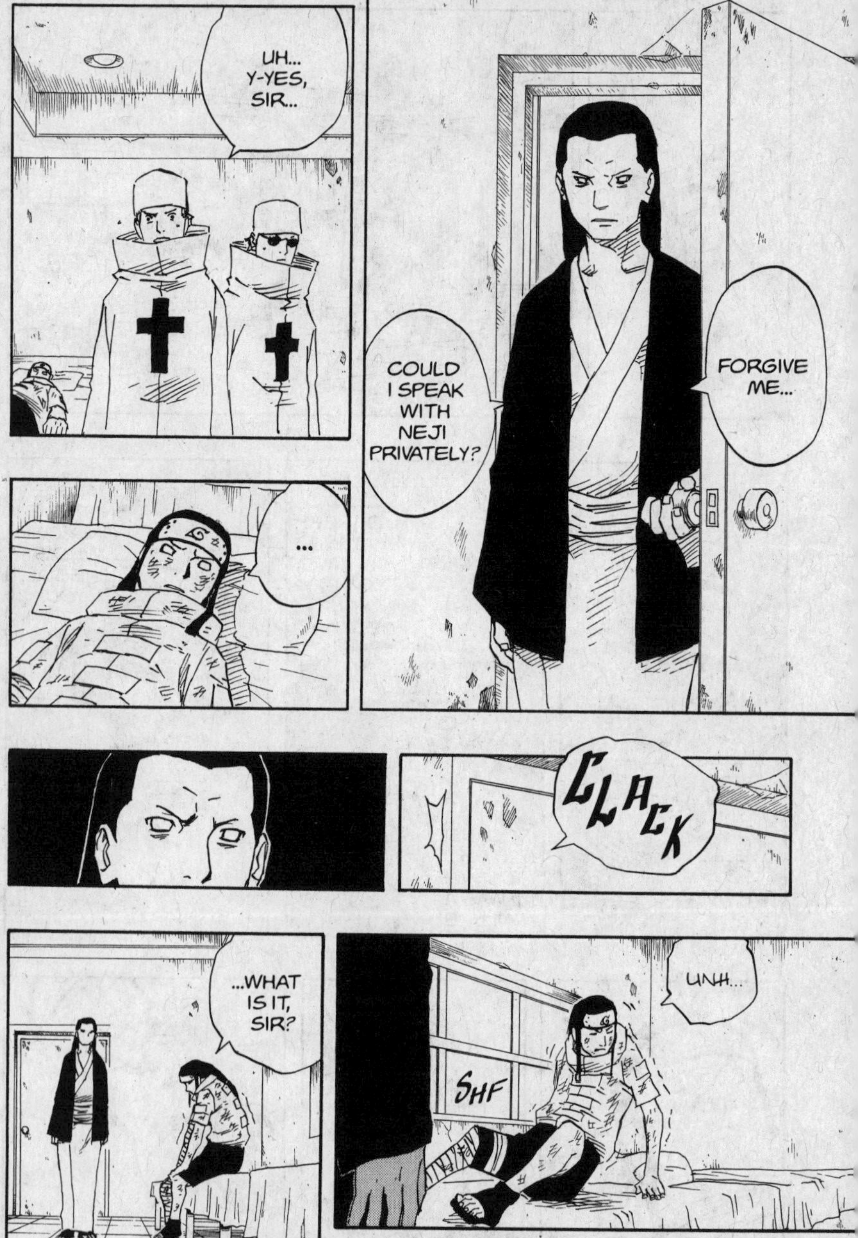
FORGIVE ME...
COULD I SPEAK WITH NEJI PRIVATELY?
UH... Y-YES, SIR...
...
CLACK
UNH...
SHF
...WHAT IS IT, SIR?

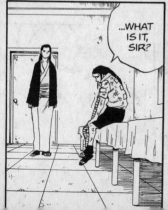

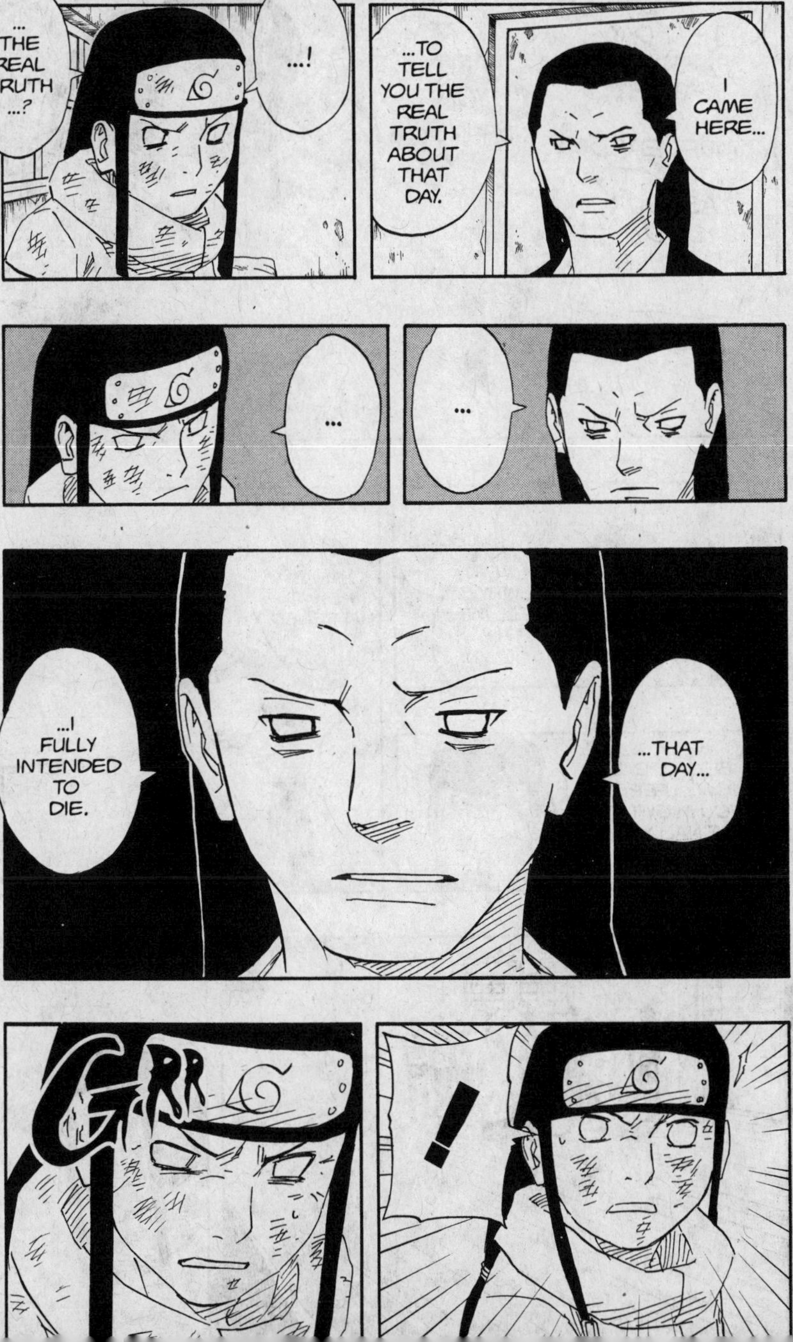
I CAME HERE...
...TO TELL YOU THE REAL TRUTH ABOUT THAT DAY.
...!
... THE REAL TRUTH ...?
...
...
...THAT DAY...
...I FULLY INTENDED TO DIE.
!
GRR

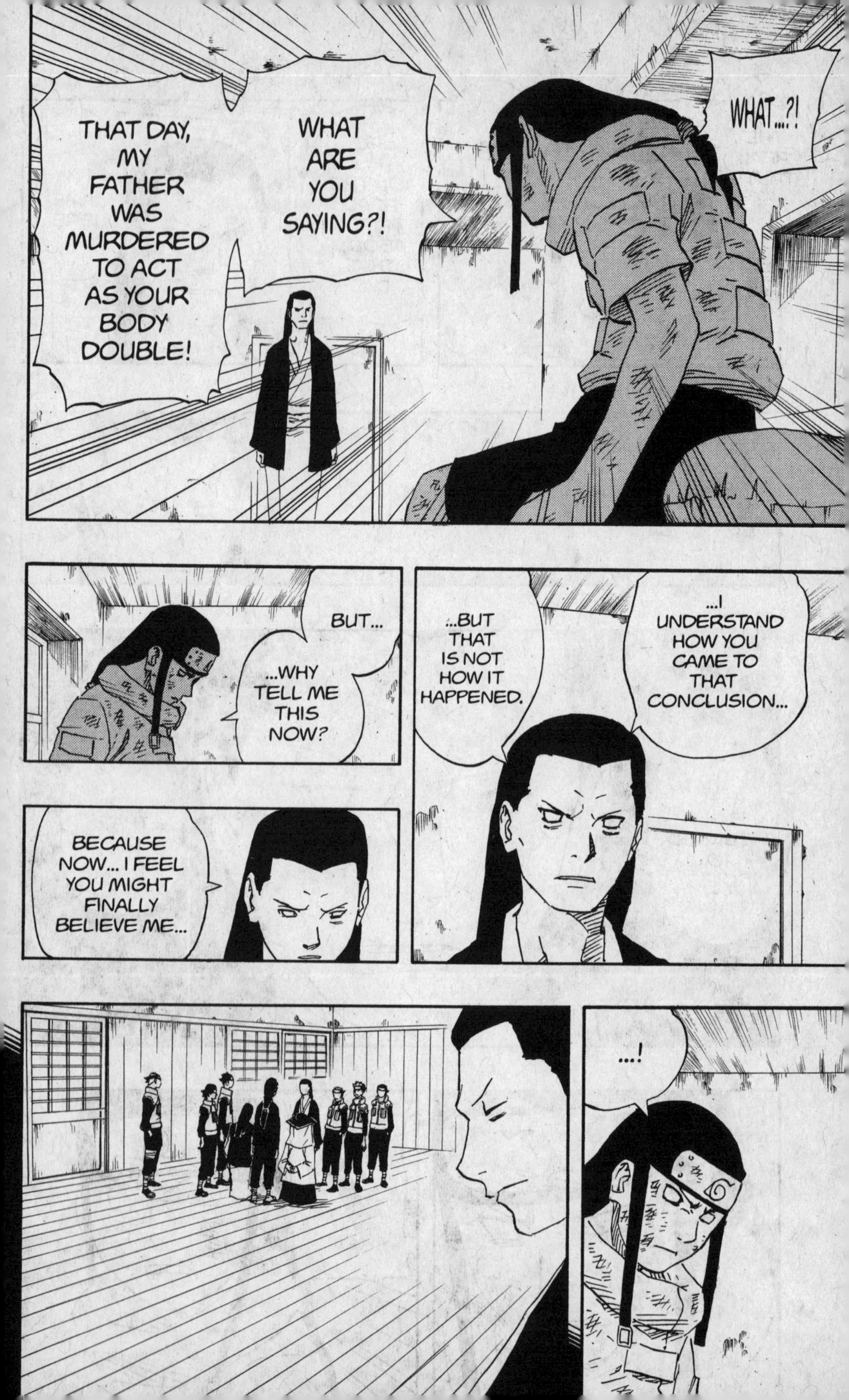
WHAT...?!
WHAT ARE YOU SAYING?!
THAT DAY, MY FATHER WAS MURDERED TO ACT AS YOUR BODY DOUBLE!
...I UNDERSTAND HOW YOU CAME TO THAT CONCLUSION...
...BUT THAT IS NOT HOW IT HAPPENED.
BUT...
...WHY TELL ME THIS NOW?
BECAUSE NOW... I FEEL YOU MIGHT FINALLY BELIEVE ME...
...!

READ THIS WAY

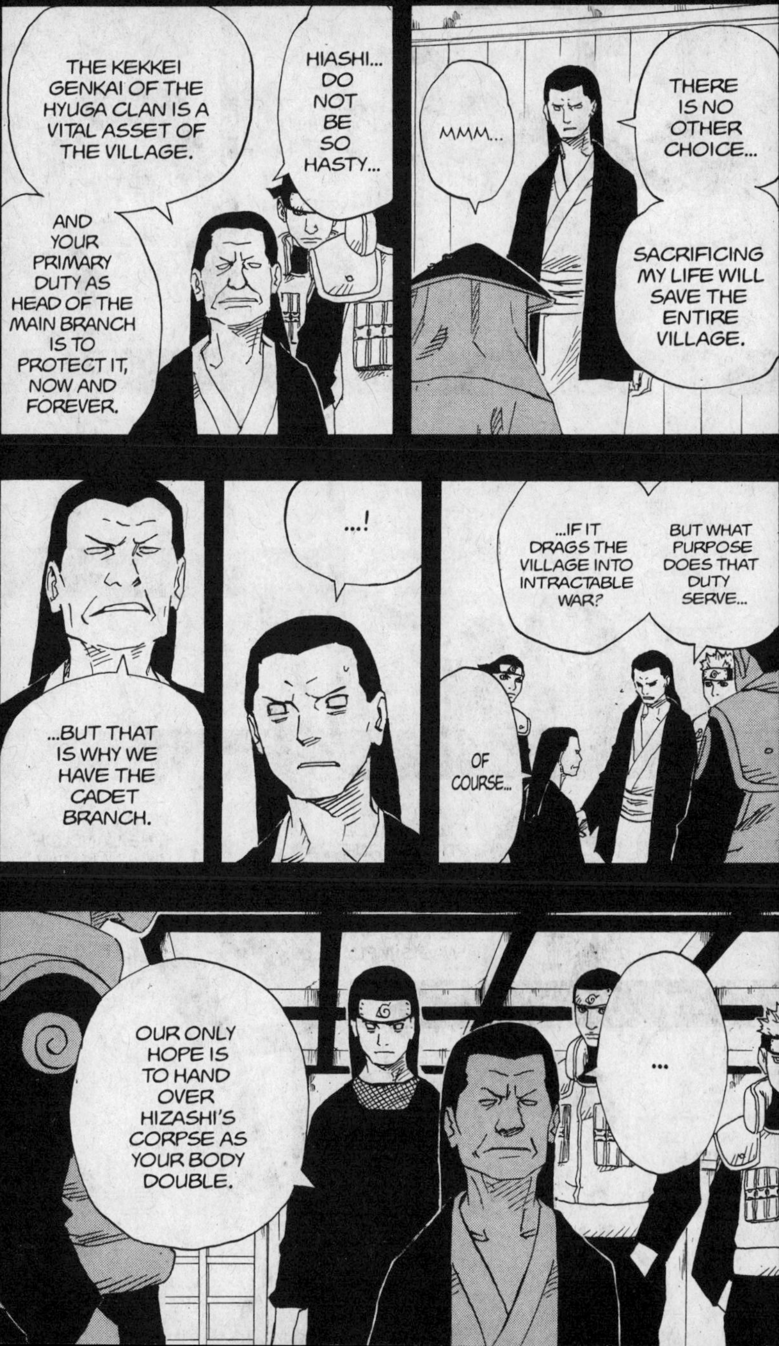
THERE IS NO OTHER CHOICE...
SACRIFICING MY LIFE WILL SAVE THE ENTIRE VILLAGE.
MMM...
HIASHI... DO NOT BE SO HASTY...
THE KEKKEI GENKAI OF THE HYUGA CLAN IS A VITAL ASSET OF THE VILLAGE.
AND YOUR PRIMARY DUTY AS HEAD OF THE MAIN BRANCH IS TO PROTECT IT, NOW AND FOREVER.
BUT WHAT PURPOSE DOES THAT DUTY SERVE...
...IF IT DRAGS THE VILLAGE INTO INTRACTABLE WAR?
OF COURSE...
...!
...BUT THAT IS WHY WE HAVE THE CADET BRANCH.
...
OUR ONLY HOPE IS TO HAND OVER HIZASHI'S CORPSE AS YOUR BODY DOUBLE.

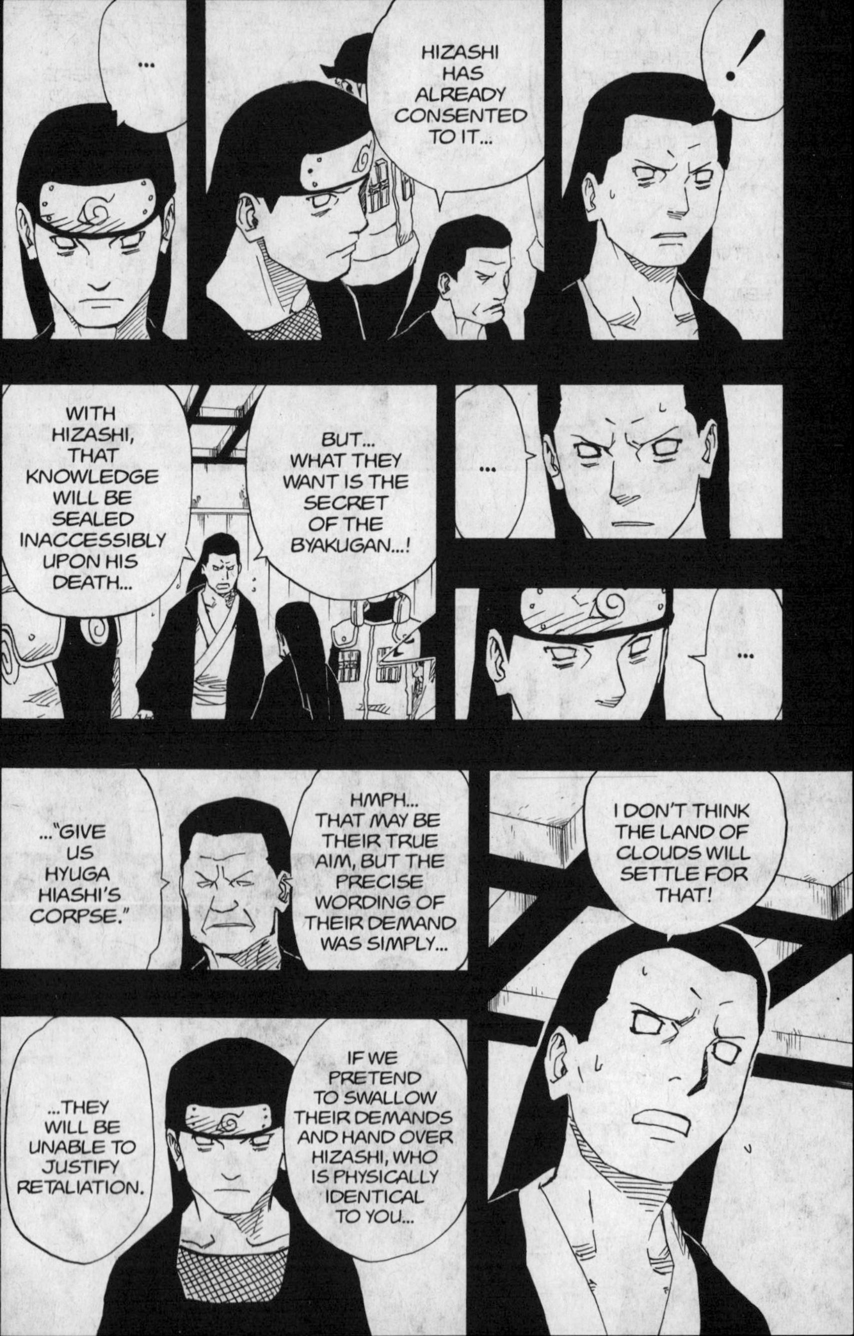
!
HIZASHI HAS ALREADY CONSENTED TO IT...
...
...
...
BUT... WHAT THEY WANT IS THE SECRET OF THE BYAKUGAN...!
WITH HIZASHI, THAT KNOWLEDGE WILL BE SEALED INACCESSIBLY UPON HIS DEATH...
I DON'T THINK THE LAND OF CLOUDS WILL SETTLE FOR THAT!
HMPH... THAT MAY BE THEIR TRUE AIM, BUT THE PRECISE WORDING OF THEIR DEMAND WAS SIMPLY...
..."GIVE US HYUGA HIASHI'S CORPSE."
IF WE PRETEND TO SWALLOW THEIR DEMANDS AND HAND OVER HIZASHI, WHO IS PHYSICALLY IDENTICAL TO YOU...
...THEY WILL BE UNABLE TO JUSTIFY RETALIATION.

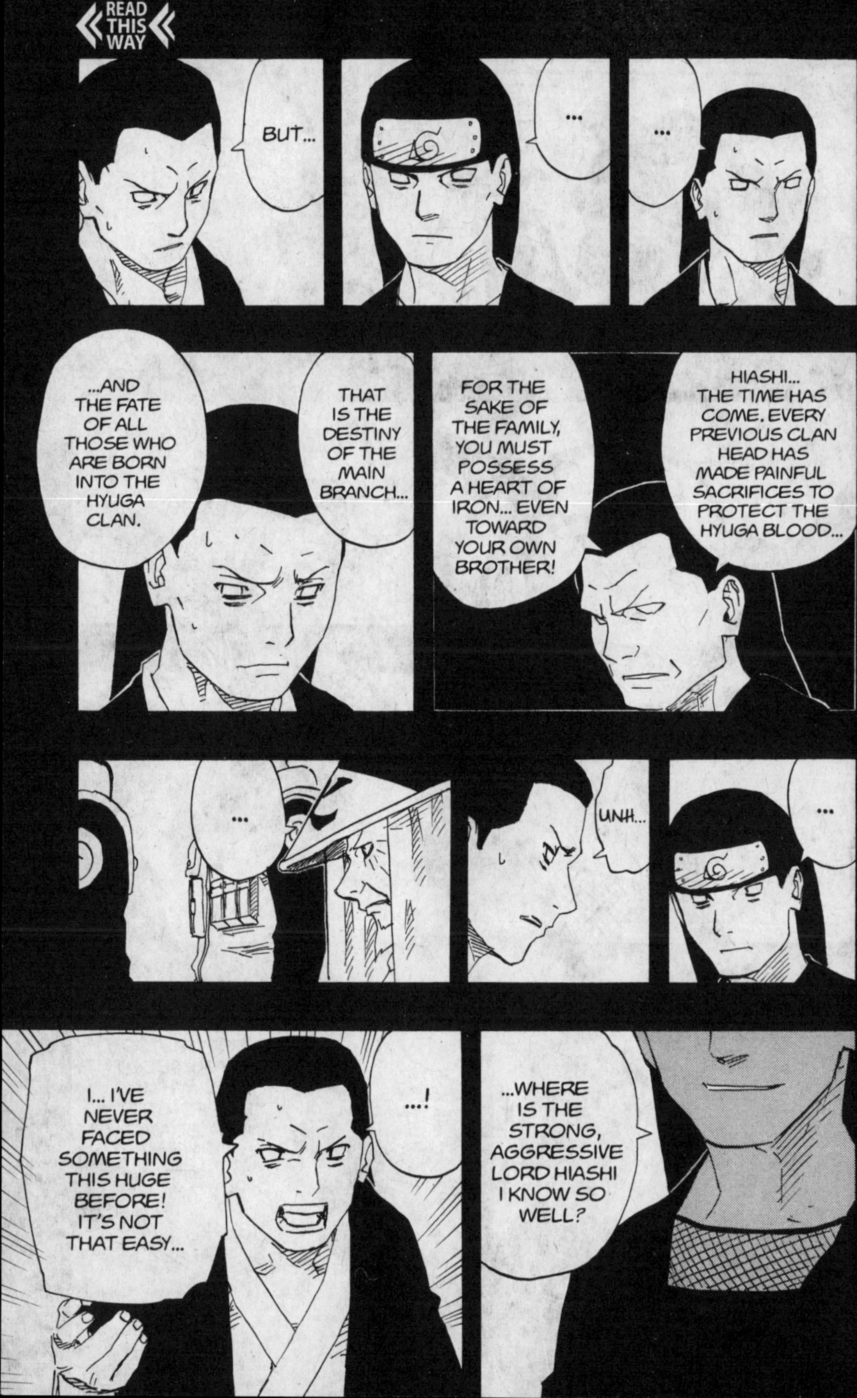
READ THIS WAY
...
...
BUT...
HIASHI... THE TIME HAS COME. EVERY PREVIOUS CLAN HEAD HAS MADE PAINFUL SACRIFICES TO PROTECT THE HYUGA BLOOD...
FOR THE SAKE OF THE FAMILY, YOU MUST POSSESS A HEART OF IRON... EVEN TOWARD YOUR OWN BROTHER!
THAT IS THE DESTINY OF THE MAIN BRANCH...
...AND THE FATE OF ALL THOSE WHO ARE BORN INTO THE HYUGA CLAN.
...
UNH...
...
...WHERE IS THE STRONG, AGGRESSIVE LORD HIASHI I KNOW SO WELL?
...!
I... I'VE NEVER FACED SOMETHING THIS HUGE BEFORE! IT'S NOT THAT EASY...

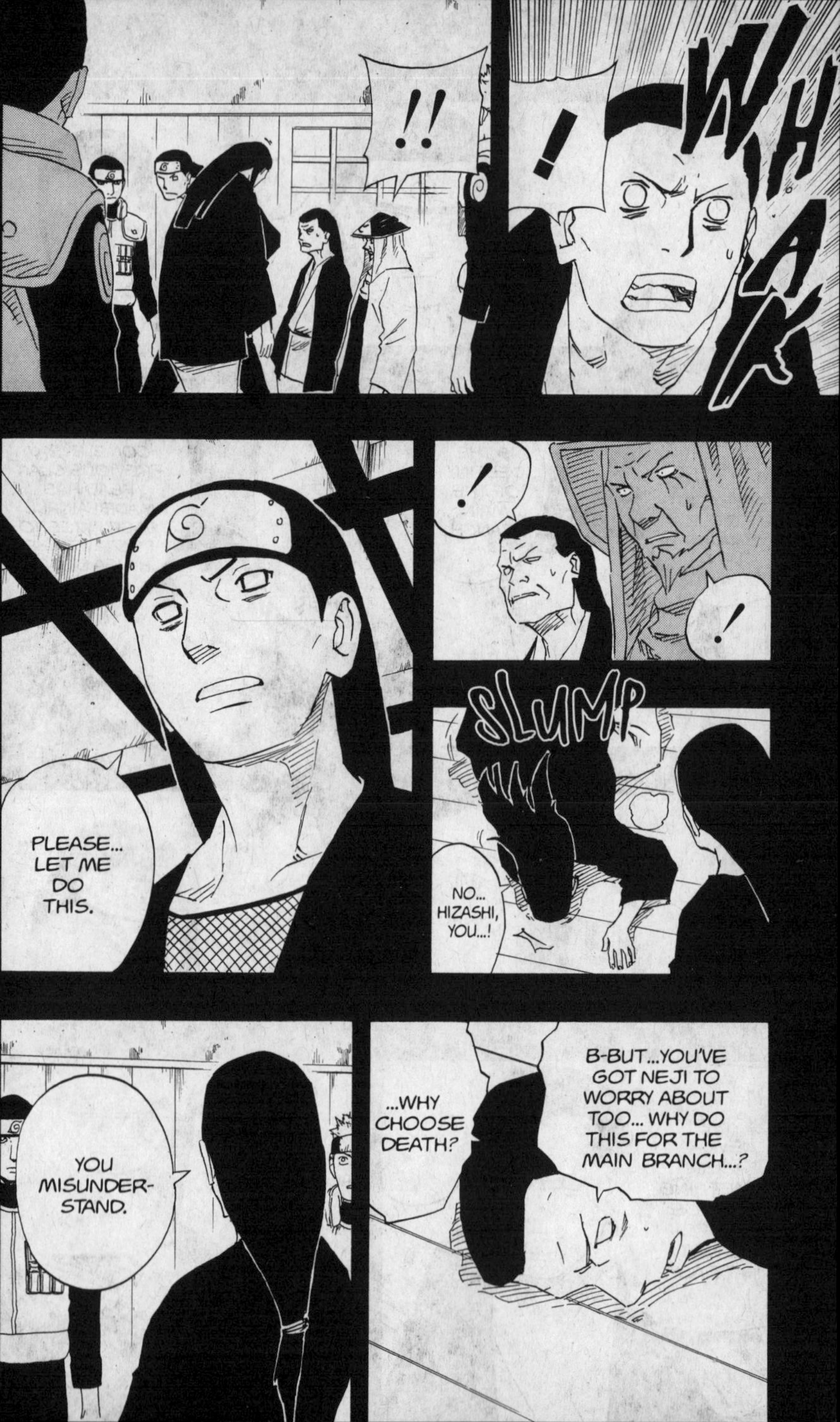
WHAK
!
!!
!
!
SLUMP
NO... HIZASHI, YOU...!
PLEASE... LET ME DO THIS.
B-BUT...YOU'VE GOT NEJI TO WORRY ABOUT TOO... WHY DO THIS FOR THE MAIN BRANCH...?
...WHY CHOOSE DEATH?
YOU MISUNDER-STAND.

READ THIS WAY

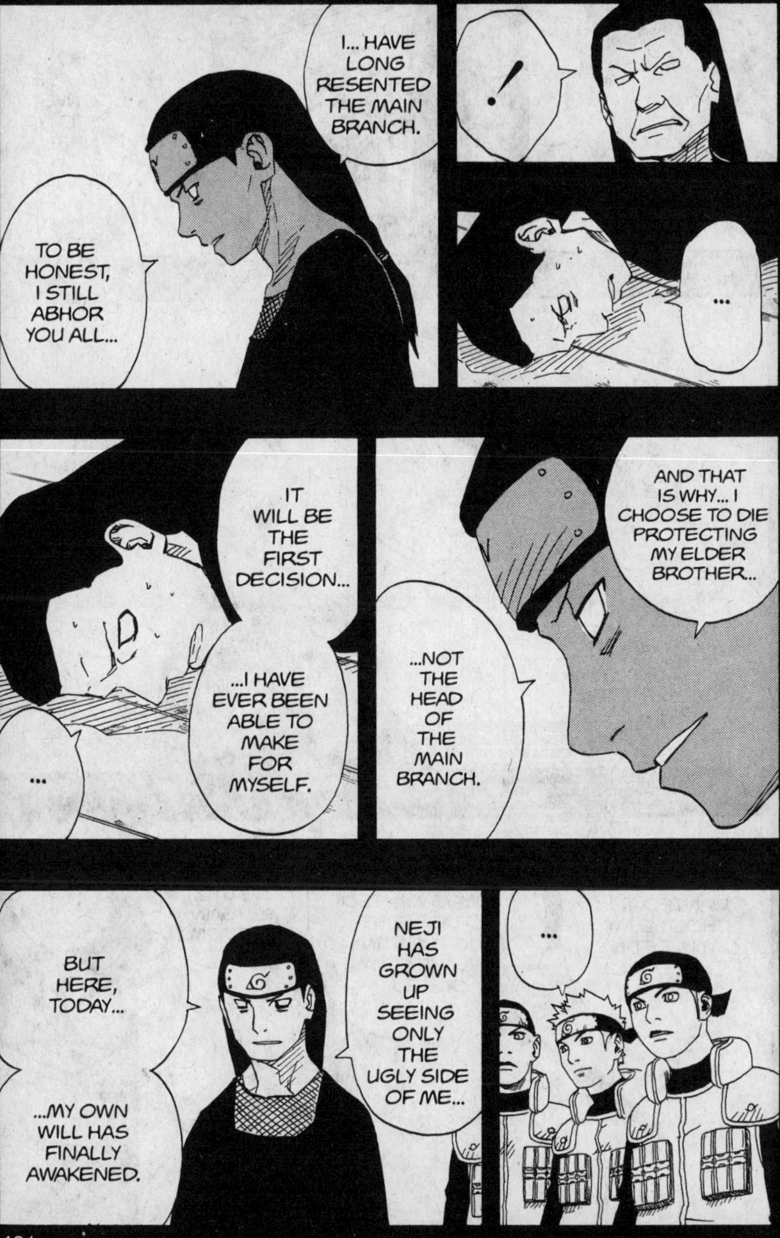

!
...
I... HAVE LONG RESENTED THE MAIN BRANCH.
TO BE HONEST, I STILL ABHOR YOU ALL...
AND THAT IS WHY... I CHOOSE TO DIE PROTECTING MY ELDER BROTHER...
...NOT THE HEAD OF THE MAIN BRANCH.
IT WILL BE THE FIRST DECISION...
...I HAVE EVER BEEN ABLE TO MAKE FOR MYSELF.
...
...
NEJI HAS GROWN UP SEEING ONLY THE UGLY SIDE OF ME...
BUT HERE, TODAY...
...MY OWN WILL HAS FINALLY AWAKENED.

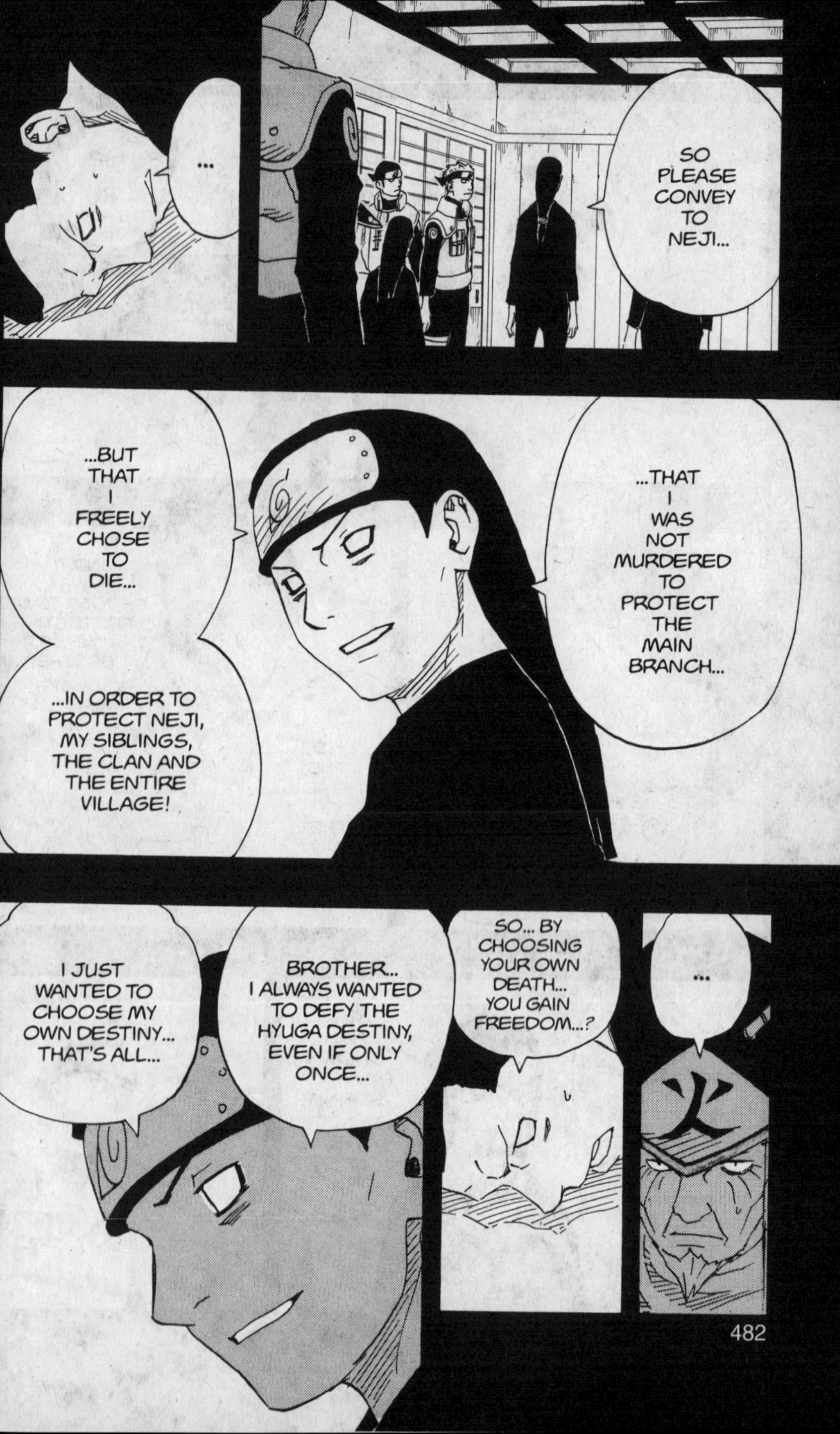
SO PLEASE CONVEY TO NEJI...
...
...THAT I WAS NOT MURDERED TO PROTECT THE MAIN BRANCH...
...BUT THAT I FREELY CHOSE TO DIE...
...IN ORDER TO PROTECT NEJI, MY SIBLINGS, THE CLAN AND THE ENTIRE VILLAGE!
...
SO... BY CHOOSING YOUR OWN DEATH... YOU GAIN FREEDOM...?
BROTHER... I ALWAYS WANTED TO DEFY THE HYUGA DESTINY, EVEN IF ONLY ONCE...
I JUST WANTED TO CHOOSE MY OWN DESTINY... THAT'S ALL...

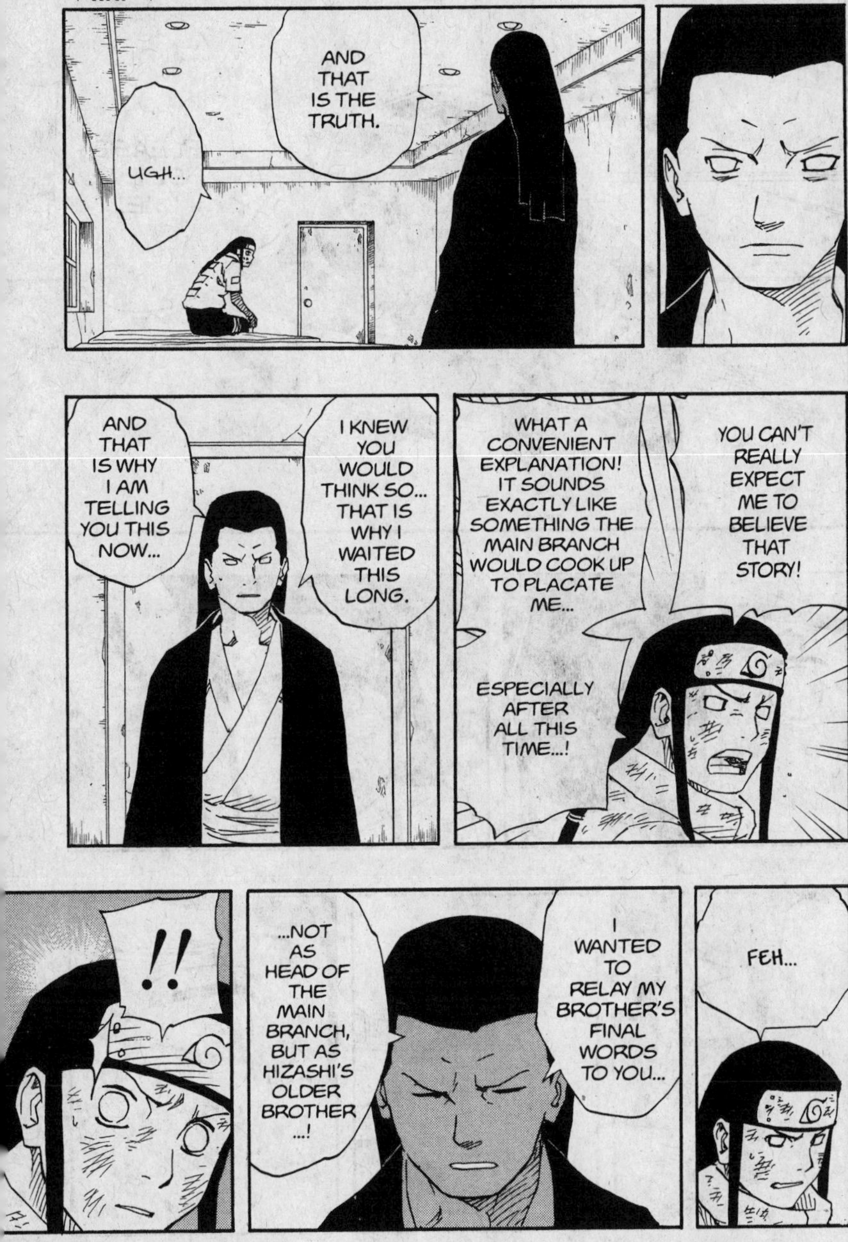
AND THAT IS THE TRUTH.
UGH...
YOU CAN'T REALLY EXPECT ME TO BELIEVE THAT STORY!
WHAT A CONVENIENT EXPLANATION! IT SOUNDS EXACTLY LIKE SOMETHING THE MAIN BRANCH WOULD COOK UP TO PLACATE ME...
ESPECIALLY AFTER ALL THIS TIME...!
I KNEW YOU WOULD THINK SO... THAT IS WHY I WAITED THIS LONG.
AND THAT IS WHY I AM TELLING YOU THIS NOW...
FEH...
I WANTED TO RELAY MY BROTHER'S FINAL WORDS TO YOU...
...NOT AS HEAD OF THE MAIN BRANCH, BUT AS HIZASHI'S OLDER BROTHER ...!
!!

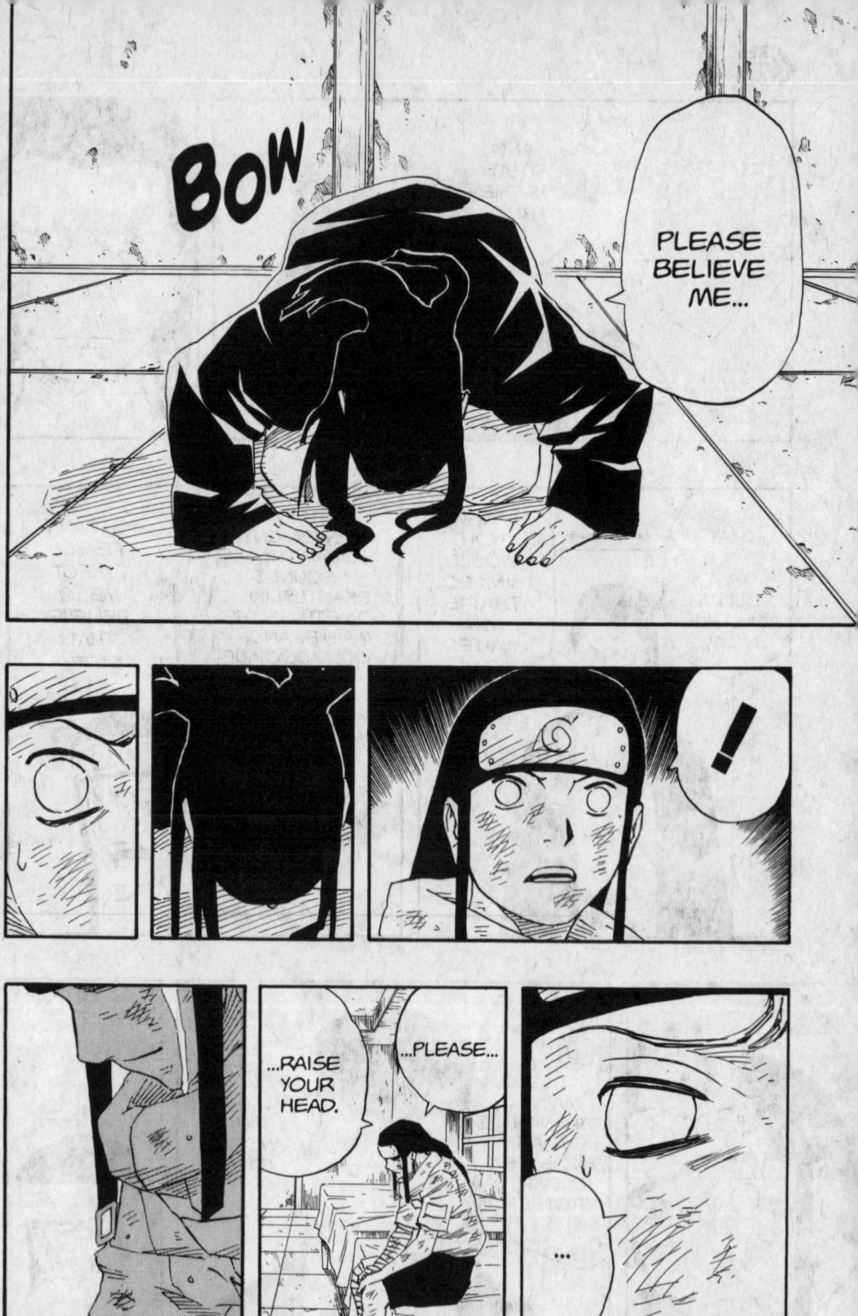
PLEASE BELIEVE ME...
BOW
!
...
...PLEASE...
...RAISE YOUR HEAD.

READ THIS WAY

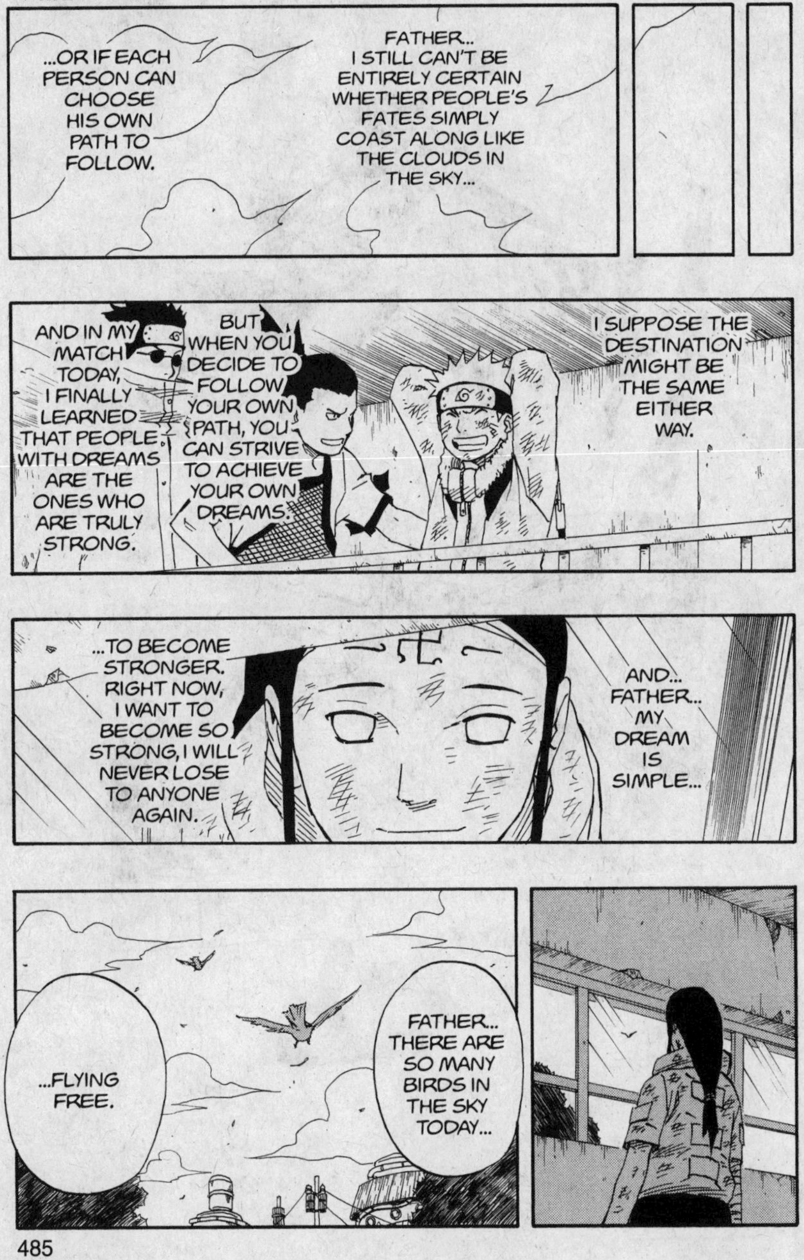
FATHER... I STILL CAN'T BE ENTIRELY CERTAIN WHETHER PEOPLE'S FATES SIMPLY COAST ALONG LIKE THE CLOUDS IN THE SKY...
...OR IF EACH PERSON CAN CHOOSE HIS OWN PATH TO FOLLOW.
I SUPPOSE THE DESTINATION MIGHT BE THE SAME EITHER WAY.
BUT WHEN YOU DECIDE TO FOLLOW YOUR OWN PATH, YOU CAN STRIVE TO ACHIEVE YOUR OWN DREAMS.
AND IN MY MATCH TODAY, I FINALLY LEARNED THAT PEOPLE WITH DREAMS ARE THE ONES WHO ARE TRULY STRONG.
AND... FATHER... MY DREAM IS SIMPLE...
...TO BECOME STRONGER. RIGHT NOW, I WANT TO BECOME SO STRONG, I WILL NEVER LOSE TO ANYONE AGAIN.
FATHER... THERE ARE SO MANY BIRDS IN THE SKY TODAY...
...FLYING FREE.

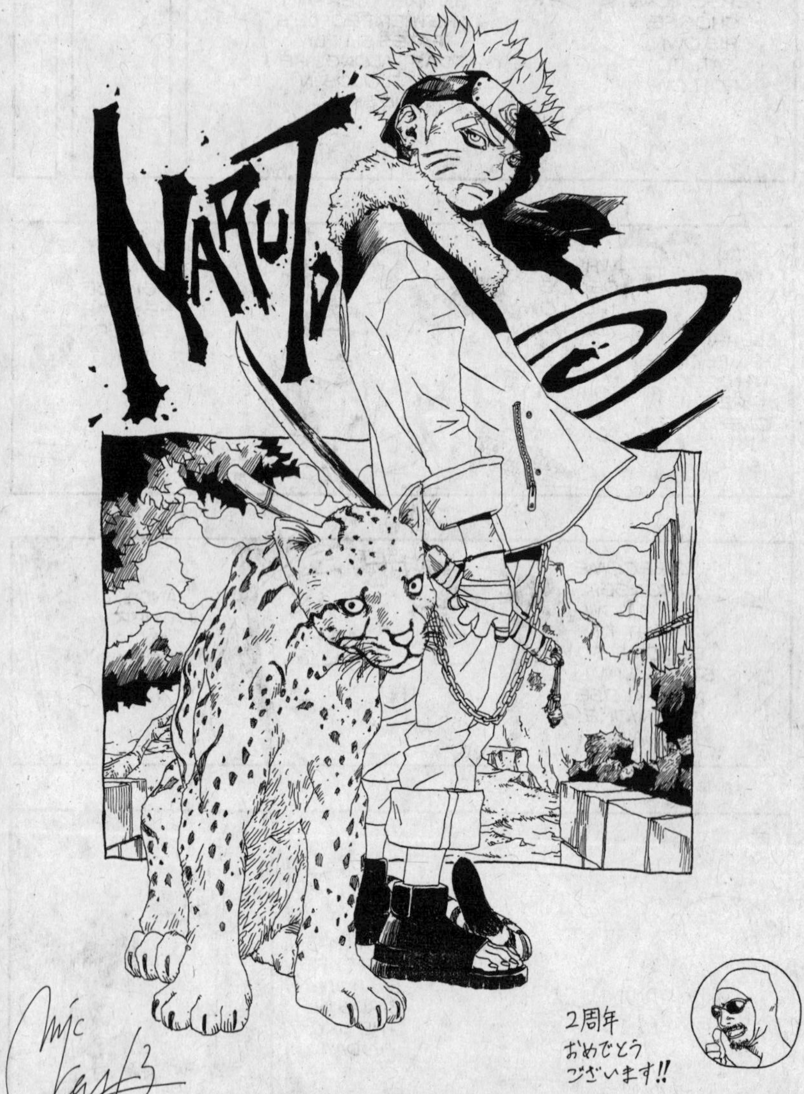
NARUTO
2周年
おめでとう
ございます!!

CONGRATULATIONS ON YOUR
SECOND ANNIVERSARY!!

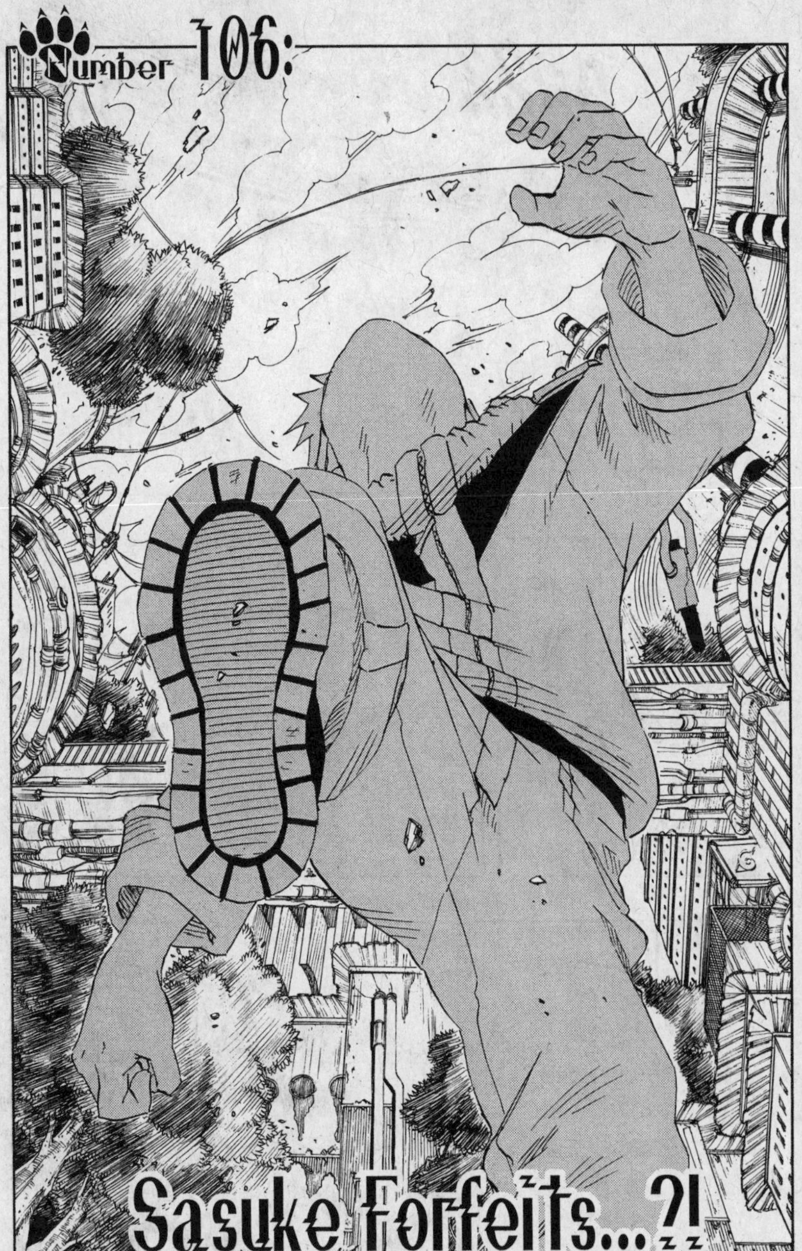
Number 106:
Sasuke Forfeits...?!

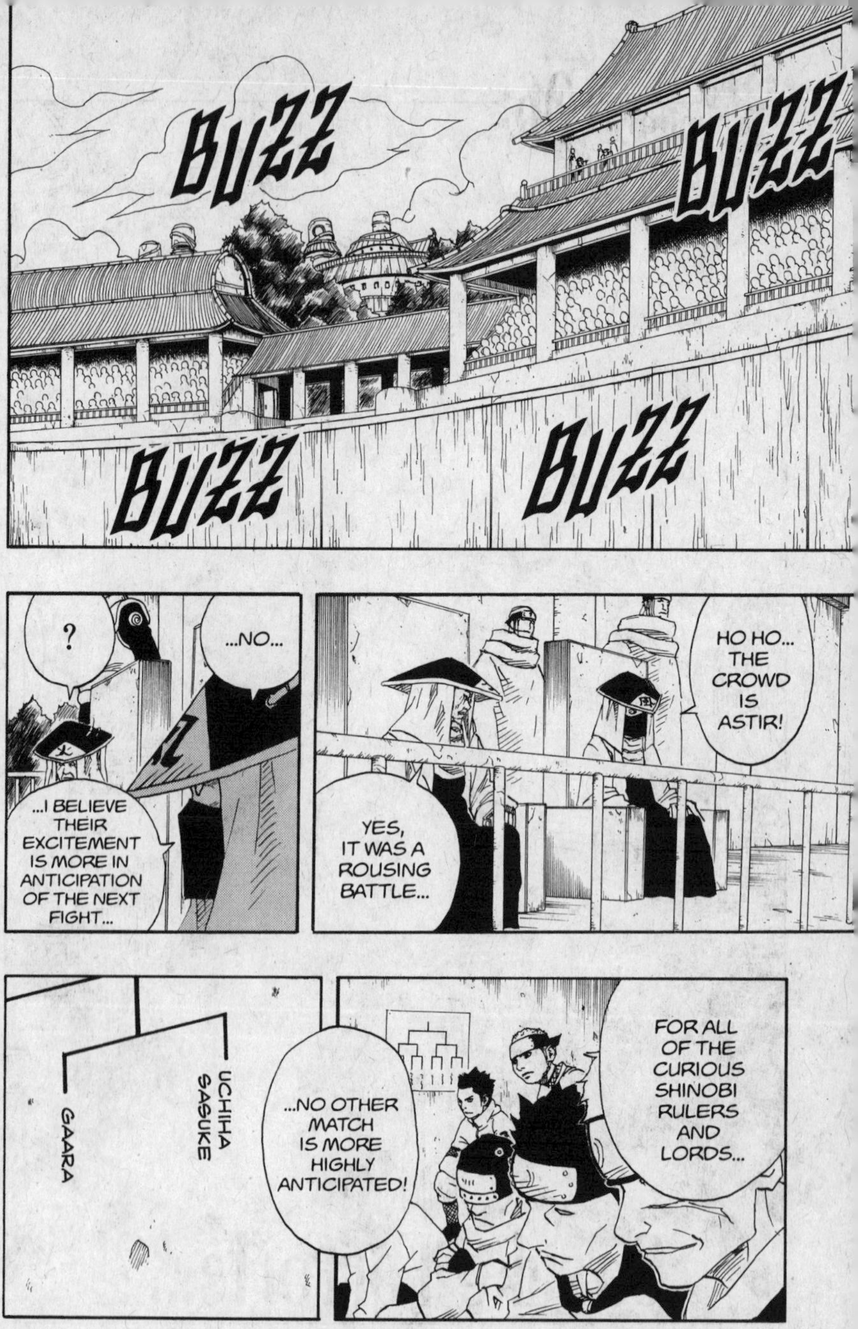
BUZZ
BUZZ
BUZZ
BUZZ
HO HO... THE CROWD IS ASTIR!
YES, IT WAS A ROUSING BATTLE...
...NO...
?
...I BELIEVE THEIR EXCITEMENT IS MORE IN ANTICIPATION OF THE NEXT FIGHT...
FOR ALL OF THE CURIOUS SHINOBI RULERS AND LORDS...
...NO OTHER MATCH IS MORE HIGHLY ANTICIPATED!
UCHIHA SASUKE
GAARA

READ THIS WAY

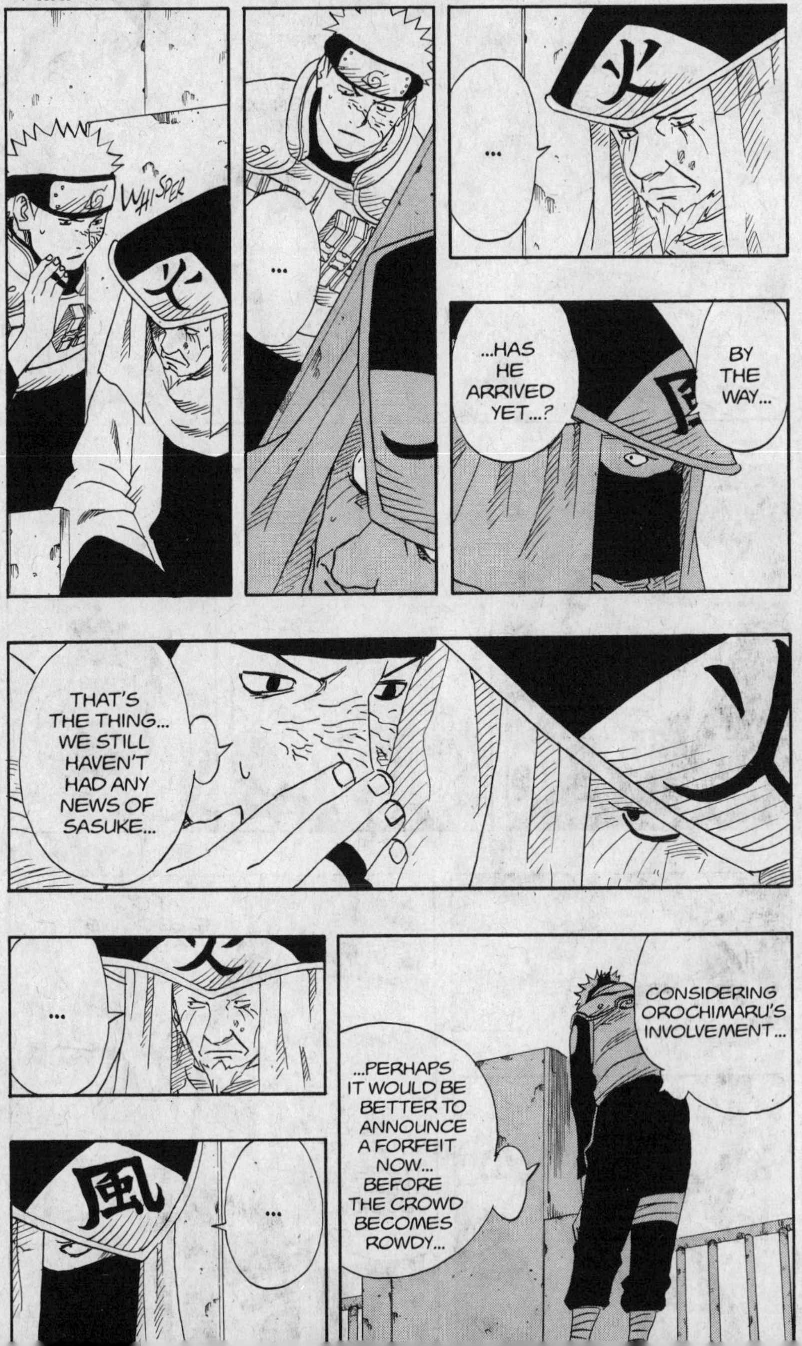
...
BY THE WAY...
...HAS HE ARRIVED YET...?
...
WHISPER
THAT'S THE THING... WE STILL HAVEN'T HAD ANY NEWS OF SASUKE...
CONSIDERING OROCHIMARU'S INVOLVEMENT...
...PERHAPS IT WOULD BE BETTER TO ANNOUNCE A FORFEIT NOW... BEFORE THE CROWD BECOMES ROWDY...
...
...

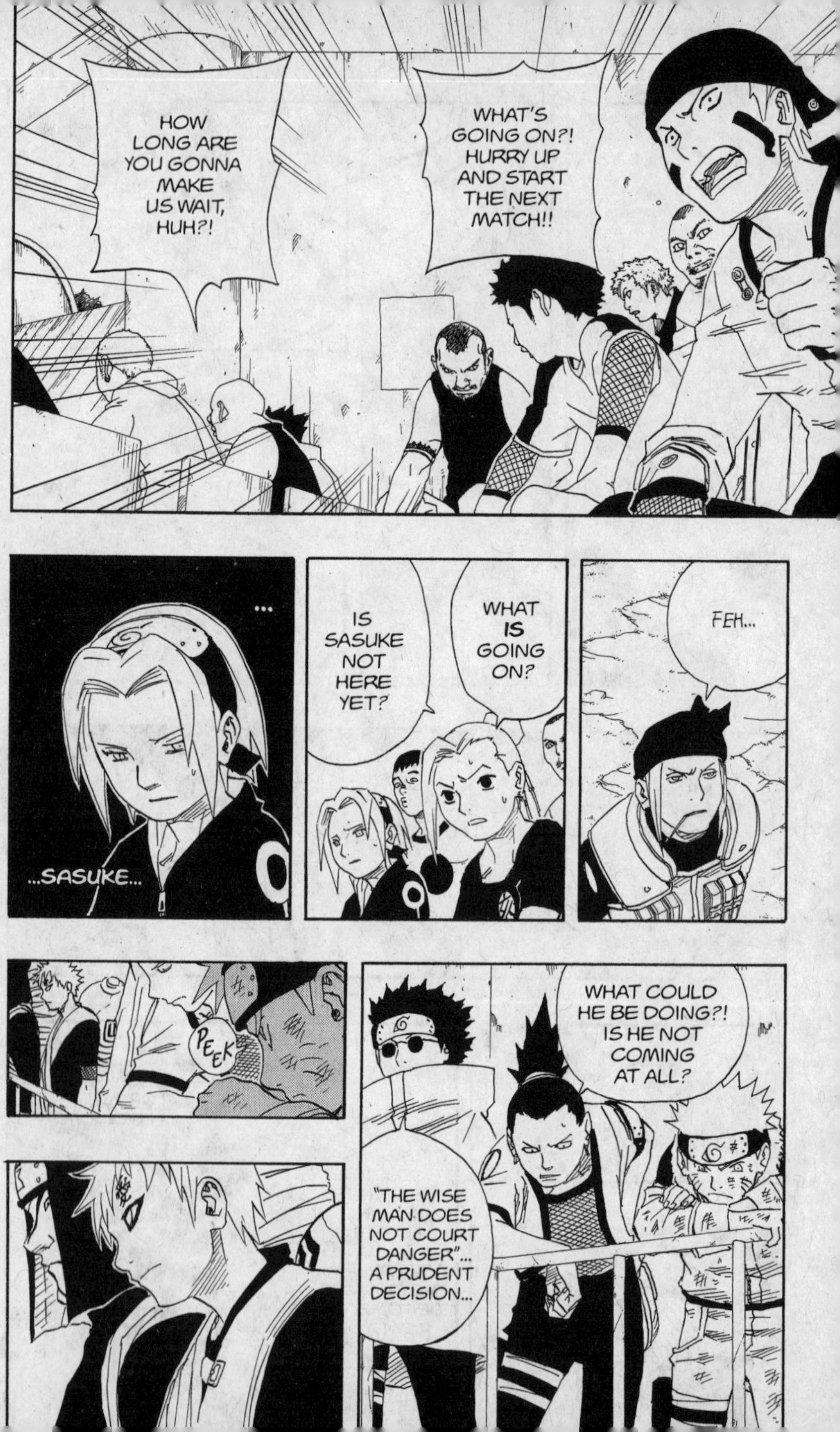
WHAT'S GOING ON?! HURRY UP AND START THE NEXT MATCH!!
HOW LONG ARE YOU GONNA MAKE US WAIT, HUH?!
FEH...
WHAT **IS** GOING ON?
IS SASUKE NOT HERE YET?
...
...SASUKE...
WHAT COULD HE BE DOING?! IS HE NOT COMING AT ALL?
"THE WISE MAN DOES NOT COURT DANGER"... A PRUDENT DECISION...
PEEK

READ THIS WAY

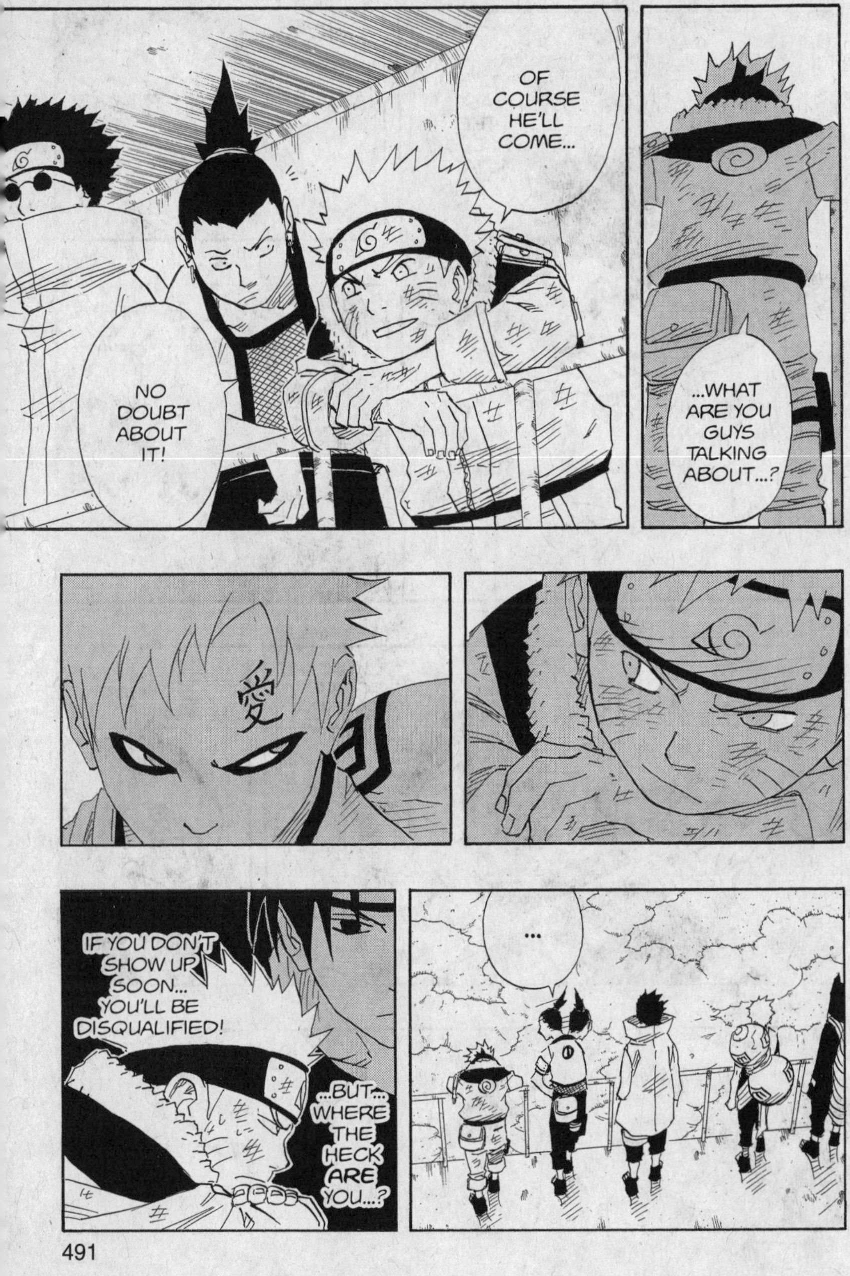
...WHAT ARE YOU GUYS TALKING ABOUT...?
OF COURSE HE'LL COME...
NO DOUBT ABOUT IT!
...
IF YOU DON'T SHOW UP SOON... YOU'LL BE DISQUALIFIED!
...BUT... WHERE THE HECK ARE YOU...?

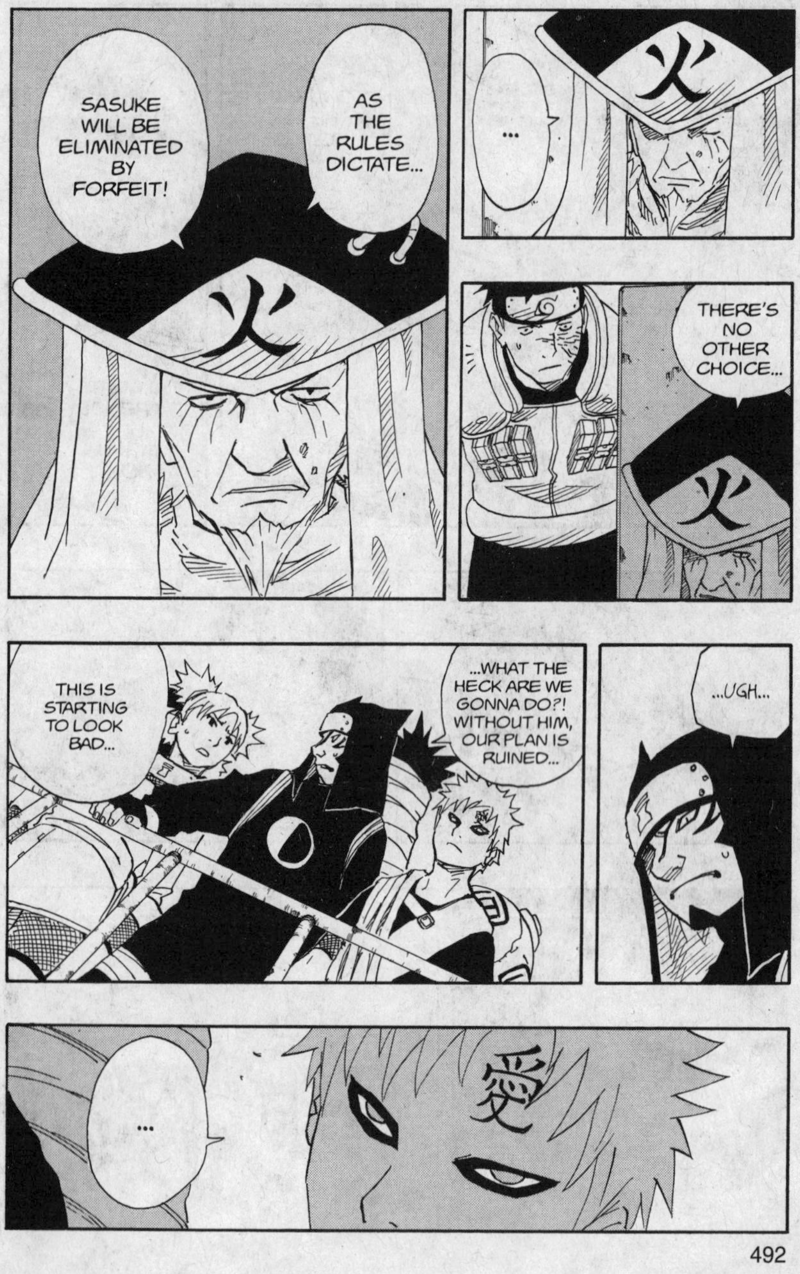
...
THERE'S NO OTHER CHOICE...
AS THE RULES DICTATE...
SASUKE WILL BE ELIMINATED BY FORFEIT!
...UGH...
...WHAT THE HECK ARE WE GONNA DO?! WITHOUT HIM, OUR PLAN IS RUINED...
THIS IS STARTING TO LOOK BAD...
...

READ THIS WAY

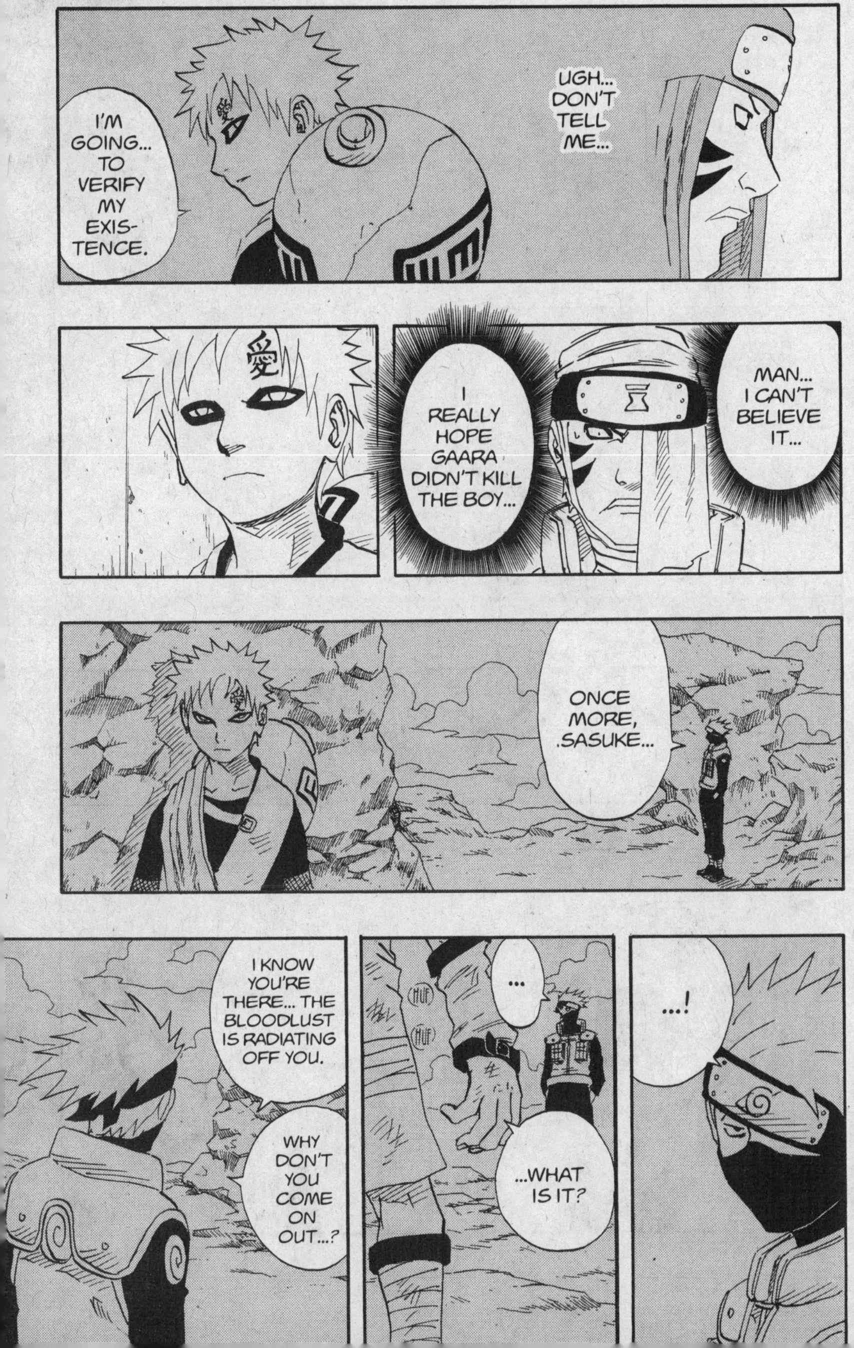
UGH... DON'T TELL ME...
I'M GOING... TO VERIFY MY EXISTENCE.
MAN... I CAN'T BELIEVE IT...
I REALLY HOPE GAARA DIDN'T KILL THE BOY...
ONCE MORE, SASUKE...
...!
...
HUF
HUF
...WHAT IS IT?
I KNOW YOU'RE THERE... THE BLOODLUST IS RADIATING OFF YOU.
WHY DON'T YOU COME ON OUT...?

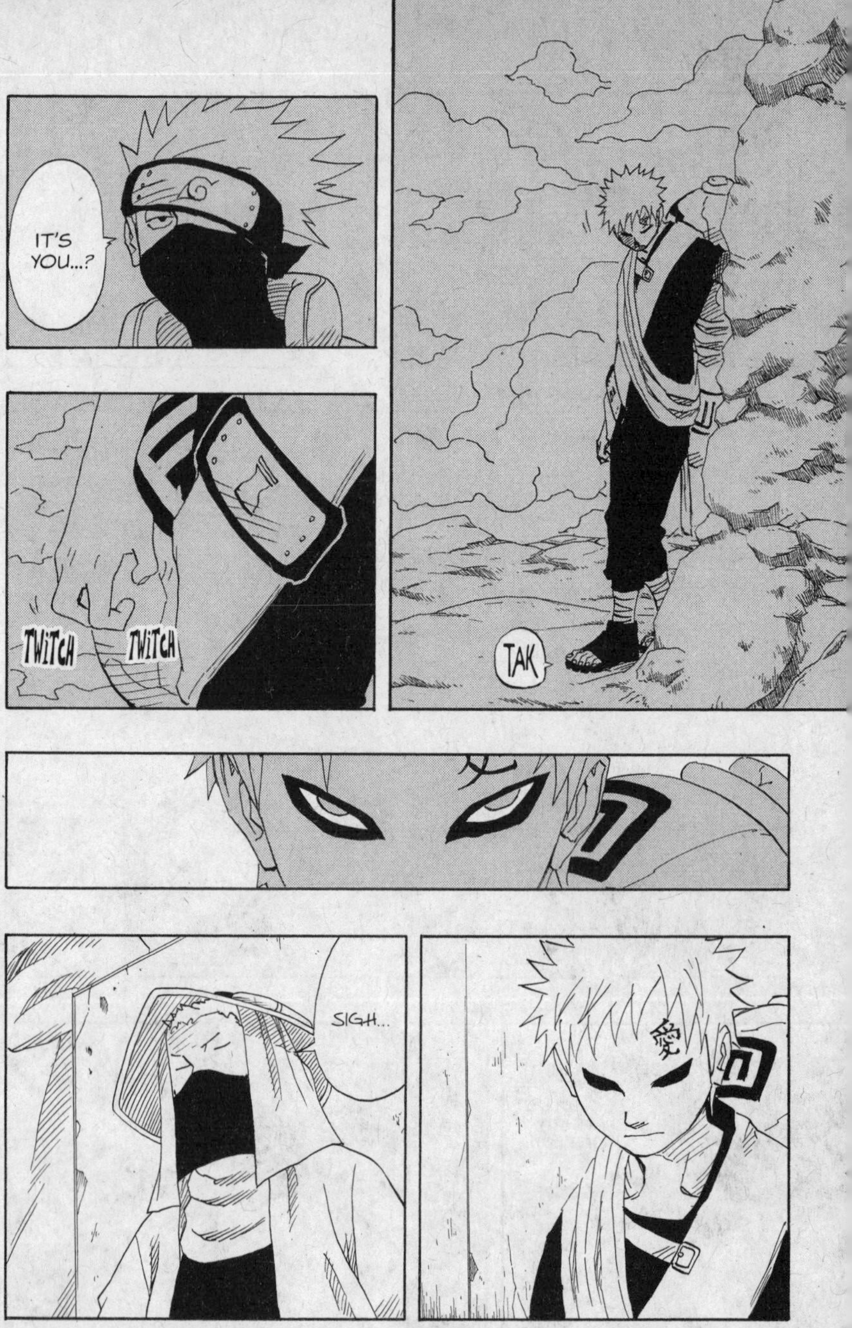
TAK
IT'S YOU...?
TWITCH
TWITCH
愛
SIGH...

READ THIS WAY

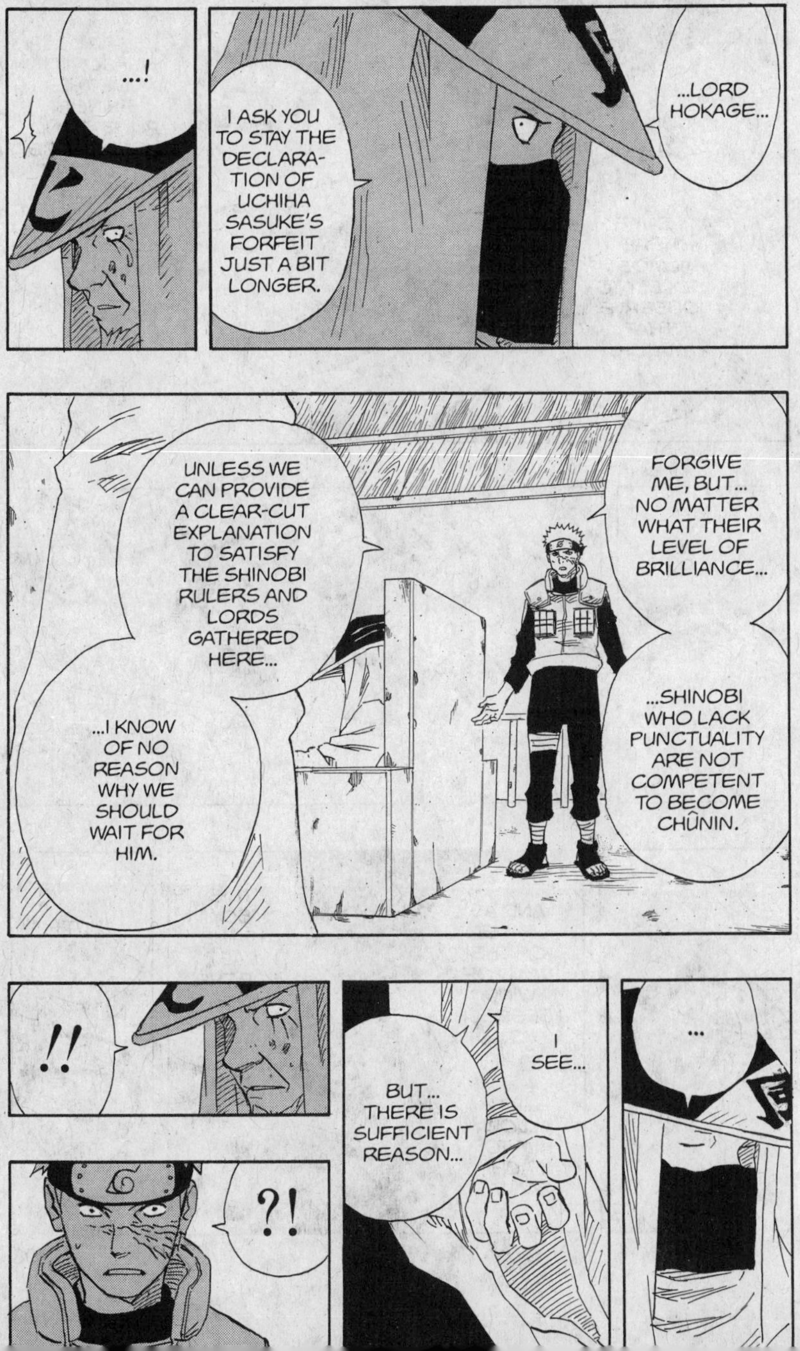

...LORD HOKAGE...
I ASK YOU TO STAY THE DECLARATION OF UCHIHA SASUKE'S FORFEIT JUST A BIT LONGER.
...!
FORGIVE ME, BUT... NO MATTER WHAT THEIR LEVEL OF BRILLIANCE...
...SHINOBI WHO LACK PUNCTUALITY ARE NOT COMPETENT TO BECOME CHÛNIN.
UNLESS WE CAN PROVIDE A CLEAR-CUT EXPLANATION TO SATISFY THE SHINOBI RULERS AND LORDS GATHERED HERE...
...I KNOW OF NO REASON WHY WE SHOULD WAIT FOR HIM.
...
I SEE...
BUT... THERE IS SUFFICIENT REASON...
!!
?!

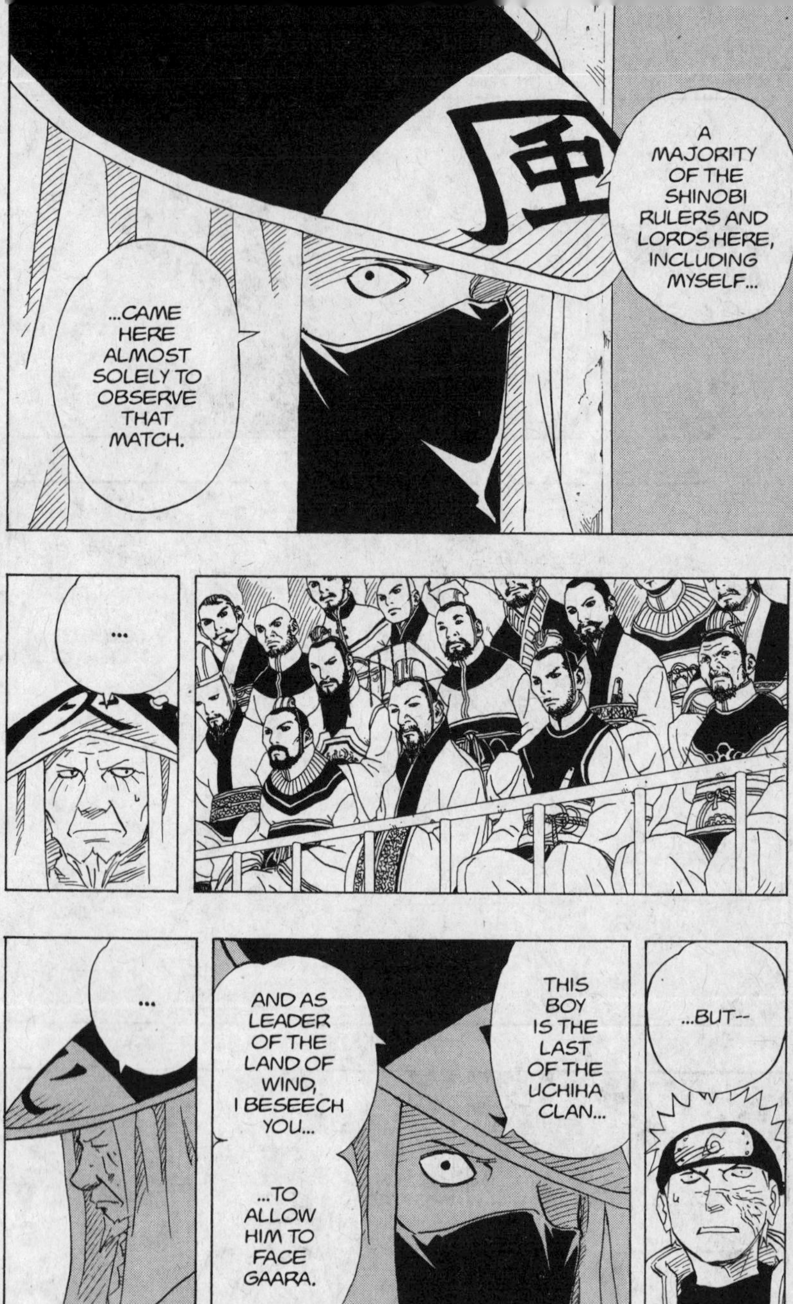
A MAJORITY OF THE SHINOBI RULERS AND LORDS HERE, INCLUDING MYSELF...
...CAME HERE ALMOST SOLELY TO OBSERVE THAT MATCH.
...
...BUT--
THIS BOY IS THE LAST OF THE UCHIHA CLAN...
AND AS LEADER OF THE LAND OF WIND, I BESEECH YOU...
...TO ALLOW HIM TO FACE GAARA.
...

READ THIS WAY

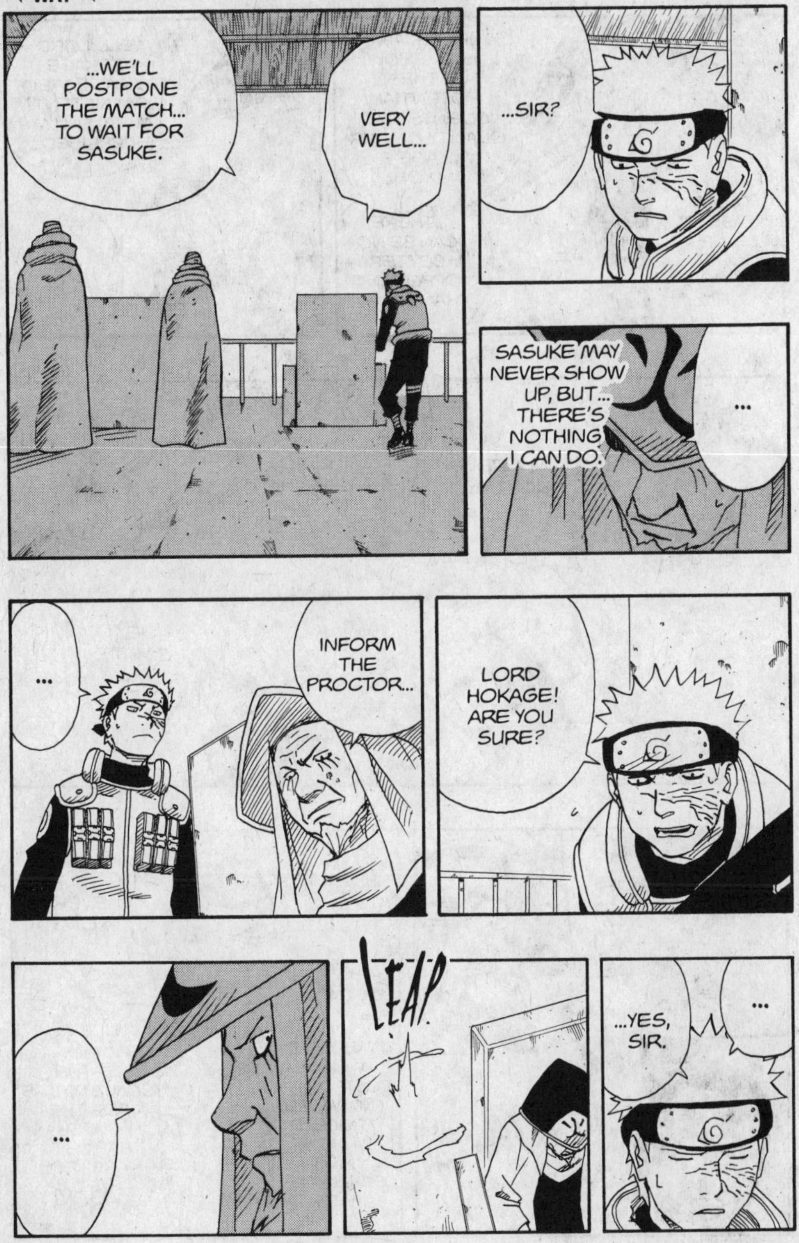

...SIR?
...
SASUKE MAY NEVER SHOW UP, BUT... THERE'S NOTHING I CAN DO.
...WE'LL POSTPONE THE MATCH... TO WAIT FOR SASUKE.
VERY WELL...
LORD HOKAGE! ARE YOU SURE?
INFORM THE PROCTOR...
...
...
...YES, SIR.
LEAP
...

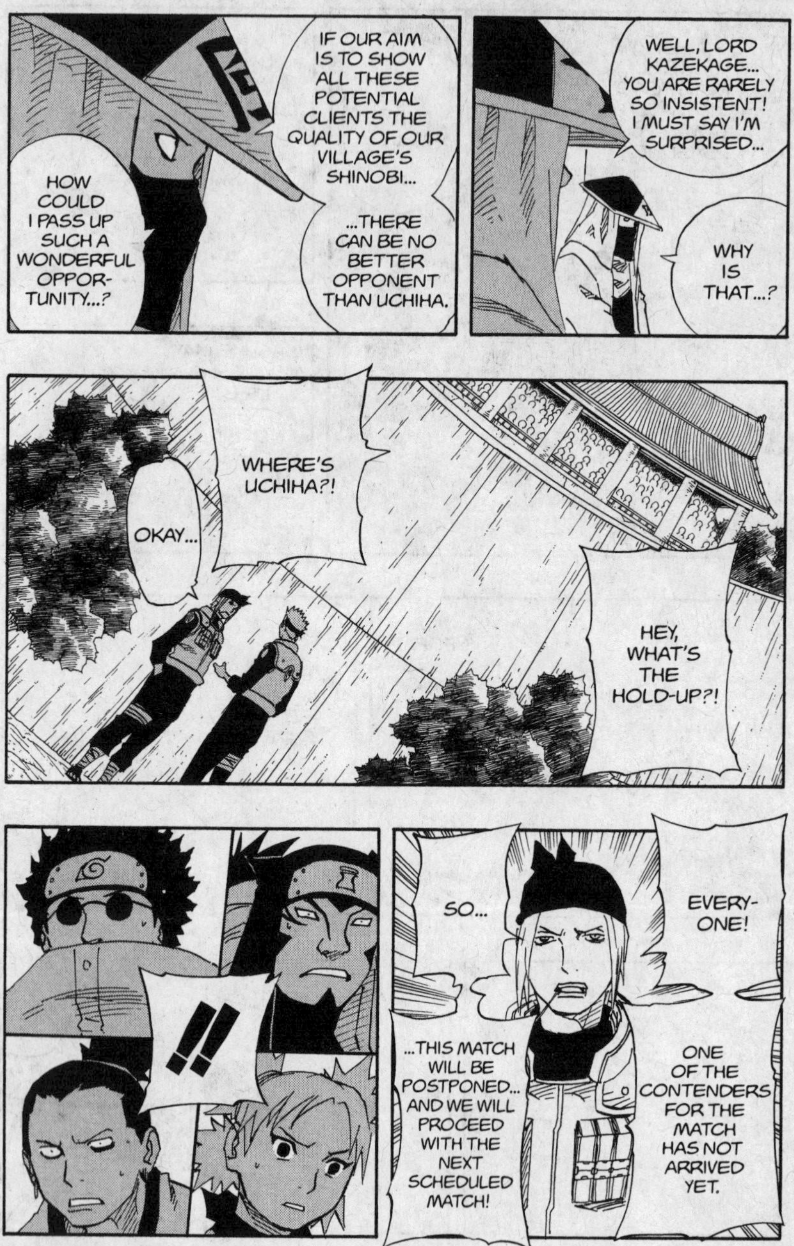
WELL, LORD KAZEKAGE... YOU ARE RARELY SO INSISTENT! I MUST SAY I'M SURPRISED...
WHY IS THAT...?
IF OUR AIM IS TO SHOW ALL THESE POTENTIAL CLIENTS THE QUALITY OF OUR VILLAGE'S SHINOBI...
...THERE CAN BE NO BETTER OPPONENT THAN UCHIHA.
HOW COULD I PASS UP SUCH A WONDERFUL OPPOR-TUNITY...?
WHERE'S UCHIHA?!
HEY, WHAT'S THE HOLD-UP?!
OKAY...
EVERY-ONE!
SO...
ONE OF THE CONTENDERS FOR THE MATCH HAS NOT ARRIVED YET.
...THIS MATCH WILL BE POSTPONED... AND WE WILL PROCEED WITH THE NEXT SCHEDULED MATCH!
!!

READ THIS WAY

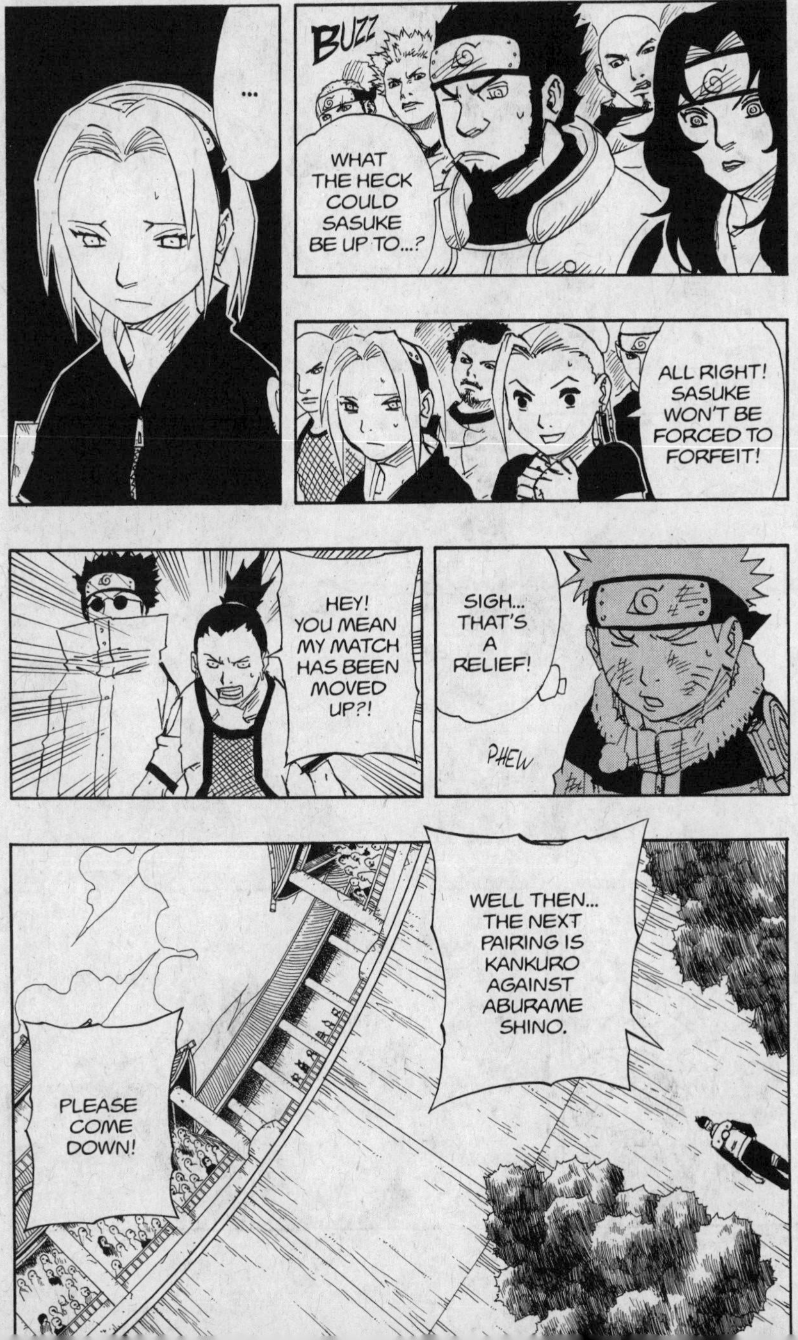
BUZZ
WHAT THE HECK COULD SASUKE BE UP TO...?
ALL RIGHT! SASUKE WON'T BE FORCED TO FORFEIT!
...
SIGH... THAT'S A RELIEF!
PHEW
HEY! YOU MEAN MY MATCH HAS BEEN MOVED UP?!
WELL THEN... THE NEXT PAIRING IS KANKURO AGAINST ABURAME SHINO.
PLEASE COME DOWN!

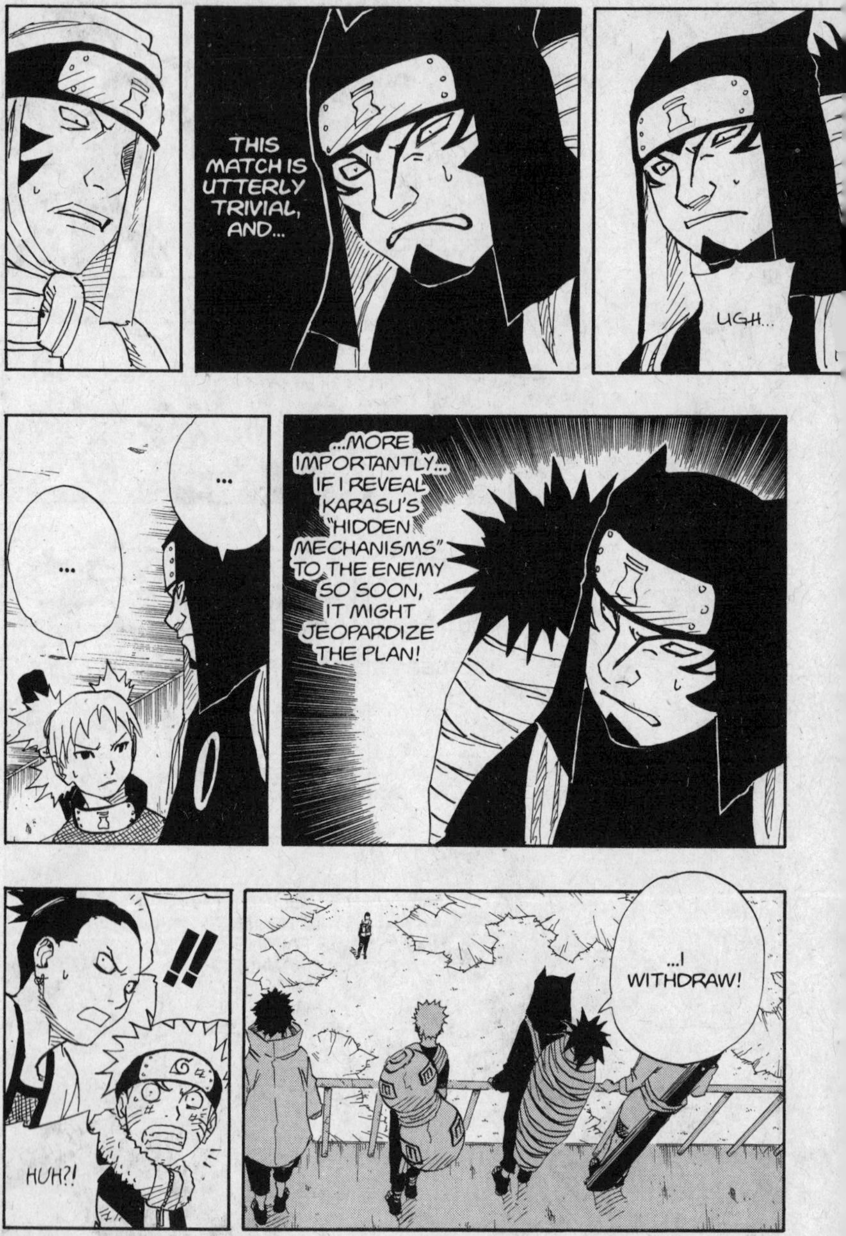
UGH...
THIS MATCH IS UTTERLY TRIVIAL, AND...
...MORE IMPORTANTLY... IF I REVEAL KARASU'S "HIDDEN MECHANISMS" TO THE ENEMY SO SOON, IT MIGHT JEOPARDIZE THE PLAN!
...
...
...I WITHDRAW!
!!
HUH?!

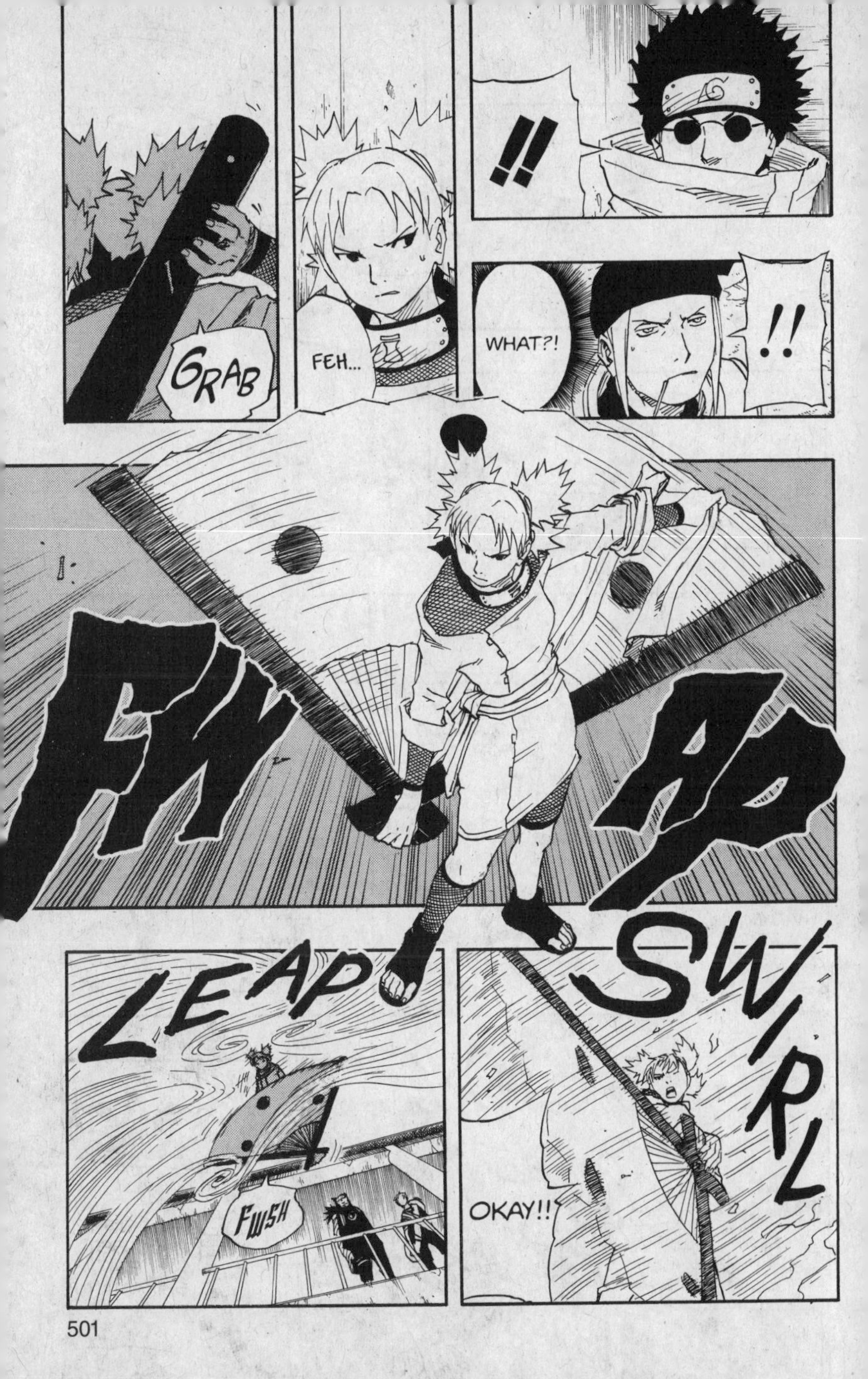
!!
!!
WHAT?!
FEH...
GRAB
FWAP
SWIRL
OKAY!!
LEAP
FWSH

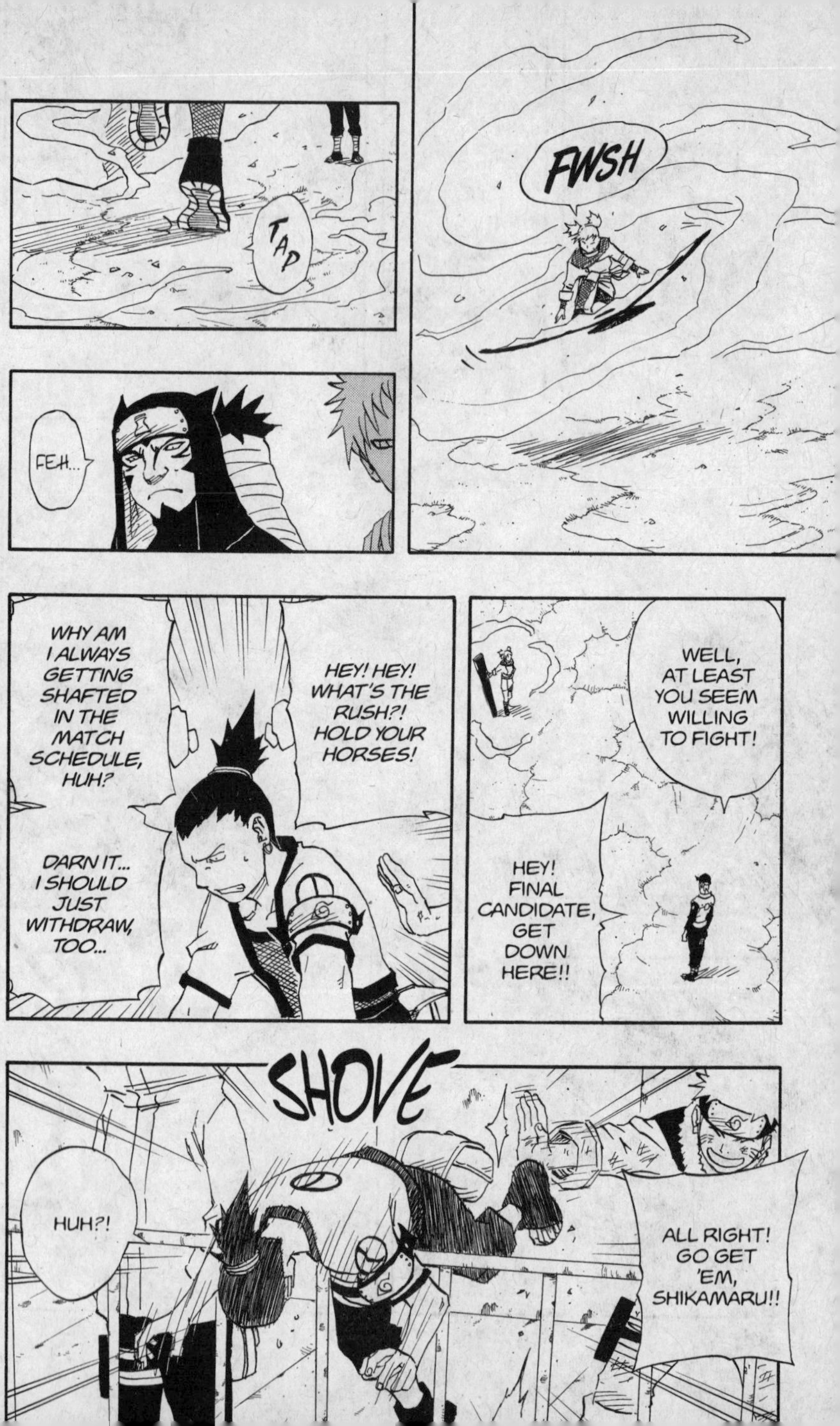
FWSH
TAP
FEH...
WELL, AT LEAST YOU SEEM WILLING TO FIGHT!
HEY! FINAL CANDIDATE, GET DOWN HERE!!
HEY! HEY! WHAT'S THE RUSH?! HOLD YOUR HORSES!
WHY AM I ALWAYS GETTING SHAFTED IN THE MATCH SCHEDULE, HUH?
DARN IT... I SHOULD JUST WITHDRAW, TOO...
SHOVE
ALL RIGHT! GO GET 'EM, SHIKAMARU!!
HUH?!

READ THIS WAY

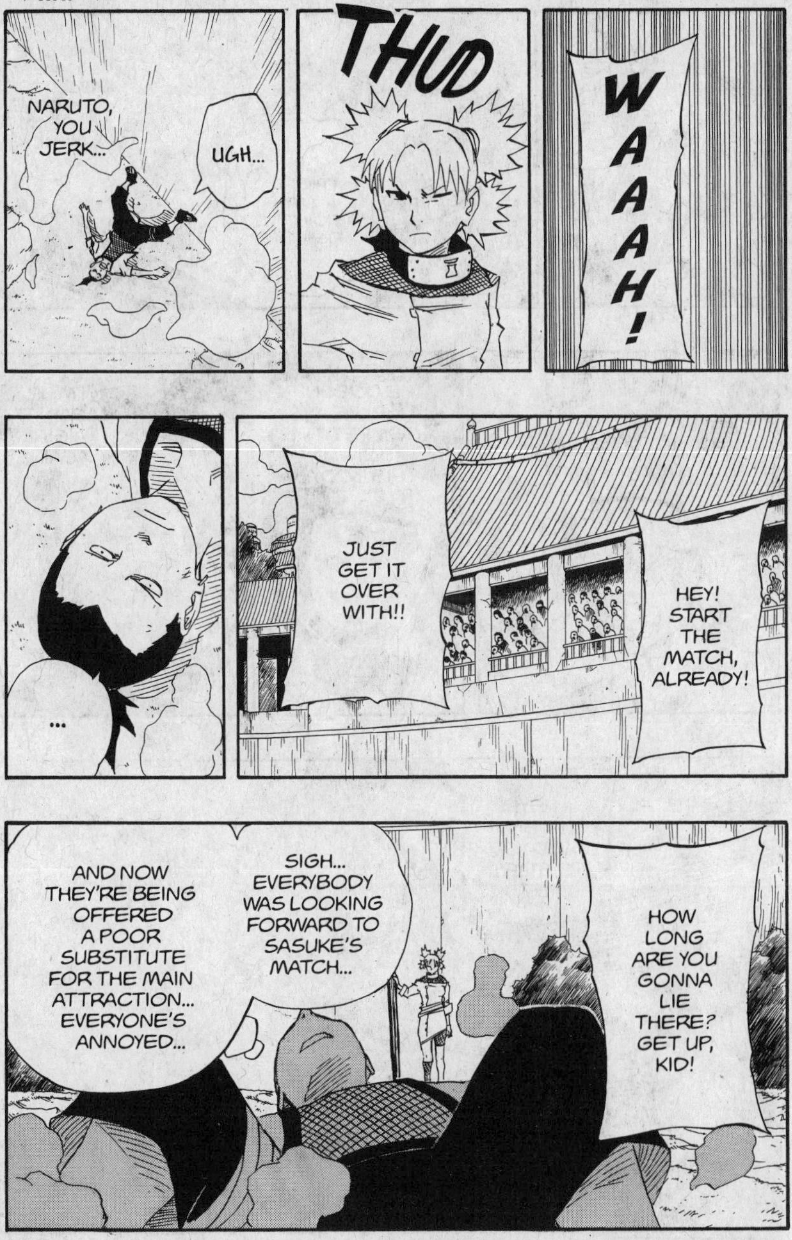
WAAAAH!
THUD
UGH...
NARUTO, YOU JERK...
HEY! START THE MATCH, ALREADY!
JUST GET IT OVER WITH!!
...
HOW LONG ARE YOU GONNA LIE THERE? GET UP, KID!
SIGH... EVERYBODY WAS LOOKING FORWARD TO SASUKE'S MATCH...
AND NOW THEY'RE BEING OFFERED A POOR SUBSTITUTE FOR THE MAIN ATTRACTION... EVERYONE'S ANNOYED...

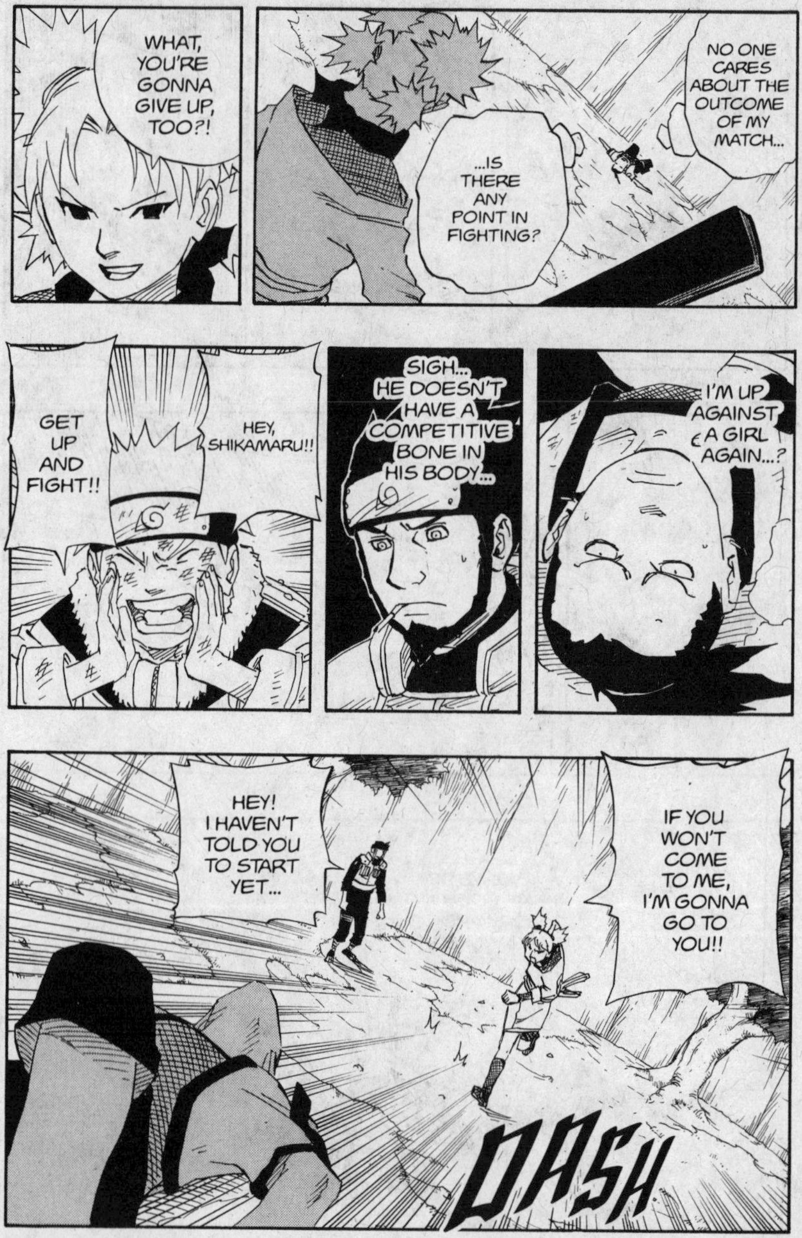
NO ONE CARES ABOUT THE OUTCOME OF MY MATCH...
...IS THERE ANY POINT IN FIGHTING?
WHAT, YOU'RE GONNA GIVE UP, TOO?!
I'M UP AGAINST A GIRL AGAIN...?
SIGH... HE DOESN'T HAVE A COMPETITIVE BONE IN HIS BODY...
HEY, SHIKAMARU!!
GET UP AND FIGHT!!
IF YOU WON'T COME TO ME, I'M GONNA GO TO YOU!!
HEY! I HAVEN'T TOLD YOU TO START YET...
DASH

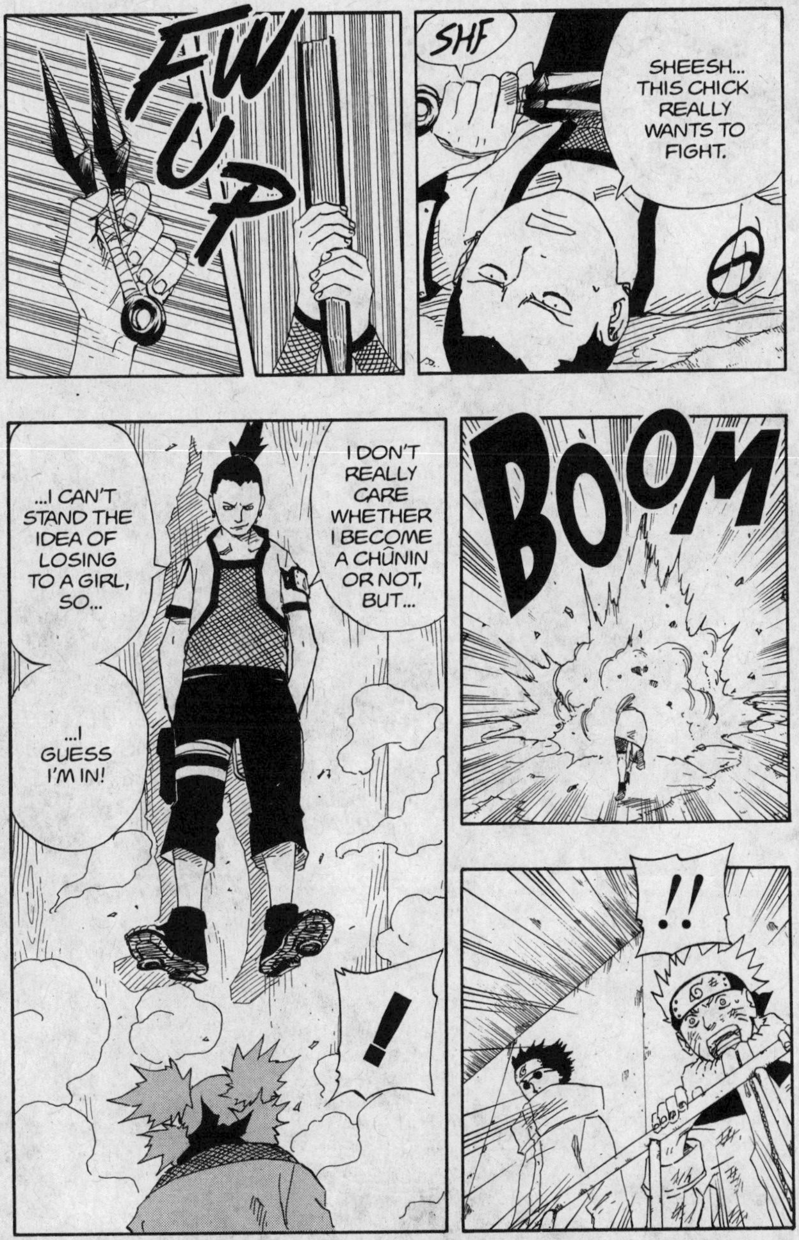
SHF
SHEESH... THIS CHICK REALLY WANTS TO FIGHT.
FWUP
BOOM
!!
I DON'T REALLY CARE WHETHER I BECOME A CHŪNIN OR NOT, BUT...
...I CAN'T STAND THE IDEA OF LOSING TO A GIRL, SO...
...I GUESS I'M IN!
!

THE RESULTS OF THE SECOND CHARACTER POPULARITY SURVEY!!

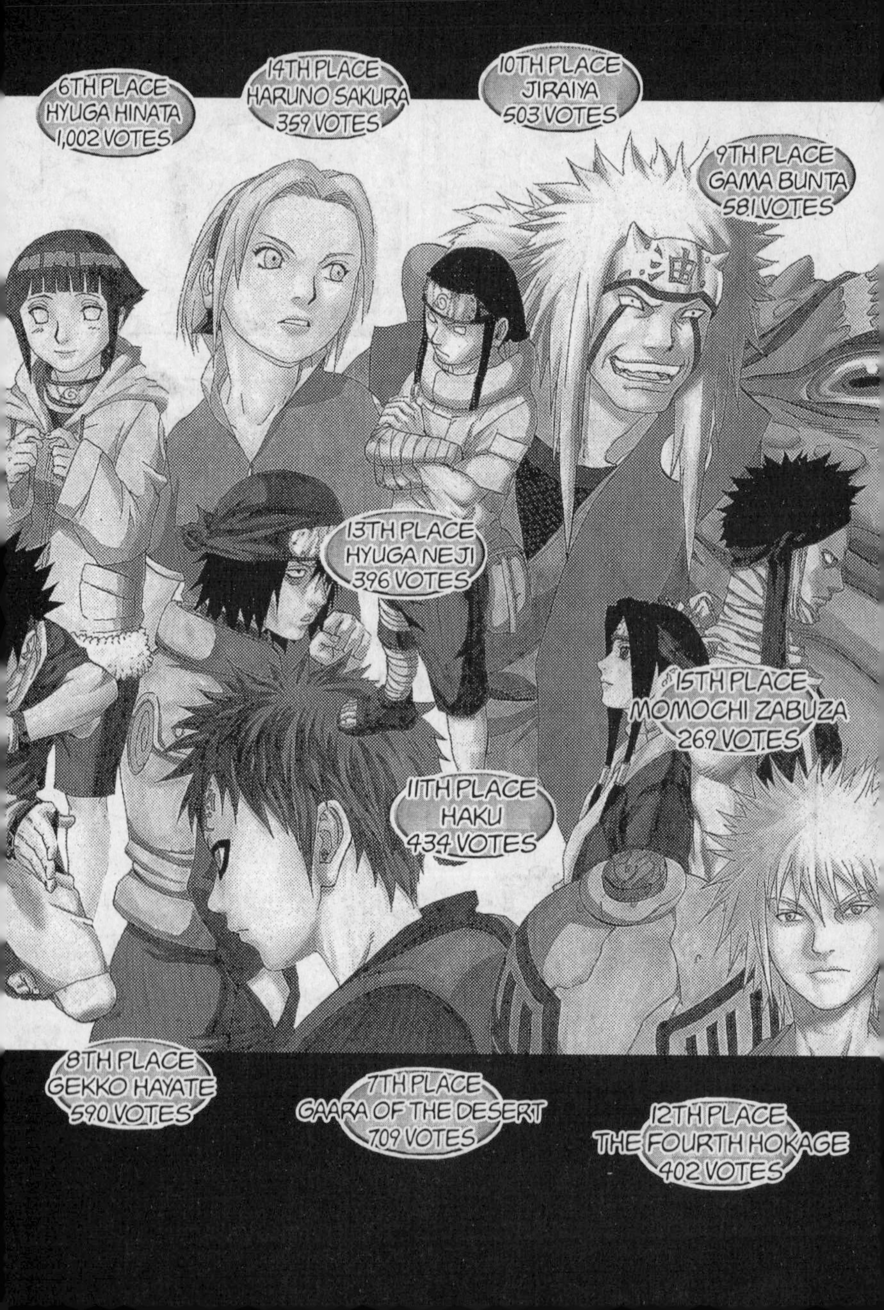

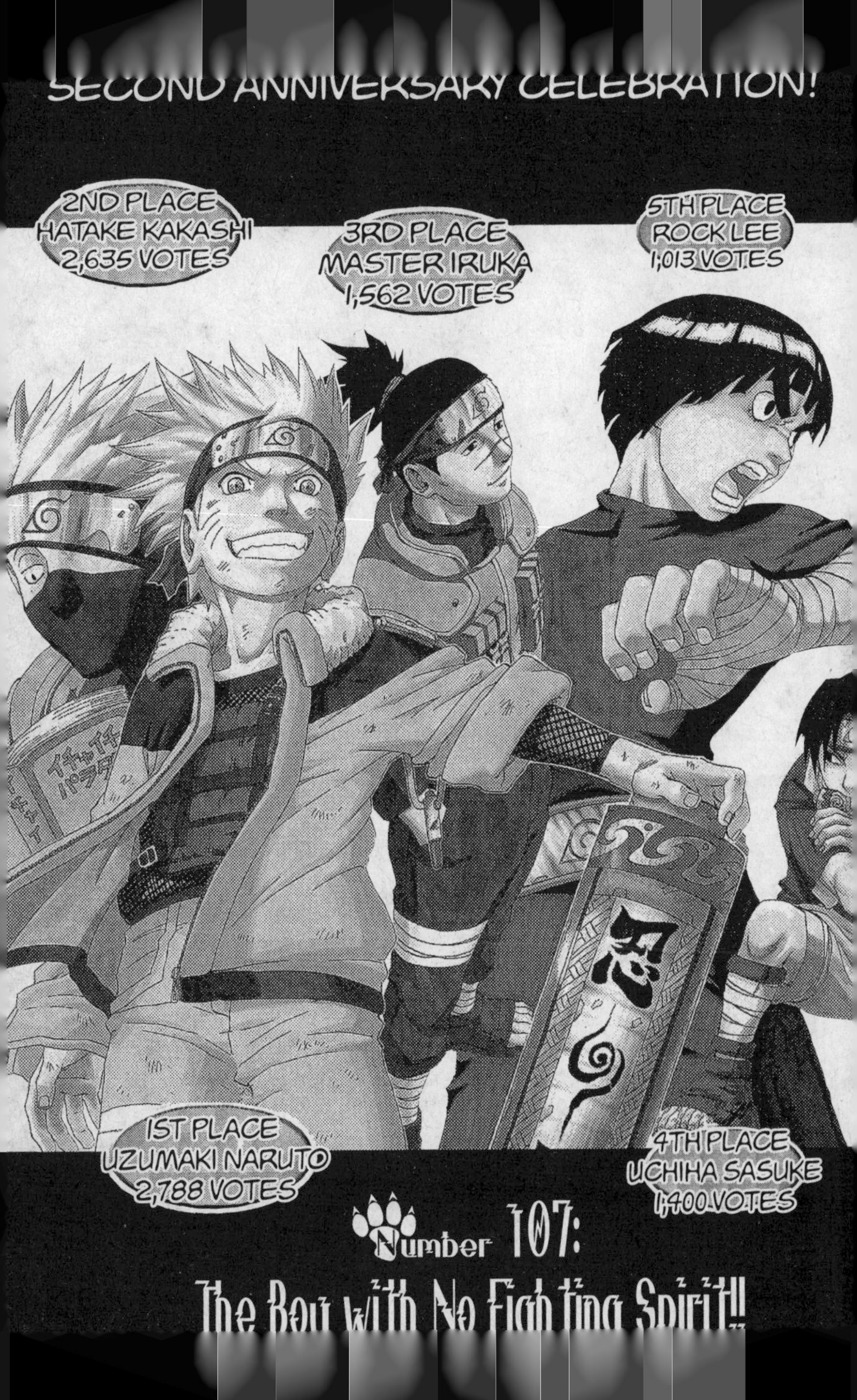
SECOND ANNIVERSARY CELEBRATION!
5TH PLACE ROCK LEE 1,013 VOTES
3RD PLACE MASTER IRUKA 1,562 VOTES
2ND PLACE HATAKE KAKASHI 2,635 VOTES
4TH PLACE UCHIHA SASUKE 1,400 VOTES
1ST PLACE UZUMAKI NARUTO 2,788 VOTES
Number 107:
The Boy with No Fighting Spirit!!

19TH PLACE
NINE-TAILED FOX
170 VOTES

18TH PLACE
MASTER GUY
172 VOTES

ROAR!

17TH PLACE
INUZUKA KIBA
199 VOTES

16TH PLACE
NARA SHIKAMARU
245 VOTES

20TH PLACE
AKAMARU
138 VOTES

TOTAL NUMBER
OF ENTRIES:
17,395 VOTES!!

THE RESULTS OF THE SECOND CHARACTER POPULARITY SURVEY!!

DISAPPOINTED?! SURPRISED?!
MAYBE YOUR FAVORITE CHARACTER IS STILL BELOW!

22ND PLACE	23RD PLACE	24TH PLACE	25TH PLACE	26TH PLACE	27TH PLACE
KABUTO 122 VOTES	TADPOLE 113 VOTES	ABURAME SHINO 110 VOTES	MITARASHI ANKO 108 VOTES	OROCHIMARU 105 VOTES	EXAM PROCTOR A 100 VOTES

28TH PLACE	29TH PLACE	30TH PLACE	31ST PLACE	32ND PLACE	33RD PLACE
TEMARI 94 VOTES	SARUTOBI ASUMA 92 VOTES	TENTEN 75 VOTES	KANKURO 64 VOTES	YAMANAKA INO 63 VOTES	UCHIHA ITACHI 62 VOTES

34TH PLACE
EXAM PROCTOR B
50 VOTES

35TH PLACE
YUHI KURENAI
49 VOTES

36TH PLACE	POOCHIE/SHOOTING STAR	33 VOTES
37TH PLACE	KONOHAMARU	29 VOTES
38TH PLACE	DOSUKINUTA	28 VOTES
39TH PLACE	SQUIRREL	26 VOTES
40TH PLACE	SNOWSHOE HARE	26 VOTES
41ST PLACE	NINJA DOGS	
	INARI	24 VOTES
43RD PLACE	MORINO IBIKI	20 VOTES
44TH PLACE	MASTER EBISU	
	SPECIAL JONIN NINJA B	17 VOTES
46TH PLACE	KONOHA BLACK OPS A	
	KIN TSUCHI	16 VOTES
48TH PLACE	NINJA TURTLE	
	JIRAIA'S TOAD	14 VOTES
50TH PLACE	AKIMICHI CHOJI	13 VOTES

21ST PLACE
KISHIMOTO MASASHI
126 VOTES

...TO THE NEXT ONE ALREADY!!

I'M LOOKING FORWARD...

KISHIMOTO-SENSEI'S THOUGHTS
IT'S A REAL CONFIDENCE-BOOSTER THAT NARUTO CAME IN FIRST... BUT TO ALL THE CHARACTERS WHO LOST TO THE TADPOLE... FOR SHAME! THANK YOU TO EVERYONE WHO VOTED.

CAST YOUR VOTE!
WRITE TO:
VIZ MEDIA, LLC
SHONEN JUMP/NARUTO CHARACTER POLL
P.O. BOX 77010
SAN FRANCISCO, CA 94107

READ THIS WAY

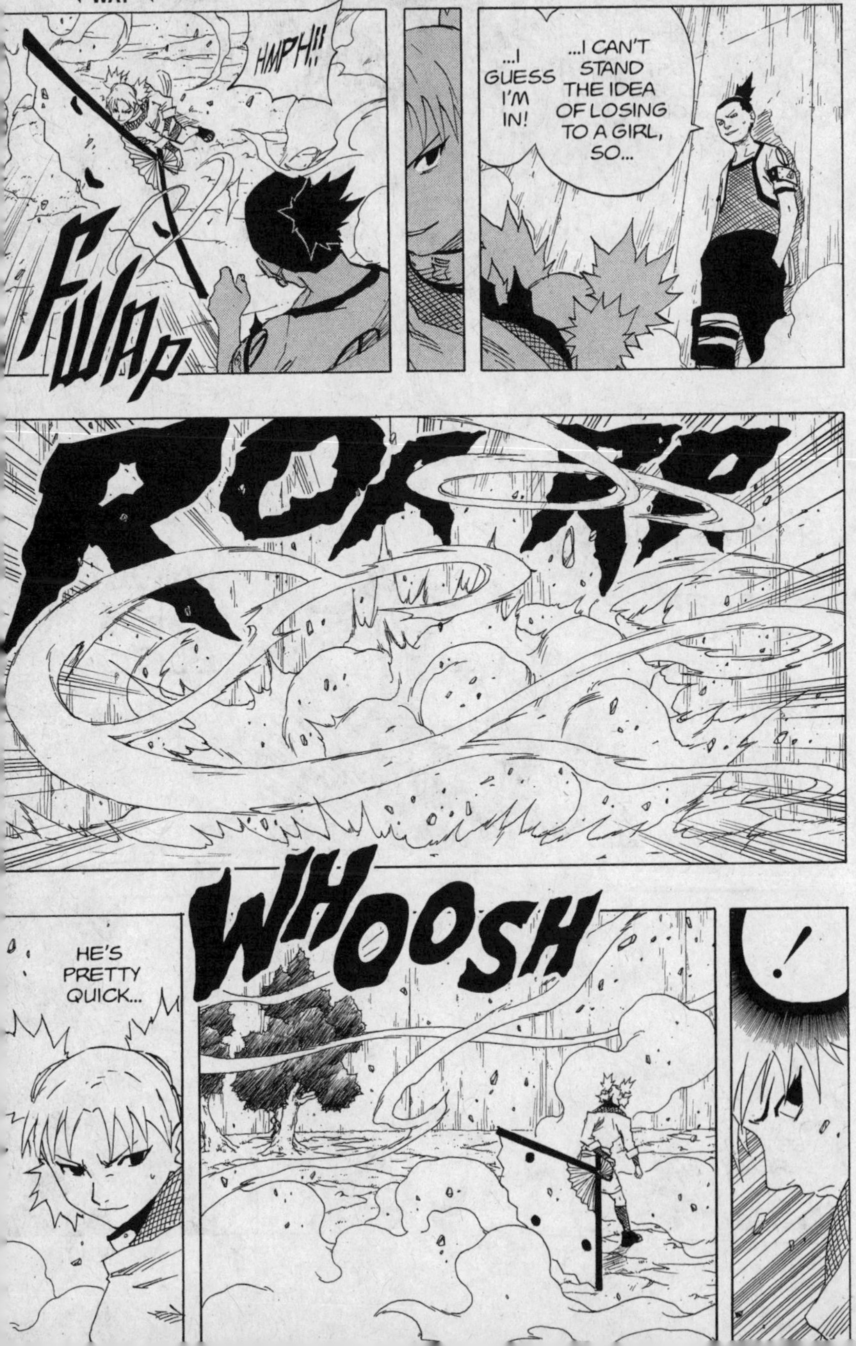
...I CAN'T STAND THE IDEA OF LOSING TO A GIRL, SO...
...I GUESS I'M IN!
HMPH!!
FWAP
ROARR
!
WHOOSH
HE'S PRETTY QUICK...

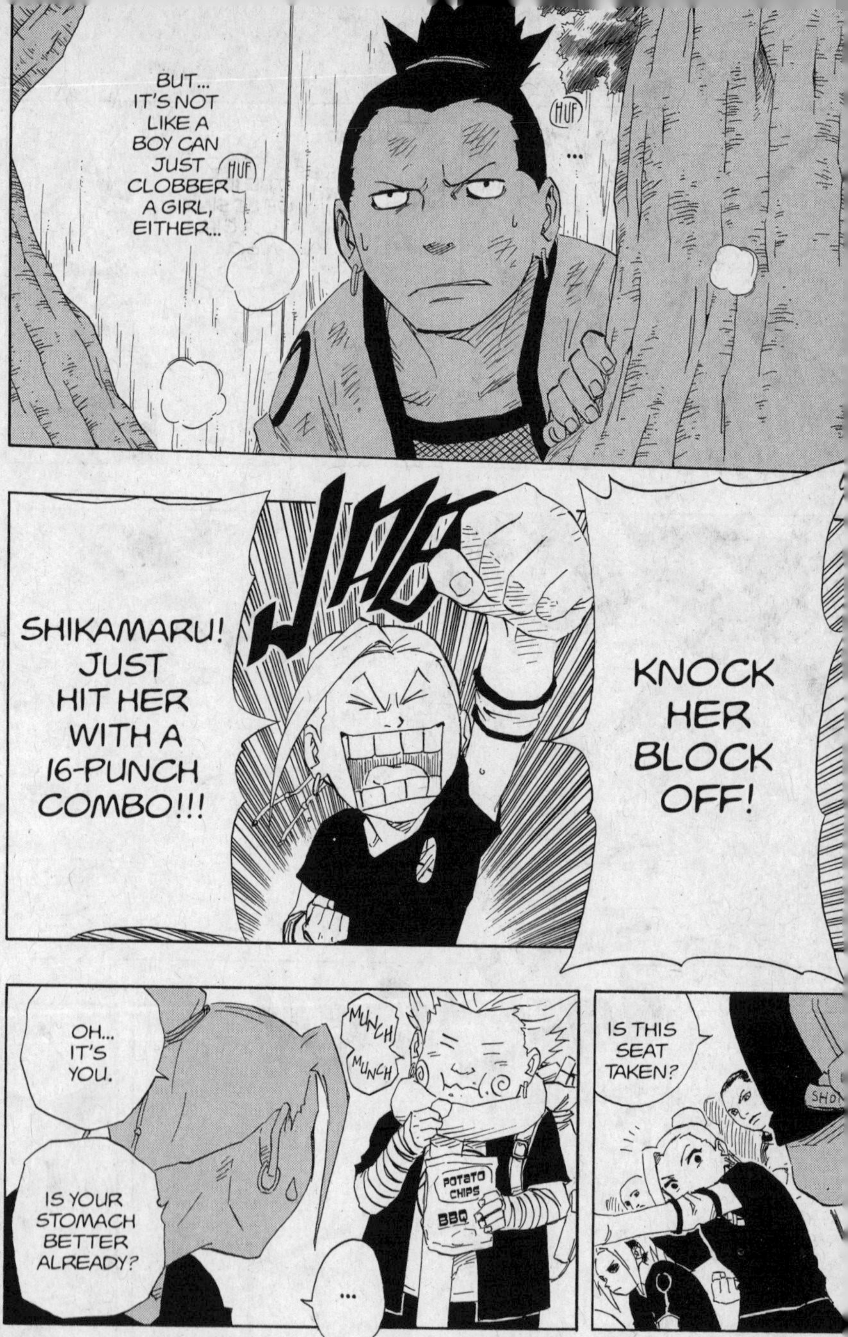
HUF
...
HUF
BUT... IT'S NOT LIKE A BOY CAN JUST CLOBBER A GIRL, EITHER...
KNOCK HER BLOCK OFF!
JAB
SHIKAMARU! JUST HIT HER WITH A 16-PUNCH COMBO!!!
IS THIS SEAT TAKEN?
MUNCH
MUNCH
OH... IT'S YOU.
POTATO CHIPS BBQ
IS YOUR STOMACH BETTER ALREADY?
...

READ THIS WAY

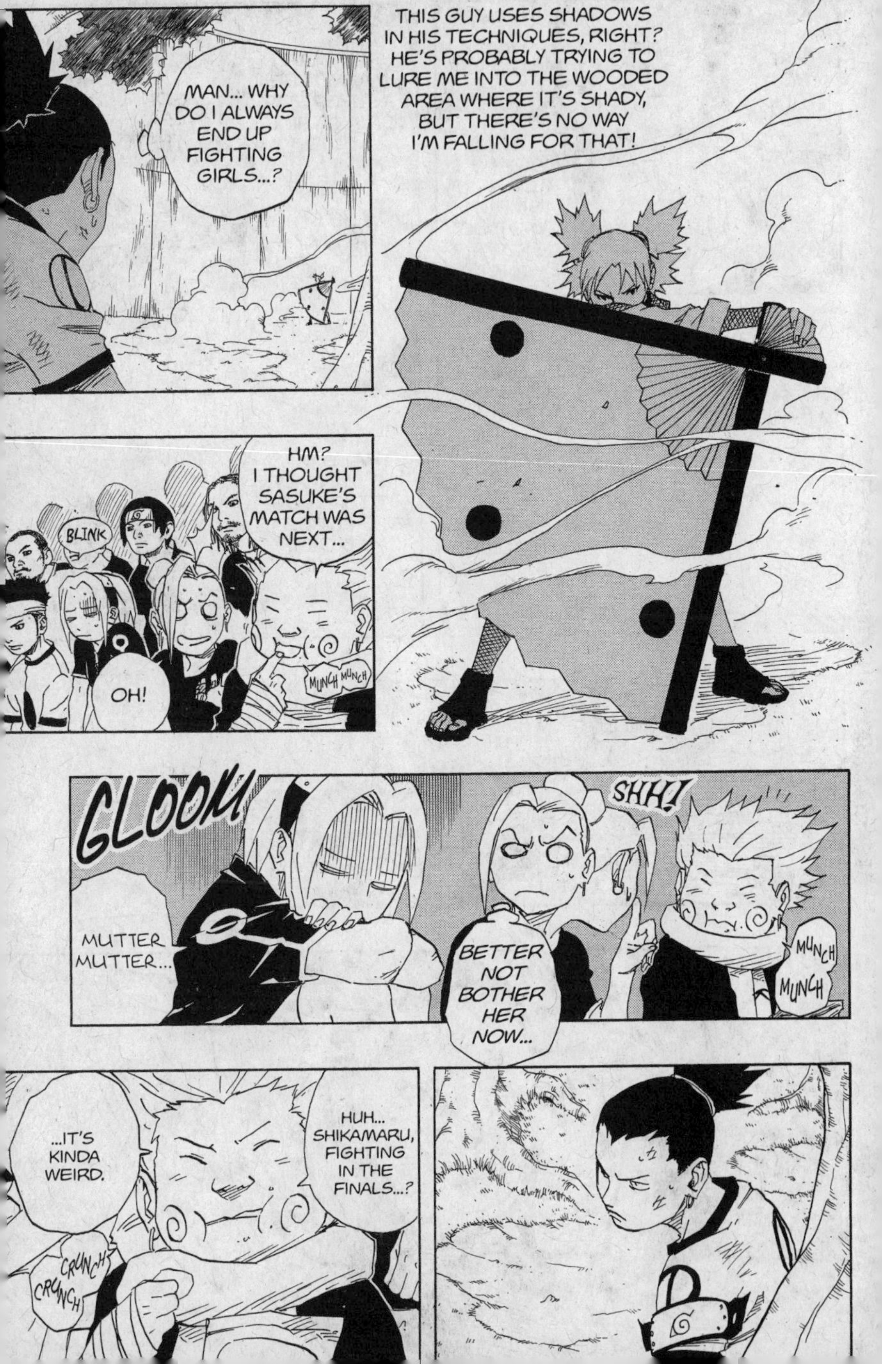
THIS GUY USES SHADOWS IN HIS TECHNIQUES, RIGHT? HE'S PROBABLY TRYING TO LURE ME INTO THE WOODED AREA WHERE IT'S SHADY, BUT THERE'S NO WAY I'M FALLING FOR THAT!
MAN... WHY DO I ALWAYS END UP FIGHTING GIRLS...?
HM? I THOUGHT SASUKE'S MATCH WAS NEXT...
BLINK
MUNCH MUNCH
OH!
SHH!
MUNCH MUNCH
BETTER NOT BOTHER HER NOW...
GLOOM
MUTTER MUTTER...
HUH... SHIKAMARU, FIGHTING IN THE FINALS...?
...IT'S KINDA WEIRD.
CRUNCH CRUNCH

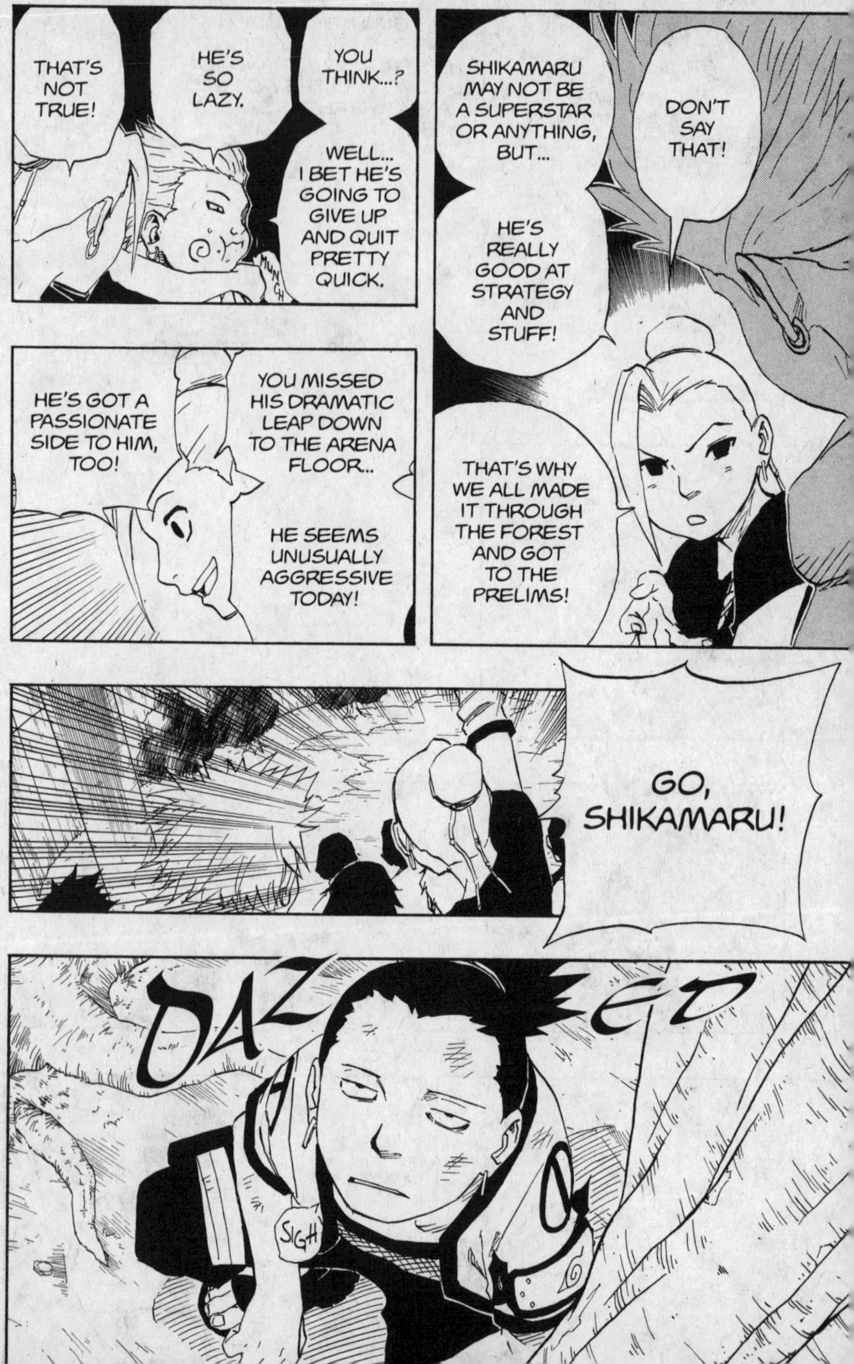
DON'T SAY THAT!
SHIKAMARU MAY NOT BE A SUPERSTAR OR ANYTHING, BUT...
HE'S REALLY GOOD AT STRATEGY AND STUFF!
THAT'S WHY WE ALL MADE IT THROUGH THE FOREST AND GOT TO THE PRELIMS!
YOU THINK...?
HE'S SO LAZY.
THAT'S NOT TRUE!
WELL... I BET HE'S GOING TO GIVE UP AND QUIT PRETTY QUICK.
MUNCH
YOU MISSED HIS DRAMATIC LEAP DOWN TO THE ARENA FLOOR...
HE SEEMS UNUSUALLY AGGRESSIVE TODAY!
HE'S GOT A PASSIONATE SIDE TO HIM, TOO!
GO, SHIKAMARU!
DAZED
SIGH

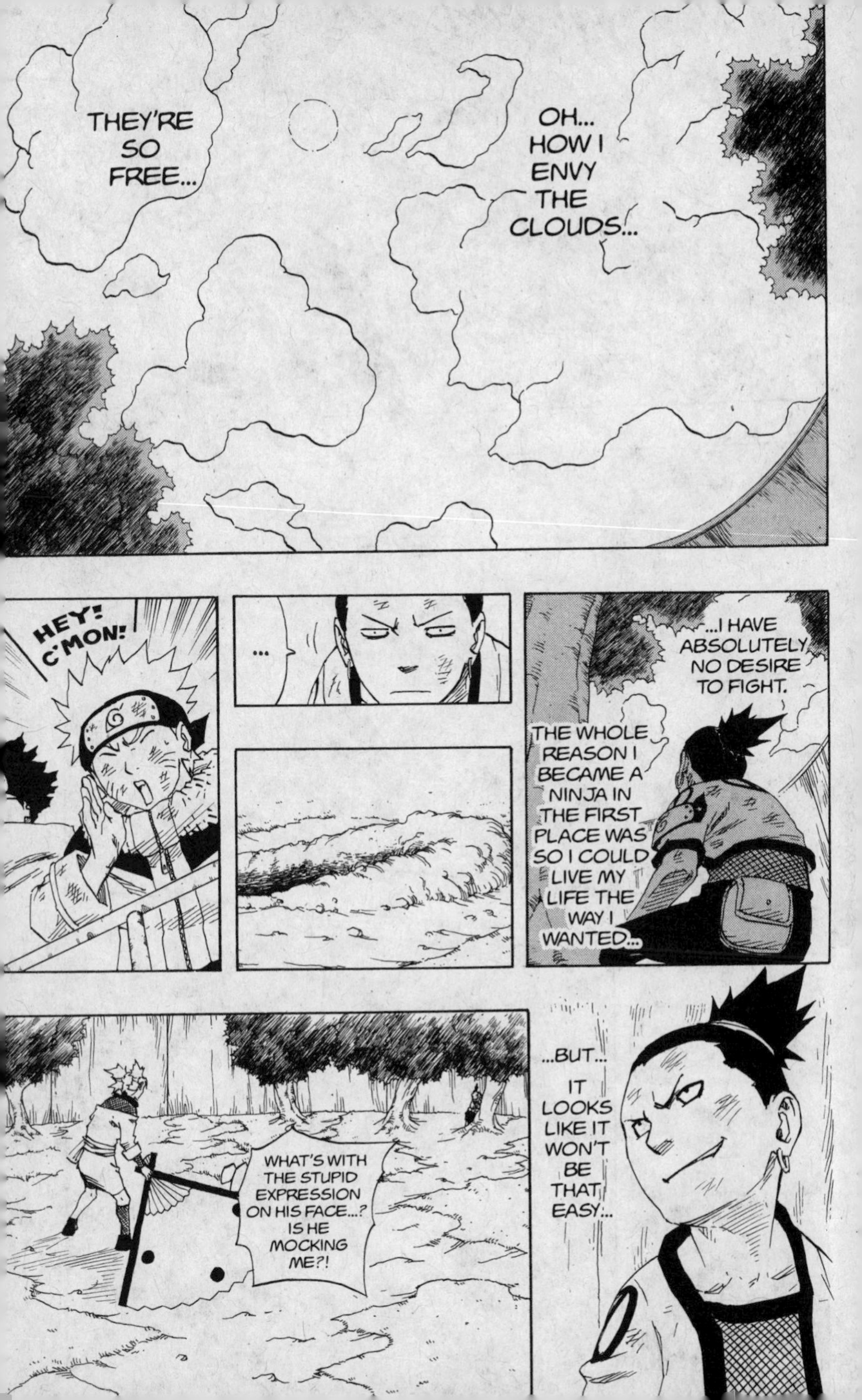
OH... HOW I ENVY THE CLOUDS...
THEY'RE SO FREE...
...I HAVE ABSOLUTELY NO DESIRE TO FIGHT.
THE WHOLE REASON I BECAME A NINJA IN THE FIRST PLACE WAS SO I COULD LIVE MY LIFE THE WAY I WANTED...
...
HEY! C'MON!
...BUT...
IT LOOKS LIKE IT WON'T BE THAT EASY...
WHAT'S WITH THE STUPID EXPRESSION ON HIS FACE...? IS HE MOCKING ME?!

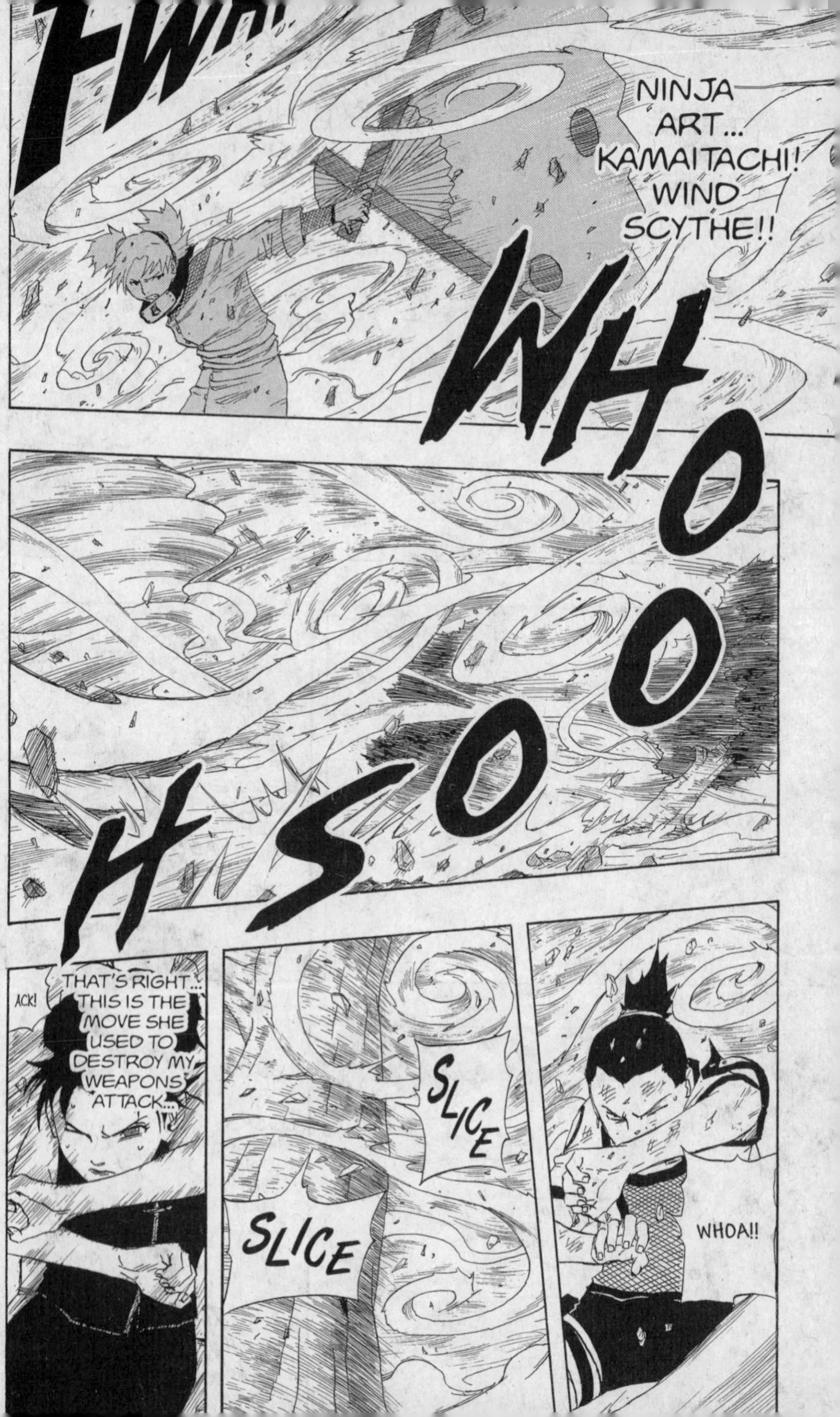
NINJA ART... KAMAITACHI! WIND SCYTHE!!
WHOOOOSH
WHOA!!
SLICE
SLICE
THAT'S RIGHT... THIS IS THE MOVE SHE USED TO DESTROY MY WEAPONS ATTACK...
ACK!

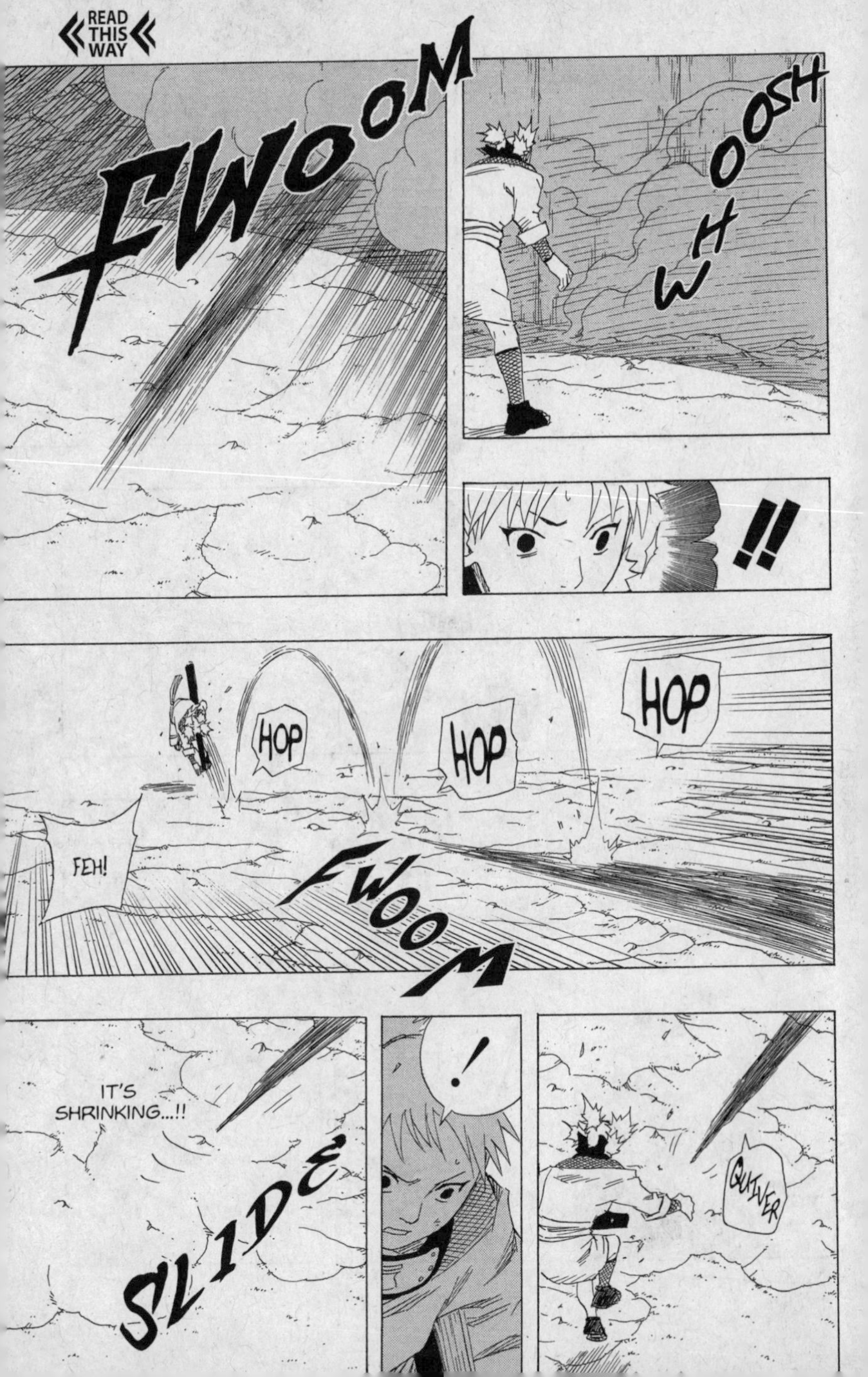
READ THIS WAY
WHOOSH
FWOOM
!!
HOP
HOP
HOP
FWOOM
FEH!
QUIVER
!
IT'S SHRINKING...!!
SLIDE

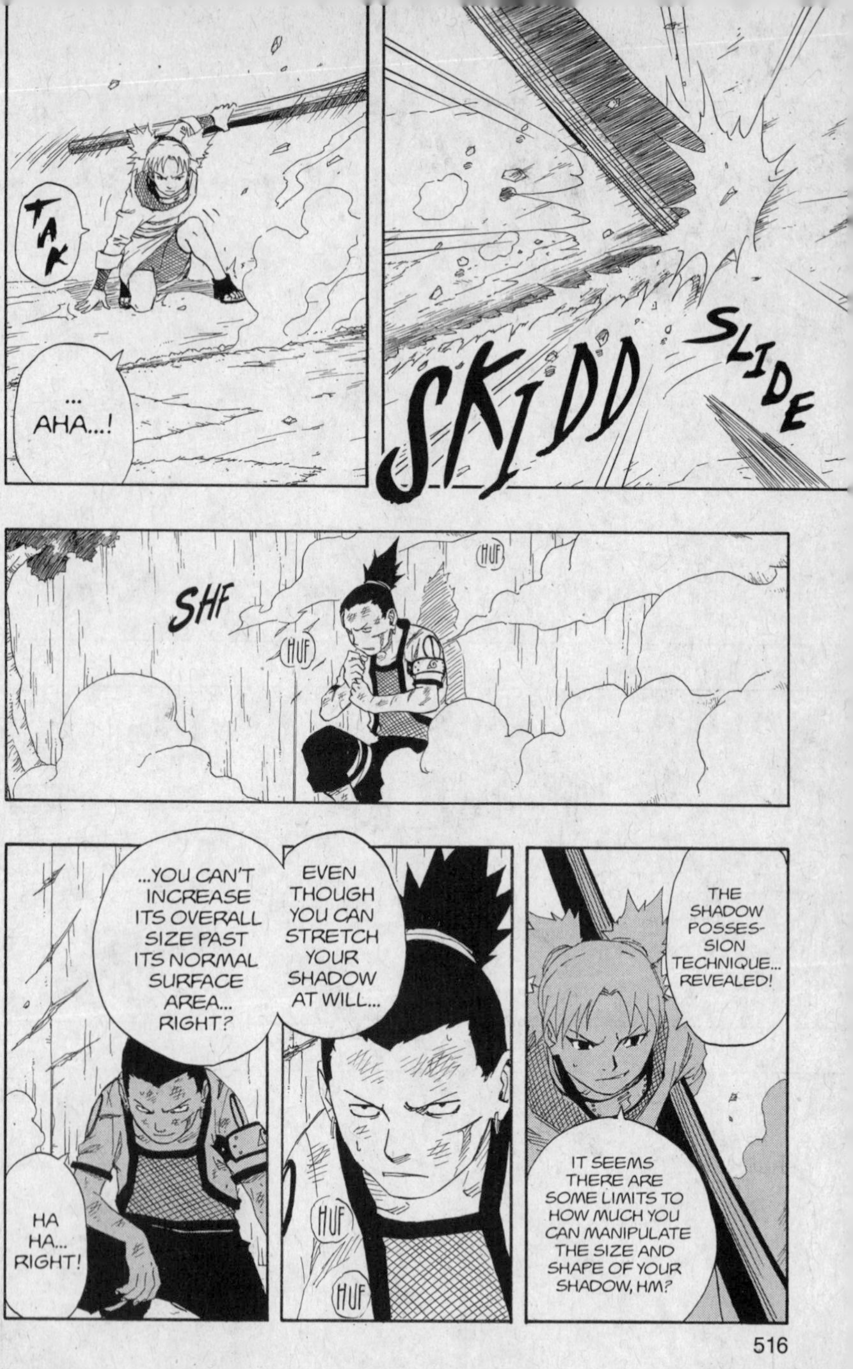
SLIDE
SKIDD
TAK
... AHA...!
HUF
SHF
HUF
THE SHADOW POSSES-SION TECHNIQUE... REVEALED!
IT SEEMS THERE ARE SOME LIMITS TO HOW MUCH YOU CAN MANIPULATE THE SIZE AND SHAPE OF YOUR SHADOW, HM?
EVEN THOUGH YOU CAN STRETCH YOUR SHADOW AT WILL...
HUF
HUF
...YOU CAN'T INCREASE ITS OVERALL SIZE PAST ITS NORMAL SURFACE AREA... RIGHT?
HA HA... RIGHT!

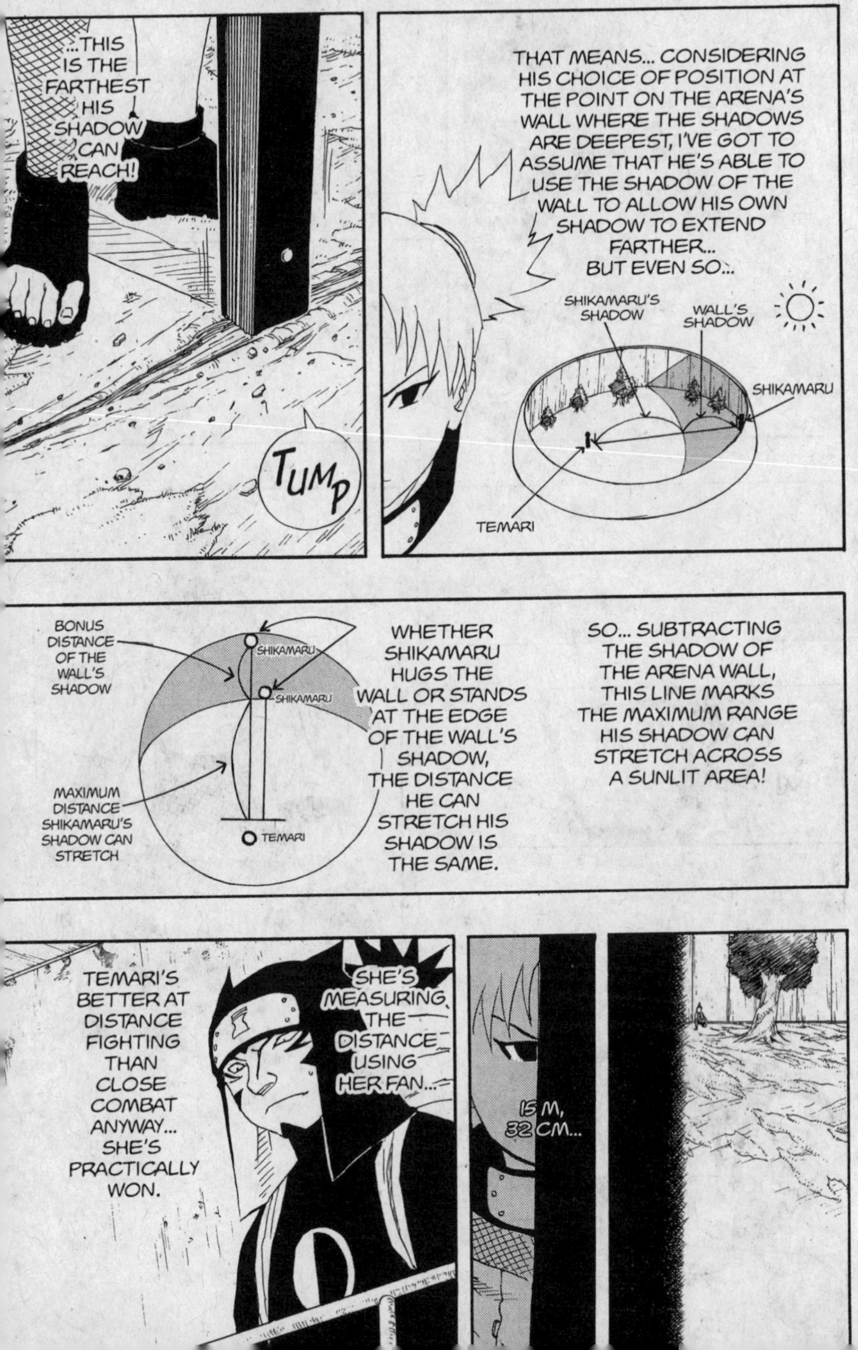
THAT MEANS... CONSIDERING HIS CHOICE OF POSITION AT THE POINT ON THE ARENA'S WALL WHERE THE SHADOWS ARE DEEPEST, I'VE GOT TO ASSUME THAT HE'S ABLE TO USE THE SHADOW OF THE WALL TO ALLOW HIS OWN SHADOW TO EXTEND FARTHER... BUT EVEN SO...
SHIKAMARU'S SHADOW
WALL'S SHADOW
SHIKAMARU
TEMARI
...THIS IS THE FARTHEST HIS SHADOW CAN REACH!
TUMP
SO... SUBTRACTING THE SHADOW OF THE ARENA WALL, THIS LINE MARKS THE MAXIMUM RANGE HIS SHADOW CAN STRETCH ACROSS A SUNLIT AREA!
WHETHER SHIKAMARU HUGS THE WALL OR STANDS AT THE EDGE OF THE WALL'S SHADOW, THE DISTANCE HE CAN STRETCH HIS SHADOW IS THE SAME.
BONUS DISTANCE OF THE WALL'S SHADOW
SHIKAMARU
SHIKAMARU
MAXIMUM DISTANCE SHIKAMARU'S SHADOW CAN STRETCH
TEMARI
15 M, 32 CM...
SHE'S MEASURING THE DISTANCE USING HER FAN...
TEMARI'S BETTER AT DISTANCE FIGHTING THAN CLOSE COMBAT ANYWAY... SHE'S PRACTICALLY WON.

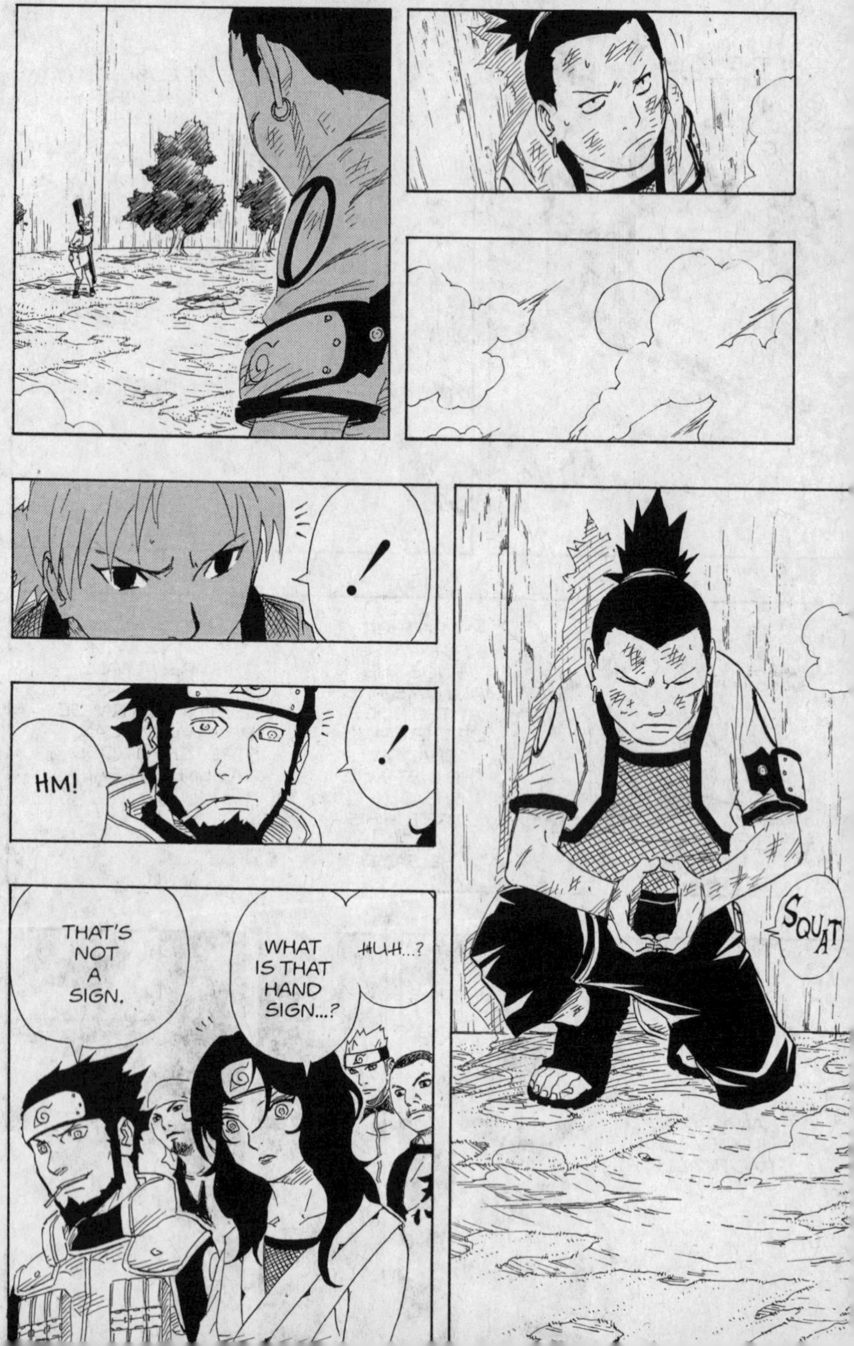
SQUAT
!
!
HM!
HUH...?
WHAT IS THAT HAND SIGN...?
THAT'S NOT A SIGN.

READ THIS WAY

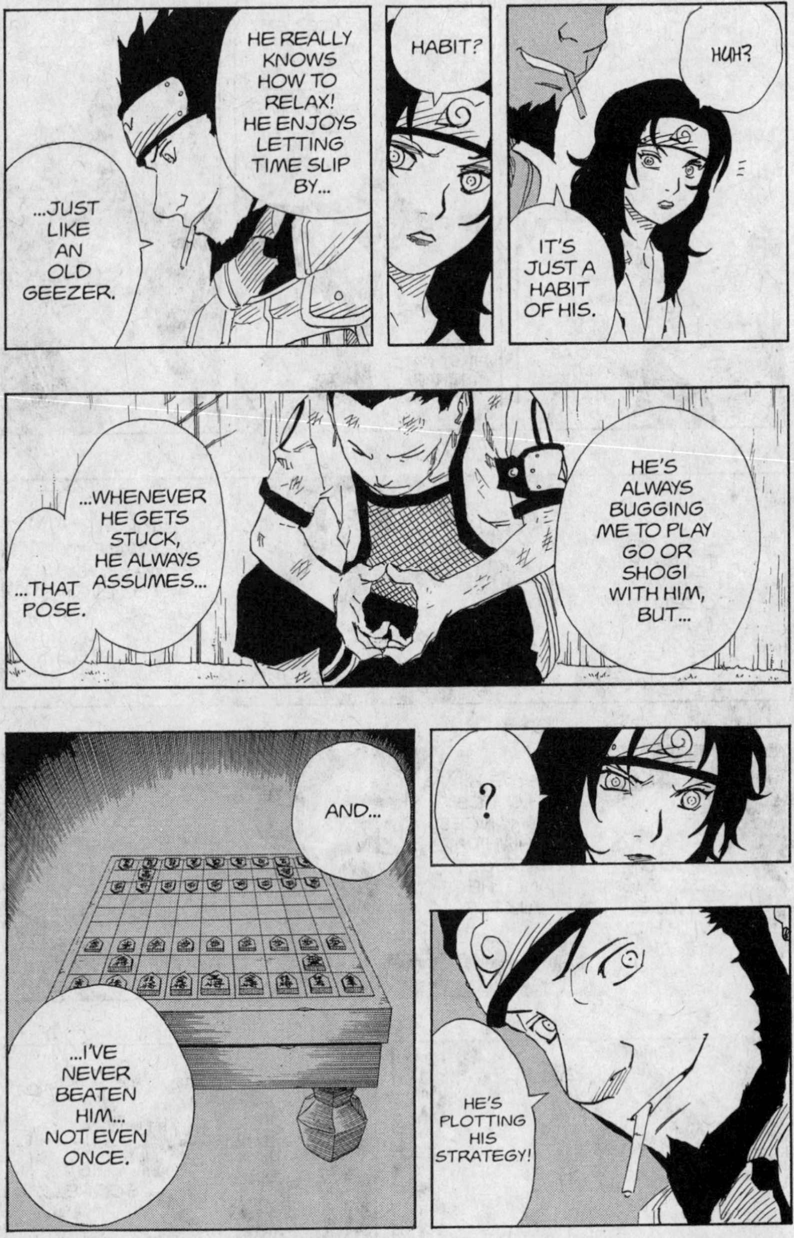

HUH?
IT'S JUST A HABIT OF HIS.
HABIT?
HE REALLY KNOWS HOW TO RELAX! HE ENJOYS LETTING TIME SLIP BY...
...JUST LIKE AN OLD GEEZER.
HE'S ALWAYS BUGGING ME TO PLAY GO OR SHOGI WITH HIM, BUT...
...WHENEVER HE GETS STUCK, HE ALWAYS ASSUMES...
...THAT POSE.
?
HE'S PLOTTING HIS STRATEGY!
AND...
...I'VE NEVER BEATEN HIM... NOT EVEN ONCE.

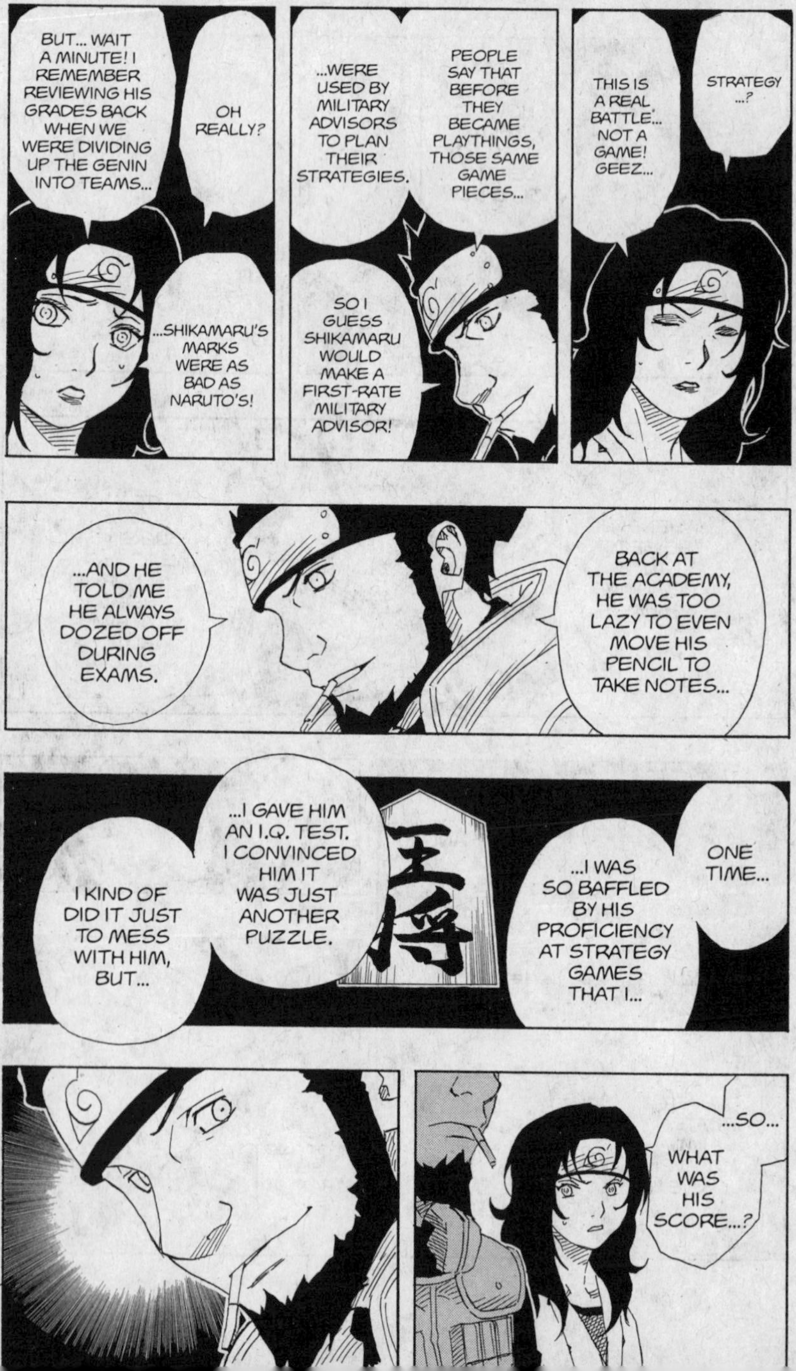
STRATEGY ...?
THIS IS A REAL BATTLE... NOT A GAME! GEEZ...
PEOPLE SAY THAT BEFORE THEY BECAME PLAYTHINGS, THOSE SAME GAME PIECES...
...WERE USED BY MILITARY ADVISORS TO PLAN THEIR STRATEGIES.
SO I GUESS SHIKAMARU WOULD MAKE A FIRST-RATE MILITARY ADVISOR!
OH REALLY?
BUT... WAIT A MINUTE! I REMEMBER REVIEWING HIS GRADES BACK WHEN WE WERE DIVIDING UP THE GENIN INTO TEAMS...
...SHIKAMARU'S MARKS WERE AS BAD AS NARUTO'S!
BACK AT THE ACADEMY, HE WAS TOO LAZY TO EVEN MOVE HIS PENCIL TO TAKE NOTES...
...AND HE TOLD ME HE ALWAYS DOZED OFF DURING EXAMS.
ONE TIME...
...I WAS SO BAFFLED BY HIS PROFICIENCY AT STRATEGY GAMES THAT I...
...I GAVE HIM AN I.Q. TEST. I CONVINCED HIM IT WAS JUST ANOTHER PUZZLE.
I KIND OF DID IT JUST TO MESS WITH HIM, BUT...
...SO...
WHAT WAS HIS SCORE...?

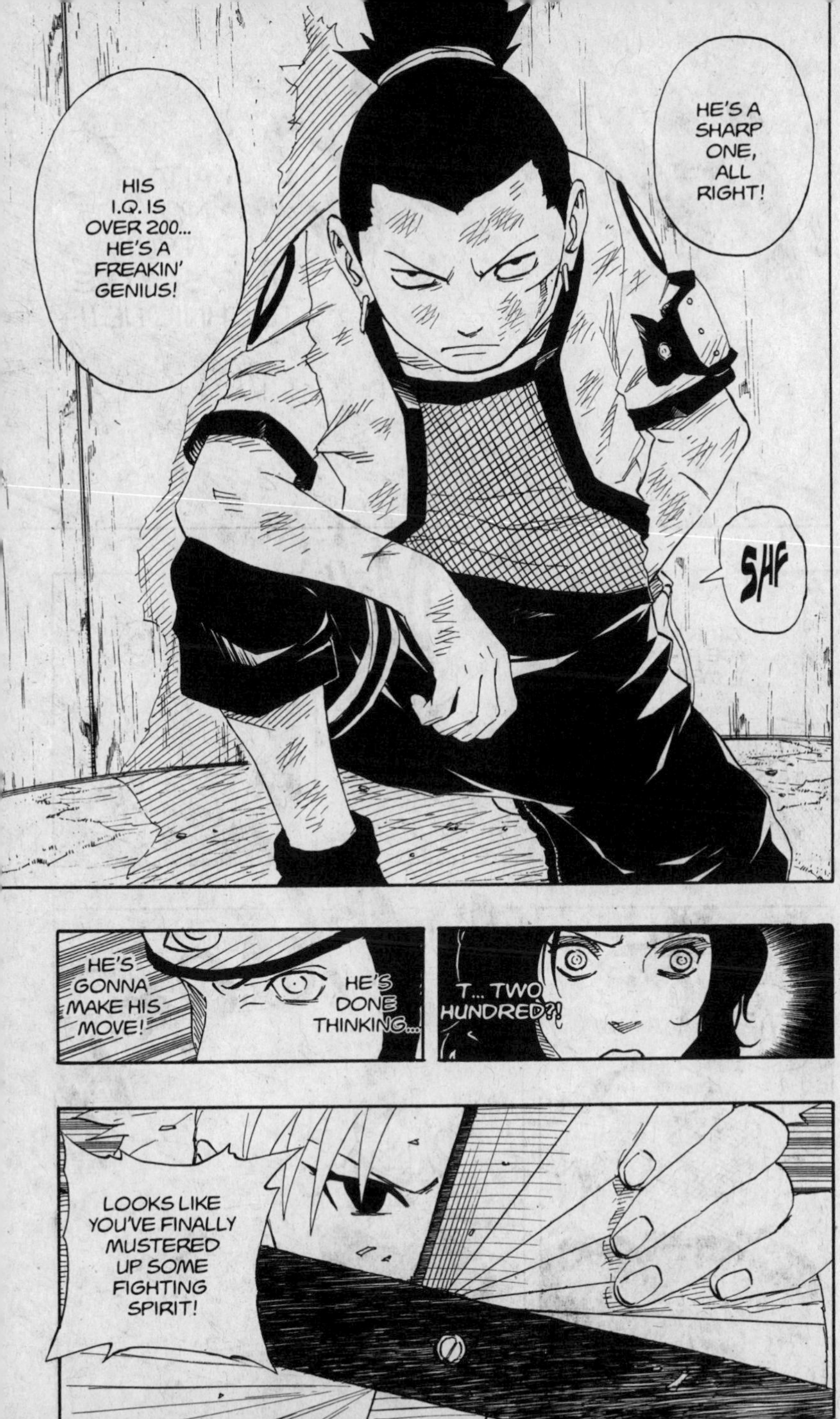
HE'S A SHARP ONE, ALL RIGHT!
HIS I.Q. IS OVER 200... HE'S A FREAKIN' GENIUS!
SHF
T... TWO HUNDRED?!
HE'S DONE THINKING...
HE'S GONNA MAKE HIS MOVE!
LOOKS LIKE YOU'VE FINALLY MUSTERED UP SOME FIGHTING SPIRIT!

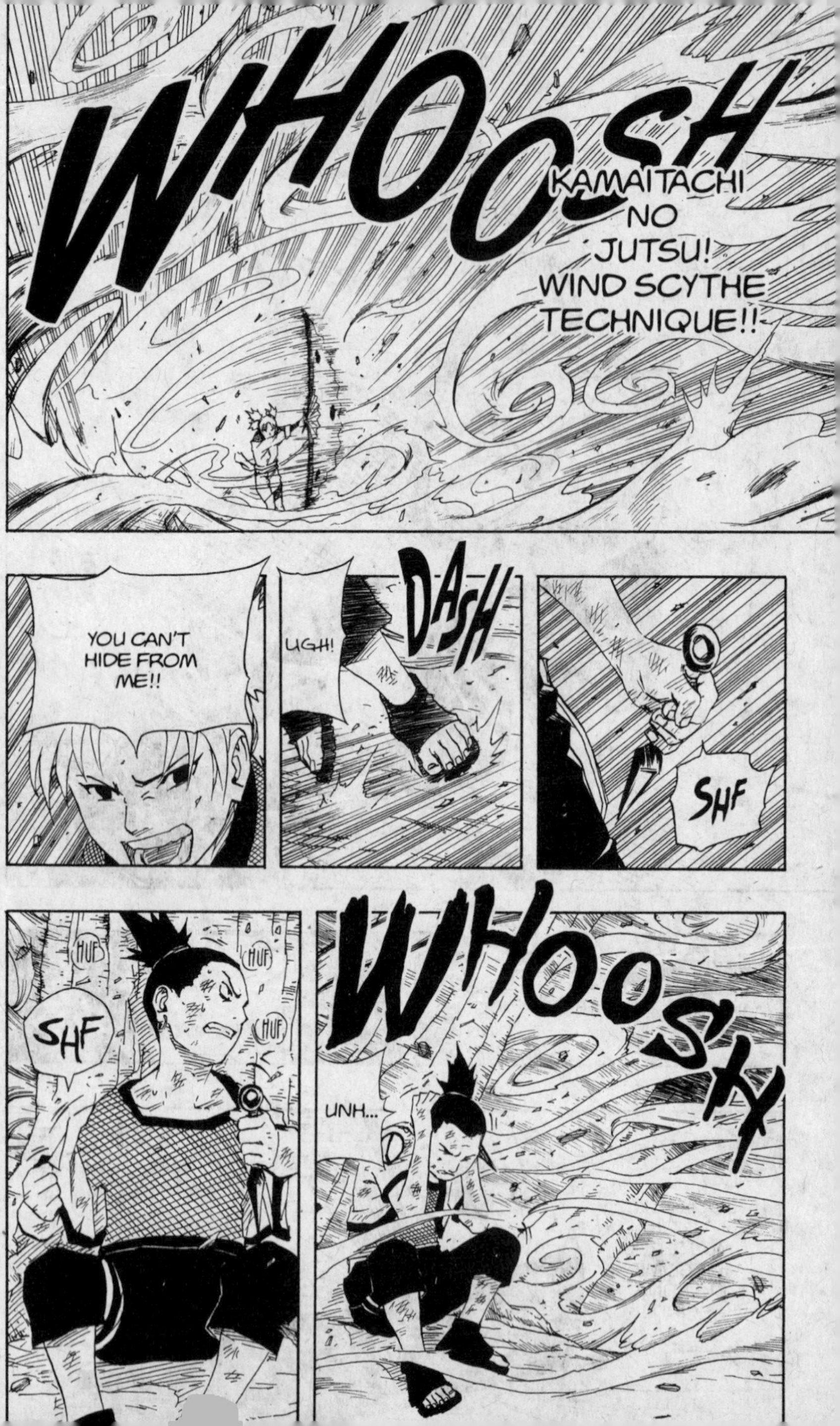
WHOOSH
KAMAITACHI NO JUTSU! WIND SCYTHE TECHNIQUE!!
SHF
DASH
UGH!
YOU CAN'T HIDE FROM ME!!
WHOOSH
UNH...
HUF
HUF
HUF
SHF

READ THIS WAY

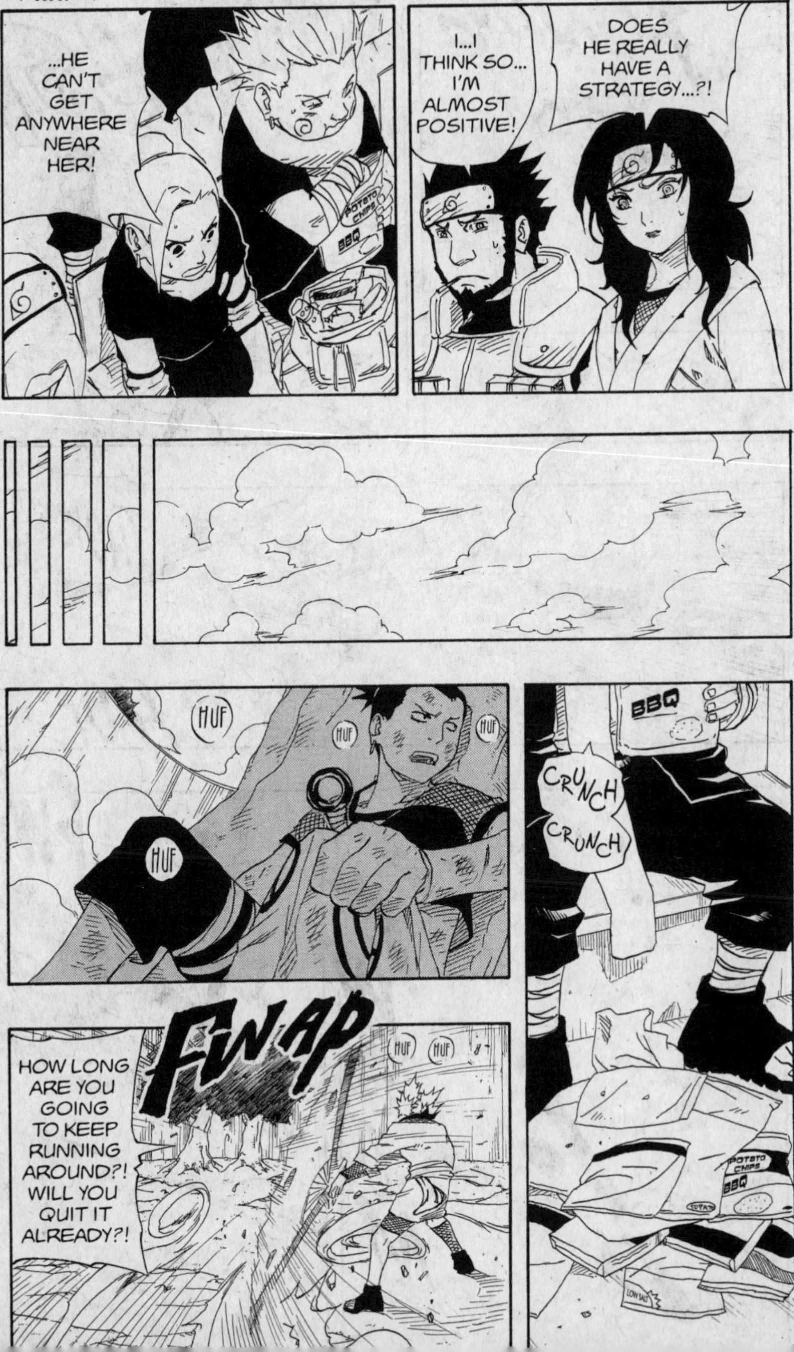
DOES HE REALLY HAVE A STRATEGY...?!
I...I THINK SO... I'M ALMOST POSITIVE!
POTATO CHIPS
BBQ
...HE CAN'T GET ANYWHERE NEAR HER!
BBQ
CRUNCH
CRUNCH
POTATO CHIPS
BBQ
HUF
HUF
HUF
HUF
FWAP
HUF
HUF
HOW LONG ARE YOU GOING TO KEEP RUNNING AROUND?! WILL YOU QUIT IT ALREADY?!

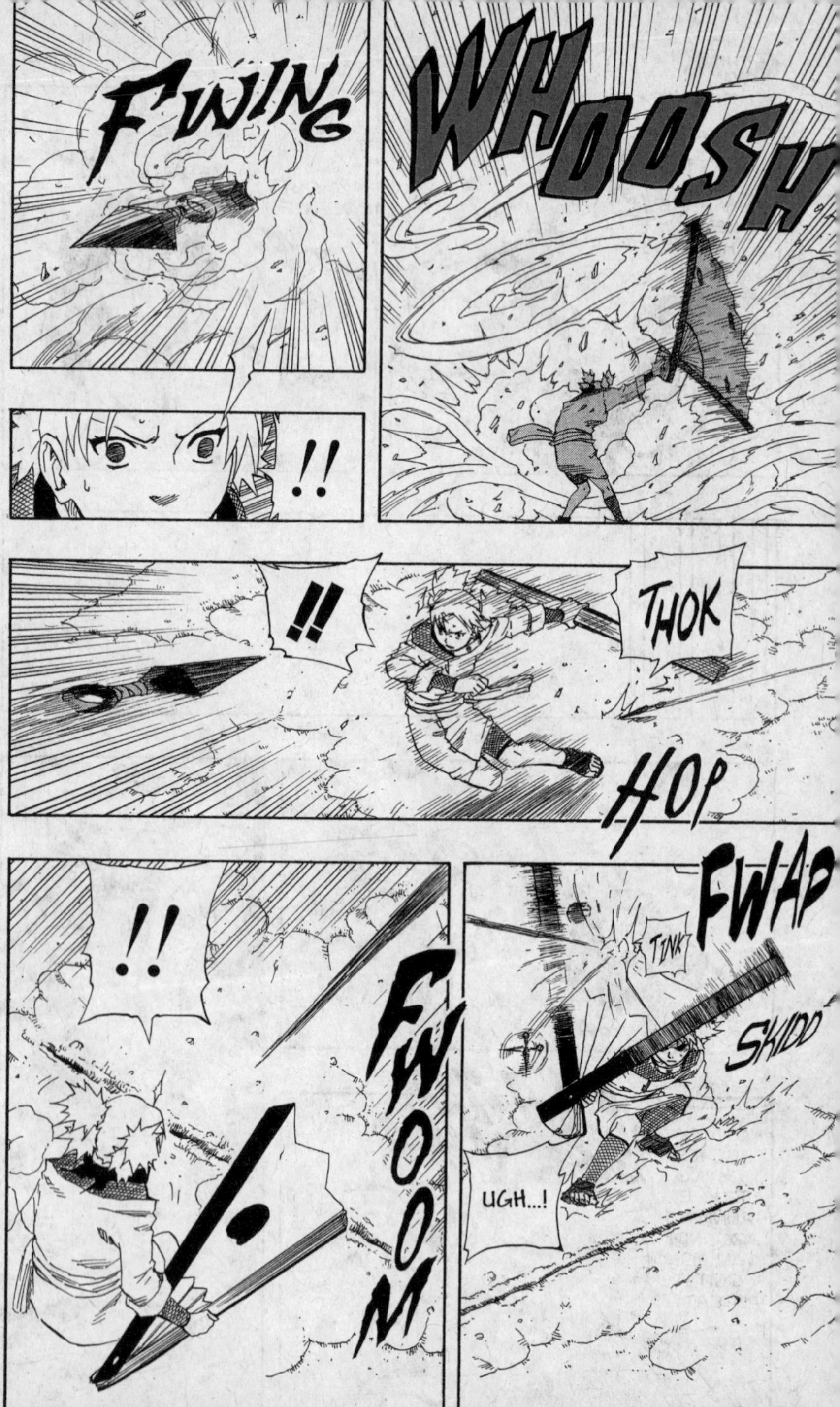
WHOOSH
FWING
!!
THOK
!!
HOP
FWAP
TINK
SKIDD
UGH...!
!!
FWOOM

READ THIS WAY

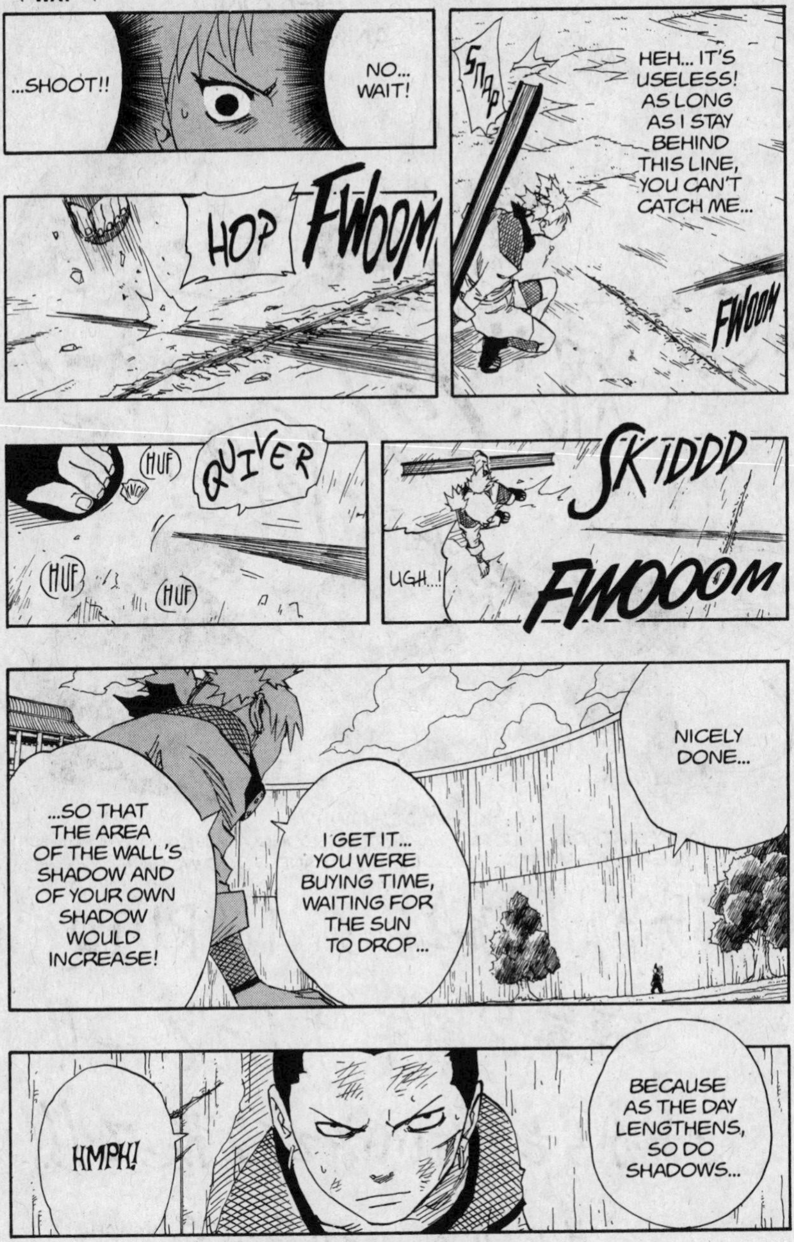
SNAP
HEH... IT'S USELESS! AS LONG AS I STAY BEHIND THIS LINE, YOU CAN'T CATCH ME...
FWOOM
NO... WAIT!
...SHOOT!!
FWOOM
HOP
SKIDDD
FWOOOM
UGH...!
QUIVER
HUF
HUF
HUF
NICELY DONE...
I GET IT... YOU WERE BUYING TIME, WAITING FOR THE SUN TO DROP...
...SO THAT THE AREA OF THE WALL'S SHADOW AND OF YOUR OWN SHADOW WOULD INCREASE!
BECAUSE AS THE DAY LENGTHENS, SO DO SHADOWS...
HMPH!

CELEBRATE!!
SECOND
ANNIVERSARY!!

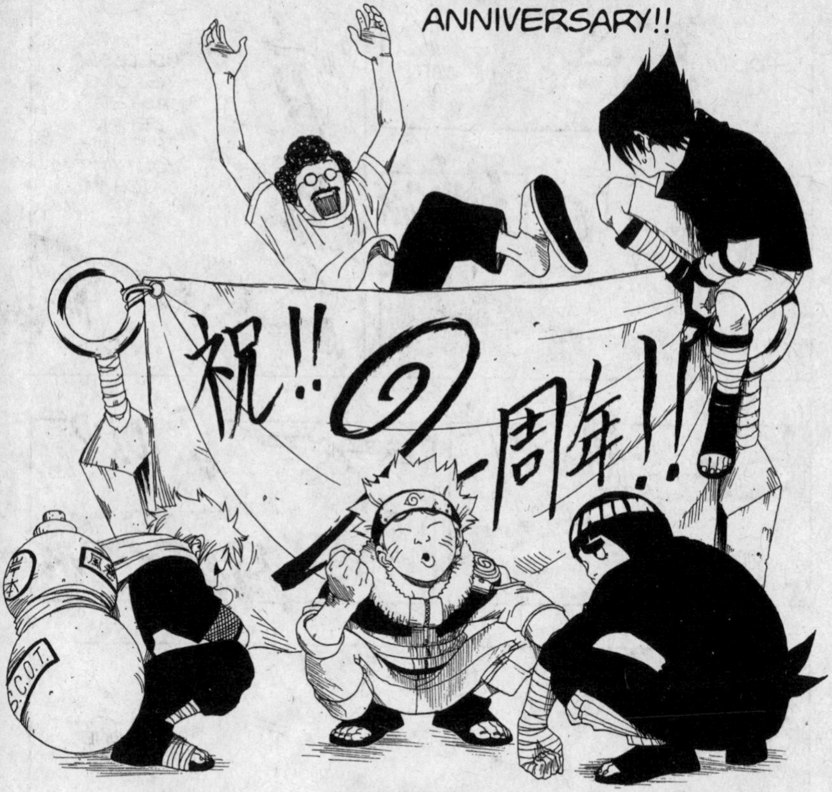
祝!!2周年!!
S.C.O.T.

KISHIMOTO-SAN!
HAPPY BIRTHDAY AND HAPPY *NARUTO* SECOND ANNIVERSARY!!
PLEASE KEEP UP THE GOOD ENERGY AND GOOD WORK!!!

岸本さん！誕生日＆「NARUTO」
連載2周年　おめでとー!!
これからも気合いいれて頑張って!!!

H.13 11.8.　河原武美 KAWAHARA TAKEMI

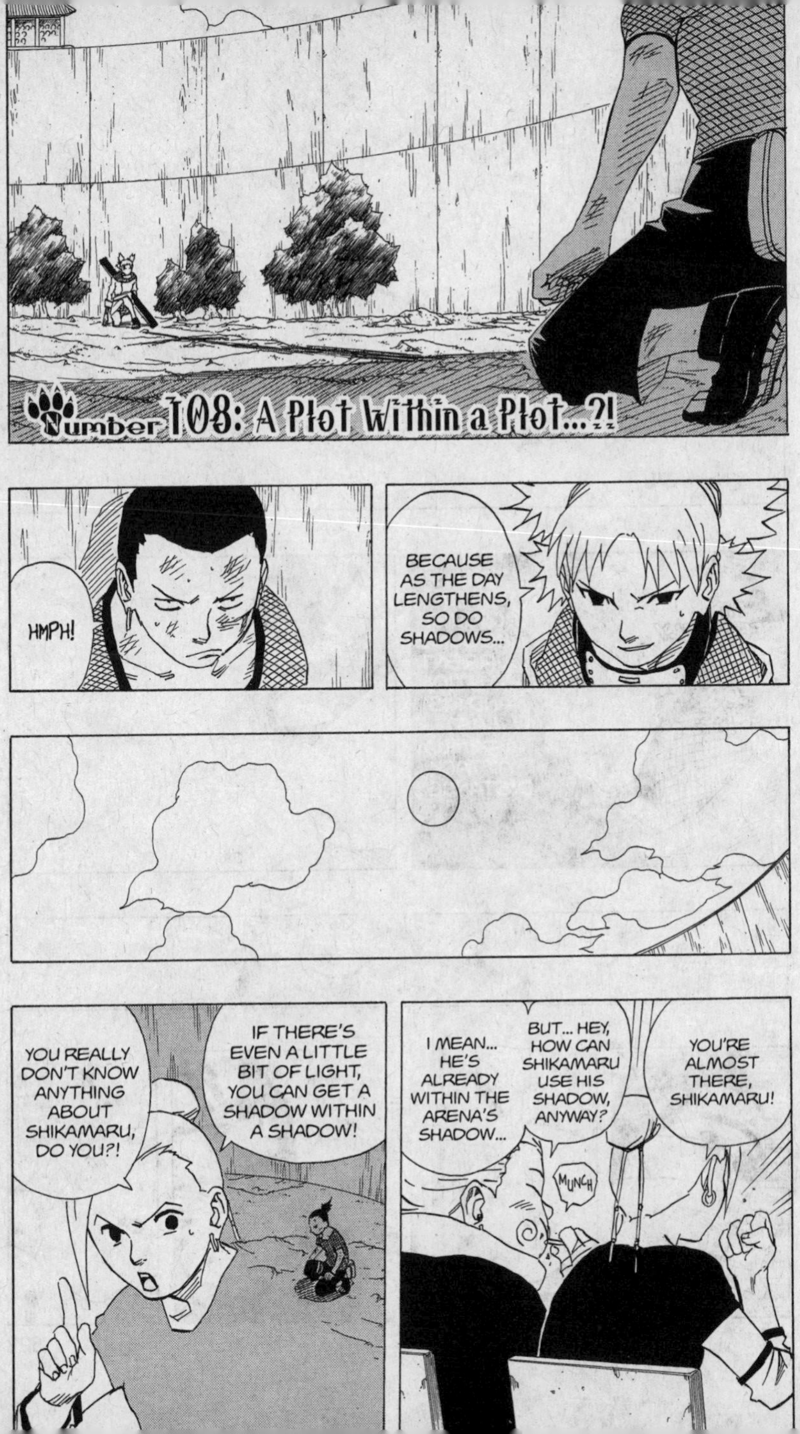
Number 108: A Plot Within a Plot...?!
BECAUSE AS THE DAY LENGTHENS, SO DO SHADOWS...
HMPH!
YOU'RE ALMOST THERE, SHIKAMARU!
BUT... HEY, HOW CAN SHIKAMARU USE HIS SHADOW, ANYWAY?
I MEAN... HE'S ALREADY WITHIN THE ARENA'S SHADOW...
MUNCH
IF THERE'S EVEN A LITTLE BIT OF LIGHT, YOU CAN GET A SHADOW WITHIN A SHADOW!
YOU REALLY DON'T KNOW ANYTHING ABOUT SHIKAMARU, DO YOU?!

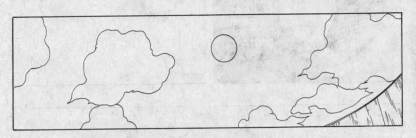

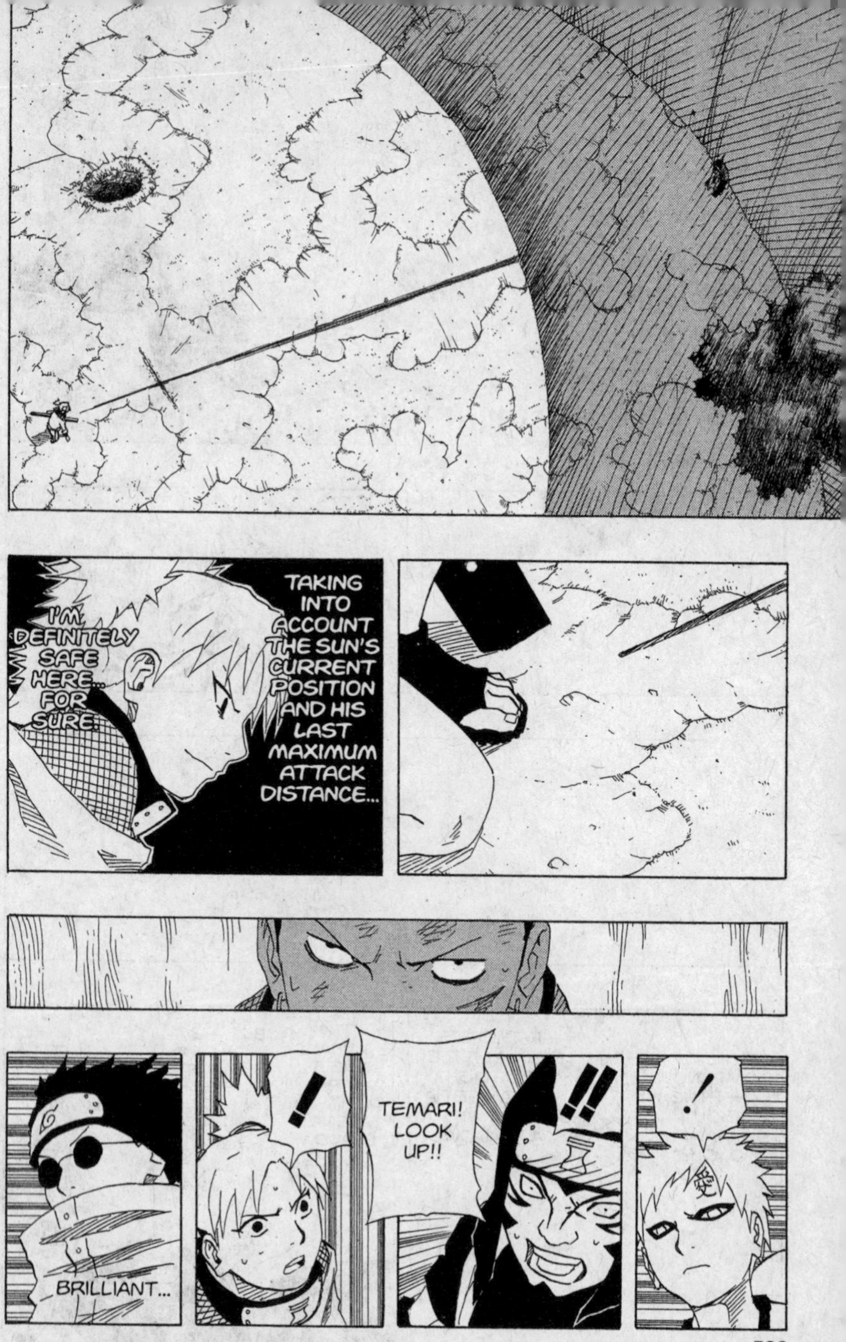
TAKING INTO ACCOUNT THE SUN'S CURRENT POSITION AND HIS LAST MAXIMUM ATTACK DISTANCE...
I'M DEFINITELY SAFE HERE... FOR SURE.
!
!!
TEMARI! LOOK UP!!
!
BRILLIANT...

READ THIS WAY

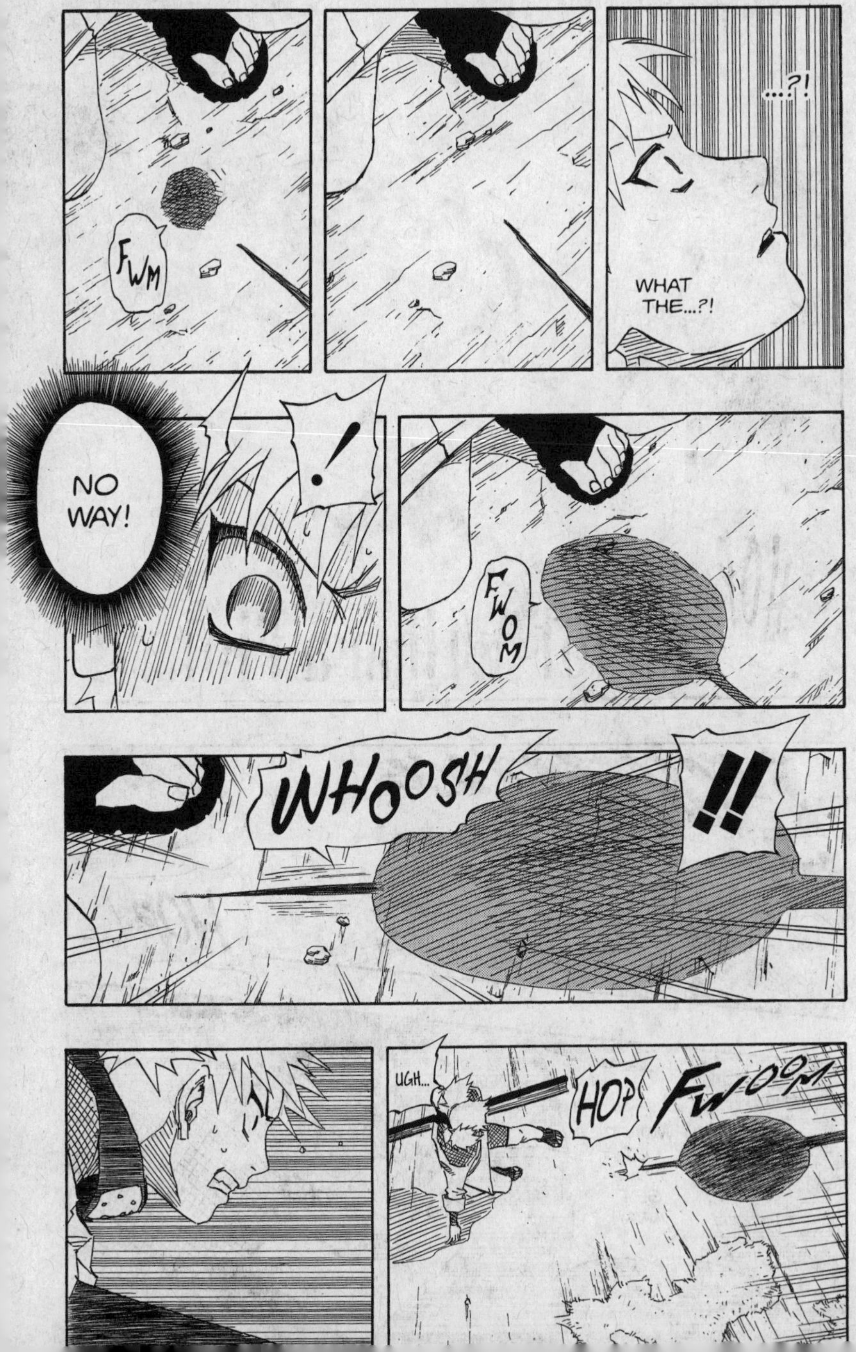
...?!
WHAT THE...?!
FWM
FWOM
!
NO WAY!
!!
WHOOSH
FWOOM
HOP
UGH...

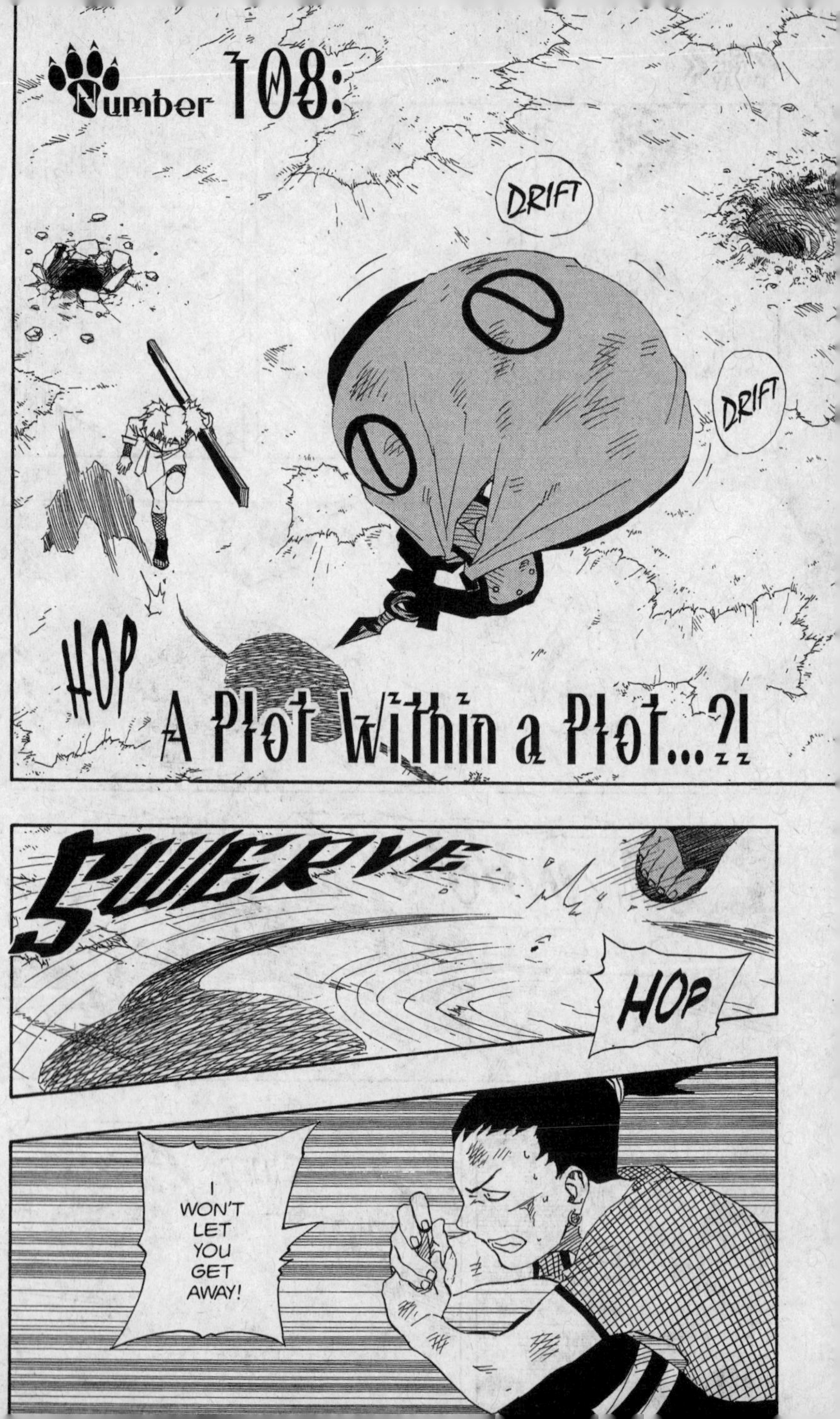
Number 108:
A Plot Within a Plot...?!
DRIFT
DRIFT
HOP
SWERVE
HOP
I WON'T LET YOU GET AWAY!

READ THIS WAY

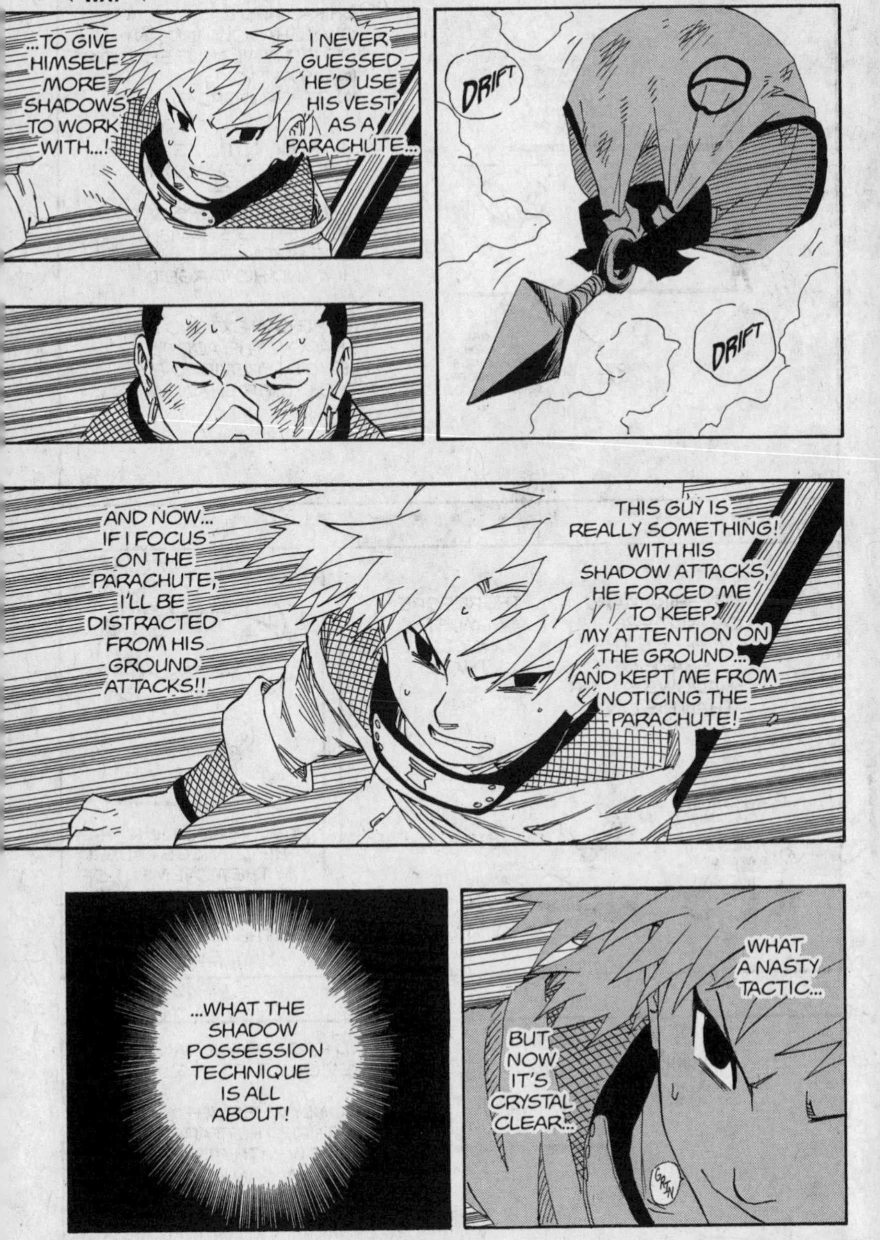
DRIFT
DRIFT
I NEVER GUESSED HE'D USE HIS VEST AS A PARACHUTE...
...TO GIVE HIMSELF MORE SHADOWS TO WORK WITH...!
THIS GUY IS REALLY SOMETHING! WITH HIS SHADOW ATTACKS, HE FORCED ME TO KEEP MY ATTENTION ON THE GROUND... AND KEPT ME FROM NOTICING THE PARACHUTE!
AND NOW... IF I FOCUS ON THE PARACHUTE, I'LL BE DISTRACTED FROM HIS GROUND ATTACKS!!
WHAT A NASTY TACTIC...
BUT NOW IT'S CRYSTAL CLEAR...
...WHAT THE SHADOW POSSESSION TECHNIQUE IS ALL ABOUT!

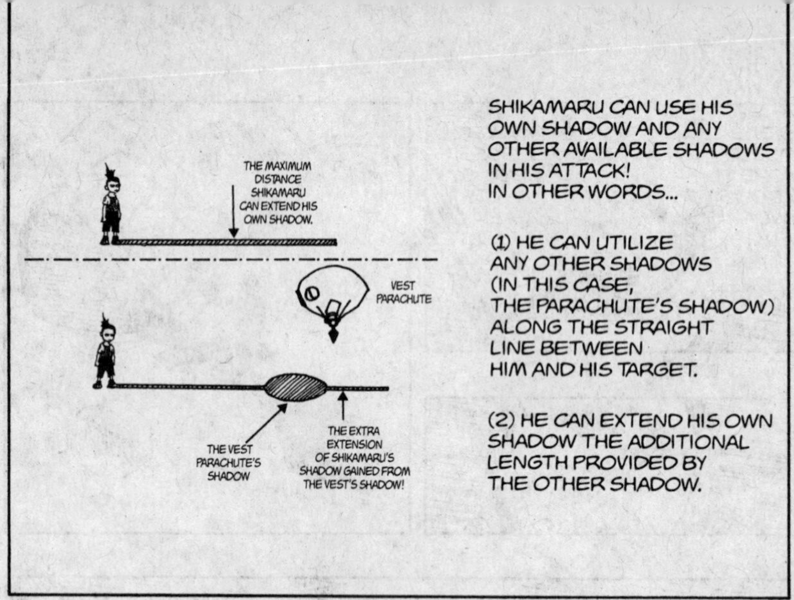
SHIKAMARU CAN USE HIS OWN SHADOW AND ANY OTHER AVAILABLE SHADOWS IN HIS ATTACK! IN OTHER WORDS...
(1) HE CAN UTILIZE ANY OTHER SHADOWS (IN THIS CASE, THE PARACHUTE'S SHADOW) ALONG THE STRAIGHT LINE BETWEEN HIM AND HIS TARGET.
(2) HE CAN EXTEND HIS OWN SHADOW THE ADDITIONAL LENGTH PROVIDED BY THE OTHER SHADOW.
THE MAXIMUM DISTANCE SHIKAMARU CAN EXTEND HIS OWN SHADOW.
VEST PARACHUTE
THE EXTRA EXTENSION OF SHIKAMARU'S SHADOW GAINED FROM THE VEST'S SHADOW!
THE VEST PARACHUTE'S SHADOW
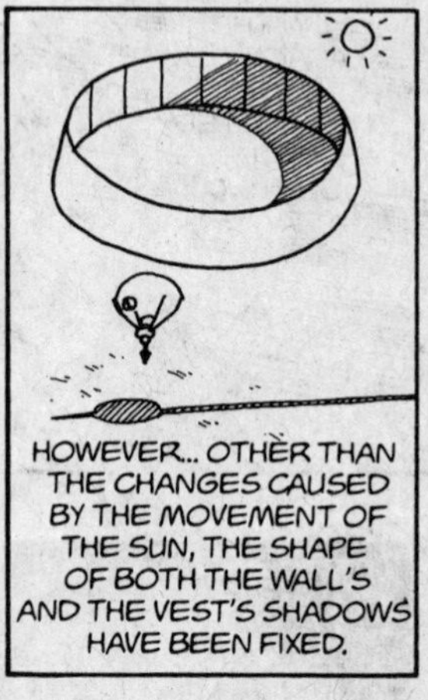
HOWEVER... OTHER THAN THE CHANGES CAUSED BY THE MOVEMENT OF THE SUN, THE SHAPE OF BOTH THE WALL'S AND THE VEST'S SHADOWS HAVE BEEN FIXED.
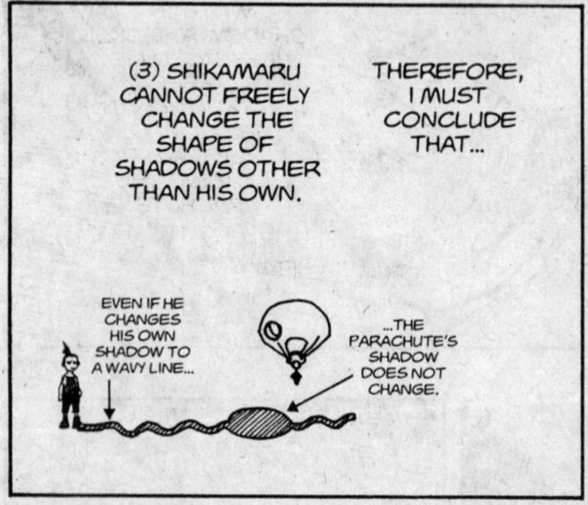
THEREFORE, I MUST CONCLUDE THAT...
(3) SHIKAMARU CANNOT FREELY CHANGE THE SHAPE OF SHADOWS OTHER THAN HIS OWN.
...THE PARACHUTE'S SHADOW DOES NOT CHANGE.
EVEN IF HE CHANGES HIS OWN SHADOW TO A WAVY LINE...
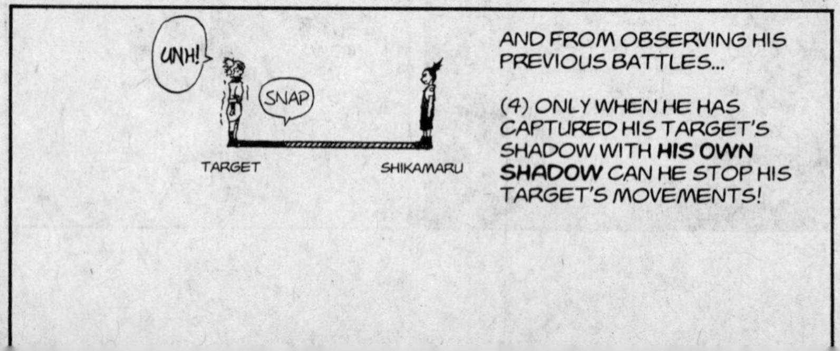
AND FROM OBSERVING HIS PREVIOUS BATTLES...
(4) ONLY WHEN HE HAS CAPTURED HIS TARGET'S SHADOW WITH **HIS OWN SHADOW** CAN HE STOP HIS TARGET'S MOVEMENTS!
UNH!
SNAP
SHIKAMARU
TARGET

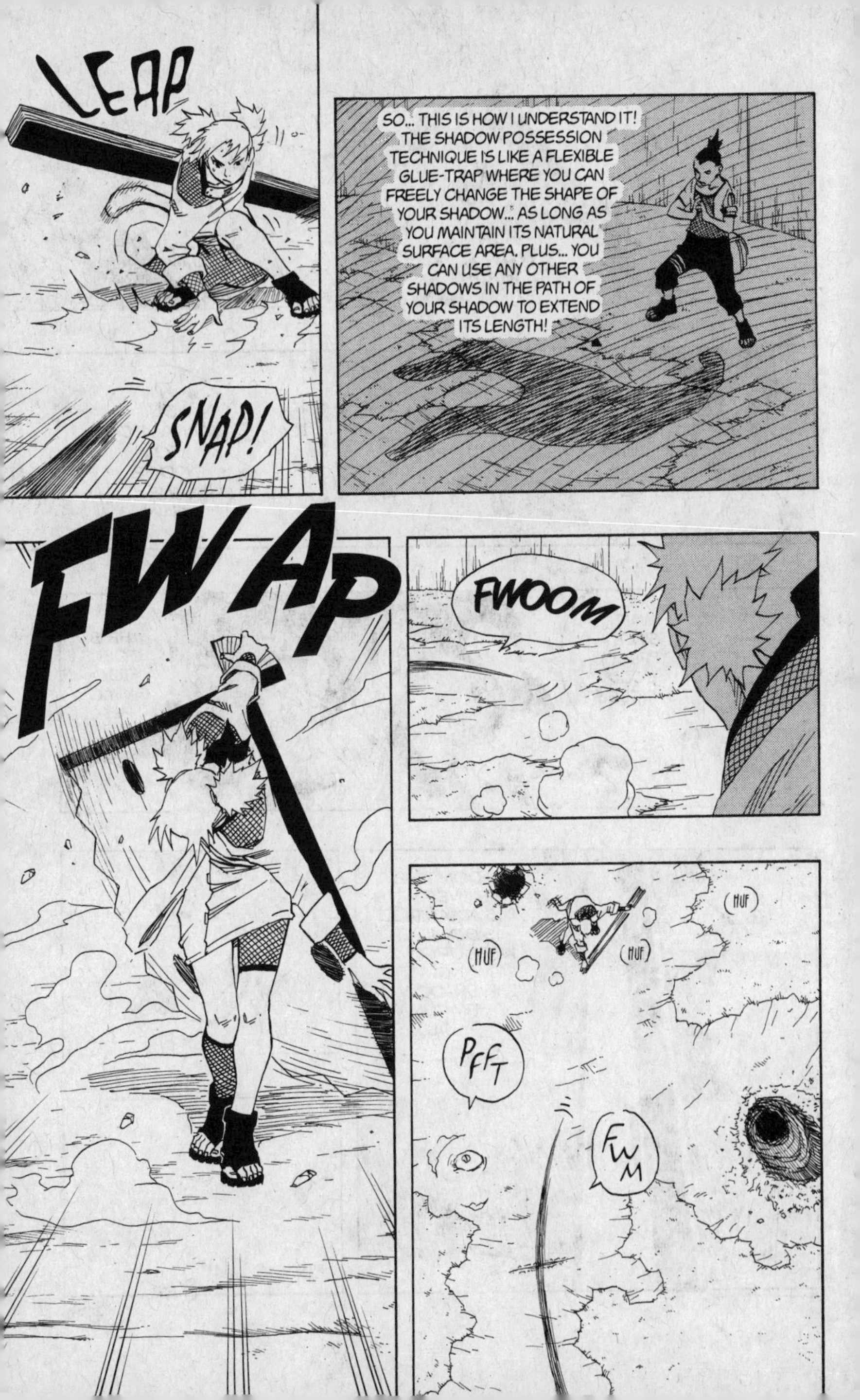
SO... THIS IS HOW I UNDERSTAND IT! THE SHADOW POSSESSION TECHNIQUE IS LIKE A FLEXIBLE GLUE-TRAP WHERE YOU CAN FREELY CHANGE THE SHAPE OF YOUR SHADOW... AS LONG AS YOU MAINTAIN ITS NATURAL SURFACE AREA. PLUS... YOU CAN USE ANY OTHER SHADOWS IN THE PATH OF YOUR SHADOW TO EXTEND ITS LENGTH!
LEAP
SNAP!
FWOOM
HUF
HUF
HUF
PFFT
FWM
FWAP

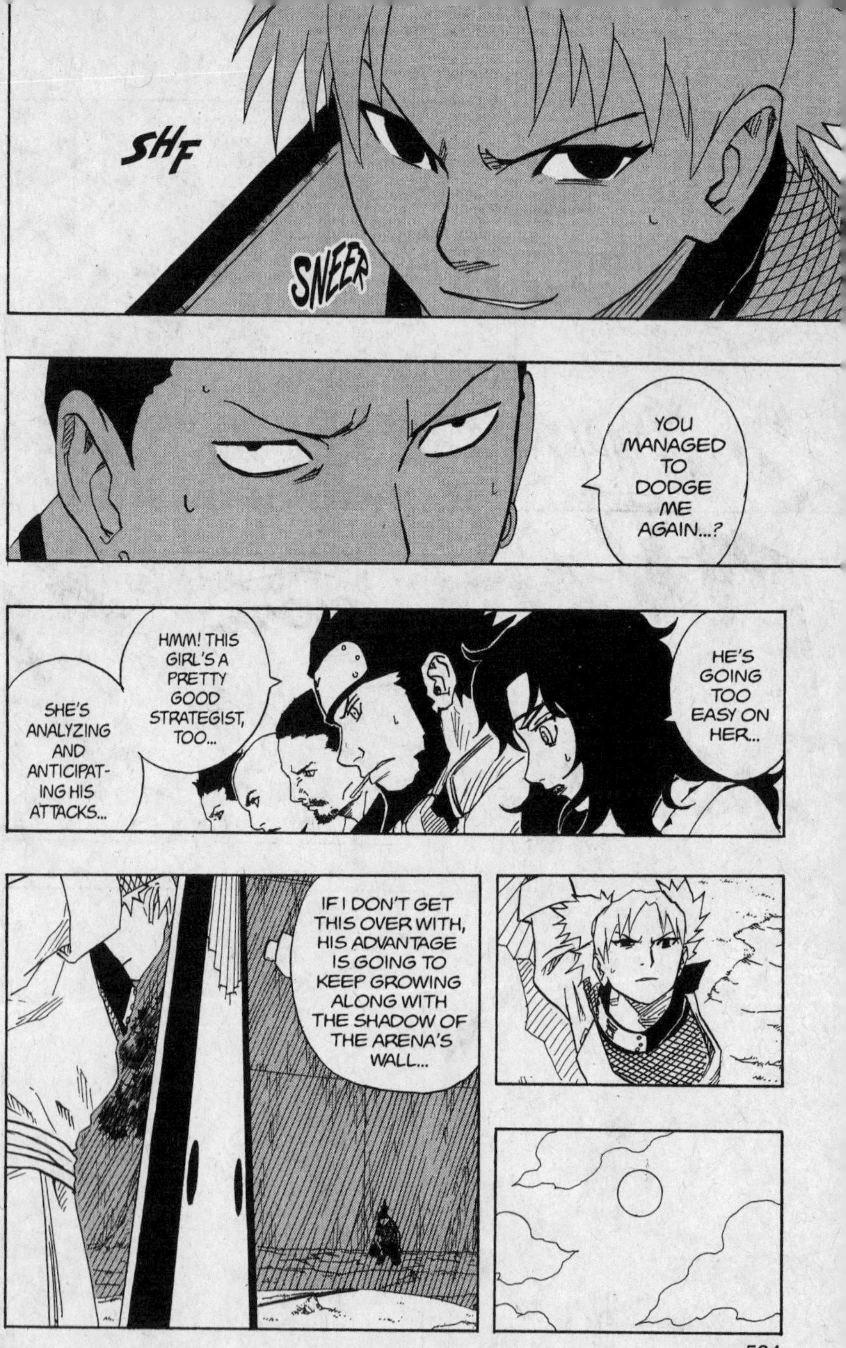
SHF
SNEER
YOU MANAGED TO DODGE ME AGAIN...?
HE'S GOING TOO EASY ON HER...
HMM! THIS GIRL'S A PRETTY GOOD STRATEGIST, TOO...
SHE'S ANALYZING AND ANTICIPAT-ING HIS ATTACKS...
IF I DON'T GET THIS OVER WITH, HIS ADVANTAGE IS GOING TO KEEP GROWING ALONG WITH THE SHADOW OF THE ARENA'S WALL...

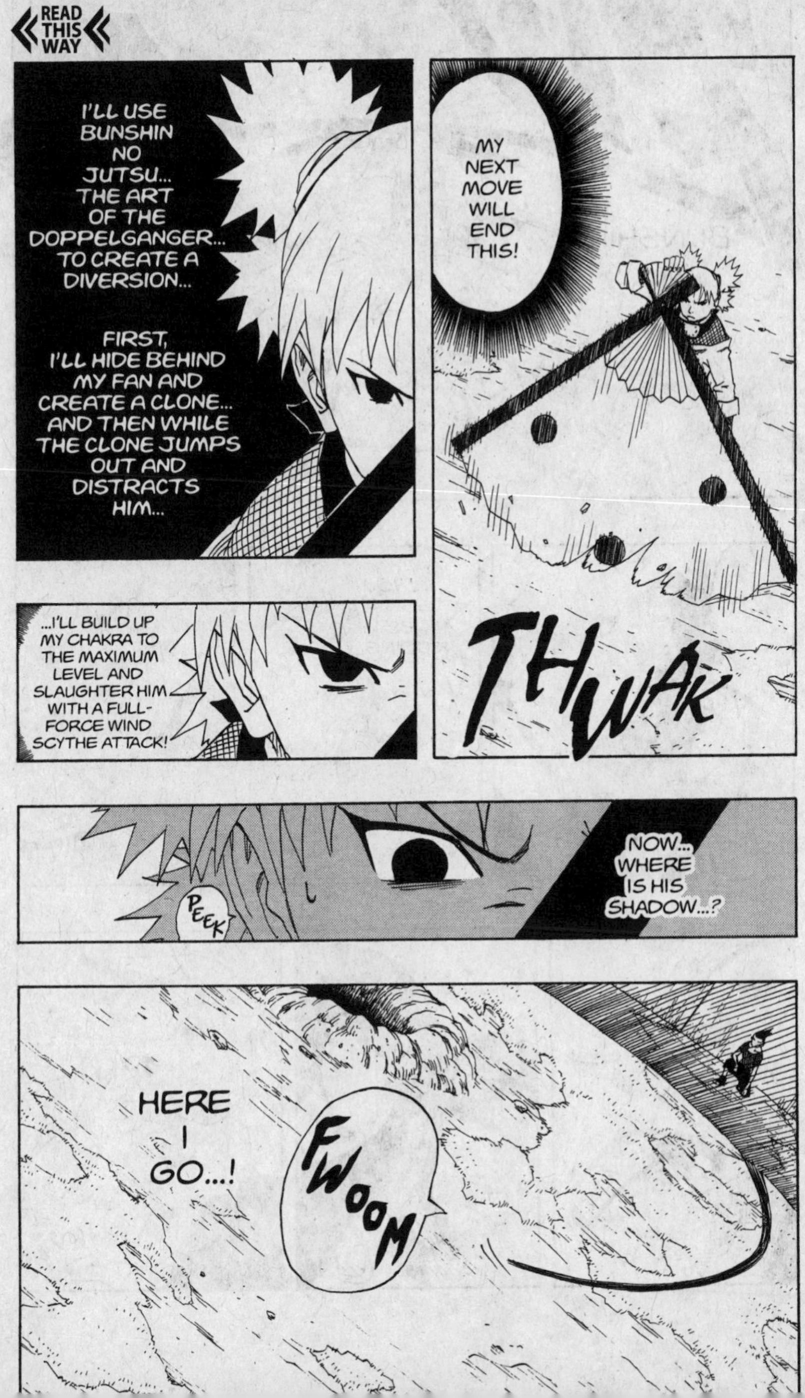
READ THIS WAY
MY NEXT MOVE WILL END THIS!
THWAK
I'LL USE BUNSHIN NO JUTSU... THE ART OF THE DOPPELGANGER... TO CREATE A DIVERSION...
FIRST, I'LL HIDE BEHIND MY FAN AND CREATE A CLONE... AND THEN WHILE THE CLONE JUMPS OUT AND DISTRACTS HIM...
...I'LL BUILD UP MY CHAKRA TO THE MAXIMUM LEVEL AND SLAUGHTER HIM WITH A FULL-FORCE WIND SCYTHE ATTACK!
NOW... WHERE IS HIS SHADOW...?
PEEK
HERE I GO...!
FWOOM

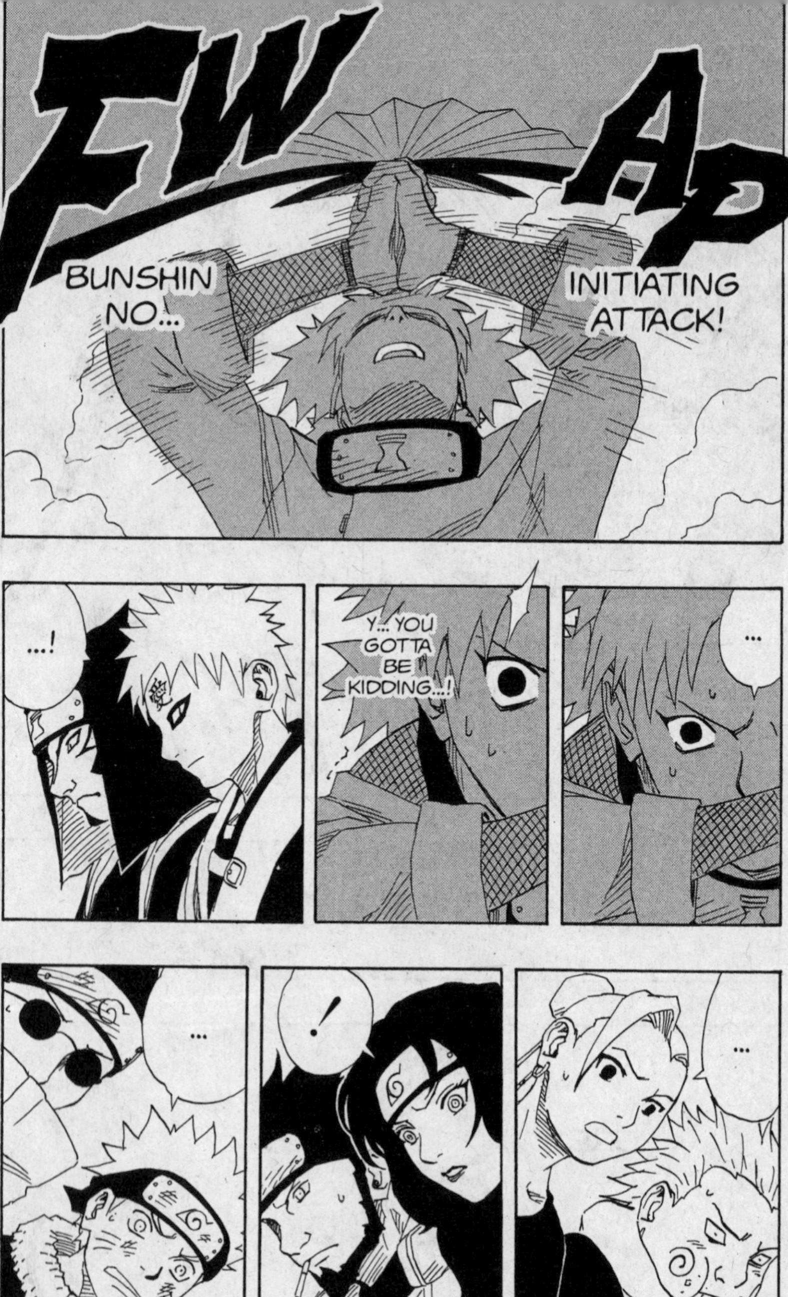
FWAP
INITIATING ATTACK!
BUNSHIN NO...
...
Y... YOU GOTTA BE KIDDING...!
...!
...
!
...

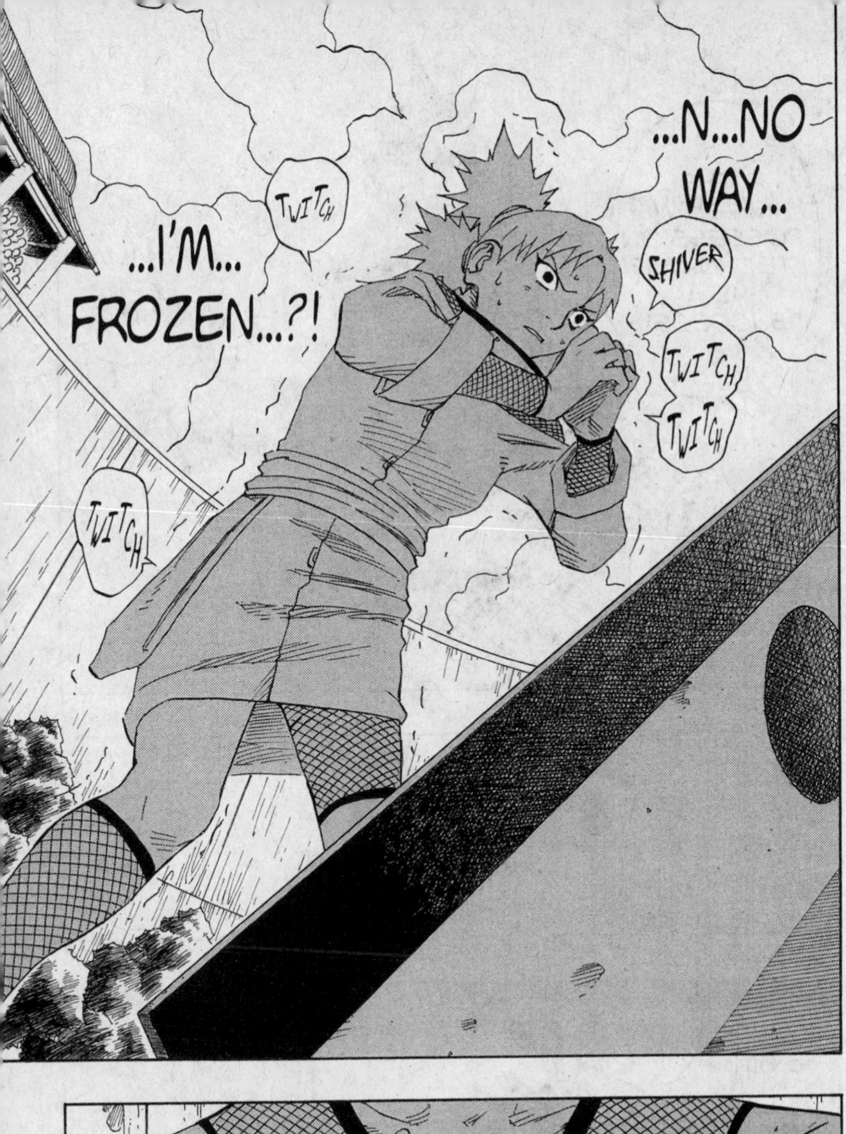
...N...NO WAY...
SHIVER
TWITCH
TWITCH
TWITCH
...I'M... FROZEN...?!
TWITCH
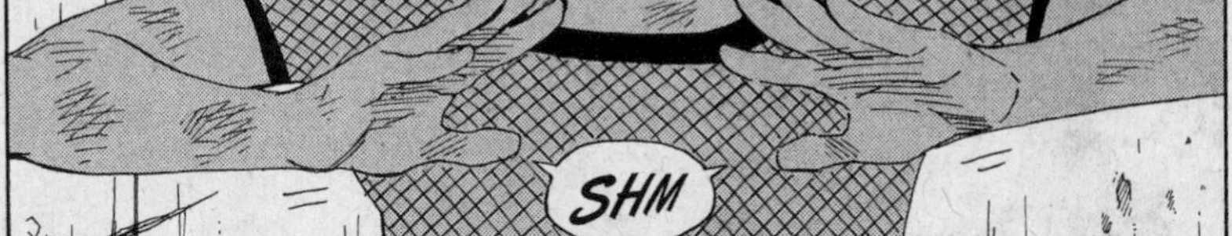
SHM

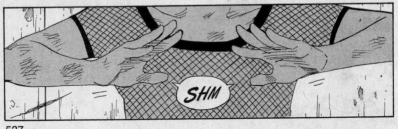

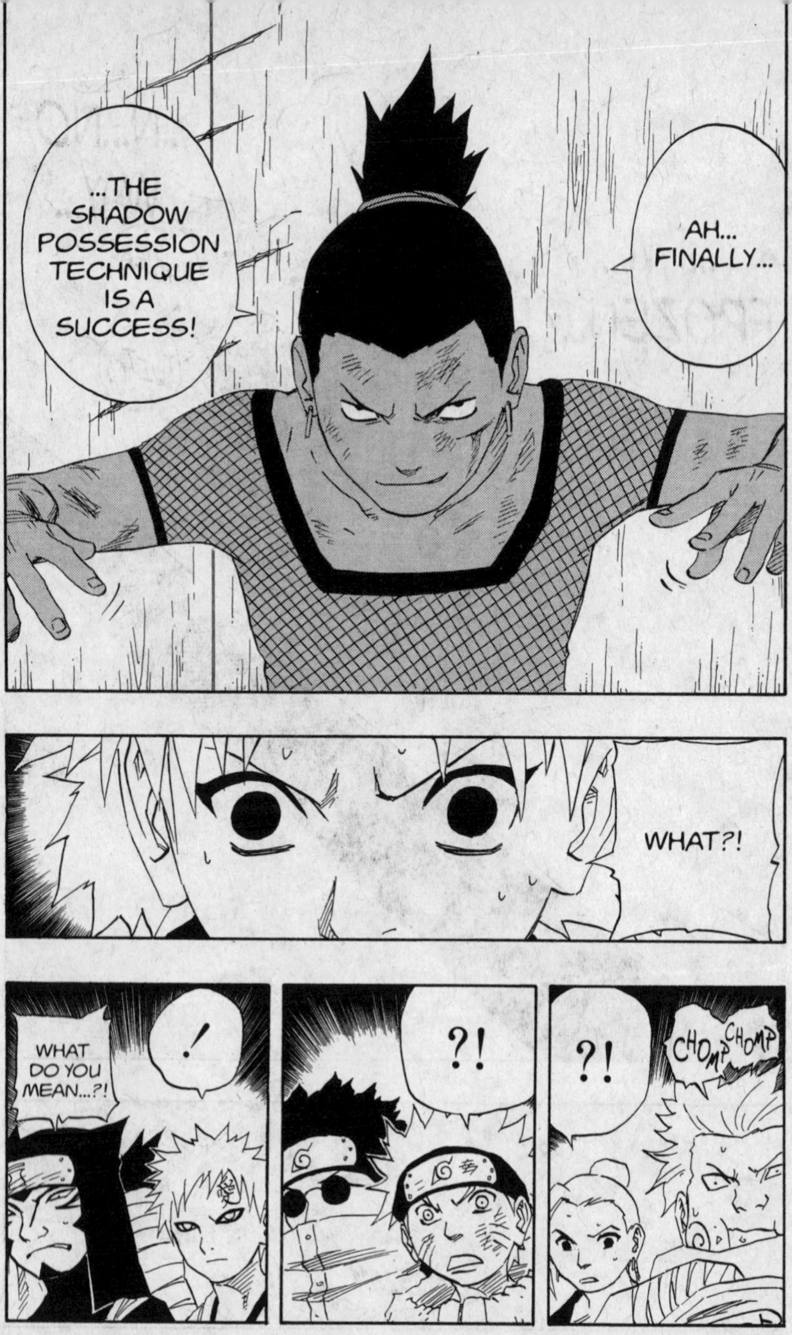
AH... FINALLY...
...THE SHADOW POSSESSION TECHNIQUE IS A SUCCESS!
WHAT?!
CHOMP CHOMP
?!
?!
!
WHAT DO YOU MEAN...?!

READ THIS WAY

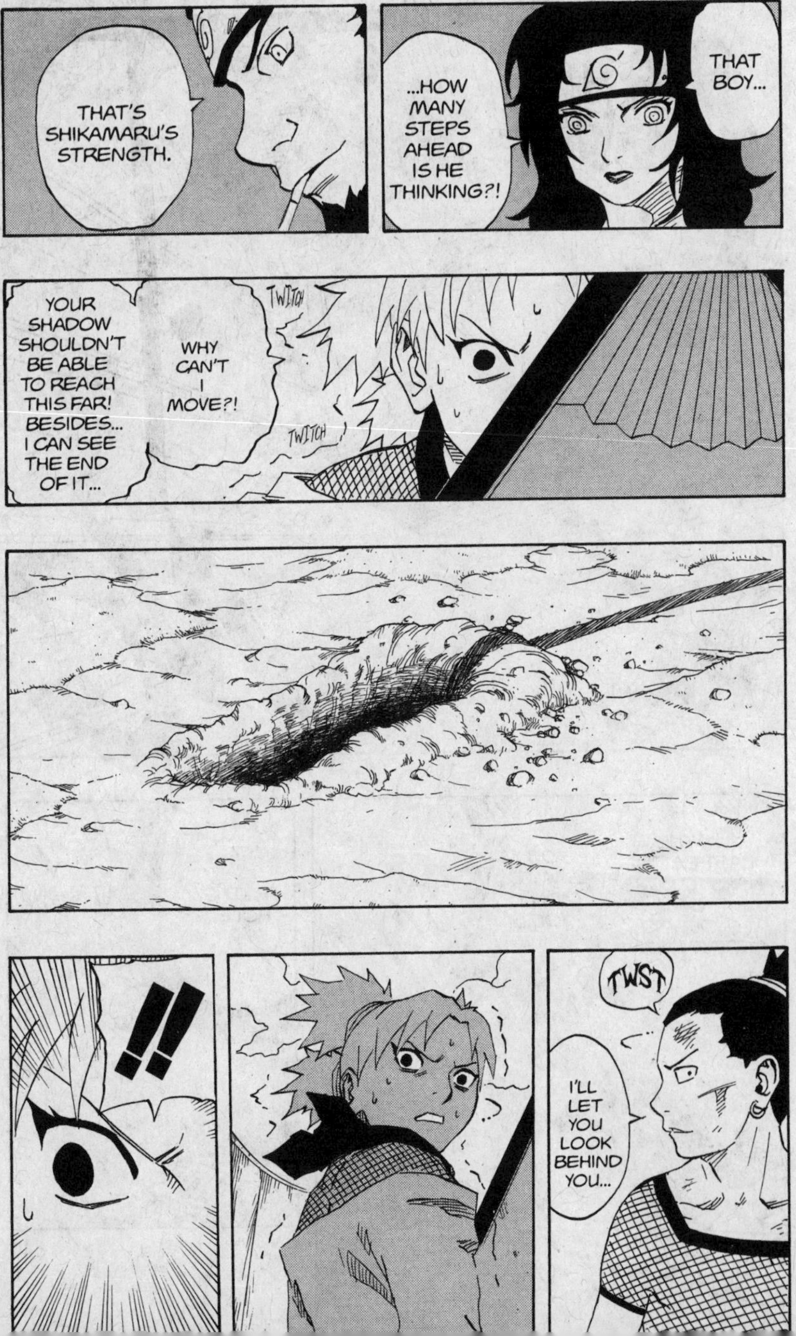
THAT BOY...
...HOW MANY STEPS AHEAD IS HE THINKING?!
THAT'S SHIKAMARU'S STRENGTH.
TWITCH
WHY CAN'T I MOVE?!
TWITCH
YOUR SHADOW SHOULDN'T BE ABLE TO REACH THIS FAR! BESIDES... I CAN SEE THE END OF IT...
TWST
I'LL LET YOU LOOK BEHIND YOU...
!!

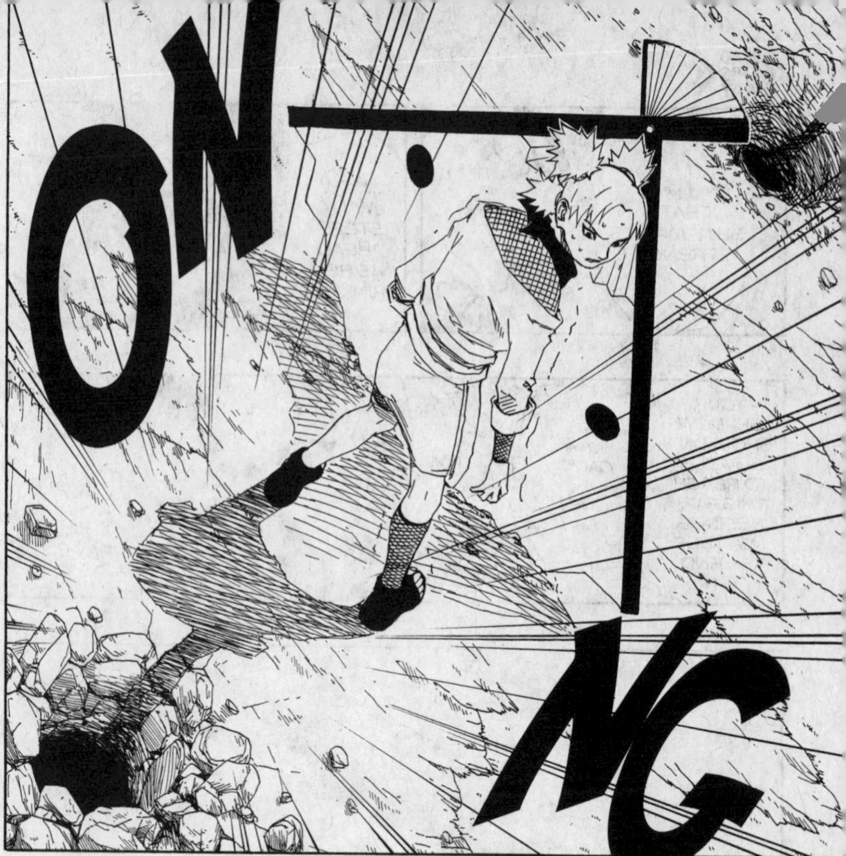
ON..NG

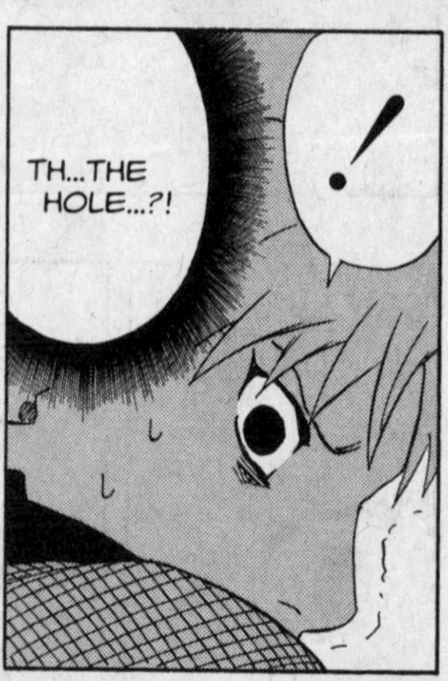
!
TH...THE HOLE...?!

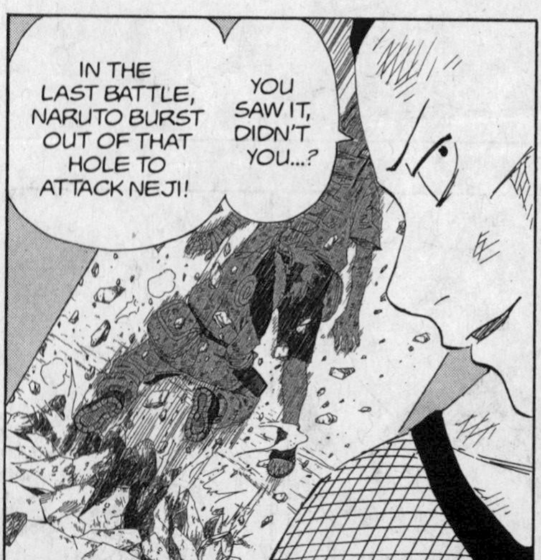
YOU SAW IT, DIDN'T YOU...?
IN THE LAST BATTLE, NARUTO BURST OUT OF THAT HOLE TO ATTACK NEJI!

READ THIS WAY

...HE TUNNELED UNDER THE GROUND FROM THAT BIGGER HOLE BETWEEN US...SO THEY'RE CONNECTED.
DON'T TELL ME... YOU USED THE SHADOW INSIDE THE TUNNEL BETWEEN THE TWO HOLES...?
BINGO.
SHF
HEH... JUST LIKE A CAREFULLY CALCULATED GAME OF SHOGI! ALL HIS PREVIOUS MOVES, WHEN HE ALLOWED TEMARI TO CALCULATE THE MAXIMUM LENGTH OF HIS SHADOW, WERE JUST SUBPLOTS LEADING TO THIS GRAND FINALE! IT'S LIKE HE TRAINED HER TO DODGE THE SHADOWS CAST BY THE SUN AND THEN COAXED HER INTO HIS TRAP, USING THE TUNNEL'S INVISIBLE SHADOW TO CAPTURE HER FROM BEHIND! IT'S A TRUE CHECKMATE...
MAXIMUM LIMIT
SHIKAMARU'S SHADOW
HOLE
SHIKAMARU
TEMARI
HOLE
THE INVISIBLE SHADOW INSIDE THE TUNNEL
UGH!
...
D...DON'T TELL ME...

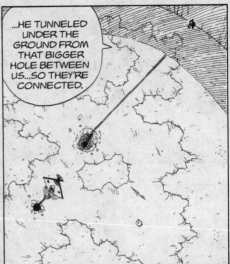

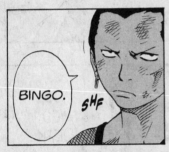

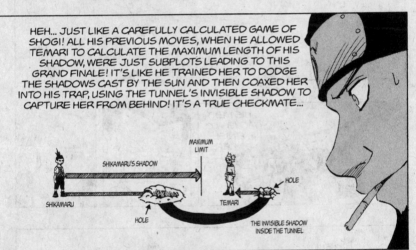

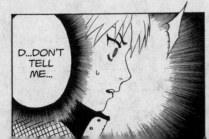

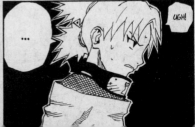

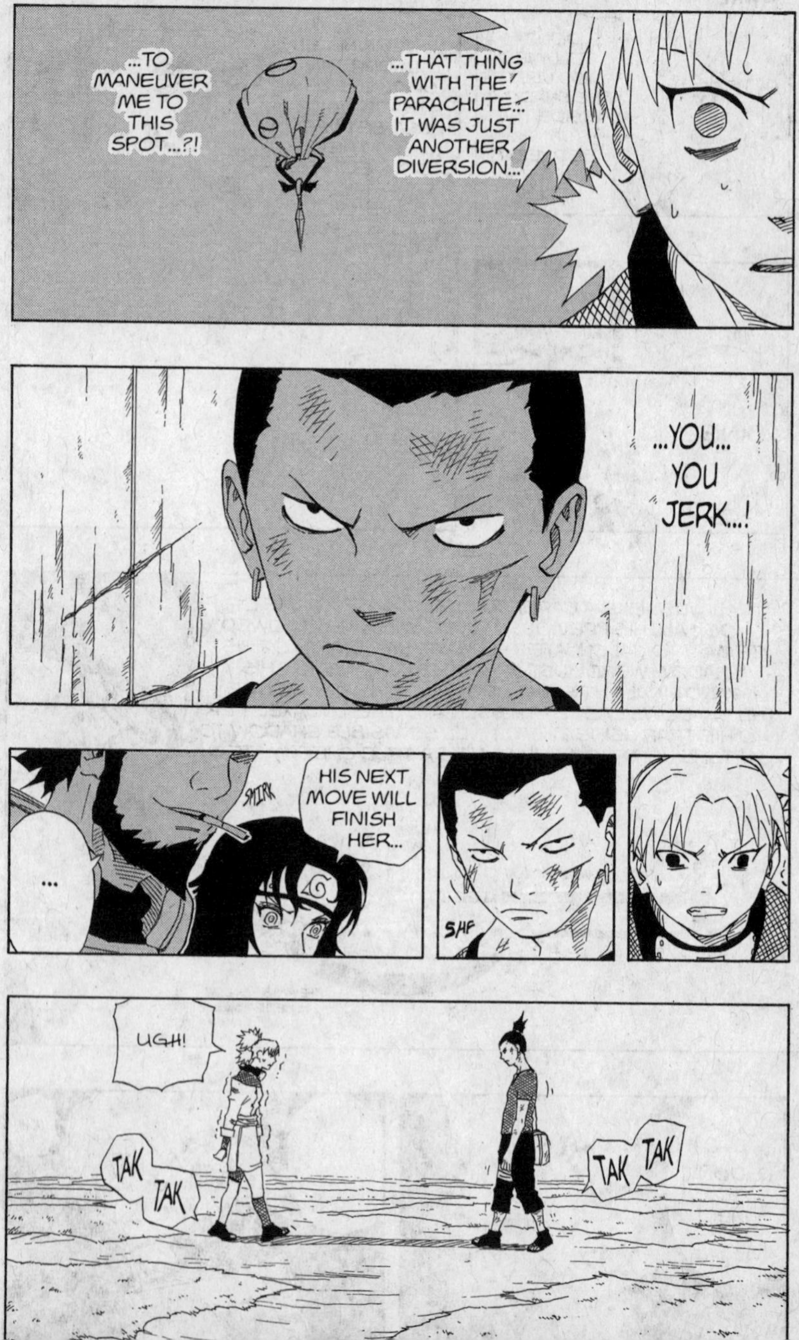
...THAT THING WITH THE PARACHUTE... IT WAS JUST ANOTHER DIVERSION...
...TO MANEUVER ME TO THIS SPOT...?!
...YOU... YOU JERK...!
SHF
HIS NEXT MOVE WILL FINISH HER...
SMIRK
...
TAK TAK
UGH!
TAK TAK

READ THIS WAY

GULP
...
!
BEFORE THEY KNEW IT, THE WHOLE CROWD GOT WRAPPED UP IN THE MATCH...
THIS KID WHO HADN'T MADE AN IMPRESSION ON ANYONE ENDS UP BEING A TOTAL DARK HORSE...
ALL RIGHT! GET HER!
GO FOR IT!
JAB
CHOMP CHOMP
CHOMP
CHOMP

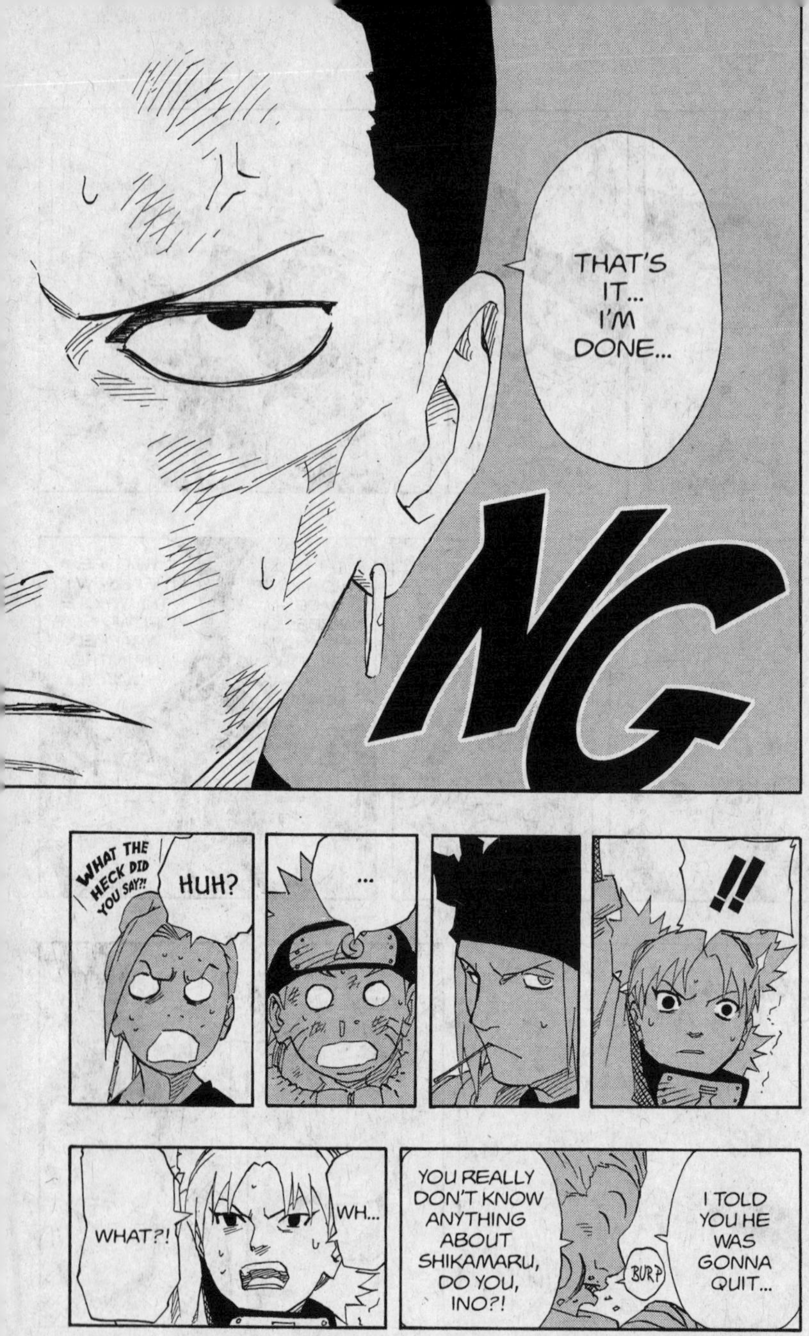
THAT'S IT... I'M DONE...
NG
!!
...
HUH?
WHAT THE HECK DID YOU SAY?!
I TOLD YOU HE WAS GONNA QUIT...
BURP
YOU REALLY DON'T KNOW ANYTHING ABOUT SHIKAMARU, DO YOU, INO?!
WH...
WHAT?!

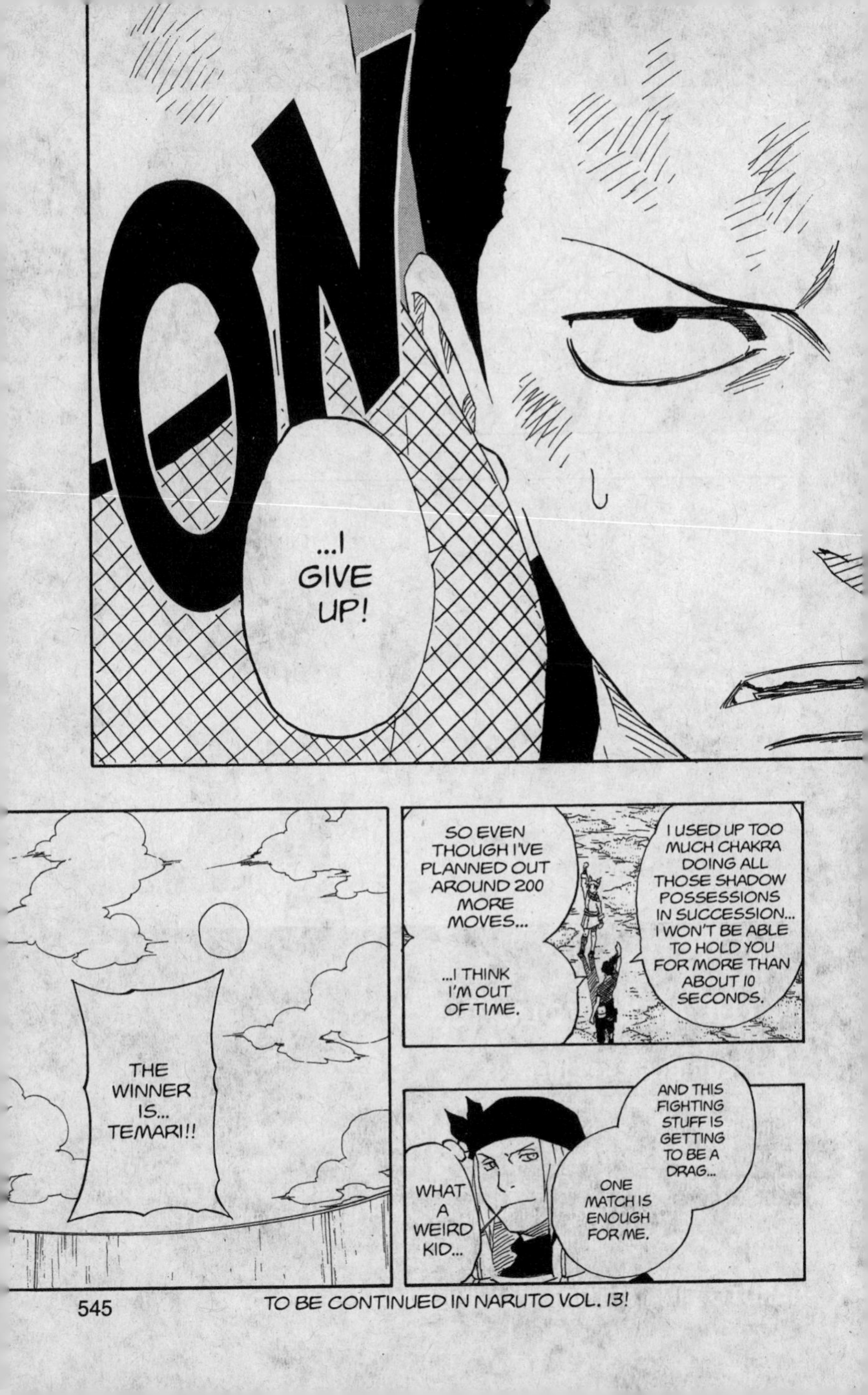
...I GIVE UP!
I USED UP TOO MUCH CHAKRA DOING ALL THOSE SHADOW POSSESSIONS IN SUCCESSION... I WON'T BE ABLE TO HOLD YOU FOR MORE THAN ABOUT 10 SECONDS.
SO EVEN THOUGH I'VE PLANNED OUT AROUND 200 MORE MOVES...
...I THINK I'M OUT OF TIME.
AND THIS FIGHTING STUFF IS GETTING TO BE A DRAG...
ONE MATCH IS ENOUGH FOR ME.
WHAT A WEIRD KID...
THE WINNER IS... TEMARI!!

TO BE CONTINUED IN NARUTO VOL. 13!

IN THE NEXT VOLUME...

THE TERRIBLE EXPERIMENT

The final battle of the Chûnin Exam is at hand, with Sasuke and Gaara facing off in the arena. Later, Naruto, Sakura and Shikamaru are on a top priority mission to track down Sasuke and the Sand ninja. Back at the village, the Third Hokage is still trapped in Orochimaru's impenetrable barrier. And the tension between Naruto and Gaara builds. As Gaara continues to mutate, Naruto prepares for the fight of his life!

NARUTO 3-IN-1 EDITION VOLUME 5 AVAILABLE NOW!

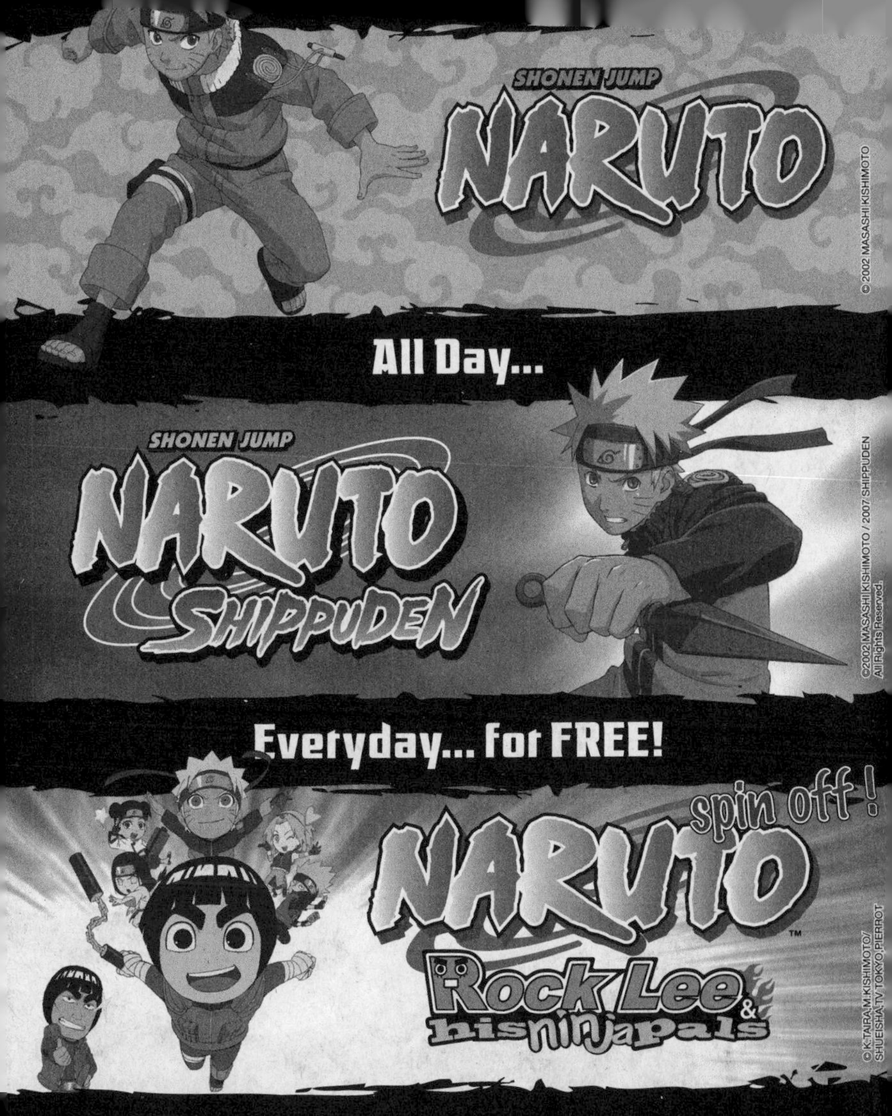
SHONEN JUMP
NARUTO
© 2002 MASASHI KISHIMOTO
All Day...
SHONEN JUMP
NARUTO SHIPPUDEN
©2002 MASASHI KISHIMOTO / 2007 SHIPPUDEN
All Rights Reserved.
Everyday... for FREE!
spin off!
NARUTO™
Rock Lee & his ninja pals
© K.TAIRA/M.KISHIMOTO/
SHUEISHA,TV TOKYO,PIERROT
Watch thousands of anime episodes officially on
neonalley.com

A PREMIUM BOX SET OF THE FIRST TWO STORY ARCS OF ONE PIECE!

A PIRATE'S TREASURE FOR ANY MANGA FAN!

STORY AND ART BY EIICHIRO ODA

Comes with **EXCLUSIVE POSTER** and the **ROMANCE DAWN** mini-comic!

As a child, Monkey D. Luffy dreamed of becoming King of the Pirates. But his life changed when he accidentally gained the power to stretch like rubber...at the cost of never being able to swim again! Years later, Luffy sets off in search of the "One Piece," said to be the greatest treasure in the world...

This box set includes VOLUMES 1-23, which comprise the EAST BLUE and BAROQUE WORKS story arcs.

EXCLUSIVE PREMIUMS and GREAT SAVINGS over buying the individual volumes!

You're Reading in the Wrong Direction!!

Whoops! Guess what? You're starting at the wrong end of the comic!

...It's true! In keeping with the original Japanese format, **Naruto** is meant to be read from right to left, starting in the upper-right corner.

Unlike English, which is read from left to right, Japanese is read from right to left, meaning that action, sound effects and word-balloon order are completely reversed...something which can make readers unfamiliar with Japanese feel pretty backwards themselves. For this reason, manga or Japanese comics published in the U.S. in English have sometimes been published "flopped"—that is, printed in exact reverse order, as though seen from the other side of a mirror.

By flopping pages, U.S. publishers can avoid confusing readers, but the compromise is not without its downside. For one thing, a character in a flopped manga series who once wore in the original Japanese version a T-shirt emblazoned with "M A Y" (as in "the merry month of") now wears one which reads "Y A M"! Additionally, many manga creators in Japan are themselves unhappy with the process, as some feel the mirror-imaging of their art alters their original intentions.

We are proud to bring you Masashi Kishimoto's **Naruto** in the original unflopped format. For now, though, turn to the other side of the book and let the ninjutsu begin...!

—Editor

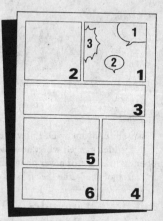